CW01663844

The Mirror of ART

This book addresses one of the key pictorial developments of Renaissance art: a conceptualisation of painting as a mirror reflection of the visible world. The idea of painting as specular was argued in Renaissance art theory, demonstrated in art practice, and represented in painting itself. Both within the artist's workshop and within pictorial representation, the mirror-image became the instrument, the emblem, and the conceptual definition of what a painting was. In this volume, Genevieve Warwick brings a dual focus to the topic through an exploration of the early modern elision of the picture plane with the mirror-image. She considers the specular configuration of Renaissance painting from various thematic points of view and offers a fully interdisciplinary analysis of the mirror analogy that pervaded not only art theory and art-making but also the larger cultural spheres of philosophy, letters, and scientific observation. Warwick's volume recasts our understanding of the inter-visual relationships between disciplines, and their consequences for a specular definition of Renaissance painting.

Genevieve Warwick is Professor of History of Art at the University of Edinburgh. The author of ten books and fifty articles on Renaissance art, from 2012 to 2017 she served as editor of *Art History*, the primary British journal for the discipline.

The Mirror of

ART

PAINTING AND REFLECTION IN EARLY MODERN VISUAL CULTURE

GENEVIEVE WARWICK

University of Edinburgh

CAMBRIDGE
UNIVERSITY PRESS

CAMBRIDGE
UNIVERSITY PRESS

Shaftesbury Road, Cambridge CB2 8EA, United Kingdom

One Liberty Plaza, 20th Floor, New York, NY 10006, USA

477 Williamstown Road, Port Melbourne, VIC 3207, Australia

314–321, 3rd Floor, Plot 3, Splendor Forum, Jasola District Centre, New Delhi – 110025, India

103 Penang Road, #05-06/07, Visioncrest Commercial, Singapore 238467

Cambridge University Press is part of Cambridge University Press & Assessment, a department of the University of Cambridge.

We share the University's mission to contribute to society through the pursuit of education, learning and research at the highest international levels of excellence.

www.cambridge.org
Information on this title: www.cambridge.org/9781009448802

DOI: 10.1017/9781009448833

© Genevieve Warwick 2024

This publication is in copyright. Subject to statutory exception and to the provisions of relevant collective licensing agreements, no reproduction of any part may take place without the written permission of Cambridge University Press & Assessment.

First published 2024

Printed in the United Kingdom by CPI Group Ltd, Croydon CR0 4YY

A catalogue record for this publication is available from the British Library

A Cataloging-in-Publication data record for this book is available from the Library of Congress

ISBN 978-1-009-44880-2 Hardback

Cambridge University Press & Assessment has no responsibility for the persistence or accuracy of URLs for external or third-party internet websites referred to in this publication and does not guarantee that any content on such websites is, or will remain, accurate or appropriate.

LEVERHULME
TRUST

The author of this work received a Major Research Fellowship award from the Leverhulme Trust.

Our art is like the effects of a mirror.

—PAOLO PINO, *DIALOGUE ON PAINTING*, 1548

Painting is the mirror of nature; it makes things that are not there appear to exist and deceive.

—SAMUEL VAN HOOGSTRATEN, *INTRODUCTION TO THE ACADEMY OF PAINTING, OR THE VISIBLE WORLD*, 1678

For my teachers and my students

CONTENTS

ILLUSTRATIONS

ACKNOWLEDGEMENTS

OVER THE COURSE OF writing this book I have incurred many debts; it is a great pleasure to acknowledge them here. First and foremost, I would like to thank the Leverhulme Trust, whose generous award of a Major Research Fellowship in 2017 made this book possible. I thank profoundly all the staff, the anonymous reviewers, and my referees, Elizabeth Cropper, Thomas Gaehtgens, and Todd Olson; without them this book could never have been realised. For two extraordinary years I travelled to museums and galleries across the length and breadth of Europe, and to collections of European art further afield, in search of the 'mirror-image within the image' that configures my subject here. I thank the museums that hosted me graciously, as I pored for hours over tiny details in the paintings of their collections, particularly the Louvre, the Prado, the Kunsthistorisches Museum in Vienna, the Metropolitan Museum of Art, and of course the National Gallery in London, home to the Arnolfini portrait and the Rokeby Venus, as the pictures that speak the thousand words of this book.

As I began to write up my findings in the spring of 2020, Covid-19 struck. All libraries and research institutes closed, travel was completely shut down, and books themselves were quarantined, so that access to the very stuff of scholarship was suddenly and relentlessly proscribed. Of course, the inevitable setbacks in writing an academic book are of very minor moment in the face of a global pandemic. Again, my sincere thanks to the Leverhulme Trust, which granted their award-holders a year's extension in order to cope with the adverse effects of Covid-19 lockdowns. What I discovered, as was surely the case for many other scholars, was the great benefit of digitisation, which made so many of the primary textual sources for this research available online. My thanks to the many libraries and museums around the world that make their rich collections available on the web. A very special word of thanks also to the London Library, of which I was privileged to be a member during the pandemic, and which was the only lending library of any kind open during that time. Although the library was closed to in-house reading, the marvellous staff continued to send out books by post to their members on request. Again, I could not have written this book without them.

I would also like to thank those who invited me to give lectures (some of necessity virtual) on my subject, as well as the conference hosts. The collections of essays that were published were where I first had the chance to test many of the most important ideas presented here and to share them with other scholars at crucial formative stages during the writing of this book. In particular, I thank Elisabeth Oy-Marra, Cristina Galassi, Eva Struhal, Denis Ribouillault, Vita Segreto, Serena Galasso, Isabelle Chabod, and Maddalena Bellavitis my fellow speakers and discussants, as well as the Accademia di San Luca, the Kunsthistorisches Institut, the Institut National d'Histoire de l'Art and their exceptional audiences. I also thank profoundly Sam Bibby and Richard Taws, who saw my earliest ideas on this into press as part of a special issue for *Art History* on early modern art and technology, and all the contributors who worked with us on this project. It was during my time as editor of *Art History*, along with Natalie Adamson and as part of that extraordinary community of art historians, that the kernel of this book first took shape in my mind, and was surely inspired by its ethos.

My sincere thanks to Beatrice Rehl at Cambridge University Press for ushering the book through to publication, and the anonymous readers for their time and careful consideration. It was a great pleasure to work with the Press again, as they were the publisher of my first book in 2000. As this book drew to a close, I prospered from the further opportunity to publish alongside it a related book with Cambridge University Press, under the expert editors of the interdisciplinary Renaissance Studies Element series, Jonathan Nelson and John Henderson, on the subject of early modern glass as a materiality of metamorphic *fortuna*. Together under the Press' imprint, these two books are intended as a complement of art-historical and interdisciplinary scholarship. Thanks are also due to the Leverhulme Trust and the University of Edinburgh for funding the photographic costs entailed. Over the years in which I wrote this book, the digital image libraries in museums and galleries around the world moved from closed to open access; I thank them all profoundly for making the once-hefty costs of art-historical publishing now readily compassed. Two exceptional postdoctoral students, Annkatrin Kaul and Elisabetta Toreno, offered invaluable practical and intellectual assistance at various stages of completion. I would also like to thank the students I taught during the final stages of this book, for their lively interest and engagement with the subject. In closing, I would like to thank my own teachers, who first set my winged thoughts on the path of scholarship. As ever I thank my family for their happy sustenance throughout life's tribulations. Finally, I thank the many authors whose writings inspired my work. I hope to have done some small justice to their example.

INTRODUCTION

The Mirror of Narcissus

I say among my friends that Narcissus who was changed into a flower, according to the poets, was the inventor of painting.... What else can you call painting but a similar embracing with art of what is presented on the surface of the water.

—LEON BATTISTA ALBERTI, *DELLA PITTURA*, FLORENCE, 1436

There was a pool, limpid and silvery.... The boy lay down, enchanted by the quiet pool ... as he drank he saw before his eyes / a form, a face, and loved with leaping heart / A hope unreal and thought the shape was real. Spellbound he saw himself, and motionless / lay like a marble statue staring down.... How often in vain he kissed the cheating pool / and in the water sank his arms to clasp.... You simple boy, why strive in vain / to catch a fleeting image? What you see is nowhere.... You see a phantom of a mirrored shape / Nothing itself; with you it came and stays / With you it too will go....

—OVID, *METAMORPHOSES*, NARCISSUS, III:402–36

IN LEON BATTISTA ALBERTI'S *Della pittura* of 1435–36, the Florentine architect and art theorist elaborated a paradigm for painting as a mirror reflection of the visible world.[1] For this he drew on classical precedents, both Platonic and Aristotelian, in conceiving of art as *mimesis*, or *imitatio* in its Latinate form. A close cognate to 'image' etymologically, Alberti understood *imitatio* as the imitation of the visible world and the artistic means by which to do so.[2] Those means comprised the methods of pictorial illusion through which to render the fiction of space and volume on the flat surface of a picture plane. Borrowing from the ancient poet Ovid as from Pliny to write the first theory of Renaissance painting, Alberti traced the mythical inauguration of this art in the reflective pool of Narcissus.[3] Indeed, Alberti recast Ovid's poetry of *Metamorphoses* into the historical origins of art:

> I say among my friends that Narcissus who was changed into a flower, according to the poets, was the inventor of painting. Since painting is . . . the flower of every art, the story of Narcissus is most to the point. What else can you call painting but a similar embracing with art of what is presented on the surface of the water of the fountain?[4]

Thus Alberti projected the mythological origin of the *imago* as a mirror reflection onto the surface of Ovid's silvered pool, *ad fonte*. This 'fount' was conceived as the source of art. In so saying, Alberti adumbrated an analogy between painting and mirroring as the foundations of a mimetic image. His analogy forms the subject of this book.

Writing from his position as humanist theorist of the arts, Alberti was heir to those cultures of classical revival patronised by the Medici that shaped a nascent Renaissance paradigm of art within a matrix of *paragone*, or comparison, inherited from Pliny, Horace, and Plutarch. Alberti's entirely new conception of painting's origins in the watery pool of Ovidian myth made art the counterpart not only to the mirror reflection but also to poetry, within the paired equivalence of the Horatian *dictum, ut pictura poesis*.[5] In Ovid's account, while Narcissus is transformed into a mirror reflection and so the flower of art, the woodland nymph Echo who desires him becomes the voice of poetry (Fig. 1). In a linked Latinate etymology, both are reflections, word and image conjoined, and so metaphors of love's longing return.[6]

In the ancient Philostratus' subsequent representation of the Narcissus myth in his *Eikones* or *Imagines* (1:23), each poetic 'image' of this mythic pool contained within it an infinite historical cascade of inset figurative imagery, like so many mirror reflections of Ovid's verse.[7] Much translated across the Renaissance, as with Ovid's *Metamorphoses*, Philostratus' *Imagines* was a literary art gallery that configured the (fictive) painted image as suffused with both poetic and pictorial recollection, each one a history of art within itself. In the sixteenth-century sculptor Benvenuto Cellini's reiteration of Alberti's specular conceptualisation of the painted image within the further context of an Ovidian *paragone*: 'Painting is nothing other than, say, a tree or a man, or anything that is reflected in a fountain's pool. The difference between sculpture and painting is great, like that between a shadow, and the thing that causes shadow to fall.'[8] Alongside this Cellini sculpted his own marbled Narcissus who casts his shadow into a fountain's pool while gazing down at his watery reflection (Fig. 2).[9] The Venetian painter Paolo Pino similarly theorised painting as the formless figurations of a specular mimesis like the shadowy reflections in Ovid's pool: 'our art is like the effects of a mirror'.[10] In both word and image, Alberti had understood art's defining characteristic as the power to 'make the absent seem present', by which he meant its illusionistic capacity of imitation to render the semblance of life where there is none.[11] As with the evocations of poetic language, art's mimetic force may cause the viewer, like Ovid's Narcissus, to love a mirrored reflection, 'nothing itself', such is the power of its veristic illusions.

Elsewhere in his *Della pittura*, Alberti described the art of painting as 'an open window, through which I see what I want to paint'.[12] This was to invoke a conceit of pictorial imitation

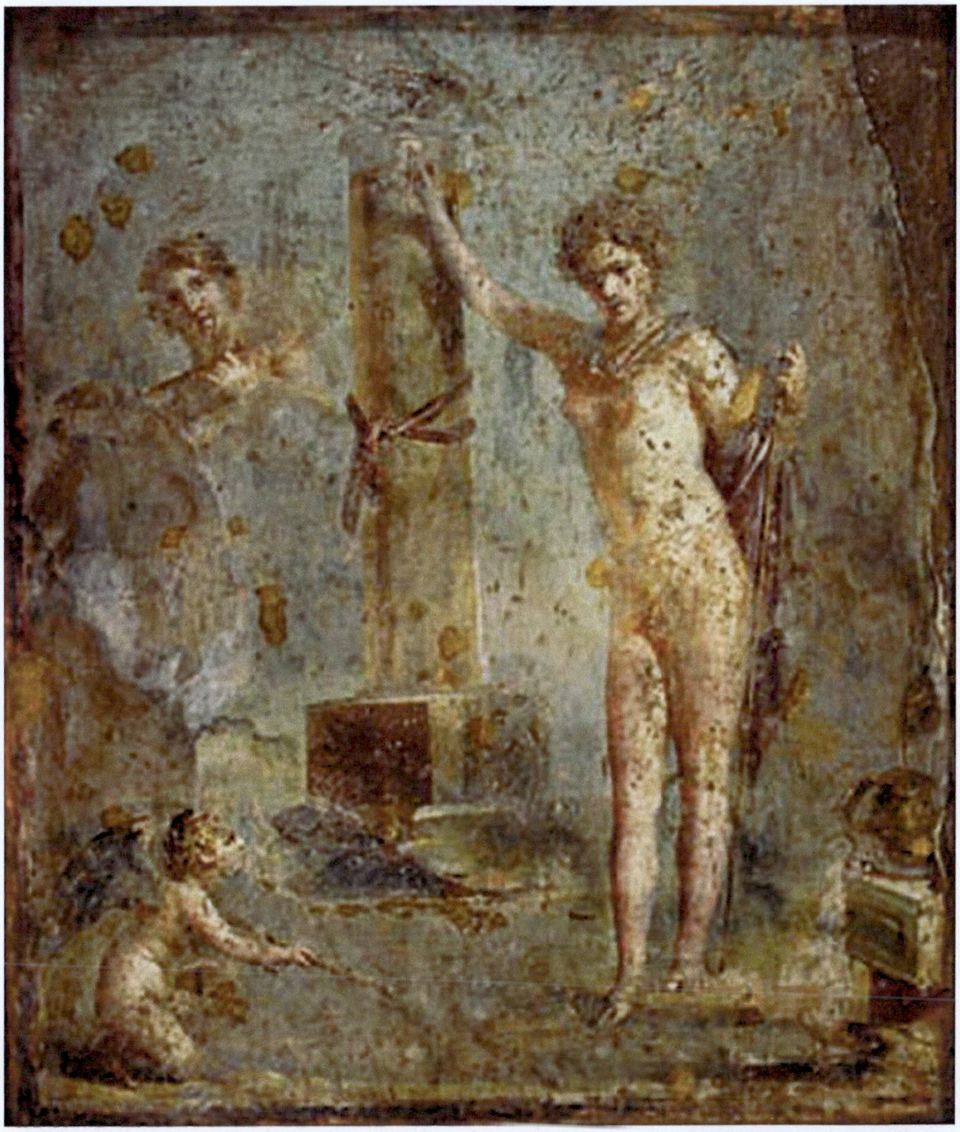

Fig. 1 'Narcissus with Cupid and Echo', before 79 CE, wall fresco, Pompeii (now Naples Museo Archaeologico). Photo: Wikimedia

within the optics of perspective as equivalent to vision itself. Alberti's reflexive conception of painting as both a mirror and a window view, in his further elaboration, comprised the optical as well as the conceptual means by which to render the image as the fiction of life, like the watery reflection that Narcissus sought to embrace on the surface of the poetic pool. Alberti's elision of the mirror-image with the window view surely derived from their shared Latin etymologies as *speculum* and *specularia,* as well as the cognate of speculation as a figure of thought. Vision, Alberti knew, had been likened to 'a living mirror' within classical and medieval optical theory. Similarly, the mirror was, Alberti argued, 'the true judge' of painting. Thus, resemblance to the mirror reflection, like Ovid's mythic pool, was the just measure of the painter's art.

While Alberti was theorising the art of painting under the sign of the mirror as specular mimesis (1434–36), in Bruges Jan van Eyck was painting the celebrated tondo mirror of his Arnolfini double portrait (1434) (Fig. 3). In this painting, which has come to define the

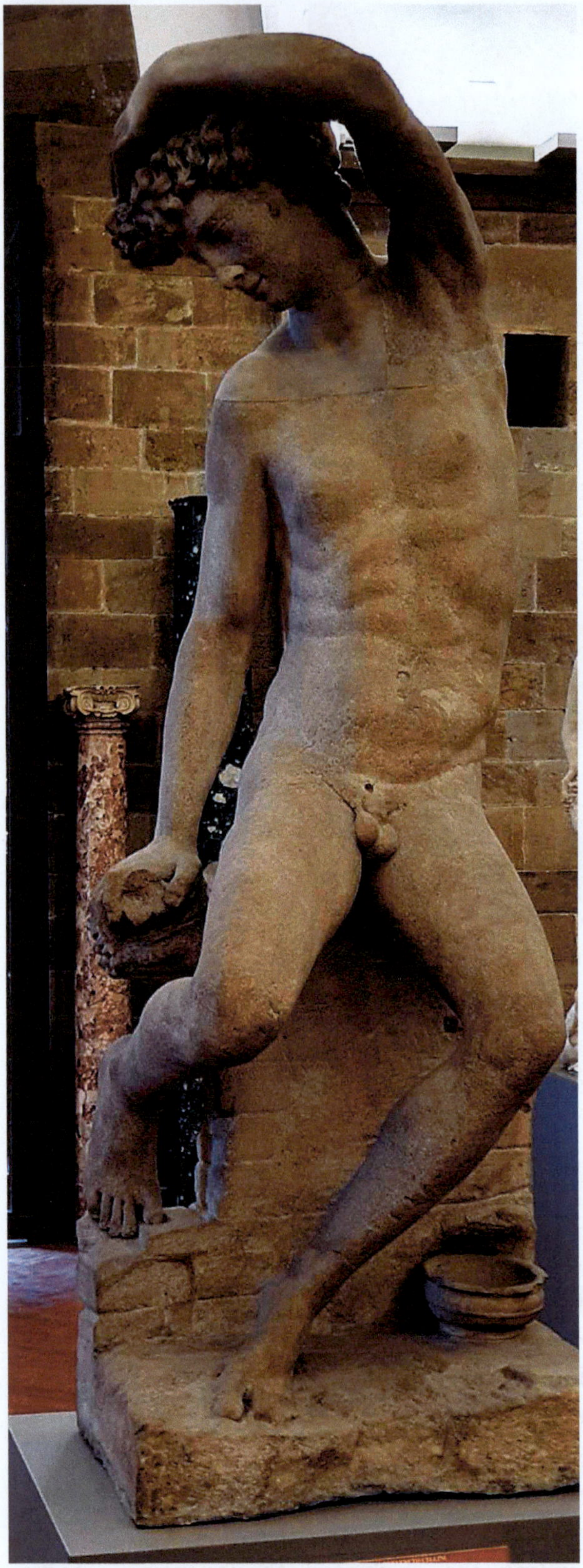

Fig. 2 Benvenuto Cellini, *Narcissus*, 1547, marble, height 149 cm, Bargello Museum Florence.
Photo: Wikimedia

inauguration of Northern Renaissance art, its inset mirror-image is the pictorial emblem of that claim. The painted reflection mirrors back the room in which it is set to show the couple within it seen from behind, the stone-mullioned window to the side, as well as a further projection of the room 'in front' of the picture plane. Van Eyck's mirror represents an illusionistic fusion of painting and mirroring, exactly as Ovid had imagined, by analogy with an Albertian 'window' of painted spatial projection. This specular pictorialisation of the art of painting was enhanced by van Eyck's highly refractive use of oil paint to heighten the capacity for optical reflection, through the application of glistening light-filled glazes suspended in translucent coloured oil. As in Alberti's text, van Eyck's lustrous mirror theorises the art of painting as a mimetic illusion like the shimmering reflection of Ovidian myth. Thus painting and mirroring were held to be commensurate forms of the Albertian 'window view' of art.

***

This book argues that the key pictorial development of Renaissance art was a new conceptualisation of painting as a mirror reflection of the visible world. In effect, the mirror became painting's sign of optics as an instrument of light and its reflection, and so of all forms of visual representation. As the emblem of vision itself, the mirror became the rebus of the painter's art. The book's temporal frame opens with the inauguration of the perspectival 'mirror-window' of painting in early fifteenth-century Italian art theory. Elaborated by Alberti, the science of perspective was demonstrated by the architect Filippo Brunelleschi by means of a mirror reflection of the view through the door of the Florentine cathedral. Alongside arose the pictorialised optical mirrors of early Netherlandish oil paint initiated by van Eyck. The book then follows the specular conceptualisation of

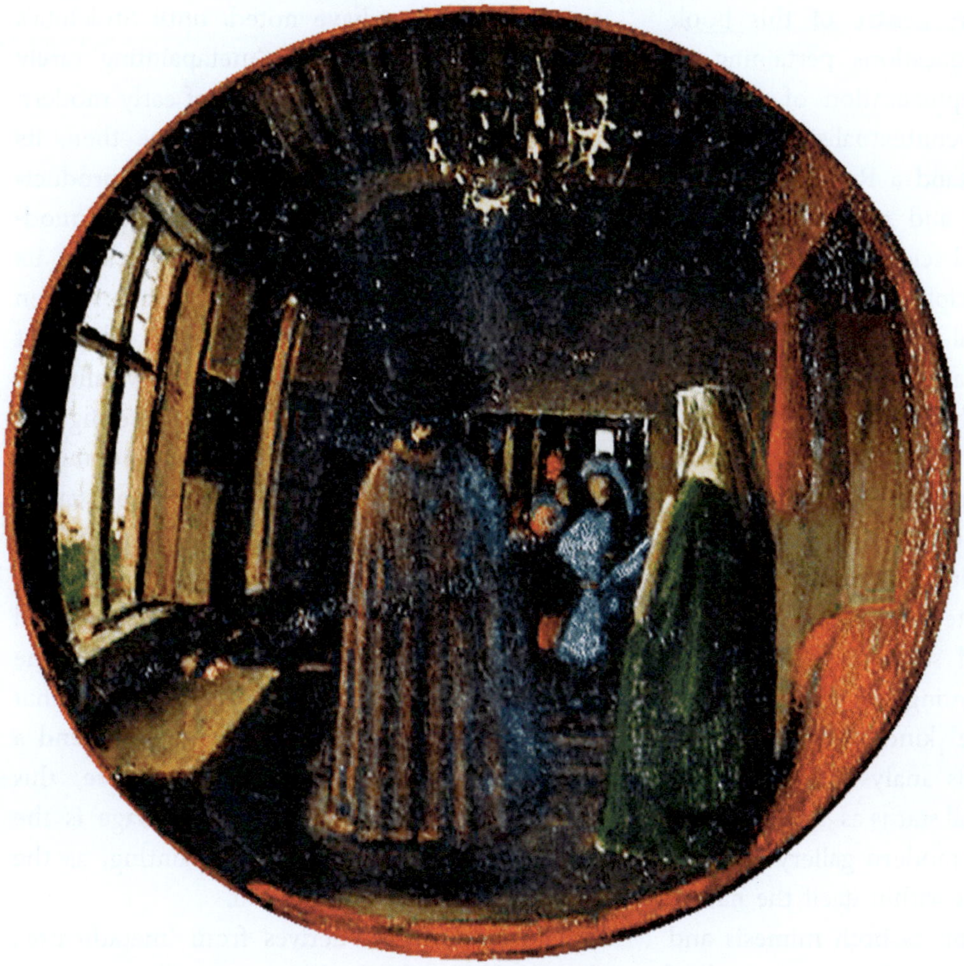

Fig. 3 Jan van Eyck, *Arnolfini Double Portrait*, detail, 1434, oil on oak panel, 82.2 × 60 cm, National Gallery London. Photo: Wikimedia

Renaissance art in the sixteenth-century rise of the easel painting as an independent work of art, in which each framed image represented in itself an Albertian 'window view' of mirroring mimetic illusion. It considers new Renaissance genres of art whose development was specifically bound to the mirror-image. This comprised self-portraiture, made by means of a mirror as its instrument, and the rise of the painted female nude with a mirror as the reigning pictorial emblem of High Renaissance art's beauty. These painted inset mirror reflections have long been acknowledged to reach a 'Baroque' apogee in the art of Velazquez, notably in his Rokeby Venus and *Las Meninas*. In effect, *Las Meninas* draws together the long Renaissance pictorial history of the embedded mirror-image as the allegory of painting itself. The Hall of Mirrors at Versailles concludes this book's account of the historical relationship between Renaissance painting and mirroring in its specular juxtaposition of mirrors, windows, and painting, just as van Eyck and Alberti had adumbrated. The example of Versailles, like *Las Meninas*, is thus the culmination of the early modern relationship between painting and mirroring that this book traces, offering *in nuce* its major themes. In sum, the book debates what defined Renaissance painting, in both artistic theory and art practice, to argue that its newly formulated techniques of optical illusion were conceived in relation to the mirror-image as the model of art's visual mimesis.

While the disciplinary centre of this book concerns art-historical questions pertaining to an early modern conceptualisation of painting as specular, the range of contextualising histories within which to understand a Renaissance analogy between picturing and mirroring extends across the literatures and sciences too. Thus the book offers an interdisciplinary account of the mirror's multiple cultural roles as an instrument and metaphor of light and vision, as of knowledge itself, within which to situate its particular address to the history of early modern art. As Hans Belting, Victor Stoichita, and Michael Fried have variously argued, this relationship between painting and mirroring is bound up with the early modern architectural development of the picture gallery, and so with the historical emergence of easel painting. As a newly independent and 'self-aware' kind of painting, the gallery picture is, in this analysis, now able to signify its own ontological status as 'art'. In such a consideration, the early modern gallery painting is understood to address within itself the nature of pictorial representation as both mimesis and illusion, like Philostratus at the poetic pool of Narcissus, or Alberti's window view. Broadly, Belting's argument concerns the historical separation of 'art' from the medieval icon or cult object wrought by religious Reformation, resulting in the nascent status of the image as a work of art in its own right. Now judged in terms of its powers of mimesis and narrative or poetic invention, rather than its resemblance to an iconic prototype as the matrix of devotional efficacy, painting was newly theorised as specular. To quote from Stoichita and Fried in turn, early modernity marks the advent of 'painting in itself', of which mirroring was its 'core modality'.[13] As such, art now reflected on itself, in theory as in practice.[14]

In the title to his book, *The Self-Aware Image*, Stoichita further invoked the term *métapeinture*, or metapainting, as the subject of his enquiry. As other scholars have noted, until Stoichita's book first appeared in 1993, 'metapainting' rarely entered the critical terminology of early modern art-historical analysis, if at all. Since then, its historical configuration continues to be productively extended – and contested – by both modernists and medievalists who also claim its theoretical mantle.[15] While this book is written in acknowledgement of the rich scholarship that Stoichita's metapainting, or image-within-the-image, has produced, its scope is configured otherwise, in its singular focus on the mirror reflection. As other scholars have argued, metapainting justly includes any pictorial device used to signal art's status as illusion. This has centred above all on inset framing devices and embedded images. In effect, together they encapsulate the double-sided aspect of Alberti's claim: that mimetic painting is both a window view and a mirror reflection. Distinctively, therefore, this book argues that the inset mirror-image is the acme of an early modern metapainting, as the very image of painting in itself.

The term surely derives from 'metatheatre', the analysis of which is generally given to Lionel Abel's 1963 book of this title. Predominantly concerned with modernist adaptations, yet Abel acknowledged its historical issue within early modernity. Centred on the study of enacted speech, Abel's study noted Elizabethan theatre's use of the dialogic aside or soliloquy, for example, in which actors momentarily 'broke' the illusion of the proscenium arch through direct address 'beyond' the confines of the play to comment on its significance.[16] The ready conflation of theatre's proscenium arch with painting's picture frame(s) that Stoichita's study intimated thus opened the way to read painting's self-aware details as 'metapainting'. Here visual art could similarly 'break' the picture plane to stage its own ontological status as illusion.

As a twentieth-century structuralist scholarship had earlier argued, the early modern inset mirror-image or picture-within-the-painting such as configures the Arnolfini portrait or, later, Velazquez' *Las Meninas* may be understood as the pictorial emblem of 'painting within itself'. That is to say, the reflexive mirror-image within and of this art functions as both imitation and illusion. As such, this book's greatest intellectual debts within the scholarship are to André Chastel's 'Le tableau dans le tableau', Daniel Arasse's 'Les miroirs de la peinture', and the rich issue of art-historical literature arising from their studied observation of the 'mirror-image' in early modern painting.[17] Such analysis rests on a matrix of word-image relations encapsulated within historical analogies of the inset mirror-image, further defined as a form of *mise-en-abyme*.

The early modern inset painted mirror-image was, in Chastel's words, an *abrégé du tableau*, or an abridged pictorial motif of painting's reflective art within itself. Identifying the perspectival 'rupture' of the picture plane with the Albertian illusion of a window-like optical recession, this conception of the early modern inset mirror-image as the emblem of painting has, in its twentieth-century scholarship, also been further theorised in relation to modernism's claim to the condition of 'art'.[18] As Lucien Dällenbach famously argued in a widely influential study of the specular double in twentieth century literature, *Le récit spéculaire: essai sur la mise-en-abyme* of 1977, the painted inset mirror-image in early modern art may be understood as a representation of the art of painting within itself.[19]

***

Distinct from a modernist account, this book instead offers a fully historical consideration of early modern painting's inset mirror-image as *mise-en-abyme*, as both a term and a concept, within Renaissance cultures of word and image. For, while the critical projection of *mise-en-abyme* onto modern art and literature has greatly expanded the theoretical valence of the term, this has tended to occlude its historical specificity within the cusp of the Renaissance. Its earliest – and defining – pictorial application was within late medieval heraldry, to denote the inset imagery at the centre of an armorial shield.[20] For this reason it retained its identification with the centre point of any image, and so with the perspectival centre point of Renaissance painting, and thus with the 'abysm' of spatial recession. From its armorial exodus, within early modern arts and letters alike, *mise-en-abyme* also came to connote the concept of any inset image or text, now likened to the inset imagery of heraldry, which was manifest across cultural genres.

Again, its prevailing matrix lay within theatre. In the Shakespearean 'play-within-the-play' of *Hamlet* or *A Midsummer Night's Dream*, inset dramatic interludes acted as emblematic commentary or 'mirror reflections' on the play proper. From Miguel de Cervantes' *Don Quixote*, Pedro Calderón de la Barca's *La vida es sueño*, and Thomas Kyd's *Spanish Tragedy* to Paul Scarron's *Roman comique*, or Pierre Corneille's *Illusion comique*, the prevailing early modern prototype was of the play-within-the-play, as an embedded 'mirror-image' within and of itself.[21]

Within Renaissance literature, *mise-en-abyme* also became an allegory of memory and so of time, or the cascading temporal reach of historical knowledge into the past represented pictorially by the optics of perspectival recession. In this regard the Albertian theory of painting as both a window and a mirror configures both temporal-spatial recession into unfathomable depth, and its specular recollection or return on itself. Thus Shakespeare's Prospero asked Miranda of her life before the storm: 'what seest thou in the ... abysm of time?' (*The Tempest*, Act 1, scene 2).[22] Such a configuration of memory was perceived as boundless in its capacities of projection and retrospection. Like the pictorially unlimited regress of perspectival spatial illusion, or an infinite cascade of inter-facing mirror reflections, memory was conceived as immeasurable. Linked to the furthest reach of time and memory, the figure of *mise-en-abyme* became the sign of knowledge itself. For this reason, it was also elided with religious conceptions of the ineffable divine, and the incommensurability of God's love. In medieval encyclopaedic texts such as Isidore of Seville's seventh-century *Etymologies,* the 'abyss' had a further ancestry from ancient Greek translations of the Hebrew bible, manifest above all in water as the fount of life's genesis, and used to signify the unfathomable source of the divine.[23] In the words of the early modern intellectual philosopher and educator John Comenius, also a theologian, the immeasurable recollective capacities of the mind are, in the image of the divine, also like an 'abysm'. Defined as a mirror, the mind reflects all that surrounds it, able to fathom into the depths of all things, to penetrate infinite space 'even to the heavens'. More broadly, Comenius argued for the pedagogic primacy of visual forms of knowledge, which he understood the mirror-image to represent. [24] As twentieth-century literary scholars of early modernity such as Georges Gusdorf and Herbert Grabes have also argued, along with historical philosophers such as Richard Rorty and Rodolphe Gasché, across Renaissance arts and letters the mirror became the emblem of reflection and so of knowledge *tout court.*[25]

Within Renaissance art theory, painting's perspectival abysm or recession of illusionistic depth was perceived as a mirror-image of the visible field. The specular inset motif within early modern painting was therefore understood as an encapsulation or pictorial metaphor of art's mirroring mimesis. Further, the emblematic figure of '*abyme*' or abysm was likened to the infinite illusionistic depth of perspectival recession, so conflating the inset image with the image proper, as an allegory of itself. Analogically, perspectival recession was conceived as a visual metaphor of chronological recession. That is to say, the temporal cast of *mise-en-abyme* as the figure of memory was, in pictorial terms, approximated to the optical configuration of spatial recession. In this way, *ut pictura poesis,* painting could rival literature in its claim to represent all forms of knowledge across time. Mirror-like, painting represented the knowledge of the world through the mathematics of optical recession, concluding in a centre point of infinite spatial regress to represent the infinitude of knowledge, *en abyme.* With the development of a window-like perspectival method for painting, as Alberti had promulgated, each image was itself both a fiction and a truth. Thus its pictorial representation of the visible field was one of conceptually infinite illusionistic depth – perspectivally 'in abysm'.

Hence in Filippo Parodi's great Narcissus mirror for the long gallery at the Durazzo Villa Faraggiana, this artist of Bernini's impress and Alberti's conception put on display the pictorial eloquence of art's mimetic illusion as specular. As the gold-carved youth bends to look at his reflection in the depths of poetry's mirroring source, yet it is the viewer's own image that is represented there, albeit as ephemeral as Ovid's account of the pool of Narcissus (Fig. 4).[26] If the perception of infinite spatial recession within the geometry of Renaissance perspective was a pictorial illusion, like metaphorical mirrors of cultural memory in the depths of time, yet its fictions were those of a demonstrable optical verity. The mirror reflection was understood as the sign of the image, while the mirror itself connoted the optics of both vision and light as the *modus* of the visible.

***

Such a historical account of early modern art's mirroring intent offers a radically historicised reframing of Ernst Gombrich's celebrated if greatly critiqued *Art and Illusion.* As Svetlana

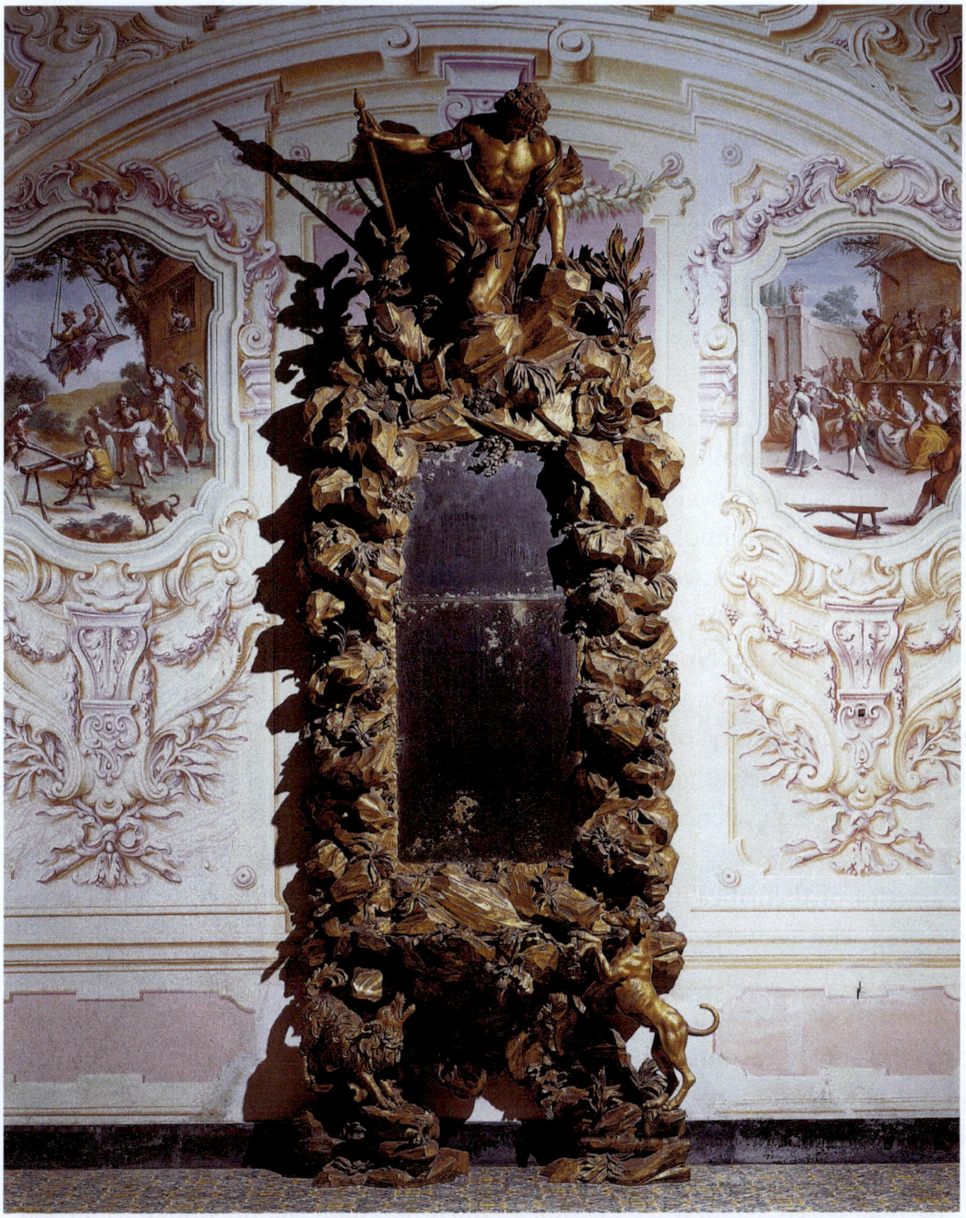

Fig. 4 Filippo Parodi, *Mirror Frame and Console Table with the Figure of Narcissus*, c. 1667, gilt wood, 450 × 170 × 70 cm, Galleria delle Stagioni, Villa Durazzo Faraggiana (Albissola Marina). Photo: Scala Images

Alpers and Norman Bryson have argued in turn, Gombrich's story of art as a progress in perception towards an increasingly precise 'matching' of painting with 'natural' vision must be recast.[27] Thus Erwin Panofsky's conceptualisation of Renaissance perspective as 'symbolic form', rather than Gombrich's psychology of perception, instead brilliantly understood the Albertian 'window view' – as the conceptual and instrumental means by which Renaissance painting was perceived to resemble a mirror – as one of historical convention. In so saying, Panofsky opened the door to a historicised reading of Renaissance art's mimesis.[28] Similarly, Alpers' address to the optical instruments of mirror magnification for the purposes of topographic illustration, from cartography to astronomy and microscopy, shaped early modern visual cultures of recording that were, in her analysis, the aegis to a newly powerful mimetic 'art of describing'. In both cases, they argued for a historical analysis of the early modern mimetic image.

Yet the subsequent wrestling of our scholarship with any chronological or geographical account of the early modern mimetic image remains unresolved notwithstanding myriad endeavours to map its development. While we recognise an increasingly diverse 'play' with the artistic deployment of the mirror-image motif, from its early fifteenth-century definition in van Eyck to the cascade of pictorial reflections at work in *Las Meninas*, as at the Hall of Mirrors at Versailles, precise temporal delineation of this pictorial development remains both open and diffuse. This book does not, therefore, attempt to map a definitive chronology of art-historical change in the theory or practice of the early modern mirror-image. Nor does it trace a history of the Renaissance mirror as directly coterminous with that of the history of painting, although it does evidence a pervasive early modern perception of an equivalence between painting and mirroring within such an account. Instead, it offers a series of thematically orchestrated chapters concerned with contextualising analyses of different aspects of the mirror's early modern pictorial manifestations. While the chapters are placed in broadly chronological order, their collective ambition is not, directly, to trace a historical progress of the early modern relationship between painting and mirroring. Rather, they take up those contexts – be they social, cultural, practice-based, scientific, literary, or intellectual history – that offer a heightened or intensified apprehension of the early modern elision between painting and mirroring. As such, the chapters can be read collectively and independently.

The temporal arc of the book runs from Brunelleschi's demonstration of geometrical perspective's visual accuracy by means of a mirror reflection at the door of the Florentine cathedral in the early 1400s to the Hall of Mirrors at Versailles in the 1680s; from the Arnolfini portrait to *Las Meninas*. In this it broadly follows longstanding art-historical convention in the periodisation of early modernity sequentially as Renaissance to Baroque. While acknowledging earlier examples of painted mirror reflections in late medieval/Renaissance manuscript illuminations, this book concerns the inset-mirror motif within the history of painting proper, independent of the illuminated page. There is no endeavour to make this a comprehensive account, for the historical examples of Renaissance 'mirror paintings' vastly exceed the scope of a single book.[29] Their quantity, in itself, testifies to the powerful historical significance of the motif as the defining metaphor of a mimetic Renaissance art. This book's concern is to analyse the broader cultural and intellectual reasons for the centrality of the mirror motif.

***

While centred in the study of painting, the book is also concerned with broader cultural interests in the mirror-image. That is to say, it offers an expanded definition of art history as a discipline bound to the study of visual culture in manifold forms, from the decorative arts of the mirror as an ornamental artefact to the scientific use of optical mirrors in the development of the Galilean telescope and the early modern box cameras that presaged the nineteenth-century advent of photography.[30] Within the sciences, it is much concerned with the documentary image, or what has become known as the epistemic image, whose purpose was mimetic 'mirror' accuracy in the representation of visual knowledge.[31] It also traces the broader cultural relationships between the significance of the mirror analogy within early modern painting and the literary arts, from theatre to poetry and philosophy, to demonstrate the central place of the mirror as the sign of the reflective intellect across myriad cultural domains.

Also at stake in the discussion that follows is the interweaving of artisanship with artistic theory in the Renaissance pursuit of visual imitation. As Alpers argued in her celebrated study of the 'art of describing', early modern scientific vision, as also painting's mimesis, was predicated on artisanal modes of viewing, from ocular lenses to the draughtsman's topographic drawing-frames and mirrors.[32] Before the advent of photography, the documentation and circulation of all forms of visual knowledge depended on the draughtsman's skill, for which the mirror was the model and the instrument. Across the pictorial arts, the mirror thus constituted the paradigm and the practice-based conduit for recording all forms of visual knowledge, comprising architecture, engineering, and science no less than painting. Eliding any neat separation between visual concept and material instrumentation, or its more familiar art-historical designations of theory and practice, this book argues that the artist's mirror was both *technē* and *logos*, at once the technical means and the exemplary model of the Renaissance mimetic image. In practice, the mirror reflection was the workshop means of translating the three-dimensional world into the two-dimensional frame of the painter's canvas or the draughtsman's page. Part of a craft knowledge of picture-making as much as the sign of Renaissance image theory, the mirror thus prevailed over the intersections between workshop technologies and patterns of visual thought. Between practice and concept, artisanal know-how and artistic theorisation, the draughtsman's mirror was both mechanical and epistemic in the production of the mimetic image, and so of Renaissance visual knowledge *tout court*. This demands our further analysis in several overlapping ways.

On the one hand, in Michel Foucault's far-reaching history of early modern thought, which he called an archaeology of human knowledge, this intellectual historian studied the vast transition between medieval and modern mentalities as epistemic shifts that structured all aspects of speculation and enquiry. Famously, he discerned a fundamental difference between Renaissance thought, which he characterised by conceptual paradigms of analogy or resemblance configured in the sign of the mirror; to an emerging 'modern' episteme of analytical distinction marked by the taxonomic classification of similarities and differences. Within such a historical construct of an emblematic Renaissance episteme, the figure of the inset mirror as *mise-en-abyme* was analogical. That is to say, and as Foucault brilliantly posited in opening *Les mots et les choses* with the painted inset mirror of *Las Meninas*, the early modern image-within-the-image was intended to signify metaphorically as an allegory of itself.[33] If the temporal boundaries of Foucault's differentiation between analogical and analytical patterns of thought may be productively questioned, in the interests of a more fully pluralist historical account, yet the reach of his analysis in its attention to a history of systems of intellectural cogitation is manifold. Thus, in Rorty's study of early modern epistemology construed as 'the mirror of nature', the figure of the speculative mirror or 'looking glasse' is considered the very emblem of thought itself. Similarly, Gasché argued that early modernity's defining metaphor of intellectual process was reflection, which he understood as the mind's mirroring return of speculative 'light'.[34] Thus the mirror-image was a rebus of mimesis and reflection as the pictorial sign of knowledge and thought.

At the same time, recent scholarship best represented in the work of Pamela H. Smith has turned our attention to Renaissance forms of craft or artisanal knowledge, and above all its material- and practice-based methods of enquiry.[35] Across the thousands of pages of Leonardo da Vinci's notebooks, this artist's central tenet was that the wisdom of books at the centre of Renaissance humanism must be measured by the knowledge of practical experience. In this regard, as Smith has argued for the history of early modern science, the artist's view was a determining one for the inauguration of modern scientific method, in its accord with the primacy of visual or demonstrable forms of knowledge. In Smith's terms as in Leonardo's, this workshop know-how founded in artisanal cultures of experiment, dependent on *technē* or 'how-to' memory over the scholastic *logos* of books, drove vast epistemic shifts in early modern scientific thought and understanding. It was the rising artisanal knowledge of glass-making that led the development of precision-cut lenses and optical mirrors, for example, which Galileo would both make himself and use in his telescope, so recasting a nascent scientific modernity within the practice-based conduct of early modern optical manufactures.

Smith's argument lends weight to a material or technological historical determinism in the formation of the new scientific observational methods of early modernity. From the artisanal philosophy of Leonardo to René Descartes' celebrated encomium of 'mechanical knowledge', or the central place of the experimental method in the advancement of all forms of enquiry, what was at stake is what we now recognise as the emergence of modern scientific methods over a medieval scholasticism. Across myriad domains of enquiry, the mirror became the sign of the probing intellect or the light of the mind. A material allegory lost to us today, it signified the artefactual function of the mirror as the locus of reflected light for the purposes of all forms of study in a pre-electric age, as historians of the decorative arts and domestic interiors have best elucidated.[36] In the work of intellectual historians such as Debora Shuger, following Gusdorf and Grabes in an analysis of textual references to mirrors pertaining to her larger study of Renaissance 'habits of thought', the burgeoning fifteenth-century technology of the glass mirror as the material emblem and instrument of a newfound source of light and so reflection may weigh as significantly in the constitution of 'Renaissance' cultures as a Burckhardtian 'individualism' or the economic determinism of a Weberian proto-capitalism.[37] It has been literary scholars and intellectual historians of early modernity who have most fully acknowledged the fecundity of the mirror metaphor as the sign of light, vision, reflection, and so of thought itself, framed in the figure of the '*imago*'. As this book discloses, the metaphor of the mirror-image is suffused throughout the painting and visual culture of early modernity, to acknowledge the centrality of this figurative paradigm. In Foucault's celebrated description of Velazquez' painted mirror-image, *Las Meninas,* it was words and things, books and mirrors, epistemes and mechanics, *logos* and *technē,* theory and practice together, which marked the transition to an emerging modernity. It is within this historical web that the Renaissance mirror – as artisanal object, conduit of light, optical sign, emblematic analogy, and, as argued here, reflected image – took on the wealth of cultural significations that made it into early modernity's central allegory of vision, and so of painting, as of knowledge itself.

***

Tracing the cultural, material, and artistic history of the early modern mirror, the interdisciplinary facets of this book's enquiry have determined its prismatic delineation into a sequence of chapters that consider its critical valence within Renaissance cultures variously: as an ornamental artefact, a technology of light, a workshop tool, an instrument of science, a pictorial rebus of illumination and reflection, and a model to the painter's brush. Thus Chapter 1, 'Halls of Mirrors', offers an over-arching discussion of the mirror's early modern conceptualisation as both a material artefact and a metaphor of illumination. To prise open early modernity's perception of an analogy between painting and mirroring, the chapter begins with the concluding monument of the book, the Grande Galerie des Glaces at Versailles. The example of Versailles elucidates the book's analysis of its subject as the relationship of painting to the mirror-image side by side. The chapter traces the early modern conceptualisation of the mirror ranging from princely magnificence and the science of light, the illuminative emblem of all forms of intellectual enquiry, and a metaphor of the soul or psyche within folklore, poetry, theatre, and faith. It further outlines the major contours of the early modern mirror motif across science, literature, philosophy, painting, and decorative art to give a full consideration of the broad parameters of this book's subject within larger intellectual and cultural histories of the period. Offering an artefactual history of the mirror as object, it maps a typology of early modern glass mirrors as variously decorative, scientific, industrial, and instrumental, marked by their ever-increasing quantity, scale, and clarity of vision, from the hand-held leaded blown-glass spheres of the early Renaissance to full-length quick-silver crystalline pier glass at the close of the seventeenth century. Further, the chapter observes the mirror's longer history from archaic usage in metallic forms, and the full cultural spectrum of its many metaphorical associations accrued over such a broad arc of time. It charts widespread developments in early Renaissance glass production, making mirrors newly prolific and so readily available across the fifteenth century as never before, as well as possessed of an evermore brilliant reflective clarity to become the modus of light itself. Acknowledging what intellectual historians such as Gusdorf, Grabes, Shuger, Rorty, and Gasché, following Foucault, have termed an early modern 'Mirror Age', it traces the rising technology of the glass mirror as the instrument of light and reflection across all domains of enquiry. Further, it suggests the mirror's brilliant materiality was perceived to usher in the heightened recognition of an equivalence between the mirror and the image that was foundational to historical development across the arts and sciences alike, so constructing the Renaissance definition of painting as mimesis.

Chapter 2, 'Armorial Mirrors', takes up the inset-mirror motif within early Netherlandish painting in the ambit of van Eyck. The insistent and symbolic representation of inset-mirror reflections in works by Petrus Christus, Metsys, and Memling in emulation of van Eyck indicate a considered artistic theorisation of the image as specular. Bound up with nascent definitions of a 'Netherlandish school' of art as founded in the manner of van Eyck, as Rudolf Preimesberger has argued, the inset mirror-image may be linked etymologically to the old Dutch term for painting as '*schild*', or shield.[38] This elision between painting and the armorial shield, as a specular surface of reflection like a metal mirror, suggests a heraldic cast to the painted inset mirror's historic configuration of fifteenth-century Flemish art in its image. Thus the rebus-like composition of armorial imagery within the painted pageant shield may represent the structuring matrix of the earliest definition of Netherlandish art as a mirror-like *mise-en-abyme*, and its pictorial manifestation in the painted inset-mirror motif inaugurated by the Arnolfini portrait.

Chapter 3, 'The Artist's Mirror', considers the early modern artist's use of mirrors, along with other visual aids, in both art theory and artistic practice. A field of art-historical analysis brought to prominence by David Hockney's acclaimed if highly controversial book, *Secret Knowledge* (2001), this entails the study of early modern optical or mirror-based artistic technologies as a mechanism for translating the visible field of three dimensions into the two-dimensional plane of painting.[39] Such devices were broadly used in all forms of land and architectural survey drawing, from military reconnaissance to early modern cartographic science and the subsequent astronomical 'mapping' of the heavens. Early Renaissance treatises on art recommended the use of mirrors as painters' aids in the accurate 'mapping' of illusionistic spatial recession, from Filarete's description of Brunelleschi's methods of perspectival rendering to Leonardo's full consideration of the mirror within painting as the 'master of art'. The mirror reflection became an acknowledged method of Renaissance artistic training precisely because it united theory with practice, just as Leonardo had argued. This is nowhere more self-evident than in what Joseph Koerner has termed 'the moment of self-portraiture' c. 1500.[40] Tellingly, this new genre of art was not known as self-portraiture until the nineteenth century; instead, it was identified in terms of the self-reflective manner of its making: '*eim spighel*' or '*allo specchio*', by means of the mirror. This intellectual firmament of artistic theory in practice reaches its fullest expression in Velazquez' *Las Meninas*, as a mirror-image portrait of the artist in the act of painting.

Chapter 4, 'Specular Sciences', analyses the relationship between specular 'truth' and optical 'illusion' in the scientific domain. It considers the new-found status of optical imagery within the observational sciences of early modernity, defined by the advent of its instruments of lens- and mirror-magnified vision, the telescope and the microscope. Just as Galileo upended the surveyor's field telescope to chart the heavens, Robert Hooke unveiled the highly detailed imagery of the microscope's magnified view. As the visible proof of scientific discovery, the mirror-image similarly laid new claims to a demonstrable verity. The chapter brings together the observational antecedents to the closely related development of the telescope and the microscope in a range of sixteenth- and seventeenth-century specular or lens-based optical instruments of vision that reconfigured artistic as well as scientific sight. The new-found vision of the optical image paved the way to an ever-greater artistic instrumentation of mimetic accuracy, but also to its 'mirror-image' double, in the extreme perspectival distortions of 'trick imagery' such as anamorphosis. This configured all manner of ludic perspectival imagery alongside trick mirrors, from the mirror-display cabinetry of the *Wunderkammer* and the Dutch *perspectyfkas* to the anamorphic picture-puzzle of Holbein's *Ambassadors*, in an early modern emblematics of optical ingenuity as pictorial wit.

Chapter 5, 'The Mirrors of Venus', considers the closely intertwined pictorial relationship between the painted representation of the mirror reflection and the female nude in High Renaissance art, from Giorgione's *bella donna* at her toilet to the Rokeby Venus. From sixteenth-century Venice to Madrid as to Rome, Paris, and Fontainebleau, across Germany and Flanders, depictions of inset mirror-images were both accompaniments to and metaphors of the perceived artistic beauty of the female form. Together, the female nude and its reflection in the mirror allegorised a newly conceived theorisation of art in terms of visual beauty. As a consequence, the mirror reflection was linked to depictions of love and desire of all kinds, from the venereal to the marital. A metaphor of beauty within the social rituals of courtship and marriage, it was displayed within painting and print as well as myriad domestic decorative arts. Yet within this imagery lay a paradoxical conceit. As in a mirror reflection, the beauty of youth was transient and fleeting, as evanescent as the passage of time. Thus the representation of love, youth, and beauty as mirror-like became a pictorial metaphor of *vanitas*, or the spiritual passing of all worldly things, like the illusionistic image of Narcissus in Ovid's shimmering pool. If, on the one hand, the allegorical relationship between the female nude and the mirror reflection was an emblem of art's beauty, yet the sign was a fully bivalent one that also contained within it the presentiment of its fleeting evanescence.

The book's conclusion draws together the cultural trope of pictorial reflection to adumbrate the future history of the early modern mirror-image within painting through modernism's refractive lens. As the ocular model for the *camera obscura*, the mirror as the figure of vision compasses an intellectual history that spans not only the subsequent development of photography but, taking a leaf from Jonathan Crary, the instrumentation of early modern visuality more broadly.[41] At the same time, the Conclusion traces a radical shift in the conception of the mirror motif as the paradigmatic early modern sign of the intellect in Cartesian mode that Stoichita posited. In the wake of the Hall of Mirrors at Versailles, the subsequent rise of the early eighteenth-century Rococo decorative mirror interior instead suggested new contiguities between painting and mirroring as interrelated forms of pictorial ornament. The mirror was not only the matrix of eighteenth-century painting, but fully its equivalent, with the introduction of large-scale halls of mirrors that could seemingly 'replace' painting entirely.

Collectively, the chapters offer a fully interdisciplinary consideration of the mirror-image as the figurative representation of the early modern visual field. Together they address the analogy between painting and mirroring as it was argued in Renaissance art theory, demonstrated in art practice, and represented in painting itself. The book takes up a double focus, between art-making and art-viewing, to argue that an early modern conceptual elision of the picture plane with the mirror reflection conflated the surface of painting with the instrument of its own mimesis. The contextualising histories advanced across the different chapters elucidate an early modern conceptualisation of the mirror metaphor as the instrument of all forms of knowledge. This is to enable a deeper analysis of the specular configuration of painting and its emblematic manifestations in literature, science, and art. Tracing the mirror-image through a range of cultural contexts, it concludes with the artist's mirror as the very image of 'art' itself. Both in the studio and in artistic representation, it argues, the mirror reflection was the method and the definition of Renaissance painting. It is the early modern conception of a perceived equivalence between painting and mirroring, manifest across all domains of visual knowledge, that forms the subject of this book.

NOTES

1 Leon Battista Alberti, *Della pittura*, and in Latin, *De pictura*. On the extant autograph Alberti manuscripts in both Italian and Latin, see Grayson, 1968; Rocco Sinisgalli's introduction in Alberti and Sinisgalli, 2011, 3–14; and the further discussion with bibliography in Chapter 3. Alberti's *De pictura* was first published in Latin in Basel in 1540, and thereafter was translated by others into sixteenth-century publications in various languages, including Italian, from the 1540 Latin edition rather than Alberti's ms. in Italian. Published editions of Alberti's manuscript in Italian date from the late eighteenth century. In the interests of clarity I have cited from John Spencer's widely used English translation from the Italian: Alberti and Spencer, [1436] 1966. The manuscripts at the Biblioteca Nazionale Centrale Firenze are usually regarded as the leading autograph ms.: https://archive.org/details/fondo-nazionale-ii.-iv.-38/page/n299/mode/2upfols.119v-136v and II.VIII.58 (Bargiacchi). Throughout, I have otherwise sought to work with first or early editions of the early modern texts under discussion in this book, many of which are now available online and therefore easier to consult than the twentieth-century critical editions that have for long stood as standard references. All translations are my own unless otherwise stated, though greatly indebted to the rich history of their scholarly translation.

2 The classic scholarship on mimesis derives from Auerbach's literary study [1946] trans. 1953; from an extensive literature see further Halliwell, 2002; Taussig, 1993; Girard, 2008; Potolsky, 2006. With respect to early modern art, see the classic essay by Marin, 1994.

3 Ovid, *Metamorphoses*, III: 356–510, 'Narcissus and Echo'. The translation at the outset of the chapter is Melville's, 1986. On the Ovidian legacy, see Consolino, 2022.

4 Alberti, 1966, 64. On the Narcissus myth in the history of art, with particular relevance to this study: Damisch, 1976; Damisch, 2010; Elsner, 1996; Frontisi-Ducroux and Vernant, 1997; Hardie, 2002; Baskins, 1993; Wolf, 1998; Kruse, 1999; Pfisterer, 2001; Bätschmann, 2013.

5 Horace, *Ars poetica*.
6 Hardie, 2002, 152–53.
7 Philostratus, *Imagines*, I:23; Rima, 2012, for a full discussion of the poetic theme of the literary art gallery.
8 Benvenuto Cellini, letter to Benedetto Varchi, 28 June 1546, published in Varchi, 1549, 152–54, with the further texts and letters pertaining to Varchi's disquisition on the *paragone* between painting and sculpture.
9 Hendler, 2010; see further Nova, 2003; Cole, 2002.
10 Pino, 1548, 5; see Bouvrande, 2017, on Pino and Alberti.
11 Alberti, 1966, 63.
12 Alberti, 1966, 56; on which see Masheck, 1991. On the mimetic concept of art as a window view, Ringbom, 1984; Wajcman, 2004. See the further discussion in Chapter 3.
13 Fried, 2010; Belting, 1994; Stoichita, 1997; Wolf, 2002.
14 Stoichita, 1997.
15 Stoichita, 1993; 1997; Pericolo, 2015, 11. See further Bokody, 2015; and Bokody and Nagel, 2020.
16 Abel, 1963. See further Fischer and Greiner, 2007.
17 Arasse, 1984; Chastel, 1967; Arasse, 1992, trans. 2013. See further, in addition to the references above, Fried, 2010 and Stoichita, 1997, as among the most celebrated studies within early modern art history; Warwick, 2016; and the instrumental texts of Vodret, 2010; Borel, 2002; Miller, 1998; De Vecchi, 1990; Bialostocki, 1988; Hartlaub, 1951. On the painted inset mirror image, see further Georgel and Lecoq, 1982; and more recently Portús, 2017, who have extended the concept into the medium of the gallery exhibition, the first reaching into modern art while the second considers the pictorial motif within the compass of Spanish art exclusively.
18 On the art-historical figuration of *mise-en-abyme* writ large, see especially Bal, 1978.
19 Dällenbach, 1977, which opens with discussion of a journal reference by André Gide of 1893 on the mirror in early modern painting from Massys to *Las Meninas* alongside Shakespeare, then applied to a study of the *nouveau roman*.
20 According to the French court heraldist, Ménestrier, 1691, 19: 'celle qui est au milieu est dite etre en abime'. On its late medieval codification, Bartolo di Sasso, *De insigniis et armis*, c. 1350; on which see Ramsay, 2022.
21 Scarron, 1651; De Cervantes, 1615; De Cervantes, 1605; Kyd, 1592; Corneille, 1639. See also Kowzan, 2006; Witt, 1975, on the Elizabethan and Stuart court masque, in which the court was in disguise as its mirror-image
22 Shakespeare, 1623, *The Tempest*, 1:2, gathers up the disjointed and illusory memories from the play's various characters of their lives before the storm. Seeking to recall their lost memories, Prospero asks: 'what seest thou else in the … abysm of time'?, so linking the figuration of limitless spatial recession with the ceaseless passing of time. See further Trimble, 2006.
23 Isidore of Seville, II, book 13, ch. 20, 'De Abysso', 1. On the Greek etymological derivation, Chantraine, 1968, I:201.
24 Comenius, [1657] 1907, 41, uses a mirror analogy throughout for the myriad powers of memory and the mind. See further Jechova, 1994.
25 Gusdorf, 1956; Grabes, [1973] 2009; Rorty, 1979; Gasché, 1986.
26 Droth et al., 2008, 40. See also Leoncini, 2022; Bruno, 2015; Magnani, 1988 and 2006.
27 Gombrich, 1960; Gombrich, 1975; Alpers, 1983a; Bryson, 1983.
28 Panofsky, [1927] 1991. See also Arasse, 2002; Damisch, [1987] 1995.
29 In a study that runs across disciplinary boundaries, artistic cultures, and geographies, bibliographic citations can only capture essential referencing, which readers may then extend more deeply.
30 Art history according to a wider definition is John Onians' phrase, in his opening editorial for the newly founded journal of *Art History* in 1978; see further Warwick with Adamson, 2013.
31 Daston, 2015. See further Chapter 4.
32 Alpers, 1983a.
33 Michel Foucault's celebrated analysis of *Las Meninas* as a painting of cascading reflection, 1964, then 1966 as the introduction to *Les mots et les choses*, trans. 1970, understood the figure of the nested self-reflexive image or inset mirror as the prevailing trope of early modernity's cultural manifestations, and which has generated an extensive literature; see the further discussion in Chapter 3.
34 Rorty, 1979; Gasché, 1986.
35 Smith, 2018; Falguières, 2006. See further the anthology by Anderson et al., 2014; and O'Malley and Welch, 2010.
36 Thornton, 1997; Thornton, 1991.
37 Shuger, 1998; Shuger, 1997. See the further discussion of Burckhardt's *persönlichkeit* in Chapter 3; and Warwick, 2021.
38 Preimesberger, 2011, 46.
39 Hockney, 2001. See also the corrective reviews, particularly Dupré, 2005.
40 The phrase is Koerner's, 1993.
41 Crary, 1990.

Chapter 1

HALLS OF MIRRORS

[I]t is as if the mirrors paint themselves. The mirrors make paintings so true to life and so brilliant as to delight and dazzle the eye in equal measure.

—JEAN-AYMAR PIGANIOL DE LA FORCE, *NOUVELLE DESCRIPTION DES CHÂTEAUX ET PARCS DE VERSAILLES ET DE MARLY*, PARIS, 1702

Mirrors, the narrated effects of which we would view as a fairy tale and a wonderment far beyond belief . . . mirrors form pictures in which imitation is so perfect that it equals nature itself in the illusion it creates before our eyes.

—ETIENNE LA FONT DE SAINT-YENNE, *RÉFLEXIONS SUR QUELQUES CAUSES DE L'ÉTAT PRÉSENT DE LA PEINTURE EN FRANCE AVEC UN EXAMEN DES PRINCIPAUX OUVRAGES EXPOSÉS AU LOUVRE LE MOIS D'AOÛT 1746*, PARIS, 1747

I. VERSAILLES

In the December 1684 issue of the Parisian monthly gazette, *Le Mercure Galant*, a lengthy review article celebrated the recent opening of the Grande Galerie de Versailles, or Galerie des Glaces as it would later become known (Fig. 5). Written under the nom de plume of 'M. Lorne, *peintre*', the essay was in fact

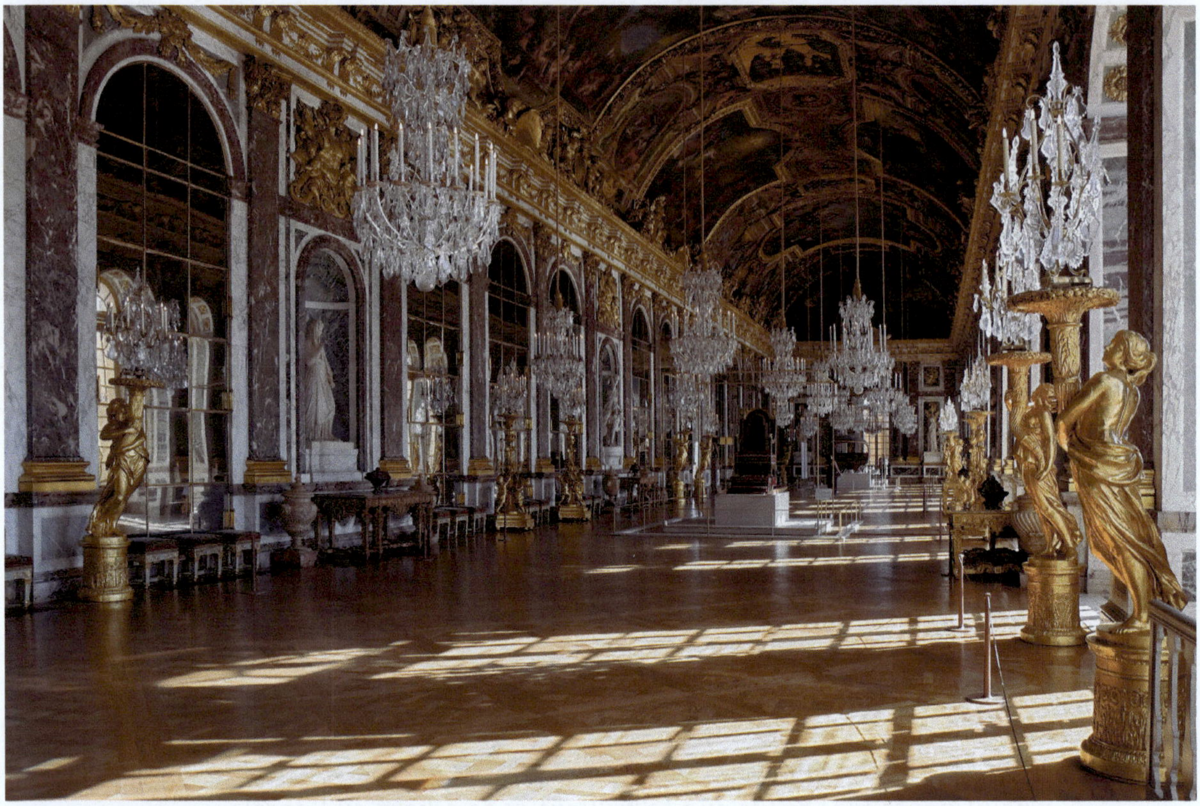

Fig. 5 Jules Hardouin-Mansart, Grande Galerie des Glaces, Château de Versailles, 1678–84.
Photo: Wikimedia

by the King's painter, academician, and decorator of this gallery's vast ceiling, Charles Le Brun, in praise and explication of his own work (Fig. 6).[1] Over the preceding few years the *Mercure*, as the official review of culture and the arts under the auspices of Louis XIV since its foundation in 1672, had published intermittent reports on the progress of the Galerie at Versailles, as with all other projects of the crown. Le Brun's text was entirely devoted to the allegorical elaboration of his painted history of Louis' rule, narrated across the great ceiling vault of the Galerie. His ceiling constituted a pictorial emulation of such panegyrics of monarchy as Rubens' cycle for Marie de Médicis and (though never completed) her husband Henri IV. The historic innovation of the Versailles Galerie, however, was the displacement of painting from its walls in favour of mirrors. For the back wall of the Grande Galerie, distinct from the painted or marbled surfaces of its architectural forebears, was instead lined with an arcade of fictive arches, each panelled with mirrors, facing onto the correspondingly arched windows overlooking the gardens.[2] As the royal historiographer, Jean-Aymar Piganiol de la Force, described in his illustrated guide book to Versailles of 1702: 'the windows of this gallery were made with such art, and placed so ingeniously to face the landscape, it is as if the mirrors paint themselves. The mirrors make paintings so true to life and so brilliant as to delight and dazzle the eye in equal measure.'[3]

To the Parisian art critic Etienne La Font de Saint-Yenne, in his considered *Réflexions sur la peinture* of 1747, such mirrored surfaces were also a source of wonderment that could rival, even surpass painting, for their capacities of imitation. Writing over half a century after the opening of

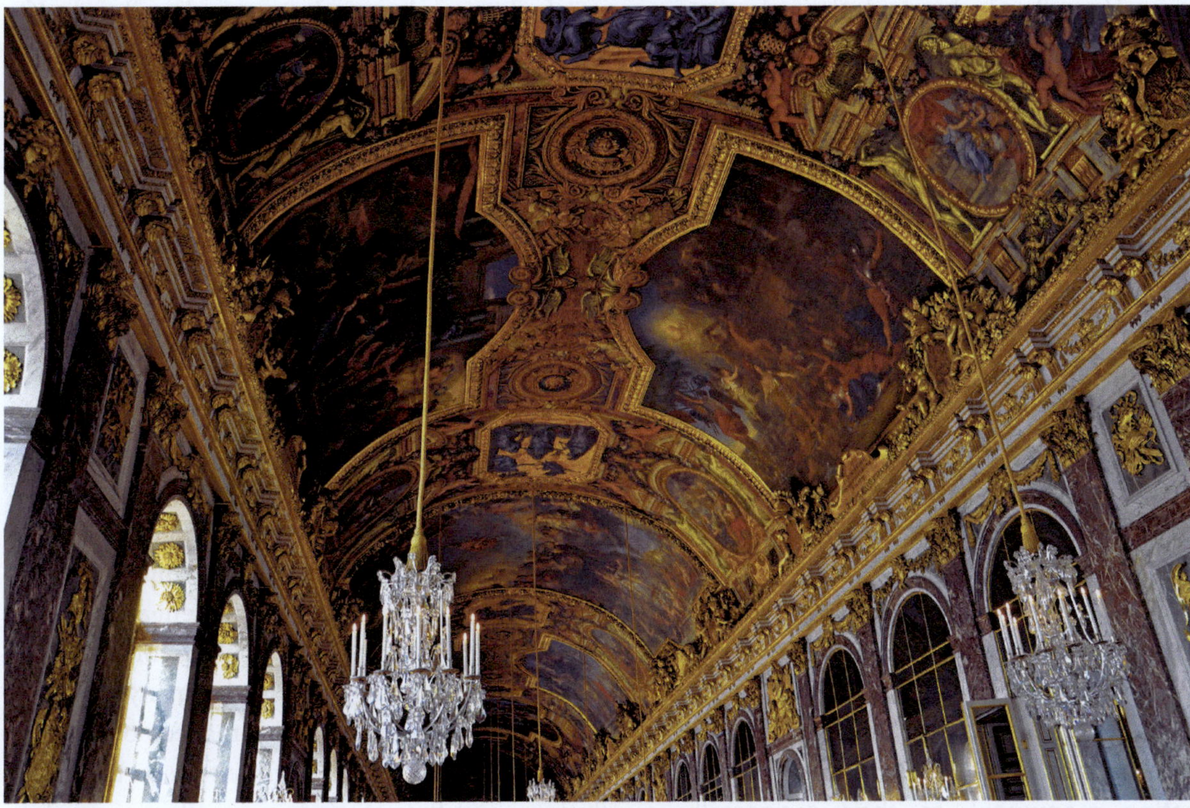

Fig. 6 Charles Le Brun, *Histoire de Louis XIV*, painted ceiling of the Grande Galerie des Glaces, Château de Versailles, 1678–86.
Photo: Wikimedia

the Galerie at Versailles, La Font de Saint-Yenne reflected critically on the usurpation of painting by mirrors in the 'Rococo' interiors that would sweep through the subsequent decoration of Versailles, other royal residences, eighteenth-century Parisian *hôtels*, and across the courts and palaces of Europe. La Font de Saint-Yenne readily perceived the intervention of the mirror-image in its transformation not only of the history of interior decoration but of painting itself. For if the mirror was deployed as a decorative replacement for painting, as at the Galerie of Versailles, then its reflected image had come to be seen as a specular simulacrum of painting's subject. At Versailles, the reflected image of the king in the Grande Galerie in his capacity as head of state in reception of foreign embassies, or the fêtes that marked royal dynastic marriage alliances and births, was a veritable counterpart to the painted images of Le Brun's ceiling above, celebrating the chief events of his reign. Painting and mirroring were thus sister arts in the encomia of the *grande manière* of the king and of history painting, defined as the illustrious deeds of great men. In the Parisian Rococo interior, however, as La Font de Saint-Yenne saw, the subject of the mirror reflection became instead that of *petit genre*. Albeit of the heightened civility of aristocratic pastimes, yet the effect of the eighteenth-century mirror interiors inaugurated by the Grande Galerie would, in his view, alter the course of painting from the grandeur of history to *petits sujets*.[4] What Paganiol and La Font de Saint-Yenne's commentary capture so powerfully is the question of the relationship between painting and mirroring, which the

Galerie at Versailles had posed through their comparative juxtaposition. Like the structuring matrix of the decorative order in the Galerie at Versailles, La Font's critical perception rested on a long-standing art-historical realisation of a conceptual equivalence between painting and mimetic mirroring manifest in the earliest theoretical treatises on art of the Renaissance inaugurated by Leon Battista Alberti's *Della pittura*. As Le Brun would also acknowledge, albeit through a considered variation of painting's illusionistic space projected onto the ceiling vault of the Galerie, painting and mirroring were commensurate forms of the Albertian specular view of art.[5]

Marking the transition to a new historical episteme for the mirror as the centrepiece of a decorative order in what would become the eighteenth-century Rococo interior, yet the Grande Galerie may also be understood as the culminating monument of their reciprocally mimetic 'Baroque' comparison. Analysis of the Grande Galerie thus rests on a full consideration of the early modern mirror in its ontology, both as a material object and as a cultural metaphor, as an artefact and as an idea. This chapter therefore divides into two parts, the first concerned with Versailles, the second with the cultural significances of the mirror. For the example of Versailles prizes open the complex cultural relations of the early modern mirror-image across a prismatic enquiry that ranges from a politics and science of light, illumination, and reflection within the spatial forms of architecture, the emblematic 'mirror reflection' of the intellect and the psyche, and its related if deeply bivalent conceptualisation as an instrument of mimesis and illusion. The mirror itself is therefore the subject, as an object and as an allegory of illumination. Across the temporal cusps of late medieval, Renaissance, and early modern conceptualisations of reflection in both word and image, the mirror was the sign of the intellect as of the psyche, and so of thought itself. To address the larger cultural parameters of the early modern mirror metaphor through its interrelated facets, which range across disciplinary as well as geographical boundaries, constitutes a vast intellectual history of the specular image.[6] The example of Versailles as the Baroque apogee of this confluence between painting and mirroring thus opens up to consideration the early modern mirror's broader histories. In its exacting mimetic reflection of the visible field the mirror-image was perceived as an optical instrument of illusion, just like painting, in which the world was both impalpably present and absent. Tracing the early modern mirror-image metaphor across this chapter is to engage a wide range of cultural contexts: the subject of scientific study in the conduct of light, the many faces of reflections in devotional and romance poetry, the instrument of spectacular light effects in theatre's illusions, and the artist's mirror reflection as the very image of 'art' itself.

THE MIRROR OF PRINCES

Among the vast royal collections inherited by Louis XIV, and in which he took direct interest, was a series of early Renaissance illuminated manuscripts concerned with classical imagery of the 'mirror of princes', or the richly elaborated ancient theme of ideal rule. Some had been prestations to Charles VI and Queen Isabeau of France, others descended from the dukes of Burgundy, as a cadet line of the Valois monarchy, including early fifteenth-century manuscripts from the ambit of Jan van Eyck. Manuscript illumination was an art form much favoured by the dukes of Burgundy, van Eyck's patrons, in which the painter was likely first trained, and which flourished to an exceptional degree at the Burgundian court. It was also one which Louis XIV particularly heralded as a historic manifestation of French royal lineage and dominion, as both a collector and a patron. Among them were a number of celebrated manuscripts on good government that included depictions of painted inset mirrors as emblems of royal wisdom. In Christine de Pizan's celebrated *Cité des dames* of 1405, Reason, alongside further personifications of regal virtue such as Rectitude and Justice, was configured with a tondo mirror upheld in her hand as the sign of tempered reflection and a cardinal virtue of monarchy.[7] Within the narrative conventions of panegyric this literary convention would also, much later, underpin Rubens' Marie de Médicis cycle for the Palais du Luxembourg and its intended counterpart of the life of Henri IV. Based on antique literary texts of exemplary virtue as prototypes, this was a genre of both literature and art titled *speculum principis*, or the 'mirror of princes', that would flourish across antiquity, the Middle Ages, and Renaissance with a major efflorescence in the Baroque.[8] It took many forms, from treatises written to princes upon accession to their throne to urge wisdom, fine judgment, and just rule, to political tracts on the exercise of power as the manifestation of magnificence, to encomiastic celebrations of the great deeds of their reign in both word and image. Such painted panegyrics of princely rule would reach an apogee across seventeenth-century court decoration, from Pietro da Cortona's Barberini ceiling in Rome to Rubens' London Whitehall ceilings. This is also the *topos* of Le Brun's heroic *Histoire du roi* series for the vault of the Grande Galerie at Versailles, and indeed the larger decoration of all royal residences under Louis XIV, as pictorial manifestations of his grandeur.

Le Brun's painted *speculum principis* took its place alongside the specular ornamentation of the Galerie's mirror arcades as an allegory of royal magnificence within the matrix of architecture and the decorative arts. Along the length of the gallery, the correspondence of mirror- and window-arcades forged a new decorative order of specular splendour predicated on the brilliance of natural light redoubled through its mirror reflection.[9] This association of the mirror with the enhancement of light was long-standing, in its capacities as an instrument and so emblem of reflection that was, from antiquity, read in cosmic allegories of the sun. The Galerie's display of specular light as an emblem of royalty was further heightened by myriad gilt chandeliers and wall sconces, magnified in their cut-crystal prism pendants. In the words of its illustrious literary visitors: 'This beautiful gallery is like a luminous walkway, lit as if by the sun itself, whose mirrors lend further perspectives that redouble its size' (Fig. 7).[10] 'The mirrors are counterfeit windows facing the real ones, and multiply this hall a million times over so that it seems almost infinite.... The lights are a thousand times redoubled in the mirrors, to form perspectives as brilliant as fire.'[11] '[The enfilade] appears of an infinite length; imagine the éclat of a hundred thousand candles . . . a July sun is less radiant.'[12] In the brilliant light of Louis' mirrors, the grandeur of the gallery was itself multiplied infinitely to form a specular cascade of glittering reflection.

As contemporaries also noted, the display of thousands of candles (at vast expense) in the Galerie's sconces and chandeliers was multiplied by their light reflection in the great mirrors of the hall.[13] For state receptions this brilliance was enhanced by the disposition of Louis' magnificent silver furnishings, no longer extant but known from descriptions in the *Mercure Galant*, as well as paintings and prints of state receptions such as the embassies of Genoa in 1685 and Siam in 1686. The display of princely silver included rows of gleaming chased vases, ewers, coffers, braziers, andirons, gilt caryatid torchères, and girandole candelabra, as well as tables inlaid with gold and precious stones along the Galerie walls. This sumptuous display culminated in the king's silver throne to signify Louis' magnificence (Fig. 8).[14] Among the king's gifts to the Siamese ambassadors were five

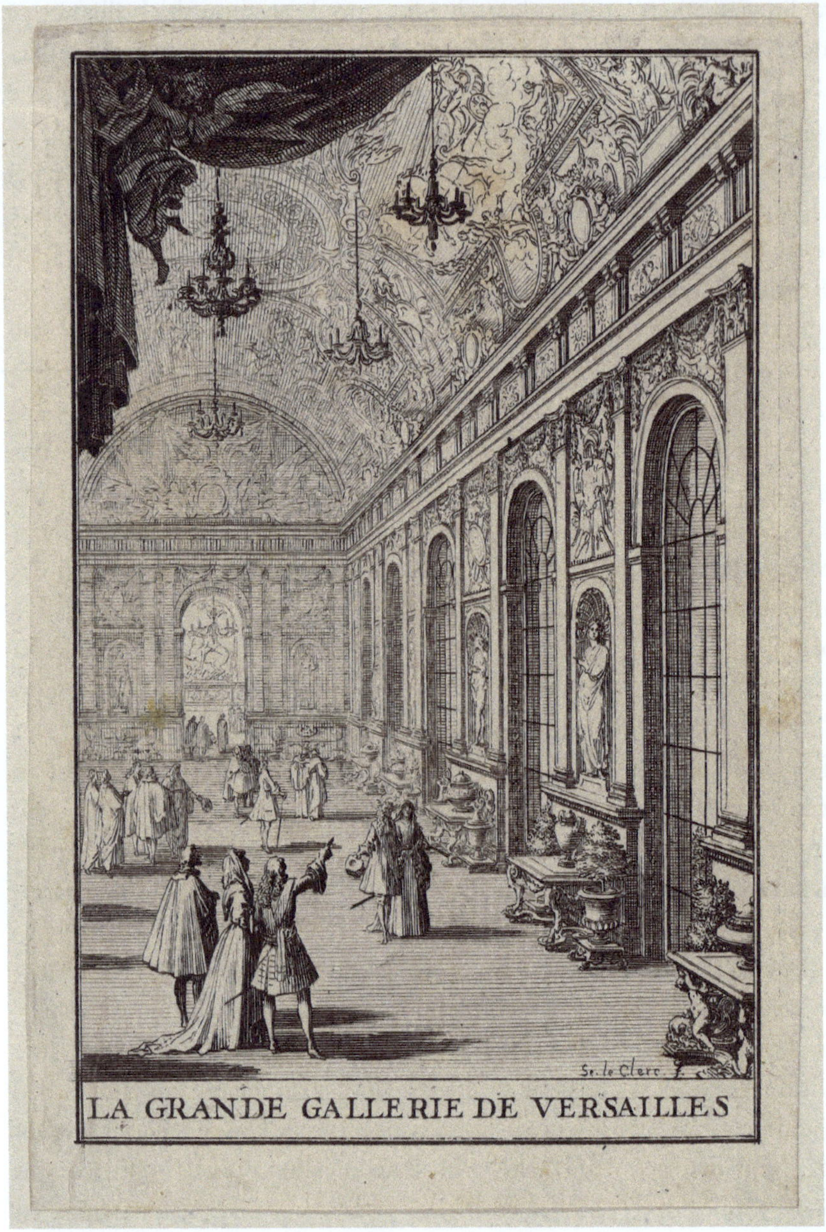

Fig. 7 Sébastien Le Clerc, *La Grande Gallerie de Versailles*, frontispiece to Madeleine de Scudéry, *Conversations*, I, 1684, etching, 15.5 × 10.2 cm.
Photo: Metropolitan Museum of Art

rock-crystal mirrors in richly worked crystal frames, as tokens of his '*splendeur*'.[15]

The king himself appeared dressed in a robe of spun-gold silk encrusted with diamonds as a further manifestation of his own devise, the sun. While the epithet of 'Sun King' was a nineteenth-century appellation for Louis XIV, yet the image of the sun was the king's chosen emblem from the inception of his personal rule in 1661 and the decision to move the court to Versailles, thus inextricably linked with the grandeur of this palace.[16] These lustrous textiles and furnishings amplified the rich effects of the Galerie's gilt architectural ornament: garlands of flowers and fruit, roses, crowns, royal devises, and trophies of arms, as well as its display of antique sculptures of sparkling crystalline white marble and rich polychrome portrait busts.[17] The painted colours of Le Brun's gallery vault are throughout of the most precious and lustrous pigments, particularly

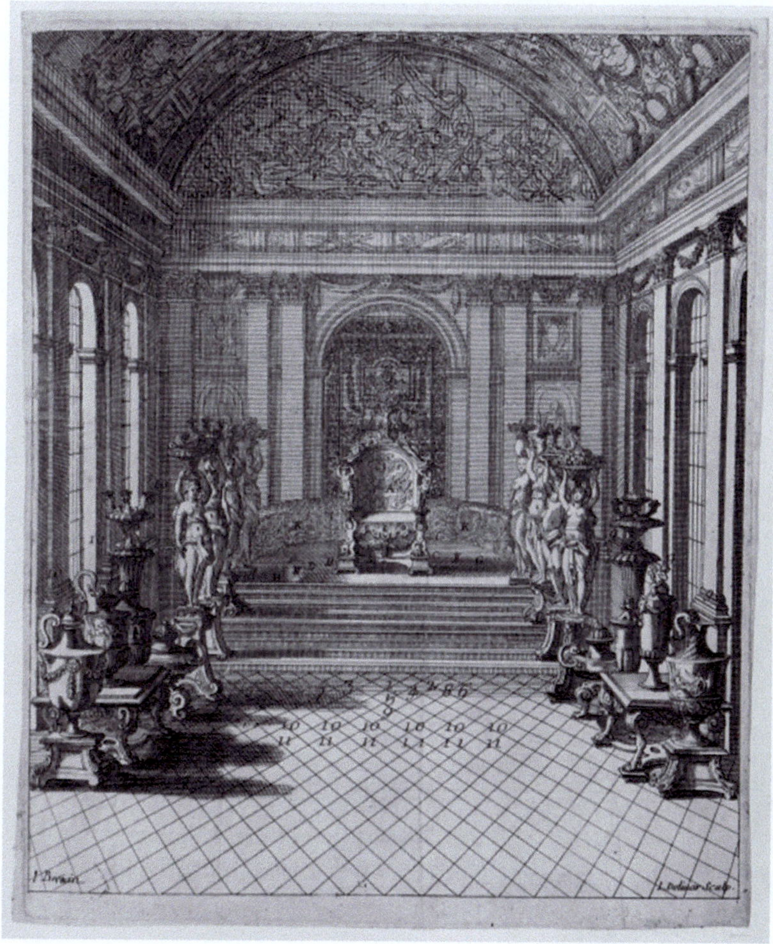

Fig. 8 Juan Dolivar (after Jean Berain), *Grande Galerie with Throne and Silver Furnishings*, September 1686 for *Mercure Galant*, engraving, 22.3 × 18.5 cm, Château de Versailles, inv. Gravures 111.
Photo: Réunion des Musées Nationaux

gilt and lapis lazuli, lit by hidden oculi to heighten their éclat.[18] Moreover, Louis' silver and gilt furnishings were themselves surfaces of scintillating light effects, furthered by their secondary reflection in the Galerie mirrors.

Most directly, the Galerie's arcade of mirrors reflected the light of the corresponding bay of windows on the opposite wall. The full-length windows of the Galerie were, in themselves, an architectural innovation of early modernity, dependent on incremental developments in glass-making to facilitate ever-greater panes and thereby increase interior light.[19] To this, the spectacular advent of the Galerie mirror arcades redoubled the fall of natural light within the hall. The mirrors also reflected the window view giving onto the gardens beyond, thus forging a 'landscape' background to the panoply of court ceremony captured in the hall's mirror reflections (Fig. 9).

Immediately beneath the windows of the Galerie, the gardens orchestrated by André Le Nôtre as part of Louis' aggrandisement of the château across the 1660s and '70s comprised a succession of *parterres d'eau*, or reflecting pools, lined with sculptures of Ovidian myth in gilt lead and bronze. These pools reflected the sky above, enhancing the light cast through the palace windows onto the mirrors of the gallery (Fig. 10). The parterres were ornamented with cascading jets of water in a sparkling display of fountains with myriad light refractions in their spray to enhance their luministic effects. Thereafter, canals of water extending into the distance shaped the celebrated perspectival axis of Le Nôtre's garden geometry as viewed from

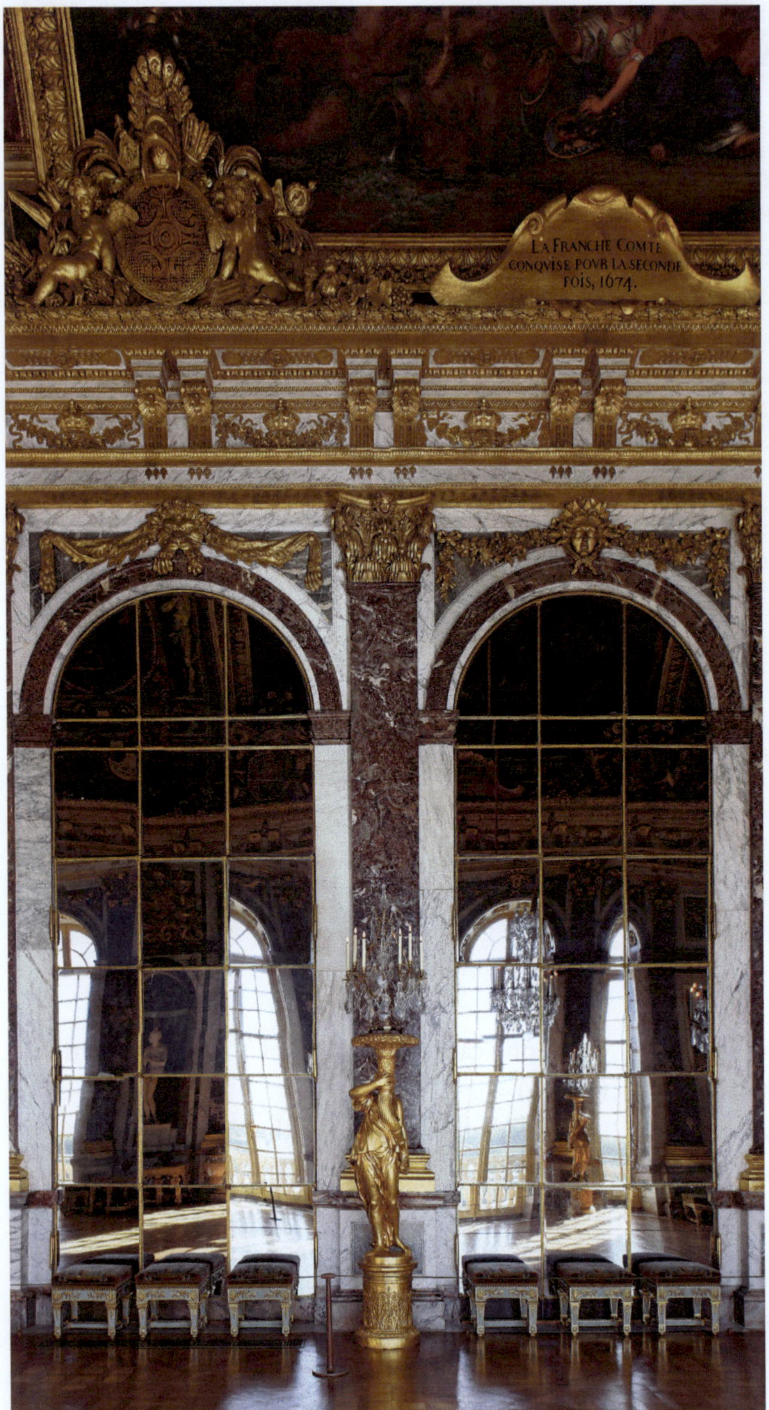

Fig. 9 Jules Hardouin-Mansart, Grande Galerie des Glaces, Château de Versailles, 1678–84.
Photo: Wikimedia

the Galerie windows. Like an Albertian window frame of the landscape, Le Nôtre's *grande allée* rendered the park in terms of a perspectivally framed optical demonstration for the dominion of the royal eye as viewed from the windows of the Grande Galerie. The compass of Le Nôtre's orchestration of the park was that of a monumental landscaped sundial as homage to the Sun King.[20]

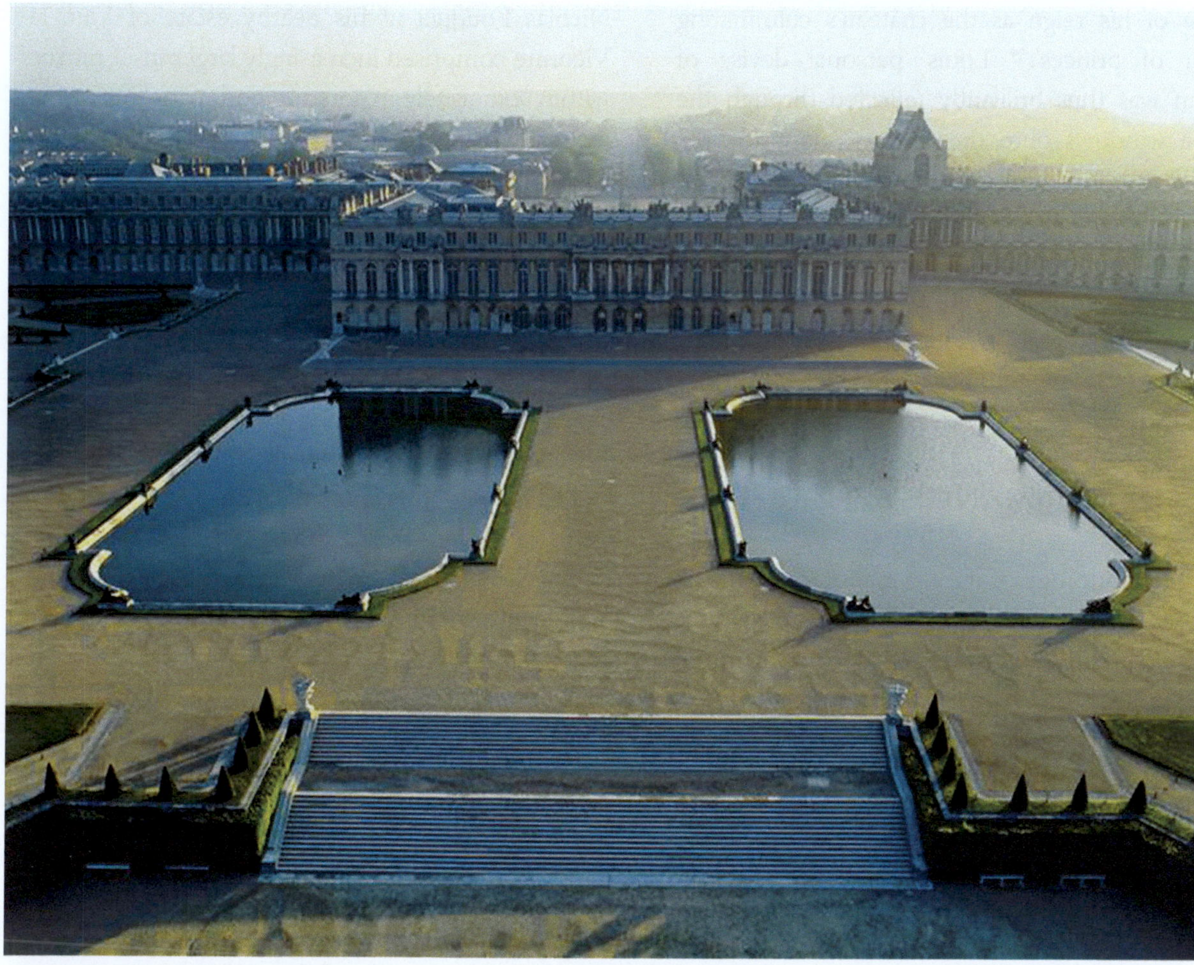

Fig. 10 André Le Nôtre, garden parterres, Château de Versailles, c. 1660s.
Photo: Réunion des Musées Nationaux

The sign of the sun was, of course, an archaic symbol of kingship and divinity as Louis surely knew from studies of Egyptology and myth. Its solar power was understood to reside in its specular reflection, as the source of Promethean fire and of Ceres' harvests. Successive sequences of fountain statuary across the garden elaborated an allegory of Louis as Apollo. The charioteer of the sun, Apollo, drove its course from dawn to dusk across the gardens of Versailles as a metaphor of Louis' *gloire* extending across the world.[21] Within the further apartments of the king's rooms beyond the Galerie, on the north side, a succession of planetary rooms to revolve around the Sun King was also conceived as a *speculum principis* in emulation of the heroic series executed by Pietro da Cortona for the Medici at the Pitti Palace in Florence.[22] The southern apartments were given over to collection cabinets (no longer extant) of the king's chosen treasures for display. These comprised books and cabinet pictures, but also the precious reflective materials so highly prized by Louis – bronze medals and armour, gold and silver filigree, gemstones and carved rock crystal, and mirrors to enhance their display.[23] Throughout, the imagery was of splendour and light, of which the Galerie's mirrors were the fullest manifestation.

Though the documentation does not permit certainty, it was likely the king's own suggestion to supplant painting with the brilliant effects of reflective mirrors in the arcades of his Grande Galerie, while Le Brun's painted ceiling above narrated the *historia* of his reign as the château's culminating 'mirror of princes'.[24] Louis' personal devise of the sun was thus brilliantly reflected through the Galerie windows onto the mirrors, alongside the specular image of himself at court and the painted panegyric above. The Galerie's alignment of mirrors with painting therefore was an architectural manifestation of royal magnificence, their cascading reflections forging an infinite multiplication of the Sun King's resplendent image.[25]

MIRROR MANUFACTURES

The technology of mirror manufacture of the size and scale of the Galerie arcades was a newly-won and much-vaunted accomplishment of the French crown under the astute direction of the king's minister of his personal rule, Jean-Baptiste Colbert.[26] The fashion for mirrors was a long-standing one at the sixteenth-century French court, however, through imports from Italy. Seemingly inaugurated by Queen Catherine de Médici's *cabinet de miroirs* (no longer extant), this dressing room panelled with over a hundred prized Venetian mirrors was considered the acme of princely decorative reflection across Europe. Catherine may have brought the taste for mirror cabinets with her from Italy; although remaining material evidence is elusive, documentary sources suggest there were Italian *camerino* cabinets of this kind already in the fifteenth century. By the sixteenth century, as Anton Francesco Doni described in his 1566 treatise on architecture, he recommended 'a small cabinet faced on all sides with the largest mirrors to be found'. Thus the principle of the mirror cabinet was an established one, even if little material evidence remains. The likelihood is that the mirrors were still very modest in size, and set within an alternating sequence of either painting, textiles, or panelling.[27] In mid-seventeenth-century Paris, both the cabinets of Louis XIV at Versailles and of his finance minister Nicolas Fouquet at his nearby estate of Vaux-le-Vicomte comprised increasingly larger inset mirrors within exquisitely painted wood panelling as an architectural ornament of princely display.[28] Louis XIV's cousin, Anne-Marie Louise d'Orléans, duchess of Montpensier, at both her apartments at the Luxembourg Palace and her country estate at Saint-Fargeau, had installed small dressing cabinets or wardrobes 'all of mirrors'.[29] If the mirror cabinets of queens were intimately associated with their dress and jewels, those of the king and his ministers were for the display of princely collectibles, comprising lightsome precious materials such as crystal, gems, gold, and silver.[30] Such inset-mirror cabinetry presaged its subsequent Rococo dispersion into wall-length interior decoration, following the great *exemplum* of the Galerie des Glaces, as La Font de St Yenne aptly described.

Mirror décor also lent lustre to early modern occasional decoration for princely celebration and entertainment of the French court. The *Gazette de France* reported an evening with dancing at the Hôtel de Chevreuse on 19 February 1633 in the presence of the Queen in which 'the rooms of this sumptuous mansion were lined with silver mirrors and tapestries'.[31] Similarly, André Félibien described a dinner set among mirrors and orange trees as floral ornament in the gardens of Versailles in 1674.[32] At a fête for Anne-Geneviève de Bourbon Duchess of Longueville in May 1651, the walls were decorated with fifty Venetian mirrors 'serving as gracious tableaux' to represent the beautiful figures of the guests. The description speaks to a perception of the mirror reflection as a pictorializing scenography of court life.[33] The extension of such mirror cabinets and courtly ephemeral decorations into a royal mirror gallery was already established with the (no longer extant) Salón de los Espejos at the Alcazar in Madrid, in which gilt-framed mirrors and royal portraits hung side by side along the great walls of this magnificent hall, as orchestrated by Velazquez in his capacity as court decorator.[34] While the Madrid gallery appears to have used mirrors of local manufacture, as the Galerie des Glaces at Versailles would also do, the call in Paris as elsewhere had been, from the early sixteenth century, for the celebrated '*cristallo*' mirrors of the Venetian Murano glass-makers as the acme of princely taste.

The exorbitant expense of importing such foreign luxuries as Venetian mirrors drove a nascent French 'nationalisation' of the arts as part of a broader cultural and economic mercantilist policy under Louis XIV and Colbert, emblematised in the Galeries des Glaces as French mirrors-of-state.[35] In this Colbert was heir to his predecessors, Cardinals Richelieu and Mazarin, for the establishment of those 'nationalising' institutions of French culture embodied in the *académies* and *manufactures* of the crown. This began with the French Academy for language under Louis XIII (of which he would himself become a member), and for painting and sculpture under Louis XIV, to which he would subsequently add academies for the sciences as well as architecture, music, and literature. In addition, in Colbert's role as minister of finance, he established the royal manufactures for the luxury decorative arts and crafts so highly prized by the king, specifically those that were, at the time, costly imports from abroad. This formed part of a larger economic policy of patriotic protectionism and cultivation of the arts at home. Among the most renowned of princely imports were mirrors from Venice, alongside tapestries from Flanders, and fine marquetry for cabinet-making in exotic woods, all of which were then vastly more expensive than painting. Thus, alongside the earlier foundation of the Gobelins for French tapestry-making, Colbert further institutionalised, among a range of such royal productions, the Manufacture royale de glaces de miroirs in 1665. Fostering a culture of technological and scientific advancement in the production of luxury goods, Louis XIV's mirror-glass manufacture would go on to produce what is perceived as one of the key historical advances in their production: the escalating development of wall-length casts for pouring molten glass into flat panes of ever-greater size.[36] An ancient technology in the production of small decorative objects such as beads and cameos, and subsequently of Renaissance ocular lenses, cast glass under Colbert's jurisdiction would be patented in 1688 and thereafter rapidly industrialised for the first time, in its extension to panes for full-length window glazing and wall-sized mirrors. By such means Colbert effectively supplanted the early Renaissance practice of blown-glass window and mirror manufacture by the end of the century. It was this development that facilitated the fabrication of single-pane windows and monumental mirrors for the interior architectural decoration of the early eighteenth-century Rococo interior.[37]

Blown glass was, however, still in use for the royal commission of the mirror panels for the Galerie at Versailles, as also for the windows. Some 70 per cent or more of the original mirror glass is still in situ, which is wholly exceptional in the artefactual history of the early modern mirror. To forge window-length mirror arcades, the blown-glass globes were slit and laid flat before hardening to form flat panes in the Venetian manner. Notwithstanding the exceptional skill of long-acquired artisanal practices in blowing and cutting glass within a craft culture of constant experimentation of glass-making from the late Middle Ages on, these methods of production had precluded larger panes, which became possible only with the industrial development of poured glass methods after 1688. Hence the mirror arcades at Versailles are composed of portrait-sized glass plates knit together by gilt bronze fillets in the form of laurel branches (Fig. 9). Thereafter the quest of French crown mirror production was for incremental technological innovation to produce ever-larger glass panels as manifestations of '*le grand goût*'.

At the same time, there was ever-accelerating demand for the technical skills of glass grinding and polishing, not only for the window and mirror plates of interior décor but also for the developing lenses and instruments of scientific vision that grew up alongside the early modern history of glass manufacture, from late medieval spectacles and magnifying glasses to seventeenth-century microscopes and telescopes. These required exacting scientific precision in the curve of the glass to the finest mathematical calculation. While the specialised skill of the oculist arose as a distinct profession of early modernity, it is also the case that scientists engaged in research on the optics of light reflection such as Galileo, Descartes, and Newton either ground their own lenses or worked in very close collaboration with a highly skilled lens-maker in this crucial aspect of their studies.[38]

Renaissance developments in mirror-silvering also converged on the much longer history of manufacture of metal mirrors, of all sizes and shapes. In the domain of the princely palace interior, the silver or silvered-glass mirror flanked by silver torchères, as at Versailles, was the hallmark of a royal décor.[39] As the metal of the highest reflective brilliance, silver was the preferred material for such luxury decorative mirrors, whether of silvered-metal plate or fronted with glass over a silver foil. Their orchestrated disposition served to augment interior light, of both lit sconces, torches, and chandeliers as well as window light. The use of mirrors and metal reflectors as a method of interior lighting was their chief purpose in an era before electricity, able to reflect and multiply both sunlight and torchlight, as well as the ornamentation of architectural interiors. While the silver furnishings designed for Versailles are no longer extant, they certainly comprised mirrors, which were displayed within the planetary rooms and apartments housing precious objects of the royal collections. A drawing by Le Brun of their design illustrates his early orchestration of their display alongside silver guéridons and above console tables also of silver. Their ornate frames, chased with an abundance of classical ornament, were surmounted by the royal crest (Fig. 11). These were evidently then made to Le Brun's design under the auspices of Girard Debonnaire in 1677 as royal goldsmith and master of the Paris Corporation des orfèvres. Apparently over three metres in height and weighing some 500 kilos each, Debonnaire described them as decorated with 'trophies and festoons of flowers and fruit, a drapery on either side to form a pavilion and above the arms of France within a cartouche surmounted by the crown flanked by angels.[40]

Metal mirrors continued to be used throughout the early modern period alongside glass, particularly for scientific and industrial uses pertaining to the concentration of light for the purposes of smelting and combustion. Generally made of burnished white steel, metal *speculae* might also be 'silvered' in the same way as glass mirrors to achieve more highly reflective surfaces, extending to the use of liquid-silver itself. Because of its inherently composite material nature, mirror-making across the Renaissance remained closely linked to both glass-making and metal-working. This is evident from the complex historical web of guild relations governing their production from the late Middle Ages. Both glass and metal mirrors were forged metamorphically through liquified forms in fiery furnaces, under the sign of Vulcan as the ancient god of armoury and metalwork. Thus the decorative unity of reflective mirrors and picture windows with the silver furnishings and gilt architectural ornament at the Galerie of Versailles was wholly in keeping with the larger history of the ornamental mirror as a decorative object, as an armorial emblem of princely valour, and as a reflector of light. At Louis' visit to the new Royal *manufacture* of mirrors in April 1666, the king was reported to be '*incantato*' – under the spell – of the mirror, whose 'enchantment' he would later bring to the orchestration of his Grande Galerie at Versailles.[41]

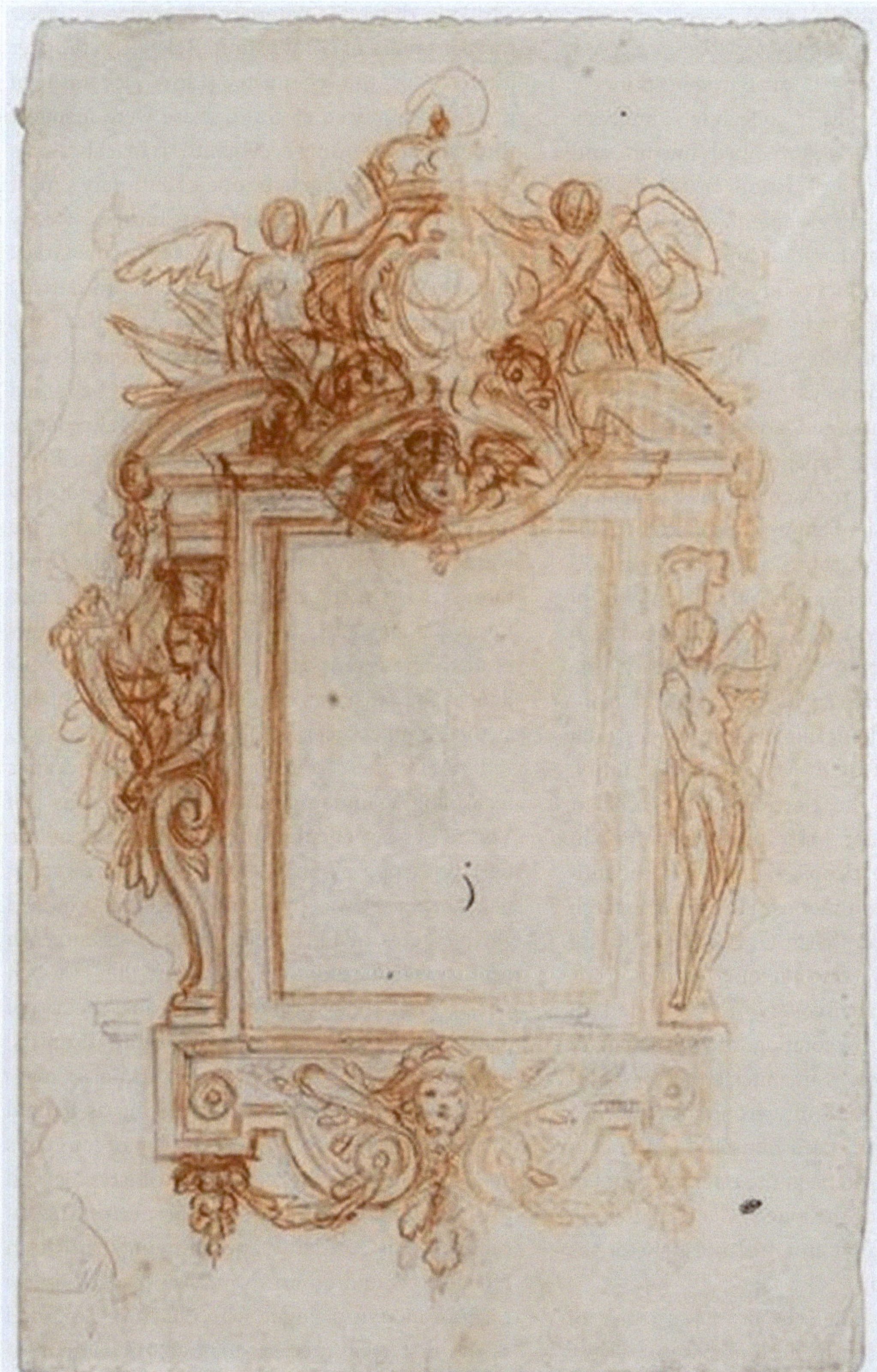

Fig. 11 Charles Le Brun, mirror frame design, c. 1677, red and black chalk drawing, 38.1 × 23.6 cm, Musée du Louvre.
Photo: Musée du Louvre

SPECULUM

As was characteristic of Baroque princely patronage, Louis' collecting interests extended to the newly developed mirror- and glass-lens instruments of vision that led early modern scientific development. These were chiefly telescopes and microscopes, arising out of late medieval optics and spectacle lenses. Astronomy, in particular, was considered the 'science of kings', through its solar and cosmic associations with astrology. Its instruments – astrolabes, quadrants, and above all telescopes made up of different types of glass lenses and mirrors – became royal collectibles made of luxury materials assembled in the collectors' cabinets of the European courts, including France.[42] Along with the establishment of an Academy of Sciences in 1666, Louis and Colbert would also establish the French Royal Observatory the following year, attracting Europe's chief astronomers to become the leading centre for research of the second half of the seventeenth century. Among them was the election of the brilliant Dutch scientist and astronomer Christiaan Huygens, whose telescopic sightings first identified Saturn's ring and moons. Huygens' research was furthered by the Italian G. D. Cassini in the early 1670s as the first director of the Paris Observatory. Their discovery was reflected in the painted ceiling decoration of the planetary rooms at Versailles, a manifestation of royal interest in the progress of astronomical science that the king also practised himself. On the ceiling of the Grande Galerie in the opening panel of the hall, the figure of the king's '*Gloire*' bathed in golden light holds aloft an astrolabe as she drives the king's chariot on.[43]

Louis' personal interests in the science of mirrors also extended to the purchase of a very costly concave or parabolic metal mirror. Termed a '*miroir ardent*', its carefully calculated curve was capable of lighting, igniting, melting, or vitrifying different materials depending on their varying points of combustion. Related to broader interests in the chemistry (and alchemy) of materials practiced at court, these were manifest throughout the king's cabinets.[44] In this Louis doubtless had recourse to one of antiquity's most celebrated accounts of 'burning mirrors' (likely metal shields), apparently deployed by the Greek mathematician Archimedes. Designed to destroy enemy ships at the siege of Syracusa, the story related to Louis' broader interests in naval warfare as well as navigation. A print by Sébastien Leclerc depicts the king's visit to the Académie des sciences in 1671, in which an astrolabe, a telescope, and a burning mirror are on display for his examination, while the view through the windows captures the building of the Royal Observatory in the distance (Fig. 12). His heirs, Louis XV and XVI, would pursue these interests even to the extent of opening up the royal residences for astronomical demonstrations, notably at the Grande Galerie.[45]

It is also the case that the advanced hydraulic technology underpinning the fountains of Versailles was effected through the use of the field telescope as an instrument of land reconnaissance, as it was by Louis' armies, and indeed all the states of Europe by the mid-seventeenth century. [46] These were precisely the years in which Isaac Newton developed his theory of prismatic light refraction in water droplets, informed by the study of mirrors and glass magnifiers, of certain interest to the king as he laid the foundations for the great display of fountains at Versailles and the collection of crystals and prisms illuminated by means of mirrors in his cabinets. His Academy appointment, Christiaan Huygens, would go on to publish his *Treatise on Light* of 1690 in dialogue with Newton. Regarded as the first early modern mathematical theorisation of light rays based on observations of mirror reflections, it was testament to the fecund cultures of research centred on mirrors, optics, and

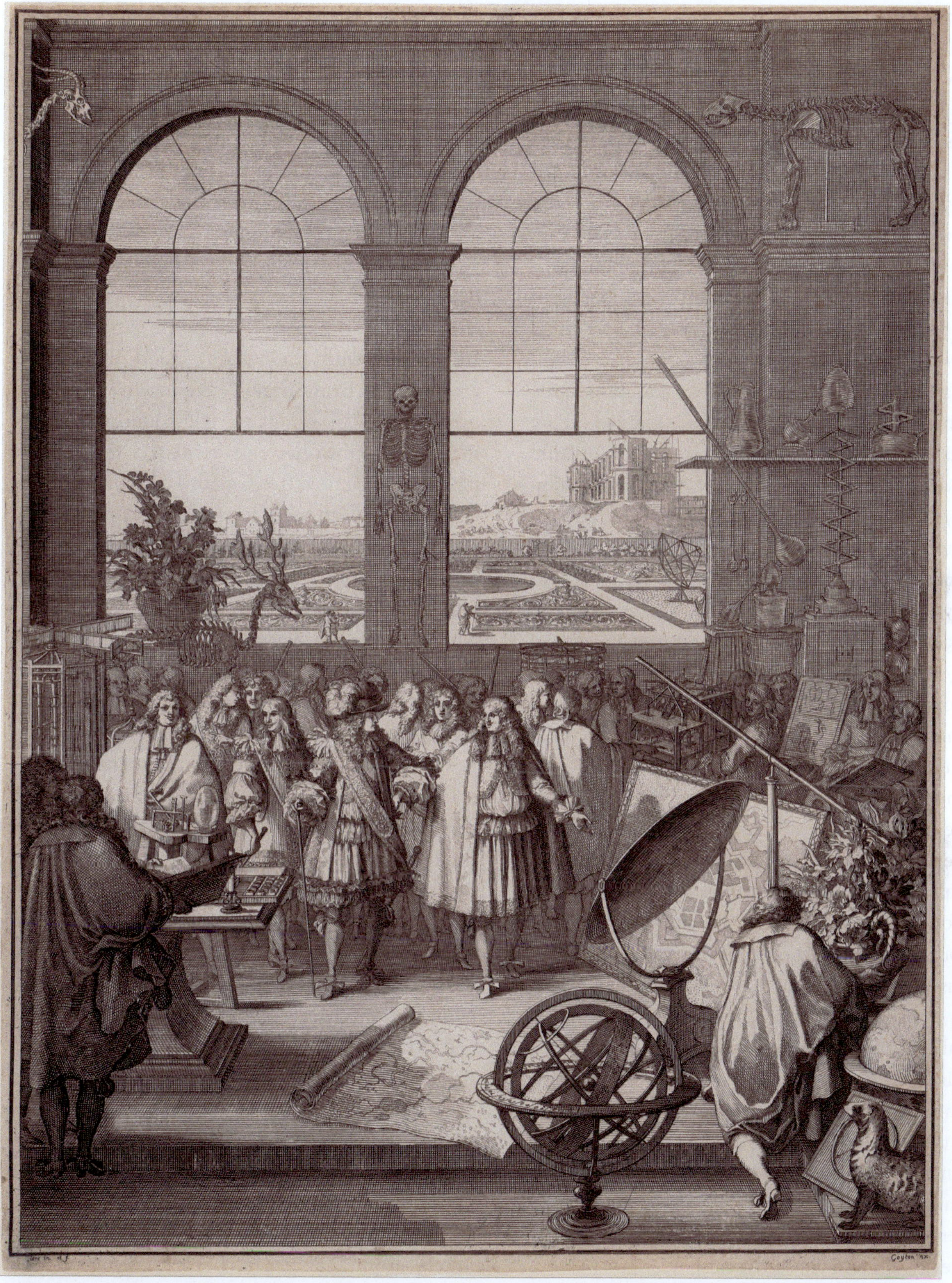

Fig. 12 Sébastien Le Clerc, *Louis XIV Visiting the Royal Academy of Sciences*, 1671, etching, sheet: 41.9 × 30.8 cm.
Photo: Metropolitan Museum of Art

light that nurtured scientific and artistic developments side by side. The nature of this research drew on, and furthered, a rich interplay between catoptrics – the study of the visual effects of reflection through mirrors – with dioptrics – the science of light's passage – instanced in the analytical calculation of its refractions. Thus the 'mirror of princes' took many forms at Versailles, across early modern arts, letters, and sciences.

In the recent spate of publications pertaining to the newly completed conservation of the *'grand décor'* of the Galerie at Versailles, curator and conservator Nicolas Milovanovic drew attention to the restoration's revelation of Le Brun's painted ceiling in its use of colour.[47] Champion of *dessein* within the debates of the Académie de peinture et sculpture, yet the full restoration of Le Brun's colours demonstrated his close interest in their optical effects. Noting the development from the painter's early, modulated use of colour in the manner of a musical harmony of tones following the precepts of his teacher and artistic model, Poussin, Milovanovic argued for a visible shift in Le Brun's compositional matrix. Increasingly structured around a concerted antithesis of lights and darks within an arrangement of colour, it emulated the style of Pietro da Cortona. As Milovanovic further observed, Le Brun's use of colour at Versailles was, in full accordance with academic precepts of artistic decorum, always in concert with the symbolic import of his imagery. It was surely also, as Poussin himself might have argued, orchestrated in a considered variation according to the architectural situation of the commission, whether a cabinet-sized easel painting or a vast ceiling painting such as that of the Galerie. Poussin was the clear model for the former. As the pre-eminent French painter of seventeenth-century cabinet paintings, Poussin was the model for works intended to be hung independently on picture gallery walls and viewed at close quarters.

Ceiling paintings, particularly those for the great spaces of palatial reception rooms such as Cortona's at the Barberini Palace or Le Brun's at Versailles, were determined by very different viewing conditions: from below, from a far greater distance, and from within a much grander architectural space. This required concerted variation as to the nature of the relationship between mirroring and painting, to pose the question of art's specular mimesis.

In the Grande Galerie, Le Brun's overarching decorative syntax was to structure the ceiling as a rhythmical progression of fictive architecture. In concert with the windows and the mirror arcades, Le Brun framed the ceiling with six broad bands of simulated gilt coffering. In the manner of Cortona, and as a 1652 treatise on painting attributed to Cortona with the Jesuit author G. B. Ottonelli advised, it is intended to offer a doubled view. An initial panoramic 'all-at-once' perception elicited awe and wonder at the richness of both the narrative and its painting. This ceded to a progressive reading 'bit by bit' as the viewer proceeded through the gallery.[48] Four painted panels on the sloping sides of the vault are rendered as *'quadri riportati'*, apparently composed of framed cabinet paintings like an illusionistic picture gallery fictively placed on the ceiling, in the manner of Annibale Carracci for the Farnese palace in Rome or indeed the Sistine ceiling. The central panels of the Grande Galerie are instead painted *'di sotto in su'*, as if illusionistically piercing the architecture of the vault with a view of the skies beyond, as well as by figures that seem to project forward into the very space of the hall. This was in keeping with the rich legacy of Italianate models of illusionistic ceiling painting exemplified in the seventeenth century by princely artists such as Pietro da Cortona for the papacy, at both the Barberini and the Medici palaces. Le Brun's strong contrasts of light and shadow rendered in rich colouring coalesce, Milovanovic noted, around a central burst of light, against which the leading narrative figures of the *historia* are pushed into visual prominence (Fig. 13).

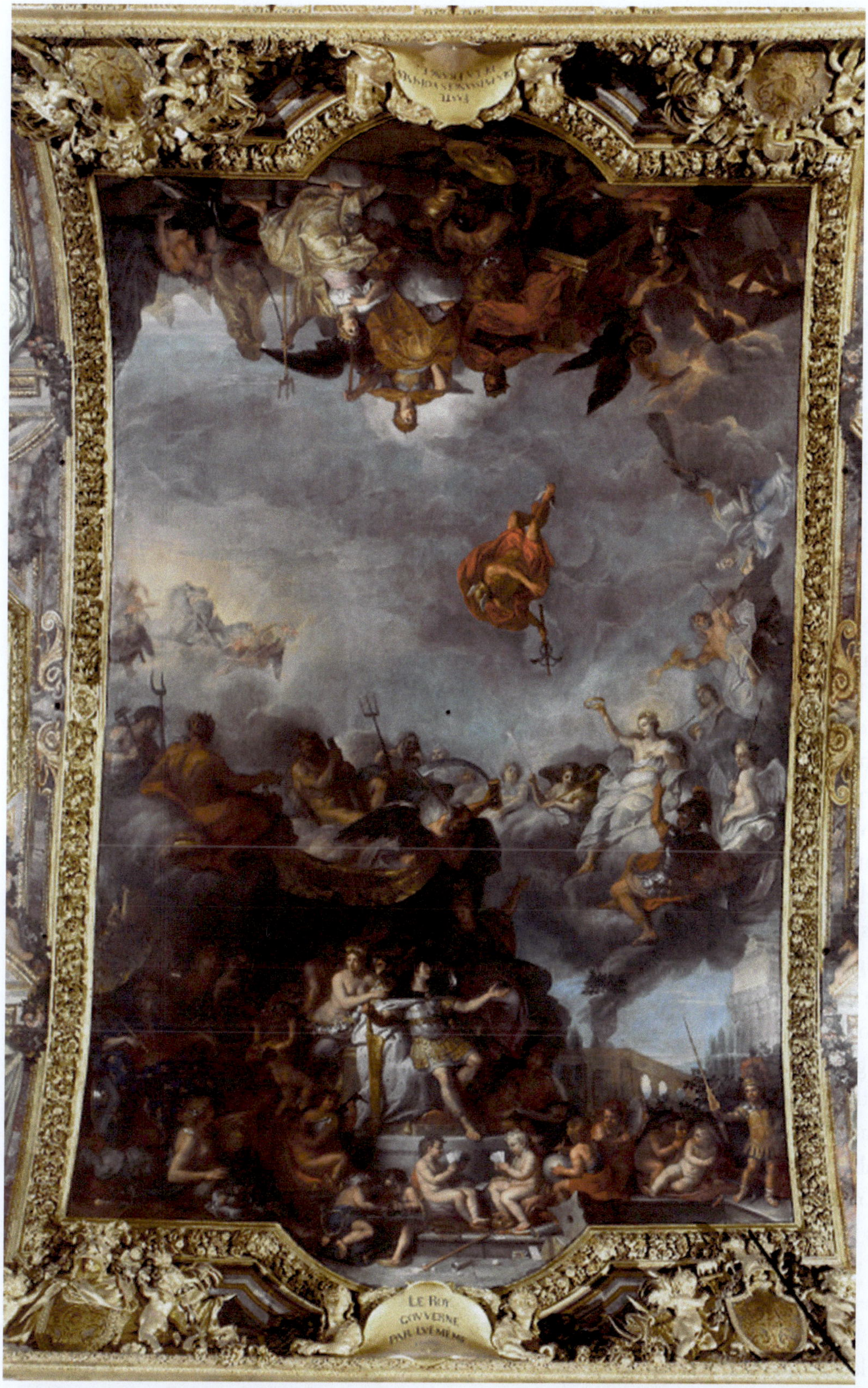

Fig. 13 Charles Le Brun, *Histoire de Louis XIV: Le roi gouverne par lui-même et fastes des puissances voisines de la France*, 1678–86, painted ceiling of the Grande Galerie des Glaces, Château de Versailles.
Photo: Réunion des Musées Nationaux

A compositional means of heightening narrative clarity within a wealth of pictorial and decorative ornament, it was a mode of picture-making perfectly in accord with the éclat of Louis' royal *gloire*. Such compositional syntax was one that Cortona had also articulated in his own princely painted ceilings in Florence and Rome, and in his putative 1652 treatise on painting.

To achieve the requisite effects of perspectival adjustment across the great vaulted space of the Grande Galerie at Versailles, Milovanovic suggested Le Brun's use of a convex or 'fishbowl' lens or mirror as an optical device. Broadly deployed by early modern draughtsmen across arts, architecture, engineering, and sciences, mirrors in general were much-used instruments in the transposition of all manner of visual information, which could then be transcribed into drawing, as Chapter 3 discusses further. Plane mirrors were optical devices of perfect perspectival rendering for both reduction and enlargement commonly used in the visual translation of scale. The mild 'fishbowl' distortion of a blown-glass spherical mirror could also render fully calibrated perspectival adjustments across spatial curvature, such as at the vault of the Galerie des Glaces. But what Milovanovic specifically postulated was Le Brun's use of a convex mirror as a means of bringing into perfectly measured optical prominence the figures at the centre of each composition of his painted 'panels' within the Galerie ceiling. The blown-glass curved mirror would, at the time, still have been as common as the flattened panes of glass being installed on the walls of the Galerie. The use of such a mirror was, moreover, a method promulgated by Le Brun's fellow academician and rival in debate, the art theorist and critic Roger de Piles, who advocated for the convex mirror as a compositional aid in his treatise for painters of 1668. Part of a larger discussion on the perspectival use of colour in order to focus the eye on the main figures of a narrative, de Piles argued that the convex mirror was a ready means of creating the illusion that the central figures of a composition appear to project forward towards the viewer from the picture plane.[49] While precise documentary evidence of such use of a convex mirror in artistic practice may be elusive, it is suggestive of the inter-related ties between the arts and sciences wrought by means of mirrors, which the rich history of the Grande Galerie as a place of art, optics, astronomy, and royal magnificence exemplifies.

Le Brun's earlier portrait of the great collector-Maecenas, Everhard Jabach, with his family c. 1660, also suggests the use of mirrors in this painter's practice, for the artist has represented himself in the act of painting in a mirror reflection directly behind his patron. It is Le Brun's pictorial homage to Jabach, but also surely to Velazquez' 1656 depiction of the Spanish royal family in *Las Meninas*, in the great mirror-picture gallery of the Royal Alcazar.[50] By the same token, the Grande Galerie's orchestrated equivalence between painting and mirroring emblematises the specular conception of painting that Alberti had inaugurated. Thus the Galerie represents the fullest spectrum of early modern painting's elision with the mirror-image, but also of its resonance across the arts and sciences, as the agent of reflected 'light'.

The summative example of the Grande Galerie as the preeminent manifestation of the early modern elision of painting with mirrors characterises the broader cultural perception of the mirror not only as the sign of the image but also as the instrument of light's conduct and reflection. In consequence of its capacities of lightsome reflection that could compose images like the mind's eye, the mirror became the metaphor of the reflective intellect, as also the inner reflections of the soul. The expanded and entwined cultural conceptualisation of the mirror metaphor, as image, as light, as inner reflection, and so of thought in all its manifold manifestations, is the province of this chapter's further analysis. This is in order to elucidate the cultural import of early modern painting's prevailing theoretical approximation to the mirror, as the potent metaphor of its representations. What follows is a fully interdisciplinary consideration of the early modern mirror as an emblem of light and reflection from its earliest archaic histories. The intention is to highlight the centrality of the mirror motif across early modern cultural domains, and so its critical configuration within painting as the sign of its own art.

II. THE ART OF THE MIRROR

> *There is a story that once a Phoenician traders' ship with a cargo of saltpetre stopped [at a beach along the Belus River near Mount Carmel] ... to make a meal. Since there were no stones suitable to support their cauldrons, they used lumps of saltpetre from their cargo. As these heated with the fire, the salt crystals mingled with the sand on the beach, from which a wondrous translucent liquid flowed forth in streams. And this, it is said, was the origin of glass.*[51]

Pliny the Elder's great compendium of the Roman world, the *Natural History* of 79 CE, set out to describe and classify all entities found in nature or derived from it in an encyclopaedia of ancient material knowledge. Comprising botany, mineralogy, metallurgy, zoology, astronomy, geography, ethnography, and physiology, it also catalogued their husbandry in mining, medicine, agriculture, and art. His tales of their historical origins were figuratively metamorphic, like the transformative materiality of glass as he described it. Pliny's perception of glass, as also metalwork, was touched by a cultural imaginary of marvellously wrought metamorphoses that extended across ancient literary forms, from Hesiod to Ovid. Pliny's account of glass epitomised the material transformations brought about by fire, in which the pale vitreous sands of the Belos melded with saltpetre crystals to form a clear and glistening liquid.[52] Cooled by the banks of the river, this flow of molten streams congealed naturally into glass.

The earliest traces of glass production, to be found along the banks of the Belos among other locations in the Middle East, lie within the obscure and diffuse histories of archaic periodisations. Like 'bronze age' metalwork, what may be reconstructed depends on the fugitive and happenstance survival of artefactual objects, all the more so in the case of glass due to its greater fragility. Obsidian or volcanic glass arising naturally from lava flows was widely used for tools and decorative objects in archaic and ancient cultures as Pliny also recorded (36:67), further complicating the little remaining archaeological evidence concerning any account of early glass manufacture.[53] Archaeologists generally agree that the earliest glass was cast, whether by nature or humankind, and then cut or carved. The technology for blowing glass appears to have emerged around the Mediterranean circa the first century BCE. Just as Pliny recounted, the marvellous metamorphosis of its 'glassy' materiality was composed of sand, mixed with saline plant ash (saltpetre or soda) to make a paste, then liquified in fire,and cast into an ice-like set of seemingly immaterial ethereality. With respect to mirrors, while glass reflectors of both volcanic obsidian and human manufacture were known and used throughout antiquity, what documentary and archaeological evidence remains is chiefly of metallic mirrors, in tempered sheets of bronze, copper, tin, or silver, as the metals with the highest degrees of reflectivity.[54] Ancient glass production appears to have been mainly for the manufacture of bottles, drinking vessels, and glass beads used as currency in trade.

Following the early origins of glass in archaic times, historians surmise a general decline in evidence for European glass-making from late antiquity to the late middle ages, before these vitreous trades and skills were again revived, above all through trade with the Levant. Concomitantly, the material history of archaic metallic mirrors is also, within the larger purview of classical archaeology, of necessity limited to their chance survival. Thus any attempt to reconstruct their uses, and so their cultural significance, lies perforce between a detailed object-based specificity to particular archaeological finds and larger contextualising histories of a more anthropological kind. At their broadest, these histories offer insight into the rich complex of cultural associations surrounding the mirror from its earliest manifestations, and which are of interest here because many of these legends survived, though often latently, into the mirrors of early modernity. To give a cultural account of early modern mirrors as artefacts thus requires us to consider their *longue durée* histories, as well as those of their Renaissance manufacture. We must also consider the history of materials, for both glass-making and metalwork. Such artefactual studies are, in scholarly terms, still in their infancy, as of general accounts of the history of mirrors more broadly, in a field that lies between the disciplines of history, archaeology, anthropology, and art-historical study of decorative arts. These interdisciplinary perspectives are brought together here, in a prismatic analysis of the mirror's polyvalent materiality and cultural reach over time and place.

***

Seemingly from earliest archaic times, sheets of polished beaten metal were used in cultic ritual, as reflectors and magnifiers of light able to ignite fire and conjure illusionistic displays of light and shadow. They were symbols of the sun as the source of life itself. In their progress from archaic to ancient cultures, like myth, mirrors were freighted with every kind of symbolic reference. Polyvalent, paradoxical, and ambiguous, they were embraced, adulated, venerated, and feared equally. In an anthropological continuum of belief from within archaic cultures, cultic and folkloric, the perceived ability to 'capture' the human image within the mirror's sphere of reflection was seen as a haunted one. Still today, the broken mirror of superstitious misfortune issues from this archaic fault line, in which the fate of the reflected image may be understood as entwined and prophetic. Across archaic cultures, archaeologists have found that burial goods often included small disc-shaped metal mirrors attached to the chest of the dead as the carrier of their reflection and so the seat of the soul, intended to safeguard its passage to the beyond in a *mythos* of specular resemblance apparently possessed of spiritual agency. For this reason, within folklore the mirror-image of the self is often regarded as the presentiment of death. This archaic belief would seem to survive within a Christian conception of 'mirroring' into early modernity. In the account of the death of Walter Devereux First Earl of Essex, in 1576, among his last acts was to call for his 'glas, that I might carie the remembrance of my countenance with me that I shall apeare with before my Lord Jhesus Christ'.[55] Similarly, the Christian pilgrim carried small metal mirrors with which to reflect and so 'capture' the image of a relic as a means of retaining its miraculous power. Such pilgrimage mirrors were made and used throughout the medieval period and well beyond, as also devotional texts titled 'mirrors' of the soul for pilgrims to carry with them. These were reportedly produced, among many others, by the Nuremberg metalsmith Johannes Gutenberg as he was developing moveable type in metalwork letters for the printing press.[56]

If mirrors may be understood as carriers of latent cosmological associations from their earliest archaic manifestations, yet they were also evidently artefacts of domestic utility across antiquity. On the one hand, they were instruments of illumination in their ability to direct and focus reflected sunlight. In this regard they were also the technology of fire and so of industry and manufacture, not least of themselves. In their form and fabrication they were close to metal armoury and particularly shields, the emblems of martial valour, so acquiring a wealth of related heraldic associations. On the other hand, they were agents of reflection, able to reproduce any visible field before them. In such manifold quotidian deployments they acquired rippling accretions of meaning over time. As Françoise Frontisi-Ducroux and Jean-Pierre Vernant have eloquently argued, the mirror-as-light became a metaphor of thought and so the sign of the scholar, while the mirror-as-reflection became the signifying emblem of beauty and thus the female domain.[57] In this latter capacity, the mirror would become an entwined trope of beauty in art and poetry coupled with the depiction of the female form.

Ancient mirrors of the female toilet made of polished precious metals with decorative backs or covers of ornamental relief commonly depicted scenes of the female nude as myth's archetype of beauty (Fig. 14).[58] Such objects were fashioned as luxury artefacts, often as gifts of courtship and marriage and so of its poetic allegorisation. Cast in the portable dimensions of hand mirrors, they were understood to manifest a close identification between the object and its bearer, as the emblem of womanhood's graced beauty and her gift in marriage. Much of their decorative imagery was self-referential, depicting themes of the female nuptial toilet and the bathing nude: of dressing the body, the hair and the face, with ornamented ewers of scented water, draperies, jewels, and attendant cupids as the preludes to love. In the sign of Venus, their tondo or disc figuration bearing the reflection of their owner's face was thus both the instrument and the emblem of her beauty. Silver-bright like the moon, her sphere was illuminated by the sun of her love. In the refrains of the poets, to capture the image of the beloved in a mirror reflection was both to captivate and to offer love's gift in return. In a cultural metaphor of marriage, the female nuptial mirror was perceived as the 'mirror-image' or specular counterpart of the circular bronze shield of male valour in emblematic reduction. The polished metallic ceremonial shield, in itself, was broadly conceived as a reflective 'mirror' of masculinity within cultures of knightly valour, and long remained a sign of his 'colours', both in arms and for his lady. Thus the idea of the mirror arose in a full complex of cultural significations. In its enduring historical reach from antiquity throughout the middle ages, dainty roundel mirrors as nuptial gifts were rendered in luxury materials of gold, silver, or finely-carved ivory. Ornamented with troubadour scenes of *amour*'s valiant pursuits, they might also be studded with small light-reflecting jewels as the 'mirrors' of love (Fig. 15).[59]

As the light of knowledge, the mirror sign was also embodied in reflective lamps as the emblem of intellectual contemplation and study. Generally circular and metallic in form, such mirror reflectors were set on small pedestals to form desk lamps as the material companions of a bookish contemplation, able to capture and focus natural or candle light onto the scholar's page.[60] They were also the agents of any type of detailed study, whether of books or objects and artefacts of all kinds. In the sixteenth-century Neapolitan polymath Giambattista della Porta's discussion of catoptrics, or the science of mirror reflection, as a utility he enlisted the use of mirrors as a method of lighting that ranged from how 'to read letters in a dark night' to lighting up a great hall for feasts and evening entertainments.[61] In this

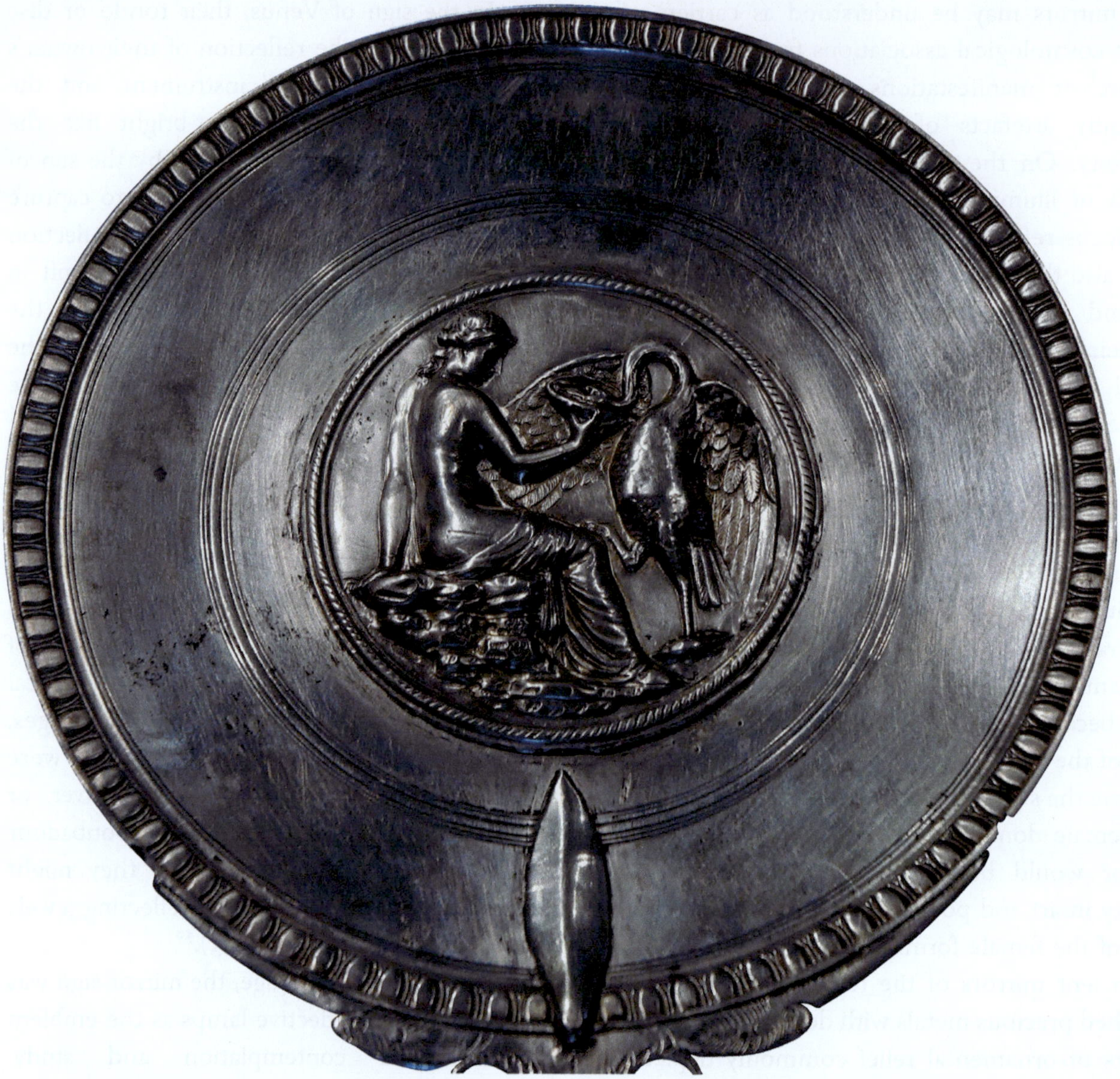

Fig. 14 Handle mirror illustrating Leda and the Swan, Boscoreale, late first century BCE to early first century CE, silver with repoussé decoration, height: 28.7 cm; diameter: 16.7 cm, Musée du Louvre.
Photo: Musée du Louvre

regard, the mirror reflector was also the locus and sign of much scientific research on the nature and conduct of light reflection throughout antiquity and beyond, best known in the writings of Euclid. In addition to Euclid's work on optics was a putative text on catoptrics as the specific study of mirror reflection and so the visible proof or demonstration of the conduct of light in the form of perspectival rays. These texts remained the most widely used and influential books on the subject up to the early twentieth century, with an exceptional history of successive elaboration and demonstration across antique, late medieval, and early modern thought.[62] From this ancient legacy of science, myth, and myriad usage, the early modern mirror emerged as suffused with a fulsome range of cultural reference. It was at once the sign of light and so the human

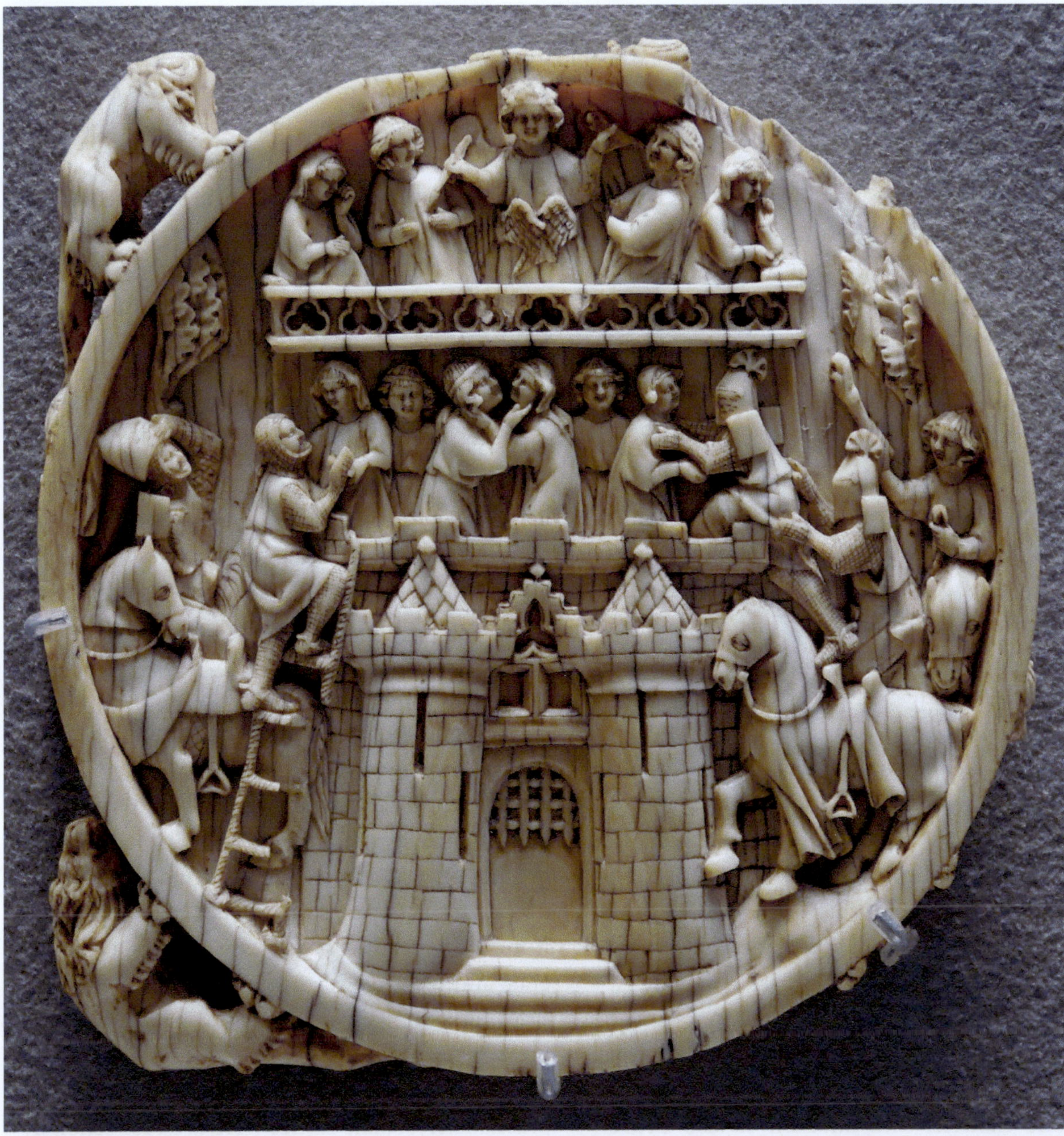

Fig. 15 German (Rhine) mirror case illustrating the *Siege of the Castle of Love*, 1325–50, ivory, height: 13.5 cm; width: 13 cm; thickness: 1.7 cm, Musée du Louvre.
Photo: Wikimedia

soul, of science and scholarship, industry and armoury, and female beauty and love.

Already the cultural locus of a vast wealth of significations within the metallic forms of ancient and medieval fabrication, the mirror's further material and hence idiomatic configuration in the medium of glass would burgeon from the fifteenth century with a gathering diffusion across early modernity. Thus conceived between bronze, silver, and glass, the cultural imaginaries of the mirror were those of a changeable and metamorphic materiality, between liquid and solid, as shifting and elusive as the mirror reflection itself to which the history of its materials was wed. In its incremental though never exclusive material translation from metal to glass, the Renaissance mirror also gathered a rich range of cultural significations pertaining to other lightsome materials. In this regard, its cultural associations ranged across a wide spectrum of related artefactual histories, from jewellery-making and metalwork to glass itself.

As an object of jewel-like reflections, the mirror's sign was drawn into the domain of gemstones and precious metals prized for their lustre. As scholars such as Sarah Dillon have argued, this apparent association with gemstones lent glass a commensurate value with the precious materials. These comprised metals and gems able to refract and reflect high degrees of light, above all silver and crystal, as well as diamond and other quartz or crystalline stones.[63] In a Plinian *paragone* of art and nature, luxury Renaissance decorative glass manufacture explicitly sought to imitate the prismatic effects of gemstones, as of other precious materials. In the words of the fifteenth-century Venetian scholar Marcantonio Sabellico, 'there is no type of precious stone in existence that has not been imitated by the glass industry; a sweet contest between nature and man'.[64] This formed part of a broader interest in the apparently alchemical properties of glass, in its seeming transformation from one material into another. It also drove much glass-making experimentation in the realm of recipes that could imitate the effects of ruby, emerald, diamond, or sapphire.

Rock crystal, in particular, represented within nature the aspirations of glass-making to produce a material of utter transparency and clarity of reflection that could magnify and refract light. Among the most plentiful of crystalline stones, crystal was always recognised for its prismatic powers of light intensification, magnification, and refraction.[65] Precious mirrors made within the domain of royal jewellery might therefore be of rock crystal itself, backed with a silver foil and framed by further gemstones in various colours – amethyst, citrine, blue or rose quartz, as well as the most valuable crystalline jewels such as emerald and diamond (Fig. 16). These were stones recognised for their light-filled refraction or 'sparkle', from archaic times. Like the earliest metal mirrors, crystals were also accreted with a full complex of mythic associations connected with rituals of sun-, moon-, and star-light. These comprised cult, love, and death's transport, as well as amuletic healing and protective properties, in a perceived magic of solar-reflected light. As gemstones they were further used in a range of decorative arts from earliest antiquity and throughout the middle ages. Crystals were also ground for the purposes of luxury glass-making and enamels, producing works of brilliant sparkle and hue. Their manifold lore was passed on through the textual tradition of the lapidaries, on the nature and meanings of minerals and stones from across the classical and medieval worlds into early modernity.[66] The allegorised perception of crystal's light-filled reflection infused every sphere of intellectual endeavour, from the perceived symbolism of majesty to science and technology, the language of poetic allusion, and religious belief in the 'crystalline firmament' of the heavens.

Within the scientific domains of optical study, prismatic crystalline stones were used for scholarly investigations into the mathematical geometry of light reflection, which would also be the case with premium lenticular glass made from fused white quartz crystal. Within the long history of optical aids, rock crystal, as among the most plentiful of the quartzes, was in continuous use from early antiquity as a means of enhancing vision due to its 'crystal' clarity and capacity for magnified enlargement. With subsequent developments in Renaissance glass-making, increasingly clear 'crystalline' glass could be precision-cut into any

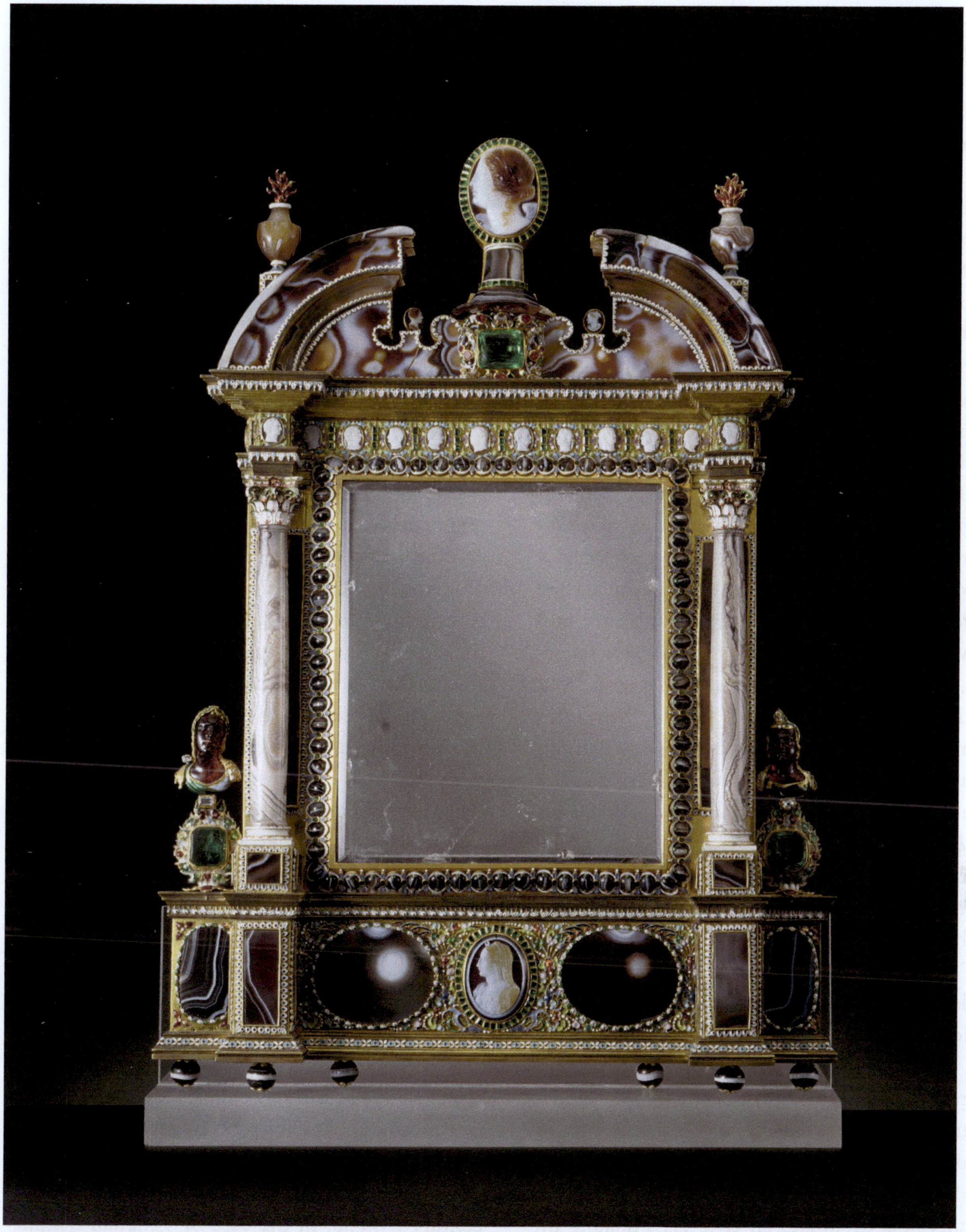

Fig. 16 French (Ile de France) mirror from the crown jewels, c. 1630–35 (so-called Marie de Médicis' mirror), gilded brass or enamelled gold (opaque white enamel, light green, light blue, purple, translucent dark blue enamel, green, orange, red, black enamel), rock crystal, agate, sardonyx, garnet, emerald, ruby, diamond; height: 40 cm; width: 28 cm; depth: 5 cm, Musée du Louvre.

Photo: Réunion des Musées Nationaux

number of curved or prismatic forms for the purposes of magnification and enlargement, enabling the development of those scientific instruments of vision of early modernity that would become telescopes and microscopes, as well as the earlier history of reading glasses or spectacles.[67] Thus optical glass, and specifically the glass lens, was as indispensable to the so-called Galilean revolution of scientific vision as to the history of reading and literacy.

Distinctively, an early modern lexicon of the mirror blurred the boundaries of its specific materiality, whether metal or glass. The specificities of its materials, from the exact type of crushed stone or sand to the sources and composition of the plant ash, or the metallic make-up of the foils, were also often obscured, as a consequence of their carefully guarded history as valuable artisanal recipes. Instead, the vocabulary for mirrors emphasised their various functions, and above all their instrumental capacities, for reflection, refraction, and combustion, but also for enlargement and reduction, and so their roles within the arts and sciences of vision and illumination. As the French Jesuit and scholar of optics Jean Leurechon put it in his *Récréations mathématiques*: 'Here I understand by the name "mirrors", not only those of glass or steel but also all reflecting surfaces that can bear images by dint of their polish.'[68]

Turning to the histories of their fabrication, while the Renaissance manufacture of premium optical glass would reside chiefly in Florence, in the production of luxury decorative glass and mirrors Venice took the lead. According to the extensive archival research of Luigi Zecchin on Venice's illustrious history of glass manufacture, the Serenissima's decision of the late thirteenth century was to situate all civic glass-making on the tiny outlying island of Murano.[69] The effect, intended or otherwise, was to create a close-knit community of glass-making island families, some of whom would rise to great wealth and renown over the next four centuries, celebrated for the exquisite luxury of their wares and for the European-wide princely admiration and wealth they brought to the lagoon. Doubtless rivals among themselves, yet to the outside world and under the protection of the Venetian governing council, Murano's glass-making workshops and their recipes remained closely guarded secrets for some hundreds of years, passed on orally within family traditions. As Colbert, who sought to break the monopoly by 'spiriting away' Murano's glass workers, astutely recognised, the question was not simply one of secret recipes for the paste, but also of a highly developed expertise in the conduct of glass through the elaborate processes of its blown facture, and above all one of reputation.

What the French crown sought, at the moment of the foundation of its own royal manufacture of glass and mirrors in 1665, was the perceived technological know-how of a great shift in the workshop chemistry of their Venetian production, generally dated to the mid-fifteenth century, and attributed to the glass-making artisanal families of Murano, particularly the Barovier. Jealously guarded by the Venetian state for centuries in order to protect its valuable exports, this was purportedly the glass-making recipe for a completely transparent glass known as '*cristallo*', on the basis of its much sought-after perceived resemblance to rock crystal.[70] For earlier glass was generally marked throughout by the imperfections of its process, resulting in a glistening light-filled material that was highly translucent but not fully transparent, greenish in tinge through the use of forest fern as flux, flecked with tiny bubbles, and of a thickness that precluded the greater clarity of fine sixteenth-century *cristallo*. In the case of Venetian *cristallo* glass, made from crushed white sand and saline plant ash, it was heralded as exceptional for its clear 'whiteness' then blown into glass of such ethereal lightness as to endow it with an unparalleled transparency. With constant experimentation across the course of the fifteenth century, the glass-makers of Murano were seen to have overcome all production difficulties to produce a glass of a crystal clarity and ethereal fineness unsurpassed elsewhere. The quest for Murano's colourless, featherweight, and flawless glass was laden with great symbolic as well as technical significance, as a manifestation of its artisanal refinement and therefore *virtù*.

Attending to the chemistry of ingredients for glass (as for its gemstone colouring) with different methods and combinations for making the paste, Murano's fifteenth-century experimentation with recipes may be likened to those that underpinned the development of oil paint in the early years of the fifteenth century in Flanders in the ambit of van Eyck. Based on the use of boiled linseed and walnut oils in combination with different mineral and herbal pigments, these painters similarly sought to create newly lustrous translucent oil glazes that could approximate the luministic effects of gemstones, enamel, and stained glass. In the case of Murano glassware, its illustrious patronage would include figures such as Isabella d'Este, Ferdinand and Isabella of Spain, and the Medicean French Queen Catherine among a constellation of European royalty. Murano's glassworks also became a celebrated attraction for courtly visitors of all kinds, according to the Venetian chronicler Marin Sanudo's diary, including the Queen of France Anne of Brittany in 1502, Charles Bourbon Duke of Vendôme in 1515, Federico Gonzaga the future Duke of Mantua in 1517, Cardinal Ippolito d'Este in 1520, Alfonso d'Este Duke of Ferrara in 1531, and Francesco Maria della Rovere Duke of Urbino in 1532.[71]

Again according to Zecchin, mirror-making was a late fifteenth-century addition to the history of Murano's glass production. In Zecchin's account, this was fostered particularly by the Ballarin, also one of Murano's long-standing families of glass-makers, and would become a leading speciality of Venetian Renaissance glass. Venetian mirror manufacture was institutionalised by the civic foundation of its own trade corporation over the course of the 1560s, the Arte degli specchiari, with responsibility for overseeing the training of apprentices. Venetian mirrors were renowned for the transparency of their glass and for the beauty of their frames, made of decorative glassworks in the form of enamel, floral, inlay, or filigree ornaments. Murano's now-burgeoning sixteenth-century manufacture of mirrors of increasing size depended on incrementally changing paste recipes and ever-developing technical skill in glass-blowing, to produce cylindrical glass 'bubbles' of greater size and above all length in the ongoing quest for larger panes.[72] This was further accompanied by improved recipes for the silvered foil backing that formed the mirror's reflective surface. The development of finely hammered tin-foil sheets softened by quicksilver or liquid mercury amalgams lent a greater milky-whiteness, lightness, and reflective clarity, also laden with a symbolic import of artisanal virtuosity. Murano's expertise would forge the mirror arcades of the Grande Galerie at Versailles, brought to Paris through the import of Venetian mirror-makers under the auspices of Colbert, in order to create national mirrors of state for France.

For Paris, as for Murano, there is extensive archival documentation surrounding the various establishments for glass mirror-making institutionalised by the crown and their ongoing governance, as well as royal patents for new 'inventions' within this larger artisanal history. Among the plethora of illustrated printed books of artisanal instruction and documentation that appeared in Paris over the course of the seventeenth and eighteenth centuries, there was an array of publications on glass- and mirror-making, so documenting an otherwise oral history of transmission of workshop technical skills. This also comprised series of illustrated prints on the manufacture and trade in mirrors, within larger sets of luxury artisanal goods. It is represented in a range of French seventeenth-century engravings such as Etienne Delaune's elaborate dressing-table mirror designs, and illustrated furniture design pattern books like Jean Le Pautre's *Livre des miroirs, tables, et guéridons*, with decorative wall mirrors for the salon or gallery (Figs. 17 and 18).[73] In lightly comic vein, Nicolas Larmessin's *Costumes des arts et métiers* depicted a range of artisans in fancy dress according to the tools and wares of their trade, including a mirror-maker fully costumed in mirrors, wittily looking through his dainty toy telescope in a playful guessing game of 'who views who' (Fig. 19).[74] In their emphasis on artisanal skill and industry such prints drew on longer textual traditions of trade representation such as Hans Sachs and Jost Amman's 1568 *Das Ständbüch* (Book of Trades), an illustrated book that comprised a full complement of craft industries, including the interior of a mirror-maker's workshop-cum-shopfront with every type and size of mirror for sale (Fig. 20). Like Larmessin, the print is humorous in its presentation, for the text below, spoken in rhyme as if in the voice of the craftsman, declares his trade as a light 'Who am I?' riddle.[75] An illustrated 1715 German edition of della Porta's 1589 *Magia naturalis*, an encyclopaedia of natural marvels including those of optical mirror illusions, included a woodcut of an optic-maker's shop with a full complement of mirrors of all shapes and sizes set among every kind of eye glass, from spectacles to telescopes. The glass-maker, in fashionable dress, stands among his mirror manufactures such that his image is reflected in a cascade of specular reflections, like a workshop optical hall of mirrors of his own making (Fig. 21).

As sixteenth-century Venice was a prominent European centre for Renaissance book publishing as well as glass-making, it too heralded good numbers of publications of a largely scientific nature that treated the production of both decorative and optical glass artefacts within them, including mirrors. Leonardo Fioravanti's *Specchio di scientia* of 1564, like the work of della Porta, described the production of glass and mirrors from the point of view of the alchemist-chemist in detailing its recipes and methods, as did Antonio Neri's *L'arte vetraria* of 1612 as the first published collection of recipes for glass. These were texts born of what would subsequently become the subject of chemistry. Within Renaissance intellectual paradigms, their interests were above all in metamorphic materials forged in fire, and therefore glass. This was also the case in Vannoccio Biringuccio's consideration of glass-making and mirrors in his study of igneous manufacturing, chiefly metalwork, *De la pirotechnia*, of 1540.[76] To commemorate the new-found French prowess in mirror manufacture, Colbert had also sought to publish an encyclopaedic series of texts with engraved plates to demonstrate national supremacy in a full range of early modern artisanal technologies. As inaugurated by Pliny, the endeavour was to showcase French encyclopaedic ambition in the production of material goods. This was in fact only achieved some 100 years after, under the broad ambit of Denis Diderot and Jean le Rond d'Alembert's mid-eighteenth-century *Encyclopédie ou Dictionnaire des sciences, arts et métiers*. Its dedicated volume on the art of glass-making and specifically of mirrors, *La fabrication des glaces* (Fig. 22), was based on the French development of these crafts since Colbert's institutionalisation of royal mirror-making in 1665.[77] Notwithstanding their respective singularities and genres, early modern textual and illustrative descriptions of glass-making for mirrors in both word and image centred largely on the representation of its tools, and the marvellous metamorphosis of its 'glassy' materiality from ash and sand into a liquid forged in fire to an ice-like set. Its seemingly immaterial ethereality produced everything from the vanity and decorative mirror to an early modern technology of light, the industrial uses of vitrification and combustion, and the instrumentation of the new sciences based on augmented lenticular vision, of the stars as of molecules.

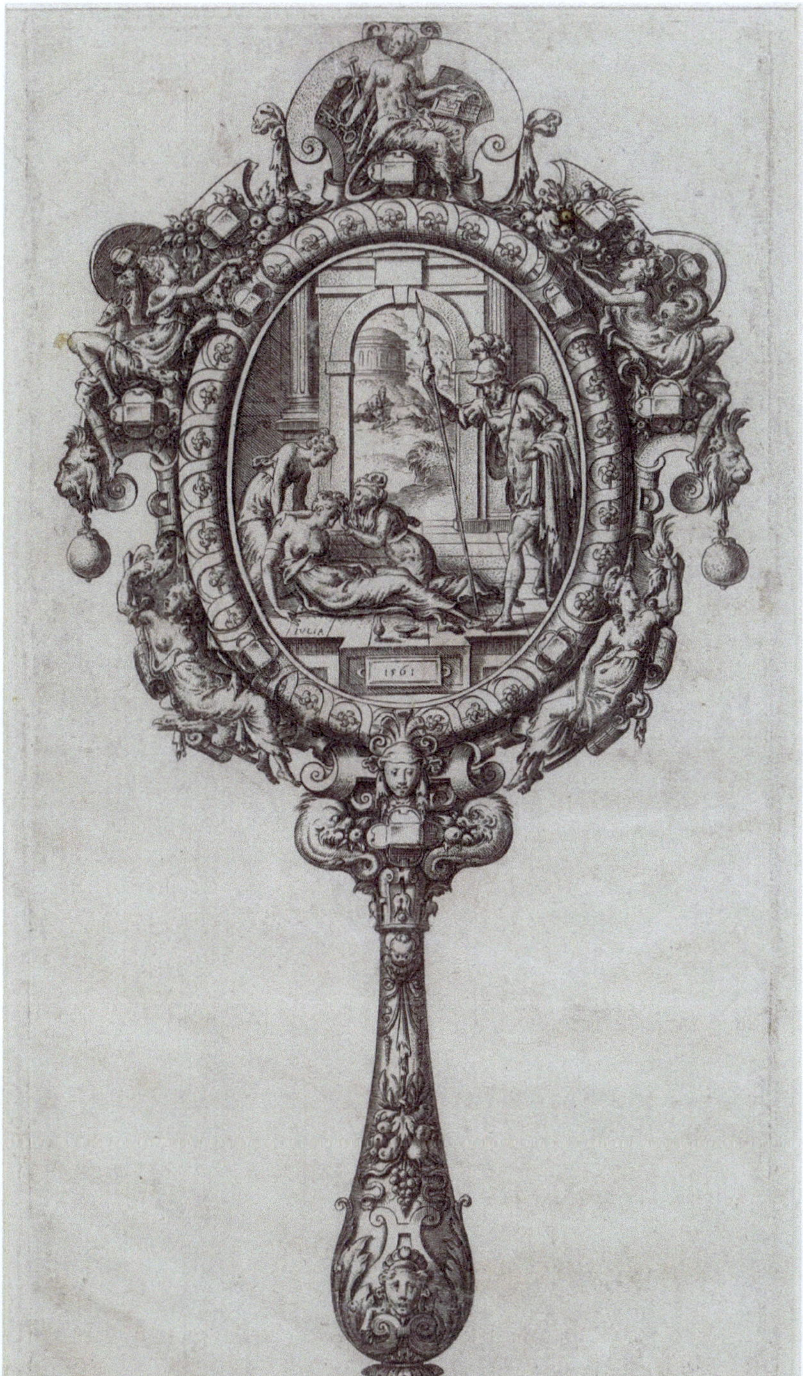

Fig. 17 Etienne Delaune, design for a gem-set gold handle mirror depicting Julia Caesar, drawing, pen and ink and wash on vellum, 13.2 × 11.5 cm, for a signed and dated engraving by Delaune of 1561, Victoria & Albert Museum.
Photo: V&A

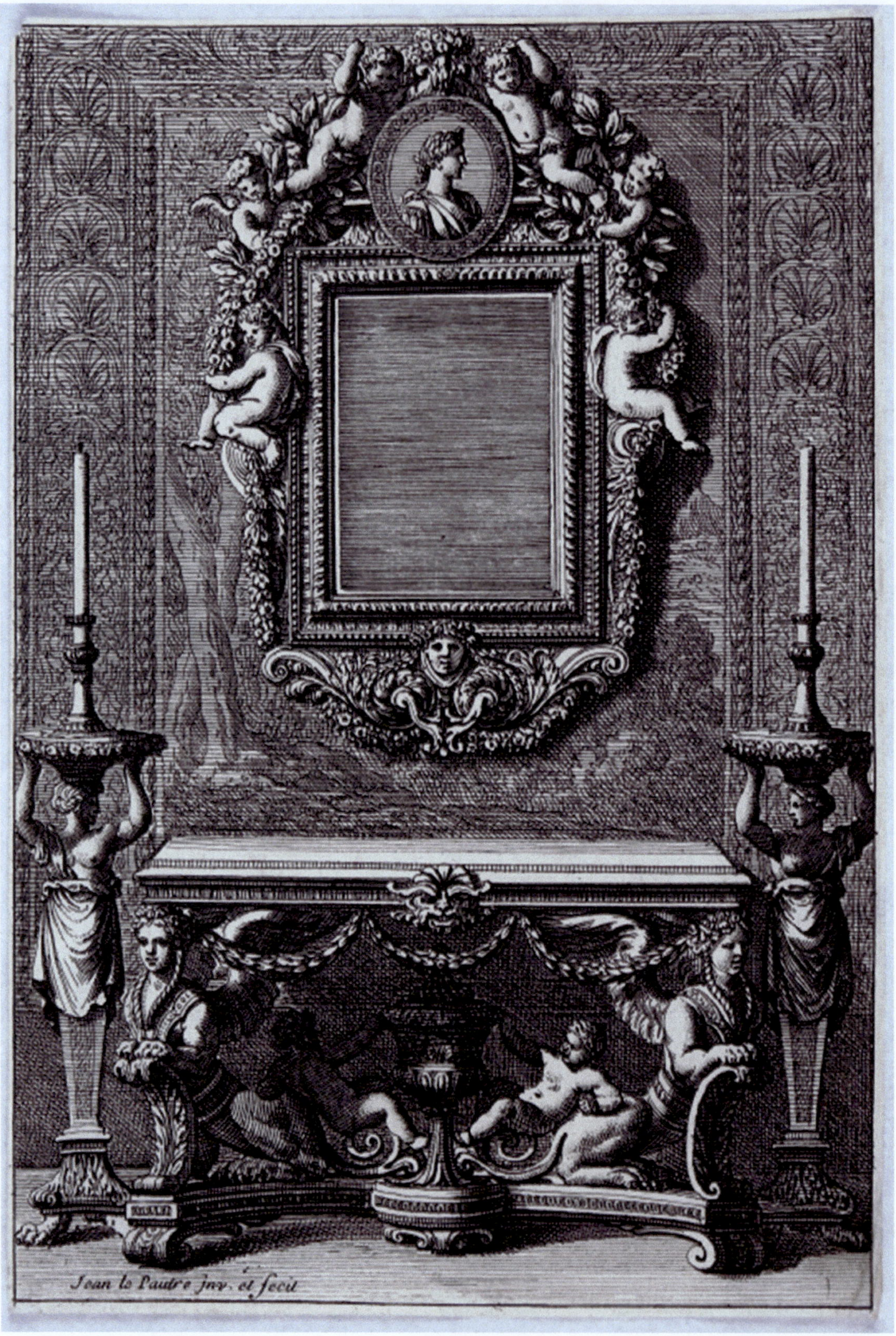

Fig. 18 Jean Le Pautre, *Livre des miroirs tables et guéridons*, Paris, c. 1670, printed illustration for a wall mirror with flanking torchères and console table.
Photo: Réunion des Musées Nationaux

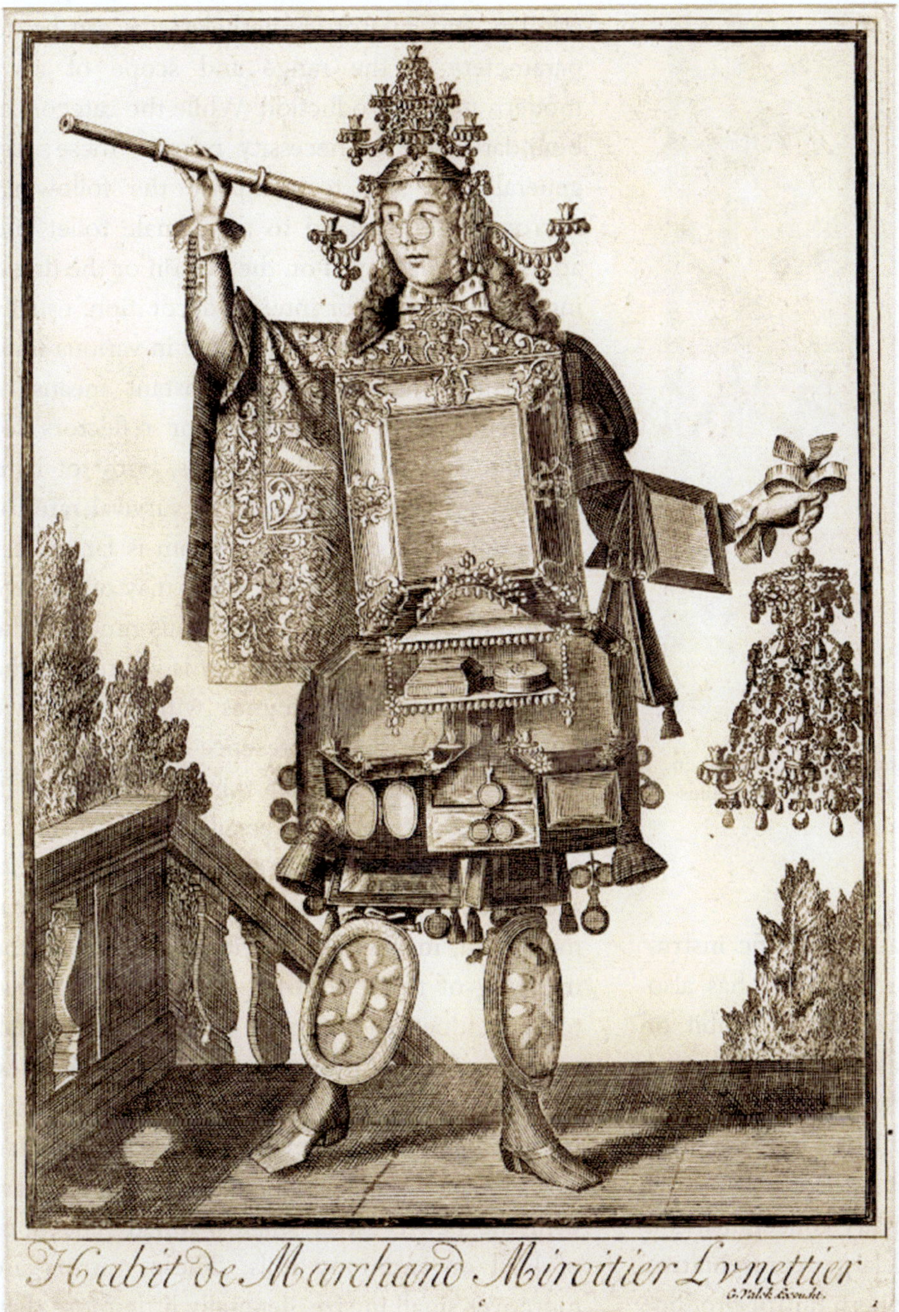

Fig. 19 Nicolas de Larmessin II, *Habit de marchand miroitier lunettier*, in *Arts et métiers*, c. 1695. Photo: Wikimedia

THE MIRROR ARTEFACT

Turning now from a history of glass mirror-making founded on archives and incunables to the material evidence of mirrors themselves, their early modern artefactual history comprises a complex grid of chronology, geography, materials, sizes, and cultural functions. The objects for study lie perforce within the holdings of divers museums: of decorative arts, early modern

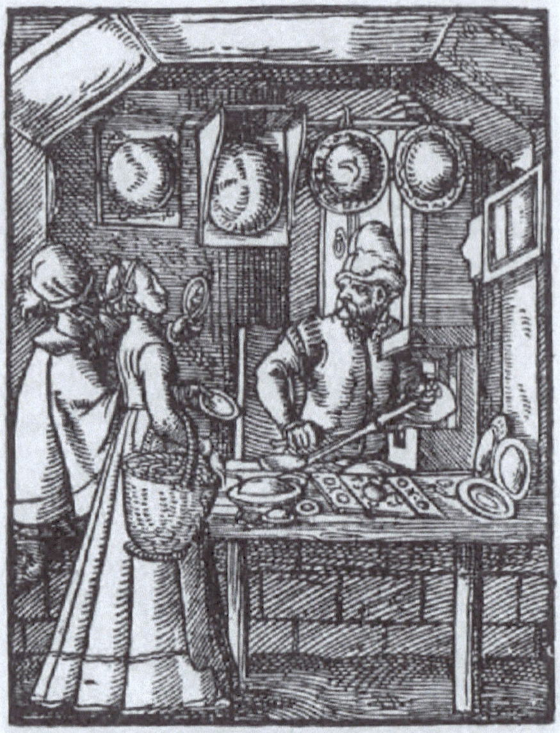

Fig. 20 Hans Sachs and Jost Amman, *Der Spiegler*, in *Das Ständbüch* (Book of Trades), 1568, woodcut illustration of a mirror-maker's shop.
Photo: Wikimedia

furnishings, and industrial and scientific instruments.[78] The history of mirror frames has also received attention within the broader ambit of picture frame scholarship, as has the industrial use of mirrors within an early modern historiography of science and optics. It is surely the case that what was kept, and subsequently found its way into museum and antiquary collections, is a tiny percentage, and by and large representative of the luxury end of early modern mirror production. This must also be qualified by the recognition that swathes of inset decorative mirrors affixed into larger interior architectural surrounds have been lost through successive histories of remodelling and refashioning. Their loss can to some extent be mitigated by surviving inventories and other types of textual description. The artefacts that do remain can only ever offer a partial history.

Within such critical caveats, antiquarian scholars and curators nonetheless discern broad parameters in the range and scope of early modern mirror production. While the categorical boundaries are of necessity porous, these may generally be said to comprise the following: mirrors closely related to the female toilet and adornment, displayed on the person or the dressing table; mirrors for interior decoration, usually but not exclusively wall-mounted in various ways and which were also an important means of enhancing light; and mirrors or reflectors for scientific and industrial purposes, both for light and for ignition. In general, the survival rate for the frames that once housed them is far greater than the mirror glass itself, which may often have been replaced multiple times. Thus much of the artefactual history of the mirror is written on the basis of its erstwhile frames within which we must read their absent presence in a now-fugitive history of their loss. For this reason, the high perdurance rate of the Versailles Galerie mirror plates and their recent conservation, with its accompanying full technical research and documentation, makes them a vital milestone in the mapping of this otherwise elusive material history, as does the chance survival of a small number of early fifteenth-century mirror glasses. These latter evidence the appearance of the mirror before the development of Venetian silver-foiled *cristallo* glass – made of a darker glass with the pewter-silver shadow-toned reflections of lead or antimony foils. These mirrors are moreover small in size, generally little more than the reach of a hand, convex in form, and self-evidently the products of a blown-glass facture (Figs. 9 and 23). While blown-glass methods would continue across the period, ever-changing expertise enabled larger bubbles that could be made into domed or flat panes of greater dimensions and increasing clarity and brightness of reflection. The advent of larger panes of cast glass c. 1700 inaugurated in Paris would replace

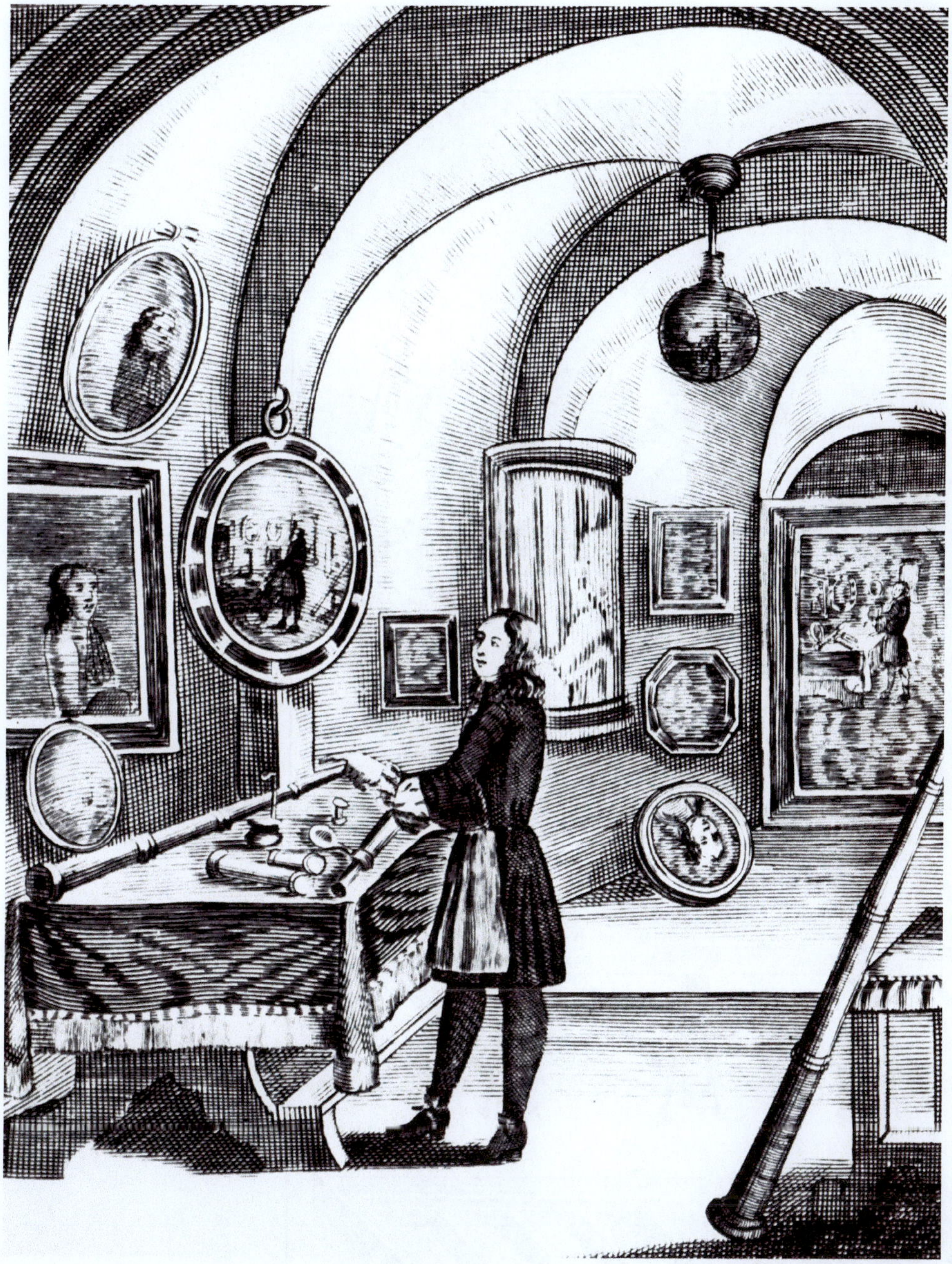

Fig. 21 German woodcut depicting an optical instrument maker in his workshop as a 'hall of mirrors', for *Magia naturalis* by Giambattista della Porta, Nuremberg, 1715 ed., 33.5 × 44.8 cm. Photo: Alamy

artisanal blown-glass mirrors almost entirely with their nascent industrialised production.

The frames for scientific or industrial mirrors were generally either rudimentary ones for safekeeping, or dictated by the instruments and machines into which they were placed. This is also the case for the mirrors kept by artists in their workshops as ready mimetic instruments in aid of painting. As nothing certain remains in object form, our knowledge depends entirely on documentary and textual references, in inventories and other descriptions, notwithstanding the fact that they were clearly ubiquitous. We can surmise their appearance on the basis of what workaday blown-glass mirrors have survived (Fig. 24) coupled with their textual description, and circumspectly from

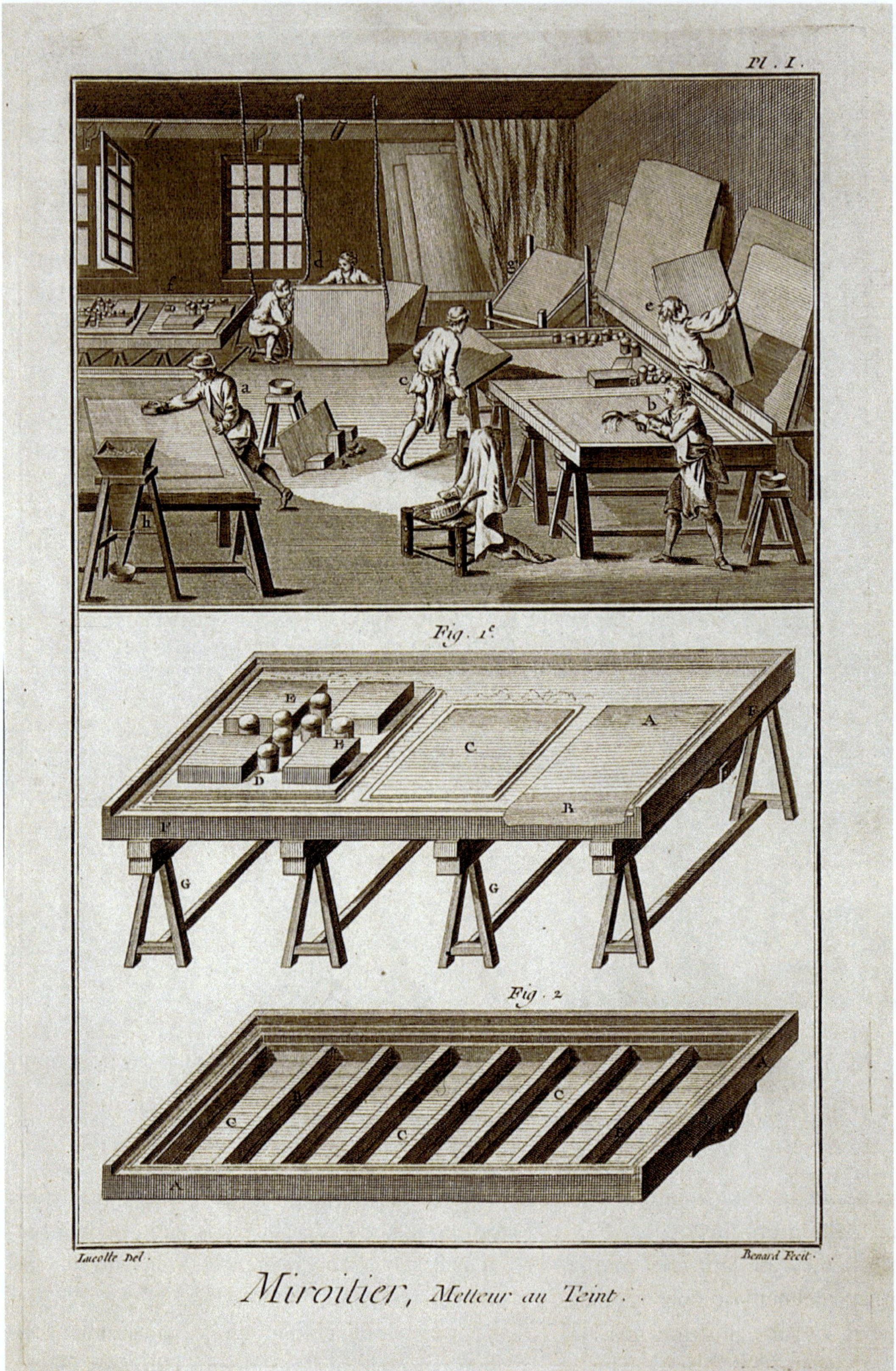

Fig. 22 Robert Bénard, after Jacques-Raymond Laclotte, *Miroitier, metteur au teint*, engraving, Denis Diderot and Jean le Rond d'Alembert, *Encyclopédie … arts et métiers, art du verre: Fabrication des glaces*, Paris, c. 1770, polishing and silvering panes of glass.
Photo: Wellcome Collection

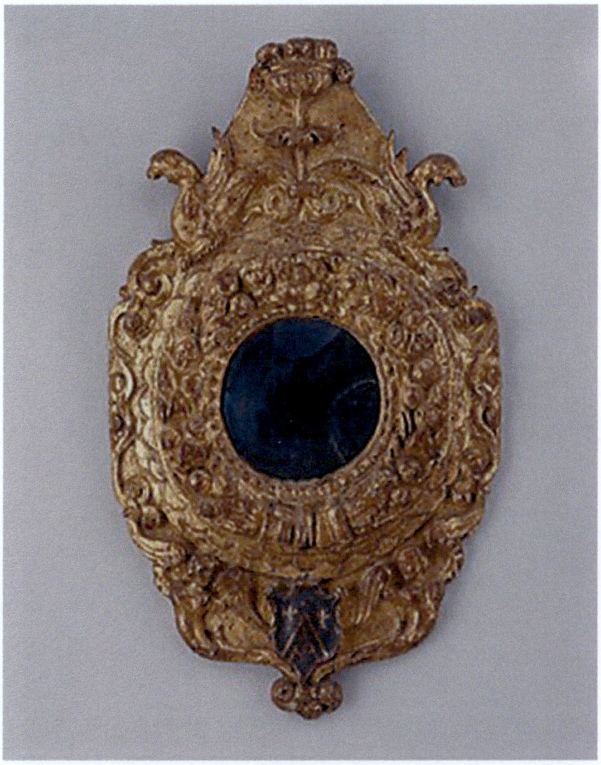

Fig. 23 Italian (Siena), tondo mirror frame with the coat of arms of the Cinuzzi family of Siena, c. 1490–1500, poplar; carved, gilt; deep red-brown bole, Metropolitan Museum of Art.
Photo: Metropolitan Museum of Art

the painted appearance of mirrors within paintings, though we cannot expect that these are necessarily direct representations of studio tools.

It is therefore the case that an object-based history of mirrors depends largely on surviving frames for the toiletry looking glass and the interior decorative reflector. In general, the compact looking glass with a protective cover has fared best, particularly those of precious materials therefore grouped with dynastic jewellery. The rate of survival of the glass itself, as against its frame alone, is also higher than for wall-mounted mirrors, presumably due to their protective covers. However it is also the case that mirrors with particularly valuable frames might have their glass replaced periodically as a matter of maintenance in case of cracking or mottling of the surface; those remaining early modern mirrors are often foxed and darkened to an extent that makes it impossible to judge their original light and reflective lustre.

We may also supplement an object-based history of the mirror with their incidence in

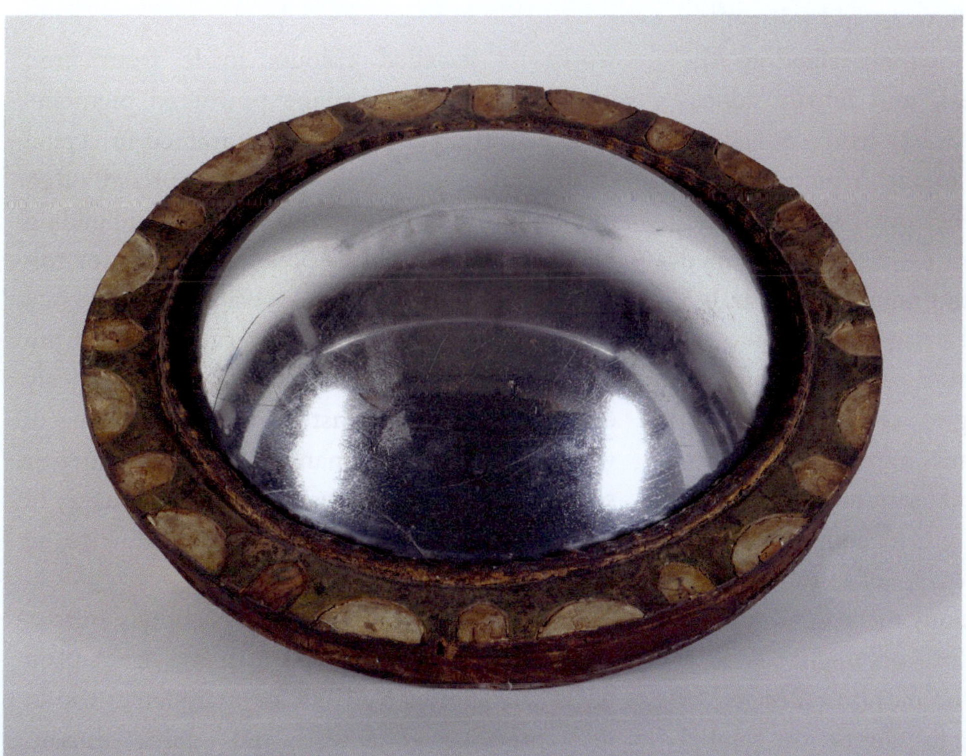

Fig. 24 German convex glass mirror, sixteenth century, wooden frame, Germanisches National Museum Nuremberg.
Photo: Germanisches National Museum

inventories. Royal inventories of the period give, in the first instance, strong quantitative indication of precious mirrors within collections of jewelled objects, luxury toiletries, and princely gifts. In the extensive inventories of crown jewels of Louis XIV, as of his royal *'présents'* to princesses, duchesses, and queens, silver-gilt toiletry mirrors were conceived as noble gifts of the first rank.[79] This was true across European courts and aristocratic households. Thus Charles II in 1672 gifted his royal favourite, Frances Teresa Stuart, Duchess of Richmond and Lennox, a French silver dressing-table toiletry service ornamented with gilt (National Museum of Scotland).[80] Within the records of Louis XIV's possessions kept by his Intendant du garde-meuble, Gédéon Berbier du Metz from 1663 to 1715 under the jurisdiction of Colbert, there were some 500 mirrors listed with every kind of frame in all manner of precious materials: engraved glass, rock crystal, silver, gilt, filigree, burnished steel, lapis, tortoise shell, agate, pearwood, walnut, and ebony, in plain fillets, figured mythologies, heraldic devices and crests, or decorative borders of cupids, birds, flowers, and foliage.[81]

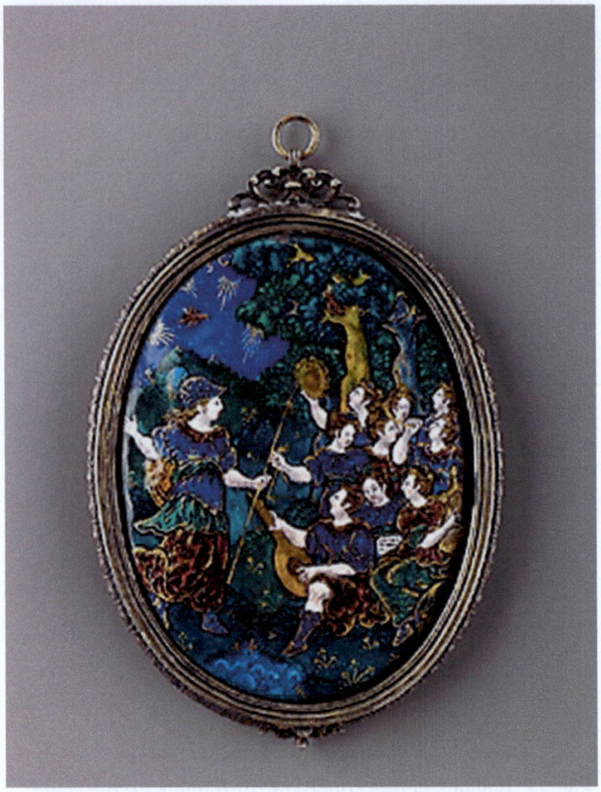

Fig. 25 Suzanne de Court, enamelled mirror with Minerva visiting the Muses on Mount Helicon, c. 1600, enamel with gilt and silvering on copper, mirror glass, 12.5 × 8.5 cm, Metropolitan Museum of Art. Photo: Metropolitan Museum of Art

The toiletry mirror is closely allied to the history of jewellery, dress, and female adornment. Bijoux examples were worn as jewels attached by silk ribbons to the feminine girdle, ever the material sign of betrothal and marriage. Thus the small and often exquisitely fashioned compact mirror was a continuing manifestation of cultures of love and marriage within the decorative arts. The painted enamels of the sixteenth-century Limoges crown workshop included jewelled pendant mirrors of mythological scenes in brilliant saturated glazes of crushed gemstones then gilded and silvered, as ornament to the colours of court dress (Fig. 25).[82] Often of precious metals and further decorated by jewels, such mirrors might also host covers with ornamental or narrative designs of poetic conceit rendered in filigree or enamel work, its jewelled colours made from fired ground glass or crystalline powdered pigments (Fig. 26a, b). Venetian mirrors framed in crystal or decorative glass were also highly prized, often in floral motifs with jewel-like colours and gilding (Fig. 27). Hand-held or pedestal mirrors for toiletry sets and dressing tables were also made in a vast range of materials of every expense, from simple wood frames to elaborate princely examples in gold encrusted with jewels, some of which were further ornamented with enamel or sculptural figures of female beauty and virtue, of both mythological and biblical scenes (Figs. 17 and 28).[83]

In the domain of the wall-mounted mirror, there was again every type of frame, from plain fillets to richly carved gilt or marquetry woods, inset precious stone work and intarsia, mosaic,

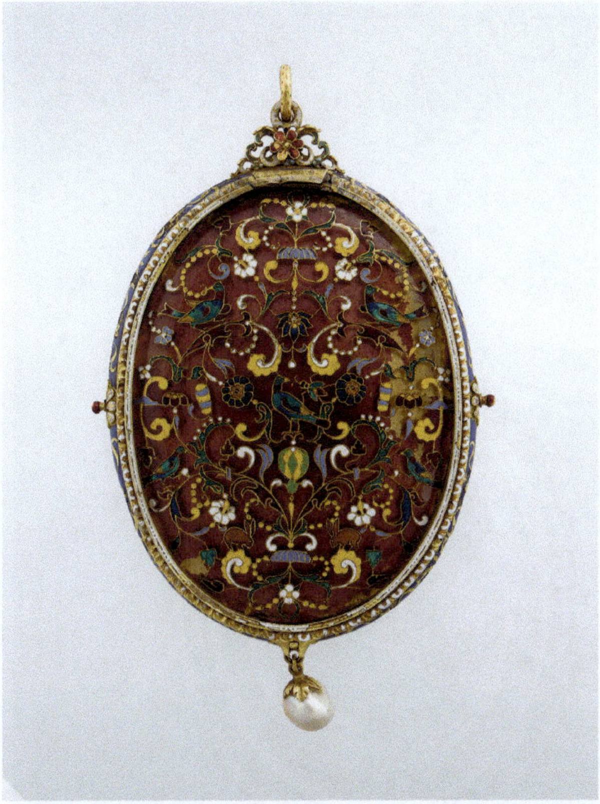

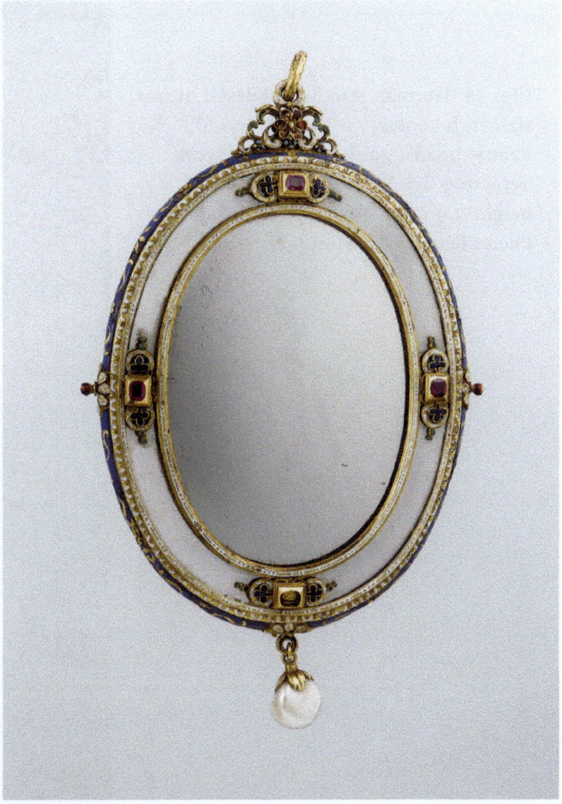

Fig. 26a, b French locket or compact mirror with gold frame, sixteenth century, inset with jewels, leather cover with enamel and filigree work, 1.2 × 0.76 cm, Ecouen, Musée Nationale de la Renaissance.
Photo: Réunion des Musées Nationaux

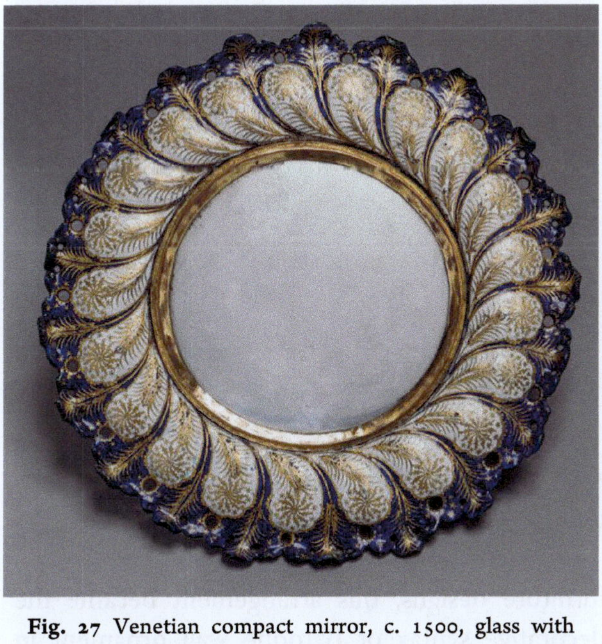

Fig. 27 Venetian compact mirror, c. 1500, glass with enamel and gilding, 2 cm diameter, Paris, Musée du Louvre.
Photo: Réunion des Musées Nationaux

enamelwork, tortoiseshell, amber, textiles such as velvet and needlework samplers, gilt leather, painted or decorated glass panels, and those adorned with silver and crystal or mirror panelling to enhance their reflective splendour. Their forms comprised everything from flat or lightly bevelled wooden struts, to architecturally styled tabernacle frames, to ornately carved wood or chiselled silver with crests, emblems, and other figurative devices. Early Renaissance examples in blown glass are circular, encased within corresponding tondo frames that ranged from simple wooden surrounds to gilt-painted stucco, papier mâché, or *cartapesta*, to maiolica ceramics, carved wood, and gilt-painted marbles (Figs. 23 and 29). Many came to include candle holders within their frames, as their primary decorative function was the enhancement of interior light. By the seventeenth century, wall mirrors placed above console

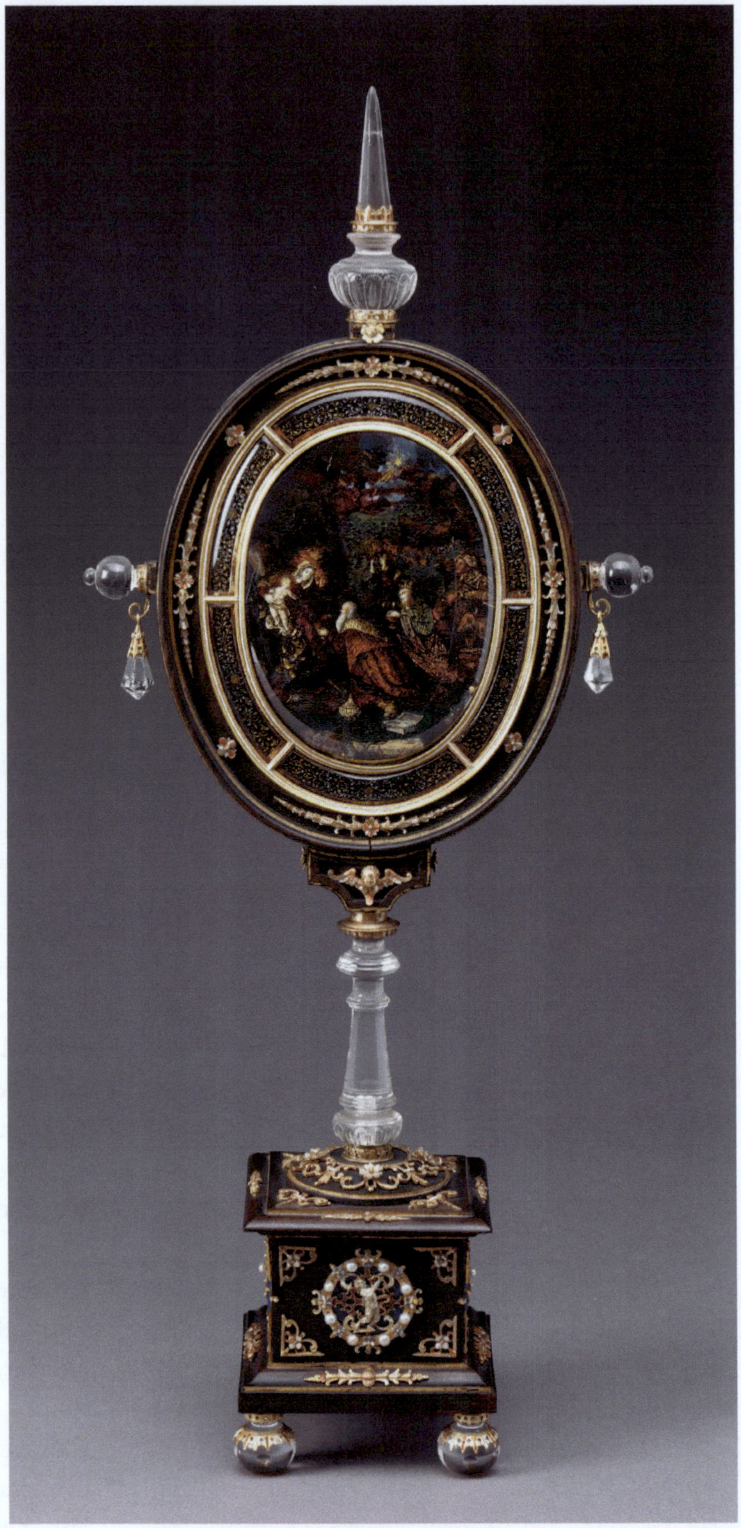

Fig. 28 German jewelled pedestal mirror, sixteenth century, with rock crystal, ebony, pearls, gold, and enamel work depicting the Adoration of the Magi, height 3.9 cm, Paris, Musée du Louvre. Photo: Réunion des Musées Nationaux

tables were often designed in a complement with adjoining sconces, torchères, or guéridons by which to augment their light through its specular reflection. As in Jean Le Pautre's 1670 manual of furniture designs, this arrangement became the decorative syntax of Baroque wall ornament in princely apartments and galleries, as a rhythmic cascade of mirrors and candelabra (Fig. 18). These

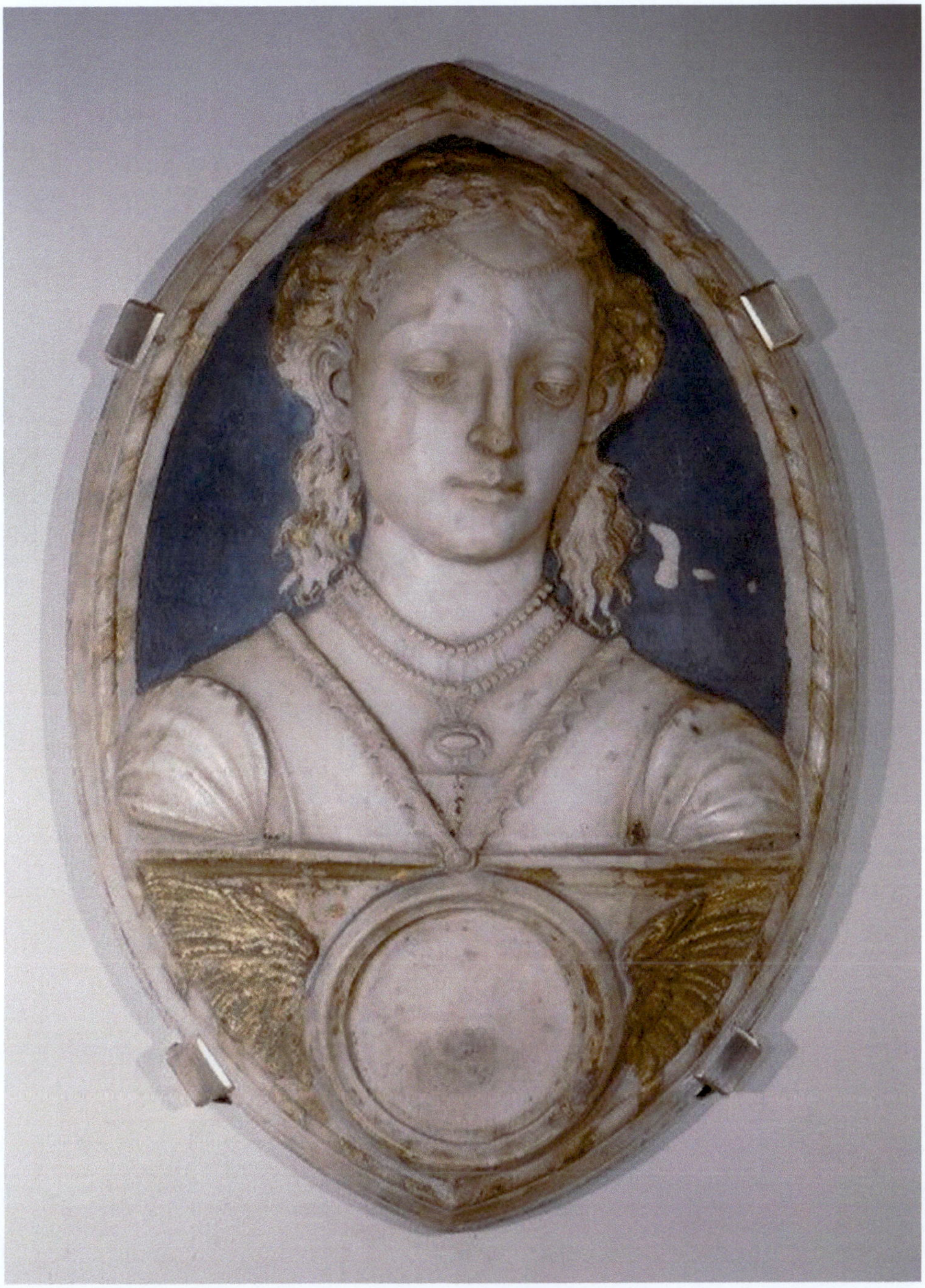

Fig. 29 Marble mandorla mirror frame in the form of a female head, c. 1470, Florence, workshop of Mino da Fiesole, marble bas-relief with gilding and blue pigment, 50 × 28 cm (mirror roundel no longer extant), Bibliothèque Nationale de France, Médailles et Antiques. Photo: BNF

were often made of precious metal, as a surety in their adjacence to candle flame, and in the case of royal apartments, of silver or silver-gilt, which lent a further resplendence of light and reflection. If the silver furnishings for Versailles, which comprised such mirrors with adjoining guéridons, have not survived, yet there are other princely examples that illustrate the place of the ornamental mirror within such Baroque courtly décor (Fig. 30). Richly ornamented with floral and mythological motifs, as well as coats of arms, they were exquisite works of silversmithing made by crown jewellers to the design of court artists such as Le Brun or Bernini. Intended for the splendour and

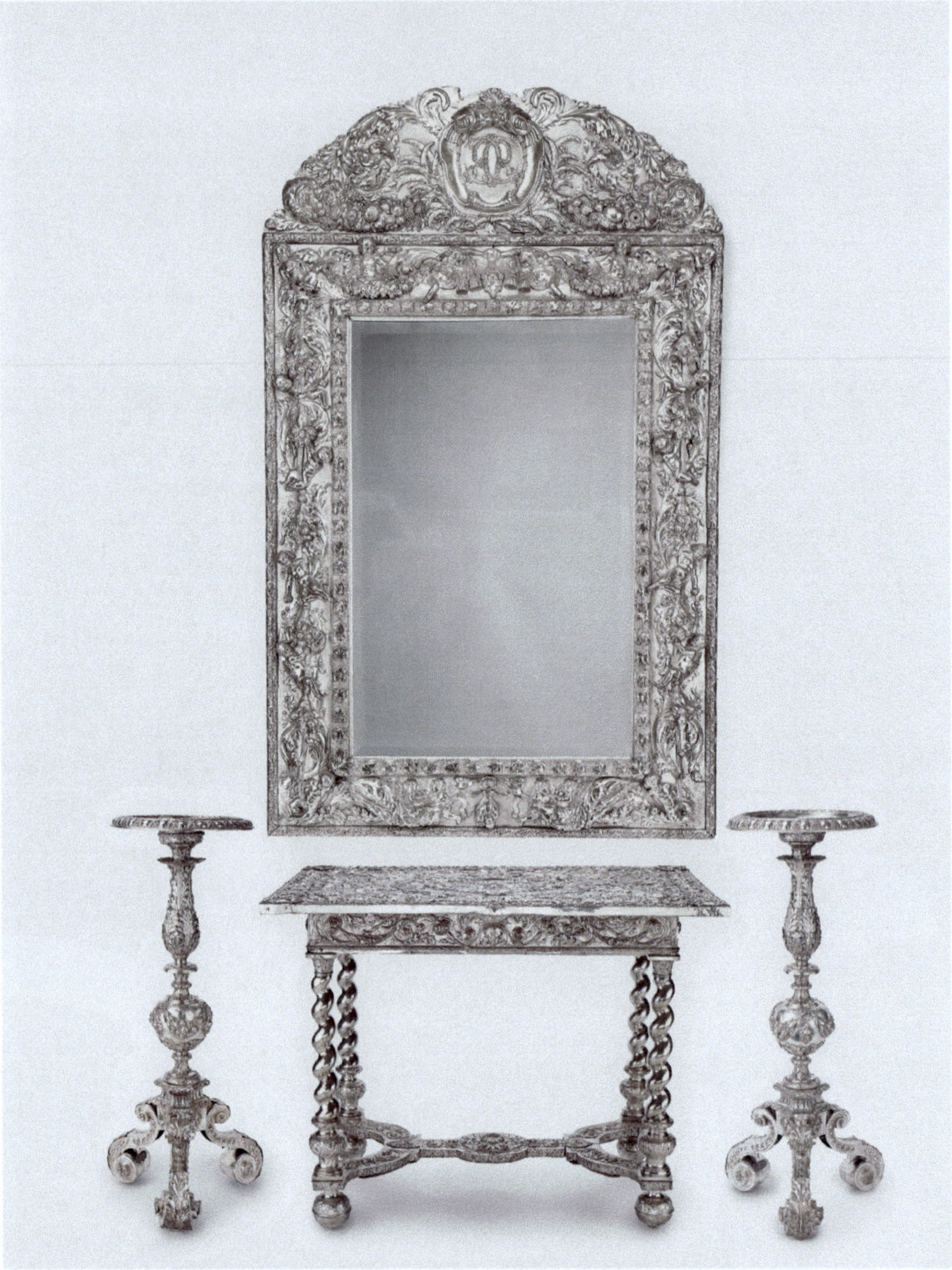

Fig. 30 English Charles II crown silver mirror, c. 1670, with torchères and console table, chased and embossed silver ornament of swags, foliage, and putti, silver, wood, mirror glass, 210 × 126 × 10 cm, Royal Collection Trust.
Photo: © Royal Collection Trust/His Majesty King Charles III 2023

illumination of the palace gallery or cabinet wall, their orchestrated display formed the matrix of the early modern interior decorative order. Designed to hang in a concerted relationship with the apartment's windows, to enhance their light, these sumptuous mirrors often formed part of a decorative ensemble with flanking torchères or sconce lights, above silver or marble console tables.[84] As in the Salón de los Espejos at the Royal Alcazar in Madrid made to Velazquez' design, now lost but known through paintings (as discussed in Chapter 3), the walls were decorated with mirrors in gilt-bronze frames of eagle wings. Set above porphyry console tables standing on lions also of gilt bronze, their orchestrated disposition along the length of the gallery in rhythmic succession became the decorative lietmotif of a Baroque princely architectural ornament (Fig. 90, Chapter 3).[85]

Throughout the long history of the mirror as a decorative object, it was closely tied to that of the decoration of its frame, and so to the adjacent history of frame-makers, from luxury silver work to stone intarsia and ornamental wood carving or inlay. Of course this object, within larger histories of the decorative arts, may be categorised according to those variations of materials and manufacture derived from sources of availability of supply that we are inclined to subsume under differences of geography. Chronologically, the history of the mirror is marked by distinctions of 'style' – in itself contingent on a broad host of contextualising matters such as changing material supply, skilled workmanship, domestic 'living' structures and habitats, forms of courtly reception and entertainment, to name only a few – that we understand as the history of art. Howsoever driven by myriad factors, ranging from the technological and material to contextualising histories of 'taste', the development of the mirror from small globe-shaped objects to flat rectangular panes that could be integrated into a grandiose wall display arose alongside the early modern advent of the gallery picture or easel painting. In practice as well as conception, their contiguous early modern histories of placement within frames as independent objects on gallery walls drew painting and mirroring into a perceived ever-closer equivalence. The parallel manners of their 'framing', in both its material and cultural aspects, in modes of facture and display, again brought painting and mirroring into a richly comparative juxtaposition within an early modern paradigm of art as mimesis.[86]

THE MYRROUR OF THE WORLD

Proceeding from the realm of objects to that of texts, the literary metaphor of the mirror was a leading bibliographic trope, and indeed title, of early modern books on every subject, as Renaissance literary scholars have long observed. Paradigmatically, William Caxton's encyclopaedic compilation of knowledge entitled *The Myrrour of the World* (c. 1480), brought out by the founder of England's first printing press, is broadly acknowledged as the earliest English illustrated printed book, appearing under the titular sign of the mirror. Along with its title, Caxton's text opens with an illustration of a scholar in his study, holding up a mirror as the source of light for his literary labours both practically and conceptually, as also the pictorial emblem of the book's contents (Fig. 31). Springing from medieval literary traditions of manuscript 'encyclopaedias' of knowledge from earlier collections generally known in Latin as *speculum mundi*, Caxton's *Myrrour* was exemplary of the genre. It was among Caxton's most successful ventures, running into multiple editions into the sixteenth century, though he is best known today as the first publisher of Chaucer. Launching his press with an edition of the *Canterbury Tales* in 1476, this text also comprised the magically prophetic mirror of the Squire's Tale, who spoke 'of quaint mirrors and of perspectives' that could read men's minds.[87] On the matter of the literary mirror motif, as the twentieth-century German scholar of early modern European literature Herbert Grabes noted, not the least of the most salient historical characteristics of Caxton's Mirror book was the title itself.

Grabes' 1973 study of the mirror trope in early modern European publishing centred on the growing ubiquity of the mirror as the emblematic title for books, which he found to be the case on all manner of subjects. From devotional tracts and courtly love poetry to political treatises and pedagogic texts to encyclopaedic compendia of all kinds, history to geography and cartography, science and cosmography, classical literature and

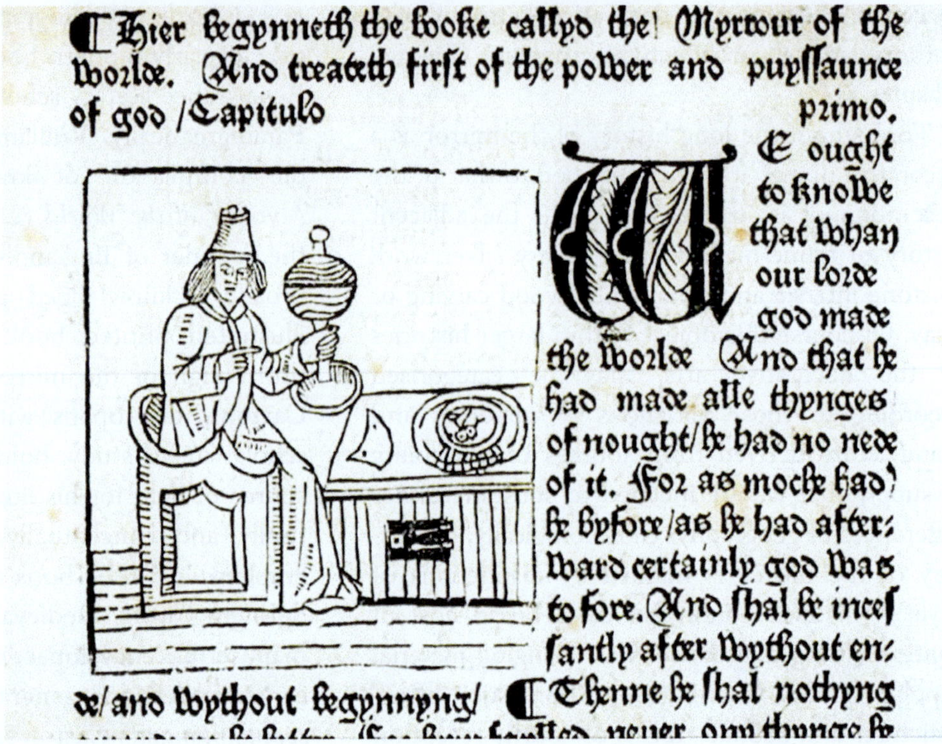
Hier begynneth the booke callyd the Myrrour of the worlde. And treateth first of the power and puyssaunce of god / Capitulo primo.
We ought to knowe that whan our lorde god made the worlde And that he had made alle thynges of nought/ he had no nede of it. For as moche had he byfore/as he had after: ward certainly god was to fore. And shal be incessantly after wythout en: de/ and wythout begynnyng/ Thenne he shal nothyng

Fig. 31 William Caxton, ed. *Myrrour of the World* (trans. Gossuin de Metz), London, c. 1480, woodcut of a scholar in his study, fol. 4v, leaf size: 23.2 × 17.5 cm, Hunterian Special Collections. Photo: University of Glasgow Special Collections

medicine, titles with the word 'mirror' – *miroir, spieghel, specchio, espejo* – configured their contents of printed knowledge. In effect, and across languages, the mirror was the ready metaphor of the light of the mind's study, emblematised in Caxton's illustrative print. The rebus of the candle and the mirror as light was profound: witness Francesco Francia's bronze medal of the Bolognese jurist, Ulisse Musotti of 1515, depicting the accoutrements of his library, for example. Comprising books, set squares, rulers, and astrolabes, at its centre the concentrated beam of a candle flame reflects onto a small convex mirror. This instrument of optically directed light was for the purposes of close study of both objects and texts and so the emblem of his *curiosité*.[88]

Within Renaissance intellectual histories of thought, Marsilio Ficino's searching philosophical enquiry into the workings of the human intellect compared thought to rays of light reflected on a mirror, so making objects appear like 'the forms of illuminated things'. In his understanding, following Plato and Theophrastus, the human eye was both the conduit and the metaphor of all intellectual perception. Mirror-like, the eye captured the forms of all illuminated objects, whose figurations thus penetrated to the mind to constitute both knowledge and speculative thought. Ficino termed the figures of ocular perception *idola*, or little images, which he understood through the conceit of the mirror-image as 'veiled' or impalpable reflections, and so the very matter of thought – as fleeting as the imagery of a mirror, or of light itself.[89]

What is signal in the case of Caxton's *Myrrour of the World*, as Grabes highlighted, was the publisher's change to the title in the process of its translation. For Caxton's text was particularly indebted to a thirteenth-century manuscript encyclopaedia by the French priest, Gauthier du Metz, titled *L'image du monde*. Whereas the thirteenth-century French manuscript used the title of *Image of the World* as an interpretive rendition of the Latin term *speculum mundi*, Caxton instead published the text as a literary 'mirror'. In his translation of Metz's *image* as *myrrour*, Caxton thus brought the pictorial field and the specular reflection into a titular equivalence as visual representations of knowledge or thought. What Grabes identified, across an extensive survey of Renaissance literary genres, was the incremental increase in the use of the metaphorical 'mirror' in all manner of book titles in every European language, first coinciding with the historical advent of the printing press. From the late Middle Ages to the end of the seventeenth century, with a particularly marked efflorescence circa 1650, according to Grabes, the circulation of books with mirror titles increased alongside the burgeoning diffusion of new specular instruments of vision. Thus Caxton's early elision of 'image' with 'mirror' stood at the inception of a broad cultural configuration of the mirror as early modernity's paradigmatic sign of knowledge and thought, as the emblem and instrument of light, and so of intellectual vision. In the words of the sixteenth-century Spanish.

Humanist Juan Luis Vives, 'Thought is, as it were, an image of things imprinted on the mind as in a mirror.'[90] In the English astronomer-astrologer John Dee's *Preliminary Aphoristic Teachings* of 1548, like Leonardo before him, Dee deployed the simile of the mirror for the visual faculties of the mind as the place where ideas appear 'as if in a mirror, showing themselves to us'.[91] Similarly, the scholar, poet, and playwright George Chapman termed 'the mind a spirit is, and cal'd the glasse ... the mirror is, in which we see the minde' in a poetic recollection of myth.[92] Similar to Caxton's *Myrrour* title for an encyclopaedia, the sixteenth-century Spanish royal cartographer Alonso de Chaves described the map of the world as its 'mirror' in his so-named *Espejo de navegantes* (Mirror of Navigators).[93] This is further exemplified in myriad book titles across all domains, as Grabes noted, such as John Swan's encyclopaedic *Speculum mundi, a Glasse Representing the Face of the World* of 1643 (using the common Elizabethan term 'glass' for mirror) in a Baroque corollary to Caxton. Among its fullest literary manifestations is surely Emmanuele Tesauro's discussion of the 'mirrors' of metaphor in his *Cannocchiale aristotelico* (Aristotelian Telescope), of 1654, in which the eloquence of Baroque wit is seen to reside in a cascading play of figurative or mirror-like literary resemblances. It is best emblematized in the scholar John Comenius' early text on pedagogic methods, the *Great Didactic* of 1657.

In Comenius' model of thought as intellectual reflection, the lucid mind is composed of myriad mirror reflections, which form the nodes of memory. The parallel Comenius draws is with the library, as the configuration of the encyclopaedia writ large, in which each book is itself a mirror of knowledge, just as the pervasive use of the book's 'mirror' title made manifest.[94] This was an ancient trope, to be found in the linked metaphorical recollection of the library at Alexandria and the legendary mirror of the lighthouse at Pharos, both of which were held to offer a view of the world in miniature.[95] Returning to Grabes' study, he found that the literary trope of the mirror or 'looking glasse' within book titles was itself emblematic, intended to signify the poetic metaphor of 'likeness' within a broader cultural paradigm of early modern mimesis. Thus the mirror title was, in Grabes' analysis, in order to demonstrate the truth of the text therein, whether worldly or spiritual. Grabes' claim was no less than to construct the matrix of early modern intellectual history as a 'mirror age'.[96] In this he both followed and led the trajectories of other literary and intellectual historians of early modernity, such as Richard Rorty's analysis of the philosophical discipline's early constitution in the metaphor of the mirror, and Georges Gusdorf, who argued that the advent of the mirror as both object and allegory precipitated the cultural rise of a new subjecthood that has long been identified as 'Renaissance'. [97]

Best known in its classic formulation by Jacob Burckhardt in his *Kultur der Renaissance in Italien* of 1860, this claim to a nascent Renaissance '*personlichkeit*' lies within Burckhardt's magisterial thesis of historical periodisation. Often seen as the founding text of cultural history writ large in its adumbration of interconnections across myriad aspects of a given historical period, Burckhardt's view of Renaissance civilization was an ambiguous one, although he recognised in it the seeds of modernity. In the political sphere its defining text was, to Burckhardt, Niccolò Macchiavelli's *The Prince* (c. 1513) as the embodiment of a nascent configuration of agonistic individualism that brought a new-found interiority to the Renaissance subject while producing the forms of competitive capitalism that would drive the development of social and economic modernity. In Burckhardt's terms, Macchiavelli's *Prince*, while nominally still in the literary tradition of *speculum principis*, entirely rewrote the genre as a justification of political authority without a 'moral mirror' of any kind; instead, the 'ideal mirror' of this Prince was the image of unfettered individual power.[98]

In Grabes' study of the literary mirror-image it is instead the other side that holds sway, of the mirror as the instrument of a morally corrective self-knowledge. Following Grabes in a brilliant essay on Chaucer's deployment of the mirror motif as the improving sign of self-knowledge, Valerie Allen further invoked the Burckhardtian thesis of a Renaissance individualism newly discernible across different cultural forms c. 1400 as the fullest manifestation of Grabes' 'mirror age'. Addressing concepts of Burckhardtian individualism within broader intellectual cultures, in Allen's view such Renaissance literary narratives turned on the process of searching individual reflection in the ethical pursuit of knowledge such as Rorty mapped in his study of the early modern mirror metaphor within the constructs of moral philosophy. Allen's literary mirror faces inward, in which Renaissance enquiry is configured like beams of the inner light of the individual mind. In her analysis, the early modern mirror-image represents a new meta-knowledge, or the paradigm of 'Renaissance' thought as illumination.[99] Similarly, Gusdorf and Debora Shuger have furthered and deepened a Renaissance configuration of the mirror as the literary emblem of self-knowledge, and so of knowledge itself.[100] Equally, Véronique Adam's study of early modern French literature highlights a figurative convergence between the optics of vision and the philosophical 'eye' of the mirror as the sign of analogical thought in a poetics of resemblance.[101] In important respects, these literary scholars also converge on Rorty's and Gasché's definition of early modern epistemology as mirror-like, in which the very processes of thought are those of specular reflection.[102] In the same vein Barbara Stafford has pointed to an early modern etymology of 'mirror' words from ancient Greek, which cluster around concepts of epiphany through light reflection, to be traced in its extensive metaphorical use throughout ancient literature and all subsequent literary forms as the sign of revelation. This quality of revelation signifies the speculative nature of thought as transformative or, to invoke Ovid once more, 'metamorphic'.[103] Hence the structure of metaphor itself is signalled in the 'light' of the mirror reflection, just as Alberti's Narcissus found it in Ovid's metaphorical pool.

Grabes' analysis of the 'mirror' motif within early modern literary cultures also studied the continuing panegyric of *speculum principis* alongside Christian devotional tracts on the reflection of divine love. In both political and devotional contexts, if in different ways, the mirror trope, as Grabes identified it, was that of a perfected double, at once mimesis and exemplum. On the one hand, the mirror shows us the subject as it is, while at the same time revealing it to us as it should be. This was inaugurated in Augustine's writings, Grabes contended, in which the mirror reflection carried a dual significance of both knowledge of the world and the moral aspiration for a 'heaven on earth'. The analogy was thus of a 'telling mirror'; whether construed as the judgment of the conscience or the intellect, the metaphor was one of moral or improving self-reflection.

This exemplarity of the mirror reflection configured not only the *speculum principis* but also the early modern encyclopaedia as *speculum mundi*, in which the acquisition of knowledge of the world is presented within the larger context of edification – often coupled with a cautionary admonition against a Faustian *vanitas*. The idealising mirror as an improving one is also discernible in the medieval literary traditions of the troubadour poets, cast allegorically in the language of devotional tracts, in which the sight of the beloved renders the lover both ardent but also chastened, above all transformed. Thus in the moral reckoning of love in Shakespeare's *Love's Labours Lost*, the princess of France has recourse to her mirror as the means of good judgment: 'Here good my glass, take this for telling true' (Act 4, scene 1).[104] Rorty likewise recalled a Shakespearian 'glassy essence' in *Measure for Measure* (Act 2, scene 2) as the literary figure of imitation and therefore learning, across all domains of knowledge.[105] As Grabes rightly argued through the choice of his own book title in English translation, *The Mutable Glass*, the Renaissance mirror metaphor was infinitely metamorphic.

What Grabes found distinctive in the early modern ubiquity of 'mirror' titles was the identification of the idealising character of the specular *exemplum* with that of art (in his case, literature). That is to say, and as Rorty also argued for the history of philosophy, the mirror's authority for trusted or ideal judgment rested on its proven capacity for true reflection, simply put, as an instrument of demonstrable veracity. As both Renaissance arts and sciences testified to, sight was accorded primacy among the five human senses as the highest form of evidential method. In this regard it is critical to recall broader shifts in Renaissance cultures of knowledge towards those of visual evidence, on which early modernity's incipient 'scientific revolution' would rest. This was foundational to Rorty's discussion. As is also evidenced in the social 'advance' of the artist from anonymous medieval craftworker to Renaissance *literato*, an intellectual equal of their counterpart in letters, the rising status of visual imagery as a form of knowledge accorded equal authority with that of texts was as central to the subsequent history of early modern science as art. The new cultural claim of Renaissance art thus rested on the demonstration of its mimetic or specular reflection. For the idealising conceit of a mirror-image made art the perfect 'double' of the 'view through the window', just as Alberti had claimed.

PSYCHE'S MIRROR

From the realm of encyclopaedias as mirror-like collections of textual knowledge to that of cultural beliefs manifest in religion, mythology, philosophy, legend, and folklore, here the mirror metaphor flourished as a representation of the inner self or psyche. Of archaic derivation, in both faith and folklore the evanescent mirror reflection was perceived as a visual corollary to the soul. Within antiquity, it was bound to the mythological figure of Psyche, and so to literary myths of the psyche's origin. In the pool of myth, this was above all configured as the reflection of the self on the surface of the water, from Dionysus to Narcissus. Further, the mirror and its paired reflection was conceived as an emblem of love, both spiritual and human, in which the reciprocity of the mirror-image was the sign both of desire and of love returned. As Chapter 5 elaborates further, the early modern inset-mirror motif within painting prospered particularly in the realm of bridal imagery, as an allegory of female beauty and its amorous pursuit. This chapter instead considers the mirror metaphor as desire's emblem within myth and folklore as the subject of a broader cultural analysis. Comprising both texts and objects, it ranges from the richly figurative imagery of secular and spiritual love poetry to enchanted specular agents of 'magical' fortune such as eye amulets, trick mirrors, optical chambers, and crystal balls to apocalyptic ocular and specular imagery as haunted configurations of myth's divided psyche, irrevocably split between the self and a 'looking-glass world'.

In the classical story of Psyche, it is Cupid's mother, Venus, whose envy of her mortal rival leads her to seek the girl's death, in a mirror-image of beauty and *invidia*. The antique story arises within classical literary conventions of metamorphic fables of changelings through love's enchantments, similar to Ovid's Narcissus, in the late Roman *Metamorphoses* of Apuleius.[106] Told by an old woman among a gang of thieves along with a terrified young female captive in a dark cave, it is a tale of *rite-de-passage*, part woven from the fabric of myth, part folklore, of a girl who is captured, and then captivated, in a metamorphosis of love's fortunes. Apuleius' Psyche is transformed into a god through her marriage with Cupid – in Greek, Eros – though she suffers abject reversals of fortune along the way. Apuleius describes the great hall of her bridal palace in an extended visual *ekphrasis*: fronted by crystal fountains, its walls are sparkling mirrors of gold and silver that shine like the sun and the moon. Psyche's fate rests on her willing suspension of disbelief: where this is broken the hall of mirrors vanishes and she finds herself alone in the wilderness. As antiquity's fabled and archaic personification of the psyche, her surety lies in the embrace of love's illusions. Hers is to delight in the mirroring simulacra of the mind without seeking to pierce their shimmering reflections, in Jean Starobinski's words, just as the Apuleian hall of psychic mirrors was the defining cultural sign of the intellect's imaginary figurations in image form.[107]

What transpires most forcibly from the story of Psyche, as Cupid's beloved, is the ancient sense of the mirror-image as the picture of desire that, howsoever fraught with the possibility of abandonment and delusion, is emotionally requited in a mythology of union. If the golden hall of mirrors is the stuff of Psyche's dreams, the mirror-image is paradigmatically the elusive face of love returned, as in the myth of Narcissus. Widely known and imitated throughout the Renaissance, the Apuleian tale of Psyche was the subject of painting at Raphael's Loggia di Psiche at the Villa Farnesina, of court masques as for opera and ballet, as well as in decorative arts such as the antique Marlborough gem and the many early modern imitations it spawned.[108]

In medieval literature of chivalric love such as the thirteenth-century French *Romance of the Rose*, itself a reworking of the myth of Narcissus as Psyche, the *Romance* is that of Psyche's love returned. As an odyssey of desire, in this text the knight/lover seeks his elusive beloved in a walled garden. He gazes on her rose-like reflection in the waters of a crystal fountain, for her union with cupidic love has transformed her into a red rose.[109] In similar *chansons* of the troubadour poets, Ovid's fountain of love, originally in the image of Narcissus, was transformed into the emblem of chivalric *amour* in which the ardent knight of romance might perceive his lady's elusive presence. Late medieval and Renaissance love poetry extended the metaphor endlessly. Thus Jean Froissart's '*Le joli buisson de jonece*' reconceived the fountain of poetic love as that of an amorous union between Narcissus and Echo, *ut pictura poesis*, while François Bérenger de la Tour's 'O saint miroir' described the face of his mistress in a mirror reflection to find it outshone by the lady herself.[110] Popular prints represented a woman alongside that of her face in a mirror reflection described as 'l'astre du jour est l'oeil de tout le monde' – the radiance of her starry light likened to the eye of all the world, as a mirror-image of the stars themselves.[111]

As the knight/lover of the *Romance of the Rose* gazes into the mirroring fountain of love, he is offered a succession of dream-like allegorical visions of his beloved, including a rose reflection, but also two crystals, like the sun and the moon, and seemingly metaphors of her crystalline eyes. The notion of the eye as a crystal or mirror is also a broad one, reflected in a wide range of literary forms. From love poetry to *Volkskunde*, such allegorisations of sight are loosely derived from the broad diffusion of Euclidean optical science and theory. In the words of the troubadour poets, suffused with the metaphorical elaborations of chivalry: 'she let me gaze into her eye / that mirror which pleases me so greatly. Mirror, since I saw myself reflected in you . . . I have destroyed myself just as the beautiful Narcissus destroyed himself in the fountain.'[112]

Within the courtly language of love the mirror-image was both captivating and a sign of acceptance or 'capture'. This was embodied in gifted nuptial mirrors of compact circular form as material metaphors of 'eye-catching'. The sixteenth-century poet of the eye as the mirror of love, Maurice Scève, described Adam's first view of himself in the wondering eyes of Eve: 'in this small place / I am reduced to a point / In the round . . . of her two eyes . . . / I am doubly reduced, I am doubled in her.'[113] Similarly, the court poet Pierre de Ronsard compared the eyes of his lover to crystals, in which he could see his shining reflection in miniature.[114] In Frederick Goldin's literary analysis of the mirror in late medieval chivalric *chansons*, the story of Narcissus became the trope of love's reflective acknowledgement. Here the recognition of the self in the eyes of another was conceived as the defining moment of youth's self-realisation in a courtly *rite-de-passage* into love.[115] In John Donne's recurrent recourse to the metaphor of the eye as the mirror of the beloved, his 'Witchcraft of a Picture' makes explicit love's ocular magic of mutual reflection: 'I fixe mine eye on thine, and there / Pitty my picture burning in thine eye.'[116] In Edmund Spenser's *Amoretti*, his anthology of love sonnets cast the 'fayre eyes' of his beloved as 'the myrrour of my mazed heart'.[117] In Milton's radical recasting of myth's *poesis* in *Paradise Lost*, it is Eve who wanders in Ovid's woods 'much wondering . . . what I was'. Seeing her own image in the liquid pool she is then awakened, her desire for her own image transposed to man, 'hee whose image thou art'. Even as she is made 'Mother of human race', yet Diana-like, Eve acknowledges she pined for that 'smooth watry image in the cleer smooth lake, that to me seemd another skie' in a vast metaphor of cosmic mirror-vision (4:448–55).[118] In Sir John Davies' poetic *Nosce teipsum* (Know thyself) of 1599, the eyes are similarly the instruments of cosmic mirror reflection: 'these mirrors take into their little space / the forms of moone and sunne and ev'ry starre'.[119] As Sarah Key has argued, the late medieval poetic metaphor of love as a mirror of the eye is surely indebted to late medieval Arabic optical theory on the science of vision, notably Hasan Ibn al-Haytham (Alhazen)'s influential demonstrations of Euclidian optics.[120] In Leonardo's searching visual observations, at the nexus of art and science and heir to the Euclidean legacy, he also noted that: 'Concerning the point of the eye . . . if you look into the eye of anyone you will see your own image there . . . your own image mirrored in the said eye.'[121]

In Euclid's ancient theorisation of vision, visual rays like light are understood to run between the eye and the object viewed. Such a model of vision was, throughout classical love poetry and myth, readily elided with Cupid's arrows casting their darts of desire, so drawing together the act of sight with that of love. Further, in Socrates' tutoring of Alcibiades, which would become a model for the later conventions of *speculum principis*, Socrates elaborates on the optics of vision in a passage concerned with relations of platonic love, yet also touching on the observation of the convex mirror of the eye. Latent within the Greek term for pupil as the centre of the eye was the recognition of its specular effect in reflecting the figure of the beholder in miniature as a *pupa*, or tiny doll.[122] This lexical elision rested on proverbial superstition concerning the eye's uncanny mirror, said to 'capture' the beloved within its gaze, but also to capture the soul, of which Psyche (Latin *Anima*) was the mythic personification.[123] It would also come to resonate within Christian devotional literature, as a metaphor of divine love but also its unknowable reach.[124] In myth, Psyche can readily gaze on the golden mirror hall but is not permitted to see her suitor, who comes to her only under the cover of night: Eros is as fleeting and elusive as a mirror reflection.[125]

Etymologically, the term *mirror*, like the French *miroir*, springs from the Latin *mirari*, meaning to look, to reflect, to admire; while in Latin *speculum* was the common term for mirror, hence the root of the German, Italian, and Spanish *spieghel*, *specchio*, and *espejo*, as well as all the cognates of spectacle and speculation, including to see, with the sense of an extended vision and therefore also to foresee. Hence perspective, as in perspicacity, which signified the transparency of optical regard and so the rays of light that came to be configured as the Renaissance painter's perspectival method in the rendering of illusionistic volume and space. The connotations of these terms were of their usage as instruments and metaphors of light, in the sense both of casting light as well as of igniting it by means of parabolic mirrors. As a reflective surface bound up with looking, the mirror made ready analogies with perception, foresight, and regard. In English the cognates of *speculum* would come to imply scientific uses as an instrument of visual knowledge as well as speculative thought or foresight. Similarly, the term *mirror* intimated the domains of beauty and renown, but also conscience or the soul – *Anima* or *Psyche* – hence the *vanitas* of vanity and the faceted reflections of the mind. From archaic usage, both the mirror object and its various histories of linguistic translations were laden with semiotic significance encompassing a full range of meanings, often deeply ambivalent, from light and truth to captivation, hubris, and delusion. In its paradigmatic reversal of left and right, and its great condensations and enlargements of scale, the mirror reflection was perceived as psychically polyvalent, as much the figure of bewitching visual deceit as of mimesis. Within convex and parabolic mirrors, with distorting distensions of scale across a 'fishbowl' reflection, it was the instrument and the emblem of a spectral deception too. It was, in Philippa Kelly's words, 'unfixed', both a 'true glasse' and a deceiving one, and haunted by the psychic bifurcations of a vexed early modern selfhood.[126]

Returning to the Burckhardtian view of the Renaissance as characterized by a new individualistic subject-hood, this comprised within it discussion of a deepening introspective interiority linked to a rising early modernity, which subsequent scholarship has greatly extended. If we have questioned the temporal boundaries and periodisation of Burckhardt's analysis, yet the adumbration of a changing individual subjectivity as the focus of historical enquiry has proved widely influential, both within the Renaissance and far beyond it. Burckhardt wrote against the backdrop of nineteenth-century German Romanticism's cultural introspection, which similarly nurtured Sigmund Freud's emerging psychoanalytic science of the psyche, whose intellectual matrices were also profoundly rooted in the study of ancient myth. In particular, Freud took up the mirror of Narcissus as the psychological metaphor of a divided subjectivity.[127] This would be greatly furthered in the ensuing work of Jacques Lacan. Lacan's own intellectual formation, like Freud's, was founded in the study of ancient mythology. The figure of the mirror, or *image spéculaire* that would form the cornerstone of Lacan's work, was transposed from archaic myth into his account of the development of the infant psyche as the *stade miroir*. Like Freud, to whom he acknowledged his influential debt, Lacan's conceptualization of the psyche's mirror was founded in the myth of Narcissus, furthered and extended by what are clearly the Dionysian and Orphic rites of the bacchanal, centred on the so-called mirror of the young god's nurture in the watery pool of Mount Nysa. Archaic accounts of the Eleusinian mystery rites in honour of the education of Dionysus in the mirroring pool of Olympian myth was, in Lacan's reading, emblematic of both early childhood's entrance into the symbolic realm and the enduring structure of human subjectivity as doubled and so divided from itself.[128] Captured and captivated by its own 'mirror-image', thus the psyche is bound and split by the manifold reflections of culture. While full scholarly exegesis of the Bacchic mystery rites would await eighteenth-century cultures of neo-classicism, yet the currency of these myths is already manifest not only in the neo-Platonic studies of fifteenth-century Medicean Florence centred around Marsilio Ficino but also, notably, in the paintings of Poussin, whose exacting representations of these rituals depicted the infant Bacchus nurtured in the thrall of myth by the woodland nymphs at the pool of Mount Nysa.

Thus the early modern conceptualization of painting as a mirror double adumbrated by Alberti in the fountain of Ovidian myth was a haunted one. Its shadowy reflection was emblematized in both art and literature, as in Charles Perrault's 1661 'romance' tale of painterly metamorphosis, *Le miroir ou la Métamorphose d'Orante*, in which the 'mirror-image' portraitist Orante is slowly transformed into a mirror himself. As a ghostly tale of metamorphosis, Perrault's story parodies the cultures of courtly imitation through the figure of Orante, who flatters his sitters by mirroring them in his images. '*Fort poli*' yet he is without memory, just like a mirror. He and his brothers, who are also mirror-image portraitists, albeit by means of 'deforming' convex and concave mirrors, are at the same time mathematicians who frequent fashionable Parisian curiosity cabinets, in a play on the illusions of perspective and those ludic mirrors of distortion that are both 'true' and false. The tale begins in the classical and courtly literary form of a conversation. In Perrault's subsequent elaboration of the genre it is revealed to be a conversation between portraits rather than people, in a further play on the spectral nature of portraiture as a 'captivated' mirror of resemblance, and so of the subject, both literal and literary.[129] Invoked by Oscar Wilde in *The Picture of Dorian Gray* (1890), it would further inflect Freud's analysis of the uncanny – both familiar and frightful – in a response to Otto Rank's psychological study of the *Doppelgänger* as a manifestation of the cultural contradictions of subject-hood as perceived in mythology's figurative pools of Bacchus and Narcissus.[130] As historians of the 'classical' formation of a divided Renaissance subject-hood, within antique texts as of their early modern exegesis and subsequently within the ongoing development of early twentieth-century psychoanalysis, the trope of the mirror-image has remained an enduring, if complicated, figure of self-knowledge as a haunted or narcissistic 'double' comprising both reflection and delusion.[131]

Above all, Psyche's mirror was perceived as an early modern metaphor of interior psychological revelation. In Shakespeare's *Richard II*, it is his monologue with his 'glass' at the moment of his unveiling and subsequent deposition in which he confronts his changed state. Dashing the mirror reflection of himself to the ground, it is 'crack'd in a hundred shivers' (Act 4, scene 1) as an allegory of his destruction. If the purpose of Hamlet's 'To be or not to be' soliloquy was to reveal his deeply conflicted private thoughts, that of *Hamlet*'s 'play-within-the-play' was 'to hold as t'were the mirror up' to the king's inner conscience (Act 3, scene 2). In this sense the 'mirror' was understood as an instrument of unmasking, as a means of penetrating to the 'privie thoughts and conceits of the mind'. Similarly in *Troilus and Cressida* (Act 3, scene 3, l. 109) the 'mirror-view' of the self lies in the looking-glass world of opinion, as the seat of reflexive introspection. In Achilles' words: 'My mind is troubled, like a fountain stirred,' so reflecting on the mirror of the mind as the fragmented fount or source of conflicted memory.[132] In the same vein, Grabes saw a bivalence in the mirror-imagery of an early modern mentality. On the one hand, the mirror-image was held up as idealizing or improving; on the other hand, it served as moral warning, admonishment, even punishment.

Theologically, the moral mirror of an omniscient divine was represented in imagery of the eye of God. In a painted representation of venal sin intended as a pair with one of virtue (in the Prado Museum, long though uncertainly attributed to Hieronymous Bosch), the central configuration is of the excoriating eye as an all-seeing mirror inscribed 'beware the eye of God'. The tiny figure of Christ appears as a '*pupa*' within the divine pupil, as a specular emblem of God's love. Set around is a succession of small scenes depicting various vices as if reflected on the iris of the eye. First documented as a *mesa*, or table top, the intended viewer and context remain unknown. Yet the imagery recalls a rich range of texts and prints on fortune, virtue, and vice, construed as exemplary 'mirrors' of improvement and admonishment, as the mirror of conscience. Among them is the representation of Superbia, or Pride, depicted in an idiomatic vernacular. A woman in a well-appointed domestic interior looks into a mirror held aloft by a 'devil'.[133] Beyond the divine eye, in a series of roundels depicting worldly sins is a further allegory of vanity as a female nude looking towards a convex mirror held by a devil while a frog nestles at her sex. The putrid and punitive elements of this imagery, howsoever delicately miniaturised and exquisitely rendered in jewel-like colours, may suggest an apocalyptic iconography of fearsome repentance c. 1500, though cast in the rich colours of courtly learning. In the teeming profusion of dream-like imagery in Bosch's *Garden of Earthly Delights*, also c. 1500, of an enigmatic complexity that continues to elude scholarly definition, a tiny convex mirror appears on the buttocks of a small devil in which a female nude in the arms of a beast must confront her captive mirror-image in a shattering 'vanity' of herself.[134] Such disturbed mirror-imagery of dreams on love between pleasure and cruelty is also present in texts such as the epic *Hypnerotomachia Poliphili*, published in Venice in 1499.[135]

The conceptualization of the early modern collective psyche as fundamentally split or divided from itself was Burckhardt's, as he read it from within such historical materials, to unsettle the historic claims of a Renaissance 'golden age'. Split into a series of faceted and competing specular images of virtues and vices, or the haunted exemplum, the psychic price of Burkhardt's early modernity came to be identified, figuratively speaking, with the infinitely cascading perspectival reflections of the mirror hall. Like Psyche's elusive golden palace of love, the human mind of Burckhardt's *individuum* was understood as irretrievably split.

Within Christian devotional literature of the period, the mirror was a frequent metaphor of the human heart, while the world was often cast as a labyrinthine perspective of mirror reflections. With a vast reach into Christian devotional literature, Paul's letter to the Corinthians (1 Corinthians 13:12) on the ineffable nature of divine love was of a mirror-reflection metaphor: 'For now we see [His love] only as a reflection in a mirror; then shall we see it face to face.' In a cascade of light as the metaphor of God, the mirror reflection of human love was but a faint imitation of divine effulgence. In the extensive Renaissance history of biblical translation, the Pauline mirror analogy as the picture of divine love returned, however dimly understood by the human soul, was a constant one. The many Renaissance elaborations of the spiritual mirror contrasted the constancy of devotional love with the 'looking glass world of opinion', as one of fractured and distorted reflections. In texts such as François de Sales' *Traité sur l'amour de Dieu* (1616) or Comenius' *Labyrinth of the World and Paradise of the Heart* (1631), the pilgrim's journey through the world of mirror illusions is characterized by the disjunctive vision of distorting mirrors, while the only 'true glass' is that of divine love.[136]

Mirrors of distortion were objects of wonder and curiosity, the subject of enquiry within optical and catoptric science, but also understood as manifestations of an ambivalent magic. Arising from archaic superstition surrounding mirror-images, they were perceived as haunted signs of the divided psyche and of a divinity configured by both love and moral judgment. Like the '*pupa*'/pupil elision of folkloric beliefs, superstition commonly understood specular reflection as a magical means of capturing the soul, whether captivated in love or caught in the snares of the 'evil eye'. Intimately linked to folkloric superstition surrounding the evil eye was the figure of the mirror, similarly able to 'capture' the soul of its viewer within its reflection, as both danger and its superstitious remedy. Hence the presence of reflective mirror tokens within archaic burial chambers was one of transport to the beyond, but also of great care in their protection, to the object as to the 'person' held within them.[137] Similarly, apotropaic charms to ward off the envious rays of the evil eye were typically of reflective metals such as gold charms, refractive quartz crystals, and reflective mirrors, including eye amulets in lustrous materials of polished metal and glass in emulation of the mirror of the eye. Within the reciprocal symmetries of mimetic magic and superstition, these were understood to return the damaging rays of envy on themselves. This was also the folklore of the mirroring shield of the Medusa myth.[138] Their fully bivalent place between Renaissance cultures of magic and myth, but also the science of optics and the seat of learning, is evident in Leon Battista Alberti's self-portrait medal, bearing the image of the winged eye as a sign of the humanist's intellectual endeavour (Fig. 32). Alberti understood the eye as 'more powerful than anything, swifter, more worthy . . . It is such as to be the first, chief, king, like a god of human parts.

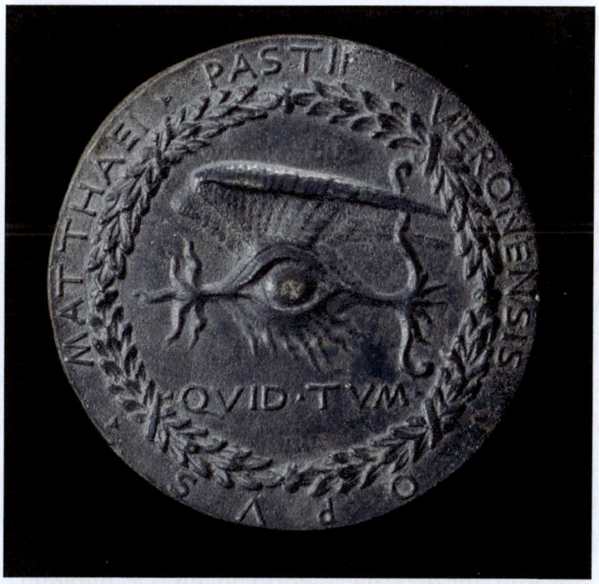

Fig. 32 Leon Battista Alberti, portrait medal/reverse side QUID TUM, with winged eye, c. 1450–55, bronze, diameter 9.25 cm, British Museum.
Photo: British Museum

Why else did the ancients consider God as something akin to an eye, seeing all things and distinguishing each separate one?'[139]

In this regard it is critical to recall the place of learned 'magic' within Renaissance cultures, as Chapter 4 will further elaborate, which comprised both the folklore of archaic superstition, astrology, and alchemy but also the very nexus of early modern scientific enquiry and humanist learning. Thus the quartz crystal ball, from archaic times regarded as 'magical' in its highly refractive powers to capture the sun's rays to ignite fire, was also a ready material metaphor of the eyeball, because of its ability both to magnify objects and to capture the visual field within itself in miniature mirror reflection. As a medieval reading aid, dome-cut crystals were placed on the page to be studied and thus moved along with the reading eye. For these reasons rock crystal was the prototype of optical lenses, as much an instrument of early science as of magic in its capacities of sight, and by analogy of foresight or prediction. In Christological depictions of crystal orbs in Salvator Mundi subjects, the miniature 'world' depicted within its sphere was understood as a metaphorical reflection of divine dominion. This extension from verifiably scientific prediction through the magnifying capacities of visual analysis to that of divination as well as its broader allegorical figuration was both long-standing and culturally ambivalent, across the realms of optics, theology, and 'magic'.

At the same time, the mirror-image was clearly understood as a metaphor of illusion or visual deception within early modern cultures of catoptric curiosity. Hence the description of mirrors that foreshorten or elongate the face by the Neapolitan polymath and playwright Giovanni Battista della Porta in his *De humana physiognomia* of 1586, surely close to the description of 'trick mirrors' of distortion, kept at Renaissance castles, palaces, and gardens, in the manner of optical jokes, such as Philip the Good's Burgundian castle at Hesdin in Artois.[140] Continuing into the seventeenth century and beyond, John Evelyn would describe the 'strange multiplication of things' by means of cascading perspectival mirrors at the Villa Borghese, in a room comprising a range of mechanical 'jokes' as equivalent curiosities of the trick mirror-image.[141]

Della Porta further described the use of mirrors of illusion in which viewers saw themselves with the head of a donkey or the snout of a pig in a specular 'metamorphosis' like that of Apuleius' Lucian or Ovid's Narcissus, but which was also part of his enquiry into the morphological differences between species to further an understanding of human physiognomy. This is elaborated by the German Jesuit scholar in Rome, Athanasius Kircher, whose interests included catoptrics, or mirror reflections, and whose museum of curiosities included prismatic 'jokes' such as a 'metamorphosis machine'. Kircher similarly instructed his visitors in the study of light reflections with specular illusions of skeletons and death's heads, touching on the theology of *vanitas* through the metaphor of the mirror's fleeting imagery.[142] The French Jesuit and astronomer-mathematician Jean Leurechon also described mirror illusions showing the face of a female beauty on one side, and a death's head on the other, in a close alignment of catoptrics with religious themes of memento mori.[143] The Bolognese scientist Leonardo Fioravanti, in his *Dello specchio di scientia universale* of 1564, described a number of trick or distorting mirrors including the celebrated '*miroir sorcière*', a specular tondo inset with smaller convex mirrors like the eyes of a sorcerer, whose cascade of reflections comprised effects of 'fishbowl' distortion, fragmentation, and perspectival multiplication.[144] An allegory of love as for thought, the early modern mirror-image and its myriad reflections turned on its swiftness, like light, but also its fleeting and illusory nature. Its capacity for infinite perspectival recession was perceived as both a source of marvelling wonder and a haunted anxiety. In the words of the seventeenth-century Parisian writer Louis d'Epinay d'Etelan, '*Sur un miroir*: [O mirror], painter of brilliance, of inimitable art / You paint, without effort, an art of inconstancy / Always *ressemblant*, never the same.'[145]

HALLS OF MIRRORS

Scattered among the extensive notes that Leonardo da Vinci made on every subject across the arts, literatures, and sciences, compiled into notebooks numbering thousands of pages together with sketches of his evolving thoughts, are the seeds of what he appears to have intended as a dedicated study on catoptrics, or the science of mirror reflection. Seemingly part of a larger prospective (never executed) treatise on optics or vision, the many uses of scientific mirrors and lenses were among Leonardo's various interests in the technological instrumentation of sight.[146] His interest in the mirror extended from the industrial to the artistic and scientific. This comprised his own production of workshop mirrors of curved metal for the purposes of heat induction for metalwork, as well as cast illumination for scientific study. He was also a student of all nature's mirroring luministic effects, including light and shadow, sun- and moonlight, stars, clouds, mists, raindrops, and rainbows. If Leonardo was exceptional in the degree of his study, yet his interest in mirrors was one that Renaissance artists broadly shared, as manifest in both artistic practice and theory, from painting to perspectival optics and catoptrics.

Across his notebooks, Leonardo documents his extensive use of mirrors as a means of observing the perspectival effects of reflection, part of his larger study of the science of vision related to his painterly practice. By means of experiment, he demonstrated the specular cross-reflection produced by a cascade of ever-smaller reflected mirrors within mirrors, in effect, a mirror chamber in the scientific domain:

> It so happens that if two mirrors be placed so as to be exactly facing each other, the first will be reflected in the second and the second in the first. Now the first [mirror] being reflected in the second carries to it its own image together with all the images reflected in it, among these being the image of the second mirror, and so it continues from image to image on to infinity, in such a way that each mirror has an infinite number of mirrors within it, each smaller than the last, and one inside another.
>
> An instance of how the images of all things are spread through the air may be seen in a number of mirrors placed in a circle, and they will then reflect each other for an infinite number of times, for as the image of one reaches another it rebounds back to its source, and then becoming less rebounds yet again to the object, and then returns, and so continues for an infinite number of times.
>
> If at night you place a light between two flat [metal] mirrors which are a cubit's space apart, you will see in each of these mirrors an infinite number of lights, one smaller than the other, in succession.[147]

Elsewhere in his notes he specified the number and dimensions for such an ocular 'hall of mirrors', followed by an illustrative sketch in the form of a polygon (Fig. 33):

> If you have eight flat [metal] mirrors, each 2 *braccia* wide and 3 high, and have them placed in a circle so as to form eight sides of 16 *braccia* of circumference and 5 of diameter, that man who stands inside will be able to see each side of himself an infinite number of times. The same happens with four mirrors, which make four sides.[148]

Leonardo's interest lay in the observation of mirroring cascades of reflections, receding to the

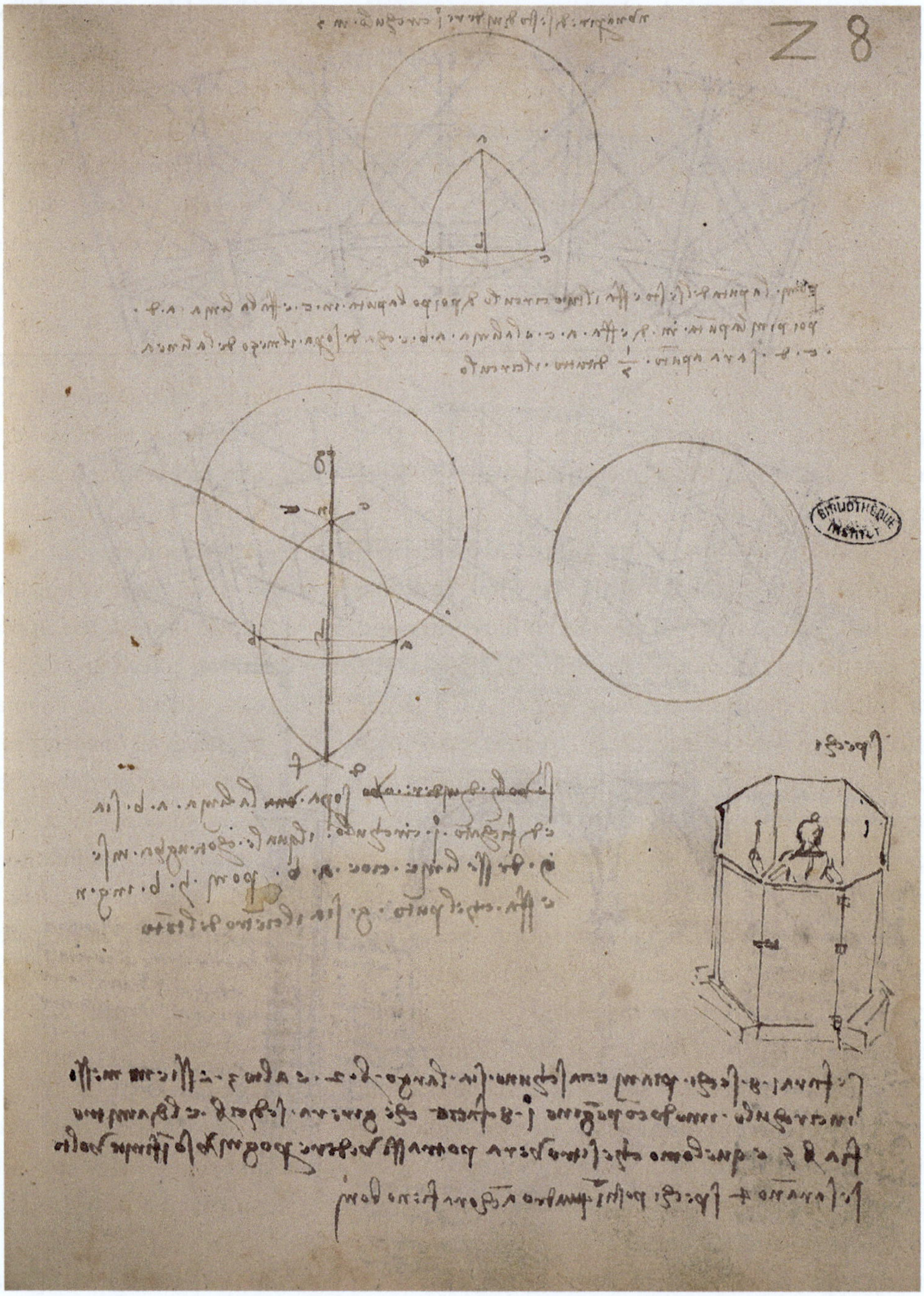

Fig. 33 Leonardo, polygonal mirror chamber (lower right), pen and ink drawing, ms. B folio 28a, Institut de France Library. Photo: Réunion des Musées Nationaux

perspectival point of infinity, for which the mirror was the proof. His study of the 'infinity' of mirror cross-reflection is, in itself, an analysis of images within an image, here in the scientific domain of optics and catoptrics. The concept of infinite specular reflection was already present in ancient catoptric manuals such as Euclid's, as Leonardo and later Louis XIV surely knew, in which angled arrangements of mirrors were assembled for their ocular effects of infinite multiplication and regress.[149] It was one that della Porta, in his book of natural science, *Magia naturalis*, which comprised much study of the mirror-image, would also pictorialise in a similar diagram of a mirror-lined

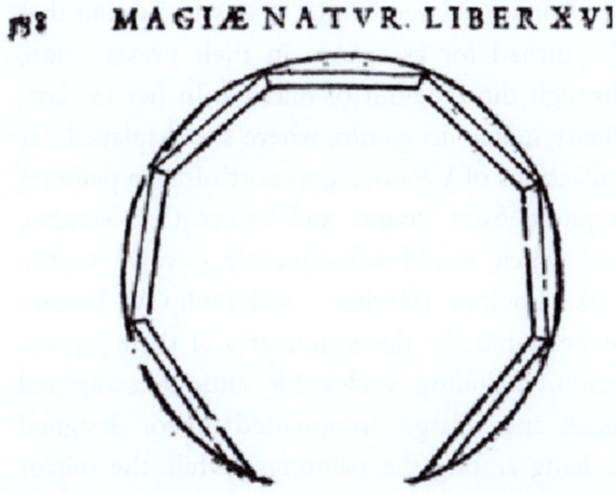

Fig. 34 Giambattista della Porta, polygonal catoptric theatre, *Magia naturalis*, Naples, 1589, book 17, chapter 3.
Photo: Hathi Trust

polygonal chamber that he termed a 'theatrical glass'. Further elaborating on its assembly, he also distinguished a more complex configuration that he called 'amphitheatrical': 'Let looking glasses be raised perpendicularly ... if you set a candle against it, you shall see innumerable candles ... you shall not see so many stars in the skies.'[150] Apparently on display in the private museum of his house and a putative design for a theatre set, its intention was to produce a cascade of infinite light reflection in the same way as Leonardo did (Fig. 34). Recalling his visit to della Porta's optical chamber when in the service of the Spanish Viceroy to Naples, the playwright Francisco de Quevedo perceived the visual effects of the catoptric theatre as a metaphor of the fleeting images of the mind or imagination – '*simulacros y formas sin materia*' – images and forms without substance.[151] Della Porta further described the infinite reflections of such a specular 'theatre', in demonstrating the effects of multiplication by setting a candle in the middle of concentrically arranged facing mirrors 'so that it will seem to multiply'.[152]

This multiplication of the mirror-image, recognisable in the early modern cultural trope of the 'hall of mirrors' that Versailles came to represent, was one of reflection but also ambiguity as to the relationship between specular mimesis and illusion. Thus of painting, whose mirroring conceit was recognised as the fiction of presence, both demonstrably visible and impalpably absent. In the words of the Roman painter and art theorist Federico Zuccaro, in his 1607 *Idea de' pittori* as a disquisition on the academic status of art, painting is commended as the 'true mirror of nature, its very portrait in all its manifestations', able to represent the 'universe of nature like a great gallery or compendium of the visible world', with seeming volume and space where there is, in fact, none.[153] In his address to Rome's Academy of St Luke, of which he was principal, Zuccaro elaborated further:

> If you place a large mirror of very fine *cristallo* in a room full of exquisite paintings and magnificent sculptures, it is clear that, when I look at it, this mirror will not only be the end of my gaze but it will also be an object which in its turn will clearly and distinctly present me with all the paintings and sculptures. And yet these paintings and sculptures are not physically present in it. They only appear in the mirror in their immaterial form. It is in this way that those who wish to have an understanding of what art [*disegno*] is should philosophise.[154]

In so saying Zuccaro defined a theory of painting as both deceit and verity, like a mirror reflection, whose verisimilitude lay in the skill of its specular fiction. Thus the true measure of art was to be judged by comparison with its exemplary double, the mirror-image. What is above all striking in this passage is Zuccaro's specular imaginary of a great gallery of pictures seen through the medium of a mirror reflection. The imagery was a pervasive one, to be found also in pedagogical texts on the structures of visual memory such as Comenius' *Great Didactic* (1657), in which the 'eye' of the mind is likened to 'a spherical mirror suspended in a room which reflects images of all things that are around it'.[155] Likewise Martin Luther, in a passage treating the ambiguity of pictures as both spiritual truth and illusion, like a reflection, described them as a *Spiegelbild* of multiple images: 'where we see stories and objects as though in a mirror'.[156] Similar to Zuccaro, the Munich *Wunderkammer* of Duke Albrecht V of Bavaria kept a great mirror 'in which you can see everything in the cabinet', as a recollective image-making instrument for collections of visual knowledge objects that Comenius also espoused in his didactic methods.[157] In the same vein, Jean-François Niceron described the Parisian cabinet of Louis Hesselin: 'there one sees such beautiful glasses for such excellent mirrors . . . that one may say it is the *abregé* to all the cabinets of Paris'.[158] Here the early modern picture gallery with its collection of independent images, as also with collection cabinets of objects of all kinds, had become a metaphor for encyclopaedic enquiry, like Caxton's *Myrrour of the World*. Moreover, in its reflected form as perceived in a mirror-image such as Zuccaro described, picture collections were seen as the intellectual equal of books, and of the early modern library too. In this regard, Zuccaro's mirror-image was an anthological one, able to collect within its reflection the gamut of paintings that a picture gallery could house. In effect, the art gallery configured in a mirror reflection was painting's exemplum, in which the academic artist that Zuccaro promulgated was instructed in the history of his art. At the same time, Zuccaro's mirror-image was the model of painting because it was both present and absent, visual truth and illusion, exactly as Alberti had prescribed. As his successor as principal of the Accademia di San Luca, Gian Lorenzo Bernini, is reported to have said in a further reflection on the paradox of painting as impalpable as a mirror-image: 'Art lies in that which is all illusion, yet appears true.'[159]

In the manner of Zuccaro's *concettismo* of art's reflections, when the Swedish Queen Christina sought to display her brilliant collection of art at her Roman palazzo Riario, it was to Bernini that she turned for assistance in their presentation, through the medium of mirrors. In her extraordinary *stanza dei quadri*, where she displayed her collections of Venetian and north Italian painting acquired from Prague and before that Mantua, and which would subsequently devolve to the Duke Philippe d'Orléans and Philip V, Bernini orchestrated the decorative arts of their presentation, including socles for antique sculptural heads and a large ornamented mirror designed to hang among the paintings. While the mirror itself is now lost, a preparatory drawing remains, doubtless made for the queen's consultation (Fig. 35). There is also an annotated sketch and a description of it by her visitor from Stockholm in 1687–88, Nicodemus Tessin the Younger, who detailed its hang above a table on which was displayed a Greek bronze head then believed to be of Alexander the Great. In Tessin's account, the mirror was designed to be of large dimensions, to the extent that it required more than one piece of glass according to the manufacturing methods of the time.[160]

Bernini's sculptural frame, carved and then gilded in full relief, was orchestrated so as to veil the joins of the glass. Depicting the figure of Time bending over the mirror, he bears a drapery in his outstretched arms as if to 'unveil' the glass behind. Surely a sculpted recollection of Parrhasios' painted curtain of ancient renown, which deceived even the great painter Zeuxis in Pliny's account (*Nat. Hist.* 35:65), the veiling drapery is both a light *paragone* of the arts and a witty Erasmian *vanitas* of Bernini's artistry, as concealed and revealed in a mirror reflection.

As with the Narcissus mirror by Filippo Parodi (Fig. 4, Introduction), also an artist of Bernini's influence, elaborately framed gallery mirrors such as Queen Christina's were designed as a specular corollary to painting. In early modern art galleries where they could also reflect the works of art within them, just as Zuccaro described.

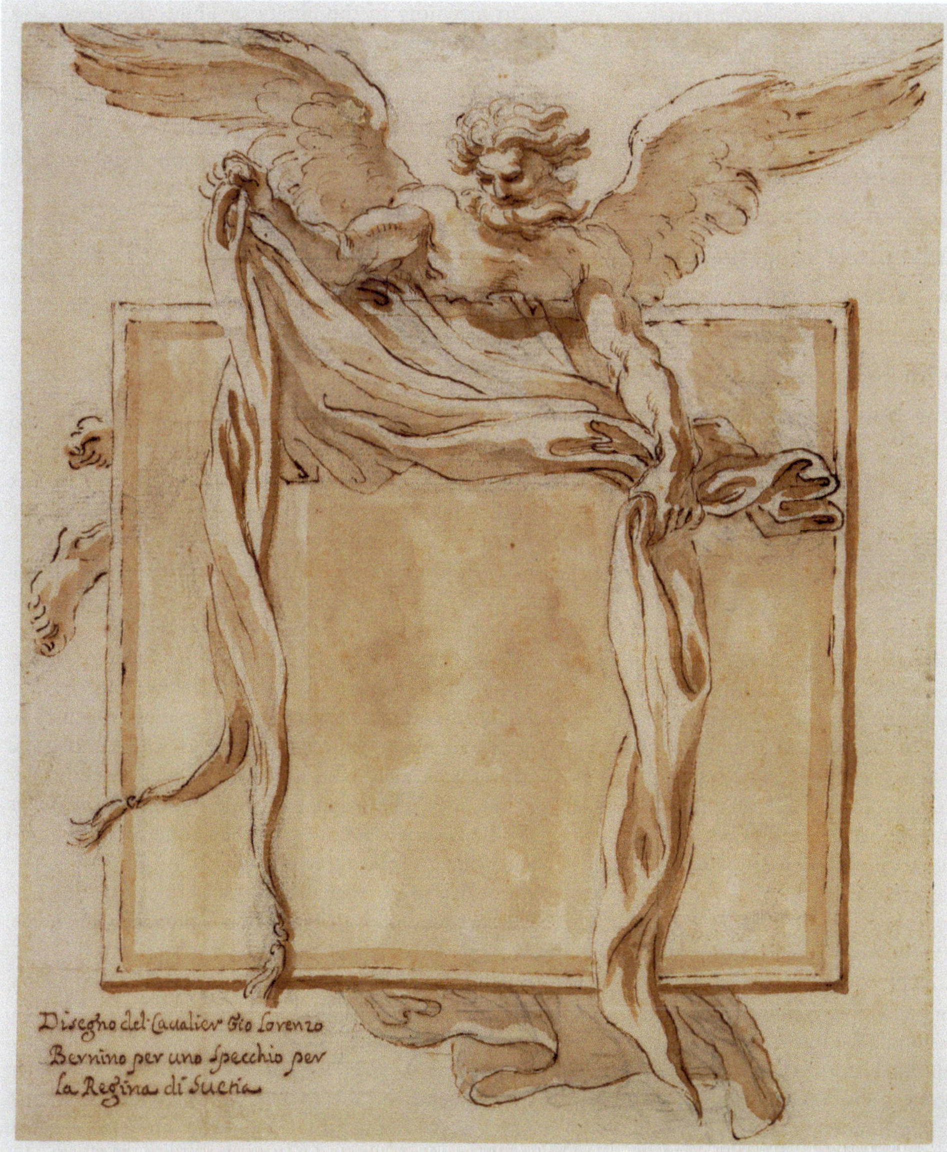

Fig. 35 Giovanni Lorenzo Bernini, *A Design for a Looking-Glass for the Queen of Sweden*, c. 1656, pen and brown wash over black chalk, 23.0 × 18.8 cm, Royal Collection Trust. Photo: © Royal Collection Trust / His Majesty King Charles III 2023

The display of such mirrors was orchestrated in respect of the pictorial composition of their reflection. That is to say, the gallery mirror was placed in order to render its surface reflection as a picture of a picture gallery, like a composite image of the collection's surrounding works of art. In both the Bernini and the Parodi mirrors, the allegory of their frames was a further commentary on this, in a doubled play on the specular motif of mimetic painting. In the Parodi mirror, the gilded youth Narcissus bends his head towards his own reflection, just as Alberti imagined in his account of Ovid's poetry as the fount of art. In the Bernini, it is winged Time who flies above the mirror, to suggest the history of art that its reflection of Christina's art collection surely represented. To borrow from Victor Stoichita's eloquent phrase, there arose within the early modern trope of painting as specular the 'self-aware' image, in which inset images signified the status of art. Concomitantly, within artistically orchestrated frames such as Parodi's and Bernini's appeared what we may also term the 'self-aware' mirror. Here the mirror surface, like a painting, reflected on itself just as Zuccaro described. Suffused with inset specular reflections of works of art, Zuccaro's *cristallo* mirror was both an anthological collection and a mimetic theorisation of painting as a mirror reflection of the visible world. It is the historical contextualisation and conceptualisation of early modern painting's specular or mimetic paradigm that constitute the subject of the book that follows.

NOTES

1 (Le Brun) M. Lorne, peintre [pseud.], 1684.

2 Following the recent restoration of the Galerie des Glaces, see Milovanovic & Volle, 2013; Milovanovic & Maral, 2007; Thuillier, 2007; and Thuillier et al., 2007, with further bibliography. On the cultural example of Versailles more broadly, see Gaehtgens et al., 2017. On Charles Le Brun, see the recent exhibition catalogue, Gady & Milovanovic, 2016; and Gady & Montagu, 2010. On the historical evolution of the early modern mirror gallery, Bazin-Henry, 2021b.

3 Piganiol de La Force, 1701, 100.

4 La Font de Saint-Yenne, 1747. On the larger histories of Versailles' eighteenth-century reception, Kisluk-Grosheide & Rondot, 2018; Ledbury & Wellington, 2020.

5 On Alberti, see the discussion in the Introduction.

6 For general literature on the history of the mirror: Anderson, 2007; Pendergrast, 2003; Melchior-Bonnet, 2002; Gregory, 1997; Melchior-Bonnet, 1994; Goldberg, 1985; Baltrušaitis, 1978.

7 On Christine de Pizan's *Cité des dames* of 1405, written in her capacity as court poet to the Valois monarchy and of which copies were dedicated to Queen Isabeau as well as other members of the royal family, from an extensive literature, see Adams, 2014; and Langdon Forhan, 2002. On the collection of illuminated manuscripts at the Burgundian court, drawing on the 1420 inventory of the library of Philip the Good, Doutrepont, 1906, cat. nos. 97, 109; and Dogaer & Debae, 1967. On the 1401 French translation of Boccaccio's *Des clères et nobles femmes*, a compilation of biographies of exemplary women in the literary tradition of *viris illustribus* and for which Boccaccio planned to write a parallel compendium of lives of illustrious men, see further Buettner, 1996, fig. 65, a depiction of the antique painter Marcia, or Iaia as cited by Pliny in his *Natural History* (35 147), who paints her portrait by means of a mirror reflection. The 1420 inventory of the library of Philip the Good also lists Christine de Pizan's *Cité des Dames*, of which there are three copies at the Bibliothèque Nationale de France (BNF) with a frontispiece illustration containing a mirror as the emblem of Reason (607, 1178, 1179). On the royal collection of manuscripts more broadly, Hamilka & Laffitte, 2009; Avril, 1991, no. 7.

8 Roskam & Schorn, 2018; Morel, 2012.

9 Gady, 2019; Balcar & Martin, 2013. On the larger architectural history of the Renaissance gallery with further bibliography, Galletti, 2016; Constans & da Vinha, 2010; Prinz, 2006; Kieven & Strunck, 2010.

10 Scudéry, 1684, 19.

11 *Mercure Galant*, Donneau ed., December 1682, 9, 61, as part of a longer text on the new decorations and entertainments at the palace.

12 Pierre Bourdelot, cited by Saule 2007, 62, and see her further discussion of contemporary reception of the Galerie; on which see also Bazin-Henry, 2021a.

13 Félibien Des Avaux, 1703, in Thuillier, 2007, 116–18, especially 117.

14 *Mercure Galant*, Donneau ed., September, 9, 1686, 306–8; Arminjon, 2007; see also the further bibliography on the Galerie furnishings below, note 17. The extant silver court furnishings with gilding, which comprise wall mirrors as well as torchères, wall sconces, and tables, in Arminjon's catalogue, on which see further below, may offer a sense of what the silver furnishings for the Galerie were once like. See also Clarke, 2022, on the making of the silver furnishings.

15 According to Boulenger, 1913, 58.

16 Milovanovic, 2009; and the broader catalogue, Milovanovic & Maral, 2009.

17 Amelot & Didier, 2013; Saule, 2013; Mabille, 2009a; Mabille, 2009c; Maral, 2009; Baulez, 2007; Didier, 2007. On the King's dress, Martin, 2015; Salmon, 2011.

18 Thuillier et al., 2007, especially the technical reports on the pigments and the discovery of the *oculi*, 311, 332, 356

19 On the development of the early modern window: Jütte, 2023; Ng, 2017; Louw, 1991.

20 Hedin, 2022, on the gardens.

21 Bouchenot-Déchin, 2013.

22 Contini 2010; Milovanovic, 2005.

23 On the cabinets for collections, and the difficulties of precise documentation concerning them because they were refashioned several times, Hans, 2010; Castelluccio, 2009. For an overview, Pérouse de Montclos, 1991.

24 As suggested by Milovanovic, 2007, 14.

25 This is underlined in the construction of a gallery of facing mirrors across the Pont-Neuf in 1686 in honour of the King's crossing, which was intended to multiply his image, cited in Melchior-Bonnet, 2002, 78; and Pendergrast, 2003, 119–20.

26 Scoville, 2008; Belhoste, 2013; Hamon, 2017. See also Philippe, 1998, for the antecedent period of French glass-making.

27 Doni, 1566, 38. See further Thornton, 1991, 238; citing Medici Invt, Florence, 1589, as well as the Florentine

Rinuccini inventory of 1499. On mirrors as decorative arts: Roche, 1956; Child, 1990; Bazin-Henry, 2021b.

28 Bazin-Henry, 2017; Bazin-Henry, 2016.

29 See Havard, 1887, III, column 795.

30 Bazin-Henry, 2021b, for discussion of French mirror cabinets.

31 *Gazette de France*, ed. Renaudot, Paris, 1633, 72.

32 Félibien, 1676, 14.

33 According to Jean Loret's report in the weekly gazette of court news, the *Muse Historique*, May 1651, as cited in Melchior-Bonnet, 2002, 26.

34 See the further discussion in Chapter 3.

35 Warwick, 2022.

36 Saule, 2010, 26, based on the archives of St-Gobain; Chaimovich, 2008. On the broader history of French early modern glass-making, based on substantial archival research, Scoville, 2008.

37 On the history of windows, Jütte, 2023. Bazin-Henry, 2021b, 122–28, gives a summary of the 1688 patent and its consequences; on which see also Maitte, 2009.

38 See the further discussion of scientific lenses in Chapter 4.

39 See Arminjon, 2007, and the further discussion below.

40 As documented in Arminjon, 2007, 46, 77, and 235 no. 13.

41 Thuillier, 2007, 31, as reported by the Venetian ambassador and future Doge Marcantonio Giustinian at the French court in the *dispacci dagli ambasciatori* in Francia, on which see further Bondue, 2010.

42 Saule, 2010.

43 Milovanovic, 2010.

44 Lehman, 2010. These were interests pursued by many princely rulers, as a demonstration of their prescience. Louis XIV's *miroir ardent* for the purposes of advancing science and industry is still extant at the Paris Observatory, by François Villette, 92 cm, of gilded bronze; at the Kunstsammlungen in Dresden made for Augustus the Strong in 1686, of copper and iron on an ebonised wood stand, measuring 230 cm in height.

45 Widemann, 2010. On the construction of the Observatory windows, Louw, 2003.

46 Mabille, 2009b; Morera, 2010.

47 Milovanovic & Maral 2007, 24–29.

48 Ottonelli, 1652; see further Frommel, 1998; Casale, 2002.

49 Milovanovic & Maral, 2007, 24, 29; Dufresnoy & De Piles, 1668, 286.

50 www.metmuseum.org/art/collection/search/626692; Wolohojian et al. 2017; Gady & Milovanovic, 2016. *Las Meninas* is further discussed in Chapter 3.

51 Pliny, *Natural History*, book 36.

52 The main ingredient of glass is sand or crushed rock, which is liquified through heat, and to which is generally added a flux composed of different types of saline ash made from saltmarsh plants or forest brushwood, referred to by a wide range of terms including saltpetre and potash. The quality of glass depends on its ingredients. This concerns the type of sand used, but also the flux of which saltmarsh plant gave the finest results, as compared with forest glass made of bracken ashes. See further the general histories of glass by Garland, 1952; Liefkes, 1997; and Cummings, 2002, with particular attention to its materials and manufacture; the useful glossary by Hess & Wight, 2005; Tait, 1991; Klein & Lloyd, 1989; Ciappi, 2006; Page, 2006; and the *Journal of Glass Studies* hosted by the Corning Museum of Glass; as well as the online catalogues of major glass collections including the Corning Museum, Toledo Museum of Glass, Glasmuseum Hentrich Kunst Palast Düsseldorf, British Museum, and other collections of decorative arts comprising glass. For a contextualising account of early modern cultures of glass-making, Warwick, 2022. On Pliny's *Natural History*, Anguissola, 2020; Murphy, 2004.

53 On the history and archaeology of ancient glass, Henderson, 2013.

54 See especially Gerolemou, 2020a; Frontisi-Ducroux & Vernant, 1997; and Schneider, 1985.

55 Cited in Kelly, 2006, 76.

56 Bechtel, 1992, 237–45; Adam, 1985, 53–54. On Gutenberg more broadly, Barbier, 2017.

57 Frontisi-Ducroux & Vernant, 1997.

58 Frontisi-Ducroux & Vernant, 1997; A. Stewart, 1996; Baratte, 1986.

59 Camille, 1988, especially 54–71. See also Williamson & Davies, 2014; Crépin-Leblond & Taburet-Delahaye 2009. The theme of the Castle of Love was also represented on medieval ivory caskets. See further the Courtauld Institute's Gothic Ivories project, www.gothicivories.courtauld.ac.uk.

60 Thornton, 1997.

61 Della Porta, 1589, book 17, chapter 4; in its 1658 English translation, 362. See the further discussion of della Porta in Chapter 4.

62 Euclid, *Optics* & *Catoptrics;* on which see Sinisgalli, 2012. This is further discussed in Chapter 4.

63 Dillon 2018.

64 Sabellicus, 1560, book III, ch. 1, 'De venetae urbis situ'. See the further discussion in Hills, 1999, 109–29; McCray, 1999, 96; and Tait, 1979, 94.

65 See further Hahn & Shalem, 2020.

66 See Bycroft & Dupré, 2020; Pointon, 2010; Scarisbrick, 2007; Evans, 1933.

67 Illardi, 2007; Bedini & Bennett, 1995; and on their princely patronage, Bedini, 1961; and Heikamp, 1986, on Medicean patronage. See the further discussion in Chapter 4.

68 Leurechon, 1642, 156.

69 Zecchin, 1987–90. See further Mariacher, 1967; Tait, 1979; Barovier Mentasti, 1982 & 1988; Judde delaRivière, 2018; Trivellato, 2000.

70 Zecchin, 1987–90, especially 1989, II, I *Barovier* 197–232, and 1990, III:131–188, 'Materie prime e prodotti della vetraria Muranese'. See further Jütte, 2023.

71 As noted by Zecchin, 1987–90, 1989, II:273–78.

72 Zecchin, 1987–90, 1990, III, especially 368–71.

73 https://collections.vam.ac.uk/item/O827182/design-for-the-back-of-drawing-etienne-delaune/; LePautre, 1670.

74 On Larmessin, see further Buck, 2019; Pullins, 2014. This type of figuration of trades was also manifest in miniature collectible figures of luxury materials for princely patrons, such as ivory 'street pedlars' studded with diamonds and gold for the collections of Augustus the Strong in Dresden, on which see Kappel, 2017, 246–47; and the broad discussion in Koeppe, 2019, 102, on the Dresden '*galanterien*' figures.

75 Amman, Sachs, & Feyerabend, 1568; trans. 2009; Stanley Smith, 1965.

76 Neri, 1612; Fioravanti, 1564; Biringuccio, 1540.

77 Diderot & D'Alembert, 1761–88, and within the larger compass of the *Encyclopédie Arts & Métiers*, the volume on glass-making, c. 1770, of which the volumes of articles and plates were published separately in facsimile ed., 2002; Knothe, 2009; Sewell, 1986. On artisanal histories of glass-making, Maitte, 2009; on windows, Jütte, 2023.

78 Of the scarce publications in this area, Roche, 1956; and Child, 1990. Crépin-Leblond & Taburet-Delahaye, 2009, offer guidance, as does and Hartlaub, 1951. On the relationship with picture frames, see Newbery et al., 1990; articles by Gilbert, 1977; the 1987 journal special issue on frames edited by Chastel; and the extensive online catalogues of museums with strong holdings in decorative arts such as Réunion des Musées Nationaux, the Metropolitan Museum of Art, the Germanische NationalMuseum in Nuremberg, and Victoria & Albert Museum.

79 Thépaut-Cabasset, 2007–8.

80 Bimbenet-Privat, 1997. www.nms.ac.uk/explore-our-collections/stories/global-arts-cultures-and-design/lennox love-toilet-service/.

81 Published by Giuffrey, 1895, I.

82 www.metmuseum.org/art/collection/search/461205?searchField=All&sortBy=Relevance&ft=suzanne+de+court&offset=0&rpp=20&pos=3.

83 Such mirrors are discussed further in Chapter 5.

84 See further Arminjon, 2007, for discussion of the silver furnishings including mirrors now at the Royal Castle of Rosenborg in Copenhagen, the National Museum of Bavaria in Augsburg, Windsor Castle, Knole, and the Esterházy collections at Castle Forchtenstein, among others, on which see also Koeppe, 2019, 16–19, 27–28.

85 See the further discussion of the Hall of Mirrors at the Royal Alcazar in Chapter 3. The cultural impact of the enclosed gallery for art collecting and its related consequences for the gallery painting is considered by Belting, 1994; and Stoichita, 1997.

86 Newbery et al., 1990, in which frames for mirrors and paintings are treated alongside each other.

87 Chaucer, 1476, *The Squire's Tale*, 234. See further Gillespie, 2006; Blake, 1976.

88 https://collections.vam.ac.uk/item/O248671/ulysses-musotti-medal-francia-francesco/. Cited by Thornton, 1997, 167, as part of a larger discussion of the role of mirrors in the Renaissance *studiolo*, citing the calligraphic treatises of Torniello (1517) and Palatino (1540). See also Lehman, 2010.

89 Ficino, 1576, *In theoprastum de somniis*, ch. 33, 1816–17.

90 Vives, 1538, 1782, III:362.

91 Dee, 1558, 41.

92 Chapman, 1614, Perseus and Andromeda, cited in Tufte, 1970, 203.

93 Chaves, (ms. c. 1536), 1983.

94 Comenius, 1657; see further Jechova, 1994.

95 Discussed in Reeves, 2008.

96 Grabes, 1973; also translated into English, Grabes, 1982. On the literary figure of the mirror, Frelick, 2016; Anderson, 2007; Shuger, 1998; Fintz, 1985; Goldberg, 1985.

97 Rorty, 1979; Gusdorf, 1956.

98 Burckhardt, 1860; on whom see the recent anthology by Bauer & Ditchfield, 2022, particularly the essays by Virginia Cox and Wietse De Boer on Burckhardt's thesis of Renaissance 'individualism'. See further Baron, 1960; and Allen, 2015.

99 Allen, 2015.

100 Gusdorf, 1956; Shuger, 1998.

101 Adam, 1985, in Fintz's larger anthological study of the literary mirror motif.

102 Rorty, 1979; Gasché, 1986.

103 Stafford & Terpak, 2001, 24.

104 Shakespeare, 1623, *Love's Labours Lost*.

105 Rorty, 1979, 42 (though Shakespeare's point was that of fickle fortune's simian imitations).

106 Apuleius, *Metamorphoses*. See further Carver, 2007.

107 Starobinski's 1965 discussion of imitation as both representation and illusion; Haig Gaisser, 2008; Kenney, 1990.

108 The Marlborough gem was an antique cameo once in the possession of Rubens, then gifted to Thomas Howard Earl of Arundel (Museum of Fine Arts, Boston). Louis XIV was said to have sought, unsuccessfully, to acquire the 'fairy tale' gem just at the time in which Charles Perrault and Jean de la Fontaine were bringing together their great literary collections of fables and *contes de fees* in imitation of Apuleius. See Penny & Haskell, 1981, 49, note 51. On Psyche in Renaissance arts and letters, Bélime-Droguet, 2013.

109 A thirteenth-century ms. with many copies, first published in 1481; see Fleming, 1969; Bel & Braet, 2006.

110 Froissart & Fourrier, 1975; Bérenger de la Tours d'Albenas & Weber, 1963, *O saint miroir*, 539.

111 Goodman Soellner, 1983.

112 Bernart de Ventadorn, 1965, vv. 17–24, 166–68.

113 Scève, 1562, I:164. See Frelick, 2018, for discussion of Scève and Narcissus emblematics.

114 De Ronsard, 1553, *Je parangonne a vos yeux ce crystalle*, 91, no. 75.

115 Goldin, 1967.

116 In Wilson, 1969, 115.

117 Spenser, 1595, Sonnet VII.

118 Milton, 1667, book 4, verses 448–55.

119 Davies, 1599b, 'Seeing' II, XIV:973–74; Tudor, 2010.

120 Key, 1983. On the influence of Alhazen on Western European art and culture, Belting, 2011.

121 Ms. A, Library of the Institut de France, sheet 37 r & v; Leonardo, 1938, II:371. Due to the great historical complexities of anthological arrangements of Leonardo's notes, initiated by the artist himself, his subsequent heirs, and thereafter by scholars and editors, the many editions and translations, as well as repetition within the notes themselves made over his lifetime, I have sought to cite directly from the manuscripts with attendant references to published translations as appropriate.

122 Plato, *Alcibiades*, 'Socrates: And have you observed that the face of the person who looks into another's eye is shown in the optic confronting him, as in a mirror, and we call this the pupil, which is a kind of image of the person looking.' The Greek κόρη and the Latin *pupilla* both mean 'little girl' or 'doll,' and were used to indicate the dark center of the eye in which a tiny image can be seen reflected, as noted in Plato, 1955, 8, 133, note 1.

123 See the classic Róheim, 1984, on mirror superstition

124 Late medieval devotional texts such as Guillaume de Deguileville's mid-fourteenth-century *Pélerinage* trilogy were broadly copied, translated, and published across the fourteenth, fifteenth, and sixteenth centuries, in which the capacity of the tiny pupil to mirror the entire figure was seen as a metaphor for the all-encompassing vision of divine love and understanding.

125 Warwick, 2017; Frontisi-Ducroux & Vernant, 1997.

126 Kelly, 2006.

127 On the relationship of early psychoanalysis with a classical mythos from within art history, Damisch, 1992, Gamwell & Wells, 1989; Kuspitt, 1989; Freud, 1957.

128 Jacques Lacan's celebrated argument on the *stade miroir* was first presented to the 1936 International Psychoanalytical Congress, and first published in 1949. See Lacan 1977; on the complex history of which see Gallop, 1982/3. On the Dionysian mysteries, see Bowden, 2010; and the classic 1790 study by Taylor, 1891.

129 Perrault, 1981.

130 Rank, 1971; Freud, 1955.

131 From a vast literature, see Porter & Buchan, 2004; Gamwell & Wells, 1989; Gallop, 1982/3.

132 Shakespeare, 1623.

133 Gibson, 1973.

134 Erwin Panofsky famously declined to comment on this work, 1958, I:358; see further Koerner, 2016, especially ch. 7, 'The Unspeakable Subject', 179–222; Belting, 2005.

135 Colonna, 1499.

136 Comenius, 1997; François de Sales, 1616.

137 Thomson de Grummond, 1981, for discussion of the archaic mirror as a metaphor of the soul as reflected in language and usage, in which such gifted betrothal objects were subsequently burial tokens as the receptacles of the spirit or soul; and the collected essays in Schneider, 1985, and especially Gottlieb, 1985, on the mirror's bewitchments.

138 Belting, 2011, 230–31: Frontisi-Ducroux & Vernant, 1997; and Roger Caillois' various writings on games of mimicry and the gorgon's gaze, concerning the *mal'occhio* and amuletic charms against it, particularly Caillois, 1960, 129.

139 Alberti, 1890, 228. The translated quotation here is from Rubin, 2007a, 93.

140 Della Porta, 1586; Hagopian van Buren, 1986; Kodera, 2014, and his further essays on della Porta.

141 Evelyn, 1827, I:183.

142 Kircher, 1646, 901. See further Chapter 4.

143 Leurechon, 1642, 160.

144 Fioravanti, 1564, book I, ch. 21, 53–56.

145 Bachelin-Deflorenne, 1869, II:52–53.

146 According to Irma Richter's reading in Leonardo, 1966, 111–12, on the basis of passages in the Codex Atlanticus that suggest a hypothetical table of contents for such a treatise, such as folio 360 r. On the layered, interwoven 'labyrinthine' nature of Leonardo's notebooks, see Zwijnenberg, 1999, especially 181–82. See the further discussion of Leonardo's interests in optics in Chapters 3 and 4, and on the editions of his notebooks with further bibliography, in Chapter 3, note 1.

147 Leonardo, Codex Atlanticus, Biblioteca Ambrosiana Milan, 138r. b, in Leonardo & MacCurdy, 1938, II:364–65.

148 Ms. B f 28, Library of the Institut de France, trans. in Leonardo, 1977, I:132, no. 65, with a reproduction of Leonardo's small diagram of the octagon chamber. It is also discussed by Zwijnenberg as the manifestation of Leonardo's 'labyrinthine gaze', 1999, 183; on which see further Desbiens, 1995.

149 Euclid, *Catoptrics*, Proposition 14; Gerolemou, 2020b.

150 Della Porta, 1589, book 17, ch. 3, from its 1658 English translation, pp. 359–60.

151 Quevedo, 1958, 1411, cited in Eamon, 2017, 11–38.

152 Della Porta, 1589, book XVII, ch. 3, from its 1658 English translation, p. 360. See further Chapter 4.

153 Zuccaro, 1607, 4, 33.

154 Zuccaro, 1607, 6–7; Heikamp, 1961, 154–56.

155 Comenius, 1907, 53. The early modern recourse to the figure of the inner eye of the mind is also noted by Rorty, 1979.

156 Luther, 1883–1929, XVIII, *Schriften*, 79, translated in Stoichita, 1997, 92.

157 Haeutle, 1881, cited in Seelig, 2017, 79.

158 Niceron 1638, 77. Thornton, 1997, 167, as part of a larger discussion of the role of mirrors in the Renaissance *studiolo*, citing the calligraphic treatises of Torniello (1517) and Palatino (1540). See also Lehman, 2010.

159 Baldinucci, 1681–1728, 5, 669.

160 The bronze head is now among the Prado Museum collections of antiquities, as with the majority of Christina's sculpture. On the annotated drawing by Tessin (Nationalmuseum, Stockholm) and his description in his travel notebook, Sirén, 1914, 182–84. On Bernini's drawing, Ebert-Schifferer et al., 2017. On Christina's collection, including the mirror: Biermann, 2017; Zirpolo, 2013; Zirpolo, 2005; Biermann, 2001. The drawing has generally been considered a workshop study, viz., Brauer & Wittkower, 1931, I:145–47; Blunt & Cooke, 1960, 24, no. 37.

Chapter 2

ARMORIAL MIRRORS

All parts are like the most beautiful and rich noble jewels, for here it seems that everything lives and rides out of the painting. These are mirrors, mirrors, not paintings.

—LUCAS DE HEERE, 'ODE TO THE GHENT ALTARPIECE', *THE COURT AND ORCHARD OF POETRY*, 1565

Soon as he bade them blow, the bellows turned
Their iron mouths, and where the furnace burned
In hissing flames huge silver bars are rolled
And stubborn brass, and tin, and solid gold
Then first he formed the immense and solid shield
Rich various artifice emblazed the field.

—HOMER, ACHILLES' SHIELD, *THE ILIAD*, XVIII, TRANS. ALEXANDER POPE

IN GIORGIO VASARI'S 1568 biography of the Venetian painter Giorgione, the Florentine art historian described a now-lost or possibly fictive painting composed of a series of mirrored effects. Apparently arising from debate with Verrocchio and the sculptors as to the artfulness of their respective arts, according to Vasari, Giorgione replied in pictorial form. Depicting a standing male nude seen from behind, Giorgione painted a figure as if it were sculpture in-the-round, through a sequence of specular surfaces comprising water, armour, and a mirror-reflection:

> It is related that Giorgione, at the time when Andrea Verrocchio was making his bronze horse, fell into discussion with certain sculptors who maintained that, since sculpture showed in a single figure a variety of aspects and attitudes to anyone walking round it, for this reason it surpassed painting, which only showed one side of a figure.... [Giorgione] painted a nude, his shoulders turned, and at his feet, a fount of ... limpid water bearing his reflection from the front. To one side was a burnished cuirass that he had removed, and this reflected his profile since the polished surface of the armour revealed everything clearly. On the other side was a mirror reflecting the further side of the nude figure.[1]

In response, Giorgione painted a work of specular reflection to trump the sculptors' claims. Whether fictive or lost, his theoretical conceptualisation of Renaissance painting centred on the idea of art as mimesis, represented by a mirror-image. It was a pictorial effect for which Giorgione was renowned, and which would have a long echo across great swathes of Renaissance painting, in Venice and far beyond.

As Vasari surely knew, the Venetian critic Paolo Pino had, some twenty years earlier, also described Giorgione's *paragone* painting as a specular trope of the pictorial arts. Pino had moreover specifically identified it as the figure of St George, which was further reflected in a constellation of reflective armour, mirrors and a mirroring pool:

> Giorgione painted St George armed, standing ... by the edge of a pool of clear water which reflected his figure in foreshortening.... He feigned a mirror resting against a tree which reflected his figure from the side, and another mirror ... in which one saw the other side of St George in profile.[2]

In its elision of reflective armour with both the surface of a mirror and a mirroring pool, Giorgione's reflected image-within was perceived as a ready metaphor for the art of painting itself, manifest in both Renaissance art theory and artistic practice. By pictorial means, Giorgione demonstrated that the shield, the mirror, and the surface of the pool, like a sequence of inset paintings, were drawn together conceptually as parallel forms of picture-making by reflection.

In their descriptions of Giorgione's lost work of mirror-images, Pino and Vasari (surely also knowingly) echoed Leon Battista Alberti's celebrated definition of painting as founded in the Ovidian pool of Narcissus. As adumbrated in the Introduction, Alberti described painting as 'embracing with art what is pictured on the surface of the water'.[3] Arising from this conceptual paradigm of painting as a shimmering paradox of truth and illusion, presence and absence, Renaissance art produced vast numbers of paintings concerned precisely with the effects of mirrored reflection. This was represented within painting by mirrors themselves and in every type of reflective surface in the manner of Giorgione – pools of water, gleaming arms and armour, and other lustrous decorative objects such as glass and jewels. The theme of painted armorial reflection was one to which Giorgione would return in works such as his Castelfranco Madonna or the Vienna *Warrior*. It would, moreover, have a great efflorescence in Venetian painting, and in sixteenth-century art more broadly, as Chapter 5 discusses, comprising paintings such as Tintoretto's *St George with St Louis and the Princess*, or Titian's *Allegory of Conjugal Love*. But the earliest pictorial manifestations of such painted reflection, as this chapter considers, are within Northern and Netherlandish painting of the fifteenth century, which couple together mirrors with mirroring shields.[4] For while Alberti was writing the first Renaissance theory of painting as the mirror-image of Ovidian myth, *Della pittura* (1435–36), Jan van Eyck was painting the celebrated inset mirror at the centre of his Arnolfini double portrait of 1434 (Fig. 3, Introduction). In this regard, the Arnolfini mirror followed the great Ghent altarpiece of 1432, with its myriad specular

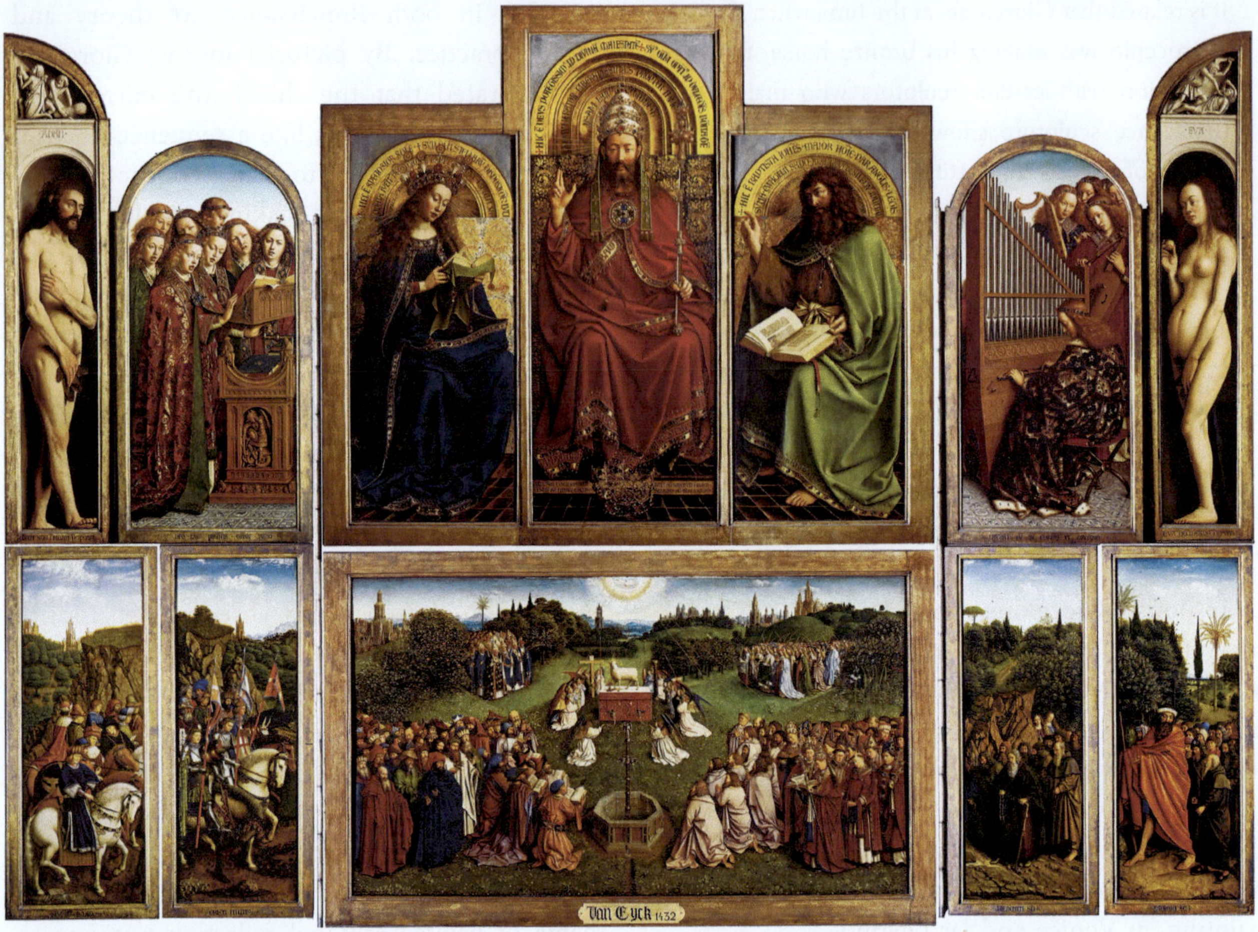

Fig. 36 Hubert and Jan van Eyck, *Ghent Altarpiece (Adoration of the Mystic Lamb)*, 1432, oil on panel polyptych, 3.5 × 4.6 m, St Bavo's Cathedral, Ghent.
Photo: Wikimedia

surfaces of gleaming armour and metal. For this was a painting that critics deemed so true to life as to be made of 'mirrors, mirrors, not paintings', in the eulogising words of the sixteenth-century Flemish painter and poet Lucas de Heere. Beginning with the Ghent altarpiece, this chapter traces the representation of reflection in fifteenth-century northern European painting, in both mirrors and other reflective surfaces, as a leitmotif of van Eyck's Netherlandish school of art.

SCHILDERKUNST

The great span of the Ghent altarpiece, composed of twelve hinged wooden panels, extends across 4.6 metres in width and 3.5 metres in height. Designed to open and close in respect of church liturgy, its folding panels are double-sided, with painted scenes on both back and front. Originally housed in an ornate wooden architectural frame of Gothic tracery (now lost), its complex iconography centres on the Adoration of the Lamb of God, flanked by angels, saints, clergy, crusaders, and the company of heaven. Across its multiple panels, as its earliest critics noted, the altarpiece depicts a fully concerted play of reflected light in the details of armour, jewels, and other ceremonial objects of crystal, silver, and gold (Fig. 36). Over a hundred years before Giorgione and Vasari, therefore, the Ghent altarpiece spoke directly to pictorial concerns on the specular nature of a mimetic art. Van Eyck's deployment of depicted armour and metalwork as reflective mirrors within his painting addressed precisely the question of pictorial imitation as a matter of specular effects that Alberti had simultaneously conceived in the shimmering pool of Narcissus.

In the armour of the Warriors of Christ in the Ghent altarpiece's lower left panel, the smooth-surfaced breast and shoulder plates of St John reflect both the garden of the Lamb and a further meadow seemingly extending before it, in a panoply of jewel-like colours – reds, blues, whites, and greens. At the same time, the large square sapphire of the singing angel's brooch in the panel above, as many scholars have recognised, reflects in miniature the long Gothic windows of the Vijd Chapel at St Bavo's Cathedral in Ghent, for which the altarpiece was originally destined. Through the study of reflection, Giorgione joined the scene of pictorial illusion with that of the painting's actual surroundings in an illusionistic continuum of architectural and painted space. This is furthered by reflections in the ornamental brass spout of the fountain at the centre of the work, whose convex surface reflects in miniature both the windows of the chapel and the groups of angels that appear on either side of its golden orb within the painting.[5]

The mirror-like quality of the Ghent altarpiece rests not only on the details of such lustrous objects as armour, precious metals, and jewels within it, however; it resides also in the manner of its making. For the burgeoning representation of such highly reflective objects in early Netherlandish painting arose alongside the historical development and diffusion of oil paint. If Vasari considered van Eyck the 'inventor' of oil painting, instead scholarship since G. E. Lessing has understood the Eyckian use of oil-based paint mixes as a historic heightening of the medium's distinctive capacity for translucent luminosity and reflection. Skilfully suspending measured quantities of coloured pigments in oil, made chiefly from boiled linseed or walnut, early Netherlandish artists in the circle of van Eyck endowed painting with new-found jewel-like colours of complex light refractions. Technical study has underscored the independent layers of each colour within the larger paint surface. Oil's glistening surfaces, applied in layers of translucent glazes, brought a new brilliance to the medium, much like the glinting light reflection of a mirror's sheen. The use of oil thus served to heighten the growing conceptual approximation between a painting and a mirror. Early fifteenth-century Netherlandish oil-based paint formed a pictorial surface of light reflection so evenly applied that, in Lucas de Heere's words, each of the Ghent altarpiece's wood panels was transformed into a seeming mirror.[6]

This specularity of paint was acknowledged to be prescient above all in the work of Jan van Eyck, which Vasari held up for emulation. He noted its heightened mimetic possibilities, particularly in the rendering of lustre and shine. The early sources on van Eyck speak to the ready analogy with the intensified properties of light refraction seen in jewels and precious gems, as well as the gleaming reflective surfaces of burnished metals, silver, and gold. These early textual sources (which are Italian) recognised that Northern painting's mimetic prowess in the detailed imitation of nature was closely tied to the increasingly luminous development of the oil medium in the early fifteenth century by Jan and his followers, notably, Rogier van der Weyden and Hans Memling.[7] This was also the case in Flemish manuscript illumination, where the increased use of gum arabic over egg white c. 1400 produced richer colours and newly shimmering light effects, as in the *Belles heures* of Jean Duc de Berry by the Limbourg brothers. The greatly celebrated limned art of the Northern courts, justly famed for its gem-like colouring, was one in which the van Eycks are also thought

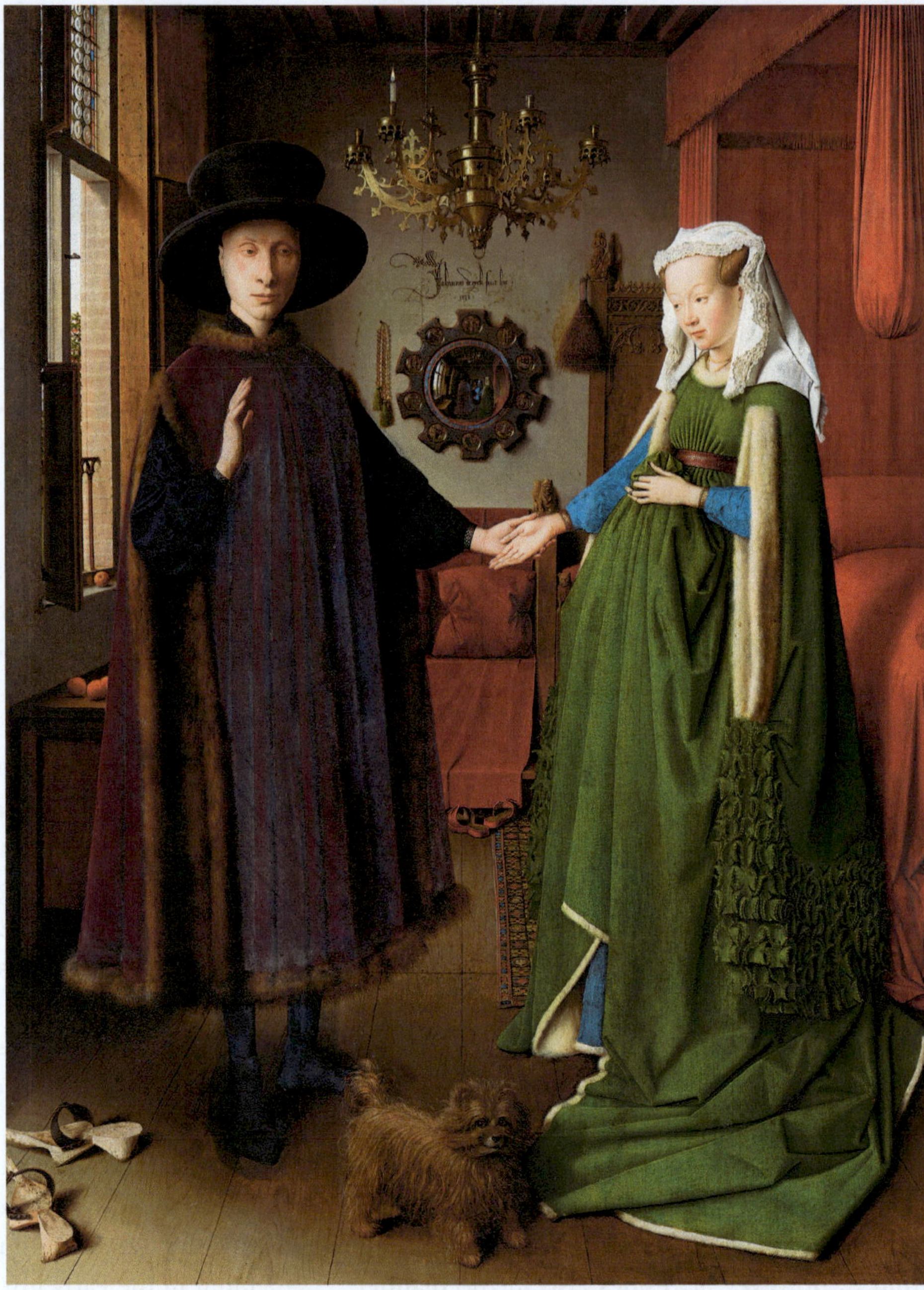

Fig. 37 Jan van Eyck, *Arnolfini Double Portrait*, 1434, oil on oak, 82.2 × 60 cm, National Gallery London. Photo: Wikimedia

to have trained.[8] So highly coveted in Italy, Netherlandish skill in the lustrous medium of oil paint was, in terms of cultural exchange, part of a great array of luxury commodities of precious and luminescent materials wrought with fine skill – gold, jewels, textiles, and decorated armour. Extensive trade links between north and south, van Eyck's Bruges and Alberti's Florence, also brought with them the ready exchange of ideas that nurtured a nascent history of art conceived in terms of the mirror-image.[9]

The pictorial trope of painting's art as specular first adumbrated in the reflective metalwork of the Ghent altarpiece is most fully manifest in the celebrated mirror at the centre of van Eyck's Arnolfini Portrait (Fig. 37).[10] Itself a product of trading relations between Florence and Flanders, this painted panel depicts the Tuscan textile magnate Arnolfini, then resident in Bruges and by whom it was commissioned in connection with his marriage.[11] The painting displays the rich accoutrements and material wealth of domestic appointment: an apartment lit by large, lead-paned windows, an elaborate brass chandelier, and a ceremonial display bed of Renaissance family estate ornamented with wood carving and a lavish display of hung textiles as the acknowledged social emblem of property and lineage. Likely a nuptial chamber, it displays the gifts of the groom to his bride in the domestic appointments of their marital dwelling. Arnolfini, as a merchant of luxury cloth, wears a tunic of silk velvet lined with sable, decorated with cuffs of silver braid; while his betrothed's ample dress of fine green wool as the colour of ardent spring, with its elaborate ruching, is lined in either ermine or miniver over turquoise sleeves cuffed in gold, with gold chains at her neck.[12]

If the Ghent altarpiece represents the pictorial metaphor of painting as mirror-like in a range of reflective surfaces such as armour, precious metalwork, and jewels, the Arnolfini portrait's specular imagery is direct. Its extraordinary perspectival centre concludes in a convex mirror of blown glass set in an ornamental wooden frame, its reflective foil in the soft lustre of lead or antimony characteristic of early fifteenth-century mirror backs. The frame displays a further series of inset images in a surrounding ring of painted glass roundels. Echoing the circular shape of the mirror in miniature, these tondo scenes depict the story of Christ's Passion. The mirror's dimensions, portrait-like, are roughly commensurate with that of a head. A large mirror for the time, when the artisanal technology of blown-glass production precluded big panes, it was certainly intended to signify a calibre of domestic decorative object whose value could rival and even exceed painting. Shield-shaped, its curving convex form produces a slight distortion of scale across the mirror-image of the interior it reflects. As other scholars have noted, this is also evident in a mild 'fish-bowl' effect of the panel as a whole. This has led to speculation that van Eyck may have used a curved mirror such as the one he depicted, from which to render his painted imitation of the Arnolfini interior.[13] If this was so, the painting's inset mirror might be understood as both the instrument and the emblem of van Eyck's closely detailed specular art. Within the artist's studio, as also the scholar's, the mirror was the instrument of 'light' in both practical and conceptual terms, able to reflect and so magnify the surrounding light in order to enable study. As such it became the ready sign of the painter's powers of reflection, of the intellect as of his art. Thus in the cuirass of St John in the Ghent altarpiece, and the Arnolfini mirror, van Eyck brilliantly inaugurated a pictorial conceptualisation of his painting's specular intent, perfectly mirrored in the glistening oil-based medium of his art. From van Eyck's mirroring example the history of early Netherlandish painting may be said to issue, as painters sought to position themselves within an Eyckian genealogy of Flemish art whose pictorial brilliance was defined as perfectly specular. Thus the inset mirror-image reflection became the abiding metaphor of early Netherlandish painting's 'art'.[14]

BRUNELLESCHI'S MIRROR

Renaissance painting's matrix of the mirror reflection as the sign of art, within the critical historiography, has been famously tied to the development of visual perspective in the story of Filippo Brunelleschi's celebrated experiment with painting and mirroring at the door of the Florentine cathedral (c. 1415–20).[15] If van Eyck was not a painter of mathematical one-point perspective like his Italian counterpart Brunelleschi, yet it is clear that both were deeply immersed in the study of optics as informing both spatial recession and the painted reflection of light. Its profound effects for the history of Renaissance art are manifest in van Eyck's attentive pictorial observation of mirror reflections.[16] The earliest sources on Jan van Eyck stressed his knowledge of geometry, which we may, within the context of late medieval intellectual cultures, understand as the study of optics.[17] Like Brunelleschi, and doubtless strengthened by the close mercantile and cultural links between fifteenth-century Florence and Bruges, van Eyck's manifest interest in the art and science of light reflection drew on an inherited knowledge of reflected light based on mirrors that underpinned the science of both optics and perspective. His was what has been termed 'an optical mode of description', distinct from Brunelleschi's mathematical conception of one-point perspective as the structuring paradigm of a mimetic art. It was surely founded in late medieval interest in the writings of Euclid as re-elaborated in tenth-century Arabic mathematical circles around the central figure of Hasan Ibn al-Haytham, which became increasingly influential in Europe across the fourteenth century. Al-Haytham's extensive writings on optics, among other things, studied the effects of light reflection on different materials and colours, or secondary light effects.[18] As recent technical research coupled with the art-historical sources of the period confirms, it is the studied imitation of reflected or secondary lights on every kind of texture and colour that distinguished van Eyck's art of optical effect in the eyes of his contemporaries. Whether the sheen of silk or the greater light absorption of velvet and fur; whether the shimmer of pearl or the full illumination of crystal; whether the specular reflections of burnished armour, the sparkle of cut diamond, or the softer scintillation of worked gold, van Eyck's virtuosity lay in their painterly rendering.[19] The legacy of Euclid's ancient geometry of light and eleventh-century Arabic experiments with light refraction issuing from the circle of al-Haytham, as it increasingly reached into late medieval European scientific thought, would touch both Brunelleschi's Florence and van Eyck's Bruges, howsoever to be interpreted variously within the respective practices of their mimetic art.

Of Brunelleschi's celebrated experiment at the door of the Florentine Cathedral, the historical evidence concurs in dating it circa 1420, precisely the same years in which Jan van Eyck was painting the Ghent altarpiece. Standing inside the Duomo looking out at the Baptistery, Brunelleschi apparently painted a panel of the scene framed by the Cathedral's doorway. The panel's square shape – reported to have been a half *braccio*, or half an arm's length, along each side – was designed to correspond in reduced scale to the view of the Baptistery as seen through the Cathedral's double doors and, crucially, the size of a mirror he had used to reflect the scene in pictorial format. Brunelleschi thus conceived of the painted panel and the mirror as a mimetic pair. To further the correlation between the panel and the mirror reflection as parallel representations of the view itself, Brunelleschi apparently burnished the sky of his painted panel with silver. In this way the panel's upper section was also a reflective surface that, when placed inside the Duomo's doorway facing outward, would reflect the actual sky with its passing clouds and changes of atmospheric effects. In this pictorial experiment, Brunelleschi's aim was to demonstrate that painting could perfectly reproduce the visible world like a mirror reflection. He deployed a mirror to advance that claim through a visible demonstration of its visual effects. It allowed the viewer to compare the view through the doorway with the mirror reflection and its painted imitation, to find them fully equivalent. The claim that painting could represent the fiction of space on a two-dimensional surface was thus made by analogy with the mirror-image.[20]

The 'mirror' that Brunelleschi used was likely of metal, as was usually the case with workshop mirrors of the period. Steel gave a particularly clear and colourless reflection, and could be tempered into sheets of considerable size as well as form, from flat to parabolic, to serve industrial uses in the workshops of architects, engineers, and smiths, among others, as a means of focussing light, as an instrument of combustion, and as the draughtsman's ready means of translating three-dimensional observation into two-dimensional form for transposition into drawing. Before either photography or electricity, drawing was broadly used for documenting all forms of visual knowledge, for which the workshop mirror was its mimetic instrument. In practice, the mirror reflection was the draughtsman's template. These metal mirrors might also be burnished with silver, as the most reflective of metals, to increase the whiteness and light of the surface finish, as was seemingly the case with Brunelleschi's panel in its reflection of the sky. Thus the metaphor of the flat squared surface of a painting as mirror-like that Brunelleschi appealed to in his view of the Baptistery was well known across the period and, equally, perceived as coterminous with the convex reflection of the Arnolfini's blown-glass mirror form, or the curving metal shields of armoury.

If the Renaissance ushered in a newly insistent approximation between painting and the mirror, yet it drew on a much longer history of their analogy and comparison. This far longer historical trajectory of pictorial mirror-imagery by poetic simile stemmed from the reflections of antique metal mirrors, forged by metal and silversmiths, of all sizes and shapes. In terms of the materials and methods of their making, metal mirrors came from the foundries and workshops for armoury of the metal, gold, and silver smiths, the art in which Brunelleschi himself first trained. The burgeoning Renaissance development of blown-glass mirrors such as Arnolfini's still required a collaboration with metalsmiths to render their reflective backs or foils, composed of varying amalgams of lead, tin, or silvering painted onto the reverse of the glass surface. As such, both metal reflectors and the glass mirrors new to the Renaissance were within the ambit of the smiths, also the fabricators of arms and armour.[21] Thus Giorgione's putative painting of reflection bringing together mirrors with armoury's shields spoke directly to the material and craft connections between them. Its purported representation of painting, pools, mirrors, and metallic shields as equivalent instruments of a reflected imagery was just as van Eyck had painted, the poets had extolled, Alberti had theorised, and Brunelleschi's Baptistery demonstration panel had claimed.

In Vasari's account of it, as scholarship has generally remarked, Giorgione painted his lost work of multiple reflections in order 'to confound the sculptors' in an emulative rivalry of the arts. By this he meant the so-called *paragone* or comparison of the arts that structured so much Renaissance art theory and criticism. Founded in antique reference, *paragone* rested on Pliny's descriptions of sculptures that rivalled paintings but, further, of emulation and comparison across the visual and the literary arts in the matter of descriptive as well as figurative imagery.[22] Hence Plutarch's epithet that 'poetry is a speaking picture, painting is mute poetry' intended to signify the correlations of word and image in their common address to the mind's 'eye'.[23] In respect of sculpture, as a mid-sixteenth-century exchange of letters from artists orchestrated by the Florentine humanist and art critic Benedetto Varchi would fully declare, the painters claimed that only they could render the effects of light and shadow, atmosphere, lustre and gleam, just as van Eyck had demonstrated in his art. The sculptors' rejoinder was that they alone could show the figure from all sides.[24] Thus the intention of the Giorgionesque St George reflected in an Albertian pool of water and a further sequence of metallic surfaces of armour, shields, and mirrors, as many scholars have argued, was to refute this claim through pictorial demonstration.

Implicit to Vasari's narrative, however, as to Giorgione's choice of subjects by which to advance his claim for painting, was surely a much deeper comparison of the arts that rested not only on the renown of ancient sculpture but also on the correlation of painting among the so-called ornamental and occasional arts that constituted the decorative order of the late Middle Ages, and notably those of armorial heraldry. The hierarchies of the arts that early modern academies would later declare, and notably by Vasari, in theorising architecture, sculpture, and painting as the principal arts under the shared sign of *disegno*, was not yet fully adumbrated. Though Vasari's paradigmatic unity of the arts under the rubric of *disegno* has largely prevailed over art-historical analysis of the Renaissance, it is in many respects teleological for discussion of the *quattrocento*. Instead, such affinities of the arts within a late medieval constellation of artisanal cultures were primarily founded in social kinships of craft instrumentation, in which what would much later be separated into the 'fine' and 'decorative' arts were then coterminous. Thus Giorgione's painting not only comments on the burgeoning *paragone* of painting and sculpture that dominated sixteenth-century art theory, but also casts back to an earlier historical legacy of comparative emulation between painters and metalsmiths, that is, between the painted figure and the precious arts of lustrous metalwork. In his depiction of armoury as of mirrors themselves, Giorgione was surely also acknowledging his attentive imitation of van Eyck's art of painted reflections.

Hence the Ghent altarpiece may, at the level of a theory of practice, be read as a fulsome *paragone* of all the late medieval arts – here are rich textiles, velvet and gold brocade, fur-lined and gold-edged, studded with glistening jewels and pearls. Jewelled and figured clasps and brooches adorn the angels, bearing musical instruments of decorated woods, while the clergy carry sceptres and mitres encrusted with precious stones, jewels, and gold filigree. The horses' harnesses and saddlery depict embossed leather with enamelled and jewelled ornament. Panels in grisaille paint sculptures in stone and wood with Gothic traceries, while in the background there are landscapes with architectures of steeples and spires. In its own great scale the Ghent altarpiece is architectural in size, its original framework of carved wooden tracery echoing the surrounding stone architecture of the Gothic cathedral for which it was destined. Within it, each object is painted with minute detail; as recent technical research has shown, for example, every pearl is layered with several coatings of silky glaze to render their nacreous iridescence, suggesting van Eyck may have painted with a crystal or glass magnifier himself as he worked.[25] In its great array of objects, of fashioned jewels, gold, wood, stone, and textile, and their myriad reflections and refractions of light, van Eyck placed the art of painting among a unison of the arts in recognition, within a late medieval conception of artisanal skill, of the deeply worked pictorial intelligence of his craft.[26]

THE GOLDSMITH'S ART

If Brunelleschi's greatest acclaim in a historiography of Renaissance art was Florence Cathedral's monumental dome, yet his training was in the miniature arts of the goldsmith. Legend has it that this ability to range across every scale was the secret to his success in winning the

Cathedral commission. The jury asked competitors to place an egg upright as a demonstration of their engineering skill. Brunelleschi's witty response was to tap the top of an egg to flatten it, thereby standing it on its tip. Apocryphal as it may be, the story goes to the crux of his claim as a universal artist, or designer, able to work across all media and 'craft', of every size and scale of commission. Similarly, van Eyck's putative training in miniature painting was, apparently, the only precedent to the monumental size of the Ghent altarpiece. The architectural reflection of the Vijd chapel within the sapphire of the Ghent altarpiece angel's morse is a ready emblem of the specular play of scale as well as light at work in van Eyck's understanding of antiquity's optical inheritance through the legacy of its late medieval textual transmission. Likewise, Brunelleschi's preparation for the great Cathedral dome lay in the fine art of jewellery. While he would go on to design not only buildings but architectural machinery, ships, and fortifications, Brunelleschi's early apprenticeship was in gold and silversmithing, which was then under the jurisdiction of the Florentine metal- and silk-workers' guild.[27] Both the (likely metal) mirror reflection of the Baptistery view and Brunelleschi's small painted panel of the same dimensions offered to the viewer the image of the Florentine Baptistery rendered in reduction. Here Brunelleschi demonstrated the function of the mirror as a method of visual translation, not only of three dimensions into a flat plane, but also in the precisely proportional reduction of scale from architecture into painting.[28] The mirror that he used at the door of the Cathedral, alongside the painted panel of its architectural view to demonstrate his theory of geometrical perspective, was surely of his own making, predicated on his early training in the arts of precious metalwork in a goldsmith's shop.

An inter-relation of skills little understood by scholarship today, which has generally only noted its curiosity, yet a goldsmith's training was also the case for Brunelleschi's close Florentine contemporaries Donatello and Ghiberti, as well as Pollaiuolo, Verrocchio, Pisanello, Botticelli, Ghirlandaio, Cellini, and Francia, among others. In Northern Europe, the Limbourg brothers were also skilled as goldsmiths as well as manuscript illuminators. Both Dürer and Holbein made jewellery designs, Dürer being the son of a goldsmith and trained in its art by his father. Johannes Gutenberg, credited with the invention of moveable type for the printing press, was by training a goldsmith, skilled in the miniaturising arts of precious metalwork out of which metal printing letters first arose. In Jan van Eyck's capacities as court artist to Philip the Good, designing the architectural decoration of princely residences as well as their festive ornament and costumes for banquets, it is likely he also practiced the art of goldsmithing, regarded as the 'noble art'. The connection is further manifest in Jan van Eyck's depiction of his fellow citizen and dean of the Bruges goldsmith's guild, Jan de Leeuw (Kunsthistorisches Museum, Vienna), in what is likely a gifted betrothal portrait. Representing De Leeuw holding a gold ring with a red gemstone between his fingers, it illustrates his bearing as a goldsmith as well as his offering to his future wife. Within the frame, itself a painted imitation of bronze metalwork, van Eyck further inscribed both their names as testament to their association, including a golden lion pictogram for De Leeuw, as lion in Dutch. Thus painter and goldsmith are linked in this pictorial representation of the goldsmith's art.[29] In Florence and Bruges, two cities closely joined by trade relations as the major fifteenth-century centres of banking and exchange, the role of the goldsmith was that of both jeweller and mint. As fabricators of currency, goldsmiths might also be merchant-bankers, brokers, evaluators of international financial exchange, and the guarantors of estimated wealth. In effect, goldsmiths were the international financiers, diplomats, and civic leaders of the late medieval political economy. Alongside Florence, Bruges was a leading centre in the early history of banking, and therefore vital to the quickening of Europe's late medieval economic growth, including trade in luxury goods so closely linked to the rise of merchant banking.[30] It is surely this civic context of interrelations between the arts – notwithstanding the guild's statutory role in protecting its members from professional encroachment as well as upholding the standards of each craft – that produced a number of Flemish fifteenth-century genre paintings or vocational portraits of a goldsmith's 'shop'.

***

According to sixteenth-century sources, Jan van Eyck apparently painted a now-lost portrait described as 'a little painting of half-length figures, of a patron making up his accounts with his factor, by the hand of van Eyck . . . made in 1440'.[31] This lost work is generally acknowledged as establishing the subject type of the banker's vocational portrait, subsequently taken up in an early example by van Eyck's successor in Bruges, Petrus Christus (Fig. 38).[32] Christus was believed to have worked for the Sforza in Milan for a time, where he might have known the great Italian goldsmith-artist, Pisanello. The encounter with Pisanello's art of smithing in this most courtly

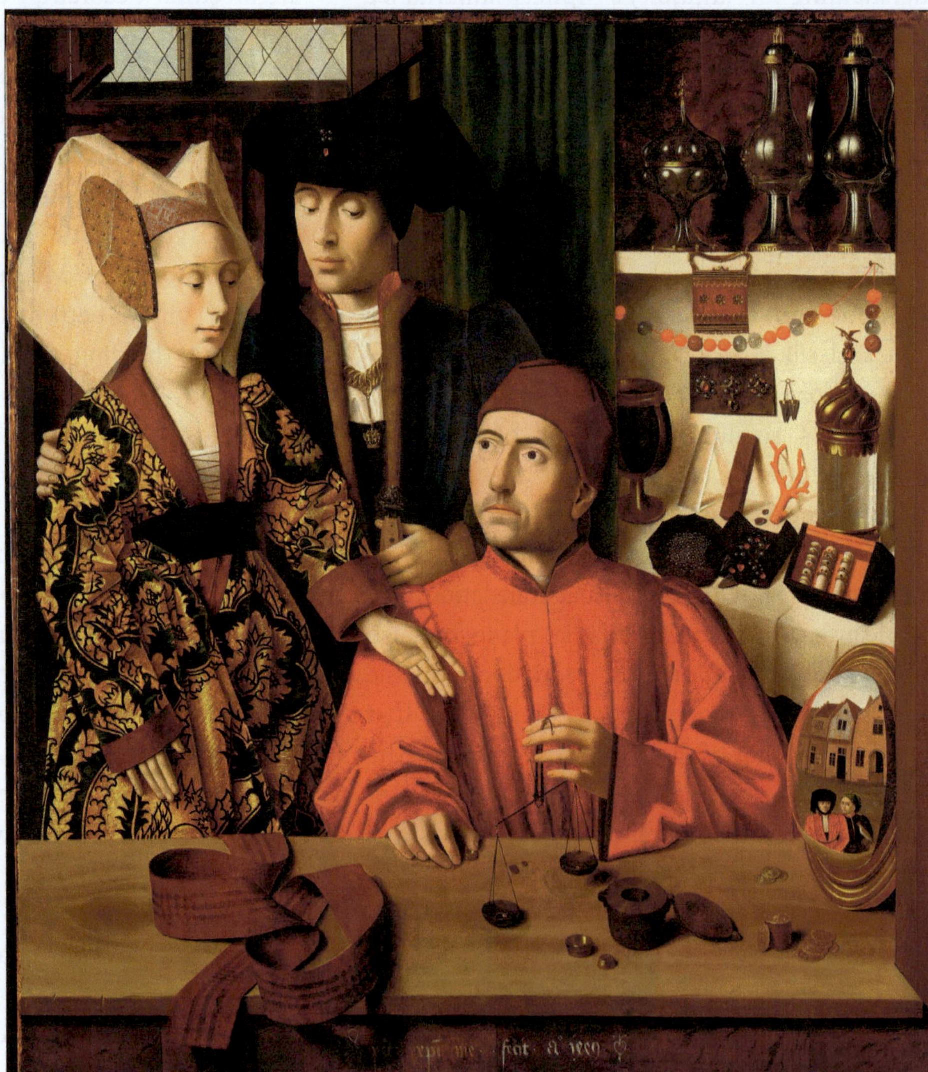

Fig. 38 Petrus Christus, *A Goldsmith in His Shop*, 1449, oil on panel, 98 × 85.2 cm, Metropolitan Museum of Art, New York. Photo: Metropolitan Museum of Art

context could have strengthened his interest in the pictorial subject matter. Within the scholarly literature the painting is often, though not universally, linked to one of the Flemish goldsmiths' guilds, likely Bruges or Antwerp.[33] Whether or not there is any specific patronage connection to be uncovered, it is unquestionably a painted evocation of Bruges' leading position in the production of luxury gold goods, and its primary status as a centre of commerce and banking too.

Earlier scholarship cast this painting as marking the emergence of genre painting, though its historical position as 'genre' is a deeply enigmatic one. It was long known as St Eligius, a seventh-century bishop of Flanders and the patron saint of goldsmiths, due to a halo above the seated figure in red. However, the halo was subsequently recognised as a later addition to the painting, and removed in 1993.[34] With its halo, nineteenth-century scholarship had linked the painting to the story of St Eligius' invitation to marry Godeberta with Clotaire III of France (though he chose instead to make her a bride of Christ in recognition of her sanctity).[35] Subsequently, the 1914 identification of the standing man's gold jewel as the coat of arms of the House of Gelders, taken together with the suggested identification of the seated man as St Eligius, led to a number of conjectured scholarly connections to the marriage between Philip the Good's ward Mary of Gelders and James II of Scotland in 1449 at Holyrood, also the inscribed date of the painting.[36] Some scholars have further suggested, on the basis of linguistic analysis of van Eyck's notes, that the painter's motherland may have been Gelderland, hence the choice of artist for such a work as a commemoration of a royal marriage.[37] The gold coins in the foreground, part of the late medieval goldsmith's art, may possibly reference the House of Gelders as a pictorial sign of '*geld*'; or simply the goldsmiths' guilds as putative patrons. While the painting's invocations of marriage are evidently manifest in the winding ribbon of the young woman's girdle in the foreground, the goldsmith's thoughtful weighing of her ring, and her outstretched left hand that gestures towards the ring she will bear, yet the absence of any royal association would seem to preclude direct representation of this particular engagement. Nonetheless, the gentle inference to marriage as a matter of estate is clearly present throughout the work. As a matter of conjecture, it may have been part of a collection of luxury objects to form a marriage gift from the goldsmiths' guilds that doubtless included jewellery, further representing the significance of the goldsmith's wedding ring as the visible confirmation of the marriage vows. Such gifts of jewellery and painted portraits, as well as a full range of domestic decorative arts including mirrors, were material agents in the diplomacy of princely and mercantile marriage, and the artefactual representation of its significance as a matter of state. It may also have been made in emulation of courtly betrothal gifts, for a marriage between merchant-goldsmith families.

The prestation of mirrors within bridal gifts, as well as their painted representation in all manner of decorative arts and painting, pervaded late medieval marriage customs of both courtly and mercantile families as the Arnolfini portrait demonstrates, and as the long-standing poetic invocations of mirrors as emblems of beauty, courtship and marriage underscore. While the starred scholarly literature on the Arnolfini double portrait has been much concerned with historical questions of the representation of a specific marital union, the larger social and cultural relations between art, marriage, and the representation of betrothal gifts in fifteenth-century painting, particularly the mirror, have been little addressed.[38] Analysis of the pictorial representation of the mirror among a host of precious artisanal goods within these paintings thus offers a prismatic key through which to address the nexus of patronage that commissioned and gifted them in respect of the social rituals of marriage and betrothal that occasioned them. Then as now, a wedding was the social locus of gifted exchanges, not only between the two families but throughout their often-extensive kinship networks, so that betrothals and marriage were of major significance to the patronage of the domestic decorative arts, including painting. In the case of the Petrus panel, its possible pictorial reference to Mary of Gelder's stately marriage further suggests the high value that Philip the Good, like the Medici, placed on the art of the goldsmith, as well as that of the painter. Philip the Good was likely versed in both arts, as among the requisite elite pastimes and the guarantor of a princely capacity of judgment in the arts.[39] Given the hypothetical patronage link with a goldsmith's guild corporation, it is also possible to conceive that this scene pertaining to marriage and estate was chosen precisely to display the spiritual and material beauty of the goldsmith's art within the exquisite diplomacy of marital alliances.

Scholarship of late medieval artisanal and mercantile guilds has generally understood the classification – and therefore jurisdiction – of their trades according to the material basis of each skill. Thus glass mirror-making, itself a relatively new trade among the late medieval guilds, might be linked with glass-makers, or with either metalsmithing or painting on account of the silvering application of the foil. This manner of material definition is undoubtedly so historically, yet it is also the case that medieval groupings of trades within guilds, companies, and corporations both elude and exceed such sensible distinctions, as also their scholarly analysis. The interconnections between trades and crafts that late medieval guild structures surely represent concerns an evolving historical basis in a range of practice-based exchanges and contingencies. These included shared materials, but also common tools and instruments, as well as the social circumstances of patronage such as collaborative productions for civic and religious festivals or court entertainments for births, deaths, and marriages, among a full range of festival occasions. In *nuce*, these ties would appear to be those of practice-based workshop contingencies among the artisanal sector, in the acquisition of materials and the often common use of instruments and tools.

Famously, the medieval Florentine guild system grouped painters with doctors and apothecaries because of their shared material use of herbs and minerals that could produce both paint colours and herbal medicines; while the sculptors were with the wood carvers and stone masons. Gold and silversmiths, however, were grouped with silk workers. The reasons for this may lie in their social position as the first rank of the merchant-artisans, the interrelations of dress and jewellery such as that of the goldsmith's painting in which the young woman bears luxury brocade textiles shot with gold, or simply through linked patronage associations for finery in the arts of social occasion such as marriage. Florentine artists of all media might also join together as fellow members of the confraternity of St Luke, who was the patron saint of painters as the purported originator of the first image of the Virgin and Child. In Flanders such companies of St Luke were more commonly also guild corporations. As such, the medieval guilds of St Luke in the North brought together painters of all kinds. This included the limners of parchment manuscript illumination, comprising also leather (and so saddlery) due to painting on vellum, and therefore closely connected with scribes, as was the case in Bruges. This was the likely background of the van Eycks, who are thought to have painted book illuminations as well as panels. It also brought together all painters on wood – comprising both panel and sign painting – with painters on cloth from processional banners to ships' ensigns and, subsequently, painting on canvas. The traditions of stained and painted glass could bring glass-makers into the painters' guild, as in Bruges, which might also include mirror-makers as glass mirrors grew more common. It is noteworthy that painters and mirror-makers belonged to the same guild in van Eyck's Bruges, as did armourers, providing an easy point of transfer between their respective crafts, from shared tools to skills and expertise. Conversely, metal mirrors and mirror silvering might just as readily be grouped with silver- and goldsmiths, also commonly including armourers, enamel workers, blacksmiths, and metalsmiths more generally. In some instances, as in Antwerp, metalsmiths and painters and their associated trades were all together, in recognition of the painter's use of precious metals and jewels in the composition of pigments and paints – gold leaf, ultramarine, lapis lazuli – also used in jewellery. The fifteenth-century advent of print making in Germany, springing from Gutenberg's goldsmith training and based on metalwork materials and tools, would alter guild associations further. Particularly in cities such as Nuremberg, as a leading centre of book production, the impact of printing was to bring metalwork into close collaboration with all aspects of the publishing trades (though this city oversaw its trades through its civic council rather than through guilds). As the example of book production – both printed and manuscript – clearly demonstrates, the material bases of a Northern renaissance of letters also rested on the mighty cultural and social relations embodied in the medieval foundations of the guilds. Guild structures were, then, historical deposits of all manner of craft and trade relations, whose ties may be seen to come together in early Flemish painted representations of a goldsmith's shop.[40]

In the Petrus panel, around the goldsmith lie the meticulous painted description of his guild's art, of a material renaissance and a world of goods.[41] The shelves behind gleam with precious jewelled objects of his craft. The scale of the panel, close to a meter in height, allows for near life-sized depiction of both the figures and objects within it. On the top shelf, two flagons of silver parcel gilt with domed lids and black letter inscriptions on their plinths, and a lobed cup on feet of crouching lions with a jewelled finial, are likely *presentkannen* for civic ceremonial occasion as befit a guild association. Their silvered convex sheen, shaped like small mirroring shields, reflects in miniature a Flemish mullioned window with a view onto the city skyline of medieval towers, so suggesting the architectural and civic space within which the goldsmith's shop is apparently situated. Half hidden behind the hanging green curtain is a further crystal vessel with a gilt metal mount, while a gilt-edged belt buckle and a string of rosary beads in semi-precious stone hang from the ledge. Behind are three gold brooches with pearls and rubies affixed to a leather swatch, beside which hangs a pair of black *glossapetrae* set in gilt mounts. These fossilised sharks' teeth, available locally, were believed to be those of ancient serpents. Like the gilt-mounted coconut cup nearby, such teeth were thought to ward off poison within a medieval medical imaginary that linked cure with cause. The branching pink coral, too, was given to children as an apotropaic charm because of its arterial form, as in coral necklaces gifted at christenings. In front lie two open packets of mixed precious stones and seed pearls, behind them two small cylinders, one a red stone, the other crystal, also considered a talismanic charm for the perceived magic of its light-refractive sparkle and rainbow prisms. Thus many of the jeweller's materials were conceived as possessed of magical properties and gifted as amulets of good fortune in the rituals of both marriage and birth. Behind is a further cylindrical crystal jar with a domed top of repoussé gold, likely for the Eucharistic host, surmounted by a finial of red stones and a tiny gold pelican feeding its young with its own blood, as a familiar emblem of Christ's passion as well as of family devotion. In front, an open box displays gold and jewelled rings arranged on parchment rolls, among them an armorial signet ring as an emblem of both lineage and marriage. Collectively, these objects represent the social position of the goldsmith as that of an esteemed civic burgher fashioning precious objects for the great ceremonies of church and state, including those of dynastic marital alliances.

Some scholars have seen possible portraits in the detailed features of the faces, particularly the goldsmith, though others note that the large size of the panel makes a private commission unlikely. Other scholars have further suggested the face of the goldsmith is modelled after the painter's own. As Maryan Ainsworth has argued, the technical evidence would seem to support the hypothesis of a possible self-portrait, based on its particularly attentive modelling and careful observation visible in the under-drawing.[42] This is suggestive of an especially close affinity between the painter and his subject. Nineteenth-century interpretations of the narrative between the figures in the manner of genre painting have also supposed the young woman is the daughter of the goldsmith and the young man her fiancé.[43] Whether self-portrait, family, or not, the goldsmith's company of the Petrus panel are dressed in the fashionable finery of his burgher estate – the woman in gold brocade of a type likely imported from Florence, coiffed in an embroidered gold net with small pearls. Her putative fiancé or guardian in dark velvet edged with ermine wears the gold chain of his office, the Gelders armorial badge of two lions affronted, with a jewel in his cap and silver chasing on the hilt of his sword. Above them are the characteristically Flemish window panes of leaded diamond-glass facets.

Before the goldsmith are the testing instruments of his trade, his means of judgment and evaluation. Holding a small scale bearing the ring in one hand, with the other he fingers a gold weight. As a painted allegory of marriage, he weighs the faith of their vows that the wedding ring represents. Fractional and further round weights with a weight box are scattered about the wooden ledge on which he performs his artisanal expertise, along with a clutch of coins. To the right is a small circular globe-shaped mirror of blown glass in a bevelled gilt frame. A diminutive starred fracture marks the edge of the mirror closest to us, marring its otherwise smoothly reflective surface with tiny cracks and bubbles so characteristic of early Renaissance glass-blowing. As Dora and Peter Thornton have argued, convex mirrors increasingly became part of the appurtenance of the Renaissance painter's workshop, and surely also the goldsmith's, as a means of shedding intensified light and magnification onto detailed workmanship such as that of a goldsmith or a manuscript scribe.[44] As such, the mirror within the painting is a miniation of the artist's methods as well as the model of his art. If we accept the identification of the goldsmith as a possible self-portrait, such a mirror may well have been the instrument of the portrait's making, by allowing the artist to study his features in its reflection.[45] It is also, as an object of silvering, one that might be among a goldsmith's wares.

Display of the goldsmith's work, in keeping with late medieval guild regulations, required its masters to practice in public view, as a symbolic surety of quality and quantity in the specification of precious materials. As Lorne Campbell has noted, the buildings in which such master-guildsmen practiced, often of great civic grandeur and situated in the main square alongside the offices of town government, were punctuated by inset shop windows on the ground floor to signify a ceremonial display of their craft, as a further consideration of the window-like disposition of this painting. The viewers of Petrus

Christus' painting look into the scene as if into the opening of a goldsmith's shop.[46] Within the mirror roundel reflection are the characteristically gabled Flemish townhouses flanking the edge of what is surely a major civic square. Their architectural ornament, seemingly a reflection of what stands behind us as we look into the 'window' of Petrus' art, frames the space of the viewer by linking it to the painting's illusionistic field. This is echoed in the miniature reflections on the parcel-gilt drinking vessels, also depicting a city view of medieval towers set against the sky. Thus the window motif in fifteenth-century painting as theorised by Alberti took painted form. As Sixton Ringbom, Gérard Wajcman, and Victor Stoichita have eloquently argued, the window motif also became a predominant pictorial allegory of Renaissance painting itself, fully commensurate with that of the mirror-image that Alberti had defined in the pool of Narcissus.[47] As with the Petrus panel, painted window frames as well as mirror frames within such works multiplied the decorative syntax of the outer picture frame, as the ornamental elaborations of a mirroring mimetic art. They served both to demarcate the field of painting as equivalent to a window or a mirror view and to demonstrate its nature as pictorial illusion. In this regard, the figurative purpose of the window-frame device was that of a mediating threshold between the field of art and the viewer, at once to distinguish and to confound the realm of painting's deceit. Thus in the Petrus panel the pictorial fiction of the window view doubles that of its inset mirror reflection, in presenting for display the artfulness of painting's illusions. The framing trope of the artifice of art as imitation is fully equivalent with its specular image.

Scholarship has sometimes suggested this painting heralded the introduction of Brunelleschi's one-point perspective system to the north, though others have argued the claim may be overstated.[48] The painter's possible sojourn to Italy, or the frequent cultural traffic between Florence and Bruges, may have familiarised him with the story of Brunelleschi's mirror experiment at the door of Florence Cathedral and with its subsequent pictorial manifestations in Italian art. Certainly, the mirror within the painting signals, among other things, the representation of illusionistic pictorial space. In this regard it is surely a recollection of the Arnolfini portrait too. If the spatial depth of the image stretches back diagonally from the mirror to the young woman's starched headdress, the specular reflection of the city square to the fore of the painting also forges a further diagonal of illusionistic space in front of the goldsmith's stand. Throughout the image, Christus has brought out the spatial volume of the many glass and silver objects he depicts – cups, flagons, bowls – and the forcible *repoussoir* of the mirror in the foreground, as the emblems of his mirroring mimetic art.

Within its miniaturising reflection, the architectural background in the mirror forges an illusionistic space in front of which appear two tiny figures. The red coat of the foremost figure echoes that of the goldsmith's, which is reflected in the edge of the mirror's curving globe. Beneath his black chaperon hat, the man looks to his companion beside him. Around his neck he bears a gold livery collar of noble privilege, identified by some as the insignia of the Order of the Golden Fleece.[49] This chivalric order was instituted by Philip the Good to celebrate his marriage to Princess Isabella of Portugal in 1430, for which he commissioned two leading goldsmiths at court to make collars for its newly appointed knights, composed of 'firesteel' motifs linked by 'flints', and commemorated in a series of portraits from the workshop of Roger van der Weyden (Fig. 39).[50] The pictorial reference suggests the nobility of the goldsmith's art, and so the painter's, through its apparent associations with an order of knights and, possibly, royal marriage. His companion, in a green cap and black jacket

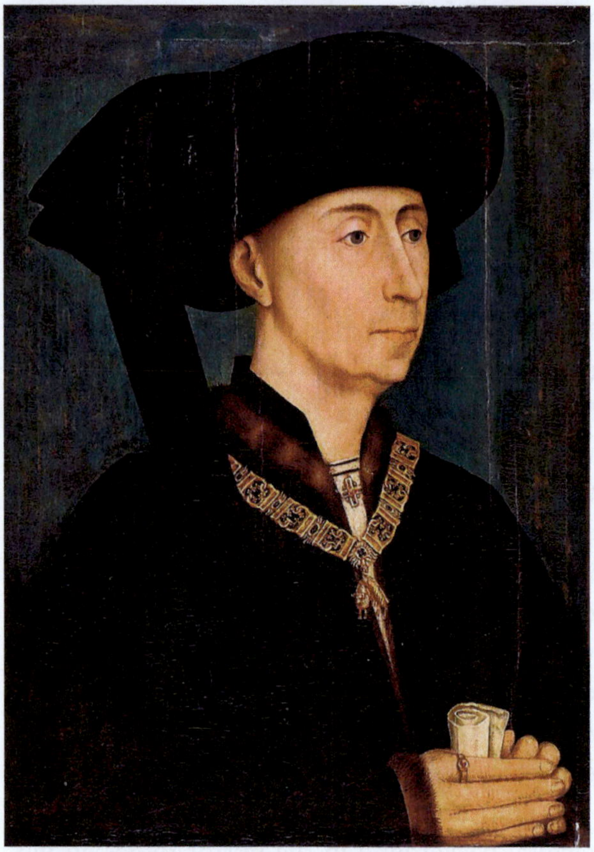

Fig. 39 *Portrait of Philip the Good*, fifteenth century, Netherlandish (after Rogier van der Weyden), oil on panel, 27 × 24 cm, Royal Museum of Fine Arts, Antwerp. Photo: Wikimedia

with a scarlet collar, carries what is generally identified as a falcon. This bird of prey was noted as a noble hunting animal possessed of exceptional eyesight and so a rebus of the painter's visual skill. It was also of particular significance to courtly love imagery as an emblem of a noble amorous pursuit, represented in manuscript illuminations, and the gifted ivory mirror cases (Figs. 40 and 15, Chapter 1) and jewel caskets of late medieval betrothal exchange.[51] In an iconography of courtly *amour*, such falcons were often depicted within decorative mirror roundels, which the miniaturising mirror *tondo* of Petrus' painting echoes.[52] Alone among the painted figures of this painting, Petrus' falconer looks towards us. As a mirror reflection, these diminutive figures bearing the attributes of courtly mores in the falcon and the gold chain emblematise the nobility of art as well as that of aristocratic marriage. Illusionistically, they must surely stand in the same spatial field as the noble viewer of the work, so eliding their position with that of the beholder as a would-be visitor to the goldsmith's shop. Thus the falconer's outward gaze links together the various realms of pictorial illusion within the image, for the view of the city square behind the reflected figures is also that which lies before the mirror, and so apparently behind us, as the viewer of the goldsmith at work.

Within the painting, the mirror is both a material object in a world of goldsmith's goods and an immaterial image reflection of light and colour, just like painting itself. The mirror's miniaturising effect reflects the visible field in reduction. Its diminutive size recalls the art of limning, or manuscript illumination, with which Petrus Christus like Jan van Eyck is also associated.[53] So highly prized at the court of Philip the Good, the art of the miniature is here underscored by the diminutive falcon and the gold pelican above. These painted miniaturisations of armorial effect give pictorial form to the nexus of guild relations in Bruges, in which panel, glass, mirror, and sign painters joined with limners in the company of St Luke. The mirror reflection is, then, an emblem of painting within itself. Christus presents his subject of the goldsmith's art as a double entendre of his own. Within it, the mirror reflection is rebus-like, like a putative armorial device of the painter's art.

The painting as a whole reflects on marriage in its worldly and spiritual dimensions. Both the mirror and the falcon within it were frequently emblems of *superbia*, or magnificence, as might befit a courtly marriage. The prominent depiction of the marriage girdle or ribbon, ever the sign of love and betrothal, is juxtaposed with the mirror as conjoined emblems of beauty's gifted adornments in matters of marriage. As the eucharistic pelican and the courtly falcon of

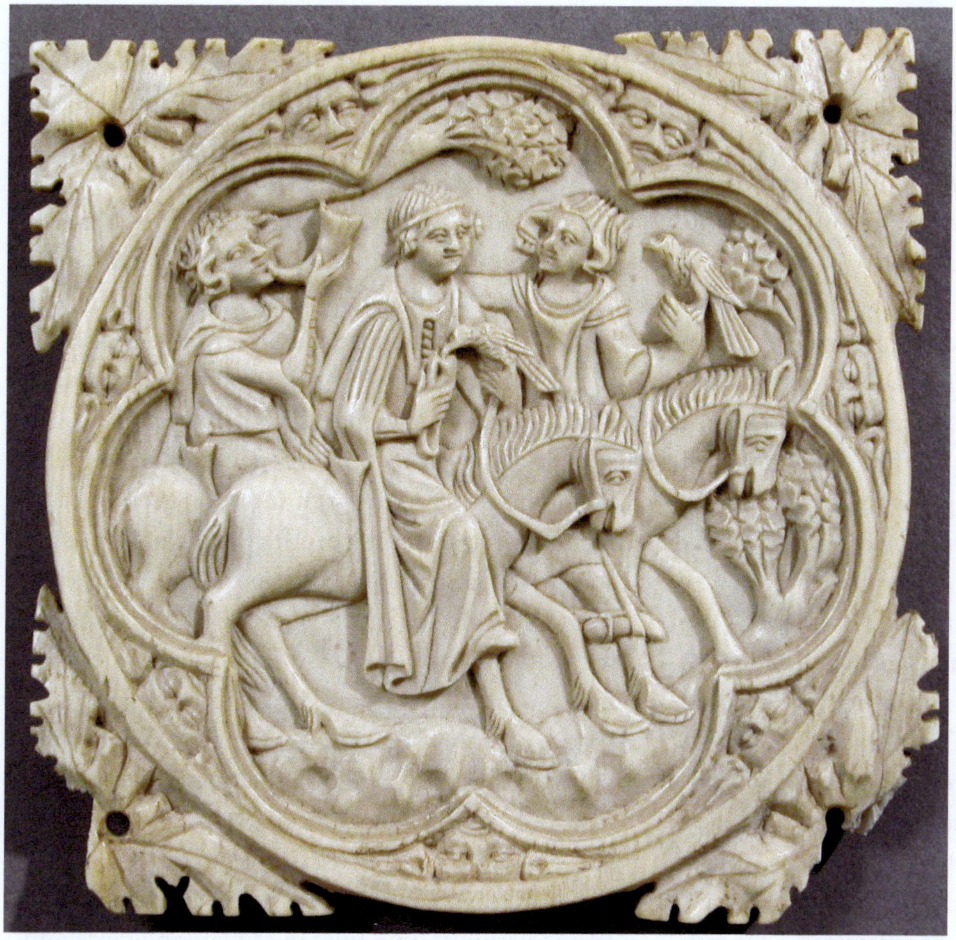

Fig. 40 'Mirror Case with a Falconing Party', 1330–60, French, ivory, 9.5 × 9.5 × 1 cm, Metropolitan Museum of Art.
Photo: Metropolitan Museum of Art

Petrus' painting together may also indicate, such a wedding was an affair of church and state – of charity and majesty. Marriage was both a dynastic and a Marian concern.

Along the bottom of the painting, beneath the tabletop on which the goldsmith practices his art, runs an inscription with the artist's signature: *m petri xpi me fecit a.o 1449*. The date in Arabic numerals was still a rarity at this time, arriving with the recent influx of Middle Eastern scribal cultures into the West over the fifteenth century.[54] To the right, the inscription concludes with a small mark, identified as that of a heart transfixed in the form of a foliot escapement, or the ticking mechanism of a clock.[55] It is a double-sided or 'valentine' heart, an emblem of human love as two hearts twined together. This pictorial motif of the love-heart (as we know it) emerged circa 1400, just then replacing earlier conical configurations of the sacred heart.[56] The ticking clock, predicated on a verge escapement, was also a technological development of the late Middle Ages. In Petrus Christus' painting suffused with the pictorial rhetoric of marital relations, it surely emblematises the beating of the heart in love – transfixed.

The force of the heart device's visual rhetoric had a ready counterpart in Flemish guilds of St Luke for painters, many of which had close associations with their city chambers of rhetoric, as further examples of such late medieval sodalities. Here, companies of artists and authors commonly joined in conceiving emblematic compositions. In this respect they were companies in the rhetorical production of word and image. This took many forms within the linked cultures of the humanist arts – in painting as in poetry, as well as recitations and theatrical dramatics, and other types of literary performance.[57] It built on a common history of manuscript production, which had traditionally brought together scribes and illuminators, and so a shared culture of word and image. These closely linked associations may lie behind the foliot heart's emblematic form. The clockwork heart may also reference the fine judgement of the goldsmith in weighing the balance of marriage in his scale, and the fine smithing of clockwork mechanics as a metaphor for the underpinning skills of his art. Moreover, the foliot heart is like a Renaissance guild-maker's mark in form, or what would later become known as a 'hallmark'. The maker's mark was the master craftsman's sign for the quality of his materials and the distinction of his craft, applied to goods through pictographic and often emblematic punch marks under guild regulations. Likewise, the lettering of the painting's inscription has been identified as one in use among guilds in Bruges, by both goldsmiths and manuscript illuminators, as the means of authenticating their work.[58] If the skill of painting is to forge pictorial illusions as powerful as a mirror reflection, the hallmark heart and signature authenticate its quality as 'art'.

The lower edge of the mirror reflects the wood of the goldsmith's worktop, and within it the topmost of the gold coins. As has long been noted, the depicted coins are largely identifiable, a mix of Flemish, French, and German mints of riders, florins, and angels, suggesting the goldsmith's role as banker in international currency exchange. Their metal faces, or 'shields' as they were commonly termed, are struck with miniature pictograms similar to those of goldsmith punches for guild-maker's marks: a Latin cross between a fleur-de-lys and a leopard, a mounted knight bearing a sword, a quartered shield with a floriated cross.[59] Then as now, coins commonly bore inscriptions as well as pictographic images, in an emblematic conjunction of word and image. Below the counter top, Petrus Christus' signature, in fact an inscription, similarly 'mints' the painting as by his hand, and declares its significance through the rebus of the beating heart, transfixed. A ready metaphor for the love and delight of art, as of marriage, it playfully proclaims the skill of its pictorial illusion, as true as a mirror reflection. In keeping with renascent literary cultures of rhetoric and recitation, the rebus of the heart as art-lover surely also suggests the speaking images of 'canting arms', or '*type parlant*', those armorial forms of pictographic play on words particularly beloved at the Burgundian court of Philip the Good.[60] In this regard, the example of van Eyck's portrait of the goldsmith De Leeuw is also telling. For the inscription on the frame naming the painter and the sitter used the pictorial hallmark of a lion for De Leeuw's name, as well as chronograms within it, in a humanist play on words and numbers as equivalent signs. It also established the genre of the speaking portrait as if declaimed by the image itself: 'I am here painted by Jan van Eyck.'[61]

ARMORIAL ARTS

Gold coins, a goldsmith's guild-mark and inscription, the jewelled coat of arms of Gelders, and the miniated gold collar of the figure in the mirror reflection all suggest an armorial bearing to the Petrus panel. Similarly, the painting's display of goods may be read as a heraldically composed play on words in a pictorial rebus of its own making. Jan van Eyck's abundant skill in the art of painted inscription and of rebus motifs, as the 'founder' of Netherlandish art, established his school as one of literary renown in the picturing play of words and images. Rudolf Preimesberger has noted that within the linguistic cultures of fifteenth-century Flanders, the common term for painting was shield – *schild*. As a combination of lower German dialects and the Netherlandish of the educated, a knight's shield, a painted sign, an armorial banner, and a panel painting were all part of this same linguistic term.[62] A medieval word, it surely sprang from the close alignments among the heraldic arts, and specifically between painters and armourers, which guild structures represented. The decorated face of a coin was also commonly termed its 'shield', or escutcheon, from the Latin cognate *scutum*, further testament to the strongly heraldic significance of the medallic arts as miniature 'shields', and within the goldsmith's realm too. Thus, the term 'shield' came to refer to the pictorial field in general, that is, the space in which imagery might be applied.

Northern painting's long connection with the arts of heraldry also resonates in the title of Carel van Mander's *Het Schilderboeck* of 1604, the first Dutch history of art, which referenced its distinctively Dutch identity through the use of this traditional term. Van Mander begins his history of art with Jan van Eyck, as the 'father' of the Netherlandish or '*schilderkunst*' style.[63] His title further demonstrates the predominance of armoury and heraldry within late medieval luxury artisanal cultures, across institutions and groups, as central to the fashioning of social identities. As Michel Pastoureau has argued, all visual imagery of the late Middle Ages was to some degree shaped by an armorial syntax as the decorative order for social and ceremonial occasions, with an apogee at the court of Philip the Good (Fig. 41).[64] It was the visual language of identity not just for noble houses, and notably of the familial alliances built through marriage, but also for ecclesiastical bodies, religious confraternities, towns, and guilds. If the painted ornament of wooden pageant shields with the colours and emblems of each dynastic family or house is surely its originating form, this decorative order with its arrangements of pictogram devices in bright colours ranged across all manner of media, from the monumental to the miniature – ceremonial shields of metal and leather, helmets and armour, bridles and falconry harnesses, horses' and soldiers' colours, banners, ship ensigns, and signs on textile, leather, and wood of all kinds, but also seals and signets, book plates and manuscript illumination, badges, coins, rings and gems, and ceremonial glassware, china, silver and plate, as well as decorated mirrors.[65] Ecclesiastical heraldry often depicted their eucharistic vessels and saints' names in rebus form, while towns and guilds, like noble houses, frequently represented their names by means of pictorial anagrams. In consequence, all structures of imagery, across cultural domains, were rooted in the emblazoned languages of heraldic impress. This was so with a

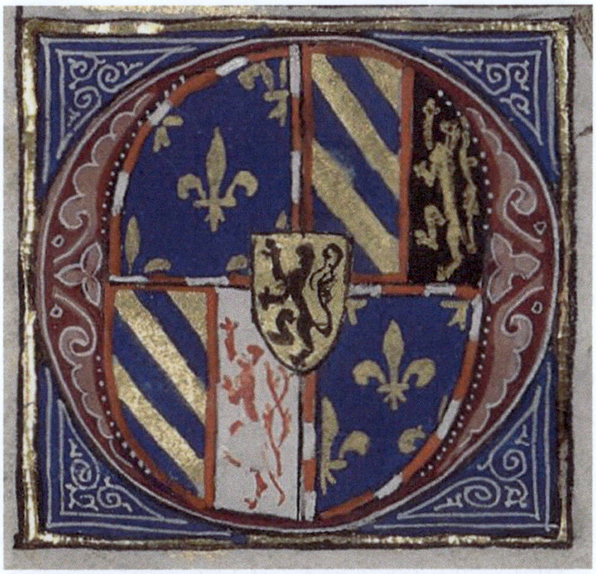

Fig. 41 'Illuminated Initial O with Philip the Good's Coat of Arms', 1401–1500, Netherlandish, for *Croniques de France, d'Angleterre, de Flandres et d'aultres contrées, commençans l'an de nostre seigneur Jhesu Crist mil deux cens quatre-vings et seze, et fenissans l'an mil trois cens soixante-dix, mises au net par David Aubert, clerc, l'an de grace mil quatre cens cinquante noeuf*, parchment 36.5 × 28.5 cm, f. 2r, Bibliothèque Nationale de France. Photo: Gallica/BNF

burgeoning efflorescence in late medieval cultures, and increasingly thereafter into the magnificently elaborated heraldry of the sixteenth and seventeenth centuries. Within antiquarian and numismatic circles as with goldsmiths in the fabrication of coinage, the shields of the medallic arts were decorated with all manner of emblems and devices. Similarly, across the festival arts of jousts, tournaments, and carousels, an emblazoned decorative imagery of word-play arose analogically from the pictorial structure of heraldry's inset rebus forms.[66] The pictorial syntax of the armorial shield was a configuring paradigm of pre-modern cultures.

Within the long medieval history of armorial devices concerned with the alliance of noble houses joined in marriage, the pictorial practice arose of placing one coat of arms within another to denote the coupled ancestry of their union. In an extended genealogy of aristocratic marriages, the possibility of ever-smaller 'shields-within-shields' arose, as markers of such a family history. Thus within late medieval heraldry emerged the pictorial convention of the sign-image within the image. In the great efflorescence of early modern court blazons, the inlay of genealogical descent was represented in the accruing collection of armorial signs, so that the pictorial shield in which they were placed became one of potentially infinite historical regress. In practice, the diminution of scale involved mitigated against such a dense pictorial working of the shield face, which was generally (though by no means conclusively) limited to one crest-within-crest only. However, this could be displayed against a quartered field in order to represent further coats of arms, as in the Valois-Burgundy heraldry of Philip the Good, to signify the accrual of titles through inheritance and marital alliance. Exceptionally, in the case of royal houses this was further multiplied in a potentially infinite cascading imagery of inset armorial signs. As also discussed in the Introduction, their long genealogical significance was referenced in late medieval French through the linguistic term *mise-en-abyme*. Denoting heraldic placement at the middle of the pictorial 'shield' as one of potentially infinite armorial recession of an ancestral aristocratic genealogy, the centre point was thereby conceived as the abyss or 'abysm', the representation of lineage conflated with the scaled diminution of the nested inset images. As Renaissance sources of court heraldry understood it, *en abyme* signified a genealogy cast as one of infinite ancestral regress into the depths of time. Thus the term *mise-en-abyme* came to mean the central picturing field of heraldic insignia as one of potentially infinite inset images-within-an-image, whether it contained further coats of arms, or any combination of armorial pictograms in its pictorial shield.[67] Such a visual conceptualisation of lineage, in its fusion of time's genealogical descent into the past with the deepest point of pictorial spatial recession, elided its temporal regress with the pictorial abyss of perspective. In the emerging visual conventions of what would become Brunelleschi's geometry of perspective, this led to a further confluence of lineage as historical time with the receding representation of spatial infinity through the optics of pyramidal vision.

Armorial decoration was a major source of occupation across all late medieval trades, with the *schilder* or 'shield' painters enjoying particularly high status among guilds for their close connections with heraldry. Guild heraldry itself was displayed in a wide range of forms and materials, from large painted ensigns for processional uses, silver plate and chargers for festive tableware, to small scrollwork motifs for documentary and epistolary ornament and identification. Within metal and leather work, armoury's pictogram motifs were embedded by means of punches, the same tool type as for gold- and silver-maker marks. Over time, punch dies became increasingly elaborate, in line with armorial decoration itself, to impress all kinds of luxury material goods with serially produced visual markers of identification and authentication. Thus there was ready exchange between these different forms of heraldic identity markers across the arts, both in concept and in practice.[68]

Turning again to Petrus Christus, the goldsmith's shop offers within it the repeated device of the image-within-the-image, in its portrait-like faces and armorial badges, but also in its pictorial reflections, and most evidently in the inset mirror-image. The reflecting surface of the mirror is also in the convex form of a pictorial 'shield', able to display within it the emblems of an aristocratic house and courtly *mise-en-abyme*: the Flemish gables, the figures' noble Flemish dress, and the falcon. The notion of art within art may, perhaps, connote a play on Petrus' own name, believed to imply a family lineage from stone sculptors of religious imagery and specifically of Christ figures as stone effigies. It surely acknowledges the art of the goldsmith as courtly and therefore armorial, as a bearer of rings and broker of aristocratic marriages. Taking together the artist's signature-inscription with its emblematic heart and the mirror reflection above it, the heraldic associations within the work may also be a pictorial declaration of the nobility of the painter's art. Presenting the goldsmith's skill as a double entendre of Petrus' own, the *schilder* paints the artist's coat of arms.

***

If Petrus Christus was reworking a lost painting of the subject by Jan van Eyck, scholarship has also argued this is the case for a later painting of a goldsmith's shop by Quentin Massys (or Metsys). Known as *De Wisselaer* in Metsys' seventeenth-century biography, it has been commonly translated as *The Moneychangers* in English, so referencing the close connections between goldsmithing and merchant banking, though recent scholarship has preferred the descriptive title of an early seventeenth-century inventory as 'a man weighing gold coins with his wife'.[69] It is a work that in turn generated much imitation across the Renaissance, and for which there are two versions generally regarded as autograph (Fig. 42, now at the Louvre dated c. 1514; and a version at Brussels Royal Museum of Fine Arts dated c. 1519). As Ursula Panhans-Bühler has argued in her analysis of early Netherlandish compositional types, *De Wisselaer* is one of a nest of closely related images along with Petrus Christus' *Goldsmith's Shop*. Part of a series of vocational portraits also stemming from the lost van Eyck 'original', the work is what Rudolf Preimesberger has aptly termed a 'paraphrase'.[70] The dress in which the figures are depicted, dating some 100 years earlier than the painting, is generically both 'Eyckian' and 'Netherlandish', reinforcing the panel's claim to this historical genealogy. It may therefore be understood as a visual statement of the 'Flemishness' of Flemish painting in the manner established by van Eyck, founded in the use of oil paint to render a meticulous exactitude in the representation of the visible world, like a mirror reflection. Declaring van Eyck the source of Flemish art and its ongoing emulation, the painting positions itself within a pictorial chain of such imitations. Like the Petrus Christus, the representation of the goldsmith's jewels may be read as an emblematic representation of the 'jewel-like' glow of Northern oil painting. Its possible provenance as a painting in Rubens' collection is suggested by its inclusion in Willem van Haecht's *Atelier of Apelles Painting Campaspe*, c. 1630 (Fig. 43). As an idealised representation of the great Flemish painter Rubens' art collection by his fellow student and later master of the Guild of St Luke in Antwerp, *De Wisselaer*'s presence within it would seem to cement its position as a statement of Flemish pictorial identity.[71]

The subject of the goldsmith too, while by no means exclusively so, was understood as a locus of an Eyckian, Flemish art by reference to his lost painting as the putative source for both Petrus

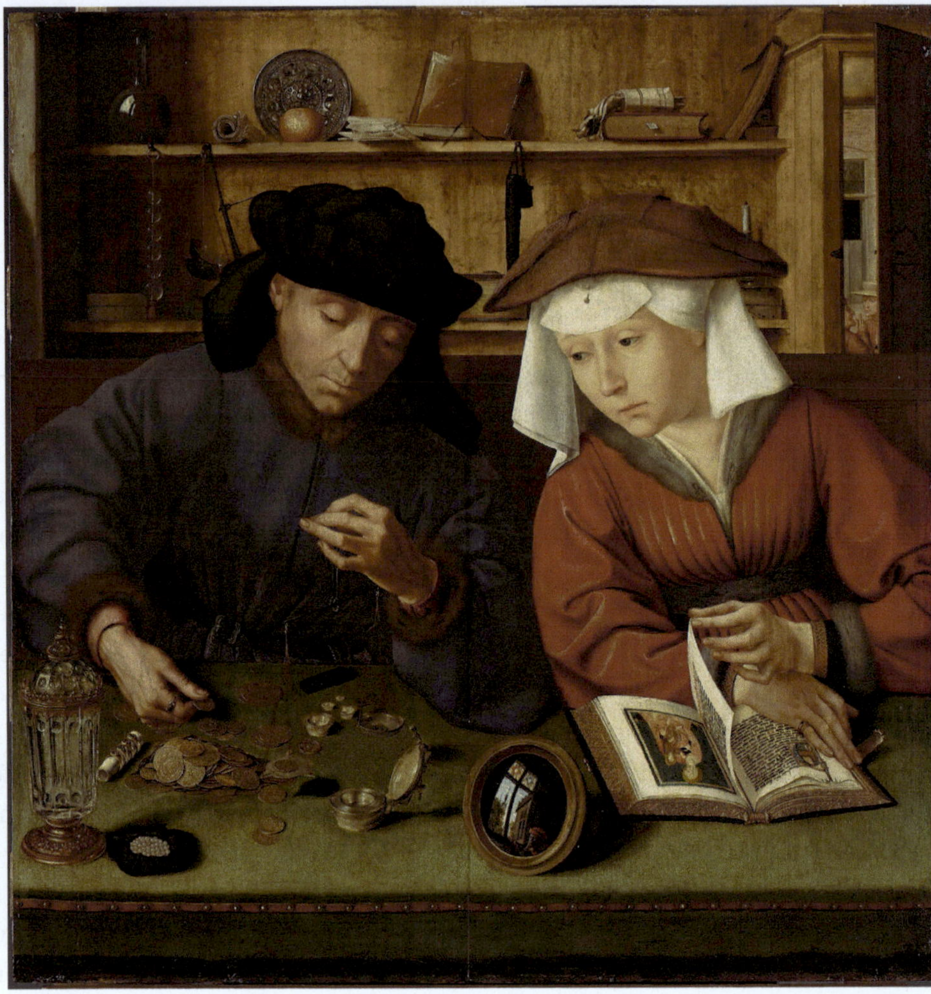

Fig. 42 Quentin Metsys, *The Moneylender and His Wife (De Wisselaer)*, c. 1514, oil on panel, 70.5 × 96 cm, Musée du Louvre, Paris.
Photo: Musée du Louvre

and Metsys. In the case of Metsys it was surely of particular significance as he is reputed to have come from a family of smiths and to have trained as a smith-turned-painter. The Antwerp Guild of St Luke, of which Metsys was a member, began as an association comprising both goldsmiths and painters, as well as painters on glass and therefore mirror makers, so the trade connections were close.[72] In the particular case of Metsys, the depiction of a goldsmith and his wife, with connections to marriage through the pictorial reference to Petrus Christus, may have had a personal significance. For sixteenth-century sources had it that Metsys became a painter to please his beloved, who preferred 'the silent play of brushes to the thundering blows of a forge'.[73]

As with Petrus Christus, the painting's Marian references accord with a marital context, suggesting a 'holy family' as a common imagery of marriage and familial concerns. The book that the young wife peruses lies open to an illumination of a mother and child bearing halos. The letter shown on the page she turns to is D, suggesting *Domine* or *Deus*, encircling an image of the lamb of God. The various light-filled glass or crystal objects within the painting are again a common pictorial metaphor for Mary's immaculacy, which also pervaded marital imagery as a sign of conjugal chastity. As other scholars have noted, the golden apple on the uppermost shelf behind them may suggest Eve as Mary's forebear, and so familial and genealogical relations, of

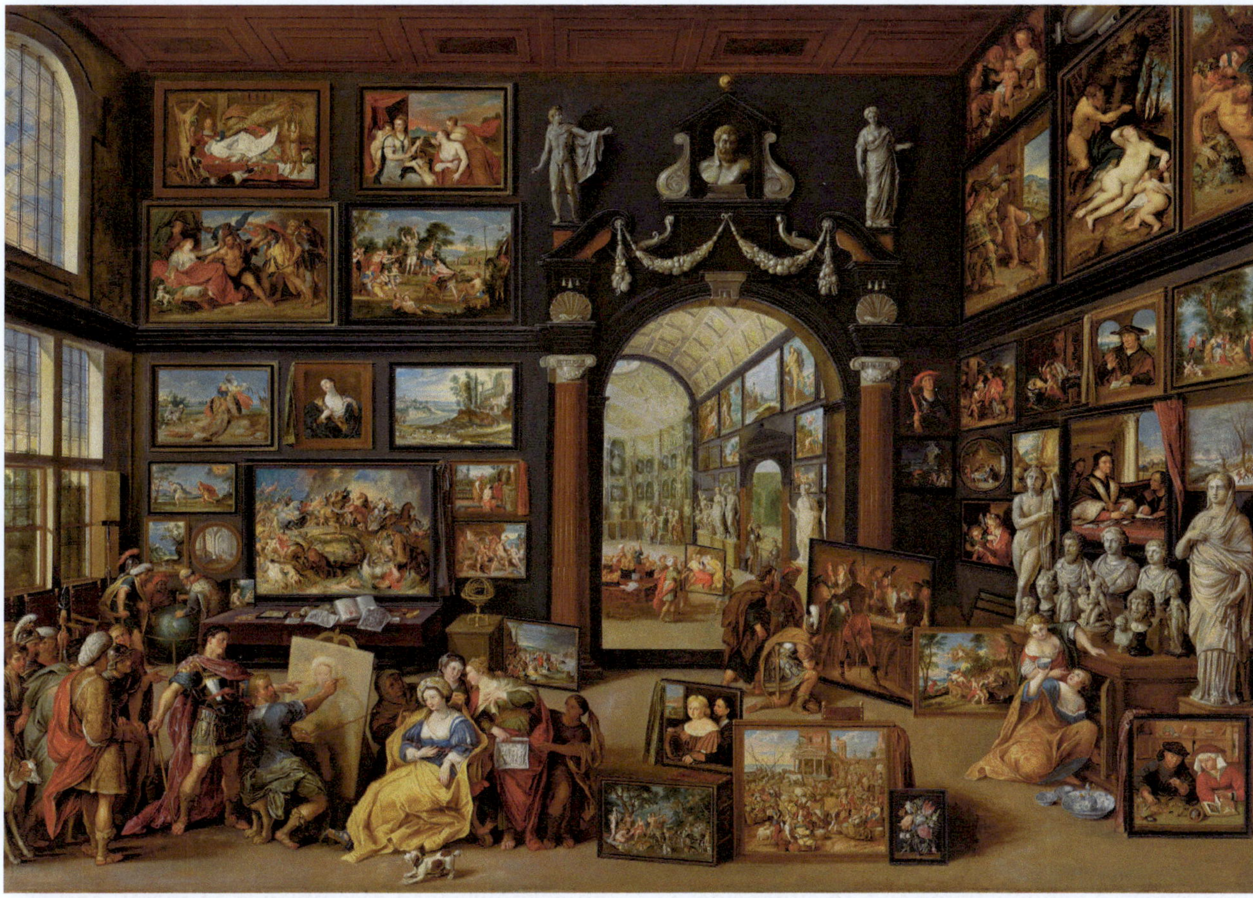

Fig. 43 Willem van Haecht, *Apelles Paints Campaspe*, c. 1630, oil on panel, 104.9 × 148.7 cm, Mauritshuis, The Hague (detail, *De Wisselaer*, lower right).
Photo: Mauritshuis, The Hague

particular significance given van Haecht's transposition of the mother and child illumination to Adam and Eve in his *Atelier of Apelles Painting Campaspe* (Fig. 43). The candle and the scales of judgment displayed on the back shelves also suggest the presentiment of conjugal chastity as a *vanitas*, alongside marriage and mother with child imagery.

Links to possible marriages as a gift have been suggested. This is resonant with the patronage and commissioning of the Arnolfini double portrait, assumed to be in connection with their marriage, and to the Petrus panel's suggested links to the social domain of marriage too. In the case of *De Wisselaer*, scholars have mooted it was a wedding gift for the celebrated 'Prince of the Humanists' Erasmus of Rotterdam's dear friend Pieter Gillis made in 1514, to whom he also dedicated his *Parabolae* of that year in celebration of this marriage.[74] As further evidence of the social ties between Erasmus, Gillis, and Metsys, a few years later Erasmus commissioned a portrait of himself from Metsys while staying with Gillis in Antwerp (1517, now Palazzo Barberini, Rome), and subsequently a portrait-medal in 1519, in recognition of the artist's capacities as both a painter and a smith, and of the circle of friendship among them.[75]

Like Petrus Christus, and in imitation of Eyckian convention, Metsys included his signature among the objects of the goldsmith's shop he depicts, in this instance interwoven with the books and bundles of papers placed on the top shelf at the back of the painting. One sheaf of paper holding a bundle bears his name as if written in ink: Quinten Matsys / *Schilder* 1514.[76] In a slip of paper acting as a bookmark below, Metsys painted a miniated hammer as if drawn by pen, within a frame of further graphic pen-marks, so equating the delicate hammers of the goldsmith's trade with the draughtsman and the calligrapher's pen, as the emblem of his craft and the hallmark of his 'Flemish' style. Linking pictorial, material, and literary forms of knowledge, here the painter's signature resembles both the goldsmith's mark and the scribe or publisher's colophon made from moveable metal type.[77]

These shelves are not, like those of Petrus, spaces of display for the goldsmith's wares, however. With the exception of the embossed silvered plate and the golden apple before it, the shelves instead bear papers and books, a set of scales, a small box, a hanging tasselled tubular device, a candlestick, and glass objects with reflective surfaces – a string of glass beads and above them a glass vase. The curving bowl of the vase reflects a window frame and, to either side, a series of reflections seemingly of the painter as he painted. Before the couple, the table on which the goldsmith undertakes his work extends to the picture plane, perspectivally raised to display a further collection of reflective objects of various kinds: a crystal cup with gold chasing, a cluster of pearls, a roll of gold rings, a mass of gold coins, and book leaves edged in gold with a metal clasp, as products of a goldsmith's facture. The goldsmith himself is depicted in the act of weighing coins, expertly holding the scale in one hand while adding a coin with the other. One coin is already in the balance, countered by a fractional weight. Around him lies an open box with a cluster of nested weights. A seventeenth-century observer noted that the painting's then-frame, now lost, apparently bore an inscription from Leviticus to link the act of weighing with that of judgment, so connecting the position of the goldsmith with an arbitrator of law under the theological sign of *vanitas*: 'Let the balance be just and the weights equal' (19:36).[78]

Closest to the goldsmith is a dark rectangular piece of stone, recognisably a 'touchstone', typically a hard lydite with a black hue known from antiquity as *iudex*, or judge, among other names. The motif was also a common literary device for the judgement of moral worth or virtue, as in the Shakespearean example of the 'Touchstone' character in *As You Like It*, whose emblematic dialogue served to disclose the true value of his interlocutors (Act 3, scene 3).[79] In the Metsys, the stone's surface bears a number of silvered marks, the residue of its function within a goldsmith's shop. As Pliny had recounted, the expert gold- and silversmith could evaluate the quantity of precious metal in a coin or other object by drawing it across such a 'testing stone', or *pietra di paragone*, and then studying comparatively the mark it left.[80] Also known as a goldstone or a streakstone – *streichstein* or *strichstone* – from the streaks of metal deposited on the surface, it bore an acknowledged resemblance to metal- and silverpoint instruments for drawing on paper. Among its many cultural analogies, from monetary to moral values, arose also a web of calligraphic associations at play in Metsys' rebus imagery. Together with the penned anvil of Metsys' signature, these pictorial references drew together smithing, penmanship, and painting, in a further *paragone* or comparison of the artisanal and scribal arts, word and image together. Similarly, Metsys' goldsmith tests each coin both for the quantity of gold by means of his touchstone and by weight through his scales. Each coin's face or shield – *schild* – is a decorated one, with the armorial style of marking that also characterised goldsmith makers' marks within guilds. Thus the goldsmith judges the quality of art as a matter of fine discernment. The art of the *schilder* weighs in the goldsmith's balance, just as he will judge the draughtsman's marks as the qualitative touchstone of his art.

The appellation of 'touchstone', the most common term for this type of rock, springs from declensions of '*toccare*', or to strike, as a reference to the striking of bells for church and civic clock-towers, also the work of metalsmiths. This implied a double meaning: of striking the metal against the testing stone, but also the striking of a chiming sound. It surely also referenced the blows of a metalsmith's hammer ringing out to shape the objects of his craft, and those of the goldsmith in striking each coin against the testing stone to gauge the quality thereof. *Touche* or touch was also the most common French term for guild-maker's marks, acknowledgement of the close tie between the act of testing metal on a touchstone and that of franking its quality. Painting, drawing, sculpting, and smithing in metal are here brought together as a pictorial rebus to celebrate the fruitful union of the arts in this most Eyckian of subjects and objects, the allegory of marriage in a goldsmith's shop.

At the centre foreground of the panel stands a mirror, similar to that depicted by Petrus Christus. Small and round as the product of blown glass, its bull's-eye form is surrounded by a gilt-painted wooden frame with a bevelled edge. Like the other objects on display, it is a likely product of a gold- or silversmith's wares due to its painted silver foil. Seemingly propped up by a hidden stand at the back, this mirror faces the viewer directly, turned very slightly on the frontally placed shelf. Its incline balances the gentle turn of the painting's perspectival recession as a whole along its opposite diagonal. Within its roundel 'eye', the mirror's reflection depicts a large mullioned window with stained glass in the upper portion, through the slight distortion of its convex surface. The lower part discloses a view onto a projecting architectural wing with a matching window surmounted by gables, and a church spire surrounded by trees set against a sky of lightly scudding clouds. It suggests the illusion of further architectural space in front of the painting in which such a window might be situated, as if behind us as viewers, so drawing us into the painting's optical illusions of fictive space. Within this reflected interior is a man, whom we see in bust length, turned in three-quarter profile, and dressed in a red tunic and chaperon. As has often been remarked, the head-dress recalls Jan van Eyck's putative self-portrait in such a red chaperon with a cornette wrapped around the head in the manner of a turban (National Gallery London), thus the Metsys reference is surely Eyckian (Fig. 44).[81]

Identified in a 1655 inventory as a '*ritratto di Gio. van Eyck de mano sua*' – a portrait of Jan van Eyck by his own hand – van Eyck's presumed portrait of himself still bears its original gilt-wood frame, on which he painted two inscriptions. Along the bottom is: JOH[ANN]ES DE EYCK ME FECIT AN[N]O MCCC 33 21 OCTOBRIS – Jan van Eyck made me in the year 1433 21 October – which is thought to be the year of his marriage, and a possible pendant to his portrait of his wife Margaret. Along the top runs the artist's device or motto, which appears in a handful of his works. In a mix of his native dialect of Limburg Dutch, it replaces some of the letters with Greek characters that are phonetically similar, as a proclamation of his humanist learning in its play with both a pictorial and aural rebus. In keeping with armorial patterns of nomenclature, it is surely a pun on his name, which declares the reach of his artistic learning and conception: ALS IXH XAN – As I can.[82] As Lorne Campbell has argued, the presence of the artist's device is itself strong evidence for the identification of this work as a self-portrait. This is coupled with the pose of the head, leaning forward with a penetrating gaze, apparently in order to study his reflection in a mirror.[83] Thus its legacy would seem to be as an image tied to the celebration of marriage as well as of artistic identity, as would typify the genre of betrothal portraiture more broadly. Seemingly made through the instrument

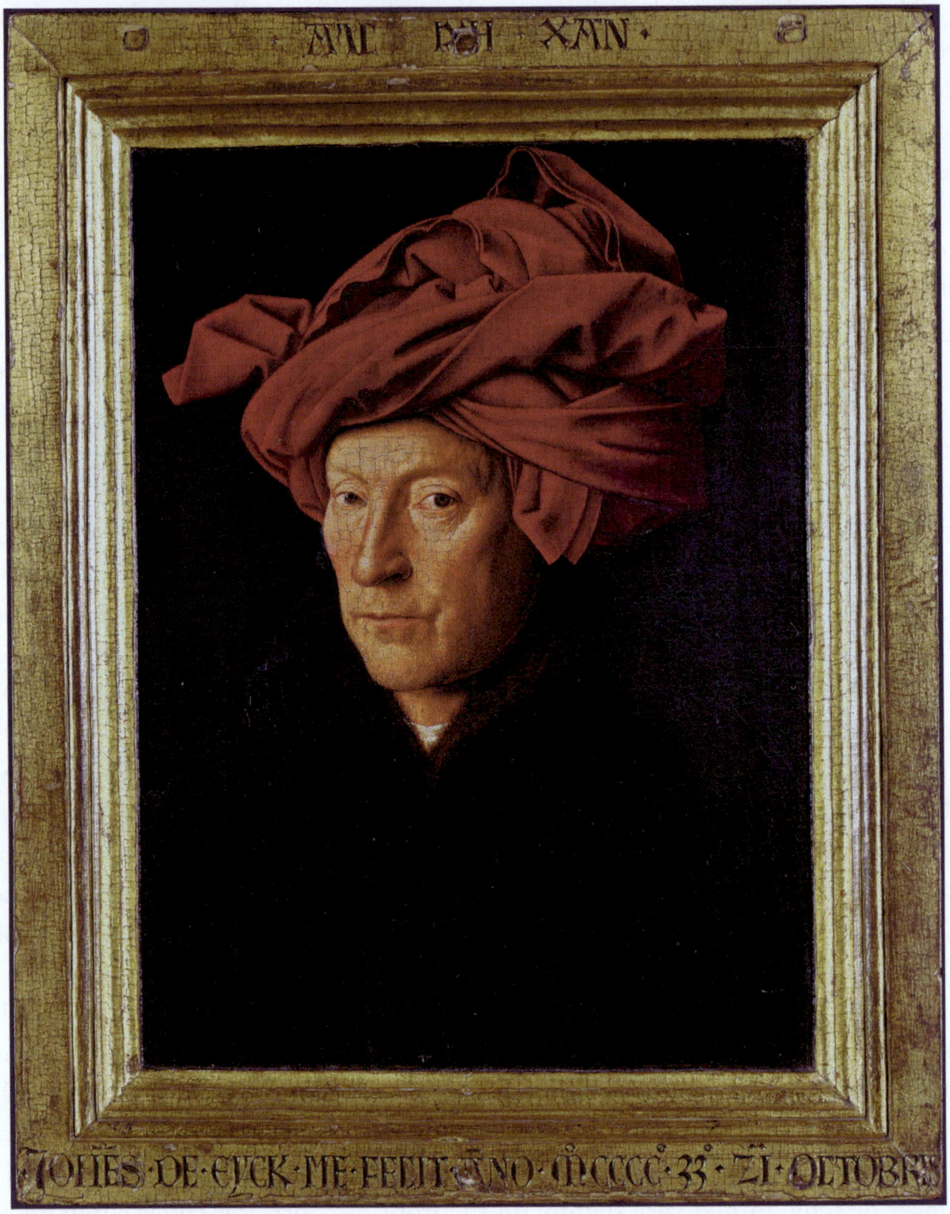

Fig. 44 Jan van Eyck, *Portrait of a Man (Self-Portrait)*, 1433, oil on oak, 26 × 19 cm, National Gallery, London. Photo: Wikimedia

of a mirror reflection, its claim is that van Eyck's painting in oil can mirror the world – and the artist who paints it – as accurately as a mirror itself. In this regard, if the mirror is the measure of the painter's skill in the arts of mimesis, it is also the instrument of its comparison, or *paragone*, as Giorgione's lost reflection-painting would later acknowledge. In his pictorial reply to the sculptors, Giorgione put the matter so as to claim an Eyckian lineage for the history of his art as a mirror-image of the visible field. Just as Alberti had theorised in the pool of Narcissus, so van Eyck also recognised the mirror-image as the painter's equal. To rival the mirror's optical claim was to argue that a painting was both a perfectly true and entirely counterfeit representation of vision, such that art and science were fully equivalent.

In *De Wisselaer*, the diminutive Eyckian mirror figure rests one hand on the window ledge, while holding an open book in the other. Situated in the fictive space of the viewer before the painting, this is also the position of the artist as he paints. The intimation of the artist's working presence within the image is repeated in the reflection of the glass vase on the shelf behind. Here is both the window to the left side of the painting and the artist in miniature, like a pictorial signature. Thus the 'artist' figure of the mirror roundel stands in thought between the window and the book. Apt metaphors for the dual sources of his knowledge, visual and textual, the window like the mirror itself may be read as a simile for the artist's observation from life, and the book as the sign of narrative and erudition of all kinds. Beside the mirror lies the open devotional book that the goldsmith's wife holds while turning the pages, though her gaze is instead directed towards her husband's action of weighing in the balance 'from life'. Behind her is a door, only slightly ajar, that opens onto the outdoors. Seemingly a courtyard facing directly onto the door and window of another house across the way, two figures stand wrapped in conversation here, one gesticulating with the hand while speaking, the other leaning in to listen. A pictorial ellipsis as a 'slice of life' window-view, it surely signals Flemish painting as genre, the artistic conventions of which Petrus Christus is said to have inaugurated with his Eyckian goldsmith's shop. In the foreground of the painting, the tacks that run across the bottom ledge of the goldsmith's worktop to fix its green baize cover in place are seemingly situated exactly at the picture plane, so that their raised heads protrude illusionistically, albeit very slightly, into the viewer's space. At either side of the painting the tacks meet the picture frame, so drawing together the fictive world of the painting into the picture frame's 'window view'. This is echoed in the specular reflection in the bowl of the glass carafe on the shelf above, which captures the light of the window to the side. Within the painting, only the far frame of the window is visible, while its reflection in the carafe is of the window-light itself, illusionistically projected as if in front of the painting, so further eliding the fiction of pictorial space with that of our own. Together these details declare the art of painting as a window, an open door, or a mirror reflection of the visible field. Thus the work may be said to contain within itself a history of Northern art in object form, from the illuminated manuscript to the medallic coins or *schild* to the mirror, the window, and the doorway view. Between the window and the door, the background shelves are burdened with books. This sequencing of the book and the window is repeated throughout the work, both within the scene and in its miniature mirror reflection, as the twin sources of pictorial imagery and artistic knowledge.

The claim to the window and the book is surely that of Renaissance art writ large, as Alberti had adumbrated. In this regard the choice of subject, that of a goldsmith and his wife reading from an illuminated book, may also recall the historical claim of Johannes Gutenberg the German goldsmith, whose skill with fine metalwork led to the development of moveable type and thus the printing press that was the means of both the Gutenberg Bible and the writings of Erasmus.[84] Metsys' Antwerp was a major centre for Renaissance book publishing and trade, hence the frequent visits of figures such as Erasmus, whose towering presence configured its literary culture, extending also to artists. At the time of Metsys' membership of Antwerp's civic guild of St Luke, it had traditionally brought together painters with smiths including mirror and glass painters, and latterly print makers as both metalworkers and image-makers for the publishing trade. Through the printmakers there were particularly close ties with the city's leading literary guild, De Violieren. Otherwise known as chambers of rhetoric, such organisations as De Violieren put on recitative literary performances and contests, including the many painters who were also members.[85] Scholars of Netherlandish painting have recently stressed the close links between book cultures and painting manifest in the material composition of fifteenth-century painted panels, often enclosed by 'covers' like those of books, and decorated in painted imitation of the marbled paper commonly used to encase them.[86] In van Eyck's Bruges this proximity produced a guild for the book trade known as the librarians' guild, as part of a Flemish literary culture joining the printed image with that of books. Within print collections, across Renaissance Europe these were largely kept within 'book covers', and often within libraries, further testament to the close cultural affinities of printed word and image.

Returning to the putative connection of the painting with the 1514 marriage of Erasmus' friend Pieter Gillis, and the great writer's offering of his *Parabolae* of that year alongside other possible wedding presents such as *De Wisselaer*, word and image together suggest an intended 'Flemishness' to these gifts. For the *Parabolae* was, as Erasmus declared in his prefatory letter, a collection of lightly ludic literary metaphors specifically in the form of proverbs. Long seen as a particularly (though by no means exclusively) Northern literary form, the proverb signified a textual equivalent to Flemish genre painting, as manifest in Brueghel the Younger's *Netherlandish Proverbs* of 1559.[87] Using seemingly quotidian language to reflect on themselves by addressing larger concerns through the light humour of the familial and the everyday, the perspicuous brevity of the proverb in both word and image was central to Antwerp's Flemish literary and artistic circles as the forum for a display of a Netherlandish wit.

As Erasmus surely knew, the proverbial title of *Parabolae* carried a specular analogy to a curved or parabolic mirror. More broadly, the parabolic curve's rhetorical valence, as Erasmus playfully acknowledged in his dedicatory preface to his friend Gillis, was one of manifold similitude. Within mathematical cultures, the parabolic plane curve, known from Greek antiquity, was one of broad U-formation; thus, it also became a rhetorical figure of doubling, as of a doubled wit. The parabolic curve's paradigmatic form was similarly likened to a rainbow, hence its early associations with allegories of light reflection and the study of optics. Within science the parabolic curve's applied calculation was fundamental to the manufacture of combustion mirrors for industrial and military purposes, whether of polished glass or metal tempered into a curving form, used to focus light for the purposes of ignition.

Calculation of the parabolic curve was also crucial to the fabrication of optical lenses. Historians of optical instruments argue that late medieval developments in lens-making grew out of the use of crystal 'reading stones' or glass magnifiers made of dome-shaped globes cut in half that were placed onto a page to facilitate greater legibility. The practice subsequently led to the thirteenth-century facture of rivet spectacles composed of twinned spherical lenses of crystal or optical glass, as with van Eyck's depiction of his Bruges patron, Canon van der Paele (Fig. 45a, b).[88] As Stephen Hanley has argued, the Canon's spectacles held over the text of an open book may further suggest the theology of the *Magnificat*, as the amplification of God's word. Scholars have also suggested van Eyck's use of such a curved magnifying lens or mirror for his painting, as the instrumental means of his art of close descriptive detail.[89] Similarly, the painted mirror reflection of the Metsys panel, like that of van Eyck's, may be read as the perspicacious optical 'eye' of a parabolic mirror and a rebus of itself. It is at once a simile of vision, of a proverbial Flemish wit, and of its mirror-like painting too.

As other scholars have pointed out in their analysis of Metsys' painting, the Antwerp book

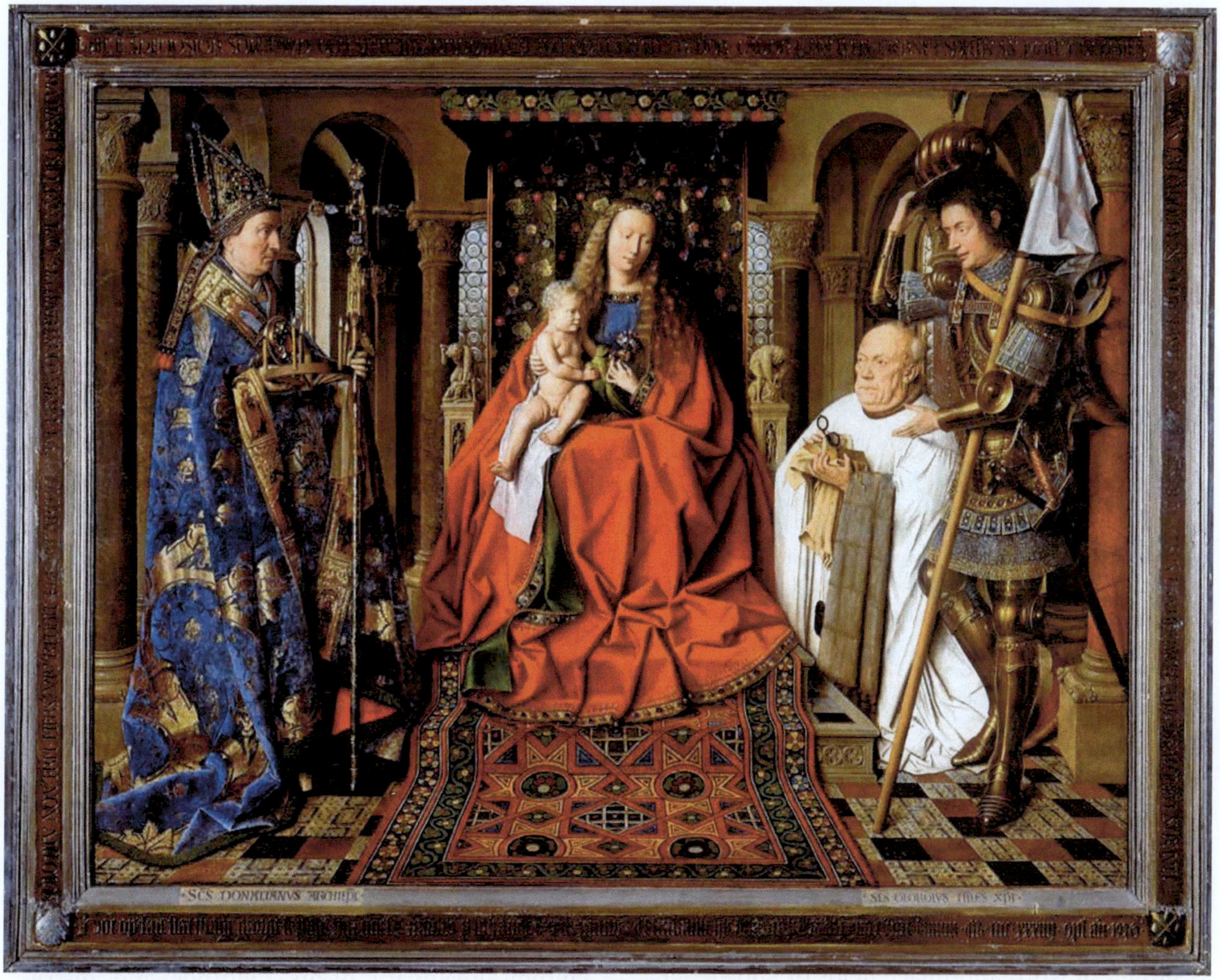

Fig. 45a Jan van Eyck, *Madonna with Canon Joris van der Paele*, 1434–36, oil on panel, 160 × 124.5 cm, Groeninge Museum, Bruges.
Photo: Wikimedia

trade in these years produced any number of books and prints under the title of 'mirror' or '*Spiegel*', in addition to those of Flemish proverbs.[90] As such, Erasmus' *Parabolae* title lightly referenced the myriad books of the period published under the broad sign of the mirror-image, as discussed in Chapter 1. Within the great mantle of the pre-modern book of knowledge conceived as a mirror of all forms of information and culture, Flemish and Netherlandish examples comprised among them the sciences and philosophies, including theology and moral instruction. This extended even to the gentle proverbial humour of moral guidance in marriage and the happy governance of the godly home, also the subject of Metsys' panel. In its reference to both the mirror of the conscience and the clear vision of an optical instrument of reflection, the parabolic mirror was thus understood as an emblem of perspicacity. As a ready metaphor for their varied contents, '*parabolae*' like '*Spiegel*' could signify both a literary collection and a collective intention to reflect, in matters of faith and morality as of knowledge more generally. Such 'mirroring' morality tales were often written in comic vein using stock burgher characters with exaggerated human foibles, or simply the domestic weal as a gentle mirror of the world, in a

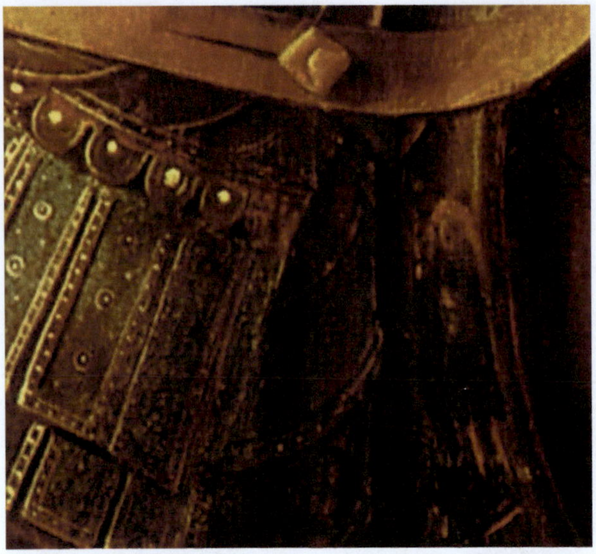

Fig. 45b Jan van Eyck, *Madonna with Canon Joris van der Paele*, detail of the putative 'self-portrait' in the shield of St George, 1434–36, oil on panel, 160 × 124.5 cm, Groeninge Museum, Bruges.
Photo: Wikimedia

literary equivalent to genre painting.[91] Hence the mirror as a metaphor was a deeply rooted one within Flemish literary production, prevalent across manifold cultural forms in both word and image. Likewise, the window and the book, as similes of word-and-image fields of knowledge, were often drawn together with the mirror in literary reflections on Netherlandish culture, and of Netherlandish art. Thus in *De Wisselaer*, the mirror reflection acts as one of a series of 'pictures within the picture': the view through the door, the illuminated page and the coin faces, and the mirror as its centre point. In effect, Metsys' *De Wisselaer* may be said to have pictorialized the literary conventions of this proverbial genre. For Metsys' painted 'mirror' of art is also convex-shaped in the manner of a parabola, like a smith's curving shield or armorial *schild*, as artefactual metaphors of an Erasmian proverbial wit. Within its reflective sphere further rebus images of Metsys and his art are encased, in a full elision of word and image, like those of armoury's *mise-en-abyme*.

SPECULUM SINE MACULA

The representation of the artist at work was, within guild structures, found most often in depictions of St Luke, as the patron saint of artists and their academies. Early Christian sources attributed to Luke the first pictorial representations of the Virgin, as portraits made of Mary by this saint.[92] As a subject that comprised within itself the image of St Luke painting within a painting, it was common to Flemish art of the period, tied particularly to those institutions bearing his name and in honour of his artistry, the guilds and academies of St Luke. Like all imagery of the Holy Family or the Holy Mother and Child, it was also tied to the celebration of marriage and childbirth through its maternal reference. As Heinrich Schwarz pointed out in his 1959 study of the fifteenth-century painted inset mirror, this imagery of St Luke painting may be supposed to depict the accoutrements of artistic practice, comprising mirrors, in Flemish Renaissance workshops.[93] While we cannot presume such paintings are social documents of artistic practice, yet they surely reflect a cultural imaginary of its methods and instruments. Like the goldsmith paintings, the typology of St Luke as painter draws on that of the vocational portrait type apparently initiated by van Eyck, with elements of genre in the rendition of artistic tools and the appurtenance of a painter's workshop. The presence of mirrors within these paintings is surely a reference to their use by artists as both instruments and emblems of their mimetic art. The mirror as the painter's emblem and so the attribute of Saint Luke is also Marian in reference to his role as the painter of her portrait. Specifically, as an object of unbroken perspicacity, the mirror was understood as an emblem of Mary's immaculacy. It is for this reason that it came to be associated with marriage imagery, as the Arnolfini double portrait most famously represents. Within paintings of

St Luke, the mirror signalled the image as made of light, fusing the representation of sunlight with its divine emanation. Within Mariological belief, the mirror reflects and contains the light of the divine, which pierces but does not break its glass as an emblem of her chastity. Again, such imagery also held valence within pictorial representations of the bonds of familial ties, in which depictions of the Holy Mother and Child were also allegories of a virtuous motherhood.[94] As other scholars have pointed out, this may also be infused by Plutarch's essay on conjugal devotion, from his *Moralia*, in which the mirror reflection is the emblem of reciprocated love.[95]

Van Eyck's contemporary and possible student, Robert Campin, painted such an image, now lost, but thought to have been for the Guild of St Luke in Tournai of which he was a leading member. Greatly celebrated, it is generally acknowledged to have prompted much emulation. Dirck Baegart's subsequent imitations of his work in a painted panel now at the Westfalisches Landesmuseum Münster, and a triptych in Stolzenhain Church, Brandenburg, Eastern Germany (Fig. 46), both dated c. 1480, may exemplify the many pictorial 'paraphrases', to borrow Preimesberger's apt term, of Campin's lost panel. The copious domestic detail of interior and outdoor scenery around the central depiction of the saint at his easel typically includes a small convex glass mirror mounted on a window mullion just above Luke as he works. Within such a richly appointed interior Mary is seated with her child swathed in abundant draperies of blue and red. The windows and loggia opening give on to a scene of water, city houses, and streets with tiny figures. In a further room beyond St Luke an angel appears, variously kneeling in prayer before a book in the Münster panel, while in the triptych version he grinds colours, accompanied by St Joseph. In both versions the mirror therefore takes its place at the centre of the work among a series of images within images: framed window and doorway views, and St Luke's painting on its easel. It also takes its place among those Flemish paintings concerned with a pictorial sequence of window and book as complementary modes of knowledge so favoured in Erasmian circles. In Baegaert's triptych, the right panel depicts St Joseph in a carpenter's workshop with the boy Christ, while the left shows a scribe at work. These panels repeat the motifs of artisanal and textual forms of knowledge as contingent to the painter's own.[96] Similarly, the St Joseph panel of the Mérode altarpiece depicts an array of carpenter's tools.[97] It may be indicative of van Eyck's lost vocational portrait, as well as Campin's lost St Luke painting that also apparently depicted a plethora of detail of a painter's workshop.

A further example of St Luke painting, also from the Antwerp workshop of Metsys (Fig. 47), depicts the saint at work in what is surely a side panel to a larger triptych with a central image of the Virgin and Child.[98] Seated before an easel on which rests the work he is painting, Luke holds a palette, extra brushes, and a mahlstick in one hand, while the other wields a fine brush towards the panel. A palette knife and jar for further brushes sit on a small table beside him. At the back of the room are shelves lined with books, and various jars and glass vessels, possibly for making pigments. A large window lights the scene from the right, picking out the details of Luke's painting, which depicts the Virgin in blue with a red mantle holding the Christ child framed by green curtains. Directly above the back of Luke's head is a wall-mounted mirror of blown glass, its small but prominent globe-shaped form surrounded by a bevelled wooden frame. Though in shadow, the mirror clearly reflects the back of the saint's head in its red bonnet with a further window reflection above, and his painting hand, raised up and holding a paintbrush, in the act of applying paint. Luke's gaze, however, looks beyond the easel to what is surely the

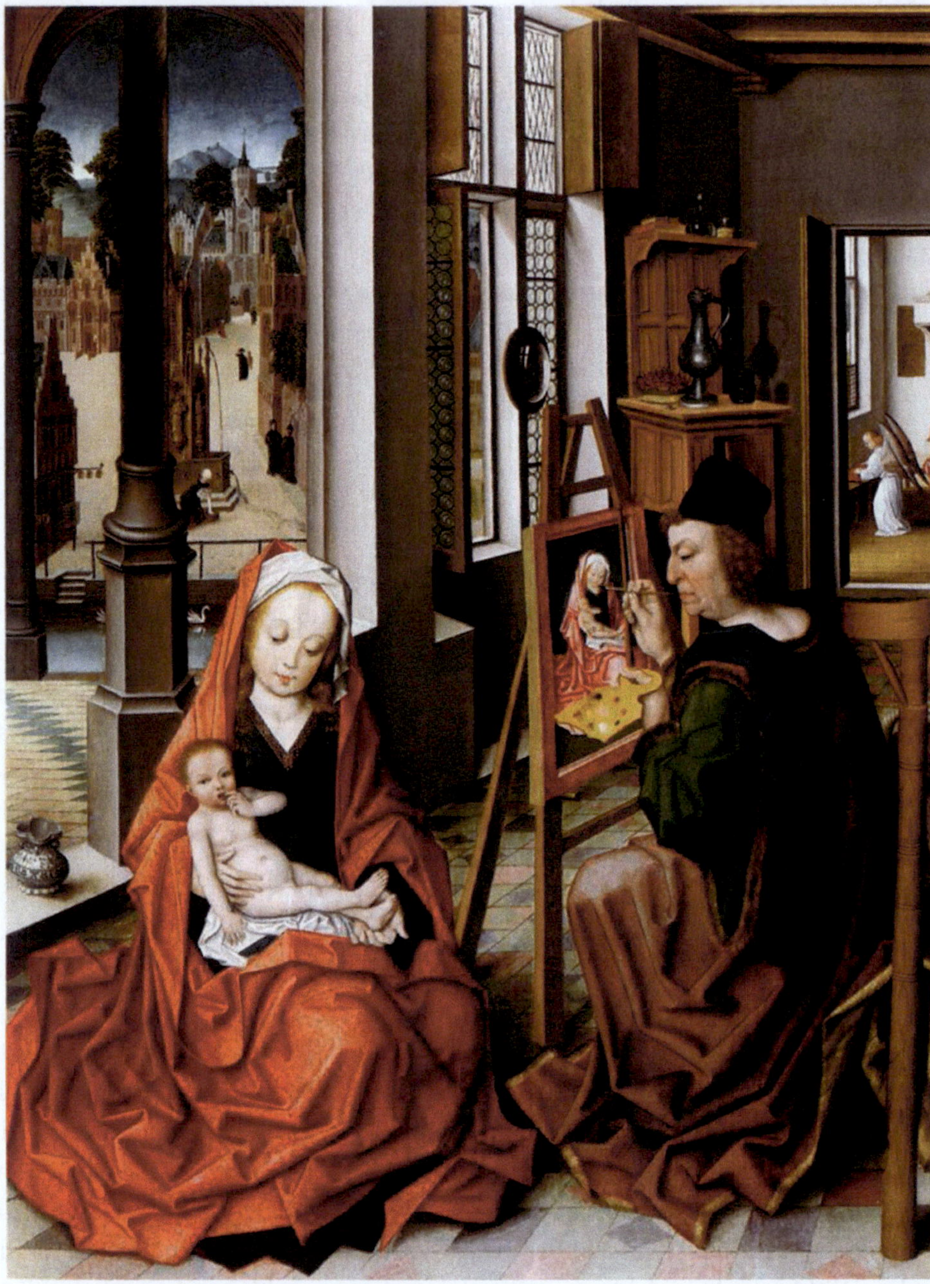

Fig. 46 Dirk Baegert, *St Luke Painting the Virgin*, after Robert Campin, c. 1480, oil on panel, Westphalia State Museum, Münster. Photo: Wikimedia

representation of the Virgin and Child of the lost central panel. Thus the triptych form must have elided the central panel of the Virgin and Child with the subject of Luke's painting, as a sequence of painted panel images, like the multiplication of a mirror reflection. The bull's-eye mirror's doubled depiction of the artist's hand is, again, like a pictorial signature, and an Eyckian representation of the act of painting within the work – ALS IXH XAN – 'as I can'.

An eight-panelled series from the late fifteenth century by the German painter Gabriel Mälesskircher depicts St Luke as one of the four gospel writers in an image replete with details of the artist-saint at work.[99] Each saint is represented twice within the series: once in the act of writing

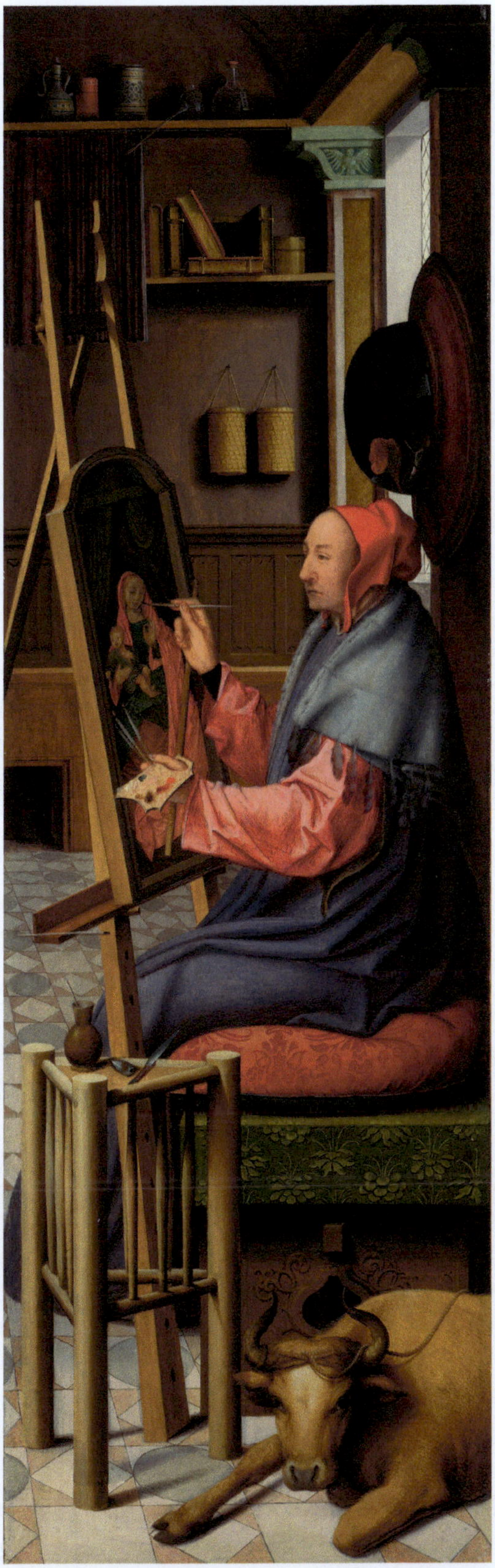

Fig. 47 Workshop of Quentin Metsys, *St Luke Painting the Virgin and Child* (side panel from a triptych), c. 1520, oil on oak, 114.9 × 35.4 cm, National Gallery, London. Photo: Wikimedia

his gospel, and subsequently in a renowned scene from his hagiography. In the case of Luke, the two panels show him seated at a desk working on his gospel account of Christ's life, and before an easel painting a panel of the Virgin and Child (Fig. 48a, b). All four gospel-writing panels depict the saints as scribes, seated at wooden writing desks of Gothic ornament, with pens, quills, and coloured inks, the book on which they work open before them as they letter the page in German Gothic script. In Saint Luke's case, his desk displays a number of leather-bound volumes with elaborate tooling, and above them a small painting of the Crucifixion with Mary and John. To the right of the inset Crucifixion scene is a stone sculpture of a standing figure under an elaborate Gothic arch. To the left, between a sequence of windows looking onto a framed landscape view, hangs a wall-mounted convex mirror in a painted frame. In miniature, like the miniated illuminations Luke may add to the page before him, the mirror reflection indicates a further room in front of the painting. Largely in shadow, this room is lit by three large cross-paned windows that echo the Crucifixion panel, and again underscore an apparent equivalence of the window and the book as the instruments of a painter's knowledge. Its fine detail suggests it was surely painted with the aid of a magnifying lens as van Eyck is also thought to have done. As such it is a miniated emblem of the painter's art.

Representations of Mary with a mirror, in both text and image, sprang from biblical accounts of her as a 'spotless mirror' – *speculum sine macula* (Book of Wisdom 7:26). The reference is also noted as a comparison of Mary's immaculacy with human flaw.[100] Certainly, Marian imagery of the period is suffused with references to her immaculate conception through the metaphor of light that penetrates glass without breaking it, as either mirrors or windows. Thus the Virgin enthroned of van Eyck's Ghent Altarpiece and his Dresden and van der Paele Madonnas all bear an inscription to her

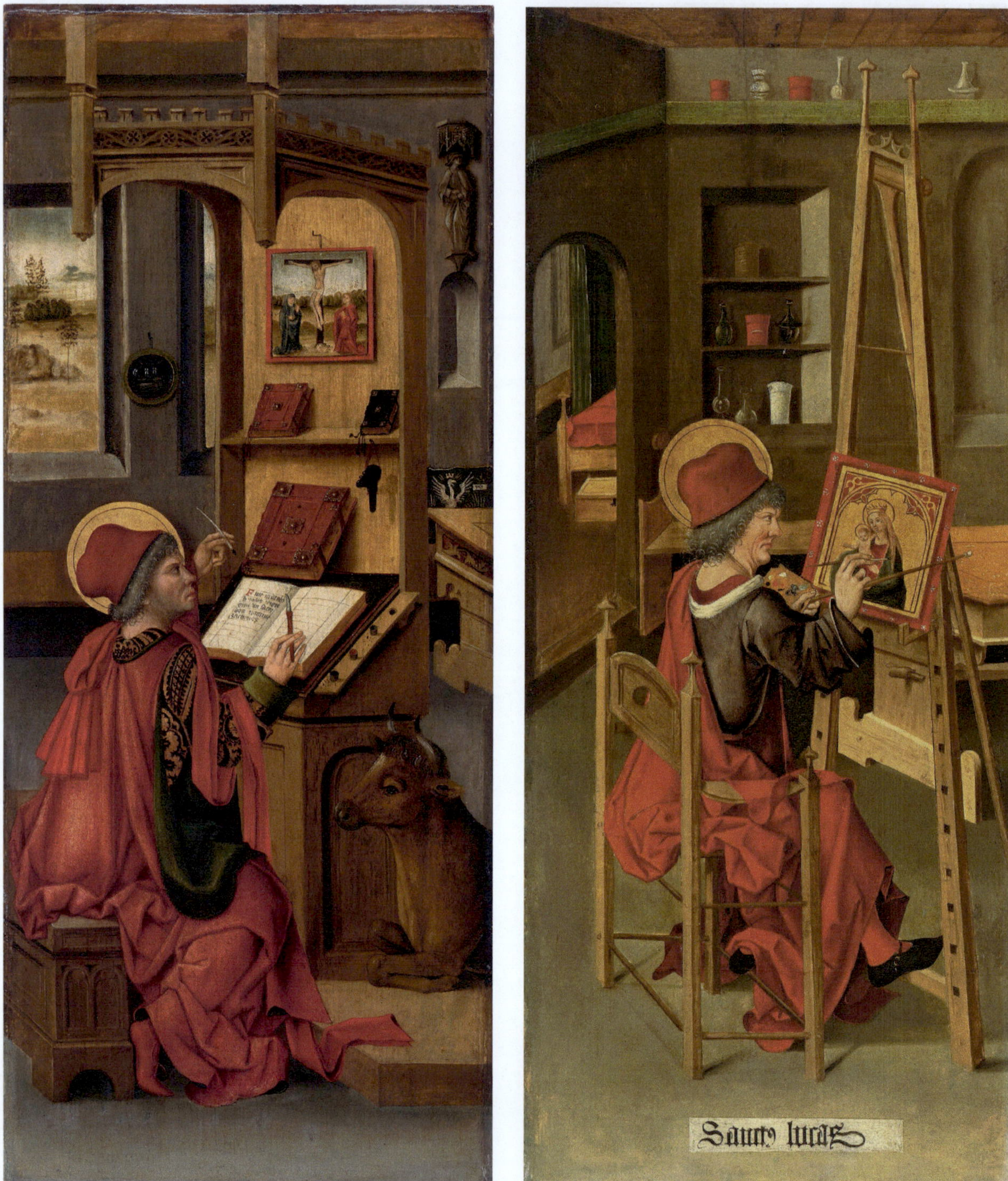

Fig. 48a, b Gabriel Mälesskircher, *Saint Luke the Evangelist*, *St Luke Painting the Virgin*, 1478, oil on panel, 77 × 32.2 cm, Museo Nacional Thyssen-Bornemisza, Madrid.
Photo: Museo Nacional Thyssen-Bornemisza

immaculacy likened to a mirror as the emblem of a cosmic or celestial imagery: 'she is more radiant than the sun and surpasses every order of star . . . she is the brightness that streams from the everlasting light, the flawless mirror of God's majesty' (Wisdom 7:29). Likewise, van Eyck's *Virgin and Child in a Church* of c. 1426–28, now in Berlin, in which golden rays of light penetrate the stained-glass windows of the cathedral-like setting as a pictorial allegory of Mary's immaculate conception, also carries this biblical inscription as well as the verse of a well-known hymn of the period: 'As the sunbeam through the glass passes without stain, Thus the Virgin as she was, Virgin still remains.'[101] This is fully explicit in the Annunciation scene of the Mérode altarpiece, where the sun's rays through the window transport a tiny child towards the Virgin. The glass window, like the mirror, became a Marian attribute.

Within devotional painting, depictions of Christ's birth often included both mirrors and other glass objects as representations of Mary's intact virginity. The motif also came to pervade marital imagery, as a conjoined emblem of a celestial Marian beauty and virtuous chastity within marriage, as well as the aspiration of maternity. Thus, painted mirrors arose within the domestic decorative arts among betrothal and marriage gifts as tokens of courtly but also spiritual love, as well as in paintings related to marriage celebrations and spousal exchange. This is exemplified in the Arnolfini double portrait as well as the works of Petrus and Metsys, which have all been linked to marriage.[102]

The round mirror reflection-image therefore flourished within Flemish and German Marian painting more broadly, as a sign of her immaculacy and the virtues of chaste womanhood. Justly celebrated examples include the Werl altarpiece panels, usually attributed to Campin, or his workshop, though sometimes to his pupil Rogier van der Weyden, of which only the outer panels of what was surely a Marian triptych remain (Fig. 49). The lost central panel undoubtedly depicted the Virgin and likely her immaculate conception, flanked by Sts John the Baptist and Barbara. Barbara sits reading before an open fire in a well-appointed interior with a large window looking onto a landscape view of a tower as her most celebrated iconographic motif. John is depicted with the kneeling patron, Heinrich von Werl, a Franciscan monk and provincial of the now lost Franciscan church in Cologne for which the painting may have been intended, and the author of a theological treatise on Mary's immaculacy as a particular Franciscan devotion. The inscription running along the bottom of the panel names Werl by both his religious and scholarly titles: 'In the year 1438, Minister Heinrich von Werl, Magister of Cologne had painted (?) his image.' The window view onto an enclosed garden with a rose bush, as well as the tondo mirror hanging beside it, also indicate a Marian iconography. Specifically, *hortus conclusus* was a further metaphor of the Virgin's immaculacy, like that of the glass mirror, as well as the devotions of the rosary prayers. The Marian theme is reinforced by the small stone sculpture of the Madonna and Child on the back wall above the mirror.

As a number of scholars have pointed out, the panels' monastic patronage suggests the structure of prayer visible in the syntax of the imagery. In particular, the visual sequencing of thresholds within the composition of the individual panels and the triptych format as a whole is suggestive of its potential function within ritual devotions. Contextualised studies of Netherlandish altarpieces within rituals of faith have drawn attention to their opening and closing tied to a conception of prayer as a progression through a series of imaginary scenes, as if in a painting, towards a growing proximity with the godhead. In this analysis, each stage of prayer is furthered through a progression into the centre of a folding panel painting. In the case of the Werl panels, as with the Mérode altarpiece, the patron is depicted kneeling in prayer at just such a threshold, before an open door through which he gazes onto the (lost) central panel's depiction of Mary, his presence in keeping with those of viewers who surely knelt in prayer before the painting.[103] Behind him, John holds a small lamb above a book as his attributes, in reference to his gospel-writing and to his recognition of Christ's future death as a

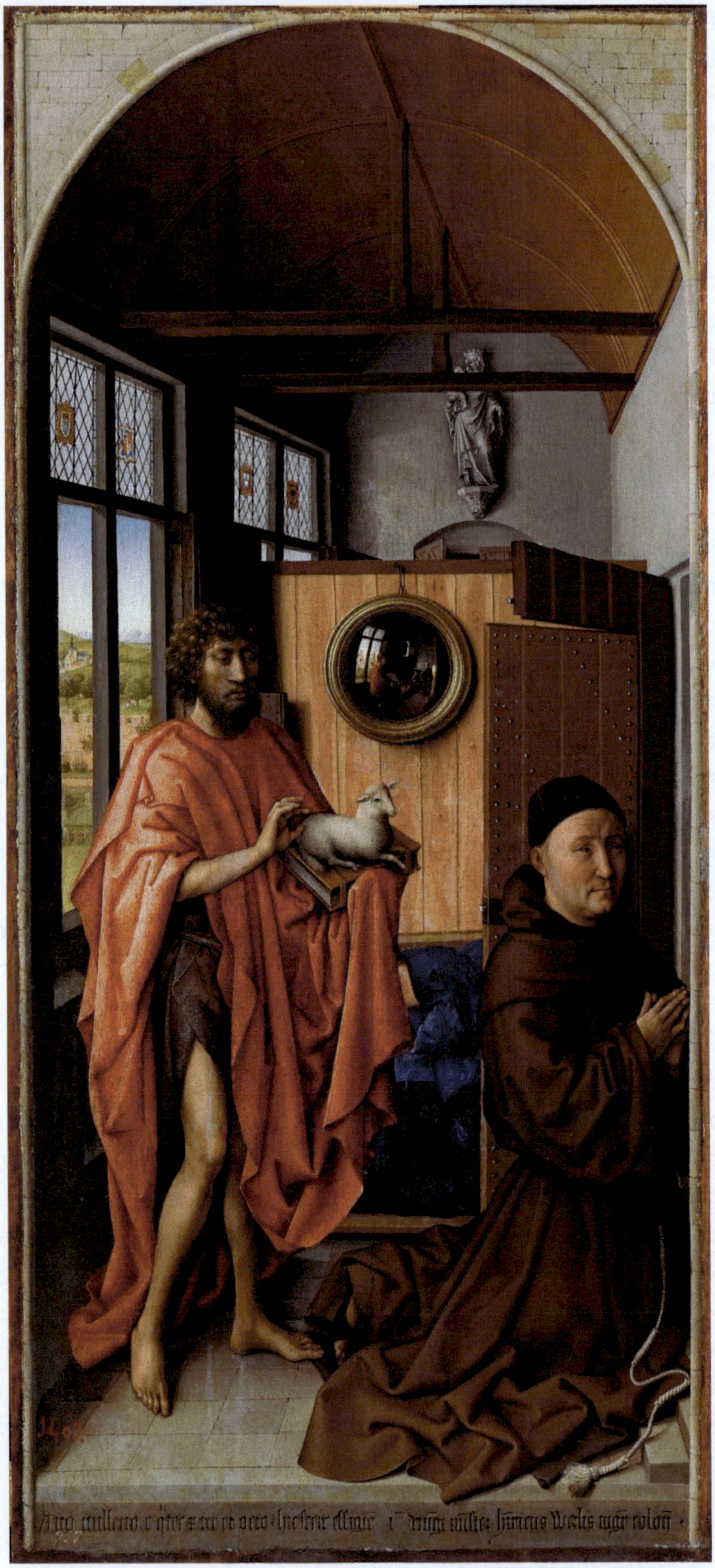

Fig. 49 Robert Campin (attrib.), *Saint John the Baptist and the Franciscan Heinrich von Werl*, 1438, oil on oak panel, 101 × 47 cm, Museo del Prado, Madrid.
Photo: © Museo Nacional del Prado

salvific lamb: 'Behold, the lamb of God.' This is reinforced by the representation of the Crucifixion above the fireplace in St Barbara's panel. The angle of the painted doorway through which von Werl gazes in adoration of Mary suggests the intended angle of the triptych panels, half open on a diagonal facing towards the centre. This is underscored by the converging diagonals of perspectival recession across both flanking panels, and in that of the mirror reflection behind St John.

The Werl mirror, wall-mounted in a bevelled gilt frame, sits at the centre of the St John panel like an armorial *schilderkunst*. Its convex shape reflects the distortions of this globe-like form, marked by a plunging recession into depth and the curving of vertical lines – the window frame and the back of the door before which Werl prays. The miniature cruciform window in the mirror's foreground gives onto a view of gabled Flemish houses, while a further raised window with shutters and an open doorway at the back let further light onto the scene. At the centre is the reflection of John holding the lamb in profile, and behind him what is surely a brazier with an open fire, echoing or possibly reflecting that of the hearth in the Barbara panel. Beyond are two further diminutive figures, seemingly monks in Franciscan habit with long knotted belts and tonsures, holding staffs as emblems of their role as shepherds like John. Within the pictorial logic of reflection they suggest the space in front of the central panel, where shepherd-monks have come to adore the depiction of Mary as we do, like viewers before the triptych itself.[104] It is, in miniature, an emblem of viewing, as also the subject of the altarpiece of Werl's adoration of the Virgin.

Two diptychs of similar portable size long attributed to Memling in the 1480s amplify the art-historical typology of the painted mirror as a Marian reflection (Figs. 50 and 51). In the case of the diptych now in the Art Institute of Chicago, the reunification of the two panels in 1953 was presaged by a long period in Spanish ownership as separate works, and brought about by the recognition of a continuous window frame with a landscape view across them.[105] In addition, they share a common perspectival viewpoint and a continuous though largely concealed parapet across the bottom foreground. In the left panel, the Virgin holds the Christ Child poised on a cushion across the sill, while on the right the unknown donor is depicted in prayer, with his elbow and his book's clasp projecting over the parapet and onto the painting's frame. Behind him is a flower vase with the reflection of a window in its convex bowl. In the opposite panel is a wall-mounted tondo mirror that similarly reflects a cruciform window. The book's clasp, prominently placed to invite touch, recalls the likely clasp for opening and closing the diptych itself, so referencing a proximity between books and paintings that the donor's painted prayer book also echoes. Its form surely issued from ancient practices of binding wooden writing tablets together, a recollection manifest in the frequent decoration of diptych covers in the manner of books, as recent scholarship has highlighted, further demonstrating the close exchange between literate and painterly cultures within Northern Renaissance humanism.[106] The reverse of the panel depicts St Anthony of Padua, possibly the donor's patron saint, who holds the Christ Child. On the panel frontal, held within the mirror reflection at the bottom, are two diminutive figures, in a yellow bonnet and red cap, generally identified as children. Possibly recalling the patron's ties of familial bonds through devotion to the Holy Mother and the Christ Child, their presence further suggests the painting's role as a marital gift and the aspiration for offspring. As Gustav Hartlaub first argued, the motif of the mirror within Marian and marital imagery surely touched on its pictorial capacity for reproduction, as a visual metaphor of family relations.[107] In this respect, it acts as an emblem of the Holy Family conflated with the promise of

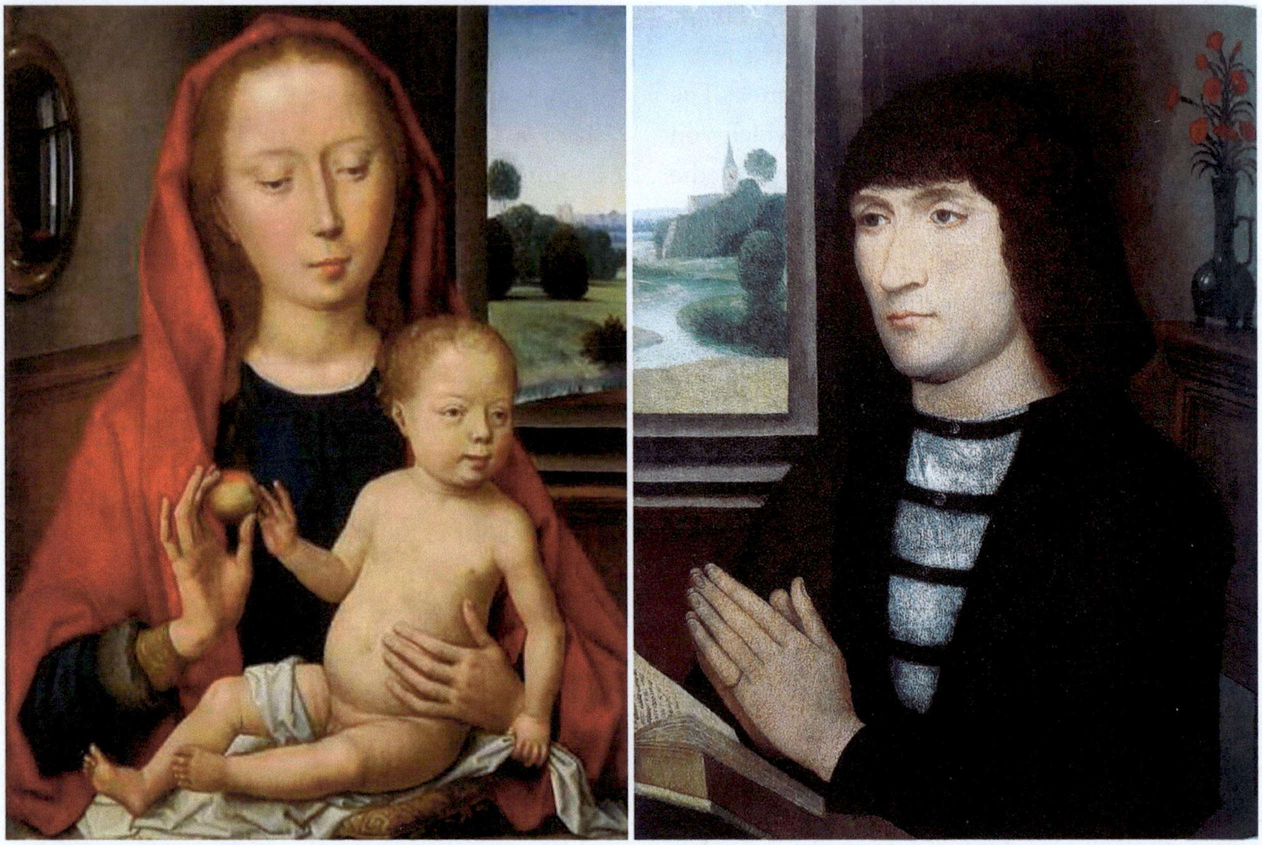

Fig. 50 Hans Memling, *Virgin and Child*, 1480–90, oil on panel, frame: 41.1 × 33.4 cm, painted surface: 34.5 × 26.8 cm, Art Institute of Chicago.
Photo: Art Institute of Chicago

marriage. The children's placement within the mirror reflection also acts as a visual anchor for the work. Seemingly standing behind Mary in reflection, their presence aligns the window in the mirror as a mirror-image of those within the panels.[108] This orchestrates the positioning of the diptych on a tabletop surface with the two panels facing each other diagonally, in concert with the common perspectival rendering across them.

Memling's Nieuwenhove diptych in Bruges, so-called after its donor whose name is inscribed on the frame along with the date of 1487, is similarly one of Marian devotion configured as prayer (Fig. 51). Again, a common parapet runs across the bottom of both panels ornamented with an oriental rug. Here Mary rests the Christ Child on a gold brocade cushion just as Nieuwenhove does his elbow and open book of prayer. Mary is draped in a red mantle over a dress with rich jewelling at the neck and a diadem of pearls, while the youthful Nieuwenhove is dressed in velvet with a jewelled ring on his left hand. A complex of diamond-paned and enamelled-glass windows runs across the panels, including representations of Nieuwenhove's name saint, Martin, as well as Sts George and Christopher. The uppermost left window represents his family coat of arms with helm, crest, and motto. The surrounding glass roundels pictorialise in rebus fashion the family name, 'new garden', through scenes of sowing flowers.[109] In this diptych the panel of the Virgin is rendered frontally, while that of the patron uses a strong diagonal perspectival recession, suggesting that viewers position themselves directly before Mary's image, and in imitation of Nieuwenhove's accompanying gesture of prayer.

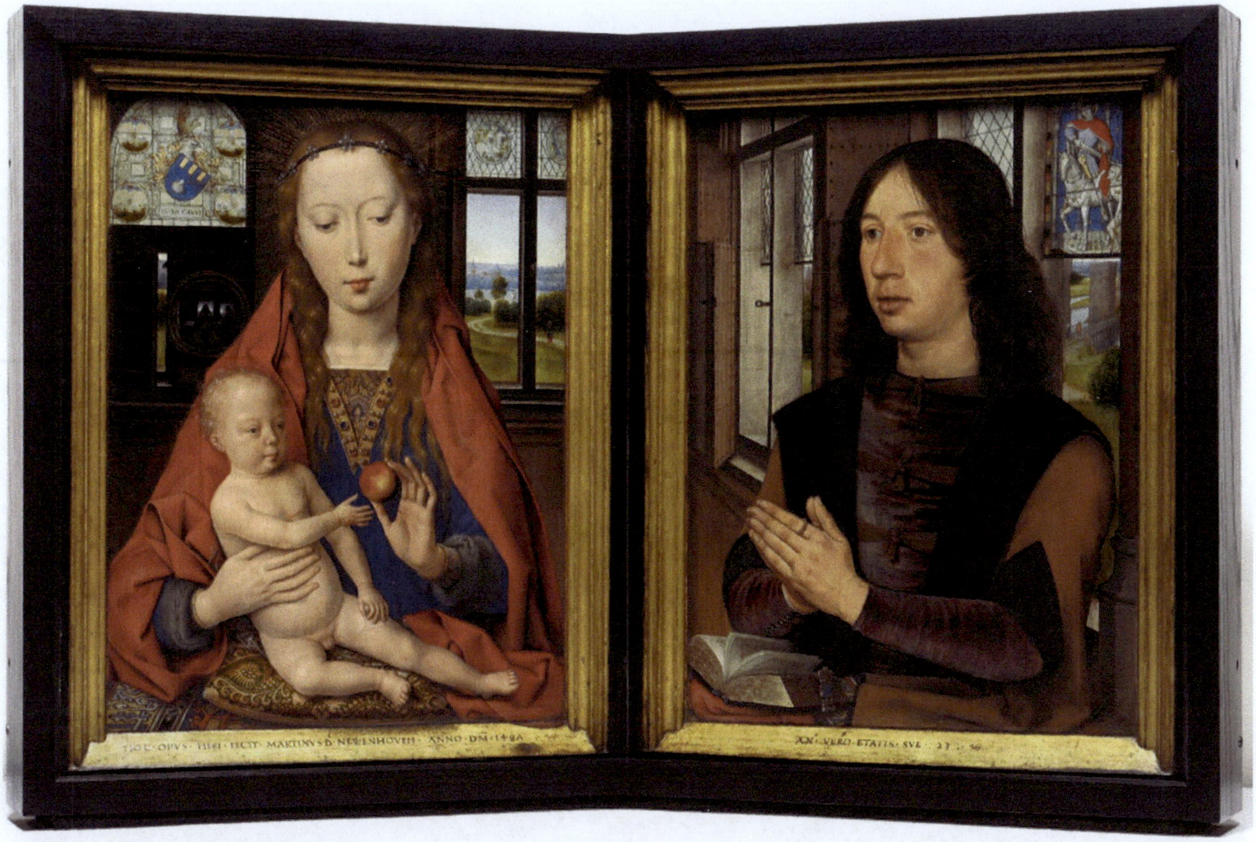

Fig. 51 Hans Memling, *Nieuwenhove Madonna,* 1487, oil on panel, 33.5 × 44.7 cm, St John's Hospital Museum, Bruges. Photo: Bruges Museums

This is reinforced by the tondo mirror above Mary's shoulder, which holds the angled positioning of the panels within its reflection, so indicating their intended placement before us in an acknowledgment of their perspectival correspondence. Though in shadow, the mirror's surface visibly captures the two diminutive figures of Mary and Nieuwenhove from behind, with a further set of double windows before them that must therefore extend illusionistically into the space of the viewer.

Within the painting's mirror reflection, Mary is seated with an open book beside her to accompany the one before which Nieuwenhove kneels.[110] Common to the pictorial traditions at work in this shield-like imagery, its armorial syntax is of images within the image, and of window and mirror views as equivalent forms of visual perception alongside the textual authority of books. The mirror's tondo form echoes that of the stained-glass roundels above, which emblematise the Nieuwenhove name in the rebus fashion of heraldry. As the sign of the artist's skills in pictorial illusion, the mirror reflection is Memling's 'hallmark' as a Netherlandish artist of Eyckian renown. It couples with the artist's painted text on the frame, in Roman letters in the manner of an Eyckian stone inscription: HOC OPUS FIERI FECIT MARTINUS DE NEWENHOVEN ANNO DM 1487 AN.O VERO ETATIS SVE 23. Together, word and image authenticate the painter's work, like a guild artist's punch mark. Memling follows each line of his inscription with a miniature stylised dragon of heraldic derivation, as if a hallmark or emblem from a coat of arms, to verify his authorial claim as the *schilder*, or shield-painter, of this work.

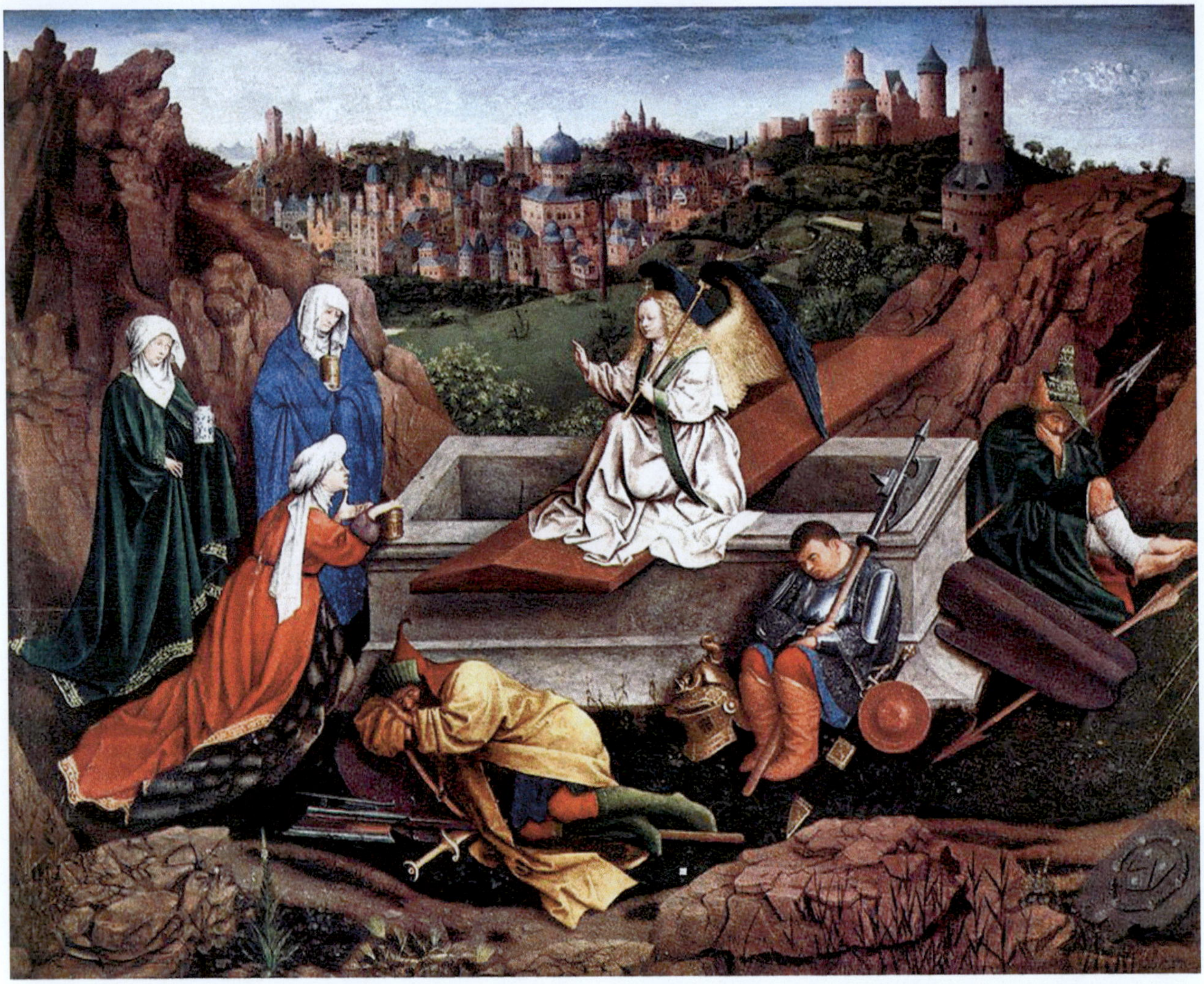

Fig. 52 Hubert and Jan van Eyck (attrib.), *The Three Marys at the Tomb*, c. 1425, oil on panel, 71.5 × 90 cm, Museum Boijmans van Beuningen Rotterdam.
Photo: Wikimedia

If the precise iconographic meaning of Memling's dragon mark is unknown, yet the overriding significance is clear. The miniature pictogram of a mythical and magical creature surely represents the magical illusions of Flemish artistic skill in the arts of *schilderkunst*. Figured in the manner of guild marks and heraldry, like the arts of miniatures in which the van Eyck brothers apparently first trained, it recalls the jewelled helmet with a gold dragon ornament of the sleeping soldier in the Eyckian *Three Maries* (Fig. 52). Like the Eyckian mirror, the tiny dragon is again a 'hallmark' of Memling's Flemish lineage from van Eyck. Tutored in the virtual representation of the visible field, Memling proclaims his ability to represent the material world in that most immaterial of forms: the shimmering reflection of the mirror image as the heraldic sign – *schild* – of painting's art.

ACHILLES' SHIELD

In Vasari's description of Giorgione's lost work of painted reflection, its pictorial *paragone* between armour and mirrors turned on a

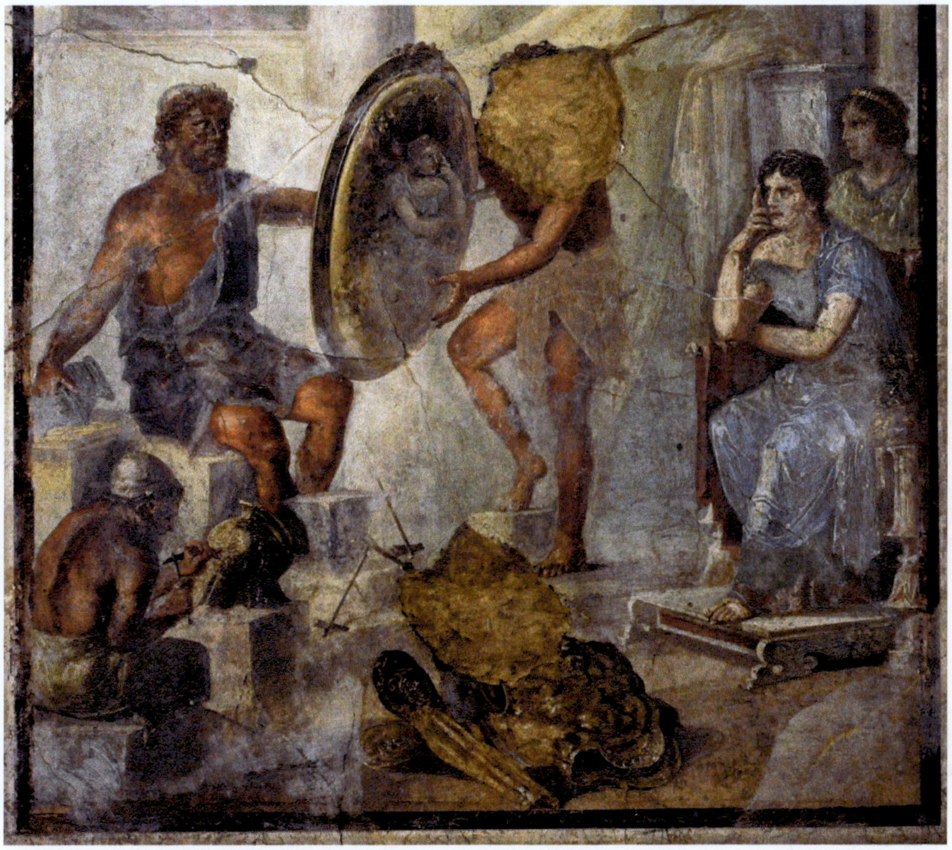

Fig. 53 'Hephaistus Presents Achilles' Golden Shield to Thetis Whose Image Is Reflected Within: "Thetis, look carefully at the golden armour that Hephaestus has made for Achilles"', first century CE, wall fresco, Pompeii, Museo Archeologico Nazionale, Naples (originally Pompeii, IX, 1,7).
Photo: Alamy

classicising but also Eyckian and Netherlandish pictorial trope. Within its comparison of painting and reflection was a long echo from the antique past, as well as into the Renaissance future of art. Its elision of painting with armoury was surely also a pictorial acknowledgement of the literary origins of *ekphrasis*, or the description of a work of art, inaugurated by Homer's evocation of the figured face of Achilles' shield. Giorgione himself was much influenced by the mimetic mirrors of fifteenth-century Netherlandish art, so that the figure of *schilderkunst*, or the reflective 'shields' of Northern painting as well as those of ancient rhetoric, formed an important part of his artistic conception of art's *paragoni*: ancients and moderns, north and south, painting and sculpture, the latter comprising also the metalwork of armoury.

Achilles' great shield of poetic memory, much represented in ancient fresco (Fig. 53), was long celebrated in word and paint both for the brilliance of its glittering light and for the epic qualities of its pictorial narrative.[111] As god of fire and so of metalwork Vulcan was said to have forged it himself, figuring it in gold and silver with scenes representing the four elements – the earth, the sea, the arial heavens, the fire of the sun with the moon and the stars. Within each quarter he depicted further ornaments, of cities, fields and pasture, vineyards and cattle. Thus the shield of Achilles was a poetic metaphor of the mirroring pictorial field founded in the ornaments of armoury. Further, it conceived of the shield face as a space of successive inset representations, of pictures within pictures as its narrative means. As Rudolf Preimesberger has noted in relation to an Eyckian rhetoric of art, the classical connotations attached to the Homeric figure of the reflective pictorial shield also included the story of the

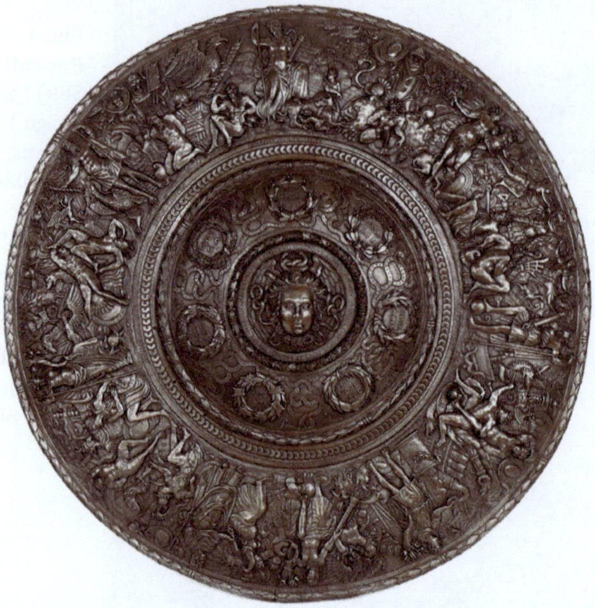

Fig. 54 Jörg Sigman, *Parade Shield with Medusa Head and Scenes from Roman History*, 1552, Augsburg, steel with bronze embossment, diameter: 61.2 cm; depth: 10 cm, Victoria & Albert Museum, London.
Photo: V&A

Greek sculptor Phidias. In his lost monumental gold sculpture of Athena in armour for the Acropolis at Athens, Phidias was said to have included his reflected self-portrait in miniature in its mirroring shield as the sign of his art. According to the classical authors Cicero, Pliny, and Plutarch, this is the first occasion of miniated self-portraiture as a form of artistic signature.[112] Thus, van Eyck's Netherlandish art of brilliant reflection arose in the mirroring shields of antique literary reference as well as those of medieval armorial heraldry (Fig. 54).[113]

As van Eyck and his courtly patrons surely knew, Homer's *ekphrasis* of Achilles' shield drew together the full range of art's skill to represent all the elements in its mirroring sheen, as the sign of the poet's mimetic sway, *ut pictura poesis*. Equally, Homer's narrative of the *Odyssey* turned on incidents of visual memory founded in the arts of armoury as the means of the hero's return to his home and family. The old nurse, Eurycleia, recognises Odysseus through a scar on his leg he bore as a youth; at the same time, Odysseus wins the trust of Penelope through his description of a great brooch she once gave him, depicting a scene of hunting wrought of figured gold whose doubled wonder lay in the force of its mimesis as much as the glittering lustre of its precious material. In Eric Auerbach's celebrated 1946 literary analysis of mimesis, Homer's ekphrastic description acted as an inset 'mirror' within the text, as a poetic form of *mise-en-abyme*.[114]

In respect of Giorgione's lost work depicting a mirror and armour, it would go on to become a founding allegory of Venetian Renaissance painting, in theory as in practice. This was defined in terms of its art of reflections – in water, mirrors, armour, and a mirroring shield. In Pino's account of the lost Giorgione, it is St George the Christian knight who represents painting's heraldic bearing in a splendour of shining armour. Within fifteenth-century Flemish art, the pictorial motif of specular reflection was announced in the inaugural painting of Renaissance Netherlandish art, the Ghent altarpiece, to be represented in an array of reflective surfaces comprising mirrors alongside armorial accoutrements proper, chiefly armour and shields. At the same time, books, inscriptions, and scrolls throughout the Ghent altarpiece laid claim to the authority of word and image together.

The Homeric reference of the art of the shield continued to ring in the metalwork of the armourers across the High Middle Ages. The armorial pageant shield bearing the inset imagery of heraldry was its sign. As the locus of the image-within-the-image in a coat of arms, the pictorial face of heraldic insignia was the shield, also the Netherlandish metaphor of painting and of its courtly esteem. As the products of metalsmithing, arms and armour were objects of great ceremonial valence as well as military utility. Often dynastic and commemorative, they were a focus of princely collecting as an aspect of family history and lineage. Jousting and parade armour, in particular, might be richly decorated in a range of precious metals including brass, silver, and gold, or with engraved and embossed relief on surfaces of gleaming tempered bronze as was surely the case with the shield of Achilles. Parade shields on wood were painted in the brilliant colours and emblems of heraldry – *azur argent vert sable gules* and *purpure*. Renaissance armoury engravers working on the decorative ornamentation of metal plates for armour were also, within guild structures and in terms of techniques and materials, close to engravers for book illustration and broadsheets, particularly those concerned with decorative design. Again, the ties within guilds brought about exchange between trades at all levels, including those of a literary conception for the arts. Thus the depiction of armoured plates within painting, particularly shields and breastplates or cuirasses, was an acknowledged locus for the representation of mirror effects in both literature and painting, and so the site for further 'paintings within paintings' as the *schilderkunst* of art.

The representation of reflective armour was, from its Eyckian inauguration in the Ghent altarpiece, a celebrated *topos* of Netherlandish art as a pictorial metaphor for the art of painting itself. Tracing the pictorial lineage of such painted reflections in art as in armour, it appears in Jan van Eyck's first emergence within the history of oil painting in the works of the van Eyck family practice such as the *Three Maries at the Tomb* (Fig. 52).[115] Here the sleeping soldier's reflective cuirass depicting the towers of a medieval cityscape appears alongside a jewelled helmet of figured gold with a miniature targe shield, and a full-sized leather-hide *scutum*, or tower shield, cut with the scrolling perimeter of a *bouché* lance-rest along the topside. The configuration of a shield as a Roman-style *scutum* with the calligraphic outline of the medieval French *bouché* in the material, scale, and form of cow hide again suggests the close ties among guilds in the production of such armorial goods across a range of materials, comprising metal- and leatherwork alongside painting. From ceremonial armour in precious metals to the painted illuminations of vellum manuscripts as themselves miniature 'shields' on leather, all the luxury goods of the Flemish trades were under heraldry's sign. Hence painted glass for windows as for mirrors, painted leather from saddlery to vellum, and painted wood from ensigns to altarpieces were also equivalent forms of *schilderkunst*, replete with heraldic insignia in Netherlandish representation. Further, the reflected cityscape of the soldier's cuirass is an apt pictorial metaphor for the painted cityscape in the background of this Eyckian panel, itself a Flemish rendering of the 'heavenly Jerusalem' of biblical event. Thus the soldier's reflective armour is the scene of painting in miniature, just as its scenic representation draws together the city of the Bible with that of the viewer's own. Reflection is the mirror-image of the Netherlandish painter's art.

In van Eyck's portable triptych of the Madonna and Child with donor and saints (Fig. 55), a

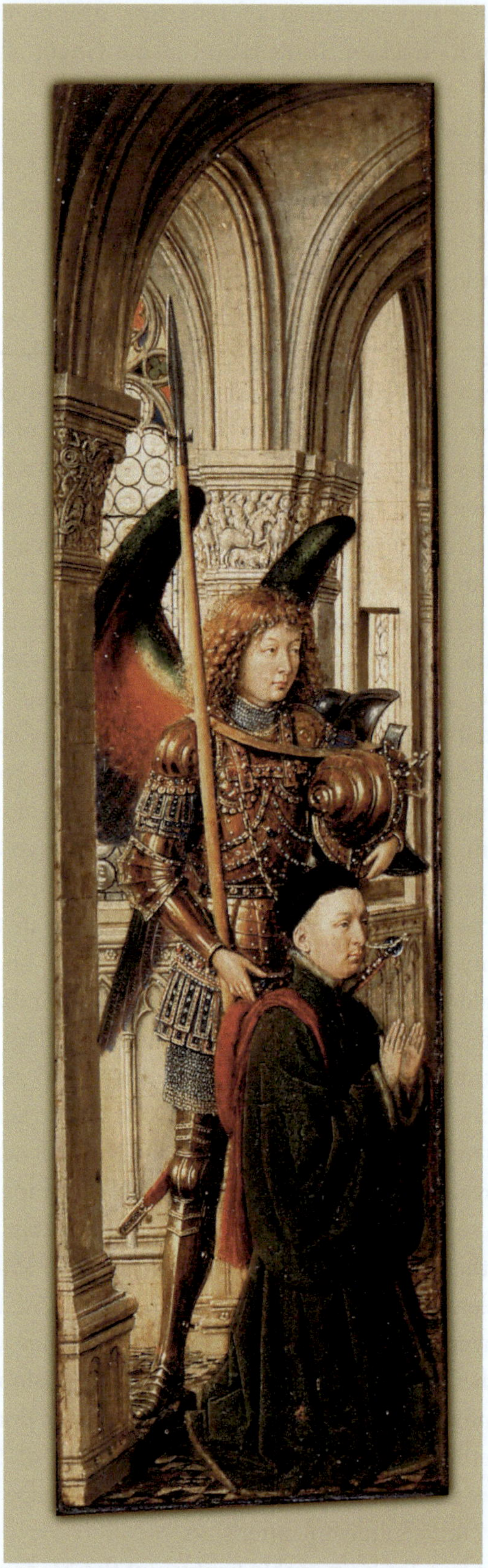

Fig. 55 Jan van Eyck, *Madonna and Child with Donor and Saints* (triptych), detail, 1437, oil on panel, central panel: 33 × 27.5 cm; each wing: 33 × 13.5 cm, Gemäldegalerie Alte Meister, Dresden.
Photo: Wikimedia

bravura of painted reflection captured in its diminutive size, St Michael's helmet brilliantly reflects the kneeling donor while his shield mirrors his rainbow-coloured wings. The trope of the reflective painted 'shield' was conceived as a pictorial theorisation of mimetic art. Hans Memling, Jan van Eyck's successor in Bruges, similarly painted a series of altarpieces and diptychs comprising the arts of reflection, both specular and armorial, as metaphors of his skill.[116] This is exemplified in his early monumental triptych with the *Last Judgment* intended for a Florentine chapel in the Badia Fiesolana, c. 1467–71 (Fig. 56). St Michael's armour is golden, like that of the globe beneath Christ's feet. The globe reflects the rainbow colours that surround it, and the setting in which Christ sits. St Michael's breastplate, too, reflects in miniature detail the architecture of the scene, the heavenly gates of Gothic ornament with Romanesque towers behind. These were luministic effects in which early modern critics recognised the greatest artifice of his art. The saint holds a decorated gold crozier in his right hand and in his left the golden scales of judgment to weigh the saved and the damned. A rich red cope with gold brocade hangs from his shoulders fastened by a large jewelled clasp. Behind, his wings are in the iridescent colours of peacock feathers. The triptych's outer panels depict the donors with saints in grisaille; their family coat of arms on curving golden shields hang beside them like emblems of the goldsmith's art, as if ornamenting the panels' closing clasp.[117]

In Memling's small portable diptych (c. 1490) of the Virgin and Child with music-making angels, on the one hand, worshipped by an unknown patron with St George, on the other, the play of reflection is also orchestrated within a pictorial field of painted armouries (Fig. 57). In the gleaming sheen of the saint's breastplate Memling painted a miniature reflection of the figures in the diptych's 'mirror' panel, the Virgin and Child with angels set against a castle landscape. The mirror-image

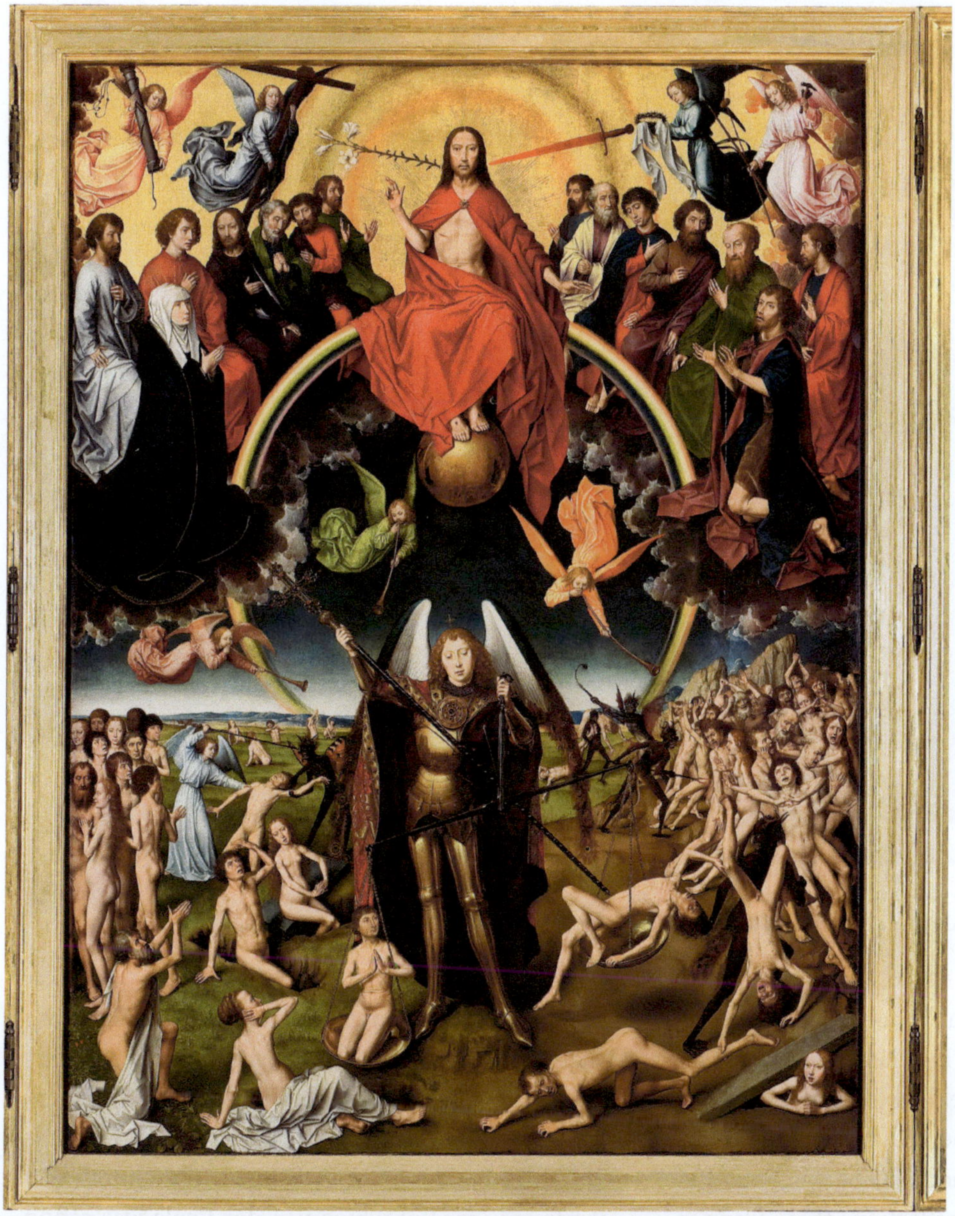

Fig. 56 Hans Memling, *The Judgement Triptych*, c. 1467–73, oil on wood, central panel: 221 × 161 cm, (Fiesole Badia) now Muzeum Narodowe, Gdańsk. Photo: Wikimedia

intimates the diptych's display, with the panels open to each other on a facing diagonal, as it would surely have been placed on a tabletop. The diptych format of two panels joined by metal hinges with a metal clasp for closure depended on close collaborations between painters and smiths, just as the painting itself represented its pictorial display of brilliant armorial reflection.

A further example of armorial mirroring by Juan de Flandes, a Flemish artist at the court of Castile, depicts St Michael defeating a dragon with a jewelled processional crozier-lance and bearing a parade shield of magnificent mimetic reflection (Fig. 58).[118] The gem-studded crimson border of the shield surrounds a burnished reflection on concave bronze, depicting the subject of St Michael's gaze towards an apocalyptic vision of a walled, burning city, surely an evocation of Gomorrah. Smoke-filled skies over the architecture are clearly rendered, reflected again in his

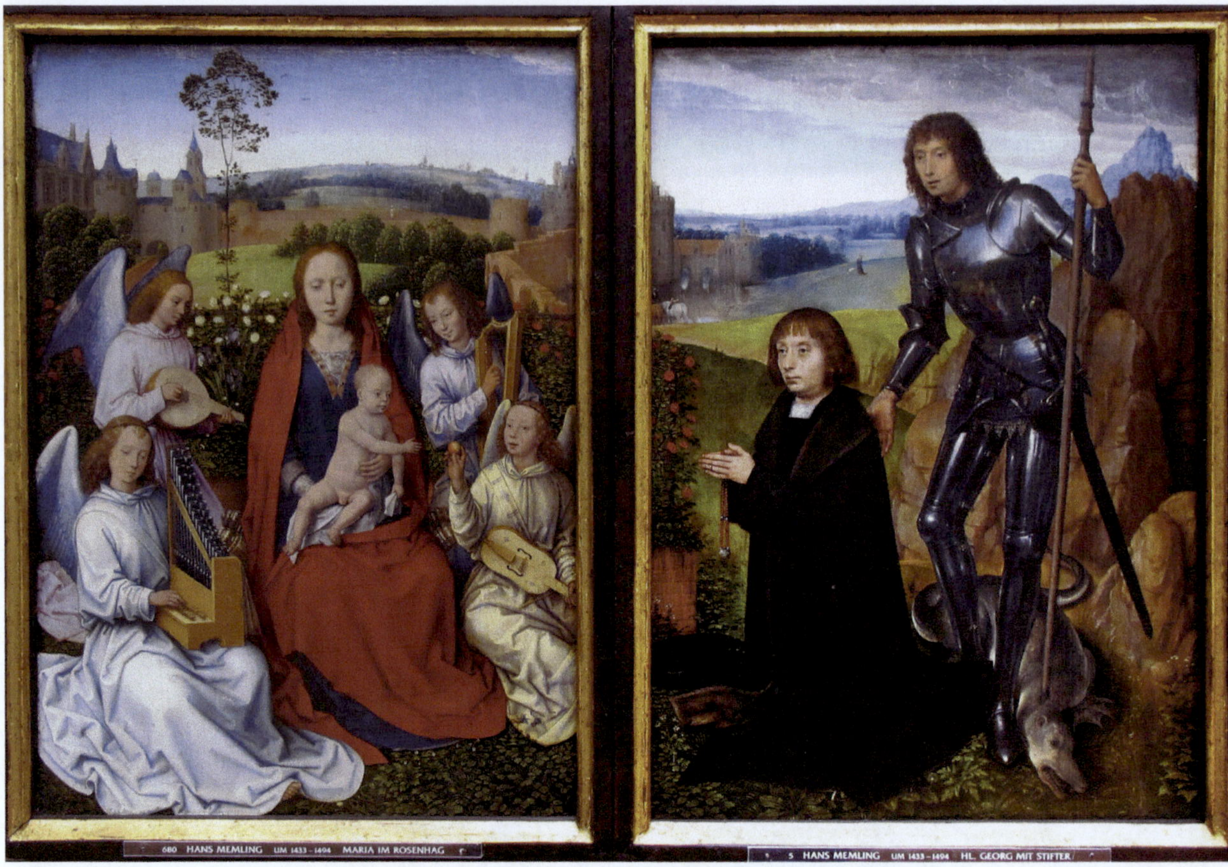

Fig. 57 Hans Memling, *Virgin and Child with Angels*, c. 1480–90, oil on panel, 43.3 × 31.2 cm, Bayerische Staatsgemäldesammlungen - Alte Pinakothek Munich.
Photo: Wikimedia

steel cuirass. It is likely a pictorial reference to this artist's Netherlandish 'Eyckian' origins and its Homeric claim to the shield of Achilles, within a large Spanish *retablo*. As the archangel and symbol of light's triumph over darkness, St Michael was a typology of armorial reflection that Flandes painted more than once for his Spanish patrons. An altarpiece of St Michael of c. 1505 for Salamanca similarly shows the saint in full armour, whose gleaming metallic cuirass and jewel-studded shield also reflect a burning city of biblical reference. His cuirass is surmounted by a jewelled gold brooch that clasps his cloak around him in a further recollection of both the Homeric forge of Vulcan's fires and Penelope's brooch for Odysseus. Metsys' *Christ before the People*, c. 1518–20 (Prado Museum), continues the Eyckian tradition in the reflections of raised lances in the soldier's helmet, which elaborate on the surrounding painted scene.

The most celebrated treatment of the mirroring shield in early Netherlandish painting is certainly van Eyck's *Madonna and Child with Sts George, Donatian, and the Canon van der Paele* for the church of St Donatian in Bruges (the church was destroyed 1779) of which van der Paele was canon (Fig. 45). Here, mother and child are enthroned, further ornamented by an array of shimmering textiles and jewels. Together they hold a trinity of small flowers whose then-familiar names were Christological in reference – the white *Cruciferae*, the red *nagelbloem* or carnation, and the blue *mannstreu* as the flower of devotion.[119] They are joined by a parakeet of bright green hue, of a type the canon could have known during his years as a papal scribe in Rome, whose bird call was then apparently reputed to resemble the *Ave Maria* of Gabriel's greeting to the Annunciate Virgin: Hail Mary full of grace, the Lord is with you (Luke

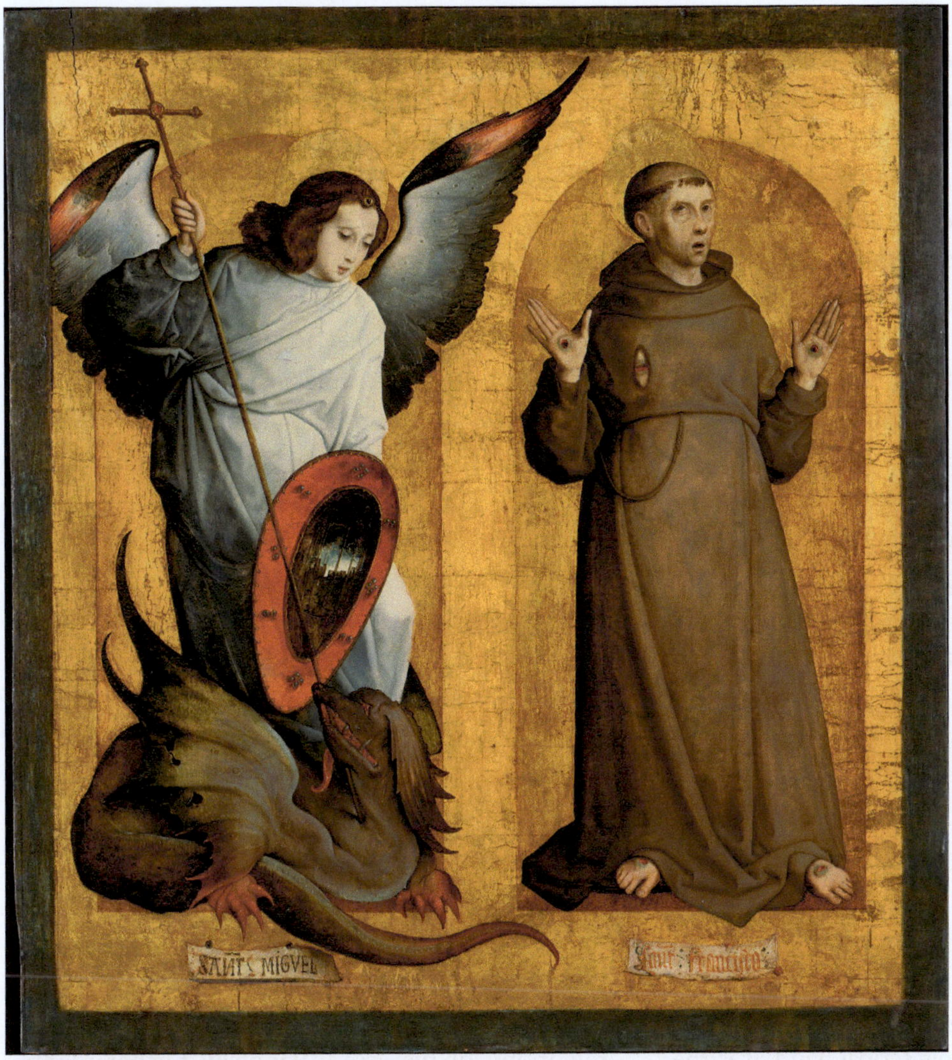

Fig. 58 Juan de Flandes, *Saint Michael Defeating the Dragon and Saint Francis*, c. 1505–9, oil on wood and gold ground; overall, with added strips at right and bottom: 93.7 × 87 cm; painted surface: 89.9 × 83.2 cm, Metropolitan Museum of Art.
Photo: Metropolitan Museum of Art

1:28).[120] The setting is an ambulatory of church architecture, with revetment in stone and wood carvings. The panel's original oak wood frame survives, its border replete with painted arms and inscriptions, both to van Eyck's artistry and to the identity of the painted figures. As patron of the work, the canon kneels before the Virgin dressed in a simple white surplice and bearing a breviary or hymn book in his hands over which he holds a crystal eyeglass. The Virgin is attended by St Donatian, in a magnificent blue brocade cope ornamented with gold edging held by a jewelled morse as the clasp, and on his head a mitre of golden cloth similarly encrusted with rubies, sapphires, and pearls. In his right hand he holds a processional cross of crystal and gold, in his left a candelabra in the form of a wheel as his attribute, whose lit candles cast their flickering light across the optical splendour of his dress. To the other side of Mary is St George, as van der Paele's name saint, with his ensign of the cross, whose left hand gestures introduction of the canon to the Virgin. The figure of St George is clad in gleaming plate armour with embossed and jewelled ornaments. Seemingly of fire-gilt steel or polished bronze, his golden armour is rendered with a multitude of reflections. As David Carter first noted in 1954, the elaborate fluted helmet of St George beside Canon van der Paele reflects in each ribbed curve a highlight of the chapel window above the seated

Madonna and Child. His breastplate reflects the Madonna's red mantle, while the curving shield strapped to his back projects the flag of the Cross at the top, and a column base at the bottom. Like the helmet and cuirass, therefore, the shield reflects the scene within the painting. Along the side, however, its burnished surface reveals a reflected image of the space before the altarpiece in which the viewer may be conceived to stand. For in the shield of St George van Eyck painted in miniature, like a manuscript *marginalia*, a small group of figures including one generally deemed to be the artist himself by association with the putative London self-portrait. Bearing a red hat and hose with a dark blue mantle, his arm is raised in the act of painting. Thus the painter signs his work in the manner of Phidias, with the hallmark of his presence in the *schild* of his art.[121]

PAINTING BY *FIDES*

Painted signatures in imitation of divers forms of text are manifest in many of the works of Jan van Eyck and his school, ranging from Roman epigraphic lettering in illusionistic imitation of stonecut inscription, as with Memling, to the courtly Gothic calligraphy of a Valois scribal hand. It is the latter that characterises van Eyck's signature mark in the Arnolfini double portrait. Conspicuously placed at the upper centre of the composition, van Eyck's Arnolfini signature runs along the back wall of the room between the mirror and the brass chandelier, both luxury artefacts of metalwork derivation. Unusually, the signature choice of verb is *fuit* rather than the more customary artists' *fecit*, denoting presence over facture: *Johannes van Eyck fuit hic / 1434* – Jan van Eyck was here / 1434. This has led to a range of scholarly interpretations on the function of the painting as the sign of 'witness' or authentication of betrothal or marriage through art.

In a leading article for the iconographic method, as celebrated as it is critiqued, Erwin Panofsky built a reading of the Arnolfini double portrait as a visual form of legal document for marriage in its pictorial authentication of their vows, the couple's hands joined in a nuptial handclasp or *impalmamento*, the man's right arm raised with an open palm in what is still the gesture of juridical oath, and which was then used in the making of wedding vows before a notary. Panofsky constructed his argument around the 1568 publication of Marcus van Vaernewijck's *Spieghel der Nederlandscher audheyt* – a further example of the many sixteenth-century books entitled 'Mirror', in this case of Netherlandish history – and repeated in van Mander's art-historical *Schilderboeck* of 1604. Panofsky's analysis centred on Vaernewijck's description of the painting 'as if contracting marriage by *fides*' – by oath. In this he referred to the social customs of marriage in an era before their sixteenth-century Catholic Tridentine reform, in which wedding rituals were conducted within family alliances, rather than at church. Panofsky read Vaernewijck's reference to the painting's gestures of marital oath as an intimation that the Arnolfini double portrait served as a pictorial form of social authentication of marriage, witnessed in Arnolfini's raised right hand as a gesture of making his marital vow. In a later reworking of his essay, Panofsky further identified the tiny figures in the mirror reflection as van Eyck and another, in his argument present as witnesses, as well as to record the event of marriage through painting it. If subsequent scholarship has cast doubt on a literal interpretation of the portrait's notarial function (pointing to the absence of a full date with day and month in the painted inscription among a host of detailed critiques), yet the historical associations with both pictorial authentication and marriage remain, if generally now recognised as pertaining to the intellectual claim of art, on the one hand, and the social ritual of marriage, on the other, rather than to any definitive legal purpose of the painting. It is also the case that much recent historical research on the social structures of marriage before Trent's sixteenth-century reform has significantly altered and extended our understanding of whether or what specific ritual, if any, might be enacted in this image.[122]

As Philip the Good's *valet de chambre*, van Eyck would have used his art and his person to serve a number of functions of witness and legitimation connected with dynastic marriage alliance. In preparation for the Duke's betrothal to Princess Isabella of Portugal, Jan van Eyck accompanied the courtiers sent to negotiate terms in order to draw her face for his patron, 'from life'.[123] Similarly, scholarly interpretation of the Arnolfini double portrait as a pictorial form within marriage or betrothal is now better understood within the elaborate social negotiations and gift exchange of goods, including portraiture, of late medieval marriage negotiations prior to Trent's institution of church marriage ceremony. Howsoever, the Arnolfini signature's declaration of van Eyck's authorship in the art of painting as 'likeness' remains. For the painted reflection that accompanies his signature declares that painting is a true counterfeit of the field of vision, as in a mirror-image. Like Brunelleschi's demonstration at the door of Florence Cathedral, van Eyck documents the making of his art by signing it just above its mirror reflection, as a verified copy 'from life'.

The script of van Eyck's Arnolfini signature is in Gothic lettering, as the form of handwriting that dominated court and church documents throughout the late Middle Ages, typifying manuscript, epistolary, and notarial hands at the Valois court and its Burgundian offshoot under Philip the Good. The interwoven scrolling lines of penmanship give rich calligraphic ornament to the opening letter 'J', in particular, extending its form into a cornucopian horn surmounted by a cadel of bountiful decorative flourish. It is close to any number of examples from notarial documents and illuminated books of the period, as has long been pointed out, as well as to the book plates and letters of Philip the Good himself.[124]

The arrangement of van Eyck's calligraphic signature and the Arnolfini mirror, as a framed conjunction of word and image, is thus both armorial and scribal in composition. For the Valois-Burgundian scriveners of documentary and book production commonly used a pictorial 'hallmark' sign alongside their signatures, just like the goldsmiths, and the heraldic seals that finalised and authorised all letters and documents of the ducal court. As with the medallic coins of princely retinue, seals were typically circular or ovoid, with an emblematic image at the centre surrounded by textual inscription of the bearer's name. Like the scrivener's or the guild-maker's mark, the seal's purpose was both to embellish and to authenticate. As an authorial signature of legal stature, the seal conveyed a surrogate form of presence as it was understood in medieval law. Within cultures of heraldry, van Eyck's Arnolfini inscription brings into the pictorial sequence a 'hallmark' of his art. For directly beneath his signature van Eyck painted, for the first time in Netherlandish art, a stunning mirror reflection as the painter's authorial sign. To either side, he disposed his figures in the manner of heraldry, as *schildwachter*, or guardian figures, to the central 'mirror shield'. In this portrait of dynastic marriage, the mirror is the painting's armorial *mise-en-abyme*.[125]

Within the mirror's shimmering surface van Eyck painted his scene again from behind, as if in a reflection. It depicts the view of the Arnolfini nuptial apartments in reverse, showing the backs of his draped figures as well as the window and the draped or hung day bed on either side, and the brass chandelier above. Deeper into the depth of the reflection are two further figures in red and blue, seen from the front. As has often been noted, these tiny figures appear to stand in a fictive space before the painting. In so doing, they bring the painted and the viewing space of the picture into a continuum, including beholders within the illusion of van Eyck's art. This doubled play of specular illusion to reflect an art of 'realism' surely confounds us.[126] We are all the more disarmed to find our reflection in the mirror is a doubled mirror-image, for the tiny figures that are somehow strangely us are also in the place of van Eyck as he painted. Thus the armorial pictograms of heraldry are transformed into the hallmarks of van Eyck's mimetic art – by *fides*. Like the shield of St George in the van der Paele Madonna, van Eyck seemingly paints himself as he paints. The signature *fuit*, like his mirror reflection, is the affirmation of his painterly witness. As with a hallmark or a wax seal, the mirror and the signature authenticate van Eyck's presence within the scene of the painting's own production, as the maker of this art.

Like a mirror, the Arnolfini reflection reduces the scale of the scene to the dimensions of a miniature, in the manner of manuscript illumination. This is further echoed in the diminutive pictorial roundels of Passion scenes that ornament the mirror frame. Coupled with the calligraphy of the inscription, it surely intends to recall French-derived Flemish cultures of illuminated manuscripts so coveted at the court of Philip the Good, and in which the van Eyck brothers apparently first trained. In this way van Eyck claimed for painting the authority of the mirror, the window, and the book, as different but equal modes of knowledge. In this regard it is notable that, just as van Eyck painted his manuscript-like Arnolfini signature above its silvered mirror reflection, Gutenberg the goldsmith was forging the letters of moveable type that would engender the Renaissance production of the printed book. Like the Homeric *ekphrasis* of Vulcan's shield for Achilles, the classical referencing of a humanist culture comprised a ready play of wit in the comparison of the 'sister arts', painting and poetry.[127] The trope became a critical *topos* of comparison for mimetic skill between the arts. Preimesberger further argued the allusion lay behind van Eyck's apparent depiction of himself in miniature in the Arnolfini mirror, as also the shield of the van der Paele St George, as equivalent forms of painted reflection.[128] Linda Seidel's emphasis on the courtly collections of a material Renaissance in relation to the Arnolfini portrait has similarly identified documentary references to illusionistic mirrors belonging to Philip the Good, whose visual reflections comprised a witty form of courtly divertissement in the science of optics as both 'truth' and illusion.[129] Bringing this to bear in a discussion of the mild distortions of form in the curving glass of the Arnolfini reflection, as has commonly been observed, the mirror reflection both miniaturises but also magnifies towards its centre, like a crystal magnifying stone. This is manifest in the slight distortion of scale between the centre and the extremities of the reflected scene. Van Eyck's acute description of this gentle convex distortion in the curving of the window and the bed suggests a ready familiarity with optical mirroring and magnifying effects. It is surely witness to the intensive study of optics, catoptrics, reflection, and refraction at play throughout van Eyck's work, as his putative self-portrait also describes. In a further form of pictorial play with the learned cultures of Netherlandish humanism, it manifests a scholarly engagement with the study of optics known through classical texts, as transmitted to Western Europe through the historic encounter with the late medieval Arabic writings of al-Haytham.[130] Here the extensive library of Philip the Good, and the court's strong bibliophile interests, were surely instrumental.[131] Among Philip's possessions was a gift of patronage from the Limbourg brothers, as the most celebrated of courtly book illuminators, of a box cover painted to look like a bound manuscript.[132] As parallel objects of visual deceit, mirrors and paintings were instruments of courtly play, along with books of optics on the science of such illusions.

The earliest textual reference to van Eyck's inset painted mirrors is that of Bartolomeo Fazio, Italian humanist and historian in the service of King Alfonso V of Aragon, in a compilation of biographies including those of artists such as van Eyck, entitled *De viris illustribus* of 1456. In Fazio's appraisal of van Eyck's celebrated artistic skills of illusion, he noted particularly the artist's ability to depict all things exactly as they are in nature by analogy with a mirror reflection: 'But almost nothing is more wonderful in this work than the mirror painted in the picture, in which you see whatever is represented as in a real mirror.'[133] The mirror reflection Fazio described was not that of the Arnolfini portrait, however, but seemingly of a now-lost work then in the collection of Ottaviano della Carda, which subsequently passed to Duke Federigo da Montefeltro, in whose collection it was noted by Vasari and subsequently van Mander.[134]

The description of this lost work is that of female nudes emerging from the bath, the painted variations of their forms apparently further enhanced by a mirror reflection of comparison. According to some scholars the Arnolfini double portrait may have originally had a similar painted cover, also attributed to van Eyck, of a bathing female nude reflected in an inset mirror to show her figure from the side and the front. If so, it may be said to typify the visual imagery of marriage gifts, in representing the bride both as the chastely Marian wife of family and estate and as the venereal beauty of the female nude, captured as if in two 'sides' of a mirror reflection of womanhood. Now lost, perhaps separated from the double portrait by Arnolfini's wife herself before her death, the image of this possible painted cover for the portrait is known from copies and its representation within the seventeenth-century 'picture gallery' painting by Willem van Haecht of Cornelis van der Geest's collection c. 1628 (Figs. 59 and 60). Here a small

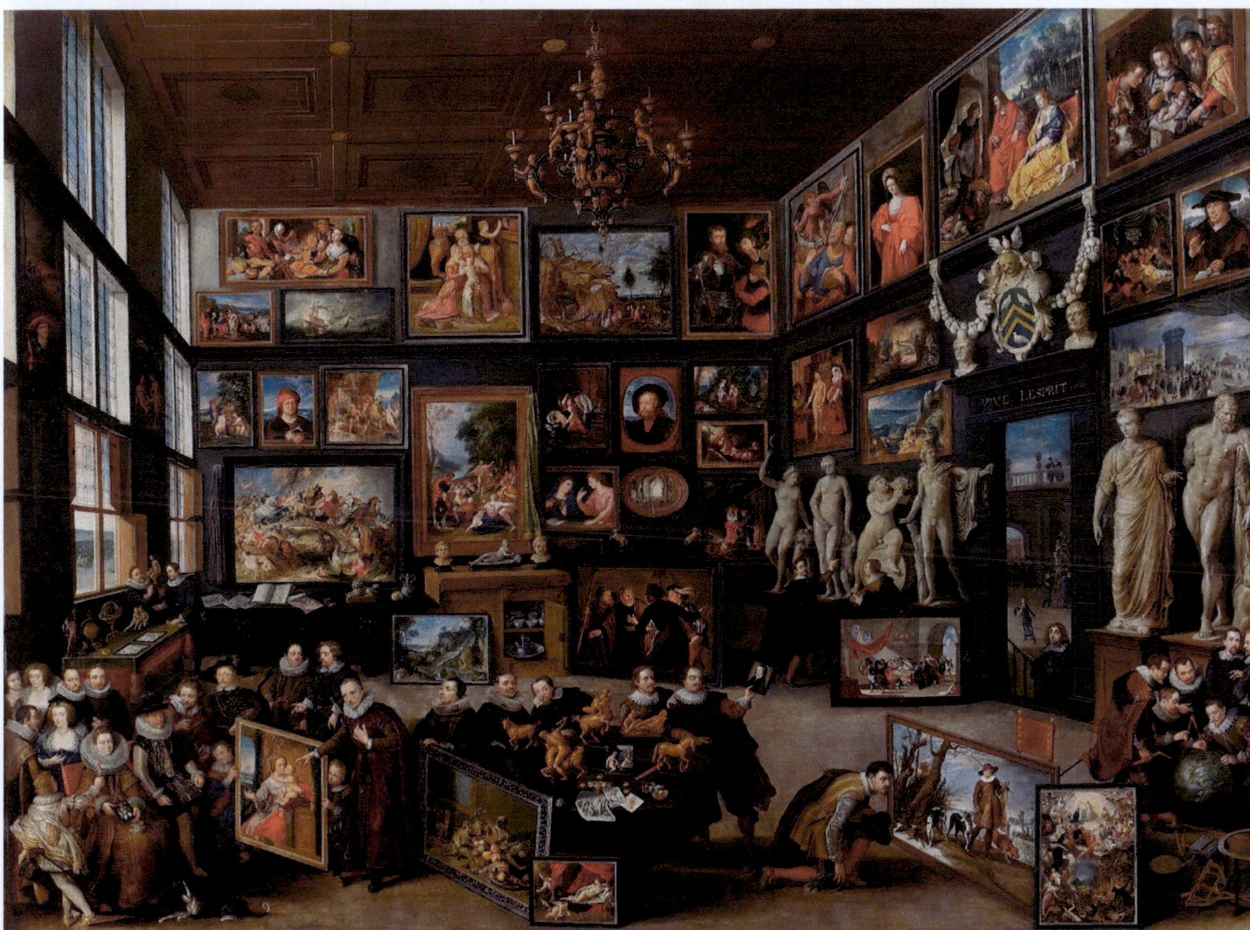

Fig. 59 Willem van Haecht, *Gallery of Cornelis van der Geest*, c. 1628, oil on canvas, 99 × 129.5 cm, Rubenshuis, Antwerp. Detail, right centre, of the putative painted panel cover to the Arnolfini double portrait of a female toilette with a mirror. Photo: Wikimedia

Fig. 60 After Jan van Eyck, *Woman at Her Toilet*, Netherlandish, sixteenth century, oil on oak panel, 27.2 × 16.3 cm, Fogg Art Museum, Harvard University. Photo: President and Fellows of Harvard College

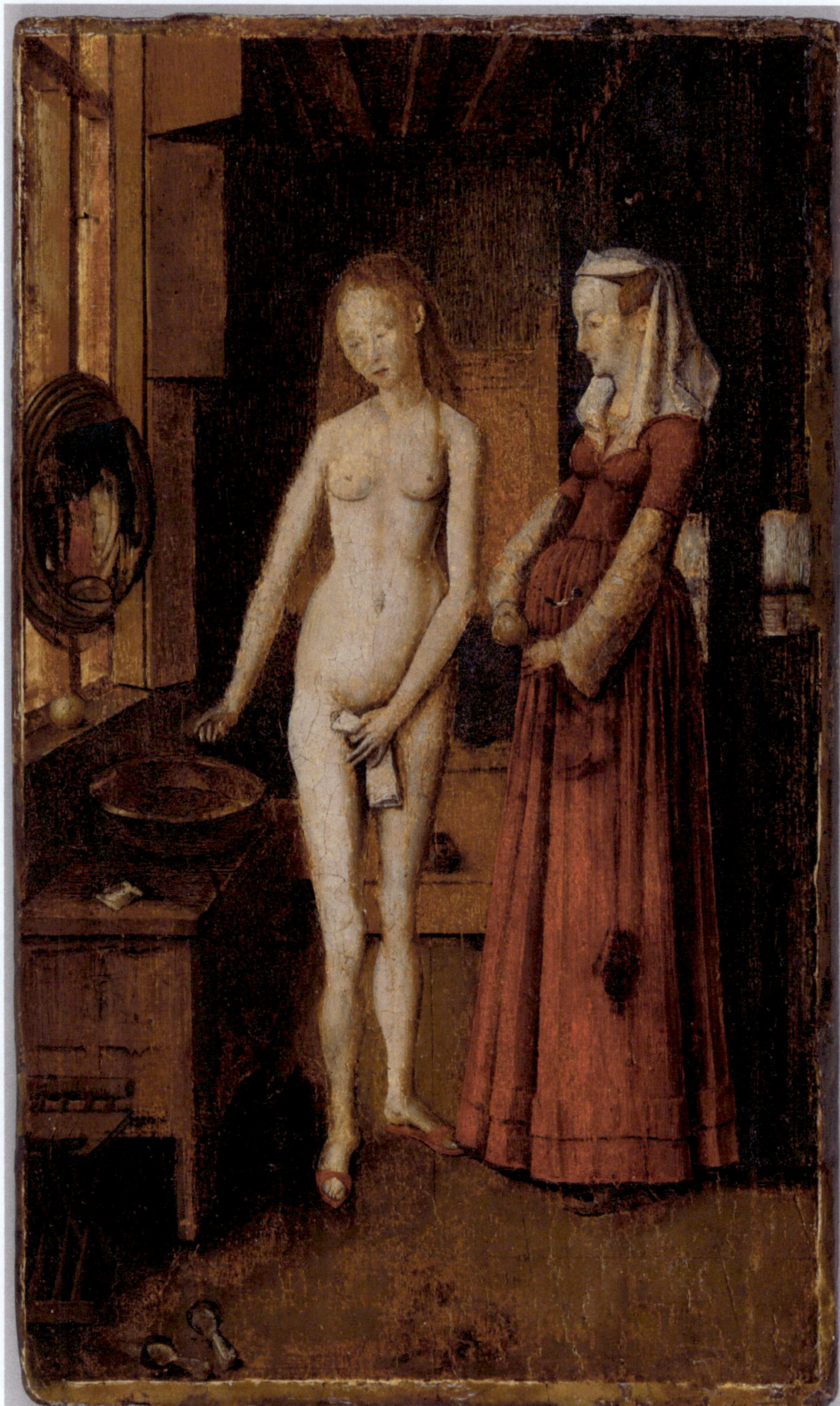

convex mirror shaped of blown glass, as in the Arnolfini portrait, mirrors the figures as if in a globe.[135] In this Eyckian image of a bath scene, known through its imitations, is the trope of painting that Vasari referred to in his description of Giorgione's lost work. In both instances the figure of the nude, reflected in a mirroring surface and rendered with the glistening refractive glazes of oil paint, may be read as the hallmark of art itself. In Fazio's words the quality of painting lies in its fiction of resemblance, for art is the mirror of nature. The very nature of the painter's skill in the depiction of resemblances is therefore occluded by the accomplishments of art. If the Arnolfini mirror demonstrates its mastery in the specular illusion of resemblance, van Eyck's signature inscription similarly declares the painter's presence, which the painting's astonishing ability to represent the world otherwise disguises. The painted mirror within a painting further represented a doubled fiction of art's mimetic power, its capacity for infinite reflection as the hallmark and touchstone of art's skill. This most celebrated of mirror images within painting was thus to become the sign of art's reflection on itself.

NOTES

1 Vasari, 1568, I, Part II, 15, in his life of Giorgione. On Giorgione's lost painting see Goffen, 2002, 60–64 and notes with further bibliography. See further the discussion in Chapter 5 of this book.

2 Pino, 1548, 27.

3 Alberti, 1966, 64. See further the Introduction.

4 See the discussion of the inset mirror in manuscript illumination touched on in Chapter 1.

5 From an extensive literature on the Ghent Altarpiece, and particularly the burgeoning bibliography arising from its recent restoration, see especially, on the question of reflection, Schneider, 2012; and further bibliography, especially on the sapphire reflection of the Vijd Chapel in the angel's morse. See further Martens, 2020a; Martens et al, 2020; Currie et al, 2019; Godfrind-Born & Martens, 2012. Its original frame was destroyed during the Iconoclasm of the Reformation.

6 De Heere, 1969, 29–32; Van der Velden, 2011.

7 Vasari, 1550, 84, 380–81, in his life of Antonello da Messina, and first questioned by Lessing, 1774. See the summary of the problem by Bochert & Huvenne, 2002; Roy & White, 2000. See also the relevant essays in Currie et al., 2019. On the development of oil painting, Ainsworth, 2017; Jones, 2011; Ames-Lewis, 2007, 47–62; Campbell, 1998, 29–31; and Campbell, 1997. For the history of documentary research on van Eyck, Weale, 1908, expanded by Paviot, 1990. On Bruges as a centre of art-making more broadly, Wilson, 1998.

8 Heyder, 2012, 59–65 and 284–89, on the Turin-Milan Hours; Lawson, 2005, 149–63. See further Kren & McKendrick, 2003; Smeyers, 1998.

9 On Florence-Bruges trade and cultural exchange, Paoli, 2012, and further bibliography.

10 From a vast bibliography on the Arnolfini double portrait, which has focused primarily on the mirror: Wedekind, 2007; Criminisi et al., 2004; Yiu, 2001. In relation to the argument presented here see especially Belting, 2016.

11 Interpretation of the painting in terms of the conduct of Renaissance marriage was launched by Panofsky's celebrated 1934 article with a long issue in the study of Netherlandish painting in terms of 'disguised meaning', on which see the larger debate in the work of Svetlana Alpers and Eddie de Jongh, among many others. On the reading of the Arnolfini portrait in terms of marriage customs, much further literature has also ensued on the complex social rituals of marriage, and therefore what stage of a Renaissance marriage the painting may relate to, betrothal or wedding, given the lengthy timespan of familial marriage customs. Much of the iconographically oriented art-historical writing on this is now superseded by historical research on marriage ceremonies and celebrations before the Tametsi decree of 1563 at the Council of Trent. Before this date, ecclesiastical involvement with marriage was very limited, it being a social contract and ritual officiated by notaries and celebrated by the families of the bride and groom, which might involve some kind of church presence. Brooke, 1989; D'Elia, 2004; Herlihy, 1985; Klapisch-Zuber, 1985; Duby, 1994; and by recent scholarship on decorative arts pertaining to Renaissance marriage customs, notably, Thornton, 1991; Musacchio, 2008. See Campbell, 1998, 174–211, for a thorough overview of the iconographical and art-historical scholarship on the Arnolfini painting; and Wedekind, 2009.

12 Seidel, 1993, offers a close analysis of the painting in terms of Renaissance material wealth and goods. Pastoureau, 2013, especially 76, reads the colour green as the emblem of love, youth, marriage, and an expectant maternity.

13 See, in particular, Hanley, 2007, 265–67, drawing on technical research conducted by Marigene Butler on the Philadelphia *St Francis*, 1997. On van Eyck's interest in optics, see further De Mey et al., 2012; Martens, 2020b. The use of mirrors by early Renaissance painters

was brought to prominence by David Hockney's visual analysis of the evidence of their use in Hockney, 2001; on which see further Dupré, 2005. See further here Chapter 3.

14 For some recent summaries of the mirror motif in early Netherlandish painting, Filippi & Schwaetzer, 2012; Malfatti, 2015.

15 As described c. 1480 by Manetti, 1927, 9–13; and its translation in Manetti, 1970, 42–44. See the further discussion with bibliography in Chapter 3 of this book. On the historical development of one-point perspective, from a vast bibliography: Edgerton, 2009, 44–53; Damisch, 1987; Edgerton, 1975; and Kemp's corrective 1978, especially 142, 159, on the practice of using mirrors in architectural surveying as posited by Krautheimer, 1952, 229–53; and its relationship to Renaissance cultures of gauging as elucidated by Baxandall, 1972. See further Dupré, 2019, on the practice of perspectival visual cultures.

16 Martens et al., 2020; Leonardi, 2019; and further bibliography. On the differences of 'mirror observation' made between van Eyck and, for example, Masaccio's pictorial demonstration of the geometry of one-point perspective in the *Trinity*, De Mey, 2012a, 83–110; Andrews Aiken, 1995.

17 Martens, 2020b.

18 Hasan Ibn al-Haytham, 1989; and in relation to Renaissance art, specifically van Eyck, Martens et al., 2020; Belting, 2011.

19 Martens et al., 2020; De Mey et al., 2012, based on van Eyck's clearly extensive knowledge of medieval catoptrics issuing from the study of al-Haytham and Euclid.

20 See the further discussion in Chapter 3.

21 On late medieval and Renaissance armour, see, from a large bibliography, Anglo, 2000; Capwell, 2018.

22 Pliny *Natural History* XXXVII:39; Isager, 2013.

23 Audy-Trottier, 2020.

24 Varchi, 1549, 120–55, on the texts and letters pertaining to Varchi's disquisition on the *paragone* between painting and sculpture.

25 De Mey et al., 2012.

26 The phrase 'pictorial intelligence' is the title of Alpers & Baxandall, 1994.

27 Vasari, 1568, Part II, vol. 1, 310, life of Brunelleschi. On the allegory of the egg, Garrard, 2010. On the play of scale that structured the medieval artistic imaginary, see especially Emanuele Lugli in Kee & Lugli, 2015.

28 See the discussion of Brunelleschi's perspective panel in Chapter 3.

29 De Vos, 1994a. The inscription is directly addressed to the viewer in a mix of letters, a pictogram of Leeuw's name, and chronograms for the dates: IAN DE [LEEUW] OP SANT ORSELEN DACH / DAT CLAER EERST MET OGHEN SACH, 1401 / GHECONTERFEIT NV HEEFT MI IAN / VAN EYCK WEL BLIICT WANNEERT BEGAN 1436, on which see Hudson, 2003. On the representation of coinage in Renaissance art and letters, Seaman & Woodall, 2022.

30 Cherry, 2011, with further bibliography; and Montias, 1990; De Roover, 1948. See also Passeri, 2014, on relations between gold coinage and artists' use of gold foils.

31 Cited by Michiel, 1800, 45, at Casa Lampognano in Milan c. 1530 as 'El quadretto a messe figure, del patron che fa conto cun el fattor, fo de man de Zuan Heic, credo Memelino Ponentino, fatto nel 1440', identified by Weale & Brockwell, 1928, 200.

32 Braune, 2020; Ainsworth, 1994; and the related 1994 conference papers, Ainsworth, 1995. See Panhans-Bühler, 1978, 91–93, on the imitation of Eyckian compositional types at issue in this work.

33 The painting is often, though not universally, linked to one of the Flemish goldsmiths' guilds, usually Bruges or Antwerp. This is based on documentation pertaining to the 1832 sale of the painting to the banker Oppenheim of Cologne stating it had belonged to the Antwerp corporation of goldsmiths, though many scholars see Bruges as more likely. See the useful summary in Ainsworth, 1994, 96–98, 101 notes 10–14. See further Upton, 1990; Shabacker, 1974, 86–91; Smith, 1915; Smith, 1914, 25 (138), 326–35; Weale & Brockwell, 1912; Ainsworth & Christiansen, 1998, 150–53; Van der Velden, 1998.

34 Ainsworth 1994, 96, 101 note 9.

35 Smith, 1915 and 1914; Weale & Brockwell, 1912.

36 Smith, 1915 and 1914, identified the badge as Gelders and suggested a connection with the marriage of James II of Scotland to Mary of Gelders at Holyrood in 1449, though he also noted the lack of royal reference in the image to conclude it was not a betrothal or marriage portrait as such.

37 Dierick, 2000, 79–82, citing discussion with Maurits Gyselinck.

38 However, Seidel's 1993 analysis of the Arnolfini portrait importantly gives much-needed attention to its representation of Renaissance goods. On the mirror as marriage gifts, and the enactment of marriage under the mirror's sign, Schneider, 1985, particularly the essays by Alexander, Gottlieb, and Baldwin; and Hartlaub, 1951. On the iconography of the mirror in Flemish painting, see the recent summary by Malfatti, 2015.

39 Campbell, 1998, 21, 33 note 22, on Philip of Burgundy, who, according to his biographer Gerard Geldenhauer, 1901, 232, learned to paint and work gold in his youth because this was seen as indispensable to the ability to judge. Campbell cites further evidence that glass painting was considered an elite pastime too (note 26). Such patrons were seen as able to intervene forcibly in the development of works of art.

40 On Bruges and Flanders, with direct reference to van Eyck and his circle, Dumolyn & Buylaert, 2020; De Munck, 2018, with further bibliography; Brown, 2011. More broadly, see Epstein, 2008. Brosens, 2019, while for a later period, evidences the exchange of tools and skills across a range of decorative arts that guilds facilitated.

41 On the influential paradigm of a material Renaissance: O'Malley & Welch, 2010; Jardine, 1996; Brewer &

Porter, 1993; Douglas & Isherwood, 1979. Seidel's study of the Arnolfini portrait is an example of the genre with regard to early Netherlandish art.

42 Ainsworth, 1994, 41, 49–53, 100, 101 note 27. See the further discussion of self-portraiture in Chapter 3.

43 Woltman, 1879; discussed by Schabacker, 1974, 87; Rothstein, 2005, 2.

44 Thornton, 1997, 62, 167–68. See also Kobi, 2021, on the use of magnifiers in early connoisseurship.

45 See the further discussion of self-portraiture in Chapter 3.

46 Campbell, 1976; Campbell, 1994, has pointed out that shop frontage to display the work was an important and jealously guarded privilege of master craftsmen, as a further consideration of the window-like disposition of this painting.

47 On the window frames of Renaissance art, see Wajcman, 2004; Ringbom, 1965, 31, 2. See also Jütte, 2023. The pictorial motif of the frame has had a much broader discussion in works such as Stoichita, 1997, following critical analysis of the pictorial structures derived from classical philosophy of the supplementary as further elaborated in ancient rhetoric's *parerga*, or supplementary ornament, in the wake of Derrida's Kantian reading, 1978; and Marin et al., 1994.

48 Schabacker, 1974, 25–26; Ainsworth 1994, 43–49, with reference to a range of his paintings summarising earlier scholarship. See the recent interpretation of an 'optical revolution' in fifteenth-century Flemish painting centred on van Eyck by Maartens et al., 2020.

49 C. H. Smith, 1915, 8.

50 A series of portraits of Philip the Good bearing the collar of his newly founded Order, and linked with his marriage to Isabella of Portugal, such as the versions at Antwerp and Dijon, are attributed to the workshop of Roger van der Weyden and are believed to be further copies after a lost original by the master, on which portrait type, see further Campbell, 2004; the useful anthology of sources in Dhanens & Dijkstra, 1999; and the recent technical study by Kemperdick, 2018. On the gold collar, see further Banjenec, 2016; Seipel, 2008; and on the history of the chivalric collar more broadly, Chefdebien & Humbert, 1997.

51 Adlin, 2013; and of which there are examples in their collections: www.metmuseum.org/art/collection/search/464248. On the efflorescence of late medieval carved ivory mirror cases within courtship rituals among a range of precious artefacts, see Camille, 1998, particularly 96–107 on the representation of falcons among other animals as courtly signs of 'love's hunt'. See the further discussion of medieval ivory mirror cases and bibliography in Chapter 1 of this book. On courtly falconry, Burnett & Abele, 2021.

52 Friedman, 1989.

53 On Petrus Christus' relationship to traditions of limning, see the summary by Ainsworth, 1994, 58–60.

54 Belting, 2011; Rotman, 1987.

55 On the heart motif: Smith, 1915, 9–11; Ainsworth, 1994, 29–30; Upton, 1995. Note the transfixed heart also on the reverse of the Grymeston portrait (Henry VI's ambassador at the court of Philip the Good) over a damaged area, generally considered to have been copied from the original frame at a later date.

56 Vinken, 2000. See the valentine heart-shaped book in the National Gallery London's *Portrait of a Man* by the Master of the View of St Gudula, c. 1480s, as testament to its reach within decorative arts and book cultures.

57 The classic study remains Yates, 1966.

58 Ainsworth, 1994, 30 note 25, identified the inscription as Burgundian *batarde* script used for makers' marks by goldsmiths and illuminators, based on hallmark dictionaries. See further Schabacker, 1974, 83–85.

59 Ainsworth 1994, 101, note 18; Smith, 1915, 6–7, in consultation with numismatists, identified the coins as golden riders minted under Philip the Good for Flanders; angels struck by Henry VI for his French dominions; gold florins of Conrad III Archbishop of Mainz struck at Hochst, noting a quartered shield with floriated cross; a mounted knight brandishing a sword; a Latin cross between a fleur-de-lys and a leopard. Schabacker, 1974, 108, suggested the reference to money-changing and currency exchange as under the jurisdiction of the gold- and silversmith's guild.

60 Pastoureau, 2009; Strohl, 1904.

61 De Vos, 1994a; Hudson, 2003.

62 Preimesberger, 2011, 23–53, especially 46.

63 Van Mander, 1604; on which see Preimesberger, 2011, 46, though his point was a different one. On the use of the term as '*schilderkonst*', see De Pauw-de Veen, 1969.

64 Pastoureau, 2009; Vaughan, 1970; Kren, 2003. Heraldry's definition within law is usually attributed first to Bartolus de Saxoferrato, *De insigniis et armis*, c. 1350; and the early codification of arms as a cultural manifestation of the late middle ages, with a rich issue across the Renaissance and Baroque. On Bartolo di Sasso, Ramsay, 2022.

65 Examples of fifteenth-century mirrors with painted stucco frames bearing coats of arms from the Metropolitan Museum collections include two from Tuscany, one attributed to the da Maiano workshop, c. 1480s; and a similar mirror bearing the Sienese Cinuzzi coat of arms dated c. 1500. The Victoria & Albert Museum holds a similar Florentine mirror in the form of a ring surmounted by a diamond point dated c. 1470 with a shield for a coat of arms.

66 Isidore of Seville, II, book 13, ch. 20, 'De Abysso', 1; Comenius, 1907, 41.

67 See further the discussion of armorial *mise-en-abyme* with bibliography in the Introduction. In medieval encyclopaedic texts such as Isidore of Seville's *Etymologies* it had a further ancestry from ancient Greek translations of the Hebrew Bible, manifest above all in water as the fount of life's genesis, and used to signify the unfathomable source of the divine: Isidore of Seville, II, book 13, ch. 20, 'De Abysso', 1. Comenius, 1907, 41, uses the figure of 'abysm' in the depths of a mirror reflection throughout for the myriad powers of memory and the mind. The

increasing codification of armorial devices may be mapped in the myriad publications of its early modern elaborations and definitions, as in the work of the French court heraldist Ménestrier, 1691, 19: 'celle qui est au milieu est dite etre en abime'. Ménestrier was also a noted numismatist and antiquary with many publications on heraldry, medals, emblems, and devices, as well as their deployment in court entertainments from jousts, tournaments, and carousels to music and ballet.

68 Pastoureau, 2009.

69 Silver, 1984, cat. no. 16, 211–12; Schütt, 2021. See also Woodall, 2015; Jones, 2011, 36–37.

70 Preimesberger, 2011, 51, note 137; Panhans-Bühler, 1978, 91–93, on the question of painted emulations of lost prototypes. See also Kühn, 2015, on the Flemish merchant portrait type. See also Kühn, 2015; and Belting, 2016, on the Flemish merchant portrait type.

71 Muller, 1989, 126, though noting the Bible page shows Adam and Eve instead of the Madonna and Child; Winner, 1957.

72 Rombouts & van Lerius, 1961; Ewing, 2018.

73 Lampsonius, 1572, cited by Silver, 1984, 1; Fickaert, 1648.

74 Erasmus, 1514; Schütt, 2021; Silver, 1984, cat. no. 16, 211–12; Woodall, 2015.

75 From a vast bibliography on Erasmus and his circle, see the classic studies by Jardine, 1993; Huizinga, 1984; and the recent MacPhail, 2023. On the Erasmian humanists including Gillis and their libraries, De Smet, 2002. On the Metsys portraits of Erasmus, Schütt, 2021; Vanautgaerden, 2010; Fehl, 1993; Campbell, 1978.

76 The 1519 Brussels version adds INVENTor. Silver, 1984, 211.

77 Verougstraete & Van Schoute, 2000, 114.

78 According to the seventeenth-century art restorer in Antwerp, Van Fornenbergh & Galle, 1658, 27, there was an inscription on the frame in a gilded compartment at the top of the picture's carved and gilded frame from Leviticus 19:35: 'Let the balance be just and the weights equal'; though Silver, 1984, 136–37, 152, note 9, points out that the frame may not be original.

79 Shakespeare, 1623; Badcock, 1677.

80 Pliny, 33.126.

81 See Campbell, 1998, 212–17, and further bibliography. On the chaperon, Jolivet, 2021.

82 Dhanens, 1980, 176–88; Jones, 2017, on van Eyck's inscriptions. On the literary claim of this inscription as well as its authenticating function, Scheller, 1968.

83 Campbell, 1998, 212–17. See the further discussion of self-portraiture in Chapter 3.

84 On Gutenberg and Renaissance printing, from an extensive bibliography, see the classic study by the *Gutenberg Museum Mainz,* 2010; Barbier, 2017; Eisenstein, 1983; Febvre & Martin, 1976; and the recent Coilly, 2023, which situates the advent of printing into a global paradigm.

85 Silver, 1984, 105–33.

86 Verougstraete & Van Schoute, 2000, 114–15.

87 Thompson, 1978, vol. 23, 123–277; Steland, 2002; Mieder, 2004. On Gillis, Tournoy, 2002.

88 On the late medieval development of eye or rivet glasses from crystal reading stones, see Ilardi, 2007; and the further discussion in Chapter 4 in this book.

89 Hanley, 2009.

90 See further the discussion of Herbert Grabes' 1973 study of early modern mirror book-titles in Chapter 1.

91 This association was noted especially by Silver, 1984; see further Woodall, 2015.

92 Bacci, 1998.

93 Schwartz, 1959. See further Nash, 2004, 157–227. On the motif of the mirror between workshop instrument and emblem of art within depictions of St Luke painting the Madonna, see also Yiu, 2005.

94 L. Schneider, 1985, especially Gottlieb and Baldwin's essays; Hartlaub, 1951.

95 Baldwin, 1985.

96 Thürlemann, 2002, 101–9: and the comprehensive article Thürlemann, 1992; Foister & Nash, 1996, on 'Copying Campin', 95–158.

97 Russell, 2017.

98 See the closely related panel painting of St Luke painting the Virgin at the Fogg Art Museum, which also depicts books, windows, and a mirror as the artist's sources of his subject as he paints; and which similarly depicts the back of the painter's head as well as the easel in the convex mirror behind him.

99 Lübbeke, 1991, 288–97.

100 Conversely, imagery of the spotted mirror was common reference to the penitent impurities of the soul, as in the late medieval hagiographical *Legenda Aurea* of Jacobus de Voragine: 'For as all things are reflected from a mirror so in the blessed Virgin, as the mirror of God, ought to see all their impurities and spots, and purify them; for the proud, beholding her humility see their blemishes; the avaricious see theirs in her poverty; the lovers of pleasure theirs in her virginity.' In light of this, scholars such as Schabacker, 1974, 89–90, have queried the Marian interpretation of the mirror due to the minor flaws in the glass.

101 Hanley, 2009; Purtle, 1982; Meiss, 1945. The hymn was translated into many languages and versions.

102 See the further discussion of mirrors and painted mirrors as betrothal and marriage gifts in Chapter 5.

103 Jacobs, 2012, 52–57; Hand et al., 2006; Jansen, 1984. Thürlemann, 2002, 303, has recently questioned whether the portrait of Werl is a later addition, though this has not been taken up by others.

104 Criminisi et al., 2004.

105 Held, 1936; De Vos, 1994a, 220–21.

106 On the inter-relations between books and diptychs, see, in particular, Jacobs, 2012; Gelfand, 2006; Hand et al., 2006.

107 Hartlaub, 1951, 64, 119.

108 De Vos, 1994a.

109 Noted by De Vos, 1994a, 279. See the discussion of enamel glass-painting for windows in Jütte, 2023, 164–87.

110 Knöll, 2019; Falkenburg, 2006; Hand et al., 2006, 178–85, 319; Borchert, 2005, 173; De Vos, 1994a, 279–83.

111 Achilles' shield, generally acknowledged as the genesis of the ekphrastic description in Western European literature, arises in the *Iliad* (18:478–608); this inspired Hesiod's description of the *Shield of Heracles*, and Virgil's of the shield of Aeneas, *Aeneid*, book 8. See further Stoichita, 1997, 221. On the Pompeii fresco, Guillaud, 1990; on the literary trope, Becker, 1995.

112 Preimesberger, 2011, 46–47, further citing classical sources on Phidias' signature self-portrait in Athena's shield including Cicero, *Tusculanae disputationes* 1:34; Pliny, *Naturalis historia*, 36:18; Plutarch, *Parallel Lives*, life of Pericles, 31.

113 On the sixteenth-century German display shield signed and dated by the Augsburg goldsmith, Sigman & Patterson, 2009, 94; and Hayward, 1956–58. On Renaissance armour in both material and literary cultures, Springer, 2010.

114 Homer, *Odyssey*, 19:225–32: 'The brooch displayed a hound that held a speckled stag in its forepaws / and watched its prey. All were amazed / to see how, though in gold, the hound strangled the stag / and how his victim / thrashed the air in vain with his feet, seeking to flee.' The literary device formed the opening chapter to Auerbach, 1953, 'Odysseus' Scar'; and Gombrich, 1960, stressed that the source of wonder is its doubled status as both a narrative scene, and a brooch of gold, being both representation and material object. On ekphrasis as literary *mise-en-abyme* originating in Homer's description of Achilles' shield, see further Becker, 1995.

115 Kemperdick & Lammertse, 2012, 293–95, for which the panel was restored.

116 Lane, 2009; De Vos, 1994a.

117 Warburg, 1902; Rohlmann, 1991; Lane, 1991; Bodart, 2010, on painted armorial reflections more broadly.

118 Weiss, 2019; Ainsworth, 2008; Maroto, 2006.

119 Koch, 1964, 73; Ward, 1994, 24.

120 Naftulin, 1971, 7, note 12. Isidore, 2009, in his *Etymologies*, book 12, section 7:24, notes that the parrot 'makes a greeting naturally, saying "*ave*" or "χαίρε"'.

121 Carter, 1954; Farmer, 1968; De Mey, 2012b, 49; Brine, 2018. See also Unglaub, 2004, on the identification of Poussin's miniature self-portrait in the armour of his Tancred and Erminia, now in the Hermitage Museums, surely in emulation of the Eyckian example.

122 Campbell, 1998, 174–211; Hall, 1994; Seidel, 1993; Panofsky, 1953, I:201–4; Panofsky, 1934. See above for further bibliography on the Arnolfini portrait, and for discussion of the historical and art-historical literature on Renaissance marriage customs as reflected in extensive gifts of art and decorative arts for the marital home, including portraits. See also Belting, 2016, who links the notarial function of authentication in Panofsky's interpretation of the Arnolfini portrait with a broader reading of portraiture's functions of legal identification in this period, as photographs do today.

123 Seidel, 1993, 214, note 66, citing documents published by Crowe & Cavalcaselle, 1879, 85. See also Fahy, 2008 on the marriage portrait; and with reference to van Eyck, Balavoine, 2021; on the role of valet-cum-artist, Rojewski, 2021.

124 Seidel, 1993, 127–69; Dhanens, 1980, 176–81; and further bibliography. See further examples in De Bouard, 1929, I, plates II, VI, VII.

125 See the introductory discussion of *mise-en-abyme*.

126 Criminisi et al., 2004.

127 The classic essay is Lee, 1940.

128 Preimesberger, 2011, 47, note 115, citing Cicero, *Tusculanae disputationes*, 1:15:34.

129 Seidel, 1993, 166.

130 Belting, 2011; Martens et al., 2020.

131 Bousmanne, 2020; Bousmanne et al., 2001–15; Dogaer & Debae, 1967.

132 Seidel, 1993, 142.

133 Bartolomeo Fazio, *De viris illustribus* ms. 1456; published by Baxandall, 1964, 102.

134 As cited by Baxandall, 1964, 103, note 27: Mehus read 'Octauianum Cardinalem' for 'octauianum cardam' and has been translated as 'Cardinal Ottaviani' (of Florence) or 'Ottaviano Cardinale' (of Genoa). The manuscript reading points firmly to Ottaviano Ubaldini della Carda, nephew and principal counsellor to Federigo da Montefeltro, previously suggested by Schmarsow 1924, 122.

135 Spronk, 1996; Held, 1982. The connection between the two panels is disputed by Campbell, 1998, 202, who notes that the double portrait had shutters by 1516. For an alternative view of the evidence, see Koster, 2003. The discussion further centres on documentation of an inscription from Ovid on the frame as recorded in a 1700 inventory, which is variously considered as pertaining to the Arnolfini or as a later addition. On an early sixteenth-century copy in oil on panel at the Fogg Art Museum Harvard University Museums: https://harvardartmuseums.org/collections/object/227899.

Chapter 3

THE ARTIST'S MIRROR

He was tempted to think, seeing as the mirror painted objects, the painter, to represent them, perhaps painted a mirror.

—DENIS DIDEROT, *LETTRE SUR LES AVEUGLES ...*, 1749

The plane mirror contains within itself true painting, and true painting is perfect in so far as it resembles the surface of a mirror; painters, you will find in the surface of mirrors your master.

—LEONARDO DA VINCI, *TRATTATO DELLA PITTURA*, BAV CODEX URBINO 1270 III:404

AT THE DEATH OF Velazquez in 1660, it fell to his son-in-law and artistic protégé, Juan del Mazo, to draw up an inventory of the artist's remaining possessions. Over two and a half weeks, Mazo worked through the great artist's studio and apartments in the Casa del Tesoro, part of the old Alcázar palace complex where Velazquez had lived as painter-courtier to the Crown. Discovered in the Madrid archives in 1925, this inventory changed the course of scholarship on Velazquez, for it revealed him to be an artist not only of shimmering colour and glittering paint surfaces but also of extensive reading and intellectual accomplishment based on the large library he kept: in short, a painter of both theory and practice. Among the many volumes listed by Mazo were works of literature and myth, classical learning and emblem books, but also scientific texts on optics, geometry, perspective, and projection, and above all treatises pertaining to the theory and practice of art, from Pliny and Euclid to Alberti and Dürer. Velazquez also owned a rare copy of Leonardo's *Trattato della pittura*, first published in Paris in 1651, testament to his lively interest in current theoretical discussion at the very intersection of early modern art and science. He was, as his early biographer and successor as a court artist Antonio Palomino described him, a painter in the manner Alberti had advised, 'learned in all the liberal arts' and in the sciences too.[1]

In addition to its extensive library, Mazo's inventory of Velazquez' possessions also disclosed a full range of workshop instruments to the painter's art. These included a number of small sculptures of classical antiquities and anatomical studies of the human body that, like his book collection, similarly reflected his conjoined interests in both art and science in object form. Velazquez' possessions further comprised a collection of instruments related to his practice, including lens-based devices for use in the studio pertaining to his study of optics for the purposes of his art.[2] He was, as Palomino further referenced in the manner of Alberti's counsel to painters, 'above all, skilled in geometry', which included the science of optical perspective as the method of the painter's art of illusion.[3] Related to these lenticular optical devices, Mazo also listed a considerable complement of mirrors among the artist's possessions, of different types, shapes, and sizes, some of steel, others of silvered glass. Thus in his library and his studio, Velazquez had assembled a range of texts and objects that together informed the science of his art.[4] Prominent among them were mirrors, as objects of both practice and theory. This chapter's purpose is the analysis of the early modern artist's instrumentation of a theory of specular mimesis, as it was expounded in art treatises, and practiced in the studio. It is manifest above all in collections of artists' mirrors, as the example of Velazquez' inventory eloquently demonstrates.

The mirror as artefact had, already by the beginning of the fifteenth century, become an increasingly pervasive visual device in artists' workshops, with a range of uses in artistic conceptualisation and studio practice. Chief among these was as an instrument of transcription. In the pursuit of an imagery that was then understood and theorized as an ever-more accurate pictorial representation of the visible field, artists turned to mirrors as a means of reflecting, and so pictorializing, the world around them. In the studio, the mirror served as a practice-based device to facilitate the transposition of the visible world of three dimensions into the flat plane of a painting. Its reflected image offered a simulacrum of painting's field of visible observation to the painter's study of his subject, already translated into a two-dimensional, pictorial format. Moreover, it rendered the scene in reduced scale; it could also be used for the purposes of enlargement. In either case, it reproduced the visual field in exactly proportional scalar adjustment. Hence the mirror reflection was both an instrument and a model of the visible world for the painter's brush. The increasingly prevalent workshop use of the mirror as a mimetic tool may be tied to what has been analysed as a growing specularisation of artists' methods from the fifteenth century on, as part of a gathering mechanisation of artisanal processes.[5] In the case of the mirror, this can be linked to developing Renaissance paradigms of visual imitation in theoretical treatises, in which painting was admired for its proximity to a mirror-reflected field of vision.

In the theoretical premise of Francisco Pacheco, the Sevillian artist and humanist who trained Velazquez, painting was to be praised for its resemblance to the 'simulacra' of vision, that is, the mirror-image of the visible world.[6] In this regard the mirror was but an instrument of imitation, to be sure. Yet its visual effect was recognized as the matrix of painting itself. To consider the mirror within the artist's studio as a tool of mimesis is therefore to invoke its place within painting as the pictorial demonstration of that claim.

The development of the mirror analogy in Renaissance artistic theory arises most prominently in the early fifteenth-century advancement of centre-point perspective, and thereafter in its subsequent elaborations throughout a vast range of early modern treatises on art as mimesis. In tracing the position of the specular image in Renaissance painting, this chapter begins with the early development of geometrical perspective as it was demonstrated by Brunelleschi and theorized by Alberti, with considered attention to the workshop instruments of its methods, notably, the use of mirrors. The extensive art-historical scholarship concerning Renaissance perspective, on the one hand, and workshop practice, on the other, serves to underscore the materiality of theory in the developing definition of Renaissance art as a mirror-image of the visible. Thereafter, Leonardo's extensive notebooks on the art and science of optics and light extend and deepen the pictorial metaphor and practice of painting as a mirror-image: in his words, 'the mirror is the master of painters'. The chapter then turns to the efflorescence of the self-portrait c. 1500 inaugurated by Dürer and Parmigianino, as the clearest demonstration of painting's mirror methods, which Renaissance theorists identified according to the method of its making as painted by means of a mirror, '*allo specchio*'. Finally, the chapter concludes with *Las Meninas* as the defining representation of painting's specular art, understood within Velazquez' magnificent though now-lost Hall of Mirrors for the Royal Alcázar. *Las Meninas* may be seen as the culminating manifestation of the early modern mirror-image, both a self-portrait of the artist as he paints and a fully theorised pictorial rebus of painting as a specular praxis.

THE OPTICAL MIRROR

A scientific conceptualization of painting as specular first took demonstrable form in Filippo Brunelleschi's mirroring experiment of visual perspective undertaken at the door of Florence Cathedral (c. 1415–20).[7] In this demonstration, Brunelleschi's aim was to give visible proof of the representational accuracy of geometrical perspective, in effect to translate the Euclidean legacy of scientific optics into the draughtsman's practice. Its genesis came from his work as an architect and surveyor, and therefore the perceived requirement to prove visually as well as mathematically that the representation of architecture in painting (or drawing) according to the principles of one-point perspective was deemed reliable, both as an accurate reflection of an edifice and as a template for the construction of buildings. While accounts of Brunelleschi's realization of perspectival design have dominated the historiography of Renaissance art, the mirror as the instrument of its demonstration has not. For the subsequent history of painting, what is signal is that Brunelleschi's chosen mode of proof was the specular reflection. By placing together a mirror and a mirror-sized painting of the view through the door of the Cathedral onto the octagonal form of the Baptistery, Brunelleschi demonstrated the pictorial accuracy of an optically construed perspectival geometry. His painting of the view was seen to be architecturally verifiable because it looked like a mirror-image. Thus the theorization of painting as specular was rooted in its scientific demonstration by means of a mirror reflection.

As Hubert Damisch has argued in a study of perspectival illusionism in *quattrocento* painting, the artist's mirror came to emblematise the theoretical turn of an early modern 'pictorial intelligence', to use Svetlana Alpers and Michael Baxandall's phrase. In effect, the mirror motif became the model of a mathematical coordination of the picture plane. In Damisch's further analysis of Renaissance perspective, the visual evidence of geometry as the structuring matrix of the mimetic image was understood to lie in its precise resemblance to a mirror reflection.[8] In this regard, the perspectival definition of Renaissance painting was heir to the legacy of transmission of antique texts on the science of optics, and particularly of Euclid. As much a theory of light as of vision, Euclid's conceptualization of optics or sight within the constructs of a mathematical ordering envisioned their conduct through a geometry of pyramidal lines or rays of light. In its manifold history of translation as of manuscript transmission, and of eventual publication in the sixteenth century in myriad languages, it would come to be titled as often 'Optics' or 'Perspective', derived from the Latin *perspicillum*.[9] In this historical confluence of terminology, sight and the science of light were fused, in a lexical but also practical elision stemming from the vast range of its applied uses in draughtsmanship, from mapping to architecture and engineering. In the fifteenth-century textual sources surrounding Brunelleschi's demonstration of perspective, as of its further applications and elaborations, what is striking is the interweave between its theoretical conceptualization and an artisanal understanding of the workshop materialities through which its quotidian practice was realized. For painters, as for draughtsmen more generally, the analogies and indeed the naming of its instruments reflect this: the double-convex lens that would play such a critical part in the early modern optical instrumentation of sight as perspectivally formulated was of the *lenticchio* – lentil; while the explications of perspective's pyramidally or conically structured sightlines would draw on quotidian examples of straw hats and of pyramids. The 'translation' of Euclidean optics into the workshop may be said to have proceeded by means of the transmission of texts, and of scientific demonstration, to be sure, but just as crucially through the material relations of artisanal tools and everyday-object analogies.[10] This synthesis of theory and practice is manifest in the instrumental mode of Brunelleschi's proof: the workshop mirror.

A key account of Brunelleschi's specular demonstration of perspective comes from a biography of the artist written in the 1480s by the Florentine scholar and architect Antonio di Tuccio Manetti, who recorded viewing the mirror reflection of the painted view of the Baptistery himself. His account describes a small eyehole Brunelleschi made at the centre of his wooden panel painting through which he was invited to view, and to compare, the facing mirror's reflection of the painted view with the view itself. A mathematician-architect, Manetti brings out the interplay between geometry, optics, and architectural surveying that underpinned Brunelleschi's historic realisation of one-point perspective. As scholars have long noted, Brunelleschi was an experienced surveyer; Manetti and later Vasari relate that he spent several years in Rome in his youth with Donatello, recording the measurements of antique buildings in order to draw their ground plans, and so was in full possession of its ancient skills and means. This comprised the critical geometrical ability to work to scale in reduction or enlargement, and to translate between two- and three-dimensional representation, from drawn ground plans into models, and then buildings. In surveying the architecture of antiquity Brunelleschi worked in reverse; that is, he used the methods of his surveying practice to effect a geometrically accurate representation of a building in the form of drawing. Manetti's account further suggests a link with land surveying too, describing Brunelleschi's perspectival method as the means to render systematic diminutions and enlargements of scale according to the viewing distance, not only for buildings but also 'plains, mountains, and landscapes, of every kind and place'.[11] This was widely used for the purposes of topographical and military reconnaissance since antiquity as well.

In Manetti's account of Brunelleschi's perspectival eye- or peephole, it ran through the centre of the panel in a conical form, like a visual pyramid. A small pinpoint on the side of the painted surface, it then widened to accommodate the viewer's eye on the reverse. As Manetti describes it, the design of Brunelleschi's eyehole was surely intended to correspond to the understanding of vision as a pyramid of light rays that formed the basis of Euclidean optics. This conceptualisation of vision as pyramidal had received further elaboration among subsequent ancient authors on optics, by means of analogy with the mirror reflection, known as the study of catoptrics. In the writings of Ptolemy and Lucretius, among others, the science of mirror reflections – catoptrics – was understood as the basis of the science of light, and also of pictorial representation, so binding the theory of the image to that of vision.[12] The ability to map a pyramid of the rays of light or vision into the mathematically coordinated recession of space on the surface of a reflecting mirror was the proof of both optical and perspectival science alike. The classical view of the image as a specular simulacrum thus drew together by analogy the view through a window or doorway, the mirror reflection, and the art of painting, just as Brunelleschi had done in the door of Florence Cathedral. The pictorial sequencing of window, mirror, and painting that would become a defining metaphor of early modern picture-making may be read as a visual reference to the optical theory of the image, howsoever differently interpreted, at the centre of Brunelleschi's experiment.

The legacy of a Euclidean understanding of vision as geometrically pyramidal was also elaborated in late medieval Arabic texts on the science of perception, chiefly the eleventh-century mathematician and astronomer Ibn al-Haytham in his *Book of Optics*. Itself founded in the study of Euclid, it was translated into Latin and widely influential throughout Western Europe from the thirteenth century on. In effect, al-Haytham's text was the instrumental link in the transmission of Euclidean optics to the early Renaissance, as Hans Belting has argued.[13] The Euclidean conceptualisation of vision in terms of pyramidal rays of light derived from al-Haytham would remain current to theorisations of the field of vision across the early modern period. This inherited body of Euclidean optics formed the basis of Alberti's first 'book' or chapter in his *Della pittura*, in which he transposed a classical theory of scientific vision into discussion of the practice of painting for the first time. Certainly, Alberti's conceptualisation of the mirroring reciprocity of Euclidean vision with perspectivist painting was founded in his observation of its practice within Florentine artistic developments emanating from Brunelleschi's foundational experiment or demonstration. It is also the case, however, that Alberti's theorisation of pictorial perspective in terms of its geometry of light derives from the legacy of Euclid as transmitted by al-Haytham.

While a theory of vision as conical or pyramidal embodied in the material form of Brunelleschi's viewing peep-hole was elaborated and disseminated in fifteenth-century treatises on perspective, the dissemination of its diagrammatic demonstration awaited the growing diffusion of printed illustrated books in the sixteenth and seventeenth centuries. Thus it is in illustrations by figures such as the seventeenth-century printmaker Abraham Bosse, in a celebrated series of plates for the French architect-mathematician Girard Desargues' 1648 treatise on perspective intended for students of the Parisian Académie, that we first find explication of the Euclidean theorem of light rays as sight-lines in visual form (Fig. 61).[14] Therefore, we must read the early diffusion of Alberti's theorisation of painting in terms of a Euclidean optics through the textual commentaries of the fifteenth century. In book III of the *Commentaries* of Brunelleschi's great rival in Florence, Lorenzo Ghiberti, the sculptor-goldsmith's discussion of perspective cites two of

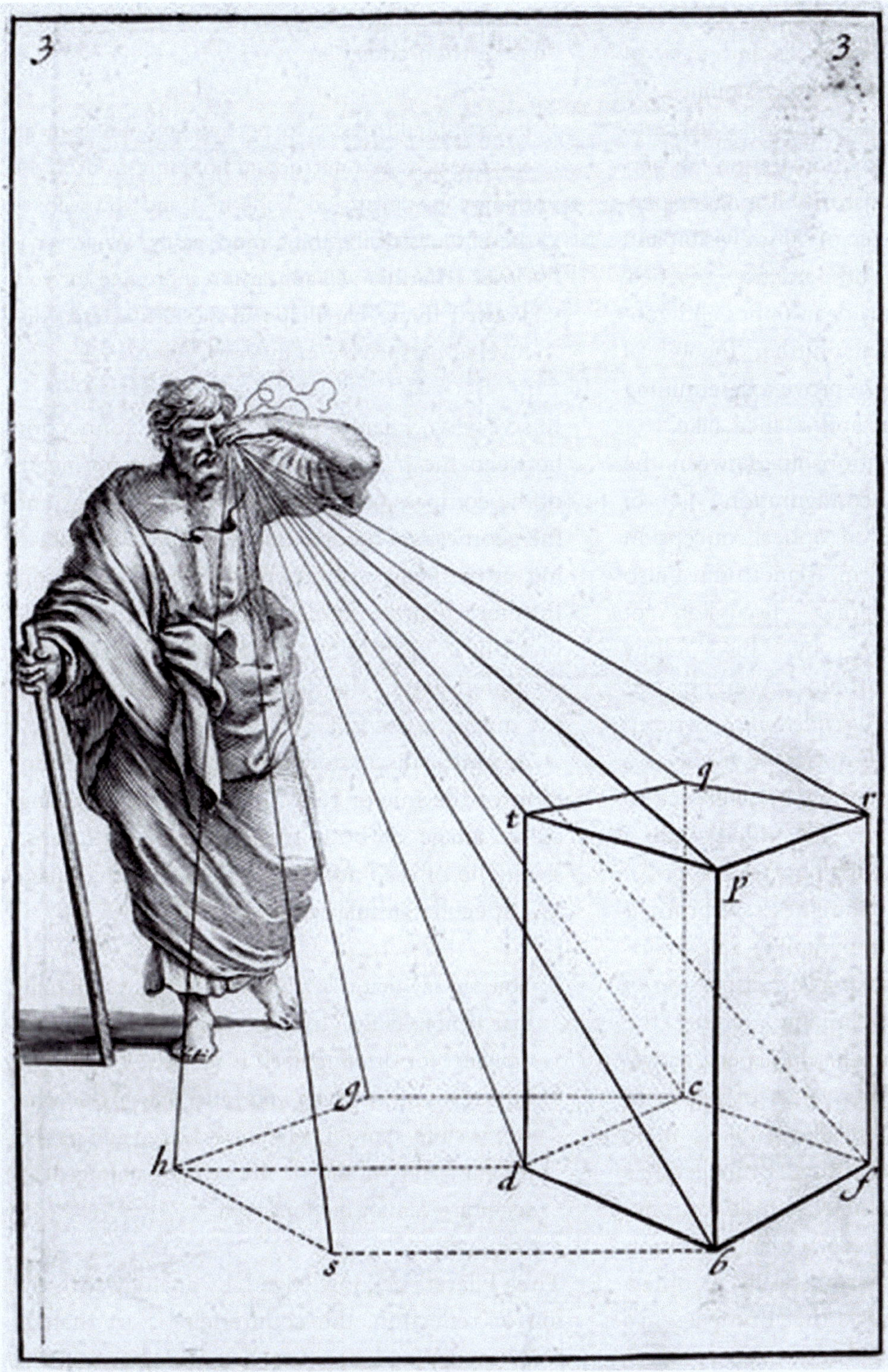

Fig. 61 Abraham Bosse, 'Le perspecteur', in Girard Desargues, *Manière universelle pour pratiquer la perspective*, Paris, 1648. Photo: Gallica / BNF

al-Haytham's experiments as demonstrations of this science, in which we witness the history of its transmission from Baghdad to Florence: the first demonstration is concerned with clouds; the second with looking through an optical eyehole at an intersection of walls. The relationship with Brunelleschi's perspectival demonstration panels, of which there were two – that of the Baptistery and a second one of the view across Piazza della Signoria, both of architectural walls and a sky of moving clouds above them – surely signifies the currency of al-Haytham's text, as Euclid's heir, into Brunelleschi's conceptual demonstration of perspective. In Brunelleschi's historic elision, perspective was now both the science of optical vision and the pictorial method of artistic practice. Brunelleschi's fusion of Euclidean optics and geometrical perspective, and its further theoretical elaboration by Alberti, was to prove a determining legacy for early modern art and science alike.[15]

In emphasising the relationship between the conceptual-material configuration of Brunelleschi's eyehole and the optical conception of vision as pyramidal in form, Manetti must also have drawn on an earlier discussion of Brunelleschi's experiment by his fellow Florentine architect Antonio Averlino, or Filarete.[16] Filarete's *Libro architettonico*, written in the 1460s, described the optics of vision as a visual pyramid in material terms, by reference to Rome's pyramid, which he illustrated with a sketch. He made further analogy to a type of conical form 'in which all [the lines] are brought to one point, exactly like a pyramid', a comparison Manetti would also make in his discussion of Brunelleschi's eyehole, so linking together the various accounts of Brunelleschi's perspectival method as founded in the science of optics as much as geometry. Filarete's account is most explicit, however, in attributing Brunelleschi's apprehension of the geometrical rule of one-point perspective to its specular demonstration in a mirror. Whether anachronistically or otherwise, Filarete further suggests that Brunelleschi's realisation of perspective arose through practice-based visual observation predicated on the use of the mirror as a specular instrument. The passage follows on from an earlier discussion of the use of compasses for the purpose of sizing different objects to be drawn to scale within architectural plans and preparatory compositions for paintings (a practice that continued).[17] In conclusion, Filarete then adds:

> If you should desire to portray something in an easier way, take a mirror and hold it in front of the thing you want to do. Look in it and you will see the outlines of the thing more easily. Whatever is closer or farther will appear foreshortened for you. Truly, I think that Pippo di Ser Brunelllesco discovered perspective in this way.[18]

In so saying, Filarete made direct the connection between the practice of measurement by means of the compass, architectural survey drawing, and the geometrical theorisation of perspectival drawing, at the heart of Brunelleschi's demonstration. Further, Filarete underscored that the visible proof of its realisation, as Brunelleschi had demonstrated, lay in the pictorializing instrument of the mirror reflection.

Filarete's discussion continued with a definition of the mirror reflection, and thus painting, as an image of both truth and illusion. In so saying he offered a full theorisation of the image as a specular simulacrum:

> You can say that it is false, for it shows you a thing that is not. This is true; nevertheless, it is true in drawing, for drawing itself is not true but a demonstration of the thing you [are] drawing or what you wish to show. Therefore, it is true and perfect for this, and without it the art of painting or of sculpture cannot be done well.[19]

Thus Filarete acknowledged, by analogy with the mirror reflection, the counterfeit of art that, in both theory and practice, had now become the definition of painting. The capacity to represent painting as specular mimesis or 'truth', in Filarete's terms, lay in the skill of its perspectival illusion, just as Alberti had said.

A further passage from Filarete elaborates the close correlations between theory and practice in the conceptualisation of painting as a view into a door frame or window, as Alberti had postulated, or a conical viewing-point through to a pyramid of vision in the manner of Brunelleschi. The discussion specifically concerns the translation of the three-dimensional visible field, as if seen through a window frame or a proscenium arch, into the two-dimensional plane of a drawing. Throughout Filarete's text, the draughtsman's sheet of paper is also described as a window view, demonstrating the depth of the Albertian analogy. In effect, Filarete's is both a theorisation of the artist's materials and a materialisation of perspectival theory in the practice-based fabrication of the specular image. Using the compass for sizing, Filarete's advice was to 'square' the draughtsman's sheet in a mirror double of the window view as seen through a squaring device, made up of a material grid of string lines over the theoretical 'window' of vision. The use of the compass embodied the confluence of mathematics and art in the draughtsman's practice. The ready instrument of geometry, it was also used by artists as a means of gauging scalar reductions or enlargements in the translation of visual perception into perspectival drawing. The squaring grid was similarly a practice-based means of transposing observation into two-dimensional perspectival form.

In Filarete's further elaboration, by means of the squaring grid the draughtsman might, with the use of a ruler on the drawing, bring together the points of a perspectival recession into convergent orthogonal lines. These are, Filarete explains, like the pyramidal lines of vision, or the mirror reversal of the rays of the viewer's eye, projected into the image. Here the ruler is the workshop instrument of a practical perspective, able to map the sight-lines of Euclidean pyramidal vision onto the draughtsman's page. In Filarete's account these lines converge at a central point. Termed by land and architecture surveyers the 'certification point', in recognition of its certifiable geometrical accuracy, Renaissance students of optics understood the centre point as the mathematical locus of infinite spatial recession, at which the horizon narrows to a point marking the furthest reach of the pyramid of vision (it was only later – 1715 – termed the vanishing point).[20] For a proof or demonstration of this geometry Filarete advocates Brunelleschi's mirror:

> If you wish to consider this more closely, take a mirror and look at [the lines of recession of a squared pavement in it]. . . . I think that Pippo di Ser Brunellesco, the Florentine, discovered the method of making the plane in this way. It was certainly a subtle and beautiful thing to discover how, by [means of a] ruler, from what the mirror shows you.[21]

Here it is clear that, as with Brunelleschi's demonstration panel of the Baptistery, geometrical perspective is understood as visually interchangeable with the view through a window, and its translation by means of a mirror reflection. Filarete brings together the tripartite method of proof deployed by Brunelleschi: window, mirror, and the plane of rendering of his painted panel.

The sequential relationship between a window view, mirror reflection, and painting runs as a continuing thread through the history of perspectival geometry in both art theory and practice. Following Brunelleschi's experiment, as scholars have successively noted, both the visual geometry of perspective and the understanding of painting as a form of specular optical reflection takes root c. 1430. This is prescient in Masaccio's geometry of foreshortening in the *Trinity* fresco for the Florentine church of S. Maria Novella of c. 1425, as has long been argued. In the historic adoption of a Euclidean science of light rays translated into geometrical form, it was as Masaccio painted this celebrated pictorial demonstration of perspective at S. Maria Novella that Alberti formulated his optical theorization of painting (1435–36), also founded in Brunelleschi's methods. Indelibly bound up with the development of one-point perspective as the new structuring logic of the picture plane, Alberti's treatise, following Brunelleschi's example of the mirror at the Cathedral door, famously conceived of painting as a mirror reflection or an open window 'through which I see what I want to paint'.[22] This analogy between painting, mirrors, and an open window is already in play, howsoever deployed optically rather than strictly mathematically, in the depiction of the window alongside the mirror within Jan van Eyck's Arnolfini portrait of 1434, and repeated in the reflection of the same window within the painting's inset mirror, as Chapter 2 discussed. The simile is also at work in Brunelleschi's conceptualization of painting as the view through a doorway transposed into the reduced size of a mirror reflection.

The widespread adoption of the window motif within Renaissance art theory, as an Albertian paradigm of painting, would become a parallel to the metaphor of the mirror-image and an equivalent definition of painting's art. At the same time, like his friend Brunelleschi to whom Alberti dedicated the Italian version of his treatise, Alberti also understood the picture plane in terms of the method of its making. He theorized the plane as what he termed the 'intersection' between the viewer and subject depicted. This intersection, as in Brunelleschi's demonstration, was the conceptual manifestation of both theory and practice, in which the science of optics was elaborated in material form. For Alberti characterized a Euclidean theory of vision by means of a perspectival 'squaring' grid. He explicated it as a drawing frame standing at a midpoint between, and intersected by, on the one side the viewer's rays of vision and on the other the converging lines of pictorial space.

In his practice Alberti advocated the use of a framed grid or squaring device such as Filarete also described, to embody his conceptualization of what he termed the perspectival intersection. In practice the drawing frame became the technological means of realizing a Renaissance painting. Standing between the artist's eye and the object to be depicted, this material grid was like a perspectival 'window'. By its means the artist could frame the composition, using it to transpose the perception of the world into two dimensions, just like a mirror. Alberti constituted this workshop-based device of his architectural practice out of a transparent veil of very finely woven cloth like muslin, marked out by parallel lines in a larger thread:

> Nothing can be found, so I think, which is more useful than that veil which among my friends I call an intersection. It is a thin veil, finely woven, dyed whatever colour pleases you and with larger threads [marking out] as many parallels as you prefer. This veil I place between the eye and the thing seen.... This veil can be of great use to you.... The veil will greatly aid you in learning how to paint.[23]

In Alberti's account, the veil of transparent cloth with a tinted colour and marked by squares was the practice-based means of a perspectival rendering. Here it is useful to recall the widespread usage of *finestre impannate* such as Alberti would have known, or the Renaissance dressed window, made of oiled or varnished textile such as canvas, parchment, or rag paper. These transparent textile windows set within wooden frames were designed to be portable. In domestic dwellings of all ranks, these were the most prevalent form of window until the advent of plate-glass casting in the final decades of the seventeenth century. Thus Alberti's conceptual elision of the artist's drawing frame with a window surely arose from their close material approximation.[24] In the materialities of artistic practice, the draughtsman's squaring device was just like a textile 'window' of the kind that predominated across Renaissance Europe. Like Brunelleschi's mirror, Alberti's intersection was both an instrument of artistic production and a virtual specularisation of the work of art in the making. This conflation of the picture plane with the workshop instruments of a mimetic art heightened the proximity between painting as representation and the processes of its own production. The painted inset mirror within a painting, as both a metaphor and an instrument of its art, directly articulated this correlation of theory and practice.

Like Brunelleschi, Alberti also conceived of painting as a mirror, for he traced the invention of painting to the myth of the beautiful youth Narcissus, who fell in love with his own reflection in a watery pool. In his treatise, Alberti therefore devoted the first book to the mathematics of geometrical perspective, conceived as the delineation of form independent of matter, as on the surface of painting. In the second book, he turned from the theorems of geometry to the instruments of perspective within artistic practice: a squaring device in the form of a window-like grid and its veil of intersecting lines of thread. His end, to be sure, was the same as the poets: the evocation of *istoria* through the methods of mimesis in both theory and practice. The story of Narcissus, in Alberti's text, marked the transition from geometrical theorems to the squaring device and the poets, because it drew together the several 'arts' of painting as one: mathematics, practice, and poetry. Ovid's watery reflection at the threshold of visual mimesis and deception was a ready metaphor for the Albertian picture plane as a surface of mere illusion, the impalpable fiction of life in its absence. It was one with a long reach into the subsequent history of Renaissance painting, conceived as a mirror effect.[25]

'HOW THE MIRROR IS THE MASTER OF PAINTERS'

Long after Alberti, Caravaggio also pictorialized the myth of Narcissus and his embrace of the mirror reflection in a work seen to repose the Albertian paradigm of painting's specular intent. The canvas in question represents both the boy and the reflection he gazes upon (Fig. 62).[26] Like Brunelleschi's Baptistery panel, Caravaggio's *Narcissus* would also appear to have been conceived through the use of mirrors as the very method of its artistic production, as Rossella Vodret has argued. In this it may be said to embody the fusion of artistic theory and practice in the Albertian conception of painting's specular claim. Here the painter seemingly worked from a model placed before two flat mirrors situated with one perpendicular to the other. One mirror was laid flat to capture the reflection of the boy in the 'water', the other upright in order to reflect the depiction of the youth leaning over the 'pool' for Caravaggio's brush. The model's arms arch in an embrace of the image, reflected back to him in the pool below. In Alberti's words: 'What else can you call painting but a similar embracing with art of what is presented on the surface of the water?', which Caravaggio paraphrased in paint.[27] Just as Alberti had adumbrated, Caravaggio fused Narcissus' act of love with the artist's gesture of painting extending towards the picture plane, figured as the reflecting surface of an Ovidian pool.

Among this artist's otherwise meagre possessions listed in a brief inventory of his property dating to 1605 were two mirrors, one large and one convex, suggesting their use as painter's aids.[28] Giovanni Baglione, an artist himself and one of Caravaggio's early biographers, observed that the painter commonly painted his figures by studying his own reflection in a mirror in his earliest works. This testimony regarding the use of mirrors within Caravaggio's working practice has always been broadly acknowledged as instrumental to his painting process of an (apparently) unmediated naturalism.[29] Thus Alberti's story of the origins of painting in the pool of Narcissus had its practice-based counterpart, which we witness in Caravaggio's specular art. In terms of both

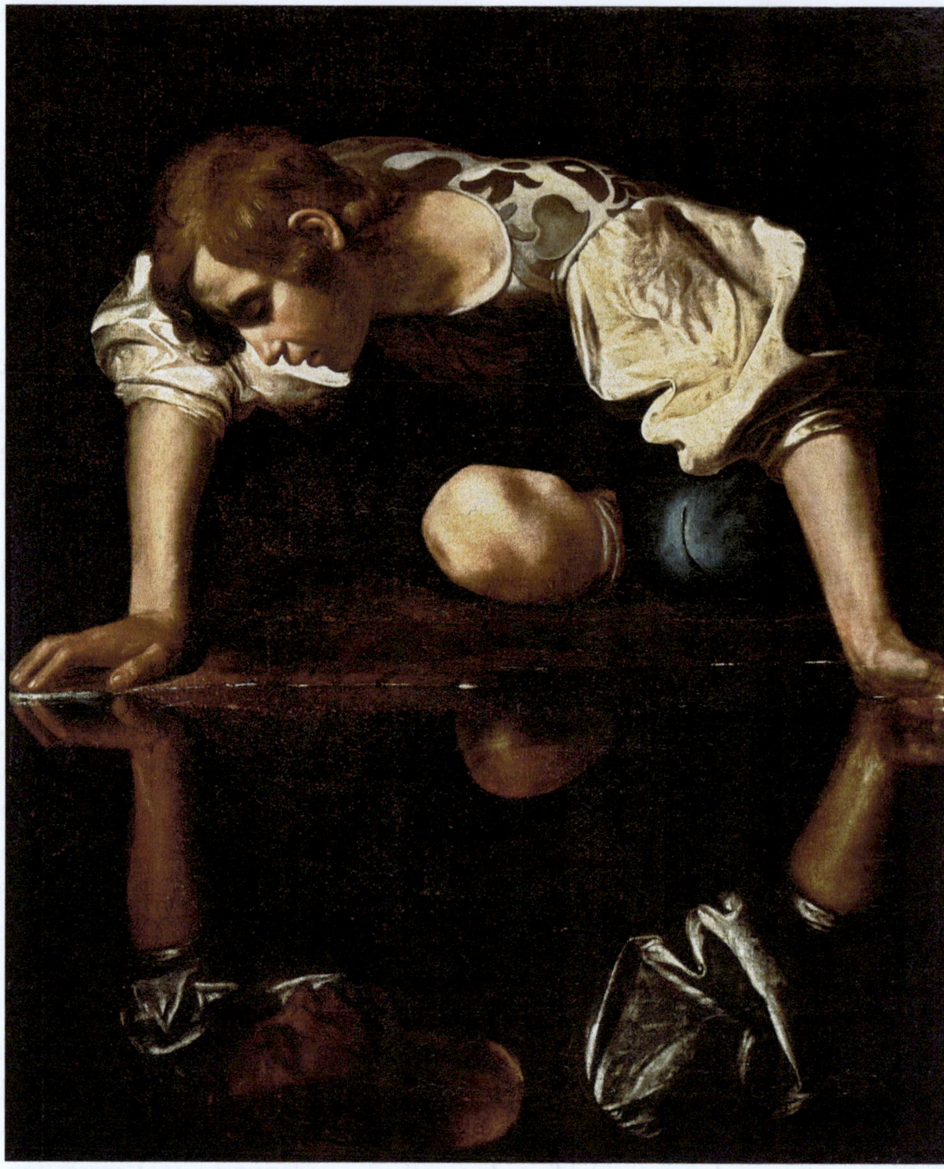

Fig. 62 Michelangelo Merisi da Caravaggio, *Narcissus*, c. 1597–99, oil on canvas, 110 × 92 cm, Galleria Nazionale d'Arte Antica Palazzo Barberini Rome. Photo: Wikimedia

representation and process, Caravaggio's *Narcissus* was precisely bound up with an extended analogy of painting as a mirror. In the studio, as per Brunelleschi's demonstration, Caravaggio's mirror was the artist's instrument for transposing the visible world into the two-dimensional surface of painting. In representation, the mirroring surface inset within the painting became the locus for the reflected depiction of its own production. The mirroring effects within Caravaggio's work are an emblem of this painter's art of realism, advancing the claim of an artist who famously purported to 'paint what I see'.[30]

In Albertian mode, artists in the studio of Leonardo in Milan had also chosen the subject of Narcissus through which to pose the question of painting's resemblance to a specular reflection in emulation of their master (Fig. 63).[31] A youth gazes down towards his reflection in a mirroring pool of water, like the fountain of Ovidian myth. A framing landscape of rock and lake-shore surrounds him in a suffused Leonardesque

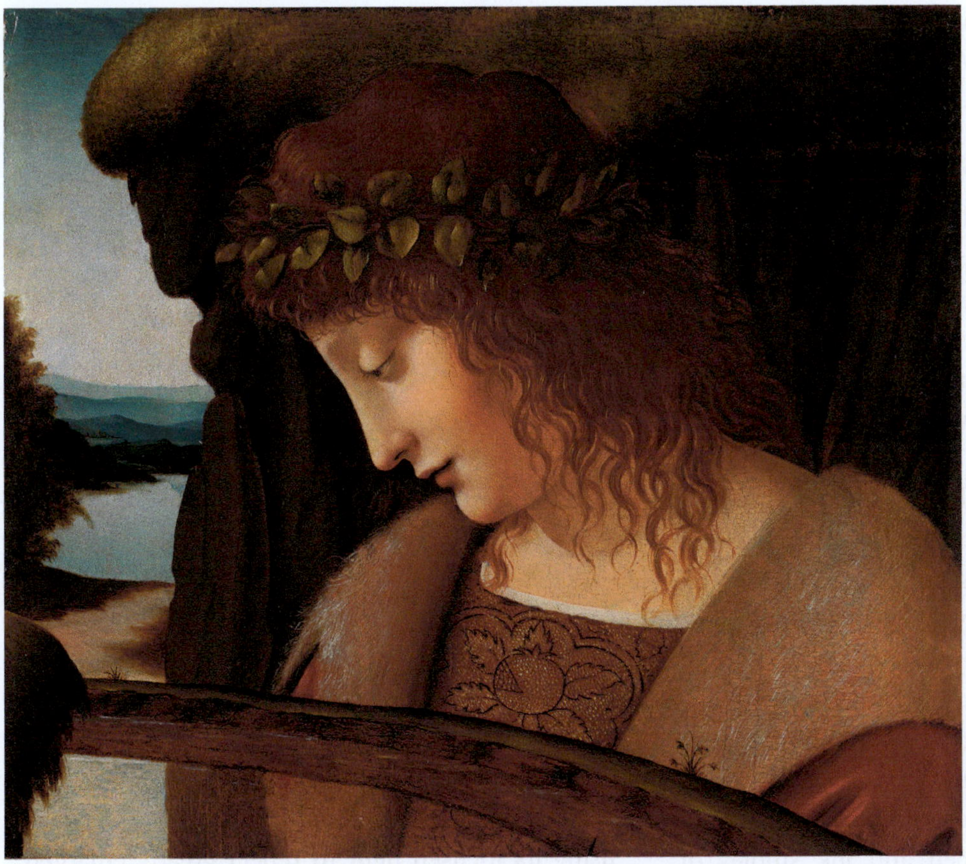

Fig. 63 Follower of Leonardo after Giovanni Antonio Boltraffio (attrib.), *Narcissus*, oil on walnut panel, 23.2 × 26.5 cm, National Gallery London. Photo: Wikimedia

perspective of deepening atmospheric effect. Dressed in gold brocade and fur, his fair hair falls to the neck in wave-like tendrils held by a band of twining leaves. Though his reflection in the water is withheld from us, we understand it through the rapt attention of his gaze. A metaphor for the visual lure of art, the occluded reflection of the beautiful youth pulls the viewer, like Narcissus, into the depths of paint's shimmering illusionistic surface.

Water, reflections, mirrors, optics, and perspective preoccupied Leonardo across his working life, as manifest in the great corpus of his notebooks and drawings. Composed of thousands of pages of drawings, sketches, and diagrams as well as extensive notes on his readings and observations, the subjects of the notebooks span the arts and sciences alike. As the history of publication of Leonardo's notebooks ably demonstrates, scholarship has often sought to order this vast corpus thematically, arranging it according to the wide spectrum of Leonardo's intellectual interests. A court artist in both Milan and subsequently Paris, he served primarily as an engineer of fortifications, weaponry, and waterways for military purposes, and as a designer of palace entertainments, theatre sets, decoration, and painting. As his celebrated letter to Ludovico Sforza, Duke of Milan, fully evidences, Leonardo understood his abilities to lie as much in engineering as in art. His notebooks reflect the full range of his scientific and artistic interests, and indeed were a key instrument of their common pursuit. They represent an ongoing account of Leonardo's daily thoughts and interests, his notes and designs for art and scientific enquiry appearing side by side, often within the same sheet. Early sketches for the figural composition of a painting may appear beside mechanical designs for water wheels, or machinery for the transport of heavy goods, for example, interspersed with further notes on their function and design. Leonardo's heirs, and indeed Leonardo himself, as well as subsequent scholars, have sought to order them into dedicated anthologies on every subject that came under his consideration, from a prospective treatise on painting to perspective, mirrors, catoptrics, optics, anatomy, astronomy, biology, natural history, hydraulics, engineering, architecture, fortifications, and weaponry. At the same time, the intertwined nature of his interests defies easy categorization, and more recent scholarship has instead preferred to maintain a dual focus in studying the notebooks collectively, as well as the early history of their anthological arrangement.[32] The wide-ranging discussion of reflections, mirrors, and perspective throughout his notes amply demonstrates the breadth of his optical interests across disciplinary boundaries. A page of pen and ink studies of sunlight reflections on water shows the close correlation between the artisanal mirror and the mirroring pool in Leonardo's theory and practice. His mix of text and sketch evidences the studied scientific as well as artistic and literary connections between water surfaces and mirror reflections that permeated his conceptual thought (Fig. 64).[33]

In his correspondence Leonardo cited his own practice in mirror-making in pursuit of building a parabolic mirror for scientific as well as military uses. Recalling Archimedes' description of the siege of Syracusa by means of 'burning mirrors' to ignite fire among enemy ships, Leonardo discussed calculation of the parabolic curve required to focus a concave mirror's reflection of the sun's rays to a single point. His interest is in casting light as much as igniting fire, in order to illuminate vision over long distances, across fields for reconnaissance purposes, and for observing clouds, rainbows, and other atmospheric configurations of water and light reflection. He also

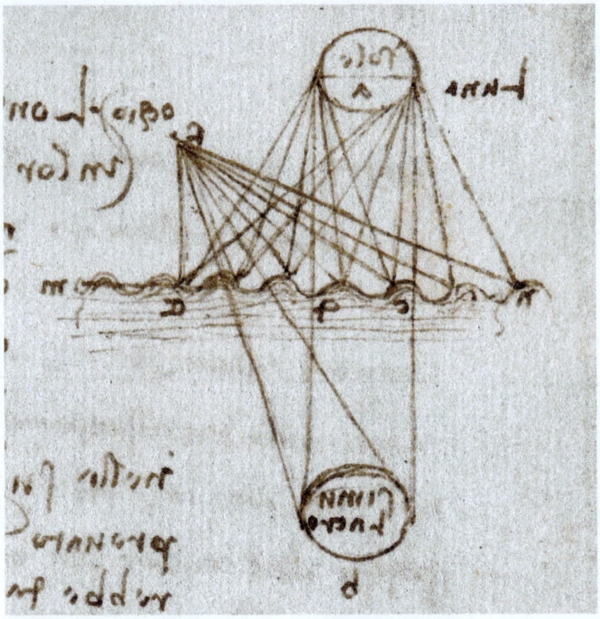

Fig. 64 Leonardo da Vinci, *Study of Sunlight on Water*, Codex Arundel, c. 1508, pen and ink, British Library ms. 263, fol. 25r.
Photo: British Library

cites turning his parabolic mirror to the stars, using its focused light to reflect greatly enlarged views of the planets for his observation. In general, the mirror served as a visual instrument of his scientific studies. For example, Leonardo studied the water droplets of a rainbow as an array of tiny mirrors, each reflecting the sun's rays in a spectrum of colours.[34] This comprised both magnification for close visual observation and, conversely, diminution in order to transpose and record his observations as drawings on paper, in which he used the mirror as an intermediary tool. His scientific method was like Brunelleschi's at the door of the Cathedral, placing the mirror between the eye and what is to be viewed, as a demonstration or visible proof of his investigation. The practice suggests a broad-based use of mirrors as the instrument of all kinds of visual observation. Leonardo's discussions of light refraction further include the observation that all objects reflect colour onto each other, 'for every object is a mirror, tinged by the colour of the thing opposite'.[35] In his frequent discussion of atmospheric perspective, the 'envelope' of coloured air through which vision occurs was of fundamental importance to his development as a painter as well as a scientist. There is reference to all manner of luminosity and light diffusion – glitter, clouds, mists, moonlight, reflections, and refractions.[36] Similarly, his extensive interest in water, from hydraulic motion to the close observation of its reflective surface, unites his artistic and scientific studies alike.

The meeting of art and science in Leonardo's notes is nowhere more in evidence than in his discussions of mirrors, as part of a possible intended treatise on catoptrics in its own right as well as in relation to his planned book on perspective.[37] The specular concept of reflection shapes the very nature of his notes, written in reverse and acknowledged by his contemporaries as legible only by means of a mirror. Notwithstanding much scholarly speculation, ranging from his left-handedness to a desire for secrecy regarding his discoveries and inventions, the reasons for his use of mirror-writing remain contested.[38] What is clear from the notes is that he understood the eye itself, the instrument of vision, as a mirror that reflects in reverse. Leonardo's study of the eye as a kind of 'mirror box' extends to what may be understood as an analogy with the early *camera obscura*.[39] Through dissection, he understood the pupil as an anatomical form of conical eyehole that collects rays of light, like the pinhole of Brunelleschi's demonstration panel. A sheet of notes and diagrams demonstrates his study of optical rays entering the eye, diagrammatically rendered as a *camera obscura* (Fig. 65). Elsewhere he noted making a model of an eyeball out of glass in order to study its mirror function.[40] Further, he pondered the eye's extraordinary powers of magnification: 'who would believe that so small a space could contain the images of all the universe?'[41] Leonardo observed that it behaved like a tiny concave mirror; he further noted that the eye also reverses images from left to right, which he elsewhere compared to the production of printed text, or the wax image of a seal.[42] The mirror-image of reversal is thus connected to both visual and textual forms of knowledge in Leonardo's thinking. Across art and science, reflection is Leonardo's instrument of intellectual enquiry.

Throughout Leonardo's notes made over many years, his thoughts encompassed a wide-ranging and varying analogy between the mirror and painting. Most profoundly, he understood the mirror as a parallel form to painting in its ability to capture the illusion of all visible things in its reflecting sheen. His longest discussion of the painter's use of the mirror occurs as part of his intended treatise on painting, in a passage entitled 'How the Mirror Is the Master of Painters':

> When you wish to see whether the general effect of your picture corresponds with that of the object represented after nature, take a mirror and set it so that it reflects the actual thing, and then compare the reflection with your picture, and consider carefully whether the subject of the two images is in conformity with both, studying especially the mirror. The mirror ought to be taken as a guide – that is, the flat mirror – for within its surface substances have many points of resemblance to a picture, namely, that you see the picture made upon one plane, showing things which appear in relief, just as in a mirror. A picture is one single surface, and the mirror is the same. A picture is intangible in that what appears round and detached cannot be enclosed within the hands, and the mirror is the same. The mirror and the picture present the images of things surrounded by shadow and light, and each alike seems to project considerably from the plane of its surface. And since you know that the mirror presents detached things to you by means of outlines and shadows and lights, and since you have moreover amongst your colours more powerful shadows and lights

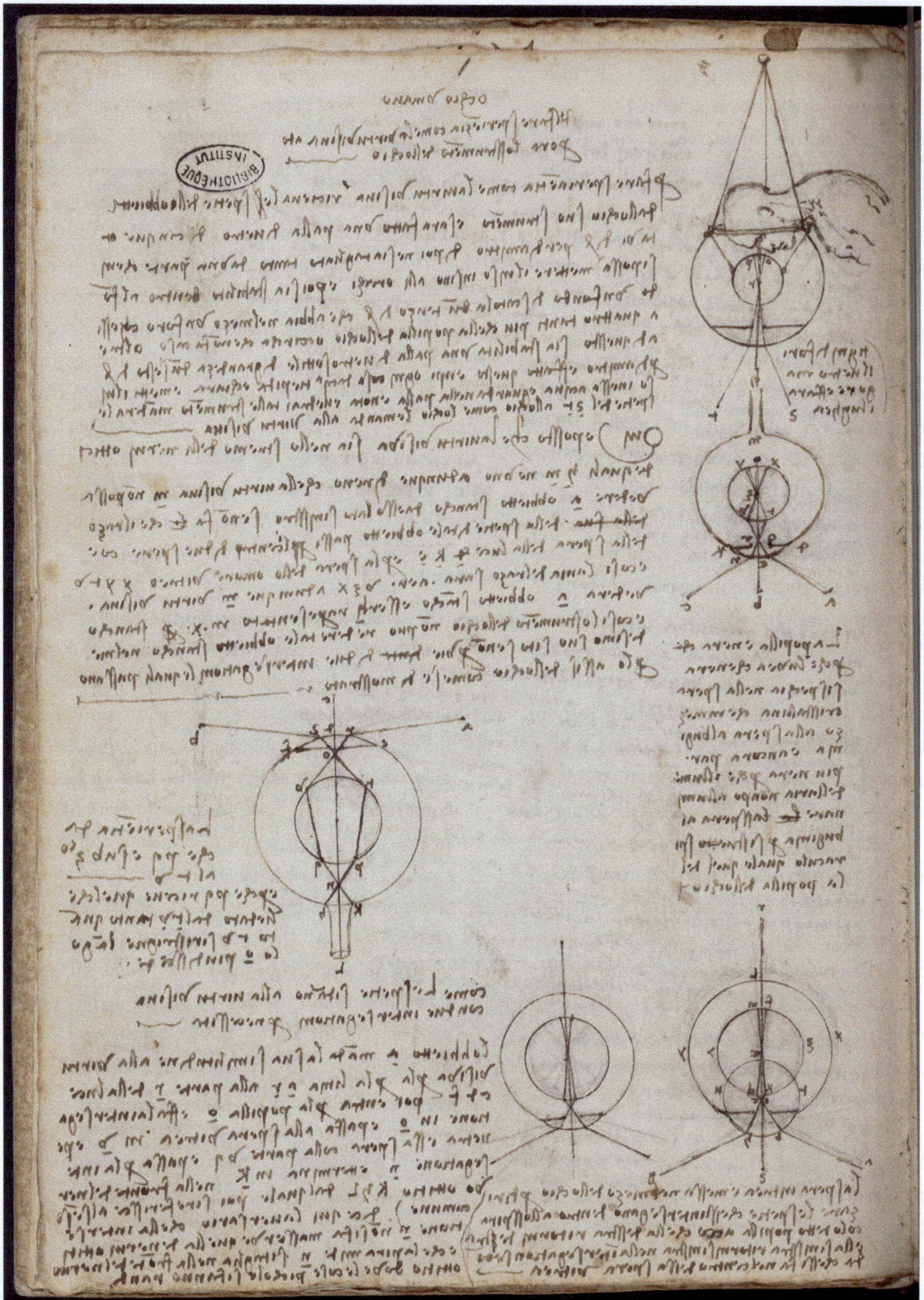

Fig. 65 Leonardo da Vinci, notebook diagram of the eye's reception of images, pen and ink, MS 2175 D folio 8 recto, Institut de France Library.
Photo: Réunion des Musées Nationaux

> than those of the mirror; it is certain that if you but know well how to compose your picture, it will also seem a natural thing seen in a great mirror.[43]

Theorisation of the picture plane in terms of a mirror is here fully intertwined with its practical application. In the first instance, the mirror is a demonstration of the veracity of painting's illusion, as with Brunelleschi, a means of comparison between the painting and the field of vision. Beyond Brunelleschi's conception, however, the mirror is for Leonardo the painter's guide. For a mirror reflection, like a painting, offers an illusion that is yet intangible. In Leonardo's thought the mirror is the metaphor and the instrument of painting, as well as the measure of its mimesis. He concludes that the well-composed painting will resemble a mirror-reflection: 'The mirror . . . contains within itself true painting, and true painting is perfect in so far as it resembles the surface of a mirror.'[44]

Elsewhere in his notes Leonardo explicated Brunelleschi's method further in considering the use of the mirror as both a practice-based mimetic aide and a demonstration of painting's specular formation. This included a discussion of the mirror as a simulacrum of painting, but also of its guidance and instruction. Here Leonardo advocated the use of a mirror as an instrument of improvement, the painter's *paragone*, as Alberti had done, who also understood it as a heightened reproduction of the work under judgment, in which the very immateriality of the reflected image was itself a model of pictorial idealization:

> A good judge for you to know is the mirror. I do not know why painted things have so much grace in the mirror. It is marvellous how every weakness in a painting is so manifestly de[-]formed in the mirror. Therefore things taken from nature are corrected with a mirror.[45]

If Alberti's story of Narcissus represented painting's claim to the mimetic powers of the mirror, the use he advocated within practice was related in concept but different in its practical orientation. In the studio, Alberti commended the mirror as an instrument of comparison and judgment, using it to reflect back the painting in progress so as to make adjustments and corrections in a *paragone* with himself. Renaissance workshop mirrors were commonly deployed as a means of verifying, even authenticating, a mimetic paradigm of art, following Brunelleschi's demonstration. Alberti's concern was to test through comparison with the mirror reflection the depiction of relief in painting, rendered through the judicious application of white and black to give the illusion of highlight and shadow and so of volume. Leonardo also advocated using the mirror this way: 'I say that when you are painting you should take a flat mirror and often look at your work within it . . . and you will be better able to judge of its faults than any other way.'[46]

Elsewhere, Leonardo described use of a drawing frame, clearly an Albertian window grid, through which to draw in correct perspectival recession, as in a mirror reflection:

> fasten a frame or loom divided into squares by threads between your eye and the nude figure which you are representing, and then make the same squares upon the paper where you wish to draw the said nude but very faintly . . . And these threads will instruct you as to all the parts of the body which in each attitude are found below the pit of the throat, below the angles of the shoulders, below the breasts, the hips, and the other parts of the body.. . . the squares you draw may be as much smaller than those of the network in proportion as you wish your figure to be less than life size.[47]

Leonardo's interests in the machinery of textile manufacture may have guided his analogy of the painter's grid with a loom, though the inference is already implicit to Alberti's description of the same instrument, suggesting the comparison was broad-based and likely founded in the common practicalities of their facture. As the fabric of painting shifted from wood panel to canvas, the reciprocity between painting and the Albertian textile veil became ever more pronounced, as also with Renaissance textile window-coverings. Whereas Alberti's account focused on the use of the grid from which then to draw perspectival orthogonals of spatial recession, as in Filarete's description of the lozenge-like configuration of pavement squares to indicate the illusion of depth, Leonardo instead describes the use of the squaring device to render the volume of bodies. 'The pit of the throat, the angles of the shoulder' – Leonardo centres on the parts of the body involving particularly complex shading to render the visual illusion of their undulating form. The purpose of the correspondence between the squaring device and the squared paper is to enable a diminution in scale as well as accuracy in proportions. In this regard it functions as a parallel to the architect's ruler and compass, and to the mirror reflection of Brunelleschi's demonstration, able to reduce in scale as well as to pictorialise the third dimension into a planar form.

In Leonardo's practice the mirror increasingly took the place of the grid. While Alberti advocated the use of the mirror as a means of comparison and correction, as Brunelleschi had demonstrated, Leonardo began to integrate it more profoundly into the conceptual development of a painting. He deployed a mirror to reflect the subject of representation in order to transcribe it onto the canvas in much the same way that Alberti's artists worked from what they saw through the squaring device. Hence Leonardo made the mirror the primary instrument of artistic mimesis. Further, the dimming reflection of the pewter-toned Renaissance mirror offered Leonardo a reduction of local colour into a unifying scale of tonal gradations in concert with his analytical understanding of atmospheric perspective, like Alberti's tinted veil. This specular shift may be joined to Leonardo's broader reconceptualization of perspective as atmospheric as well as linear, and so the art of painting itself.[48]

Throughout his notes Leonardo advocated a thinking mirror, not merely a mimetic one, asking the painter to imitate by practice and judgment of the eye coupled with the use of reason. Elsewhere Leonardo so fused painting with the reflection of the mirror that he urged the painter to liken his mind to its surface.[49] 'The mind of the painter should be like a mirror . . . which is filled by as many images as there are things placed before it.'[50] Here Leonardo touched on the related issue of artistic memory, which he understood as a compendium of 'mirror' reflections. This is to suggest an equivalence between the mirror metaphor and the practice of drawing, which Leonardo counselled for the formation of artistic memory of figural form. He therefore advocated training the artist's visual memory through the repeated practice of drawing, conceived as a specularised form of imitation. He touched on the practice of drawing as the instrument of a mirroring mimesis both in terms of the sketchbooks he advised the painter to carry with him, as he did himself, and as the instrument of an artist's academic study conducted through drawing, so 'filling the mind with as many images as there are things placed before it' in the visual study of:

> all the varieties of the forms which nature produces – which indeed you will not know how to do unless you see them and retain them in your mind – look to it, O painter! That when you go into the fields you give your attention to the various objects, and look carefully in turn first at one thing and then at another.[51]

In the studio, Leonardo advised drawing as a form of study practiced through the use of

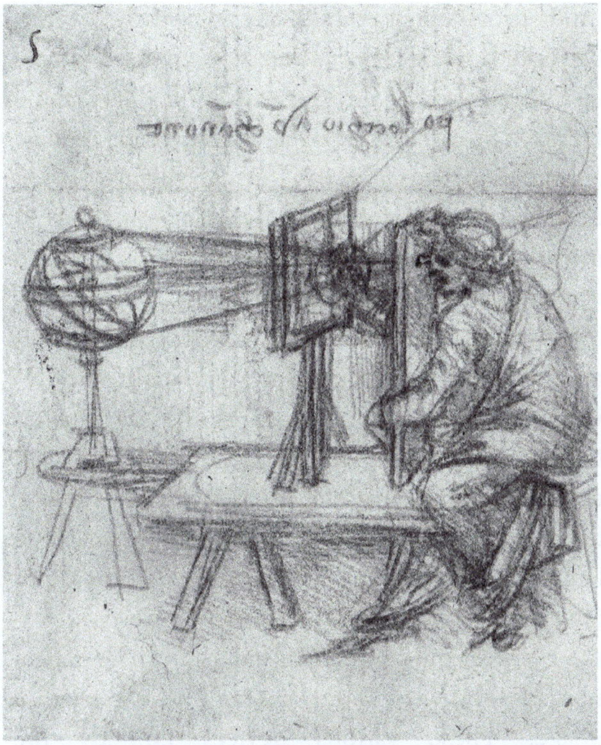

Fig. 66 Leonardo da Vinci, detail from a page of sketches illustrating a draughtsman drawing an armillary sphere as seen through a perspectograph, Codex Atlanticus f. 5r, c. 1480–82, Biblioteca Ambrosiana Milan.
Photo: Veneranda Biblioteca Ambrosiana

various mirror-like instruments, through which to train the judgment of the hand and eye. These included an 'exemplar traced on to a thin flat plane of glass. Place this on top of the drawing you have done without the exemplar, and note carefully where the tracing does not match up with your drawing.'[52] A sketch among his notes in the Codex Atlanticus illustrates Leonardo's device. It is a flat pane, like a window or a sheet mirror, on which to trace the outlines of what he saw. Recalling its theorization as a perspectival instrument, Leonardo termed it a 'perspectograph' (Fig. 66).[53] In the figure, a seated draughtsman sketches a globe-shaped armillary sphere, an astronomical model of the circuits of the planets used to derive mathematical measures of space and time. It was perceived as particularly adept to a draughtsman's training, both metaphorically and practically, requiring the ability to translate a complex three-dimensional object into its illusionistic rendering on a flat plane. Leonardo's reverse 'mirror' writing titles the diagram. It is the instrument through which the draughtsman views the sphere that brings together Leonardo's converging interests in the Albertian problem of geometrical perspective and a painterly practice of the picture plane. In order to render the visual appearance of the armillary sphere's three-dimensional volume into the two-dimensional surface of a diagram, the draughtsman works by means of the vertically placed viewing plane. The artist looks through the sighting device to steady the eye, onto a framed viewing pane placed before the object to be depicted. By this means the perspectograph allows the draughtsman to establish the outline and geometrical relation of the parts directly onto the viewing device before him. In effect, it is a technology of visual translation, through which the draughtsman maps the perspectival outline of a complex spherical volume onto a flat plane. In Leonardo's practice, the viewing plane takes the place of the Albertian grid, or window, through which to draw, as a direct equivalent to a Brunelleschian mirror reflection. Through its field of vision Leonardo's draughtsman can compare his drawing on paper with the view itself. It is a practical application of Alberti's conceptualisation of a painting as a planar intersection of the visual pyramid of rays between the viewing eye and the field of vision.

Further deepening the analogy between the viewing pane and the plane of intersection, Leonardo understood perspective as:

> nothing else than the seeing of an object behind a sheet of glass … on the surface of which all the things may be marked that are behind this glass; these things approach the point of the eye in pyramids, and these pyramids are cut by the said glass.[54]

Leonardo's viewing pane is Alberti's theoretical window in material form. Collectively, Leonardo's notes on the mirror and the window view theorize their conceptual equivalence with painting as well as their practical use as instruments of imitation. This, in turn, drew on his larger interests in optics, the science of reflected light, and the relationship between reflection and vision.

THE PRACTICE OF MIMESIS

As Leonardo was collecting his notes for an intended treatise on painting, Albrecht Dürer was preparing his multi-volume book on artistic measurement, the *Underweysung der Messung mit dem Zirckel und Richtsheyt* (Manual of Measurement with the Compass and Ruler) of 1525.[55] This treated the geometry of figural forms in art, and specifically the representation of complex volumes, in the two-dimensional medium of drawing. Aptly described as a revolving door in its accommodation of theory with practice, in Erwin Panofsky's words it familiarized 'coopers and cabinet-makers with Euclid and Ptolemy . . . [and] professional mathematicians with what may be called workshop geometry', or its material instrumentation.[56] At the close of the volume Dürer included a plate depicting an artist drawing a three-dimensional object through the use of various glass-pane instruments. As with Brunelleschi's mirror, Alberti's grid, and Leonardo's glass perspectograph, which Dürer surely knew, this technological apparatus was evidently the draughtsman's ready means for translating the appearance of volumes into two dimensions. In the first illustration, a draughtsman draws the outline of a vase onto an upright sheet of glass framed like a picture, or indeed a window, using also a sighting device to keep the position of the viewing eye constant (Fig. 67a, b). The sighting device corresponds to the point of the visual pyramid as a mirror reflection of the centre point within the perspectival image. These various devices embody the Albertian concept of the window 'intersection' in material form, for the distance between the viewing eye, the panel, and the object to be depicted effected the same transpositions of perspectival distance as the corresponding squares of the draughtsman's squaring device. Like a preparatory drawing, the outline on the glass forms the first

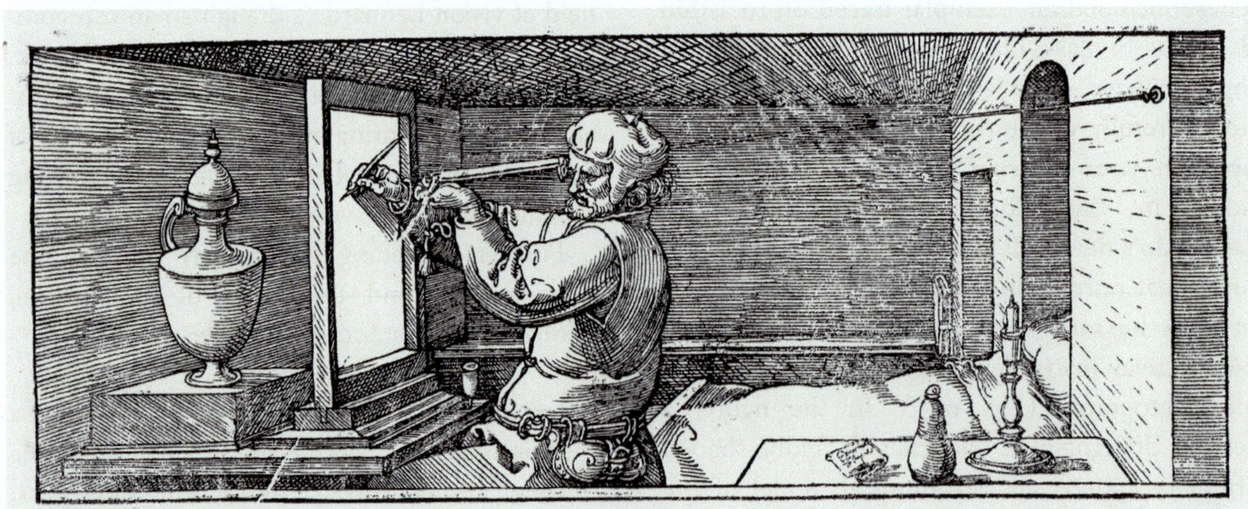

Fig. 67a Albrecht Dürer, woodcut illustration for *Underweysung der Messung mit dem Zirckel und Richtscheyt,* Nuremberg, 1538, 31.9 × 21.5 cm.
Photo: Wikimedia

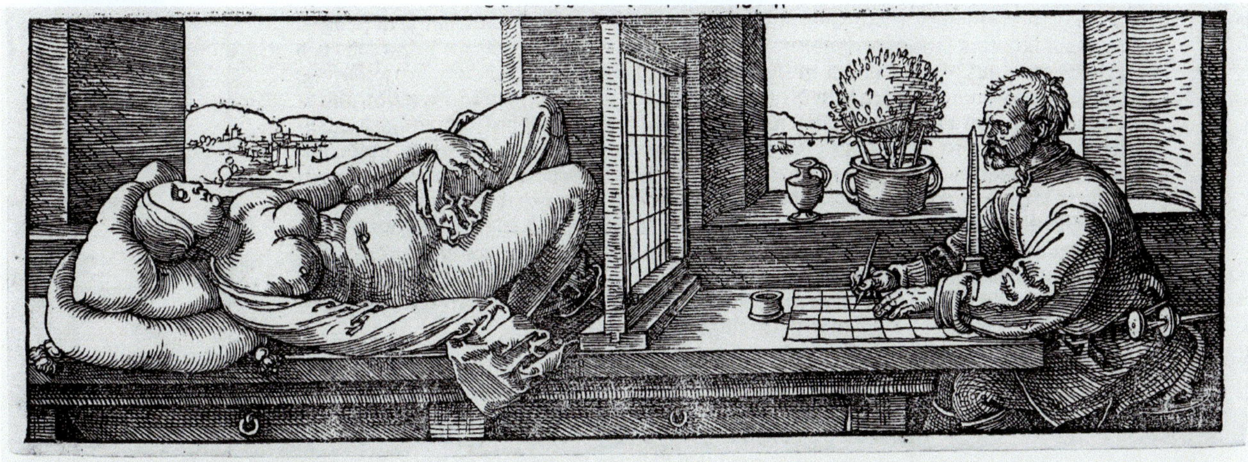

Fig. 67b Albrecht Dürer, woodcut illustration for *Underweysung der Messung mit dem Zirckel und Richtscheyt*, Nuremberg, 1538, 31.9 × 21.5 cm.
Photo: Wikimedia

stage in the artistic translation of the world into the flat field of a painting. As with Leonardo's description and sketch of his glass 'perspectograph' exemplar, Dürer's illustrations visibly demonstrate the use of a range of optical devices in Renaissance artistic practice to facilitate the translation of observed volume and space into the plane of drawing or painting.

In this regard Dürer's second illustration is particularly instructive. It shows a draughtsman seated at a table with a large sheet of squared paper before him on which he has begun to draw. However, his eyes do not follow his hand at this moment; rather, he looks through a sighting device onto an upright framed grid, whose squares correspond to those on the artist's sheet of paper below. Looking through the grid to what lies beyond it, we/the artist observe a life-size female nude awkwardly recumbent across the further half of the table, seemingly a sculpture. Clearly, the artist is using the framed grid to establish within its squares where each part of this female anatomy lies, in order to transpose its three-dimensional form onto the squares of his paper. Again, the framed viewing device – in this instance, a grid – acts as the method of artistic translation from three into two dimensions. As Dürer stressed in his notes, the grid enabled the artist to alter the scale, rendering the imitation either larger or smaller, as wished.[57] Here Alberti's celebrated metaphor of the picture plane as a 'window' or intersection has become the artist's working instrument.[58]

The practice was explicitly illustrated in treatises of perspective such as *Eyn schön nützlich Büchlin und Underweisung der Kunst des Messens*, of 1531, by Hieronymus Rodler of Simmern, apparently a one-time pupil of Dürer. To demonstrate the method, Rodler depicted a draughtsman seated before a squared drawing surface in front of a window view overlaid with a grid, tracing the contours of the landscape before him 'square by square' (Fig. 68).[59] Such images appeared subsequently in similar publications across the sixteenth and into the seventeenth century for the purposes of the draughtsman's education, whether artistic or for a wide range of practical applications from engineering to science. This included texts such as the mathematician and philosopher Robert Fludd's 1617 *Metaphysical History of the Two Worlds*, the draughtsman and inventor John Bate's 1638 *Mysteries of Art and Nature*, the mathematician Jean Dubreuil's *Perspective pratique* of draughtsmanship of 1642, or the engraver Abraham Bosse's celebrated 1648 artists' manual on

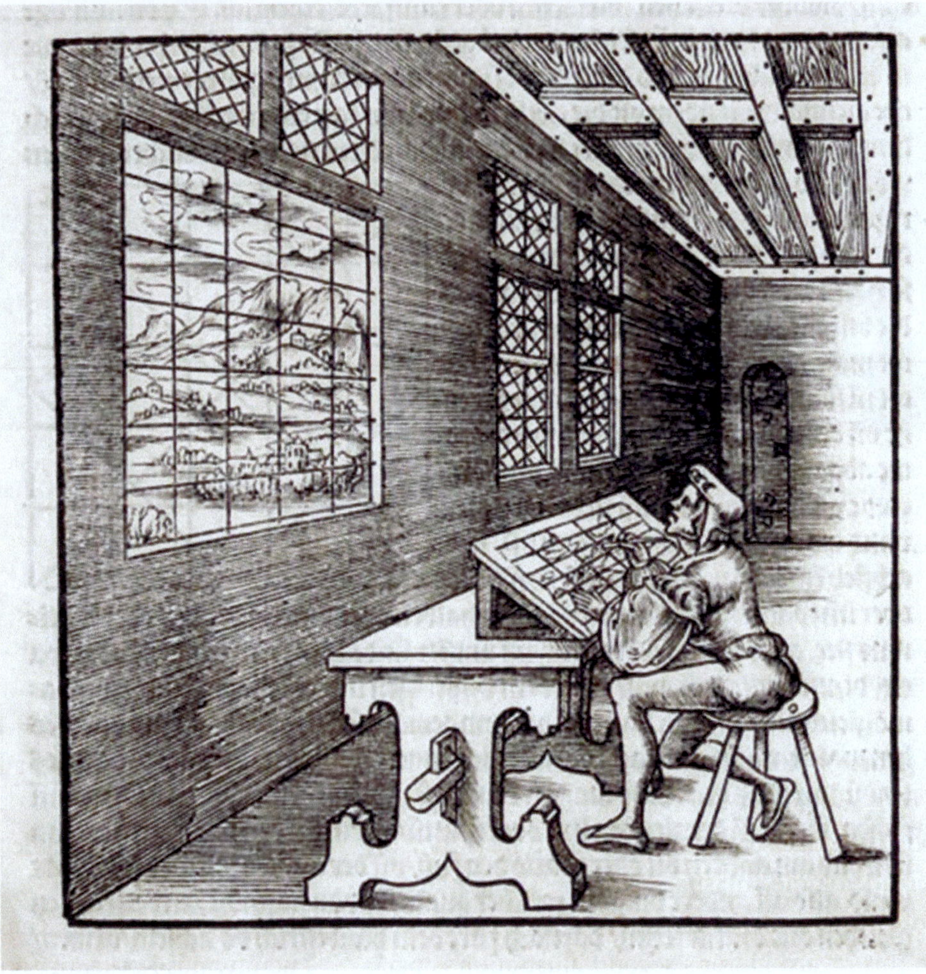

Fig. 68 Hieronymus Rodler, 'A Draughtsman before a Squaring Device', woodcut illustration for *Eyn schön nützlich Büchlin und Underweisung der Kunst des Messens*, Simmern, 1531. Photo: Internet Archive

perspective based on the teachings of the architect Girard Desargues.[60] Bate's manual, intended for the layman, specifically illustrated the squared drawing frame as well as the 'little glass' on the sighting device before it, designed to direct vision according to the sight-lines of optical perspective. Similarly, the Dubreuil book, as a 'how-to' textbook in perspectival design, illustrated the use of a glass window and grid such as Dürer's, also fitted with a sighting device (Fig. 69). It was a practice fully articulated as theory in the writings on perspective of the Dutch mathematician Samuel Marolois: 'Perspective is an art which contemplates all objects through a perspicuous [window or mirror] onto which all visual rays may be projected.'[61] The continuing illustration of such devices in sixteenth-century prints in manuals on perspective testifies to their common and indeed recommended use for draughtsmen. This history of early modern art's technologies of perspectival practice would culminate in the extensive range and development of optical and geometrical devices described by Galileo's friend and fellow Florentine artist-mathematician Ludovico Cardi il Cigoli in his *Trattato pratico*, which illustrated the growing complexity and elaboration of artists' instruments originating in Dürer's glass and grid (Fig. 70).[62] In effect, such practice is the material and practical embodiment of an Albertian theory of painting as a reflective window. The workshop technologies of Dürer's craft are thus fully entwined with the broad conceptualization of painting as a window or

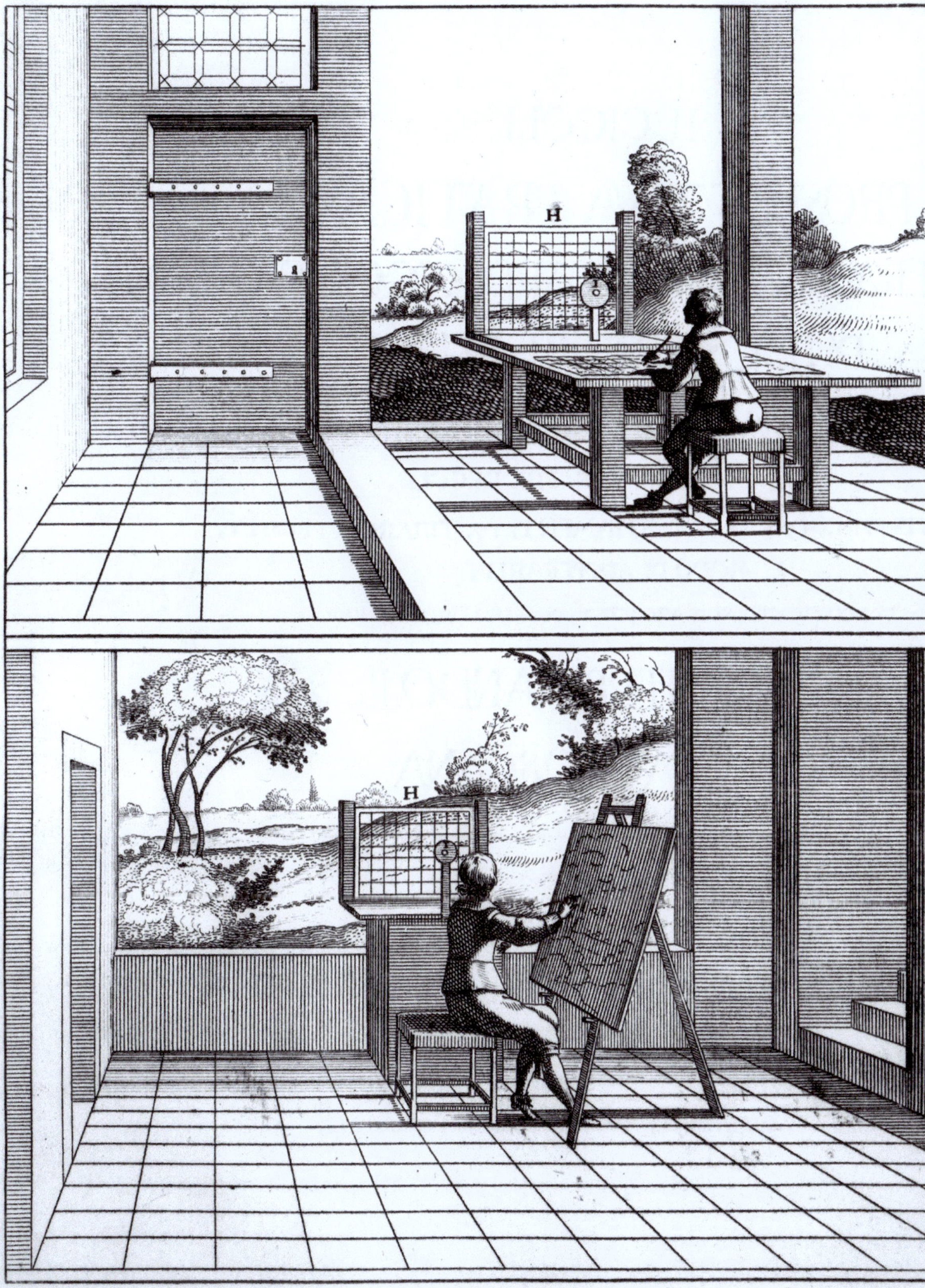

Fig. 69 Jean Dubreuil, *La perspective pratique,* III XCIV 119, engraved bookplate, Paris, 1679.
Photo: Metropolitan Museum of Art

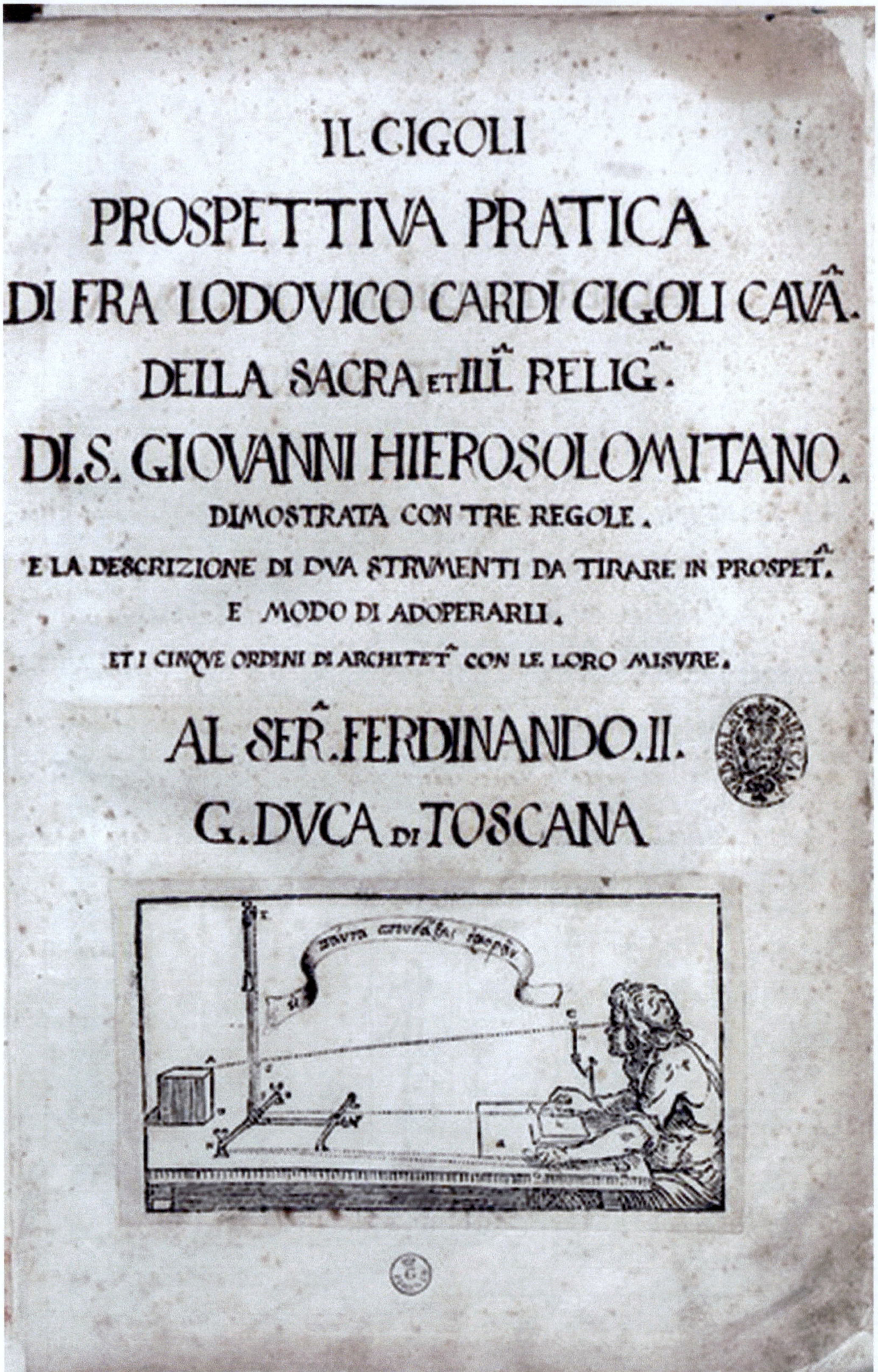

Fig. 70 Ludovico Cardi (il Cigoli), *Prospettiva pratica* frontispiece ms., pen and ink, Florence, 1613, Gabinetto dei Disegni e delle Stampe degli Uffizi 2660A.
Photo: Gabinetto dei Disegni e delle Stampe Uffizi Museum

mirror, as Brunelleschi had demonstrated, and Alberti and Leonardo had theorized. What we witness in Dürer's prints is the practice-based, technological counterpart to a Renaissance theory of mimesis as a mirror reflection.

FATTO AL SPECCHIO

Turning now from the specular instruments of pictorial mimesis to their painted results, the preeminent genre in which we witness the use of the mirror as the Renaissance artist's aid is the self-portrait. This was an artistic development of the sixteenth century, which may be said to have arisen directly as a consequence of the mirror's newly pervasive role in the artist's workshop. Here the use of the mirror as the technology of a mimetic process was clearly instrumental to the self-portrait's developing configuration. The picture-making functions of the mirror thus take on a particular significance.

If the advent of self-portraiture has been the focus of a considerable art-historical scholarship, however, the mirror's role as the instrument of its making has not. What is therefore under discussion is the burgeoning efflorescence of self-portraiture alongside the growing dispersion of the mirror as a workshop tool, deployed in order to translate visual perception into studied artistic form. Tracing the Renaissance rise of self-portraiture, its early examples in the work of the young Dürer and Parmigianino are those of study and instruction, in which these artists first sought out the mirror in order to depict their own features as an exercise in close artistic observation and a demonstration of their mimetic skill. The encomia with which they were heralded fomented the sixteenth-century efflorescence of the genre, collected and celebrated precisely for its closely mimetic specular effects. By the close of the century the self-portrait had consequently become the locus of a concerted theorisation of painting's mirror mimesis, in which artists used their own features to represent the mimetic claims of their art as a form of artistic signature.

The advent of the self-portrait c. 1500 has long been recognized as pivotal not only for the history of art but for the very definition of Renaissance culture itself. For in the emergence of self-portraiture scholars since Jacob Burkhardt's *Die Kultur der Renaissance* (1860) have identified a new, 'renaissance' *individuum* predicated on the closer identification of the self, effected by the mirror-image.[63] Burckhardt further defined this with the term *persönlichkeit*, in which 'people became individuals, and recognised themselves as such'.[64] Critiques of Burkhardt's Renaissance '*persönlichkeit*' by subsequent generations of scholarship have productively complicated both questions of periodisation and the place of self-portraiture within such a teleological account. In acknowledging renewed definitions of Renaissance 'self-fashioning', in Stephen Greenblatt's now-classic reconceptualisation of Burckhardt's *individuum*, scholarship on the self-portrait has been much concerned with adjacent cultural manifestations of individual subject-hood and identity that the rise of self-portraiture may indeed suggest.[65] This has ranged from the extensive revival of historical biography as a literary form of emulation inherited from antiquity to the rise of literary memoirs and autobiography, from the introspective address of the dramatic soliloquy to the inwardly reflective *Essais* of Montaigne, as textual evidence of an apparently new-found early modern interiority. The case of artistic self-representation as the manifestation of a Renaissance authorial identity also perforce draws on larger historical narratives of an emerging 'selfhood' further evidenced across a vast swathe of changing social forms.[66] Within a history of Renaissance art, as Omar Calabrese has argued, the rise of Renaissance individualism manifest in the self-portrait also comprises the ubiquitously acknowledged though greatly understudied transition from a medieval history of anonymous craftsworkers to the complex figure of the Renaissance 'artist' and indeed the very notion of individual style.[67]

While the vast cultural underpinnings of a renaissance selfhood must surely frame the larger analysis of self-portraiture, the direct concern here is with the method of its conception as of its practice, and specifically with the specular instruments of a Renaissance 'auto-mimesis', in Leonardo's phrase.[68] In this regard, the turn of recent scholarship towards a history of Renaissance artisanship at the intersection of a theory of practice and the workshop means of its execution by scholars such as Pamela H. Smith and Patricia Falguières is instrumental.[69] As 'every painter paints himself', in Leonardo's words, so the methods of a mimetic art lay in the mirror image as the basis of a new-found Renaissance self-portraiture. The use of mirrors was the practice-based means of rendering an exactingly specular mode of imitation, certainly predicated on their increasingly plentiful supply across the fifteenth century, but also deeply bound to a Renaissance theorisation of the image as mimesis. The self-portrait represents an artisanal quest for a painted likeness of the self within the larger cultural conventions of its literary invention as authorship. Such images of the reflected self may be understood as both demonstrative and declarative. That is to say, they are self-portraits that turn on the methods of their making in theory and practice, and so on their status as mirror-images. While some bear inscriptions that relate the manner of their making by means of a mirror, others evidence the process of their production pictorially, by visual reference to the artist's presence before its specular gaze.

Among a wide-ranging literature on self-portraiture, scholars have noted that the term itself is a nineteenth- (or even early twentieth-) century one, seemingly born of the same moment as Burkhardt's master narrative of Renaissance historical development in terms of *persönlichkeit*.[70] What has passed largely unremarked is that Renaissance sources instead defined such images of the self by the instrumental means of their making: *'fatto al specchio'* – made from a mirror. In Jennifer Fletcher's prescient survey of this terminology, Venetian inventories of collections by Marcantonio Michiel, Gabriele Vendramin, and Alessandro Vittoria exactingly described such images in terms of the manner of their making: *'fatto al specchio'*.[71] Further, in Vasari's formative account of Renaissance art he acknowledged the use of a convex mirror for the purposes of self-portrayal as the defining characteristic of the genre. Noting it first within fifteenth-century representations of the self embedded within larger works, in examples by Masaccio, Filippo Lippi, Ghirlandaio, and Raphael's *School of Athens*, Vasari also explicitly identified these self-portraits as *'fatto al specchio'*. In addition, Vasari noted a self-portrait by Alberti then in Palazzo Rucellai as 'a portrait of himself made in the mirror'. Although of uncertain attribution today, as Lukas Madersbacher has recently argued, Vasari's evidence should be viewed alongside Alberti's self-portrait medal, to suggest an emerging genesis of the self-portrait in Florence in the 1430s. Coterminous with Alberti's *Della pittura*, this is suggestive of a new conceptualisation of art as specular. Vasari further noted examples of independent painted self-portraits made in a mirror c. 1500 as various kinds of artistic demonstration of optical skill for interested patrons, such as a request made to Gentile Bellini 'to paint himself from a mirror', or a self-portrait made from a mirror by Andrea del Sarto intended as a companion piece to a portrait of his betrothed, Lucrezia del Fede. Vasari also described making his own portrait in such a pictorial demonstration of mimetic skill, 'made by my own hand, of my face, by means of a mirror'.[72]

Vasari's lexicon for the specular self-portrait further comprised '*fatto alla spera*' or 'made by sphere', by which he meant a convex mirror whose blown-glass form was shaped like a half-globe. Such curving mirrors were as common to the period as those of a plane formation. As elaborated in Chapter 1, the craft technologies of glass-making until the late seventeenth century were largely of blown glass; while the still-soft globules could be slit and flattened, they were just as often factured into domed or convex formations. In either case, the size of a single pane was limited by the artisanal capacity for blowing glass, so that Renaissance mirrors were generally no more than the size of a head. This surely intimated a ready equivalence between the portrait head and the mirror reflection as the instrument and the image of its making. The larger suggestion, as literary scholars of early modernity have advanced most forcefully, is that the growing prevalence of mirrors in the fifteenth century forged a new recognition of selfhood that Burckhardt called Renaissance 'individualism'.[73]

Dürer's youthful depiction of himself drawn in a mirror of 1484 brilliantly announces the self-portrait genre, howsoever documented retrospectively. With this sheet he inaugurated a sequence of portrayals of himself in both drawing and painting that span his artistic career (Fig. 71). In his mature annotation of the drawing Dürer ascertained: 'This I fashioned after myself out of a mirror in the year 1484 when I was still a child. Albrecht Dürer.'[74] If earlier examples such as van Eyck's supposed self-portrait of 1433 (Fig. 44, Chapter 2) continue to be interrogated,[75] the evidence of Dürer's inscription confirms both the drawing's status as self-portraiture and the specular means of its making, for the later annotation in the artist's hand affirms this. The drawing itself is the size of a small Renaissance mirror, material testament to the inferred equivalence between them. With his later inscription, Dürer sought to ensure the self-portrait's transmission to historical memory, as Joseph Koerner has argued, in an act of *gedächtnis* long subsequent to the drawing itself. For the destiny of this drawing by a child was not foreseen at the moment of its making; rather, it may be linked to a portrait of the same year of Dürer's father, the Nuremberg goldsmith.[76] While Dürer the Elder holds a small silver statuette as the emblem of his art, the young artist's hand is instead held in what is surely an act of 'sizing'. With his fingers he gauges the dimensions of a detail of his body as seen in the mirror to capture it accurately in his drawing. In effect, it is a pictorialisation of the draughtsman's ready 'compass of the hand', for the translation of proportions from visual perception to the drawn page. It is a gesture he would repeat in a further drawing of himself dated to 1493, in which his outstretched hand with closed thumb and forefingers are seemingly also gauging his own features in a mirror reflection in order to transpose this to the paper on which he draws (Fig. 72).[77] Here too, his intent gaze scrutinises his reflection in order to draw it, noting the slight distortion of the nose and right cheek in what is surely the bowl of a convex mirror. As the drawing documents, hand, eye, and mirror are the instruments of his auto-mimesis. It is a draughtsman's exercise in the methods of specular imitation.

Parmigianino's early self-portrait of 1525 is, like the 1484 Dürer drawing, the work of a young adolescent, dating to the same moment as Dürer's later inscription of his sheet (Fig. 73). The conjunction of dates suggests a new-found historical awareness of the specular self-image in the early *cinquecento* as a ready means of training the draughtsman's judgment of hand and eye. While of oil paint on wood panel, its conceptual genesis was similar to that of a drawing, for it was made as what Vasari understood as a pictorial experiment. Vasari tells us the young Parmigianino painted it as a virtuoso display of skill in the observation of reflections:

> With a view to investigating the subtleties of art, one day he decided to portray himself, looking in a

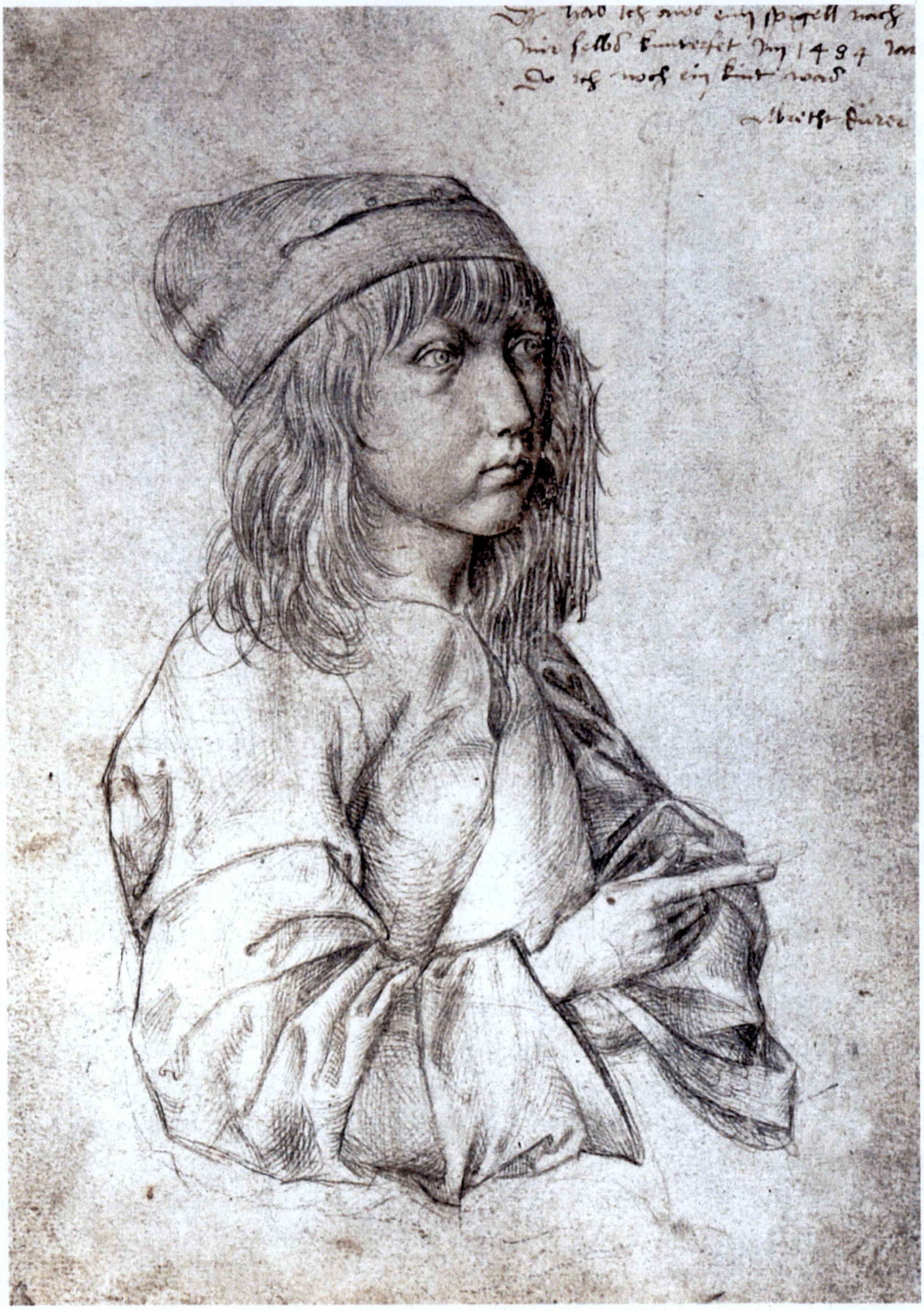

Fig. 71 Albrecht Dürer, *Self-Portrait Drawing Age 13*, 1484, silverpoint on prepared paper, 27.5 × 19.6 cm, Albertina Museum Vienna. Photo: Wikimedia

barber's mirror of a half-globe type. In doing this, he studied the bizarre distortions made by the curve of the mirror's shape, such as of the beams of the ceiling and the strange vanishing point of the doors and architectural features as reflected in the mirror. In play, he sought to imitate it all as he saw it. He then had turned a wooden ball split in half to the same size as the mirror, on which he depicted himself and all that he could see in the mirror with great skill, and particularly himself, in so natural a way it is difficult to believe. And because everything near to such a mirror appears enlarged, while everything in

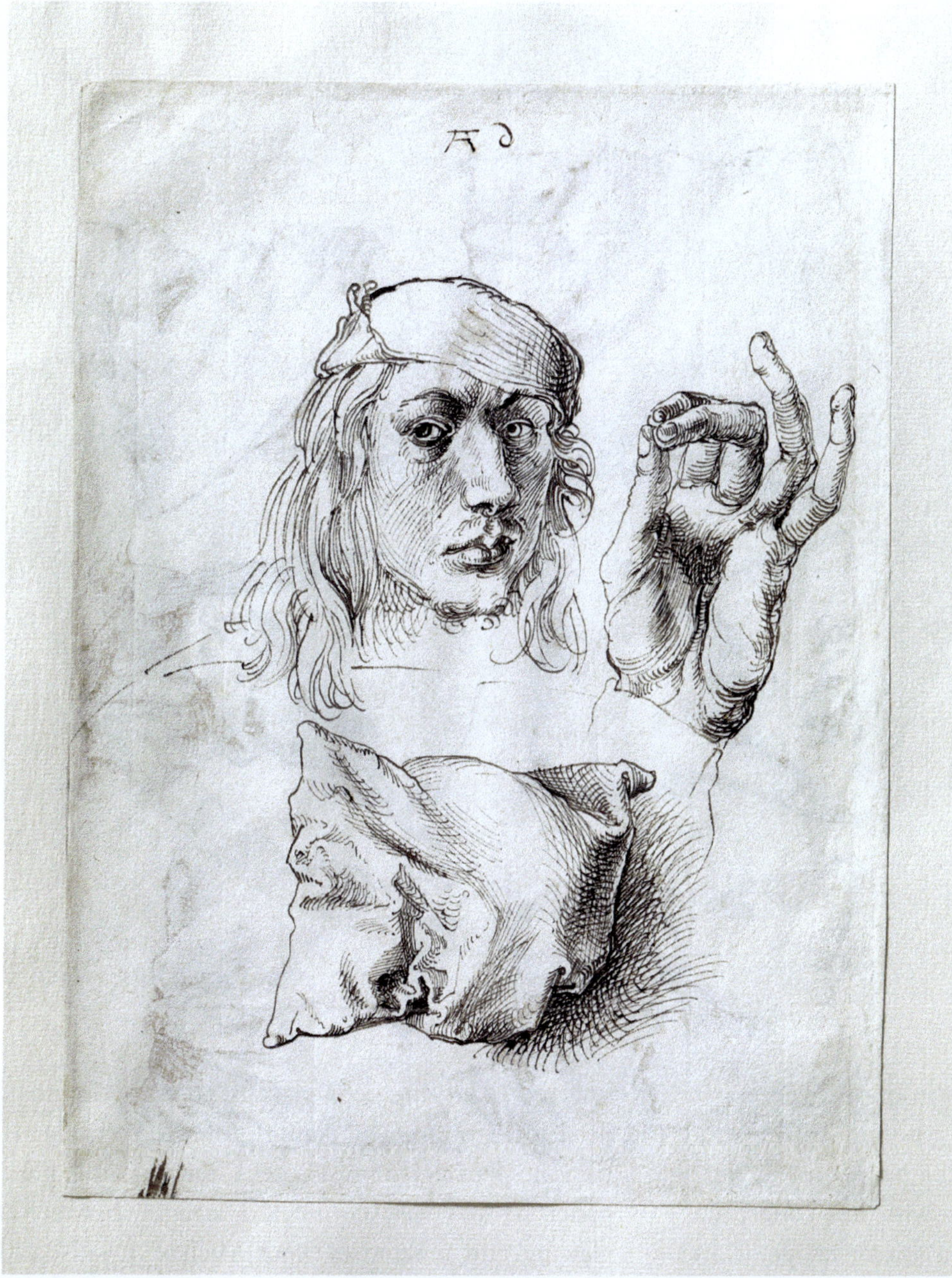

Fig. 72 Albrecht Dürer, *Self-Portrait* (recto), 1493, drawing, pen and brown ink, 27.8 × 20.2 cm, Metropolitan Museum of Art. Photo: Metropolitan Museum of Art

> the distance is in miniature, he made his drawing hand of a great size, as it was in the mirror, so beautiful and lifelike ... his work was so excellent that it was ... life itself: the sparkle of the glass, each reflection, shadow and light so accurate and true that there can be no picture more ingenious.[78]

Here Parmigianino rendered his image on a small convex wood panel he had fabricated to the same dimensions as the convex mirror in which he studied his face, so reinforcing the visual equivalence between them. The image meticulously observes the distortions of the mirror's reflection caused by the rise of the blown glass. This is particularly pronounced in the lozenge-shaped window on the upper left, recognisably that of a reflection in a spherical mirror; and in the exaggerated size of the artist's hand in the foreground.

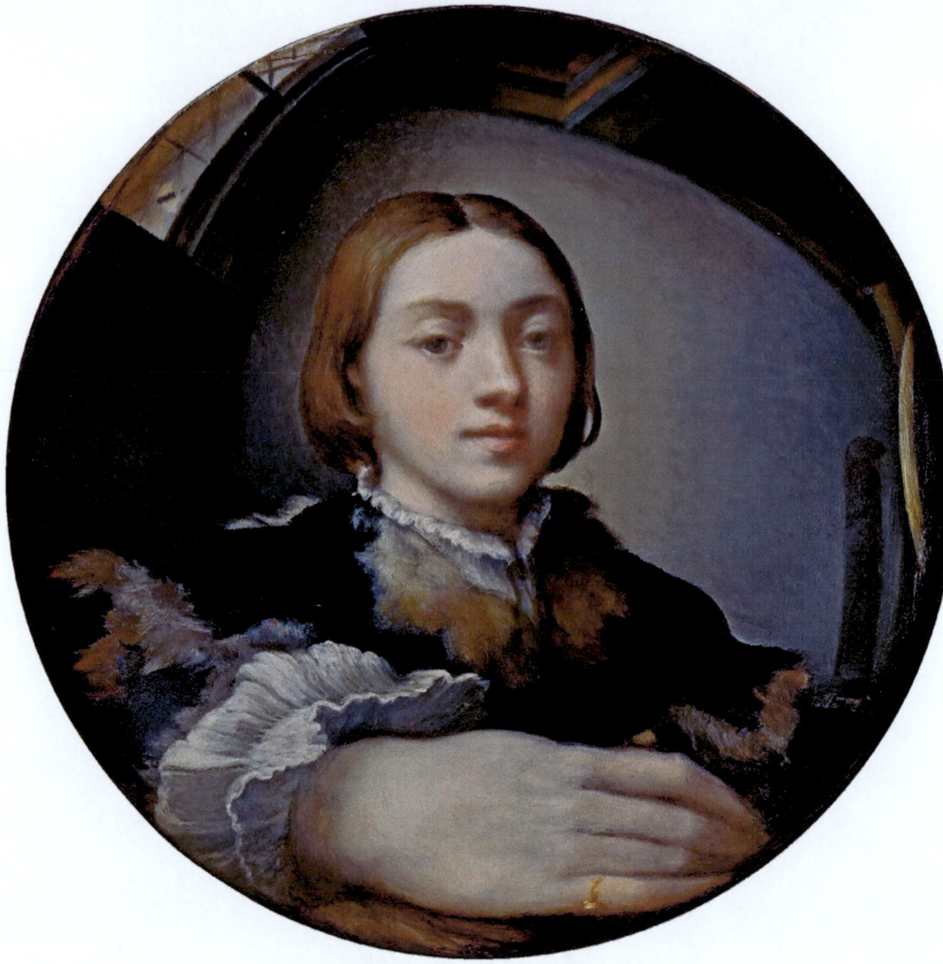

Fig. 73 Parmigianino (Girolamo Francesco Maria Mazzola), *Self-Portrait in a Convex Mirror*, c. 1525, oil on poplar wood, 24.4 cm diameter, Kunsthistorisches Museum Vienna. Photo: Wikimedia

Thus the image conflates the mirror, which constitutes the means of the painting's production, with the material form of the panel on which it is painted. In a doubled play with this conceptualisation of the painting as a mirror image, it also severs the two. To the right side of the painting we see the edge of a tondo-shaped frame, seemingly the mirror from which Parmigianino, according to Vasari, had worked. This has the effect of recalling to mind the temporal processes of the painting's production, for we are witness to the artist studying the canvas on which he paints as if he has just turned from looking in the mirror to observe what he means to depict. Both hand and eye reach forward to what must be the canvas before him, the gaze slightly lowered to its apparent placement in the immediate foreground. The painting is both the reflection in Parmigianino's round mirror and the panel he has just completed, caught between viewing and making in what Michael Fried has argued was the core modality of a fully reflexive early modern specular art, practice and theory intertwined.[79]

A red chalk self-portrait drawing by Pontormo that dates from the same time as the Parmigianino and the Dürer inscription of his earlier self-portrait shows a similar pictorial fusion between the mirror and the sketch, in a confluence of viewing and making (Fig. 74).[80] Here Pontormo stands in a three-quarter profile pose. With his lower arm he draws himself on a

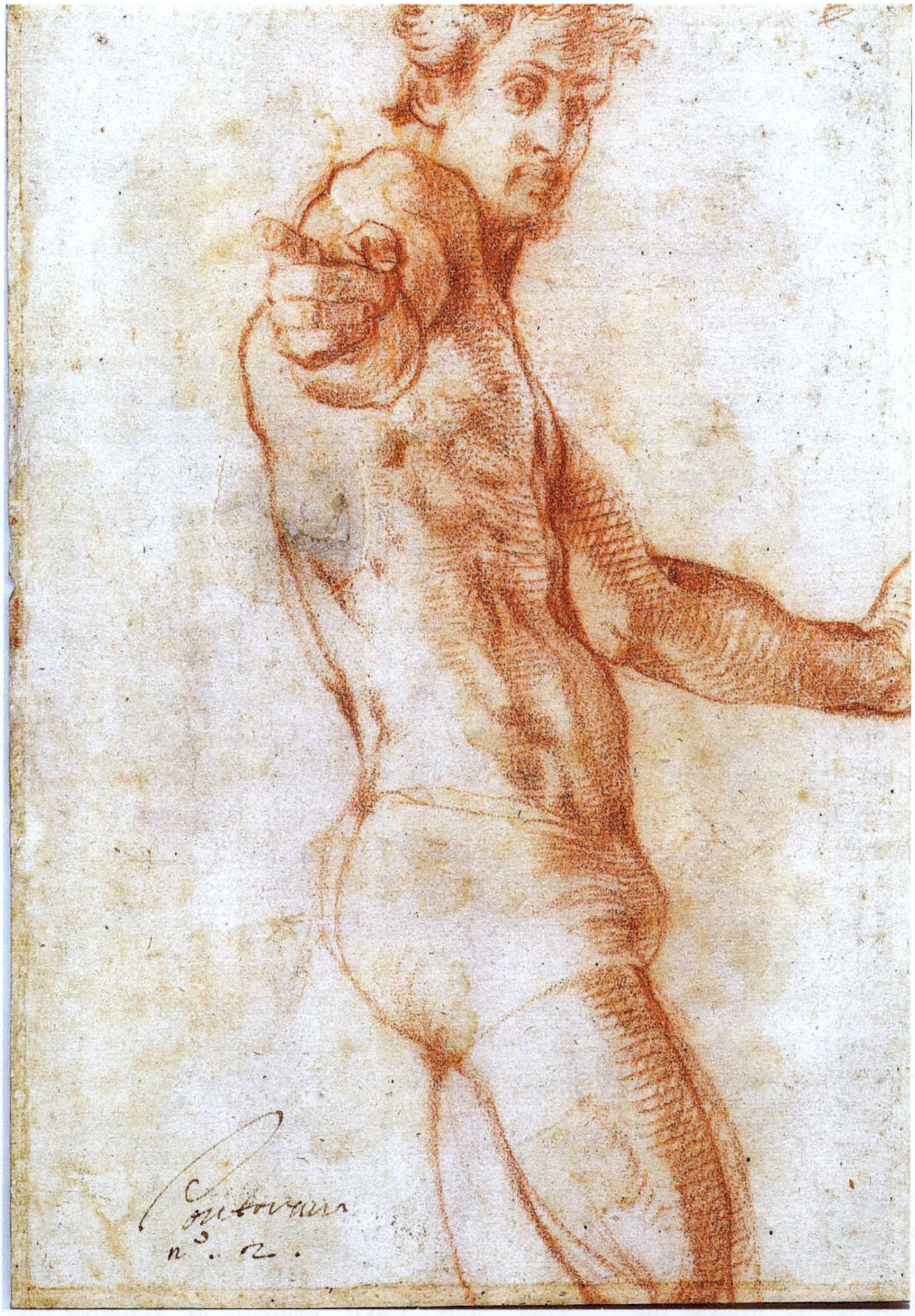

Fig. 74 Jacopo Carucci da Pontormo, *Self-Portrait Drawing*, c. 1525, red chalk on paper, 28.1 × 19.5 cm, British Museum, London.
Photo: British Museum

sheet of paper directly in front of him, placed just outside the image to the right. The other hand extends forward towards the surface of the picture plane, seemingly touching it with the tips of his fingers. The lower fingers are loosely curled into the fist, while the index finger and thumb extend forward in a gesture of sizing. His gaze is directed towards the tips of those fingers. Like Dürer's early self-portrait drawing, Pontormo is apparently measuring what he sees in a mirror, his fingers spanning a detail in a compass of hand and eye. Pontormo would seem to practice

Michelangelo's famed *giudizio dell'occhio*, that the artist's true compass should lie in the judgment of the eye, rather than depending on the mechanical devices and grids that Dürer had elaborated for draughtsmen in his treatise on measurement, also of 1525.[81] As the study of a reflection in a flat mirror Pontormo's image is reversed, with the consequence that the drawing hand appears to be left but in fact would have been right. Like the Parmigianino, a bifurcation is at play in the pictorial logic of the composition. On the one hand, there is an elision of the drawing with the mirror, in its representation of what Pontormo saw. On the other hand, we understand the drawing as a process occurring to the right of this sheet as we regard it. Hence its temporal structure moves from mirroring to drawing, like the Parmigianino, so pictorializing the practical means of its own production.

Alessandro Allori, a pupil of Pontormo's student Bronzino, took up the pictorial theme of mirror-image making in a youthful painted self-portrait of c. 1555 that would presage his future as court portraitist to the Medici (Fig. 75). Here he depicts himself in the act of painting, a fine brush held up to a canvas occluded by the edge of the picture that we view, with a fragmentary representation of a palette in the other hand. He gazes into the foreground with considered intent, eyes half lowered, at what must surely be a small Renaissance mirror on a table before him, in which he studies his features in order to paint his own image. The slight distortion of the line of the nose suggests the rise of a convex mirror. As in the Pontormo drawing, we witness the artist as he works between the attentive observation of his image in a mirror reflection and the raised hand's translation of vision into the concerted application of paint. As Fabiana Cazzola-Senkpiel has argued, the painting demands we read it not only in terms of a rising Burkhardtian individualism that has dominated scholarly discussion of Renaissance self-portraiture, but also as an artistic theory of the mimetic image in its representation of the act of painting.[82] The panel was seemingly intended as a presentation piece, sent by the youthful artist into Florentine court circles and thereby making its way into the Medici collections. Here it would later form part of a nucleus of self-portraits that would over time come to define the genre. This was also the case with the Parmigianino that was gifted to the pope, Clement VII, in order to vouchsafe this youthful artistic career, and then in turn to the Venetian art critic Pietro Aretino, in whose house Vasari saw it. Further promoting its acclaim, Aretino's ownership of the Parmigianino subsequently led to its acquisition by Rudolf II for the imperial collections in 1608 as a particularly brilliant exemplification of the specular self-portrait as the display of mimetic skill.

Similarly, the Uffizi self-portraits, along with a cognate group at the Accademia di S Luca in Rome, would establish the category of self-portraiture as an independent genre of art through the concerted display of their collection.[83] Leopoldo de Medici and his curator Filippo Baldinucci initiated the collection of artists' self-portraits, seemingly in the 1670s. They were not displayed as an ensemble until the eighteenth century, however, and their move to the Uffizi *corridoio* was in the late nineteenth century, apparently coterminous with the rise of the self-portrait term. From the sixteenth century on, much of the Uffizi's self-portrait collection was the result of gifted portraits by artists in homage to the Medici as patrons and collectors. They were often painted in response to Medicean request and rewarded with honorific counter-gifts. Howsoever defined in language, it suggests the painted image was understood as a gift of selfhood within ties of patronage, as both subject and author, in an artistic genre fully bound to the demonstration of its specular method. It was the painter's most eloquent *exemplum* of auto-mimesis in theory as in practice.

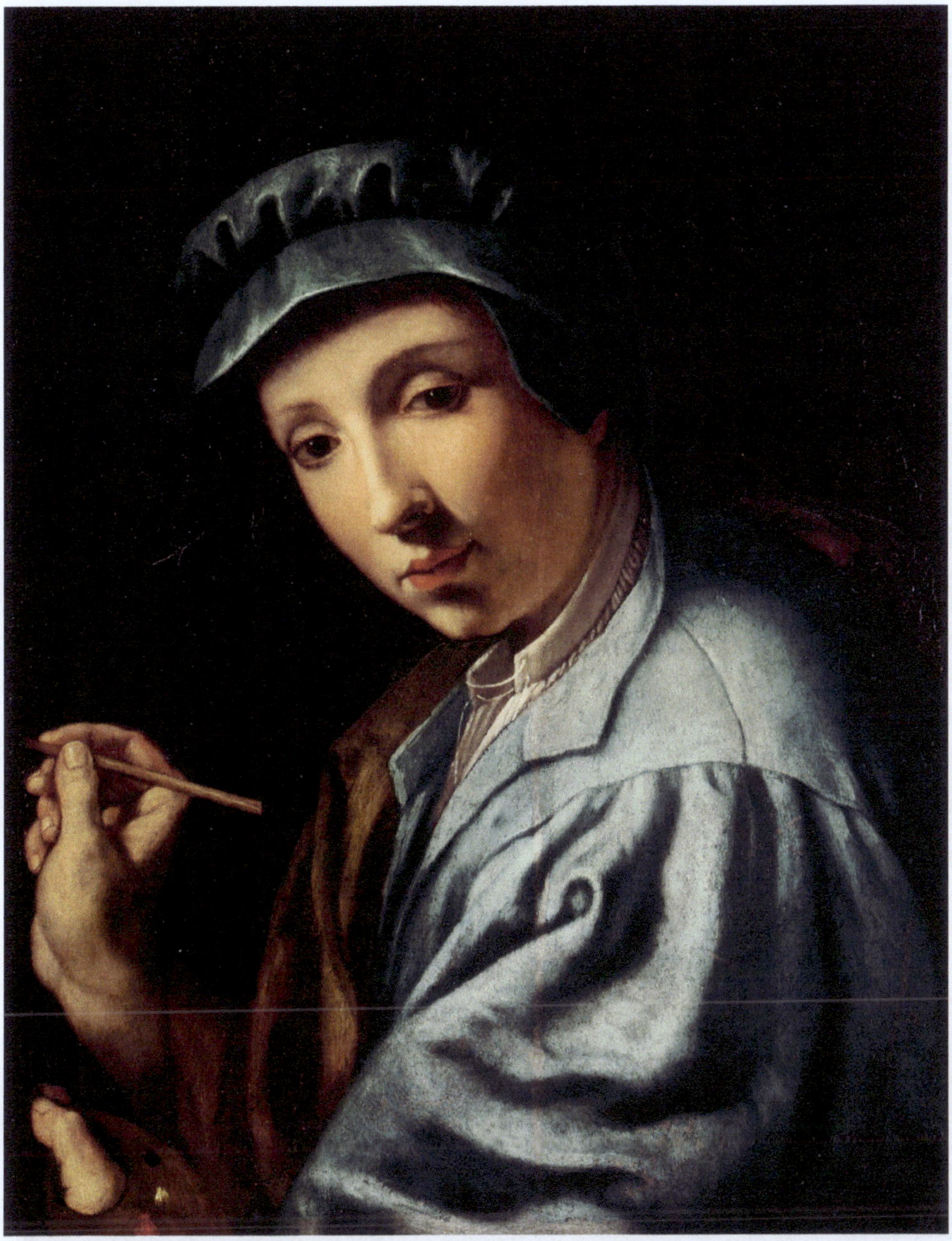

Fig. 75 Alessandro Allori, *Self Portrait*, c. 1555, oil on panel, 60 × 47 cm, Uffizi Gallery, collection of self-portraits, Florence. Photo: Wikimedia

Closely contemporaneous with Allori, the Cremonese noble and subsequently court painter in Madrid, Sofonisba Anguissola, painted a series of self-portraits in the mid 1550s including a miniature in a locket format (Fig. 76). In varnished watercolour on parchment, the portrait is set in an oval metal frame with a pendant surmount (though its current locket enclosure is a later one, and the portrait itself likely was originally in a tondo form). In Anguissola's hands she bears a circular shield or medallion with heraldic decoration of her father's name as if in embossed gilt and bronze. Around its circumference she painted a further inscription: SOPHONISBA ANGUSSOLA VIR[GO] IPSIUS MANU EX [S]PECULO DEPICTAM CREMONAE (Painted from a mirror with her own hand by the Cremonese maiden Sofonisba

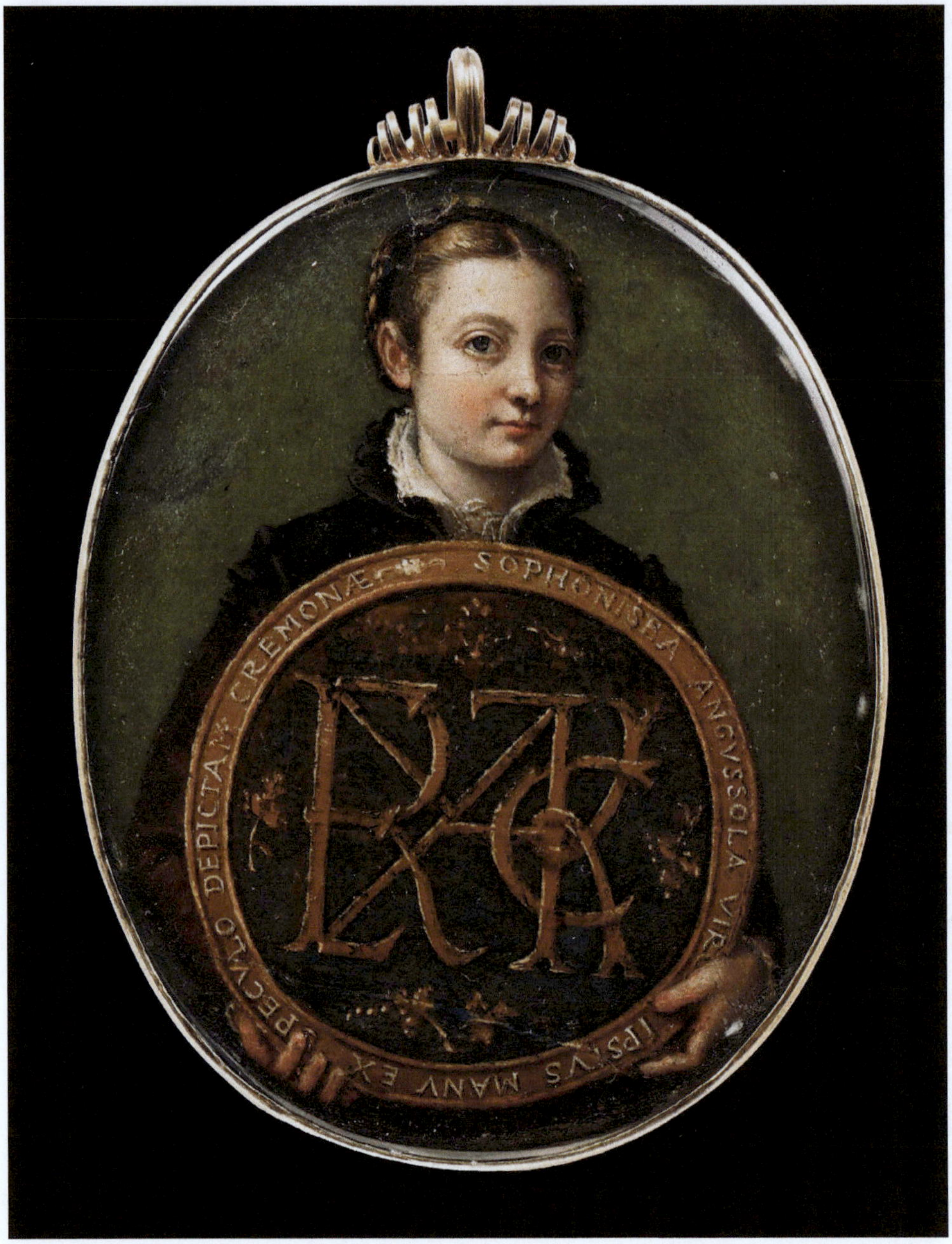

Fig. 76 Sofonisba Anguissola, *Self Portrait in a Locket Frame*, c. 1555, varnished watercolour on parchment, 8.3 × 6.4 cm, Museum of Fine Arts, Boston. Photo: Museum of Fine Arts, Boston

Anguissola), so acknowledging the specular means of its making. In size the portrait imitates the use of small mirrors as pendant jewels in this jewel-like specular portrait, and so the means of its making. Its glowing colours and sparkling varnish further suggest a seeming mirror reflection of the artist, like a compact mirror. At the same time, the reference to the medallion she holds in her hands claims the ancient art of medallic portraiture as her own. Other self-portraits depict her variously: as an artist painting a scene of Mother and Child, wielding a fine brush before the easel as an allegory of *Pittura* herself (Łańcut Castle, Poland), or in a witty reversal where she becomes the subject of the painting-within-the-painting as if depicted by her master before the easel, Bernardino Campi (Pinacoteca Nazionale, Siena). In both of these, the artist's right hand is raised high to the canvas about to engage in the act of painting while the gaze is directed towards the artist-viewer or the apparent though absent mirror, as the source of the portrait's making.[84]

Also painter to the Spanish court, the Netherlandish artist Anthonis Mor depicted himself in the same year, 1555, in a picture destined for the Medici gallery of self-portraits as with the Parmigianino and the Allori. Within a large easel painting, Mor sits before a painted easel, with brushes, palette, and mahlstick in hand. The canvas-within-the-canvas is completely blank, however, but for a sheet of paper pinned to it, bearing a poem penned in Greek, so that text takes the place of image here, while the image of the artist is instead before the canvas about to paint. Testament to his humanist learning, along with his fine clothes of silk and velvet, the poem is surely witness to the exalted standing of the artist at court. Like Anguissola, Mor uses text within the image emblematically to disclose the specular means of his portrait's making:

> Yes, he has made this portrait of himself.
> He painted it with his own skilled hand.
> He studied himself in a metal,
> In front of the mirror,
> Oh what an excellent artist!
> The counterfeit Mor which you now behold,
> Mor . . . presently speak![85]

Mor's tribute to the mirror and the brush as the methods of his mimetic art is to the illusionistic power of its seeming presence, so lifelike as to lack only speech.

Lavinia Fontana, a Bolognese painter active in Rome, also painted self-portraits, including a self-portrait in the studio in a roundel image on copper (Uffizi, dated 1579). Like the Anguissola, Fontana here engages with the self-portrait genre through recourse to a jewelled metaphor of its typology, denoted in the lustre of her copper support and its miniature size. Here she depicts herself as a scholar-painter whose studio is reminiscent of the humanist's *studiolo*. As other scholars have argued, this was a defining paradigm of the sixteenth-century self-portrait, tied to the intellectual claims of the Renaissance painter's art.[86] Gazing directly at us, apparently into the mirror from which she works, she conflates her painting with the mirror roundel that the copper tondo support suggests. Her hand holds a quill pen poised above a page of paper at her desk, with an ink well beside her and a multitude of classical sculptures by which she claims her artistic authority. Also destined for the Medici self-portrait collection at the Uffizi, though originally for the Roman collection of the Spanish Dominican antiquarian scholar Alfonso Chacon, it asserts Fontana's historical presence within the self-portrait genre. A further diminutive self-portrait of herself playing the clavichord, now in the Accademia di San Luca in Rome but likely made as a betrothal gift for her marriage in 1577, similarly portrays the artist in a marital allegory of painting's musical harmony. Behind, an easel stands beside a window to illustrate the Albertian nature of painting's art. Alongside, an inscription testifies to her self-portrait's specular means: 'Lavinia, Prospero Fontana's virgin daughter, depicted herself using a mirror in the year 1577' (Fig. 77).[87] Again, both of Fontana's self-portraits turn around the conjunction of the painter's eye and hand.

The Brescian painter Girolamo Savoldo, a pupil of Paolo Pino who worked in Venice, also took up the pictorial trope of the artist's eye and hand depicted in the mirror in a specular self-portrait in armour of c. 1529 (Fig. 78). Depicted in a seated three-quarter pose, mirrors behind and to the side capture the artist and his accoutrement of gleaming armour and rich velvet from further points of view. This is set within an enveloping atmospheric perspective that further recalls Venetian painting's debt to Leonardo. It is surely also a pictorial manifesto of Venetian painting's

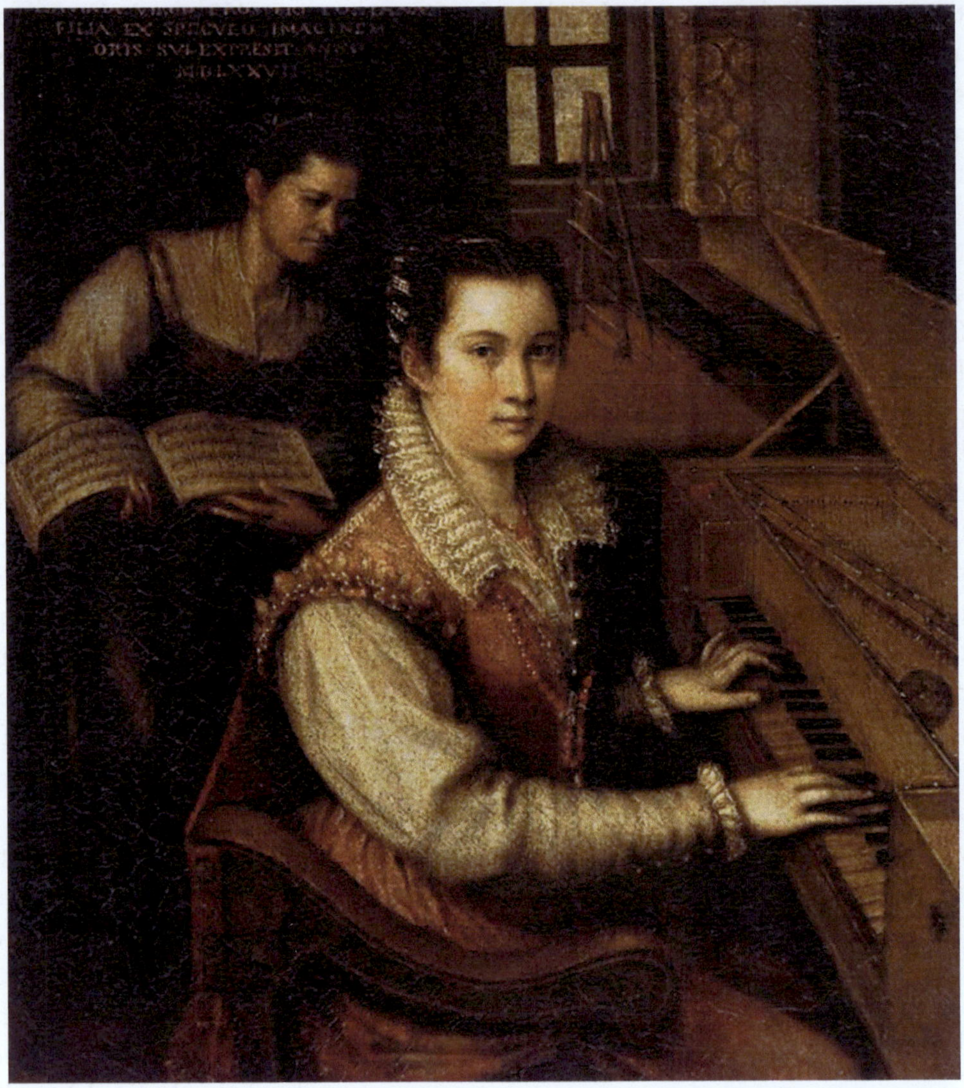

Fig. 77 Lavinia Fontana, *Self-Portrait at the Spinet*, 1577, oil on canvas, 27 × 24 cm, Accademia di San Luca Rome.
Photo: Wikimedia

giorgionismo. For the depiction of mirrors and armour is a demonstrative recollection of Giorgione's lost work of specular reflection, apparently of a St George, discussed in Chapter 2. It was a work that both Pino and Vasari described as Giorgione's intended *exemplum* of painting's specular means, and with which Savoldo's armorial portrait was long confused. In the image of Giorgione, the mirror on the left reflects a range of textiles and textures – velvet, muslin, gleaming steel – in a pictorial declaration of Savoldo's *venezianità*. In the foreground, his right hand gestures towards a further piece of armour, a cuirass, casting myriad metallic reflections. His outstretched left arm points to the mirror to his side, where both hands are further reflected. This is corroborated by the *cartellino* bearing his signature, which is present only in a mirror reflection, alongside the portrait of the artist himself.[88] This specular doubling of the representation heightens both hand and eye, and mirror, as the instruments of Savoldo's mimetic art.

Artemisia Gentileschi's allegorical self-portrait as an *Allegory of Painting* of the late 1630s is structured by a similar pictorial trope, which speaks to the ongoing significance of this

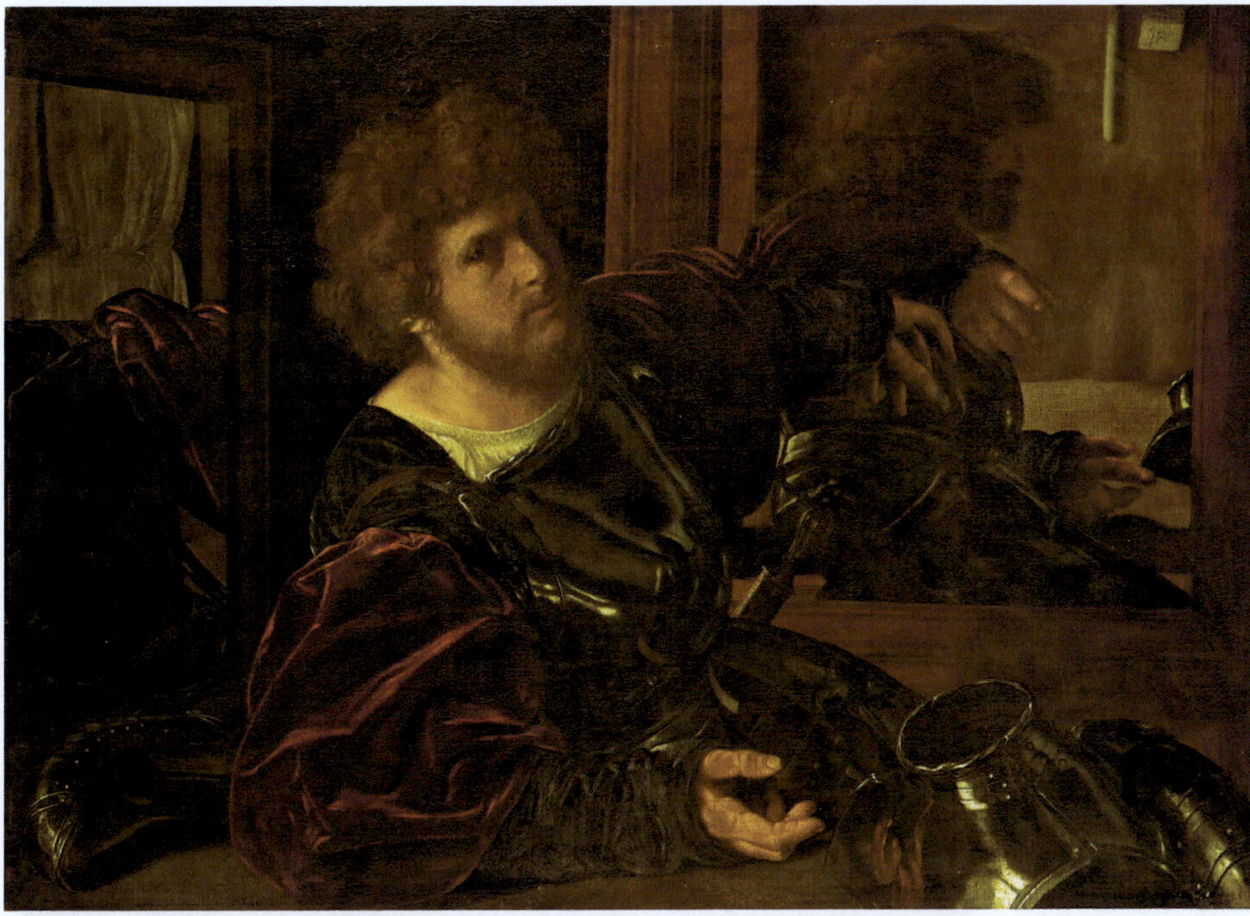

Fig. 78 Girolamo Savoldo, *Self Portrait or Portrait of a Man in Armour (so-called Gaston de Foix)*, 1529, oil on canvas, 91 × 123 cm, Musée du Louvre, Paris.
Photo: Musée du Louvre

specular conception of the self-portrait, in both representation and process, across the century divide (Fig. 79).[89] Her many self-portraits were heralded by the poets for their specular address: in the verse of the Neapolitan Girolamo Fontanella: 'Gaze in the mirror, and then, on the canvas / With your lovely brush, paint yourself.'[90] In this instance, the elision of painting with its mirror reflection is an elliptical one, for the mirror is 'present' only beyond the boundaries of the frame. The image shows Gentileschi in the act of painting. As many scholars have noted, she has depicted herself in the guise of the allegory of *pittura* taken from the well-known iconological handbook of Cesare Ripa, bearing 'a chain of gold from which hangs a mask inscribed "*imitatio*"'. The mask motif, as Ripa identified it, was to represent the conjunction of painting with poetry.[91] The canvas on which Gentileschi paints is before her, her right hand holding a brush raised and about to mark the surface, while in her left hand she holds a palette. That celebrated hand holding a fine brush was commemorated in a drawing by the French portraitist Pierre Dumonstier as the artist's defining instrument, inscribing it: '*apres la digne main de l'excellente e sçavante Artemise*' (after the worthy hand of the excellent and wise Artemisia).[92] As in the Pontormo drawing, and also in Sofonisba Anguissola's portrait-on-an-easel as if by Campi, Gentileschi's painted gaze is directed beyond her hand to the edge of the canvas. What she

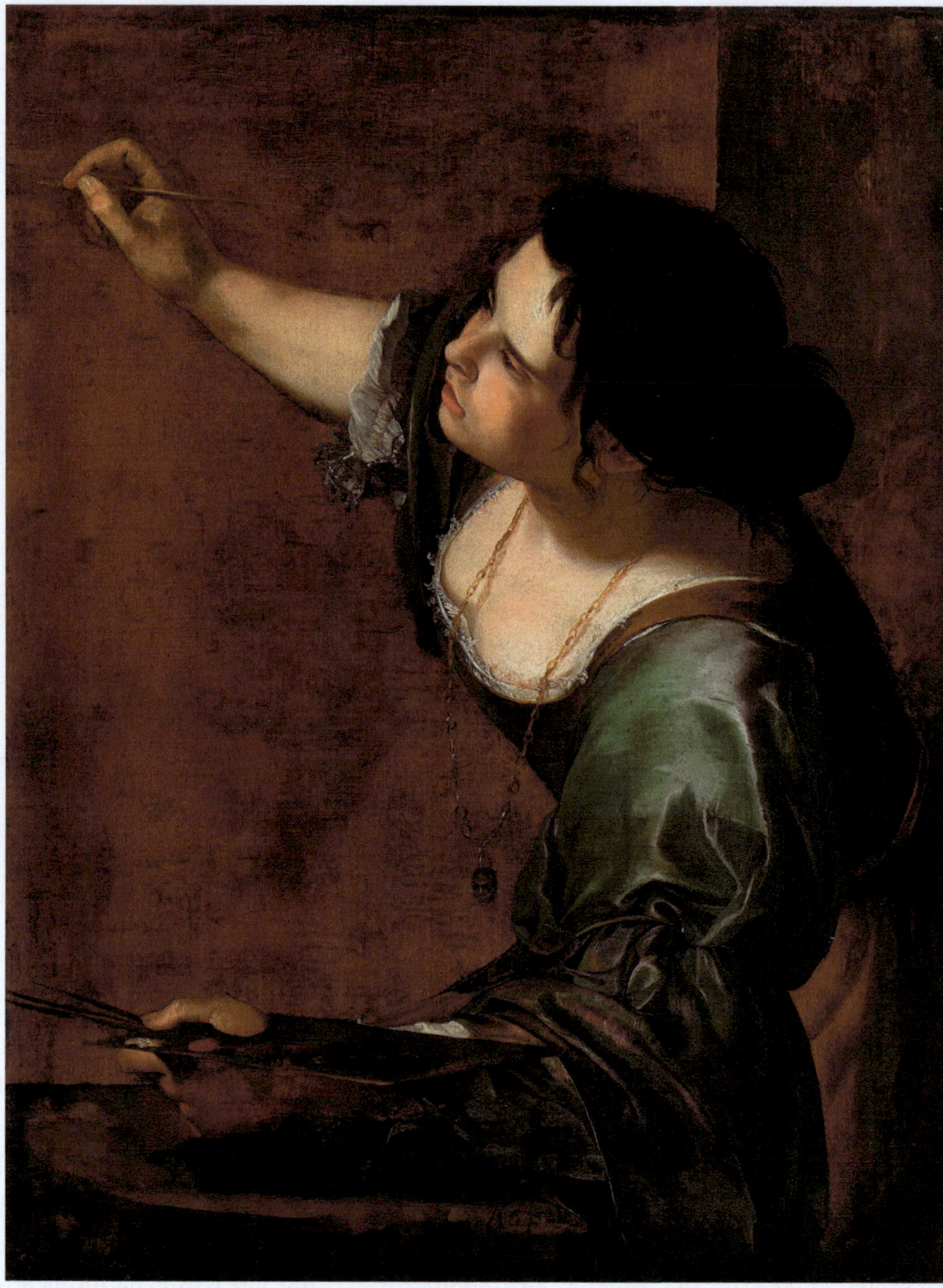

Fig. 79 Artemisia Gentileschi, *Self-Portrait as the Allegory of Painting (La Pittura)*, c.1638–39, oil on canvas, 98.6 × 75.2 cm, Royal Collection Trust. Photo: © Royal Collection Trust/ His Majesty King Charles III 2023

contemplates is surely the mirror in which she studies her reflection before applying her paint. Here too, the absent mirror is both the instrument and the matrix of pictorial representation. In mirror-image, Gentileschi paints the process of her portrait's own production.

A series of self-portraits by Annibale Carracci also give pictorial demonstration to the painter's art bound to the mirror reflection. In an early example by Annibale in the company of the painter's family, he stands in the foreground with his palette of colours in one hand and a brush in the other (Fig. 80).[93] His painting hand, near the bottom right of the picture, is suspended before the canvas-within-the-canvas on which he apparently works. Only the side of his canvas within

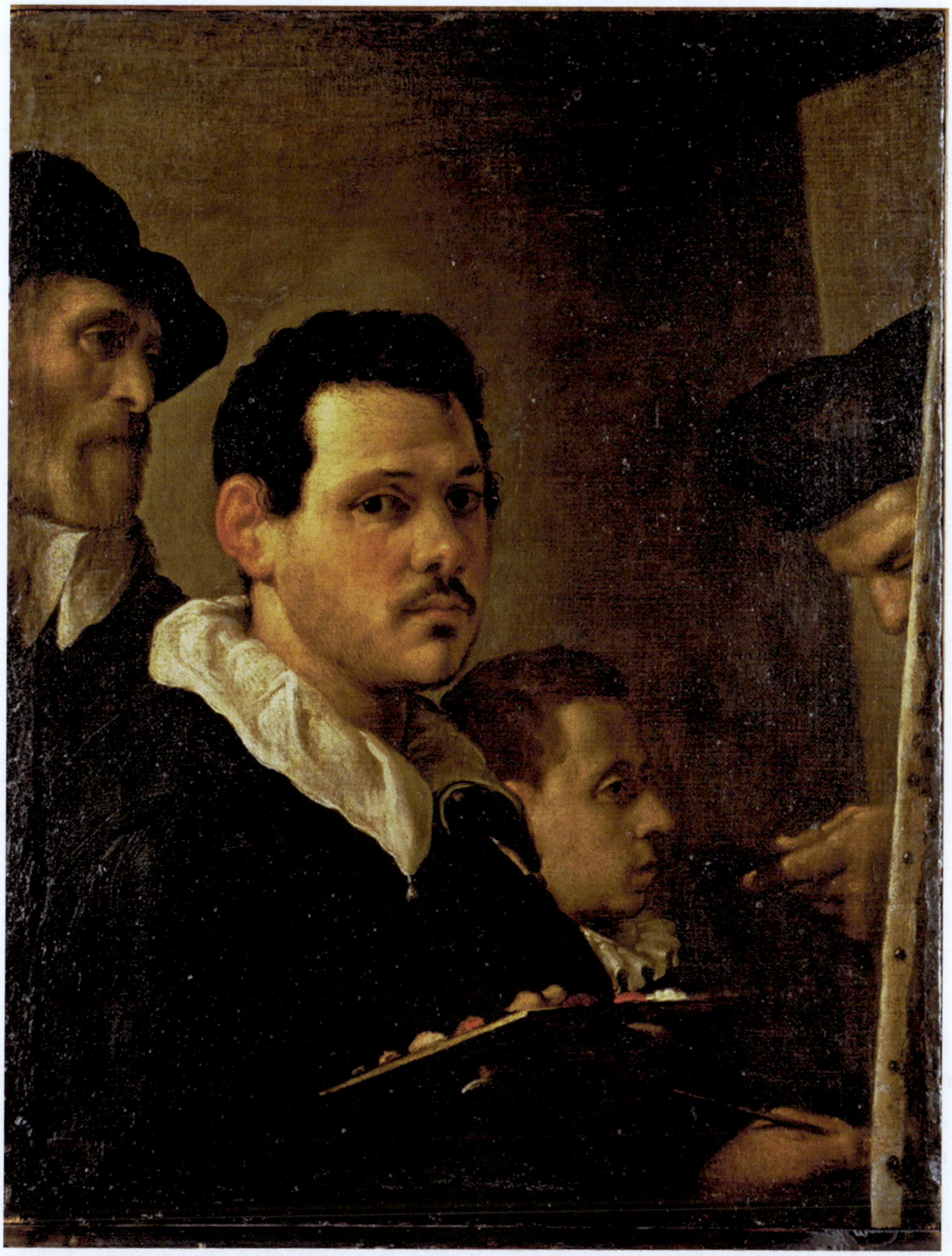

Fig. 80 Annibale Carracci, *Self-Portrait with Other Figures*, c. 1593, oil on canvas, 60 × 48 cm, Brera Pinacoteca Milan. Photo: Wikimedia

the painting is visible, as a white-edged slip marked by nails to hold the cloth in place on its stretcher, placed at a slight angle to suggest that its dimensions are the same as the picture we regard. He faces toward his painting yet his gaze is outward, which is surely the locus of the mirror he apparently uses to depict himself and the scene surrounding him. Like the Gentileschi *Allegory*, the presence of the mirror just beyond the painting is implied by the pictorial logic of the picture itself. Diagonally opposite to Annibale stands his brother Agostino, in a cap, his head bent down towards his raised hand, which bears a spatula loaded with black pigment. Annibale's painting hands appear one above the other to display their primacy in the act of

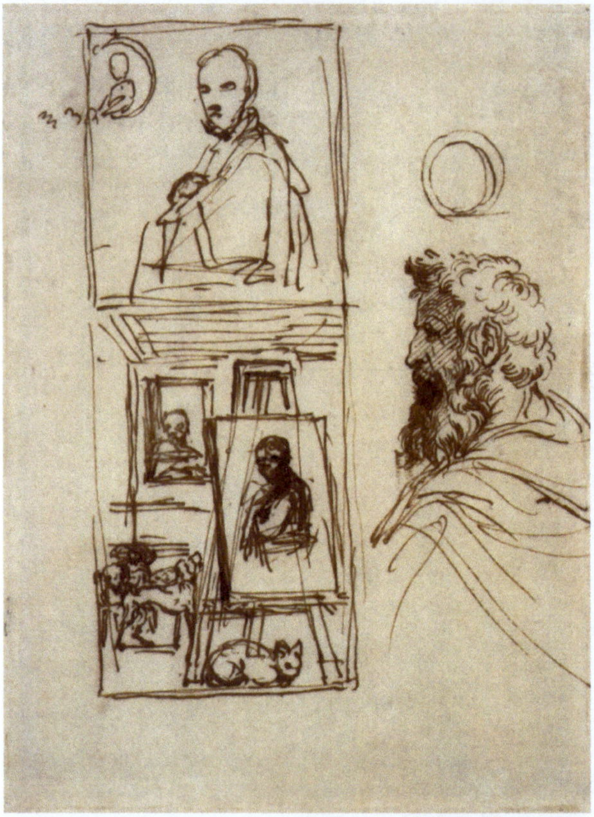

Fig. 81 Annibale Carracci, *Study for the Self-Portrait on an Easel*, c. 1603–4, pen and ink, 24.5 × 18 cm, Windsor Castle Royal Library, Royal Collection Trust.
Photo: © Royal Collection Trust/His Majesty King Charles III 2023

painting. Yet the manual practice of their art is ever yoked to the painter's eye, which we regard in Annibale's gaze towards us. As we are thus elided with the mirror that must surely have been the optical means of the painting's production, so our gaze upon the painting becomes the mirror-view of Annibale's in return. Annibale's considered attention to the hand and the eye as the conjoined instruments of his art is further underscored by the rapt attention of the young boy beside him, and the older man to the left, as they watch his painting take form.

A preparatory drawing of c. 1604 by Annibale shows a succession of compositional ideas for a self-portrait similarly bound up with its own specular address (Figs. 81 and 82).[94] To the right is a bust of a man in classical garb surmounted by a roundel form. The left side is devoted to two sketches for a painting of himself. Above, he depicts himself in a three-quarter pose, his torso also enveloped in a cloak from which only his right – painting – hand protrudes, looking out to what must be his mirror reflection. To the left just above him, the same cloaked figure appears again within a tondo in reduced scale, so repeating the roundel motif on the drawing's right. As other scholars have suggested, this is surely a notation of Annibale's own reflection in a circular mirror, thus identifying the source of his self-portrait's means. It suggests a Leonardesque doubled reflection of his figure, seen from behind as well as from the front, as a further conceit of the specular image. Its tondo form is also that of the compass and so the sign of mimetic art's perspectival geometry. It may also suggest Vasari's account of the young Giotto, apparently discovered by Cimabue for his precocious draughtsmanship, manifest in the execution of a perfectly mathematical circle performed before a wondering papal audience.[95]

The tondo form as the sign of art recurs in a number of specular self-portraits, configured variously as both mirrors and circles. For the story of Giotto's perfect circle surely comprised within it the artistic authority of the compass, sizing tool of artists and architects as Filarete had explicated, but also mathematicians following Euclid's geometrical forms, as the full title of Dürer's *Underweysung* made clear – by the circle of the compass and the ruler's line. In Filarete's bronze relief self-portrait of 1445 with members of his workshop, he depicted himself with a circle just above his head, the sign of the architect's compass he holds before him as the emblematic instrument of his art. The noble Genoese artist G. B. Paggi also chose to represent himself in a painted portrait of c. 1580 that brings together the compass, the mirror, and the painter's brush as the conjoined implements of art (Fig. 83).[96] In the foreground of the painting stands a

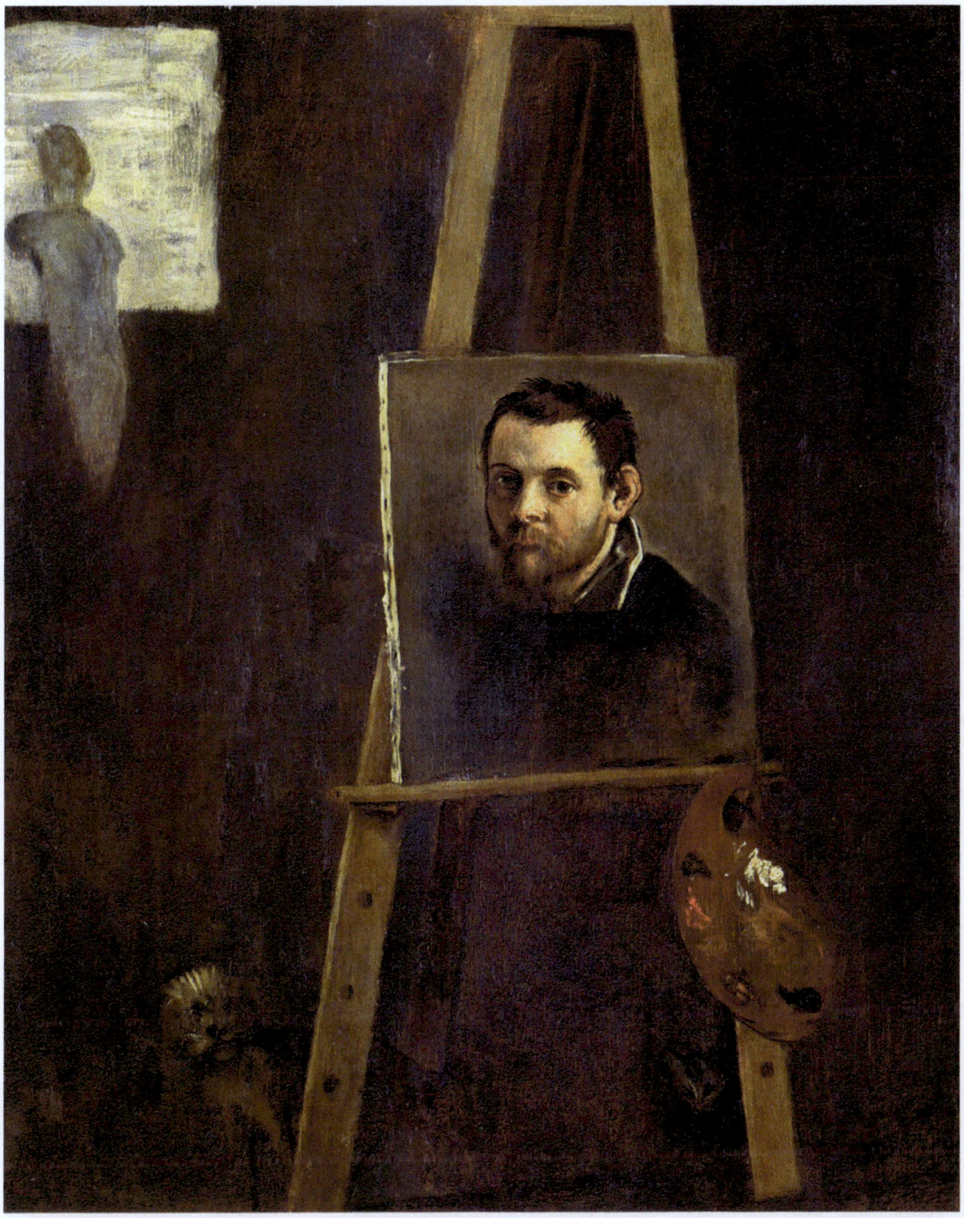

Fig. 82 Annibale Carracci, *Self-Portrait on an Easel in the Artist's Studio*, c. 1604–5, oil on wood, 37 × 32 cm, Galleria Uffizi Florence. Photo: Wikimedia

fellow-artist in three-quarter back profile, in black tunic and hat, before a drawing table. In his right hand he holds a compass to the paper on which he is drawing a circle. His left hand is raised in a rhetorical gesture, as if elucidating the point of his drawing to his companion. On the wall behind hangs a framed flat mirror in which we see the reflection of his face from the front. The mirror also displays what the portrait otherwise withholds: his companion, and the painter of the piece, who must therefore stand in the space before the painting as both viewer and maker of the image. Paggi is in three-quarter view, his gaze intently fixed on what he sees in the mirror. At the same time, his brush-wielding hand is raised, just touching the 'frame' of the mirror, to suggest the edge of the painting on which he works.

Similarly, Rembrandt's late self-portrait among circles of c. 1665 (Fig. 84), one of some eighty

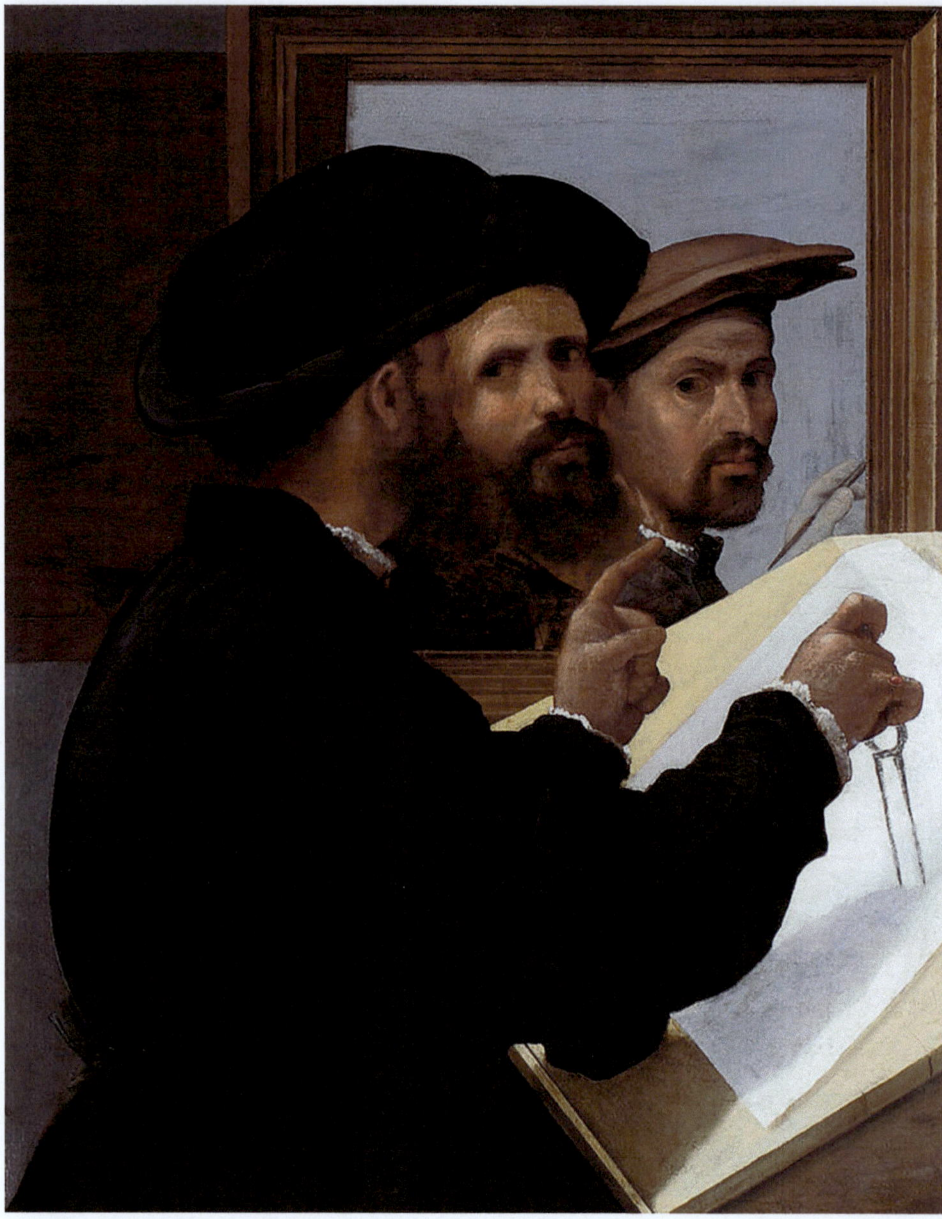

Fig. 83 Giovanni Battista Paggi, *Self-Portrait with an Architect Friend*, 1580s, oil on canvas, Martin von Wagner Museum, Würzburg. Photo: Wikimedia

self-portraits in painting, drawing, and etching, from across his working life, depicts the aging artist set against a configuration of circular outlines, wearing a painter's smock, tabard, and linen cap with a palette, brushes, and mahlstick in his left hand. Technical research on the picture's surface suggests this was originally sketched in with the brush in his left hand held up to the canvas, according to the direct reflection of a mirror image, then transposed, so documenting materially the use of a mirror by which to compose. Behind him, his head is loosely positioned between the outlines of two great circles, both of which are elliptically intercepted by the canvas edge. One runs through the figure of the artist from the head through the painting arm; the other seems to encircle the canvas-within-the-canvas as the emblem of its art. The nailed edge of the canvas on which he works runs along the upper right of the canvas we view.[97] In a full

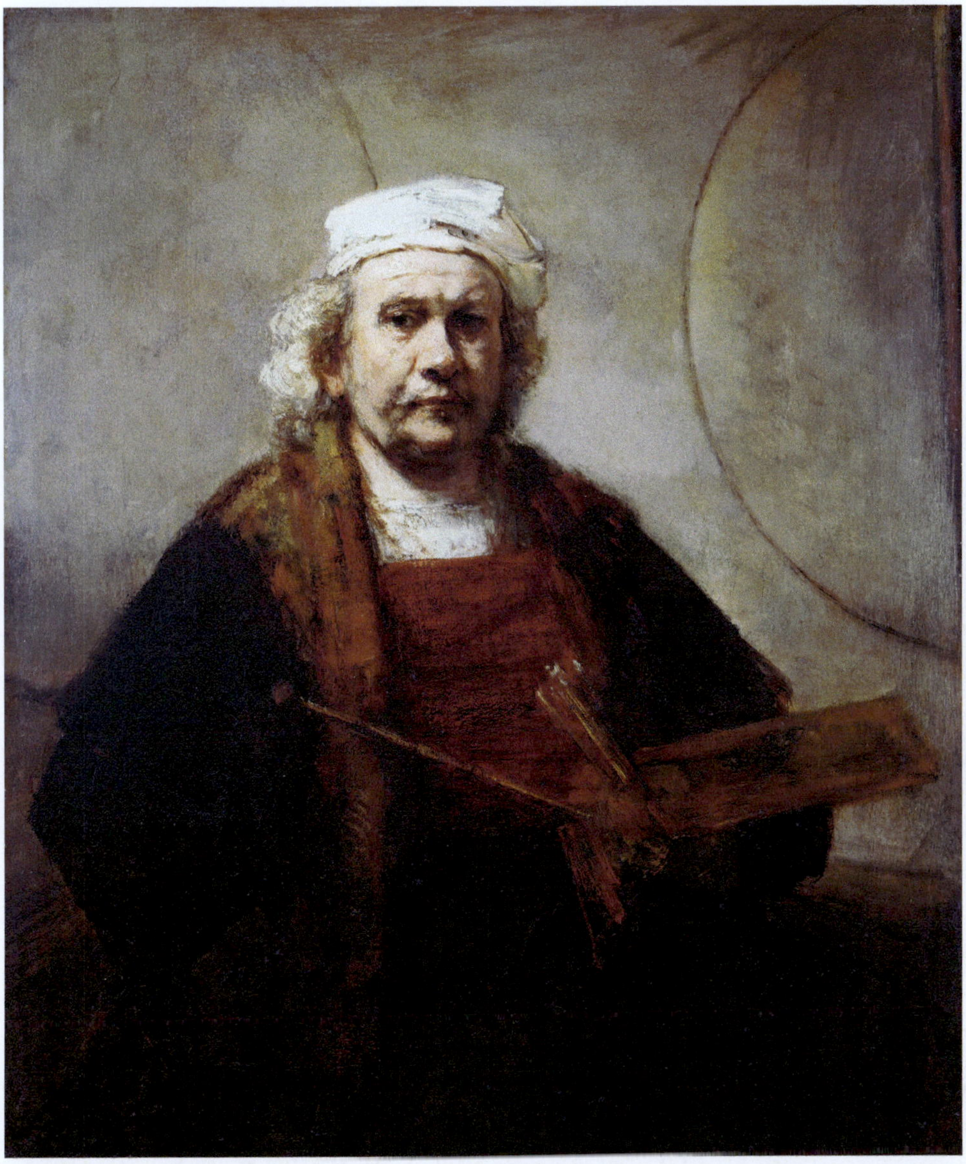

Fig. 84 Rembrandt Harmenszoon van Rijn, *Self-Portrait with Circles*, c. 1665, oil on canvas, 114.3 × 94 cm, Iveagh Bequest, Kenwood House, London. Photo: Wikimedia

elision of painting and reflection it seems to pictorialise the injunction of Rembrandt's pupil, the painter and art theorist Samuel van Hoogstraten in his *Academy of Painting* of 1678, to paint 'in front of a mirror, so that you are both performer and observer'.[98]

In his early self-portrait of c. 1628, Rembrandt painted himself before an easel in the studio (Fig. 85).[99] Here he is a diminutive figure in the shadowy back of the room, enveloped in thick robes, a wide-brimmed Dutch hat, and heavy leather boots. The canvas before him, by contrast, assumes a monumental size in relation to the artist, its edge picked out in bright sunlight. The marked shift of scale and 'fishbowl' curve to the perspective suggest the use of a convex mirror through which to paint. The studio is otherwise bare but for a few jars on a trestle table. In Rembrandt's left hand he holds a mahlstick and a clutch of brushes, in his right hand a small palette and brush. Behind him are further painter's palettes hanging on the wall, as if in the

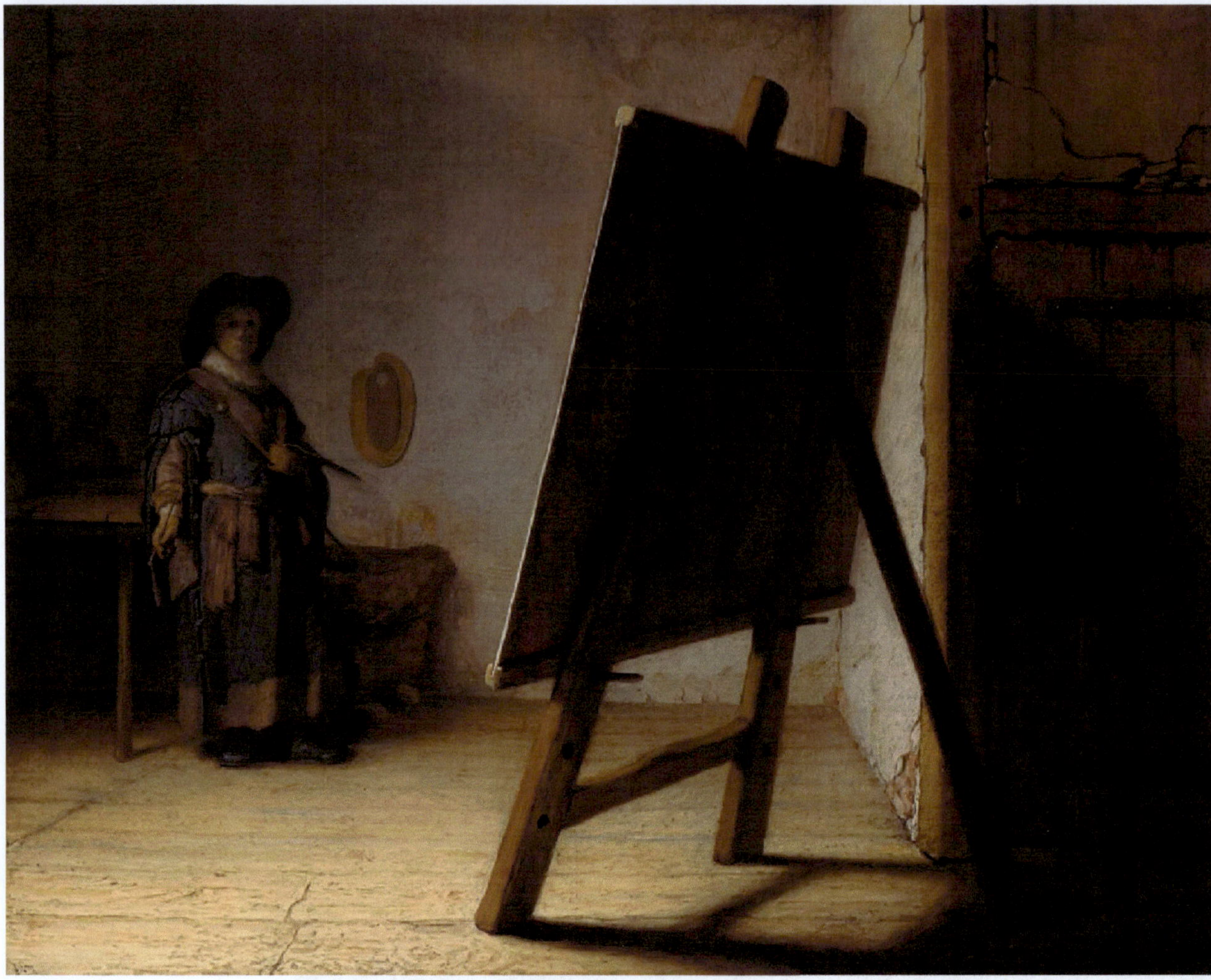

Fig. 85 Rembrandt Harmenszoon van Rijn, *Self-Portrait of the Artist in the Studio*, c. 1628, oil on panel, 24.8 × 31.7 cm, Museum of Fine Arts Boston.
Photo: Museum of Fine Arts, Boston

shape of small shields, to carry the painter's distinctive earthy pigments.[100] The canvas looms before him, as for us, though we see it only from the back. The wooden slats of the easel, like those of the closed panelled door beside it, underscore that our view of the picture he paints is withheld from us. The juxtaposition of the painter and his canvas imply that it is himself he is painting, standing back to regard the picture as we do. In this moment he turns his gaze from the canvas towards us. This is surely in order to consult the mirror from which he paints, in which he beholds as we do the object of his art – himself painting. It is a full elision of painting with its subject, as reflected in the artist's mirroring gaze.

Returning to Annibale's drawing (Fig. 81), the compositional sketch of the lower half of the sheet depicts his developing conception of the self-portrait on an easel that would form the basis of his painted self-portrait for which this is a preparatory sketch. The pen and ink figure in the sketch seems to hold a collection of brushes under his arm. Behind is, again, a repetition of the bust-length portrait, now shown frontally. Seen through a squared frame, it suggests both a further painting and a mirror reflection in what is surely a purposeful elision of the two. In the painted versions of the composition, the background figure is transformed into what has been identified as a sculptural herm or terminus figure. As other scholars have argued, it may be a possible reference to *vanitas* but also to a kind of immortality in art, recalling Alberti's evocation of portraiture as that which makes the absent 'present', as the counterfeit of a mimetic art. The term stands before a silvered square opening that recalls the mirror of the drawing, here surely a window, so underscoring the Albertian theory of their equivalence. In the painted version of the composition (Fig. 82), in the foreground stands an easel from which a palette hangs, daubed with colours of white, red, and black. The canvas on the easel is itself in a three-quarter view, like the self-portrait within it. To the left the tacked edge of the canvas is visible, emphasising its status as a work in the making and still without a frame. The surface of the painting throughout is sketch-like, as is the demeanour of the self-portrait: the careless creases of the painter's collar and the ruffled hair underscore the daub-like character of the painting's finish, further echoed by the palette below. The painter's gaze is direct, however; surely that of his own reflection as he studied it in a mirror. The metaphor of painting as reflection is repeated through the luminosity of the mirror-like silver window behind. The sequence of compositional development in the preparatory sketch further manifests the conceptual proximity between window, mirror, and painting, that underlies the self-portrait form.[101]

A red chalk portrait-drawing of Poussin (British Museum) long attributed to the artist himself was, according to a later inscription by a subsequent collector of this work, also '*fatto nello specchio*' – made by means of a mirror. As the inscription further relates, it was a gift of the self in effigy to his beneficent patron Cardinal Camillo Massimi, to whom he gave lessons in drawing. Here he is dressed in a painter's cap and open shirt, as if in artistic homage to the materialisation of theory that Annibale had also propounded: 'we painters speak with our hands'.[102] Perhaps a reference to his patron Cardinal Massimi's own gesture of decorum in deference to the arts, in taking up apprenticeship in the artisanal drawing instruments of a painter, it was an image of the figure of the artist that Michelangelo had also drawn in his own self-portrait in a turban (Louvre Museum), and that Bernini would later emulate in receiving Queen Christina of Sweden dressed in a sculptor's smock.[103] In a twin set of self-portraits for his closest Parisian patrons, Poussin chose to depict himself variously, according to his differing modes of address for each: on the one hand, the courtly Paul Fréart de Chantelou, celebrated patron and critic of the arts (Fig. 86); on the other, the wealthy merchant-banker and art collector Jean Pointel.[104] For Chantelou, Poussin represented himself in classical dress, with a scroll in his right hand, which bears a ring surmounted by a pyramidal point diamond as an emblem of the art of light and shadow in the representation of volumetric geometrical form. First delineated as an element of painting's theory by Alberti, the representation of volume through the application of light and shade was critical to the practice of a mimetic art of painting, and elaborated in all subsequent treatises of perspective, just as it was central to the teaching precepts of early modern art academies. Behind Poussin's academic figure stand an array of canvases framed in bevelled gilt, the first of which, otherwise blank, bears his signature-inscription. It serves both to occlude and to disclose the canvas behind it, of which we see only a fragment to the side, depicting a female allegory of *Pittura*, her diadem crowned by a winged eye in direct imitation of her own below. From outwith this canvas-within-the-canvas, two arms extend in an embrace towards her. The embrace of art is surely that of the *amateur*, or art-lover, in which the viewing patron Chantelou

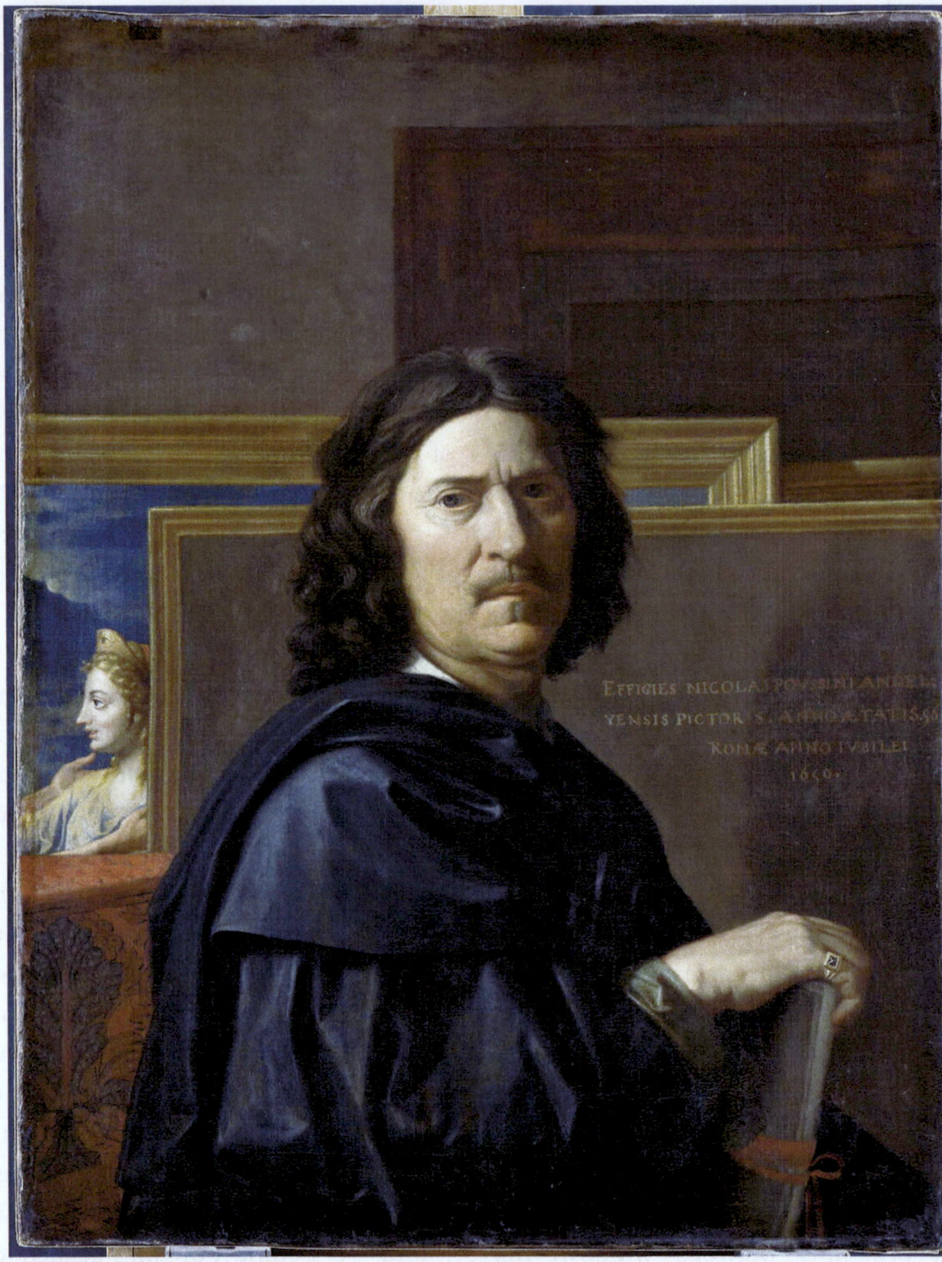

Fig. 86 Nicolas Poussin, *Self Portrait for Chantelou*, signed and dated 1650, oil on canvas, 0.98 × 1.165 m, Musée du Louvre Paris. Photo: Musée du Louvre

and the artist are here joined, like a *Narcissus*, in a further Albertian reference to the love of art reflected in the Ovidian pool of classical myth that so fully nurtured Poussin's art. The winged eye of this *Pittura*'s diadem, as an antique reference, may further recall this motif as the emblematic winged eye of Alberti's portrait medal (Fig. 32), as well as the 'eye' of Poussin the painter that she surely personifies.

In a further coupling of myth and self-portraiture, Annibale's contemporary and sometime rival Caravaggio was famously said to have depicted his own features as a Medusa head. The beautiful yet terrifying gorgon was a further allegory of the captivations of art whose gaze could transfix the viewer into stone, recast as the marbled forms of sculpture (Fig. 87). This painting would also join the Medici-Uffizi

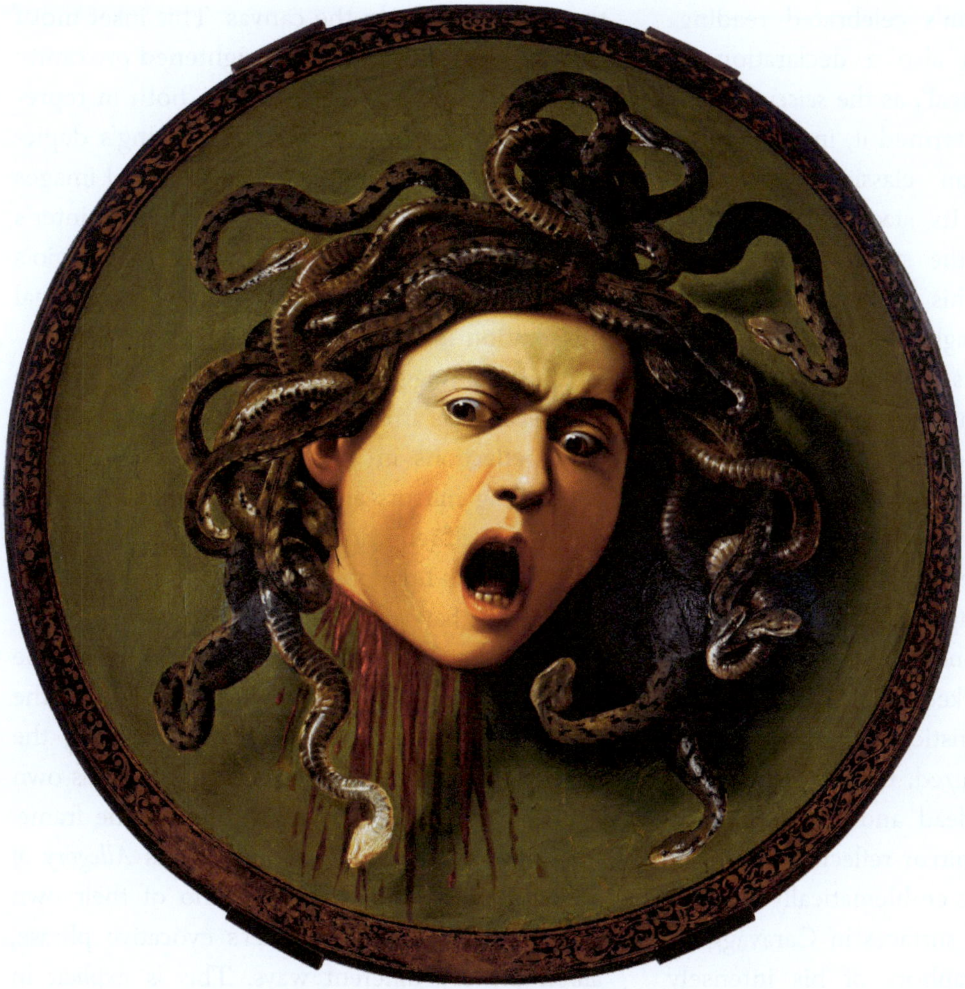

Fig. 87 Michelangelo Merisi da Caravaggio, *Medusa*, c. 1597, oil on canvas mounted on wood, 60 × 55 cm, Galleria Uffizi Florence. Photo: Wikimedia

collections, though not as a self-portrait but as a piece of ceremonial armour, where decorative representation of a gorgon head was the classical sign of a valorous *terribilità*. For Caravaggio's Medusa was painted onto the surface of a wooden parade shield, tondo in shape, convex in form, like a mirroring shield of Homeric renown. Thus its material basis recalled the Netherlandish linguistic elision of *schild* – shield – with painting, in a pictorial acknowledgement of painting's emblematic history within heraldic art, as elaborated in Chapter 2.[105] It surely also recalls the art-historical trope of painted armour as a mirror reflection within sixteenth-century *paragone*-comparisons of painting with sculpture issuing from Giorgione's lost work of armorial reflections, like Medusa's petrifying gaze. Medicean patronage circles would also have understood it as a reference to the ancient sculptor Phidias, who carved his self-portrait as well as a Medusa head into the shield of his cryselephantine Athena Parthenos sculpture, as a 'signature' of the transfixing beauty of his art. Further, it would have recalled the young Leonardo's lost 'Medusa' shield, which he similarly painted onto the wooden buckler of a huntsman, depicting a fiery serpentine creature of such specular verism as to induce both terror and wonder in the viewer in equal measure. In Rome it would also have been seen comparatively, in relation to Annibale Carracci's depiction of the Medusa head in Perseus' mirroring shield at Palazzo

Farnese. In Louis Marin's celebrated reading, Caravaggio's *Medusa* is also a declaration of Caravaggio's art of the 'real', as the *seicento* critic Giovanni Pietro Bellori termed it, in considered contrast to the Roman classicism of both Annibale and Poussin. Its startling mimesis is intently mirror-like in the studied observation of the face, recalling his seventeenth-century biographer Giovanni Baglione's testimony that Caravaggio used mirrors to draw his own features. Like the Parmigianino, also painted on a wooden roundel to approximate a convex mirror, close specular observation is notable in the slight distortion of the cheek over the rise of the panel's centre. Medusa was the mythological sign of a 'captivated' mirroring, capturing the subject in its gaze by turning it to stone, as in Ovid's account, which Caravaggio reworked as an allegory of the arresting force of his veristic art. As poets of the day immediately recognized, the *Medusa*'s art is to be at the same time 'dead' and 'alive' – both as real and as fictive as a mirror reflection.[106]

Self-mirroring extends emblematically across a range of reflective glass surfaces in Caravaggio's work, as pictorial metaphors of his intensely specular mimetic art. Since the celebrated cleaning of Caravaggio's Uffizi *Bacchus* in 1922, the finest detail in the reflections depicted in the carafe, according to Mina Gregori, included 'the reflected head . . . of a male who wears a contemporary costume with a white collar; there also seems to be a painting seen from the back, as though on an easel'.[107] Both versions of Caravaggio's *Boy Bitten by a Lizard* (Uffizi/National Gallery London) similarly suggest the reflection of a window in the carafe of water, with the intimation of the room in which the work was painted. In Caravaggio's attentive art of visible realism, he seemingly rendered a reflection of himself and his surroundings as he worked. Through the prism of the reflective glass carafe, Caravaggio pictorialized his own artistic process in front of a mirror whose reflection he could then transpose onto the canvas. This inset motif furthers the intimation of a heightened proximity between painting and specularity, both in representation but also, crucially, in painting's depiction of its own production. The reflected images in *Boy Bitten by a Lizard* suggest the painter's studio, lending further credence to Caravaggio's use of the mirror as a means of translating visual observation into art.

Like Caravaggio, Vermeer also intimated the presence of the artist as he painted, through studied inset reflections in a series of specular surfaces comprising mirrors and other glass objects. Such mirroring self-reflection of the artist is most clearly defined in his London *Music Lesson* (Fig. 88). The mirror that hangs above the virginals reflects not only the face and bust of the woman who plays the instrument but also, at the top of the image, the stand of the artist's easel, so corroborating the painter's presence. Here Vermeer painted his own act of painting elliptically, just beyond the frame. Vermeer's *Allegory of Painting* and his *Allegory of Faith* also pictorialize the 'scenario of their own production' in André Chastel's evocative phrase, albeit in very different ways. This is explicit in Vermeer's *Allegory of Painting* or *De Schilderkunst* (Kunsthistorisches Museum, Vienna), where the artist sits at his easel in the act of painting the model before him. In the *Allegory of Faith* we also see the artist's working space, but here in the miniaturizing reflection of the blown globe of clear glass that hangs from the timbered ceiling (Fig. 89). The glass globe resembles the Christological depictions of crystal orbs in *Salvator Mundi* subjects, but the miniature 'world' depicted here instead lies on its reflecting surface rather than within. Further, it reflects optically the locus of the painting's production, that is, the mullioned window of Vermeer's studio, which must surely lie behind the tapestry curtain, in which one shutter is open, the other closed. Like Caravaggio, Vermeer's pictorial address is to a range of reflective surfaces within his painting by which to declare the specularity of his art.

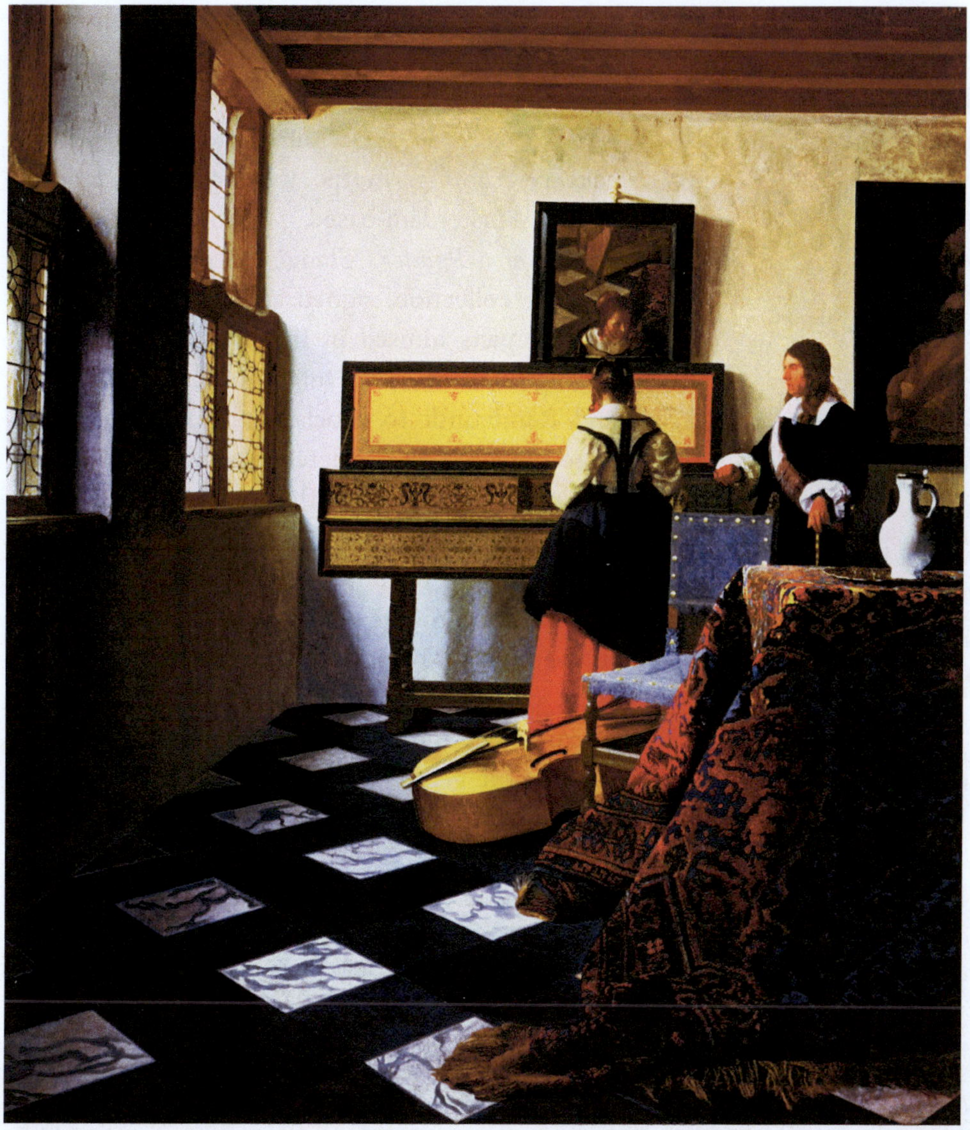

Fig. 88 Johannes Vermeer, *The Music Lesson or Lady at the Virginal with a Gentleman*, c. 1665, oil on canvas, 74.1 × 64.5 cm, Royal Collection Trust. Photo: © Royal Collection Trust/His Majesty King Charles III 2023

As Daniel Arasse has argued, the pictorial structure of the work produces a theoretical, rather than any iconographic, meaning for the painted reflection as the artistic mirror of its own mimesis.[108]

As representations of the artist's studio with the artist at work developed into a distinct genre of self-portraiture over the seventeenth century, so did its reflexive *exemplum*. This was particularly pronounced in Dutch art, surely an acknowledgement of its Eyckian genealogy as *schilderkunst*, as Carel van Mander's title to his 1604 history of Netherlandish art explicitly proclaimed. It was manifest in van Eyck's purported 'signature portraits' in the shield of St George of the Canon van der Paele altarpiece and the Arnolfini mirror, and subsequently in Vermeer's 'allegory' of his art.[109] This signature presence of the artist was pictorialised in miniature in such inset reflective surfaces as glass vessels and globes, metallic shields and *tazze*, as well as mirrors themselves. Vermeer's close contemporary from Haarlem, Pieter Gerritsz. van Roestraten, would paint himself before a canvas in his studio repeatedly, into a range of reflective surfaces in still-life pictures of silver and glass objects, as a manifesto of his skill in the art of reflection. Often coupled with emblems of *vanitas*, or the fleeting pleasure of his patrons' wealth, the fragile glass sphere is as ready a metaphor for the fugitive nature of a reflection, in both thought and image, as for the illusions of art. The theme was a considered one within Dutch seventeenth-century painting. In the work of the London-born Amsterdam-based Simon Luttichuys' *Corner of a Painter's Studio: Allegory of the Arts* (private collection, signed and dated 1646), the artist depicts himself in the orb's convex globe among a collection of Dutch portraits by Lievens and Rembrandt to proclaim the Netherlandish genesis of his art.[110] Pieter Claesz' *Vanitas with Violin* further represents the genre. Depicting the artist in a silvered glass orb standing before an easel with a window behind him, he looks towards the still-life objects laid out on a table in the studio as he paints them onto the canvas in front of him (Fig. 90). In a demonstration of specular skill, he paints the violin and the clock both in the geometrical perspective of a cabinet

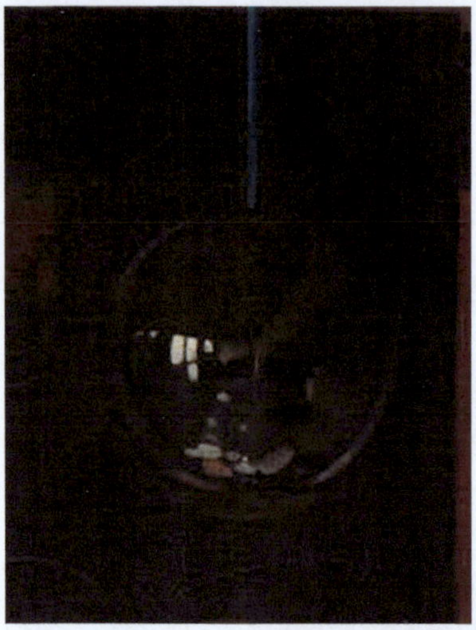

Fig. 89 Johannes Vermeer, *Allegory of Faith*, detail, c. 1670, oil on canvas, Metropolitan Museum of Art. Photo: Metropolitan Museum of Art

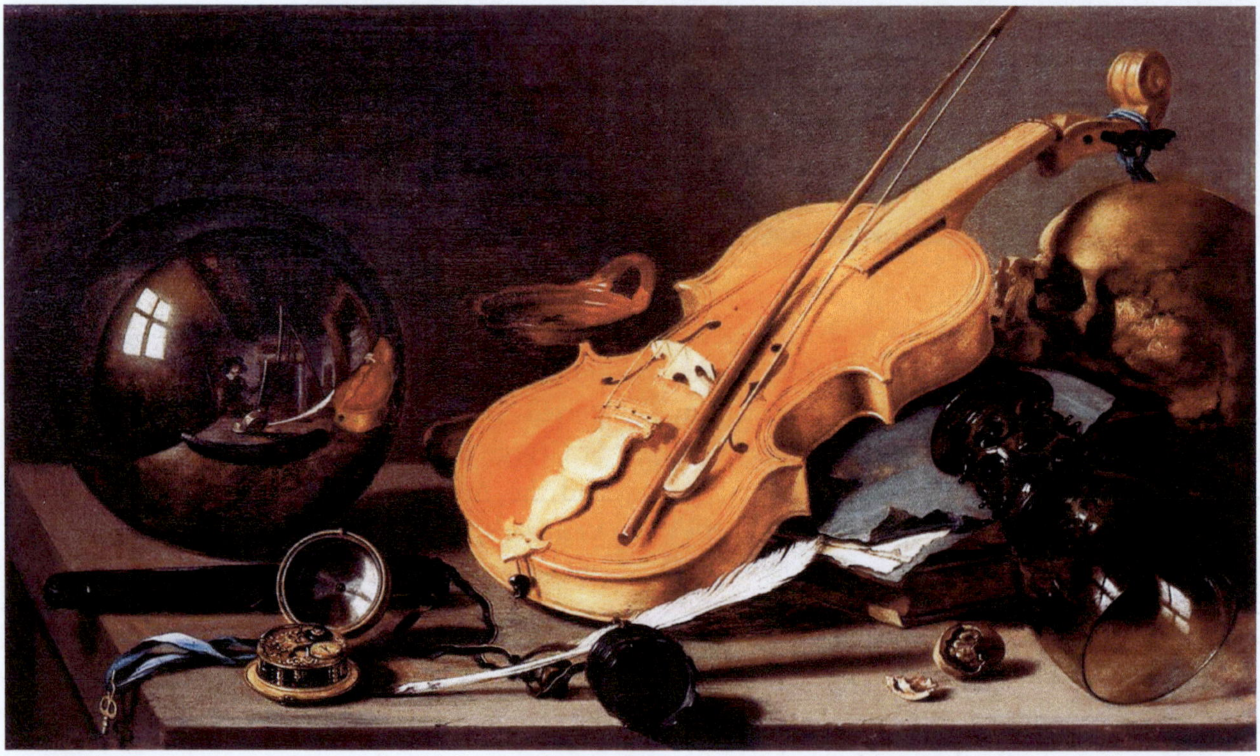

Fig. 90 Pieter Claesz, *Vanitas with Violin*, c. 1630, oil on wood, 39.9 × 59 cm, Germanisches Nationalmuseum, Nuremberg. Photo: Wikimedia

picture, and in the 'fishbowl lens' of the painter's glass. In a related example by the Antwerp artist Clara Peeters, *Ceremonial Cups and Flowers*, of 1612 (Staatliche Kunsthalle Karlsruhe), the artist painted herself into a convex ornament on an elaborate silver cup, bearing her palette and paintbrushes as she prepares to paint the work that we behold. Similarly, Maria van Oosterwijck painted her studio with her own self-portrait reflected in the bowl of a wine carafe in a vanitas still life of 1668 (Kunsthistorisches Museum, Vienna) as an artistic signature of her skill in the arts of imitation. These inset reflections of the artistic self are both a recollection of Phidias' portrait signature in the shield of his Athena Parthenos and an Erasmian vanity of the arts. Just as they commemorate the artist's presence within the work, so they also reference its evanescence, as fugitive as a mirror-image. As pictorial *Pensées* or *Essais* in the manner of Blaise Pascal or Michel de Montaigne, they articulate the painter's skill in the passing ephemera of light, depicting the self in the medium of the glass bubble or the fleeting reflection of the mirror's sheen.[111]

SALÓN DE LOS ESPEJOS

Velazquez' *Las Meninas* is the culminating example of the baroque self-portrait conceived as one of an infinite specularity. The portrait is set within the apartments of Madrid's Royal Alcázar, which Velazquez was charged with decorating in those same years. For during the last decades of his artistic career Velazquez served as much as director of the royal collections and their courtly display throughout the palace, as he did as a painter himself. This entailed not only acquisitions, but also extensive work on the decorative remodelling of the old Alcázar specifically to create opulent new galleries for the King's picture collection. Lost in a fire of 1734, Velazquez' decorative work in the Alcázar was recognised by his contemporaries as among his most significant artistic legacies. The interiors notably included mirrors, particularly in its major reception rooms, known as the Salóns Dorado and Espejos or 'Hall of Mirrors', a clear precursor to the Grande Galerie at Versailles. Like Versailles, the Hall of Mirrors at the Royal Alcázar was to become the ceremonial centre of Habsburg rule, host to court festivities of royal and diplomatic occasion and so to the choicest display of the princely art collections. Lined with glittering pendant mirrors, mythological allegories, and dynastic portraits of Habsburg lineage by Europe's court artists of the first rank, it was Madrid's gallery-within-a gallery, like the Uffizi Tribuna, and among the most celebrated museums in early modern Europe.[112] A room that inaugurated a new decorative order for the early modern palace interior, the grandeur of its mirroring art became a leitmotif of the seventeenth-century court. In these magnificent halls, facing mirrors produced a cascading play of reflection alongside painting, whose opulent optics came to be recognised as the princely paradigm of the early modern palace.

A series of court portraits by Velazquez' assistant at court, Juan Carreño de Miranda, give a partial view into this lost Hall of Mirrors, for the figures are posed against it as the backdrop to their majesty (Fig. 91). Its resplendent display was a ready metaphor for the magnificence of the Spanish crown. In respect of its key dynastic role Velazquez oversaw all aspects of the gallery installation himself, including bespoke frames for both the mirrors and the paintings. Each mirror-pair was set within richly ornamented gilt-bronze frames in the form of outspread eagle wings, the imperial bird of the Habsburg emperors, above gold torchères and marble consoles resting on gilt-bronze royal lions as the heraldic emblems of Spanish power. Its elaborately framed mirrors

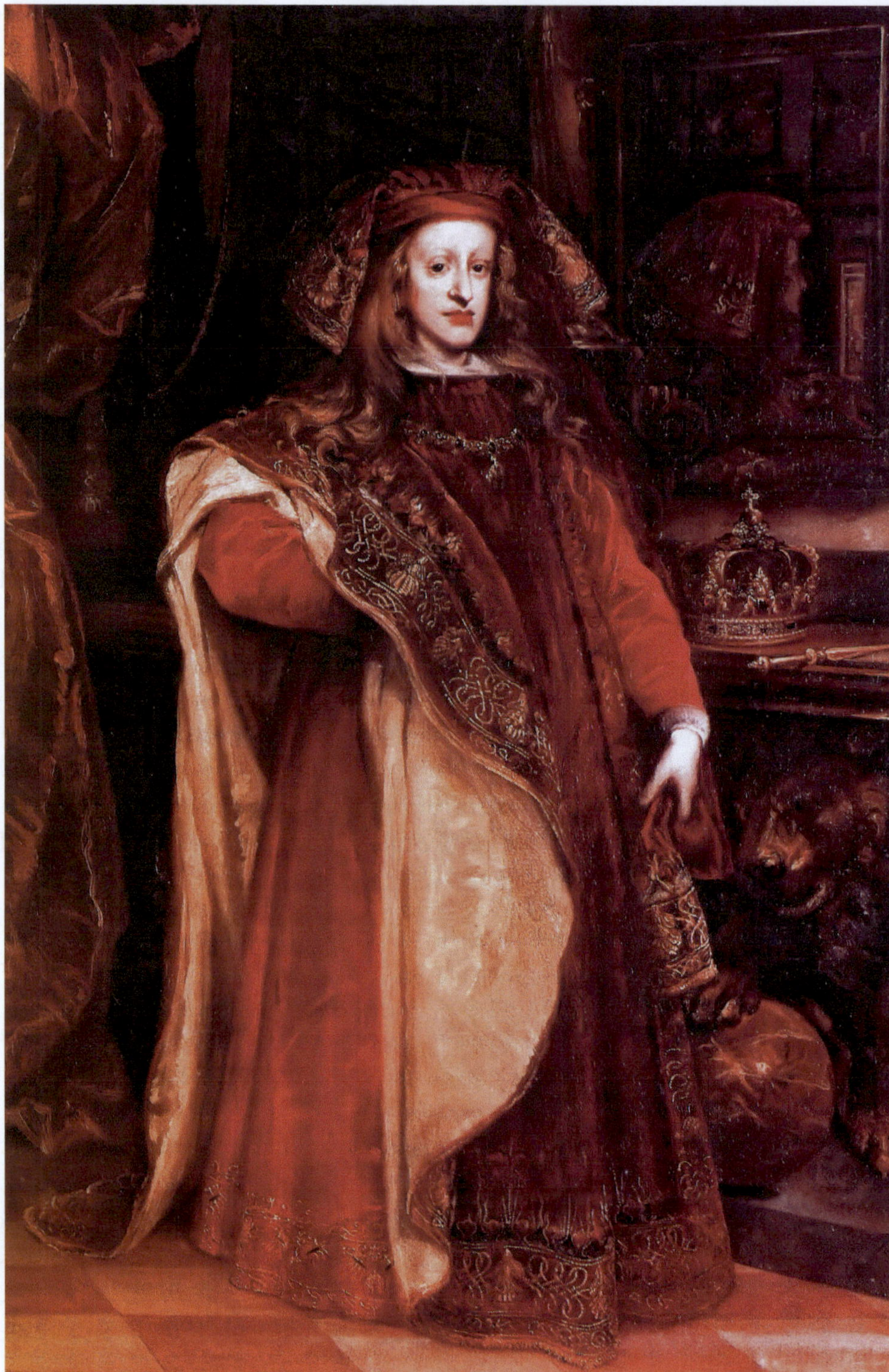

Fig. 91 Juan Carreño de Miranda, *Carlos II of Spain as Grand Master of the Golden Fleece in the Salón de los Espejos*, 1676, oil on canvas, 217 × 141 cm, Schloss Rohrau, Austria.
Photo: Wikimedia

were displayed on the gallery walls as if to equal painting itself.

De Miranda's court portraits further disclose the manner in which the mirrors of this great hall were displayed. Within each portrait, we see captured in reflection not only the king, but also the gallery hang of the royal picture collection.[113] In portraits of the 1670s of Carlos II as Hapsburg monarch and Grand Master of the Order of the Golden Fleece, the young king stands in the elaborate dress of his office depicted both before and within the mirror reflections of the hall. The mirror behind him multiplies his image further, in its splendour of gold-edged red silk draperies. The gallery wall visible in the mirror reflects the paintings on the opposite side of the hall: in Fernando Checa Cremades' account these are Titian's *Tityus* (as a common allegory of the triumph of faith) and Rubens' equestrian portrait of Philip IV. The portrait is testament both to the magnificence of monarchy and to the great riches of the picture collection on display in this ceremonial hall of mirrors. In a related series of portraits of Carlos II dressed in black silk in the Salón de los Espejos, de Miranda similarly painted into the mirrors that frame the young prince a reflection of Velazquez' own equestrian portrait of the Spanish monarch as well as the corresponding mirrors of the opposite wall with its further cascade of reflections.[114] On occasions of state, members of the court appeared as a series of further 'living portraits' in mirror reflection, alongside their painted counterparts.

De Miranda's princely portraits were a painted emulation of Velazquez' orchestration of the gallery's mirroring ornament. Within these painted princely mirrors we witness the reflexive motif of the early modern specular image as a cascading splendour of reflection construed as a pictorial manifestation of grandeur. They were surely a pictorial homage to the great artist's most celebrated late works, known and eulogised across the European courts through all manner of imitations, in which the art of painting was itself pictorialized by means of the inset mirror reflection. For Velazquez' princely hall of mirrors for the Alcázar took form over the same years as he painted his *Rokeby Venus* and *Las Meninas*, both of which centre on the fiction of a painted inset mirror reflection.[115] In Daniel Arasse's apt term, these are *miroires-peintures*, configured by the reflexive trope of painting as a mirror reflection, and undoubtedly the most renowned mirror paintings of early modernity.[116]

Velazquez' celebrated address to painting as a mirror-image in *Las Meninas* (Fig. 92) is, in the first instance, a self-portrait of the artist at work. Here the artist depicted himself as he painted in a picture gallery of the Royal Alcázar surrounded by the Spanish court. As the extensive scholarship on this painting avers, in the mirror reflection of *Las Meninas* Velazquez may be said to gather together a history of the early modern inset-mirror motif, in a brilliantly condensed pictorial reflection on its theoretical elaboration as the paradigm of painting's art. For in this work Velazquez compasses the Hapsburg-Netherlandish heritage of an Eyckian *schilderkunst*, the plunging geometry of Florentine mathematical perspective, and the optical reflections of Leonardo's aerial perspective enveloped in painterly *sfumato*. It is at the same time the artist's most considered reflection on the position of his art within the royal Alcázar's magnificent display of Spain's court culture. The painting's renown rests on its complex pictorial conceptualisation as a specular image that multiplies the artifice of its reflexive illusion serially, as if itself a hall of mirrors. In the wake of reception of Michel Foucault's greatly vaunted analysis of *Las Meninas* as an infinitely cascading mirror reflection of optical and reflective vision, it has come to be regarded as encapsulating both a cultural definition of early modernity and the art of painting itself. In effect, Foucault read *Las Meninas* as a pictorial theorisation of artistic *mise-en-abyme*.[117]

At an initial level of signification *Las Meninas* represents the Spanish Infanta, or princess, at play with her maids of honour while Velazquez paints. It therefore comprises a self-portrait of the artist within the royal portrait genre.[118] Antonio Palomino's 1724 treatise on Spanish history of art, *El parnaso español pittoresco laureado*,

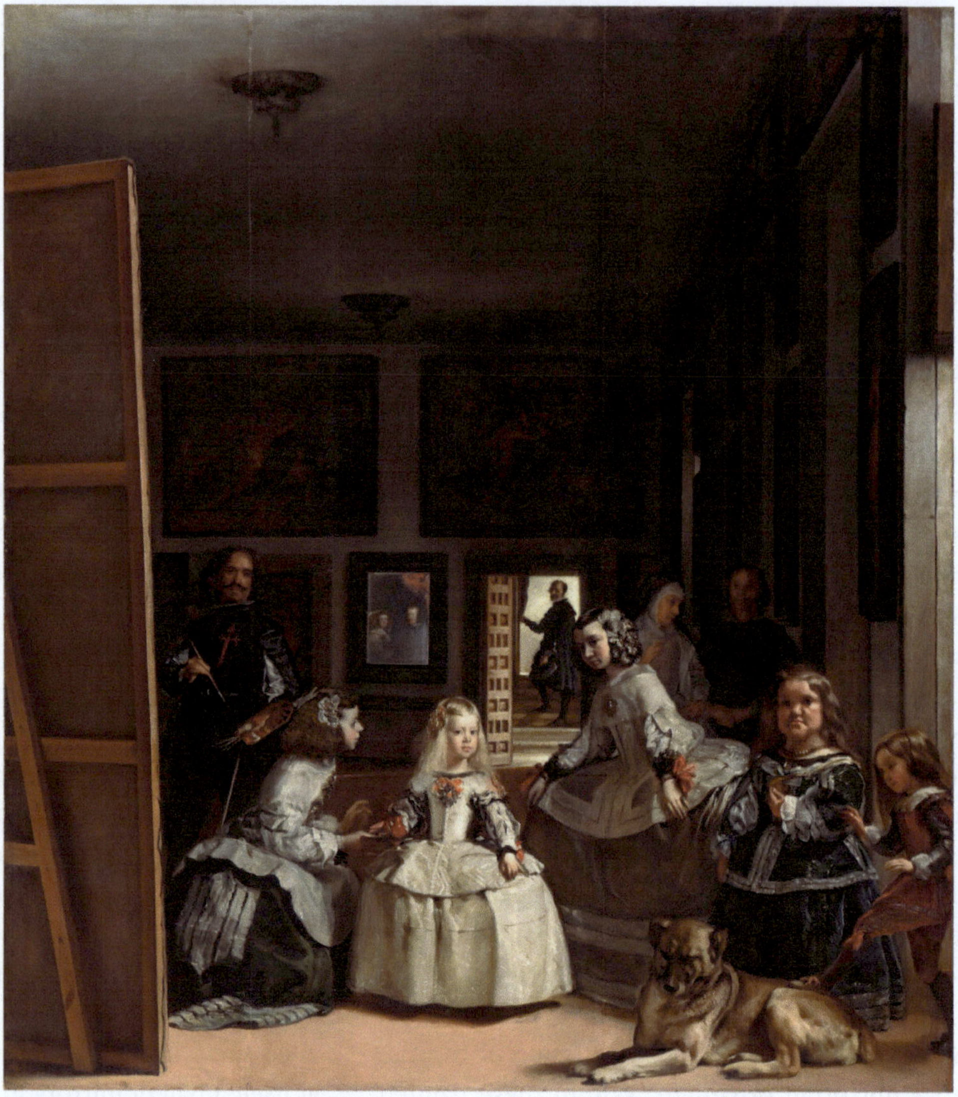

Fig. 92 Diego Velázquez, *Las Meninas*, c. 1656, oil on canvas, 320.5 × 281.5 cm, Museo del Prado, Madrid.
Photo: © Museo Nacional del Prado

gives an extensive description of the work, based on the author's prodigious knowledge derived from his position as court painter to Carlos II, which remains fundamental to any interpretation of this painting.[119] The great hall in which Velazquez depicted the courtly scene was, according to Palomino, in fact the one in which Velazquez painted the royal portrait. Situated within the princely quarters of the Alcázar, it also served as a further palace picture gallery for the royal art collections that Velazquez oversaw.[120] Thus Velazquez' great canvas, like the Salón de los Espejos, is of both portraits within portraits and a picture gallery within a gallery at the Royal Alcázar.

On the back wall of *Las Meninas*, displayed alongside a group of paintings, hangs a mirror, picked out by the shimmer of light across its surface and most intensely at its bevelled edge. In the reflecting surface of this mirror we see what Palomino identified for us as the king and queen.[121] The reflection implies the presence of the royal couple before the canvas, apparently in the space of the viewer, but also of Velazquez as he painted this work. The king and queen are surely the subject of Velazquez' large easel painting within the painting. As viewers, however, we see this great canvas only from the back. Through the mirror Velazquez reveals to the viewer what he also withholds – his art. For the mirror appears to capture a double perspective, as an extensive scholarship avers: the view of the royal couple as they sit for their portrait, but also the canvas that Velazquez paints. The complexity of mirror images at play pulls the viewer into the labyrinth of reflections that this painting seems to contain within it. As well as the mirror depicted within the painting, there is also the implication of a further mirror surrounding this work – the mirror that Velazquez surely used to paint his self-portrait. As a portrait of the artist at work in the company of the Infanta, the mirror reflection that *Las Meninas* holds within it is a portrait-within-a-portrait, as the canvas-within-the-canvas on which Velazquez paints must also be.[122]

In fact, *Las Meninas* was not destined to hang among the formal royal portraits in the ceremonial halls of the Alcázar such as the Salón de los Espejos, or indeed the court gallery that it depicts and in which it was painted. Instead, it was displayed for Philip IV alone, within his *studiolo* or office *del despacho*, for his exclusive view in a cabinet of inner sanctum for his private study. Here it hung among some thirty choice paintings of the royal collections including celebrated Italian and Flemish works by Correggio, Tintoretto, Veronese, Guercino and Guido Reni, Rubens, and van Dyck, among others, largely of mythological themes, in a concerted display of Velazquez' curatorial orchestration. This exquisite princely cabinet was further ornamented with seven great mirrors and buffets of inlaid stone marquetry in a visual display of royal opulence.[123] Both within the mirror surroundings of the *despacho* and within the pictorial space of *Las Meninas* as the artistic recollection of the princely gallery in which it was painted, the work was conceived and surely was received as one of painting's reflection on itself. Moreover, it reflects on Velazquez' vast knowledge of the history of art and of the inset mirror-image as its emblem, founded in his extensive travels in Italy and, centrally, his position as curator of the royal collections. These extraordinary collections comprised not only Titian's much-copied Toilet of Venus (discussed in Chapter 5) critical to the genesis of Velazquez' own Rokeby Venus as well as those of Rubens, but also, by Habsburg descent, the Arnolfini portrait.[124] Thus from its earliest Eyckian manifestation in portraiture to its extensive elaboration within the painting of Titian and Rubens, and to the hall of mirrors for the Alcázar, the mirror-image lay at the conceptual centre both of the royal collections and of Velazquez' art.

As a Hapsburg artist, Velazquez' representation of Flemish art's nobility as a historical antecedent to *Las Meninas* was richly layered, comprising the Eyckian mirror device as well as Rubens' further elaborations. While the paintings along the side of the painted gallery of *Las Meninas* are a mere ellipsis of frames, the lower reaches of the back wall display two further paintings-within-the-painting that Palomino specifically identified as compositions by Rubens, which is further corroborated in royal inventories.[125] The Rubensian scenes, from Ovid's *Metamorphoses*, depict, on the one hand, *Apollo and Marsyas* and, on the other, *Minerva and Arachne*, stories of contest with the gods. As other scholars have argued, such inset paintings of Ovidian myth within a royal portrait manifest a pictorial form of *speculum principis*. The cultural practice of such veiled citation was of both ancient pedigree and courtly Habsburg decorum.[126]

Palomino's further account of *Las Meninas* is itself emblematic of the play of veiled or ambiguous meanings attributed to the work, in his narrative of its genesis as a royal '*divertissement*': while Velazquez worked on *Las Meninas* the king 'went frequently to see it being painted. So did [the queen] ... and the Infanta and ladies-in-waiting, who came often, considering it a delightful ... entertainment'.[127] It was a form of courtly diversion that treatises on painting such as the Flemish Carel van Mander's *Schilderboeck* of 1604 commented on, terming them '*storykens*', or the incidental anecdotes that animate the scene.[128] Palomino's description is resonant of much early modern court pastime, which comprised such visits to the studios of their artists to watch them at work, often in the company of visitors, from Rubens to Bernini and Velazquez. As related by their respective biographers, these visitations on the part of princes were in themselves often instrumental to the further elaboration of the work in execution.[129] In *Las Meninas*, however, the painting is a seeming mirror-reversal of the work of art in the making. Apparently a sitting by the king and the queen for their royal double portrait, Velazquez has transposed his canvas instead into a representation of its making in the company of the Infanta. The princess and her retinue, an apparent diversion for the king and queen as they sit for Velazquez, have instead become the central subject of his portrait. A mirror-like structure of courtly counterpoint pervades the work.

As much brilliant scholarship on *Las Meninas* has debated, there is a further apparent pictorial paradox at stake, between the rigorous geometrical accuracy of its perspectival representation and its ambiguous perception as '*a capricho*', in Palomino's words.[130] This pictorial puzzle is seen to lie above all in the conundrum of its mirror image as the painting it apparently depicts. Within the pictorial narrative of its own making, this mirror purportedly reflects both the canvas on which Velazquez works, as the one we regard, and the king and queen as they sit for their portrait, which we see in mirror reflection. Further, their seeming pictorial presence before the painting elides with our position as viewer, which is also that of the king's gaze.

Within the painting would seem to lie a further series of judiciously balanced pictorial antitheses. If the mathematical perspective is so assured that, in Palomino's words, 'it looks as if one could walk on it', yet the great size of the gallery cast in the pictorial medium appears to veil the representation of spatial depth into the shadowy *tenebroso* reaches of its lofty height, as critics and scholars have long acknowledged. In the foreground, the extended scale of the back of the canvas on which Velazquez paints, which is twice his height, stands in marked visual juxtaposition to the small jewel-like reflection of the king and queen in the mirror's specular reduction at the back. Further, the resonant fall of light and shadow, like a Leonardesque atmospheric perspective, seems to exceed the rigorous geometry of its perspectival construction. Already Palomino signalled these counterpoints within the work in his description of the painting's play of illusion in the representation of shadow and scale.[131] Light scatters visual attention across the canvas into a multitude of pictorial reflections, from the princess to the other members of her retinue, the artist and the lit parameters of his great canvas, the ellipses of the windows, and the bevelled sheen of the mirror edge beside the silhouette of the queen's doorman against the fully lit doorway. Velazquez thereby casts his royal viewer, the king, before a luminous cascade of specular reflection, just like a hall of mirrors. The work appears to confound any clear distinction between mimesis and illusion; it is everywhere both a court portrait and a fiction of painting's deceit.

In Pedro Calderón's great court play of the 1630s, *La vida es sueño* (Life Is a Dream), the prevailing *mise-en-scène* is of a shimmering twilight indeterminacy. Staged at the Royal Alcázar for the court of Philip IV, it displayed all the luministic effects of Baroque theatre by means of reflected candles and torches. Its dazzling scenic effects of cascading light – sunrise, sunset, moonrise, dawn and twilight, storm and tempest, as in Shakespeare's homonymous play of that name – signified the cosmic indices of fate. The premise of Baroque court theatre was, like *Las Meninas,* of an inset performance within a larger spectacle of princely entertainments.[132] For court itself was a theatre, as many scholars have argued, its fetes and entertainments indelibly cast in the image of '*speculum principis*' to reflect the splendour and *exemplum* of princely grace, by which royalty was itself circumscribed.[133] Both Velazquez and Philip IV appeared in court theatrical productions, which were the centre of princely entertainment under his rule.[134] Thus the apparently fluctuating patterns of surface light in *Las Meninas,* which puzzle the surety of the painting's perspectival geometry in a display of sparkling pictorial antithesis, suggest that a painting is indeed both a mirror-image and a painted deceit. In a dazzling sequence of pictorial 'play' with the Albertian definition of painting, Velazquez argues that even as his art is as true as a window or a mirror view, yet it is all illusion, a theatre, an optical fiction of light and shade.

In its mirroring perspective of illusionistic space, Velazquez' painted picture gallery may be said to summon the history of art – past, present and future – to consideration of his work. In Palomino's words, citing his fellow court artist Luca Giordano, it is a painting that contains within itself a 'theology' of reflection, as a *summa* of pictorial knowledge. Palomino's treatise is titled a 'Museo pitorico', like a pictorial museum of the history of art; so too is Velazquez' great canvas in homage to the collections he oversaw. A painting destined to hang among the extensive artworks of the Spanish monarchy, *Las Meninas* also, reflexively, mirrors those works within it. At the same time *Las Meninas* reflects on its own production, and on the central figure of the mirror within that process. The painted mirror that is also a royal portrait hangs on a wall of further paintings-within-the-painting, which makes of it a picture gallery-within-a-gallery of the royal collection where, then as now, it was displayed. If the painted surface of this mirror-reflection double portrait is sketchy in comparison with the rest of the canvas, it is fitting, for it reflects a painting in the process of its making. Here reflecting what is apparently represented on the artist's canvas, the metaphor of the inset mirror within the painting is direct. Distinct from the miniaturised details of Caravaggio's carafe or Vermeer's glass globe, this reflexive vision of art as a mirror is central to the work. As a summation of the pictorial trajectory of the Renaissance '*miroire-peinture*', *Las Meninas* declares itself the mirror of art. Depicting a painted mirror, by means of a mirror, *Las Meninas* recalls within itself the long history of the painted mirror reflection. In Velazquez' rendering, a painting may indeed be both a perfect mimesis and an entirely fictional reflection of the mirror method of its own production.

NOTES

1 Palomino, 1795, vol. III, no. 106, VII:321–54, notably I:324. Palomino was royal painter at the Spanish court in the 1680s, giving him access to key materials that informed his work, on which see further the introduction by Ayala Mallory to her translation of Palomino, 1987, vii–xviii. For the inventory, Sanchez Canton, 1925, III, 379–406, for a full list of his books; on which see further Cacho Casal, 2020. As suggested by Fernando Marías, 2003, 128, note 63, his library's books on optics and lenses included an '*especularia*', surely Rafael Mirami, 1582. On the larger question of Velazquez' intellectual and literary culture, and in light of his training with the noted humanist scholar as well as painter Francisco Pacheco, see the recent essay by Aterido, 2007; and Pacheco, 1649 and 2018.

On Leonardo's *Trattato della pittura,* the manuscript and publication history of Leonardo's treatise on painting is complex. It was first published in an abridged version by Raphäel Trichet du Fresne in Paris in 1651 in Italian and French, which was widely consulted by artists thereafter, as with Velazquez. But it also circulated in manuscript copies made by Leonardo's heirs over the course of the sixteenth and early seventeenth centuries. The BAV ms. Codex

Urb. 1270 is generally regarded as the top version. It was likely a copy of Leonardo's own definitive version made by his heir and pupil, Francesco Melzi. First published in full in 1817, see the now-classic edition by Milanesi (Leonardo, 1890); and the recent facsimile edition by Carlo Vecce (Leonardo, 1995). Martin Kemp's 1989 translation, *Leonardo on Painting*, has become the authoritative English edition; see also Farago et al., 2018. As Leonardo's treatise on painting evidently developed out of ideas he developed across his notebooks, I have cited manuscript references from the notebooks, Italian editions of the notebooks, and English translations, particularly MacCurdy, 1938; Richter (Leonardo, 1970); and Richter and Pedretti (Leonardo, 1977), as appropriate.

The bifurcation of Baroque studies under the sign of theory/practice takes its origins from G. P. Bellori's presentation of the history of art as a dialectic of idealism/realism, in his *Idea* lecture of 1664, subsequently published in his canonical *Vite*, Bellori, 1672. It resonates across twentieth-century study of the period, in classic works by Mahon, 1947; Panofsky's *Idea*, 1924, and its subsequent history of republication and translation as the debate unfolded; and further in the work of Elizabeth Cropper and Charles Dempsey. For a recent restatement, notably in light of current interests in the materialities of art as the locus of both theory and practice: Cropper, 2018a. See also literature on the embodiment and materialities of practice respectively: Smith, 2004; Falguières, 2006.

2 Sanchez Canton, 1960, vol. 2, 391–400; Sanchez Canton, 1942. As Velazquez' wife died only days after him, the inventory of goods in their palace quarters comprises objects belonging to both, as well as to the Crown, so that caution must be exercised in attributing all such objects to Velazquez himself.

3 Palomino, citing after Alberti, 1724, III, *Vida* no. 106, I:324.

4 From an extensive bibliography on Velazquez' practice: Garrido Pérez, 2022; Ferino-Pagden, 2018; Portús et al., 2018; Portús, 2018; Stoichita, 2018; Knox & Tiffany, 2017; Garrido Pérez & Brown, 1998; McKim-Smith et al., 1988.

5 See the further discussion in Warwick, 2016; Warwick, forthcoming 2023.

6 Pacheco, 1649 and 2018, whose theorization of imitation arises out of the traditions of icon painting, but is also clearly endebted to Federico Zuccaro's conceptualization of imitation, as of *disegno*, in terms of a Catholic spirituality of the vision of the immaterial.

7 See also the discussion in Chapter 2. From an extensive literature, in addition to the below, see Gentil Baldrich, 2013; Grave, 2010.

8 Damisch, 1995; Damisch, 2002. The phrase pictorial intelligence is Alpers & Baxandall, 1994.

9 For an example of an early modern translation into Italian, Euclid (c. 300 BCE) 1573.

10 As Damisch, 1994, has noted, the analogical models through which to describe and conceptualise the use of the lens are those of the lentil – *lenticchia*, as resembling the form of a two-sided convex optical lens – and the conical form of a straw hat through to describe the cone of vision, as also the form of the peephole or sighting device, on which see below. The play of resemblances between the diminutive and the material, on the one hand, and the monumental and conceptual, on the other, is in Damisch's argument characteristic of an early modern theorisation of artistic practice between the particular and the abstract, the historical residue of which remains in the etymology of the term 'lens'.

11 Manetti, 1927, 9–13. Vasari, 1568, Part II, vol. 1, 305–6, life of Brunelleschi, on Brunelleschi's archaeological surveyance of Roman antiquities; on which see especially Kemp, 1978. From an extensive secondary literature on the development of Renaissance perspective: Belting, 2011; Dupré, 2019; Edgerton, 2009; Trachtenberg, 1997; Panofsky, 1991; Kemp, 1992; Dalai Emiliani, 1980; Edgerton, 1975; Damisch, 1994 and 2002; White, 1957. See also Sinisgalli, 2012.

12 Gerolemou, 2020; Sinisgalli, 2012.

13 Belting, 2011; Lindberg, 1976. This has generated much recent work; see Paravicini Bagliani, 2021.

14 Bosse & Desargues, 1648. See Dauvois, 2016; Dhombres, 1994; Da Costa Kaufmann, 1975.

15 Belting, 2011; Smith, 2014; Smith, 2011; Ghiberti, 1998.

16 On Filarete, Hub, 2020; see also Warwick, forthcoming 2023.

17 On the use of the compass, Warwick, forthcoming 2023.

18 Averlino, 1972, book 23; Filarete & Spencer, 1965, I:305.

19 Averlino, 1972, book 23; Filarete & Spencer, 1965, I:305.

20 The term 'vanishing point' appears to originate with Taylor, 1715. See further Belting, 2011, particularly on the rise of Arabic numerals in the fifteenth century in Western Europe and therefore the concept of 0, on which see further Rotman, 1987; Field, 1997.

21 Filarete, book 23; Filarete & Spencer, 1965, I:303–4.

22 Alberti, 1966, 56. On the Alberti manuscripts, see Grayson, 1968; and Sinisgalli, 2011, 'Introduction', 3–14. See further the Introduction to this book.

23 Alberti, 1966, 68–69. See Edgerton's discussion of Alberti's window or velum in Edgerton, 2009, 126–32; Moffitt, 2002; Pardo, 1997.

24 Jütte, 2023, 113–27, on the Renaissance fabric window.

25 See also the opening discussion of Alberti's Narcissus in the Introduction.

26 Vodret, 1996; and Vodret, 1995, for a discussion of the painting's composition by means of mirrors. On Caravaggio's use of mirrors more generally, see also Lapucci, 2005; for his art of specular address, Fried, 2010.

27 Alberti, 1966, 64.

28 Published in Corradini & Marini, 1993.

29 Baglione, 1642, 136–39. This has been taken to mean that Caravaggio painted his self-portrait within these early mythological works, on which see the helpful corrective by Gregori et al., 1985, 241–42: 'What Baglione records is the widespread practice of

employing a mirror as an aid in achieving a realistic representation – a method that, as a painter, he was certainly familiar with.'

30 As related by Bellori, 1672, 212, with reference to Caravaggio's depiction of a gypsy. On the larger question of Caravaggio's art of visible realism, see especially Warwick, 2017; and Bologna, 2006.

31 Fiorio, 2000, cat. no. C4, 166–67. The National Gallery painting is usually seen to be an imitation of the Narcissus painting attributed to Boltraffio in the Uffizi, while both are thought to be after a Leonardesque work no longer extant.

32 From a vast literature on Leonardo's notebooks and their complex anthological history, see Bambach, 2019; Laurenza & Kemp, 2019; Farago et al., 2018; the useful summary in Kemp, 2006, 207–8; and Kemp, 1989. See also Farago, 1992; and Galluzzi & Nova, 2022, on digital editions of Leonardo's notebooks. Wherever possible I have cited both the manuscript source and an authoritative English translation of his notes.
Leonardo's letter to Ludovico Sforza appears in Codex Atlanticus, fol. 1082r (Biblioteca Ambrosiana, Milan), c. 1480s, as cited by Kemp, 1992, 170–71.

33 The theme was a constant preoccupation across Leonardo's notebooks; see also the related diagram published in Heydenreich, 1954, II, no. 150; and Leonardo, 1938, II:338–39, for an anthology of Leonardo's notes on sun reflections on water from ms. C, Institut de France Library, fol. 17 r&v. On Leonardo's interests across arts and sciences, see especially Kemp, 2011; Kemp, 2006; and Kemp 2004; for his interests in the representation of ephemeral effects, see Nova, 2011; and the further anthologies, Galluzzi, 2018; Frosini, 2015; Fiorani, 2013.

34 Leonardo, 1977, I:183, 190, 216, and II:19, 20, 120, for notes by Leonardo on his industrial and scientific uses of mirrors; and Leonardo, 1938, II:43, 537; Dupré, 2005. On the parabolic mirror or *ignea*, see further Bambach, 2019, III:259–62; on the raindrop mirror, see further Markovic, 2020.

35 Leonardo, Institut de France Library, vol. A, 19 v, in Leonardo 1938, II:295.

36 Leonardo, Bibliothèque Nationale de France (BNF), ms. 2038, 24v–25v, in Leonardo, 1938, II, 'Paragone', 229.

37 Leonardo, 1977, II:119–20, with reference to a planned treatise on perspective. Leonardo's Codex Atlanticus, fol. 360r, suggests a putative table of contents for a treatise on mirrors, as part of a discussion of optics and catoptrics.

38 Luca Pacioli, 'De viribus quantitatis', ms. University of Bologna, c. 1496–1508, fol. 239v, cites using a mirror to read Leonardo's notes, as did Vasari, on which see Bambach, 2003.

39 See the further discussion of the *camera obscura* in Chapter 4.

40 Leonardo, Institut de France Library, vol. K, 118[38]v, in Leonardo, 1938, I, 266. On the manufacture and uses of glass eyeballs, Levkoff, 2015.

41 Leonardo, Codex Atlanticus, fol. 345v, in Leonardo, 1938, I:253.

42 Leonardo, Institut de France Library, vol. D, fol. 2v, in Leonardo, 1938, I:235–36, 241–43.

43 Leonardo, BNF ms. 2038, fol. 24v, in Leonardo, 1938, II, 254. The passage also appears in the 1651 Du Fresne edition of the *Trattato della pittura*, no. 275.

44 Leonardo, Codex Urbinate Lat. 1270, Vatican Library, in Leonardo, 1890, III:404: 'Come la vera pittura stia nella superficie dello specchio piano: "lo specchio ... contiene in se la vera pittura ... E la perfetta pittura ... e simile alla superficie dello specchio"'.

45 Alberti, 1966, 83, from Spencer's translation. The interpretation of Alberti's *diforme* surely suggests unformed as much as deformed, in the sense of painting's composition of impalpable form. Panofsky, 1915, 41, references also Leonardo showing his use of both the grid and the glass pane method.

46 Leonardo, BNF ms. 2038, 28r, in Leonardo, 1938, II:263

47 Leonardo, BNF ms. 2038 24v in Leonardo, 1938, II:254.

48 From a vast literature, see Kemp, 1989, on the ordering of Leonardo's notes around themes of perspective and the relation between linear, colour, and atmospheric perspective, 47–116.

49 Leonardo BNF 2038 2r; Codex Urbinas 33v and 50v–51r; Codex Atlanticus 184vc/505v, brought together in Kemp, 1989, 202, 205.

50 Leonardo BNF ms. 2038, fol. 2r, in Leonardo, 1938, II:235.

51 Leonardo BNF ms. 2038 fol. 2r, in Leonardo 1938, II:235.

52 Leonardo BNF 2038, fol. 24r, in Leonardo, 1938, II:353.

53 Kemp, 1990, especially 170–71. See also the compendium of Leonardo's notes on painters' aids in Kemp, 1989, 191–217. See further Warwick, 2016.

54 Leonardo Institut de France Library, vol. A, fol. 1v in Leonardo, 1938, II:369; Leonardo, 1970, II:83.

55 Dürer & Strauss, 1977.

56 Panofsky, 1943, 257. See further Cache, 2016; Schröder, 1980.

57 Durer & Strauss, 1977, 435.

58 Edgerton, 2009, 126–32; and Kemp, 1990, 167–88.

59 Rodler & von Simmern, 1970, 88.

60 Bate, 1638, III:109: 'A verie easie way, to describe a Towne, or Castle: being within the full sight thereof': 'you must have a frame made, and crossed into equall squares with lute strings, and figured at the end of each string ... You must divide your paper that you are to draw upon into so many equal squares as your frame containeth.... Before this frame must be placed a style or bodkin having a little glasse on the top of it for to direct the sight.' Dubreuil, 1765, 286–87, illustrates two types of Dürer's devices, a glass window and an Albertian grid like Bate: 'Many lovers of painting, and who entertain themselves in drawing after nature, would willingly be excused the trouble of opening the compasses, or taking up the ruler, and in this method neither the one nor the other are required; and yet the proportions and distances of objects will be exactly

preserved.... The principal requisite is a large piece of fine clear glass, fitted in a wooden frame.... Place the instrument before the object you would draw, look through the little hole or sight ... draw on the glass everything that you see thereon.... With pen and ink, then ... laying a moist sheet of paper on ... the design, rub or press ... and the whole draught will be ... transferred from the glass upon the paper.'

61 Marolois, 1614, republished in 1625, 1, as the opening definition.

62 Cardi & Profumo, 1992; and Camerota, 2010; and the useful summary in Kemp, 1990, 167–88.

63 Burckhardt, 1860; on whose work see the recent anthology by Bauer & Ditchfield, 2022. From an extensive literature on self portraiture defined by Koerner, 1993; see further the expansive Woods-Marsden, 1998; Bond & Woodall, 2005; Calabrese, 2006; Galassi & Maffei, 2021. On the concept of selfhood as manifest in self-portraiture centred on Dürer's Munich self-portrait, Didi-Huberman, 1993. See also Didi-Huberman, 1994, and, from a vast literature on Renaissance portraiture more broadly, Pommier, 1998. On the purported van Eyck London self-portrait, seemingly a betrothal portrait, see the further discussion in Chapter 2 in this book and Gentili et al., 1989.

64 Burckhardt, 1860, Part II, 131–32.

65 Greenblatt, 2005.

66 For example, in the late medieval rise of surnames, usually of place. Vasari's *Vite*, as has long been noted, exemplifies the rise of biographical writing in the realm of art history, in which each biography is framed by a portrait, though it is also historically salient to observe, on the question of surnames, that his index of artists' names proceeds by first name. This is still current in the continuing usage of, for instance, Leonardo da Vinci.

67 Calabrese, 2006. From an extensive literature on Renaissance identity, Rogers, 2020; and Ciappelli & Rubin, 2000. See also Bedford et al., 2006. On the figure of the Renaissance 'artist' the classic study remains Kris & Kurz, 1979; see further Barker et al., 1999.

68 Zwijnenberg, 2003; Zöllner, 1992; Kemp, 1976. More broadly, see Marin, 1989.

69 Notably, Smith, 2004; Falguières, 2006.

70 Bonafoux, 2007.

71 According to Fletcher, 1992, based on her study of Venetian inventories; and De Vecchi, 1990. See further Warwick, 2021.

72 Vasari, *Vite* ..., according to Bellosi & Rossi (Vasari, 1986): Masaccio, 288, 'fatto da lui medesimo, allo specchio'; Alberti, 372, 'un ritratto di se medesimo fatto alla spera'; Filippo Lippi, 398, 'ritrasse a lo specchio se stesso; Gentile Bellini, 444, on request 'di dipinger se medesimo ... ritrattosi a una spera ... lo presente'; Domenico Ghirlandaio, 472, 'ritrattosi in un specchio da se medesimo'; Raphael, 623, 'ritrattosi da se medesimo nello specchio'; Andrea del Sarto, 741, 'tolse una spera, e ritrasse se medesimo in un tegolo, che è vivissimo naturale, oggi appresso alla donna sua'; Parmigianino, 816, on which see further below. Vasari also wrote of his own self-portrait in a letter of 20 September 1567: 'stamani ho fatto di mio mano il mio viso, ritratto dallo specchio', Frey & Frey, 1982, DCVII, 351. On Alberti's self-portrait as described by Vasari, Madersbacher, 2017, part of his larger research project on fifteenth-century embedded self-portraits; see also Aurenhammer, 2014, on Alberti's 'autobiographical imagination'.

73 See especially Shuger, 1998, and the further discussion in the Introduction.

74 The translation is taken from Koerner, 1993, 43.

75 See the discussion of van Eyck's putative self-portrait (National Gallery London) in Chapter 2; and Madersbacher, 2017, for the above discussion of the uncertain pictorial identification of a painted self-portrait by Alberti as described by Vasari.

76 Koerner, 1993, 43–44. The portrait of Dürer the Elder, also in the Albertina collection, has been identified both as a self-portrait and as a portrait by the young Dürer of his father; in both cases it is seen as linked to Dürer's 1484 self-portrait drawing.

77 www.metmuseum.org/art/collection/search/459214. Alsteens et al., 2012, 12–16; Koerner, 2006, 37, 40.

78 Vasari, 1568, 3:I, 232, life of Parmigianino. See David Ekserdjian's discussion of Vasari's slightly differing accounts of the painting from the 1550 to the 1568 edition of his *Vite*, in Ekserdjian, 2006, 130. See also Rubin, 2007b; Ferino-Pagden, 2002. The portrait was gifted to Pope Clement VII and then to the Venetian art critic Pietro Aretino, in whose house the Aretine Vasari saw it, and then into artists' collections, acquired by Rudolf II for the imperial collections in 1608.

79 Fried, 2010, 96.

80 https://collections.mfa.org/objects/32665. Carol Plazzotta in Campbell et al., 2008, cat. no. 83, 256.

81 On Michelangelo and the *giudizio dell' occhio*, see especially the discussion by Summers, 1981, 332–79; Winner, 1986; Wivel, 2022. On the place of the compass in artistic theory and practice, Warwick, forthcoming 2023.

82 Cazzola-Senkpiel, 2020, based on the analysis of the 'moment' of painting by Michael Fried, 2010; Bond & Woodall, 2005, cat. no. 3, 88; Pilliod, 2001, 256; Woods-Marsden, 1998, 229–30; Pizzorusso, 1982.

83 On the Uffizi self-portrait collection, initiated by Cardinal Leopoldo de' Medici in discussion with his curator of collections Filippo Baldinucci, see Rosen, 2020, Giusti, 2007; Langedijk, 1992; Berti, 1976; Prinz, 1971. See also the publication of archival sources pertaining to the Medici self-portraits in *Memofonte*: www.memofonte.it/ricerche/collezionismo-mediceo/. The self-portraits were brought together in a dedicated room (of which there is an engraving by Benedetto Felice de Greyss, who was tasked with a pictorial inventory of the Medici collections) only after Leopoldo's death in 1681, as the interest in their collection was also taken up by Cosimo III, and were moved to the Vasari corridoio in the late nineteenth century.

84 https://collections.mfa.org/objects/33656/selfportrait?ctx=9d72e2fc-3adb-44d1-b5a8-9915a25c8064&idx=0. Ruiz Gomez, 2019; Cole, 2019, 33–39; Woods-Marsden, 1998, 187–214; Ferino-Pagden & Kusche, 1995. On her portraiture more broadly, the recent Rijksmuseum exhibition by Jonker, 2023.

85 Translation from Woods-Marsden, 1998, 232; see further Woodall, 2007.

86 Woods-Marsden, 1998; Calabrese, 2006.

87 https://artsandculture.google.com/asset/self-portrait-at-the-spinet-lavinia-fontana/_gH8Qmx8fVJNgA?hl=en inscribed: LAVINIA VIRGO PROSPERI FONTANAE / FILIA EX SPECULO IMAGINEM / ORIS SUI EXPRESIT ANNO / MDLXXVII. Ruiz Gomez, 2019; Bohn, 2004; Murphy, 2003; Woods-Marsden, 1998, 215–21; Ghirardi, 1994. On the question of scale in these self-portraits by women, Tostmann, 2021.

88 https://collections.louvre.fr/ark:/53355/cl010066782. Passamani, 1990, no. 26, 164–67, where it is titled man in armour, and with discussion of its provenance within the royal painting collection of François I in his *cabinet des peintures*, then attributed to Giorgione, with a further copy in the *appartement des bains*; Goffen, 2002, 62–64. The painting was identified as a self-portrait by Gilbert, 1955, 48, who drew attention to the signature and its rebus-like character. The work is signed: opera/opus de Jovani Jeronimo de Bressa/Brisia di Savoldi, lower left, and also Savoldo on the scrap of paper at the top of mirror. It is one of a handful of signed works, all of which are embedded into the illusion of the work, i.e., on wall or paper, etc. Alternatively, the painting has also long been identified as a possible portrait of Gaston de Foix, on which see Fagnart, 2015. There is also much scholarly debate as to date. On the armour, see further Rossi, 1984. De Vecchi, 1990, 63, argues for Savoldo's self-portrait as the closest pictorial commentary on the lost Giorgione, with reference to the Leonardesque/Venetian envelope of atmospheric perspective, the play of reflections and refractions on armour and textiles in a virtuoso display. See also Bialostocki, 1988, 93–98. As Savoldo's pupil and close imitator, Paolo Pino's definition of painting as a mirror may be related to this work: 'L'arte nostra fa l'effetto che fa lo specchio', Pino, 1548, 5, as cited by De Vecchi. Savoldo has enjoyed renewed attention following Fried's 2021 monograph, which attends to the representation of face and hands in the painter's works; and also Barilli, 2021.

The motif of a mirror-canvas equivalence is rendered most literally in a portrait of himself at work by the Austrian artist, Johannes Gumpp, signed and dated 1646, also destined for the Uffizi self-portrait collection (in tondo format, while the Innsbruck version is in portrait format). The painting shows the artist from the back, before a canvas on which he paints himself based on a mirror reflection to his left. It takes up the pictorial conventions of the trope in depicting the painting arm raised to the canvas with brush in hand, while looking in the mirror with intent gaze as we see it in reflection. Rave, 1960; Tudor, 2010.

89 www.rct.uk/collection/search#/1/collection/405551/self-portrait-as-the-allegory-of-painting-la-pittura. Treves, Barker et al., 2020, cat. no. 34, 217–19; Treves, 2020; Barker, 2017, which extends knowledge of the intellectual contexts in which she worked; Locker, 2015, 125–60, on the larger parameters of Artemisia's self-representation, particularly the 'costume' self-portrait; and the fundamental publications by Garrard, 1989, especially 'The Allegory of Painting', 337–70. See further Mann, 2005, 51–77; Christiansen, Mann, et al., 2001.

90 Girolamo Fontanella, 'Alla stessa' in Fontanella & Contarino, 1994, 155–58; trans. Locker, 2015, 156.

91 Ripa, *Iconologia*, 1603, 429–30.

92 www.britishmuseum.org/collection/object/P_Nn-7-51-3. Treves, Barker et al., 2020, cat. no. 17, 160–61; Garrard, 2005, 99–120; and the recent Straussman-Pflanzer & Tostmann, 2021. The drawing is further inscribed on the back: 'Les mains de l'Aurore sont louées et renomées pour leur rare beauté. Mais celle cy plus digne le doit estre mille fois plus, pour scavoir faire des merveilles, qui ravissent les yeux des plus Judicieux.'

93 https://pinacotecabrera.org/en/collezione-online/opere/autoritratto-con-figure/. See Zapperi, 1986 for a discussion of this painting as a family portrait.

94 There are two versions of the painted self-portrait, at the Uffizi Gallery and the Hermitage Museum. See further notes below.

95 Vasari, life of Giotto, *Vite*, 1568, Part I, vol. I, 123.

96 On the sign of the compass, Warwick, forthcoming 2023.

97 www.english-heritage.org.uk/visit/places/kenwood/history-stories-kenwood/rembrandt-self-portrait/. The many scholarly interpretations are summarised by Chapman, 1992, 97–101. See also Wetering (van de), 2005; and Small, 1996. On his painting materials and methods, Bomford et al., 1989. On the O of Giotto, see Ladis, 2008; Moffitt, 1984.

98 Van Hoogstraten, 1678, 110; trans. in Jacobs, 2012, 157; as cited by Chapman, 1992, 20.

99 https://collections.mfa.org/objects/32665. Smith, 2015; Slive, 1964, in addition to the above bibliography.

100 On the Netherlandish *schild*, see Chapter 2; van Mander, 1604.

101 Feigenbaum, 2020; and Feigenbaum, 2010; Sparti, 2001; Winner, 1989, II:509–15.

102 Malvasia, 2000, 286.

103 www.britishmuseum.org/collection/object/P_1901-0417-21, https://collections.louvre.fr/en/ark:/53355/cl020003571. On Queen Christina's visit to Bernini's studio in 1663, Warwick, 2012, with further bibliography.

104 See especially Unglaub, 2004, on Poussin's affective recourse to reflections, and the persuasive suggestion of an Eyckian self-portrait in the armour of the Hermitage *Tancred & Erminia*; the classic literature by

Cropper, 1992b; and Cropper, 2018b, on his thoughtful eschewal of the mirror metaphor in these images; Marin, 1999; Revel, 1997; Bätschmann, 1990; Winner, 1983.

105 See the further discussion in Chapter 2, based on Preimesberger, 2011.

106 Heikamp, 1966; Fontana, 2004. On the relationship with the poetry of Gaspare Murtola and Giambattista Marino, see Cropper, 1991. On the Murtola Medusa, Zoffili, 2011; and on the larger question of 'doubles', Ebert-Schifferer, 2007. On Bellori's view of Caravaggio's 'realism', Bellori, 1672, 212, and Marin, 1977; Bologna, 2006, in response to Calvesi, 1990. See also Warwick, 2017; Warwick, 2006.

107 The reflected image in the Uffizi *Bacchus* is famously difficult to read, though much clearer in the *Boy Bitten by a Lizard*; Gregori's analysis also takes account the discussion of Caravaggio's use of mirrors by Baglione, 1642, 136–39. This has been taken to mean that Caravaggio painted his self-portrait within these early mythological works, on which see the helpful corrective by Gregori et al., 1985, 241–42: 'What Baglione records is the widespread practice of employing a mirror as an aid in achieving a realistic representation – a method that, as a painter, he was certainly familiar with.' See also her useful summary, 236–41. See further Fried, 2010, 60; the implication of the mirror reflection is at the centre of Fried's study.

108 Arasse, 1994, 22–23; Stoichita, 1997, 260–62; Chastel, 1967. With regard to the *Allegory of Painting*, some have attempted to reconstruct an arrangement of mirrors that would have allowed Vermeer to see himself from behind, for example, Hultèn, 1949. See the important new technical research from the National Gallery of Art Washington in Gifford et al., 2022. On Vermeer more generally, see further the recent Rijksmuseum exhibition, Roelofs & Weber, 2023, particularly the essay by Sabine Pénot; Koja et al., 2021.

The scholarly literature on Vermeer has been much preoccupied with the question of whether the artist used a *camera obscura* as his primary painting method, based on meticulous observation of its visual effects of halation in his work; circumstantial evidence that he may have known the celebrated Delft scientist and lensmaker, Leeuwenhoek, who was the executor of his will, particularly given the consensus that he did meet Constantin Huygens; and Van Hoogstraten, 1678, 263, which refers to his own use of a *camera obscura* in his text, as a mode of instruction for young artists in their study of nature. See, in particular, Liedtke, 1979; Larsen, 1977; Fink, 1971; Schwartz, 1966; Seymour, 1964; and the key works by Wheelock et al., 1995; Wheelock, 1988; Wheelock 1977a & 1977b. Steadman, 2001 and Nash, 1991 are particularly strong on the historical reconstruction of artistic practice under discussion in this question. See also the corrective Chapman, 2005; and the useful survey by Wadum, 1995; and Kemp, 1990. As Arasse has argued, it seems incontestable that he knew and used the instrument; the question is how. There is every reason to suppose that an artistic use of the device might vary greatly from the cartographic needs of an architectural surveyor or military mapmaker. See the further discussion of the draughtsman's use of mirrors and optical devices in Chapter 4; and of Vermeer's inset mirrors represented in domestic interiors in Chapter 5.

109 See the further discussion of '*schilderkunst*' in Chapter 2.

110 Ebert, 2009; Chong, 1999, no. 37, 186–88.

111 The motif is addressed in Stoichita, 1997, 222–25; following Chastel, 1967; Brusati, 1990–91, and further bibliography; and Arasse, 1984. On the signature portrait of Phidias in the shield of the Athena Parthenos, Preimesberger, 2011, 46–47. On the relationship of self-portraiture to Montaigne and Pascal, Small, 1996. The theme of genre and still-life painting's double-bind as a demonstration of mimetic skill and at the same time a *vanitas* is the direct subject of Pascal's 1670 *Pensée* 134: 'How useless is painting, which attracts admiration by the resemblance of things, the originals of which we do not admire.' See further Bryson, 1990. On Peeters, Vergara, 2016.

112 On the decoration of the Hall of Mirrors of the Alcázar: Orso, 1986; Brown, 1986, 192–256; Checa Cremades, 1994; Lopez-Rey, 1996, 221–24; Cruz Yábar, 2016; Barrio Moya, 1989, 43–48. The extensive archival work yields surprisingly little about the manufacture of the mirrors themselves, while there is considerable detail about the making of the frames.

113 Checa Cremades, 1994, 391–94; Portus, 2014, both with excellent illustrations. On Carreño de Miranda, see Lopez Vizcaino & Carreño, 2007, 282, 52, for these works.

114 Checa Cremades, 1994, 381–84. There are multiple versions of this portrait, at the Prado and the Escorial, among others, with varying degrees of legibility of what can be seen of the gallery hang through the mirror reflection behind the young king. Juan Carreño de Miranda also painted portraits of Doña Mariana de Austria, which show something of the Salòn de los Espejos, of which there is a version in the Prado, another in the Palacio de Linares in Madrid. Remaining lions of gilt bronze as supports for the console tables from the hall of mirrors are preserved in the Prado in the Rubens gallery. The lions were commissioned by Velazquez in Rome in 1650. As can be seen in the portrait their paws rest on red porphyry balls.

115 Both paintings are also addressed in Chapter 5, with further bibliography. It is worthy of note that both paintings acquired these titles long after they were painted. *Las Meninas*, so-named when it entered the Prado Museum collections, is included here in relation to self-portraiture; the question of its title as of its genre – royal portrait, self-portrait – has in itself produced an extensive literature, on which see further the notes below.

The vast bibliography on this painting cannot be treated in full; I have cited those works pertaining to particular aspects of the subjects under discussion. Scholarly literature on this work is in itself prismatic, representing a wide spectrum of art-historical trajectories as well as formative interventions from adjacent disciplines. Stratton-Pruitt, 2003, offers a useful survey of the literature up to 2003; Karelis, 1985, 101–14, offers a critical overview; while Marías et al., 1995, publishes an important cross-section of the scholarly literature up to 1995, as do Greub, 2001; Nova, 1997. On the publication of the 1984 conservation of the painting, Brealey & Mena Marqués, 1984. See further above on Velazquez' technique and artistic practice more broadly. The earliest extensive discussion of the painting, which remains the authoritative source, is Palomino, 1987, vol. III, *Vida* no. 106, VII:342–43.

116 Arasse, 1984.

117 From a celebrated bibliography on *Las Meninas*, in addition to the notes below, Foucault 1964; republished as the prologue to *Les mots et les choses*, Foucault, 1966, 7–16; and for a summary of its enormous impact on the art-historical literature, Dubreuil-Blondin, 1993; and the larger discussion on the specularity of the work stemming from Foucault's 'Les suivantes' in Nova, 1997. On *mise-en-abyme*, see the Introduction to this book and Chapter 2, with further bibliography.

118 The question of the painting within the conventions of royal portraiture has received much scholarly attention from many points of view. This has generally centred on the dynastic roles of royal portraiture, notably in Portùs 2014, particularly the essay by Andrea Sommer-Mathis, 'Dynastic and Cultural Relations between the Two Lines of the Habsburg Dynasty and Their Effect on Velazquez's Work', 61–73; and the work of Fernando Marías, notably Marías, 1995. The thesis is further complicated by the politics of succession at the Spanish court at this time, which had implications for the future marriage negotiations surrounding the Infanta. At the moment of the portrait's making the Infanta was under serious consideration as heir to the throne, subsequently overtaken by the birth of a male heir. This had far-reaching implications for the cultural productions of the court in these years, as in *Las Meninas*. Dressed in the distinctive *guardainfante* of Spanish costume, she decorously takes a small ceramic *bucaro* of water proffered to her on a silver tray, the material emblems of her queenship extending to those colonies in the Americas over which she would then also preside. See further Martínez i Albero, 2016; Pereda, 2010; Codding, 2006, 102.

The related question of *Las Meninas* as a painting concerned with the claim to ennoblement for art, as represented in the painter's depiction of himself beside the presumed heir to the throne, both individually in Velazquez' own pursuit of knighthood and collectively on the part of Spanish painters in their bid to free themselves from the demeaning tax on painting as a manual craft, has won general consensus as a central concern, if not the exclusive one of this complex work. The thesis is referred to by a great number of Velazquez scholars and notably in the work of Tolnay, 1949; and most extensively Brown, 1986.

119 Palomino, 1987, vol. III, *Vida* no. 106, VII:342–43.

120 An extensive literature based on archival and collections-based research on Velazquez' role as keeper of the royal collections and as chamberlain of all court and palace decoration has yielded much information on both the interior setting within the painting and subsequent display of *Las Meninas* within the Alcázar, and on Velazquez' wide art-historical knowledge: Brown, 1986; Orso, 1986; Serrera, 1995; Greub, 2019; Greub, 2015. See further the publication of Spanish royal inventories: Martínez Leiva & Rodríguez Rebollo, 2015; Burke & Cherry, 1997. For bibliography pertaining to Velazquez' quarters within the Alcázar, see note 2 above.

121 Palomino, 1987, vol. III, *Vida* no. 106, VII:342–43.

122 Whether the mirror reflects the king and queen as they sit for the painting, or whether it reflects what is painted on Velazquez' canvas, has been greatly debated, with a general though by no means universal consensus for the former, on which see especially Steinberg, 1981; Searle, 1980; and Snyder & Cohen, 1980.

123 As Palomino noted, 1987, vol. III, *Vida* no. 106, VII:343, *Las Meninas* hung in the king's office or study. See further Greub, 2019, for discussion of the paintings displayed in this room, which included a strong number of exceptional works.

124 For discussion of the sources regarding Velazquez' interest in the Arnolfini double portrait, see Checa Cremades and Saenz de Miera, 1994, 223. On his travels in Italy, Luzón Nogué, 2022.

125 Palomino, 1987, vol. III, *Vida* no. 106, VII:343, identified both works as by Rubens; see further Mallory's note 144, 182. The paintings were first identified by Francisco Sánchez Cantón as copies by Juan del Mazo for the Prado collections of two works painted by Rubens and his workshop (*Pallas and Arachne*, now lost) with the assistance of, among others, Jordaens (*Apollo and Marsyas*, now in the Prado Museum) for the Torre de la Parada, Sanchez Canton, 1943, 14; and then tied to seventeenth-century royal inventories of the painting collection then on display in the *pieza principal* of the *cuarto del principe* (Baltasar Carlos, d. 1646) in a series of five articles by Bottineau, 1958, 451, which inspired much further scholarship on the relationship between the painting and the royal collections in Velazquez' care; see further the notes above.

126 Stoichita, 1986; Snyder, 1985; Emmens, 1961; Tolnay, 1949.

127 Palomino, 1987. vol. III, *Vida* no. 106, VII:343. This spawned a considerable art-historical literature on the genre-like quality of *Las Meninas*, beginning with the great nineteenth-century scholar Justi, 1889, 414. Glen, 1993, reread the pictorial moment further as that of the king and queen preparing to leave from their portrait sitting, hence

the opening of the door at the back of the gallery through which they will exit, and the dawning acknowledgement of their departure from the other figures in the painting. On Justi, Marten & Kanz, 2016. Justi's suggestion of a photographic quality to *Las Meninas* has spawned a further literature on the question of the painting's verifiable 'realism', much of which has centred on the mathematical accuracy of its perspective, and thus of the relation between the inset mirror-image and what it reflects within the pictorial logic of the painting, on which see especially Snyder & Cohen, 1980 (in response to Searle, 1980); and Moffitt, 1983, who suggested the use of optical aids in the painting of the room. Alpers, 1983b, also addressed the question of optical description in *Las Meninas* while drawing different conclusions as a response to Searle, 1980; and Steinberg, 1981.

128 Van Mander, 1604, fol. 250r.

129 See further Warwick, 2012, 187–229, on the interventions of court visitors to the development of the work of art in the making as documented in Chantelou's account of the making of his bust of Louis XIV.

130 Palomino, 1987, vol. III, *Vida* no. 106, VII:343. On interpretation of the painting as *capricho*, Marías, 1995. Whether the mirror reflects the king and queen as they sit for the painting, or whether it reflects them as painted on Velazquez' canvas, has been greatly debated. See especially Steinberg, 1981; Searle, 1980; Snyder & Cohen, 1980. See further Alpers, 1983b; and Stoichita, on the question of the 'puzzle-picture'.

131 Palomino, 1987, vol. III, *Vida* no. 106, VII:343–44.

132 On Calderón and court theatre, Burton, 2017; and Greer, 1991; and Forcione, 2009, for a nuanced understanding of the cultural complexities of representations of monarchy in seventeenth-century Spanish court theatre. On the Coliseo Theatre at the Buen Retiro, see further Brown & Elliott, 1980. The relationship between Velazquez and court theatre remains surprisingly understudied, although see Portús, 2017b, for discussion of the literary contexts surrounding the Surrender of Breda including Calderón. On the larger question of relations between Baroque art and theatre, Warwick, 2012.

133 Greer, 2017; Antonucci, 2020; Brown & Elliott, 1980.

134 Velazquez himself appeared in theatrical events at court, on which see Bergman, 1974. Philip IV also appeared on the stage of court as a prince, for example, playing the part of Cupid descending from clouds in a masque of 1617, on which see Deleito y Piñuela, 1935.

Chapter 4

SPECULAR SCIENCES

O telescope, instrument of much knowledge, more precious than any sceptre!

—JOHANNES KEPLER, *DIOPTRICS*, AUGSBURG, 1611

At last we come to the structure of the eye, which is like a small world in another small world, a dark chamber of infinite art and without which all the beauties of the world would be as nothing. . . . God formed the eye, which we will compare to a camera obscura, *in which exterior objects – trees, men, and the perspective of a whole countryside – are perfectly represented on a white paper.*

—JOHAN JAKOB SCHEUCHZER, *PHYSICA SACRA*, 1731–35, PSALM 94:9

ON 13 MARCH 1610 the Venetian publisher Tommaso Baglioni produced a pamphlet of some sixty unbound pages that would, through its demonstrative methods of visual enquiry, chart the future course of modern experimental science. Titled *The Starry Message* (*Sidereus nuncius*), it was the first early modern scientific treatise based on documented visual observation. Undertaken by the then-emergent astronomer and mathematician Galileo Galilei, its evidence rested on his newly devised instrument of specular magnification, the telescope. Galileo's early drafts disclose the title was chosen specifically to clarify the methodological purpose of his book. Rather than a philosophical statement on the nature of astronomy based on classical texts in the manner of his predecessors, Galileo's *Message* instead was written in the form of a documentary report, founded on empirical visual observation made with a telescope. The text that follows is precisely that: it charts his nightly telescopic sightings and the conclusions he was able to draw from what he saw. By looking through his telescope, Galileo identified the starry composition of the Milky Way, Jupiter's moons, the opaque and cratered nature of the lunar surface, and its 'strange brightness' as a reflection of Earth's light. Further to his notes, Galileo included some seventy drawings, diagrams, and charts of his telescopic observations in order to demonstrate the visual evidence for the scientific basis of his work.[1]

Taking up the example of Galileo's telescopic vision, this chapter studies interconnections between scientific and artistic imagery made by means of early modern optical instruments, including scientific mirrors, to uncover the proximate relations between them. For according to Galileo's earliest biographer and assistant, Vincenzo Viviani, the scientist's first wish was to become a painter, suggesting their close inter-relations within his work. Though he studied medicine and then mathematics at university, he also learned draughtsmanship, a critical skill for scientific study in a pre-photographic age, in order to record visual evidence. Galileo subsequently took lessons in perspective – comprising drawing – with Ostilio Ricci, professor of mathematics at the Florentine Accademia delle Arti del Disegno, under the auspices of the court architect, Bernardo Buontalenti. His fellow students included Giuliano de' Medici, and the artist who would become Galileo's lifelong friend and collaborator on the telescope, Ludovico Cigoli. Whether artist or scientist, the study of cast shadow was central to a draughtsman's training in perspectival rendering, that is, the application of shade and highlight in order to render the visual impression of volume in the graphic medium. It was this that enabled Galileo to comprehend the patches of light and dark he observed on the moon's surface as evidence of its relief.[2] The philosophical traditions of natural history, founded in Aristotelian studies, had conceived of the moon as a perfectly smooth mirroring sphere made of pellucid glass, crystal, alabaster, or diaphanous cloud; thus, Galileo's telescopic observation of a rough cratered surface characterised by hills and valleys, like Earth, posed a direct challenge to enshrined perceptions. This fundamental shift in scientific method that we call 'Galilean' arose through the contiguities of early modern art and science, both predicated on the skill of the draughtsman in the representation of the visible as the means of its documentary record, and on the shared specular instruments of optically assisted vision, from magnifiers, lenses, and mirrors to the telescopic view.

If only one page of drawings by Galileo survives, his abilities as a draughtsman were clearly recognised in his election to the Florentine Accademia del Disegno in 1613.[3] The remaining sheet, now in the Bibliotheca Nazionale in Florence, comprises a succession of moon 'faces' in pen and ink wash that formed the basis for the engraved illustrations of *The Starry Message* (Fig. 93).[4] Through the disposition of light and shade on the page, Galileo recorded his visual perception of the changing 'face' of the moon's demonstrably cratered surface. Knowledge of his further sketches of the moon rests on the resulting printed illustrations to *The Starry Message*. These engravings of Galileo's scientific drawings record sightings he made over a sequence of night observations, depicting the changes in its lunar phases waxing and waning between a crescent and a half moon. As Horst Bredekamp has noted of Galileo's preliminary drawings, each moon's perimeter was outlined with a compass, to which the draughtsman-

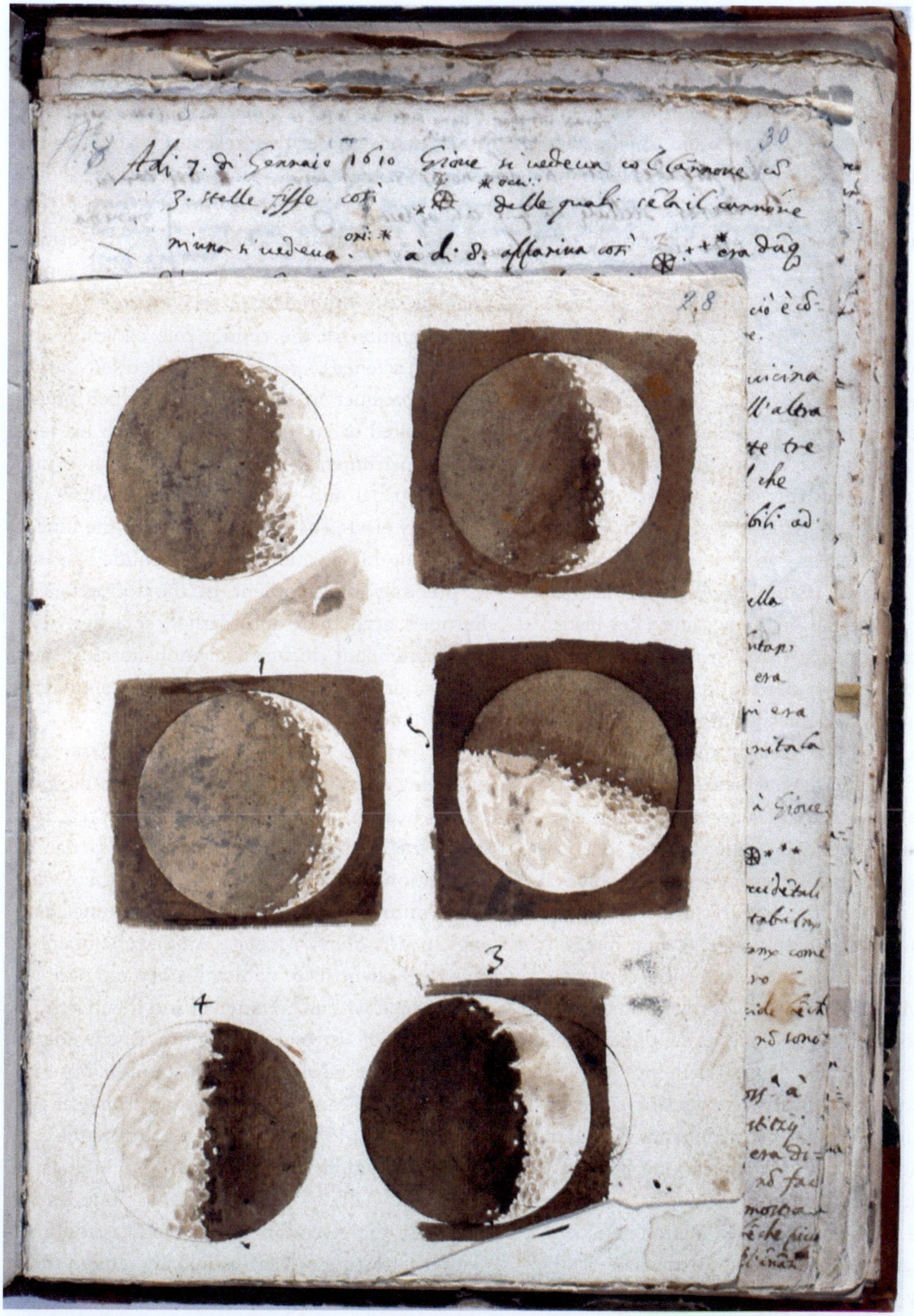

Fig. 93 Galileo Galilei, *Drawings of the Moon*, November–December 1609, pen and ink wash, Florence, Biblioteca Nazionale Centrale Firenze, Ms. Gal. 48, f. 28r.
Photo: Wikimedia

scientist then applied brush and ink to render its cratered surface. At the point in which light gives way to darkness, Galileo meticulously observed the raised mountain tops or relief that catch the light first. The more linear medium of engraving into which Galileo's drawings were translated for the purposes of book publication served only to underscore the perceptible transition between light and dark as one marked by the spotted lights of the moon's craggy relief.[5]

The immediate fame of *The Starry Message* meant that Galileo's star-gazing telescope went from being the purview of a small number of scientists to a leading collectible in both princely and scholarly *studioli* across the early modern world. Thus this instrument, composed of varying sequential combinations of precision-ground optical glass lenses and lenticular mirror-reflectors encased within a tube of leather-covered wood or cardboard, became a key instrument of early modern visual enquiry, resulting in a manifold increase in scientific observation of the heavens by its quickly burgeoning numbers of owners.[6] As Rolf Willach and Eileen Reeves have evidenced, the achievements of early modern astronomy that Galileo's career encapsulates crucially depended on incremental advances in optical glass-making, from the late medieval advent of spectacles to the crystalline silica-glass recipes and precision cutting tools and methods of the late fifteenth and sixteenth centuries.[7] As A. Mark Smith has further postulated, sixteenth-century developments in optical glass meant that spectacle lenses were not only of greatly increased efficacy but also of far wider manufacture, as the key instrumental precedent to the lenticular and specular viewing devices of Galilean scientific vision.[8]

On the basis of his newly minted telescope, Galileo had been appointed to a chair at the University of Venice; with the appearance of *The Starry Message* dedicated to Grand Duke Cosimo de' Medici he soon secured the appointment of chief mathematician and philosopher at the Florentine court he coveted.[9] As a means of procuring patronage, Galileo made princely gifts of telescopes he fabricated himself, ornamenting the leather cases with gold tooling as befitting their noble status, so securing his own ascent (Fig. 94).[10] In 1611, Prince Federico Cesi, director and founder of Rome's newly formed scientific academy, the Accademia dei Lincei (named after the reflective cats' eyes of the lynx in recognition of the central role of vision and optics in science),[11] celebrated Galileo's invention with a banquet in his honour at which guests were invited to view the moon through his telescopic instruments, so extending his fame into Rome's papal and scientific circles. Galileo was then duly elected as an academician to the Lincei, cementing his position within scientific research at precisely the moment of the formation of Europe's academies and learned societies, with their attendant lectures, demonstrations, and publications for the discussion and dissemination of new knowledge.

Yet within the encomia there was also gathering approbation on Galileo's scientific view of the heavens. While this would only reach its most tragic consequences in Galileo's trial by inquisition and condemnation of 1633, there were more immediate refutations of his celestial findings in *The Starry Message*. Among members of Europe's scientists of natural history and philosophy trained within Aristotelian and then Catholic traditions of astronomy, there was considered dissent to the new methods of scientific observation over the canonical authority of biblical and classical texts. Johannes Kepler, court mathematician to Rudolf II in Prague, by and large endorsed Galileo's lunar sightings, but others such as the German Jesuit and astronomer Father Christopher Clavius initially refuted them entirely (though he would later come to cautious acceptance), continuing to uphold the standing view of the heavens as crystalline, and the moon

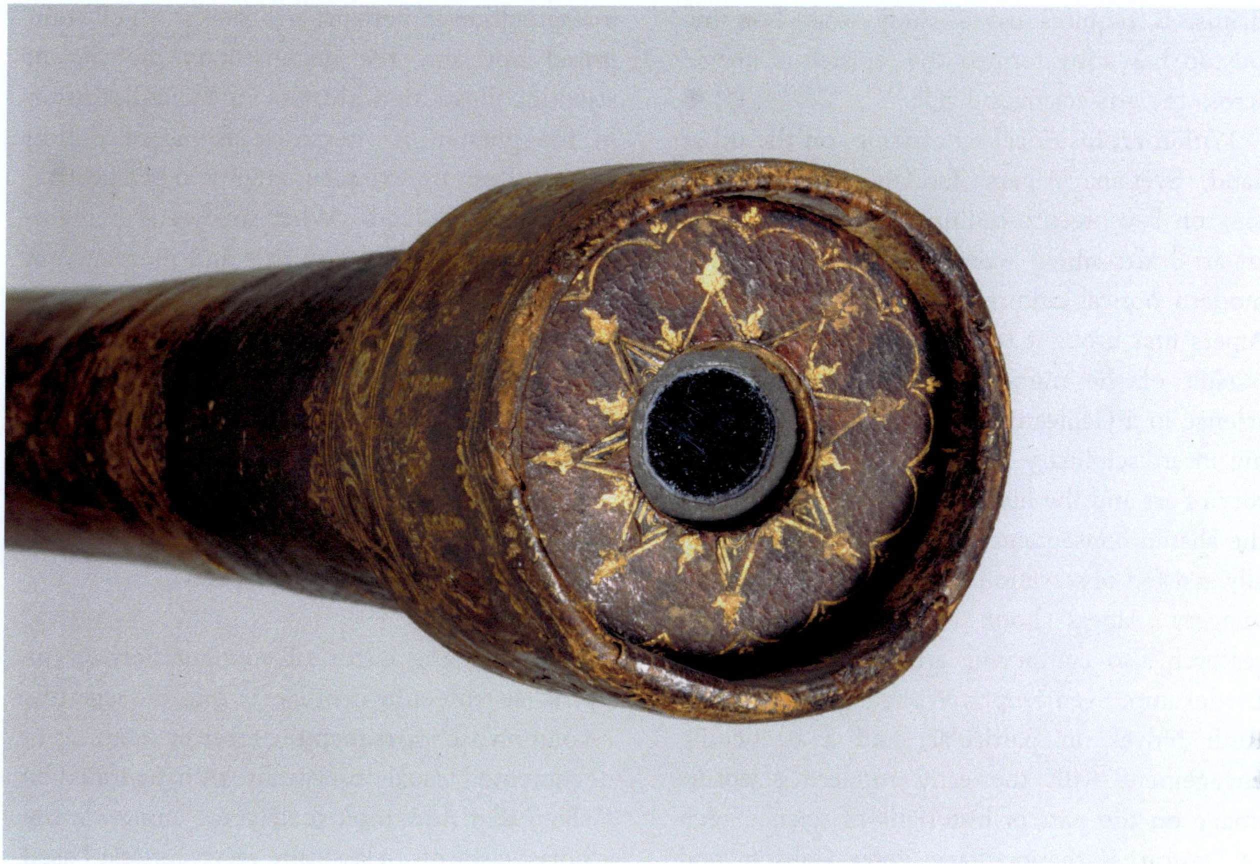

Fig. 94 Galileo Galilei, *Telescope*, late 1609, wood, leather, glass, 127.3 cm, Museo Galileo Florence, inv. no. 2428. Photo: Alamy

as either glassy or cloud-like, a perfectly smooth and spherical reflective surface symbolising Marian immaculacy. For Father Clavius would declare that Galileo's observations were nothing but illusions: the product either of optical distortion arising from the use of curved or clouded lenses or of painted images implanted into the lenses.[12] Howsoever Father Clavius was wrong in his initial judgment of Galileo, as he later acknowledged himself, his comment speaks to the historical array of competing views at the time, as to both the nature of the moon and, more broadly, the intellectual place of optically assisted visual imagery as a scientific method.

What is significant, in mapping the early history of negative response to Galileo's telescopic findings, is the recourse to another parallel if much-debated form of early modern enquiry also arising from the use of mirroring lenses and consultation of the stars: that of the optics of 'magical' illusions. This chapter's concern is thus to address the complex folds of early modern scientific imagery, founded in the perspectival skills of the draughtsman coupled with the new magnifiers, reflectors, and projectors of optical science. On the one hand, it includes a vast imagery of ludic visual illusion, in both art and visual culture, which was understood as a learned *divertissement* and as a demonstration of the 'natural magic' of optics. On the other hand, it takes up the early modern mimetic images of scientific documentary observation as witnessed through optically assisted instruments of vision such as Galileo's telescope. This documentary imagery of Galilean scientific observation is here understood as companionate to painting's mimetic claims. It requires us to study what Lorraine Daston has aptly termed the 'epistemic image' across the arts-sciences divide.[13]

Within art-historical scholarship, on the other hand, Svetlana Alpers' fundamental study of 1983 on seventeenth-century Dutch painting as an 'art of describing' was also predicated on early modern optical cultures of vision. In this book Alpers first brought to prominence the cognate pursuit of the mimetic image across art and science in a Galilean age.[14] Inaugurating a growing interdisciplinary proximity between the history of art and the history of science, centred on the shared consequences of early modern optically assisted observational vision and its resulting imagery, Alpers' book nurtured a wealth of research also comprising art historians such as Bredekamp, Sven Dupré, Wolfgang Lefèvre, and Ruth Noyes, in particular; and a deepening engagement with the early modern scientific image on the part of historians of science such as Daston, Katharine Park, Peter Galison, and Christoph Lüthy.[15] This chapter's subject is therefore to map the place of the mirror-image as the matrix of visual mimesis within early modern science, and then to consider its implications for the arts.

Taking up the historical advent of the Galilean telescope in light of existing research on art-science imagery, the chapter pursues the interrelated material histories of scientific mirrors and lenses in the development of optically assisted vision, and its manifold cultural consequences for all forms of image-making, both mimetic and illusionistic. Alongside the first telescopes and microscopes, it studies the earliest catoptric museums and panorama theatres, anamorphoses and perspective cabinets, scientific images as well as every kind of optical trick or *trompe-l'oeil* imagery, and the illusionistic Baroque ceiling paintings of the heavens that accompanied Galileo's now-scientific view of the skies. Further, it turns to their broader cultural interpretation in both art and letters, which comprised not only the documentary drawing of scientific illustration but also its ludic distension in the pursuit of alternative forms of optical illusion, from theatre scenography to perspectival painting of all kinds. What follows is a multifaceted account of the mirror and its reflection across a wealth of objects and images, to evidence the proximity of early modern art and science in the shared study of optics as the science of light and vision, but also of optical illusion as the scientific basis of mimetic painting.

NATURAL MAGIC

Within any historical configuration of the seventeenth century as one of 'scientific revolution', scholars map the forensic methods of documented visual observation as inaugurated by Galileo that now took their place alongside the scholasticism of a classically received, text-based wisdom. At the same time, scholars of the history of science acknowledge the co-existence of other epistemes, or what Pamela H. Smith has termed 'pseudo-sciences', alongside the emergence of what we now recognise as the prevailing scientific paradigms of a nascent modernity. These 'pseudo-sciences' centred on optical illusion or 'magic', as the study of optical effects, in both art and science. Entirely separate fields today, their interwoven histories within the early modern development of scientific vision emerged from a larger cultural firmament of intellectual 'curiosity'. Thus alongside what we recognise teleologically as proto-science, 'magic' was an equally weighty field of research within early modernity, which juxtaposed astronomy alongside astrology; alchemy with chemistry; optical science and optical illusions. For within the early modern study of so-named natural magic was the weighty realisation of a new scientific vision, forged by means of optically assisted observational methods that shaped the future course of all visual enquiry. As Catherine Wilson and others have argued, modern scientific methods based on empirical observation nonetheless arose within Renaissance intellectual frameworks of the analogical and the magical.[16] The illusions of which Father Clavius accused Galileo were apparently those of 'natural magic' precisely because of their shared interwoven configuration in the history of early modern optically assisted vision.

Thus the Renaissance term 'natural magic' continued to be used across the seventeenth century in the domain of scientific enquiry, to signify those aspects of empirical observation seen as marvellous or wondrous. From the astronomical as well as astrological study of the stars, the study of nature was understood as both scientific and magical. This is epitomised in the title to the sixteenth-century best-selling, republished, and much-translated book on the subject by the Neapolitan polymath Giambattista della Porta, *Magia naturalis* (Natural Magic) (1558), and notably in his greatly expanded 1589 illustrated edition with dedicated chapters on the illusions of optics.[17] With still-evident ties to late medieval 'books of secrets' in its assembly of recipes and how-to instructions in 'natural magic', yet it is also kin to emerging scientific concerns of natural history in the Galilean age. In this respect the very purpose of the title may be said to demonstrate the scientific basis of what had heretofore been seen as nature's wonders, and to disseminate broadly through the printed medium those 'occult' recipes so long kept secret. Indeed, della Porta's title was explicitly intended to suggest the equivalence and adjacence of these fields of study, by designating nature's 'magic' as an aspect of natural history precisely within experiment- and observation-based science.

The intertwined consideration of these spheres was manifest across intellectual and political domains. Thus Queen Catherine de Médicis was patron of scientific learning, but also governed through the astrological predictions of Nostradamus; while at the Elizabethan court, both Francis Bacon and the astrologer John Dee acted as chief advisors to the Queen on account of their recognised knowledge across all aspects of intellectual enquiry, including mineral, optical, and astronomical science but also alchemy and astrology. Like other magi of the pre-modern era, Dee apparently made his astrological predictions by means of instruments of vision close to those of lens-based scientific enquiry: a crystal ball or prismatic lens, and a 'shew-stone' mirror of obsidian or black volcanic glass through which he claimed to describe the portents of nature and the stars. Thus the very materials of magic and science were contiguous.[18] The prismatic crystal ball of the type Dee consulted was an ancient amulet form deemed to 'divine' or descry illusionistic images in its bi-convex lens; its visual 'magic' in fact resided in its scientifically demonstrable ability to refract clearly to a focal point in bowl-shaped reduction the reflections of its surroundings, which were interpreted as celestial signs. Similarly, della Porta authored not only his book of *Natural Magic*, which comprised the study of both scientific and 'magical' optics, but also a treatise on light refraction observed in the passage of light through glass ampoules of water.[19] This proximity of early modern optical science with 'magical' illusion may be understood to culminate in the figure of Isaac Newton, as the father of modern optics and indeed of scientific research more broadly, who also sustained career-long interests in the scientifically verifiable optics of visual illusion, understanding both as parallel manifestations of natural wonder.[20] The science of optics developed alongside the magic of optical illusions, nowhere more so than in the early history of the lens-based instruments of observation that were to constitute the very method of modern scientific research.

Scholars have compassed this early history of modern optics between Newton, on the one hand, and late medieval optical research, on the other, inaugurated by the thirteenth-century development of crystal magnifiers and the first lenses for spectacles to produce optically assisted extensions of human vision. Thus the interwoven development of the scientific instruments of modernity lies within a much larger field of the intellectual history of the visible, as this chapter traces, from late medieval magnifiers and spectacles to the microscopes and telescopes of the Galilean 'revolution' of sight.[21] The range of premodern scientific enquiry also engaged in the study of 'magic' encompassed medicine as well as mathematics, optics, and perspective. The thirteenth-century papal and royal doctor Arnauld de Villeneuve or Villanova, for example, studied the development of optical lenses in their medical capacity for improved sight as well as their use in courtly displays of magical illusions. Sixteenth-century forms of optical theatre also meshed with the highest circles of scientific enquiry. Girolamo Cardano, Milanese, was professor of mathematics at the university, family doctor to the cardinalate Borromeo family, and author of a tract on optics entitled *De subtilitate* (1550); at the same time he was deeply engaged with courtly displays of the 'magic' of optical illusion.[22]

Endebted to the ancient legacy of Euclidean texts on both optics and catoptrics, or the science of mirror reflection, early modern ocular science also regarded the mirror and the lens as equivalent instruments of light's conduct, and so of vision itself. Rafael Mirami's 1582 *Specularia*, dedicated to *'la scienza de gli specchi'*, brought together the science of spectacle glasses with mirrors, as the title proclaimed. While scientific in its orientation towards the geometry of light reflection, it nonetheless acknowledged the 'miraculous' and 'marvellous' effects of mirror reflections, able to make the faraway appear present, to distort, reverse, or miniaturise. Yet these illusions, Mirami qualified presciently, were not occult, arising instead from the science of light, howsoever apparently magic.[23] The Jesuit Athanasius Kircher's books, *Primitiae gnomonicae catoptricae* (First Principles of Gnomonics and Catoptrics) of 1635 and *Ars magna lucis et umbrae* (Great Art of Light and Shadow) of 1646 treated the subject of light and shade within various domains and specifically within specular and optical projection, from the legendary burning mirrors of Archimedes to the science of reflection to catoptric shows of specular illusion with mirrors and lenses. Great polymath of the age with interests across every domain, Kircher's writings and collections bespeak his understanding of science and natural magic as conjoined wonders.[24] Charles Patin, a French physician and numismatist visiting Nuremberg, witnessed an optical illusion show that led him to coin the term 'deceptive art' to describe it;[25] while Jean-François Niceron's treatise, *La perspective curieuse, ou Magie artificielle des effets merveilleux* (The Curious Perspective, or The Artificial Magic of Marvellous Effects), first published in 1638 and appearing in an expanded edition in 1652, specifically brought together optical illusions in the study of science and perspective as an aspect of magic's crafted illusions.[26] Thus the relationship between science and natural magic, as the study of wonder, pervaded the visual and literary arts in the twinned pursuit of illusion. The seventeenth-century Scots poet William Drummond of Hawthornden, who also devised optical devices and mirrors, described perspective as a form of 'alchimie' in its manner of visual deceit. Shakespeare's *Twelfth Night* termed such imagery 'a natural perspective that is and is not' (5:1), following Emanuele Tesauro's literary disquisition on perspective as that 'which makes you see what you do not see'.[27] Equally, John Dee saw optics – which he called perspective – and scrying or divining as one and the same in his

Preliminary Aphoristic Teachings, a text dedicated to explication of celestial forces within nature, and particularly of astrological interpretations of astronomical observation.[28]

Thus Father Clavius' refutation of Galileo's telescopic observations as nothing but optical illusions sprang from a closely entwined if often contested early modern history of optical science with apparent magic, of astronomical sighting with visual deceit. Galileo too worked within this fused history of early modern optics, with a sure understanding of his telescope as an instrument of both science and wonder. He frequently gave demonstrations of his telescopes to princely and scholarly audiences, as a performed 'curiosity' within precisely those cultures of the marvellous that characterised the interwoven histories of early modern science and technology, spectacle and showmanship, magic and illusion, even if he also criticised their sometime confusion.[29] Clavius' objections had valence precisely because the use of optical lenses for the purposes of illusionistic display was equally pervasive as their use in the search for scientifically observed 'truth'. More broadly, early modern cultures of 'curiosity' nurtured both, with an interest towards the exceptional, rare, curious, wondrous, or marvellous. A much-debated term within scholarship as to its precise designation and significance, early modern 'curiosity' may here be understood as informing the quest for all forms of knowledge through a process of investigation, just as Galileo proposed in *The Starry Message*.[30]

In Galileo's correspondence, however, we witness his clear distinction between the domains of optical illusion within science and those of curiosity, even if he also practiced across them in the interests of princely patronage. In a letter of 1612 to the artist Lodovico Cigoli, his close collaborator in study of the moon, Galileo set forth his scientific analysis of light and shade as the visual signs of a lunar relief surface, appealing to his knowledge of optics in the art of the draughtsman as well as the observations of an astronomer.[31] As various scholars have noted, the study of optics and particularly the branch concerned with cast shadow informed early modern art and astronomy alike. If astronomers mapped the cast shadow of the sundial, and later the patterns of light and dark on the moon's surface through Galileo's telescope, artists studied the effects of light and shade in the illusionistic rendering of volume and form. Equally, it was by means of draughtsmanship that early modern astronomers mapped the heavens of astronomical observation through its specular instrumentation.[32] Galileo's letter to Cigoli concerns precisely the science of optics and perspective as it pertains in painting in which he argues the case for drawing as a specular medium of visual truth, while also recognising its capacities as an instrument of illusion. Bringing together his perceptual observation of the moon through his telescope, and his practice-based knowledge of the art of drawing, Galileo demonstrated that the visible perception of relief is founded in the science of optics:

> if we were to expose a . . . figure to the light and were then to proceed to color it in such a way that we paint it dark wherever it is light until its color [tone] is completely unified, the figure would appear devoid of relief altogether.[33]

In so saying, Galileo clarifies that visual observation is fundamental to all scientific method, such that optics must be a primary tool in any form of intellectual enquiry. At the same time, the letter eloquently evidences Galileo's broad engagement with the arts. As Erwin Panofsky noted in publishing this letter with his commentary, Galileo came from a family of musicians, and his comparative analogies are with the arts: music, literature, sculpture, and painting. Across disciplines, Galileo's comparisons rest on different forms of visual illusion, both scientific and artistic. The scientist fully recognised that art's mimetic power lay in the profundity of its deceit. Thus the art of painting's perspectival illusion lay in the skill of its feigned presence of volume and space. Panofsky understood this as Galileo's acknowledgement of optical or perspectival science as a kind of 'magic' or visual acuity inherent within representational form.[34]

Elsewhere, however, Galileo was critical of those types of art taking up the pictorial conventions of perspective to what were in his view anti-illusionistic ends, as with paintings predicated on perspectival 'tricks' of distortion such as anamorphoses, which 'show a human figure when looked at sideways but when observed frontally . . . display nothing but a welter of colors and strange chimerical shapes'. He valorised instead the veristic illusions of mimetic painting in which 'the contours are softly dissolved, and by virtue of smooth transitions from one color to the other the picture becomes soft, round, and rich in relief'.[35] His commentary indicates the prevailing cultural adoption of the ludic telescopic view as a metaphor of perspectival vision in its doubled sense, of both scientific truth and optical illusion.

Just as Galileo the scientist turned to the arts to enrich his comparison between scientific vision as a form of demonstrable 'truth' and anamorphic or 'trick' perspective as distortion, so the poets took up the Galilean telescope as a literary device of rich metaphorical valence. As Galileo also surely understood, the term 'illusion' arises from *ludere*, to play. Thus John Donne, in 1611, wrote of 'Galileo . . . who of late hath summoned the other world, the stars to come nearer to him, and give him an account of themselves'.[36] The telescope's perceived 'magic' lay in the play of distance, able to make present what was otherwise invisible to the eye, bringing the distant stars into view. Galileo's fellow-astronomer, Kepler, would compose a work of fiction about a trip to the moon as if through a telescope, which he titled 'The Dream' (*Somnium*), so launching the literary genre of imaginary space travel.[37] By 1654, in the publication of the Jesuit literary theorist Emanuele Tesauro, *Il cannocchiale aristotelico* (The Aristotelian Telescope), the telescope had become a widely used figure of speech to signify the marvellous wonders of metaphor and literary wit with the ability to 'see' by allusion. The frontispiece to the definitive 1670 edition of Tesauro's literary *cannocchiale* depicts two women, one holding a telescope up to the sun, the other painting a sundial, so pictorializing the relations between the arts and sciences in the study of astronomy (Fig. 95). Throughout, Tesauro celebrates the figurative force of allegorical witticisms by likening figures of speech to perspectival illusions – hyperbole, clever deceits, and unexpected counterpoints. Metaphor, like perspective, is a mirror of the mind for Tesauro, in which it is more pleasing and curious to view objects in a perspective view than in unmediated nature, in recognition of their greater 'artfulness'. As Tesauro's frontispiece indicates, the abiding literary tropes of his text are those of telescopic viewing and painting, as parallel forms of marvellous deceit and figurative ingenuity within the picturing 'shield' of art's noble devices. The telescope, product of practice-based research centred on the optics of glass lenses and specular light reflections, had become, alongside the mirror, the visual sign of both knowledge and wit, truth and illusion. In John Milton's *Paradise Lost*, the spotted moon of Galileo's optic glass is conflated with the Achillean shield of classical myth and Homeric verse, marked by the blows of angelic battle like the cratered lunar surface of scientific observation (I.284–91). Taking sight as the central allegory for the discovery of knowledge, yet Milton balances the authority of scientific vision with textual exegesis, of ancients and moderns, of 'picturing and poesie'. Milton's view of the moon's light, now understood as the secondary

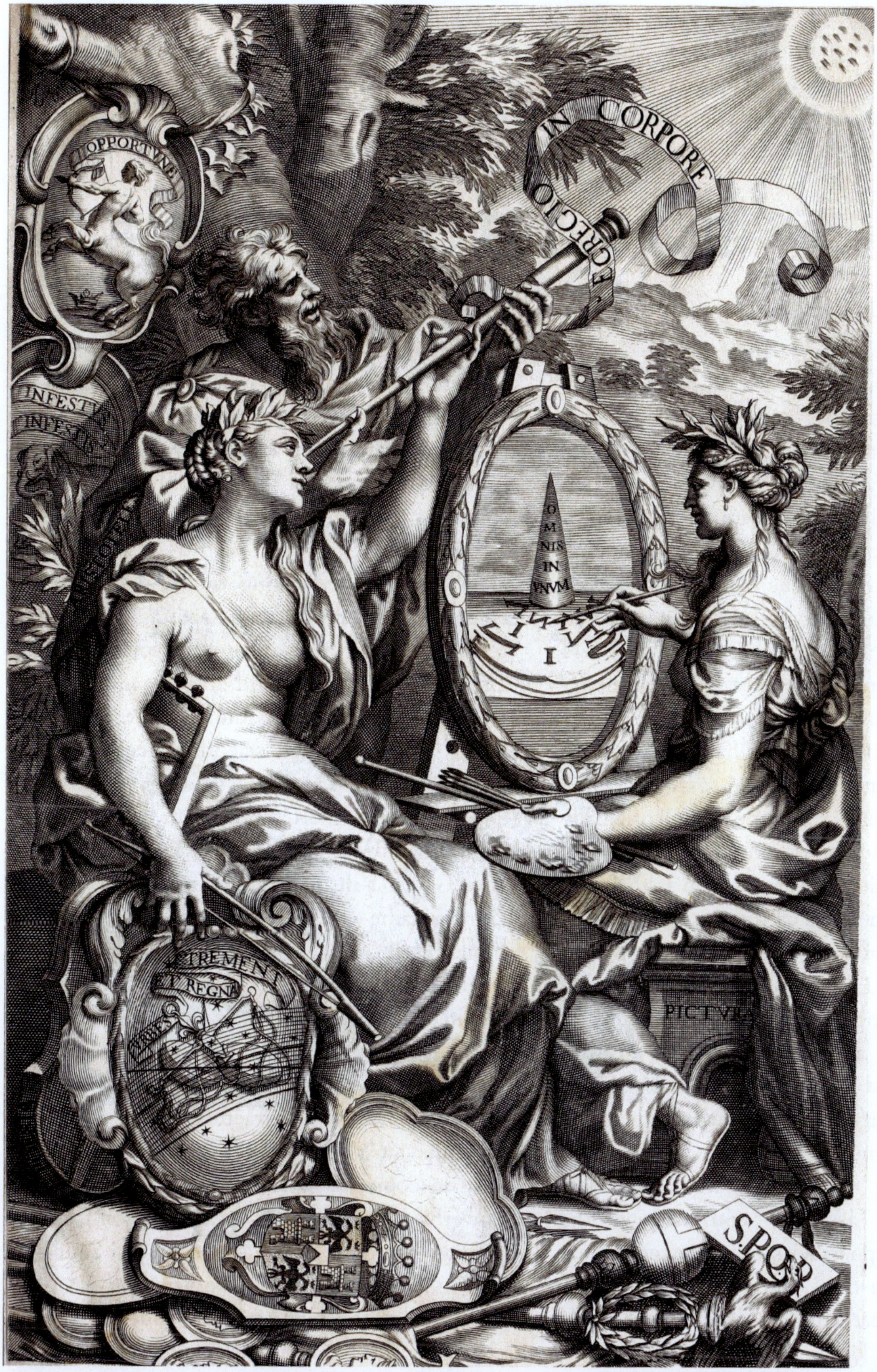

Fig. 95 Domenico Piola and Giorgio Tasnière, frontispiece for Emanuele Tesauro, *Il cannochiale aristotelico*, Torino, 1670.
Photo: Wikimedia

reflection of sunlight on Earth, is of a 'mirror, with full face borrowing her light from him, for other light she needed none'. Through the metaphorical telescope the poet pictorialises vision itself, in the name of that 'Tuscan artist' Galileo.[38]

CHAMBERS OF VISION

The early history of the telescope as an object is a layered and contested one, emerging from long-standing craft-based expertise in blowing glass and grinding lenses in pursuit of a variety of optical instruments for magnification, from magnifying stones to spectacles. While Galileo is generally credited with the full realisation of the telescope's astronomical uses, its first emergence appears to issue from the quest for optical aids in land surveying and military reconnaissance, closely related to binoculars and field glasses. Like Filippo Brunelleschi's demonstration of perspective at the door of Florence Cathedral (discussed in Chapter 3), also indebted to land surveying practices, the seventeenth-century telescope was originally designed as an aid for viewing across territorial distances. Its earliest documentation is that of a patent application made by the Dutch spectacle- and lens-maker Hans Lippershey to the States-General at The Hague dated 2 October 1608. Lippershey described it as an instrument 'for seeing things far away as if they were nearby'. This he proposed to develop for the benefit of the state in military reconnaissance, immediately arousing governmental interest.[39] The demonstration of the instrument was reportedly encomiastic: an assembly convened at the Hague to test Lippershey's claim gained a clear view of both the clock tower in Delft and the windows of the cathedral at Leiden, respectively nine and sixteen kilometres away. In the weeks that followed, other lens-makers came forward with similar claims: if Lippershey did not, as a consequence, receive his patent, the advent of the telescope as an instrument of long vision had clearly arrived. As news of the exceptional sighting abilities of the instrument spread, others set about designing their own, including Galileo. While Lippershey's telescope could reportedly magnify up to three times, Galileo swiftly engineered a capacity for twenty times, so enabling him to turn his instrument to the stars.[40]

In the *Starry Message*, Galileo described his instrument as *perspicillum*, the singular form of a magnifying eyeglass, so reflecting the close links with ancient instruments of magnification, from rock crystals to medieval lenses. Throughout his notes, however, he more commonly referred to it simply as '*il cannone*', or the viewing tube. Early translations include 'perspective glass' and 'spy glass', together indicating the close links with land surveying and military reconnaissance. The term 'telescope' was apparently coined by the Greek mathematician and theologian Giovanni Demisiani, present at the banquet held at Rome's newly formed scientific Accademia dei Lincei in 1611 in which guests observed the night sky through Galileo's 'tube'. From the Greek *tele*, for far, and *skopein*, for looking, Demisiani's term gave Galileo's instrument the mantle of a classicising name within a celebration of its modernity.[41]

Historiography of the telescope has generally credited to Lippershey and Galileo the development of a tubular telescope using two spectacle-type lenses at either end as its means of magnification, known as a refracting telescope. While accounts vary, the realisation that two lenses used in conjunction could produce much more powerful magnification was apparently the guiding principle of its construction. Similarly, Newton is generally acknowledged as the 'inventor' of the reflecting telescope for greater clarity of chromatic focus in 1668, built with mirrors in lieu of lenses – one concave and one flat – at either end of the viewing tube. However,

Galileo and indeed many of his predecessors working with optical magnifying devices of many kinds had been experimenting with both mirrors and lenses – reflective and refractive, convex and concave, metal and glass – for at least a century and likely much longer.[42] In effect, the telescope arose out of a lengthy historical process of experimentation with both lenses and optical mirrors as instruments of magnification, reflection, and projection, to result in the first scientific view of the heavens.[43] Its destiny is at no time more apparent than in the extraordinary mirrors of the James Webb Space Telescope today.

The historical evidence is further complicated by changes in terminology. In English and French, the terms '*glasse*' or '*verre*' were used interchangeably for both lenses and mirrors, indicative of their ready reciprocity within the fabrication of such instruments; while in Italian '*la sfera*' indicated convex lenses and convex mirrors interchangeably by describing their shared form. In Dutch, '*brillen*' similarly drew together mirrors with lenses, the term centring on their shared lightsome capacities. The generic English term for all manner of lenses and reflectors was thus 'glass', hence 'perspective glass' for concave or convex mirrors; 'burning glass' for parabolic mirrors (usually made of metal); even 'steel glass' for metal mirrors; magnifying glass for a magnifying lens, as also for field glasses; and 'looking glass', which would subsequently become identified with toiletry mirrors but which originally designated any type of mirror for close observation, while the equivalent term '*glace*' for mirror alongside *miroir* also remains in French.[44] Optical lenses and mirrors alike were readily available for sale both as spectacles and as instruments of vision from glass-lens makers, as a business card of 1683 from John Yarwell's optician shop in St Paul's churchyard London illustrates, displaying a range of lenses and optical devices (Fig. 96). In early modern scientific discourse they were regarded as largely interchangeable in their shared capacity for both magnification and projection. The most advanced scientists made and ground their own lenses in close collaboration with highly skilled optical glassmakers, from Galileo to Newton; indeed, much of their success in astronomy and microscopy depended on their skill in the specific composition of optical glass for precision-cut lenses and reflectors.[45]

Galileo himself used both spherical and plane mirrors alongside his lens-based telescope in his astronomical studies, and his correspondence with Gian Francesco Sagredo and Cesare Marsili testifies to their discussion of mirror-based as well as lenticular telescopes. The Roman Jesuit Niccolò Zucchi claimed to have thought of using a concave mirror in a telescope in 1616 as the means of magnification, which Galileo also considered, as well as the Minim monk and mathematician in Paris, Marin Mersenne. In 1632, Galileo's associate Bonaventura Cavalieri, professor of mathematics at Bologna, published a design for a reflecting telescope within a larger compendium of experiments with parabolic mirrors, in his *specchio ustorio*.[46] The mirror-based or reflecting telescope was perceived to offer greater clarity of vision through a reduction in chromatic variation. For this reason, the Scottish professor of mathematics and astronomer James Gregory revived Mersenne's reflecting telescope in Edinburgh, in pursuit of enhanced vision; while in his *Optica promota* of 1663, Gregory illustrated the geometry of differing chromatic light reflection through a variety of differently shaped lenses comprising glasses and mirrors: convex, concave, parabolic (Fig. 97).[47] These optical experiments constitute the background to Newton's mirror-based reflecting telescope, taking up Mersenne's and Gregory's ideas, as well as the parallel development by Laurent Cassegrain, which was published in the dedicated journal of the French Académie des Sciences in 1672.[48] Newton's

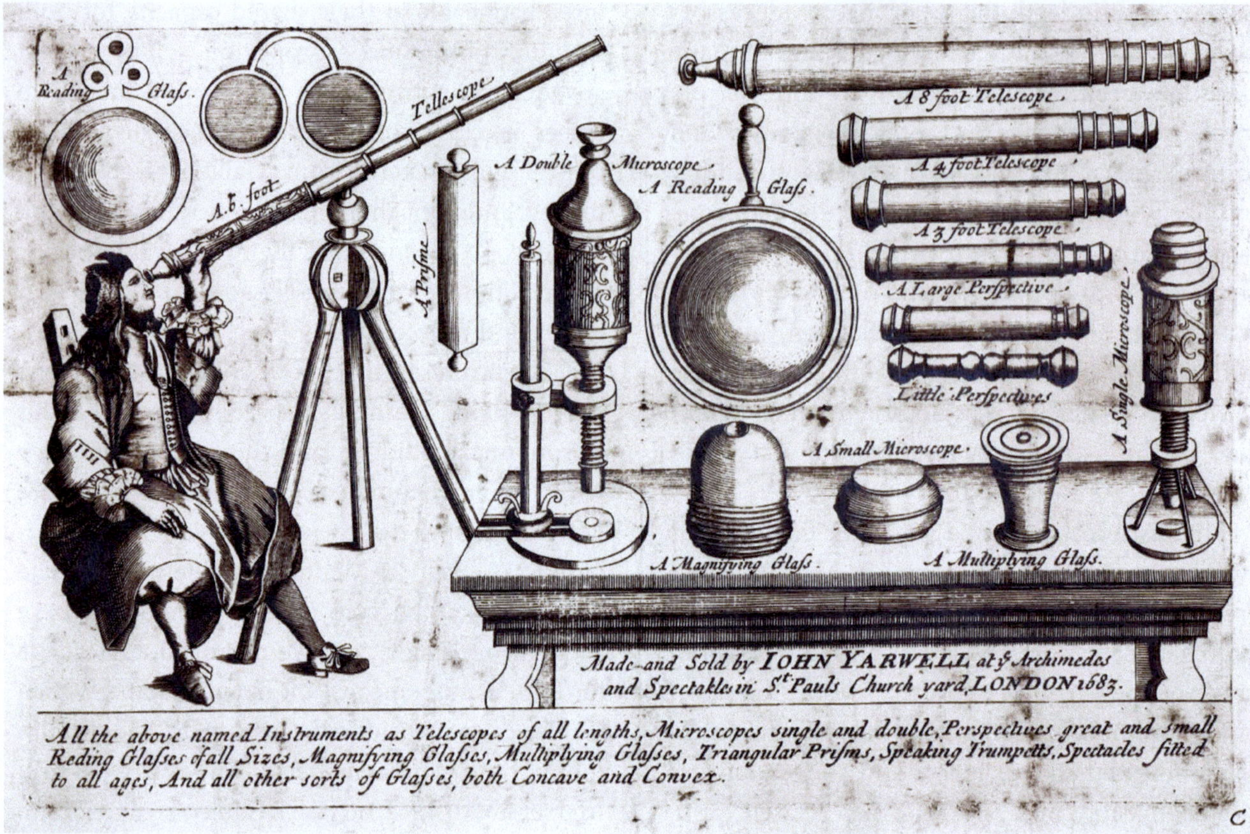

Fig. 96 John Yarwell, trade card: *John Yarwell, St Paul's Churchyard, London*, 1683, print, Science Museum London, Object No. 1951-687/45.
Photo: Science Museum Group

model succeeded in delivering the lowest chromatic aberration on the basis of greater precision in glass-lens and mirror-making technology to avoid irregularities of reflection, so underscoring the vital importance of its material manufacture alongside optical research. This he presented to the Royal Society in 1671, and to the king Charles II the following year (Fig. 98).[49]

As scholars such as Rolf Willach have pointed out, much depends on the definition of what constitutes a telescope, and what forms part of a wider range of now-obsolete instruments of early modern magnification. Out of the broad field of enquiry into early modern viewing instruments, including spectacle glasses and mirror reflectors, arose both the telescope and the microscope in the same historical moment. Howsoever they would become recognisably distinct instruments over the course of the seventeenth century – one for long vision and the other for close-up magnification – their early history as instruments of enlargement is a shared one. The development of the telescope was much more rapid because of its initial uses within military surveying; in other respects the two instruments arose side by side.[50] Scholarship has often considered Galileo as the 'inventor' of the compound or multi-lens microscope, in which two or more lenses were fitted into a tube made of wood or fortified paper. Further, Galileo is documented as having used a small telescope, which he termed '*occhiolino*' (little eye) or *cannoncino* (little tube) for the close-up purposes of microscopy, by adjusting the types of lenses fitted into the viewing tube. Again, members of the Accademia dei Lincei were apparently

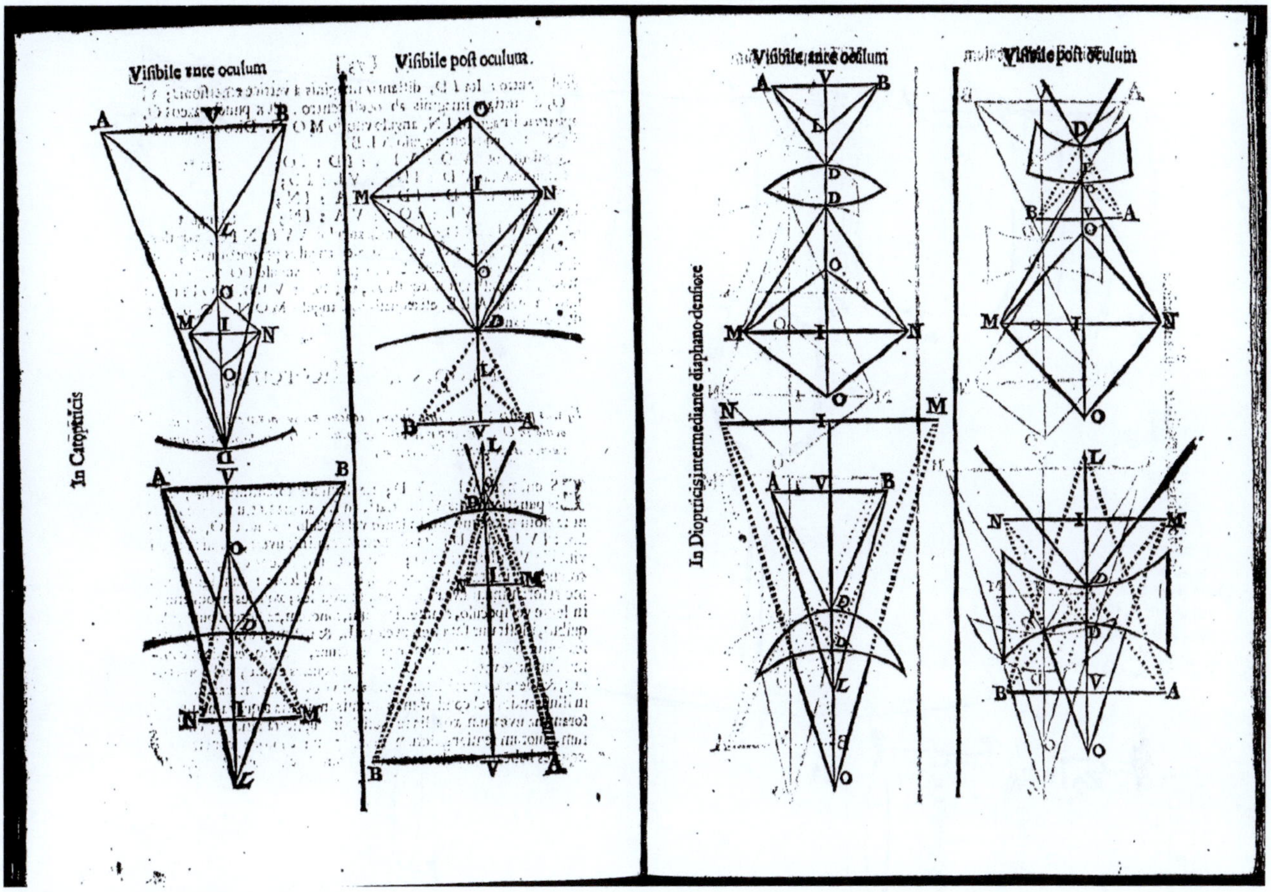

Fig. 97 James Gregory, cross-section diagram of lenses within tubular viewing instruments, in *Optica promota*, London, 1663. Photo: Proquest EEB

responsible for conceiving the title 'microscope', meaning small, by Lincean Giovanni Faber just one year after Demisiani had coined the term 'telescope', clearly intended to suggest an analogous relation between the two instruments.[51]

It is also apparent from Galileo's letters that he and Cigoli made use of a type of *camera obscura*, or 'darkened chamber', as a means of transcribing their astronomical observations of sunspots onto paper.[52] Often seen as the early modern origins of nineteenth-century photography, this was in fact an ancient method of image reflection using a pinhole to admit focussed light into a darkened chamber for the purposes of documentary transcription, and commonly deployed in land surveying and mapping from antiquity. Its early modern development was greatly extended through the increasing use of lenses and mirrors at the point of the pinhole in order to 'right' an otherwise reversed and upended cast image. The earliest documented use of biconvex mirrors or lenses placed as a glass eye at the pinhole of a room-sized *camera obscura* is generally given to Girolamo Cardano, as he describes in *De subtilitate* (1550): 'If you wish to see what goes on in the street when the sun is bright, place in your windows a glass disc and, the window having been closed [shuttered], you will see images projected through the aperture onto the wall.'[53] This is confirmed by Daniele Barbaro's description of using spectacle lenses at the pinhole of a *camera obscura* in his *Pratica della perspettiva*, first published in 1568; while his fellow Venetian, Giovanni Battista Benedetti, suggests the use of a flat mirror to correct the natural

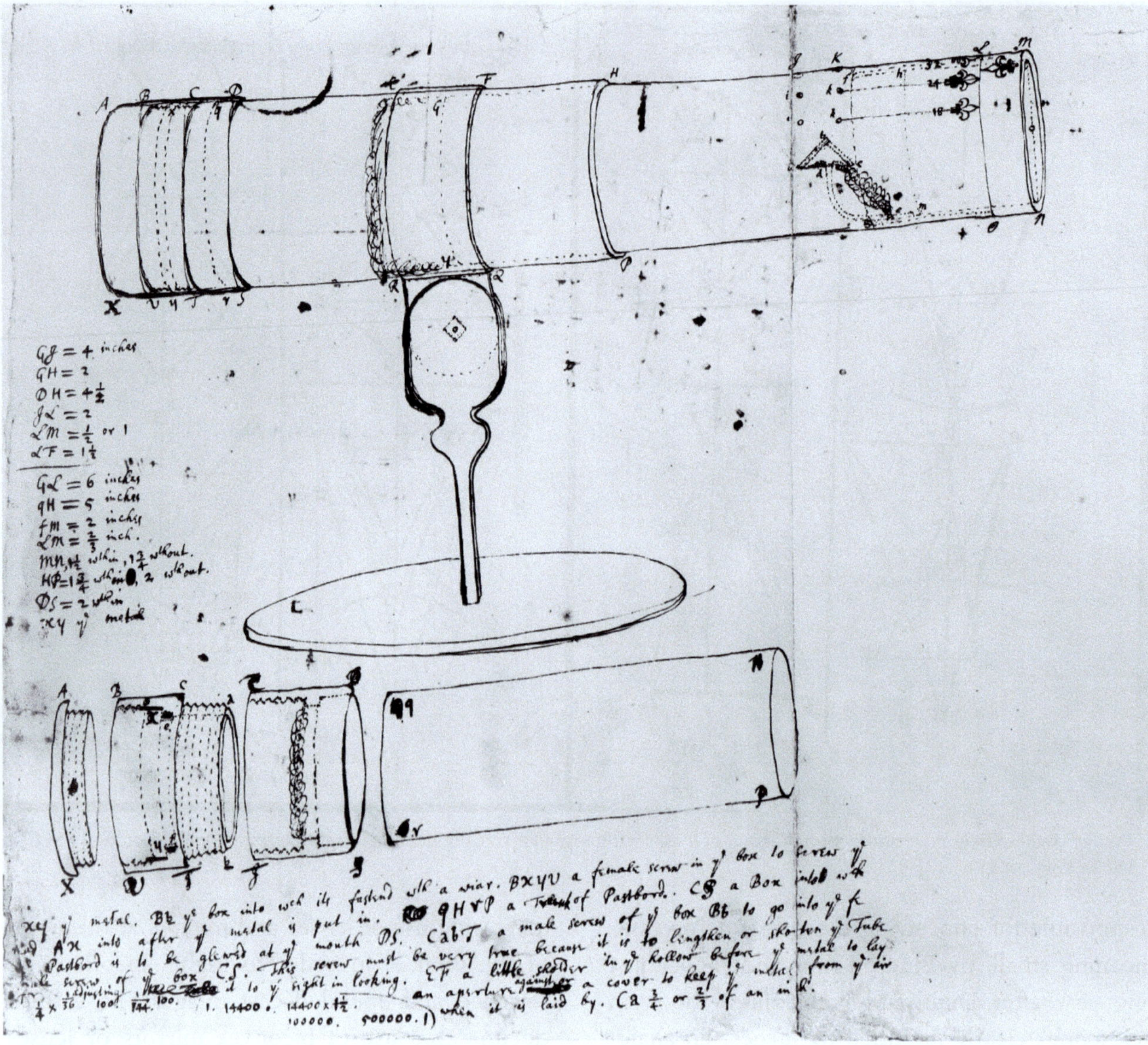

Fig. 98 Henry Oldenburg, *Newton's Reflecting Telescope*, 6 January 1672, drawing, pen and ink, 26.3 × 21.3 cm, Royal Society, London.
Photo: Alamy

inversion of the reflected image in his *Diversarum speculationem* of 1585.[54] The practice seems to have become broad-based among early modern astronomers, who used the *camera obscura* interchangeably with the telescope, and with varying combinations of lenses and mirrors, as a further means of corroborating their findings through tracing them, as graphic documentation of their observations. There is also evidence that Galileo used the lenses of large telescopes just like Dürer's glass window for painters or Leonardo's perspectograph (discussed in Chapter 3), that is, by drawing directly onto the glass the outlines of what it made visible as a primary record of his astronomical observations, a method also widely in use among cartographers.[55] It is clear that these now-distinct instruments were, in the moment of their first formation, used interchangeably and experimentally in pursuit of different visual enquiries and effects, across a range of purposes in science and surveying, magical illusion and art.

If the telescope induced wonder by bringing the distant stars into proximate view, the microscope also brought forth a rhetoric of the marvellous in its great magnification of scale. The earliest sure description of a compound microscope pertains to the Dutch inventor, lens-maker, and magus in London, Cornelis Drebbel, though its development owed much to Galileo's experimentation with lenses for viewing both near and far.[56] By 1624, Galileo was said to have built a compound or multiple-lens microscope that could multiply up to 50,000 times, able to show 'a fly as big as a hen'.[57] Such reflection on the wonders of scale were clearly commonplace, as the Ingolstadt Jesuit scientist Christoph Scheiner's *Rosa ursina* described: 'that wonderful instrument the microscope, by means of which a fly is magnified into an elephant, and a flea into a camel'.[58] Exemplifying the interest of the instrument to princely patrons as an object of wondrous courtly diversion as well as of scientific enquiry, Galileo gave one to Cardinal Eitel Friedrich von Zollern in May of that year for presentation to the Duke of Bavaria, and in September, he sent another to Prince Cesi of the Roman Lincei.[59] Similarly, Louis XIV's physician Pierre Borel's 1655 description of 100 microscopic anatomical observations included in his *De vero telescopii inventore* again dwelt on the wondrous play of scale in its objects of study. Tellingly, Borel drew together microscopes and telescopes in his book, surely based on the similarities of their construction. He also illustrated his history of these instruments with a cross-section diagram of a variety of lenses within a tube to show the multiple reflections and refractions of light rays they effected as devices of intense magnification, and of an expanding telescope of multiple nesting tubes to demonstrate its ocular reach. He further described both the results of their magnifying vision, and the mode of their construction:

> A microscope, whether it be a flea glass or a fly glass, whereby a flea is enlarged the size of a camel, and a fly to the size of an elephant, is made out of two glasses inclosed in a small tube: the glass nearest the eye is convex and made out of a small segment of a spherule, whose diameter should be two inches: the other glass is plane.
>
> A microscope can also be made of two convexes, and is superior.
>
> Some are made of a single spherule inclosed in a tube, opposite the end of which either a small glass box is arranged for the reception of sundry tiny objects, or a saucer is applied for the examination of liquids.
>
> Or the model of the tube may be a system of pipes, which can be shortened and lengthened at pleasure, and under which objects may be applied: also, more glasses, even three or four, can be mounted, and so objects appear enlarged.[60]

One of the earliest illustrated books of microscopy was also by an astronomer, Giovanni Odierna, whose *L'occhio della mosca* of 1644 produced startling 'close-up' printed images dedicated to the study of the insect eye; though the defining text would be Robert Hooke's *Micrographia* of 1665. Hooke offered the reader thirty-eight finely detailed copper-plate illustrations, including the eye of a drone-fly, the body of a louse, and a large fold-out page of a flea described as 'adorn'd with a curiously polished suit of sable [black] armour'.[61] As lecturer and curator of experiments at the Royal Society, Hooke demonstrated the results of his experiments in both writing and oral presentation, with the illustrations of his observations as proof of his methods, as well as a diagram of his microscope instrument whose fabrication he described in his preface (Fig. 99).[62] Hooke concluded his book by turning his lenses to the stars, demonstrating again the close ties between the early modern microscope and the telescope, as parallel instruments of visual science and natural wonder.

Reception of Hooke's illustrations renewed and intensified the recognition of marvel in the

Fig. 99 Robert Hooke, diagram of microscope with flanking candle holder of glass ampoules and lenses for enhanced light and magnification, in *Micrographia*, London, 1665. Photo: Granger.com

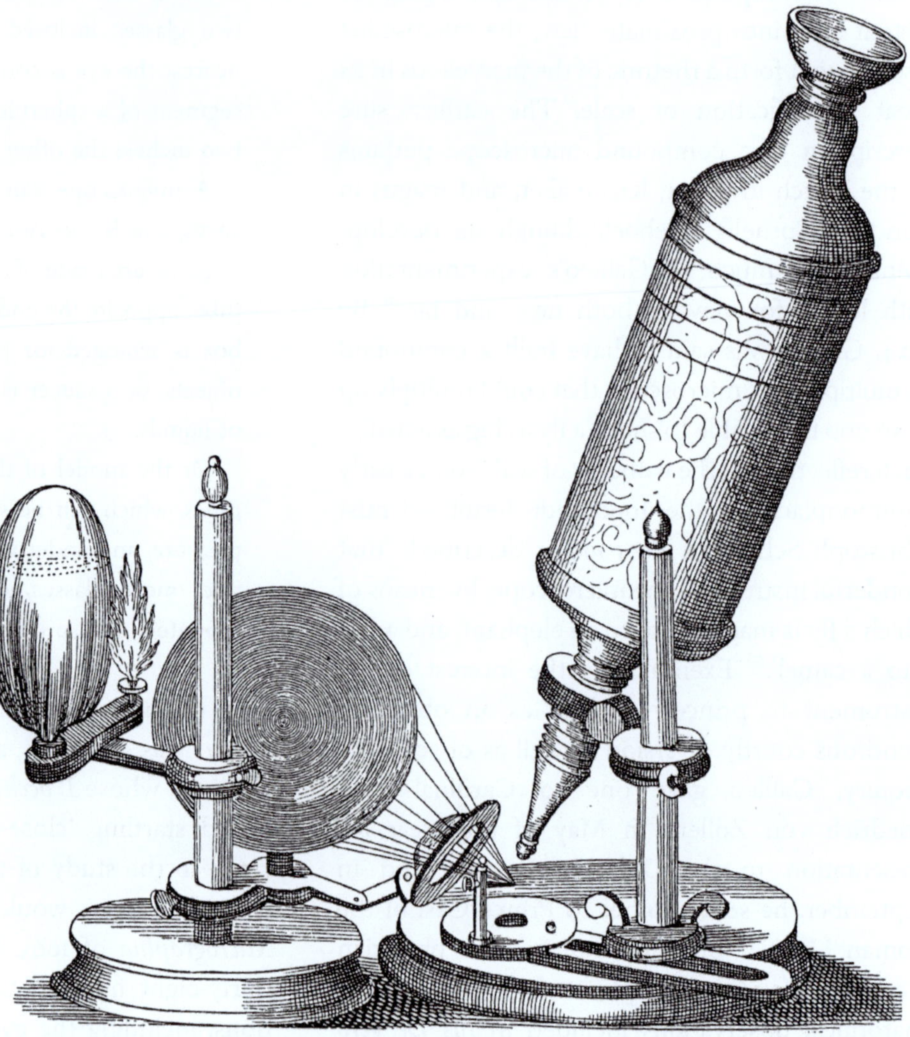

visual results of magnification, uncovering a heretofore 'invisible world discovered to the understanding'.[63] Texts such as della Porta's influential *Natural Magic* explicitly presented the effects of mirroring and magnification as a scientific or 'natural' form of magic, constituting part of the study of natural history proper. Among other things a playwright as well as a scientist, Neapolitan aristocrat, and lay Jesuit, della Porta also kept a museum of natural wonders including mirrors and catoptrics for the display of optical projection, with shared interests in displays of optics and magic alike, and wrote specifically on the use of lenses and mirrors for the purposes of scientific observation as well as theatrical wonder in his book. The book in its entirety may be read as a collection of early modern knowledge forms, ranging from magic to science, including optics and illusions.[64] Similarly, authors such as the German Jesuit Gaspar Schott, in his *Magia universalis naturae et artis*, published in Würzburg in 1657, explicitly presented microscopy as a display of natural magic or illusionism founded in a wondrous magnification:

> [fill a receptacle fitted with a lens with] minute fragments of stones of various colours, with gold and silver filings, with little balls of coriander and such like trifling things . . . If you now look into the vase you will think you see great pieces of

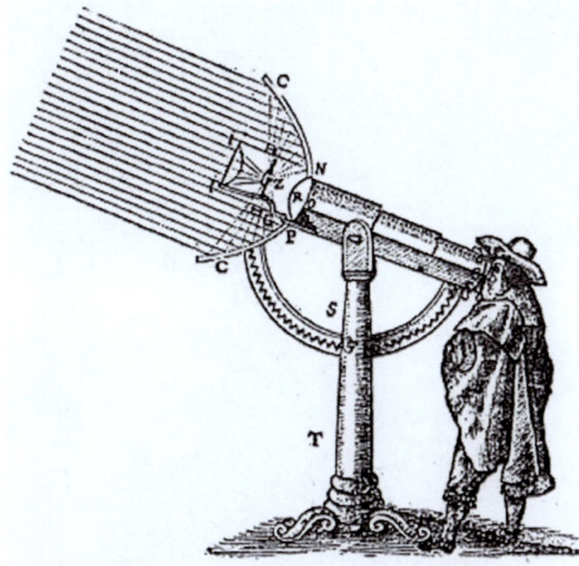

Fig. 100 René Descartes, engraved illustration of Descartes' giant compound 'microscope', in *La dioptrique*, Leiden, 1637.
Photo: Wikimedia

> stones, gold, and silver twigs, pumpkins, rosy apples, and you will wonder.[65]

As objects, early modern microscopes varied greatly in size and composition: the leading natural philosopher René Descartes was also a considered microscopist whose most famous giant microscope design was larger than human, with lenses of every dimension including a parabolic mirror (Fig. 100).[66] Early compound or multiple-lens microscopes were more often in the form of short, hand-held telescopes or tubular chambers, made of a similar range of materials including tooled and gilded leather over wood and pasteboard as in the case of Hooke; or of turned wood or ivory, or brass for smaller instruments as Italian examples tended to be.[67] The plate from Hooke's *Micrographia* illustrates his tubular compound microscope with further reflective magnifiers including both mirrors and a phial of water, along with a candle for light, designed to enhance the clarity of instrumental vision (Fig. 99).

By contrast, the simple or single-lens microscope-magnifiers used by the Delft lens maker Antoni van Leeuwenhoek were the size of small eye-pieces, like magnifying monocles of miniature proportions. Leeuwenhoek also used precious metals such as silver and gold for his jewel-like monocle-sized magnifiers, for patrons including Peter the Great, William of Orange, and Mary II of England. Considered the leading lens manufacturer of the era, Leeuwenhoek produced magnification up to a conjectured 500× by mounting globe-shaped single lenses the size of pinheads into small metal plates made to fit the socket of the eye. He was also the leading early modern microbiologist for his conclusive observation of the microbe and the circulation of blood.[68]

It is also the case that microscopes and magnifiers were developed and used for purposes well beyond the strictly scientific; Leeuwenhoek, for example, deployed them in his textile production business, as was true of many other industrial concerns. Magnifying instruments were also used for examining artworks, as in Raphael's portrait of Pope Leo X (Fig. 101), in which he holds a lens for examining manuscript miniatures.[69] There is evidence to suggest lens- and glass-cutting first emerged for the purposes of enlargement and clarification of vision within late medieval jewellers' workshops, both because they had the requisite tools for cutting and grinding crystals as magnifying stones, and because they had a direct interest in magnification for their own detailed work. It is from this sphere, historians have argued, that eyeglasses first arose for the same purposes, fitted with crystal magnifying lenses, and later supplanted by precision-ground optical glass as its artisanal technology superseded the use of crystal (in Fig. 45a, Chapter 2, Canon van der Paele holds rivet spectacles). Such practical, industrial, and artisanal uses of magnification greatly preceded and subsequently informed the composition of the early modern scientific microscope.

Della Porta would later write a manuscript treatise specifically on the telescope, likely c. 1610–15 (which remained unpublished until its rediscovery in the twentieth century).[70] As with Galileo, and later Leeuwenhoek, it is clear that

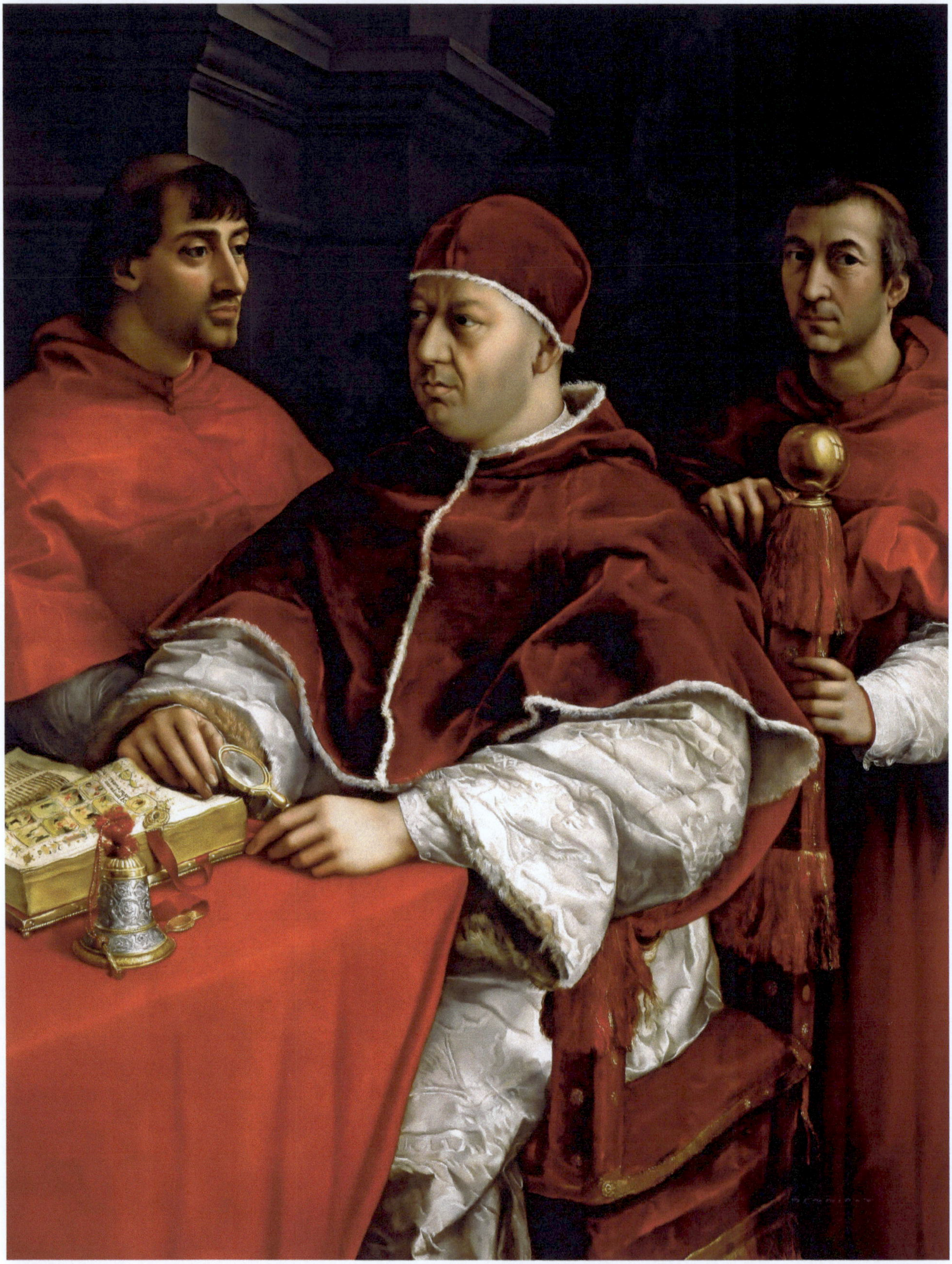

Fig. 101 Raphael Sanzio, *Portrait of Leo X with Cardinals Luigi de' Rossi and Giulio de' Medici,* (detail), c. 1518, oil on panel, 155.5 × 119.5 cm, Galleria degli Uffizi Florence.
Photo: Wikimedia

della Porta is using *avant-la-lettre* telescopic and microscopic magnifiers, and other similar optical instruments interchangeably, for the purposes of both optical science and illusion. Della Porta was, together with Galileo, a founding member of Rome's academy of science, the Accademia dei Lincei. For the Neapolitan humanist academy that della Porta also sponsored, the Accademia Secretorum Naturae, he demonstrated his experiments with mirrors and optical illusions, including one that apparently displayed the viewer as if suspended in mid-air. Such visual effect is treated extensively in his book *Magia naturalis.* A section devoted to mirror optics, titled in its 1658 English translation 'Of Strange Glasses', comprised both lenses and concave mirrors of distortion. In the expanded text on optics of his 1589 edition della Porta describes a chamber of vision where images hang in the air 'as if by magic', effected by placing an inclined mirror in a darkened room in order to reflect light-cast imagery from a small aperture onto a blank wall:

> How in a Chamber you may see Hunting, Battles of Enemies, and other [illusions]:
>
> . . . then which nothing can be more pleasant for great men, and scholars, and ingenious persons to behold; that in a dark Chamber . . . one may see as clearly and perspicuously, as if they were before his eyes, Huntings, Banquets, armies of Enemies, Plays, and all things else that one desireth. Let there be over against that Chamber, where you desire to represent these things, some spacious Plain, where the sun can freely shine. Upon that you shall set trees in order, also woods, mountains, rivers, and animals, that are really so, or made by art, or wood, or some other matter. You must frame little children in them, as we use to bring them in when Comedies are acted, and you must counterfeit stags, bores, rhinoceress, elephants, lions, and what other creatures you please, then by degrees they must appear, as coming out of their dens upon the plain. The Hunter must come with his hunting pole, nets, arrows and other necessaries, thet may represent hunting. Let there be horns, cornets, trumpets sounded. Those that are in the Chamber shall see trees, animals, hunters, faces, and all the rest so plainly that they cannot tell whether they be true or delusions. Swords drawn will glitter in at the hole, that they will make people almost afraid. I have often shewed this kind of spectacle to my friends, who much admired it, and took pleasure to see such a deceit, and I could hardly by reasons, and reasons from the Opticks, remove them from their opinion when I had discovered the secret. Hence it may appear to Philosophers, and those that study Opticks, how vision is made.. . . The image is let in by the pupil, as by the whole of a window, and that part of the Sphere that is set in the middle of the eye stands instead of a crystal table. I know ingenious people will be much delighted in this.[71]

Della Porta is certainly referring to a thaumaturge type of *camera obscura.* Already in his first, much shorter edition of the *Magia naturalis* of 1558 he cited his scientific deployment of this instrument, together with a convex mirror to project the image upright onto paper for ease of transcription into documentary drawing.[72] Here we have the material origins of the projected mechanical image.

Della Porta's near-contemporary, Gemma Frisius, Dutch physician and mathematician who made lenses for use in astronomy as well as medicine, illustrated such a device particularly clearly in his *De radio astronomico e geometrico* of 1545, generally acknowledged as the first published diagram of a *camera obscura* and surely of his own instrumentation (Fig. 102). It demonstrates the passage of light through a small aperture into a chamber such that the image appears in reduction on the white wall opposite. The object of his study was a solar eclipse, which he recorded and dated 24 January 1544.[73] By this means the optical reproduction can readily be transcribed and recorded as a documentary drawing. In della

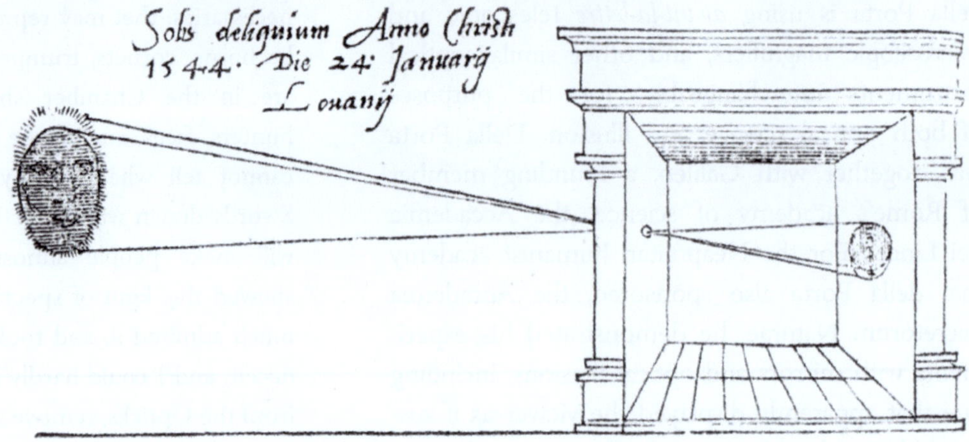

Fig. 102 Gemma Frisius, illustration of a solar observation through a camera obscura dated 24 January 1544, in *De radio astronomico e geometrico*, Antwerp, 1545. Photo: Wikimedia

Porta's further elaboration, he understood it as a ready means of transcribing visual appearances into documentary drawing:

> This is an Art worth learning. Let the Sun beat upon the window, and there about the hole, let there be pictures . . . put a white paper against the hole . . . until the sun cast a perfect representation upon . . . it. One that is skill'd in painting must lay on colours where they are . . . so the image being removed, the picture will remain.[74]

If fitted with lenses and mirrors, della Porta added, the *camera obscura* could reverse and therefore correct the naturally occurring inversion of a light-reflected image as both upside-down and back-to-front.[75] Christoph Scheiner's *Oculus hoc est* of 1619 illustrated this in the book's frontispiece with small details showing the role of a suspended lens in 'righting' the reflected image; this is most clearly illustrated in a diagram by Johann Zahn (Fig. 103).[76] Equally, field telescopes were often used as the pinhole lens within a *camera obscura*, again suggesting the hybrid and interchangeable nature of these early modern instruments. While Galileo and Cigoli employed such a device within astronomical study, della Porta's reflects a more broad-based use in keeping with the nature of his interests in theatrical stage illusions and magical displays as well as optical science. He further described how to multiply the visual effects of what is reflected so that 'if you see a galley you think it a fleet; if a soldier, an army', as illusionistic games of ludic multiplication it produced.[77]

Together these examples testify that the wide-ranging use of the *camera obscura* across arts and sciences was well established, certainly by the mid-sixteenth century and likely much earlier.[78] In the technological development of lens-based viewing instruments lies a cultural history of early modern vision as optically constructed. Already by the mid-seventeenth century in Paris, a large chamber-sized *camera obscura* was in use as a form of public spectacle of optical illusions of the type that would come to predominate across eighteenth-century Europe. Around 1630 a *camera obscura* opened to the public near the Samaritaine at the Pont-Neuf (demolished in the nineteenth century), from which point it captured a panoramic view of the Seine, the Louvre, the bridge, and all its passers-by. By 1678 the Dutch perspective painter and theorist Samuel van Hoogstraten would describe having seen such entertainments in both Vienna and London, 'with countless people walking about . . . hundreds of boats with people, and the entire river, landscape, on a wall, and everything capable of movement was moving'.[79] At the same time, the *camera obscura* became the

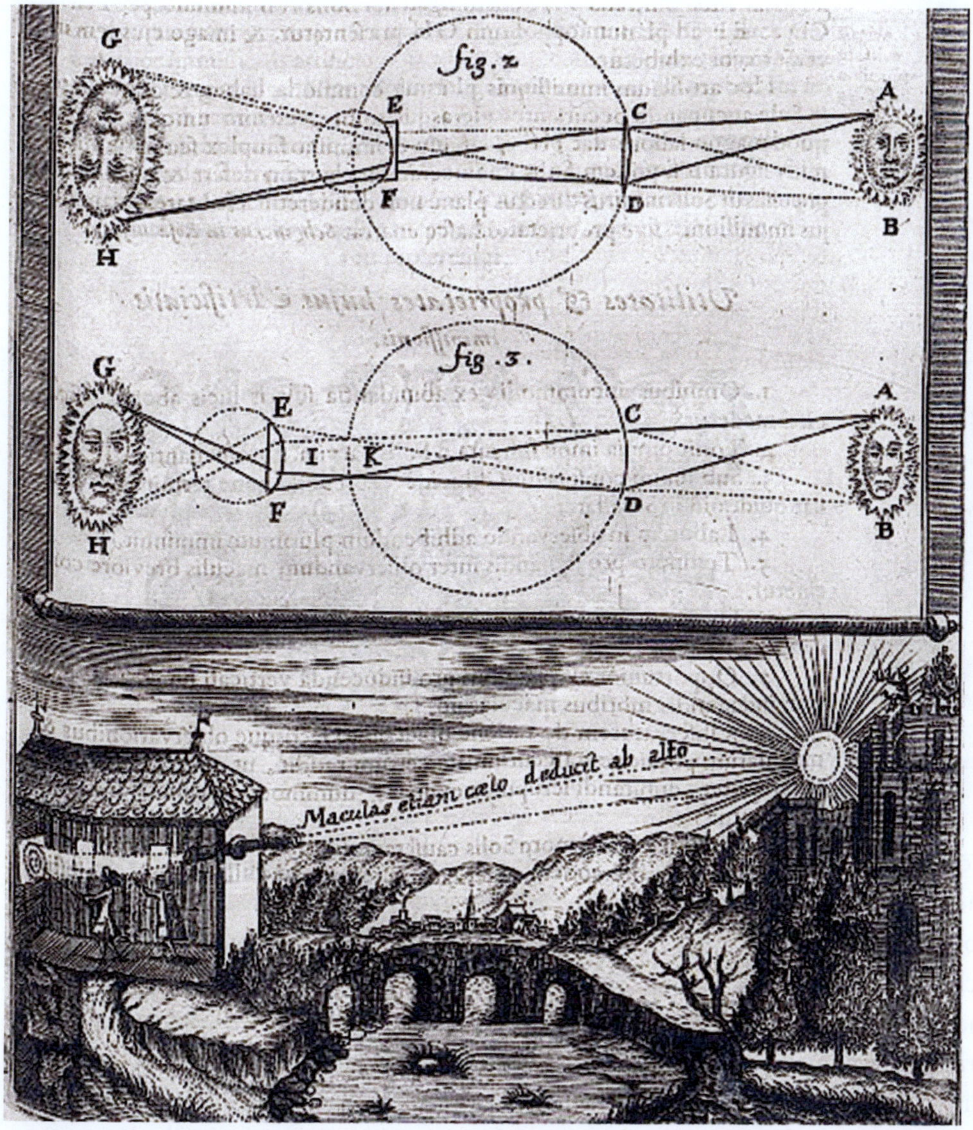

Fig. 103 Johann Zahn, diagram showing lenticular correction of the inverted image in a camera obscura, in *Oculus artificialis teledioptricus sive telescopium*, vol. 2, Würzburg, 1686.
Photo: Deutsche Fotothek / Wikimedia

paradigmatic visual instrument of scientific documentation. With rapidly expanding uses and types in tandem with the Galilean 'revolution' of instrumental viewing, it was a ready means of seeing in depth and across distance, and of capturing and translating its optical effects into drawing. Used to project imagery of all kinds, it comprised the scientific and the scenic, the theatrical and the apparently magical.[80] In this regard, it marked the origins of mechanical picture-making, with vast consequences across the arts and sciences alike.

The early modern *camera obscura* came to be constructed in a full range of sizes, from dedicated chambers as public entertainments or ante-rooms within noble houses and palaces of a classicising architecture, as in the Frisius illustration, to portable box-rooms for plein-air or fieldwork by surveyors, scientists, and artists. The German astronomer Johannes Kepler's *camera obscura* was described as a tent-like portable construction that could be taken into the field, within which its lens could apparently rotate in order to capture the outside view in a 360-degree radius.[81] This capacity for in-the-round viewing was greatly extended by the German professor of mathematics Daniel

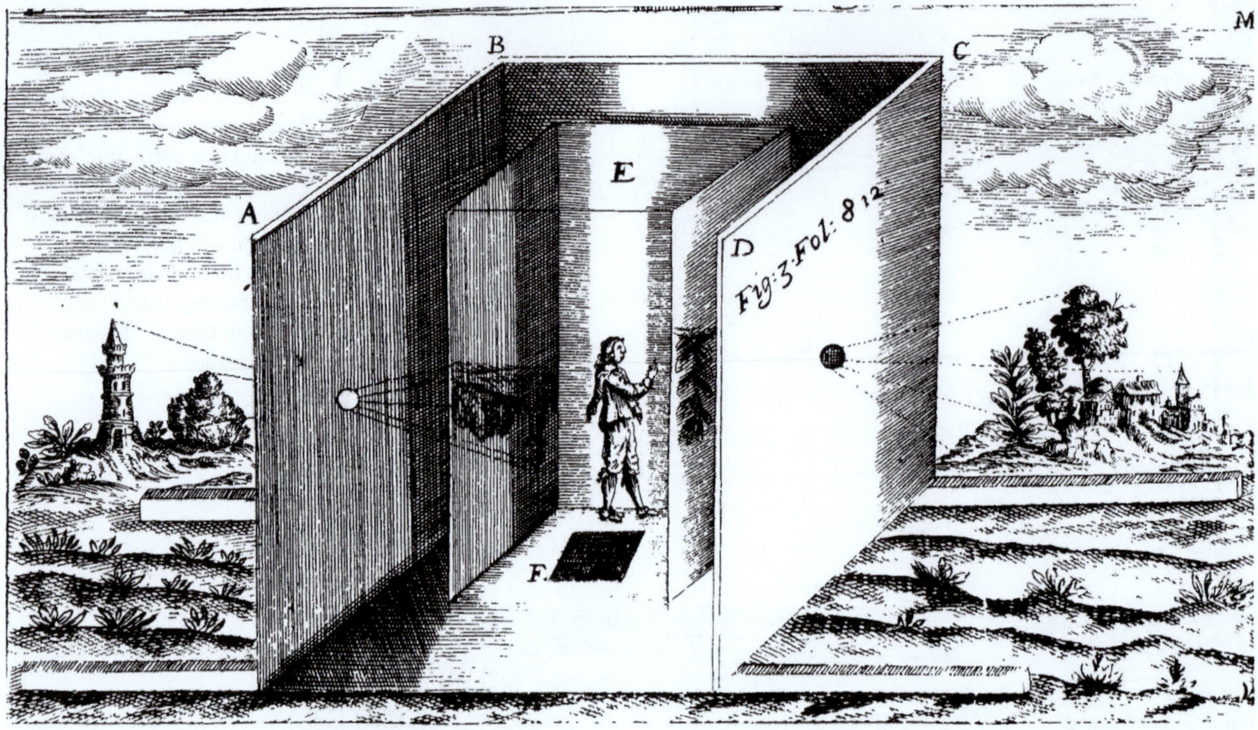

Fig. 104 Athanasius Kircher, illustration of a portable, full-sized camera obscura, in *Ars magna lucis et umbrae*, Rome, 1646. Photo: Wikimedia

Schwendter, whose *Deliciae physico-mathematicae* (Scientific and Mathematical Delights) of 1636 illustrated what would become known as a fully rotating 'sky optick', or scioptic ball, into which fitted lenses enabled panoramic views. It was known as *oeil artificiel* in French, due to its evident foundation in the study of the eyeball.[82] Similarly to Kepler, Kircher illustrated a portable *camera obscura* on wooden struts for ease of transport. In a life-sized chamber, a draughtsman stands within the room between two projected images on hanging screens that enter from pinhole apertures on either side. Picturing a steeple and trees, respectively, the draughtsman within the portable camera transcribes through drawing (Fig. 104).[83] Johann Zahn, German canon and lecturer on both astronomy and anatomy, subsequently published a number of diagrams of box-sized *camera obscura* in his three-volume treatise on ocular devices of 1685–86, *Oculus artificialis teledioptricus sive telescopium* (Fig. 105).[84] Niceron similarly constructed a type of box camera in the form of a 'portfolio', surely a precursor to the type of book-shaped box camera of the early eighteenth century in which the equivalence between book knowledge and visual observation that characterised the early modern 'scientific revolution' took material form.[85] The box-sized *camera obscura* type that would prevail across the eighteenth century (and come to inform the development of the nineteenth-century daguerreotype camera) was, however, that of the German professor Johann Sturm as described in his *Collegium experimentale* of 1676, the academy proceedings of Altdorf's '*Collegium curiosum*' of which he was the founder. It used a moveable eye made up of lenses as well as a mirror and a sheet of paper onto which the mirror-image was then cast, within an extending portable box-chamber of fortified paper:

> This dioptric and catoptric machine is then placed in front of an open window, such that the face of the objective lens is directed towards the street. All objects in the street will be presented first to the objective lens, which throws them up onto the paper. This represents the best and most realistic

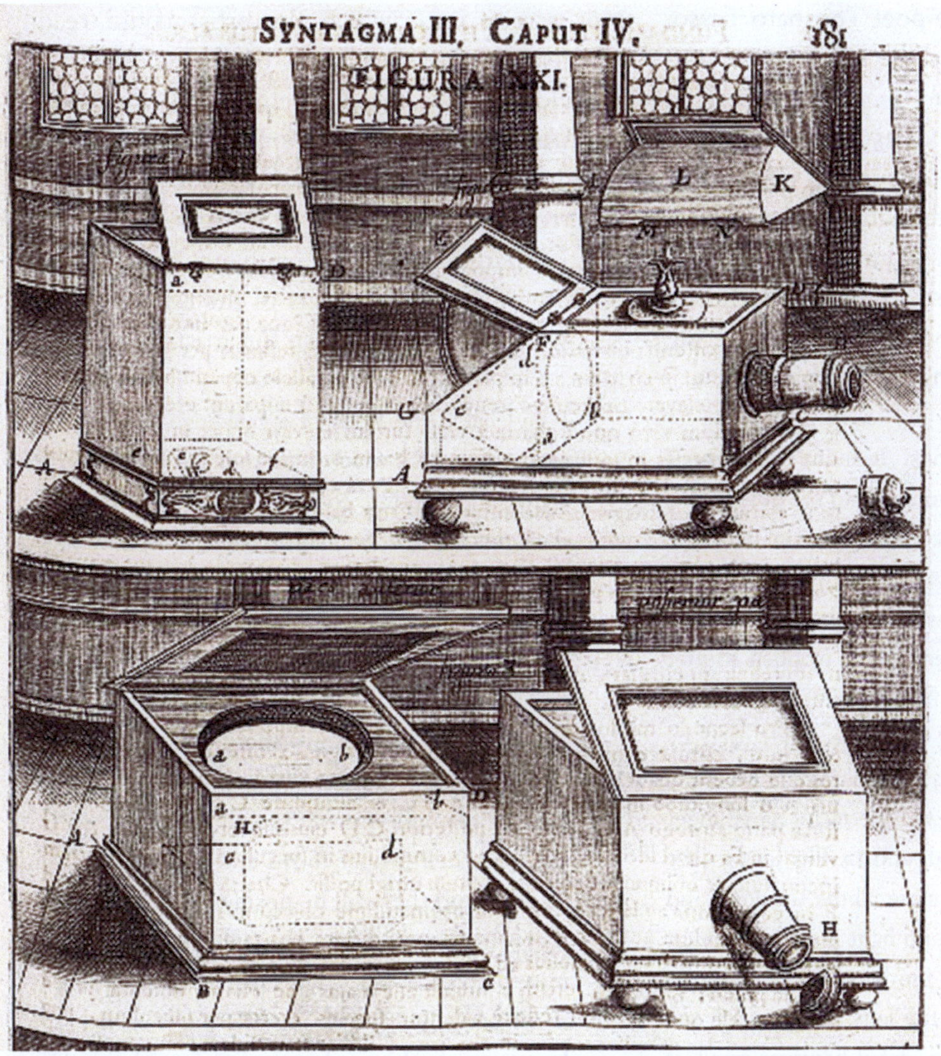

Fig. 105 Johann Zahn, illustration of early modern tabletop box 'cameras', in *Oculus artificialis teledioptricus sive telescopium*, Würzburg, 1685–86. Photo: Google ebooks

> 'paintings', in which one can recognise and perfectly distinguish the faces and clothes of the people passing by from over a hundred feet away.[86]

The term *camera obscura* is considered to arise first with Kepler's *Optics* of 1604. Kepler's use was chiefly astronomical, deploying it as a form of telescope-cum-draughtsman's aid in order to record by drawing his perception of the gibbous moon. The English diplomat Sir Henry Wotton also wrote to Francis Bacon of the possibilities of its application to matters of chorography, or topographical drawing for legal purposes of proprietorship, following a visit to Kepler's astronomy theatre.[87] As Galileo's use of this device also exemplifies, the *camera obscura* had a broad deployment in practical matters of field surveying for land and architecture, and also cartography, as a means of accurate transcription in the field. Its proximity to Brunelleschi's perspectival experiment at the door of Florence Cathedral is clear, and likely grounded in a range of similar surveying instruments resembling the single-lens magnifier or microscope, and close to the *camera obscura*.

The earliest reference to a *camera obscura* device in treatises devoted to art is generally acknowledged as by Daniele Barbaro, Venetian patriarch and architect, patron to Palladio, also humanist and friend to the poet Torquato Tasso, with broad interests across the arts. His *La pratica della perspettiva, opera molto profittevole a pittori scultori et architetti* of 1568 describes and illustrates his manufacture of such an instrument and its functions within a draughtsman's practice. Barbaro discusses its use as a drawing aid particularly with reference to the accurate transcription of proportions, or correct perspectival rendering of figures and objects within any visual field:

> Now I will describe a most beautiful experiment concerning perspective. If you wish to see how nature shows us the various aspects of things not only the outline of the whole but also of their parts as well as of their colours and shadows, you must make a hole of the size of a spectacle lens in the wooden shutter of a window of a room from where you wish to observe. Then take a lens from spectacles used by old men, that is to say a lens which is fairly thick at the centre and not concave like the spectacles for younger men who are short sighted, and fix this lens in the hole you made. After that close all the windows and doors of the room, so that no light is present except that which enters through the lens. Take a sheet of paper and hold it behind the lens and you will see on the sheet of paper every detail however small of everything outside the house and this will happen most distinctly at a given distance from the lens. By moving the sheet of paper towards or away from the lens you will find the most suitable position.[88]

Galileo's collaborator, the Florentine painter Ludovico Cigoli, cites the *camera obscura* in the introduction to his treatise *La prospettiva pratica* (The Practice of Perspective), written for artists in the practical application of perspectival devices. Of the *camera obscura*, he argues by analogy to art that it is 'nature painting' by light through a dark hole to reflect onto a white surface.[89] Kircher too described a type of *camera obscura* expressly intended for landscape or topographical painters, characterised by a paper wall or screen onto which the artist could readily transpose the view from outdoors, and which could also be used 'plein air'.[90] Equally, in Sturm's account of his *camera obscura*, analogy with the 'best and most realistic painting' is, mirror-like, the measure of its visual efficacy.

Leonardo, extensive student of light, also wrote of the visual effects of the *camera obscura*, as well as its practical use for artists:

> I say that if the front of a building – or any open piazza or field – which is illuminated by the sun has a dwelling opposite to it, and if, in the front which does not face the sun, you make a small round hole, all the illuminated objects will project their images through that hole and be visible inside the dwelling on the opposite wall which may be made white; and there, in fact, they will be upside down. . . .
>
> Then, you will receive these images on a white paper placed within this dark room and rather near to the hole and you will see all the objects on the paper in their proper forms and colours, but much smaller; and they will be upside down by reason of that very intersection. These images being transmitted from a place illuminated by the sun will seem actually painted on this paper which must be extremely thin and looked at from behind.[91]

Among the most compelling descriptions of the visual impression made by the *camera obscura* is surely that of the Dutch diplomat and patron of the arts Constantin Huygens when in London. Huygens had acquired such a device from the Dutch inventor-philosopher and optical lens-maker at the Stuart court, Cornelis Drebbel, who had wide-ranging interests across the arts and sciences. Evidently, Huygens transported the device, suggesting it was in a portable or box-chamber format, and used the instrument himself for the admiration of his guests as well as a painter's aid:

> I have at home that other instrument of Drebbel's which certainly produces admirable effects by

painting the reflection in a *camera obscura*; it is impossible for me to describe to you the beauty of it in words; all painting is dead, for here is life itself, or something more, if words don't fail me. For the figure, the contour, motions, are here seen as in nature.... 13 April 1622 from London.[92]

The French Jesuit astronomer and mathematician Jean Leurechon also observed the capacity of the *camera obscura* to capture the visual impression of life, like a painting. What is pertinent is the informed comparison such scholars of science made between the reflected images of the *camera obscura* and the art of painting:

> Choose a chamber ... closing all light openings save one that must be left open to design [*dessein*]; it will make all the images whereby exterior objects enter by this aperture, where you will see them projected onto the wall, or more surely onto white paper ... and even better if you apply a convex glass to the aperture, that is to say, a lens that thickens towards the centre, such as burning mirrors and spectacle glasses for the aged ...
>
> Above all there is the pleasure of seeing the movement of birds, men, or other animals and the quivering of plants waving in the wind; for although all that is reversed, nevertheless, this beautiful painting [*peinture*], beyond being fore shortened in perspective, represents ingeniously well that which no painter has ever been able to represent in his painting, to realise movement continued from place to place.[93]

If the majority of sixteenth-century documentation concerning the *camera obscura* comes from the scientific domain, within this realm there is also ready recognition of the instrument's 'picture-making' capacities, indicative of a developing perception of the profound visuality of scientific method. Thus Ettore Ausonio (c. 1520–70), Venetian mathematician and alchemist to the Duke of Savoy famous for his mirror-making and author of the *Discourse on the Concave Spherical Mirror*, described the *camera obscura*'s projected image 'as if a painting', as well as the use of mirrors within it:

> If a man should close himself in a dark room and let the light of the sun enter only through a small hole, and place above this hole a white paper, arranging a mirror in front of the hole at a certain distance from it, he will then represent on the paper a fine, clear, tiny painting, in which everything to be seen outside is represented in perspective view: and should there be men or animals which are moving, in the painting the images will move, to our great delight.[94]

Correspondence within Galileo's circles included letters from Georg Stengel to a Karl Stengel on the use of the *camera obscura* for astronomical observation, also with a clear analogy to painting, and with the ready ability to transcribe those observations by means of paint:

> And thus when the chamber had been entirely closed [to light] and solar rays are admitted through a single small aperture the size of a marble, if these fall on blank paper in the more distant parts of the moon they will depict these very spots.... And when the face of the observer comes between the paper and the aperture, then all things beyond the window come together on the paper clearly positioned and with their true colours, and thus they can be made out exactly and in their proper relation, and they can even be painted.[95]

Among the many correspondents of René Descartes on astronomical observation and the use of optical devices, he wrote often to Scheiner, addressing him according to the Jesuit scientist's pseudonym of 'the antique painter Apelles', in whose name Scheiner also published a short treatise on sunspots. Their correspondence comprised detailed exchanges on the nature of their solar observations, accompanied by small sketches of what they saw by means of a *camera obscura* projection onto a white surface, which Scheiner termed the 'apellean canvas', like his nom de plume, 'Apelles hidden behind the painting' – *Apelles latens post tabulam*.[96] His epistolary sketches of the moon traced from the *camera obscura* closely resemble those that formed the basis of the engraved illustrations for Galileo's *Starry Message*, testament to the documentary draughtsmanship on which the transmission of early modern scientific knowledge depended. The appeal to the pseudonym of Apelles just as clearly designates the close scientific links with the visual arts. In this regard it also salient that Milton's poetic reference to Galileo in *Paradise Lost* was not to a scientist but to the 'Tuscan artist', for the telescopic view of heaven and earth 'to descry new lands'.[97]

Descartes' own writings on optics were particularly rich in analogical *exempla* surrounding the *camera obscura*. For example, he illustrated the path of visual rays by comparison to tennis balls, gunshot, and the passage of light through a glass bowl of water. A further disquisition of his *Dioptrique* of 1637 famously turns to the structure of the eye itself. By conducting an anatomical investigation of the eyeball – the 'peephole' pupil that admits light, passing through the eyeball like light through a glass as an analogy for the 'crystalline' of the eye onto which the visual field is projected as an image – Descartes demonstrated, as Leonardo had also thought, that the eye is structured like a *camera obscura* (Fig. 106). Descartes further elaborated on the mind's capacity to 'see' in images, making sense of the fall of light on the eye as if looking at paintings, just as Galileo had done in his telescopic observations of the moon. Descartes' comparison is with a pen and ink drawing on paper, in which the optical manipulation of line and wash could represent 'forests to the eye'. Further, he compared the image on the retina to a scene in a mirror, so approximating both painting and optics to the specular reflected image.[98]

The early modern analogy between the eyeball and the *camera obscura* was a constant one. Already present in Leonardo's study of the eye, the artist speculated further, using his knowledge of light apertures, reflective glass ampoules filled with water, and mirrors, to demonstrate the process of vision with the *camera obscura* as his model. Like the late medieval theorists of optics before him, Leonardo used the effect of light through a pinhole into a chamber to show how vision works (Fig. 64, Chapter 3).[99] Della Porta also had recourse to the analogy, further comparing the white of the eye to the crystal of a glass or lens, and the aperture of the pupil to a window: 'the image is let in by the pupil, as by the hole of a window; as that part of the sphere, that is set in the middle of the eye, stands instead of a crystal'.[100] As Alpers has noted, it was Johannes Kepler's *Optics* of 1604 that first published the observation of the retinal image which is cast by vision onto the back of the eye. In Kepler's analysis, the means of sight is also understood in terms of the chamber of the eye, by comparison with the *camera obscura*. Kepler further theorised the eye as both a mirror and a painting (Fig. 107). He understood optics as a theory of image production by light, whether on the eye or a *camera obscura*, through a mirror or lens. Here is the first full elision in print between the *camera* and the eyeball.[101] In the optical writings of the mathematician Marin Mersenne, the image on the retina is compared to a painting as with Descartes, and the eye itself to a chamber or *camera obscura* with a pinhole of light.[102] This analogy also underpins the Capuchin physicist Cherubin d'Orleans' *La dioptrique oculaire* of 1671, in which he referred to his own collection of optical devices springing from the *camera obscura*, also comprising glass models of the eyeball, which he termed his *oeil dioptrique*, or optical 'eye'. Like many of these authors who also undertook research on the optimal manufacture of lenses as the basis of visual instruments

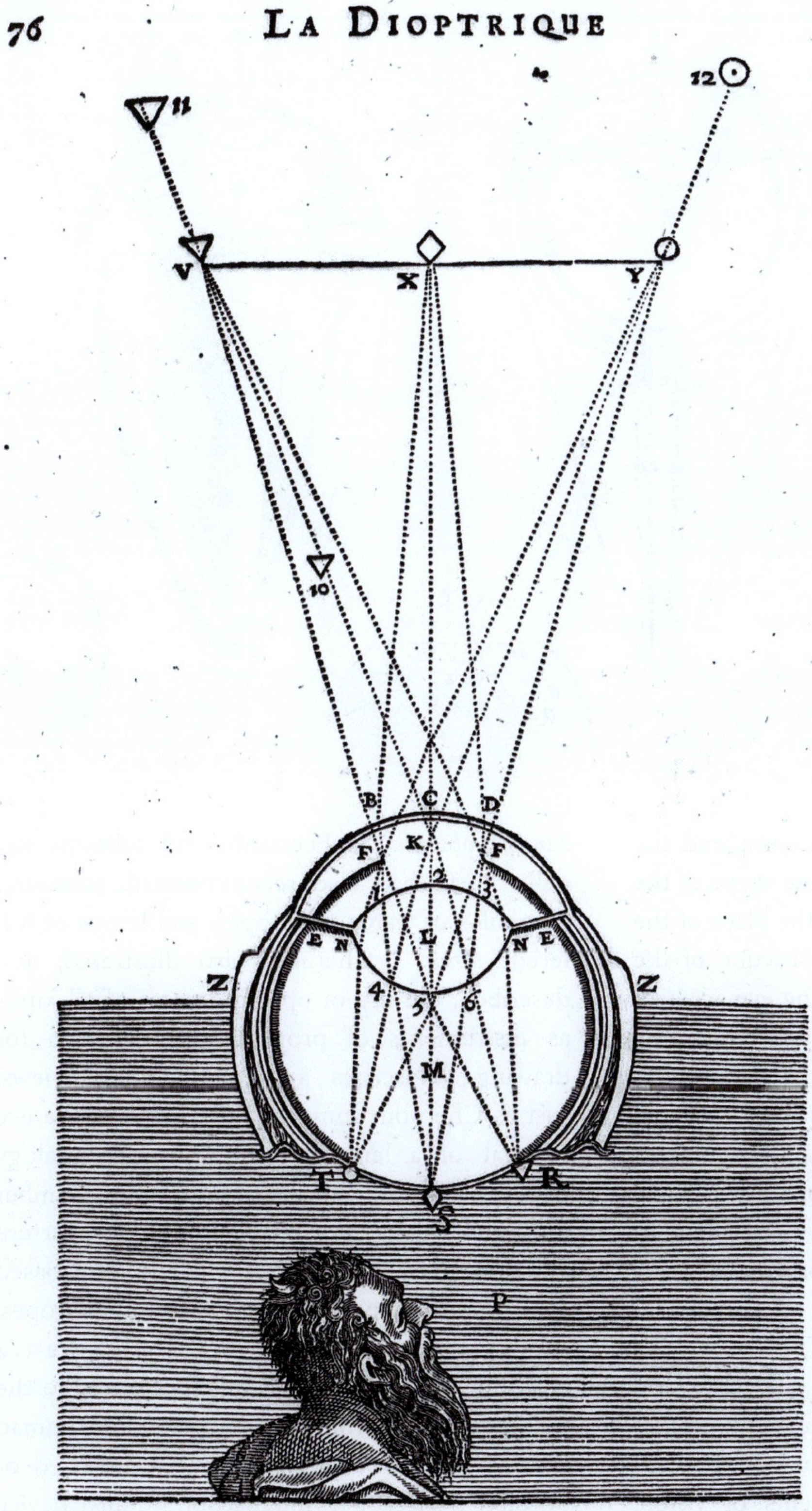

Fig. 106 René Descartes, printed diagram of the eyeball as a 'camera obscura', in *La dioptrique*, Leiden, 1637. Photo: Wikimedia

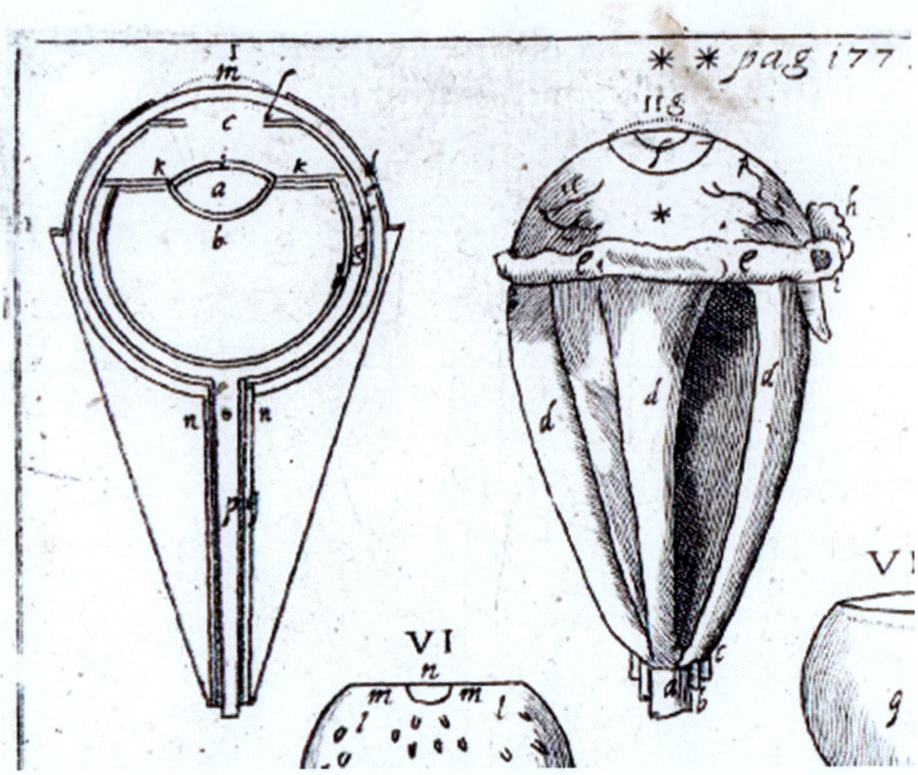

Fig. 107 Johannes Kepler, illustration of anatomical eyeballs, detail, in *Astronomiae pars optica*, Frankfurt, 1604. Photo: Google ebooks

they made themselves, Cherubin compared the form of a curving convex lens to the shape of the eyeball, and of concave lenses to the place of the retina within it. In the 'camera obscura' of the eyeball, the 'crystalline' white of the eye acts like the convex lens or sphere in receiving the 'painting' of objects it sees, in Cherubin's words.[103] The much-repeated analogy with the eye would also lead to the material configuration of optical devices in the form of one, as illustrated in treatises such as Zahn's *Telescopium*, in which the *camera obscura* is constructed as a mechanical eyeball (Fig. 108).

With ever-finer developments in lens-making for spectacles and subsequently telescopes and microscopes, the early modern *camera obscura* also underwent further development through interchange with other instruments of vision. Illustrations to Kircher's student Gaspar Schott's *Magia universalis* of 1657 exemplify Kircher's varying and experimental uses of mirrors and magnifiers of all kinds within a *camera obscura*, as Leonardo and subsequently della Porta had also recommended, including ampoules of water, telescopes, and lenses of different sizes.[104] Cherubin also illustrated, and described, the use of optical devices of all kinds as instruments of proportional reduction for drawing landscapes and topographical views. Just as Cherubin compared the shape of the eye to that of a lens, so he also made analogy between a room-sized *camera obscura* or chamber into which light may enter through an aperture and the tubular chamber of any lens-based viewing device such as field glasses, microscopes, and telescopes.[105] Thus the model of the eye as a chamber of vision applied metaphorically to the full range of instruments that extended human sight – *camera obscura*, whether room-sized or portable; telescope; microscope – any device with a 'chamber'-like construction used to house optical lenses and mirrors acting as a visual aid. In this it may be tied to broader analyses of an early modern 'mechanical philosophy', manifest

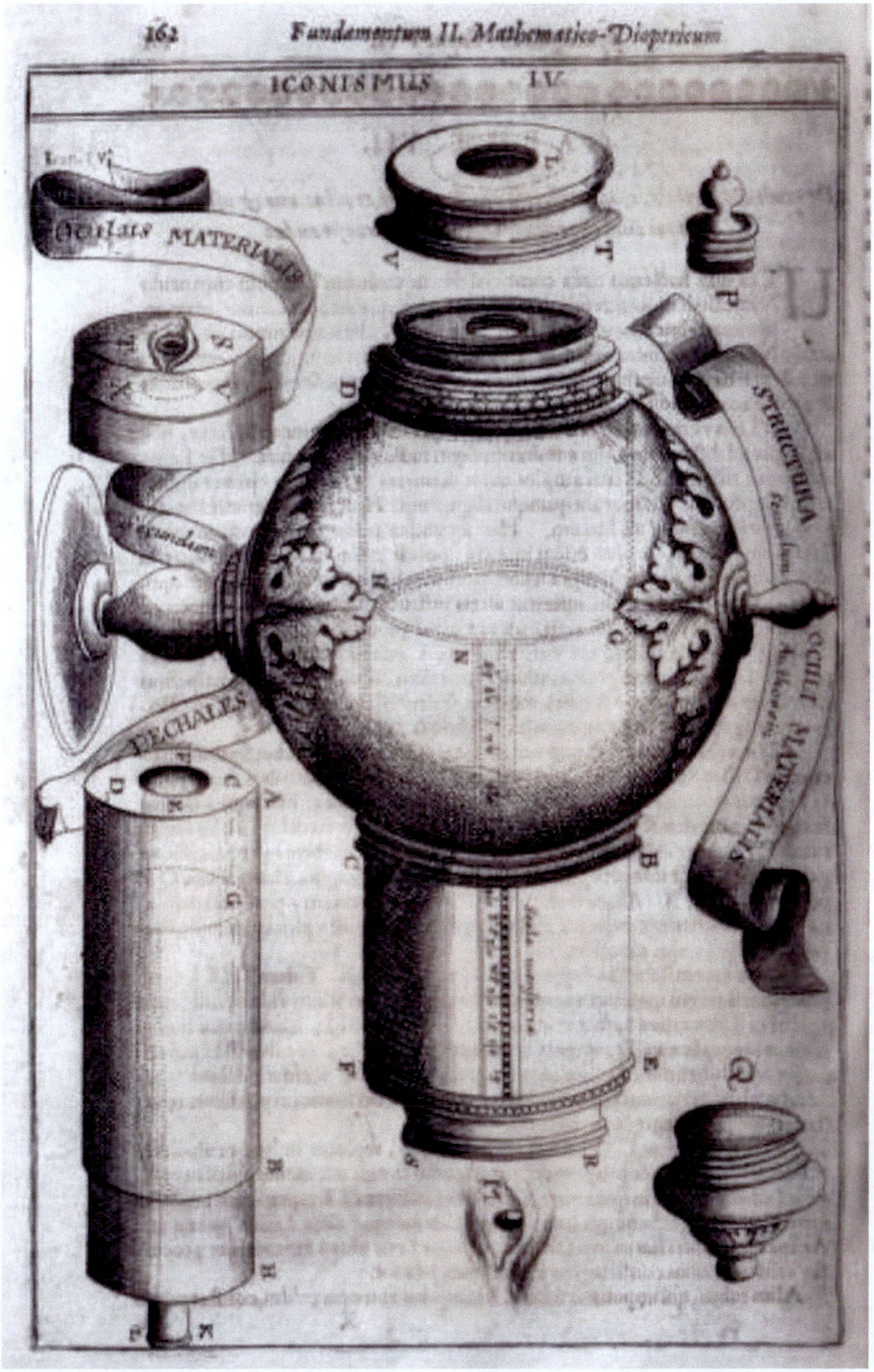

Fig. 108 Johann Zahn, diagram of a tabletop camera with internal lenses in the form of an artificial eye with a further range of ocular lenses and lenticular instruments, and a 'viewing eye', in *Oculus artificialis teledioptricus sive telescopium*, Würzburg, 1685–86. Photo: Wikimedia

above all in the work of Descartes, to signify an undergirding analogy between nature, artisanal manufacturing, and scientific method.[106] Undoubtedly for this reason, the term '*camera obscura*' came to represent the broad category of early modern mirror- and lens-based optical instruments, as a metaphor of the mechanical eye, and so of scientific vision writ large. [107]

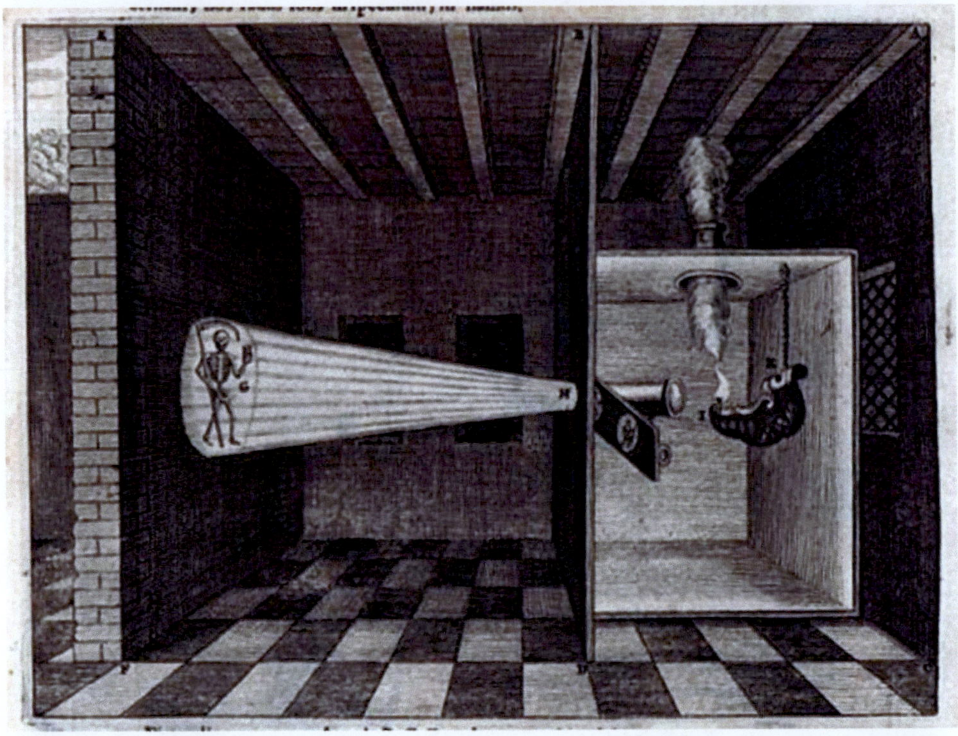

Fig. 109 Athanasius Kircher, illustration of a lantern slide projection using candlelight for illumination of a painted glass roundel slide of a 'Grim Reaper', in *Ars magna lucis et umbrae*, 1671. Photo: Wikimedia

Johann Zahn's *Telescopio* of 1685–86 further comprised a plethora of illustrations of all manner of optical devices, including a range of *camera obscuras* of every size and function, to chart its development as an instrument of illusion alongside science. Many of Zahn's engraved plates further illustrate what may be termed generic 'magic' lantern, box-sized *camera* devices, used to project painted-glass slide images onto a screen lit by candlelight and metal reflectors or concave mirrors. Such devices arose historically within the broad ambit of the seventeenth-century development of optical instruments in the wake of the telescope. Particularly pluriform were the box-sized cameras fitted with lenses circa 1650 in the circle of Kircher and Huygens. Their range is illustrated most brilliantly in the writings of Kircher, particularly his *Ars magna lucis et umbrae* (Fig. 109). Among an array of illusionistic optical devices Kircher describes, there are *camera* types used for the extension of scientific vision, but also a tabletop box-*camera* lit by candle and reflector, through which to project glass slides. An early modern precursor to lantern slide projection, their imagery was often of landscape views painted onto glass roundels or lenses, cast in enlarged form onto a white wall, though Kircher also used them for both scientific demonstration and religious imagery. The Dutch astronomer and mathematician Christiaan Huygens, son of Constantin, similarly used a candle-illuminated projector, both for scientific purposes, including anatomical demonstrations, and for spectral imagery of wonder such as animated skeletons after Holbein's 1538 'Dance of Death' prints.[108] Thus the instrument was, from its inception, one of pictorial and even magical illusion as much as visual documentation, with a broad range of uses convergent with the *camera obscura* for the purposes of chorography and topography, as well as painted fiction. It was also, within the draughtsman's practice, an optical instrument of scaled enlargement of any image, in its projection from a miniaturised glass slide to a wall-sized extension. Within its multivalent appropriations lies a cultural history of early modern visuality, and so a changing understanding of epistemic imagery as both demonstrably evidential and optically illusionistic at the dawn of the mechanical image.

ANAMORPHOSIS

It has often been suggested that, already in the early fifteenth century, Leon Battista Alberti had developed a type of optical *camera* mechanism for showing images painted on glass; if some have termed it a *camera obscura*, other scholars have preferred to call it a *camera ottica*, or optical chamber. While definitive conclusion remains elusive, the various interpretations of textual sources pertaining to Alberti's device certainly suggest a type of optical chamber, and possibly a medium of artistic translation akin to the drawing frame he describes in *Della pittura*, discussed in Chapter 3. Like Brunelleschi's experiment at the door of the Florentine Duomo, it is surely derived from architectural surveying methods and instruments pertaining to Alberti's work as an engineer. Whether it was a box cabinet containing a mirror reflection of a painting or a sheet of glass between a peephole sighting point and an object placed within it, it would seem that Alberti used it for architectural purposes as well as a medium of 'wonder' in its display of scenic effects. Like Brunelleschi's mirror-image view of the Florentine Baptistery, Alberti's camera was apparently intended as a demonstration piece for a one-point perspective system. The sighting point situates the eye in the appropriate place from which to view 'in perspective' the painted or reflected scene within. There is some indication that the interior scene was a changeable one, also suggesting the use of glass slides, apparently including painted architectural views and seascapes. A reference from Alberti's biography indicates the visual power accorded to it in effecting the illusion of three dimensions within a flat pictorial surface:

> he drew great admiration from certain Greek captains, to whom the sea was well known, for when he showed them this artificial immensity of the world through, as I have said, a little opening, and asked them what they saw there, this is how they responded: 'Ah', said they, 'we see a fleet of ships in the midst of the waves. It will be here by noon, unless that cloud to the East and that awful approaching storm stops them. We see, too, that the sea has grown wild, and a sign of danger are the rays of the sun too sharply reflected from the sea.'[109]

If Alberti's '*camera*' device was, like Brunelleschi's mirror, concerned to give proof of the visible veracity of a geometrical perspectival system, the subsequent early modern development of this instrument would be two-fold. That is to say, as well as 'legitimate perspectives' such as Alberti's, it would also encompass the purposeful distortion of perspective to forge 'trick' imagery of various kinds. Thus early modern 'trick' images stood alongside scientifically 'true' ones within perspectival treatises and collections of curiosities. Notwithstanding Galileo's light censure, trick imagery was understood as demonstrations of the science of optics, to be sure, but also the wonders of visual illusion. Kircher, for example, used a number of objects to demonstrate science, magic, and above all the magic of science through further types of *camera obscura* and other optical devices of illuminated projection. These included 'magic' mirrors of distortion and animation alongside accurate or 'truthful' mirrors. Of course, both were in fact products of catoptric science; at the same time, in cultural terms, the juxtaposition opened up a wide field of semantic play on the veiled significance of their apparently doubled meaning. For this 'doubled' imagery was understood as metaphors for the doubled meaning of ludic wit, as also in the double entendres of literary form. Thus early modern optical instrumentation became the subject of much literary metaphor. In the words of George Puttenham in his *Arte of English Poesie* of 1589, the literary metaphor was perceived to surpass the norms of language through a cloaking in deception, 'drawing it from plainnesse and simplicitie to a certain doublenesse whereby our talke is the more guilefull'.[110] The double-faced image was readily reconciled with such literary conceits of metaphorical wit, as in Tesauro's praise for allegories in both text and image in his book the *Cannocchiale* (Telescope). For wit was understood to reside in the double entendre of language, just like the double image of perspectival illusion, to show simultaneously its truth and fiction:

> A metaphor, all at once, pulls everything tightly into a word: and in a miraculous way makes you see one thing inside another. Hence the greater is your delight: in the same way as it is a more curious and pleasing thing to see many objects together through a perspective than the originals themselves in a succession. A work . . . not of the dull, but of the sharpest wit.[111]

Collectively, these texts directly reflect the interests of those cultures of curiosity that nurtured early modern science, analogical magic, and visual illusion alike. Among the many forms of perspectival illusion such texts illustrate, the clearest corollary to metaphor in the orchestrated play of double vision were those of a doubled perspective.[112] This 'doubleness' was at the crux of a burgeoning anamorphic imagery celebrated in early modern art, optical science, and literary allegory alike. Reflected in manifold illustrations in printed books, it extended to a wide range of painted imagery from the merely curious to the acknowledged masterpiece, such as the anamorphic skull of Hans Holbein's great *Ambassadors*. Early modern anamorphic imagery was widespread and widely regarded, as the visual equivalent of the literary metaphor in its ability to pictorialize veiled or coded, even hidden meanings. Both made and revealed by means of mirrors, anamorphic imagery was consequently classed alongside distorting mirrors, as a type of picture-puzzle imagery concerned with the visual double entendre or pun. Its inclusion, in a chapter on early modern optical imagery, is to demonstrate, on the one hand, the rippling cultural significations read into the optically assisted image and, on the other, its tight relationship, howsoever apparently in reverse, with the exacting specular claim of Renaissance painting's mimetic art.

Engravings from the Parisian Jesuit Jean Dubreuil's *Perspective pratique*, published in successive editions from the early 1640s, give a particularly rich account of the early modern anamorphic image. Dubreuil illustrates the display and use of anamorphic devices within early modern science museums, often in dedicated catoptrics rooms that he described as set with mirrors all around (Fig. 110). Conical viewing lenses and pyramids with anamorphically painted interiors placed on tables, walls, floor, and ceiling invited visitors to uncover the hidden or distorted images within, while mirrors were also used to resolve the picture-puzzles or to multiply their visual effects. The instruments on display were intended as examples of lessons in the science of optics, as well as the witty ingenuity of metaphor, similar to those of Kircher's catoptrics chamber, which Dubreuil, long in Rome, surely knew. In this regard collections and treatises on the science and wit of optics were closely linked. In another illustrated example from Dubreuil, two *curieux* view a range of anamorphic images through sighting devices to the side of each picture. The oblique side view is the viewing point through which the perspectival distortion may be resolved.[113] Thus the viewer is presented with both the anamorphosis, and its resolution, as a witty lesson in the science of optics, and in the veiled nature of metaphor too.

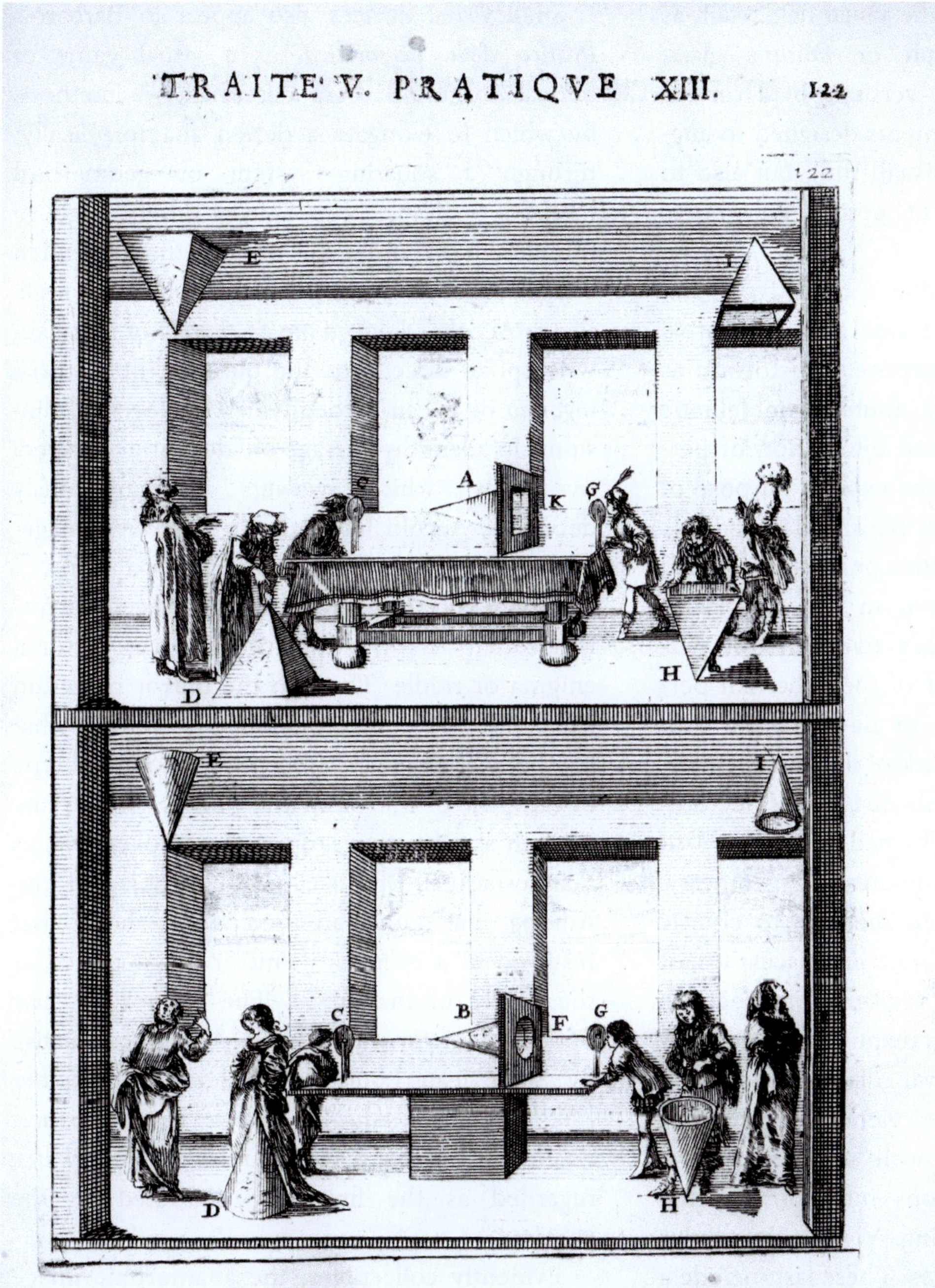

Fig. 110 Jean Dubreuil, illustration of a catoptrics chamber with a range of optical and catoptric devices, in *La perspective pratique*, 2nd ed., Paris, 1647.
Photo: Gallica BNF

In early modern treatises for the draughtsman's practice also, the double use of geometrical perspective for the purposes of visual accuracy and its playful distortion are often presented together. Indeed, Renaissance perspectival treatises, written by artists and mathematicians alike, generally included examples of both, as instruction in draughtsmanship, perspective, and the ingenuity of pictorial play. Equally, perspectival drawing aids for the draughtsman in the mimetic reproduction of the visual field, such as Leonardo's perspectograph or Dürer's glass, could be integrated with versions of a *camera obscura* to produce instruments designed to augment the perception of visual truth, but also to distend it into images of optical illusion as pictorial wit.

Thus perspective became a cognitive metaphor of itself, of acts of vision and conceptual thought but also of its purposeful distortion as the pictorial emblem of a doubled emblematic wit. Indeed, such calculated bifurcation of perspectivist deployment is the express purpose of treatises such as Giacomo Barozzi da Vignola's *Le due regole della prospettiva pratica* (published in 1583 but largely written in the 1530s with Vincenzo Danti). Vignola's two rules of perspectival practice are that of the Albertian perspective box, and its re- or de-formation into chimerical form as the mark of illusionistic play. Many texts referred to this division as 'legitimate perspective' and 'de-formed perspective' to signal their common foundation in geometry, howsoever distended from mimetic to cryptic effect. Thus Vignola follows his discussion of perspectival 'windows' of legitimate perspective with methods for their transposition into various types of perspectival distension. These included stage sets with accelerating or decelerating perspectives, as well as perspectival elongations and extensions into monumental illusionistic ceiling painting. Vignola concludes with a series of trick images. These last include a 'staircase' or folding structure in which two images are superimposed in alternating strips to produce a double image that can only be resolved into unified form by the use of an angled mirror; and the squaring method for an anamorphic distortion or elongation, which can then be resolved by placing the image within a viewing box or cabinet with a lenticular peephole sighting device at the side, from which viewpoint the elongation is corrected.[114]

Such visual devices also appear in Barbaro's *Pratica della perspettiva,* as a visual game of optical 'magic'. Barbaro describes two methods by which to elongate a design anamorphically: through a squaring system or geometrical method, or by placing a light at a right angle to the design in order to project the distended image onto a larger surface such as a wall. Pietro Accolti's *Lo inganno de gl'occhi* of 1625 likewise spoke directly to the question of pictorial *inganno* or deceit through such perspectival illusions. In a lengthy passage on 'delightful perspectives' by which viewers are'marvellously deceived', Accolti like Barbaro describes image-puzzles that can only be resolved with a mirror.[115] In such works, it is the judiciously placed mirror-image that acts as the solution to the pictorial enigma or riddle. Through the mirror reflection the image takes on recognisable form from what is otherwise shapeless splotches of colour, a type of catoptric or mirror anamorphosis that became a much sought-after early modern collectible, as manifestations of visual wit in object form. Among the most admired were those that resolved in a cylindrical mirror when placed at the centre of the image. The science of their optical geometry was elaborated in a 1630 treatise by Sieur Jean Louis de Vaulezard, *Perspective cilindrique et conique ou traicté des apparences veuës par le moyen des miroirs cilindriques,* regarded as the first text dedicated to the subject.[116]

Evidently collectibles, the anamorphic image or object was therefore to be found in early modern displays of catoptrics, whether of science or art. The inventory of William Cartwright's London Picture Gallery at the point of its 1686 bequest to Dulwich College documents the collection as having a number of boxed or 'closit peeces' including six 'perspective pictures', five of which were to be viewed by means of a 'Sellinder glass put in y.e midst of y.e bourd' including 'a paintin of y.e king of France his

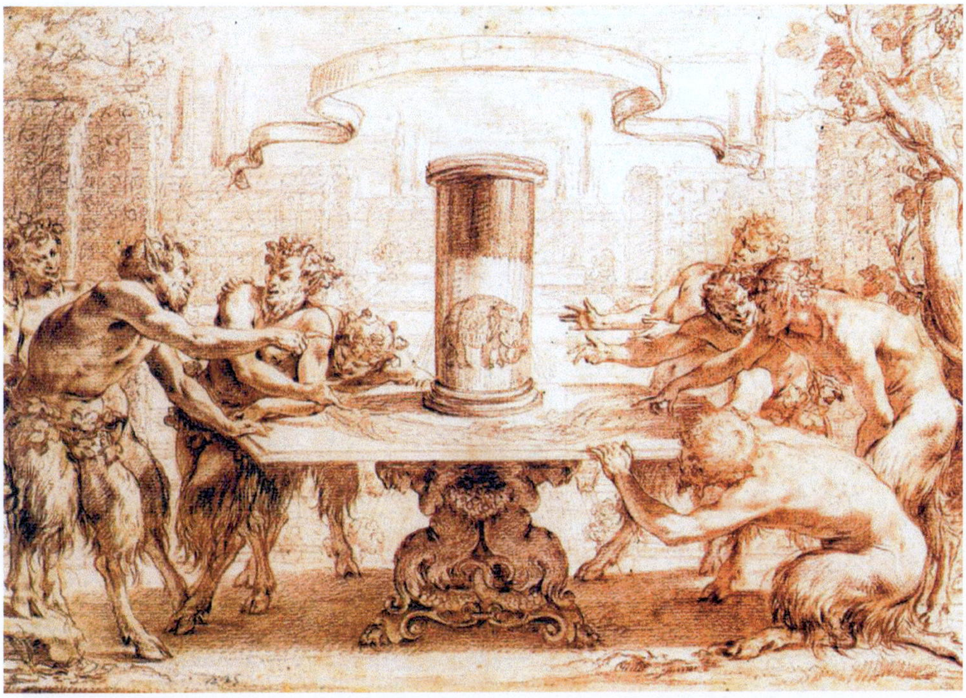

Fig. 111 Simon Vouet, drawing of 'curieux-satyrs' viewing a cylinder anamorphosis of an elephant, c. 1625, red chalk, printed as the frontispiece to Jean-François Niceron's *La perspective curieuse* (1652), Hessiches Landesmuseum Darmstadt. Photo: Wikimedia

head . . . & looke in y.er glasse, you may see him perffetly'. Another had an attached moveable eyepiece, 'a thing to pull out, & at y.e end of it a brass playt with a Lickell hole in it, Look through that hole with on[e] eye . . . and you may perfitly see them'.[117] When the reflecting cylinder or sighting device of such an anamorphosis was removed from view, the image was hidden, making it an ideal vehicle for prohibited or risqué imagery of a political or erotic nature, as well as all manner of veiled pictorial illusion cast as metaphorically doubled wit.

According to Dubreuil, 'these pieces are extremely entertaining in that, from a melange of colours that seem to be thrown onto the surface without any order, one sees a beautiful image in the cylinder'.[118] A drawing attributed to Simon Vouet, later printed and used as the frontispiece for the expanded edition of Niceron's *Perspective curieuse*, dedicated to the mathematical study of anamorphosis (1652), illustrates the genre in comedic form. A group of '*curieux-savants*', here rendered as satyrs, gaze in wonder at an anamorphosis of that most exotic of beasts of the period, an elephant (Fig. 111).[119] Niceron further illustrated in a diagram the draughtsman's geometry of a cylinder anamorphosis, showing it both in distention and in resolution (Fig. 112). The genre was a common divertissement for the perspectival artist: Domenico Piola, the great Baroque Genoese painter of *quadrature*, or illusionistic ceilings, also painted such a tabletop catoptric anamorphosis that both reproduces and distorts Rubens' *Erection of the Cross* into a comically erotic scene, revealed only when the reflective tubular viewing cylinder is in place (Rouen Musée des Beaux Arts).[120] In anamorphic imagery, such doubling of pictorial illusion could extend from the drawing manual to the gallery wall, but also to miniature or tabletop pieces. An anamorphic portrait of the lately beheaded Charles I, now at Castle Gripsholm near Stockholm, indicates with a death's head where the cylinder tube should be placed in

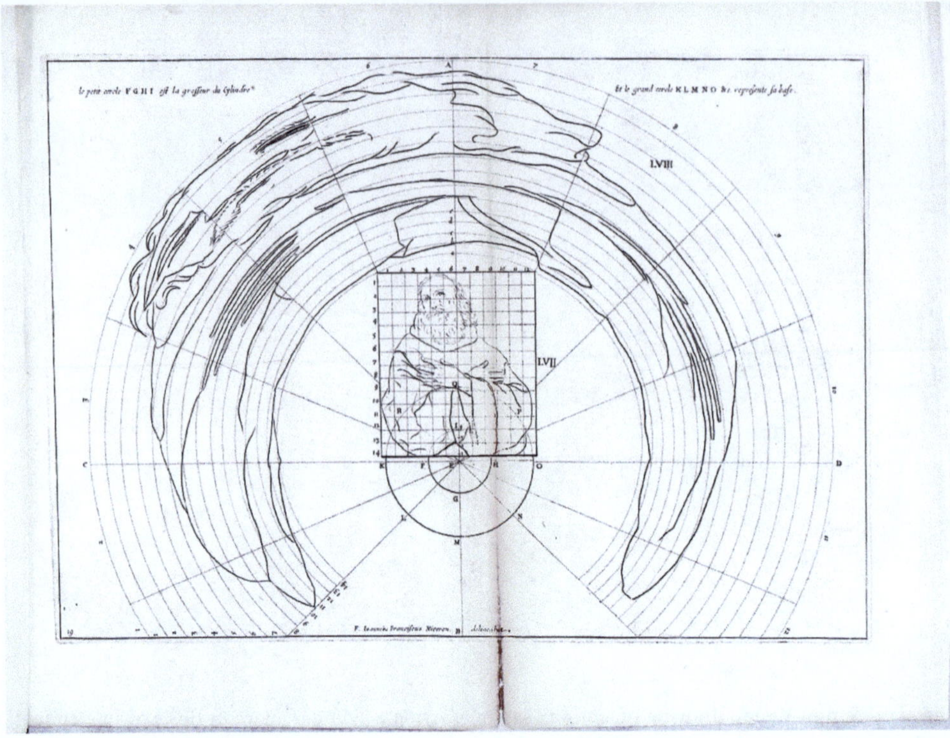

Fig. 112 Jean-François Niceron, diagram of a cylinder anamorphosis of S. Francesco di Paola showing the image in circular distention and in resolution, in *La perspective curieuse*, Paris, 1638.
Photo: Gallica / BNF

order to reveal the king's image, so acknowledging the lightly constructed cultural *vanitas* of such clever objects of curiosity.[121] Another example of a distended catoptric eye, by the Jesuit mathematician and astronomer Mario Bettini, served to illustrate his *Apiaria universae philosophiae mathematicae* of 1645, an encyclopaedic collection of mathematical curiosities including trick perspectives (Fig. 113).[122] Bettini adds a further level of metaphorical double play in an image representing two forms of anamorphosis: by the geometry of cylinder catoptrics and by torchlight. Directly behind the upright image of an eye is a flame that casts its rays through the cylinder onto the extended version of the eye below. This is surely visual reference to those types of anamorphic images rendered by cast illuminations, like magic lanterns, for example, projecting pictures painted on oiled-paper lampshades onto surrounding ceilings, walls, and floors. Reportedly depicting the eye of Cardinal Colonna, whose election was apparently foretold by means of optical magic, Bettini wittily suggests both the Cardinal's clear vision and his abilities to navigate the specular eddies of politically doubled metaphor at the papal court.[123]

Texts such as Niceron's *Perspective curieuse*, or *Thaumaturgis opticus* in its 1646 Latin edition, attended directly to the anamorphically perspectival bifurcation of form as a type of optical riddle or magic, as the use of the Greek term '*thauma*' was intended to signify. Niceron's textual examples of anamorphoses range from miniatures to tabletop devices of optical illusion to monumental wall and ceiling imagery. This is also the case in his own artistic output, which included a range of small images and objects as well as wall frescoes undertaken for his religious order, the Minims, in commemoration of their founder S. Francesco di Paola.[124] Both friar and artist, Niceron was a celebrated mathematician, trained under the tutelage of Marin Mersenne, also of the Minims in Paris. Like Kircher, Niceron produced a range of optical toys as

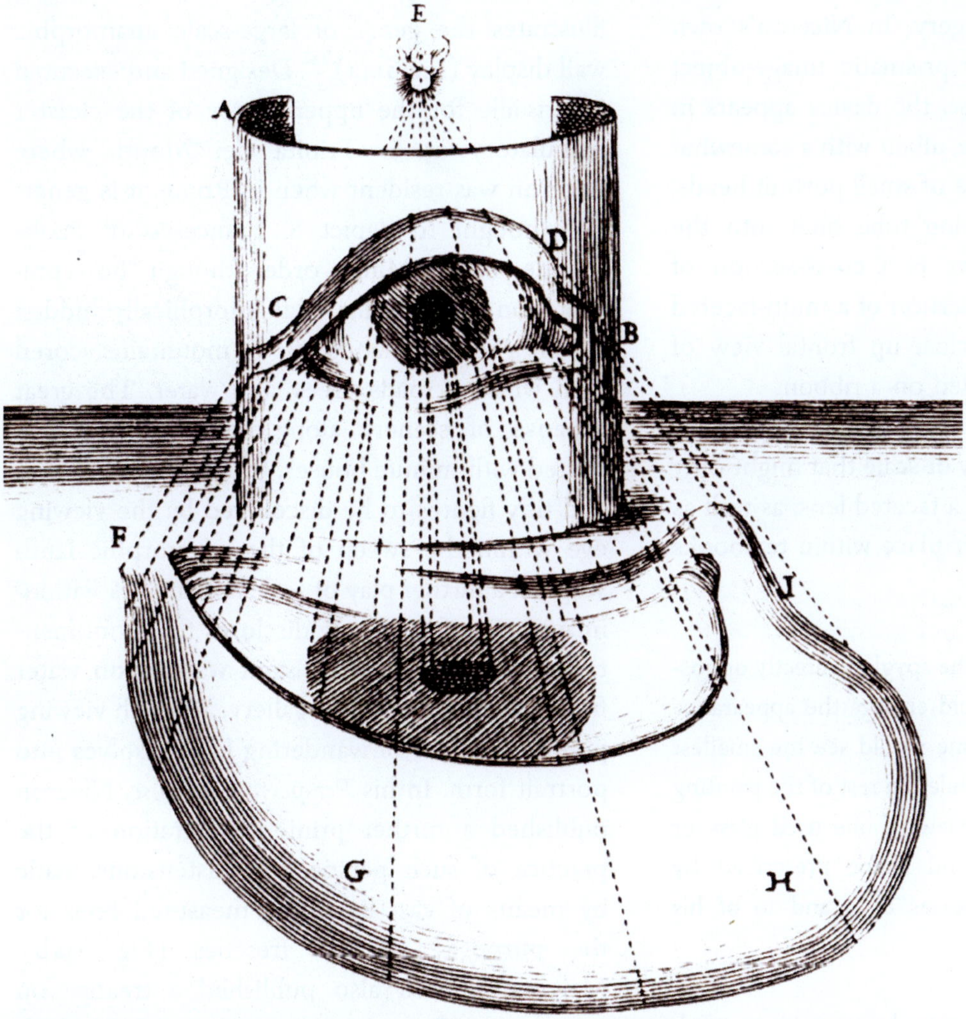

Fig. 113 Mario Bettini, diagram of 'Cardinal Colonna's' anamorphic eye, in *Apiaria universae philosophiae mathematicae*, Bologna, 1645.
Photo: Fototeca Gilardi

object-illustrations of his perspectival mathematics and their anamorphic extensions. For example, an optical toy by Niceron of a prismatic or trick portrait was designed as a small wooden cabinet piece for tabletop viewing, which he also illustrated in his treatise. The device was once part of the Medici collections of optical devices at the Uffizi Palace, intended as a type of witty toy for use by visitor-viewers, to delight and amaze as well as to instruct playfully in the art of perspective and the science of optical illusion. With an unmediated view, the small painted panel appears as a series of revolving turbaned heads with a flag displayed in their midst. However, the wooden stand within which it is set comprised a faceted polyhedral viewing lens through which to resolve the whirligig painting into a portrait of Ferdinand II de' Medici. Seen through the refractions of such a prism, the viewing apparatus generates an optical illusion similar to anamorphosis.[125] This metaphor of the prismatic or multiplying image surely lay behind Thomas Hobbes' image of the body politic composed of multiple bodies within the body of the king for his *Leviathan* of 1651, as Barbara Stafford has suggested.[126] It highlights not only the widespread diffusion of the genre, but also its valence as political imagery. In Niceron's own illustration of a similar prismatic image-object for his *Perspective curieuse*, the device appears in the lower half of the page, albeit with a somewhat different image of a circle of small portrait heads. Before it stands a viewing tube built into the tabletop platform. Above is a cross-section of the tube showing the insertion of a multi-faceted refraction lens, with a close-up frontal view of two such lenses suspended on a ribbon.

Niceron further described miniature images-within-an-image in a play of scale that might only be revealed by means of a faceted lens, as well as a keen awareness of their place within textbooks on optics:

> By putting your eye to the spyglass directly opposite, this tiny object would enlarge the appearance to such a degree that one would see the smallest details very distinctly, while the rest of the painting would disappear from view, if one used glass or crystals of the form and shape prescribed by M. Descartes in Discourses 8, 9, and 10 of his *Dioptrics*.[127]

Niceron's own wall frescoes have not survived, but an example he cited by his fellow Minim, Emmanuel Maignan, using Niceron's methods, illustrates the genre of large-scale anamorphic wall display (Fig. 114a).[128] Designed and executed in grisaille for the upper storey of the cloister ambulatory at S. Trinità dei Monti, where Niceron was resident when in Rome, it is generally thought to depict S. Francesco di Paola, founder of the Minim order, though the representation of the saint is anamorphically hidden within a seeming landscape of mountains scored with winding roads, trees, and water. The great expanse of scenery along the gallery wall is dotted with minute houses, turrets, domes, ships, and tiny figures to be discovered by the viewing eye within the sweep of the anamorphic landscape in a further play of scale and images-within-images. The fresco only discloses the monumental representation of the saint walking on water from the entrance to the gallery, at which viewing point the welter of wandering lines resolves into portrait form. In his *Perspective curieuse*, Niceron published a further printed illustration of the practice of such perspectival distensions made by means of cast light and measured lines for the purposes of wall frescoes (Fig. 114b). Maignan himself also published a treatise on perspective, *Perspectiva horaria*, in 1648, which includes a technical description of the

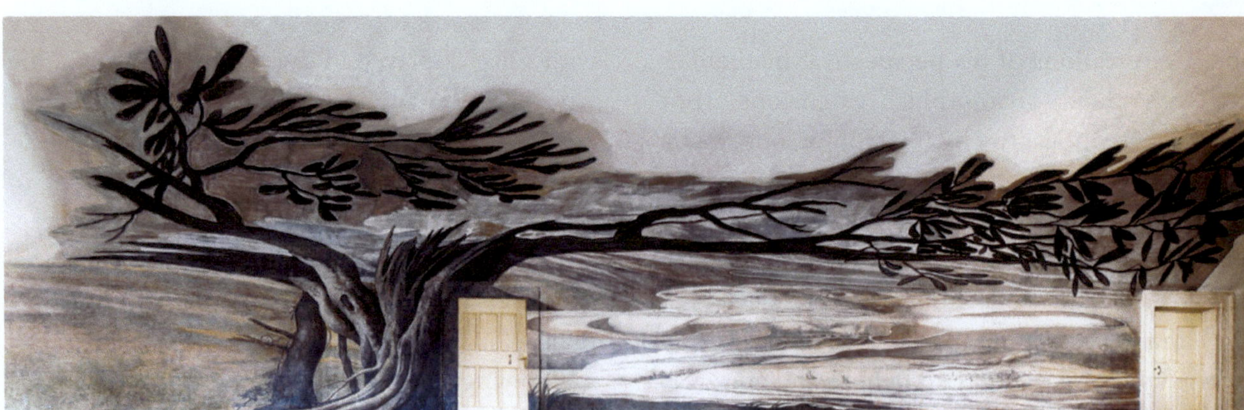

Fig. 114a Emmanuel Maignan, with Jean-François Niceron, *S. Francesco di Paola*, anamorphic wall fresco, Sta Trinità dei Monti, Rome.
Photo: Araldo de Luca

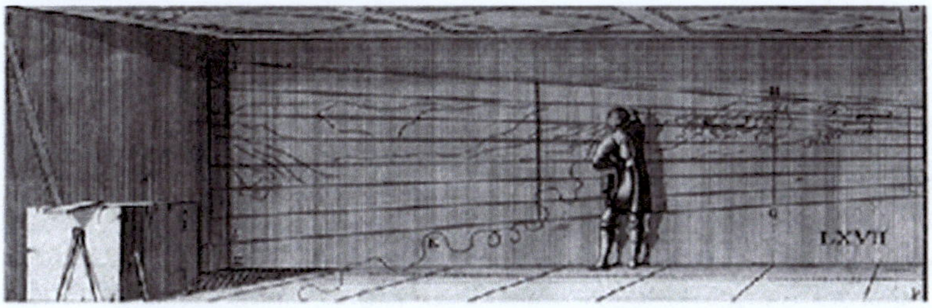

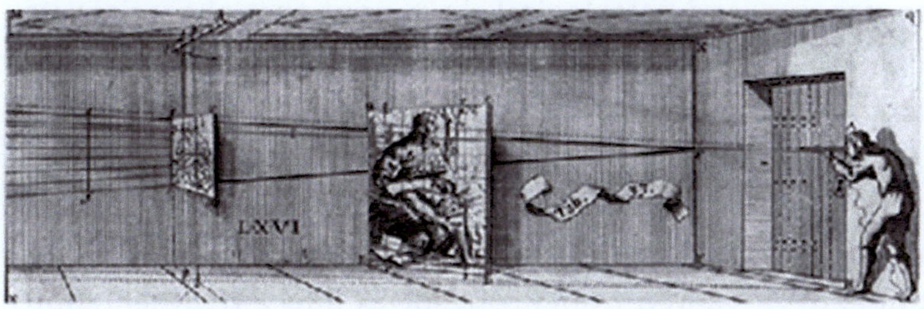

Fig. 114b Jean-François Niceron, diagram of the practice of an anamorphic perspectival distention for a wall fresco, in *La perspective curieuse*, Paris, 1638.
Photo: Google ebooks

anamorphic methods he used at S. Trinità dei Monti. The text is chiefly concerned with sundials and gnomons, with mirrors of all kinds throughout, used to capture cast shadows as a means of measuring the arc of the sun, and closely related to his design of the catoptric sundial for the Meridian Gallery at Palazzo Spada, in which the targeted reflection of sunlight onto a mirror effects a moving sunbeam dial.[129] His anamorphic method for draughtsmen is similarly concerned with shadow projection, using string, mirrors, and a gemstone lens to project an elongated image from a shuttered panel onto a vaulted ceiling or wall.[130] Like the eye of Bettini's Colonna anamorphosis, representations of such optical devices and images used the figure of the disembodied eye to 'fix' the viewer spatially, in order best to witness the double play of perspectival illusion. While Bettini illustrated the light of a torch or candle as the source of a cast anamorphic image, many perspectival treatises adopted the emblem of the viewing eye as the focal point of visual perception, in a demonstration of perspective as the instrument of vision. In Zahn's *Telescopio* a telescopic illuminated projector in the form of a scioptic eye is pictured with a viewing eye, while the frontispiece to Descartes' *Dioptrique* pictures a viewing eye alongside its anatomical representation as a type of camera (Figs. 108 and 106, respectively).[131] There is surely recollection of Alberti's celebrated self-portrait medal with a winged or demiurge eye, as the emblem of his perspectival art and the dominion of vision as the instrument of all knowledge (Fig. 32, Chapter 1).[132] It is also a theorisation of the draughtsman's sighting device as the practice-based means of 'fixing' the viewing eye at the point of perspectival resolution, and a pictorialisation of the place of the viewer within an Albertian one-point perspective system of vision.

If the term 'anamorphosis', meaning to reshape or re-form, awaited dictionary definition in Denis Diderot's *Encyclopédie* of 1751, its practice and theory arose in the fifteenth century alongside the development of mathematical perspective itself. The term as such appears first in seventeenth-century treatises on perspective, seemingly with Gaspar Schott's *Magia universalis* (Universal Magic) of 1657,[133] but must already have been in use in oral discussion and certainly in pictorial practice. For the visual practice of anamorphosis is the obvious extension of a mathematical perspective system, because of the optical adjustments needed for depicting objects as if seen from an angle or at a height. Taken to its mathematical extreme as a form of pictorial ingenuity, perspectival distortion produced doubled images read as visual emblems or metaphors of an inventive wit, sometimes referred to as 'secret perspectives' in a further play on conceptions of the multi-perspectival point of view. Scholars of anamorphosis have suggested Dürer was an early practitioner on the basis of a letter from Venice of 1506 in which he writes to the Nuremberg humanist Willibald Pirckheimer that he is going to Bologna to learn the art of 'secret perspective', seemingly from the revered mathematician Luca Pacioli. Pacioli had translated Piero della Francesco's writings on perspective and collaborated with Leonardo in such studies in Milan, so his engagement with artists was renowned.[134] The same term was also used by the Venetian Daniele Barbaro for 'secret' devices of proportional elongation similar to the perspectival 'windows' Dürer illustrated in his *Underweysung* (Fig. 67a, b, Chapter 3) as a type of visual game or 'secret part of perspective', suggesting an oral and practice-based link between the two.[135] Further early examples emanate from the circle of Dürer in Nuremberg, in the form of woodcuts by his pupil Erhard Schön. Dating from the 1530s, this oeuvre comprises humorous images known as *Vexierbild* or picture puzzles that play between religious representation, the erotic, and scatological. In a print that allegorises its own manner of hidden imagery between anamorphic distention and perspectival resolution, titled *Was Siehst Du?* (What Do You See?), of 1538, what appears an allegorical 'dream' seascape with Jonah and the Whale, when viewed frontally, resolves into a representation of defecation seen from an oblique viewing point to the left of the inscription (Fig. 115).[136] Further, Leonardo is often cited as providing the first example of an anamorphic or perspectivally extended image, a drawing of an eye in his Codex Atlanticus. In his treatise on painting Leonardo reflected on the art of perspectival distortion depending on the position of the eye viewing the image askance through a sighting device:

> and if you were to paint this on a wall in front of which you can move freely, the effect would appear out of proportion to you because of the great

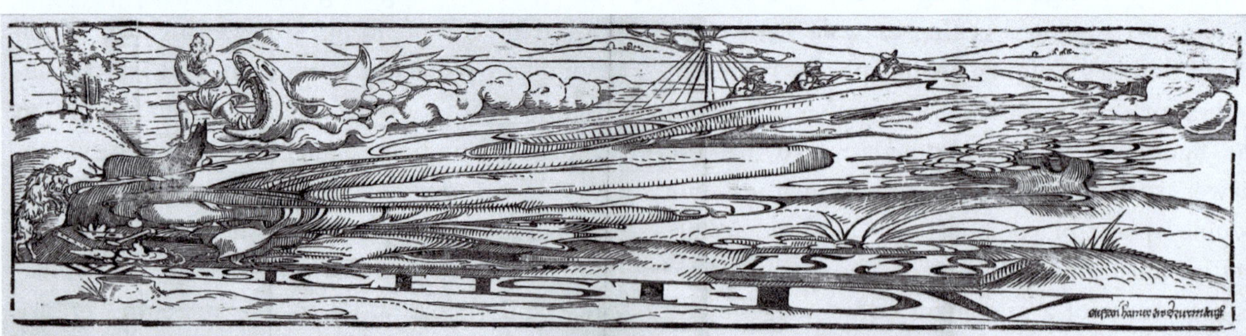

Fig. 115 Erhard Schon, *Was Siehst Du?*, 1538, woodcut, 21.2 × 85.1 cm, Nuremberg. Photo: British Museum

> difference between [the intervals]. This happens because the eye is so close to the wall that the painting appears foreshortened. And if you wished to paint that, your perspective would have to be viewed through a single hole.[137]

Like fresco, Renaissance panel painting was also a locus of anamorphic play, notably in court portraiture, where pictorial wit was part of a princely '*speculum ludens*'. Such imagery was clearly designed in the form of doubled or 'trick pictures', displays of ingenuity between portraiture and courtly jest, like a veiled rebus or encoding of mimetic recognition. Hence the Flemish Guillim Scrots, as court artist to Henry VIII and subsequently the boy king Edward VI, depicted the young monarch frequently, including in an anamorphic portrait as a courtly *ludens* of pictorial wonder. The painting is on a wood panel mounted into a deep box frame that originally had a hinged lid in the manner of a small cabinet picture of visual curiosity (Fig. 116).[138] Viewed frontally through the open shutter, the picture's elongations render the image and surrounding text illegible. However, a remaining hollow in the side of the frame indicates it was intended to be viewed from an oblique position, in a 'double' of perspectival vision, frontal confusion yielding to resolution when seen from a sighting device at the right.

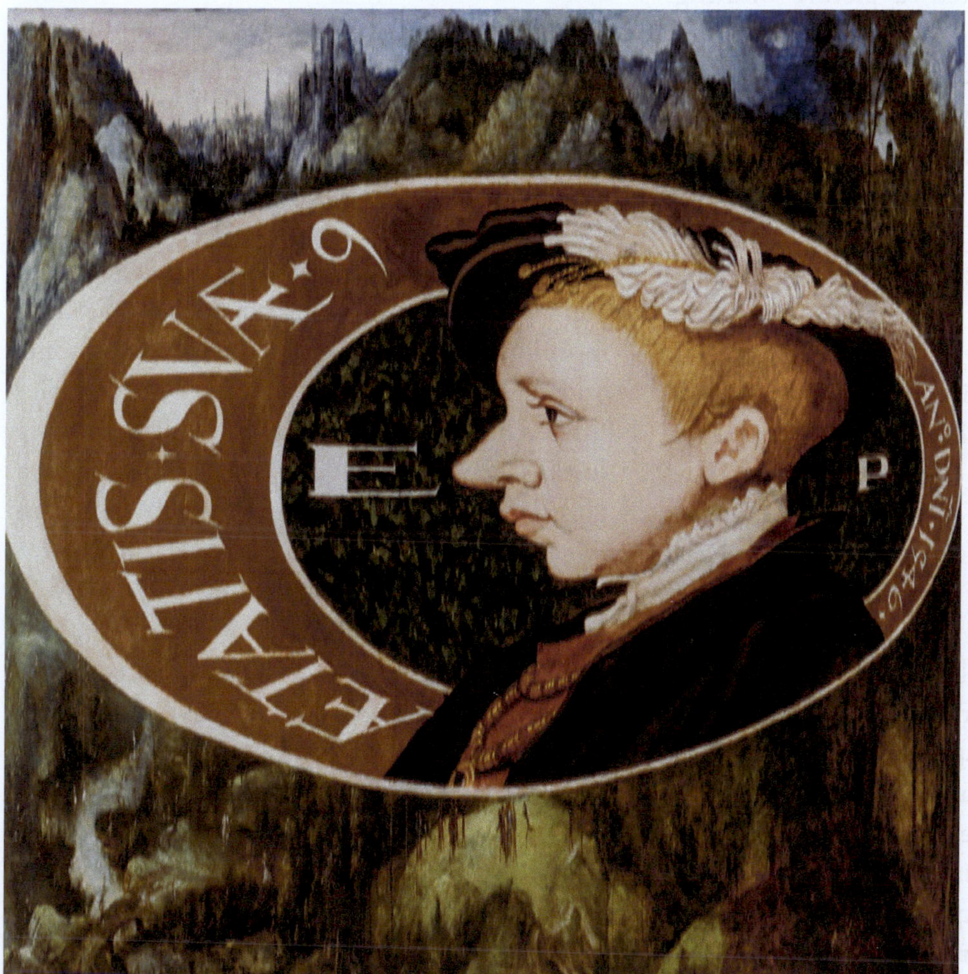

Fig. 116 Guillim Scrots, anamorphic portrait of King Edward VI, 1546, oil on panel, 42 × 160 cm, National Portrait Gallery London. Photo: NPGL

A German traveller, Lupold von Wedel, who saw the portrait in Whitehall Palace in 1584, described the use of the 'double view' through an attached sighting mechanism:

> If you stand before the portrait, the head, face, and nose appear so long and misformed that they do not seem to represent a human being, but there is an iron bar with a plate at one end fixed to the painting; if you lengthen this bar for about three spans and look at the portrait through a little hole made in the plate in this manner – O – you find the ugly face changed into a well-formed one.[139]

Another German visitor, Paul Hentzner, viewing it in 1598, noted 'a picture of King Edward VI, representing at first sight as something quite de-formed, till by looking through a small hole in the cover which is put over it, you see it in its true proportions'.[140] Mathematical analysis finds the portrait is perfectly resolved from the determined viewing point to the side, when the elliptical extension of the image becomes legible as a circle framing the boy's head.

The perspectival precision of the image's resolution point indicates the fixity of the viewing eye, as determined by the picture itself. The painting exemplifies a mathematical anamorphosis in which the viewer is invited to engage with the image through a doubled view. At first sight incomprehensible, from a second 'perspective' it is rendered legible, in a pictorial game of occlusion and disclosure intended to astonish with its pictorial-perspectival wit. Vignola's engraving of a box anamorphic portrait in his *Due regole*, written in the 1530s, illustrates a frame like Scrots' with its viewing 'peephole' to the side. Above, he places the squaring grid of both the corrected and the distended image to show the arithmetical means of its making.[141] Similarly, Niceron illustrated in diagrammatic form a series of portrait heads both in perspective and in anamorphic distention (Fig. 117). As with all such imagery, an angled mirror will reflect the corrected image such that both the distorted and the resolved perspective may be viewed simultaneously. As the German mathematician and logician, Gottfried Leibniz, would later describe:

> It is as in those devices of perspective, where certain beautiful drawings appear only as confusion until one finds their true point of vision, or views them by means of a certain glass or mirror. It is by placing and using them properly that they serve as adornment for a room.[142]

Scholars of Shakespeare have speculated that his company, the Chamberlain's Men, may have performed at Whitehall in 1598 where Scrots' portrait of Edward VI then was. Certainly, Shakespeare's plays deploy the trope of the anamorphic image as a sign of the doubled or metaphorical play between 'truth' and 'fiction' that is theatre. In fact, the anamorphic literary device was a pervasive one. Such split images were termed 'couzening pictures' that show two ways: in Shakespeare's further elaborations, 'painted one way like a gorgon / the other way's a Mars', these are 'Like perspectives which, rightly gaz'd upon / show nothing but confusion, ey'd awry / Distinguish form'.[143]

Anamorphosis was also the pictorial carrier of deeply meditated if necessarily hidden thoughts and beliefs on articles of faith, politics, philosophy, and culture in encrypted form. Its most celebrated early modern manifestation is undoubtedly Holbein's so-called *Ambassadors* of 1533, a double portrait of life-sized dimensions on a great oak panel in oil (Fig. 118a, b).[144] Painted by the German artist in the employ of the Tudor

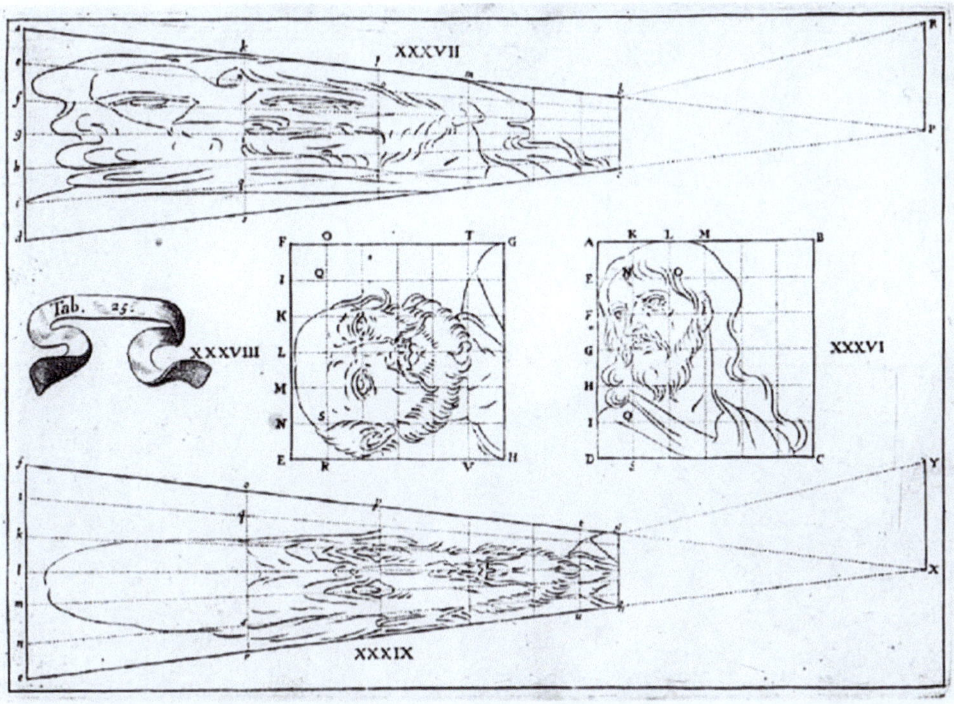

Fig. 117 Jean-François Niceron, diagram of portrait heads in perspective and in anamorphic distention, in *La perspective curieuse*, Paris, 1638.
Photo: Gallica/BNF

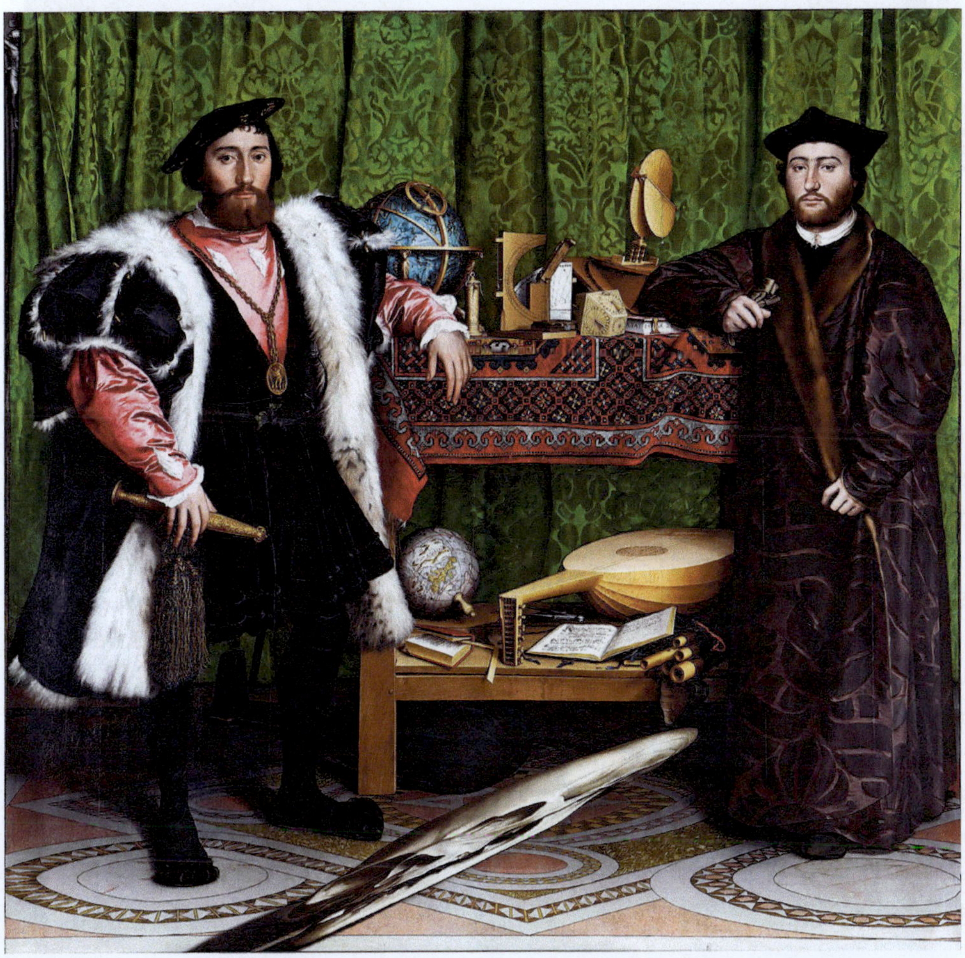

Fig. 118a Hans Holbein the Younger, *Jean de Dinteville and Georges de Selve as the Ambassadors*, 1533, oil on oak, 207 × 209.5 cm, National Gallery London.
Photo: Wikimedia

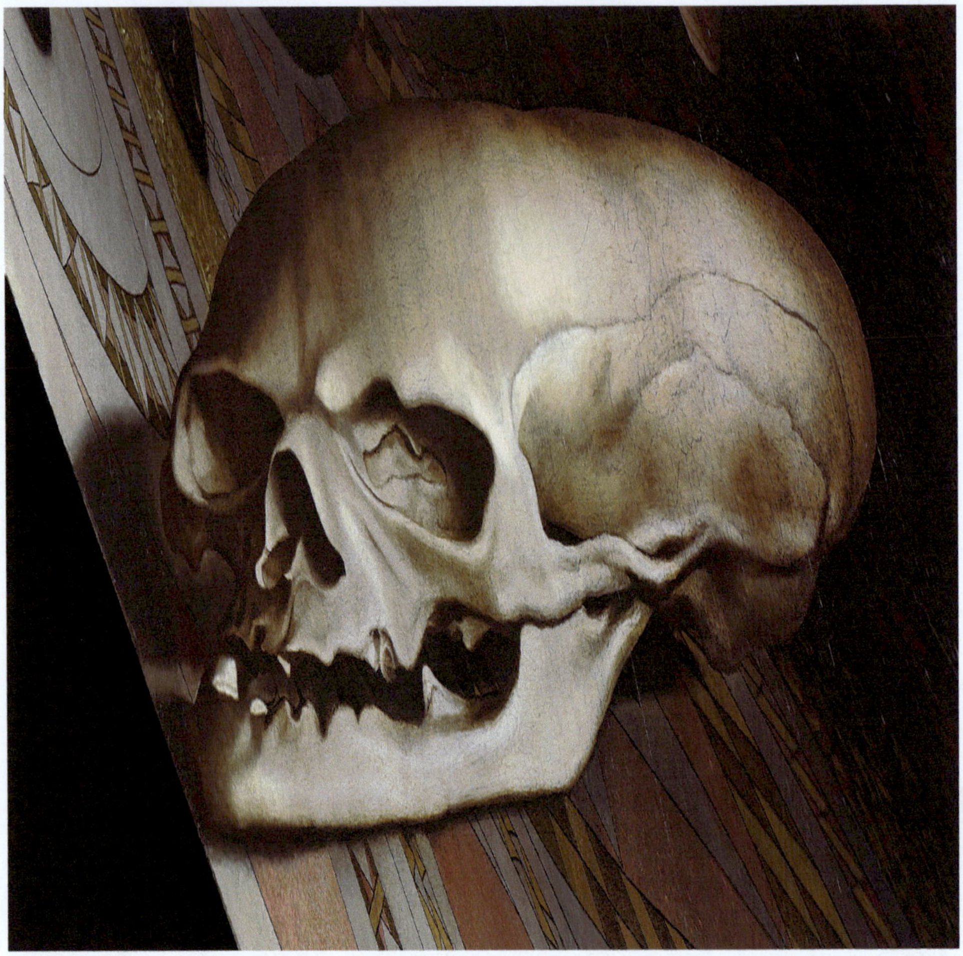

Fig. 118b Hans Holbein the Younger, detail of the anamorphic skull from the side/in resolution, from the *Ambassadors*, 1533, oil on oak, 207 × 209.5 cm, National Gallery London.
Photo: Wikimedia

court, of French ambassadors then present in London at the court of Henry VIII, it is a double portrait with a doubled perspectival viewing point. It was the year of Henry's VIII's marriage to Anne Boleyn and break with Rome, which François I's ambassadors were there to report on. Diplomatic correspondence, in matters of both *gravitas* and *ludus*, was written in code as a matter of ambassadorial protocol. The advent of moveable type and the printing press produced a burgeoning Renaissance literature on ciphers of encryption inaugurated by Alberti and furthered by humanist cultures concerned with philological linguistics, logic, and mathematics.[145] This diplomatic culture of encryption, like veiled metaphor, took pictorial form in the figure of anamorphosis. Holbein's wittily doubled art may thus be read as the pictorial device of their diplomatic code.

Often cast as a friendship portrait, it is testament to the relations of the two men as ambassadors at the Henrician court. Between the two stands an open cabinet of objects of their *virtù*. If extensive iconographical research on this painted collection has yet to reach full consensus, it is broadly recognised as an ensemble of objects concerned with the mapping of both heaven and earth, geographically and temporally.[146] Astronomical, cartographic, and mathematical, these objects of knowledge comprise an earthly and celestial globe of the heavens, with an array of instruments for measuring its longitudes and latitudes, and the passing of time, by means of the stars. They have often been linked to representations of the medieval university curriculum; they were also, in their day, the most up-to-date scientific instruments of their kind, comprising quadrant, torquetum, and an array of dials along the upper shelf, fit for a princely *Kunstkammer*. Below are two open books: on the left, a treatise on arithmetic next to Jean de Dinteville, courtier to François I and Seigneur of Polisy near Fontainebleau, and, on the right, a hymn book next to Georges de Selve, classics scholar and Bishop of Lavaur. In keeping with the painting's many cartographic instruments, the arithmetic primer is surely a reference to the mathematical knowledge that informed both Renaissance maps and perspective. The terrestrial globe marks the Dinteville estates of Polisy, as well as mapping the most recent endeavours at global circumnavigation, thus charting the worldly place of the ambassadors' elevated position at the centre of early modern knowledge.[147]

The arithmetical primer is by Peter Apian, a German humanist, like Holbein, who was a mathematician, cartographer, and astronomer, as well as a designer of astronomical instruments such as sundials, on which he also published.[148] As a map-maker, Apian's best-known image was a heart-shaped or cordiform mathematical projection of the world, published in 1530, which Holbein surely knew from his own interests in cartography. Within the *Ambassadors*, Apian's book is propped open to a page on division, a possible reference to the politics of the French embassy during the period of Henry VIII's breach with Rome. Coupled with the knowledge of Apian's heart-shaped map, this may suggest the royal *amour* that would bring about the division of the church.

The hymn book, as has often been noted, is in German, likely in reference to the German Holbein himself, surely also an allusion to the impending separation of the English church from Rome as had already taken place in Martin Luther's Germany, possibly in a pictorial call for Christian unity in the face of the break-up of Catholic Europe. For the hymns depicted at the book's open page are traditional verse of the Catholic Church, howsoever newly translated from Latin into Luther's German. A case of pipes or flutes and a lute accompany the hymn book as instruments of music. Music may be understood both as a dimension of learning and the arts and as an allusion to the classical astrological harmony of the spheres aspired to in overseeing the politics of Henry VIII's marriage to Anne Boleyn that year. As a portent for de Selve's ambassadorial position at court and at home during the period of the king's marriage and the break with Rome, as has often been noted, the lute's broken string, suggests discord within the political harmony of the day. Similarly, the equivocal significance of the pipes, of which one appears to be missing, may suggest both the *amour* and conflict of Henry VIII's marriage.[149] The inscription on the quadrant, '*Umbra Versa*', may also suggest the role of diplomacy in righting the shadows of Henry's marital straits, here depicted upside-down as an ambassadorial aspiration rather than its realisation. As a textbook example of perspectival rendering in every Renaissance treatise on draughtsmanship, the lute may also represent the arts of design that are Holbein's. This is reinforced by the representation of tools such as the compass and set-square, the shared instruments of artists and mathematicians alike as fellow students of perspective, and the geometrical patterning of both the Cosmatesque floor tiles and the Turkish rug that lines the cabinet shelves.

Directly beneath the lute and in a diagonal alignment with it lies the 'double picture-puzzle' of the painting. Seemingly arising from within the geometrical patterns of the floor, the greatly elongated grisaille ellipsis in the foreground is anamorphic. If the painting as a whole is a virtuoso display in Holbein's ability to render the very semblance of materials and objects in pictorial illusion, the picture-puzzle at the fore of the painting is the symbolic representation or hallmark of that skill, as if in reverse. Its display against the rigorous perspectival representation of the Cosmatesque floor underscores the geometry of the skull's anamorphic distention. Seen from an oblique position to the side of the panel, as with the Scrots portrait of Edward, its pictorial 'chaos' is resolved. Perspectivally rendered in oblique form, as a metaphor of diplomacy, it is recognisable as a skull that floats above the floor, surely also a ludic sign of *vanitas* of the arts. Thus the painting comprises within it two viewpoints, from the front and from the side, as a doubled perspective of its own art.[150] As the example of the Wittenburg professor of mathematics Lucas Brunn's *Praxis perspectivae* of 1615 demonstrates, the skull motif would itself become a textbook example of anamorphism, with the 'legitimate' and the elongated views placed side by side (Fig. 119), just as they are in the *Ambassadors*.[151] It has been argued that the key to the resolution of Holbein's anamorphosis is also by mirror reflection: that is, by observation through a cylindrical glass or mirror. Though there is no further evidence beyond that of visual perception, it suggests the possible application of such a device by the ambassadors in decoding Holbein's *Vexier-bild*.[152]

Together the *Ambassadors*' collected and figured objects are signs of the painting's patron and the politics of court, to be sure, but also of the court painter. For as Panofsky remarked, the skull is, at one level, an emblem of the painter's name, 'hollow bone or *hohle bein*', as a pictorial rebus of Holbein.[153] Thus Holbein's artistic signature resides precisely in this capacity for pictorial-perspectival play. His many portraits of Erasmus explicitly link him to his fellow-German's learned humanism and wit in a shared conception of 'knowledge as a whole to be of two kinds, of things and words'.[154] A rebus-like syntax pervades the work, and notably in its 'picture-puzzle' collected objects and ornaments. Equivocal signs of the politics of religious breach, they are also like a painted curiosity cabinet or *Wunderschrank*, a collection of wonders, as a microcosm-museum of encyclopaedic knowledge. Further, de Dinteville bears a small gold badge embossed with a silver death's head as a personal device in his cap, an ornamental double of the anamorphic head at his feet. Holbein the painter was also a goldsmith, crafting jewels as well as portraits for the Henrician court; the meticulous detail of painted jewellery such as de Dinteville's badge, sword hilt, and gold chain testifies to his interest and knowledge of its art. Though both the death's heads are undoubtedly a light reference to concepts of *memento mori* and *vanitas*, their ludic and decorative depiction also suggest a witty Erasmian playfulness within its representation. The vanity is the pleasures of worldly learning and the arts, emblematised in the cabinet display of scientific objects. It has often been suggested that the painting is, like the Arnolfini portrait (see the further discussion in Chapter 2), heraldic in composition with the two flanking figures and its array of pictorialized object-signs like images-within-the-image on an armorial painted shield. Thus the anamorphic skull is the picture's own disquisition on itself. In a fluent display of pictorial wit, Holbein's skull – *hohle bein* – is the 'rebus sign' of his painting within the *Schilderkunst* of his Germanic, Northern art. As a pictorial image-within-the-image, it is also heraldic in conception, and so the temporal figure of an aspired-to genealogical lineage, to represent its royal *mise-en-abyme*.[155]

THEATRUM CATOPTRICUM

Among the renowned objects of wonder in Athanasius Kircher's *musaeum* at the

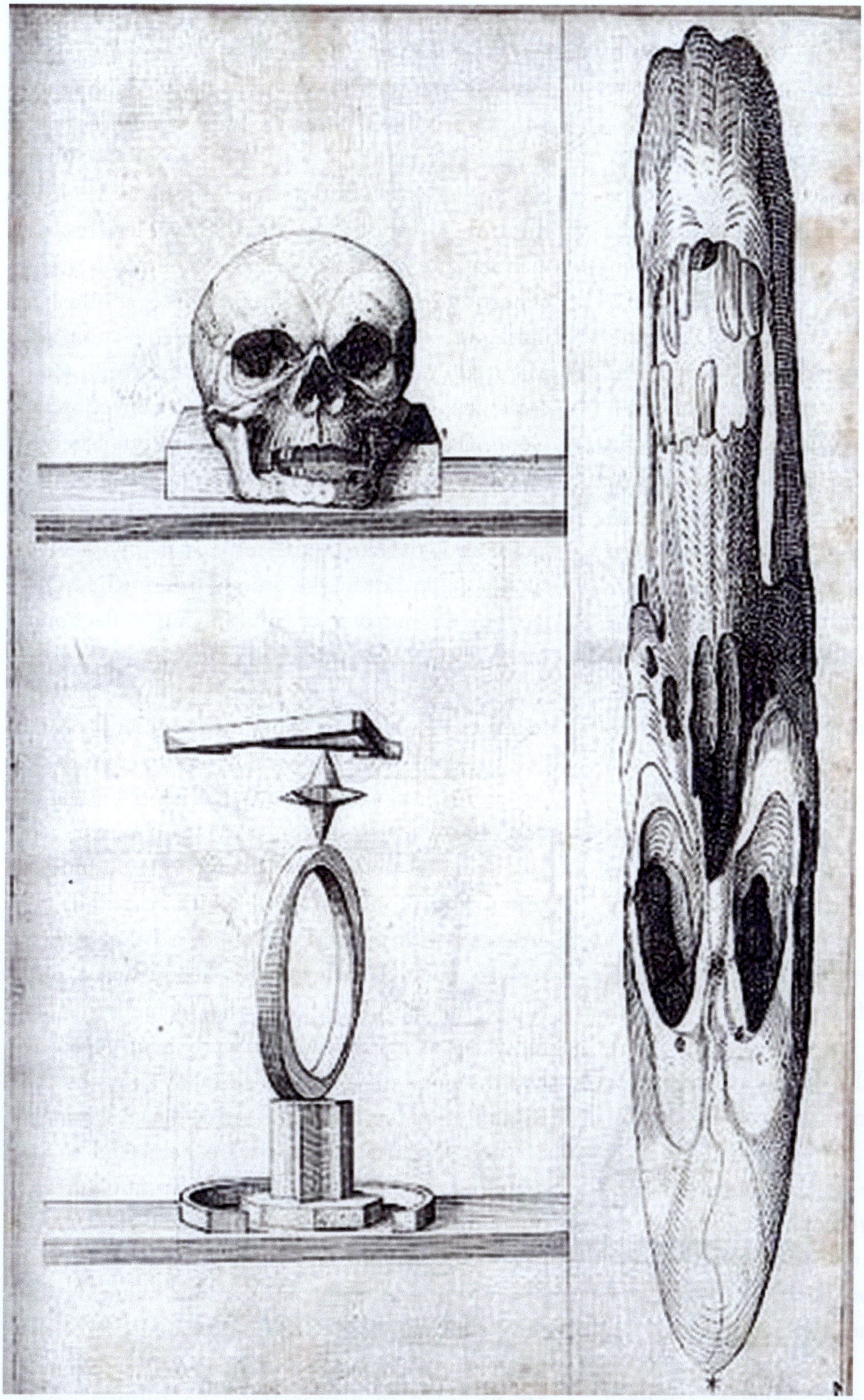

Fig. 119 Lucas Brunn, illustration of a skull in perspectival and inverted anamorphic distention, in *Praxis perspectivae*, Leipzig, 1615.
Photo: Wikimedia/ Deutsches Fotothek

Collegio Romano that he described in his *Ars magna lucis et umbrae* (Great Art of Light and Shadow), of 1646, was a much-celebrated room of catoptrics, or mirror devices, for the demonstration of optical science. Now completely dispersed, it apparently comprised a *camera obscura* along with other machines of illuminated projection for the purposes of science, experiment, education, amusement, and display. Kircher's book illustrations to the *Ars magna* illustrate some of the catoptric devices he kept, with instructions on how to assemble them as well as how to use them in order to conduct the experiment-lessons he set in his text. A 1678 illustrated catalogue of the museum prepared by his fellow Jesuit, Giorgio de Sepi, the *Romani Collegii Societatis Jesu musaeum celeberrimum*, offers a further guide to the collections, itemising such specular and prismatic objects as crystal-domed clockworks, and a parabolic mirror 'of both convex and concave form projecting an infinite number of luminous images into the air', in a display of specular multiplication and reconfiguration.[156] Among Kircher's own illustrations of his catoptric devices is a plate titled a '*theatrum catoptricum*', or mirror theatre, of particular note (Fig. 120).

The *theatrum catoptricum* was a desk-sized optical cabinet lined with a multitude of small mirrors onto which chosen objects were reflected. Designed for the display of curious or marvellous objects, the intention was a spectacular mirroring effect: 'by continuously gathering up the same images they [the mirrors] break them up optically, so that it is impossible to count them'. In this it surely resembled the parabolic mirror and reflectors described by de Sepi, in its confounding prismatic multiplication of specular reflections. A crank on the side of Kircher's illustrated mirror cabinet activated movable reflective plates embedded within the tabletop to effect a similar specular multiplication of any selected object displayed on it, in order to heighten the sense of wonder.[157] By this means, miniature models of trees might appear as a forest; a few wax flowers as a garden; miniature books of coloured paper a library; small pieces of jewels and gold as vast hordes of treasure. Kircher's example and design for such a catoptric theatre of display appears to have led to the manufacture of similar specular cabinets in other collections: one at the Villa Borghese, another in imitation of Kircher's in the collection of Manfredo Settala in Milan according to its 1664 catalogue, and one in the German collection of Georg Philipp Harsdörffer, who also published it in his *Delitiae philosophicae et mathematicae* of 1652.[158] According to Niceron, the Parisian collector and courtier Louis Hesselin also possessed such a catoptric theatre among a renowned collection of mirrors of multiplying reflections. In his description Niceron particularly praised 'the combination of many mirrors placed together in a chest to show medals, coins, pearls and precious stones . . . multiplied to infinity'.[159] As an earlier example, Michel de Montaigne described viewing a similar type of mirror box belonging to the ancient Orsini family during his sojourn in Rome in 1581, which was 'artfully arranged with mirrors all round [so that] when it was opened it appeared much wider and deeper in every direction, and seemed to hold ten times as many jewels as were in it, since one and the same thing were seen many times by the reflection of the mirrors'.[160] The visual wonders of such specular cabinets were perceived to be manifold: in the play of scale, from miniature to magnified; in the infinite mirror multiplication of the objects therein; and in the visual presentation of any object with in-the-round viewing by means of mirrors.[161] In this chapter on early modern optical imagery and its instruments, they are included to demonstrate the cultural reach into perspectivally constructed catoptric museum displays, from collection cabinets to chambers of every subject, size, and scale.

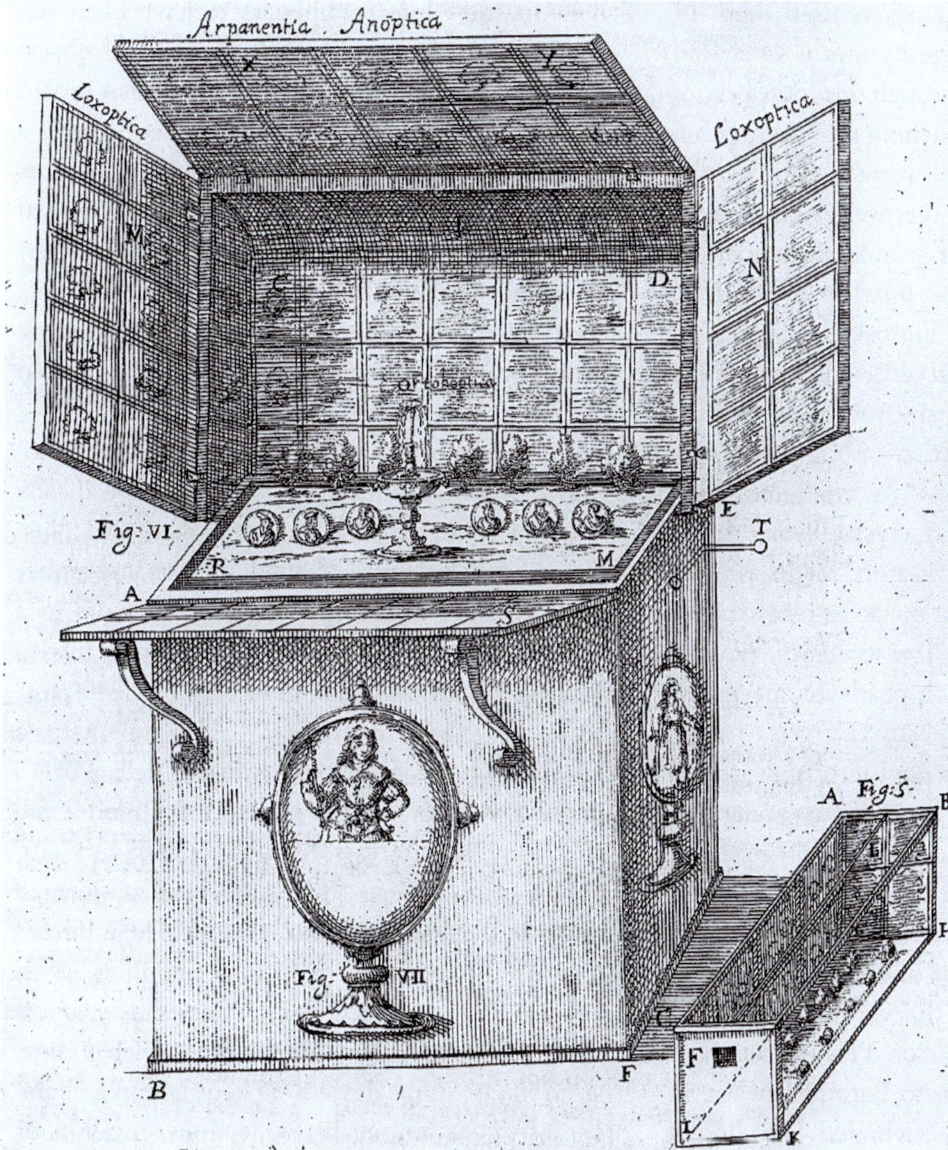

Fig. 120 Athanasius Kircher, diagram of a mirror-display cabinet titled '*theatrum catoptricum*' with prismatic mirror ball and other optical devices above, in *Ars magna lucis et umbrae*, Rome, 1646. Photo: Wikimedia

While Kircher's museum at the Collegio Romano opened to the public only in 1651, it was a much sought-after destination by the curious from its inception in the 1630s. Among its illustrious visitors, John Evelyn noted in his Rome diary of 1644 its encyclopaedic disposition, particularly its scientific instruments and inventions, including devices of optics and catoptrics.[162] Among the collections was also the archives of Kircher's extensive correspondence, with other Jesuits globally but also with the burgeoning learned societies of the sciences across Europe: the Royal Society in London, the Académie Royale des Sciences in Paris, the Accademia del Cimento in Florence, and of course Rome's Accademia dei Lincei. The correspondence, in particular, indicates the nature of Kircher's museum as both a research collection and a laboratory. The experimental paradigm of his museum was distinctive: the objects in active use as instruments of knowledge production in an enquiry- and observation-based method of scientific research. He and others used them to advance scientific knowledge by means of shared reports of experiments through his network of correspondence, and for teaching purposes within the Jesuit curriculum. But it was also, as the descriptions of the objects themselves make readily manifest, a museum of wonders intended to delight, full of rebus-like puzzles to decode, emblems to resolve, and curiosities to ponder. Nowhere was the combined sense of experimental method with a ludic curiosity more in evidence than among the catoptrics, which de Sepi described as 'object experiments' conducted with glass or metal mirrors and crystal lenses lit by daylight or candles. Here visitors might witness optical conundrums such as magic lanterns able to cast fantastic illusions of 'forests, cities, houses, libraries, gold and silver with pearls' or specimens of scientific research now greatly enlarged to allow for group consultation. De Sepi further described catoptric visual effects such as 'a mirror scene rich in every kind of fitting and furnishing', 'an architectural perspective representing the disposition of rooms in a magnificent palace', and a catoptric cat. One scene forged the effect of rushing water from above about to inundate the viewer, only to be revealed as a trick of the mirror. This was a type of special effect also common to Baroque theatre in those years, as in Bernini's celebrated 'Flooding of the Tiber' stage set.[163] If Kircher's museum presentation was both ludic and theatrical, yet it was also the locus of the most advanced research on optics and catoptrics as of every other branch of early modern natural history.

The use of mirrors as agents of a cascading specular multiplication was already long established within the broad legacy of Euclidean optics and catoptrics, as also evidenced in the writings of Leonardo and della Porta. As discussed in Chapter 1, in his notebooks Leonardo described optical experiments with chambers of facing mirrors in order to study their effects of cascading reflection (Fig. 33, Chapter 1).[164] If Leonardo's interest appears to have been scientific in the first instance, in the optical observation of light and reflection, mirrors also served his artistic study of *chiaroscuro*. Among artists and scientists alike, such chambers of mirrors were clearly understood as visual displays of specular illusion in the manner of painting's perspectival configuration of space and volume. As at Kircher's *musaeum*, early modern catoptric cabinets were at once scientific and illusionistic in their specular effects.

In della Porta's second expanded edition of *Magia naturalis*, in the sections specifically devoted to optics, he also described and illustrated a full-scale mirror-lined polygonal chamber close to Leonardo's optical hall of mirrors in a chapter entitled '*De speculo theatrali*', or 'How to Make a Theatrical Glass' in its 1658 English translation (Fig. 34, Chapter 1).[165] As a polymath, a collector, and a playwright himself, della Porta's interest in such devices similarly spanned a full spectrum of interests from scientific and academic catoptrics to the courtly and performed realm of illusionistic optical display. Della Porta's own use of specular effects also extended across every scale of object, from room-sized *camera obscuras* to specular cabinets to tabletop box-sized *thaumaturge* devices he kept within a chamber of optics among his collections. In all sizes, della Porta's means of forging specular theatres of wonder were, like Leonardo and later Kircher, based on systems of mirror magnification and multiplication: 'so that if you see a galley you will think it a fleet; if a soldier, then an army'.[166] Della Porta further described the infinite reflections of a tabletop, box-sized specular 'theatre' of mirror-images. Seemingly similar to the *theatrum catoptricum* in Kircher's catoptrics chamber, here della Porta demonstrated the effects of specular multiplication as Leonardo had also done, by setting a candle in the middle of concentrically arranged facing mirrors 'so that it will seem to multiply . . . you can never wonder enough'.[167]

Such notions of specular theatre as the display of wonder similarly extended to Kircher's *musaeum*, and specifically in his display of catoptrics including his *theatrum catoptricum*. As the title of Kircher's *theatrum catoptricum* also suggests, mirror chambers such as della Porta described were a form of early modern 'theatre' for the marvellous display of art and science alike. Here it is critical to recall that the term 'theatre' historically encompassed not only staged performance but also a broad range of cultural events, from court social occasion and religious devotion to those of scientific demonstration such as the anatomy theatre (a term that survives today). Early modern court entertainments used mirrors in elaborate scenographic displays of illusionistic lighting effected by multitudes of candles whose lights were magnified, multiplied, and intensified by metallic mirror reflectors just as Leonardo described. If Leonardo's notes on catoptrics arise among his scientific interests in optics and technology, he may also have practiced such specular effects of lighting in his orchestrations of princely theatrical interludes, in his work as court artist to both the Sforza in Milan and subsequently François I, king of France.

Specular display was clearly pervasive across the great early modern curiosity collections of universal knowledge objects, where mirrors were in use as instruments of light, as the sign of the intellect, and as a means of heightened optical illusionism in exhibitions of catoptric science such as Kircher's. Thus Joseph Furttenbach, architect and author, whose design interests extended from stage sets to monumental architecture, including theatre lighting of reflective metal mirrors, was also owner of one of the most celebrated cabinets of curiosities in seventeenth-century Germany.[168] Such shared interests between science and curiosity nurtured the use of mirrors as specular theatres of knowledge across these cultural domains, and particularly in the display of collections, as well as theatre scenographies. In a 1565 description of Duke Albrecht V of Bavaria's extensive musaeum, including mirrors and catoptrics, by his advisor Samuel Quiccheberg, he titled the work *Theatri amplissimi*. Within the text, Quiccheberg termed the ducal collections both a *theatrum sapientiae*, or universal theatre of knowledge, and a *Wunderkammer*, or chamber of wonders.[169] Among the earliest texts to use the term, Quiccheberg further defined the *Wunderkammer* as a microcosm or 'theatre' of the world. In so doing he sought to make demonstrable not only its marvellous objects, but also the link between the production of knowledge and its display. Quiccheberg's terms have led the extensive scholarship on early modern cabinets of curiosity or wonder, inaugurated by Julius von Schlosser's magisterial *Die Kunst- und Wunderkammern der Spätrenaissance* of 1908, which studied the links between collecting and broader intellectual histories of the period bound to its methods of object-based enquiry.[170]

Much of the early modern collection's theatrical wonder was seen to reside in the play of scale. From Kircher's '*theatrum catoptricum*' to entire princely collections as with Quiccheberg, this comprised both magnified and miniature objects within them; indeed, Quiccheberg privileged models and 'tiny' objects within Duke Albrecht's collections as the greatest source of marvelling ingenuity. Like a theatre set able to represent 'all the world' as 'a stage', the *Wunderkammer* itself was held to encapsulate all the world in a small chamber. As the English statesman and natural philosopher Francis Bacon purportedly wrote in a discussion of knowledge theatres in 1594, the ideal prince should keep a museum 'to have in small compass a model of universal nature', thus including a library, garden, menagerie, as well as a 'goodly huge cabinet, wherein whatsoever the hand of man by exquisite art or engine has made rare in stuff form or motion . . . whatsoever Nature hath wrought in things' and 'furnished with . . . instruments . . . as may be a palace fit for a philosopher's stone'.[171] What is of interest here, in addition to the often-noted juxtaposition of natural and artificed wonders, is the range of scale for the display of collections and collectibles, from monumental to life-sized chambers to tabletop cabinets such as the *theatrum catoptricum*, or even miniatures. In this connection lies a shared history of visual magnification and optically constructed shifts of scale intrinsic to the optical view through the telescope and microscope, as also those of a perspectival picture-making. The argument therefore concerns a shared preoccupation with the optics of scaled reflection, for perspectival enlargement or reduction.[172] Here the mirror played a critical role. Whether for the purposes of housing miniature collectibles, a scenographic stage set, or an anamorphic-perspectival painting, the optically adjusted mirror was a ready means of proportional scaling. As such it was instrumental to all forms and sizes of perspectival display.

Similar to Kircher's *theatrum catoptricum*, many early modern *Kunstschrank*, or display cabinets, were designed with miniature catoptric theatres built into the cabinetry and further lit by surrounding mirrors as a centrepiece for display. In addition to their illumination of any object placed within, they offered a comparative juxtaposition of viewing points, simultaneously front, back, and sides. Further, they were constructed as miniature examples of stage sets of the optical sciences of light and perspective also used in theatre. A fine Dutch curiosity cabinet made in Amsterdam in precisely the years of the formation of Kircher's Collegio Romano museum comprises a central mirror display or catoptric theatre within a miniature architectural surround of a type that came to exemplify the curiosity-collector's '*theatrum catoptricum*'. Made of oak veneered with a range of precious tropical woods, including ebony, snake wood, rosewood, kingwood, and cedar, it is further inlaid with mother-of-pearl, ivory, and horn stained to an aquamarine green (Fig. 121).[173] It is thus a Baconian world-in-a-box by the very nature of its luxury materials. An array of small drawers with richly decorated fronts surround the central mirror-display unit, which is hidden behind two sets of hinged cupboard doors. Any viewing of the cabinet was thus a sequential one, which involved the opening of its panelled doors to reveal the mirrored treasure at the centre. Within, the catoptric theatre, known as the 'perspective' of the piece, is laid out like a Renaissance stage set in miniature. Receding colonnades of ivory columns line each side, with a black-and-white checkerboard floor of ivory and ebony inlay of the type favoured by perspectival treatises. The back wall is framed by two further ivory columns and a tripartite arch in ebony inset with small mirrors designed for magnification and multiplication, just like Kircher's '*theatrum catoptricum*' display table, as also that of Hesselin.[174]

Among the most coveted of such cabinets were those orchestrated by the Augsburg ambassador, dealer, and collector Philipp Hainhofer, who used them as princely gifts in the conduct of diplomacy, with superlative examples inlaid with precious stones and encrusted with jewels.[175] The magnificent cabinet now at Uppsala University, gifted to King Gustav Adolf II of Sweden in 1632 by Hainhofer on behalf of the city fathers of Augsburg, exemplifies their exceptional luxury. An encyclopaedic or universal museum in miniature, it was designed in exotic woods and precious stones to house over 1,000 objects from every domain of knowledge.[176] Composed of fold-up or retractable writing and display desks, a multitude of small box drawers, glass display cases, and other types of cabinets-within-a-cabinet, it housed mirrors and optical devices of every kind, including an anamorphic

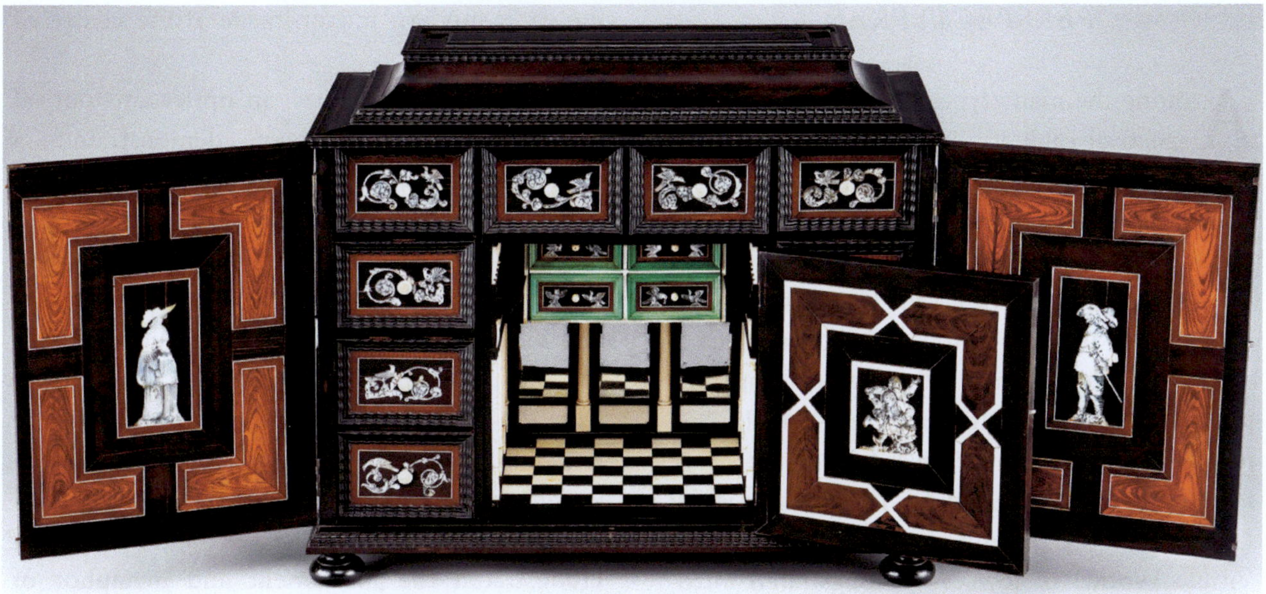

Fig. 121 Herman Doomer, attrib., collector's cabinet with catoptric theatre, Amsterdam c. 1640–50, oak veneered with ebony, snakewood, rosewood, kingwood, and cedar, inlaid with mother-of-pearl, ivory, green-stained bone, and mirrors, Metropolitan Museum of Art.
Photo: Metropolitan Museum of Art

engraving on copper of a cavalier whose image is corrected in a cylindrical mirror, and a pair of fragmenting metamorphic eyeglasses. Small silvered mirrors and telescopic viewing instruments were also included, to enhance the collection's modes of observation and display.

Here it is useful to recall that treatises on perspective often included instructions for the design of wooden stage sets for all manner of theatrical occasion and of all sizes and dimensions, from life-sized to miniature, orchestrated according to Alberti's one-point perspective system. As many scholars of Renaissance perspective have pointed out, the art of the stage set was itself a critical arena for the development of perspectival theory, for the theatrical stage represented an architecture 'in reduction' or, conversely, a perspective box writ large.[177] The defining example of the genre, an illustrated treatise on perspective of 1545 by the sixteenth-century architect-painter Sebastiano Serlio, concluded with a series of theatrical stage sets of architectural design built for the purposes of occasional performances, also used as models for a range of tabletop decorative arts, including the cabinet-sized catoptric 'stage set' cabinets for the display of collectibles.[178] Hence perspectival theatre sets, themselves the products of fine carpentry and decorative arts, suffused the model miniature architectural theatres of the *Wunderkammer* museum and its cabinets, notably the *Kunst-* and *Wunderschranke*, as also the perspectival marquetry of the Renaissance studiolo, for encyclopaedic displays of knowledge in object form.[179] Thus the realms of perspectival theatre sets, architecture, and cabinetry were proximate, and deployed in all sizes for the purposes of early modern museum and cabinet display. In this regard the metaphor of theatre was, in *nuce*, that of a perspectival scenography, to be deployed across a wide range of cultural artefacts as well as arts of occasion, from anatomy to collecting to performance. For the Renaissance theatre set, like the *Wunderkammer*, was conceived as a dazzling mirror metaphor of the world.

PERSPECTYFKAS

Among the many types of early modern perspectival cabinetry in the mid-seventeenth-century Netherlands was the *perspectyfkas*, of which Samuel van Hoogstraten was the acclaimed master. As a man of letters as well as painter of perspectives, van Hoogstraten was both a poet and a theorist of his art, with interests in the optics and catoptrics of painting's perspectival means. In his great treatise on painting as illusion, the *Inleyding tot de hooge schoole der schilderkonst anders de zichbaere werelt* (Introduction to the Academy of Painting or the Visible World) of 1678, van Hoogstraten introduced his discussion on the theory of practice with a fully specular definition of painting as a marvellous fiction: 'For a perfect painting is like a mirror of nature; it makes things that are not there appear to exist and deceive.'[180] As his title proclaimed, the specular definition of painting was intended as the reflection of the visible world.

Written from within the canons of Dutch art as inaugurated by the mirroring mimesis of Jan van Eyck's Ghent Altarpiece, van Hoogstraten's treatise was certainly part of a larger defence of Dutch painting as *fijnschilder* in its illusionistic art of finely detailed painting, following the example of Carel van Mander's *Het Schilder-Boeck* of 1604. More broadly, van Hoogstraten's text was also a defence of painting as the mirror-image of the 'visible world'. As such it was a celebration of Hoogstraten's own art of *trompe-l'oeil*, founded in the notion of painting as a perfectly specular counterfeit, fully intended to deceive the eye. For van Hoogstraten, painting was an ingenious optical deceit, just like a mirror – *spiegeling* – 'in what diminishes or magnifies / darkens and lightens, comes forth or recedes / Justly then, she [painting] governs shadows and lights'.[181] In many respects, van Hoogstraten's treatise, like his painting, offers a concerted theorisation of the early modern mirror-image at the centre of this book.

In a dedicated chapter on optics and optical devices, van Hoogstraten demonstrated a developed theoretical interest in the use of mirrors and lenses in artistic practice. In this regard his work was close to Niceron in its theoretical conception of the place of optics and optical devices in the artist's studio, as also the play of scale it enabled. Such instruments were the means of rendering a perfectly specular imitation of all 'the visible world' or *zichbaere werelt*, as he titled art's purpose. Lens- and mirror-based optical devices were to van Hoogstraten the instrument and metaphor of both vision and art. He advocated their use as a training method for apprentice painters and as a practical means of transposing the perception of three dimensions into the flat plane of painting. This advice came along with a general consideration of mirrors, lenses, and magnifiers as the optical instruments of artistic translation more broadly, which may be understood to represent the generic category of the painter's aid.[182] From his discussion of mirrors and optics there follows a passage on the '*perspectyfkas*', as a genre of painted illusionistic cabinetry. As Celeste Brusati has argued, the *perspectyfkas* was a demonstration of van Hoogstraten's optical theories in practice.[183]

The *perspectyfkas* was a tabletop, cabinet-sized optical toy composed of a number of anamorphically painted panels inserted into a wooden box. In some respects similar to Scrots' box-panel portrait of Edward VI discussed above, yet the *perspectyfkas* was generally closed on all sides so that the painted interior panels could only be viewed through a peephole or viewing device at the point of perspectival resolution (while Scrots' portrait commanded two viewing positions, anamorphically from the front and in resolution from the side). Van Hoogstraten's own perspective cabinets are acknowledged as the most

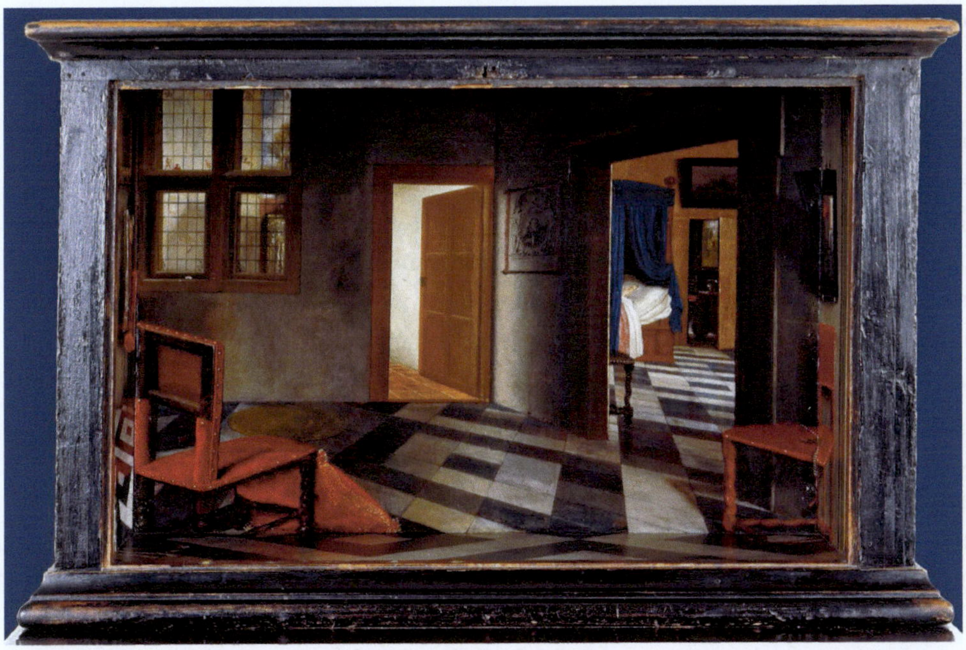

Fig. 122 Samuel van Hoogstraten, painted perspective box of a Dutch domestic interior, c. 1655–60, oil on wood, signed, 58 × 88 × 60.5 cm, National Gallery, London. Photo: Wikimedia

accomplished of the genre, led by the superlative example now in the National Gallery in London (Fig. 122).[184] Unusually, this cabinet appears to have been made with sighting holes on either side, as well as an open front, so offering three viewpoints onto its interior. Set on a pedestal of carved wood, it is of greater proportions than the other remaining examples, suggesting it was intended as a display centrepiece. Interpretations of its possible signification have always taken note of the theme of love that pervades its painted scenes. In the manner of 'veiled meanings' this has been read variously, and most recently as that of van Hoogstraten's own marriage of 1656, in which the cabinet is interpreted as a wedding gift to his bride as the emblem of his love and his art.[185] The painted decoration of the wood exterior comprises a succession of linked scenes of Cupid assisting the artist at work on the side panels, for the sake of love, fame, and wealth, respectively. The top of the box figures an anamorphic image, surely Venus and her infant son Cupid, seemingly in a birthing bed. As Jun Nakamara has recently argued, it is likely this was intended to be seen through a peephole, specular, or lenticular viewing device, like the Scrots portrait of Edward, as a visual correction of the anamorphosis.[186] Within the *perspectyfkas*, from viewing holes on either side of the cabinet, the image of a Dutch burgher home in miniature extends to either side through an enfilade of rooms adjoining a central front hall or *voorhuis*, paved in its typically perspectival black-and-white tiles. Paintings ornament the walls and door frames, to forge a cascading series of pictures-within-pictures, composed of the views through framed doorways and surrounding framed works of art. Stained-glass windows display a coat of arms, identified as those of van Hoogstraten's bride, Sara Balen, while a painted portrait bears the van Hoogstraten crest. In the front hall, a further framed mirror hangs above a chair, attached to the wall by brass fittings and a black ribbon. Its reflection casts back the tiled floor and the red chair, as well as a window or doorway beyond. On the chair is a small collection of toiletry objects comprising a comb and a string of pearls that, taken with the mirror above, surely suggest a nuptial toilet of Venus for the young 'bride' as well as the gentle (and entirely conventional) reminder of *vanitas*. The poised ambiguity of the depicted objects throughout the painting, as Herman Colenbrander has argued, suggests a playful picture-puzzle from van Hoogstraten to his bride like that of Samson's marriage riddle: 'out of the strong, something sweet' (Judges 14:14).[187] The ceremonial broom to represent domestic cleanliness, the well-kept house, the Bible, and the woman reading by a window all encode the ideals of the godly Dutch home, while the woman in the marriage bed and the boy at the far window suggest the hope of offspring from their marital relations. Thus the riddle of marriage, like van Hoogstraten's perspective painting, is not difficult to resolve. On the tiled floor of the front hall van Hoogstraten has left a letter of his love and pride in their marital home, addressed to himself as the signature of himself for her: Samuel van Hoogstraten in Dordrecht. The *perspectyfkas* is thus the pictorial embodiment of Hoogstraten's art as of his love.

Within the *perspectyfkas*, light enters through its viewing holes, which would likely have been further amplified by inset mirrors that augmented and directed the light in the manner of model stage-set cabinet scenographies. As van Hoogstraten explicitly acknowledged, the art of perspective was like that of the theatre stage set, whether in a painting or a perspective box. Within the *perspectyfkas*, such inset mirror lights might be adjusted in order to spotlight different areas of the painted scenes they contained. This is evidenced in another example also attributed to van Hoogstraten, now in Detroit, which still houses its original light-reflecting mirrors (Fig. 123).[188] The Detroit cabinet is of modest dimensions compared with the more elaborate London example, its walnut exterior only roughly planed as a simple wooden chest, painted as if with fictive drawers along the front. Within, however, it presents in miniature a magnificent feast set in a monumental banqueting hall ornamented with elaborate sculptural reliefs, monumental columns, and stained-glass windows. The play of scale in the representation of 'entire palaces within a tiny chamber' was the considered source of its specular wonder, as the early modern Dutch art historian Arnold Houbraken remarked in his *Great Theatre of Dutch Painters* in 1719.[189] In the foreground of the scene a table is set with opalescent oysters, flanked by a range of reflective surfaces such as a gold pocket watch, a silver candlestick holder, silver plate, and a crystal goblet festooned with ornamental grapes that reflects a series of window lights in its bowl. A cat playfully presides, gazing directly towards the viewer with lynx-like eyes. These lustrous objects are emblems of the painter's skill in the art of reflection as the means of pictorial illusion. Together they represent luxury and fleeting pleasure, as well as acknowledged symbols of a Christological *vanitas*, or the passing of all worldly things that the inscription above the central doorway proclaims: *Memento mori*. Above the door hangs a silvered glass orb that gleams with further reflections, of window lights and the suggestion of a figure before the painted scene as if in the space of a viewer. Within the hall the central doorway frames a view of a gracious architectural ensemble beyond, while two side doors give on to further apartments. Above each door is a hanging cabinet picture, one of an angel appearing to the shepherds, the other a still-life painting of an open book. On the right, the view through the doorway depicts a standing figure in a chapel-like room of sculptural revetment; while the left reveals a well-appointed domestic interior with a seated figure writing at a table before a hearth with a further picture above it, alongside a mirror and a window. Together the sequence of tiny pictures-within-the-picture is of perspectival views: windows, doorways, inset

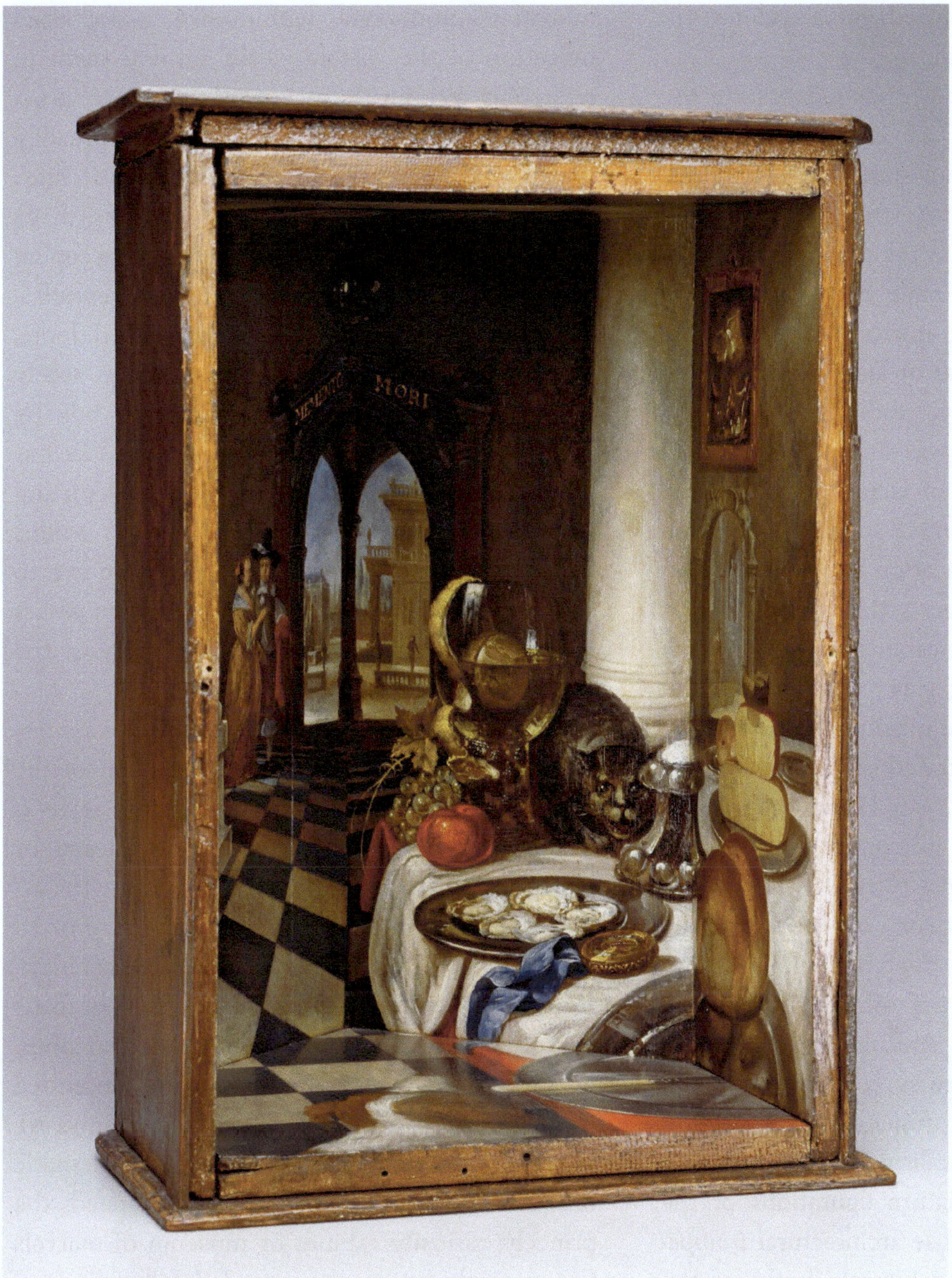

Fig. 123 Samuel van Hoogstraten, painted perspective box of a Dutch domestic interior, 1663, oil on walnut panel with mirrors, 41.9 × 30.2 × 28.3 cm, Detroit Institute of Art. Photo: Detroit Institute of Art

paintings, and mirror reflections. At the foreground of the cabinet, flanking mirrors cast illumination from the peephole across the scene as well as reflecting the painting on either side. Thus, the table of fine oysters and crystal on the one side is matched by the reflection of simple Dutch fare on the other: bread and the rounded form of a Dutch cheese, in a playful declaration of proverbial Netherlandish pictorial wit and parabolic skill. The couple at the back, dressed in Dutch finery, together with the sumptuous feast, suggest the cabinet was also a betrothal or marriage gift, coupled with a visual declaration of 'Dutchness'. This is manifest in an opulence married with modesty, of the *'fijnschilders'*, or finely painted Netherlandish art of miniaturisation, captured in a cabinet of exquisite perspectival skill.

If the cabinet's flanking inset mirrors are the means of illumination, as well as reflection, within the scene, they are surely also an intimation of the painter's instrument in its execution. For the skill of the artist in the placement of each brushstroke must only have been possible by means of a magnifying mirror as he worked. Similarly, the perspectival or anamorphic distortion within the painting, resolved only at the peephole viewing point, was surely also achieved through a configuration of facing mirrors in the construction of the painted scene.[190] The fine detail of the paint application within the miniature scene further suggests that viewers might have looked through the cabinet's peephole with the aid of a magnifying glass. Thus lenses and mirrors pervade both the making and viewing of its perspectivally orchestrated imagery.

In his treatise on art, van Hoogstraten drew together the use of the mirror for painting the diminutive scale of the *perspectyfkas*, on the one hand, with the grandeur of perspectivally rendered painted ceilings of architectural illusionism or *trompe-l'oeil*, on the other. Through the skilled mastery of such specular perspective, a painter of fine knowledge such as himself could paint accurately both in miniaturising reduction and in monumentalising enlargement. He contrasted the miniature figurations of the *perspectyfkas* with grandiose architectural *trompe-l'oeils* such as he painted himself, both for the court in Vienna and in London. On the one hand, he could make 'finger-length figures as if life-sized'; on the other, a full-scale doorway so illusionistic as to invite the viewer's 'entrance'.[191] Within the *perspectyfkas* cabinet the tiny interior painted scenes are, without exception, of grand architectural interiors in miniature: Dutch homes, halls, and churches. As van Hoogstraten further noted in his commentary, the delight of their illusionism lay in the perception of a miniature monument within, like a doll-sized reflection of the 'visible world' around them in reduction. Within the perspective cabinet, however, its painted 'finger-sized' illusion was readily understood to represent the full scale of 'life'. The visual wit attendant to such imagery, in its play of miniature and monumental, of sweeping architectural vistas seen through tiny peepholes, of grand doorways as diminutive cupboard doors, is pictorialized in a drawing of a design surely intended to ornament such a viewing box by Leonaert Bramer, c. 1655. As Walter Liedtke has suggested, such a painted cover depicting gathered spectators peering through an oculus keyhole must have intended to draw the eye to the actual peephole of the viewing box on which it appeared, so redoubling the ingenuity of the *perspectyfkas*, both without and within.[192]

Fabricated as if would-be chests or cabinets made of wood, the exterior construction of the *perspectyfkas* took a number of forms: as rectangular chest-cabinets raised on a pedestal or table legs, in some instances decorated with further painted scenes; as squared cabinetry of all dimensions; or as triangular standing cabinets, sometimes with painted illusionistic drawers half-open as if containing coins, precious stones, or jewels. Their decoration was surely intended to suggest a painted *Wunderkammer* cupboard, which were often configured with emblematic ornament to signify their contents. Indeed, the princely curiosity cabinet or museum of marvels was certainly among the intended collocations of the *perspectyfkas*, as corroborated by what is known of their provenance history. Van Hoogstraten himself was a protégé of the Habsburg Emperor Rudolf II, with an intimate knowledge of the extensive *Kunst- and Wunderkammer* collections at Vienna and Prague, comprising all manner of scientific instruments and devices, including lenses and mirrors alongside arts and armour, minerals and gemstones. In such a setting they might be wittily confounded with an actual cupboard of artefacts, in a double play of their Zeuxian cabinetry.

As at the Rudolfine court in Prague and Vienna, the royal collections of King Frederick III in Copenhagen took particular delight in the visual wit of the Dutch *perspectyfkas*. In the Danish capital, these were housed within a dedicated room of optical, catoptric, and perspectival devices, kin to the Kircherian museum of catoptrics at the Collegio Romano and to the illustrated display of such viewing instruments in the pages of Dubreuil. A succession of early modern inventories of the Danish royal *Kunstkammer* describe its celebrated perspective chamber as a room of intellectual wit predicated on the display of a range of optical devices of advanced geometry, including five Dutch *perspectyfkas*, as tabletop or furniture-sized standing cabinets with painted architectural perspectives within. Here the painted perspective chamber was understood as a miniature of the *Wunderkammer* or room chamber as a whole, able to capture all the principles of optics and geometry within a box.[193] Their exteriors were designed to resemble the furniture cabinets of a *Wunderkammer*, with its range of cupboards and drawers used to house its artefacts and specimens of natural history, while within they displayed the science and art of optical illusion.

Within the Copenhagen perspective chamber (still extant, now a storage room for maps and drawings in the Danish National Archive), the *perspectyfkas* appeared alongside a display of *trompe-l'oeil* paintings by Cornelis Gijsbrechts as painter to the crown, as well as scientific instruments, including the observation chair of the great sixteenth-century Danish royal astronomer Tycho Brahe. As Justina Spencer has argued, the display was surely an acclamation of study based on optical observation, from Tycho's early lenticular telescopic viewing instruments to Gijsbrechts' *trompe l'oeil* and the Dutch *perspectyfkas*. In the case of the *perspectyfkas* depiction of a Dutch domestic interior, Spencer further contends that the box was sent as an empty painted interior, which Gijsbrecht then decorated with objects from the Danish royal collections, including miniature portraits of figures from the king's court entourage.[194] The effect was thus a further 'mirroring' of the palace, pictured within the miniaturising prism of the painted perspective box.

As in the Danish royal perspective chamber, van Hoogstraten's discussion of the *perspectyfkas* in his treatise arises alongside a passage on the artistic use of optical mirrors as the instruments of perspectival science. Thus the optical *perspectifkas* appears as part of a broader discussion on the instruments of enlargement, reduction, and distortion by means of reflective spherical globes, cylinder anamorphoses, and a conjunction of mirrors placed at right angles to one another, which is the basis of a perspective-box construction. In this sense, the *perspectyfkas* represented a painted demonstration of the artist's perspectival knowledge. Van Hoogstraten further promised to disclose his methods for painting the anamorphic panels within a *perspectyfkas* by means of such optical mirrors (a promise he never fulfilled). However, he did allude to the use of diminishing mirrors, for the purposes of miniaturising reduction from life in order to render 'truly natural painting'. This is surely a reference to the use of the concave lens or mirror as the painter's instrument of mimetic reduction, able 'to draw a large plain into a small compass' in della Porta's words, as well as the translation of three dimensions into two for the purposes of painting the *perspectyfkas*.[195] Van Hoogstraten further alluded to the celebrated lost mirror-painting of Giorgione's, discussed in Chapter 3, depicting a nude from behind, then reflected from one side in a mirror, from another in a shield, and in a smooth reflective pool from the front. Van Hoogstraten made direct equivalence with his own art of in-the-round specular imagery in the miniaturised *perspectyfkas*.

In the same passage van Hoogstraten also touched on the perspectival contrivances and artistic means of scaling up, for painting monumental illusionistic, frescoed ceilings. These required the same optical adjustment in reverse, to enable their perspectival illusionism within a greatly increased enlargement. In an earlier passage, he described the reflected images of a room-sized *camera obscura* 'with which one can picture . . . all the things that are outside . . . in miniature'.[196] Throughout the great shifts of scale between the monumental and the miniature entailed in van Hoogstraten's examples, the painter's anticipated use of mirrors and lenses as the means of artistic imitation in enlargement and reduction is manifest:

> I shall pass over the methods by which the reflections of globe, right angle, and cylindrical mirrors can yield corrected form to anamorphic figures; for these are more artifice than necessary science. But nonetheless a master has to understand . . . these amusements so as not to be at a loss when he has to paint an oblique-angled, curved, or otherwise strangely shaped building or vault. Vaults or walls may be as angular as you wish, [but] by using this art one can always break them down in such a way that they appear to have a completely different form . . . even to paint the corners and foreshortened walls as if they were not there.. . . It is possible through this knowledge to make a very small place appear very large, as was shown by Giulio Romano in the Palazzo del Te at Mantua where he painted the Battle between the Gods and the Giants in a vaulted room. Although the room was only fifteen feet, by means of diverging perspectival views he made it appear as an expansive space, as if by magic.[197]

Van Hoogstraten's example by which to encapsulate the painter's specular lesson in optical enlargement is Giulio Romano's frescoed Sala dei Giganti at Palazzo Te near Mantua of the early 1530s (Fig. 124). This palatial villa, built and decorated for the Gonzaga by Giulio and his workshop, comprised a series of rooms of stunningly illusionistic fresco decoration after mythological subjects. As van Hoogstraten describes, the most celebrated was a small chamber displaying mighty Jove's thundering expulsion of giants from Mount Olympus.[198] The subject, of monumental proportions fitting to a gigantomachy, is in witty contrast with the intimate scale of the room. This play of scale produces an intensified effect of perspectival wonder in the plunging thrust of its greatly foreshortened forms, as gigantic bodies and architectures seem to fall from the heavens above. Giulio's sweeping frescoed illusion concludes in the apex of the ceiling vault, a fictive oculus and surely an homage to Mantegna's *Camera degli sposi* for the Gonzaga's Mantuan palace, which playfully redoubles the mimetic counterfeit of Giulio's art.

Whether or not the case, in van Hoogstraten's account, Giulio's perspectival artifice was understood to have been made by means of optical mirrors, as if a room-sized perspective chamber. The use of such mirrors was also the compositional method promulgated by van Hoogstraten's French contemporary, the art theorist and critic Roger de Piles, who advocated for the mirror as a compositional aid in illusionistic ceilings in his treatise for painters of 1668 (as Chapter 1 discussed in relation to Le Brun's ceiling for the Grande Galerie at Versailles). In particular, de Piles argued for the use of convex mirrors as the painter's ready means of forging the illusion that the central figures of a composition appear to project forward towards the viewer from the picture plane, just as Giulio had effected in the tumbling giants at Mantua.[199] What van Hoogstraten singled out in his discussion of the Mantua chamber was the great play of scale, 'to make a small place appear very large'. This skill was also the mirror's, able to reflect in a perfect reduction or enlargement of scale.

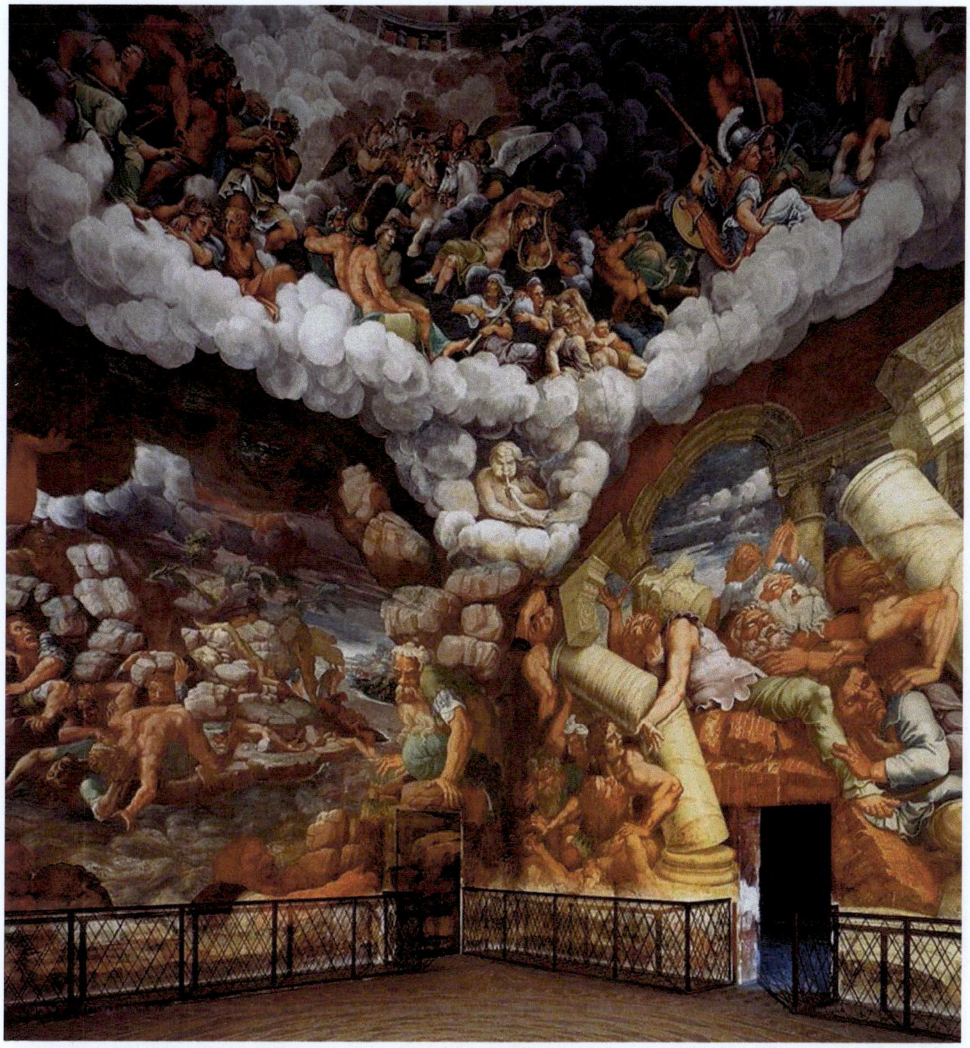

Fig. 124 Giulio Romano, Sala dei Giganti, wall and ceiling fresco, 1532–34, Palazzo del Te, Mantua. Photo: Wikimedia

In della Porta's further elaboration: '[B]y opposition to a concave lenticular, those things that are in a great plain are contracted into a small compass by it; so that a painter that beholds it, may with little labour and skill, draw them all proportionable and exactly' – that is to say, employ the concave mirror for scaled enlargements, the convex for diminutions.[200] Like della Porta and de Piles, van Hoogstraten also stressed the optical capacities of mirrors to aid the painter in feigning the pictorial dissolution of the right angles of the walls into a seeming circle through specular adjustments of perspective. In van Hoogstraten's case, the comparison rested on analogy with the painted optical chambers of his own pictorial practice, the miniaturising Dutch *perspectyfkas* and monumental architectural *trompe-l'oeil*. In van Hoogstraten's terms, if the early modern *camera obscura* might be both room-sized and box-sized, a *camera* or a cabinet, so too the painted perspective chamber could range from a frescoed palace hall to a room-in-a-box – *perspectyfkas*. Whether an entire room or a tabletop viewing device, in van Hoogstraten's understanding these were all equivalent painted optical *Wunderkammern* of a specular art.

Giulio Romano's pictorial subject of Ovid's fallen giants would, like Mantegna's *oculus*, become a *topos* of Italian illusionistic ceiling painting, as a visual demonstration of

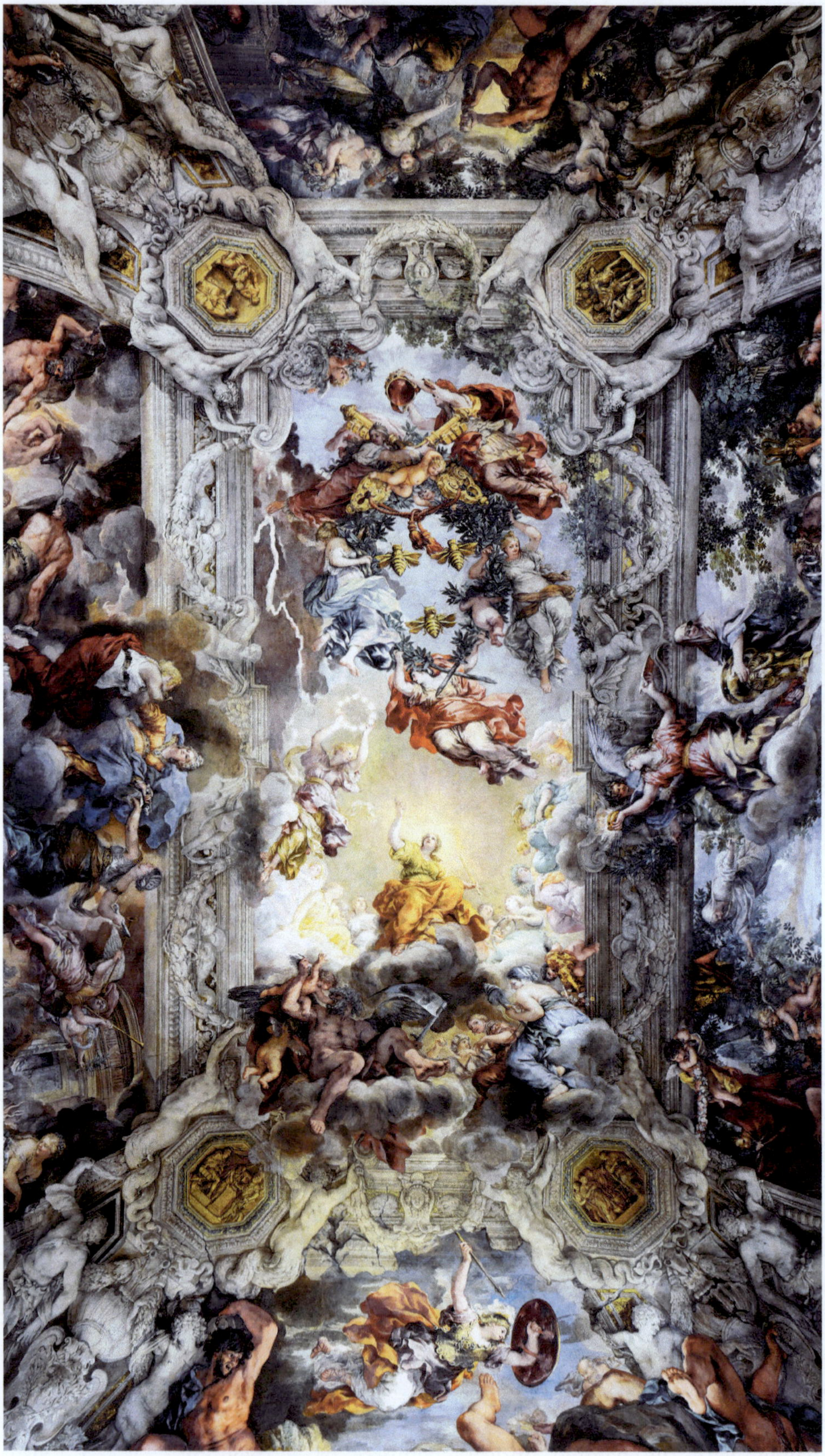

Fig. 125 Pietro da Cortona, *Allegory of Divine Providence*, 1633–39, ceiling fresco, Barberini Palace Rome. Photo: Wikimedia

perspectival skill with a long issue into the seventeenth century, as has long been acknowledged. The most celebrated example is undoubtedly Pietro da Cortona's great ceiling fresco of Divine Providence for the monumental audience chamber of the Barberini Palace in Rome of the 1630s, which represents the tumbling fall of their gigantic bodies as part of a magnificent illusionistic panoply of princely splendour.[201] At the centre of Cortona's vast ceiling is a fictive architectural pergola that, like Mantegna's Mantua *oculus* though now on a monumental scale, seems to open up an expansive view of the sunlit heavens, where painted allegories crown the Barberini coat of arms with the starry diadem of immortality (Fig. 125).

Cortona's Barberini ceiling is, within the canons of the history of art, recognised as a leading exemplar of painted Baroque illusion, in which perspectival optics seemingly dissolve the hall's shallow vault into a glittering splendour of infinite celestial light. Within any art-historical account of illusionistic perspective, these Baroque ceilings are the acme of an art of stunning mimetic illusion. In its empyrean view of the heavens, the Barberini ceiling may also compare to Milton's poetry of the sky's now-boundless infinitude, the 'thousand thousand stars' the poet saw through Galileo's telescope in a metaphor of its 'illimitable perspective'.[202] While the years in which Cortona painted his (utterly Catholic) vision of the skies were deeply troubled ones in the history of their scientific observation, marked by the trial and condemnation of Galileo for heresy in 1633, the will to view them is a shared one. Pope Urban VIII Barberini's own position within the polemic of science and faith was irrevocably marked by the shifting eddies and complexities of the debate over heliocentrism; if he would be the pope to authorise Galileo's condemnation, yet he was also a leading patron of the scientific 'revolution' launched by the view through the Galilean telescope.[203] As the artist and the scientist looked through the specular lenses of their early modern viewing instruments, or 'chambers of vision', Cortona and Galileo both understood what they saw through a shared training as draughtsmen in the observation of light and shadow as the visual sign of perspectival volume. In van Hoogstraten's words, the perspectival 'chamber' and the perspective box, the optical mirror and its illusionistic effects, were linked manifestations of early modern specular vision, across art and science alike.

NOTES

1 Galilei, 1610; Galilei & Helden, 1989; Drake, 1983, which also includes a translation of Galileo's *Sidereus nuncius*. See further Reeves, 2008; Strano, 2008; Gingerich & van Helden, 2003; Rosen, 1950.

2 Edgerton, 1975 and 2009. See further Lipking, 2014; Reeves, 1997; Edgerton, 1984; Bredekamp, 2007; Bredekamp, 2011–14; the corrective review by Wilding, 2014. See also DaCosta Kaufmann, 1975; Warwick, 2014 on light and shadow in the perception of relief.

3 Reeves, 1997; Chappell, 1975.

4 See the lavish reproductions of these drawings in Bredekamp, 2007, and his attendant descriptions of these works; and Galluzzi, 2009; Bredekamp, 2000.

5 The engravings of Galileo's drawings were executed by Mathias Greuter; see further Bredekamp, 2007; and Noyes, 2022, 25–55, on the illustrations for Galileo's 1613 *Macchie solari*.

6 Willach, 2008; Helden, 2010; Ilardi, 2007; Reeves, 1997. On the interface with instruments for technical and scientific drawing: Bredekamp et al., 2015; Payne, 2015; Taws & Warwick, 2016.

7 Willach, 2008; Reeves, 2008. The history of Renaissance glass-making is discussed in Chapter 1.

8 Smith, 2017, lxxvii.

9 Biagioli, 1993.

10 Strano, 2008, 45, on Galileo's presentation telescope for Cosimo II de Medici; Biagioli, 2006.

11 As pictorialized on the cover of Giambattista della Porta's *Magia naturalis*, 1589, with lynx eyes, and of which della Porta was a founding member, Freedberg, 2002.

12 Bredekamp 2001. See further Vasconi, 2015; Lattis, 1994, as Clavius was subsequently persuaded of Galileo's lunar observations, though he remained highly cautious about their further implications on the issue of heliocentrism. On early modern philosophy of doubt of visuality, Clark, 2007.

13 Daston, 2015.

14 Alpers, 1983a.

15 Bredekamp, particularly his study of technical imagery (Bredekamp et al., 2015); and Bredekamp, 2018; Dupré, especially 2003, 2005a, in addition to Dupré & Lüthy, 2011; Lefèvre, 2003 and 2007; Noyes, 2022; Daston & Lunbeck, 2011; Daston & Galison, 2010; Daston & Park, 1998; Lüthy et al., 2018. See also the collections of essays brought together by Faye & Jardine, 2013; Payne, 2015; Henderson et al., 2015.

16 Smith, 2009; Wilson, 1995. From an extensive literature on the so-called scientific revolution and its critique: Gal & Chen-Morris, 2013; Shapin & Schaffer, 2011; Shapin, 1996; Cohen, 1994; Gooding et al., 1989; and further work by Lorraine Daston, Sven Dupré, James Elkins, Paula Findlen, Peter Galison, Michael Hunter, Katherine Park, among others. Yates, 1972, and Kuhn, 1962, remain classic texts. See also the leading literature on historical theories of vision by Bryson, 1983; Clark, 2007; Crary, 1990; and Jay, 1993, among others.

17 Della Porta's *Magia naturalis*, 1558, written at the age of fifteen, comprised four books, in which optics are discussed in book 4, ch. 2; while della Porta's 1589 edition comprises twenty books, in which the section on optics appears in book 17. The publication history of the *Magia naturalis* is a complex one, appearing in multiple editions and translations across the early modern period, with some variation between editions and translations, out of which I have cited from the seventeenth-century English translation, Porta, 1658. See further Verardi, 2018; Borrelli et al., 2017; Balbiani, 2001; Muraro Vaiani, 1978; and the extensive work of Vasco Ronchi, notably Ronchi & Naldini, 1962.

Throughout the following notes referencing early modern texts on astronomy, dioptrics, and catoptrics, the reader is reminded that their publication histories are complex, often comprising multiple editions and translations with varying degrees of variation, including the titles. Ensuing editions might also comprise expansions of illustration programmes in various formats. These texts often also have parallel histories as manuscripts, with complex histories of various anthological arrangements of their own. There is also often substantial repetition or citation from author to author in the early modern circulation of emerging scientific knowledge, such that the history of these texts is densely interwoven, characterized by a high degree of intertextuality among authors, the degree of unacknowledged citation from another author at times problematizing any discrete consideration of them as independent texts. Conversely, within the same author there may be significant variation across different editions, thus raising the question as to when they should be considered as different texts rather than expanded re-editions or translations. See further the discussion of early modern publishing concerning expanded re-editions by Chartier, 1994, among others. I have cited from first editions or early English translations as far as possible.

18 Tadié, 2014; Rossi, 2009; Yates, 2001; French, 1972; Tait, 1967.

19 Della Porta (1593) in Smith, 2017.

20 Newman, 2018; Cohen & Smith, 2016.

21 On the history of lenses and magnifiers, Dupré, 2014; Reeves, 2008, Willach, 2008. See further Payne, 2015; and Ilardi, 2007.

22 Cardano, 1550; see Grafton, 2001a.

23 Mirami, 1582. (The author's name is surely a pseudonym.)

24 Kircher, 1646; Kircher, 1635. See Findlen, 2004; Lo Sardo, 2001; Rowland, 2000.

25 In a letter of 1672, as cited by Mannoni et al., 2004, 42, 60.

26 Niceron, 1638, in French; its expanded posthumous edition in Latin, edited by his tutor, Marin Mersenne, Niceron & Mersenne, 1646: and its subsequent Paris 1652 expanded French edition. See further notes below.

27 Tesauro, 1670, 89, and Tesauro, 1654; Drummond of Hawthornden, 1656; Shakespeare, 1623. See Thorne, 2000; and Gilman, 1978, whose 'curious perspective' importantly opened up to further research the vestiges of such scientific enquiry within early modern literature.

28 Dee, 1558; Shumaker, 1978.

29 Discussed extensively in Drake, 1978.

30 The culture of curiosity is Krzysztof Pomian's phrase, 1987, 'La culture de la curiosité', 61–80, drawing on Blumenberg, 1966, on the trial of theoretical curiosity, though the notion of a direct link to modern scientific method has been much critiqued and revised, especially by Daston & Park, 1998. From an extensive literature Kenny, 2004 and 1998, traces shifts in meaning from an early Renaissance term for knowledge acquisition to an increasing connection with knowledge objects; with a focus on collections, see also Findlen, 1996; Bredekamp, 1995; Kenseth, 1991.

31 Erwin Panofsky published the letter in Italian and English translation in Panofsky, 1954, 17–18. See also Warwick, 2014; Panofsky, 1956.

32 On relations between art and science pertaining to Galileo and his friendship with Cigoli, see Chappell, 2009; Bredekamp, 2007, especially 283–93; Reeves, 1997; and Edgerton, 1984. For a more general discussion of relations between art and astronomy, see DaCosta Kaufmann's 1975 discussion of shadow projection. On Panofsky and Galileo's letter on the *paragone*, see Tongiorgi Tomasi, 2007. On the early modern sundial, Feist, 2016.

33 Panofsky, 1954, 17–18.

34 Panofsky, 1954.

35 Panofsky, 1954, 13.

36 Donne, 1611, 2–3. See Nicolson, 1948, on a new sense of space that pervades seventeenth-century English literature after the publication of Galileo, 1610.

37 Kepler, 1634, although written in 1608. The Jesuit scientist Kircher would also take up the allegory of space travel in Kircher, 1656. As also Milton's 1674 space travel in *Paradise Lost*, these texts may be indebted to

Lucian's *True Histories*, in which the ancient author 'travels' to the moon from where he views Earth by means of a great lunar mirror, on which see Ní Mheallaigh, 2020.

38 Milton, 1674, books 7:377–78; I.284–91 in twelve books and the earliest edition in ten books, Milton, 1667; Cowan, 2018; Lipking, 2014, and further bibliography.

39 Hans Lippershey, letter of patent application to the States General, 2 October 1608, Minute Book of the States General of the Netherlands, The Hague, ms. Staten-Generaal, 33, f. 169r, reproduced in Strano, 2008, 130.

40 Reeves, 2008; Strano, 2008; Willach, 2008, 90–91.

41 Gingerich & Van Helden, 2003; Rosen, 1947.

42 Willach, 2008; Ilardi, 2007.

43 Willach, 2008; Reeves, 2008; Ilardi, 2007.

44 See further the discussion in Chapter 1.

45 Willach, 2008; Strano, 2008. See also the many articles by Silvio Bedini, notably, Bedini, 1966.

46 Cavalieri, 1632, ch. 32, 125–97, figs. xxi and xxii.

47 Gregory, 1663.

48 Cassegrain, 1672.

49 https://pictures.royalsociety.org/image-rs-15841; Del Santo & Strano, 2008.

50 On the shared yet differing histories of early telescopes and microscopes as instruments of magnification: Payne, 2015; Daston & Lunbeck, 2011; Helden, 2010; Willach, 2008; Lüthy, 1996; Wilson, 1995.

51 Carpenter & Dallinger, 1901, 124–25, publishing a letter from Faber to Cesi on the name, 13 April 1625. On the early modern history of the microscope: Helden, 2010; Schickore, 2007; Bovi & Capparoni, 2002; Fournier, 1996; Ruestow, 1996; Wilson, 1995.

52 Galilei, 1613; see further Reeves & van Helden, 2010, 31, 40, 47.

53 Cardano, 1550, book IV, 107.

54 Barbaro, 1568, part 9, ch. 7 (193); Benedetti, 2019, 94, 198–203, 335.

55 Camerota, 2005; Dupré, 2005a. See the further discussion of artists' aids in drawing in Chapter 3.

56 Ruestow, 1996, 7. See further Fournier, 1996. Drebbel came to prominence in the art-historical literature with Alpers, 1983a.

57 Wilson, 1995, 76, citing a letter from Nicolas Claude Fabri de Peiresc published in Govi, 1889, 577.

58 Scheiner, 1630, 130.

59 Drake, 1978, 289, 286.

60 Borel, 1655, 43; trans. Borel, 1658.

61 Hooke & Wren, 1665, 210; Odierna, 1644. See further Hunter, 2013; Purrington, 2009; Neri, 2008; Hunter & Schaffer, 1989.

62 Hooke & Wren, 1665, preface.

63 Hooke & Wren, 1665, preface; as per Catherine Wilson's title, 1995.

64 On della Porta's *Natural Magic*, Balbiani, 2001; on his dramatics, Clubb, 1964; and further, Kodera, 2014; Borrelli et al., 2017; and Smith, 2017, on della Porta's 1593 *De refractione*. See also the related Bell, 2018, on the 'Apparenze diverse del specchio concavo' ms. attributed to Matteo Zaccolini.

65 Schott, 1657–59, I, *Optica*, 534–35, of which he published an abridged version of all four volumes in Schott, 1659.

66 Descartes, *Dioptrique*, published as a tripartite series on light, refraction, and dioptrics, in Descartes, 1637b, Discourse 19. See further Burnett, 2003; Gaukroger, 1995.

67 Bovi & Capparoni, 2002.

68 Fransen, 2023; Ruestow, 1996; Ford, 1985. See further Fournier, 1996; and Wilson, 1995.

69 From an extensive bibliography on this painting, Serra, 1996, and with attention to the depiction of a window reflection in the brass ornament of the Pope's chair back. On the use of optical lenses in then-emerging early modern art-connoisseurial methods, Kobi, 2021.

70 Published by Ronchi & Naldini, 1962. See also Borrelli et al., 2017.

71 Porta, 1658, book 17, 364–65.

72 Porta, 1558, book 4, ch. 2.

73 Frisius, 1545, 31. See Gessner, 2019.

74 Porta, 1658, book 17, 365.

75 Porta, 1658, book 17, 365.

76 Scheiner, 1619, frontispiece detail, among a series of inset images of light reflection.

77 Della Porta, 1589, book 17, ch. 4, translation from the 1658 English edition, 369.

78 Dupré, 2008b.

79 Van Hoogstraten, 1678, 263; Brusati & Jacobs, 2021, 294–95.

80 Mannoni 2000, 3–27. See Väliaho, 2022; Lefèvre 2007; Hammond, 1981; Delsaute, 1998.

81 Pearsall Smith, 1907, 2, 206, cited by Alpers, 1983a, 51.

82 Schwendter, 1636. See further Stafford & Terpak, 2001; and Warwick, forthcoming 2023.

83 Kircher, 1646, II:X:II, 807 facing. See further Lo Sardo, 2001; and in the same volume, Camerota, 2001; and Gorman & Wilding, 2001. See also Vermeir, 2007.

84 Zahn, 1685–86.

85 Niceron in Mersenne, 1652, 21–22, as noted by Mannoni, 2000, 14 and note 19, with further discussion of the book-shaped *camera obscura* c. 1700; on which see further Stafford & Terpak, 2001, on remaining eighteenth-century book-box *camera obscura*, 307–14, which would seem to reproduce the long-standing analogy between the window and the book as equivalent knowledge forms.

86 Sturm, 1676, I:161–62. See further Mannoni, 2000, especially 17, note 23; and Stafford & Terpak, 2001.

87 Kepler, 1604, 56; trans. in Kepler & Donahue, 2000; Dupré, 2008a; Alpers, 1983a, 51; Smith, 1907, 2, 206; Chen-Morris, 2016. Wotton's letter is published in Smith, 1907, II:206.

88 Barbaro, 1568, 192–93. See further Ronchi, 1970, 79, note 6; Lemerie et al., 2017. See also the discussion of draughtsman's aids in Chapter 3.

89 Cigoli, ms., Uffizi, 6v, c. 1613 (Cigoli, 1992); Camerota, 1987; and subsequently Camerota, 2010.

90 Kircher, 1646, 811–12; Mannoni, 2000, 14, note 22.

91 Leonardo, c. 1502, 135v b, with further citations in ms. D, Paris, Institut de France Library; see the translation in Leonardo, 1970, book II, chs. 70 and 71, 141–42.

92 Huygens & Worp, 1911–17, I:94; Alpers, 1983a, 12. See further Wheelock, 1977b.

93 Leurechon, 1642, 98–99.

94 Cited by Dupré, 2005b. See the further discussion in Reeves, 2008.

95 Cited by Reeves & van Halden, 2010, 40.

96 Scheiner, 1612. This was a pamphlet publication of three letters on sunspots from Scheiner to Mark Welser, prior to his definitive work on sunspots in Scheiner, 1630. See further Reeves & van Helden, 2010; Dietz Moss, 1993.

97 Milton, 1674, 1.284–91; 5.260–63.

98 Descartes, 1637b. His analogy of the eye with a machine and the metaphor of the 'mind's eye' for thought have, famously, been the subject of much critique, on which see Massey, 2007, in surveying the critical literature from Lacan to Merleau Ponty and Heidegger. For further discussion of the relationship between the designation of the retinal image as 'painting' and seventeenth-century painting, see Alpers, 1983a; and Kitao, 1980.

99 As Kemp, 2006, 326, notes, the Institut de France Paris Library ms. D contains a short treatise on the eye, seemingly written c. 1508. Leonardo's discussion of the eye as a camera obscura arises c. 1502 in the Codex Atlanticus, Milan, 135v b; also in Leonardo, 1938, I:248; Leonardo, 1970, book II, chs. 70 and 71, 141–42. See further Ackerman, 1978; in response to Kemp, 1977.

100 Della Porta, 1658, book 17, 363–64. See also Smith's 2017 discussion of della Porta's 1593 *De refractione* as a study of vision and the fall of light on the eye by analogy with the passage of light rays through glass ampoules of water.

101 Kepler, 1604; Alpers, 1983a, 40.

102 Mersenne, 1652, especially book II, 112.

103 Cherubin, 1671, especially 16.

104 Schott, 1657–59, I, *Optica*, 292, and illustrated plates. On della Porta's *De refractione*, 1593, which takes up similar ideas to Leonardo's experiments with light refraction through liquids in glass ampoules, Smith, 2017.

105 Cherubin, 1671, especially plate 35.

106 The classic bibliography on 'mechanical philosophy', as in the mechanical or clockwork universe, comprises its mathematisation within late medieval and early modern philosophies of science: Dijksterhuis, 1950; Koyré, 1957; in relation to the early modern industrialisation of artisanal practices, see further Taws & Warwick, 2016. The question of Cartesian and instrumental visuality has received considered treatment by critics such as Jay, 1993; and Crary, 1990, among others. In relation to seventeenth-century painting, see further Wolf, 2001; and the broader discussion in Foster, 1988.

107 Gasché, 1986, in particular, linked the philosophical trope of reflection as a mode of thought to Descartes.

108 Stafford & Terpak, 2001, 297; Väliaho, 2022; Mannoni, 2000; Wagenaar, 1980; Wheelock, 1977b; Huygens, 1950, XXII, 197. Huygens' drawing is preserved at the University of Leiden, ms. Hug 10 fol. 76v.

109 Fubini & Menci Gallorini, 1972, 73. See further Grafton, 2001b, 90.

110 Puttenham, 1968, 128.

111 Tesauro, 1670, 301; see further Alberti & Bodart, 2018; Bowen, 2004; Findlen, 1990; Barolsky, 1978; Gilman, 1978.

112 Zirpolo, 2016; Massey, 2007; Leeman, 1976; *Anamorfosen*, 1975; and the classic study by Baltrušaitis, published in various editions with modifications to the title from 1955 to 1984 and in translation (Baltrušaitis, 1976). See also his related Baltrušaitis, 1978. See further Pérez-Gómez & Pelletier, 1995.

113 Dubreuil, 1647, 6, 124–25, 143; see further Gilman, 1978, 44–46. This was an immensely popular treatise on perspective with a correspondingly complex history of re-editions.

114 Barozzi da Vignola & Danti, 1583, 95–96. See further Tuttle et al., 2002. On Vignola's architectural writings, Strunck & Scheidel, 2020. On the pleated image, see Shickman, 1977.

115 Barbaro, 1568, 159; Accolti, 1625, 48–49.

116 Vaulezard, 1630.

117 Waterfield et al., 1988, especially 'Transcript of Mr Cartwright's Inventory', 20–27, nos. 36–41.

118 Dubreuil, 1647, 6.

119 Baltrušaitis, 1976, 146–47, within a larger discussion of cylinder anamorphoses, 131–58; Gomez Lopez, 2016; Maaz, 2010; Thuillier et al., 1990, especially 106–7.

120 https://art.rmngp.fr/en/library/artworks/domenico-piola-l-ancien_anamorphose-d-apres-l-erection-de-la-croix-de-rubens_huile-sur-bois. On Piola, see the recent publications by Sanguineti, 2017 and 2019.

121 Knoppers, 2003.

122 Bettini, 1645.

123 Baltrušaitis, 1976, especially 116.

124 De Rosa, 2013; Bessot, 2005, I:91–129.

125 Truci, 1976.

126 Stafford & Terpak, 2001, 185.

127 Niceron, 1638, 119.

128 Niceron's fresco is illustrated in Niceron, 1646, 176–78. John Evelyn described the excellent perspective of the anamorphic frescoes at S. Trinità dei Monti when in Rome in 1645, 22 February, in De Beer, 1955, II, 373. See further De Rosa, 2019.

129 Farroni, 2019; De Rosa, 2019.

130 Maignan, 1648, 438.

131 Zahn, 1685, 162.

132 www.britishmuseum.org/collection/object/C_G3-IP-1, www.nga.gov/collection/art-object-page.43845.html#overview. Schneider, 1990.

133 According to Baltrušaitis, 1976, 1, in Schott, 1657–59, *Magia*, I, *Optica*, ch. III.

134 Dürer, 1977, 7, 13.10.1506.

135 Barbaro, 1556, 58; discussed in Baltrušaitis, 1976, 34. See also Massey, 2007, 49.

136 On Schön's woodcuts, see the Hollstein print catalogues vols. 48 and 50 in Hollstein et al., 2000.

137 Leonardo, *Codex atlanticus*, c. 1510, fol. 35, citation in translation in Baltrušaitis, 1976, 33; see also the related discussion in Leonardo, 1977, I, 149–50. See further the discussion of anamorphic imagery, or 'prospettiva inversa', among Leonardo's followers in Milan, and of two lost anamorphic pictures by Leonardo for François I, Lomazzo, 1584, ch. XIX, 335–36.

138 www.npg.org.uk/collections/search/portrait/mw02032/King-Edward-VI?search=sp&sText=Scrots+Edward&firstRun=true&rNo=0.

Hunt & Sharp, 2015; Strong, 1969, I:88–90; Foister et al., 1997, 50; Gilman, 1978, 55; Shickman, 1977.

139 Von Wedel, 1895, 235.

140 Hentzner, 1757, 32. Hentzer saw the portrait in the Royal Library, item VI.

141 Barozzi & Danti, 1583, 96.

142 Leibniz, 1710, 147, where he used the analogy of multiple perspectives to exemplify the mathematical point of infinity in a discussion of the godhead. On Leibniz and art, see further Bredekamp, 2020.

143 George Chapman's *All Fools* performed for James I, in 1605. See Chapman, 1605, I.1.47; Shakespeare, 1623: *Antony and Cleopatra*, Act 2, scene 5; *Richard II*, Act 2, scene 2. See further Thorne, 2000; Gilman, 1978, 88–128; Shickman, 1977.

144 From an extensive bibliography: Woollett, 2021; Nelson, 2019; Foister, 2004; North, 2002; Bätschmann & Griener, 1997; Foister et al., 1997.

145 Alberti, 'De componendibus cifris', ms. c. 1466, 1568, trans. 2010. The genre engaged humanists, mathematicians, philologists, and logicians alike, such as della Porta, Kircher and Leibniz, on which see further Sherman, 2014.

146 Dekker & Lippincott, 1999.

147 On Polisy, see Frommel, 1998, 321–23, though the palace was built after Holbein's painting but the estate was already theirs.

148 Apian, 1527.

149 Rasmussen, 1995.

150 See Faust, 2018, on a German painted panel anamorphosis of the same moment, read as dynastic, with particular attention to the viewer's bodily engagement in reading the panel from different viewpoints.

151 Brunn, 1615, unpaginated illustration.

152 Samuel, 1963; Foister et al., 1997, based on cleaning of the painting and computerised testing of critical viewing points and viewing with a glass cylinder.

153 Panofsky, 1954.

154 Erasmus, 1517, 105v.

155 Hamlyn, 1979, for a reading of the skull anamorphosis as *mise-en-abyme*. See the further discussion of the term in the Introduction and Chapter 2.

156 Kircher, 1646; De Sepi & Kircher, 2015, 35–40. Schott, 1657–59 (I, *Optica*), Kircher's student and assistant, also included illustrations apparently pertaining to Kircher's catoptric devices; while his fellow Jesuit Dubreuil, 1647, also illustrates the display of such perspectival objects, on which see further below. On Kircher's museum more broadly, see Godwin, 2015, especially 191–214 on the museum's optical machines; Vermeir, 2007; Findlen, 2004; Lo Sardo, 2001; Rowland, 2000.

157 Kircher, 1646, book 10; Stauffer, 2016; Gorman & Wilding, 2001, 223; Stafford & Terpak, 2001, 256–66, though with some differences of interpretation. Kircher's fellow Jesuit de Sepi's catalogue of the museum, 1678, details the catoptrics room, though it describes this device more in terms of a box of illusionistic views, 36 (De Sepi & Kircher, 2015, 148).

158 Settala, 1664; Aimi et al., 1984, cited in Stafford & Terpak, 2001, 261. Harsdörffer, 1652. See further Gerstl, 2005.

159 Niceron, 1638, 77.

160 Montaigne's *Journal du voyage*, of his travels of 1580–81, was discovered and first published in Paris in 1774. See Montaigne in Frame, ed., 1983, 164.

161 The play of scale in mirror reflections, comprising reduction and enlargement, was much commented on in early modern treatises on catoptrics, along with mirror reversal, as an aspect of specular 'magic'. See, for example, Niceron, 1638.

162 De Beer, 1955, 8 November 1644, II:230.

163 De Sepi & Kircher, 2015, 18–19, 35–40; Lo Sardo, 2001; Findlen, 2004; Gorman & Wilding, 2001, 217, 222. Surprise water effects were also a feature of Renaissance gardens, as at Tivoli, and theatre, as in Bernini's celebrated 'flooding of the Tiber' scenographic effect, on which see Warwick, 2012, 30–31.

164 Leonardo, Codex Atlanticus, Milan, Biblioteca Ambrosiana, 138r. b, and Leonardo, 1938, II:364–65; Leonardo, ms. B f 28, Paris, Library of the Institut de France (Leonardo, 1977, I:132, no. 65, with a reproduction of Leonardo's small diagram of the polygon chamber). It is also discussed by Zwijnenberg, 1999, 183, as the manifestation of Leonardo's 'labyrinthine gaze'. See also the discussion of this passage in Chapter 1.

165 Della Porta, 1589, book 17, 579–81.

166 Della Porta, 1658, book 17, 369.

167 Della Porta, 1589, book 17, 550–55.

168 Furttenbach, 1627, unpaginated; Lazardzig & Rössler, 2016; Gess et al., 2015; Warwick, 2012.

169 Quiccheberg, 1565; Meadow & Robertson, 2014. See further Yates, 1969, concerned with the links between science and performance in the early modern term 'theatre', and closely tied to her earlier Yates, 1966, and based on Camillo, 1550. See further Bolzoni, 1984.

170 Von Schlosser, 1908. From an extensive and exceptional field of scholarship, see, in particular, Impey & MacGregor, 2017; Bredekamp's extensive publications in this area including Bredekamp, 1995; DaCosta Kaufmann's many publications on the subject brought together in 1993; Wheelock, 1998; Findlen's many publications in the field, including Findlen, 1994 and 2013; and the recent Chipps Smith, 2022.

171 Bacon, 1914, 34–35.

172 On the question of scale in terms of wonder, see especially S. Stewart, 1996; Kee & Lugli, 2015.

173 www.metmuseum.org/art/collection/search/238523?searchField=All&sortBy=Relevance&ft=doomer+cabinet&offs. Further examples of cabinets with inner mirror theatres include V&A Antwerp cabinet, Alfred Williams Hearn Gift, 1640–60, of which the first layer of interior decoration of the cabinets has oil scenes of the Prodigal Son parable; Ghent Museum of Fine Arts, inv. 3877, curiosity cabinet, seventeenth century, wood, tortoiseshell, ivory, glass; Musée National de la Renaissance, Château d'Ecouen, inv. 30476, ebony cabinet with interior marquetry and mirror recess; V&A Endymion cabinet, https://collections.vam.ac.uk/item/O34065/the-endymion-cabinet-cabinet-on-stand-unknown/.

174 Fabri, 1991.

175 Wenzel, 2020; Emmendörffer & Trepesch, 2014; Boström, 1975.

176 Boström, 2017; Böttiger, 1909–10. As a further example: www.metmuseum.org/art/collection/search/188830?searchField=All&sortBy=Relevance&ft=hainhofer+cabinet&offset=0&rpp=20&pos=1.

177 Damisch, 1994. See also Hénin, 2003.

178 Serlio, 1545, II, in bilingual French and Italian with woodcut illustrations, of his 1537, *Le regole generali di architettura*, published in successive volumes over Serlio's lifetime. See further Carpo, 2004; Hewitt, 1958. For a complete edition of Serlio's books on architecture: Hart & Hicks, 1996; Hart & Hicks, 2001. For an overview of Serlio, Frommel, 2003. On the subsequent translations of Serlio, Nan Rosenfeld, 2003. On the classical antecedents of scenography, particularly Vitruvius, Sinisgalli, 2012. There is an extensive literature that touches on the diffusion of Serlio's 'scenographic' architecture, particularly through Barbaro, 1568; and Barbaro's patronage of Palladio, particularly of the Teatro Olimpico at Vicenza, with the subsequent formative influence on Inigo Jones, British architectural 'Palladianism', and the Stuart court masque. On the Teatro Olimpico in Vicenza, a wooden theatre made for the Accademia Olimpico of which Palladio and Daniele Barbaro were members, see, most recently, Avagnina, 2011. For a discussion of early modern theatre as an art of occasion, Warwick, 2012.

179 On the intarsia marquetry of Urbino and Gubbio, Cheles 1986; Wood, 2003; Kirkbride, 2008; Trevisan, 2011.

180 'Want een volmackte Schildery is al seen Spiegel van de Natuer, die de dingen, die niet en zign, doet schijnen te zijn, en op een geoorlofde vermakelijke en prijslijke wijze bedriegt.' Van Hoogstraten, 1678, 25; trans. Brusati & Jacobs, 2021, 79. See further Weststeijn, 2013; Blanc, 2008; Weststeijn, 2008; Brusati, 1995.

181 Van Hoogstraten, 1678, 243; trans. Brusati & Jacobs, 2021, 279.

182 Van Hoogstraten, 1678, book 7, ch. 7.

183 Liedtke et al., 2001, 115–29; Liedtke, 2000, ch. 2, 39–79; Brusati, 1995, ch. 5, 169–217; Wheelock 1973; Koslow, 1967. The fashion for the Dutch perspective cabinet was short-lived, and whatever the numbers made at its height, only six are known today. For a view of the technical evidence suggesting other methods of scaling additionally/alternatively in use, see Bomford, 1998; Bomford et al., 1987.

184 www.nationalgallery.org.uk/paintings/samuel-van-hoogstraten-a-peepshow-with-views-of-the-interior-of-a-dutch-house.

185 Colenbrander, 2013, 139–60.

186 Nakamura, 2020.

187 Colenbrander, 2013, 157.

188 www.dia.org/sites/default/files/tms-collections-objects/35.101.A-S1_02.jpg. At present, only one remaining cabinet still has its original lighting with mirrors, on which see further Bomford, 1998, 126.

189 Houbraken, 1718–21, II:156.

190 See the extended discussion with attendant bibliography in Liedtke, 2000, 39–79.

191 Van Hoogstraten, 1678, 264; trans. Brusati & Jacobs, 2021, 304, on the one hand, arguing that, by means of the art of perspective, the skilled painter can fashion perspective boxes that make 'a figure the size of your finger appear to be life-sized' and, on the other, referring to his *trompe-l'oeil* paintings such as that of a threshold, painted for Thomas Povey's London house and now at Dyrham Park.

192 Liedtke et al., 2001, cat. no. 108, 458; Liedtke, 2000, 23.

193 Spencer, 2018, points to the influence of Samuel Marolois' illustrated perspectival treatises on Dutch artists in particular, following Brusati, 1995, 190, with specific reference to van Hoogstraten; and Wheelock, 1973, 66–67.

194 Spencer, 2018; Koester, 1999; Gundestrup, 1991–95.

195 Della Porta, 1589, book 17, ch. 10, 269.

196 Van Hoogstraten, 1678, 262; trans. Brusati & Jacobs, 2021, 294–95.

197 Van Hoogstraten, 1678, 274. The translation draws on those of Brusati & Jacobs, 2021, 303–4; and Wheelock, 1973, 71.

198 Ovid, *Metamorphoses*, I:151–76. On Giulio Romano, see the recent Furlotti et al., 2019 and 2022.

199 Dufresnoy & De Piles, 1668, 286. See the further discussion in Chapter 1.

200 Della Porta, 1589, book 17, ch. 10, 269.

201 Cicconi, 2023; Lo Bianco, 2004, with further bibliography.

202 Milton, 1674, 3:590, 7:383. Milton described his visit to the aged Galileo on his trip to Florence in Milton, 1674. Though some have questioned the veracity of the encounter, the influence of the Galilean vision of the heavens fused with Milton's Puritan humanism is generally acknowledged, as elaborated in a series of publications by Nicolson, 1948. See also Belting, 2011; Field, 1997; Damisch, 1995. Rotman, 1987, takes up further the relation between the history of perspective and the notion of infinity as expressed mathematically, of which see also Leibniz, 1710.

203 On Galileo's trial, see Heilbron, 2010; Finocchiaro, 1989.

Chapter 5

THE MIRRORS OF VENUS

Here lies a she sun, and a he moon here,
She gives the best light to his sphere
Or each is both, and all, and so,
They unto one another nothing owe.
—John Donne, *St Valentine's Day Epithalamion for the Marriage of Elizabeth Stuart and Frederick V Count Palatine*, 1613 (1633)

Beauty's but a vain and doubtful good, a gloss, a glasse, a flower.
—*THE PASSIONATE PILGRIM* XIII (1599)

WHEN THE SEVENTEENTH-CENTURY Roman art critic and theorist Giovanni Pietro Bellori wrote his celebrated *Idea*, or discourse on the immortality of ideal form, he opened his essay with a print of a reclining female nude to represent the figure of art. Classically draped, she is the representation of an idealising art theory coupled with practice to which Bellori's text is wed. Bellori further illustrated his book of artistic biographies with an allegorical print of *imitatio sapiens*, or 'knowing imitation', as a woman who gazes into a mirror (Fig. 126).[1] The emblematic elaboration of these prints intended to signify Bellori's idealising conception of art founded in a selective *imitatio*, according to the celebrated precept of Raphael's *Galatea*, or the composite beauties of the classical Maids of Croton. Bellori furthered his argument through the figure of Helen of Troy as the beauty that 'launched a thousand ships' to open his discussion of artistic

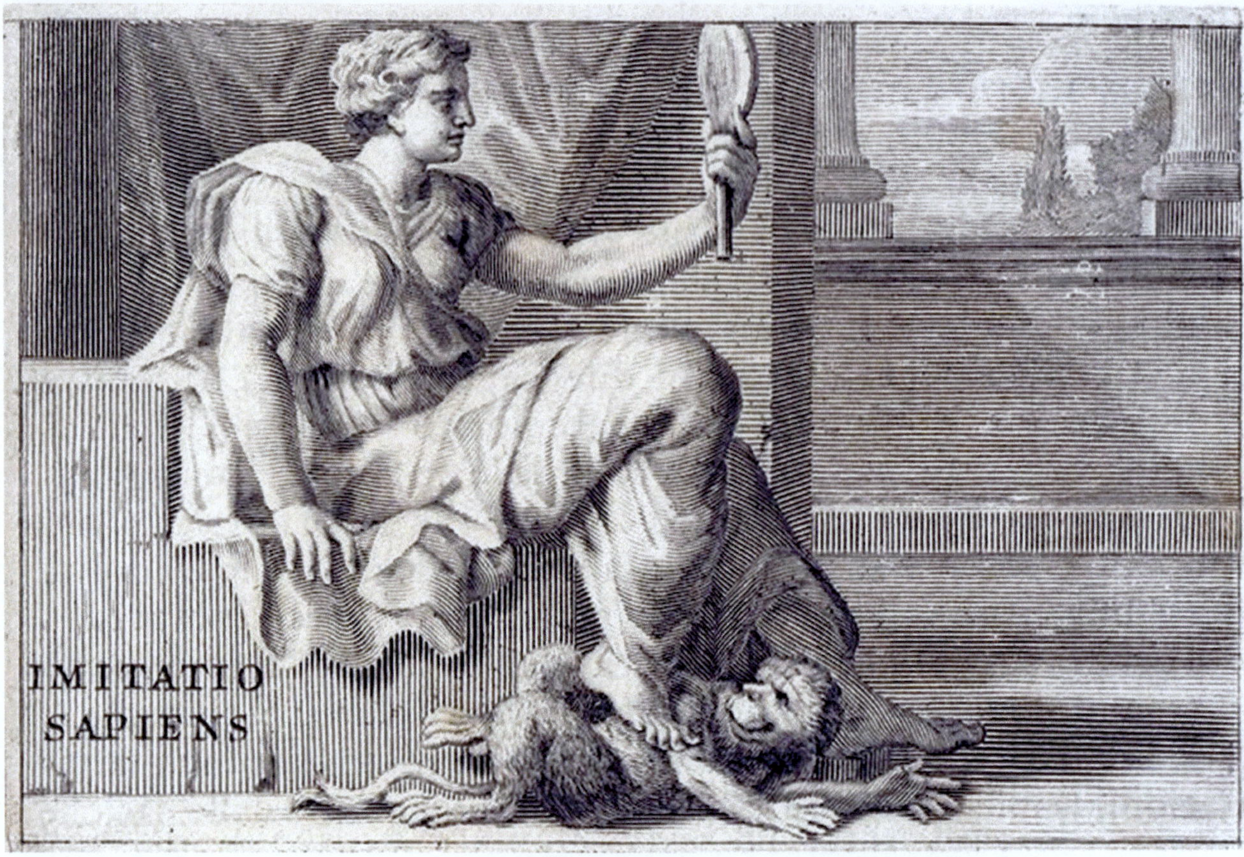

Fig. 126 Charles Errard, *'Imitatio sapiens'*, engraving for G. P. Bellori, *Le vite de' pittori . . .*, Rome, 1672. Photo: Gallica/BNF

idealisation. In legend, Helen was an earthly Venus given to Paris in return for his award of beauty's prized golden apple. Yet in Bellori's reworking of Helen's story he concluded that the power of her beauty so transcended the merely mortal she must instead have been a work of art.[2] It is this conflation of art's beauty with the representation of the female and the mirror, often termed *belle donne* painting, which forms this chapter's subject, through a faceted analysis of its many social forms.

***

Lost already within antiquity, it was Praxiteles' sculpture of Venus for her temple on the island of Cnidos that cast the longest art-historical reflection across the subsequent history of the female nude, through her insistent imitation in both ancient and Renaissance art. In her setting at Cnidos, Praxiteles' originary Venus apparently stood in a sanctuary high on a coastal terrace surrounded by mirroring fountains. Accounts of her cult, celebrated above all in spring, describe ritual bathing in the sea, for archaic myths of origin relate she was born of a divine congress with water. While Pliny described in-the-round views of her monumental marble figure, according to Lucian her earliest architectural surroundings framed two points of encounter, as viewed from the front and from the back.[3] The approach to the Cnidia's shrine, as Lucian described it, was that of the view through a doorway or window, the very analogies Filippo Brunelleschi and Leon Battista Alberti would later adopt in their theorisations of painting as a window view. Her shrine, according to Lucian, framed her figure pictorially, making her into a sculpture-painting. The Cnidia's mode of display and the ancient sources that describe it may be read within a structure of comparison, or *paragone*, between sculpture and painting, as also the window views of her front and back. Such comparisons of the arts suffused Pliny's art-historical descriptions, between sculpture and painting, but also between painting and poetry, as 'sister arts' yet also rivals in the mirroring mimesis of beauty.

Subsequent emulations of the Cnidia, as one of antiquity's most widely imitated sculptures, were often displayed within themes of bathing and reflection. Her figure was frequently set within fountains in reference to her sea-borne genesis, the 'reflection-painting' cast in the waters surrounding her to form a further pictorialisation of her figure. Such reflections could, unlike sculpture, reveal each Venus from only one side at a time, but in supplement could show the surrounding sky, cloud, sea, landscape, fountain, or garden as ornaments to her beauty, just like a painting. In this respect, her display resembled that of Alberti's Narcissus reflected in the pool of Ovidian myth.[4] Moreover, the representation of Venus in both sculpture and painting was common to ancient bath houses, depicting her emergence from the sea like the bathers surrounding her. Among the many Venus typologies of antique statuary were those with a mirror as her attribute, held by the goddess herself or by an attendant cupid, in which to view her form.[5] These mirrors, often of shining precious metals, complemented the range of reflections of her figure in the surface of the pool around her. She might also be appointed with shimmering textiles, sparkling jewels, and the glitter of gold or silver vases as references to her bathing. These lightsome objects of her toilet further elaborated the beauty of Venus as the mirroring ornaments of her femininity.

Bellori's idealised evocation of art's beauty elaborated in his *Idea* undoubtedly paid homage to earlier treatises on the ideals of art, such as that of the Milanese artist-theorist Gian Paolo Lomazzo's *Idea* of 1590, founded in Leonardo's precepts on art; or the 1607 *Idea* of Federico Zuccaro, who at the time was president of Rome's Accademia di San Luca.[6] Lomazzo's ideal turned on the celebrated but lost or fictive painting of mirror-images by Giorgione, already a *topos* of Renaissance art theory in the work of Paolo Pino and Giorgio Vasari as discussed in Chapter 2. While the earlier theoretical elaborations of this lost work had described it as a male figure in armour, Lomazzo instead transformed it into an allegory of the art of painting now configured as a female nude:

> 'Giorgione da Castelfranco [represented] painting as a nude [reflected] in a fountain, with a mirror behind her to show her from the back, and a polished cuirass at her side that reflected her in profile.'[7]

Lomazzo brought together the depiction of the female nude with her reflection into a pictorial allegory of painting itself, as a metaphor of art's ideal.

Throughout these texts, the abiding conceit of Giorgione's theoretical image as the definition of painting was of mimetic specular reflection. Whether of gleaming martial shields and armour, the shimmering pools of Ovidian myth, or the looking-glass of a venereal toilet, each specular surface was accorded a pictorial equivalence with painting itself as the image of reflection. In earlier accounts of its genesis, this lost work by Giorgione was apparently born of a *paragone*, or comparison, of the relative merits of sculpture and painting, ancients and moderns, to which this painter made pictorial response 'to the perpetual confusion of sculptors'.[8] In the words of Pino, the sixteenth-century Venetian painter and critic: 'our art is like the effect of a mirror'.[9] In so saying he bound the definition of painting to the reflected image. Painting could rival and even surpass the sculptures of antiquity in its ability to show the human figure from multiple viewpoints, as well as the ephemeral effects of nature's mirroring reflections. Thus armour, water, and the mirror itself had become a Renaissance paradigm of painting as a mirror-image. It was, however, Lomazzo's critical reworking of this celebrated pictorial trope that drew together the mirror view with the female form as the defining metaphor of High Renaissance painting. The subject of this chapter, *pace* Lomazzo and Bellori, is to explicate how the definition of painting's beauty came to reside in the mirror of Venus, as the metaphor of the painted female form.

THE TOILET OF VENUS

By the time of his writing, Lomazzo's conflation of painted reflection with the beauty of the female figure was long manifest in a wealth of High Renaissance paintings, inaugurated in Venice c. 1500 and swiftly emulated across Europe. The sixteenth-century Venetian representational typology of the 'Venus reflection' was to become the definition of the painter's art, in an artistic equivalence with female beauty that configured High Renaissance painting.[10] Cast as both venereal and conjugal to comprise the flower of maidenhood in courtly love as well as marriage and maternity, such paintings of feminine beauty were understood to emblematise the trope of art above all in the inset mirror reflection of the female form. Sometimes simply termed paintings of *belle donne*, these depictions of Venetian *cinquecento* female beauties in mirror reflection approach the typology of a toilet of Venus, so weaving together the subject of myth with the poetry of love and the social occasion of nuptials. For these paintings were also held to reflect the idiomatic language of the poets in the allegorical description of *amour* and courtship.

Across the painted, sculptural, decorative, literary, and theatrical arts, within prints and illustrated books, the sign of the silvered mirror waxing like the moon in the name of female beauty, as of nuptials and marriage, was one of myriad social reflection. Thus the mirror of Venus was at once the emblem of an idealised womanhood as the matrix of Eros; and an allegory of marriage and motherhood under her venereal protection: both the *Rokeby Venus* and the Arnolfini double portrait. Hence the Venus mirror of female beauty appeared in a full range of Renaissance domestic decorative arts pertaining to rituals of nuptial bathing, dressing, the female toilet, courtship, marriage, and childbirth. It was conventionalised and domesticated within a great swathe of imagery pertaining to women, to mark the rituals of transition from maidenhood into motherhood. From the religious figurations of Marian devotions of the Holy Family to the social rituals of courtship and childbirth, the mirror motif crossed the bounds of family with both romantic and devotional love.

As scholars of the Renaissance have long recognised, interpretation of the *bella donna* subject is defining for any account of Renaissance art's history, in no small measure because of the great profusion of its representation. If the sheer plethora of examples will always defy any attempt at its exhaustive analysis, yet their reach into every cultural domain manifests its paradigmatic position: of love, marriage, and family; the history of the home and its domestic décor; and the complex of cultural relations surrounding adjacencies between beauty, sexuality, and desire, on the one hand, and art, on the other. This comprises the most celebrated works of the art-historical canon, such as Titian's *poesie* paintings, and the costly jewels, dress, furnishings, decorative arts, and exquisite toiletries of royal marriage. But it also encompassed vast swathes of images and artefacts extending to almost every social estate, manifest in an outpouring of illustrated printed books for women on love, family, and conjugal faith; and a plethora of domestic artefacts for and of women concerned with courtship, marriage, and childbirth. Imagery of the female figure with a mirror therefore ranged across the quotidian domestic realm, from wood-carved or painted earthenware toiletry items; patterned crockery, glass, and textile ornament; as well as any number of Marian devotional prints, illustrated books, and decorated ritual objects of every kind. Comprising the rich legacy of newly translated classical myth and verse on the loves of the gods, and the great range of poetic literatures it inspired in chivalric romance as well as Christian devotion, it also drew on ancient ethical and political philosophy and its familial early modern manifestations in the form of books of commonplaces, proverbs, and emblems that counselled women in the good and prudent government of the home as of marriage. As Andrea Beyer has rightly argued, any scholarly analysis of the early modern Venus and her mirror-image as subject matter consequently carries with it the defining weight of a Renaissance periodisation precisely because of the vast range of objects at stake. Over the past fifty years or more, interpretation has broadly ranged from neo-Platonic readings of a Christianised mythology to those of social practice concerning sexuality. Out of this binomial interpretive divide, recent scholarship has argued for the more tempered consideration of the *bella donna* within the domestic decorative arts of marriage.[11] Such a reading accords with the great numbers of images to which it pertains. The polyvalent role of the feminine mirror inset within a Renaissance imagery of *amour* is therefore framed by the study of courtship, women, sexuality, marriage, childbirth, and the home, in themselves extensive fields of scholarly enquiry. Following the rich polyvalence of mirror imagery in its allegorisation of female beauty as a prevailing metaphor for art itself, the figure of the *bella donna* that issued from Venetian painting c. 1500 with immediate efflorescence thereafter was bound to the broad cultural figuration of love in all its manifold forms.

Two closely related paintings from Venice stand at the inception of the genre, a late work by Giovanni Bellini on wood panel, signed and dated, and a somewhat larger canvas by his pupil, the young Titian, that scholars have conventionally assigned to the same year, 1515. Both depict women with a mirror; both arise in the immediate ambit of the celebrated silvered *cristallo* mirrors of Renaissance Venetian facture (detailed in Chapter 1), whose renown surely heightened the poetic analogy of the mirror's pictured beauty.[12] Both deploy the pictorial trope of a doubled mirror reflection, which contemporaries undoubtedly understood as a *paragone* of art within the structure of painting itself; both play with a poetic ambiguity as to genre and so meaning, *ut pictura poesis*.

Bellini painted a young woman at her toilet, holding a small looking-glass through which she views her hair by means of a further mirror on the wall behind her (Fig. 127). Both mirrors are roundels seemingly framed in wood gilt, the larger being the size of the woman's head, to suggest their pictorial equivalence. Such Venetian sixteenth-century mirrors as toiletry sets were made explicitly for the purpose of dressing the hair with jewels and textile ornaments in luxury frames, just as Bellini pictorialised in this work.[13] The view of the back of the woman's head reflected in the mirror on the wall is apparently the view that the subject herself observes in the small looking-glass she holds in front of her. Thus the picture calls into play the motif of the mirror as an instrument of observation, but also as a 'painting within a painting': that is, both a direct reflection on artistic practice and a metaphor of Renaissance painting's specular definition. The force of the picture lies precisely in its doubled structure, signifying both its status as representation and the mirroring instrument of its making. As other scholars have suggested, it is a profound artistic meditation on the sense of sight as an allegory of art and beauty, emblematised in the mirror motif.[14]

Bellini's toilet scene is both one of minor domestic moment, in which a woman arranges

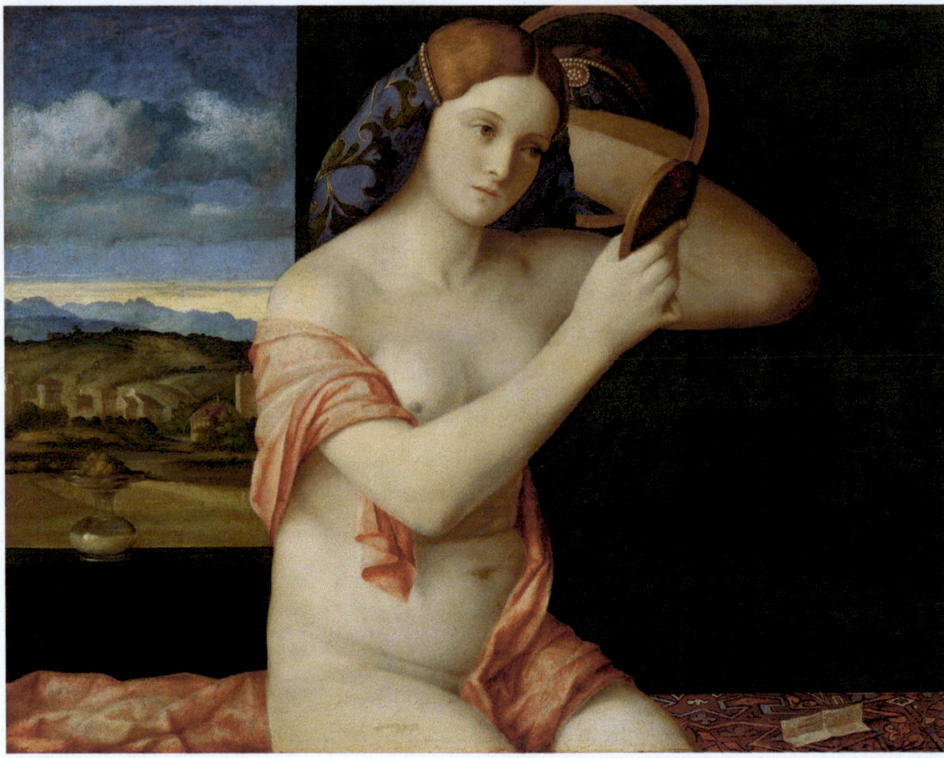

Fig. 127 Giovanni Bellini, *Young Woman at Her Toilet*, 1515, oil on panel, 78.3 × 62.9 cm, Kunshistorisches Museum, Vienna. Photo: Wikimedia

her hairpiece by means of a mirror; and a deeply meditated pictorialisation of painting's theoretical claim as mimesis. Beside the wall mirror a window opens onto a landscape of rolling hills, a further picture-within-a-picture to extend the metaphor of the mirror's mimetic art. On the window sill is a small glass scent bottle of curving form, hinting at the figure of a bathing Venus.[15] From Homeric hymn, the bath of Venus was long associated with rich perfume, ranging from flowers to aromatic oils.[16] In verse too, perfume was an evocation of the beloved, recalling her elusive presence in swathes of sonnets and madrigals arising around Petrarch's *'Quel, che d'odore'*.[17] As in the Ovidian name for Narcissus, and Alberti's celebrated reworking of the myth as the origins of painting (invoked in the Introduction), the heavy scent of this flower was likened to the poetic passion of love's desires, and the allure of art's mimetic enchantments. The flower that Narcissus became was thus the metaphor of his defloration. Painted representation of the scent bottle was therefore fully bivalent in signification. Linked to Venus and to bridal adornment but also the figure of the Magdalen in the washing of Christ's feet, it was a *vanitas* of both pleasure and presentiment of the social boundaries of *amour* as well as the shattering of desire beyond such constraints.

In keeping with Bellini's *sfumato* use of the oil medium, to which he lately came, light glances gently off the glass of the jar, suggesting the *specula immacula* of the Virgin's conception and so the chaste relations of the marital bed, but also the closely detailed observation of Gentile's art in emulation of van Eyck.[18] The silken modelling of the body through imperceptibly soft transitions of light and shade, coupled with her monumental proportions, readily suggest an emulation with smoothly modelled antique marbles.[19] Bellini's signature, in Latin in Roman cursive lettering on the small folded card or *cartellino* beside her, heightens the comparison with the classical past. The artist's use of the imperfect tense – *faciebat* –

which Pliny had praised among Greek artists, surely underlies an artistic *paragone* with the ancients.[20] It must also have intimated a Venetianising rivalry with Michelangelo, for his celebrated use of the term as for his Tuscan *maniera statuina*, or sculptural mode of painting, in emulation of ancient statuary. About her are the deeply saturated hues of Venetian *colorito* – greens, blues, reds. She is flanked, on the one hand, by the rich colours of a Persian carpet and, on the other, by a red-shot silk that twines about her shoulder. Her abundant fair hair is caught up in a pearl-edged brocade of gilt-lined ornamental lilies in deep green on blue. Its colouring echoes the Leonardesque blue of the horizon in the landscape beyond her, so binding her to the forms of nature as well as art. It readily invokes the image of a Venetian Renaissance 'Venus' as the figure of love, decorated in silk and pearl ornament. Bellini's *cartellino* bearing his name beside her further suggests a love letter from the artist as her *amateur*, so invoking the realm of female beauty as art's emblem in a re-enactment of her classical past. It may also intimate a painterly rivalry with van Eyck's now-lost painted cover to the Arnolfini portrait, depicting a female nude emerging from the bath with a mirror reflection of her form (discussed in Chapter 2). A testament to Bellini's interests in Netherlandish art, this suggests a tribute to his great predecessor's inaugural image of a feminine '*pittura*' with the inset mirror motif, now painted *alla veneziana*. The very structure of the composition, as it revolves around two facing mirrors, further suggests a pictorial matrix of *paragone* comparing the front and back view, like Lucian's description of the Cnidian Venus, or Giorgione's lost work of multiple reflections.[21]

In turn Titian depicted a young woman whose loose hair falls across her shoulder to her waist, which she also tends by means of a doubled mirror reflection. At her side a young man steadies a gilt-framed convex mirror with his left arm while holding up a smaller rectangular mirror in his right hand for her gaze (Fig. 128).[22] The typology suggests both homage and *paragone* with Bellini's work. The woman here is dressed in dark green gold-shot silk over a white lawn chemise that falls from her shoulder, her gown fastened by a translucent blue chiffon ribbon, with a sumptuous ultramarine drapery over her arm. Her hair is simply adorned by a twining blue ribbon, while her hand gesture recalls a Venus Anadyomene dressing her hair after bathing. Her left hand bears a gold ring on her finger, while gently touching a glass vessel of what is surely perfume on the window ledge before her. The woman gazes at her face in the small mirror which, as with the Bellini, is seen only from the reverse side. Here she must also see her reflection from the back, like the viewer. In the mirror behind her we can trace the shadowy outline of her head and shoulders set just under the strong reflection of what appears to be a window, casting its light on her face from the left. To her side in the reflection image is the profile of the man holding the mirrors, with his arms extended towards her in an act of courtship, to suggest both an embrace and the act of painting. This doubled caress, which Poussin would later use in a specular self-portrait of his own within an allegory of *pittura* (Fig. 86, Chapter 3), links the gestures of painting with those of love to configure the artist, like the viewer, as an art-*amateur*.[23]

Thus the Venetian painters' subject of the *bella donna* as a toilet of Venus grafted the mirror reflection to the female nude as intertwined emblems of the beauty of art.[24] If the female form was the very picture of desire, the inset mirror reflection was the figure of art within itself. As painting's trope it was swiftly emulated across the courts of Europe, often used to depict celebrated beauties as allegories of their renown, as well as the beauty of art itself. In its myriad elaborations, the subject generically depicted the goddess and her followers amid jewels, silks,

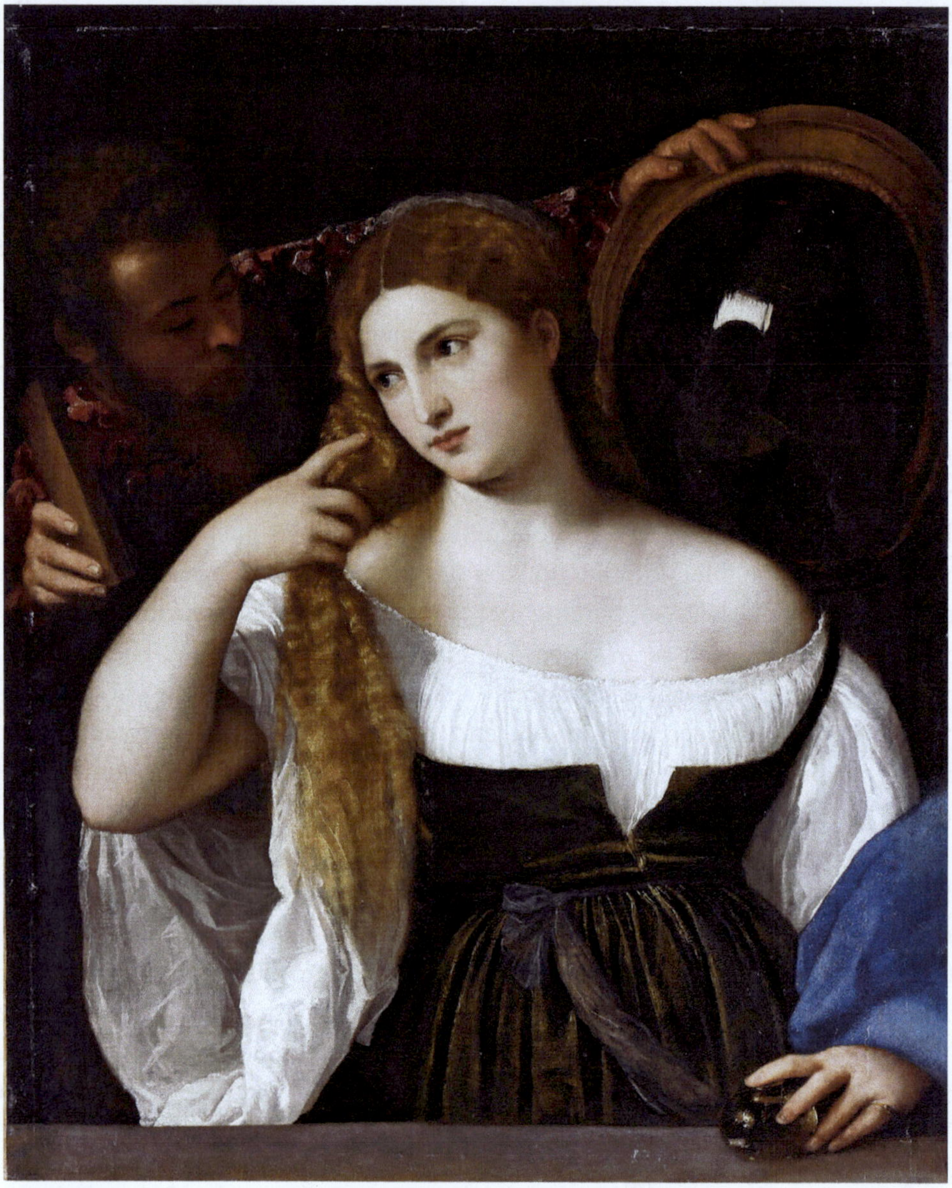

Fig. 128 Titian, *Woman with Mirror*, c. 1515, oil on canvas, 99 × 76 cm, Musée du Louvre, Paris. Photo: Musée du Louvre

blossoms, and other emblems of her flowered allure, her passing youth and beauty allegorised as the captivating yet fleeting image of her mirror reflection.

The pictorial motif was closely tied to poetic tropes of love and the beauty of women, exemplified in the verse of Petrarch and his many imitators as well as those of epithalamic poetry of ancient derivation in celebration of marriage. In a cultural representation of love as treasured, the female face and body were anthologised like so many jewels – coral or ruby lips, pearlized cheeks, golden hair, ivory teeth.[25] In a sonnet of love apparently for Lucrezia Borgia in the manner of Petrarch, Pietro Bembo cast her as a woman made of jewels – hair like pure amber, ivory hands, her mouth of ruby and pearls.[26] Like Zeuxis' composition of ideal form from the various beauties of the maids of Croton, such venereal beauty was understood as a collection of perfect parts, assembled like a series of metonymic reflections of details of the female body.

As Raphael purportedly wrote to Baldassare Castiglione concerning the figuration of ideal beauty for his *Galatea* (c. 1512–14), the anthological method enshrined by Zeuxis and echoed by Bellori lay in the finely concerted arrangement of parts, howsoever also in the idealising conceptualisation of the mind's eye as the artist's measure of judgment: 'to paint a beauty, I should have to see a number of beauties, provided your Lordship were with me to choose the best. In the absence of good judges of beautiful forms, I use an *idea* that comes to my mind.'[27] This idea, as Bellori fully theorized, was composed from visual memory suffused with the recollection of the most beautiful forms of art, like an anthology of mirror-images.

PICTURA POESIS

Like Raphael, Renaissance poets drew on a classical legacy of poetic love, as emblazoned in Ovid's description of his mistress unveiled to him in her parts – shoulders, arms, breasts, legs – each of a modelled perfection to rival the sculptors.[28] In poetry it became the trope of courtly conversation on the arts of love, as in Mario Equicola's *Libro di natura d'amore*, or Pietro Bembo's *Asolani*, itself written on the occasion of marriage of Caterina Cornaro as Bembo's graced patron.[29] Baldessare Castiglione's renowned *Cortigiano* (Book of the Courtier) similarly evoked the evanescent beauties of art in evening conversations on noble love set at the court of Urbino in 1507 (published in Venice in 1528).[30]

Within such courtly paradigms of love, the motif of viewing female beauty arose most presciently from its specular reflection. In Sperone Speroni's *Dialogues* on love as the mirror of beauty, the literary evocation of women imitated the ancient Lucian's *Imagines* as 'painted' mirror-image word-portraits of beauty's delights, every perfect part enumerated in succession. The iterations of a woman's beauties further comprised such texts as Giangiorgio Trissino's *Ritratti* as a composite portrait of female beauty and Agnolo Firenzuola's *Dialogue on the Beauty of Women* of 1542 as a living canon of Petrarchan female beauty. In a Raphaelesque enumeration of beautiful features like so many jewels, the theme is similarly treated in Ludovico Dolce's and Federigo Luigini's tracts on the figure of the *bella donna*.[31] Like the inset mirrors of Bellini and Titian, these courtier-amateurs mirrored each other in describing each beautiful part of their beloved one by one in a poetry of ellipsis. Thus the painted inset mirror that captured such beauty in its various parts became the artist's sign of *pictura poesis.* As in poetry, so in painting, according to the Horatian dictum: the specular reflection of beauty's detail, be it of the face, the arch of the back, the details of the cheek, the lips, the throat, or the hair, was recognised as the emblem of painting's art. The mirror's prismatic image reflections, like faceted diamonds, furthered the anthological collection of female beauty by offering the otherwise hidden or occluded view of that which would not otherwise be seen. In this way, it only deepened the poet's catalogue of love's intimate pleasures, like an array of mirror reflections of veiled beauties in the manner of Zeuxis.[32]

Titian continued to paint a great spectrum of mirror-image venereal toilets across his career, as artist to all the courts of Europe and particularly of Spain. Among the most widely imitated, both within his own production and well beyond by assistants and artists working in emulation of his example, is a representation of a seated female nude attended by young putti who playfully hold up a mirror into which she gazes at her own reflection (Fig. 129).[33] Among its many variations (some fifteen), the version remaining in Titian's possession until his death was, according to the

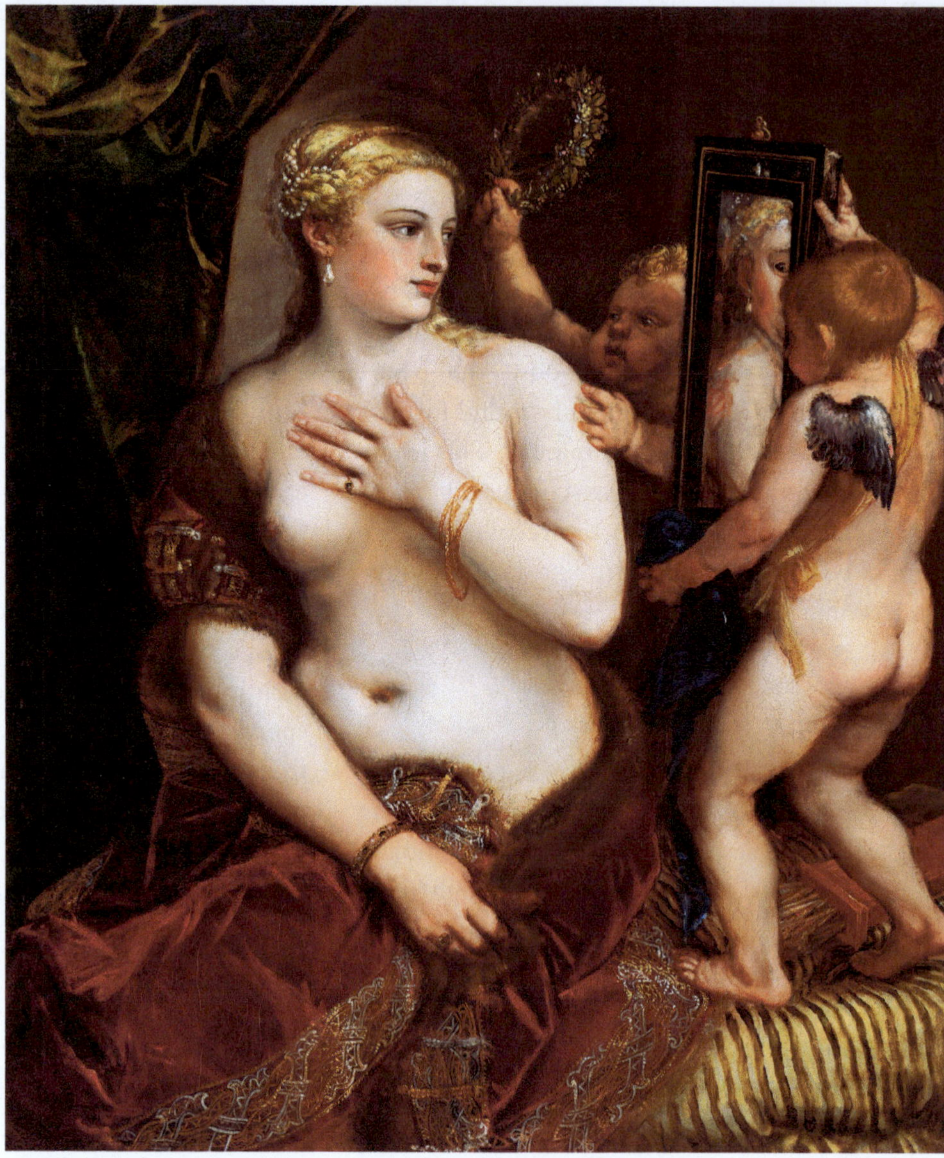

Fig. 129 Titian, *Venus with Mirror*, c. 1555, oil on canvas, 124.5 × 105.5 cm, National Gallery of Art, Washington, DC. Photo: NGA Washington

Venetian art biographer Carlo Ridolfi, to become acknowledged as a particular pictorial demonstration of his art. Now in the National Gallery in Washington, DC, it enjoys scholarly consensus as autograph. X-rays reveal another compositional variation underneath, also autograph, indicative of the multivalence of this pictorial motif for Titian as also the principle of variation at work in his art. The underpaint depicts a woman in a white chemise, similar to that of a further variant of this compositional type (now lost) painted for Philip II, and described by the artist as a 'Venus with Amor who holds the mirror for her'.[34] Titian's first or underlying composition is best known today through a subsequent imitation made by Rubens in emulation of his great predecessor at the Spanish court (Fig. 130).[35] It forms part of a celebrated artistic dialogue between them that centred on the depiction of the female nude and her mirror reflections. While the Washington painting covers the legs of the goddess but reveals the stomach and breasts, the Rubens version after Titian at Madrid, like the X-rayed version, veils the lower torso and

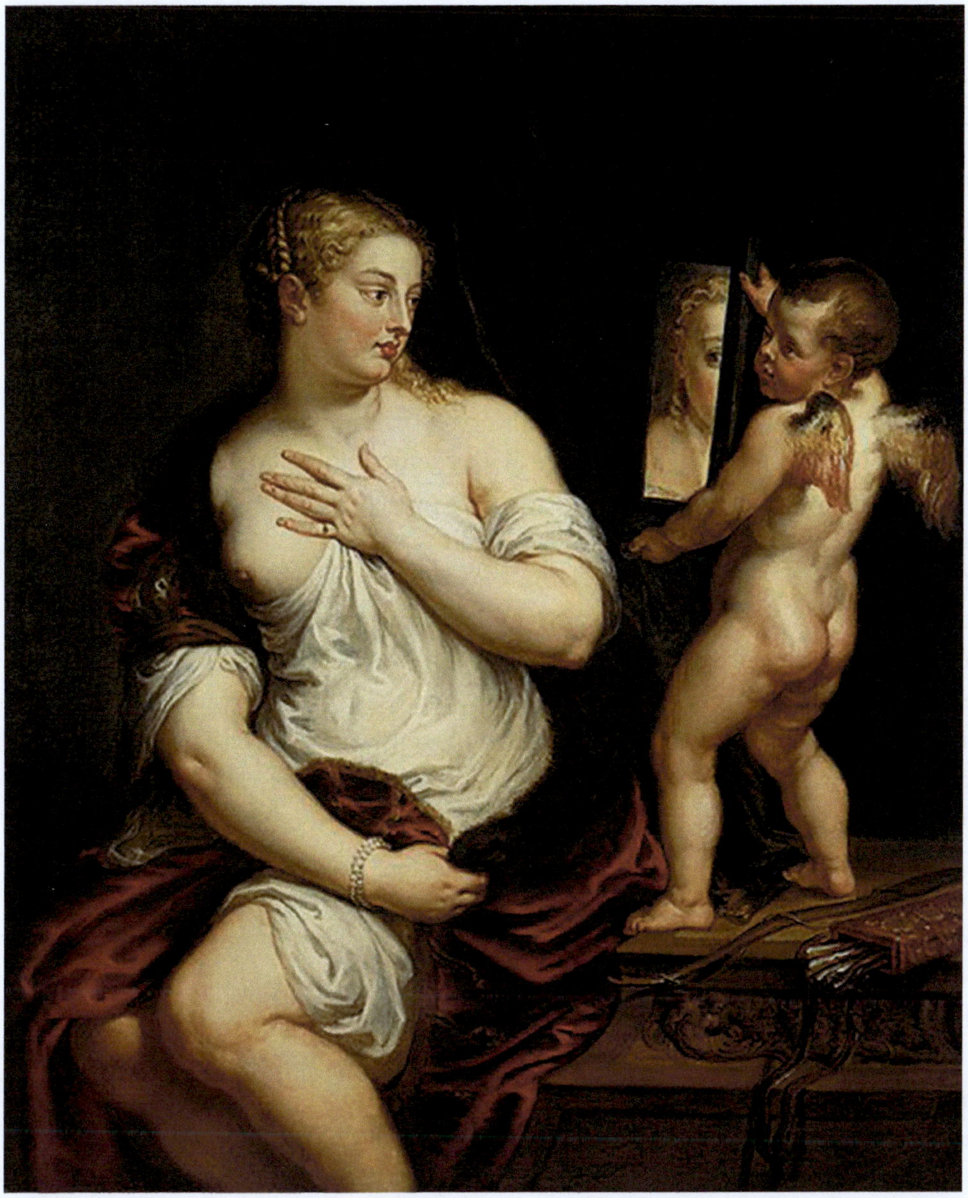

Fig. 130 Peter Paul Rubens, *Venus and Cupid*, 1606–11, oil on canvas, 137 × 111 cm, Thyssen-Bornemisza Museum, Madrid. Photo: Thyssen-Bornemisza Museum

displays her legs. In both instances, and in a mirror-image of each other that was surely intended to invite *paragone* between the two artists on the part of Rubens, these paintings thematise the act of viewing the female form as a composite of beautiful parts according to the conventions of classical *imitatio* and Petrarchan love poetry. In each instance, and heightened by comparison, Titian's composition invokes those parts of her form that are veiled by inviting the viewer to supplement with the imagination what the painter has withheld.

Castiglione had similarly evoked the ideal beauty of art as of women through the poetic metaphor of the veil. Here the exquisite gentility of the courtier-amateur was one of a lightly cloaked significance, suggesting a comparison between veiled beauty and veiled meaning that came to underpin the cultural metaphors of the Renaissance venereal image in both poetry and painting. It was also seen to reside in a Leonardesque *sfumato*, or the gentle fusion of painted lights and shadow that swept through early sixteenth-century painting. From Milan to Venice and beyond, *sfumato* served as a pictorial 'veil' of art's beauty like its poetic intimation.[36]

Thus, in Titian's Venus the inset mirror reflection captures elliptically the side of the face otherwise withheld from view. Its surface is sketchier than the rest of the canvas, as if of a painting in the making. Throughout, Titian suspends his colours in glistening layers of glaze, so that if her face is well defined by a creamy *impasto*, the outline of her limbs seems to fade gently into the half-light behind her in painted veils of *sfumato*.[37] As other scholars have suggested, the composition takes up the ancient theme of *paragone* between painting and poetry, as well as the great sixteenth-century comparison between painting and sculpture that structured so much art criticism of the period. Just as Petrarchan love poetry suggested the beauties of the beloved one by one – hair, eyes, brows, lips, neck, breasts – so the painter might deploy a pictorial syntax of textile veils and mirror views to alternate between revelation and occlusion.[38] In the ancient myths of Leucippe and medieval Acritic song of Maximou, transparent textiles of gossamer both veiled and displayed female nuptial beauty 'as if in a mirror', like a transfixing light to the courtly viewer's eye.[39] Hence in Titian's Washington painting the legs are draped in rich red silk velvet that also wraps around her right arm, edged with embroidery in gold and silver thread and lined with sable fur. Her arms cross over her torso in imitation of the Cnidian Venus, in a pose that simultaneously 'covers' and gestures to the breasts and the sex. Her body turns in a pose of variation that acknowledges the classical trope of *contrapposto*, like an artful display of the figure in a mirror-like counterpoint.

The pearls and rubies that twine through her hair, and the drop pearl earrings that frame her visage, are also captured in a mirror reflection that shows the side of her face a painting must occlude, so rivalling the sculptors and the poets in the rendition of beauty's ideals. Like reflections in a statuary fountain's pool, Titian here lays claim to painting's art in the full representation of the visible field, as if a mirror-image of itself. Iridescent pearls, the highlight of the eye, the soft swell of the cheek and shoulder, light tendrils of hair, are all encompassed within this specular conceptualisation of painting's ineffable beauty. The gambolling cupids are further ornament to her venereal figure, in the display of their pearlized flesh offset by silks and feathered wings, and the emblems they hold up to her: a large mirror of silvered Venetian glass edged in gilt-lined ebony to frame an additional view of her face, and a flower garland to adorn her hair. Bracelets and rings of jewelled gold embellish both arms and hands, while all around she is framed again by a wealth of sumptuous fabrics – deep green curtain swags behind her, and the gold-striped silk bed covering on which she rests. Together with her rich surrounds Titian's Venus is both a mirror and a metaphor of an opulent Renaissance, of exquisite precious materials predicated on luxury trade – Chinese silks, Russian furs, Indian pearls, Burmese rubies, African ebony and gold.[40] It is also pictorial invocation of poetic verse written in celebration of love and betrothal as connoted in the epithalamia that accompanied princely marriage, and which extolled the beauties of jewels, flowers, and silken veils as ornament to the bridal bower. Titian's pictorial orchestration of beauty thus comprises both Venus and her decorations, which act like so many mirror reflections of her own. Artfully arranged throughout the composition, each one is a further ornament to the painter's venereal theme. Like the splendour of poetic episodes from the ancient verses of marriage song from Homer to Claudian, and of epic romance exemplified by Matteo Maria Boiardo and Ludovico Ariosto's tales of Orlando's chivalric love, Titian's richly ornamented venereal toilet cast a lasting light of beauty as a shimmering mirror-image across Renaissance art.[41]

VENERALIA

Like Rubens and Velazquez, Veronese too would paint in emulation of Titian's reflecting Venus, now turning her figure in order to display her from the back in a counterpoint to Titian's pose. As in Lucian's description of viewing the Cnidian Venus from the front and the back, Veronese's work (*Venus with a Mirror*, c. 1580, at the Joslyn Art Museum) was surely intended as a *paragone* of his art with Titian, and with the broader Venetian tradition. Set between silks, furs, and lace amid carved gilt-wood furnishings, her fair hair is twined with ribbon and pearls offset by drop earrings and further bracelets of gold at her wrists. A childish cupid steadies the mahogany mirror she holds up to herself, to show her face both from the front and in profile in a specular multiplication of her form.

Celebrated for his painterly skill in rendering every visual effect of cloth, jewel, and skin, Veronese was the consummate artist of Venetian luxury. His marvelling seventeenth-century Venetian critic, Marco Boschini, described his work as a kind of painted alchemy of materials by which to give them seeming presence: 'he has mixed gold with pearls, rubies, emeralds, and sapphires of the best quality, and the purest and most perfect diamonds', as if jewels were the very matter of his paints, in a *paragone* of Petrarchan love poetry on the jewel-like forms of female beauty. Boschini playfully acknowledged Veronese's primacy among painters in the portrayal of Venus as if in the voice of the goddess herself: 'When I wanted to be portrayed, I went to Paolo [Veronese], who knows how to imitate my beautiful parts better than anyone.'[42] The Venetian toilet of Venus would become the pictorial typology of the goddess of beauty and art across the European courts, subsequently manifest above all in the lush paints of Rubens and Velazquez.

As court artist to Albert VII, Archduke of Austria, and the Spanish Infanta Isabella Clara Eugenia, also sovereigns of the Low Countries, Rubens painted a full range of Venus images with mirrors, among them the *Venus and Cupid* now at the Thyssen-Bornemisza Museum and long acknowledged as founded in emulation of Titian (Fig. 130). In the documentation of his trip to Madrid in 1628/9, Rubens' encounter with Titian's work for the Spanish monarchy was profound, and particularly in the artistic company of the newly appointed painter at the Spanish court, Velazquez. The artistic encounter between the three artists took place through the prism of Venus and her mirror, as the emblem of painterly beauty, and the *paragone* of their art. Hence in Rubens' emulation of his Venetian predecessor, the white chemise imitates that of Titian's underpainted composition, while the pose of the body clearly recalls Titian's reworking of the Cnidia, here also ornamented with pearls and sumptuous sable-lined red velvet.

In a related Venus at the mirror now housed in the Liechtenstein Museum in Vienna, Rubens made explicit use of the specular reflection to reveal what the painting itself occludes. Here the artist pictorialises the female form from behind, lightly draped in shimmering white voile to complement her iridescent skin and hair. While the painting captures her face in profile, the mirror shows her frontally, where her eyes meet the viewer's gaze. The exchange of glances within the mirror renders the viewer – the patron – into an art-lover, configured by the love of a Venus reflection. In the bevelled edge of the mirror beside her reflected face, Rubens painted the suggestion of himself as he painted her. In an Eyckian recollection of his Flemish lineage, like the figure of the artist in the shield of St George in the van der Paele Madonna, it is a pictorial signature of his presence. Artist and viewer are here joined in an *amitié* of art.

A further celebrated example of Rubens' emulation of Titian in the representation of Venus and her mirror comprises their respective depictions of the *Worship of Venus* (1518, now at the Prado Museum, and 1630s, now at the Nationalmuseum, Stockholm). One of a series of mythological paintings undertaken for Alfonso d'Este's *camerino d'alabastro* at Ferrara, Titian's *Worship of Venus* was thus destined for this choice princely collector's cabinet, which was in itself an exquisite jewel box of alabaster walls with a gilded ceiling. The subject springs from the ancient Greek Philostratus' *Eikones or Imagines* (I, VI), a text composed of a collection of short ekphrastic essays on imaginary works of art of mythological themes. The *camerino d'alabastro* was surely intended to recall both an antique picture cabinet and its classical literary evocations. Epithalamic verse often comprised descriptions of bridal gifts made of precious materials, figuring the loves of the gods in wrought silver or gold-thread embroidery. In Titian's *Worship of Venus*, childish cupids playfully gather apples into jewelled nuptial baskets as a votive offering to the goddess of love, who is represented in sculptural form. Beside her ornamented pedestal two richly draped nymphs prepare the ritual offering, one proffering to the goddess a framed *tondo* mirror as an emblem of her beauty and of Titian's art. According to Philostratus, such votive mirrors were offered by the nymphs to Venus in thanks for the gift of motherhood of the infant cupids, as a metaphor of reproduction.[43] The subject arises from the annual Roman rites of spring worship conducted in honour of Venus as the patron of marriage in which women made offerings to the goddess for beauty, and its purification. The *veneralia* ritual was the particular preserve of married women as a celebration of desire within the bounds of wedlock and family. It centred around a ritual bathing and dressing of her cult image to invoke her help in the happy regulation of conjugal love, in imitation of a bridal toilet. Rubens would imitate Titian's work closely in a painting he kept in his private collection until his death, as a pictorial emblem of his art. Further, he subsequently adapted it in another variation, as a *Feast of Venus* (Kunsthistorisches Museum, Vienna), in a fulsome celebration of marital relations apparently including his own, in the image of his young wife.[44]

A further series of paintings by Rubens on the theme of the mirror reflection and the allures of the female nude turned on representations of the shield of Perseus. Like Giorgione's lost work of mirror reflections, which Vasari and Lomazzo had described as a male in armour, the motif comprised a painted counterpoint of martial valour with venereal beauty as the conjoined emblems of a specular art. In a witty layering of painterly deceptions to decorate the loggia of the Rubenshuis, the Italianate villa in Antwerp that was his home, studio, and place of reception for the princes he served, Rubens included in fresco a fictive canvas of Perseus, resplendent in shining armour, alongside the naked Andromeda chained for a beauty that dared to rival the gods. In this he claimed the laurels of his art, like Zeuxis, as founded in an ideally beautiful *imitatio*. Similarly, in subsequent representations of the Judgment of Paris, the contest of beauty among the goddesses that led to the abduction of Helen and so the Trojan War, Rubens brought together the loveliness of the painted female nude with the valorous emblem of his artistic skill in the mirroring shield of Perseus (Fig. 131). Suspended from a tree branch, the shield's convex form is mirror-like, yet its reflection is a counterfeit, depicting instead the gorgon's head that Perseus used to turn his enemies to marbled stone. A painted acknowledgement of both Caravaggio's Medusa shield

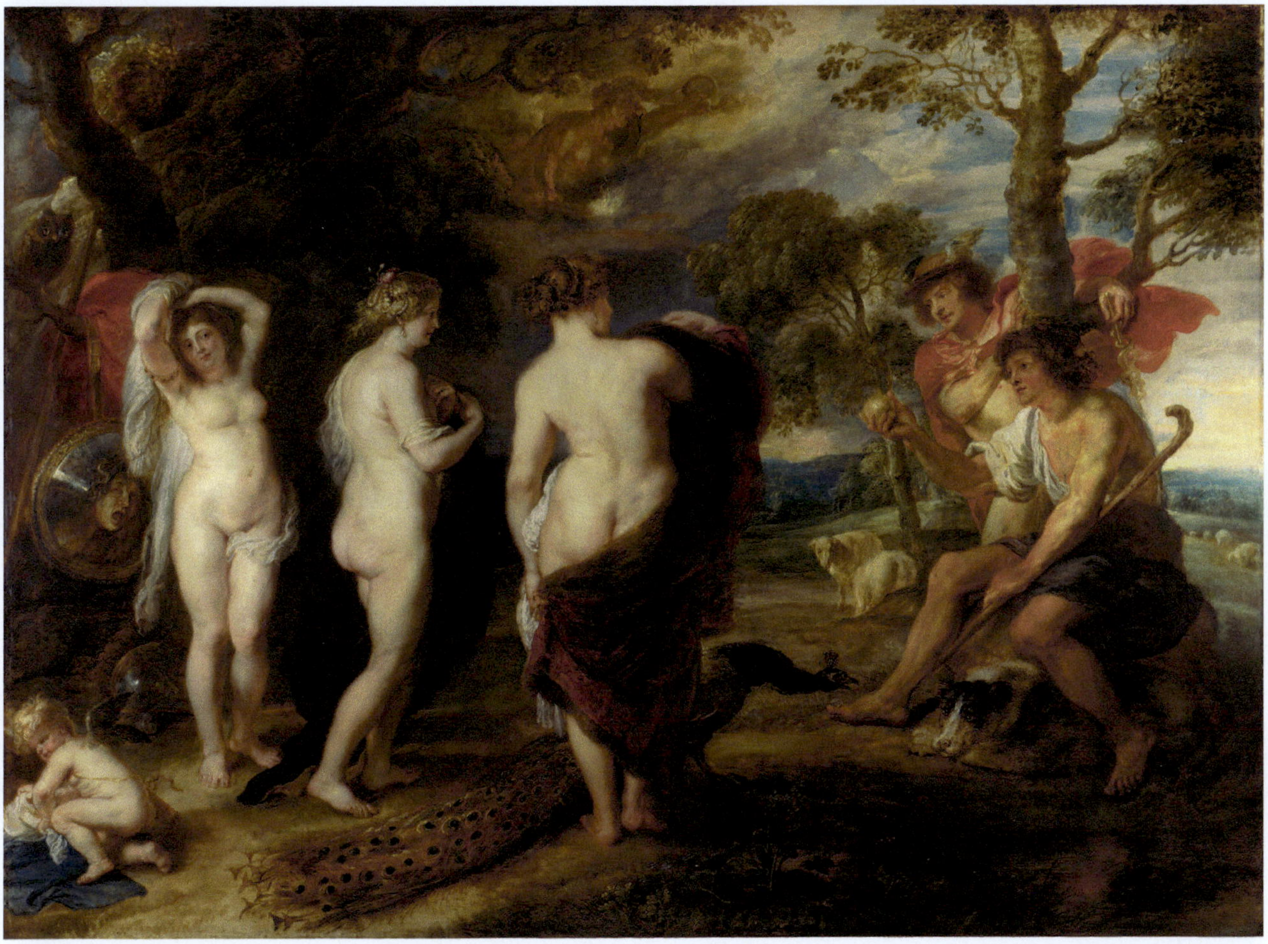

Fig. 131 Peter Paul Rubens, *The Judgement of Paris*, c. 1632–35, oil on panel, 144.8 × 193.7 cm, National Gallery, London. Photo: Wikimedia

gifted for a Medici wedding and Annibale Carracci's pictorial account of the myth in the frescoed epithalamia of the Farnese-Aldobrandini marriage in the great gallery of their palace, Rubens' painting also cited the trope of the gorgon's shield to represent the force of his art's mimetic illusions. If 'love conquers all', so also does art. In Rubens' painted renditions of the goddesses' beauties, as palpably Titianesque invocations of classical statuary, the viewer is transfixed and conquered. Turned to 'stone' by Medusa's gaze as the emblem of art's valiance, Rubens' art is as beautiful and haunting as her mythic head.[45]

Rubens' considered play with the viewer's attention by means of the painted mirror reflection of Venus as allegory of the love of art was something that Velazquez, sometime student of Rubens during the Flemish painter's trip to Madrid, also observed in his emulation of the Antwerp master. Equally, Velazquez made profound study of Venetian painting, through his travels in Italy and his position as keeper of the Spanish Royal collections, which then included the now-lost toilet of Venus and her mirror reflection by Titian. Velazquez' knowledge of this pictorial tradition and of Titian further inflected by Rubens, in particular, informed his own great painting of Venus at her mirror, c. 1650, known as the *Rokeby Venus* for reasons of her subsequent provenance (Fig. 132).[46] Though the details of the painting's genesis remain unclear, by

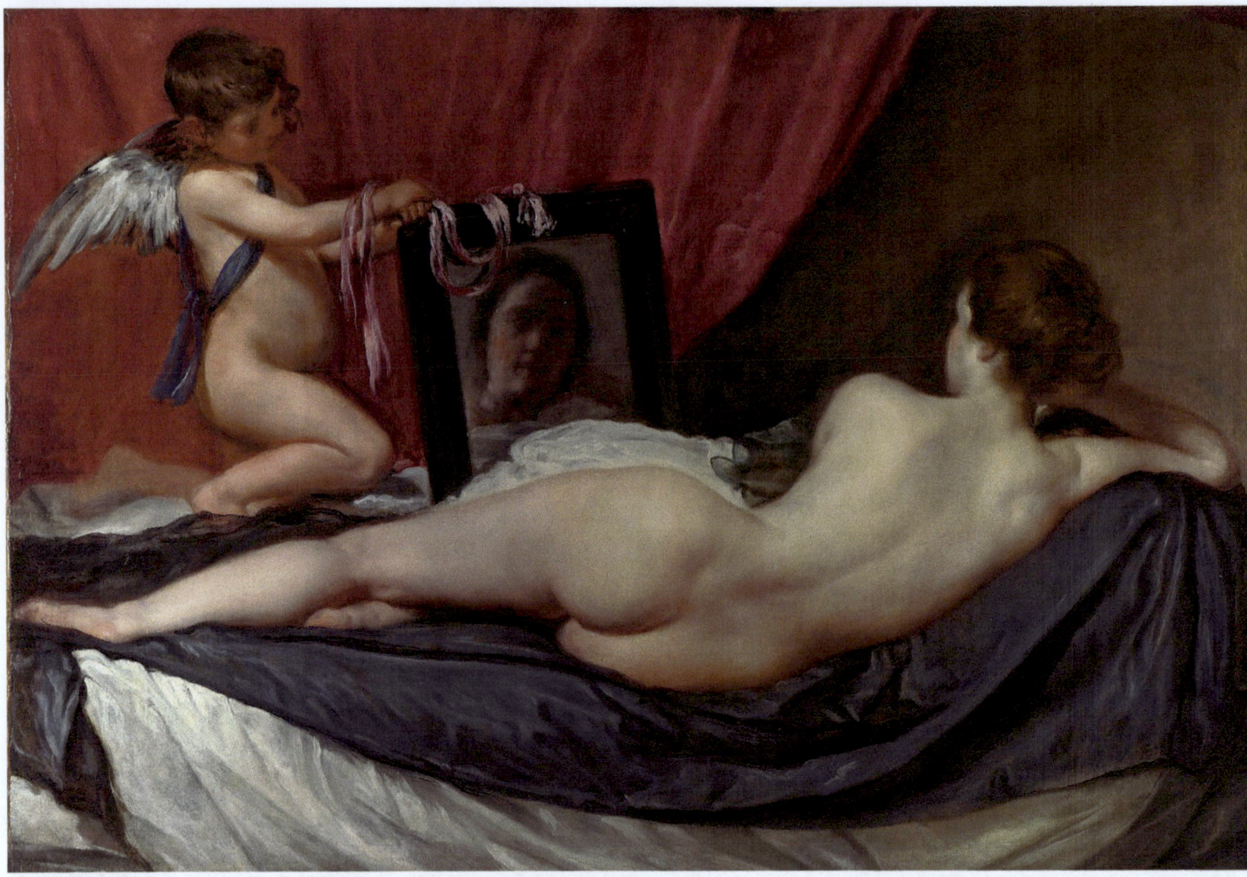

Fig. 132 Diego Velázquez, *The Toilet of Venus* (*'The Rokeby Venus'*), 1647–51, oil on canvas, 122.5 × 177 cm, National Gallery, London.
Photo: Wikimedia

1 June 1651 it was in the possession of the Spanish noble Gaspar de Haro, nephew of the line of Olivares who, as royal favourites, possessed wealth and position manifest in art collections of the highest rank. If the painting has been connected to Velazquez' 1649–51 voyage to Italy made at the time of the king's marriage for the purpose of art acquisitions, 1650 was also the year of Gaspar de Haro's ducal marriage for which it may conceivably have been a royal bridal gift. The affective beauty of Velazquez' Venus has also been held to lie in a Roman *amour* of the painter's own.[47]

A reclining female nude seen from behind, Velazquez' rendition is unusual as a Venus without jewels, her identity instead manifest in the beauty of her form and colour alone. In a concert of damson tones, Velazquez renders his Venus as a recollection of Venetian *pittura*, of Giorgione's *Sleeping Venus* infused by Titian's later elaboration in the *Venus of Urbino*, above all in the liberal *macchia* of brushwork as the signature of his art. Her undulating form is framed by satins of saturated reflection and hue, further echoed in an array of filmy, gossamer fabrics. This is lightly accentuated in a range of textile surfaces – satin sheen and the airy feathers of Cupid's wings – as ornament to the gentle beauty of her curving form.

At the heart of the painting's composition lies the reflecting surface of a mirror, its ebony frame a pictorial reflection of the painting's own in a counterpoint to the pearly colouring of her skin. The mirror captures the face of Venus in its shimmering surface, displaying frontally what would otherwise be occluded from our sight. The painting presents the viewer with a *paragone* of views, in emulation of both Lucian's Cnidia and its Titianesque elaborations. Yet the mirror reflection presents a further inset pictorial paradox. For the reflection is seemingly inflected: the angle of the mirror should properly reflect the viewer rather than Venus. As this is so, the image within its courtly viewing context suggests a flattery of the princely viewer as either a Venus herself or as her lover. The intimation is surely that the circuit of gazes includes Venus regarding the viewer as well as the viewer looking at Venus.

Notable also are the differences in paint surfaces. While a creamy impasto forges the figure of Venus herself in a palpable recollection of classical marble statuary now transformed into seeming flesh, in comparison the mirror-image is rendered with a thinner, more fleeting application of paint. Its sketchy surface finish suggests the passing beauties of a mirror reflection, in a metaphor of painting's art, as of youth and love. Hence Velazquez' mirror reflection becomes a further variation of the painter's subject – his art. In this it is surely also a paean to the poetics of sight, as the agent of love and art conjoined. The complex of viewing relations held within the mirror-reflected image further suggests its use as the optical instrument of his painted variations. If this is so, then Velazquez' contrast between the smoothly modelled *impasto* surface of the body and the gauze-like sketchiness of the glazes in the mirror-image intimates a considered critical engagement with a specular theory of painting.[48] The polished body figures painting like a sculpted marble *all'antica,* while the sketchy *alla macchia* image of the face is Velazquez' signature – *al borrón.* As court art, the painting's conceit is its artfulness, and it is in this, the play of its pictorial illusionism, that its status as an allegory of *pittura* resides. Nowhere might this be more so than in a rendition of Venus and her mirror as confluent signs of the beauty of art and the specular means of its mimesis. The life-sized representation of her form heightens the elision between art and viewer, Venus and her *amateur,* at the centre of this painting's declaration of viewing art like an act of love.[49] Through the reflection of the inset mirror, Velazquez paints the specular definition of his art.

The mirror-image of Venus as an allegory of painting and metaphor of sight was further taken up by Rubens in collaboration with Jan Brueghel the Elder, in a series of works depicting the five senses also for Archduke Albert VII and Isabella. Set within palatial interiors and gardens resembling their court, those scenes dedicated to sight are staged in collectors' galleries of art comprising cabinet paintings, sculptures, decorative arts, medals, prints, and drawings, but also optical and scientific instruments of vision. A five-part series treating each sense individually depicts Sight as a female nude attended by Cupid (Fig. 133).[50] Together they contemplate a small cabinet painting of Christ restoring sight to a blind man, surrounded by viewing glasses of various kinds as well as medals and jewels. Behind the nude a further table displays a range of objets d'art in precious metal and stone, ivory and porcelain, comprising astrolabes and compasses, small bronzes, and a painted ebony cabinet for their storage before which sit two mirrors: one in a wooden frame like a further cabinet painting, the other a small, double-sided convex glass mounted on a gilt pedestal. Abiding over all these is a portrait of the Archdukes Albert and Isabella, as the figure of marriage and sovereignty, and the love of art manifest through their patronage. Beyond the great gallery of their collections – tapestries, prints, paintings, and sculptures of all sizes – stretches a view onto gardens with fountains and ornamental pools as further 'mirrors' to the beauty of art and the opulence of vision. Framed by flowers and exotic birds throughout the composition, this venereal 'Juno-Optica' is swathed in a sumptuous ultramarine drapery

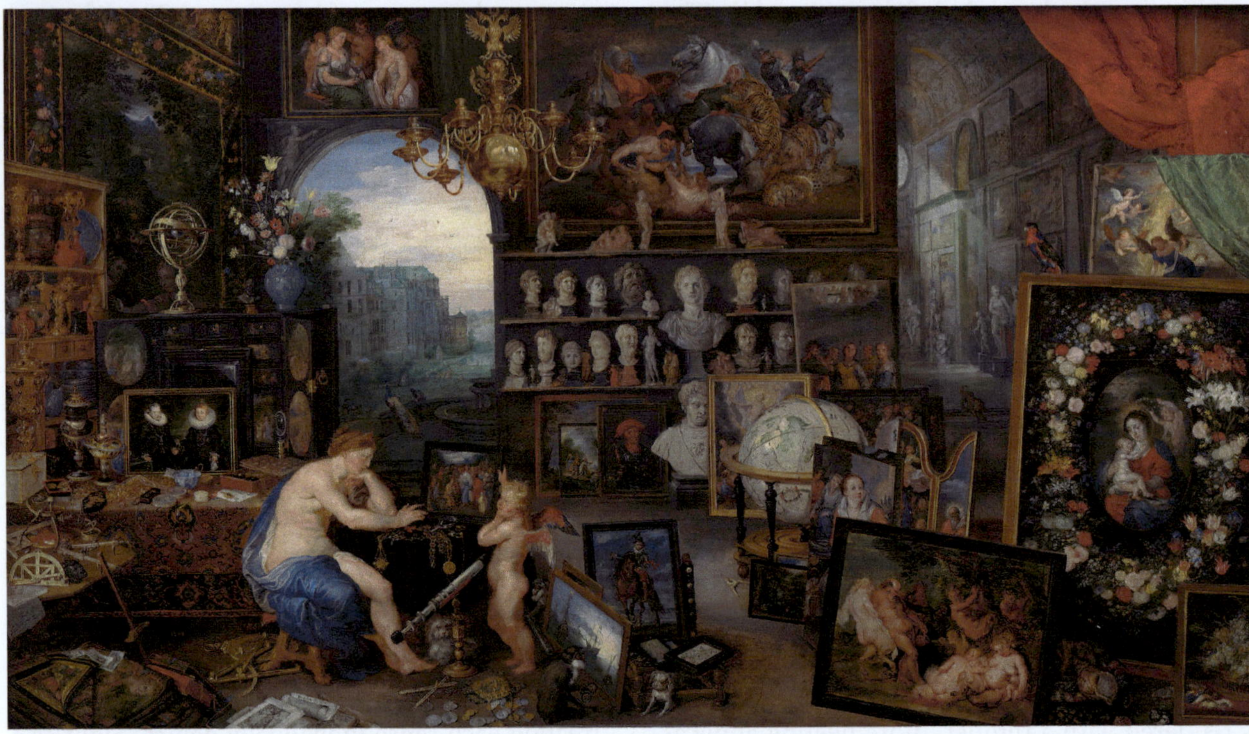

Fig. 133 Peter Paul Rubens and Jan Brueghel the Elder, *The Sense of Sight*, 1617, oil on panel, 64.7 × 109.5 cm, Museo del Prado, Madrid.
Photo: © Museo Nacional del Prado

and a diadem of pearls fronted by a large cut gem as the prism or diamond-shape of an eye, an allegory both of sight and of the art-amateur, or the lover of painting. In the gilt bowl of the chandelier above her, its convex reflection intimates the reach of the gallery to the front of the picture plane, configured by further windows and paintings, as the space in which the viewer, like the painter before, surely stands. The golden cast of its reflection offsets that of the silver clouds seen through the arch, to suggest the precious lustres of paint as the artist's means of mimetic illusion. This is manifest in the myriad gallery paintings on display in this painted hall of art.[51] Just as the painted picture gallery represents a collected history of art, so the chandelier's painted reflection in emulation of van Eyck makes this an emblem of Rubens' Flemish *schilderkunst.*

A further pair of paintings of the senses by Brueghel in collaboration with other Flemish painters brings together *Sight with Smell* (Prado Museum, c. 1620). Depicting cupids attending two women, one studies her face in a dressing-table mirror reflection as an allegory of sight and painting, while the other is surrounded by flowers and an elaborately chased perfume basin in gold and silver as the personification of scent and smell. Behind them, the gallery walls are marked by receding rays of light, while around are instruments of vision by which to measure their power of reflection and refraction. In their several versions, Brueghel's paintings sit within a larger historical typology of allegories of sight as one of the five senses, with a rich issue in seventeenth-century Northern painting in emulation of his work: in the oeuvre of his son Jan Brueghel II, grandson Jan van Kessel, and artists such as Frans Wouters, Jan Rombouts, and Frans Francken. It was also a subject much represented in prints, as in the work of Adriaen Collaert, Jean Couvay, and Abraham Bosse, each of which address sight and its instrument the mirror respectively in conjunction with a theology of light, its *paragone* with music in the arts of love, or the female dressing table alongside the optics of science.[52] It was equally celebrated by the poets, in a *paragone* with painting, as in the words of Pietro Bembo, who, like Couvay, compared the sense of sound with sight as equivalent overtures to the art of love: 'The flight of virtuous love has two windows: one is hearing, which sends it to the beauty of the spirit: the other is that of sight, which leads love's flight to the beauty of the body.'[53]

As other scholars have noted, the typology of the senses in which sight is identified by a figure with a mirror is an ancient one. Its early manifestations were, however, with the male figure, as also in Vasari's and Pino's descriptions of Giorgione's lost work of mirror reflections.[54] Its pictorial embodiment as female arises historically as a genre of the High Renaissance, exemplified in Bellini's *Woman at the Mirror*. Articulated in the shifting critical identification of Giorgione's theoretical 'reflection' painting from male to female by Lomazzo, over the course of the sixteenth century the mirror-image bound the allegorisation of viewing artistic beauty to the female form.

ARTS OF LOVE

In the concluding tapestry of the Lady and the Unicorn series, a graced lady in jewelled silk brocade of red and gold stands in an embroidered *millefleurs* landscape of flowers, fruits, trees, and birds reminiscent of epithalamic poetry and of armorial *animalia* in the rich colours of heraldry. She is depicted with a maidservant who proffers a chest of betrothal jewels while a heraldic lion and unicorn attend her on either side. Among the most celebrated of French examples c. 1500 to link the representation of courtly love with an elaboration of feminine graces, the Cluny tapestries are also emblematic devices of the five senses. The tapestries of each sense embroider their pleasures variously. As these tapestries are surely connected with aristocratic marriage alliance, even if their precise armorial representation remains contested, scholarly consensus has understood them as allegories of courtly love in which the heraldic unicorn represents both the object and the affect of her sentiment. If connected with the Le Viste family, as has generally been postulated, their representation of the senses may be in emblematic play with the sense of sight – *viste* – as the ruler of the senses and so the heart. They have also long been seen as lightly Mariological in inference, given that the unicorn may only be captured by a chaste woman as an emblem of marriage's singular love. Further, the Mariological cast of much imagery pertaining to noble marriage carries an intimation of the Holy Family and so to the aspiration of dynastic lineage.

In the allegory of sight, the seated lady allows the unicorn to kneel before her, touching her as she does him, while looking into a richly worked gold hand mirror she holds (Fig. 134). The mirror's convex tondo form framed by jewels echoes her face offset by pearls throughout her hair, while her sumptuous dress of gold brocade is in fact woven in silk tapestry thread.[55] Facing frontally at the centre of the pictorial field, the inset mirror-image serves as a heraldic rebus or armorial 'portrait' pertaining to betrothal. Its form may recall Burgundian-Valois manuscript illuminations for early fifteenth-century French copies of Boccaccio's *Des clères et nobles femmes* in its encomium of the ancient painter, Marcia, who paints her portrait by means of a hand-held mirror; and Christine de Pisan's 1405 reply in her *Cité des dames*, on the virtuous renown of women as the figurative architects of civility. Configured by means of an emblematic mirror of perspicacity and gifted to the royal princes of Charles VI in

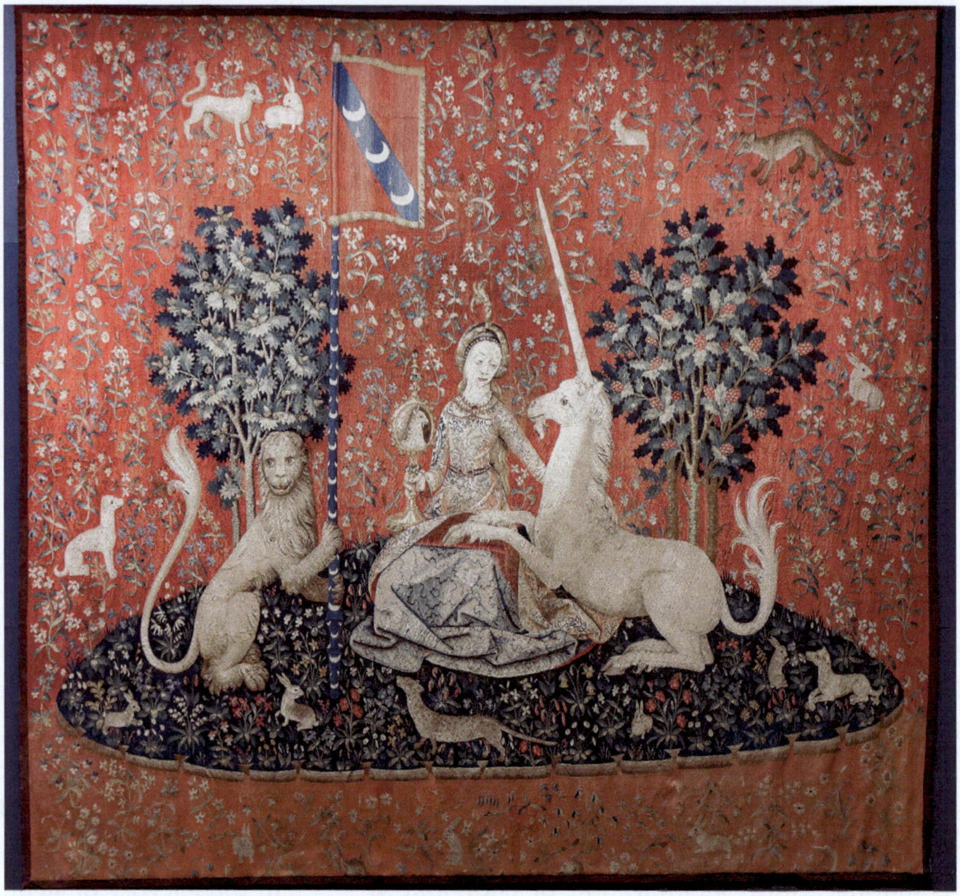

Fig. 134 *La dame à la licorne*, late fifteenth to early sixteenth century, French tapestry, Musée de Cluny.
Photo: Wikimedia

Christine's capacity as court poet, the *City of Ladies* became a defining image of French aristocratic identity for the illustrious court lady.[56] Within the Cluny tapestry, the mirror face does not reflect the lady, however, but rather the unicorn, as the chivalric image of her beloved and surely the intended viewer of these works. This mirror reflection sits beside her portrait head as a pendant 'pair', like courtship portraits, framed by the lion and the unicorn as emblems of their heraldic bearing. Thus the courtly viewer looks on the Lady and the Unicorn as the image of his knightly claim to her, both lover and art-lover entwined.

Imagery of the arts of love flourished at the French court, issuing both from High French Gothic conventions of noble and chivalric *amour* such as the Cluny tapestries and from the nascent emulation of Italianate Renaissance forms. In particular, the Italian 'toilet of Venus' genre became a celebrated typology for the representation of royal consorts as of queens, in painted emulation of the '*bella donna veneziana*' portrait. In this it was deeply indebted to Giorgionesque and Titianesque examples, as well as the Raphaelesque representation of ideal female beauty emblematised above all in the *Galatea* at the Chigi Villa in Rome (later Farnesina) as the painted paradigm of a renascent 'classicism' and its figural pleasures. Here the wealthy banker to the popes, Agostino Chigi, built an architectural pledge on the pleasures of love to the celebrated Venetian beauty and his future wife Francesca Ordeaschi as painted invocation of the epithalamic poets of *amour*. The scene of Alexander and Roxana's

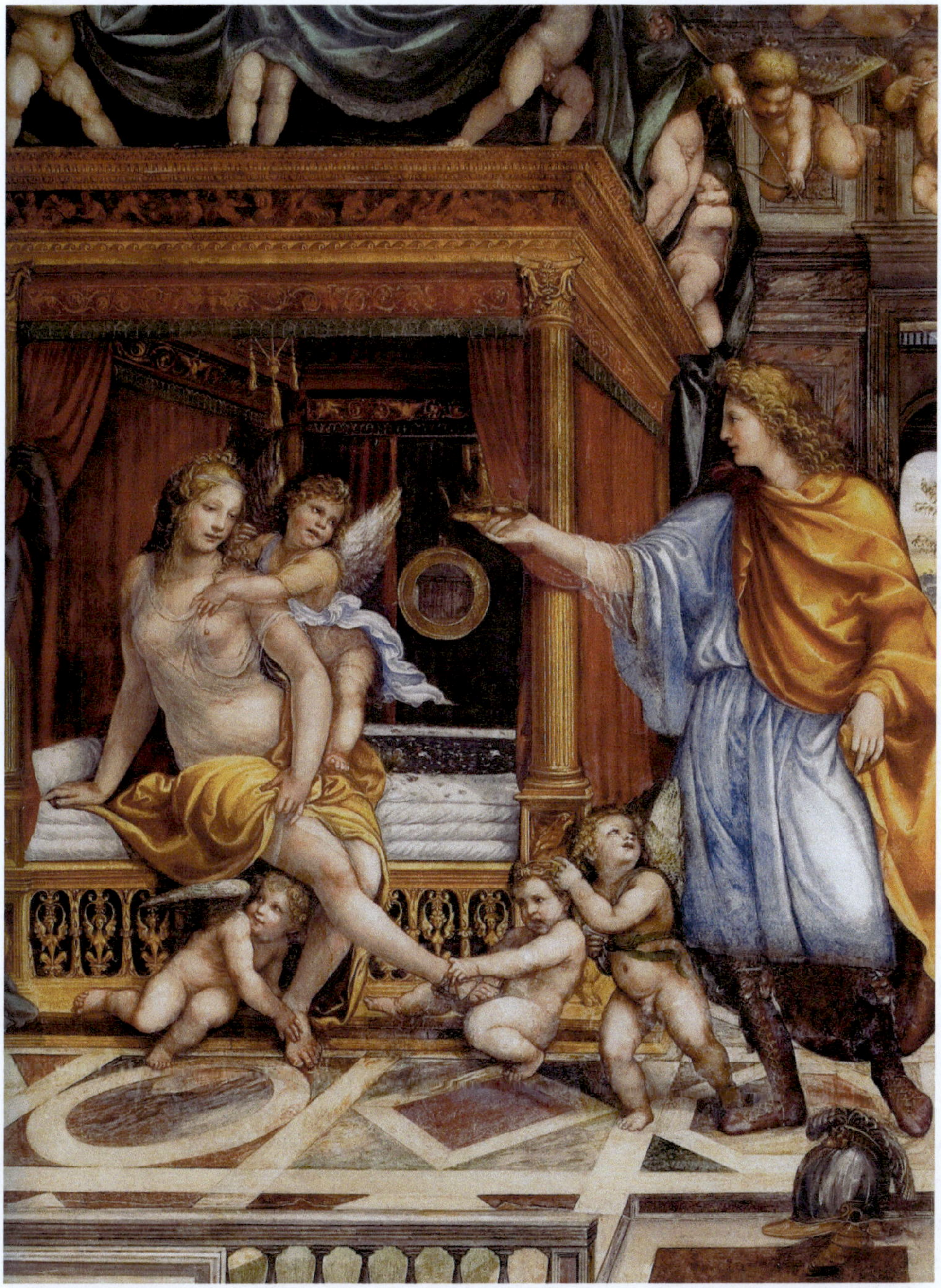

Fig. 135 Giovanni Antonio Bazzi (Il Sodoma), *The Marriage of Alexander and Roxanna*, c. 1511–19, wall fresco, Villa Chigi-Farnesina Rome. Photo: Wikimedia

amorous consummation was surely a pictorial 'mirror' of the great Chigi bed before it, in imitation of classical poetic descriptions of the nuptial couch ornamented with embroidered silks (Fig. 135). Roxana is depicted as a Venetian beauty in emulation of Chigi's Francesca, her fair hair dressed with a filmy ribbon that encircles her brow above the modesty of her downcast eyes, while cupids undress her figure, veiled only by a transparent silk chiffon of nuptials, for Alexander's delight. Their courtly swaying figures frame the painted mirror at the centre of the composition as if heraldically, over which hangs the crown he proffers to his consort and queen.[57]

At the court of François I too, such veiled 'portraits' of the king's consorts were an acknowledgement of these women's royal alliance and its dynastic significance, as well as the refined pleasures of the king's bed. Princely venereal paintings flowered at the court of François I and his successors, among the artists of Fontainebleau, in emulation of both Venetian and Raphaelesque examples. The subject touched on lineage in its reference to the issue of children from royal wives as well as mistresses whose features were often lightly inferred or mythologised in such works.[58] This apparent fusion of queen and consort surely reflects a cultural understanding of marriage as an alliance independent of church law, in which the companions of princes might enjoy a recognized social role at court in many respects equivalent to marriage itself.[59] The paintings to commemorate such alliances often also pictorialized the decorative arts of the venereal or nuptial toilet as those fit for a queen. Within these images, a range of lustrous toiletry objects including elaborately worked gold and jewel-framed mirrors were fitting ornament to their representation of an ennobled feminine beauty. The subject reflected aristocratic cultures of the bath, in emulation of antique precedents, which was a social occasion of court. Its luxury was manifest in the noble ornament of the dressing table – exquisite chased ewers and vases in precious metals, decorated ivory combs, jewelled scent bottles containing valuable perfumes, and mirrors set in richly carved gold frames.[60]

The refined pleasures of the royal bath and female toilet as the site of a luxuriant delight in beauty was particularly cultivated at Fontainebleau. The name of the palace was of a woodland spring, echoed in myriad figurations of the bathing nude in painting and sculpture. Embodying the renascence of antiquity, the arts, and the mythological loves of the gods, Fontainebleau represented what François I's artistic patronage sought to claim for France. Within, the celebrated *appartements des bains* at Fontainebleau (and subsequently Versailles) were built in emulation of antiquity. Richly decorated with mythological scenes of Venus, bathing, and the loves of the gods, they were in keeping with courtly cultures of the king's *amour*.[61] Hence the Renaissance rise of the venereal toilet as an occasion of court denoted the king's claim to the pleasures of the ancients, in both art and beauty.

Such refined cultures of the royal bath brought with them the rise of the dressing table as a noble furnishing, a princely pastime, and a poetic preoccupation. It further produced toiletry objects made of the finest materials – ivory, ebony, precious metals and jewels – and kept in richly ornamented caskets for the court lady's marriage trousseaux. This in turn was depicted in paintings of venereal bathing and ritual dressing of queens as for royal mistresses in emulation of the nuptial toilet of antique epithalamia. The subject was also one of female adornment in elaborately worked luxury textiles, or *'toile'*. The decorated surface of the noblewoman's embroidered sampler as the pastime of queens thus became a synonym both for the display of the feminine toilet and for the artist's painted canvas, in a further linguistic elision of art with its subject conceived as an allegory of feminine beauty.

This figuration of the arts of the trousseau with that of female beauty in a mirror reflection was manifest above all in the aristocratic genre of lightly mythologised nuptial portraits. These were paintings that stood between the so-called fine and decorative arts (a distinction generally acknowledged as arising only in the eighteenth century), wedded to the social rituals of courtship and marriage that formed their subject. At once visual representations of bridal wealth and of the dynastic place of women, they are imagery of female beauty as family estate.

Thus the English portrait of Elizabeth Vernon, Countess of Southampton, depicts this royal favourite of the queen before her dressing table, or 'vanity' as it would also be known (private collection, Duke of Buccleuch). Dressed in silk-embroidered cloth, she combs her loose hair before a gilt-painted table with a tasselled-silk cloth on which her open jewel box of ebony and mother of pearl displays a mirror.[62] Within the decorative arts of the female toilet, aristocratic dressing-table sets in silver, ivory, tortoise-shell, and other precious materials comprised framed mirrors with candelabra and matching combs, pins, and brushes, along with caskets and boxes for jewellery, perfume, toiletries, hair-pieces, and makeup, such as the silver-gilt Lennoxlove service gifted by Charles II to Frances Teresa Stuart as a celebration of their romance.[63] Such jewelled toiletry objects constituted courtly gifts to consorts, as also brides, accompanied by great painted betrothal chests of clothes, linens, and silks, as well as caskets of nuptial jewels themselves. The vanity of the mirror, like the woman, is set about with a sumptuous display of fabrics – velvets, lace, silk – with exquisite applique needlework as well as pearls, precious stones, and gold.

The richly decorative mirror at the centre of the venereal toilet became both the possession and the emblematic sign of female beauty, and the envy of poets in its captivation of their beloved. This is exquisitely rendered in Jan Gossart's *Toilet of Venus* for Philip IV of Burgundy, a cabinet painting on panel for this Valois Duke's collection of mythological works, or possibly a courtly gift. Depicting a female nude in the pose of the Cnidia, she contemplates her reflection in a gilt-framed tondo mirror (Fig. 136).[64] Both the Venus and the mirror are richly jewelled in crystal, pearl, and gold ornament, so complementing the polished marbling of her form and the gold-flecked tendrils of her softly curling hair. At her feet, a vase of gilt-chased classicising ornament holds a flowering carnation as the emblem of profane love, paired with a decorated helmet *all'antica* as the sign of martial triumph here amorously 'disarmed', while Cupid's winged quiver, arrow, and bow declare his victory. Philip's patronage of armoury was as renowned as that of painting, and his court feted equally for the arts of war and love, as well as a newly renascent classicist humanism; hence Gossart's panel compliments his patron's conquests in arms, antiquity, and *amour* alike. The gleaming metallic surfaces are foils to the sheen of her body, as are the jewels that frame her face.

In this *paragone* of painted pleasures, Venus looks into a mirror that she holds in her hand, its roundel form surmounted by a cluster of jewels as if in imitation of her dressed hair. A looped silk ribbon suggests the mirror might also hang at her dressing table, or from her marriage garter, as a trophy of her nuptial toilet, which the painting surely represents. It is an invitation to the love of art, in the Cnidian figure of Venus and her mirror. Girthed by a gilt-metal framing band apparently bearing an ornamental inscription, the mirror's frame intimates the painted text of the frame in other works such as Gossart's 1521 *Venus and Cupid* (Royal Museums of Fine Arts of Belgium, Brussels). Spoken as if in the voice of Venus on her surrender to love, the work and its frame were seemingly displayed in Philip's *studiolo* for his private delight.

In Gerard Geldenhouwer's 1529 court biography of Philip, this historian in the circle of Erasmus praised the duke's study of the ancients, particularly his patronage of *versificatores*, 'who decorated pictures . . . with poems, so that he could display each picture as both talking and silent'.[65] Paintings such as the Brussels *Venus and Cupid* were thus dressed with a double frame, of which the outer border, ornamented by inscriptions, could also be removed so that the image might indeed be both 'talking and silent', according to its changing display within courtly Renaissance cultures of humanist eloquence.[66] As this is so, the seeming letters that border the mirror of Gossart's venereal toilet may also

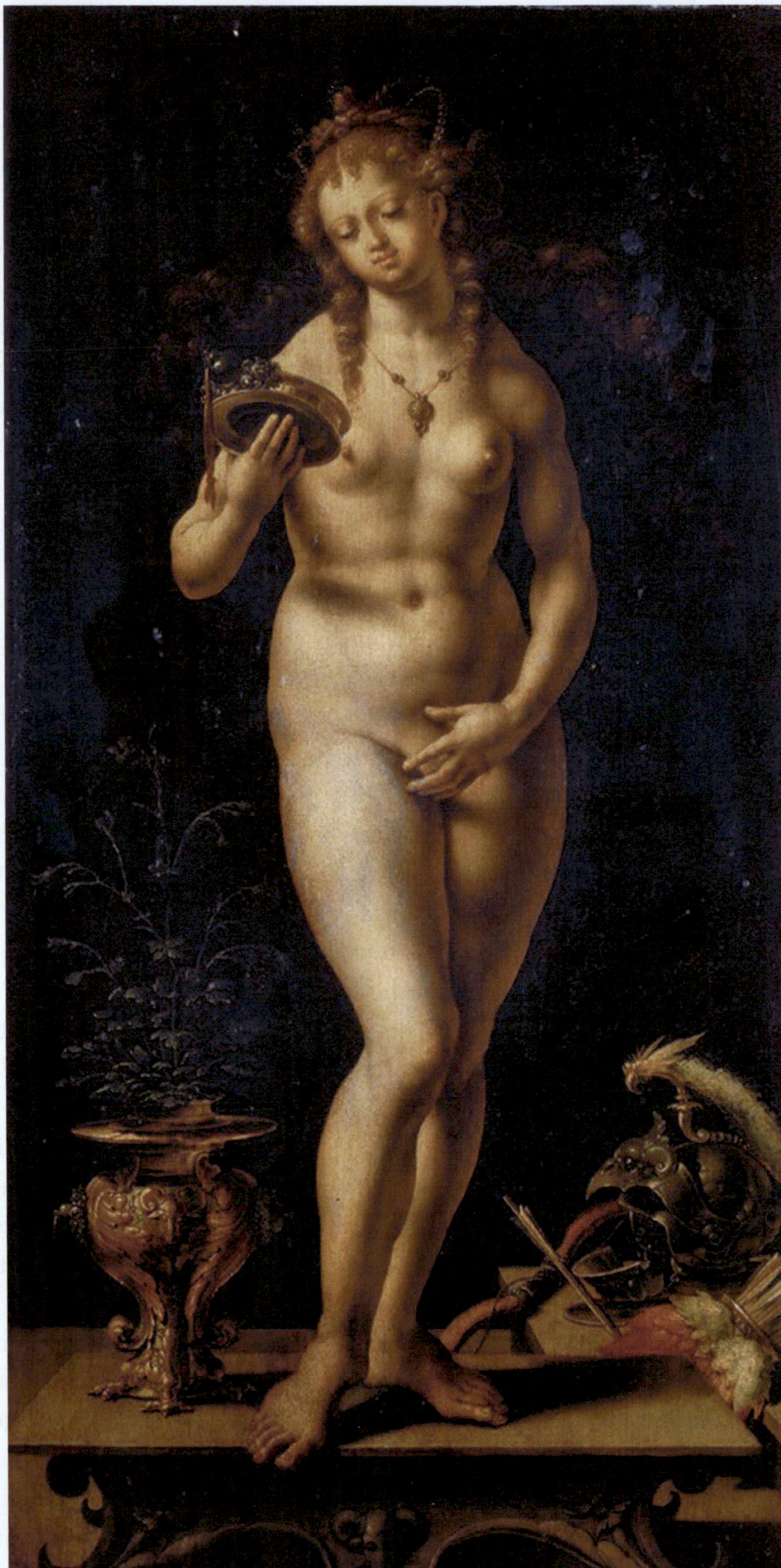

Fig. 136 Jan Gossart, *Toilet of Venus*, c. 1521, oil on panel, 59 × 30 cm, Pinacoteca dell'Accademia dei Concordi Rovigo.
Photo: Artstor/Scala Images

intimate the mirror-image of art as a 'speaking picture', in homage to the goddess whose reflected image it represents.

At the Valois court of François I, too, the female toilet and its exquisite accoutrements were particularly celebrated by the Pléiade poets in the circle of Pierre de Ronsard, writing in Petrarchan vein. Envying even as they admired, the poets longed to rival their lady's instruments of beauty – her comb, her jewels, her mirror, her *'heureux joyaux'* – for admission into her intimacy. The mirror was adulated above all for its ability to capture the image of their beloved. In Petrarch's 'il mio adversario' the mirror is his rival in love, while poets such as François Bérenger de la Tour also addressed their verse to their mistress' *'heureux miroire'*. But however bright, the poetic conceit parried, a mirror could only cede its light to the lady herself.[67] The refined pleasures of the courtly bath as one of a poetic elision of female beauty with the gorgeous objects of her toilet was particularly cultivated at Fontainebleau. In one of its most renowned if anonymous paintings is depicted the venereal nuptial bath as one of every conceivable luxury (Fig. 137).[68] Its rich material lustre is ornament to her beautifully marbled form. The iridescent pearls that adorn the hair are ready metaphors for the soft glow of the nude body, like the sumptuous sheen of the draped velvet behind that frames her. Gold ornament *all'antica*

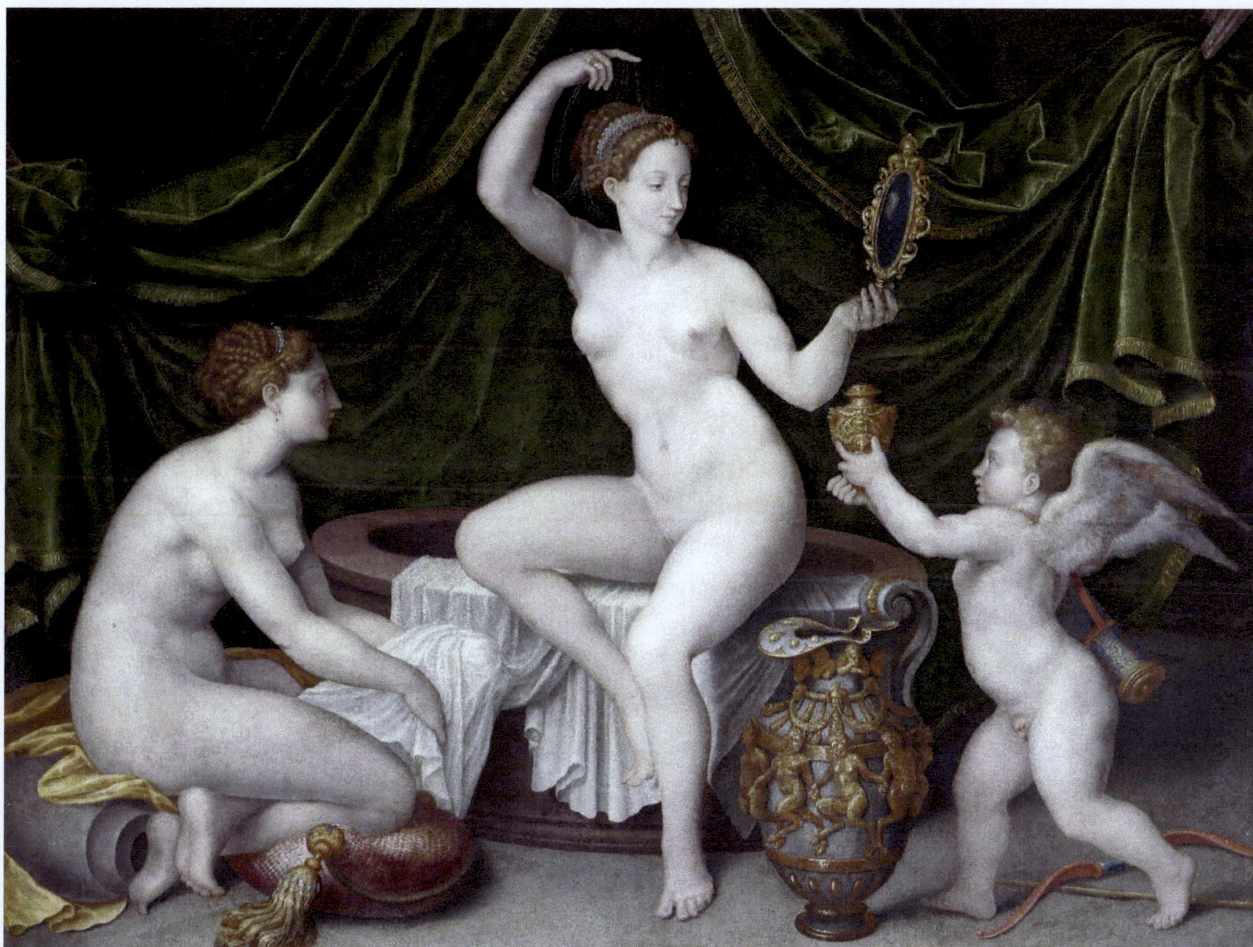

Fig. 137 Anonymous, *Venus at the Toilet*, second quarter of the sixteenth century, oil on canvas, 97 × 126 cm, Musée du Louvre, Paris.
Photo: Musée du Louvre

embellishes the beauty of this courtly Venus throughout the work: the setting of the ruby jewel at her forehead, the delicate scent bottle her cupid proffers, gold-thread silk textiles and tassels, the rose marble bath, the elaborately embellished water vase at her feet, and the decorated mirror frame she holds up before her face as she arranges a diaphanous veil across her hair. Here the mirror reflection withholds what it seems to disclose, for its shimmering surface offers only the gleam of a light reflection across her face, like a luminescent 'veil', as if in witty pictorial reply to the poets' claims.

The cultural mores of the French court produced a plethora of such nuptial painting in imitation of the artists of the king, and in celebration of royal *amour*. Many of these compositions are broadly typological, recurring in series of the same imagery by a wide variety of hands in emulation of renowned works. Their representation of the courtly arts of love, in many instances based on now-lost prototypes by the most celebrated royal painters, was a measure of their broader cultural diffusion in homage to the king.[69] Hence courtiers styled their own betrothal and nuptial gifts in the image of royalty, the mythological loves of the gods lightly infused by those of the king. In the Venetian manner of the *Venus of Urbino*, such works often depict a further scene-behind-the-scene in the background. They are thus a double- or diptych-image of the lady as both Venus of beauty in the foreground and mistress of her domain at the back. The domestication of the feminine realm of the background generally centres on representations of nuptial luxury goods. Painted marriage chests, or *cassoni*, housed valuable textiles pertaining to dowry gifts of betrothal, matrimony, and *amour*, often of trousseaux, dress, and bridalwear. These elaborations of a feminine domesticity were also within the domain of Venus as the patron of marriage. In this regard these paintings surely display a composite social genre: part myth, part painted poetry, part mythologised portrait, part pictorial invocation of marriage and its dynastic gifts. Like the Arnolfini portrait and its putative cover of a bathing Venus, this imagery conjoins marital with venereal beauty.

An example in emulation of the Dresden Venus displays, in the foreground, a recumbent female nude on an exquisite textile bed of embroidered flowers. Surely in imitation of a *mille-fleur* tapestry or a flowered nuptial bower as the poets proclaimed, behind her a lady-in-waiting stitches a sampler as the pastime of a feminine nobility (*Vénus endormie*, Musée des Beaux-Arts, Strasbourg).[70] Her seated figure is flanked by a great Renaissance fireplace of carved stone putti *all'antica*, the ready emblem of familial heraldry as well as the fires of love. Between lies a wall-mounted mirror within a gilt-wood carved frame. Though it too bears no reflection, its significance is surely that of love's alliance, for a winged cupid adorns the base while the top is framed by a male portrait head, as a further manifestation of the ornaments of love. In other examples in imitation of French courtly mores, the mirror reflection of Venus instead offers her nude figure again in a miniated double of herself, while the background scene elaborates other aristocratic pastimes, such as the figure of a beautifully dressed young woman on horseback set in a verdant landscape (*Vénus au miroir*, Musée des Ursulines, Mâcon).[71] This female nude ornamented with pearls similarly tends to a diaphanous train of cloth that suggests her nuptial 'unveiling'. She is further set within the luxury toiletries displayed beside her and the sumptuous gold-edged drapery to offset her pearlized skin, as the 'first jewel among jewels' of her bridal bed.

Other works in imitation of the French court similarly present the subject of female beauty through a poetics of objects, veiled metaphors, and mirror reflections. In a series of mythologised paintings apparently after a lost work by the royal painter François Clouet of Diane de

Poitiers, as official mistress to Henri II, the female nude is celebrated as the goddess Diana both for her waxing beauty, like the moon, and for the chastity of her exclusive relations with her king. In some variations of this courtly image, a woman in noble dress in the background kneels at a trousseau chest, surely a recollection both of the *Venus of Urbino* and of the social rituals of a lady-in-waiting who attends to her mistress' robing.[72] In other works these 'mirroring' background figures are engaged in needlework, as the noble pastime of queens and a further metaphor of the picture's making.

Throughout such 'Diane/Diana' painted variations in homage to the goddess as namesake to the royal consort Diane de Poitiers, there is abundant use of transparent textile veils, both to cover and to reveal the female body in a poetic play of refined amorous pleasures that are alternately given and deferred (among several versions are those now at Musée des Beaux-Arts de Dijon and at Worcester Art Museum).[73] Shot with gold thread, these fabrics echo the rich ornament of her hair and throat, as well as the casket of jewels she fingers. Strewn flowers further adorn her beauty while hinting at its transience, like the painted *poesie* of lustre and gleam. At the dressing table of her cabinet, the reflected image of this apparent Diana's face in the mirror before her is like the jewels that surround her and the mirror's echoing frame. Her face is doubled, though elliptically, in the flat glass of this elaborately decorated pedestal mirror beside her which stands on *all'antica* nudes figured in gold, as the cultivated emblem of her regal toilet. Her fleeting mirror-image, stilled by the artist's act of painting, becomes the very picture of her poetic 'captivation' for the art-lover's delight.

Such jewelled mirrors as those pictured for the venereal toilet of queens were rare court possessions of the highest rank. Princely inventories of crown jewels across the Renaissance detail their form and fabrication. Of silvered crystal framed in gold and further ornamented with ivory, sapphires, rubies, and pearls, they possessed the same status as dynastic jewellery. Again, their design might be typologically diffused throughout the ranks of courtiers for their imitation, as gifts to their brides in emulation of royalty. Renaissance mirrors of any size or configuration were, in themselves, highly valuable objects, as their inventoried descriptions exemplify, and redolent symbols of family estate. Jewelled mirrors, in particular, were princely gifts of exquisite luxury. Among the most valued possessions of Princess Isabelle of France and Queen of England were gold mirrors decorated with pearl and precious stones given to her by the Count Mareschal Godfrey d'Estrades, and another in the form of a marguerite flower. François I commissioned mirrors of rock crystal or Venetian *cristallo* glass from his royal jewellers, decorated with precious stones and framed in ebony or gold to be used as gifts; while Henri IV's minister, Maximilien de Béthune the Duke of Sully, recounted in his *Mémoires* a gift to Elizabeth I of a Venetian mirror encased in a gold cover encrusted with diamonds. A mirror of silvered crystal given to Henriette of Savoy the Duchess of Mayenne in 1579 stood on a silver pedestal ornamented with figures of nymphs and satyrs around an inset rock crystal figured as a poetic emblem of the moon's crystalline light. At the marriage of Marie de Médicis to Henri IV the banquet decorations apparently comprised table ornaments of mirrors with lapis lazuli to lend heightened brilliance to the occasion, while her bridal gifts included a princely '*miroir de toilette*' presented to her by the Republic of Venice.[74] A further looking-glass of royal inventory once thought to have belonged to Marie de Médicis may be identified with an exquisitely jewelled crystal mirror in the French royal collections set in a pedestal frame (Fig. 16, Chapter 1).[75] Of agate and sardonyx, it is bordered with a succession of large emeralds mounted in goldwork and a scrolling filigree of flowers composed of enamels, rubies, and diamonds. A frieze of cameos of the Caesars flanked by larger female heads of a lightly mythological cast may also have been veiled portraits of the queens or consorts such a mirror was intended to reflect, in a jewelled mimesis of courtly love. Similarly, the inventory of jewels of royal mistress to Henri IV, Gabrielle d'Estrées, lists 'a mirror all of gold . . . and on the inside cover a portrait of the king garnered with diamonds and rubies' as pendant to the mirror's 'portrait' of herself.[76] As Cervantes' *Don Quixote* later described, in emulation of Petrarch, such courtly mirrors were perceived as metaphors of their lady (I:33)[77] Like a mirror reflection, the poets claimed the beauty of woman was both captivating and impossible to capture, itself a mirroring 'beauteous light'.

Among the most celebrated if enigmatic paintings of the Fontainebleau School is a series linked to Clouet, apparently of Gabrielle d'Estrées as official consort to Henri IV, with her sister or her children at their bath (Fig. 138).[78] If one that eludes definitive meaning, it surely represents aristocratic cultures of the refined pleasures of the royal bath as a courtly occasion in a painted recollection of antique *nuptialia*, accompanied by the rich ornaments of a princely toilet. In the painted representation of

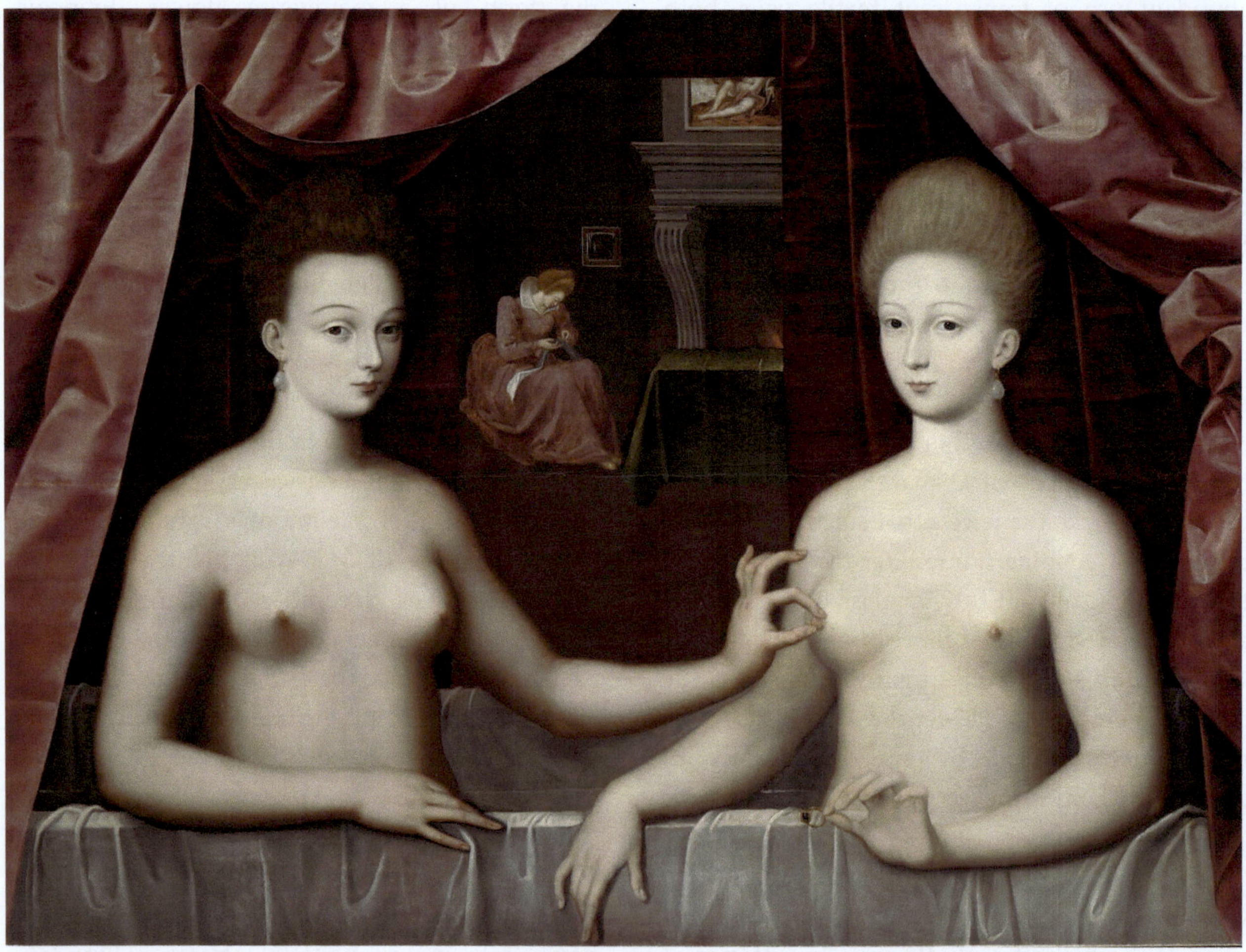

Fig. 138 School of Fontainebleau (formerly attrib. to François Clouet), *Presumed Portrait of Gabrielle d'Estrées and One of Her Sisters*, oil on wood, 96 × 125 cm, Musée du Louvre, Paris.
Photo: Musée du Louvre. Photo: Musée du Louvre

Gabrielle and her sister, the female nudes in the foreground bear only light jewellery – pearl drop earrings and a ring thought to be that of the king, which Gabrielle holds between her fingers to signify the nature of her exclusive relations. Her sister's parallel gesture to the nipple of the breast surely suggests both the poetic beauty of love's rubies or roses and the anticipation of dynastic lineage. The nacreous lustre of pearl jewels emblematises the sisters' exquisitely pearlized skin, echoed in the sheen of crimson satin drapes around them. A further scene-behind-the-scene depicts a domestic counterpoint to the venereal representation of the foreground. A small mirror in a simple square frame hangs beside her, bearing only the coloured reflections of its surrounding light. The monumental stone fireplace is surmounted by an elliptical view of a painted reclining male nude of heroic anatomy, like a mythologised representation of a kingly presence. Other versions stress the issue of Gabrielle's alliance with the king, with inset portraits of their children as ornament to her femininity, such as the painting also given to Clouet in imitation of Gabrielle in the bath with her infant offspring (National Gallery, Washington, DC). This work presents the soft sheen of her skin in a counterpoint to that of the ruddy wet-nurse and the lady in waiting behind her, set against the edge of a great stone hearth. An embroidered chair back represents a unicorn as a heraldic symbol of her exclusive relations with the king, while the framed mirror directly above is surely also an emblem of her beauty. On her left hand she displays a ring as symbol of their relations, while in her right she holds a red carnation, the emblem of their union in love.[79]

DOMESTIC ARTS

Within ennobled cultures of the female toilet also arose a great array of decorative arts tied to the nuptial grooming of brides and consorts, both at court and beyond, in emulation of royal mores. This is manifest in a multitude of decorated mirrors, where the imitation of aristocratic exemplars in luxury materials could extend across a full range of social ranks. Their conceit, elaborated in a variety of representation, is the mirror of beauty in the manner of Petrarch's sweet 'adversary'. A series of late fifteenth-century Tuscan mirror frames depicting female heads with dressed hair and jewels in imitation of a Botticellian Venus thus depict together the 'picture' of beauty alongside its specular reflection (Fig. 29, Chapter 1). Among the decorative arts of the female toilet with the mirror as its centrepiece, they were fabricated in a wealth of materials including courtly gilded marble, but also in those of a broader emulation such as maiolica and painted *papier mâché*.[80] Likely made as wedding gifts for women's trousseaux, these objects entwined the mirror reflection with both pictorial and decorative effect. For the roundel mirrors they once contained were at the same time necklace 'pendants' to the ideal beauty depicted above and looking-glasses in which their noble owners might dress their hair and don jewels in imitation of the figured form in the frame above their reflection. Texts such as the Venetian Giovanni Marinelli's *Ornamenti delle leggiadre donne* or *Ornaments for beautiful women* of 1562 were not simply manuals of recipes on the dressing of hair and the preparation of the female toilet of bathing, scents of musk and flowers, and colouring of the eyes, lips, face, and skin, but treatises on ideal beauty in practice.[81] Thus much of the decorative arts of courtship, marriage, the female toilet, and dress arose within such Renaissance cultures of the bridal Venus, of which the mirror was both the material instrument and the social metaphor.

A painted mirror dated to the 1470s in the form of a Medicean diamond ring, further ornamented by stucco reliefs of Venus crowned by cupids beside a recumbent Mars and surmounted by heraldic insignia, makes manifest the cultural ties of marriage alliance within a domesticated nuptial imagery in the realm of decorative arts.[82] Such examples of the domestic mirror of the female toilet fully elided the reflected image with the painted representation of female beauty in a tribute to the 'decorative arts' of the noble lady and the poetic canons of ideal beauty within Renaissance cultures of love and marriage. More broadly, decorative furniture and furnishings and particularly the nuptial bedchambers of the domestic interior that were commissioned as spousal wedding gifts might bear painted imagery pertaining to the mirroring pictorialisation of ideal beauty in poetry and myth, as in the venereal toilet.

Venus was, throughout antiquity, the patron goddess of marriage, her poetic presence summoned at weddings in the epithalamic verse sung before the bridal chamber. As a celebration of love, the epithalamia were an invocation of good wishes to the lasting pleasures of the marriage bed.[83] Such rituals were, throughout antiquity and in Renaissance marriage ceremony also, accompanied by the presentation of gifts for the bridal chamber that were intended both as objects of the domestic toilet – mirrors, dressing tables, toiletry items, jewel boxes, and bedroom furnishings – and as painted recollections of the matrimonial celebration of love. The mythic and poetic allusions of nuptial verse, as for the painted imagery pertaining to it, might range from easily evident domestic iconographies of female graces to highly complex veiled references to the enchanting powers of beauty as of love. The pleasures of longing and an imagery of pleasure were intertwined. This pertains to a wide range of painted panels formerly part of furnishings for the Renaissance bridal bed, trousseau chest, and dressing table c. 1500, at the cusp of the High Renaissance. In the noble home, such imagery might be painted by artists of the first rank – Botticelli, Bellini, Giorgione, even the young Titian.

Considered scholarly reconstruction by historians of early modern household architecture, painting, and the decorative arts as well as by scholars of marriage, the noble home, and family has deepened understanding of these works within the domestic interior and as part of the cultural mores of Renaissance love. Originally built into the panelling of their bedchamber settings as nuptial or bridal suites, these paintings were subsequently detached from the furnishings or interior decors for which they were originally made as the locus of princely art patronage shifted from the nuptial suite to the dedicated art collection or gallery. They were then reframed to become gallery paintings within noble collections of art. This would appear to be the case not only for such celebrated works as Botticelli's *Venus and Mars,* Giorgione's *Concert champêtre* or Titian's *Sacred and Profane Love,* all depicting the transformation of a bride into a goddess of love, but also for vast swathes of smaller painted panels (as well as other decorative arts) once part of domestic and decorative nuptial settings.[84]

Such provenance must surely include the putative cover of a bathing nude to the Arnolfini double portrait, as it was later depicted in Willem van Haecht's painting of Cornelis van der Geest's art gallery (Fig. 59, Chapter 2). Once apparently a painted panel cover to van Eyck's celebrated portrait of a marriage, this image is redolent of Renaissance nuptial imagery in its invocation of the bridal toilet. Severed from its original setting as a painted marital furnishing, the Eyckian cover became instead a framed picture in its own right within the context of the early modern art collection, as van der Geest's painted gallery represents. In this regard it encapsulates the larger history of such artworks pertaining to Renaissance marriage and the bridal chamber, as well as their subsequent transformation into gallery paintings, as Hans Belting and Victor Stoichita have argued, and art historians concerned with Renaissance decorative arts such as Anne Barriault, Peter Thornton, Jacqueline Musacchio, Marta Ajmar-Wollheim and Flora Dennis, Cristelle Baskins, and Andrea Beyer have also shown.[85]

Though depicting female beauty as a venereal nude in the realm of the royal consort or mythologised courtesan, these paintings also commonly recall within them domestic aspects of imagery pertaining to the social and familial rituals of courtship, marriage, and childbirth, so suggesting the cultural intertwining of these amorous spheres. The mirror is a particular locus of this, manifest in representations of a venereal beauty not only in mythological works but also in those pertaining to the domestics of marriage and family. As chapter 2 argued, mirror-imagery by painters such as Memling and Metsys fused representation of the Holy Family with marriage. As the emblem of a Marian devotional immaculacy and so the religious prototype of the Holy Family, the 'spotless mirror' also appears in depictions of childbirth, notably in nativities of John and Christ as the light of divine love, particularly of the Florentine and Flemish Renaissance. Such imagery of biblical childbirth transposed into the decorative interiors of the Renaissance elided the Holy Family with the social realm of motherhood. Hence the mirror motif in a domesticated Renaissance nativity scene was a constant one among artists such as Jan Rombouts and Jan de Beer, who practiced in Leuven and Antwerp, respectively, as painters on both glass and wood.

Rombouts' birth of the Baptist depicts Elizabeth's lying-in surrounded by a wealth of Renaissance domestic detail, including a maidservant who prepares a ritual meal for the newly delivered mother while other women prepare to wash the infant in a richly ornamented bathing pool. One is swathed in an abundance of jewelled red and gold silk; the other is a Marian figure draped in blue in a white veil with the child in her arms to intimate the forthcoming birth of Christ. Above this Mary's head hangs a convex blown-glass mirror in a figured frame of bronze arabesque design, which reflects a further mullioned window in the form of a cross to signify his Passion as the 'light of the world' (Fig. 139).[86] Similarly, Jan de Beer's birth of the Virgin of the same moment (c. 1520, Thyssen-Bornemisza Museum, Madrid) also depicts the biblical nativity set amid a wealth of Renaissance decorative detail of a mother's lying-in, including two ornamental mirrors above the heads of 'Mary' and the child, respectively, as ready emblems of their devotional light.[87] The specular motif also appears in de Beer's Annunciations (private collection and Thyssen-Bornemisza):[88] in one, a small convex mirror in a wrought-gilt frame hangs on the wall above a vase of lilies to signify Mary's immaculate birth; in another, the large convex jewel at the centre of the annunciate angel's morse or clasp reflects its architectural surroundings in miniature. It is surely an Eyckian recollection of the angel's morse in the Ghent altarpiece, which also reflects the architecture of the chapel for which the painting was intended (discussed in Chapter 2). Such mirroring jewels featured in betrothal and marriage portraits of the period, in which bridal gems might also reflect emblematic imagery in jewel-like reduction. In the companion portraits of Ursula Rudolph with her husband Ruprecht Stüpf, signed and dated 1528 by Barthel Beham, Ursula is depicted in a wealth of velvet brocade and jewellery, her gold chains alluding to the gentle yoke of marriage while the large jewel at the centre of her dress reflects in miniature the light of the cross as the metaphorical window of the soul (Thyssen-Bornemisza Museum).[89] The specular reflection, in the domesticated sphere of marriage and family, might touch on both venereal beauty and holy matrimony as the conjoined allegory of their devotional and social conflation.

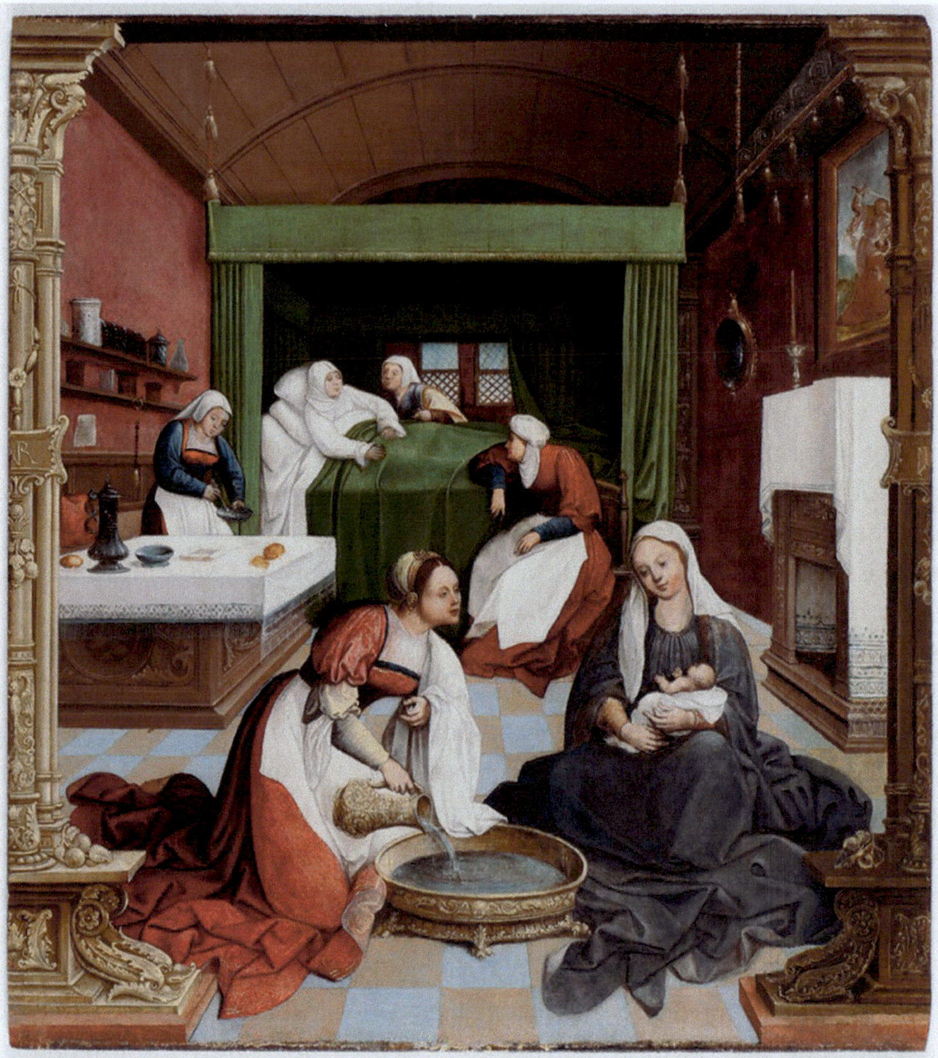

Fig. 139 Jan Rombouts the Elder, *The Birth of St John the Baptist*, c. 1515–20, oil on panel, 58.1 × 52.7 cm. Carnegie Museum of Art, Pittsburgh. Photo: Wikimedia

MARIAN MIRRORS

In the spiritual poetry of biblical epithalamia arising from the canticle of Solomon, the Book of Kings, and the *Eructavit cor meum* of the Psalms in celebration of mystical marriage, Marian devotions might configure her betrothal and motherhood in princely terms as the 'Queen of Heaven' in a further elision of faith and monarchy. The metaphor of Mary as bride and mother thus appeared as a constant in royal marital imagery, for the emulation of queens as for every estate. Works such as Juan de Flandes' diminutive panel of the *Marriage Feast at Cana* painted for Queen Isabella of Castile as part of a series on the life of Christ and Mary seem to fuse together biblical narrative and royal genealogy in the name of a Catholic Marian queenship. For this 'jewelled' work appears to comprise within it a veiled allusion to her son Prince Juan and Margaret of Austria on the occasion of their marriage in 1497, as other scholars have suggested, so manifesting the cultural intertwining of these spheres of royal marriage and Catholic faith (Fig. 140).[90] The seated couple's heads of biblical account incline towards each other,

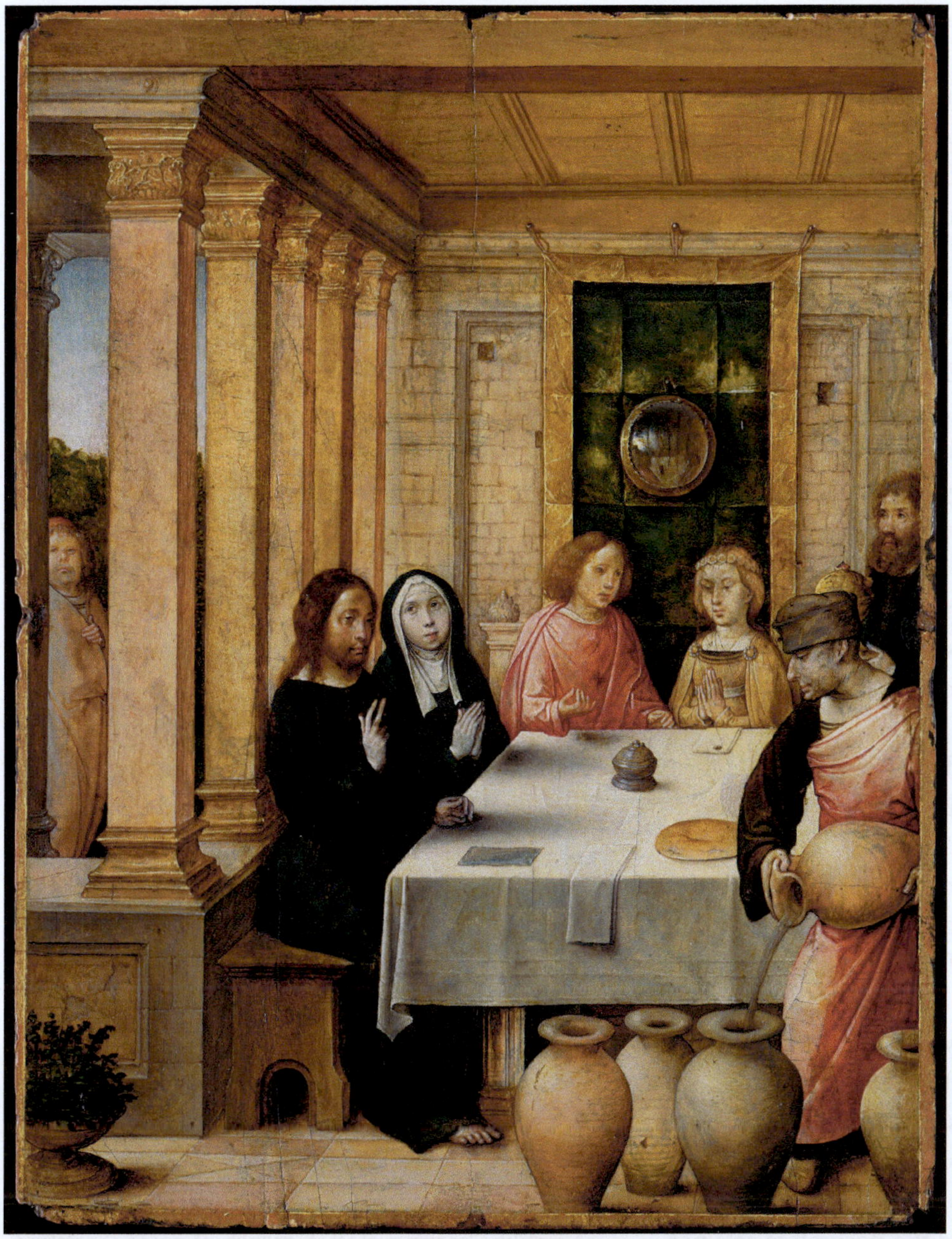

Fig. 140 Juan de Flandes, *The Marriage Feast at Cana*, c. 1500–1504, oil on wood, 21 × 15.9 cm, Metropolitan Museum of Art.
Photo: Metropolitan Museum of Art

surmounted by a small convex mirror in a gilt frame. The mirror hangs on a presentation cloth of green and gold whose folds suggest the usage of ritual occasion. The clear glass of the mirror reflects the biblical couple from behind, and the white nap of the table before them, with the mild distortion of its curved form. The bride's head is wreathed in pearl roundels that echo the mirror's shape, composed in the form of marguerite daisies like the jewelled clasps at her shoulders, to reinforce the allusion to Margaret of Austria as her namesake. Her hands are held in prayer as witness to the miracle of Christ and Mary's presence among them, and testament to the place of queenship within both spiritual and royal patronage. Another panel by Juan de Flandes similarly weaves together the regal with the biblical in a *Birth of the Baptist* (Cleveland Museum of Art) for a panelled altarpiece commissioned by Queen Isabella for the monastery of Miraflores and site of the royal tombs of Castile. Such imagery of marriage and the intimation of the royal marital bed was the pictorial province of queens and their progeny of kings to come. Like the Rombouts, the painted scene depicts the mother in the birthing bed of a fifteenth-century Flemish interior.[91] In recollection of her lineage as both biblical and royal, Elizabeth is dressed in the modesty of a white bonnet and chemise, while the lying-in bed of estate is hung with abundant green textiles. Her cousin Mary attends to her and her child, whom she presents to Zacharias the father in a confirmation of his name. Directly above Elizabeth's head hangs a convex mirror in an ornamental brass frame. Its unbroken glass that yet transmits the reflected light is clear reference to the immaculacy of Elizabeth's conception; at the same time it is a Renaissance artefact of domestic appointment, to reflect and magnify interior light, as an allusion to the coming of Christ. Within its sheen is a close mimetic depiction of a window reflection in front of the picture plane looking out onto the landscape beyond. In its detail it is also surely an inset emblem or signature of Flandes' specular art. Hence the decorative arts and family heirlooms that attended social rituals of childbirth frequently elided the representation of Renaissance domestic interiors with their lightsome mirrors, and the biblical narratives of the birth of Mary and John as of Christ.

Domestic artefacts and the decorative arts pertaining to rituals of marriage and childbirth also juxtaposed mother and child imagery with lightly Marian inferences to the holy family. Within such imagery the mirror could again reflect the realms of marital chastity, as well as the decorative appointment of the domestic interior to lend Christian light to the home. Birthing trays and maiolica-ware pertaining to the social occasions of gifting mothers and their new-born children commonly depicted such scenes of women 'lying in' configured in a Marian vein. Maidservants attend the new mother to bathe and swaddle the child and to serve food to her and her guests, in the manner of a domesticated nativity scene.[92] Within, depicted mirrors as decorative objects of the birthing chamber interior connoted the celebration of childbirth within marriage, as emblems of happy conjugal relations in a domesticated femininity.[93]

Hence the pictorialisation of a venereal beauty within both matrimonial and nativity scenes carried a full array of associations pertaining to the social rituals of marriage and childbirth. The sway of the venereal realm is represented in the young Titian's oeuvre, from the *belle donne* of the nuptial toilet to the epithalamic bride of his 1533 *Conjugal Love* (Fig. 141). Seemingly a marriage gift for Alphonso d'Avalos Marquis of Vasto, of Spanish Neapolitan descent in the retinue of Charles V, to Maria d'Aragona, granddaughter to King Ferdinand I of Naples and childhood friend of Vittoria Colonna, it represents the coupling of marriage through the figures of Mars and Venus. He stands in armour with his hand to her breast, while she is depicted in modesty with downcast eyes, holding a glass sphere as an attribute of marital union, suffused with Marian inference to the unspotted mirror of the Holy Family as well as cosmic mythological allegories of the sun's light and the waxing moon. They are accompanied by personifications of love, marriage, and childbirth: the infant cupid, the figure of Hymenaeus as the god of marriage song for the procession of the bride, and the figure of fertility bearing aloft a casket of roses. Swathed in draperies of shimmering silk and gold-shot gauze, this Venus' hair is dressed in the manner of beauty's prescriptions, braided through with pearls. Together the painting's attributes speak to the arts of love as to those of art itself. The reflections in the glassy sphere, which have been read as the figure of the artist as he paints, may be interpreted as allegories of art's figurative conception, in a further metaphor of human fecundity. In the play of reflections, in the sphere of Venus' mirror as of Alphonso's armour, Titian also surely recalls Giorgione's lost *paragone* painting of specular

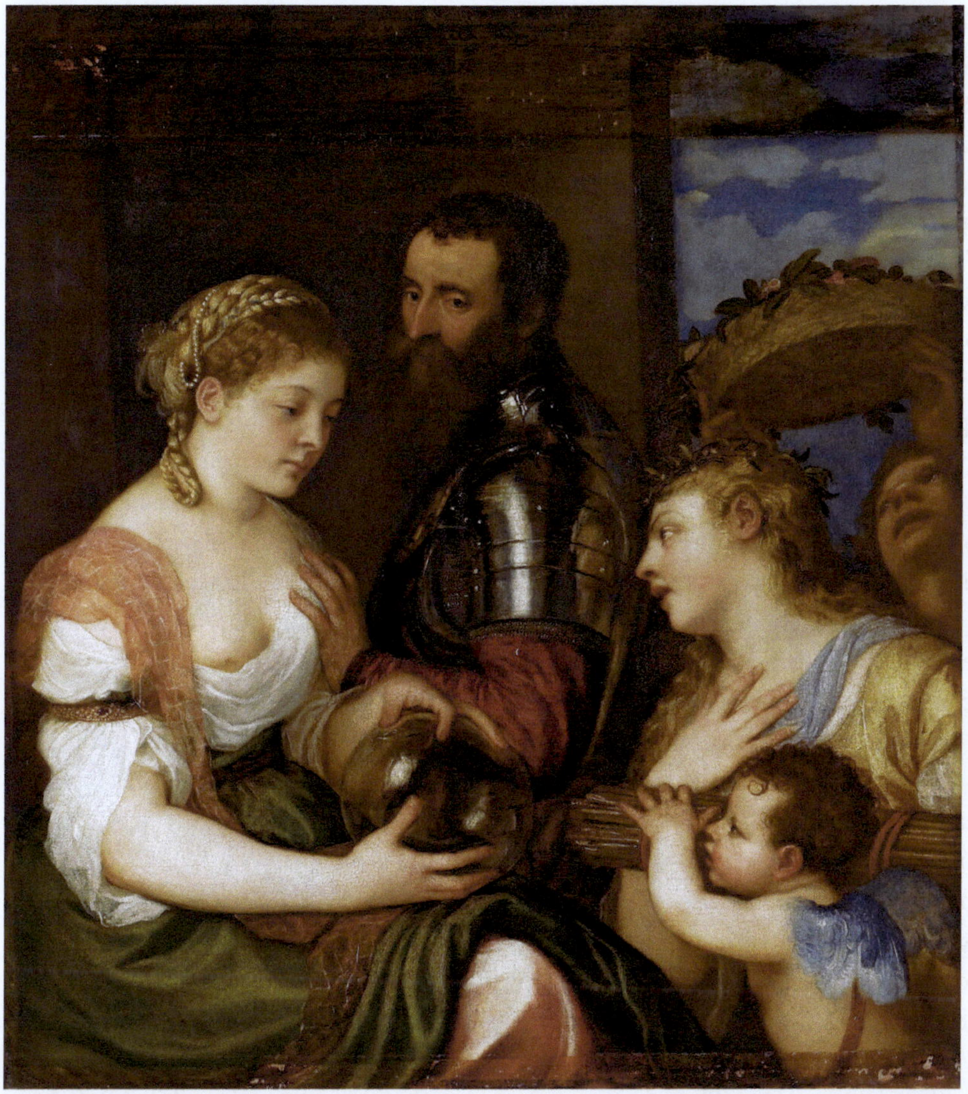

Fig. 141 Titian, *Allegory of Marriage*, c. 1530, oil on canvas, 123 × 107 cm, Musée du Louvre, Paris. Photo: Musée du Louvre

reflection as both male and female, martial and venereal, in a fully pictorial theorisation of art, like love, as a mirror-image of itself.[94]

VANITAS

Among Titian's most celebrated works for the Habsburg king Philip II of Spain, he undertook a series of mythological paintings of the female nude that also claimed for painting the mirroring pool of Venus. Terming them *poesie* in a full *paragone* of painting with poetry in the Venetian manner elaborated by Giorgione, these works turned on mirror-like depictions of the female nude.[95] In a much-cited letter to Philip II, the artist explained his mirroring theme of specular antithesis as a meditated figural variation:

> Since the *Danaë* that was sent to Your Majesty was seen from the front, in this other *poesia* [*Venus and Adonis*] I wanted to vary and show the figure from the opposite side so that the small chamber [*camerino*] where they are to be placed will be more beautiful.[96]

In this letter Titian brought the many threads of the *paragone* debate to bear – ancients and moderns, painting and sculpture, art and literature. By terming these works *poesie* he acknowledged his understanding of painting as a 'mute poetry' charged with the *ekphrases* of the ancient writers such as Philostratus. Together the paired paintings for Spain afforded the binary viewing points of Lucian's *Cnidia*, from the front and from the rear. The other three paintings in the *poesie* series for Philip II – *Diana and Actaeon, Diana and Callisto*, and the *Rape of Europa* – also make eloquent use of a pictorial poetics of variation, through a counterpoint of figured female forms. Thus the paired Diana paintings of the goddess and her nymphs bathing depict the female nude from a multiplicity of viewpoints, dressed with pearls and set against rich velvets and brocades, in a further polyphony of *colorito*. As Mathias Wivel has recently argued, the Diana paintings are themselves a *poesia* of variation, in which their 'collection' of bathing nymphs as emblems of different female beauties may be read as further pictorial couplings for a royal *camerino*. In a pair, the framing figures of Actaeon, on the left, and Diana, on the right, serve as the *varia* of an antithesis for the pictorial presentation of the male and female form. This is further heightened by the painted *paragone* of Diana's ivoried skin beside that of her ebony-hued attendant. The principle of *paragone* as variation then ripples out across the paired paintings like a sequence of mirror reflections in the figures of the nymphs – reclining, crouching, bending, kneeling, pictured from front and back, they are so many *varia* of Titian's art.[97] The Venetian art critic and Titian's friend, Ludovico Dolce, further described Titian's *poesia* Venus depicted from the back as a painted recollection of Praxiteles' *Cnidia*, by soliciting the viewer to imagine the view of the front that the painting itself withholds: 'not for lack of art . . . but to display a doubled art'.[98] Within the intimate and exquisite luxury of Philip's anticipated *camerino*, the paintings must have seemed an art-historical fount of juxtaposed 'mirror reflections'. Together they figured the loveliness of the female form in pictorial tribute to ancient marbles and their poets, like Alberti's poetic definition of art in the mirror-image of Ovid's pool.[99]

In a closing letter-memorandum of 1574 on his work for Philip II, including the *poesie* paintings, the artist recalled the series as a whole as well as the individual pieces within it. As a further recollection of the ancient sea-borne Venus type at the shores of Cnidos, Titian described the Diana painting as 'Actaeon stumbles upon the bath'.[100] The shared theme of bathing that reaches across the two canvases was underscored by the Spanish painter and art historian Francisco Pacheco. In his *Arte de la pintura* of 1649 Pacheco described Rubens' subsequent imitations of the Venetian painter as 'all the things by Titian that belong to the king, [including] the two baths'.[101] They are elsewhere referred to as 'Diana's fountain', to suggest the water reflections as the very source of painting's art.

Manifestly, the Diana *poesie* were conceptualized as painted mirror reflections of Venus statuary captured in pooled water, to claim the palm for painting in a *paragone* of the arts. The figures are framed by *all'antica* sculptural ornament, but also the shimmering luministic effects of reflected sky and water as pictorial qualities beyond the reach of sculpture's art. A small mirror, alongside an elaborate glass vessel, sits beside the young nymph at Actaeon's feet, like a miniature inset painting of Titian's skill (Fig. 142). On the one hand, it is in part a harbinger of Actaeon's fate, for he will be transformed into a stag by the wrathful Diana as which he will then recognize himself in the reflection of a woodland pool. On the other hand, it is Titian's emblem of his venereal art, born of the watery reflections of the Cnidian form. For the small inset mirror reflects the girl's ultramarine blue drapery, recognizable in the sweeping strokes of Titian's brush as the hallmark of his

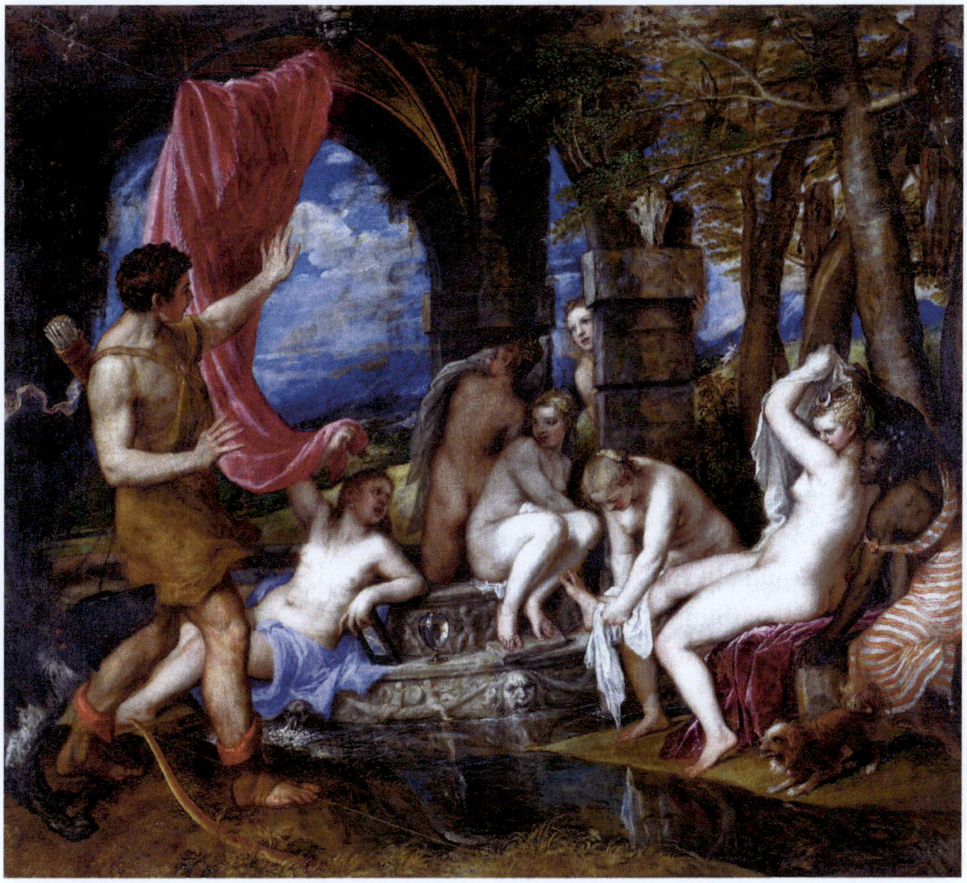

Fig. 142 Titian, *Diana and Actaeon*, 1556–59, oil on canvas, 184.5 × 202.2 cm, National Gallery, London. Photo: Wikimedia

painterly style like a painted signature of the 'art' of his art. As Titian's friend the Venetian critic Pietro Aretino described, the liquid ripples and ribbons of colour rendered by the mottled impasto and veiling glazes of Titian's brush depicted the atmospheric effects of nature, as if reflected in Alberti's mirroring pool of poetic myth.[102]

Within this imagery, as inherent to the myths related by it, are pictorial declarations of female beauty and love's pleasures, to be sure, but also portents of its fleeting transience and poignant loss. Actaeon and Adonis will meet savage deaths at the hunt as a consequence of their visual and amorous pleasures with Diana and Venus; while Callisto, Danäe, and Europa will be destroyed in the thrall of Jupiter. Like accounts of Narcissus as a statue gazing into a pool at his own reflection, the ancient cult of the Cnidian Venus was heralded as the manifestation of spring and rebirth, but also of myth touched by death. Just as Narcissus reached out to embrace his love of the painted image on the surface of the mirroring pool, so young men who came to worship at the shrine of the Cnidian Venus apparently threw themselves into the sea below, as the legendary source of her beauty.[103] To seek to 'capture' the semblance of art's mirroring but illusory allure was a metaphor of life's flowered passing. It further touched on the myriad classical and Christian philosophies of *vanitas*. The metamorphic nature of love, like the fleeting transience of youth and beauty, as Ovid had told, was swift and changeful. Like the passing of spring, the flowers of an ardent passion might transform Helen's Trojan beauty into the marbled lustre of stone; thus the imagery of Renaissance love was shot through with the presentiment of loss. It was a theme to which the poets insistently returned, in celebrating both the delights and pleasures of love but also its shimmering transience, like the flower that Narcissus became, the passing gloss of reflected light on water, or the fleeting image of the looking-glass. The mirror reflection, as captivating as it is ephemeral, at once fully mimetic and impalpably absent, was a ready metaphor for the swift metamorphoses of desire. So too the mirror as object, whether of metal or glass, was conceived as both ardent and glacial in its poetic conception. Forged in fire, its cooling metamorphosis from molten liquid to icy stillness was apt emblem of the classical marbling of the poetic passions of eros wrought by the passage of time.

In the watery pools of Titian's *poesie* are a further array of painted inset-reflections on his art. Just as Actaeon, like the viewer, seems to draw back the Parrhasian curtain to disclose the nude Diana at her bath, her loveliness elaborated in an ornament of velvet and pearls, so the waters below reflect the object-landscape of Titian's painting. In an art-historical recollection of the Cnidian Venus, as also reflected in the royal nuptial toilet, Titian's 'mirror' is an elliptical one. Fragments of sculpture and drapery, as of bodies, float across the shadowy depths of the water like so many painted echoes of Titian's brushwork. At the centre stands a small glass vase reflected in the water below. Its curving form is surely a pictorial metaphor of the female figure, venereal in its reference to bathing and lightly Marian in its unbroken specular reflection of Diana's chastity. Its brightly coloured, reflected highlights, further echoed in the water below, are also a ready emblem of the painter's mimetic means. Above Diana's regal hand gesturing to Callisto, a brilliant spray of tumbling water issues from the sculptural fountain of a Cupid vase into the shadowy pool below. Equally, Titian's Europa is carried out to open sea in a further pictorialisation of mythological love. Here the variegated colouring of the sea swell is marked by cresting ripples of highlight around her. Set against the vast reflection of the heavens above, the ocean and the sky are as shifting and changeable as Jupiter's desire.

The metaphor of venereal bathing embodied in the pictorial representation of the female nude was also that of Ovid's pool. In a classical theology of myth, water marked the passage to the underworld, whether the pool of Narcissus or the rivers of Lethe and Styx. In the poetic imaginary of ancient burial practices, the underworld was conceived as 'sleep' and so of dreams, the source of myth. The shadowy reflections on the surface of the water's pool were within the domain of Psyche, whose god-like lover of Amor came to her only in her sleep. If the reflection of Venus in the realm of art was that of a quest for perfect beauty, it was also haunted by the intimation of love's loss, and the swiftly poignant passage of desire as of youth. Like poetic accounts of Narcissus as a statue gazing into a pool at his own reflection, the ancient cult of the Cnidian Venus was heralded as the manifestation of spring and rebirth, but also of myth touched by death. To seek to 'capture' the illusion of art's mirroring but illusory beauty was a metaphor of life's passing. Hence the cultural sign of the venereal mirror was a deeply bivalent one, suffused by the pleasures and ruses of love, beauty, and transience, of heart's ache and heart's ease. Its Renaissance representations in art, as in poetry, were richly faceted, though consistently figured within cultural canons of female beauty as the mirror reflection of art itself.

In Alberti's retelling of the story of Narcissus as a paradigm of art's *storia*, its closure of immortal 'death' as the origins of art is of a poetic indeterminacy. In the great sixteenth-century debate over literary genres inaugurated by Ariosto, such mythical reference might be both 'tragical and pastoral' in Shakespeare's words, of a classicism tinged with longing and a refined wit as varied and mutable as love itself.[104] Ovid's mirroring pool as the fount of art, like Echo's poetic cry, became the *vanitas* of love's fleeting pleasure marked in the brief presence of a flower. As the Introduction of this book adumbrates, the first theory of art, Alberti's, was founded – *ad fontes* – in the Ovidian pool of the Narcissus myth. Like Narcissus' love of a fleeting reflection, the swift passing of youth and desire is, however, stilled and immortalized in the marbling power of Titian's mimetic art.

***

A range of Old Testament subjects also led painters to reflect on the bivalent pleasure and poignancy of a star-crossed beauty, as fleeting as time, as ephemeral as a mirror reflection, in figurations of the venereal bath, particularly the stories of Susannah and Bathsheba. Tintoretto's *Susannah and the Elders* (Fig. 143), for example, paints a plethora of pictorial pleasures, of luministic effect and their transience as a metaphor of youth and beauty. The gentle modulations of light across the soft sheen of her marbled skin are offset by an ornament of pearls and white silk, a silver scent bottle, and the play of reflection in the pool of water at her feet. She gazes into a

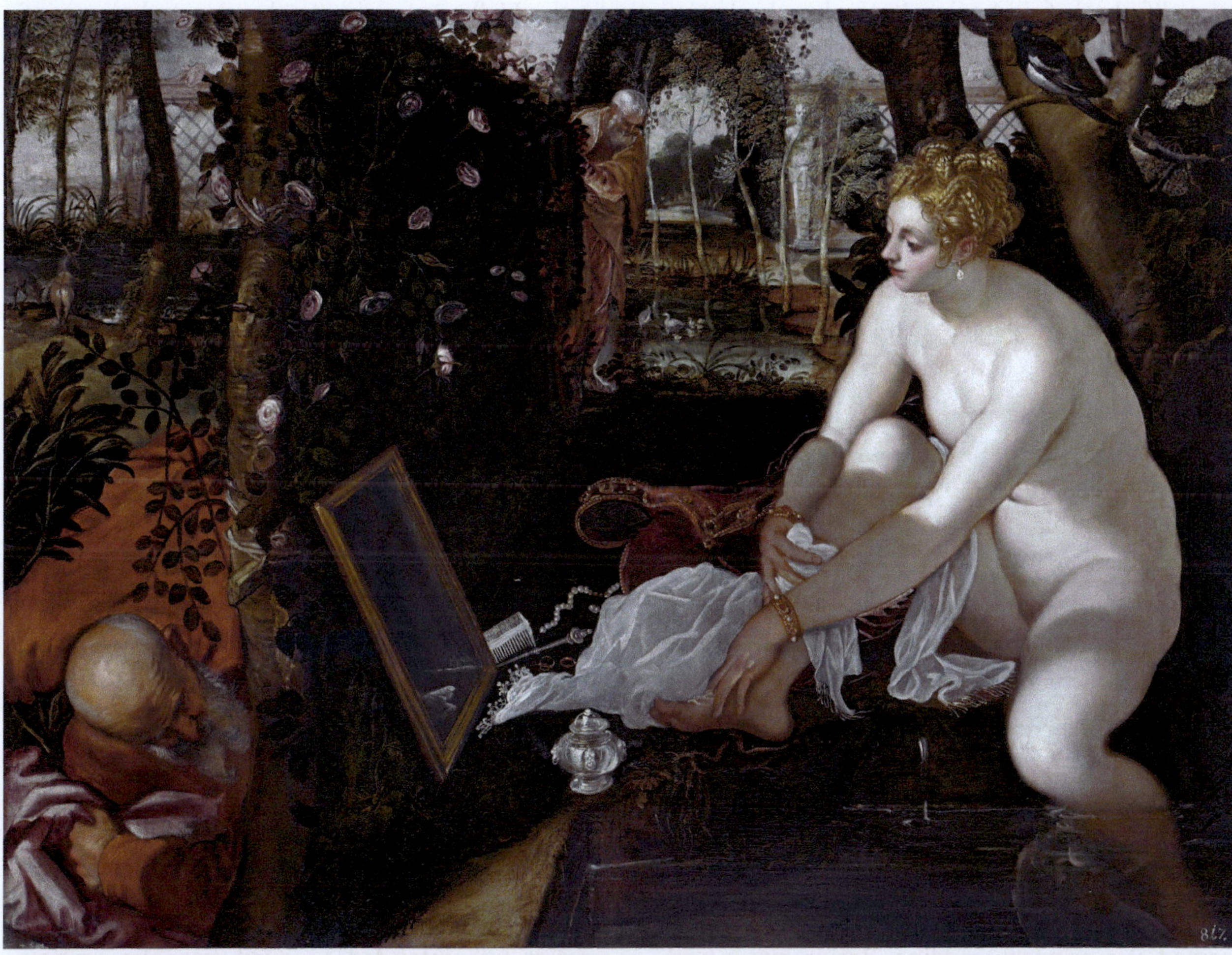

Fig. 143 Jacopo Robusti (Tintoretto), *Susannah and the Elders*, 1555–56, oil on canvas, 146 × 193 cm, Kunsthistorisches Museum, Vienna.
Photo: Wikimedia

looking-glass propped against a rose trellis as the flower of love's passion; like the empty mirror reflection she is innocent, as yet unaware of the portentous figures just behind.[105] If the composition recalls the poetics and ornaments of a nuptial bath, yet she is also a Callisto, captured in the mirror of innocence and desire.

The story of Bathsheba similarly elicited pictorial representation of a beauty fraught with turbulence. Both were stories of married women desired by others, and of divine punishment. Yet both also figured in the epithalamic festivities of princely Renaissance marriages, howsoever lightly turned. In verse, in performed entertainments, and in painted and decorative arts pertaining to marriage, these stories were used to exemplify both female chastity and male desire, as well as the pleasures of the marital bed. In the case of Bathsheba, King David's desire for her led him to seek her husband's death in battle, which resulted in the loss of their first-born child, though it would be followed by the redemptive birth of Solomon. In a pictorial version by Jan Metsys, it is the visual pleasures of her beauty, however, that the painter extolls as the demonstration of his art. The loveliness of Bathsheba's face and breasts is offset by pearls and shimmering cream silks edged with gold (Fig. 144). He painted this subject more than once, of which the 1562 painting (Louvre Museum) is like a courtly marriage proposal. The gold chain about her neck surely suggests the gilded yoke of her amorous royal alliance. Her right hand holds the sponge with which she bathes herself, recalling a venereal nuptial toilet as well as the Magdalen's washing of Christ, while her left bears a small mirror that we see only from the back. Directly behind stands David on a balcony, resembling those theatre stage sets for stories of love in the manner of Romeo and Juliet that might be performed at a princely wedding. Beside him a bird recalls bridal song. He gazes onto her bathing form, which Bathsheba has surely seen in her mirror reflection. Her visual address, however, is towards us, in witty acknowledgement of what she sees in the mirror with the presentiment of her destiny, but also in a pictorial elision of the viewer with the king, who views her nude beauty. Above her are two miniature figures in sculpted grisaille: a soldier as *memento mori* of her husband's fate, and Moses holding the tablets of God's law to recall the commandments that David will break, as the cautionary terms of marital epithalamia often also lightly recalled. Yet the pictorial allusions of the painting are overwhelmingly those of love's delight in the 'conquest' of beauty, as the manifestation of David's valour in arms of which Bathsheba will be the Hellenic trophy. In the visual pleasures of paint's mimesis, we as viewers are poetically implicated, also caught in the spell of her bathing beauty.[106]

Other painted mirror imagery of the anguish and pleasures of love turns to the apparent snares of its enchantments, as in the fifteenth-century German so-called Niederrheinischer Master's *Love Spell* (Fig. 145), or the perilous enchantments of passion. Intimating the force of love as one of Shakespearean 'sorcery' such as Desdemona's for Othello (Act 1, scene 3), the panel casts its spell upon us.[107] The young woman at her nuptial toilet, nude but for a diaphanous veil and fine leather slippers, tends to a heart she has placed in a jewel casket. Alternately kindling the flames of love and quenching them with drops of water, she conjures what is seemingly a sequence of incantations over this captive heart, whose sorcery apparently summons the young man at the door behind. The painted banderoles have remained blank; though we have no details of the panel's history of ownership or audience, this may suggest it was intended to elicit bespoke written response on the part of its owner, perhaps as an

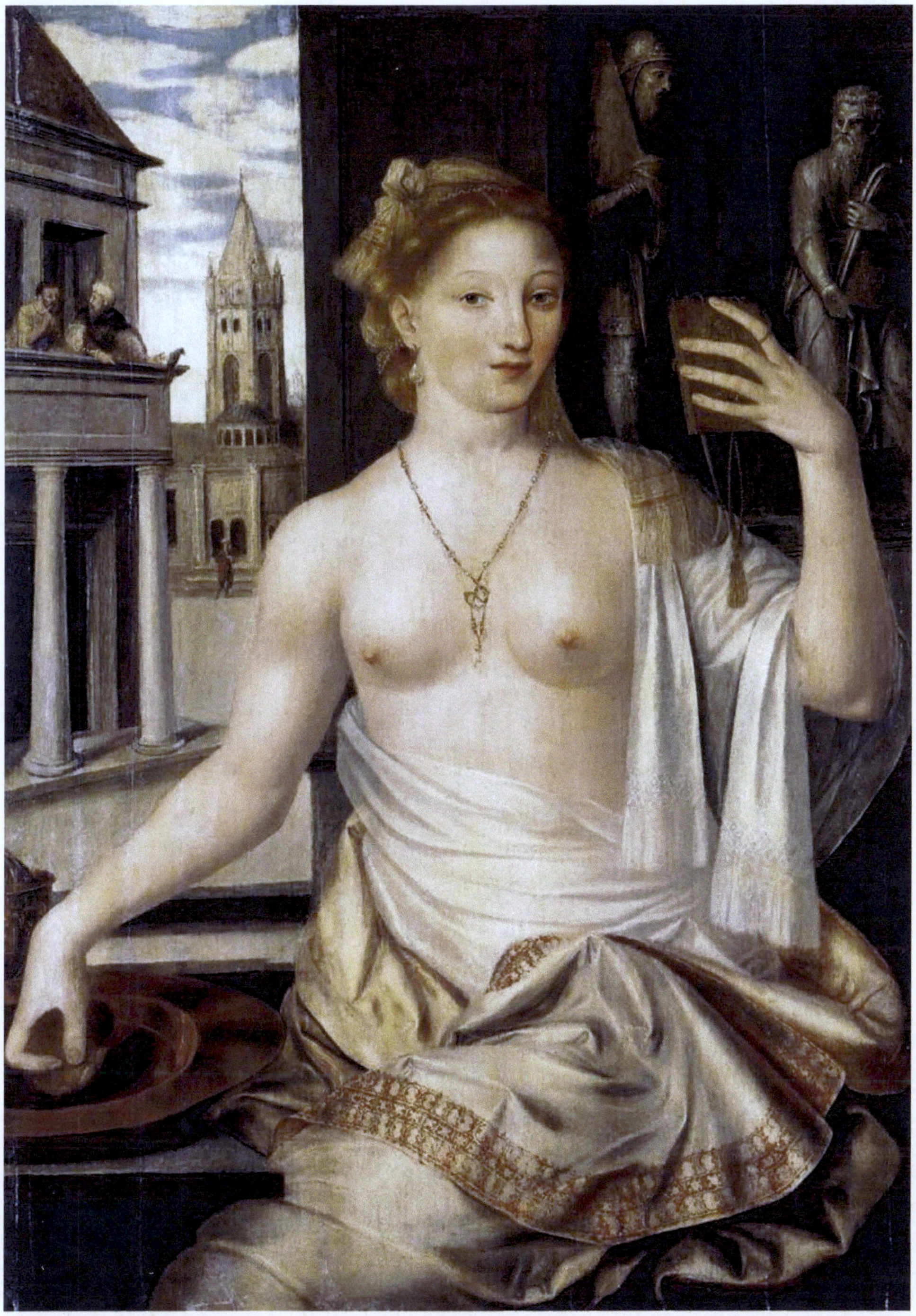

Fig. 144 Jan Metsys, *David and Bathsheba,* sixteenth century, oil on panel, 110 × 76 cm, private collection. Photo: Wikimedia

exchange of epithets on the perilous enchantments of love of a painted kind like Gossart's double-framed Venus inscription. The richly appointed paneled room is replete with emblems of love and desire: flowers, birds, the small dog at her feet, a range of domestic objects in lustrous precious metals, a fan of peacock feathers, and the small jewel-like, gold-framed convex mirror that hangs between the window frames, which must surely reflect her from the side. Michael

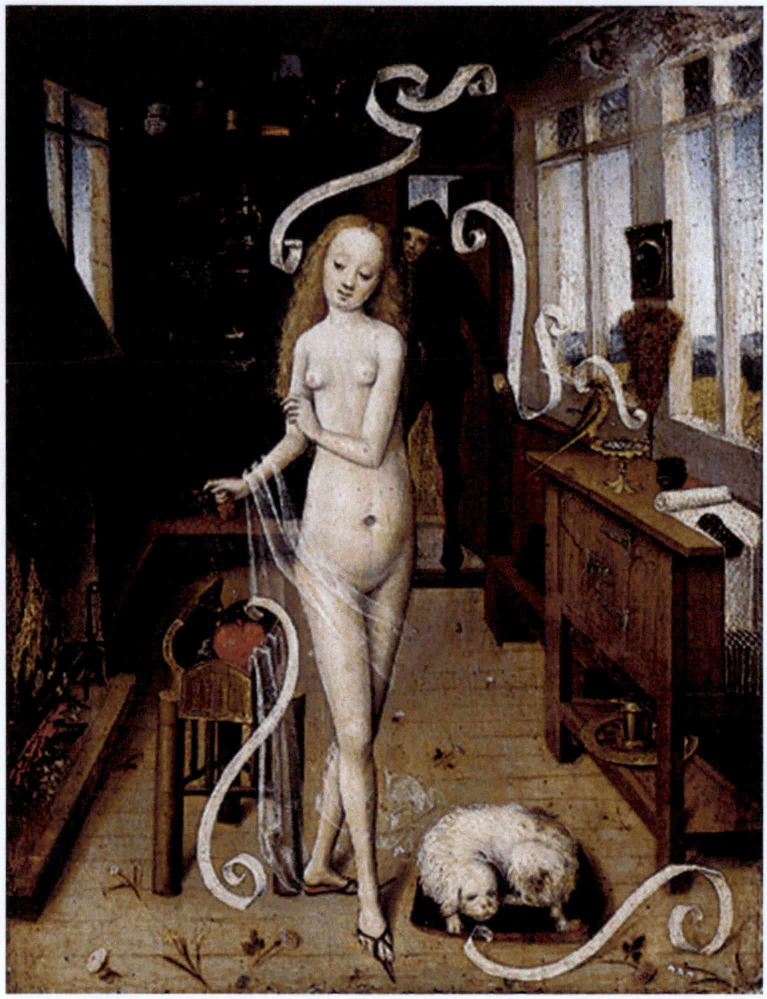

Fig. 145 Anonymous, *Love Spell (Love Magic)*, first half fifteenth century, German, oil on panel, 24 × 18 cm, Museum der Bildenden Künste Leipzig. Photo: Wikimedia

Camille and others have tied the imagery to the aphrodisiacal magic and folklore of the midsummer solstice as the rites of spring, or St John's Eve; while others have seen it as an erudite allegory on the literary trope of love's wiles in which a capricious 'Lady Love' alternately fires and quenches a young man's heart. As a painted allegory of love's bewitchments, like painting itself, its spell lies in the pleasure of its exquisitely detailed rendering that is both a meticulous mirror-image and a captivating deceit.[108]

In a representation of beauty's dangers from ancient history, to complement those of biblical account, poetic allegory, and classical myth, a painting of a Venetian woman as Cleopatra attributed to Paris Bordone represents a further extension of the *vanitas* theme (Walters Art Gallery). It depicts the great queen as a Venetian beauty sumptuously dressed in glowing silks and jewels within a richly appointed *palazzo* interior. Lover to both Caesar and Mark Antony, yet her destiny was the demise of the Egyptian pharaohs and thus the dispossession of her children as well as her consequent death. Bordone casts her in the role of stoic tragedy, caught up and lost in the 'doubled kisses' of fate. Beside her hangs a wall mirror of jewel-like cut with an elaborately carved and gilded frame. While light glints off its beveled edges, it bears no reflection, in contrast with the sumptuous surroundings of the room. The counterpoint recalls the biblical mirror of Ecclesiastes (1:2): 'vanity of vanities, all is vanity', of the generations of Egypt to come and go with her demise. Similarly, her face, as she contemplates her suicide in the wake of Antony's death and their defeat, carries no trace of turmoil.[109]

In a lighter genre, further painted consideration of the mirror of beauty as a dangerous enchantment arises in pictorialisations of Torquato Tasso's epic poem of the First Crusade, the *Gerusalemme liberata* of 1581, in which knights are misled from their true cause by the lure of beautiful 'Saracens'. Itself a poetic mirror of Ariosto's *Orlando furioso* of 1516, both poems were the subject of much painted imagery as well as performance, in the literary genre of chivalric romance. An early illustrated version of *Gerusalemme liberata* published in 1590 included a print by Tasso's friend, the Genoese painter-engraver Bernardo Castello, of the Christian knight Rinaldo seduced by the sorceress Armida, who holds up a decorated mirror to him as the emblem of her beauty.[110] In the foreground, however, Rinaldo's knightly companions approach armed with mirroring shields of diamond virtue in which they will show him his 'true' face as a Christian soldier. Thus the story turns on a mirroring pair, in which truth and beauty are opposed, casting the first as the path of virtue, and the latter as an illusory enchantment. In Tasso's verse, Rinaldo and all nature cry that no earthly mirror can hold Armida's image, such is her beauty that only the sky and the stars may reflect her enchantments. This is in contrast with the knight's shield, whose polished virtue represents the true face of valorous reflection; while that of Armida is the bewitching mirror of beauty's deceptions. The coupling of the venereal mirror with the armorial shield is central to emblematic reflection on painting's art that runs through the early modern imagery under discussion. A range of painted works by the Carracci and their pupils, and subsequently Poussin, Van Dyck, and Tiepolo, further elaborated Tasso's theme of beauty as the mirroring illusion of seduction, depicting the lovers in Armida's enchanted garden of flowers, birds, and flying cupids.[111]

Insistently, such imagery posited the mirror reflection and the female form at the deeply multivalent threshold of love and the fragility of desire, the contemplation of which later drove Tasso to repent his work as a vanity. Found in marriage portraits, in imagery of the Virgin's immaculate conception and birth, as well as in the shattering presentiments of *vanitas* and *memento mori*, the mirror was at the same time a pictorial metaphor of love's spell, within marriage but also beyond, from the consort to the courtesan and enchantress, and the pleasures of the flesh. As a literary trope too, the figure of the mirror was both pervasive and deeply bivalent in early modern love poetry and letters. It was the attribute of beauty, but also of the lover captured and transfixed. This ranged from the familial pleasure of marital relations to representations of *lascivia*, the anguished sufferings of love's cut, but also the spiritual ardors of devotional love.

***

As a cultural category, Renaissance wedding and betrothal portraits also bear the traces of a deeply meditated theological view of marriage as a *rite-de-passage*. It was thus a joyful celebration marked by the affects of love and the epithalamia of Eros to be sure, but also the constitution of family as social order and the cycle of life that heraldic genealogy mapped. Hence the often-poignant connections between marriage and *vanitas* imagery, like Eve's apple as the emblem of generation of both eros and family. Further, early modern marriage imagery, in both painting and poetry, often touched on the intertwined presentiment of love with loss and death that the consummation of desire and then childbirth could bring. As part of a greater historical *mentalité,* life and death were ever-proximate realms within pre-modern cultures of *amour* and childbearing. The classical literature of consolation was of such grieving, from the deeply moving letters of Cicero to his young wife at the death of their young daughter, or Seneca's to Marcia to console her for the loss of her infant son. Such meditations on the fragility of life at the very threshold of its reproduction produced a rich literature on grief and suffering across the middle ages and early modernity in the *ars moriendi* and beyond, with which the mirror texts of piety and Christian devotion were fully consonant.[112]

A portrait of the Augsburg painter Hans Burgkmair and his wife Anna by Lukas Furtenagel is a particularly vivid pictorialisation of this intertwined mentality of marriage and *vanitas* conjoined. It depicts the couple before a mirror 'reflection' apparently of themselves, as a pictorial memento of their union (Fig. 146). The convex hand-held mirror Anna holds before them bears an inscription as the prophecy of *vanitas* but also of Christian salvation: 'Know thyself / o death / hope of the world.' In the *banderole* above is a further reflection on the theology of *vanitas* as a mirror-image of life's temporal passing: 'This is how we looked. But in the mirror, nothing remains.' Hans' outstretched hand bears a ring, while his wife's wedding girdle is ornamented with delicate gold buckles of cloud-borne winged figures between a heraldry of floral motifs, as emblems of marriage. Yet the mirror-image double-portrait of themselves is of coupled death's heads, together in death as in life, as the token of an enduring loyalty.[113] If the perceived proximity between marriage and death of this period is now strange to us, yet it is readily evidenced historically within early modernity. We witness it most intimately in Renaissance wedding portraits and rings as well as *memento mori* jewellery, the decoration of toilet mirrors for marital trousseaux, and interwoven with the classical traditions of epithalamic verse that accompanied noble marriage. A redolent example within nuptial jewels is one early modern 'gimmal' wedding ring, consisting of coupled or twinned hoops with a jewelled bezel enclosing in gold miniature motifs of both an infant and a skeleton, as presentiments of birth and death within the full cycle of familial life rites.[114]

Similarly, betrothal and conjugal portraiture often reflected on *memento mori* through the miniature inclusion of a rebus-like death's head. A portrait painted of Thomas Gresham, merchant and financier to Henry VIII, in the year of his marriage, 1544, depicts him with a skull at his feet, his heart-shaped merchant's mark, and an inscription of their marriage vows: 'love serve and obei' (Mercers' Company City of London collection).[115] Such imagery pervaded every social estate, from merchants to kings. Holbein's great *Ambassadors* of 1533, as discussed in Chapter 4, may also be linked to international diplomacy surrounding Henry's VIII's marriage to Anne Boleyn (Fig. 118, Chapter 4). Painted by the king's painter, it commemorates the French ambassadors' engagement at the English court during the period of the marriage, coronation, and birthing of the new queen on the part of the French crown. Its many emblems of vanity depicted in the objects displayed on the shelves behind the ambassadors elaborate the patron's motto, *memento mori.* This is further embellished by his jewelled hat badge in the form of a skull, and the celebrated anamorphic skull in the foreground. The death head's prominence is both occluded and enhanced by a distorted perspectival illusionism, which may be resolved by a mirror or viewpoint to the side

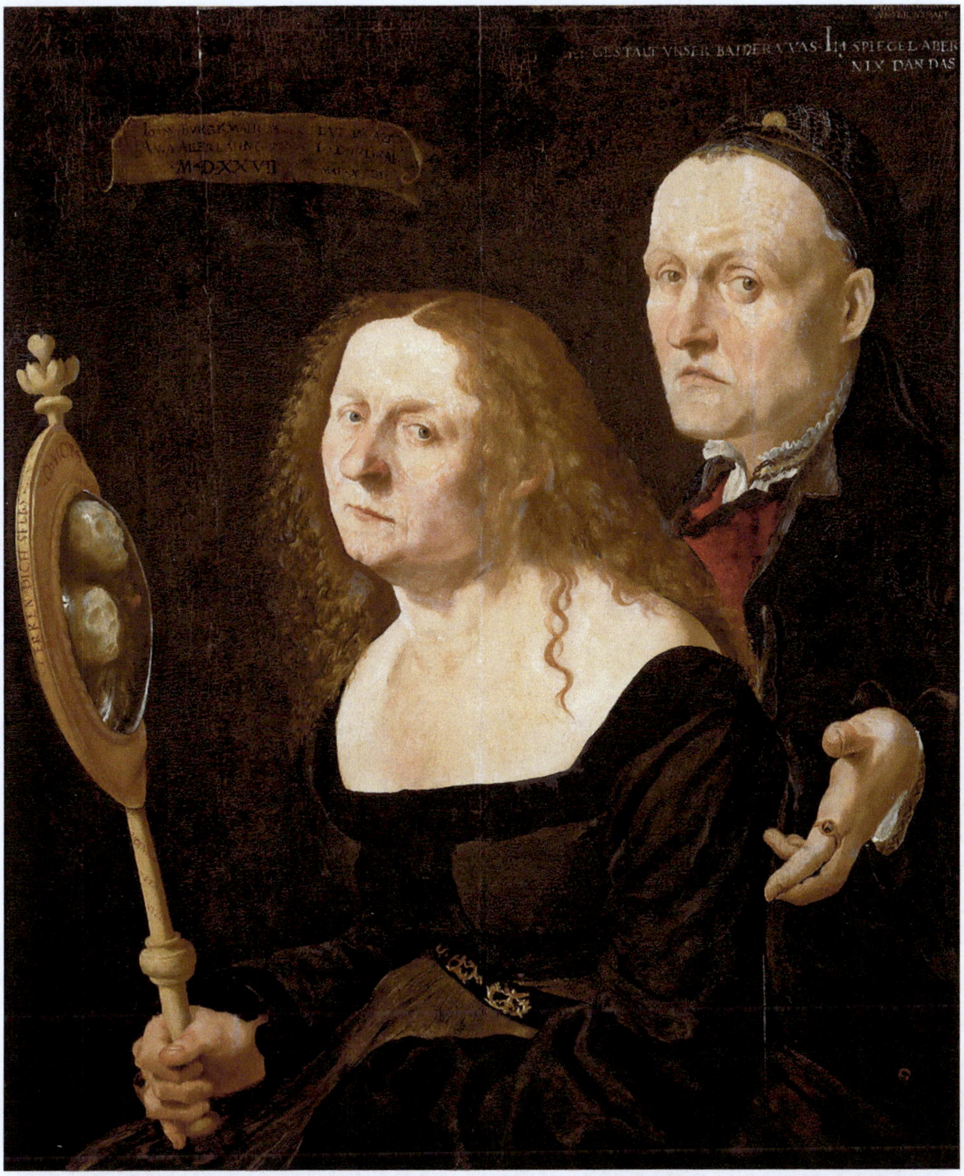

Fig. 146 Lukas Furtenagel (after lost original by Hans Burgkmair), *The Painter Hans Burgkmair and His Wife Anna*, 1529, 60 × 52 cm, Kunsthistorisches Museum, Vienna. Photo: Wikimedia

of the panel, as part of a court fashion for the diplomacy of such veiled or doubled imagery.[116]

Equally, within pictorial typologies of *vanitas* allegories, the female nude with a mirror might be coupled with a death's head or skeleton to signify the transience of worldly beauty, as a parallel to that of the *Ambassadors*' Erasmian vanity of worldly knowledge. These were pictorial meditations on the transience of youth and beauty as of life's passing. Hans Memling's *Earthly Vanity*, c. 1485 (Fig. 147), is an early Renaissance example of this.[117] A double-sided triptych of hand-held dimensions, it is surely a meditative work on the theme of youth's *vanitas*. Its central panel depicts a standing female nude, her loose hair held by a diadem of pearls, holding a gilt-framed oval mirror. The glass seemingly reflects her face, although its frontal viewpoint does not accord with hers, suggesting an elision between a mirror reflection and a painted portrait miniature. She stands in a *mille-fleur* landscape flanked by dogs – a greyhound couple and

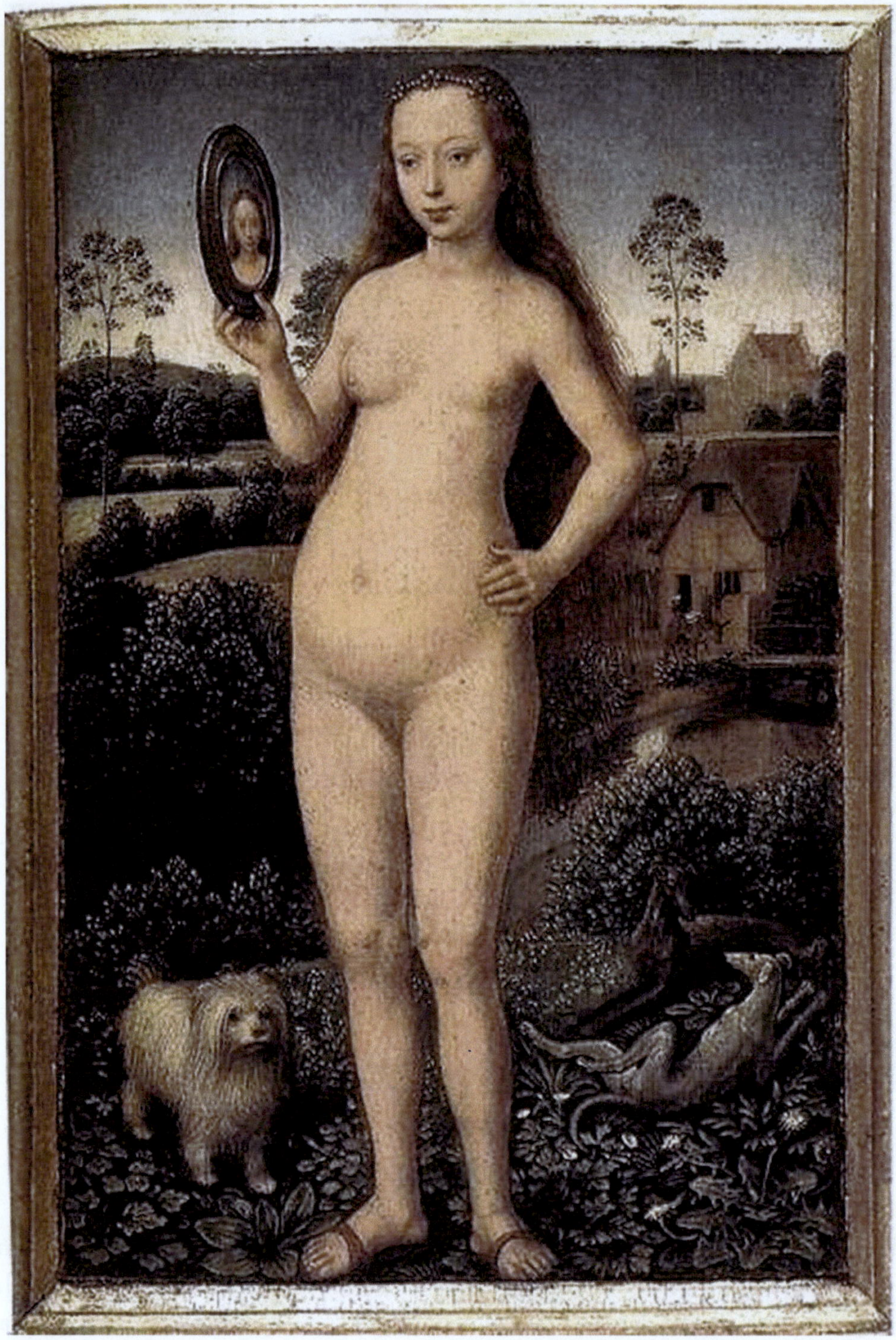

Fig. 147 Hans Memling, *Triptych of Earthly Vanity and Divine Salvation*, c. 1485, oil on panel, 22 × 15 cm (each wing), Musée des Beaux-Arts, Strasbourg. Photo: Wikimedia

a griffon dog like that of the Arnolfini double portrait – as emblems of both marital fidelity and the fleeting flower of physical love. The house and mill behind her similarly connote the domestic weal. A small canal projects further reflections of trees and sky to underscore a conceptualisation of painting as specular, like the mirror-portrait she holds in her hand. The flanking panels depict death as a corpse, and hell in the form of a devil. In a full arc of Christian belief, the reverse represents a *Salvator Mundi* in the centre, between the commissioning family's coat of arms and motto – *Nul Bien sans Peine* – and a skull on the other.[118]

Similarly, Hans Baldung's *Three Ages of Youth Age and Death*, c. 1510 (Kunsthistorisches Museum, Vienna), depicts in one panel a female nude holding a convex mirror in which she regards her haunted reflection, flanked by a baby at her feet and a corpse beside her, who holds an hourglass above her head to signify the ravages of beauty by time. Such imagery had a proximate type within the decorative arts, of Renaissance domestic mirrors known as '*miroirs de mort*', whose wooden covers were of painted death's heads in an admonitory counterpoint to the mirror-image of the woman's face encased within.[119] It is also manifest in Low Country manuscript illuminations of the fifteenth century, as James Marrow has argued, in representations of the death's head accompanied by a mirror as conjoined emblems of *memento mori*.[120] It was a death-like mirror-motif Baldung would echo, in his 1529 *Allegory of Prudence* (Alte Pinakothek, Munich) in which a female nude holds a convex mirror bearing a reflection of a skull in a further recollection of time's triumph over youth and beauty as *vanitas*.[121]

***

The theology of *vanitas* as penitence was most directly manifest in pictorial representations of the Magdalen, as the personification of both feminine beauty and repentance. In devotional writings, as in painting, she was frequently depicted with the attributes of the mirror and the candle, as emblems of life's fleeting passage, and of the skull as *memento mori*. The tradition may be exemplified in the writings of Pierre de St Louis, in a devotional text entitled *La Madeleine* of 1668. In a poetic personification of the penitent's attributes, the skull addresses the saint at her mirror of contemplation with a reminder of time ravaging beauty: 'I am now nothing more than that which you can see / Make good use of me thus, as you do your mirror.'[122] In both word and image, the Magdalen's reflection was a deeply bivalent one: of spiritual revelation as truth, but also of vanity and so of her past as a venereal beauty. As other scholars have noted, the sixteenth century witnessed a renewed veneration of the Magdalen within Catholicism as the figure of penance, manifest in an outpouring of devotional tracts, poetry, prints, illustrated books, and religious imagery of this saint, bound to the larger Catholic defence of sainthood and the sacraments in the face of Protestant diatribe.[123] The spiritual emblem of the repentant sinner, the Magdalen was also, however, the image of devotional love 'because she loved much', in the words of Pope Gregory the Great.[124] In the devotional poetry of Vittoria Colonna, Marchioness of Pescara, lay Benedictine, friend, and patron of Michelangelo, Titian, Pietro Bembo, and Pietro Aretino, the Magdalen was a spiritual mirror of the Lord as a figure of passionate devotion and radiant spiritual love:

> And desire arrested, arrested her steps
> Atop a great mountain
> whence I mirror myself and back
> In the beautiful example, and straighten and raise up my soul
> Following in the blessed footsteps and the saintly deeds.[125]

Such verse dedicated to the Magdalen, written in the sonnet form of lyric love poetry, was extensive across the sixteenth century, as in the further example of the English Catholic poet Henry Constable's *To St Mary Magdalene* of 1592, in which the beauty of this saint is the object of an intense if ineffable longing of 'winged affection'.[126] In the manner of Petrarchan verse, the Magdalen was a spiritual metaphor for the impossible striving of the human heart in the ways of God's love. Fully suffused by the Pauline conception of human understanding as no more than a dim reflection in a mirror of the true force of divine effulgence 'through a glass darkly' (1 Corinthians 13:12), it was a poetry of searching, affective devotion. Spiritual love was the mirror of God. In Vittoria Colonna's sonnets, the Magdalen's capacity for 'the pure flame of burning love' is her mirror, or *exemplum*, of an ardent faith's constant heart.

Vittoria was gifted with an image of the penitent Magdalen by Federigo Gonzaga in 1531, commissioned of Titian (generally linked with the version now in the Pitti Gallery). Representing the saint as the figure of what has been termed 'heavenly beauty', Titian's painting for Vittoria, as with his many depictions of the Magdalen, dwells on the pictorial elaboration of the loveliness of her form as a metaphor of her capacity for the ardent love of Christ.[127] In Titian's oeuvre, the representation of the Magdalen became indelibly linked with that of female beauty, in a pictorial heightening of her spirituality of love. Thus, in a devotional counterpoint to Titian's representations of *belle donne* such as the Louvre's *Woman with Two Mirrors*, c. 1515, Titian's *Vanitas*, generally dated to the same year on the basis of their similarities, fuses the two pictorial genres (Figs. 128 and 148). Here a similarly clad young woman wears a white chemise that falls from her shoulder surmounted by a deep green silk tunic. Rather than a specular reflection of herself as in the *Woman with Two Mirrors*, however, this Magdalen holds a mirror that apparently reflects the scene before her, in a display of her vanities. The pearls, gold, and jewels are at once the attributes of beauty and the source of her repentant contemplation as the mirror-image of her former *bellezza*. Behind stands the diminutive figure of a serving woman, possibly an attendant to the Magdalen's toilet, as characterised also in the great *Venus of Urbino*. The proximity of the two works has even led some scholars to group the *Woman with Two Mirrors* among Titian's Magdalens; if the ties to Bellini's *bella donna* at her toilet must take precedence, yet the similarities serve to underscore Titian's confluence of genres in forging a new pictorial language of devotional ardour.[128] In effect, the Magdalen in contemplation of a mirror-image is the devotional representation of the toilet of Venus.[129] It further illustrates the underlying *vanitas* of the toilet motif, and of the mirror, as the sign of beauty and love, both spiritual and secular.

Out of many subsequent pictorial examples of the repentant Magdalen, Simon Vouet's *Mary with Her Sister Martha*, c. 1620 (Kunsthistorisches Museum, Vienna), takes up Titian's emblem of repentance coupled to beauty's ornament in the motif of the mirror reflection. The abundant shot-silk iridescence of her dress is repeated in the lustrous toiletries laid out on a flowered textile including pearls, jewels, an ivory comb, a perfume jar, and a richly figured standing mirror reminiscent of those depicted in Fontainebleau's venereal toilets. This proximity in the imagery of Venus with its *vanitas* speaks to the rich polyvalence of the mirror as the feminine trope. Within the Vouet, the mirror face details Mary's reflection in its convex bowl, echoing the colours of her dress in a further elaboration of visual pleasure as the emblem of art.[130] Among the most celebrated examples of this pictorial theme is surely Caravaggio's *Martha and Mary*, c. 1598 (Detroit Institute of Arts), which Vouet may have known from his years in Rome. In contrast to Vouet's glowing palette of cast gems, Caravaggio uses earthen colours of a greater pictorial *humilitas* in his depiction of a Magdalen without jewels. Here the large, convex, gilt-framed mirror of dark glass is marked by the strong highlight of a window-light reflection, as a

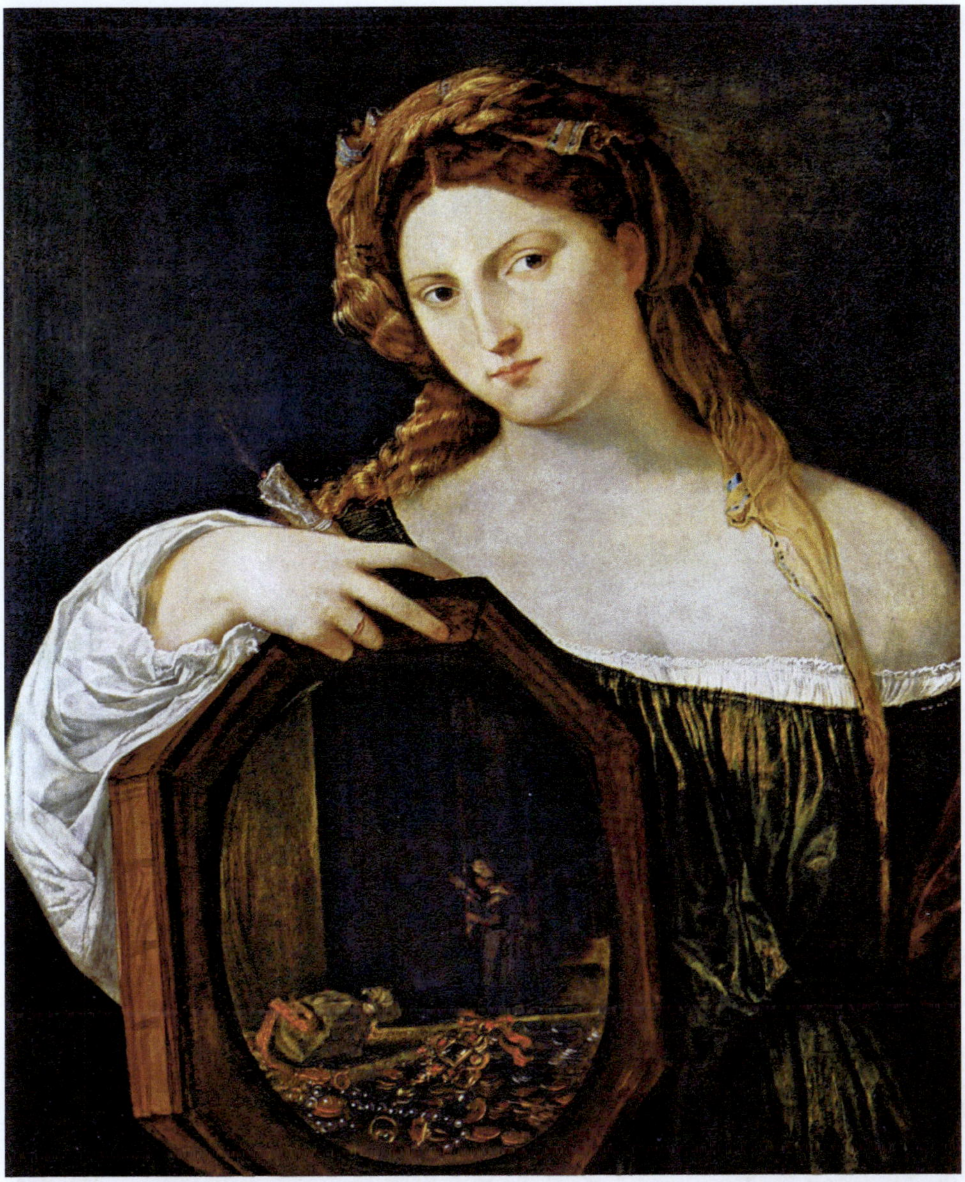

Fig. 148 Titian, *Vanitas*, c. 1515, oil on canvas, 97 × 81.2 cm, Bayerische Staatsgemäldesammlungen, Munich. Photo: Wikimedia

ready metaphor of her coming redemption.[131] As such, it is a pictorial counterpoint to the use of the mirror as an unstained glass through which light penetrates in Marian representations of her immaculacy. In the case of Caravaggio's Magdalen, the pronounced light reflection within a darkened mirror surely emblematises her salvation through love. Recalling again Paul's epistle to the Corinthians, in its Renaissance translations the mirror light was understood as a comparison of itself, between the pure light of God's love and the imperfect or dim reflection of human understanding.[132]

This theology of specular light is most evident in a series of penitent Magdalens by Georges de la Tour, one of which depicts the saint in rapt meditation before a candle reflected in a mirror, in which the bright flame of divine love stands out against the darkening glass (Fig. 149). Both the candle flame and its reflection are ready

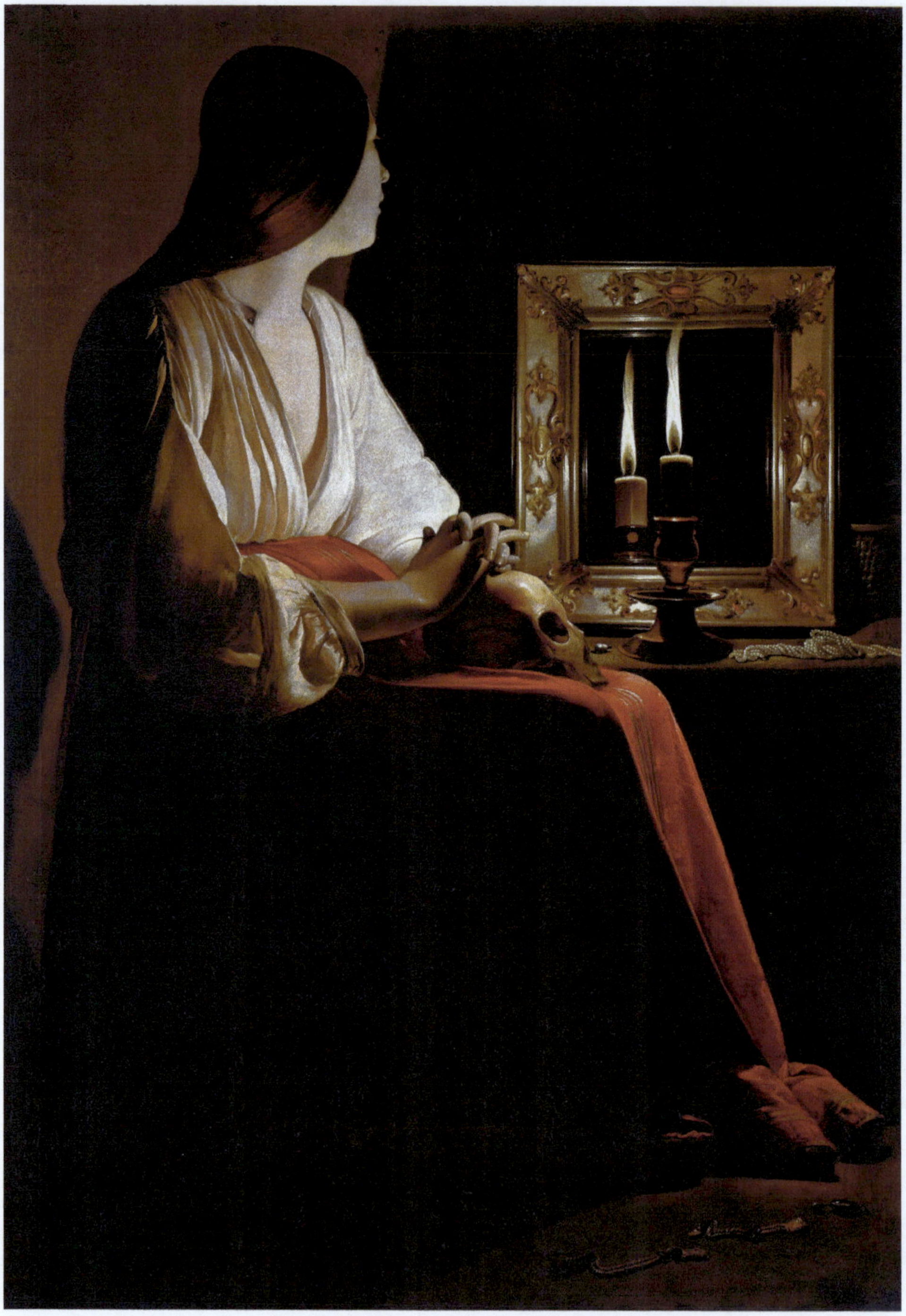

Fig. 149 Georges de la Tour, *The Penitent Magdalen before a Candle and a Mirror with a Skull as Memento Mori*, c. 1640, oil on canvas, 133.4 × 102.2 cm, Metropolitan Museum of Art.
Photo: Metropolitan Museum of Art

emblems of the fleeting transience of worldly beauty and pleasure that the Magdalen has renounced, bending her hands in prayer upon a skull as the metaphor of *memento mori* within the visual idioms of *vanitas*. De la Tour's imagery is fully infused with the theology of light and dark, in which the candle flame is apt allegory of the Magdalen's ardent love for Christ as 'the light of the world' (Matthew 5:14) 'shining in the darkness' (John 1:15). Jacques Thuillier and others have brought these paintings together with seventeenth-century devotional texts on the

Magdalen as the spiritual embodiment of divine love and the longing of the soul for union with the godhead in both word and image. In particular, Thuillier recalled the mystical poetry of Cardinal Pierre de Bérulle's *Elévations à Jésus-Christ sur la sainte Madeleine* of 1625, in which the pain of her separation from Christ at the tomb became the beginnings of her spiritual journey to perpetual union with the godhead through an imagery of light and darkness.[133] Scholarship has further linked de la Tour's Magdalens with a set of sermons by a Father André de l'Auge, published in Paris in 1623. Here Christ is conceived as a mirror with two sides, one dark and opaque as the human condition, the other the crystal and brilliant of the divine. This duality of reflection may be read as a metaphor for the human soul between sin and repentance at the very moment of the Magdalen's conversion.[134] The force of de la Tour's *chiaroscuro* further suggests the Pauline mirror within spiritual allegory more broadly, as a metaphor of divine light and its dim reflection in the face of human comprehension. For if the painted mirror casts back the candlelight, it is but a dim reflection of God's splendour. The light of divine love, instead, shines as bright radiance across the Magdalen herself, bathing her heart in its effulgent glow. In the medieval compilation of apocrypha, Jacobus de Voragine's *Golden Legend*, the Magdalen's capacity for love makes her a lantern in the darkness, a giver of light.[135] As Paul further wrote to the Corinthians, in a recollection of the burning radiance surrounding Moses following his spiritual union with God in prayer, 'we all, with unveiled face beholding in a mirror the glory of the Lord, are transformed into his image, from glory to glory, even unto the Lord' (2 Corinthians 3:18).

VALIANT MIRRORS

The mirror of female virtue was also an iconography of queens in their political capacity as guardians of the state as of their household. Across arts and letters, the imagery of the mirror of state was of royal sagacity and foresight; in the case of queens this turned much on marital matters. In Edmund Spenser's 1590 poetic epic of the *Faerie Queene* dedicated to Elizabeth I, it is the magician Merlin's enchanted glass globe, also termed a Venus looking-glass, which can foretell the future for the virgin queen's consultation. In what Spenser himself described as a text of 'continual allegory', Elizabeth I is lightly personified as the fairy monarch Queen Gloriana, who presides over the book *in absentia*, as well as a series of young females whom Spenser calls further 'mirrours' of his Queen. Chief among these is Britomart, the 'sweet maid' whose destiny is to found a united kingdom in her name: Britain. As the Greek term for a virgin nymph of Artemisia's retinue, Britomart is also a lady knight of valorous Marian chastity, in honour of Elizabeth too. Spenser's book, like Merlin's glass, is offered to the queen as the guiding light of princely wisdom, or *speculum principis*, 'Like to the world itself and seemed a world of glas' (III:2).[136] As in Tasso's Christian epic, the *Faerie Queene* is both a Virgilian pastoral and a literary invocation to the *Aeneid*. Ovidian poetry as well as chivalric romance and Petrarchan verse are united in its playful parody of Ariosto, Chaucer, and Arthurian legend. Merlin's 'wondrous mirror' will also reveal to Britomart the '*semblant*' of her elusive spouse as a shadow 'faded to a watry flower', like the Ovidian pool of Narcissus. Within Spenser's poetic epic, Merlin was also the maker of Arthur's arms and armour, which Britomart will bear as a 'mayd martial'. This included a shield of diamond whose mirror-like brilliance dazzles all her opponents into suppliance. Through this jewelled armorial figure Spenser brought together the parallel enchantments of mirror, shield, and diamond 'glass' within his chivalric romance, all parallel metaphors of Elizabeth's queenship as one of magnificent illusion, both venereal and martial.[137]

Such dynastic and princely connotations of the mirror metaphor are fully redolent within the broad literary trope of '*speculum principis*' or 'the mirror of princes'. As discussed in Chapter 1, these were literary texts of comparison intended to guide the good judgment of monarchs.[138] The genre comprises celebrated examples of Renaissance political theory such as Machiavelli's *Principe* as well as the 'clowdily enwrapped allegorical devises' of Spenser's poetic queen. Spenser acknowledged his poem as such, describing its conceit as a 'fayre mirror' to Britomart in tribute to the valorous reign of Elizabeth I. In effect, Spenser's 'mirrour' for Britomart is itself an emblem of *speculum principis*, as an inset device of good guidance within the story it reflects.[139] In such literature, the mirror was a common metaphor of clear and tempered judgment. This was reflected in book plates to '*speculum principis*' texts such as the celebrated frontispiece, depicting the prince looking into a mirror as an emblem of his perspicacious rule, for the 1655 Brussels edition of Pedro Belluga's fifteenth-century manuscript on good government.[140] Thus the Spenserian metaphor of the mirror or 'glasse' as the attribute of monarchy was a ready one, much used in Elizabethan poetry (as of other royalty) as an emblem of the queen's sagacity. In John Davies' *Hymns of Astraea* of 1599, the poetic figure of Astrea carries a perspicacious mirror of her government as the instrument by which to discern truth from illusion and error, to suggest the fulfilment of Virgilian prophecy in Elizabeth's queenship: 'By this straight rule she rectifies / . . . / This is her cleare true mirror / Her looking-glasse'.[141] Shakespeare's many uses of the 'glass' as metaphor similarly encompassed the literary figure of the princess not merely as beauty, virtue, or royalty but in her capacity as ruler, as a tribute to his queen. In *Love's Labours' Lost* (IV:1) the Princess of France calls for her mirror in order to consult it as an instrument of verity in affairs of love as of state: 'Here good my glass, take this for telling true.'[142] Matters of royal marriage were also inextricably those of alliance, and indeed the means of political union for centuries. From the marriage of Ferdinand of Aragon with Isabella of Castile and Portugal to the accession of James VI and I of Scotland and England, princely marriage and its dynastic issue were acts of state-making.

Spenser and Shakespeare both authored marital epithalamia inset within their texts for 'marriages' of literary occasion in mirror-like emulation of those at court. Likewise, the masques of Ben Jonson, as first poet laureate to James I and VI, were often performed within the festivities of court marriages under royal patronage. In such instances, Jonson's epithalamic masques made specific mythological allegory of the new union of the crowns of 1613 as the archetype of dynastic marital alliance. Marriage was thus a metaphor of the recent act of union in 1603, according to the Spenserian prophecy of Britomart. This was the case with Jonson's 1616 *Masque of Hymen*, and the *Hue and Cry after Cupid* of 1608, both of which concluded in a 'theatre' of marriage as a mirror-image of its social occasion. Performed by members of court, and interwoven with court dancing, their scenographic centrepieces by Inigo Jones were of a great silvered sphere to represent the union of marriage as of Britain in a perceived coupling of the specular image with its mirror reflection. In the *Hue and Cry after Cupid* of 1608, composed for a marriage of Scottish and English nobilities and performed in the banqueting hall at Whitehall, such a cosmological silvered spherical mirror is Vulcan the metalsmith's prestation to his wife, Venus. In Jonson's stage directions for Vulcan's presentation of the gift it is represented as a symbol of the 'heaven of marriage', of court as of state. Drawing together the silvered globe with the cosmological realm:

> with loud, full music, the cliff parts in the midst and discovers an illustrious concave, filled with an ample and glistering light, in which an artificial sphere is made of silver, eighteen feet in diameter, that turns perpetually; the colours are heightened with gold.[143]

Embedded within Elizabethan theatre more broadly are the concluding 'marriages' that surely mirrored those at which they were performed, from *As You Like It*, *A Midsummer Night's Dream*, and *The Tempest*.[144] In the same way as *La vida es sueño*, these plays confound any simple distinction between art and audience, so conflating the play, the play within, and the intended viewers on the boundaries of illusion. Similarly, Spenser's 1579 pastoral poem the *Shepherd's Calendar* included a spring eclogue in the flowered imagery of bridal song, eliding literature's fictions with its social mirror. Fusing the red rose of love with the bride's blushing cheek, as the manifestation of her chaste desire, the sphere of her cheek is also that of a mirror:

> The red rose medled with the white sphere
> In either cheek depicting lively cheer
> How the red roses flush up her cheeks
> And the pure snow with goodly vermilion stain.[145]

The metaphor of marriage as a silver-tained reflective sphere was a constant one in theatre and poetry alike. It appears also in John Donne's St Valentine's Day poem for the marriage of Elizabeth Stuart and Frederick V Count Palatine in the royal chapel of Whitehall Palace in 1613, here cast within cosmic imagery as a complement of mirroring pairs that marriage should surely be:

> Here lies a she sun, and a he moon here
> She gives the best light to his sphere
> Or each is both, and all, and so
> They unto one another nothing owe.[146]

Donne's friend Sir Henry Goodere also composed royal epithalamic verse on the bridal couple as a complement of mirroring pairs, like two sides of a blown-glass sphere. In a succession of similes ranging from the miniature forms of coupled jewels of royal estate to the monumental claims of a global dynastic imperialism engendered through the lineage of their political union, Goodere wove together the metaphor of the crown jewels with the union of the kingdom through princely marriages, in a recurring metaphor of the reflective image in the mirroring spheres of love:

> Now like two half-spheres set . . .
> As half-spheres make a globe by being met.[147]

As Goodere declaimed, metaphors of princely perspicacity as a mirror compendium of specular light so central to all early modern forms of *speculum principis* also extended to the royal collections of crystalline objects such as Elizabeth espoused.[148] Thus the great jewels of the Crown were understood as both the pellucid reflection of natural marvel and the magnificent brilliance of majesty. This is manifest in descriptions of Tudor and Stuart state jewels, perceived as the national emblems of monarchy, of which the most celebrated were termed 'mirrors' as the very image of kingship. These large jewels of state were shaped in the form of tiny flat mirrors trimmed by bevelled edges, with so-called mirror- or tablet-cut faces. Thus Elizabeth I's Mirror of Portugal, the Mirror of France, or the Mirror of Great Britain in celebration of the union of the crowns of Scotland and England in 1603 were crown jewels all presented as specular reflections on the brilliance of their rule.[149] State portraits further displayed the emblems of monarchy through the material devises of dress, of which jewellery was its clearest sign. Elizabeth's portraits as queen present the monarch configured by the materials of royal magnificence – gold cloth encrusted with pearls, rubies, and diamonds, further ornamented by large jewels set as pendants at her throat, waist, and hair. A late portrait of c. 1590 now at Compton Verney is emblematic of her queenly portraiture (Fig. 150). On her bodice, appliqued jewels are arranged in the shape of Diana's crescent moon to signify her watch over her nation as well as her chastity, while her open-work crown represents the sovereignty of her rule. Such jewels were often configured as mythological, as emblems of a princely authority over every domain of classical learning as well as exquisite material splendour in the refinements of their faceted brilliance. At the crest of her brow, she carries a great 'mirror' diamond of her rule framed by a pearl pendant.[150] These 'mirror' diamonds were the

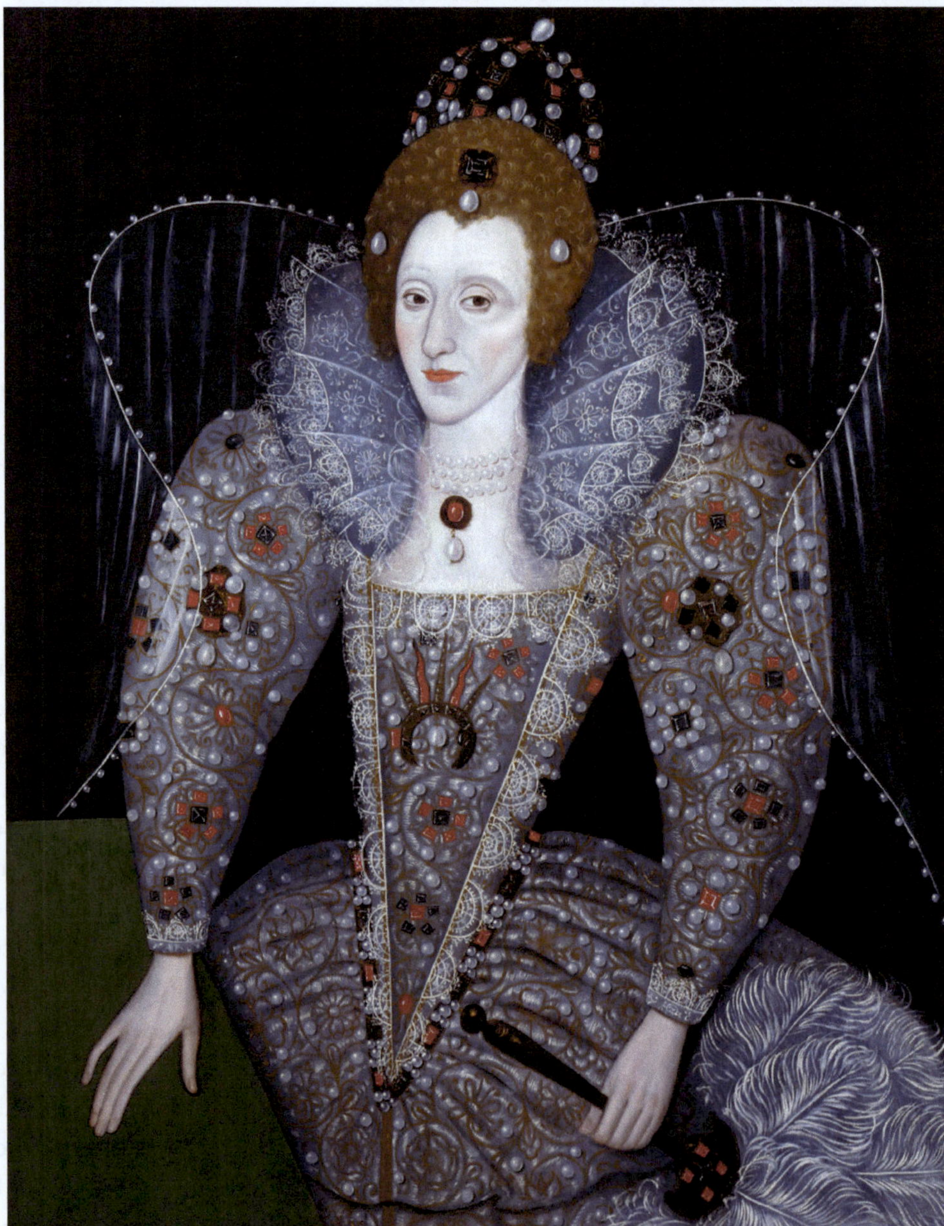

Fig. 150 Anonymous, *Portrait of Queen Elizabeth I with Mirror-Jewel Headpiece*, c. 1590, oil on wood, 114 × 88 cm, Compton Verney Art Gallery, Warwickshire. Photo: Compton Verney Art Gallery

material emblems of Elizabeth's prescient queenship.

If the princely hall of mirrors such as at Versailles awaited the seventeenth century, the paradigm of a courtly amplification through the use of mirror reflection was an established one, in both texts and images of the sixteenth century, and specifically in the realm of noble portraiture pertaining to marital alliance. A representation of the child Anna Eleonora Sanvitale, ward of the Este court and future Countess of Scandiano, by Girolamo Mazzola Bedoli of 1562, posed his young subject against such a stately mirror of magnificence (Fig. 151).[151] The child, then age four, is depicted in court dress of red silk with gold and black velvet trim, a white lace collar offset by a pearl pendant necklace, with ribbons in her hair. In her right hand she holds a pink,

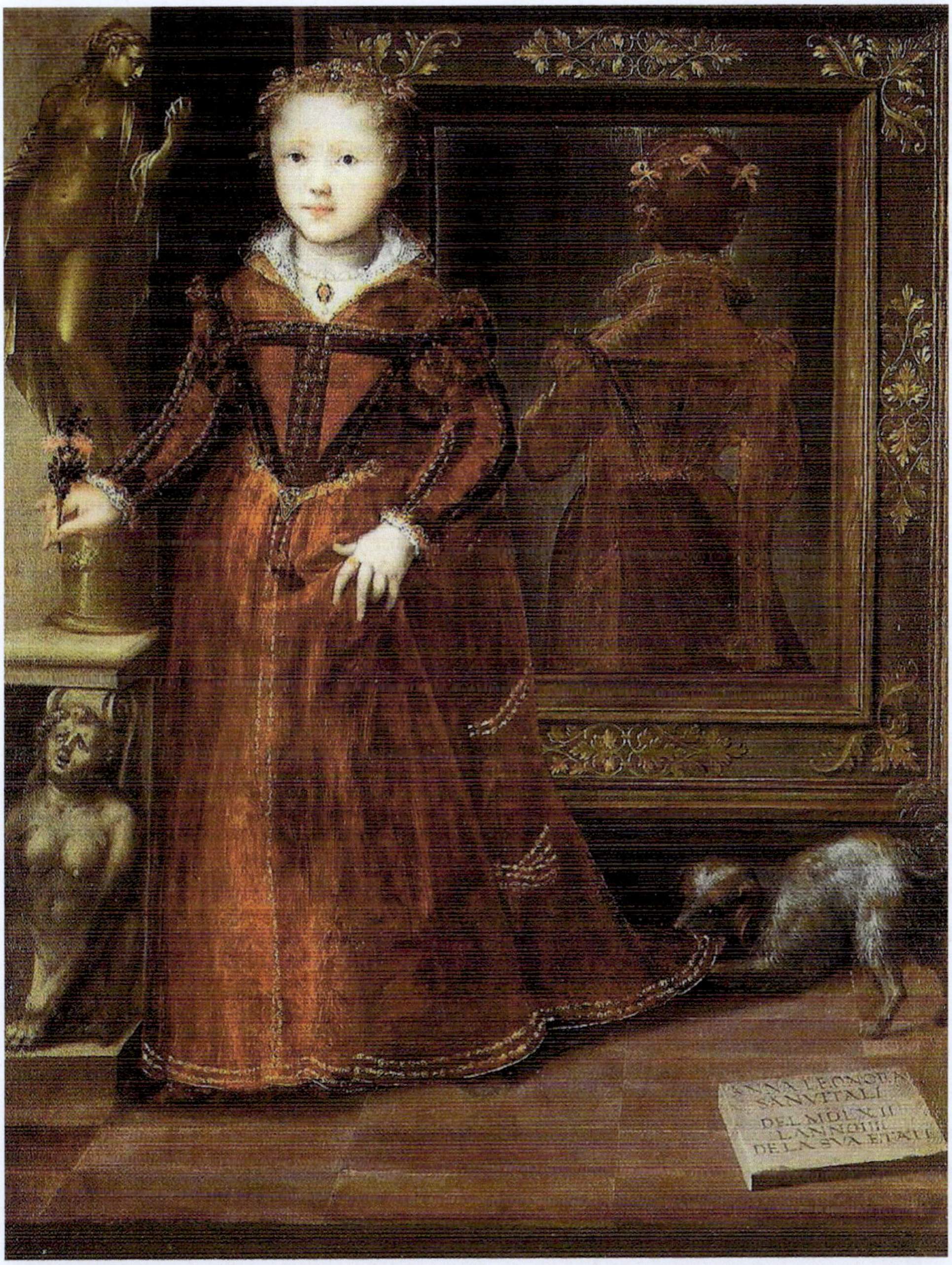

Fig. 151 Girolamo Mazzola-Bedoli, *Portrait of Anna Eleonora Sanvitale*, 1562, oil on canvas, 121.5 × 92 cm, Galleria Nazionale, Parma. Photo: Wikimedia

while a small dog playfully lifts the hem of her dress, both ready emblems of female fidelity in marriage, so suggesting a portrait of betrothal. Such portraits, particularly of women, played a critical part in the early modern diplomacy of courtly marriage, as veritable effigies of exchange in the lengthy courtesies of gift-giving that characterised the aristocratic conduct of marital alliances. In Bedoli's representation of the young Eleonora, gilt statuary comprising a venereal female nude holding up a small looking-glass frames the left side of the painting. Behind Eleonora stands the mirror, of exceptional size for the period, set within an ornate wood and gilt frame. Its reflection displays the noble carriage of the shoulders and head from the back, in a Cnidian counterpoint to the painting's frontal depiction. The two mirrors of the painting signify prismatically on the social place of women in courtship and marriage. The looking glass of the sculpted Venus is a metaphor of female beauty, while the large mirror 'presents' Eleonor within the mores of display pertaining to noble marriage negotiations. The painting testifies to the ready approximation between the nubile noblewoman and the mirror as her accoutrement. The mirror accessory was also an element of female court dress, as seen in the jewellery of Elizabeth's state portraiture.

As Elizabeth wore great 'mirror' diamonds, her court wore small decorated mirrors like jewels, as lustrous embellishments of their attire and mirror complements to the radiance of their queen. As Ben Jonson described in accounts of noble attire for the royal masques, court fashion included small ornamental mirrors attached by ribbon to the girdle or waist of aristocratic dress.[152] These were often exquisite jewels of fine goldsmithing, and frequently betrothal gifts. Some 'girdle glasses' were fashioned as miniature books or as optical lenses for reading and study, in a courtly acknowledgement of patronage of all forms of learning. An example of the dowager consort to the French king, Diane de Poitiers (formerly at Château de Versailles, now Château d'Écouen Musée Nationale de la Renaissance), apparently after a portrait by Clouet, illustrates the looking-glass magnifier pendant as jewelled ornament to her courtly dress in black, attached by a silver chain about the waist and bearing a reflection of the room around her with its mullioned window light.[153] Among English portraits, one of Elizabeth I (now at Charlecote Park) similarly depicts a small crystal or mirror roundel framed in jeweller's precious metalwork and attached to the dress by ribbon.[154] Such ornamental mirrors or magnifying looking-glasses for dress were of miniated and jewel-like dimensions, often of polished silver, rock crystal, or Venetian *cristallo* glass, elaborated with frames and covers of precious metals, inlay, filigree, jewels, or enamels (Figs. 14, 15, 25, 26, and 27, Chapter 1). While many frames for small looking-glasses or magnifying glasses for reading and other detailed study are purely decorative, others depict mythological narratives in elaborate enamelling or damascened metal. Such miniature imagery was often of Venus, both of her beauty but also as a gentle forewarning of its unbounded passion. Many figured Diana as the poetic conceit of the moon's mirroring light, waxing and waning like women's youth and beauty, and so of her protection of female chastity. Others figured Minerva as the personification of wisdom in a paean to the mirror's perceived powers of knowledge and revelation, a subject often figured by the celebrated Limoges enamellist Suzanne de Court for her female patrons at the French court (Fig. 25, Chapter 1).[155] As betrothal gifts these were surely intertwined emblems of feminine beauty as a vanity coupled with erudition and knowledge in a light Erasmian *vanitas*. At the Whitehall court the diminutive jewelled mirrors women carried on their girdles were, in miniature, political allegories of Britain's state of union, like the silver-sphered emblems of their unions in marriage under Cupid's sway, as nuptial poetry celebrated. In the dress of Elizabeth herself, as of the noble women of her retinue, they were also a material metaphor of the queen's clear vision, with ordained perspicacity and knowledge. Thus the composition of early modern jewellery, as ornament to female beauty and sagacity, comprised the mirror-like reflection as the emblem of women's majesty over affairs of marriage, of the state as of the heart.

MIRRORS OF PRUDENCE

Early modern allegories of female sagacity took many forms, in myriad elaborations of queenly virtue as a model for emulation. These were diffuse across early illustrated books, prints, and decorative arts connected with female conduct in love and marriage. In print, Cesare Ripa's celebrated iconographical handbook of allegorical personifications, the *Iconologia*, was widely influential. First published in textual form in 1593, it reappeared in 1603 with illustrative woodcuts that would become its definitive edition.[156] Stemming from Renaissance traditions of printed commonplace books, on the one hand, and emblem books in the wake of Andrea Alciati's *Emblemata* of 1531, on the other, the metaphorical representation of ideas through a puzzle-like oscillation between word and image had strong roots in classical and medieval allegorical modes, including those of heraldry, and was widely diffuse across all forms of early modern knowledge enquiry.[157] In Ripa's hands, the *Iconologia* displayed a complex of abstract thought through the literary figure of personification. The images were presented to the reader using the compositional matrix of an emblem book, combining together an inscription or motto, a figurative personification, and a short text by way of elaboration of their collective meaning. Among a cluster of much-repeated attributes throughout the text, a number of Ripa's allegorical figures comprise women with mirrors. While some are representations of love's light and fire, as well as female beauty, others present a quite different feminine mirror face. As the metaphor of intellectual and moral light, the mirror sign appears in Ripa's allegories of knowledge, theory, and practice, and also as the perspicacious figure of Prudence (Fig. 152).

Thus Ripa's '*Incendium* of Love' depicts a young beauty holding a round mirror up to the sun, with a torch in her other hand as the attribute of burning ardency. It is an allegory of female beauty in which eros is represented through the light of optical knowledge. The accompanying text below describes the sight of her beauty like the rays of sun caught in her mirroring glass, with the power to light a torch. Like men's eyes regarding a beautiful woman, which can kindle a flame in the heart, it is a full *poesie* of the *miroir ardent*. Ripa's figure of Prudence, by comparison, wears the gilded helmet of Minerva to signify her sagacity armed by wise counsel. The ruminating stag beside her advises careful consideration before coming to any resolution. She bears a mirror-image of her face in her left hand to bid us examine ourselves well as the foundations of circumspection. Similarly, the figure of 'perfect work' – '*operatione perfetta*' – holds a mirror of knowledge in one hand and a compass of true measure in the other, as does Ripa's personification of '*disegno*', to signify the unity of the arts in conception as well as practice. Ripa's image-signs for subjects of theory and science similarly include mirrors, to denote the intellectual capacity for abstraction and the knowledge of things, which are also aspects of the wise or prudent mirror.[158]

Painted personifications of Prudence with a mirror are long antecedent to Ripa's allegories, in celebrated examples such as Giotto's Arena Chapel frescoes or Pollaiuolo's figuration of Prudence and her mirror reflection within a

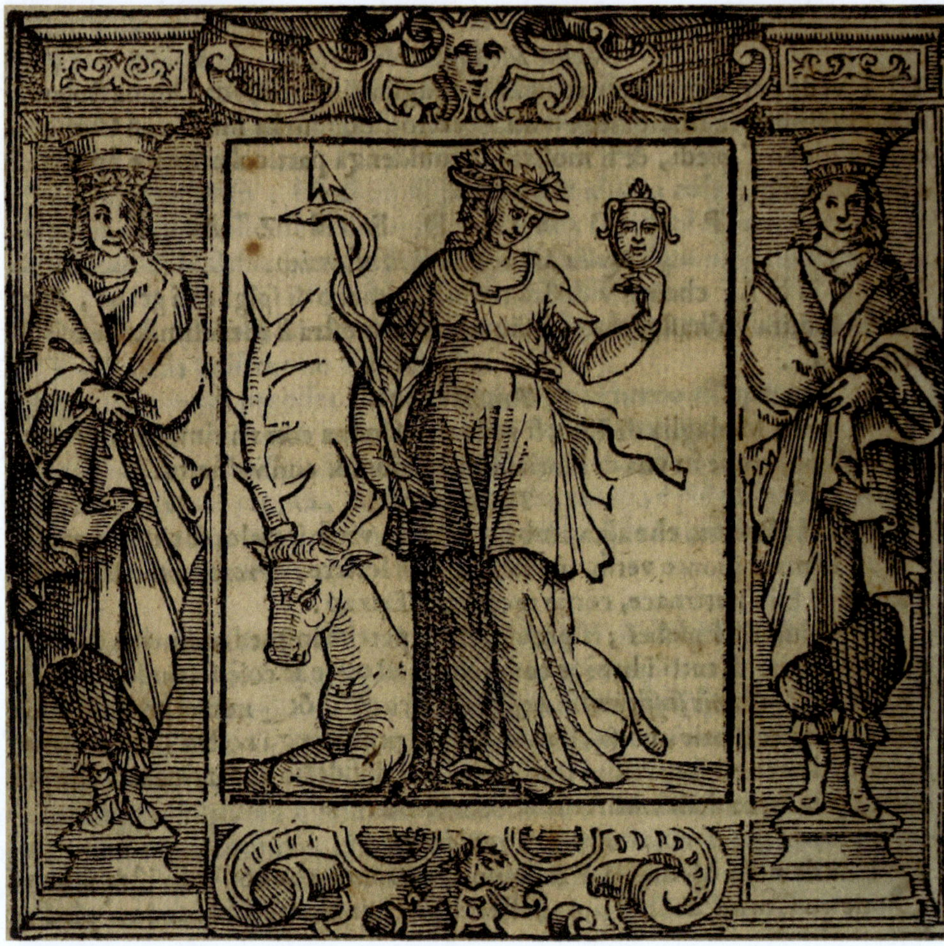

Fig. 152 Cesare Ripa, *Prudence with a Mirror*, engraving in *Iconologia*, Rome, 1613. Photo: Wikimedia

larger series of Cardinal Virtues, as of Veronese's *trompe-l'oeil* frescoes of allegory and *famiglia* at the Villa Barbaro. Prudence also figures in a full range of decorative arts, and across all aspects of print culture, from broadsheets to playing cards and illustrated books.[159] Her etymological origins lie in close alignment with wisdom, knowledge, reason, prescient forethought, and circumspect judgment, (its modern association with caution is a secondary definition historically) and therefore with good governance, of the self as of others. In both classical and Christian thought she was the *auriga virtutem*, or charioteer of all the virtues, as the personification of the rule of wisdom. She was a key allegory of princes as of queens, manifest throughout the *speculum principis* tradition, but also more broadly of the realm of women in the good governance of family and home, as the social foundations of statehood.[160] Consequently, the many treatises on the good conduct of women at every social level were often configured as mirrors of prudence – of modesty, but also great perspicacity in the management of men as of marriage and family.[161]

If the mirror of Prudence was common imagery within all manner of prints and printed books dedicated to the good governance of the family, she also figured within the domestic decorative arts as an emblem of virtuous womanhood. Such artefacts of quotidian use were decorated in tandem with texts of advice on circumspection and good conduct as a further branch of *speculum prudentiae et virtutis* books for women. Mirror decorations themselves often included the figure of Prudence, as an allegory of female self-reflection. Catherine de Médicis in particular favoured Prudence as an emblem of her sagacity as queen, which inspired much imitation in sixteenth-century French Renaissance decorative arts. The queen herself commissioned and designed state jewellery, both for her own ornament and as courtly diplomatic gifts, including jewelled pendant mirrors for Marguerite of Angoulême the Queen of Navarre and Margaret of Austria the Duchess of Savoy. The extent of her correspondence with her appointed goldsmiths details her close involvement in the development of jewellery elaborately coded with emblematic devices to signify the attributes of her reign.

Gold court jewellery of Catherine's rule often figured the image of Prudence in particular emulation of the Queen's chosen emblem. A mid-sixteenth-century French pendant of chalcedony and enamel displays the virtuous mirror of Prudence set as a diamond in a golden frame within the larger jewel face, while the reverse depicts Diana in enamels as the 'mirror-image' of female beauty and chastity (Fig. 153).[162] Beyond court circles, any number of mid-sixteenth-century French ornamental mirrors included the figure of Prudence holding a mirror in homage to Catherine as queen. Seemingly made after lost court pieces gem-set in gold, such design was then published as engraving by the court goldsmith Etienne Delaune for broad circulation and emulation. As a consequence, the figure of Prudence appeared as mirror decoration in all manner of dressing-table and toiletry mirrors for women in imitation of Queen Catherine. Some were embossed repoussé covers of gilt leather, for example, similar to luxury book bindings, again suggesting the emblematic devices of text and image that characterised

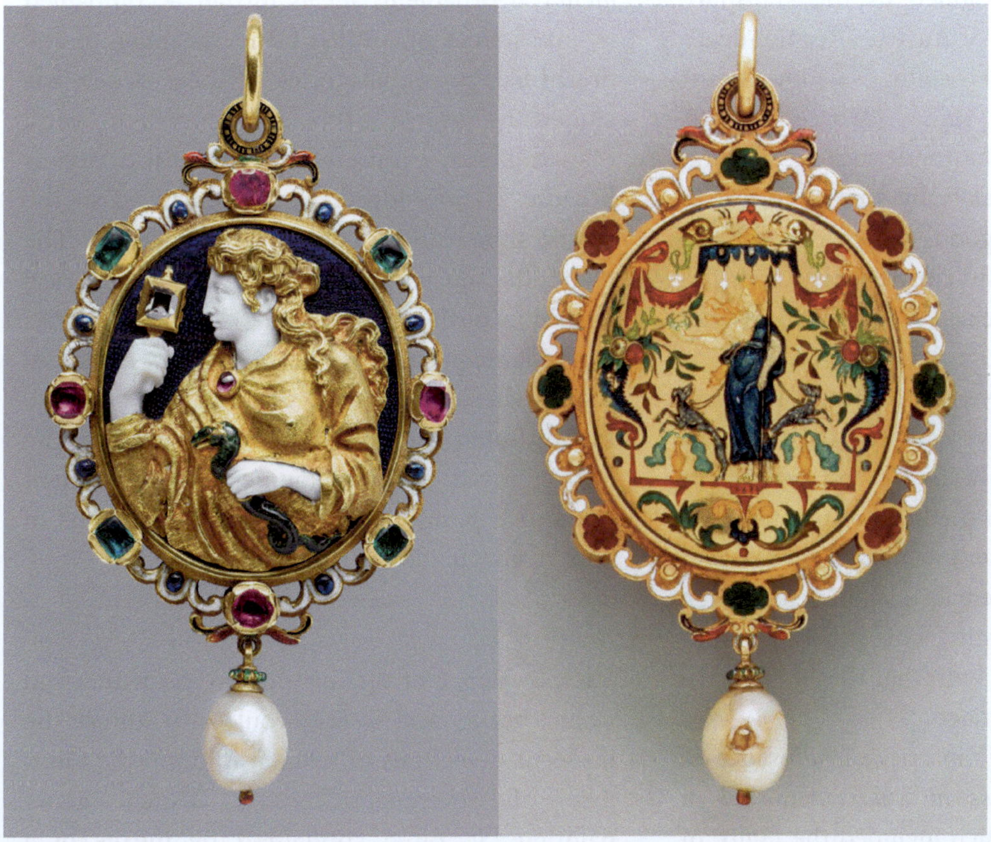

Fig. 153 'The Mirror of Prudence', c. 1550–60, French pendant jewel, chalcedony mounted in gold with enamel, rubies, emeralds, diamond, with pendant pearl, nineteenth-century enamel reverse after a design of Diana by Etienne Delaune, 8.2 × 4.8 cm, Metropolitan Museum of Art, New York, acc. no. 17.190.907. Photo: Metropolitan Museum of Art

Catherine's patronage.[163] Another of Delaune's mirror designs for print circulation and in emulation of the queen's wise rule depicted Julia Caesar, Caesar's daughter. Greatly loved by the Roman populace for her beauty as for her prudent virtue, she became an emblem of ideal queenship such as Catherine's, her mirror-image configured in precious metals or carved in wood, with pearl, crystal, or glass pendants (Fig. 17, Chapter 1).[164] Thus the mirror imagery of the queen's decorative arts set at court might have a significant diffusion into early modern dress and domestic interiors more broadly in emulation of her rule, in the particular domain of jewels and ornamented female toiletries, as of books for women on the happy governance of their marriage and home.

As the imagery of queens, Prudence also figured among the great decorative paintings commissioned at court in homage to the good graces of wise female rule. Thus Simon Vouet's figure of Prudence was commissioned by the Hapsburg queen of France Anne of Austria after the death of Louis XIII and her new status as widow-regent to represent her rule (Musée Fabre, Montpellier). In Vouet's rendering, the decorative gilt mirror held aloft by the three graces suggests the queen's good governance was by virtue of the beauty of Venus coupled with the perspicacity of Prudence.[165] Venus and her myriad reflections across the arts were seen as conducive to the happy government of marriage as of state, in a beauty tempered by measured reason. The figure of Prudence and her mirror therefore also graced a plethora of painted decorative arts of betrothal and marital gifts alongside Venus and other female allegories of beauty, virtue, and marital chastity. This is best exemplified in the great gilded betrothal chests of aristocratic Renaissance marriage.

For the Morelli-Nerli marriage in Florence of 1472, the nuptial trousseau was transported in magnificent *cassoni*, which included the figure of Prudence and her mirror among a series of painted triumphs, coats of arms, and allegories befitting their customary place in the bridal procession of marital gifts (Courtauld Gallery).[166] Such imagery also configured the painted decoration of bridal furniture, including dressing tables and mirrors alongside trousseau chests. In Giovanni Bellini's celebrated if deeply enigmatic allegorical paintings once part of a walnut-panelled domestic mirror stand, thought to have been a wedding gift, this included a figure of a female nude with a mirror as an emblem of truth and virtue as prudence (Fig. 154). Alongside the painted panels, the cabinetry would have housed luxury toiletry items such as ivory combs and bottles of scent. Within the image, Bellini's nude holds aloft a convex mirror in a gilt-edged arabesque frame. She points to the mirror's miniaturising shadowy reflection, in which we dimly see a face in a seeming pendant pair to her own as the coupling of marriage. Standing on a pedestal of *all'antica* ornament, she is further accompanied by music-making putti. If the meaning of the dream-like poetic allegories of these panels has eluded the extensive scholarship on them, yet a refined literary culture of metaphorical devices is broadly acknowledged, as emblematised in the arcane significance of the mirror reflection. The recondite and elusive nature of their allegorical invention further suggests the close artistic links with Mantegna and others of Bellini's circle, on the intellectual sources of their art. Bellini's domesticated yet elliptical significance of the mirror motif in a personification of prudent virtue is a *paragone* on the poetic inventions of artistic imagination as of fortune itself.[167]

***

Such bivalence of the mirror sign as fortune and virtue, beauty and vanity, would also suffuse the insistent depictions of women in domestic interiors of seventeenth-century Dutch genre painting. So often configured by means of a

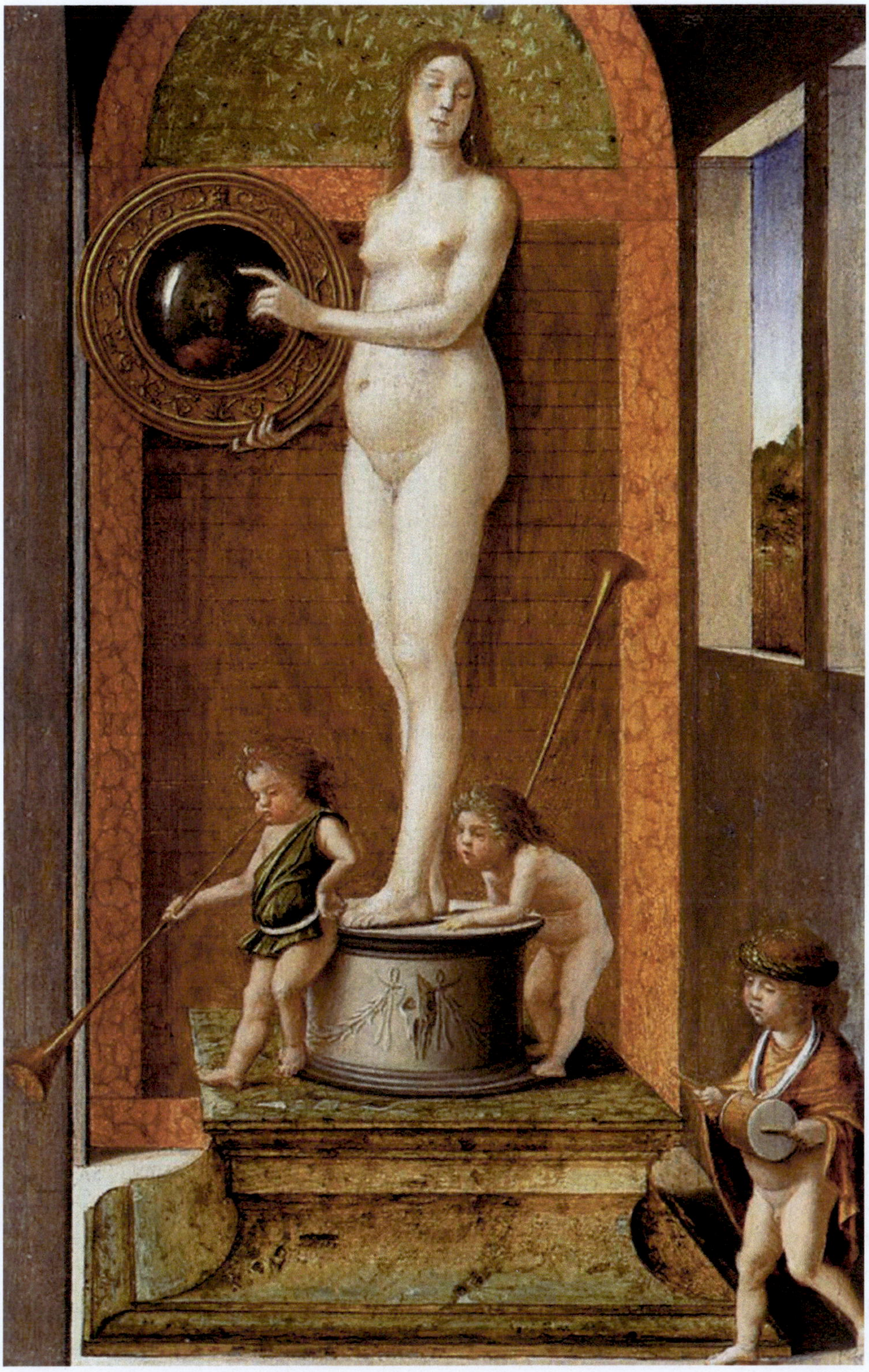

Fig. 154 Giovanni Bellini, *Allegory with a Mirror*, c. 1490, *restello*, oil on panel, 32 × 22 cm, Gallerie dell'Accademia, Venice.
Photo: Wikimedia

mirror reflection in the image of female prudence, yet this domestic imagery of women was also deeply enigmatic, as its extensive and often bifurcated scholarship attests to. A burgeoning of paintings depicting the Dutch domestic interior after 1648's Treaty of Westphalia that inaugurated Dutch independence configured an emerging cultural identity of prudence within the 'homestead' of its national values. Thus the subject of Dutch nationhood perforce centred on the myriad representations of women as guardians of the home as of the state. Whether of mothers and children, courtship and love, or its antithesis in depictions of courtesans and merry company, women were emblems of *amour* of different kinds held up as exemplars in a comparative relationship of gently moralised pictorial types.[168] As the scholarship has generally noted, the apparent 'double-face' of such Dutch domestic imagery is a mirror-image of itself, in which the painted admonitions against the sins of vanity and lust were an often-humorous counterpoint to those that eulogized the sanctity of Dutch motherhood, as well as the visual pleasures of art. Scholars have long and famously argued as to the signifying codes of these works, which are generally seen as cloaked in a pictorial ambiguity of disguised meaning, between a mirroring mimesis of an 'art of describing' and a metaphorical mirror of moral instruction.[169] A structure of veiled comparison also pervaded early modern Dutch emblematic literature of advice and guidance to women, as scholars wedded to a moralised interpretation of this painted imagery have much recourse to. This is noted especially in the widely published and much-read familial and gently humorous proverbial homilies of the Dutch jurist and moralist Jacob Cats.

In Cats' great Dutch emblem book, titled *Spiegel* (Mirror) of 1632, the author acknowledged his domesticated veiling of the subject's attributes 'to explain something in a hidden way'.[170] His title was intended as the gentle mirror of conscience, like a great profusion of early modern books entitled as 'mirrors' offering moral and ethical guidance of various kinds. This literature, much of which was aimed at the instruction of women in the arts of marriage as of beauty, had broad recourse to the metaphor of the mirror, albeit a bivalent one: if women were enjoined to the artful preparations of beauty's pleasures, yet they were also lightly admonished as a vanity, and thus gently reproved by the 'true' mirror of modesty as the gauge of a feminine grace. Cats' epithets, illustrated in roundel form as the pictorial mirrors or *spiegel* of custom, were the most widely circulated texts of seventeenth-century Dutch book culture and fully commensurate with Ripa's book of allegorical personifications of a moral cast.[171] Testament to their wide cultural reach, many of Cats' emblems passed into a wealth of Dutch proverbs to become household phrases. Gentle lessons in self-reflection and self-improvement, they were intended as both humorous and exemplary. Among them were such epithets as 'Everyone's mirror is a reflection of themselves.' Touching on what has become known as the Dutch Golden Age 'embarrassment of riches', this was the perceived analogy between a vanity of possessions and character. The accompanying 'mirror figure' illustration to Cats' text depicts a familial couple amid a wealth of domestic objects in which the woman, seated at a dressing table with a toilet mirror, turns to listen to his kindly admonishment of her conspicuous display of vanity, while it is the man's face that figures in the mirror's reflection (Fig. 155).

If the question of Cats' formative influence on the rise of Dutch genre painting is an open one in the scholarship, yet the cultural matrix of such popular visual emblematic imagery as a humorous 'mirror' of self-improvement was so pervasive that it surely touched contemporaneous reception of painting, and so its intentions, even if the

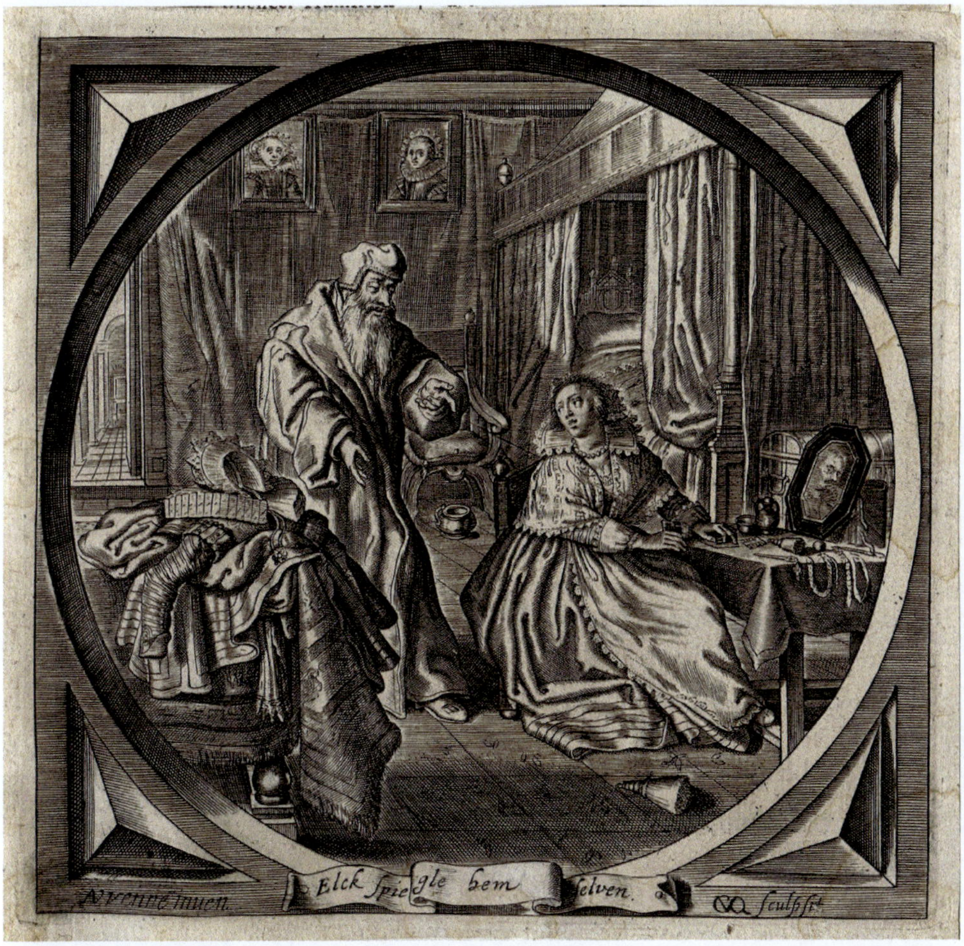

Fig. 155 Crispijn van Queborn after Adriaen van de Venne, *Elck spiegelt hem selven*, etching in Jacob Cats, *Spiegel van den Ouden ende Nieuwen Tijdt*, 1632. Photo: British Museum

precise nature of the relationship remains ambiguous. The 'art of describing' that Svetlana Alpers identified in seventeenth-century Dutch painting may itself be interpreted as possessing a moral cast, of artistic industry and care, and so the mirror of Dutch propriety. This is in keeping with the prevalent use of 'mirror' book titles concerned with moral instruction, such as Cats'. As Dutch printed emblematic imagery discloses, the prevailing paradigm is one of comparison between the representation of life and its mirror image, of which its specular reflection is the telling sign. Much of it also reflects on the representation of the Dutch domestic interior, itself the subject of great debate both then and in current scholarship because of its perception as the locus of a nascent Dutch moral identity in the political construction of its newly formed republic. While we cannot assume that the painted representation of domestic mirrors in art is measurable historical evidence of their material display within the early modern Dutch interior, we can argue that their insistent depiction within paintings of Dutch homes and women – as in prints and the decorative arts – signifies the mirror-image's perceived critical position in the representation of Netherlandish art and culture. This surely encompasses both the mirror as a moral trope of beauty and its judgment, in all senses, and the specular reflection as the metaphor and measure of a justly celebrated Dutch art of description.

Thus, Cornelis de Man's *Game of Cards* (Fig. 156), for example, depicts a couple at a card table covered in deep blue cloth edged with gold, behind which a wooden-framed mirror sits against a leaded window. The young woman in the foreground appears from behind, seated on a red tapestry stool complemented by her scarlet bodice and shoe. As she turns her head, the view of her face offers a Titianesque *paragone* with the mirror view of the back of the head but also, tellingly, of her décolleté neckline framed in a white ruffle. It is both a minor scene of domestic genre and a proverbial pictorialisation of the 'playing cards' of love as of beauty's seductions, for she is like a Cnidian Venus, viewed from the front as from the back. In this sense such images may be understood as polyvalent and often ambivalent reflections on the perils of love

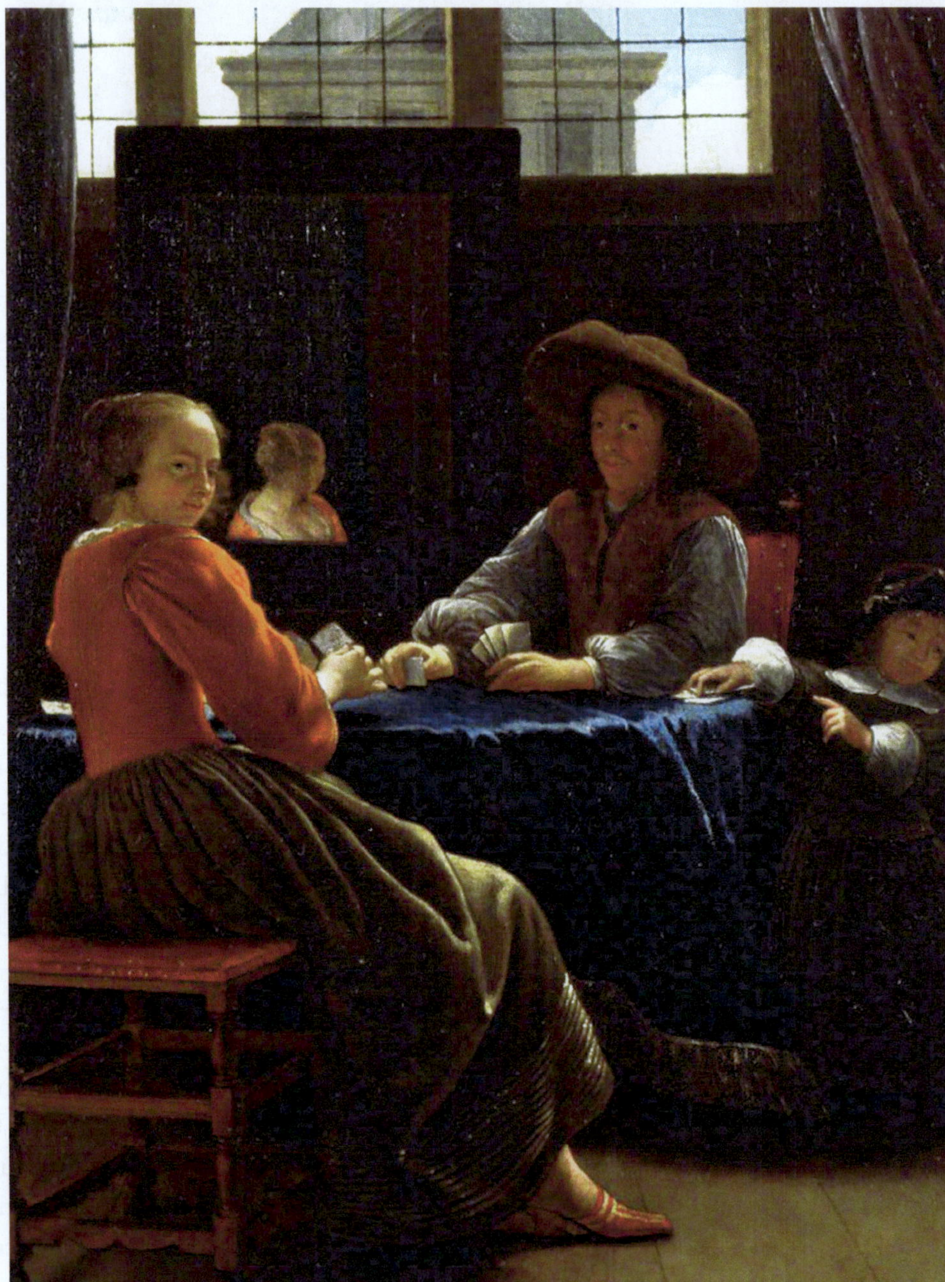

Fig. 156 Cornelis de Man, *The Game of Cards*, c. 1655, oil on panel, 43.2 × 33 cm, Polesden Lacey, Surrey, NT 1246498. Photo: Wikimedia

embodied in the evanescent beauty of woman, like the mirror reflection, but also as painted emblems of the love of art. Just as youth and beauty are fleeting, so too are the illusions of paint. Like the mirror of Narcissus, painting's shimmering deceit is only ever an absent presence, a beauty as ethereal as a mirror reflection.[172]

Many seventeenth-century Netherlandish painters took up the Venetian *cinquecento* theme of the female toilet, transposing this Renaissance *bella donna* subject *all'antica* into early modern Dutch homes. Here it became both a celebration of the modern Dutch homestead as the moral foundation of the state but also a gentle reminder of beauty's ephemerality, as a *vanitas*, like all worldly things. In this respect, the exquisite mimeticism of a Dutch art of describing – its satins, furs, Turkish rugs, porcelain, pewter ewers, and lustrous brass chandeliers – depicts interiors of a shimmering feminine luxury to convey the domestic pleasures of a newfound Dutch opulence but also a warning of fortune's fleeting evanescence, like the passing sheen of a mirror reflection.[173]

Gabriel Metsu, as a preeminent artist of the Dutch home, painted the subject frequently, and variously, in the modest dimensions of cabinet pictures for the Dutch burgher house. In the meticulous jewelled surfaces of his paintings, each work is itself a seeming mirror-image. For example, in *The Huntsman Visiting the Lady at Her Toilet* (private collection), a young woman in a splendour of white satin sits before a table at an open window with a covering of Turkish rug. Before her lie a richly chased silver casket for toiletries and a dressing-table mirror in ornately carved gilt, as the emblems of a venereal toilet in a Petrarchan idiom here transposed into a Dutch display of mercantile luxury. These jewel-like objects frame the beauty of the woman, set within the minor domestic narrative of courtship from a gentleman caller, and so intimating her forthcoming transformation from maidenhood.[174] In other examples, Metsu depicts a woman in a sober dress of earthen hues at her dressing table seemingly lost in thought (private collection). She gazes into her mirror, gently touching its ornate gilt frame to adjust her view as she straightens her white bonnet in a scene of tranquil domestic interiority. Beside the mirror is the glint of a silvered casket, suggesting these are the toiletries of her marriage trousseau, and so a cherished recollection of her passage into womanhood. The intimacy of the scene as one of quiet reflection is surely mirrored by that of the viewer's regard, for in beholding the woman we are like the looking-glass in which she sees herself. Her profile head is further framed by the picture hanging on the wall behind her, of which we can read only the intimation of a green curtain before it, recalling both the skill of Parrhasios as the measure of Metsu's mimetic art, but also the composition of her mirror-like 'portrait'.[175] The subject was also a recurring one in the work of Gerard ter Borch, whose paintings touched lightly on the line between pleasure and prudence in the female toilet. In one example, Ter Borch represents the theme as a gentle *vanitas* that both celebrates and hints at the passing of youthful beauty (c. 1652, Rijksmuseum). A young woman in fashionable dress of shimmering satin and gold trim, with her hair elaborately coiffed by means of ribbons, sits before an ebony-framed mirror held up to her in which we see her reflected face. Together the painting offers her to the viewer from the front and the back, like a Cnidian Venus. Her gaze, however, is directed not towards us but to her older companion beside her, soberly dressed as a figure of Prudence, to recall the effects of time on youth and the constant vigilance of sound judgment. Thus the work both celebrates and gently cautions female beauty through the medium of painting, like Cats' bivalent 'mirror' of Dutch wealth. This is emblematised in the inset image or painted reflection of the young woman's face as the mirror of an evanescent art of beauty.

In another example the young woman is washing her hands in a pewter basin with the assistance of a maid as a metaphor of Dutch cleanliness but also of the venereal toilet (Fig. 157). On the walls are two cabinet pictures in chased silver frames that echo the satin sheen of her dress. Behind her, a small framed mirror stands on a dressing table beside a silver box and a leather-bound book. Their arrangement together may suggest a gentle *vanitas* in the contiguity of biblical study and the instruments of beauty's adornments; yet the mirror and the book, like the paintings (of which she is one), are also conjoined metaphors of knowledge in which viewing and reading are linked modes of meditated reflection.[176]

The mirror and the book arise together in a range of such scenes of Dutch domesticity, in further allegorical elaborations of the painter's art as *pictura poesis*. Pieter Jannsens Elinga depicted the theme variously, also representing himself in the act of painting from these joint foundations of his art (Fig. 158). The artist, with palette in hand, is in a further room seen through a doorway; the brightly lit windows contrast with the

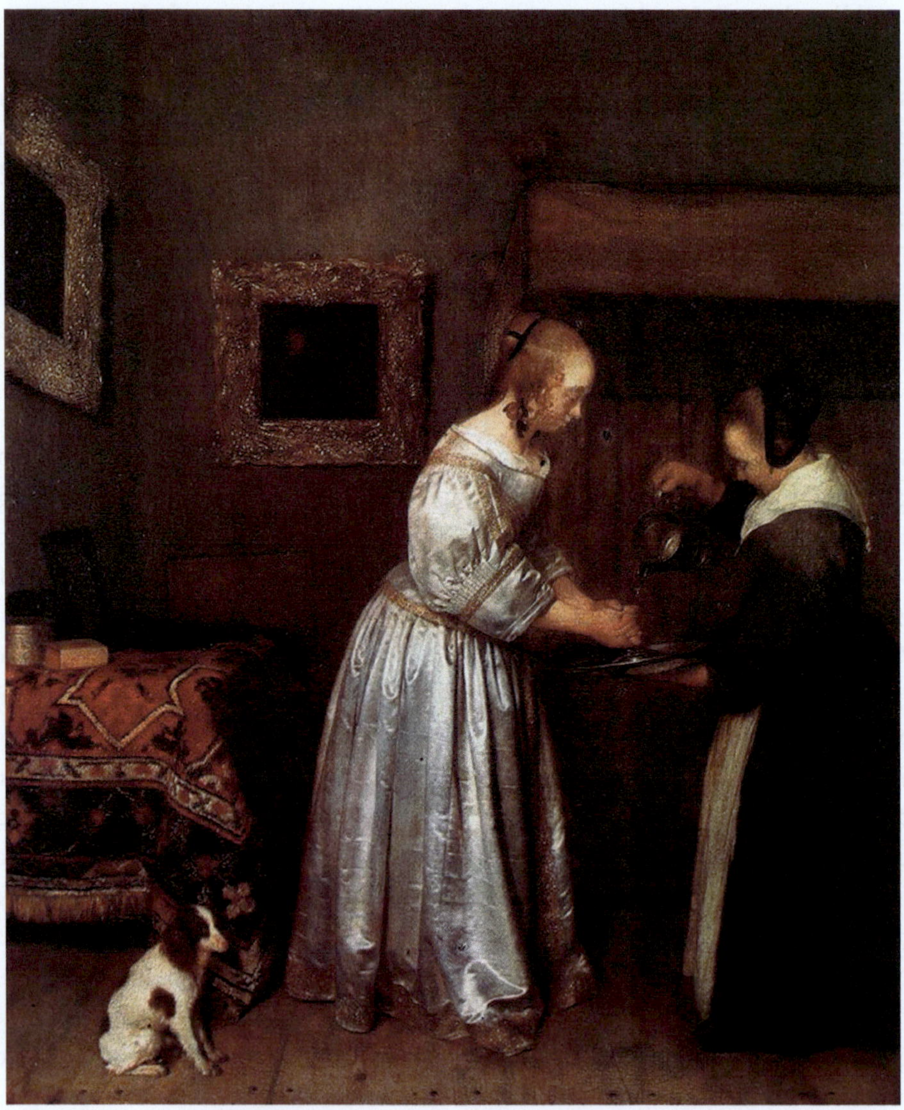

Fig. 157 Gerard ter Borch, *A Woman Washing Hands*, c. 1665, oil on oak wood, 53 × 43 cm, Staatliche Kunstsammlungen Dresden. Photo: Wikimedia

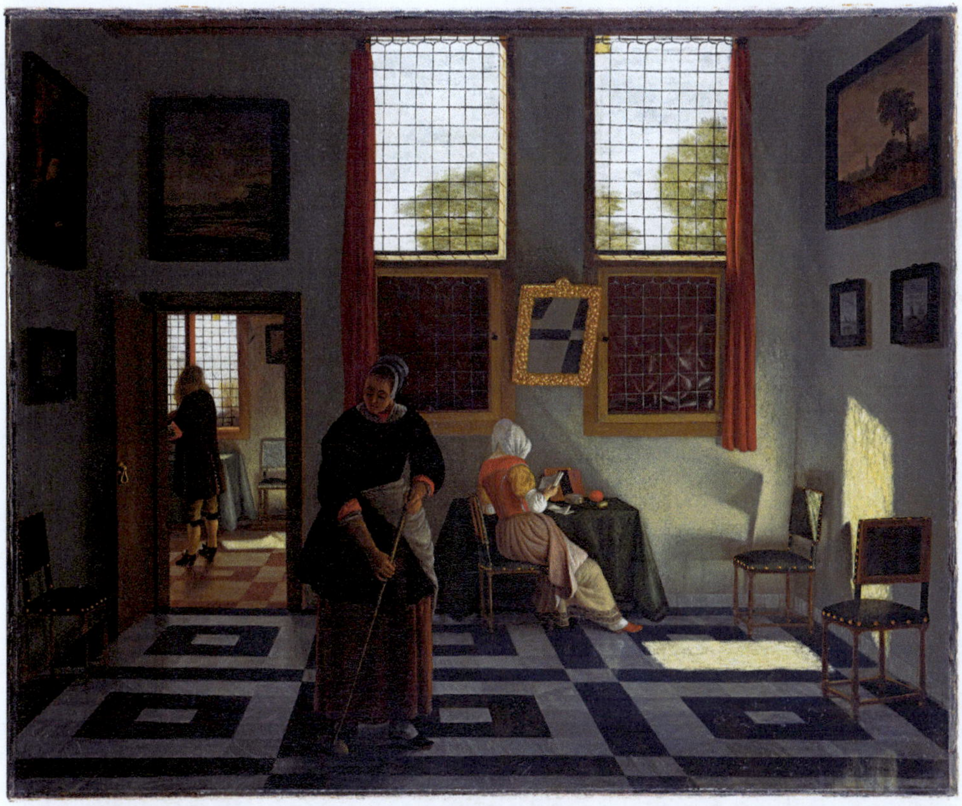

Fig. 158 Pieter Janssens Elinga, *Interior with Artist, Woman Reading, Maid Sweeping,* c. 1665–70, oil on canvas, 82 × 99 cm, Städel Museum, Frankfurt. Photo: Städel Museum, Frankfurt am Main

shaded light of the main salon where a maid sweeps while a woman reads at a table surmounted by a gilt-framed mirror. The downward angle of the mirror's face reflects back the black-and-white tiles of the floor, just as the woman's face is modestly covered by a white bonnet, and the maid's eyes downcast, while the artist turns away from the viewer towards the light of the window beside him as he paints. The painting both depicts and veils the intimated wealth of a measured Dutch domesticity, in which the brightest object on display is the mirror's gold-painted frame.

Equally pervasive in seventeenth-century Dutch depictions of women reading in interiors was the subject of the love letters of courtship. It formed one of a range of pictorial subjects associated with women and the conduct of marriage. As authors of the period extolled, courtship was a critical step in the biography of women. A further text by Cats, his influential 1625 treatise on marriage and family titled *Houwelyck* (Matrimony), was arranged into chapters according to the stages of a woman's life, from maiden to sweetheart, then bride, housewife, and mother. Paintings also pictorialized this progress of ritual events in women's lives, of which courtship, with its opportunity for all manner of veiled moral and social comment, formed a significant category.[177] An example by Gabriel Metsu makes full emblematic use of the picture-within-the picture motif to clarify the nature of love's epistolary relations (Fig. 159). A young woman who is both expensively yet modestly dressed in coloured silks and furs with a white bonnet to cover her hair sits by a window, in the light of which she reads a letter just received from the maid beside her. At her feet are both a dog and a shoe, generally regarded as familiar and even colloquial emblems of love and marriage for Dutch viewers of the day, as cultural tropes of fidelity and coupling.[178] She turns the letter to the window

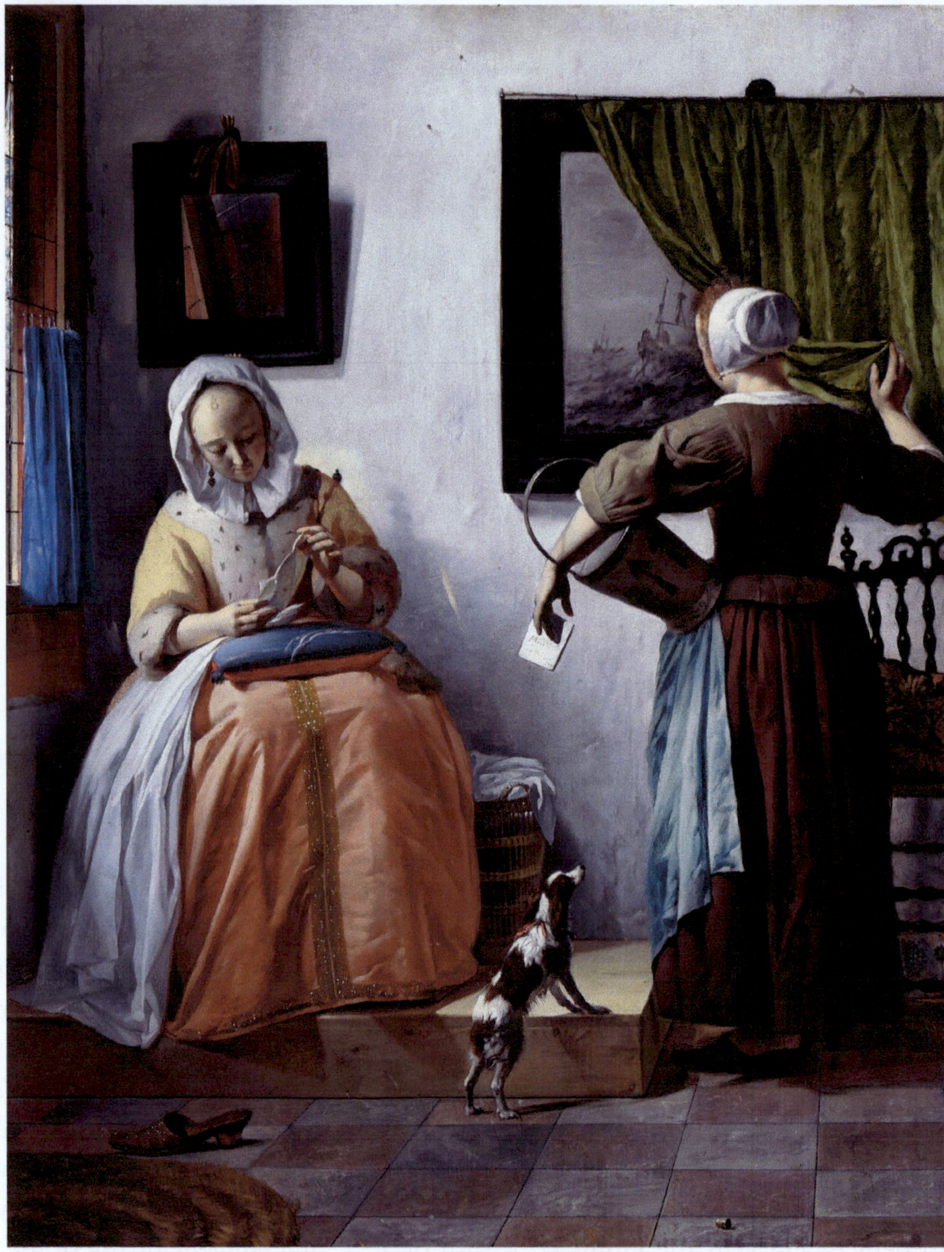

Fig. 159 Gabriel Metsu, *Lady Reading a Letter*, 1662–65, oil on canvas, 53 × 40 cm, National Gallery of Ireland, Dublin. Photo: Wikimedia

and away from the maid so as not to disclose its contents. Yet the maid, whom we see from behind in a counterpoint to her mistress, is nonetheless aware. She draws back a green curtain over a painting, from the corner of which we perceive it to depict a ship in stormy seas, as a common metaphor both for the transmission of letters and the travails of love as of fortune. To the left, and directly above the young woman's head, is a mirror, framed in ebony like the seascape it hangs beside, attached to the wall at an angle. Its reflection faces us, like the mistress, displaying an elliptical slice of quotidian domesticity, the edge of the leaded window beside. Such reflections are frequent within the depiction of Dutch domestic interiors, suggesting the mirror's means as an instrument of descriptive imitation of the painter's visible field. The sequence of window, mirror, and painting is also common reference to art's mimetic sway, following van Eyck's Arnolfini example. In her other hand, Metsu's maid holds a further letter, though this one is addressed to the viewer, for here the artist has artfully rendered his signature: Mr / Metsu / tot Amst[erdam] / Port. Thus Metsu infers that if art is like a window or a mirror, it is also like a letter to the viewer: in the manner of emblems it is both an image and a text.[179] Artist and viewers are similarly art-lovers, joined in the representation of feminine beauty as the cultural sign of painting's pleasures in the mirror-image of art.

Vermeer's *Girl Reading a Letter at an Open Window* (Fig. 160) also invokes the sequential arrangement of window, reflection, and painting as a pictorial meditation on the art of love as of paint, emblematised in the representation of female beauty. Dressed in lemon and black silk

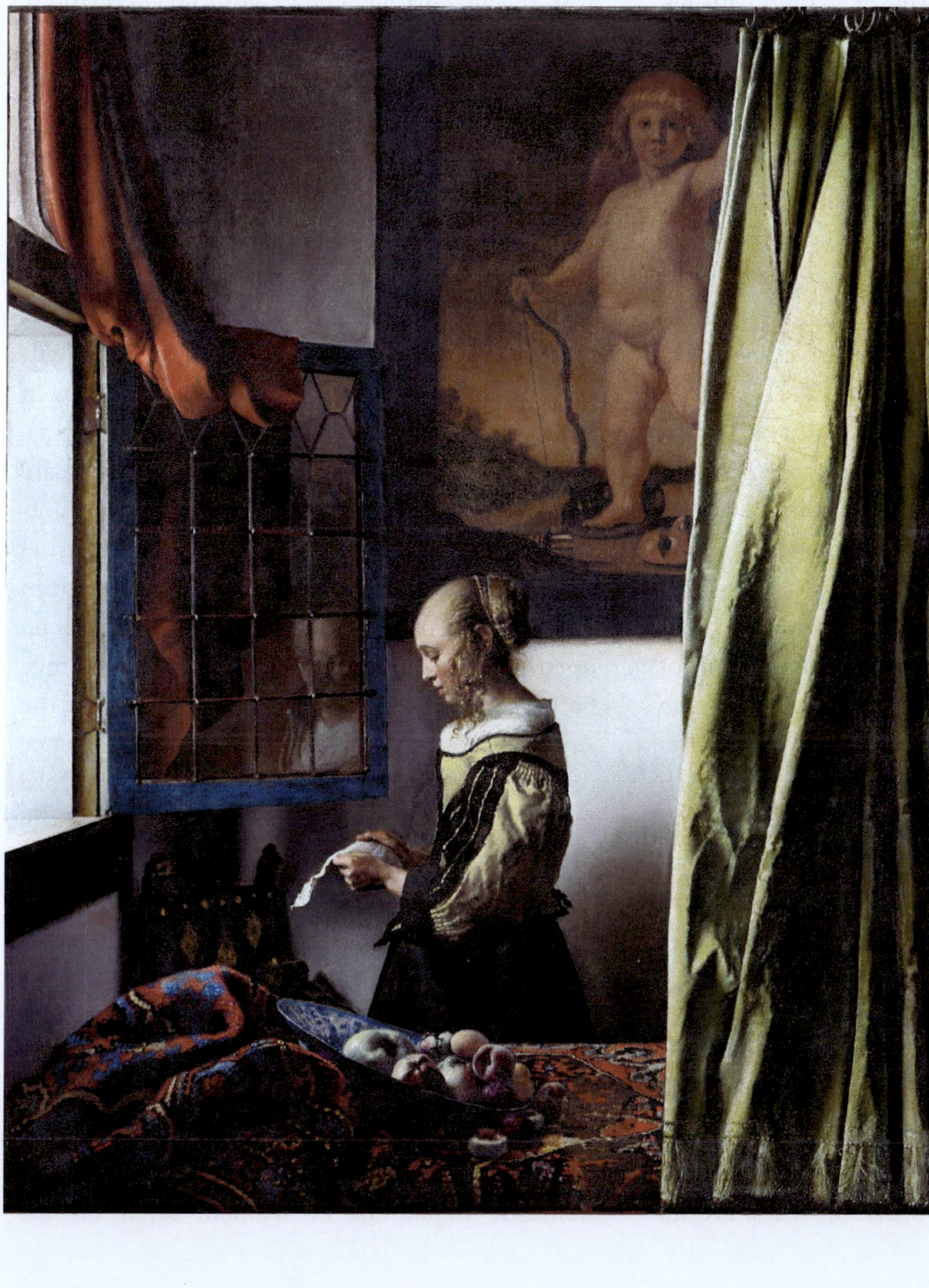

Fig. 160 Johannes Vermeer, *Girl Reading a Letter by an Open Window*, 1657–59, oil on canvas, 64.5 × 83 cm, Gemäldegalerie Alte Meister, Dresden. Photo: Wikimedia

ruched with velvet ribbon, the young woman stands in profile before the leaded panes of an open window in which her face is depicted frontally in muted reflection. The window's red curtain is draped behind the pane, so framing this 'reflection painting' of her face. In the immediate foreground there falls a further curtain of shimmering green silk, to suggest both a covered cabinet painting and a momentary view into an otherwise private domestic interior. Recent conservation has restored a further painting-within-the-painting on the back wall, of a cupid with his bow, whose direct gaze is a counterpoint to the downcast eyes of the young woman before him. With his raised left arm, he seems to draw back the curtain as if to reveal the woman to her viewer, so putting her painted beauty on display. The cupid's painted presence articulates not only the nature of her letter but also the relationship between the painter, the viewer, and the painting itself, as the mirroring reflection of mimetic art lightly allegorised as an act of love.[180]

A further elaboration of the amatory relationship between the pictorial representation of female beauty and the art-lover within seventeenth-century Dutch genre painting was that of music-making scenes. This took on particular significance in the depiction of young women playing a virginal as the instrument of their virtue. The instrument itself provided the occasion for further paintings-within-the-painting, as common pictorial decoration to such pieces of cabinetry furniture. Thus in Metsu's *Lady at a Virginal* (Museum Boijmans van Beuningen, Rotterdam) the instrument is decorated with painted grisaille ornament *all'antica*, further bearing two painted devotional inscriptions to signal music as a form of praise, to which Metsu adds his signature.[181] The slipper and the dog are, again, readily identified cultural metaphors of love and marriage within Dutch imagery. In the adjoining room a maid sits on a chest, surely a wedding trousseau, with a broom to the side as a metaphor of the home's cleanliness, both material and spiritual. Between the two windows hangs a wall-mounted mirror in a carved gilt frame facing directly to the viewer. Yet its powers of reflection are veiled by the curtain suspended across it, just as the faces of the two women are wrapped in the soft shadow of modesty. It would seem to emblematise a concept of veiled pictorial meaning as it was expounded in Netherlandish art theory by writers such as Carel van Mander and Samuel van Hoogstraten, as well as in the allegorically coded word-image relations of emblem books such as that of Cats. Emanuel de Witte's *Woman at a Virginal* (Fig. 161) similarly depicts the mistress of the house making music while a maid sweeps in a further apartment behind. Throughout, the measured space of the home is marked out by patterns of reflected sunlight that fall across the inlaid perspective floor, cast by large leaded windows. At the front, the mistress plays the virginal. Above her, a gilt-carved frame encloses a mirror that, as in Vermeer's *Music Lesson* (Fig. 88, Chapter 3), reveals the top of her head in its modest white bonnet. Beyond, the reflection dims, tracing outlines of a further window and an over-mantel painting frame. The mirror hangs between windows, paintings, and the view through an open doorway, suggesting an equivalence between them, in a Netherlandish lineage of the Arnolfini portrait's specular claim. The sequence of window and mirror perspectives they afford further allegorises the Dutch art of painting as a mirror window view.

As also discussed in Chapter 2, other images of the Netherlandish home similarly draw together mirrors, paintings, and views through windows and doorways, like a sequence of pictorial or 'window-frame' motifs within the pictorial field or '*schild*' of Netherlandish art that van Mander's 1604 *Het Schilderboek* commemorated. Such mirror-images act as metaphorical frames to domestic depictions of women, often on the

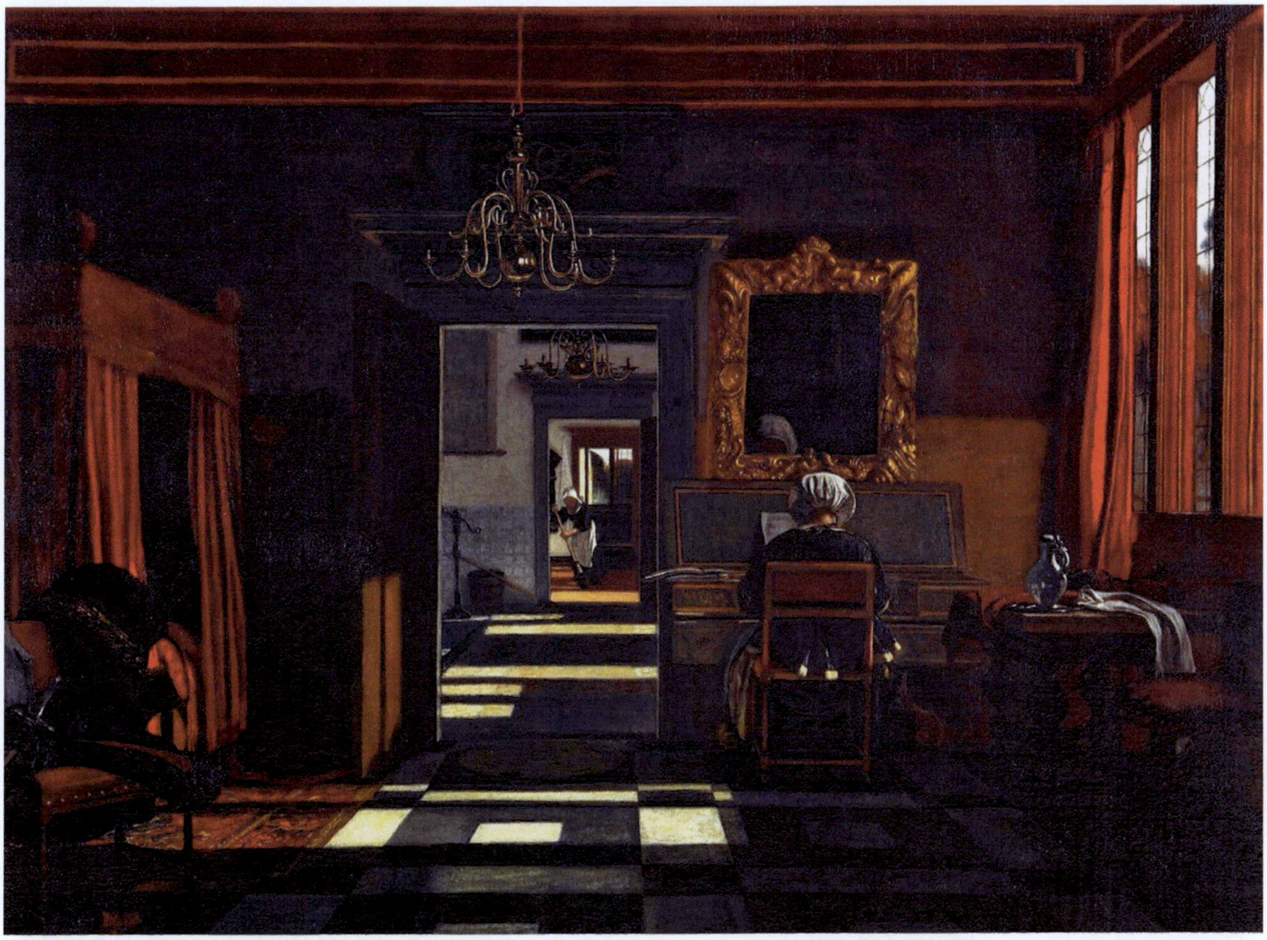

Fig. 161 Emanuel de Witte, *Interior with a Woman at the Virginal*, c. 1665–70, oil on canvas, 77.5 × 104.5 cm, Museum Boijmans Van Beuningen, Rotterdam.
Photo: Wikimedia

theme of maternity with children as the foundations of the Dutch home. Pieter de Hooch, contemporary to Vermeer in Delft, depicted the subject in a number of works of Dutchifying interiors. In one painting, a young mother in a white bonnet makes up a box bed, while a child enters from the open view behind, framed by a succession of doorways. Above the door hangs a landscape painting, so highlighting the pictorialisation of the view itself. Small mirrors mounted on the walls on either side face into the interior space of the room, framed in ebony and gilt, respectively. In other examples, de Hooch paints domestic interiors of Turkish rugs and Chinese porcelain as emblems of Dutch wealth through trade, coupled with minor familial narratives of motherhood – nursing or putting an infant to sleep, or teaching a young child to walk – the scene pictorialized within itself by means of a mirror reflection. At one level, such images are pictorial descriptions of homely Dutch domesticity, yet they are also meditations on the art of painting as a mirror reflection, like a view through a doorway or window.[182] In de Hooch's *Woman Giving Money to a Servant Girl*, c. 1668–72, a mother, seated by a window, looks up from her needlework to give her maid a coin to take to market while a small child plays before an open hearth (Fig. 162). The large gilt-framed mirror suspended by a ribbon above her further reflects the appurtenances of the home: the Turkish rug and the handsomely shaped water

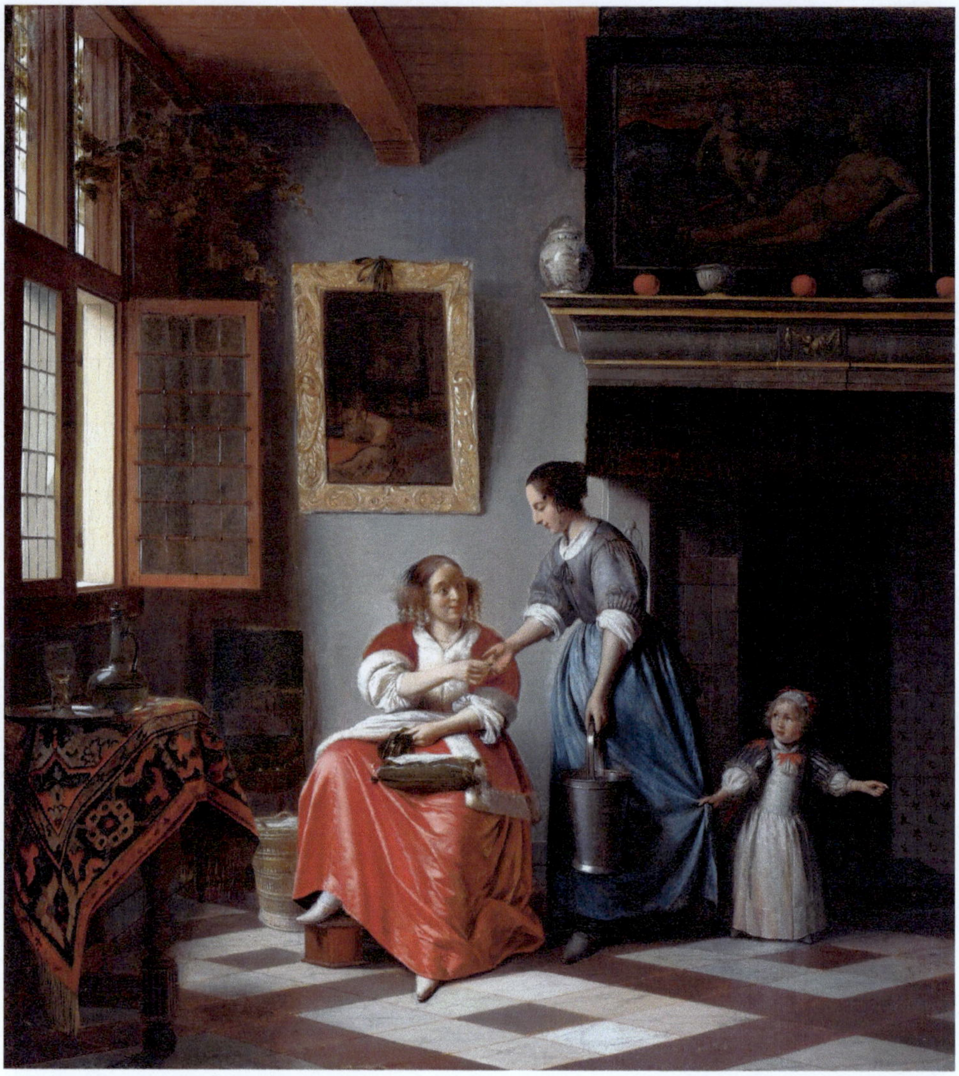

Fig. 162 Pieter de Hooch, *Woman Giving Money to a Servant Girl*, c. 1668–72, oil on canvas, 67.5 × 59 cm, private collection.
Photo: Wikimedia

jug that rests on the table beside her, like a fragment of still life. Laden with signs, yet these images also echo the place of painting simply to describe a world of objects within the Dutch home, whether of virtue or its gently humorous ambivalence, as the veritable 'mirror' on which its nascent national culture was understood to rest.[183]

Such familial imagery might also include family portraits in the domestic interior of a Dutch home, as in Emanuel de Witte's *Portrait of a Family* (1678, Alte Pinakothek, Munich), of a prosperous and lavishly appointed burgher house. Mother and father are seated at a table covered by a Turkish rug on which rests a glass vase of flowers. Richly yet soberly dressed in black silk and white lace, they receive their daughter, who wears an overdress embroidered with flowers and further roses in her hair and offers them a platter of fruit. Through the open door behind her we view an enclosed courtyard garden with a portico, an ornamental arch, and marble statuary. A number of paintings hang above the gold-embossed leather wall covering. Only one is frontally displayed, surely intended as de Witte's pictorial 'signature' in depicting a church interior of the kind that typified his artistic output, further singled out by a fictive green curtain drawn back to allow viewing. To the other side of the *all'antica* hearth, a gold-framed mirror captures a fragment of the carved capital but is otherwise in shadow, facing inwards to the interior of the room in an ellipsis of its own art. The other paintings visible from their frames are similarly occluded from view. Again, de Witte draws together a sequence of mirror, paintings, and the view through a door frame as a pictorial statement on the equivocal nature of a Dutch mimetic art. Across the range of this genre of painting, of women pictured within domestic interiors at every social level, the female figure is a further metaphor of the beauty of art, in this example heightened by the ornament of flowers and the enclosed garden of Marian virtue, also a trope of love within the bounds of marriage and family.[184]

The insistent mimetic representation of the well-appointed Dutch home and family was also manifest in a range of decorative arts, including collectors' cabinets of all kinds. Among the most prized of such collectibles were the *puppenhaus*, models in miniature of Dutch houses equipped with every accoutrement of domestic appointment and peopled by tiny figures representing the *familias* of a burgher house. Like the myriad seventeenth-century paintings of the Dutch home, these were highly coded signifying spaces of emblematic representation, to use Martha Hollander's phrase, of a Dutch identity bound to the homestead.[185] Thus, among the luxury possessions of the fashionable Amsterdam merchant Johannes Brandt and his wife Petronella Oortman was a large *puppenhaus* cabinet of tortoiseshell and pewter inlay with glass-fronted doors, measuring some 2.5 by 2 metres. Crafted by a French cabinet maker in 1686 according to Petronella's bespoke request, it was designed to house in miniature replica the apartments and accoutrements of their own home, as in the proverbial Dutch 'mirror' of themselves. Employing expert craftworkers in textiles, joinery, metal-, and glass work, readily accessible to her through her husband's position in the lucrative Amsterdam silk trade, Petronella commissioned miniature copies of the range of goods that characterised their home, from silk upholstery to porcelain, silverware, carved furniture, paintings, and mirrors. Material representations of the world of goods of Dutch early modern trading and trades, collectors like Petronella commissioned in miniature thousands of pieces of the same materials as their own houses, and reputedly at the same costs – silver, glass, silk, linen, ebony and cherry woods, brass, leather, gilt, Chinese porcelain, Turkish rugs. As cabinet-sized encapsulations of the domestic realm, like seventeenth-century genre paintings of interiors, the *puppenhaus* offered a further mimetic 'mirror' or emblematic exemplification of the Dutch home. Like early modern collections of arts and crafts within princely *Wunderkammern*, they were surely conversation pieces within Dutch social forms but also material repositories of national ideals of domesticity and labour as the cornerstones of both family and state.[186] Some, such as the Stromer *haus*, contained over a thousand objects, artfully laid out as if in present use by its occupants – clothes and toiletries, playing cards and opened letters. In a further mimetic display, even miniature emblem books might be left open on tables, as with a Haarlem example, suggesting that allegorical readings in the manner of Cats were intended in the arrangements of *puppenhaus* furnishings. Further examples such as the *haus* of Petronella de la Court represented a birthing chamber in miniature and a small sitting room with a dressed day bed as the customary reception room for female visitors following family births. Mirrors in elaborately carved gilt frames ornament the walls throughout the wealthy de la Court *puppenhaus*, in the bedrooms, the study, and in the

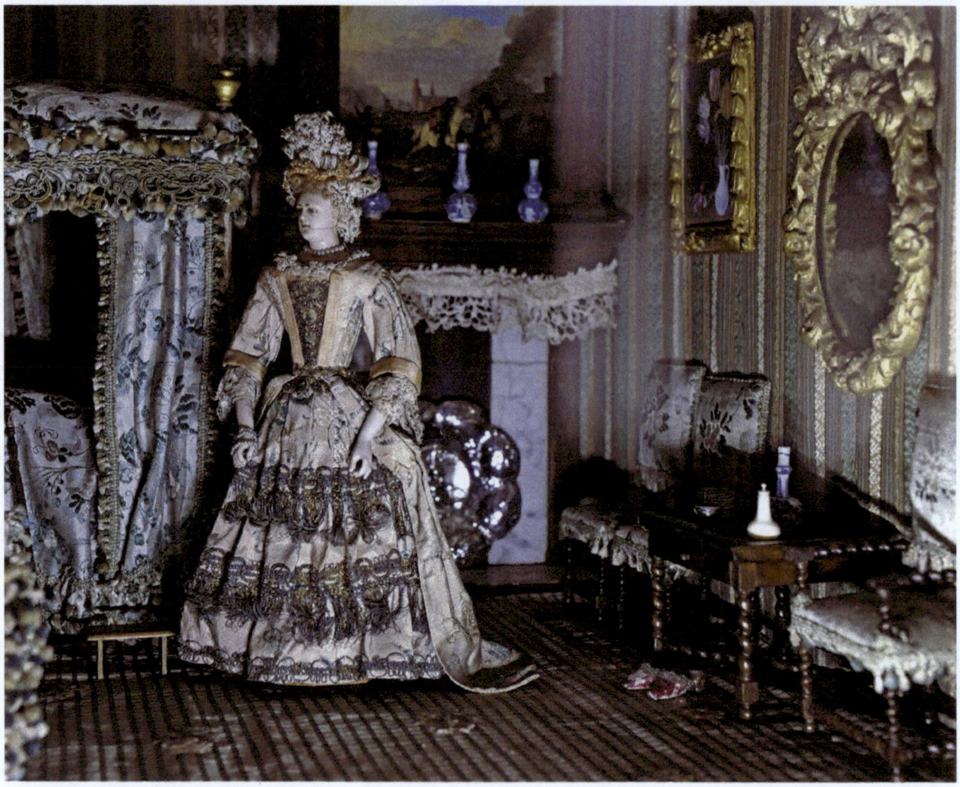

Fig. 163a Petronella de la Court, detail of the master bedroom, *puppenhaus*, 1670–90, oak and walnut wooden cabinet, 206.5 × 189 × 279 cm, Centraal Museum, Utrecht. Photo: Alamy

salon, set against artfully painted walls of classical landscapes (Fig. 163a, b). As imitations of the Dutch home in miniature, the *puppenhäuser* were broadly understood as 'mirrors' of emblematic instruction in the *bienséance* and good governance of the home, as a mimetic metaphor of a 'homely' and domestic Dutch identity.[187]

Yet, beside the conspicuous display of wealth in the burgher interior as configured in the *puppenhaus*, and in its pictorial manifestations, these mirror-images of the Dutch home display a recurring pictorial conundrum. For many of the inset mirrors in these paintings occlude any further view. In myriad examples they bear no visible reflection. Turned toward the interior of the painting rather than to the viewer, their mirror reflections are elliptical, captured in a perspectival alignment that renders them as nothing other than a patch of silver-gold paint to indicate a surface of reflected light. As such, they may be read as metaphors of a deep interiority within the art of painting that the late nineteenth-century critic and theorist of the history of art Alois Riegl identified in Dutch art.[188] This pictorial paradox is particularly evident in the art of Vermeer, as Daniel Arasse has brilliantly argued.[189]

In Vermeer's c. 1664 pendant pictures *Woman with a Pearl Necklace* and *Woman Holding a Balance*, a wall mirror hangs between windows and opposite a woman tending to her jewels (Figs. 164 and 165). The compositions preclude a view of the mirror's surface, offering only a shimmer of light as a sign of its reflective sheen. Together they present a considered variation of reflections on the theme of female beauty and the love of painting, yet in company with the larger pictorial trope of the early modern inset mirror-image, here configured as an ellipsis of light. Depicted in what would seem to be the same space in both paintings (likely Vermeer's studio), it is recognisably the corner of a room beside a window, hung with a yellow curtain. The

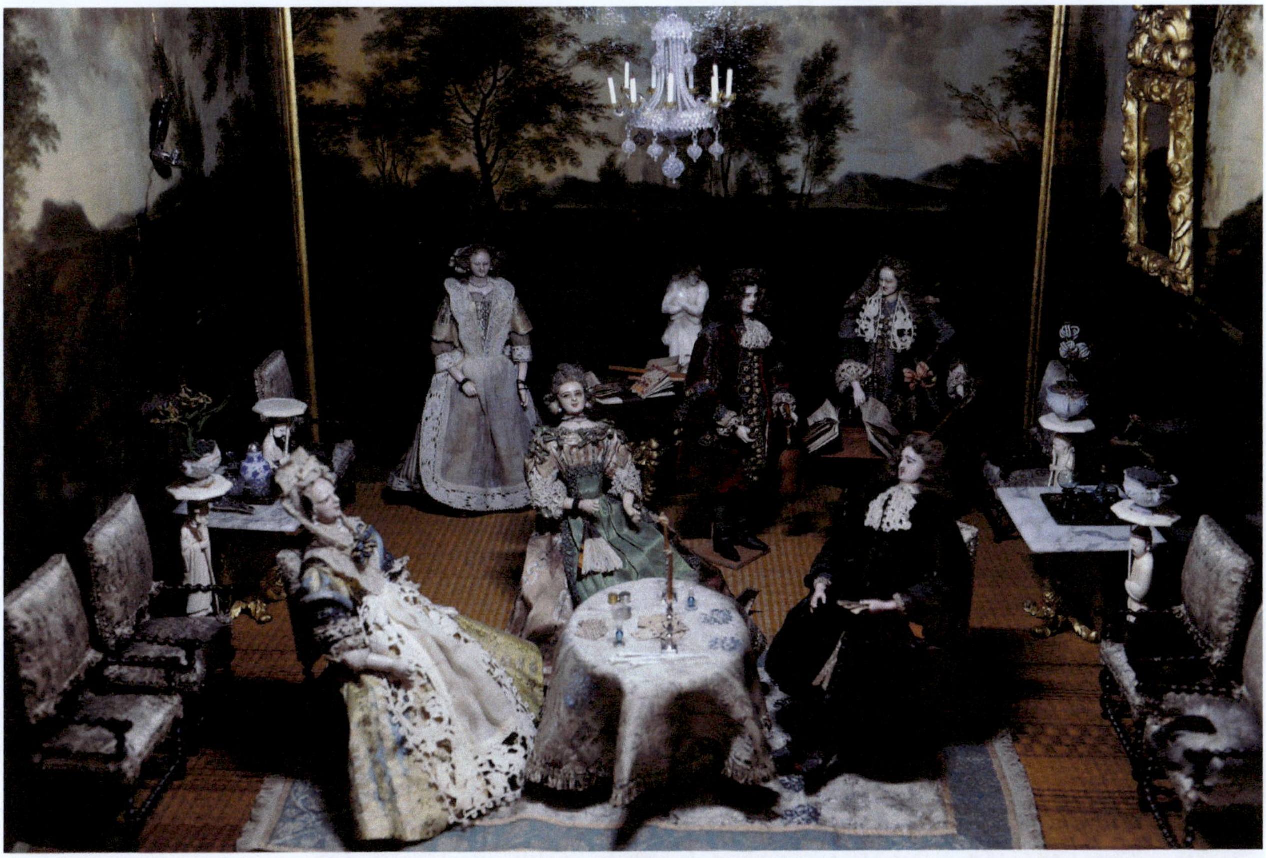

Fig. 163b Petronella de la Court, detail of the drawing room, *puppenhaus,* 1670–90, oak and walnut wooden cabinet, 206.5 × 189 × 279 cm, Centraal Museum, Utrecht.
Photo: Alamy

concerted variation between the two works in the presentation of both the place and the women suggests a spectrum of amorous relations, as the common trope of such art. In *Woman with a Pearl Necklace,* the subject stands in profile before the mirror as she ties the ribbon of her pearl necklace. Their soft lustre is echoed in the reflection of her drop earring and the painted highlights of her nose and cheek. Her slightly parted lips are accentuated by the flower-shaped scarlet ribbon of her hairpiece. Her jacket is of yellow-patterned silk edged with a white-flecked fur, offsetting her arms raised to tie the yellow ribbon at her throat. On the table before her are the items of her toilet – an ivory comb, a silver box – and ample folds of ultramarine drapery beside a curving porcelain jar. Daylight from the leaded window throws full light on her face and torso. To the side, the curtain echoes the colour of her dress to suggest the possibility of both opening and closing our view onto her. Like the sliver of reflected light on the surface of the mirror, the scene is also cut elliptically through the chair at the right side, to emphasise the chance view of a private domestic scene that genre painting purports to represent.

Woman Holding a Balance similarly depicts a standing woman with her hair modestly covered by a white veil in a pictorial recollection of a Madonna type (Antonello da Messina, Sassoferrato), furthered by the deep blue of her jacket. Though she bears no jewellery herself, she holds up a fine jeweller's scale before a table with open cases of shimmering pearls, gold chains, and minted coins enveloped by an abundant drapery of lapis lazuli dye. The jewel-like richness

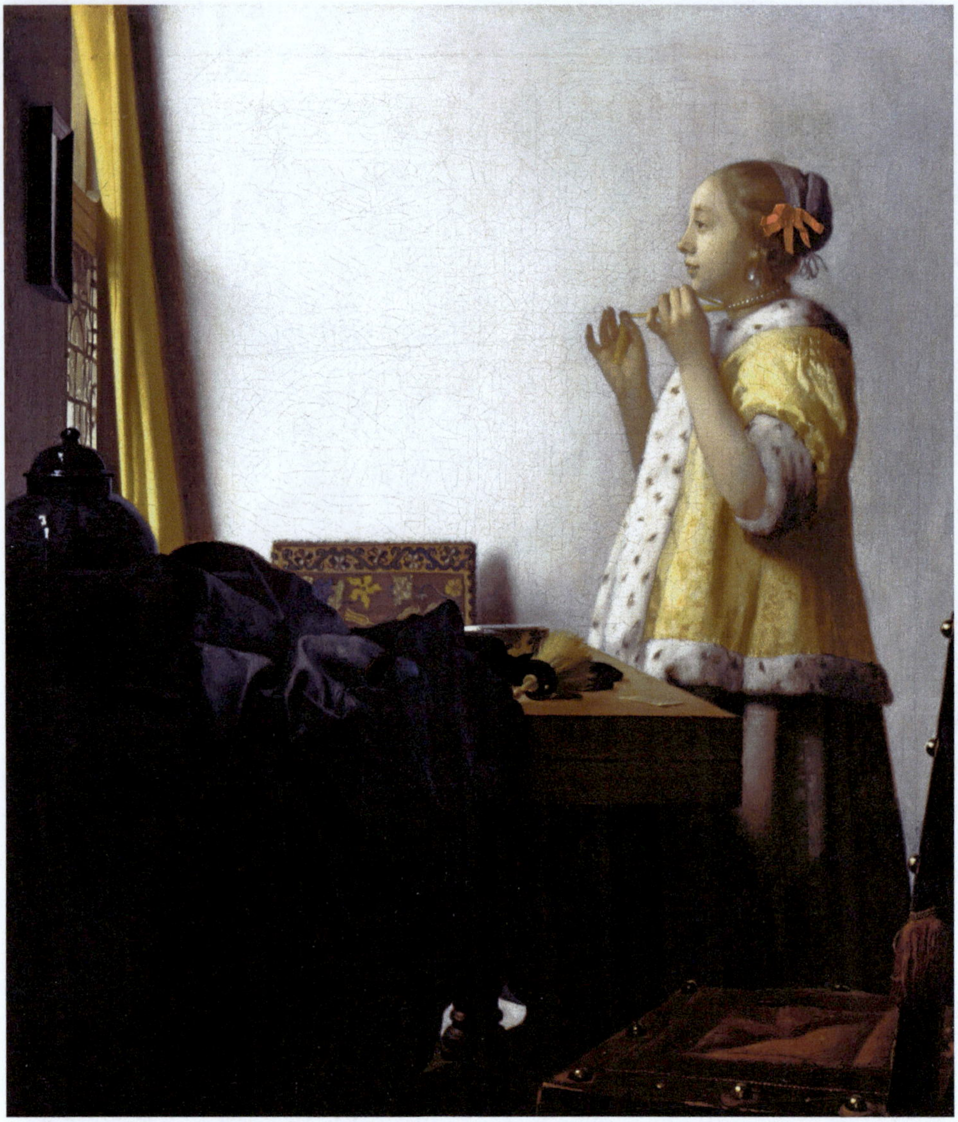

Fig. 164 Johannes Vermeer, *Woman with a Pearl Necklace*, c. 1662–65, oil on canvas, 55 × 45 cm, Staatliche Museen Preußischer Kulturbesitz, Gemäldegalerie, Berlin.
Photo: Staatliche Museen Preußischer Kulturbesitz, Gemäldegalerie, Berlin

of the work is, perhaps, underlined by its apparent seventeenth-century display within a casket, like a jewel-box itself.[190] The woman's right hand that lifts the scale is poised directly at the edge of the painting that hangs behind her, a representation of a Last Judgment. The association between the weighing of the woman's balance and divine judgement is both articulate yet veiled. As Jacob Cats proposed and Eddy de Jongh and Ivan Gaskell have argued, this is an image of gentle reflection on the theme of *vanitas*. It is surely also an art-historical recollection of fifteenth-century Flemish paintings of a goldsmith's shop (discussed in Chapter 2), here transposed into a woman before a jewel-box in a domestic interior: 'now you weigh precious stones and gems, one day you in turn will be weighed and judged'.[191] Yet the opacity of the mirror reflection confounds any direct iconographic resolution to the question of the painting's representation as to whether she is judge or judged. As an emblem of painting, the mirror's glinting unreadability is

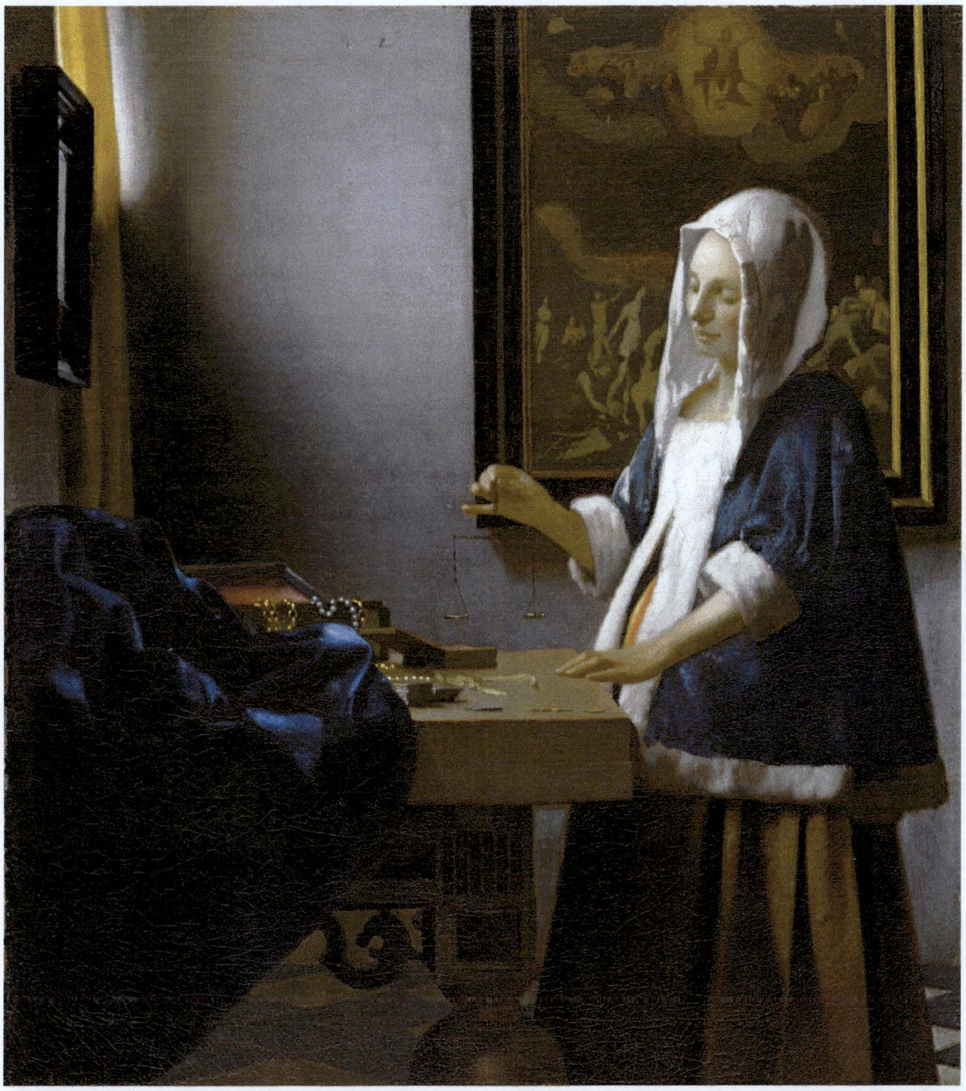

Fig. 165 Johannes Vermeer, *Woman Holding a Balance*, c. 1664, oil on canvas, 39.7 × 35.5 cm, National Gallery of Art, Washington, DC.
Photo: National Gallery of Art

like the woman herself. This is echoed in the modelled blankness of the wall behind the woman in Vermeer's *Woman with a Pearl Necklace*, as Victor Stoichita has noted, as also by the bared nail and nail holes between the painting and the window frame in the *Woman Holding a Balance*, which similarly suggest the traces of a further painting that is no longer there. Through the detail of the nail Vermeer thereby further intimates the movable display of the painting that currently hangs on the wall – that of judgment – and so of the early modern cabinet or easel painting in general. The empty nail, like the empty mirror are, in Hoogstraten's words, those telling details that endow the work with a pictorial eloquence that is all the greater for being veiled in an ambiguity of signification.

As Eddy de Jongh has argued, such mutable meanings are like the painted curtain that might be drawn to give a partial view of the scene, or the luxury textiles of Titian's 'petrarchan' Venus types that both disclose and occlude the beauty of her painted form.[192] If there are earlier works of the sixteenth-century 'Venus' at her toilet that similarly display an inset mirror reflecting only the intimation of light reflection rather than an image-within-the-image, yet their compositional structure would still seem to be bound to the

Albertian definition of painting as forever held in an equivalence, or *paragone*, to the mirror or the window view. In the case of Vermeer, the judgment of vanity suggested by the mirror-image-within-the image is gently suspended. The pictorial contiguity of the mirror's sheen, like that of the jewels, and the display of a woman in a Dutch interior, instead compose Vermeer's considered pictorial reflection on the specular beauty of his art. For Vermeer has displaced the image in the mirror with the image of painting itself. As Arasse and Stoichita have both suggested, Vermeer paints at the threshold of the classical trope of *paragone*, the blank sheen of his mirror reflections intimating the limits of painting's readable meanings, or of the image as text.[193]

Likewise, Poussin, consummate artist of *pictura poesis*, painted a modest mythological woodland scene alongside his monumental *St Erasmus* (his only Vatican commission) that seems to question the narrative mirror of his art just at the moment in which he was establishing it in his name (Fig. 166). For as the satyr drinks at cupid's behest, the woman beside him, surely an emblem

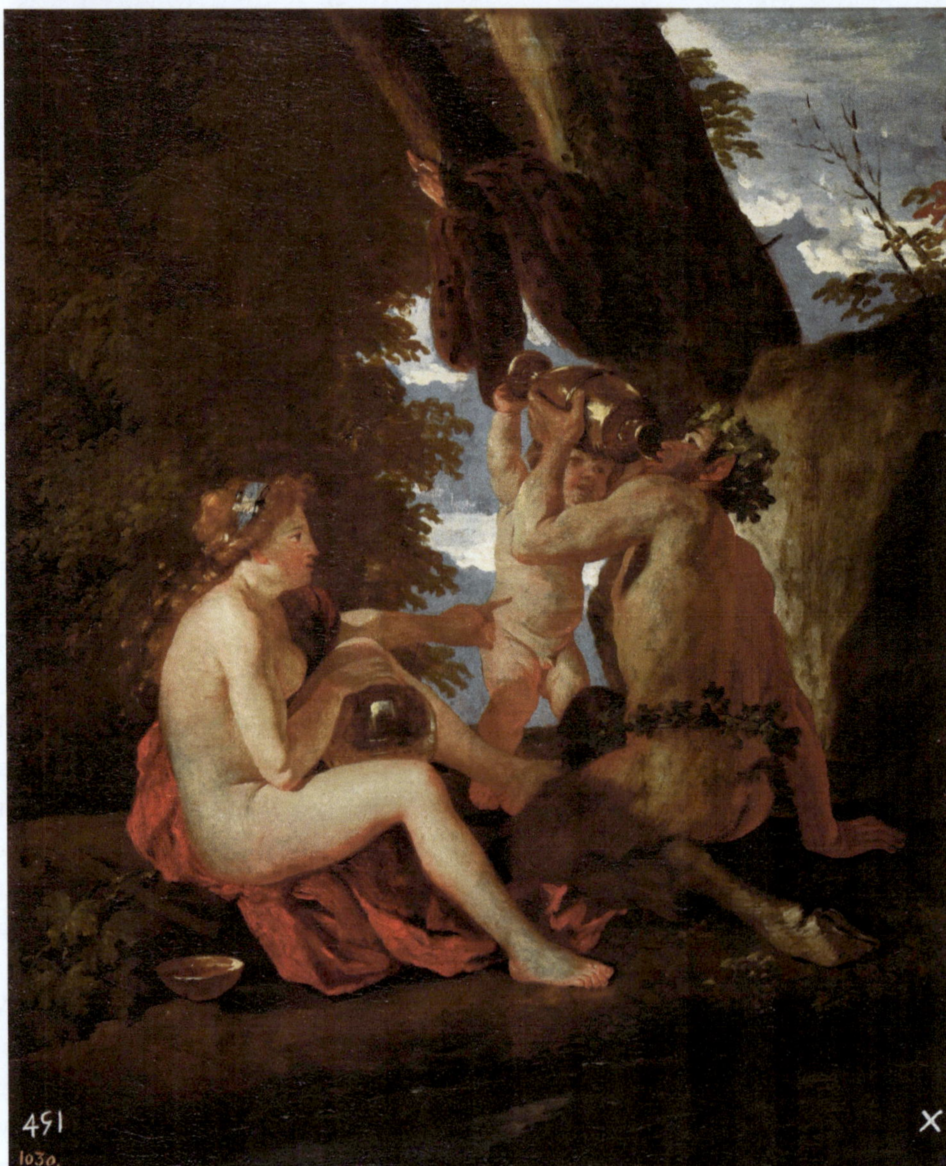

Fig. 166 Nicolas Poussin, *Bacchic Scene*, 1626–28, oil on canvas, 74 × 60 cm, Museo del Prado, Madrid. Photo: © Museo Nacional del Prado

of *pittura* in Bellorian fashion, seems to gesture to the past and future of painting. Her left hand points into the arcadian depths of the painting, while her right rests on a reflecting metallic sphere in whose bowl we see what must lie in its foreground, as if in our place: an oblique mirror view through a garden archway looking onto an Ovidian fountain of poetic memory – *ad fontes*.[194] Prospero-like, Poussin poses this classical nymph looking into the mirroring depths of art's illusions as if into its distant source in the 'abysm of time', as Shakespeare's *Tempest* understood it in his theatrical *mise-en-abyme*.[195] Similarly, Rembrandt's self-portrait of c. 1628, surely painted by means of a convex mirror in respect of its great diminution of scale and curving perspective, shows us the artist in the studio before his canvas, which we see only from the back (Fig. 84, Chapter 3). Thus the subject of Rembrandt's canvas back, like Poussin's obliquely placed mirror, withholds from us its subject, in a pictorial counterpoint to Alberti's definition of painting as a window or mirror view.

It could be said that Velazquez, too, in *Las Meninas*, brought the Albertian equivalence between painting and mirroring in Ovid's poetic fount into questioning pictorial play (Fig. 92, Chapter 3). Like Petrarchan veils, the image of the painting-within-the-painting is thus withheld. It may be that Velazquez, as a painter possessed of great art-historical familiarity through his curatorship of the Spanish royal collections and his voyage to Italy, made pictorial acknowledgement not only of the Arnolfini mirror but also his extensive knowledge of Venetian mirror painting. *Las Meninas* seems also to recall such examples as Bellini's Woman at Her Toilet (Fig. 127) and Titian's *Woman with Mirror* (Fig. 128), in which the structure of the doubled mirror offers the viewer both the front and the back of the mirror object. Yet in the Bellini we regard a pictorial consideration of painting as a manifestation of the early modern science of specular perception; in Velazquez, instead, it is, as Giordano is reported to have said, a 'theology' of painting, as a full concert of visuality and its veiling, to reconfigure entirely the early modern question of the specular nature of painting's art.[196]

NOTES

1 Bellori, 1672, 3, 253. The first image opens the text of the *Idea*, while the second pertains to his account of van Dyck, where the personification of imitation holds a mirror to represent ideal imitation, while her foot is placed upon a monkey to signify ideal art's triumph over mere simian imitation.

2 Bellori, 1672, 'L'Idea', 3–13; see also Bellori & Wohl, 2005; Panofsky, 1968 and 1924. See further Bell & Willette, 2002; Borea & Gasparri, 2000. On the letter to Baldassare Castiglione attributed to Raphael dictated via Pietro Aretino, with regard to his fresco of *Galatea* for the Villa Farnesina, c. 1512–14, published by Ludovico Dolce, *Lettere*, 1544, 226–28, cited below. See further Arasse & Nitti, 2001; and Hubert Damisch's extensive discussion of *The Judgement of Paris* in relation to the sensibility of aesthetic and desire, in Damisch, 1996. On Zeuxis' depiction of the legendary Helen of Troy and the composite beauties of the Maids of Croton, Mansfield, 2006; and Catoni & Settis, 2008. The epithet of Helen as 'the face that launched a thousand ships' was Christopher Marlowe's, in *The Tragical History of Doctor Faustus*, 1604. Research for this chapter originated in a series of publications undertaken for an AHRC award in 'Translating Cultures'; Warwick, 2019; Warwick, 2017; Black and Warwick, 2014; and subsequently further developed in Warwick, 2022.

3 Pliny, *Naturalis Historiae*, book 36:4; Lucian, *Amores*, 11–17. For the ancient sources on the Venus of Cnidos, see Pollitt, 1990, 84–89. See the more recent discussions of the textual and physical evidence in Stewart, 1997, 97–99; Mitchell Havelock, 1995. On Pliny's art history, Isager, 2013. See further Arscott & Scott, 2000; Neer, 2017. Her widely imitated figural form is best known today in the Venus de Milo. On the myth of ancient art, Hénin & Naas, 2018.

4 See the discussion of Alberti's Narcissus metaphor in the Introduction.

5 Bober & Rubenstein, 2010, 18, 63–69, for a typology of classical Venus poses and their attributes, including mirrors.

6 Lomazzo, 1590; see further Tantardini & Norris, 2020; Zuccaro, 1607; Lukehart, 2009.

7 Lomazzo, 1590, 59. On Giorgione's poetics, see Anderson, 1997; and on Giorgione's lost painting, see especially Goffen, 2002, 60–64 and notes. See the further discussion in Chapter 2.

8 Vasari, 1568, in his life of Giorgione, Part III, vol. I:15.
9 Pino, 1548, 5, 27.
10 Damisch, 1992.
11 Bayer, 2008, and further bibliography from which see especially Sylvia Ferino Pagden's summary of a complex literature on the '*belle donne*': Ferino-Pagden, 2022 and 2006 and Brown & Ferino-Pagden, 2006. Goffen, 1997a, launched the interpretation of these pictures within the domain of the courtesan and the history of sexuality. See also her volume of essays in Goffen, 1997b. Interpretation of these works as erotica is evidenced in Giovanni della Casa's much-cited letter on Titian's *Danae*, 20 September 1544, on which see Zapperi, 1991 (interestingly, his letters to Alessandro Farnese also comprise the acquisition of jewels and a mirror); critical analysis of the *Venus of Urbino* encompasses both courtesan and bride, as indicative of the gamut of readings these works have received. De Tolnay, 1943–60, best represents the neo-Platonic interpretation of Renaissance art.
12 On the Venetian *cristallo* mirror, see Chapter 1.
13 http://collections.vam.ac.uk/item/O125620/mirror-unknown/, of Venetian origin, dated c. 1570.
14 Goffen, 1991, for discussion of the use of two mirrors in relation to the *paragone* as a pictorial means of showing views not otherwise seen, thereby showing both direct vision and indirect reflection, based on a letter from Alfonso d'Este's agent in Venice, Jacopo Tebaldi to the duke in Ferrara, 14 October 1522, (cited from Gronau, 1928, 246, no. 2). See also Ferino-Pagden, 2006; Roman d'Elia, 2006; the recent discussion in Grave, 2018, 258–62; and Rowley, 2023, for the recent Musée Jacquemart-André exhibition.
15 As elaborated in Cropper, 1976.
16 *The Homeric Hymns*, 5, 'To Aphrodite'. See McHam 2008, 169, note 32.
17 Petrarca et al., 1964, 420.
18 Lucco, 2004.
19 Fletcher, 1990, on Bellini's responses to antiquity including ownership of an antique mirror; and the further discussion by Brown, 2019, 217–29.
20 McHam, 2008.
21 McHam, 2008, 163.
22 On this painting, see Vodret, 2010; Wethey, 1975, III:162–65, for other versions in Barcelona and Prague.
23 See the discussion of Poussin's self-portraits in Chapter 3.
24 Damisch, 1992, on the theme and its Renaissance expansion as an allegory of art.
25 See the classic essay by Cropper, 1976, on the Petrarchan enumeration of beautiful parts; Vickers, 1982, who analyses this as a poetic 'mirroring'; and recent bibliography in Brown et al., 2002.
26 Bembo, 1544, V.
27 Letter to Baldassare Castiglione attributed to Raphael dictated via Pietro Aretino, with regard to his fresco of *Galatea* for the Villa Farnesina, c. 1512–14, published by Dolce, 1544, 226–28.
28 Ovid, *Amores*, 1.5. On the classical synaesthesia of poetry and art, and of a *poesis* of beauty in fragments, Boymel Kampen, 1996, especially the essay by Dubois, 1996.
29 Equicola, 1525; Bembo, 1544; Bembo, 1505.
30 From a vast literature on Baldassare Castiglione's *Il cortegiano*, 1528, and particularly of the aesthetic as well as social concept of dissimulation as *sprezzatura* or *non so chè* of grace (I:26), see the authoritative edition by Singleton & Javitch (Castiglione, 2002). See also Peacock, 2021: Richards, 2001.
31 Lucian's *Imagines (Eikones)*; Luigini, 1554; Dolce, 1545; Speroni, 1542; Trissino, 1524; Firenzuola, 1552, and the translation Firenzuola, 1992.
32 Kelso, 1959, gives a comprehensive history of treatises on women's beauty; on which see also Tonelli, 1933.
33 Brown, 1990; Humfrey, 2015; and his comprehensive catalogue entry on Titian's *Venus with Mirror* for the National Gallery of Art catalogue in Echols & Humfrey, 2019, 392–417, with further bibliography. On Titian and Spain, Falomir, 2003a; and on the question of Titian's 'repetitions' and variations, Falomir, 2003b; see also Loh, 2007. From an extensive literature on Titian as painter of Venus, see especially Ferino-Pagden's exhibitions on the subject, 2021 and 2022; Calabrese, 2003; and Goffen, 1997a. Hope's 2023 publication of Titian documents appeared as this book was going to press.
34 Ridolfi, 1648, I:200; Crowe & Cavalcaselle, 1877, 2, 334–36, 540, citing Titian's letter to Antonio Perez, 22 December 1574, 'Venus con Amor gli tien il specchio.'
35 Checa Cremades, 2002. Titian's lost work is known through Rubens' imitation of it on his visit to Madrid (now in the Thyssen-Bornemisza Museum), which Velazquez would also have known. On the larger subject of Rubens' emulation of Titian in Madrid, most recently, Portùs, 2020; Moràn Turina, 2004. The Rubens *Venus with a Mirror* now at the Liechtenstein Museum, Vienna, is also closely connected with this group of paintings on specular beauty.
36 From an extensive literature on Leonardo and sfumato, see especially Shearman's classic 1962 article.
37 On Titian's paint surfaces, see especially the work of Jill Dunkerton, notably her studies of Titian with Marika Spring in Dunkerton & Spring, 2013, 2015a, and 2015b.
38 On textile veils, Hills, 2006, 29; and Hills, 2018. See also Pardo, 1997. On the manifold Renaissance references to veiling, Castiglione's Duchess of the *Cortigiano*, 1528, book I, 26, gives the greatly quoted phrase on the definition of true art, like beauty and courtly grace, as 'that which does not appear to be art', or an art that veils the artfulness of its making, thus adding a further artful veil while at the same time seemingly presenting its art as 'natural'. See also Wolf 2002 on veils and mirrors.
39 See the discussion by Afentoulidou, 2020.
40 From an extensive literature on Renaissance luxury dress: Warwick, 2022; Monnas, 2012; Dolin, 2010;

Schoeser, 2007; Jones & Stallybrass, 2000; Weiner & Schneider, 1998; De' Marinis, 1994; Scott, 1993; Joyce & Addison, 1992; Arnold, 1988; Thornton, 1965; Scarisbrick, 1995 and 2007.

41 On the history of epithalamic verse, Tufte, 1970. See also D'Elia, 2004. Matteo Maria Boiardo's *Orlando innamorato*, though remaining unfinished, was published in parts across the 1480s and 1490s, with the first complete edition published posthumously in Scandiano, 1495. Ariosto's *Orlando furioso*, first published in 1516 and in its complete version in Venice, 1532, took up Boiardo's embroidered structure and characters, greatly surpassing Boiardo's in fame. Torquato Tasso, like Ariosto also a courtier at the d'Este court of Ferrara, in his *Gerusaleme liberate*, 1581, would also use the structure of the embroidered plot established by Boiardo, which was broadly influential on subsequent epic poetry such as Spenser's *Faerie Queene* 1596 and Milton's *Paradise Lost*, 1674 and 1667.

42 Boschini, 1660, 364, 664, as recently discussed in Salomon, 2014; on Boschini, Dal Pozzolo, 2014.

43 Philostratus *Imagines* (I, VI). Jaffé et al., 2003, centred on a reconstruction of the *camerino d'alabastro*; see also the related Titian exhibition curated by Falomir, 2003a, 162; and Hope, 2012; Ballarin, 2002–7.

44 Van Hout & Balis, 2012; Geraerts, 2011; Rosenthal, 2005; Brown et al., 1999; Cavalli-Björkman, 1987.

45 Rubens depicted the *Judgment of Paris* more than once, of which the most celebrated are the versions now at the National Gallery London and the Prado Museum. The painting at the National Gallery since its acquisition in 1844 was previously in the collection of Richelieu, where it is thought to have been overpainted, on which see Oliver, 2005; and further Healy, 1997; Wood, 2010; and on the *Three Graces* and *Judgment of Paris*, McGrath, 2016, I:449–69. Rubens' *Judgment of Paris* depicts the rival goddesses from front, side, and back in a clear *paragone* with Raphael as also in his related depictions of the *Three Graces*, and further reflective shields, some with gorgon's heads, which may be read as classicizing references, as a *paragone* with Caravaggio, and as an Eyckian identification with the lineage of his Flemish art. On Rubens' representation of the shield of Perseus at the Rubenshuis in relation to Annibale Carracci and Italian art, see Beldon Scott, 1988; and Muller, 1981–82; and on Rubens' house, De Poorter & Baudouin, 2022. See further the discussion of Flemish 'Eyckian' shields of art in Chapter 2.

46 Prater, 2002; and more broadly, Carr & Bray, 2006, cat. no. 37, 214–17, with further bibliography.

47 Velazquez travelled to Italy with the party dispatched to meet Mariana of Austria, the royal bride to Philip IV in 1649, the official purpose of his trip being to augment the royal collections as part of the programme of redecoration of the royal palaces he would oversee. On his voyage to Italy, Luzón Nogué, 2022. Gaspar de Haro's 1650 marriage was to the daughter of the Duke of Medinaceli, Antonia Maria de la Cerda, renowned as a great beauty, though Gaspar de Haro himself was a notorious libertine. Jennifer Montagu, 1983, uncovered documentary evidence to suggest Velazquez was father to a love child while in Rome. In the complexities of the painting's origin unanswered questions remain as to whether it was a requested work and, if so, by whom, and indeed whether it was executed while Velazquez was in Rome. As a royal appointment Velazquez did not receive commissions as such. The earliest reference to the painting in de Haro's collection arises in the 1651 inventory first published in Pita Andrade, 1952.

48 From an extensive literature on Velazquez' celebrated paint application: Brown, 1998; McKim-Smith et al., 1988.

49 Prater, 2002, especially 95 on the question of the figure's life-sized presence and its acknowledged debt to Victor Stoichita's 1986 analysis of the mirror-image in *Las Meninas*. Pomian, 1982, for discussion of the figure of Venus as a representation of the art-amateur. On the philosophy of love in relation to this painting, see Cherry, 2007.

50 Honig, 2016; Woollett & Van Suchtelen, 2006; Von Berswordt-Wallrabe et al., 2003; Padron et al., 1992; Ertz & Nitze-Ertz, 1998. On the five senses, Wagener et al., 2016.

51 Müller-Hofstede, 1984.

52 Lothe, 2008, no. 317; Goldstein, 2012.

53 The passage is much cited in the scholarly literature on Titian's Venus in the company of music-making; see further Bayer et al., 2008, 328–29.

54 Nordenfalk, 1985.

55 Boehm, 2020; Delahaye & Bardelot, 2018; Pastoureau & Delahaye, 2013; Teodorescu, 2010; Delahaye, 2007; Erlande-Brandenburg, 1989; Joubert, 1987; Campbell, 2002; Cavallo, 1998; Ackerman, 1933.

56 Leisch-Kiesl, 2021. See also the discussion in Chapter 1. On the 1420 inventory of the library of Philip the Good in Doutrepont, 1906, 109, (cat. no. 97); and Dogaer & Debae, 1967. On the Bocaccio BNF ms. 12420, fol. 101v depicts the ancient female artist Marcia or Iaia, who is portrayed painting her portrait by means of a small convex mirror. This was gifted to Philip the Good Duke of Burgundy in 1403 and subsequently devolved to the French royal collections through the Valois inheritance. See further Buettner, 1996, fig. 65. The 1420 inventory of the library of Philip the Good also lists Christine de Pisan's *Cité des Dames*, of which there are three copies at the BNF (607, 1178, 1179) with a frontispiece illustration on the conceit of the book, of a city built by and in celebration of the great deeds of women, with a small tondo mirror as the emblem of foresight. In a dream, three personifications of feminine virtue visit Christine in her study to suggest the book's subject: Justice, Rectitude, and Reason, the last of which holds up a mirror as an attribute of the perspicacious mind. On the royal collection of manuscripts more broadly, see Hamilka & Laffitte, 2009, 297–300; Avril, 1991, no. 7.

57 Turner, 2022; Bartalini, 2014; Henry et al., 2013, especially the essay by Bartalini, 2013; Frommel, 2003, I:123–24, 193.

58 On the 'School of Fontainebleau', see the landmark exhibition led by Sylvie Beguin et al., 1972. See also Capodieci & Brouhot, 2019; Crépin-Leblond et al., 2019; Broomhall, 2018, with further bibliography; Mansfield, 2016; Elsig, 2012; Zorach, 2005.

59 See further the discussion with bibliography of Renaissance marriage customs in Chapter 2 in relation to the Arnolfini portrait; here the larger point is the permeable relation between the position of royal wives and consorts at the French court, and what has been termed the 'institutionalisation' of the king's mistress.

60 Crépin-Leblond & Taburet-Delahaye, 2009; Fagnart, 2016.

61 Eschenfelder, 1993; Le Gillou, 2014.

62 Adlin, 2013.

63 See the discussion of the Lennoxlove toilet set in Chapter 1, www.nms.ac.uk/explore-our-collections/stories/global-arts-cultures-and-design/lennoxlove-toilet-service/.

64 Ainsworth et al., 2010, 229–32 (no. 34), and related depictions of Venus, bathing female nudes, and men in armour, as well as the essay by Schrader, 2010.

65 Geldenhouwer, 1529, 235, as discussed by Schrader, 2010, 62; see also Bass, 2016, on Netherlandish classicism at the court of Philip IV, especially 8, 12–13, 109–11.

66 Ainsworth, 2010, 70, and Ainsworth et al., 2010, 226–29 (cat. no. 33).

67 Francesco Petrarca, 'Il mio adversario in cui veder solete', in Petrarca et al., 1964, 45; Scève, 1544; De Ronsard, 1553; François Bérenger de la Tour d'Albenas, 'O saint miroir' in Weber, 1963, 539. See Goodman Soellner, 1983; Eymard, 1975; Forster, 1969.

68 Crépin-Leblond & Taburet-Delahaye, 2009, 300–301; Zorach, 2005. https://collections.louvre.fr/ark:/53355/cl010062789.

69 See the thoughtful discussion by Jollet, 1997, on the question of the typological disposition of these works, and so of the open-ended question of their attribution.

70 Musée des Beaux-Arts, Strasbourg, MNR 496. On textiles, Jones & Stallybrass, 2000, 134–71.

71 Musée des Ursulines, Mâcon, Inv. A 700.

72 On the artistic imagery of Diane de Poitiers: Ruby, 2007; Ruby, 2017a; Ffolliott, 1989; Chastel, 1966; Béguin, 1956; Dimier, 1913, with a catalogue of portraits of Diane de Poitiers. On François Clouet: Deldicque, 2019 and 2022; Elsig, 2012; Jollet, 1997.

73 http://mba-collections.dijon.fr/ow4/mba/voir.xsp?id=00101-5175&qid=sdx_q0&n=6&e=, Ecole de Fontainebleau, *Dame à sa toilette* (Diane de Poitiers), Musée des Beaux-Arts Dijon CA 118; https://worcester.emuseum.com/objects/5956/woman-at-her-toilette, School of Fontainebleau, *Woman at Her Toilette* (Diane de Poitiers), Worcester Art Museum 1932.23.

74 The documentary references to aristocratic jeweled mirrors are cited by Havard, 1887, under 'glace' and 'miroir', II:1100–115 and III:887–912. On royal gifts, which often comprised jewelled mirrors, see Thépaut-Cabasset & Warner, 2007–8.

75 The documentary citation to a mirror bearing this description was, from eighteenth-century inventories, identified with this jewelled rock crystal pediment mirror ornamented with cameos in the royal collections, and believed to have been a gift to Marie de Médicis, on which see Alcouffe, 2001, 391–93; *Un temps d'exubérance . . .*, 2002, 282–83.

76 On Gabrielle d'Estrées' inventory of jewelled mirrors: De Fréville, 1842, 170.

77 De Cervantes, 1605, book I, ch. 33 (its subsequent books were published in 1615).

78 Of the many versions of this typology, see especially the National Gallery, Washington, DC, version below, in addition to the Louvre painting. These works have attracted a wide range of interpretations. See Crawford, 2018; Zorach, 2001; and the further notes below.

79 www.nga.gov/collection/art-object-page.46112.pdf. Hand, 2012; Ruby, 2017b.

80 http://medaillesetantiques.bnf.fr/ws/catalogue/app/collection/record/ark:/12148/c33gbf2rs. On the decorative arts of domestic mirrors, Crépin-Leblond & Taburet-Delahaye, 2009; Bayer et al., 2008; Musacchio, 2008; Ajmar-Wollheim & Dennis, 2006; Thornton, 1991. Further examples include: https://collections.vam.ac.uk/item/O161874/mirror-frame-unknown/ in maiolica; https://collections.vam.ac.uk/item/O93438/mirror-frame-landi-neroccio-de/ in carta pesta.

81 Marinelli, 1562. See further Merlini & Storti, 2010, particularly the essay by Nocentini, 2010, for discussion of Renaissance collections and books of recipes for the toilette such as soap, perfume, make-up, skin bleach, and hair dyes.

82 The face of the coat of arms is abraded so that it is impossible to identify; the flanking dragon and goose are surely heraldic also. The diamond ring has been identified as Medicean, though it may simply be generic. http://collections.vam.ac.uk/item/O93042/mirror-frame-in-the-form-mirror-frame-none.

83 Tufte, 1970; Pinto, 1971; Dean & Lowe, 1998; D'Elia, 2004.

84 Ferino-Pagden, 2022; Bayer et al., 2008; Bernardini, 1995; and the further bibliography below.

85 Baskins, 2008; Bayer et al., 2008; Musacchio, 2008; Ajmar-Wollheim & Dennis, 2006; Barriault, 1994; Thornton, 1991. On the question of the gallery painting see further the Introduction; on the Arnolfini portrait and its purported cover, Chapter 2.

86 Bruijnen, 2011.

87 Ewing, 2016.

88 www.museothyssen.org/en/collection/artists/beer-jan/annunciation; private collection, Christie's, Sale 17655, New York, 29 October 2019, *Old Master Paintings and Sculpture*, lot 708, Property of a Distinguished American Private Collector.

89 Löcher, 1999.

90 Ishikawa, 2004; Weiss, 2018.

91 Madou et al., 2010; Maroto, 2006.

92 Musacchio's work remains fundamental on the decorative arts of Renaissance birthing imagery. See also Bayer et al., 2008, 172–74.

93 www.dia.org/art/collection/object/childbirth-set-25798; and the special issue of the DIA Bulletin on Italian Renaissance ceramics, Darr & Wilson, 2013.

94 Unger, 2022, offers a prismatic range of interpretations, see especially Kodera and Unger's essay on the reflections in the glass orb. See further Herrmann-Fiore, 1995, for discussion of the different versions and possible sources.

95 Wivel, 2020; Dalla Costa, 2019; Falomir, 2014; Puttfarken, 2005.

96 Fabbro, 1977, 158; or Puppi, 2012, 203; published in English translation by Dalla Costa, 2020, 195.

97 Wivel, 2020.

98 Roskill, 1968, 214–15, from Dolce, 1557, 66, letter to Alessandro Contarini.

99 See the further discussion in the Introduction.

100 Puppi, 2012, 337, published in English translation by Dalla Costa, 2020, 203, with an indicative date of 22 December 1574.

101 Pacheco, 1649, ch. 8, 100, trans. in Portùs, 2020, 94. On the poetics of water in Venetian painting, Oettinger, 2015.

102 Aretino in Procaccioli, 1999, notably the celebrated letter to the artist on Titian's brushwork and colour in the pictorial evocation of atmospheric effects as nature's own, May 1544, III:78–80. See further Ferino-Pagden et al., 2007; Woods-Marsden, 2007. See also the recent technical research on Titian by Dunkerton et al., 2020; Dunkerton & Spring, 2013, 2015a, and 2015b.

103 Pollitt, 1990, 84–89. For discussion of the violence of desire in both ancient and early modern art and poetry with reference to Venus, Didi-Huberman, 1999; Salomon, 1996. On the antique synaesthesia of word and image in the representation of desire, see Boymel Kampen, 1996, especially the contribution by Elsner, 1996.

104 Shakespeare, 1623, *Hamlet*, Act 2, scene 2.

105 Echols & Ilchman, 2019, especially the essay by Falomir, 2019, 252, and notes; Falomir et al., 2009 especially the essays by Aikema, 2009; and Wald, 2009, with further bibliography; and the 2007 exhibition to which the conference pertained, detailed in Falomir, 2007.

106 Galassi, 2015; Buijnsters-Smets, 1995; Marlier, 1954. On epithalamic entertainments, including of Old Testament subjects, of which Erasmus was author, Tufte, 1970; and Barriault, 1994, especially 122–23.

107 Shakespeare, Othello, 1623, I:iii.

108 Zamani et al., 2019, and particularly Dechant, 2019. Camille, 1998, 119, following Hermann Lücke; Lymant, 1994.

109 *Paris Bordon*, 1987, for an overarching discussion of relationships between poetry and portraits of women in relation to Bordon; Pisot et al., 2017, and the accompanying conference publication of the same title, Pisot, 2017. It may be compared with Bordone's *bella donna* portrait in the KHM Vienna, see further the recent exhibition, Facchinetti & Galansino, 2022.

110 Tasso, 1590.

111 Tasso, 1581, canto 14:22. Careri, 2005; Unglaub, 2006; Careri, 2021.

112 On the arts of dying, see the classic work of Ariès, 1981 and 1974; and, more recently, Laqueur, 2015. On consolation theology, Rittgers, 2012; Gregg, 1975. On the representation of love, childbirth, and death in art, Warwick, 2017.

113 Bournet-Bacot, 2014; Augustyn & Teget-Welz, 2018.

114 www.metmuseum.org/art/collection/search/667863; Hindman et al., 2015. See also Perkinson, 2017, on skull and death imagery in jewelry and prints.

115 Blanchard, 1997; Ames-Lewis, 1999.

116 Nelson, 2019; Foister et al., 1997. See further Chapter 4.

117 De Vos, 1994a, 245–47; and the review by Campbell, 1995, who argues for a workshop attribution. See also de Vos, 1994a and 1994b; Lane, 2009 331–33. On the diptych, Verougstraete, 2006. On the theme of death and the maiden especially in sixteenth-century Germany, Wirth, 1979.

118 This reconstruction is commonly accepted but not definitive. The coat of arms has been identified as of the Bolognese Loiaini family. The text on the skull is from Job: 'I know that my redeemer lives and that I shall rise again on the last day when, wrapped in my skin and flesh, I will see God my saviour'; Death's banderole: 'Behold the end of man. Clay I was and to dust and ashes I returned; the devil's banderole: in hell there is no salvation.' See Borchert, 2014; Lane, 2009.

119 Havard, 1887, III:912.

120 Marrow, 1983, with reference to Furtenagel's portrait and the Huntington Library's ms. HM 1165 fol. 105r.

121 On Baldung Grien and imagery of death as *vanitas*, Koerner, 1985. On the arts of death as vanity, see also the classic essay by Białostocki, 1966. On Baldung Grien, Holger, 2019. In this image she is an allegory of sagacity, whose reflection comprises the wisdom of Eve's serpent under her feet and the ruminating stags in the woodlands behind her, so that her nudity, like the mirror, is here the clear glass of truth and chastity.

122 Pierre de Saint-Louis, 1668, 45.

123 The early history of the figure of the Magdalen is much bound up with that of the Bible's early transmission; she is generally regarded as a later conflation of several people within the Gospels who tended to Christ. Like much of the Apocrypha, sixteenth-century religious controversy brought Protestant repudiation of saints, and Catholic defense, in which the Magdalen was the particular focus of the sacrament of penance. See further Haskins, 2005; Jansen, 2000.

124 Gregory the Great, *Homily on the Gospels*, XXV.

125 Citation from Gibaldi, 1987, 34; published in Colonna, 1538, on which see the recent bilingual edition by Targoff & Tower, 2021.

126 Constable, 1592.

127 Goffen, 1997a, 170–92; Debby, 2003; Graham, 2008; Puppi & Baccaglini, 2016.

128 On the mirror-image relationship between genres of beauty and *vanitas*, Pericolo, 2009.

129 In this regard, see also Bernardo Licinio's portrait of a *bella donna* (Salamon Collection), usually held to be a courtesan, whose mirror reflection is surely of blind Tobit and Anna, as an allegory of the pleasures but also vanities of sight with reference for the intended viewer of the work.

130 From the scholarship on Vouet, Bonfait, 2011; Thuillier, 1990, and its associated conference, Loire 1992.

131 The early provenance of Caravaggio's Mary and Martha now in Detroit is uncertain, but it seems probable that it remained in Rome until at least the 1620s when Vouet may have known it or of it. See the collected articles on this painting in the *Burlington Magazine*, 1974, 116, special issue on Caravaggio's Detroit Magdalen, particularly Spezzaferro, 1974. On Caravaggio's *vanitas* imagery more broadly, Ruffino & Tristan, 2013; Floridi, 2011.

132 Conisbee, 1997, esp. 102 and 112; Choux, 1973; Salmon & Ubeda de los Cobos, 2016; Judovitz, 2018.

133 De Bérulle, 1625; Thuillier, 1992, 152–67.

134 Père André de l'Auge's sermons, 1623, as cited by Choux, 1973, 109–12, in a broader consideration of a theology of light in de la Tour's deep *chiaroscuro*; as also by Conisbee et al., 1997, as an enduring theme in de la Tour scholarship from Thuillier's pioneering exhibition, illustrated in Thuillier, 1972, especially 177–83; to the more recent Salmon & Ubeda de los Cobos, 2016; and Judovitz, 2018.

135 De Voragine, 1995, I:375, as discussed recently by Judovitz, 2018, 24–27; see also Fohr, 2018.

136 Spenser, 1596 edition of VI books, with an unfinished seventh book at his death. Elizabeth is also allegorized in a number of other characters including Gloriana, the faerie queene. See further Headlam Wells, 1983; Hadfield, 2001.

137 Spenser, 1596, I–III. From an extensive literature concerned with the politics and allegory of Spenser's text, see the recent Stump, 2019.

138 See the discussion of 'speculum principis' in Chapter 1, including Machiavelli's *Principe*, 1532.

139 Ibid.

140 Belluga, 1530. Belluga was a Spanish jurist and author of the fifteenth century in Valencia.

141 Davies, 1599, XXII, 'Of her wisedome'.

142 Shakespeare, 1623, *Love's Labours Lost* IV:1.

143 Jonson, 1616 and 1608, for the marriage of John Lord Ramsey, Lord Viscount Haddington to Lady Elizabeth Radclyffe in Whitehall banqueting hall.

144 Shakespeare, 1623.

145 Spenser, 1579, IV, Aprill.

146 Donne, 1633, VII.

147 Published in Case, 1896, 51.

148 See further Chapters 1 and 4.

149 Strong, 1966; Tillander, 1995, 99–121; Scarisbrick, 2007. See also Bycroft & Dupré, 2019; Tallis, 2023; Pointon, 2010.

150 Identified as the Portugal mirror diamond. From an extensive literature on the portraits of Elizabeth and the iconography of queenship in her representation: Riehl, 2010; Connolly & Hopkins, 2007; Doran & Freeman, 2003; Strong, 1987 and 2003; and further bibliography. On her dress, see also Arnold, 1988.

151 On Bedoli, Fadda & Milanesi, 2019; Bertini, 1977.

152 Grabes, 1982, 71, 330, 375–76, gives a full list of citations. See the further discussion of compact mirrors in Chapter 1.

153 RMN MV 3118 Inv 9762. See note 72 above on Diane de Poitier's portraits, especially Ruby, 2007.

154 Arnold, 1988, 37. The literature has generally assimilated this ornament to Elizabeth's portraits with a sieve as an emblem of her chastity in the name of the Vestal Virgin Tuccia; the suggestion here is that it may be an ornamental crystal mirror or a magnifying glass: www.nationaltrustcollections.org.uk/object/533882. See also the anonymous portrait of a lady dated 1569 at Emmanuel College, Cambridge. In this respect it is also noteworthy that, according to Zecchin, 1987–90, III:167, sixteenth-century shop inventories of Venetian *specchiari*, or spectacle makers, referred to these reading aids interchangeably as *'specchi'* and *'libreti'* (little books), so reinforcing the approximation between looking and reading that spectacle-magnifiers facilitated.

155 See the further discussion of these types of mirrors in Chapter 1.
www.metmuseum.org/art/collection/search/461205?searchField=All&sortBy=Relevance&ft=suzanne+de+court+minerva&offset=0&rpp=20&pos=1, www.metmuseum.org/art/collection/search/460520?searchField=All&sortBy=Relevance&ft=suzanne+de+court+minerva&offset=0&rpp=20&pos=3.

156 Ripa, 1603; Mino et al., 2013. On personification in word and image, Melion & Ramakers, 2016; Leuschner, 2014.

157 Alciati, 1531. Moss, 1999; Rolet & Rolet, 2013; and more broadly the publications of emblem book scholars such as Daly, 2014; and Enenkel, 2019, with further bibliography.

158 Ripa, 1603, 226, 416–18, 367.

159 www.metmuseum.org/art/collection/search/342646?searchField=All&sortBy=Relevance&ft=Raimondi+Prudence&offset=0&rpp=20&pos=1. The representation of Prudence in Renaissance prints is vast. On Renaissance playing cards, many of which comprised series of personifications of different types of classical and ethical knowledge such as the cardinal virtues, including Prudence, O'Bryan, 2019; Alligo, 2017. The literature on Raimondi is chiefly concerned with his role as reproductive printmaker to Raphael, on which see Pon, 2004; more generally, see Lincoln, 2000.

160 Rice, 1958, for discussion of the virtue of prudence as foresight in rulership as argued in Renaissance political theory.

161 Sanson & Lucioli, 2016; Maassen & St Clair, 2000. See also Janson's, Alexander's, and Baldwin's discussions of prudence, mirrors, and marriage in Schneider, ed., 1985.

162 Draper, 2008. On Catherine's extensive patronage of the arts, Fonkenell et al., 2022; Frommel, 2008. On her extensive and detailed correspondence with her chosen

goldsmiths, Bimbenet-Privat, 2007. On her representation as Prudence, Crouzet, 2018.

163 On the mirrors, see Crépin-Leblond & Taburet-Delahaye, 2009, 308–9. On Delaune, Pollet, 2001; Rohou et al., 2019.

164 Pollet, 2001, I, 264–67; https://collections.vam.ac.uk/item/O999534/second-miroir-à-main-la-print-etienne-delaune/second-miroir-à-main-la-print-etienne-delaune/, https://collections.vam.ac.uk/item/O827182/design-for-the-back-of-drawing-etienne-delaune/.

165 Thuillier et al., 1990, 62.

166 https://courtauld.ac.uk/highlights/pair-of-marriage-chests-the-nerli-chest/. Laaser, 2009; De Marchi et al., 2015. See the further bibliography on *cassone* and bridal gifts in notes above.

167 A possible figure of Prudence with a mirror, Giovanni Bellini's *restello* panels have long been considered a marriage gift to his fellow-artist Vincenzo Catena, though precise iconographical identification of these allegories has eluded the extensive scholarship on them, recently summarized in Brown, 2019, 24–33, who argues that the *restello* was Bellini's own, passing to Catena only at the older artist's death, and that the music-making putti surround the female nude suggest this is an allegory of Fame rather than Prudence or Vanity.

168 Schama, 1987, for a discussion of a then-prevailing scholarly focus on the representation of 'fallen' women in Dutch painting with a correcting view through attention to images of motherhood and domestic virtue as defining emblems of an emergent Dutch culture; Franits, 1993; Salomon, 1998; de Jong et al., 2000; Wieseman, 2011. On the rise of Dutch genre painting more generally, including the question of typological repetition, recent titles include Ho, 2017; Franits, 2004.

169 The celebrated scholarly debate on the question of 'veiled' meaning in Dutch art originating in Panofsky, 1953. See also De Jongh, 2000; Alpers, 1983a, who famously argued instead for an 'art of describing'; and the extensive further scholarship these texts have generated.

170 Cats, 1632, iv–v. The interpretation of this text is central to debate on the emblematic nature of Dutch imagery in general, including Vermeer scholarship discussed below.

171 The case for Cats' significance for Dutch genre painting is made primarily in De Jongh, 2000. On the further discussion of early modern books bearing the title of 'mirror', see Grabes, 2009; and the further discussion in Chapter 1.

172 Lambrechtsen, 2005; Bassett, 2003.

173 De Vries, 2003.

174 Waiboer & Franits, 2010, 69 (no. 38).

175 Waiboer, 2011, A-121, 261–62.

176 Wheelock et al., 2004; McNeil Kettering, 1997 and 1998.

177 Cats, 1625; Cohen & Reeves, 2018, especially van Tilburg, 2018, 255–74; Westermann, 2000; Snell, 1994; Franits, 1993.

178 De Jongh, 2000b. On the shoe as the emblem of marriage, as a pair, see Warwick, 2022.

179 Waiboer, 2011; Waiboer & Franits, 2010.

180 Arasse, 1994, 65; Blanc, 2014 and 2017. On the conservation, Neidhardt, 2019; Koja, 2021. The recently revealed picture of a cupid, a motif taken from Otto van Veen's 1608 emblem book, *Amorum emblemata*, which Vermeer used in a number of paintings, keys the tenor of the letter she reads. The technical evidence suggests the painted curtain at the right-hand side was a second thought: https://hnanews.org/gemaldegalerie-restoring-johannes-vermeers-girl-reading-letter-open-window/. The curtain underscores the partially withheld view in a counterpoint to that of the window.

181 Waiboer, 2012, 263–64 (no. A-123). See also his discussion of the virginal in 'Gabriel Metsu and the Art of Luxury' in Waiboer & Franits, 2010, 53–71, (63), referring to an example by Johannes Ruckers of 1640 now in the Koninklijk Oudheidkundig Genootschap Amsterdam.

182 Kersten et al., 1996, 150–62. On De Hooch's art of interiors, Hollander, 2000; see also Charbonnier, 2019.

183 The argument here draws on Alpers' 'art of describing' and Stoichita's reading of the *parerga* of art in the inset image. Jansen, 2019; Söntgen, 2016.

184 Wuestman & de Groot, 2017.

185 Hollander, 2002, her opening discussion of Fromentin's perception of Dutch painting's condensation effect being particularly apposite to the *puppenhaus*.

186 Petronella Oortman's *puppenhaus* at the Rijksmuseum is dated 1686–1710, the date of Jacob Appel's painting of it as commissioned by Petronella, where the arrangement differs from the house itself, suggesting objects were rearranged: www.rijksmuseum.nl/en/collection/BK-NM-1010; www.rijksmuseum.nl/en/collection/SK-A-4245; on which see Braamhorst & Visser, 2014. There are also leading examples at the Germanisches National Museum Hallersches Haus in Nuremburg and in Utrecht Centraal Museum (Petronella de la Court, on which see Hut, 2020). On the early modern dollhouse more generally, Broomhill, 2011; Müller, 2007; Loughman & Montias, 2000.

187 Such miniature cabinet-houses would also take their place among early modern princely collections more broadly, as an aspect of the cultivation of objects of wonder between the arts and sciences. This was the case within the extensive collections of Albrecht V, Duke of Bavaria, and his wife Anna, which contained such a house of miniatures in imitation of their apartments. Subsequently lost in a fire and known today only through textual description, it formed part of a large collection of miniatures within a cabinet of wonders, numbering some 6,000 objects. See Seelig, 2017; Warwick, 'Playing with dolls', forthcoming; and the discussion of scale and miniature objects in *Wunderkammern*, including Albrecht's, in Chapter 4.

188 Riegl, 1999, though Riegl's point was a different one, pertaining to early modern subjecthood. See the further discussion of Burckhardt on Renaissance subjecthood in Chapter 1.

189 Arasse, 1993. Out of an oeuvre of some thirty works, five contain inset mirrors, of which only one reflects back an

image, that of the *Music Lesson*, while the others are visibly blank. See Chapter 3, note 108, for bibliography on Vermeer's possible (and contested in the scholarship) use of optical devices.

190 As discussed by Stoichita, 1997, 165, though to different ends; the painting was apparently presented in a *kastje* at auction in 1696. Stoichita tied this to the seventeenth-century Dutch *perspectyfkas*, discussed here in Chapter 4. On Vermeer's pigments, Gifford, 2022.

191 Wheelock, 1995, 374–76; De Jongh, 1988; Serres, 1988; Arasse, 1993, 51–75; Gaskell & Jonker, 1998; Liedtke et al., 2001; Gaskell, 1984; though Thoré-Burger, 1866, 460, instead saw the Last Judgment as a condemnation of the *Woman with Scales*, who weighs her jewels as she will also be weighed and judged, a thesis that continues along with interpretations of the scene as one of Justice and family as per Alpers, 1976; Salomon, 1983. On fifteenth-century Flemish goldsmith's shop paintings, see Chapter 2, with attendant bibliography.

192 Stoichita, 1997, 165, for discussion of the blank wall, and for the larger argument concerning the relationship between the image-within-the-image and the rise of the cabinet painting. De Jongh, 2000, 130, on the use of poetic-pictorial veils from Petrarch to Hoogstraten.

193 Stoichita, 1997, 171.

194 www.museodelprado.es/en/the-collection/art-work/bacchic-scene/6b90cod9-4456-424e-8acb-99f99ff0f89b. More generally, the recent essay by Hui, 2020; Falomir, 2021; and Unglaub's 2004 discussion of Poussin's art of reflections.

195 Shakespeare, *The Tempest*, I:2, 1623. In a metaphor of reflective recollection, Shakespeare's *Tempest* gathers up the disjointed and illusory memories from the play's various characters of their lives before the storm. Seeking to recall their lost memories, Prospero asks: 'what seest thou else in the . . . abysm of time' (*The Tempest*, 1:2), so linking the figuration of limitless spatial recession with the ceaseless passing of time, Trimble, 2006. See further the Introduction.

196 The argument is indebted to Stoichita's discussion of Cornelius Gijsbrecht's *Reverse Side of a Painting*, in Stoichita, 1997, ch. 9, 268–79. See the further discussion of Rembrandt's self-portrait in the studio and *Las Meninas* in Chapter 3, with attendant bibliography.

CONCLUSION

To hold, as t'were, the mirror up to nature
—WILLIAM SHAKESPEARE, *HAMLET* (ACT 3, SCENE 2), FIRST QUARTO 1603

The pool paints Narcissus, and the painting paints the pool.... Do you then expect the pool to enter into conversation with you? Nay, this youth does not hear anything we say, he is immersed, eyes and ears alike, in the water and we must interpret the painting for ourselves.
—PHILOSTRATUS, *IMAGINES*, NARCISSUS, 1:23

ACCORDING TO PHILOSTRATUS, the ancient author of an imaginary picture gallery configured in verse, art's history first arose in the mirror-image of *imitatio*: 'for one who is . . . seeking the origin of art, imitation is an invention most ancient and most akin to nature; and wise men who invented it, call it now painting'. In Philostratus' poetic invocation of the story of Narcissus, it is the mirror reflection that paints the youth, while painting itself paints, like the poets, from the *imagines* of myth: 'the pool paints Narcissus, and the painting paints the pool'.[1] As Leon Battista Alberti, the fifteenth-century architect and humanist, would later perpend, painting was nothing other than the mirroring surface of the image, as it was reflected in the pool of Ovidian myth.[2] In the fictive word-gallery of the Baroque poet Giambattista Marino, itself in imitation of Philostratus, the myth of Narcissus was also the image of painting reflected in the 'liquid mirror' of its poetic sources.[3] In this Alberti and Marino echoed the precepts of the ancients, from Ovid to Philostratus, so positing a mimetic genealogy for the history of the image as a mirror reflection of the visible world.

The burden of this book has been to uncover an early modern conceptualisation of painting as a mirror reflection, as it was advanced in art theory, demonstrated in art practice, and represented within painting itself. It argues that the mirror-image, as an object and as a metaphor, was critical to the mimetic definition of painting that we recognise as the key pictorial development of Renaissance art. Distinct from the symbolic forms of medieval painting, Renaissance artists turned to the mirror reflection of antique emulation as the matrix of pictorial representation. Art-historical narratives of the shift in representation from a medieval to a Renaissance idiom of form have generally – and rightly – been configured through a history of mathematical perspective.[4] This book's analysis differs in its emphasis on the mirror reflection as the metaphor of a renascent artistic *imitatio*. In Alberti's account of painting's theoretical genesis, perspective is painting's means, but the mirror is its *exemplum*. In Alberti, as in the painting of Jan van Eyck, and the scientific demonstration of perspective by means of a mirror by Filippo Brunelleschi, arose a concerted theorisation of the painted image as specular imitation. Tracing the conceptual elaboration of the reflective image, this book's argument has centred on the prolific representation of the inset-mirror motif within early modern painting as both the rebus and matrix of its own pictorial representation. That is to say, the inset-mirror image was understood to configure in visual form the theorisation of painting as specular mimesis.

If this book has eschewed charting a chronology of temporal change to the early modern representation of painting within itself as a mirror-image, it has sought to suggest that there were significant paradigm shifts in art's visual representation of the world. The early fifteenth-century conceptualisation of painting within a Euclidian construct of vision as theorised by Alberti and demonstrated by Brunelleschi formulated a geometrical definition of painting's capacity for representational mimesis as a mirror reflection. Howsoever reconfigured and elaborated in manifold ways over time, as this book suggests, its continuing re-composition and reinvention is testament to the longevity of the pictorial paradigm of specular mimesis. For the mirror would remain painting's conceptual matrix, not only for early modernity but up to the early twentieth century, superseded only by the advent of abstraction.

Notwithstanding the paradigmatically pictorial construct of the mirror-image analogy, it has been literary scholars and historians of science who have most presciently brought the mirror metaphor to the fore in accounts of early modernity's intellectual and cultural histories. Across the sciences and literatures, this scholarship has noted both the critical valence of the mirror as the key metaphor of reflective thought and its central place within an early modern technology of scientific vision that would enable entirely new forms of knowledge. This book draws together their analyses of early modern intellectual history concerned with the prevailing figure of the mirror as the light of the mind's reflection, with its pictorial representation in the history of art. It argues that, within painting, the figure of the mirror-image became the model and the metaphor of art itself.

Of course, as this book has traced, the mirror as a metal reflector is an archaic artefact; it is nonetheless the case that the period we term 'Renaissance' heralded its burgeoning materiality, as historians of thought have long recognised. Within intellectual and literary histories of the period, as Richard Rorty and Rodolphe Gasché, in particular, have argued, the mirror paradigm prevailed as the figuration of light and so of thought itself.[5] Moreover, the early modern ascent of the mirror arose alongside new technologies of prosthetic vision that would altogether reconfigure human capacities of sight. Predicated on the manufacture of glass mirrors that subsequently produced the speculum and lenses instrumental to the Galilean 'revolution' of scientific vision, this brought vast consequences for the visible field as the locus of an evidential or demonstrable 'truth'. Within this account, as other scholars have argued, the efflorescent availability of mirrors over the course of the fifteenth century, as well as their ever-greater brilliance and clarity of reflection, offers a practice-based, technological, or materialist account of Renaissance imagery's newfound mimesis. While this book is written in acknowledgement of historical argumentation for a technological determinism, it does not seek to force close temporal ties between the history of the mirror-image and the history of painting, however. Instead, it traces a broad early modern perception of their mimetic equivalence. Within the larger history of painting, this was surely furthered by the concomitant development of oil-based paints able to reflect and refract light in an enhanced materialist approximation of the mirror's specular sheen. More widely, as historians of science have argued, the growing prevalence of optical mirrors and lenses suggests new epistemes of knowledge based on specular instruments for 'seeing'.

Until the nineteenth-century development of electricity, mirrors remained the instrumental agents of light, able to focus and thus to 'shed light' on every type of enquiry, whether scientific, literary, or artistic. Doubtless for this reason (like the lightbulb icon today), the mirror emblem was the ready rebus by which to signify the 'light' of intellectual reflection or speculative thought. Arising from the materialities of an artefactual history, as intellectual historians have argued, the mirror-glass became the sign of illumination in the literal and figurative sense of the word, and across myriad cultural forms and contexts. Within the history of the image, the mirror's valence was a doubled one, to represent both the light of intellectual enquiry and the primacy of visual knowledge alongside that of texts, as Leonardo's notebooks repeatedly proclaimed. In a Euclidian construct of the science of light, the mirror was the emblem of vision itself, as well as the visual field. Within the figure of the painted mirror reflection, art's mimetic claim was nothing less than to embody both the literary and the visual arts, and the observational sciences, as theory and practice, logos and technē, fully intertwined.

To posit the place of visual technology within any account of the history of art is thus to argue for the central place of vision in the extension of knowledge enquiry, as prosthetic sight enabled new ways of seeing the world. If this book, bound to the centuries of early modernity, can only adumbrate the vast changes to image production (including art) that nineteenth-century photography would later forge, it can underscore the longer reach of such a shared history of the visual domain, between art and its instruments. As Martin Kemp, Svetlana Alpers, Barbara Stafford, and Jonathan Crary have critically argued, in various ways, an early modern conceptualisation of the image as mimetic rested on the history of its instruments of vision, just as the pursuit of the perfectly specular image surely drove the means of its mechanisation.[6] Through the figure of the mirror reflection, painting was bound to a specular conception of vision and the visible field.

As Alberti had theorised, painting was the mirror of Narcissus, a fully mimetic yet wholly impalpable image of light reflection captured on the surface of the water. In his conception, painting was also a window view. This double view of the image as both a window and a mirror configured not only the conceptual theorisation of vision, as of painting, but the very structures of early modern thought. To cite from Joseph Koerner, Herbert Grabes, and Victor Stoichita in turn, the 'moment' of self-portraiture is precisely that of a renascent 'mirror age', bound to a Burckhardtian 'individualism'. Thus the early modern inset mirror-image within a mimetic paradigm of painting may be understood as painting's 'title', to use Grabes' method: that art like all knowledge is a mirror-image of the mind's 'eye'.[7] In Alberti's portrait medal of himself, it is surely this sense of 'vision' that configures its celebrated image of a winged eye, the emblem of optical perspective and the dominion of sight as the instrument of all knowledge (Fig. 32, Chapter 1).

To put the argument emblematically, in the manner of painters: the convex tondo reflection of van Eyck's Arnolfini portrait reflects back to us the space in which the viewer must surely stand illusionistically, so demonstrating the status of painting as a mirror. At the same time, it elides the space of the viewer with the painter as he painted, apparently depicting the image of the artist within its specular 'eye' in order to authenticate the method of his extraordinary mimetic art. In *Las Meninas*, as Luca Giordano had recognised and Michel Foucault would argue, the Renaissance theorisation of the image as specular is fully represented in the metaphorical lens of the mirror reflection.[8] Equally, in Federico Zuccaro's specular analogy of painting, each individual work within an early modern art gallery was constituted as a mirror-image of vision.[9] Through a skein of reflecting sight lines, the perspectival painting pictorialized its conception of the viewing eye optically, just as Brunelleschi had demonstrated and Alberti had argued. Thus the early modern mirror reflection within the image of a mirroring art is the very metaphor of painting as mimesis. Like Alberti's summoning of the Ovidian pool of Narcissus, the mirror reflection became the definition and the instrument of what a Renaissance painting was.

***

In closing, it is fitting to adumbrate the subsequent history of painting's inset-mirror motif within a larger view of art's complex histories of visual imitation. As the new wall-sized mirrors of the late seventeenth century swept through the decorative order of the Parisian Rococo interior, so the inset-mirror motif of early modern painting's pictorial definition would cede, apparently, to the place of the mirror itself. As Etienne La Font de Saint-Yenne brilliantly observed of the subsequent history of art in the wake of the Galerie des Glaces at Versailles, painting yielded its place to the mirror as the matrix of the eighteenth-century decorative interior.[10] To be sure, a mimetic and specular theoretical definition of painting would continue to prevail well into the nineteenth century. Yet the motif of the inset-mirror image as the acme and definition of its art, with notable exception in the painted domestic interiors of François Boucher, would otherwise all but disappear from eighteenth-century painting. In effect, Boucher painted its transition from intellectual metaphor into decorative ornament.

The inset-mirror motif would recur again as an insistently prevailing metaphor of painting in the art of the nineteenth century. While its early modern efflorescence that this book has traced may be linked to the development of those lens-based scientific instruments of vision that produced the first spectacles, plentiful mirrors, the Galilean telescope, and the microscope, that of the nineteenth century is surely imbricated within the advent of photography, howsoever the myriad complexities of tracing such historical relationships remain debated and elusive. If Dominique Ingres' portraits of women set against a mirror image of themselves – Marie Marcoz, Louise de Broglie, Mme Moitessier –

suggest both a recollection of the Renaissance *bella donna* and the exactingly specular claim of his 'classically' mimetic art, Edouard Manet's *Bar at the Folies Bergères* instead troubles the very question of its specular relation, in an art that would recast the question of painting itself. Subsequently, Pablo Picasso's encounter with the masks of African art at the Trocadero would bring him to the radical shattering of mimetic form into prismatic anamorphoses in the *Demoiselles d'Avignon*, so rupturing the mirror of Renaissance art in perpetuity. Yet just as Clement Greenberg's 1940 *Newer Laocoon* would apparently sever painting from the mirror irrevocably in the name of abstraction, René Magritte's *Condition Humaine* would, in pictorial terms, pose once again the question that Brunelleschi had done at the door of the Florence Cathedral: of painting as a perfectly specular reflection of the window view.

NOTES

1 Philostratus, 2022, *Imagines*, I: Introduction and 23, 3.
2 Alberti, 1966, 64; Ovid, *Metamorphoses*, III:356–510. See the discussion of Ovid and Alberti in the Introduction.
3 Marino, 1620, 8, 'liquido specchio'.
4 In relation to this argument, see especially Edgerton, 2009, in which he retitled his 1975 study of Renaissance linear perspective as *The Mirror, the Window, and the Telescope*.
5 Rorty, 1979; Gasché, 1986.
6 Kemp, 1990; Alpers, 1983a and 1983b; Stafford, 2001; Crary, 1990.
7 Koerner, 1993; Grabes, 1982; Stoichita, 1997.
8 Foucault, 1970.
9 Zuccaro, 1607, 6; in Heikamp, 1961, 154.
10 La Font de Saint-Yenne, 1747, as discussed in Chapter 1.

BIBLIOGRAPHY

Abel, Lionel. (1963) *Metatheatre: A New View of Dramatic Form*. New York: Hill & Wang.

Accolti, Pietro. (1625) *Lo inganno de gl'occhi*. Florence: Pietro Cecconcelli.

Ackerman, James. (1978) 'Leonardo's Eye'. *Journal of the Warburg & Courtauld Institutes*, 41, 108–46.

Ackerman, Phyllis. (1933) *Tapestry: The Mirror of Civilization*. New York: Oxford University Press.

Adam, Véronique. (1985) 'Le miroir alchimique: objet analogique, objet taxonomique'. In Claude Fintz, ed., *Le miroir: une mediation entre imaginaire, sciences et spiritualité*. Valenciennes: Presses universitaires de Valenciennes, 49–63.

Adams, Tracy. (2014) *Christine de Pizan and the Fight for France*. University Park: Penn State University Press.

Adlin, Jane. (2013) 'Vanities: Art of the Dressing Table'. *The Metropolitan Museum of Art Bulletin*, 71(2), 3–48.

Afentoulidou, Eirini. (2020) 'The Unspotted *Dioptra* of Prophecy: A Mirror Metaphor in Byzantine Literature.' In Maria Gerolemou, ed., *Mirrors and Mirroring from Antiquity to the Early Modern Period*. Exeter: Exeter University Press, 127–38.

Aikema, Bernard. (2009) 'La Casta Susanna.' In Miguel Falomir et al., eds., *Jacopo Tintoretto: actas del congreso internacional Jacobo Tintoretto*. Proceedings of the International Symposium, Madrid: Museo Nacional del Prado, 26–27 February 2007. Madrid: Museo Nacional del Prado, 45–49.

Aimi, Antonio, Vincenzo De Michele, & Alessandro Morandotti. (1984) *Musaeum septalianum: una collezione scientifica nella Milano del seicento*. Exhibition catalogue, Milano: Museo Civico di Storia Naturale, 1984. Florence: Giunti Marzocco.

Ainsworth, Maryan W. (1995) *Petrus Christus in Renaissance Bruges: An Interdisciplinary Approach*. Turnhout: Brepols.

Ainsworth, Maryan. (2008) 'Juan de Flandes, Chameleon Painter'. In Julien Chapuis, ed., *Invention: Northern Renaissance Studies in Honor of Molly Faries*. Turnhout: Brepols, 104–23.

(2010) 'Observations Concerning Gossart's Working Methods.' In Maryan Ainsworth et al., *Man, Myth, and Sensual Pleasures: Jan Gossart's Renaissance*. Exhibition catalogue, New York: Metropolitan Museum of Art, 6 October 2010–17 January 2011; London: National Gallery, 23 February–30 May 2011. New Haven, CT: Yale University Press, 69–87.

(2017) *Workshop Practice in Early Netherlandish Painting: Case Studies from Van Eyck through Gossart*. Turnhout: Brepols.

et al. (2010) *Man, Myth, and Sensual Pleasures: Jan Gossart's Renaissance*. Exhibition catalogue, New York: Metropolitan Museum of Art, 6 October

2010–17 January 2011; London: National Gallery, 23 February–30 May 2011. New Haven, CT: Yale University Press.

Ainsworth, Maryan, & Keith Christiansen. (1998) *From Van Eyck to Bruegel: Early Netherlandish Painting in the Metropolitan Museum of Art*. Exhibition catalogue, New York: Metropolitan Museum of Art, 22 September 1998–3 January 1999. New York: Metropolitan Museum of Art.

Ainsworth, Maryan, with Maximilliaan P. J. Martens. (1994) *Petrus Christus: Renaissance Master of Bruges*. Exhibition catalogue, New York: Metropolitan Museum of Art, 14 April–31 July 1994. New York: Metropolitan Museum of Art.

Ajmar-Wollheim, Marta, & Flora Dennis. (2006) *At Home in Renaissance Italy*. London: Victoria & Albert Museum.

Alberti, Francesca, & Diane Bodart, eds. (2018) *Rire en images à la Renaissance*. Turnhout: Brepols.

Alberti, Leon Battista. (1540) *De pictura* (c. 1435). Basel: Bartholomaeus Westheimer.

Alberti, Leon Battista. (1568) *Opusculi morali*. Venice: Francescho Franceschi, mss c. 1466 'De componendibus cifris', translated as *The Mathematical Works of Leon Battista Alberti*, ed. Kim Williams et al. Basel: Springer, 2010, 169–200.

(1890) 'Anuli'. In Girolamo Mancini ed., *Leon Baptistae Alberti: opera inedita et pauca separatim impressa*. Florence: Sansoni, 224–35.

(1966) *On Painting* (1436). Translated by John Spencer. New Haven, CT: Yale University Press.

(2011) *Leon Battista Alberti: On Painting, a New Translation and Critical Edition* (1436). Translated by Rocco Sinisgalli. Cambridge: Cambridge University Press.

Alciati, Andrea. (1531) *Emblemata*. Augsburg: Heinrich Steyner.

Alcouffe, Daniel. (2001) *Les gemmes de la couronne*. Exhibition catalogue, *Les gemmes de Louis XIV*, Paris: Musée du Louvre, 27 April–23 July 2001. Paris: Réunion des musées nationaux.

Alexander, Robert L. (1985) 'The Mirror, Tool of the Artist'. *Source: Notes in the History of Art*, special issue on mirrors, ed. Laurie Schneider, 2(3), 55–58.

Allen, Valerie. (2015) 'The Self'. In Ian Johnson, ed., *Geoffrey Chaucer in Context*. Cambridge: Cambridge University Press, 187–93.

Alligo, Pietro, ed. (2017) *Tarocchi dal Rinascimento a oggi*. Exhibition catalogue, Turin: Museo Ettore Fico, 4 October 2017–14 January 2018. Turin: Lo scarabeo.

Alpers, Svetlana. (1976) 'Described or Narrated? A Problem in Realistic Representation'. *New Literary History*, 8, 15–41.

(1983a) *The Art of Describing: Dutch Art in the Seventeenth Century*. Chicago: University of Chicago Press.

(1983b) 'Interpretation without Representation, or, The Viewing of *Las Meninas*.' *Representations*, 1, 34–46.

Alpers, Svetlana, & Michael Baxandall. (1994) *Tiepolo and the Pictorial Intelligence*. New Haven, CT: Yale University Press.

Alsteens, Stijn, Freyda Spira, et al. (2012) *Dürer and Beyond: Central European Drawings 1400–1700*. Exhibition catalogue, New York: Metropolitan Museum, 3 April–3 September 2012. New Haven, CT: Yale University Press.

Amelot, Arnaud, & Frédéric Didier. 'L'éclairage de la Grande Galerie: naturel/artificiel'. In Nicolas Milovanovic & Nathalie Volle, eds., *La galerie des glaces après sa restauration: contexte et restitution* (XXVI Rencontres de l'Ecole du Louvre, June 2015). Paris: Ecole du Louvre, 97–109.

Ames-Lewis, Francis, ed. (1999) *Sir Thomas Gresham and Gresham College: Studies in the Intellectual History of London in the 16th–17th Centuries*. Aldershot: Ashgate.

(2007) 'Sources and Documents for the Use of the Oil Medium in Fifteenth-Century Italian Painting'. In Ingrid Alexander-Skipnes, ed., *Cultural Exchange between the Low Countries and Italy (1400–1600)*. Turnhout: Brepols, 47–62.

Amman, Jost, Hans Sachs, & Sigmund Feyerabend. (1568) *Das Ständbuch*. Frankfurt am Main: Aarthus University Press.

(2009) *A Sixteenth-Century Book of Trades*. Translated from the German by T. Rabb. Palo Alto, CA: Society for the Promotion of Science and Scholarship.

Anamorfosen: Spel met Perspectief (1975) Exhibition catalogue, Amsterdam: Rijksmuseum; Paris: Musée des arts décoratifs, 1975. Köln: M. DuMont Schauberg.

Anderson, Christy, Anne Dunlop, & Pamela H. Smith. (2014) *The Matter of Art: Materials, Practices, Cultural Logics, c. 1250–1750*. Manchester: Manchester University Press.

Anderson, Jaynie. (1997) *Giorgione: The Painter of Poetic Brevity*. Paris: Flammarion.

Anderson, Miranda, ed. (2007) *The Book of the Mirror: An Interdisciplinary Collection Exploring the Cultural Story of the Mirror*. Newcastle: Cambridge Scholars.

Andrews Aiken, Jane. (1995) 'The Perspective Construction of Masaccio's *Trinity* Fresco and Medieval Astronomical Optics'. *Artibus et Historiae*, 16, 171–87.

Anglo, Sydney. (2000) *The Martial Arts of Renaissance Europe*. New Haven, CT: Yale University Press.

Anguissola, Anna, ed. (2020) *The Nature of Art: Pliny the Elder on Materials*. Turnhout: Brepols.

Antonucci, Fausta. (2020) *Calderón de la Barca*. Rome: Salerno editrice.

Apian, Peter. (1527) *Ein Newe und Wolgegründete Underweisung aller Kauffmanns Rechnung in Dreyen Büchern, mit Schönen Regeln und Fragstücken Begriffen*. Ingolstadt: G. Apianum.

Apuleius. (1989) *Metamorphoses* or *The Golden Ass*, trans. J. Arthur Hanson. Cambridge, MA: Harvard University Press (LOEB).

Arasse, Daniel. (1984) 'Les miroirs de la peinture'. *L'imitation: aliénation ou source de liberté, rencontres de l'Ecole du Louvre*, 9 (September), 63–94.

(1992) *Le détail: pour une histoire rapprochée de la peinture*. Paris: Flammarion.

(1993) *L'ambition de Vermeer*. Paris: Biro.

(1994) *Vermeer: Faith in Painting*. Translated from the French by T. Grabar. Princeton, NJ: Princeton University Press.

(2002) 'Perspective régulière: rupture historique?' In J. Galard, ed., *Ruptures: de la discontinuité dans la vie artistique*. Paris: Ecole Nationale Supérieure des Beaux Arts, 58–71.

(2013) *Take a Closer Look* (1992). Translated from the French by A. Waters. Princeton, NJ: Princeton University Press.

Arasse, Daniel, Patrizia Nitti, et al. (2001) *Raphael: grâce et beauté*. Exhibition catalogue, Paris: Musée du Luxembourg, 10 October 2001–24 February 2002. Milan: Skira; New York: Rizzoli International Publications through St. Martin's Press.

Aretino, Pietro. (1999) *Lettere*, 5 vols., ed. Paolo Procaccioli. Rome: Salerno Editrice.

Ariès, Philippe. (1974) *Western Attitudes toward Death from the Middle Ages to the Present* (1949). Reprint. Baltimore MD: Johns Hopkins University Press.

(1981) *The Hour of our Death* (1977). Reprint. New York: Knopf Doubleday.

Ariès, Philippe, Georges Duby, Roger Chartier, & Arthur Goldhammer. (2003) *A History of Private Life: Passions of the Renaissance*, 5 vols. Cambridge, MA: Belknap Press of Harvard University Press.

Ariosto, Ludovico. (1532) *Orlando Furioso*. Venice: Francesco Rosso da Valenza.

Arminjon, Catherine, ed. (2007) *Quand Versailles était meublé d'argent*. Exhibition catalogue, Versaille: Château de Versailles 21 November 2007 – 9 March. Paris: RMN.

Arnold, Janet. (1988) *Queen Elizabeth's Wardrobe Unlock'd*. Leeds: W. S. Maney.

Arscott Caroline, & Katie Scott, eds. (2000) *Manifestations of Venus: Art and Sexuality*. Manchester: Manchester University Press.

Aterido, Angel. (2007) 'La cultura de Velázquez: lectura, saber y red social'. In Javier Portús Pérez, ed., *Fábulas de Velázquez: mitología e historia Sagrada en el siglo de oro*. Exhibition catalogue, Madrid: Prado Museum, 20 November 2007–24 February 2008. Madrid: Prado Museum, 72–93.

Audy-Trottier, Andréane, et al., eds. (2020) *Ut pictura poesis: dialogues entre les arts à l'epoque modern (XVe–XVIIIe siècles)*. Paris: Hermann.

Auerbach, Eric. (1953) *Mimesis: The Representation of Reality in Western Literature* (1946). Translated from the German by W. R. Trask. Princeton, NJ: Princeton University Press.

Auge, Père André de l' (1623) *La Saincte Apostasie*. Paris.

Augustyn, Wolfgang, & Manuel Teget-Welz, eds. (2018) Special issue *Hans Burgkmair – Neue Forschungen Veröffentlichungen des Zentralinstituts für Kunstgeschichte in München*, 44.

Aurenhammer, Hans. (2014) '*Liberalitas*: the image of a friendly virtue as a hidden self-portrait in Leon Battista Alberti's *Della pittura*'. In Jeanette Kohl, Marianne Koos, & Adrian Randolph, eds., *Renaissance Love: Eros, Passion, and Friendship in Italian Art around 1500*. Berlin: Deutscher Kunstverlag, 149–62.

Avagnina, Maria Elisa. (2011) *Il Teatro Olimpico Vicenza*. Venice: Marsilio.

Averlino, Antonio di Piero. (1972) *Trattato di architettura* (mss 1461–64) (c. 1460), ed. Anna Maria Finoli, Anna Maria, & Liliana Grassi. Milan: Polifilo.

Avril, François. (1991) *La passion des manuscrits enluminés: bibliophiles français: 1280–1580*. Exhibition catalogue, Paris: Bibliothèque Nationale, 2–21 September 1991. Paris: BNF.

Bacci, Michele. (1998) *Il pennello dell'evangelista: storia delle immagini sacre attribuite a San Luca*. Pisa: Gisemets.

Bachelin-Deflorenne, Antoine. (1869) *Le bibliophile français: gazette illustrée des amateurs de livres, d'éstampes et de haute curiosité*, vol. 3. Paris: Libraire Bachelin-Deflorenne.

Bacon, Francis. (1914) *Gesta grayorum* (1594). Reprint of 1688 ed. Oxford: Oxford University Press.

Badcock, William. (1677) *A Touch-Stone for Gold and Silver Wares, or, A Manual for Goldsmiths* London: Thomas Bassett.

Baglione, Giovanni. (1642) *Le vite de' pittori, scultori, et architetti dal Pontificato di Gregorio XIII del 1572. Fino a' tempi di Papa Urbano Ottavo nel 1642*. Rome: Andrea Fei.

Bakhtin, Mikhail. (1968) *Rabelais and His World*. Translated by Hélène Iswolsky. Cambridge, MA: MIT Press.

Bal, Mieke. (1978) 'Mise en abyme et iconicité'. *Littérature: Revue trimestrielle*, special issue, 'Le travail des mots', 29, 116–28.

Balavoine, Ludovic. (2021) *Jan van Eyck: als ich can.* Villeneuve-d'Asque: Presses universitaires du Septentrion.

Balbiani, Laura. (2001) *La magia naturalis di Giovan Battista Della Porta: lingua, cultura e scienza in Europa all'inizio dell'età moderna.* Bern: Lang.

Balcar, Nathalie, & Elizabeth Martin. (2013) 'L'éclairage de la grande Galerie: naturel/artificiel'. In Nicolas Milovanovic & Nathalie Volle, eds., *La Galerie des Glaces apres sa restauration: contexte et restitution,* XXVI Rencontres de l'Ecole du Louvre, June 2013. Paris: Ecole du Louvre, 97–110.

Baldinucci, Filippo. (1681) *Notizie dei professori del disegno da Cimabue in qua,* 6 vols. Florence: Santi Franchi.

Baldwin, Robert (1985). 'Plutarch's Wife as Mirror in a German Renaissance Marriage Portrait'. *Source: Notes in the History of Art,* special issue on mirrors, ed. Laurie Schneider, 2(3), 68–71.

Ballarin, Alessandro. (2002–7) *Il camerino delle Pitture di Alfonso I,* 6 vols. Padua: Bertoncello Artigrafiche.

Baltrušaitis, Jurgis. (1976) *Anamorphic Art.* Translated from the French by W. J. Strachan. New York: Abrams.

(1978) *Le miroir: révélations, science-fiction, et fallacies. essai sur une légende scientifique.* Paris: Seuil.

Bambach, Carmen C. (2003) 'Leonardo, Left-Handed Draughtsman and Writer'. In Carmen C. Bambach et al., eds., *Leonardo da Vinci, Master Draftsman.* Exhibition catalogue, New York: Metropolitan Museum of Art, 22 January–30 March 2003. New Haven, CT: Yale University Press, in association with the Metropolitan Museum of Art, New York, 59–78.

(2019) *Leonardo da Vinci Rediscovered,* 4 vols. New Haven, CT: Yale University Press.

Banjenec, Elise. (2016) 'Philippe le Bon et les orfèvres: les orfèvres du XVe siècle d'après les comptes du duc de Bourgogne'. In Elisabeth Antoine-König & Michele Tomasi, eds., *Orfèvrerie gothique en Europe: production et reception.* Rome: I Libri di Viella, 173–85.

Baratte, François. (1986) *Le trésor d'orfèvrerie romaine de Boscoreale.* Catalogue, Musee du Louvre. Paris: RMN.

Barbaro, Daniele. (1556) *I dieci libri dell'architettura di M. Vitruvio, tradutti et commentati.* Venice: Francesco Marcolini da Forli.

(1568) *La pratica della perspettiva; opera molto profittevole a pittori scultori et architetti.* Venice: Borgominieri.

Barbier, Frédéric. (2017) *Gutenberg's Europe: The Book and the Invention of Western Modernity* (2006). Translated by J. Birrell. Cambridge: Polity Press.

Bargagli, Girolamo. (1581) *Dialogo de Giuochi che nelle veggie Sanesi si usano di fare.* Venice: Alessandro Gardane.

Barilli, Renato. (2021) *Savoldo.* Florence: Giunti.

Barker, Emma, Nick Webb, & Kim Woods. (1999) *The Changing Status of the Artist.* New Haven, CT: Yale University Press.

Barker, Sheila, ed. (2017) *Artemisia Gentileschi in a Changing Light.* London: Harvey Miller.

Barocchi, Paola, ed. (1960) *Trattati d'arte del cinquecento fra manierismo e controriforma.* Bari: Laterza.

Barolsky, Paul. (1978) *Infinite Jest: Wit and Humour in Italian Renaissance Art.* Columbia: University of Missouri Press.

Baron, Hans. (1960) 'Burckhardt's "Civilization of the Renaissance" a Century after Its Publication'. *Renaissance News,* 13(3), 207–22.

Barovier Mentasti, Rosa. (1982) *Mille anni di arte del vetro a Venezia.* Exhibition catalogue, Venice: Palazzo Ducale & Museo Correr, 24 July–24 October 1982. Venice: Albrizzi.

(1988) *Il vetro veneziano dal medioevo al novecento.* Milan: Electa.

Barozzi, Giacomo da Vignola, & Ignazio Danti. (1583) *Le due regole della prospettiva pratica.* Rome: Francesco Zanetti.

Barriault, Anne. (1994) *Spalliera Paintings of Renaissance Tuscany: Fables of Poets for Patrician Homes.* University Park: Penn State University Press.

Barrio Moya, José Luis. (1989) 'El escultor Domingo de Rioja y las águilas del Salòn de los Espejos del Alcázar de Madrid.' *Boletin del Museo del Prado* 28, 43–48.

Bartalini, Roberto. (2013) 'Da Raffaello al Sodoma: Sulla camera nuziale di Agostino Chigi alla Farnesina'. In Tom Henry, Paul Joannides, et al., eds., *Late Raphael.* Exhibition catalogue, Madrid: Prado, 12 June–16 September 2012; Paris: Louvre, 11 October 2012–14 January 2013. London: Thames & Hudson, 80–89.

(2014) 'Sulla camera di Alessandro e Rossane alla Farnesina e sui Soggiorni Romani del Sodoma (con una nota su Girolamo Genga a Roma e le sue relazioni con I Chigi)'. *Prospettiva: Rivista di Storia dell'Arte Antica e Moderna,* 153–54, 39–73.

Barthes, Roland. (1964) 'Image, raison, déraison'. In *L'univers de l'encyclopédie,* 9–16. Paris: Libraires Associés.

Baskins, Cristelle. (1993) 'Echoing Narcissus in Alberti's *Della Pittura*', *Oxford Art Journal,* 16(1), 25–93.

(2008) *The Triumph of Marriage: Painted Cassoni of the Renaissance.* Exhibition catalogue, Boston: Isabella Stewart Gardner Museum, 16 October 2008–18 January 2009; Sarasota, FL: John and Mable Ringling Museum of Art, 14 February–17 May 2009. Boston: Isabella Stewart Gardner Museum; Sarasota, FL: John and Mable Ringling Museum of Art; [Pittsburgh]: Gutenberg Periscope Publishing.

Bass, Marisa. (2016) *Jan Gossart and the Invention of Netherlandish Antiquity*. Princeton, NJ: Princeton University Press.

Bassett, Laura. (2003) 'The Paintings and Career of Cornelis de Man: Art and Mercantile Culture in Seventeenth-Century Delft'. PhD thesis, University of Michigan.

Bate, John. (1638) *The Mysteryes of Nature and Art*, 4 books. London: Harper.

Bätschmann, Oskar. (1990) *Nicolas Poussin: Dialectics of Painting*. London: Reaktion Books.

(2013) 'Narcisse, le découvreur de l'image'. In Frédéric Elsig et al., eds., *L'image en questions*. Geneva: Dros, 86–92.

Bätschmann, Oskar, & Pascal Griener. (1997) *Hans Holbein*. London: Reaktion Books.

Bauer, Stefan, & Simon Ditchfield, eds. (2022) *A Renaissance Reclaimed: Jacob Burckhardt's Civilisation of the Renaissance in Italy Reconsidered*. Oxford: Oxford University Press.

Baulez, Christian. (2007) 'L'ammeublement de la Grande Galerie de Louis XIV à nos jours'. In Jacques Thuillier et al., eds., *La Galerie des Glaces: histoire et restauration*. Dijon: Editions Faton, 84–95.

Baxandall, Michael. (1964) 'Bartholomaeus Facius on Painting: A Fifteenth-Century Manuscript of the *De Viris Ilustribus*'. *Journal of the Warburg and Courtauld Institutes*, 27, 90–107.

(1971) *Giotto and the Orators: Humanist Observers of Painting in Italy and the Discovery of Pictorial Composition 1350–1450*. Oxford: Warburg Studies with Oxford University Press.

(1972) *Painting and Experience in Fifteenth-Century Italy*. Oxford: Oxford University Press.

Bayer, Andrea, et al., eds. (2008) *Art and Love in Renaissance Italy*. Exhibition catalogue, New York: Metropolitan Museum of Art, 11 November 2008–16 February 2009; Fort Worth, TX: Kimbell Art Museum, 15 March–14 June 2009. New Haven, CT: Yale University Press in association with the Metropolitan Museum of Art.

Bazin-Henry, Sandra. (2016) 'Mirror Galleries and Their Diffusion in Europe during the 17th and 18th Centuries'. In Linda Hinners, Martin Olin, & Margaretha Rossholm Lagerlöf, eds., *The Gallery of Charles XI at the Royal Palace of Stockholm in Perspective*. Stockholm: Kungl. Vitterhets Historie och Antikvitets Akademien Kungliga Vitterhets, 97–112.

(2017) 'Charles Le Brun et les décors de miroirs'. *Bulletin du Centre de recherche du château de Versailles*, 14. http://journals.openedition.org/crcv/14600.

(2021a) 'La Galerie des Glaces: Un modèle emblématique? De la reception des décors de miroirs français par les voyageurs allemends aux Spiegelkabinette et Spiegel galerien dans les cours de l'Empire'. *Bulletin du Centre de recherche du château de Versailles*, 21. https://doi.org/10.4000/crcv.22764.

(2021b) *Tromper les yeux: miroirs dans le grand décor en Europe*. Paris: Editions Faton.

Bechtel, Guy. (1992) *Gutenberg e l'invention de l'imprimerie: une enquête*. Paris: Fayard.

Becker, Andrew Sprague. (1995) *The Shield of Achilles and the Poetics of Ekphrasis*. Lanham. MD: Rowman & Littlefield.

Bedford, Ronald, Lloyd Davis, & Philippa Kelly, eds. (2006) *Early Modern Autobiography: Theories Genres Practices*. Ann Arbor: University of Michigan Press.

Bedini, Silvio. (1961) 'The Optical Workshop Equipment of Giuseppe Campani'. *Journal of the History of Medicine and Allied Sciences*, 16(1), 18–38.

(1966) 'Lens Making for Scientific Instrumentation in the Seventeenth Century'. *Applied Optics*, 5(5), 687–94.

Bedini, Silvio, & Arthur Bennett. (1995) 'A Treatise on Optics by Giovanni Christoforo Bolantio'. *Annals of Science*, 52(2), 103–26.

Béguin, Sylvie. (1956) 'Note sur un portrait de Diane de Poitiers'. *La Revue des Arts*, 6, 82–84.

et al., eds. (1972) *L'Ecole de Fontainebleau*. Exhibition catalogue, Paris: Grand Palais, 17 October 1972–15 January 1973. Paris: Éditions des Musées nationaux.

Bel, Catherine, & Herman Braet. (2006) *De la rose: texte, image, fortune*. Louvain: Peeters.

Beldon Scott, John. (1988) 'The Meaning of Perseus and Andromeda in the Farnese Gallery and on the Rubens House'. *Journal of the Warburg & Courtauld Institutes*, 51, 250–60.

Belhoste, Jean-François. (2013) 'La glace dans la Galerie et le décor français'. In Nicolas Milovanovic & Nathalie Volle, eds., *La Galerie des Glaces apres sa restauration: contexte et restitution* (XXVI Rencontres de l'Ecole du Louvre, June 2013). Paris: Ecole du Louvre, 145–66.

Bélime-Droguet, Magali. (2013) *Psyché à la Renaissance*. Actes du Lille Colloque internationale d'études humanistes 2009. Turnhout: Brepols.

Bell, Janis. (2018) 'A Treatise on Mirrors Attributed to Matteo Zaccolini'. *Nuncius*, special issue, 'Visual Representation in Early Modern Earth Sciences', ed. Luca Ciancio & Domenico Laurenza, 33(3), 563–84.

Bell, Janis, & Thomas Willette. (2002) *Art History in the Age of Bellori*. Cambridge: Cambridge University Press.

Bellori, Giovanni Pietro. (1672) *Le vite de' pittori, scultori et architetti moderni*, 2 vols. Rome: Mascardi.

(2005) *The Lives of the Modern Painters, Sculptors, and Architects: A New Translation and Critical Edition*, ed. Hellmut Wohl. Cambridge: Cambridge University Press.

Belluga, Petrus. (1530) *Speculum principum ac iustitiae*. Paris: Galliot du Pres.

Belting, Hans. (1994) *Likeness and Presence: A History of the Image before the Era of Art*. Translated from the 1990 German edition by E. Jephcott. Chicago: University of Chicago Press.

(2005) *Hieronymus Bosch: Garden of Earthly Delights*. London: Prestel Publishing.

(2011) *Florence and Baghdad: Renaissance Art and Arab Science*. Cambridge, MA: Harvard University Press.

(2016) *Specchio del mondo: l'invenzione del quadro nell'arte fiamminga*. Rome: Carocci Editore.

Bembo, Pietro. (1505) *Gli asolani*. Venice: Aldus.

(1544) *Rime*. Venice: Francesco Marcolini da Forlì.

Benedetti, Giovanni Battista. (2019) *Science in Court Society: Giovanni Battista Benedetti's Diversarum speculationum mathematicarum et physicarum liber*. Facsimile of Giovanni Battista Benedetti, *Diversarum speculationem mathematicarum et physicarum liber* (1585), ed. Pietro Daniel Omodeo & Jürgen Renn. Turin: Nicolo Bevilaqua. Edition Open Sources 11: epub. 203–644.

Bérenger de la Tours d'Albenas. (1963) *Les amours*, ed. François Weber & Henri Weber. Paris: Garnier.

Bergman, Hannah. (1974) 'A Court Entertainment of 1638'. *Hispanic Review*, 42, 67–81.

Bernardini, Maria Grazia, ed. (1995) *Tiziano amor sacro e amor profano*. Exhibition catalogue, Rome; Palazzo delle Espositioni, 22 March–22 May 1995. Milan: Electa.

Bernart de Ventadorn. (1965) *The Songs of Bernart de Ventadorn*, ed. Stephen G. Nichols. Chapel Hill: University of North Carolina Press.

Bernini, Domenico. (1713) *Vita del Cavaliere Gio. Lorenzo Bernini*. Rome: Rocco Bernabò.

Berti, Luciano. (1976) *The Uffizi: The Vasari Corridor*. Florence: Becocci.

Bertini, Giuseppe. (1977) *La quadreria farnesiana e judgment quadri confiscati nel 1612 ai feudatari parmensi*. Parma: La Nazionale.

Bessot, Didier. (2005) 'Synthèse et développement de techniques d'anamorphoses au XVIIe siècle: les traités du Père Jean-François Niceron'. *Mélanges de l'Ecole Française de Rome. Italie et Méditerranée*, 117(1), 91–129.

Besterman, Theodore. (1924) *Crystal-Gazing: A Study in the History, Distribution, Theory and Practice of Scrying*. London: William Rider & Son.

Bettini, Mario. (1645) *Apiaria universae philosophiae mathematicae*. Bologna: G. B. Ferroni.

Biagioli, Mario. (1993) *Galileo, Courtier: The Practice of Science in the Culture of Absolutism*. Chicago: University of Chicago Press.

(2006) *Galileo's Instruments of Credit: Telescopes, Images, Secrecy*. Chicago: University of Chicago Press.

Białostocki, Jan. (1966) 'Kunst und Vanitas'. In *Stil und Ikonographie Studien zur Kunstwissenschaft*. Dresden: Verlag der Kunst, 269–317.

Bialostocki, Jan. (1988) *The Message of Images: Studies in the History of Art*. Vienn a: IRSA.

Biermann, Veronica. (2001) 'The Virtue of a King and the Desire of a Woman? Mythological Representations in the Collection of Queen Christina'. *Art History*, 24 (2), 213–30.

(2017) 'Der unbeherrschte Korper der Konigin und sein Geschlecht: Christina von Schweden im Spiegel Gian Lorenzo Berninis'. *Zeitsprunge*, 21, 137–63.

Bimbenet-Privat, Michèle. (1997) 'Pierre Fourfault and the Lennoxlove Toilet Service'. *Burlington Magazine*, 139, 11–16.

(2007) 'Catherine de Médicis et ses orfèvres: autorité, précision, exigence'. In Kathleen Wilson-Chevalier, ed., *Patronnes et mécènes en France à la Renaissance*. Saint-Etienne: Publications de l'Université de Saint-Etienne, 545–55.

Bindman, David, & Lionello Puppi. (1970) *Canaletto: The Complete Paintings*. London: Weidenfeld & Nicolson.

Biringuccio, Vannoccio. (1540) *De la pirotechnica*. Venice: Venturino Roffinello.

Bisceglia, Anna. (2016) *Buffoni, villani e giocatori alla corte dei Medici*, ed. Anna Bisceglia et al. Exhibition catalogue, Florence: Uffizi Gallery, 19 May–11 September 2016. Leghorn: Sillabe.

Black, Peter, & Genevieve Warwick. (2014) *Picturing Venus in the Renaissance Print*. Exhibition catalogue, Glasgow: The Hunterian, 9 March–29 June 2014. Glasgow: The Hunterian.

Blake, N. F. (1976) *Caxton: England's First Publisher*. London: Barnes & Noble.

Blanc, Jan. (2008) *Peindre et penser la peinture au XVIIe siècle: la théorie de l'art de Samuel van Hoogstraten*. Berne: Peter Lang.

(2014) *Vermeer: la fabrique de la gloire*. Paris: Citadelles & Mazenod.

(2017) *Vermeer et les maîtres de la peinture hollandaise: plongée au spejr du mystère Vermeer*. Issy-les-Moulineaux: Beaux Arts.

Blanchard, Ian. (1997) *Sir Thomas and the 'House of Gresham': Activities of a Mercer-Merchant Adventurer*. Edinburgh: Newlees.

Blumenberg, Hans. (1966) *Der Prozess der theoretischen neugierde*. Suhrkamp: Taschenbuch, Wissenschaft.

Blunt, Anthony, & Lester Cooke. (1960) *The Roman Drawings of the XVII and XVIII Centuries in the Collection of Her Majesty the Queen at Windsor Castle*. London: Phaidon Press.

Bober, Phyllis, & Ruth Rubenstein. (2010) *Renaissance Artists and Antique Sculpture: A Handbook of Sources* (1998). Reprint. London: Harvey Miller.

Boccaccio, Giovanni. (1401) *Livre des femmes nobles et renommees* (c. 1360–74). Anonymous French translation. Paris, BNF, ms. Français 12420.

Bodart, Diane. (2008) 'Tiziano e l'ultimo lustro'. *Venezia cinquecento*, 18(36), 65–90.

(2009) 'Le reflet et l'éclat: jeux de l'envers dans la peinture vénitienne du XIVe siècle'. In Frederick Ichman, ed., *Titien, Tintoret, Véronèse: rivalités à Venise|Titian Tintoretto Veronese: Rivals in Renaissance Venice*. Exhibition catalogue, Boston: Museum of Fine Arts, 15 March–16 August 2009; Paris: Musée du Louvre, 14 September 2009–4 January 2010. London: Lund Humphries, 216–59.

(2010) 'Le reflet, un detail-emblème de la representation en peinture'. In Frédéric Cousinié, ed., *Daniel Arasse, historien de l'art*. Paris: Editions des Cendres, 43–61.

Boehm, Barbara Drake. (2020) 'Blessing of Unicorns: The Paris and Cloisters Tapestries'. *The Metropolitan Museum of Art Bulletin*, 78(1, Summer).

Bohn, Babette. (2004) 'Female Self-Portraiture in Early Modern Bologna'. *Renaissance Studies*, 18(2), 239–86.

Boiardo, Matteo Maria. (1495) *Orlando innamorato*. Scandiano: Camillo Boiardo.

Bokody, Péter. (2015) *Images-within-Images in Italian Painting (1250–1350): Reality and Reflexivity*. Farnham: Ashgate.

Bokody, Péter, & Alexander Nagel, eds. (2020) *Renaissance Metapainting*. Turnhout: Harvey Miller Publishers.

Bologna, Ferdinando. (2006) *L'incredulità del Caravaggio e l'esperienza delle 'cose naturali'* (1992). Reprint. Turin: Bollati Boringhieri.

Bolzoni, Lina. (1984) *Il teatro della memoria: studi su Giulio Camillo*. Padua: Liviana.

Bomford, David. (1998) 'Perspective, Anamorphosis, and Illusion: Seventeenth-Century Dutch Peep Shows'. In Ivan Gaskell and Michiel Jonker, eds., *Vermeer Studies*. Studies in the History of Art, Washington, DC, National Gallery of Art, 55, XXXIII. New Haven, CT: Yale University Press, 125–35.

Bomford, David, Christopher Brown, Joyce Plesters, & John Mills. (1987) 'Samuel van Hoogstraten: Perspective and Painting'. *National Gallery Technical Bulletin*, 11, 60–84.

Bomford, David, Christopher Brown, & Ashok Roy. (1989) *Art in the Making: Rembrandt*. Exhibition catalogue, London: National Gallery, 12 October 1988–17 January 1989. London: National Gallery.

Bonafoux, Pascal. (2007) 'Autoritratti o tratto autori, trattoria tuo'. In Giovanna Giusti, ed., *Artists' Self-Portraits from the Uffizi*. Exhibition catalogue, London: Dulwich Picture Gallery, 22 May–15 July, 2007. Milan: Skira, 63–64.

Bond, Anthony, & Joanna Woodall. (2005) *Self-Portrait: Renaissance to Contemporary*. London: National Portrait Gallery.

Bondue, Didier. (2010) 'La guerre des miroirs: Colbert et Murano au regard de deux fonds des Archives d'Etat de Venise (1665–67)'. *Revista Arhivelor*, 2, 179–210.

Bonfait, Olivier. (2011) *Simon Vouet en Italie*. Rennes: Presses universitaire de Rennes.

Bonifacio, Giovanni. (1616) *L'arte de' cenni con la quale... si tratta della muta eloquenza*. Vicenza: Francesco Grossi.

Borchert, Till-Holger. (2014) *Hans Memling: rinascimento fiammingo*. Exhibition catalogue, Rome: Scuderie del Quirinale, 11 October 2014–18 January 2015. Milan: Skira.

et al. (2005) *Memling's Portraits*. Exhibition catalogue, Madrid: Museo Thyssen-Bornemisza, 15 February–15 May 2005; Bruges: Groeningemuseum, 8 June–4 September 2005; New York: Frick Collection, 12 October–31 December 2005. Ghent: Ludion; New York: Thames & Hudson.

Borchert, Till-Holger, & Paul Huvenne. (2002) 'Van Eyck and the Invention of Oil Painting: Artistic Merits in Their Literary Mirror'. In Till-Holger Bochert, ed., *The Age of Van Eyck: The Mediterranean World and Early Netherlandish Painting, 1430–1530*. Exhibition catalogue, Bruges: Groeningemuseum, 15 March–30 June 2002. Ghent: Ludion, 221–25.

Borea, Evelina, & Carlotta Gasparri. (2000) *L'idea del bello: viaggio per Roma nel seicento con Giovanni Pietro Bellori. Cinque itinerari nella città seicentesca*. Exhibition catalogue, Rome: Palazzo delle Espozioni, 29 March–26 June 2000. Rome: De Luca Editori d'Arte.

Borel, Françoise. (2002) *Le peintre et son miroire*. Turnhout: La Renaissance du Livre.

Borel, Pierre. (1655) *De Vero Telescopii Inventore*. The Hague: Vlacq.

(1658) *A new treatise proving a multiplicity of worlds ...* London: John Streater.

Borrelli, Arianna, Giora Hon, & Yaakow Zik, eds. (2017) *The Optics of Giambattista della Porta (ca. 1535–1615): A Reassessment*. Cham: Springer International.

Boschini, Marco. (1660) *La carta del navegar pitoresco*. Venice: Baba.

Bosse, Abraham, & Girard Desargues. (1648) *Discours sur la manière universelle pour pratiquer la perspective Par Petit-Pied, Comme le Geometral*. Paris: Pierre Des-Hayes.

Boström, Hans-Olof. (1975) *Fünf Egerer Kabinettschränke des 17. Jahrhunderts in Schwedischem Besitz*. Uppsala: Almquist & Wiksell.

(2017) 'Philipp Hainhofer & Gustavus Adolphus's Kunstschrank in Uppsala'. In O. R. Impey & Arthur MacGregor, eds., *The Origins of Museums: The Cabinet of Curiosities in Sixteenth- and Seventeenth-Century Europe*. Oxford: Ashmolean, 90–101.

Böttiger, John. (1909-10) *Philipp Hainhofer und der Kunstschrank Gustav Adolfs in Upsala*, 4 vols. Stockholm: Verlag der Lithographischen Anstalt des Generalstabs.

Bottineau, Yves. (1958) 'L'Alcázar de Madrid et l'inventaire de 1686: aspects de la cour d'Espagne au XVIIe siècle (5e et dernier article)'. *Bulletin hispanique*, 60–66, 450–83.

Bouchenot-Déchin, Patricia. (2013) *André Le Notre in Perspective*. New Haven, CT: Yale University Press.

Boulenger, Jacques. (1913) *L'Ameublement Français Au Grand Siecle* (1907). Reprint. London: Wentworth Press.

Bournet-Bacot, Marianne. (2014) 'Lucas Furtenagel (Augsbourg 1505–avant 1563), peintre luthérien'. *Zeitschrift für Kunstgeschichte*, 77(1), 42–72.

Bousmanne, Bernard. (2020) *The Library of the Dukes of Burgundy*. Turnhout: Harvey Miller.

et al. (2001–15) *La librairie des ducs de Bourgogne: manuscrits conservés à la Bibliothèque Royale de Belgique*, 5 vols. Turnhout: Brepols.

Bouvrande, Isabelle. (2017) 'Le "Dialogo di pittura" de Paolo Pino: une reception remarquable du "De pictura" autour de 1550 à Venise', *Albertiana*, 2(1), 243–73.

Bovi, Tina, & Angelo Capparoni. (2002) *Lenti e antichi microscopi*. Rome: Museo storico Nazionale dell'Arte Sanitaria.

Bowden, Hugh. (2010) *Mystery Cults of the Ancient World*. Princeton, NJ: Princeton University Press.

Bowen, Barbara. (2004) *Humour and Humanism in the Renaissance*. Aldershot: Ashgate.

Boymel Kampen, Natalie, ed. (1996) *Sexuality in Ancient Art: Near East, Egypt, Greece, and Italy*. Cambridge: Cambridge University Press.

Braamhorst, Karin, & Marlies Visser. (2014) *Het poppenhuis van Petronella Oortman*. Amsterdam: Uitgeverij Luitingh-Sijthoff.

Brauer, Heinrich, & Rudolf Wittkower. (1931) *Die Zeichnungen des Gianlorenzo Bernini*, 2 vols. Rome: Bibliotheca Hertziana.

Braune, Sandra. (2020) 'Von der äusseren zur inneren Reflexion: ein Goldschmied in seinem Geschäft von Petrus Christus als Spiegelbild des Gottesbundes'. In Sandra Braune & Jürgen Müller, eds., *Alltag als Exemplum: religiose und profane Deutungsmuster der frühen Genrekunst*. Berlin: Deutscher Kunstverlag, 24–45.

Brealey, John, & Manuela Mena Marqués. (1984) 'La restauración de *Las Meninas* de Velázquez.' *Boletín del Museo del Prado*, 5, 87–108.

Bredekamp, Horst. (1995) *The Lure of Antiquity and the Cult of the Machine: The Kunstkammer and the Evolution of Nature, Art, and Technology*. Translated from the German by A. Brown. Princeton, NJ: Princeton University Press.

(2000) 'Gazing Hands and Blind Spots: Galileo as Draftsman'. *Science in Context* 13(3–4), 423–62.

(2001) 'Gazing Hands and Blind Spots: Galileo as Draftsman'. In Jürgen Renn, ed., *Galileo in Context*. Cambridge: Cambridge University Press, 153–92.

(2007) *Galilei der Künstler: Die Zeichnung, der Mond, die Sonne*. Berlin: Akademie Verlag.

(2011–14) *Galileo's 'O'*, 4 vols. Berlin: Akademie Verlag.

(2018) *Image Acts: A Systematic Approach to Visual Agency*. Berlin: De Gruyter.

(2020) *Die Fenster der Monade: Gottfried Wilhelm Leibniz' Theater der Natur und Kunst*. Berlin: De Gruyter.

et al., eds. (2015) *The Technical Image: A History of Styles in Scientific Imagery*. Chicago: Chicago University Press.

Brewer, John, & Roy Porter, eds. (1993) *Consumption and the World of Goods*. London: Routledge.

Brine, Douglas. (2018) 'Reflection and Remembrance in Jan van Eyck's van der Paele Virgin'. *Art History*, 41 (4), 600–23.

Brooke, Christopher N. L. (1989) *The Medieval Idea of Marriage*. Oxford: Oxford University Press.

Broomhall, Susan. (2011) 'Imagining Domesticity in Early Modern Dutch Dolls Houses'. In Susan Broomhall & Jennifer Spinks, eds., *Early Modern Women in the Low Countries: Feminizing Sources and Interpretations of the Past*. London: Routledge, 99–122.

(2018) *Women and Power at the French Court, 1483–1563*. Amsterdam: Amsterdam University Press.

Brosens, Koenraad, et al. (2019) 'The Brussels Guild of Painters, Goldbeaters, and Stained-Glass Makers, 1599–1705: A Multi-faceted Aanalysis'. *Zeitschrift für Kunstgeschichte* 82(4), 531–53.

Brown, Andrew. (2011) *Civic Ceremony and Religion in Medieval Bruges c. 1300–1520*. Cambridge: Cambridge University Press.

Brown, David Alan. (1990) *Titian: Prince of Painters*. Exhibition catalogue, Venice: Palazzo Ducale, 1

June–7 October 1990; Washington, DC: National Gallery, 28 October 1990–27 January 1991. Venice: Marsilio Editori.

(2019) *Giovanni Bellini: The Last Works*. Milan: Skira.

Brown, David Alan, & Sylvia Ferino Pagden, eds. (2006) *Bellini, Giorgione, Titian and the Renaissance of Venetian Painting*. Exhibition catalogue, Washington, DC: National Gallery of Art, 18 June–17 September 2006; Vienna: Kunsthistorisches Museum, 17 October 2006–7 January 2007. New Haven, CT: Yale University Press.

et al. (2002) *Virtue and Beauty: Leonardo's Ginevra de' Benci and Renaissance Portraits of Women*. Exhibition catalogue. Washington, DC: National Gallery of Art.

Brown, Jonathan. (1986) *Velazquez: Painter and Courtier*. New Haven, CT: Yale University Press.

(1998) *Velazquez: The Technique of Genius*. New Haven, CT: Yale University Press.

Brown, Jonathan, & J. H. Elliott. (1980) *A Palace for a King: the Buen Retiro and the Court of Philip IV*. New Haven CT: Yale University Press.

et al. (1999) *Velazquez, Rubens, y Van Dyck: pintores cortesanos del siglo XVII*. Exhibition catalogue, Madrid: Prado Museum, 17 December 1999–5 March 2000. Madrid: Museo Nacional del Prado.

Bruijnen, Yvette. (2011) *Jan Rombouts: the Discovery of an Early Sixteenth-Century Master in Louvain*. Turnhout: Brepols.

Brunn, Lucas. (1615) *Praxis perspectivae*. Leipzig: Lorenz Kober.

Bruno, M. (2015) 'Intrecciando arabeschi, e fogliami': Filippo Parodi as intagliatore in wood'. In C. Milner, ed., *The Eternal Baroque: Essays in Honour of Jennifer Montagu*. Milan: Skira, 345–58.

Brusati, Celeste. (1990–91) 'Stilled Lives: Self-Portraiture and Self-Reflection in Seventeenth-Century Netherlandish Still-Life Painting'. *Simiolus* 20, 168–82.

(1995) *Artifice and Illusion: The Art and Writing of Samuel van Hoogstraten*. Chicago: University of Chicago Press.

Brusati, Celeste, & Jaap Jacobs, eds. (2021) *Introduction to the Academy of the Art of Painting; or, The Visible World*. Los Angeles: Getty Publications.

Bryson, N. (1983) *Vision and Painting: The Logic of the Gaze*. New Haven, CT: Yale University Press.

Bryson, Norman. (1990) *Looking at the Overlooked: Four Essays on Still Life Painting*. London: Reaktion.

Buck, Sarah. (2019) 'Bodies of Work in the Ancien Regime: The 'Costumes Grotesques' by Nicolas I de Larmessin'. In Tara Zanardi & Lynda Klich, eds., *Visual Typologies from the Early Modern to the Contemporary*. New York: Routledge, 31–44.

Bucklow, Spike. (2009) *The Alchemy of Paint: Art, Science and Secrets from the Middle Ages*. London: Boyars.

Buettner, Brigitte. (1996) *Bocaccio's Des Clères et Nobles Femmes: Systems of Signification in an Illuminated Manuscript*. Seattle: College Art Association with University of Washington Press.

Buijnsters-Smets, Leontine. (1995) *Jan Massys: een Antwerps Schilder uit de Zestiende Eeuw*. Zwolle: Waanders.

Burckhardt, Jacob. (1860) *Kultur der Renaissance in Italien*. Basel: Schweighauser'sche Verlagsbuchhandlung.

Burke, Marcus, & Peter Cherry. (1997) *Collections of Paintings in Madrid 1601–1755*. Los Angeles: Getty Information Institute.

Burnett, Charles, & Baudouin Van den Abele. (2021) *Falconry in the Mediterranean Context during the Pre-modern Era*. Geneva: Droz.

Burnett, Graham D. (2003) *Descartes and the Hyperbolic Quest: Lens Making Machines and Their Significance in the Seventeenth Century*. Philadelphia: American Philosophical Society.

Burton, Grace. (2017) 'Painting and Politics in *El Pintor de Deshonra*: Monarch as a Work of Art'. *Bulletin of Spanish Studies*, 94(5), 745–70.

Bycroft, Michael, & Sven Dupré, eds. (2019) *Gems in the Early Modern World: Materials, Knowledge, and Global Trade, 1450–1800*. Cham: Palgrave Macmillan.

Cache, Bernard. (2016) *Toujours l'informe ... Géometrie d'Albrecht Dürer*. Lausanne: PPUR.

Cacho Casal, Marta. (2020) 'Courtiers, Compasses, Fables, and Dictionaries: Italian Books in the Collections of Velazquez, Carducho and Guerra Coronel'. In Kelley Helmstutler Di Dio, ed., *Artistic Circulation between Early Modern Spain and Italy*. New York: Routledge, Taylor & Francis, 152–72.

Cahan, David. (2018) *Helmholtz: A Life in Science*. Chicago: University of Chicago Press.

Caillois, Roger. (1960) *Méduse et cie*. Paris: Gallimard.

Calabrese, Omar. (2003) *Vénus dévoilée: la Vénus d'Urbino di Titien*. Exhibition catalogue, Brussels: Palais des Beaux Arts, 11 October 2003–11 January 2004. Gand: Snoeck; Milan: Silvana.

(2006) *L'art de l'autoportrait*. Paris: Citadelles.

Calderón de la Barca, Pedro. (1635) *La vida es sueño*. Madrid & Saragoza.

Calvesi, Maurizio. (1990) *Le realtà di Caravaggio*. Turin: Einaudi.

Camerota, Filippo. (1987) 'Dalla finestra allo specchio: la prospettiva pratica di Ludovico Cigoli alle origini di una nuova concezione spaziale'. PhD thesis, University of Florence.

(2001) 'Ricostruire il seicento: macchine ed esperimenti'. In Eugenio Lo Sardo, ed., *Athanasius Kircher*

S.J. Il Museo del Mondo. Exhibition catalogue, Rome: Palazzo Venezia, 28 February–28 April 2001. Rome: De Luca, 239–55.

(2005) 'Looking for an Artificial Eye: on the Borderline between Painting and Topography'. *Early Science and Medicine*, 10(2), 263–86.

(2010) *Linear Perspective in the Age of Galileo: Ludovico Cigoli's Prospettiva pratica*. Florence: Leo Olschki Editore.

Camille, Michael. (1998) *The Medieval Art of Love: Objects and Subjects of Desire*. London: Laurence King.

Camillo, Giulio. (1550) *Idea del teatro*. Florence: Lorenzo Torrentino.

Campbell, Lorne. (1976) 'The Art Market in the Southern Netherlands in the Fifteenth Century'. *Burlington Magazine*, 118, 188–98.

(1978) 'Quentin Matsys, Desiderius Erasmus, Pieter Gillis and Thomas More'. *The Burlington Magazine*, 120, 716–24.

(1994) 'Roger van der Weyden and His Workshop'. *Proceedings of the British Academy*, 84, 1993 Lectures & Memoirs, 1–24.

(1995) '*Hans Memling, the Complete Works* by Dirk de Vos.' *Burlington Magazine*, 137, 253–54.

(1997) 'The Methods and Materials of Northern European Painting, 1400–1550'. *National Gallery Technical Bulletin*, 18, 6–25.

(1998) *The National Gallery Catalogues: The Fifteenth-Century Netherlandish Schools*. London: National Gallery; New Haven, CT: Yale University Press.

(2004) *Roger van der Weyden*. London: Chaucer Press.

Campbell, Lorne, Miguel Falomir, et al. (2008) *Renaissance Faces: Van Eyck to Titian*. Exhibition catalogue, London: National Gallery, 15 October 2008–18 January 2009. London: National Gallery; New Haven, CT: Yale University Press.

Campbell, Thomas P., ed. (2002) *Tapestry in the Renaissance: Art and Magnificence*. Exhibition catalogue, New York: Metropolitan Museum of Art, 12 March–19 June 2002. New Haven, CT: Yale University Press.

Capodieci, Luisa, & Gaylord Brouhot. (2019) *Il sogno d'arte di François Ier: l'Italie à la cour de France*. Rome: Bretschneider.

Capwell, Tobias. (2018) *Arms and Armour of the Medieval Joust*. Leeds: Royal Armouries Museum.

Cardano, Girolamo. (1550) *De subtilitate*. Nuremberg: Johann Petreius.

Cardi, Ludovico detto Il Cigoli, & Rodolfo Profumo. (1992) *Trattato pratico di prospettiva di Ludovico Cardi detto Il Cigoli: manoscritto MS2660A del Gabinetto dei disegni e delle stampe degli Uffizi* (c. 1613). Rome: Bonsignori.

Careri, Giovanni. (2005) *Gestes d'amour et de Guerre: la Jérusalem Délivrée, images et affects (XVIe–XVIIIe siècle)*. Paris: EHESS.

(2021) *The Making of the Affetti: Torquato Tasso's 'Jerusalem Delivered' from the Carracci to Tiepolo*. Turnhout: Harvey Miller.

Carlino, Andrea. (1994) *La fabbrica del corpo: libri e dissezione nel Rinascimento*. Turin: Einaudi.

(2009) *La bella anatomia: il disegno del corpo fra arte e scienza nel Rinascimento*. Milan: Silvana.

Carpenter, William B., & William H. Dallinger, eds. (1901) *The Microscope and Its Revelations* (1856). Reprint. Philadelphia: Blakeston's Sons.

Carpo, Mario. (2004) 'Le "secondo libro" traduit par Jean Martin (Paris: Jean Barbé, 1545), edition bilingue'. In Sylvia Deswarte-Rosa, ed., *Le traité d'architecture de Sebastiano Serlio*, vol. 1. Lyon: Mémoire Active, 131–36.

Carr, Dawson, & Xavier Bray. (2006) *Velázquez*. Exhibition catalogue, London: National Gallery, 18 October 2006–21 January 2007. London: National Gallery.

Carson Pastan, Elizabeth, & Brigitte Durman-Schwarz, eds. (2019) *Investigations in Medieval Stained Glass: Materials, Methods, and Expressions*. Leiden: Brill.

Carter, David. (1954) 'Reflections in Armor in the Canon van der Paele Madonna'. *Art Bulletin*, 36(1), 60–62.

Carver, Robert. (2007) *The Protean Ass: The Metamorphoses of Apuleius from Antiquity to the Renaissance*. Oxford: Oxford University Press.

Casale, Vittorio. (2002) 'L'idéologie du baroque dans le *'Trattato della pittura e scultura'* di Gian Domenico Ottonelli et Pierre de Còrtone'. In Jean-Marc Olivesi, ed., *Les cieux en gloire: paradis en trompe-l'oeil pour la Rome baroque: bozzetti, modelli, ricordi et memorie*. Exhibition catalogue, Musée Fesch, Villa d'Ajaccio, 17 May–30 September 2002. Ajaccio: Musée Fesch, 211–31.

Case, H. Robert. (1896) *English Epithalamies*. London: John Lane; Chicago: A. C. McClurg & Co.

Cassegrain, Laurent. (1672) *Recueil des mémoires et conférences concernant les arts et les sciences*. Paris: Jean-Baptiste Denys.

Castelluccio, Stéphane. (2009) 'La présentation des collections royales durant le règne de Louis XIV'. In Nicolas Milovanovic & Alexandre Maral, eds., *Louis XIV: l'homme & le roi*. Exhibition catalogue, Versailles: Château de Versailles, 20 October 2009–7 February 2010. Paris: Skira (Flammarion), 64–71.

Castiglione, Baldassare. (1528) *Il libro del Cortegiano*. Venice: Heirs of Aldus Manutius and Andrea Torresano d'Asola.

(2002). *The Book of the Courtier: The Singleton Translation* (1959), ed. Charles S. Singleton & Daniel Javitch. New York: Norton.

Catoni, Maria Luisa, & Salvatore Settis. (2008) *La forza del bello: l'arte greca conquista l'Italia*. Exhibition catalogue, Mantua: Palazzo Te, 29 March–6 July 2008. Milan: Skira.

Cats, Jacob. (1625) *Houwelyck*. Middelburg: Jan Pietersz van de Venne.

(1632) *Spiegel van den Ouden ende Nieuwen Tijd*. The Hague: Isaac Burchoorn

Cavalieri, Bonaventura. (1632) *Specchio ustorio*. Bologna: Clemente Ferroni.

Cavalli-Björkman, Görel, ed. (1987) *Bacchanals by Titian and Rubens*. Symposium: Stockholm, 18–19 March, 1987. Stockholm: National Museum.

Cavallo, Adolfo Salvatore. (1998) *The Unicorn Tapestries at the Metropolitan Museum of Art*. New York: Metropolitan Museum.

Cazzola-Senkpiel, Fabiana. (2020) 'L'atto del divenire dell'immagine: medialità e temporalità nell'autoritratto poietico di Alessandro Allori (1555)'. *Imagines*, 3.

Chaimovich, Felipe. (2008) 'Mirrors of Society: Versailles and the Use of Flat Reflected Images'. *Visual Resources* 24(4), 353–67.

Chantraine, Pierre. (1968) *Dictionnaire étymologique de la langue grecque*. Paris: Klincksieck.

Chapman, George. (1605) *All Fools*. London: Thomas Thorpe.

(1614) *Andromeda liberata*. London: L'Isle.

Chapman, Perry H. (1992) *Rembrandt's Self-Portraits: A Study in Seventeenth-Century Identity*. Princeton, NJ: Princeton University Press.

(2005) 'The Imagined Studios of Rembrandt and Vermeer'. In Michael Cole & Mary Prado, eds., *Inventions of the Studio, Renaissance to Romanticism*. Chapel Hill: University of North Carolina Press, 108–46.

Chappell, Miles. (1975) 'Cigoli, Galileo, and "Invidia"'. *The Art Bulletin*, 57, 91–98.

(2009) '"Il vero senza passione": Proposte su Cigoli e Galileo'. In Lucia Tongiorgi Tomasi & Alessandro Tosi, eds., *Il cannocchiale e il pennello: nuova scienza e nuova arte nell'età di Galileo*. Exhibition catalogue, Palazzo Blu, Pisa, 9 May–19 July 2009. Florence: Giunti, 131–42.

Charbonnier, Jean-Michel. (2019) *Pieter de Hooch à Delft: dans la lumière de Vermeer*. Exhibition catalogue, Delft: Prinsenhof Museum, 11 October 2019–16 February 2020. Paris: Société Française de Promotion Artistique.

Chartier, Roger. (1994) *The Order of Books: Readers, Authors, and Libraries in Europe between the 14th and 18th Centuries*. Stanford, CA: Stanford University Press.

Chastel, André. (1953) 'Marquetrie et perspective au XVe siècle'. *Revue des Arts*, 3, 141–53.

(1966) 'Diane de Poitiers: "l'Eros de la Beauté Froide"'. In Vittorio Gabrieli, ed., *Friendship's Garland*, 2 vols. Rome: Edizioni di storia e letteratura, vol. 1, 95–104.

(1967) 'Le tableau dans le tableau'. In *Stil und Überlieferung in der Kunst des Abendlandes, Akten des 21 Internationalen Kongresses für Kunstgeschichte in Bonn*. Epochen europäischer Kunst. Vol. 1. Berlin: Mann, 15–29.

ed. (1987) *Revue de l'art*, special issue on frames, 76.

Chaucer, Geoffrey. (1476) *The Canterbury Tales*. London: William Caxton.

Chaves, Alonso de. (1983) *Quatri partitu en cosmografia práctica, y por otro nombre Espejo de navegantes* (ms. c. 1537), transcribed and ed. Paulino Castañeda Delgado, Mariano Cuesto Domingo, & Pablo Hernández Aparicio. Madrid: Instituto de Historia y Cultura Naval.

Checa Cremades, Fernando. (2002) *Tiziano/Rubens: Venus ante el espejo*, Contextos de la Colección in permanente, no. 13. Exhibition catalogue, Madrid: Museo Thyssen-Bornemisza, 24 September 2002–26 January 2003. Madrid: Fundación Colección Thyssen-Bornemisza.

Checa Cremades, Fernando, with Jesus Saenz de Miera. (1994) 'La corte Española y la pintura de Flandes' In Fernando Checa Cremades et al., *El real Alcázar de Madrid: dos siglos de arquitectura y coleccionismo en la corte de los reyes de España*. Exhibition catalogue, Madrid: Palacio Real, 16 September–13 November 1994. Madrid: Nerea, 220–35.

et al. (1994) *El real Alcázar de Madrid: dos siglos de arquitectura y coleccionismo en la corte de los reyes de España*. Exhibition catalogue, Madrid: Palacio Real, 16 September–13 November 1994. Madrid: Nerea.

Chefdebien, Anne, & Jean-Marcel Humbert. (1997) *Grands colliers: l'orfèvrerie au service d'un idea*. Exhibition catalogue, Paris: Musée national de la Légion d'honneur et des orders de chevalerie, 3 June–16 November 1997. Paris: Musée national de la Légion d'honneur et des orders de chevalerie.

Cheles, Luciano. (1986) *The Studiolo of Urbino: An Iconographic Investigation*. University Park: Penn State University Press.

Chen-Morris, Raz. (2016) *Measuring Shadows: Kepler's Optics of Invisibility*. University Park: Penn State University Press.

Cherry, John. (2011) *Medieval Goldsmiths*. London: British Museum Press.

Cherry, Peter. (2007) 'Velázquez y el desnudo'. In Javier Portús Pérez, ed., *Fábulas de Velázquez: mitología e historia sagrada en el siglo de oro*. Exhibition catalogue, Madrid: Prado Museum, 20 November 2007–24 February 2008. Madrid: Prado Museum, 241–70.

Cherubin d'Orléans. (1671) *La dioptrique oculaire*. Paris: Jean Cusson.

Child, Graham. (1990) *World Mirrors, 1650–1900*. London: Sotheby's Publications.

Chipps Smith, Jeffrey. (2022) *Kunstkammer: Early Modern Art and Curiosity Cabinets in the Holy Roman Empire*. London: Reaktion Books.

Chong, Alan, with Wouter Th. Kloek & Celeste Brusati. (1999) *Still Life Painting from the Netherlands, 1550–1720*. Exhibition catalogue, Rijksmuseum Amsterdam and Cleveland Museum of Art, 1999. Zwolle: Waanders.

Choux, Jacques. (1973) 'Le miroir de la Madeleine chez Georges de la Tour'. *Le pays lorrain*, 54(2), 109–12.

Christiansen, Keith, Judith Mann, et al. (2001). *Orazio and Artemisia Gentileschi: Father and Daughter Painters in Seventeenth-Century Italy*. Exhibition catalogue, Rome: Palazzo Venezia, 15 October 2001–6 January 2002; New York: Metropolitan Museum of Art, 14 February 2002–12 May 2002; St Louis Art Museum, 15 June–15 September 2002. New Haven, CT: Yale University Press.

Ciappelli, Gianni, & Patricia Rubin, eds. (2000) *Art, Memory and Family in Renaissance Florence*. Cambridge: Cambridge University Press.

Ciappi, Silvia. (2006) *Il vetro in Europa: oggetti, artisti, e manifatture dal 1400 al 1930*. Milan: Electa.

Cicconi, Maurizia, et al. (2023) *L'immagine sovrana: Urbano VIII e I Barberini*. Exhibition catalogue, Rome: Palazzo Barberini, 18 March–30 July 2023. Rome: Officina libraria.

Cicero, *Tusculanae disputationes*.

Cigoli, Ludovico. (1992) *Trattato pratico di prospettiva di Ludovico Cardi detto il Cigoli: Manoscritto Ms 2660 A del Gabinetto dei disegni e delle stampe degli Uffizi* (1613), ed. Rodolfo Profumo. Rome: Bonsignori.

Clark, Stuart. (2007) *Vanities of the Eye: Vision in Early Modern European Culture*. Oxford: Oxford University Press.

Clarke, Christina. (2022) 'Reanimating the Goldsmith: An Artisanal Reading of the Archive'. *Journal 18*, 14, unpaginated. www.journal18.org/past-issues/14-silver-fall-2022/.

Clayton, Martin. (2012) *Leonardo da Vinci: Anatomist*. Exhibition catalogue, London: The Queen's Gallery, 3 May–7 October 2012. London: Royal Collection Publications.

Clemens, Claude. (1635) *Musei sive bibliothecae tam privatae quam publicae extructio, instruction, cura, usus*. Lyon: Jacques Prost.

Clubb, Louise George. (1964) *Giambattista della Porta, Dramatist*. Princeton, NJ: Princeton University Press.

Codding, A. Michell. (2006) 'The Decorative Arts in Latin America 1492–1820'. In Joseph J. Rishel & Suzanne L. Stratton-Pruitt, eds., *The Arts in Latin America 1492–1820*. Exhibition catalogue, Philadelphia: Philadelphia Museum of Art, 20 September–31 December 2006. New Haven, CT: Yale University Press, 98–143.

Cohen, Bernard, & George Smith, eds. (2016) *The Cambridge Companion to Newton*. Cambridge: Cambridge University Press.

Cohen, Elizabeth, & Margaret Reeves, eds. (2018) *The Youth of Early Modern Women*. Amsterdam: Amsterdam University Press.

Cohen, Floris H. (1994) *The Scientific Revolution: A Historiographical Inquiry*. Chicago: University of Chicago Press.

Coilly, Nathalie. (2023) *Imprimer! L'Europe de Gutenberg 1450–1520*. Exhibition catalogue, Paris: Bibliothèque nationale de France, 12 April–16 July 2023. Paris: Bibliothèque nationale de France.

Cole, Michael W. (2002) *Cellini and the Principles of Sculpture*. Cambridge: Cambridge University Press.

(2019) *Sofonisba's Lesson: A Renaissance Artist and Her Work*. Princeton, NJ: Princeton University Press.

Colenbrander, Herman. (2013) 'A Pledge of Marital Domestic Bliss: Samuel van Hoogstraten's Perspective Box in the National Gallery, London'. In Thijs Weststeijn, ed., *The Universal Art of Samuel van Hoogstraten (1627–1678): Painter, Writer and Courtier*. Amsterdam: Amsterdam University Press, 139–60.

Colonna, Fancesco (attr.). (1499) *Hypnerotomachia poliphili*. Venice: Aldus Manutius.

Colonna, Vittoria. (1538) *Rime*. Venice: Gabriel Giolito de Ferrari.

Colonna, Vittoria, Ramie Targoff, & Troy Tower. (2021) *Poems of Widowhood*. New York: Iter Press.

Comenius, Johann Amos Komensky. (1907) *The Great Didactic* (1657). Translated from the Czech by M. K. Walter. London: Adam and Charles Black.

(1997) *Labyrinth of the World and Paradise of the Heart* (1631). Translated by Howard Louthen & Andrea Sterk. New York: Paulist Press.

Conisbee, Philip. (2007) 'Life and Art of La Tour'. In Philip Conisbee et al., eds., *Georges de la Tour and His World*. Exhibition catalogue, Washington: National Gallery, 6 October 1996–5 January 1997; Fort Worth: Kimbell Art Museum, 2 February–2 May 1997. New Haven, CT: Yale University Press, 102–12.

et al., eds. (2007) *Georges de la Tour and His World*. Exhibition catalogue, Washington: National Gallery, 6 October 1996–5 January 1997; Fort Worth: Kimbell

Art Museum, 2 February–2 May 1997. New Haven, CT: Yale University Press.

Connolly, Annaliese, & Lisa Hopkins. (2007) *Goddesses and Queens: The Iconography of Elizabeth I*. Manchester: Manchester University Press.

Connors, Joseph. (1990) 'Ars Tornandi: Baroque Architecture and the Lathe'. *Journal of the Warburg and Courtauld Institutes*, 53, 217–36.

Consolino, Franca. (2022) *After Ovid: Aspects of the Reception of Ovid in Literature and Iconography*. Turnhout: Brepols.

Constable, Henry. (1592) *To St Mary Magdalene*. London: I. C. for Richard Smith.

Constans, Claire, & Mathieu da Vinha. (2010) *Les grandes galleries européennes XVIIe–XIXe siècles*. Paris: Maison des Sciences de l'Homme.

Conticelli, Valentina. (2007) *Guardaroba di cose rare et preziose: lo studiolo di Francesco I de' Medici: arte storia e significati*. Lugano: Agorà.

Contini, Roberto, ed. (2010) *Una gloria europea: Pietro da Cortona a Firenze (1637–47)*. Milan: Silvana.

Corneille, Pierre. (1639) *Illusion comique*. Paris: Francois Targa.

Corradini, Sandro, & Maurizio Marini. (1993) 'Inventarium omnium et singulorum bonorum mobilium di Michelangelo da Caravaggio "pittore"'. *Artibus et historiae*, 14(28), 161–76.

Cowan, Jacqueline. (2018) 'Milton, the Royal Society, and the Galileo Problem'. *SEL*, 58(3), 569–89.

Crary, Jonathan. (1990) *Techniques of the Observer: On Vision and Modernity in the Nineteenth Century*. Cambridge, MA: MIT Press.

Crawford, Katherine. (2018). '"Gabrielle d'Estrées et l'Une de ses Soeurs" and the Pleasures of Proliferative Criticism'. In Angeliki Pollali & Berthold Hub, eds., *Images of Sex and Desire in Renaissance Art and Modern Historiography*. New York: Routledge, 209–21.

Creighton, Gilbert. (1955) 'The Works of Girolamo Savoldo'. PhD dissertation, New York University.

(1977) 'Peintres et menuisiers au debut de la Renaissance en Italie'. *Revue de l'Art*, 37, 3–28.

Crépin-Leblond, Thierry, Étienne Faisant, et al. (2019) *Dossier de l'art: Henri II et les arts: expositions du 500e anniversaire*. Dijon: Faton.

Crépin-Leblond, Thierry, & Elisabeth Taburet-Delahaye, eds. (2009) *Le bain et le miroir: soins du corps et cosmétiques de l'antiquité à la Renaissance*. Exhibition catalogue, Paris: Musée de Cluny, 20 May–21 September 2009. Paris: Gallimard.

Criminisi, Antonio, Martin Kemp, & Sing Bing Kang. (2004) 'Reflections of Reality in Jan van Eyck and Robert Campin'. *Historical Methods: A Journal of Quantitative and Interdisciplinary History*, 37(3), 109–22.

Cropper, Elizabeth. (1976) 'On Beautiful Women: Parmigianino, Petrarchismo, and the Vernacular Style'. *The Art Bulletin*, 58(3), 374–95.

(1991) 'The Petrifying Art: Marino's Poetry and Caravaggio'. *Metropolitan Museum Journal*, 26, 193–212.

(1992a) 'Marino's Strage degli Innocenti: Poussin, Rubens, and Guido Reni'. *Studi secenteschi*, 33, 137–64.

(1992b) 'Painting and Possession: Poussin's Portrait for Chantelou and the Essais of Montaigne'. *Der Künstler über sich in seinem Werk, Acta Humanoria*, 6, 485–509.

(2018a) 'Theory and Practice Revisited: Francesco Scanelli between Giovanni Battista Agucchi and Carlo Cesare Malvasia'. In Sybille Ebert-Shifferer et al., eds., *Arte dal naturale series: quaderni della Bibliotheca Hertziana*, 2. Rome: Campisano editore, 129–50.

(2018b) 'Visages: les miroirs de Poussin'. In Alan Cantillon et al., eds., *A force des signes*. Paris: EHESS Editions, 365–86.

Crouzet, Denis. (2018) 'Catherine de Médicis Tested by the Virtue of Charity: Discourse and Metadiscourse'. In Susan Broomhall, ed., *Women and Power at the French Court, 1483–1563*. Amsterdam: Amsterdam University Press, 357–76.

Crowe, J. A., & G. B. Cavalcaselle. (1877) *Titian: His Life and Times*, 2 vols. London: J. Murray.

(1879) *The Early Flemish Painters*. London: J. Murray.

Cruz Yábar, Juan Maria. (2016) 'La primera etapa del Salón de los Espejos y las intervenziones de Carbonel y Velázquez (1639–1648)'. *Anales de Historia del Arte*, 26, 141–69.

Cummings, Keith. (2002) *A History of Glassforming*. Philadelphia: University of Pennsylvania Press.

Currie, Christina, et al., eds. (2019) 'Part I: The Ghent Altarpiece'. In Christina Currie et al., eds., *Van Eyck Studies: Underdrawing and Technology in Painting, Symposium XVIII, the Royal Institute for Cultural Heritage Centre for the Study of the Flemish Primitives*. Leuven: Peeters, 3–194.

Da Costa Kaufmann, Thomas. (1975) 'The Perspective of Shadows: The History of the Theory of Shadow Projection'. *Journal of the Warburg & Courtauld Institutes*, 38, 258–87.

(1993) *The Mastery of Nature: Aspects of Art, Science, and Humanism in the Renaissance*. Princeton, NJ: Princeton University Press.

Dal Pozzolo, Enrico Maria, ed. (2014) *Marco Boschini: l'epopea della pittura veneziana nell'Europa barocca*. Treviso: Zel Edizioni.

Dalai Emiliani, Marisa, ed. (1980) *La prospettiva rinascimentale: codificazioni e trasgressioni*. Florence: Stampa Stiav.

Dalla Costa, Thomas. (2019) *'Venere e Adone' di Tiziano: arte, cultura e società tra Venezia e l'Europa*. Venice: Marsilio.

(2020) 'The *Poesie* in Correspondence'. In Matthias Wivel, ed., *Titian: Love, Desire, Death*. Exhibition catalogue, London: National Gallery, 2 December 2020–17 January 2021. London: National Gallery, 193–202.

Dällenbach, Lucien. (1977) *Le récit spéculaire: essai sur la mise-en-abyme*. Paris: Editions du Seuil.

Daly, Peter. (2014) *The Emblem in Early Modern Europe: Contributions to the Theory of the Emblem*. Farnham: Ashgate.

Damisch, Hubert. (1976) 'D'un Narcise l'autre'. *Nouvelle Revue de Psychoanalyse*, 13, 108–46.

(1987) *L'origine de la perspective*. Paris: Flammarion.

(1992) *Le jugement de Paris*. Paris: Flammarion.

(1994) *The Origin of Perspective* (1987). Translated from the French by J. Goodman. Cambridge, MA: MIT Press.

(1996) *The Judgement of Paris*. Chicago: University of Chicago Press.

(2002) *A Theory of |Cloud|: Toward a History of Painting* (1972). Translated from the French by J. Lloyd. Stanford, CA: Stanford University Press.

(2010) 'The Inventor of Painting'. *Oxford Art Journal*, 33 (3), 301–16.

Darr, Alan, & Timothy Wilson, eds. (2013) 'Italian Renaissance and later ceramics'. *Bulletin of the Detroit Institute of Arts*, 87.

Daston, Lorraine. (2015) 'Epistemic Images'. In Alina Payne, ed., *Vision and Its Instruments: Art, Science, and Technology in Early Modern European Art*. University Park: Penn State University Press, 13–35.

Daston, Lorraine, & Peter Galison. (2010) *Objectivity*. Princeton, NJ: Princeton University Press.

Daston, Lorraine, & Elizabeth Lunbeck. (2011) *Histories of Scientific Observation*. Chicago: University of Chicago Press.

Daston, Lorraine, & Katharine Park. (1998) *Wonders and the Order of Nature, 1150–1750*. New York: Zone Books.

Dauvois, Daniel, ed. (2016) *Les règles et les manières: Abraham Bosse et les arts du dessin*. Paris: Hermann.

Davies, Sir John. (1599a) *Hymns of Astraea in Acrosticke Verse*. London: Richard Field for John Standish.

(1599b) *Nosce teipsum*. London: Richard Field for John Standish.

De Beer, E. S. ed. (1955) *The Diary of John Evelyn*, 6 vols. London: George Philip & Son.

De Bérulle, Pierre. (1625) *Elévations à Jésus-Christ sur la Sainte Madeleine*. Paris.

De Bouard, Alain. (1929) *Manuele de diplomatique française et pontificale*, 2 vols. Paris: A. Picard.

De Brosses, Charles. (1858) *Lettres famileres écrites d'Italie*. ed. M. R. Colomb. Paris: Didier.

De Ceglia, Francesco Paolo. (2020) *The Body of Evidence: Corpses and Proofs in Early Modern European Medicine*. Leiden: Brill.

De Cervantes, Miguel. (1605) *El ingenioso hidalgo Don Quixote de la Mancha*, Part I. Madrid: Juan de la Cuesta.

(1615) *El ingenioso hidalgo Don Quixote de la Mancha*, Part II. Madrid: Juan de la Cuesta.

De Fréville, Ernest. (1842) 'Notice historique sur l'inventaire des meubles de Gabrielle d'Estrées'. *Bibliothèque de l'Ecole des Chartes*, 3, 148–71.

De Heere, Lucas. (1969) *Den hof Emboomgaerd der Poësien* (1565), ed. W. Waterschoot. Zwolle: Tjink Willink.

De Jong, Jan, ed. (2000) *Nederlands Kunsthistorisch Jaarboek*, special issue, 'The Art of Home in the Netherlands 1500–1800', 51.

De Jongh, Eddy. (1988). 'On Balance'. In Ivan Gaskell & Michiel Jonker, eds., *Vermeer Studies*. Studies in the History of Art, Washington, DC: National Gallery of Art, 55, XXXIII. New Haven, CT: Yale University Press, 351–65.

(2000a) *Questions of Meaning: Theme and Motif in Dutch Seventeenth-Century Painting* (1995). Translated from the Dutch by M. Hoyle. Leiden: Primavera Press.

(2000b), 'A Bird's Eye View of Erotica: Double-Entendre in a Series of Seventeenth-Century Genre Scenes'. In *Questions of Meaning: Theme and Motif in Dutch Seventeenth-Century Painting* (1995). Translated from the Dutch by M. Hoyle. Leiden: Primavera Press, 21–58.

De Marchi, Andrea et al. (2015) *Le Opere e i Giorni: exempla virtutis, favole antiche e vita quotidiana nel racconto dei Cassoni rinascimentali*. Exhibition catalogue, Florence: Museo Stibbert, 26 September 2015–6 January 2016. Florence: Masso delle Fate.

De' Marinis, Fabrizio. (1994) *Velvet: History Techniques Fashions*. Milan: Idea Books.

De Mey, Marc. (2012a) 'The Lines and Lustre of the Light'. In Marc (de) Mey et al., *Vision and Material: Interaction between Art and Science in van Eyck's Time*. Royal Flemish Academy of Belgium Conference 2010. Brussels: KVAB, 28–63.

(2012b) 'Within and beyond a Computer Reconstruction of Masaccio's *Trinity*'. In Rocco Sinisgalli, ed., *Ut pictura poesis: per una storia delle arti visive*. Prato: CB Ed., 83–110.

et al. (2012) *Vision and Material: Interaction between Art and Science in van Eyck's Time*. Royal Flemish

Academy of Belgium Conference 2010. Brussels: KVAB.

De Munck, Bert. (2018) *Guilds, Labour, and the Urban Body Politic: Fabricating Community in the Southern Netherlands, 1300–1800*. New York: Routledge.

De Pauw-de Veen, Lydia. (1969) 'De begrippen "schilder", "schilderij" en "schilderen" in de zeventiende eeuw'. *Verhandelingen van de Koninklijke Vlaamse Academie voor Wetenschappen, Letteren en Schone Kunsten van België*, 31(22), 1–3, 96–203.

De Poorter, Nina, & Frans Baudouin. (2022) *Rubens: Architecture and Sculpture: Rubens's House*, 2 vols. Turnhout: Harvey Miller.

De Ronsard, Pierre. (1553) *Les amours*. Paris: Maurice de la Porte.

De Roover, Raymond. (1948) *Money, Banking and Credit in Medieval Bruges: Italian Merchant-Bankers, Lombards and Money-Changers: A Study in the Origins of Banking*. Cambridge, MA: Mediaeval Academy of America.

De Rosa, Agostino. (2013) *Jean François Niceron: prospettiva, cattotrica e magia artificiale*. Rome: Aracne.

ed. (2019) *Roma anamorfica: prospettiva e Illusionismo in epoca barocca*. Rome: Aracne.

De Sepi, Giorgio, & Athanasius Kircher. (2015) *The Celebrated Museum of the Roman College of the Society of Jesus* (1678), ed. Peter Davidson & Jane Stevenson. Facsimile of the 1678 Amsterdam edition of Giorgio de Sepi's description of Athanasius Kircher's *Museo Musaeum Celeberrimum Collegii Romani Societatsis Jesu*. Amsterdam: Ex officina Janssonio-Waesbergiana; Philadelphia: St Joseph's University Press.

De Tolnay, Charles. (1943–60) *Michelangelo* (5 vols.). Princeton, NJ: Princeton University Press.

De Vecchi, Pierluigi. (1990) 'La mimesi allo specchio'. In Bruno Passamani, ed., *Giovanni Gerolamo Savoldo tra Foppa, Giorgione e Caravaggio*. Exhibition catalogue, Brescia: Monastero di Santa Giulia, 3 March–31 May; Frankfurt: Schirn Kunsthalle, 8 June–3 September 1990. Milan: Electa, 59–64.

De Voragine, Jacobus. (1995) *The Golden Legend*, 2 vols. Translated by William Granger Ryan. Princeton, NJ: Princeton University Press.

De Vos, Dirk. (1994a) *Hans Memling: The Complete Works*. London: Thames & Hudson.

(1994b) *Hans Memling: Five Centuries of Fact and Fiction*. Exhibition catalogue, Bruges: Groeningemuseum, 1994. Brussels: Ludion.

(2005) 'Van Eycks vernuft: het opschrift van het "Portret van Jan de Leeuw"'. In A. Balis et al., *Florissant. Bijdragen tot de kunstgeschiedenis der Nederlanden (15de–17de eeuw)*. Liber Amicorum Carl Van de Velde. Brussels: VUB Press, 45–49.

De Vries, Jan. (2003) 'Luxury in the Dutch Golden Age in Theory and Practice'. In Maxine Berg & Elizabeth Eger, eds., *Luxury in the Eighteenth Century: Debates, Desires and Delectable Goods*. London: Palgrave Macmillan, 41–56.

Dean, Trevor, & Kate Lowe, eds. (1998) *Marriage in Italy 1300–1650*. Cambridge: Cambridge University Press.

Debby, Nirit Ben-Aryeh. (2003) 'Vittoria Colonna and Titian's Pitti *Magdalen*'. *Women's Art Journal*, 24(1), 29–33.

Dechant, Lyle. (2019) 'Fascinated by Fascination: Female Privacy and the Leipzig "Love Magic" Panel'. In Daniel Zamani et al., eds., *Visions of Enchantment: Occultism, Magic, and Visual Culture*. Lopen: Fulgur Press, 39–49.

Dee, John. (1558) *Propaedeumata aphoristica*. London: Henry Sutton.

Dekker, Elly, & Kristen Lippincott. (1999) 'The Scientific Instruments in Holbein's Ambassadors: A Re-examination. *Journal of the Warburg & Courtauld Institutes*, 62, 93–125.

Del Santo, Paolo, & Giorgio Strano. (2008) 'From Galileo to Newton'. In Giorgio Strano, ed., *Galileo's Telescope: The Instrument That Changed the World*. Exhibition catalogue, Florence: Museo Galileo, 4 March 2008–31 January 2009. Florence: Museo Galileo, 103–20.

Delahaye, Elizabeth Taburet. (2007) *La dame à la licorne*. Paris: Réunion des Musées Nationaux.

Delahaye, Elizabeth Taburet, with Beatrice de Chancel Bardelot. (2018) *La dame à la licorne*. Paris: Réunion des Musées Nationaux.

Deldicque, Mathieu. (2019) *Clouet: le miroir des dames*, Dijon: Editions Faton.

(2022) *Clouet à la cour des petits Valois*. Chantilly: Fondation d'Aumale.

Deleito y Piñuela, José. (1935) *El rey se divierte*. Madrid: Espasa Calpe.

D'Elia, F. Anthony. (2004) *The Renaissance of Marriage in Fifteenth-Century Italy*. Cambridge, MA: Harvard University Press.

Della Porta. Giambattista. (1558) *Magia naturalis sive de miraculis rerum naturalium*, vol. 4. Naples: Cancer.

(1586) *De humana physiognomia*, 3 books. Vico Equense: Giuseppe Cacchio.

(1589) *Magia naturalis*, vol. 10. Naples: Orazio Salviani.

(1658) *Natural Magick*. Translated from the Latin. London: T. Young and S. Speed.

Delsaute, Jean-Luke. (1998) 'The Camera Obscura and Painting in the Sixteenth and Seventeenth Centuries'. In Ivan Gaskell & Michiel Jonker, eds., *Vermeer Studies*. Studies in the History of Art,

Washington: National Gallery of Art, 55, XXXIII. New Haven, CT: Yale University Press, 111–23.

Derrida, Jacques. (1978) *La vérité en peinture*. Paris: Flammarion.

(1995) 'Catoptrique et illusions spatiales'. *Espace Sculpture*, 31, 36–39.

Descartes, René. (1637a) *Discours sur la méthode*. Leiden: Ian Maire.

(1637b) *La dioptrique*. Leiden: Ian Maire.

Dhanens, Elisabeth. (1980) *Hubert and Jan van Eyck*. New York: Alpine Fine Arts.

Dhanens, Elisabeth, & Jellie Dijkstra. (1999) *Rogier de la Pasture van der Weyden*. Tournai: La Renaissance du Livre.

Dhombres, Jean, ed. (1994) *Desargues en son temps*. Paris: Librairie Scientifique A. Blanchard.

Diderot, Denis, & Jean Le Rond D'Alembert. (1761–88) *Encyclopédie: arts et métiers*, 28 vols. Paris: Académie des Sciences.

(2002) *Art du verre: fabrication des glaces* (c. 1770). Facsimile ed. Paris: Bibliothèque de l'Image, Inter-Livres.

Didier, Frédéric. (2007) 'Eclairages et ambiances lumineuses dans la Galerie des Glaces'. In Jacques Thuillier, ed., *La Galerie des Glaces: chef-d'oeuvre retrouvé*. Paris: Gallimard, 110–13.

Didi-Huberman, Georges. (1993) 'L'autre miroir: autoportrait et mélancolie christique selon Albrecht Dürer'. In Augusto Gentili, Philippe Morel, & Claudia Cieri Via, eds., *Il ritratto e la memoria. Materiali 2*. Rome: Bulzoni, 2, 207–40.

(1994) 'Ressemblance mythifiée et ressemblance oubliée chez Vasari: la légende du portrait "sur le vif"'. *Mélanges de l'Ecole Française de Rome: Italie et Méditerranée*, 106(2), 383–432.

(1999) *Ouvrir Vénus: nudité, rêve, cruauté*. Paris: Gallimard.

Dierick, A. L. (2000) 'Jan van Eyck's Handwriting'. In Susan Foister, Sue Jones, & Delphine Cool, eds., *Investigating Jan Van Eyck: Jan van Eyck Symposium, the National Gallery, London, 13–14 March 1998*. Turnhout: Brepols, 79–82.

Dietz Moss, Jean. (1993) *Novelties in the Heavens: Rhetoric and Science in the Copernican Controversy*. Chicago: University of Chicago Press.

Dijksterhuis, D. J. (1950) *De mechanisering van het wereldbeeld*. Amsterdam: J. M. Meulenhoff.

Dillon, Sarah. (2018) *Seeing Renaissance Glass: Art, Optics, and Glass of Early Modern Italy, 1250–1425*. New York: Peter Lang.

Dimier, Louis. (1913) 'An Idealized Portrait of Diane de Poitiers'. *The Burlington Magazine*, 24(128), 89–93.

Dogaer, Georges, & Marguerite Debae, eds. (1967) *La librairie de Phiippe le Bon: exposition organisée à l'occasion du 500e anniversaire de la mort du duc*. Exhibition catalogue, Bruxelles: Bibliothèque Albert I, 9 September–12 November 1967. Brussels: Bibliothèque royale de Belgique.

Dolce, Ludovico. (1544) *Lettere*. Venice: Paolo Gerardo.

(1545) *Dialogo delle donne*. Venice: Gabriele Giolito.

(1557) *Dialogo della pittura intitolato l'Aretino*. Venice: Gabriele Giolito.

Dolin, Eric Jay. (2010) *Fur, Fortune, and Empire: The Epic History of the Fur Trade in America*. New York: W. W. Norton.

Doni, Anton Francesco. (1969) *Le ville* (1566), ed. Ugo Bellocchi. Reprint. Modena: Aedes Muratoriana.

Donne, John. (1611) *Ignatius, His Conclave*. London: N. Okes for R. Moore.

(1633) *An Epithalamion or Marriage Song on the Lady Elizabeth and Count Palatine Being Married on St Valentine's Day 1613*. London: William Stansby.

Donneau de Visé, Jean, ed. (1672–1710) *Mercure Galant*. Paris.

Doran, Susan, & Thomas S. Freeman. (2003) *The Myth of Elizabeth*. Basingstoke: Macmillan.

Douglas, Mary, & Baron Isherwood. (1979) *The World of Goods: Towards an Anthropology of Consumption*. London: Routledge.

Doutrepont, Georges. (1906) *Inventaire de la Librairie de Philippe le Bon (1420)*. Brussels: Kiessling.

Drake, Stillman. (1978) *Galileo at Work: His Scientific Biography*. Chicago: University of Chicago Press.

(1983) *Telescopes, Tides, and Tactics: A Galilean Dialogue about the Starry Messenger and Systems of the World*. Chicago: University of Chicago Press.

Drake, Stillman, & Paul Rose. (1971) 'The Pseudo-Aristotelian Questions of Mechanics in Renaissance Culture'. *Studies in the Renaissance*, 18, 65–104.

Draper, James David. (2008) 'Cameo Appearances'. *The Metropolitan Museum of Art Bulletin*, 65(4), 1–56.

Droth, Martina, et al. (2008) *Taking Shape: Finding Sculpture in the Decorative Arts*. Exhibition catalogue, Leeds: Henry Moore Institute, 2 October 2008–5 January 2009; Los Angeles: Getty Museum, 31 March–5 July 2009. Leeds: Henry Moore Institute; Los Angeles: Getty Publications.

Drummond of Hawthornden. (1656) *A Cypress Grove*. London: Richards.

Dubois, Page. (1996) 'Archaic Bodies-in-Pieces'. In Natalie Boymel Kampen, ed., *Sexuality in Ancient Art: Near East, Egypt, Greece, and Italy*. Cambridge: Cambridge University Press, 55–64.

Dubreuil, Jean. (1647) *La perspective pratique necessaire a tous peintres, graveurs, sculpteurs, architects, orfèvres, brodeurs, tapissiers, & autres se servans du pessein*. Paris: François d'Anglois.

(1765) *The Practical Perspective* (1647), 4th ed., ed. Ephraim Chambers. Translated from the French. London: J. and C. Bowles.

Dubreuil-Blondin, Nicole. (1993) 'Le philosophe chez Velazquez: l'intrusion de Michel Foucault dans la fortune critique des Ménines'. *RACAR*, 20(1–2), 117–29.

Duby, Georges. (1994) *Love and Marriage in the Middle Ages*. Translated by Jane Dunnett. Cambridge: Polity Press.

Dufresnoy, Charles-Alphonse, & Roger de Piles. (1668) *L'art de peinture traduit en François, avec des remarques necessaire et tres-ample par Roger de Piles*. Paris: Nicolas L'Anglois.

Dumolyn, Jan, & Frederik Buylaert. (2020) 'Van Eyck's World: Court Culture, Luxury Production, Elite Patronage and Social Distinction within an Urban Network'. In Maximiliaan Martens, Till-Holger Borchert, et al., eds., *Van Eyck: An Optical Revolution*. Exhibition catalogue, Ghent: Museum voor Schone Kunsten, 1 February–30 April 2020. Ghent: Museum voor Schone Kunsten, 84–125.

Dunkerton, Jill, & Marika Spring. (2013) 'Titian's Painting Technique to 1540'. *National Gallery Technical Bulletin*, 34, 1–136.

Dunkerton, Jill, & Marika Spring, eds. (2015a) *Titian after 1540: Technique and Style in His Later Works*. National Gallery Technical Bulletin, 36. London: National Gallery.

(2015b) 'Titian's Painting Technique from 1540'. *National Gallery Technical Bulletin*, 36, 1–136.

Dunkerton, Jill, Marika Spring, et al. (2020) 'Modes of Painting: Titian's Technique in the *Poesie*'. In Matthias Wivel, ed., *Titian: Love, Desire, Death*. Exhibition catalogue, London: National Gallery, 2 December 2020–17 January 2021. London: National Gallery, 61–90.

Dupré, Sven. (2003) *Renaissance Optics: Instruments, Practical Knowledge, and the Appropriation of Theory*. Berlin: Max-Planck-Institut für Wissenschaftsgeschichte.

ed. (2005a) *Early Science and Medicine*, special issue, 'Optics, Instruments, and Painting, 1420–1720: Reflections on the Hockney-Falco Thesis', 10(2).

(2005b) 'Ausonio's Mirrors and Galileo's Lenses: The Telescope and Sixteenth-Century Practical Optical Knowledge'. *Galilaeana: Journal of Galilean Studies* 2, 145–60.

(2008a) 'Inside the *Camera Obscura*: Kepler's Experiment and Theory of Optical Imagery'. *Early Science and Medicine*, 13(3), 219–44.

(2008b) 'Images in the Air: Optical Games, Magic and Imagination'. In Christine Göttler & Wolfgang Neuber, eds., *Spirits Unseen: The Representation of Subtle Bodies in Early Modern European Culture*. Leiden: Brill, 71–92.

(2014) 'Galileo and the Culture of Glass'. In Andrea Albrecht, Giovanna Cordibella, & Volke R. Remmert, eds., *Tintenfass und Teleskop: Galileo Galilei im Schnittpunkt wissenschaftlicher, literarischer und visueller Kulturen im europäischen 17. Jahrhundert*. Berlin: De Gruyter, 297–319.

ed. (2019) *Perspective as Practice: Renaissance Cultures of Optics*. Turnhout: Brepols.

Dupré, Sven, & Christoph Lüthy, eds. (2011) *Silent Messengers: The Circulation of Material Objects of Knowledge in the Early Modern Low Countries*. Berlin: LIT.

Dürer, Albrecht. (1977) *The Painter's Manual of Measuremen: A Manual of Measurement of Lines, Areas, and Solids by Means of Compass and Ruler . . .* (1525), ed. Walter L. Strauss. Facsimile and translation. New York: Abaris Books.

Eamon, William. (2017) 'A Theatre of Experiments: Giambattista della Porta and the Scientific Culture of Renaissance Naples'. In Adrianna Borelli et al., eds., *The Optics of Giambattista della Porta (ca. 1535–1615): A Reassessment*. New York: Springer Books, 11–38.

Ebert, Bernd. (2009) *Simon und Isaack Luttichuys: Monographie mit kritischem Werkverzeichnis*, Berlin: Deutscher Kunstverlag.

Ebert-Schifferer, Sybille, et al., eds. (2007) *Caravaggio e il suo ambiente*. Milan Cinisello Balsamo (Milan): Silvana.

et al. (2017) *Bernini disegnatore*. Rome: Campisano.

Echols, Robert, & Peter Humfrey. (2019) *Italian Paintings of the Sixteenth Century*. Washington, DC: National Gallery of Art.

Echols, Robert, & Frederick Ilchman, eds. (2018) *Tintoretto: Artist of Renaissance Venice*. Exhibition catalogue, Washington: National Gallery, 24 March–7 July 2018; Venice: Palazzo Ducale, 7 September 7, 2018–6 January 2019. New Haven, CT: Yale University Press.

Edgerton, Samuel Y., Jr. (1975) *The Renaissance Rediscovery of Linear Perspective*. New York: Basic Books.

Jr. (1984) 'Galileo, Florentine Disegno, and the "Strange Spottedness" of the Moon'. *Art Journal*, 44, 225–32.

Jr. (2009) *The Mirror, the Window, and the Telescope: How Renaissance Linear Perspective Changed Our Vision of the Universe*. Ithaca, NY: Cornell University Press.

Eisenstein, Elizabeth. (1983) *The Printing Revolution in Early Modern Europe*. Cambridge: Cambridge University Press.

Ekserdjian, David. (2006) *Parmigianino*. New Haven, CT: Yale University Press.

Elsig, Frédéric, ed. (2012) *Peindre en France à la Renaissance: Fontainebleau et son rayonnement*, vol. 2. Milan: Silvana.

Elsner, Jaś. (1996) 'Naturalism and the Erotics of the Gaze: Intimations of Narcissus'. In Natalie Boymel Kampen, ed., *Sexuality in Ancient Art: Near East, Egypt, Greece, and Italy*. Cambridge: Cambridge University Press, 247–61.

Emmendörffer, Christoph, & Christof Trepesch. (2014) *Wunderwelt: der Pommersche Kunstschrank*. Exhibition catalogue, Augsberg: Maximilianmuseum, Augsburg; Berlin: Deutscher Kunstverlag, 2014. Berlin: De Gruyter.

Emmens, J. A. (1961) 'Les Ménines de Velázquez: miroir de princes par Philippe IV'. *Nederlandisch Kunsthistorisch Jaarboek*, 12, 51–79.

Enenkel, Karl. (2019) *The Invention of the Emblem Book and the Transmission of Knowledge ca 1510–1610*. Leiden: Brill.

Enggass, Robert, & Jonathan Brown, eds. (1970) *Italy and Spain 1600–1750: Sources and Documents*. Hemel Hempstead: Prentice-Hall.

Epstein, Stefan, ed. (2008) *Guilds, Innovation and the European Economy, 1400–1800*. Cambridge: Cambridge University Press.

Equicola, Mario. (1525) *Libro de natura de amore*. Venice: Lorenzo Lorio da Portes.

Erasmus of Rotterdam, Desiderius. (1514) *Parabolae sive similia*. Basel: Nicolaum & Eusebium Episcopios.

(1517) *De duplici copia verborum ac rerum* (1512). Antwerp: Froben.

Erlande-Brandenburg, Alain. (1989) *The Lady and the Unicorn*. Paris: Réunion des musées nationaux.

Ertz, Klaus, & Christa Nitze-Ertz. (1998) *Breughel-Brueghel: Pieter Breughel le jeune (1565–1637/8) – Jan Brueghel l'ancien (1568–1625), une famille des peintres flamands vers 1600*. Exhibition catalogue, Antwerp: Koninklijk Museum voor Schone Kunsten, 3 May –26 July 1998. Lingen: Luca Verlag.

Eschenfelder, Chantal. (1993) 'Les bains de Fontainebleau: nouveaux documents sur les décors du primatice'. *Revue de l'Art*, 99, 45–92.

Euclid. (1573) *La prospettiva di Euclide* (c. 300 BCE; also comprising *La specularia*). Translated from the Greek by I. Danti. Florence: Giunti.

(1957). *Optica et catoptrica* (c. 300 BCE). Greek with Latin translation by J. Pena. Paris: Andreas Wechel.

Evans, Joan. (1933) *English Medieval Lapidaries*. Early English Text Society. London: Oxford University Press.

Evelyn, John. (1827) *Diary* (1644), 5 vols., ed. William Bray. London: Henry Colburn.

Ewing, Dan. (2016) *Jan de Beer: Gothic Renewal in Renaissance Antwerp*. Turnhout: Brepols.

(2018) 'Guild Work, Guild Glory: Sixteenth-Century Antwerp Artists' Work for the Antwerp Saint Luke's Guild'. In Andreas Tacke et al., eds., *Material Culture: Präsanz und Sichtbarkeit von Künstlern, Zünften und Brüderschaften in der Vormoderne*. Peterberg: Michael Imhof Publishers, 56–75.

Eymard, Julien. (1975) 'Le thème du miroir dans la poésie française'. PhD thesis, Université de Lille III.

Fabbro, Celso, with Clemente Gandini. (1977) *La corrispondenza diretta di Tiziano Vecellio tratta dalla Silloge di documenti tizianeschi*. Belluno: Magnifica comunità di Cadore.

Fabri, Ria. (1991) *De 17de-eeuwse Antwerpse Kunstkast. Kunsthistorische Aspecten*. Exhibition catalogue, Brussels: Paleis der Academie, 1991. Brussels: Paleis der Academien.

Facchinetti, Simone, & Arturo Galansino, eds. (2022) *Paris Bordon 1500–1571: Pittore divino*. Exhibition catalogue, Museo Santa Caterina Treviso, 16 September 2022–15 January 2023. Venice: Marsilio.

Fadda, Elisabetta, & Giorgio Milanesi, eds. (2019) *Quaderni della Societa storica viadenese*, special issue, 'Girolamo Mazzola Bedoli, "eccellente pittore, e cortese e gentile oltre modo"', 13.

Fagnart, Laure. (2015) 'Le 'Portrait d'Homme en Armure' de Giovanni Gerolamo Savoldo, un portrait présumé de Gaston de Foix'. In Joana Barretto, ed., *Voir Gaston de Foix (1512–2012)*. Paris: Sorbonne Publications, 132–51.

(2016) 'L'appartement des bains et le cabinet des peintures du Château de Fontainebleau sous le règne d'Henri IV'. In Colette Nativel, ed., *Henri IV: art et pouvoir*. Tours: Presses universitaires de Rennes, 53–65.

Fahy, Everett. (2008) 'The Marriage Portrait in the Renaissance, or Some Women Named Ginevra'. In Andrea Bayer et al., eds., *Art and Love in Renaissance Italy*. Exhibition catalogue, New York: Metropolitan Museum of Art, 11 November 2008–16 February 2009; Fort Worth, TX: Kimbell Art Museum, 15 March–14 June 2009. New Haven, CT: Yale University Press in association with the Metropolitan Museum of Art, 17–28.

Falguières, Patricia, (2006) 'Poétique de la machine'. In Philippe Morel, ed., *L'art de la renaissance entre science et magie*. Actes du colloque international, 20–22 June 2002, Paris, Institut d'Art et d'Archéologie, Académie de France à Rome. Paris: Éditions Somogy, 401–52.

Falkenburg, L. Reindert. (2006) 'Hand Memling's Van Nieuwenhove Diptych: The Place of Prayer in Early

Netherlandish Devotional Painting'. In John Oliver Hand & Ron Spronk, eds., *Essays in Context: Unfolding the Netherlandish Diptych*. Cambridge, MA: Harvard Art Museums and Yale University Press, 92–109.

Falomir, Miguel. (2003a) *Titian*. Exhibition catalogue, Madrid: Prado Museum, 10 June–9 July 2003. Madrid: Museo Nacional del Prado.

(2003b) 'Titian's Replicas and Variants'. In Charles Hope et al., eds., *Tiziano*. Exhibition catalogue, Madrid: Prado Museum, 10 June–7 September 2003. New Haven, CT: Yale University Press, 60–68.

ed. (2007) *Tintoretto*. Exhibition catalogue, Madrid: Prado Museum, 30 January–27 May 2007. Madrid: Museo Nacional del Prado.

ed. (2014) *Titian: Danaë, Venus and Adonis: The Early Poesie*. Exhibition catalogue, Madrid: Prado Museum, 19 November 2014–1 March 2015. Madrid: Museo Nacional del Prado.

(2018) 'Mythologies'. In Robert Echols & Frederick Ilchman, eds., *Tintoretto: Artist of Renaissance Venice*. Exhibition catalogue, Washington: National Gallery, 24 March–7 July 2018; Venice: Palazzo Ducale, 7 September 7, 2018–6 January 2019. New Haven, CT: Yale University Press, 191–99.

(2021) *Mythological Passions: Titian, Veronese, Allori, Rubens, Ribera, Poussin, Van Dyck, Velázquez*, Madrid: Prado Museum.

et al. (2009) *Jacopo Tintoretto: actas del congreso internacional Jacobo Tintoretto*. Proceedings of the International Symposium, Madrid: Museo Nacional del Prado, 26–27 February 2007. Madrid: Museo Nacional del Prado.

Farago, Claire, ed. (1992) *Leonardo da Vinci's Paragone*. Leiden: Brill.

Farago, Claire, Janice Bell, & Carlo Vecce, eds. (2018) *The Fabrication of Leonardo da Vinci's 'Trattato della pittura'*, 2 vols. Leiden: Brill.

Farmer, D. (1968) 'Further Reflections on a Van Eyck Self-Portrait'. *Oud Holland Journal for Art in the Low Countries*, 83, 107–9.

Farroni, Laura. (2019) *L'arte del disegno a Palazzo Spada: l'astrolabium catoptrico-gnomonicum di Emmanuel Maignan*. Rome: De Luca.

Faust, Marta. (2018) 'Eyed Awry: Blind Spots and Memoria in the Zimmern Anamorphosis'. *Journal of Historians of Netherlandish Art*, 10(2, Summer).

Faye, Isla, & Nicholas Jardine, eds. (2013) *Early Science & Medicine*, special issue, 'New Light on Visual Forms in the Early Modern Arts and Sciences', 1.

Febvre, Lucien, & Henri-Jean Martin. (1957 1976) *The Coming of the Book: The Impact of Printing 1450–1800*. Translated from the French by D. Gerard. London: NLB.

Fehl, Philipp. (1993) 'Dürer's "Portrait of Erasmus" and the medal by Quentin Massys: 2 Types of Mimesis'. *Künstlerischer Austausch*, 2, 453–72.

Feigenbaum, Gail. (2010) 'A Likeness in the Tomb: Annibale's Self-Portrait Drawing in the J. Paul Getty Museum'. *The Getty Research Journal*, 2, 19–38.

(2020) 'An Evanescent Corpus of Self-Portraits by Annibale Carracci in the Uffizi'. *Imagines*, 4, 76–97.

Feist, Ulrike. (2016) 'The Reflection Sundial at Palazzo Spada in Rome'. In M. Nancy Frelick, ed., *The Mirror in Medieval and Early Modern Culture: Specular Reflections*. Turnhout: Brepols, 271–86.

Félibien, André. (1676) *Les divertissements de Versailles donnez par le roy à toute sac our au retour de la conqueste de la Franche-Comté, en l'année MDCLXXIV*. Paris: Imprimerie royale.

Félibien Des Avaux, Jean-François. (1703) *Description sommaire de Versailles ancienne et nouvelle*. Paris: Antoine Chrétien.

Ferino-Pagden, Sylvia. (2002) 'L'autoritratto del Parmigianino: la consistenza (im)materiale dell'autoritratto di Vienna'. In Lucia Fornari Schianchi, ed., *Parmigianino e il manierismo europeo*. Atti del convegno internazionale di studi, Parma, 2002. Cinisello Balsamo (Milan): Silvana Editore, 67–82.

(2006) 'Pictures of Women, Pictures of Love'. In David Alan Brown & Sylvia Ferino-Pagden, eds., *Bellini, Giorgione, Titian and the Renaissance of Venetian Painting*. Exhibition catalogue, Washington, DC: National Gallery of Art, 18 June–17 September 2006; Vienna: Kunsthistorisches Museum, 17 October 2006–7 January 2007. New Haven, CT: Yale University Press, 190–235.

(2022) *Tiziano e l'immagine della donna nel cinquecento veneziano*. Exhibition catalogue, Milan: Palazzo Reale, 23 February–5 June 2022. Milan: Skira.

Ferino-Pagden, Sylvia, & Maria Kusche. (1995) *Sofonisba Anguissola: A Renaissance Woman*. Exhibition catalogue, Washington: National Museum of Women in the Arts, 7 April–15 June 1995. Washington, DC: National Museum of Women in the Arts.

et al., eds. (2007) *Late Titian and the Sensuality of Painting*. Exhibition catalogue, Vienna: Kunsthistorisches Museum, 17 October 2007–6 January 2008; Venice: Gallerie dell' Accademia, 26 Janauary–4 May 2008. Venezia: Marsilio.

et al. (2018) *Velàzquez: Anregungen, Vorschläge*. Lösungen Series: Schriften des Kunsthistorischen Museums, 18. Turnhout: Brepols.

et al. (2021) *Titian's Vision of Women: Beauty, Love, Poetry*. Exhibition catalogue, Vienna: Kunsthistorisches Museum, 5 October 2021–23 February 2023. Milan: Skira.

Ffolliott, Sheila. (1989) 'Casting a Rival into the Shade: Catherine de' Medici and Diane de Poitiers'. *The Art Journal*, 48, 138–43.

Ficino, Marsilio. (1576) *Opera omnia*. Basel: Froben.

Fickaert, Franchoys. (1648) *Metamorphosis, ofte wonderbaere veranderingh ende leven vanden vermaer den Mr Quinten Matsys constigh grof-smit, ende schilder*. Antwerp: Fornenbergh.

Field, V. John. (1997) *The Invention of Infinity: Mathematics and Art in the Renaissance*. Oxford: Oxford University Press.

Filarete and John Spencer. (1965) *Filarete's Treatise on Architecture* (c. 1460), 2 vols. New Haven, CT: Yale University Press.

Filippi, Elena, & Harald Schwaetzer. (2012) *Spiegel der Seele: Reflexionen in Mystik und Malerei, Texte und Studien zur Europäischen Geistesgeschichte*. Münster: Aschendorff.

Findlen, Paula. (1989) 'The Museum: Its Classical Etymology and Renaissance Genealogy.' *Journal of the History of Collections*, 1, 59–78.

(1990) 'Jokes of Nature and Jokes of Knowledge: The Playfulness of Scientific Discourse in Early Modern Europe'. *Renaissance Quarterly*, 43, 292–331.

(1996) *Possessing Nature: Museums, Collecting, and Scientific Culture in Early Modern Italy*. Berkeley: University of California Press.

ed. (2004) *Athanasius Kircher, the Last Man Who Knew Everything*. New York: Routledge.

(2013) *Early Modern Things: Objects and Their Histories, 1500–1800*. Abingdon: Routledge.

Fink, Daniel. (1971) 'Vermeer's Use of the Camera Obscura: A Comparative Study'. *Art Bulletin*, 53, 493–505.

Finocchiaro, Maurice. (1989) *The Galileo Affair: A Documentary History*. Berkeley: University of California Press.

Fintz, Claude, ed. (1985) *Le miroir: une mediation entre imaginaire, sciences et spiritualité*. Valenciennes: Presses universitaires de Valenciennes.

Fiorani, Francesca, ed. (2013) *Leonardo da Vinci and Optics: Theory and Pictorial Practice*. Venice: Marsilio.

Fioravanti, Leonardo. (1564) *Specchio di scientia universale*. Venice: Andrea Ravenoldo.

Fiorio, Maria Teresa. (2000) *Giovanni Antonio Boltraffio: un pittore milanese nel lume di Leonardo*. Milan: Jandi Sapi Editori.

Firenzuola, Agnolo. (1552) *Delle bellezze delle donne*. Venice: Giovanni Griffio.

(1992) *On the Beauty of Women* (1542), ed. Konrad Eisenbichler & Jacqueline Murray. Translated from the Italian. Philadelphia: University of Pennsylvania Press.

Fischer, Gerhard, & Bernhard Greiner. (2007) *The Play within the Play: The Performance of Metatheatre and Self-Reflection*. Amsterdam: Ferdinand Schoeningh.

Fleming, John. (1969) *The Roman de la Rose: A Study in Allegory and Iconography*. Princeton, NJ: Princeton University Press.

Fletcher, Jennifer. (1990) 'Harpies, Venus, and Giovanni Bellini's Classical Mirror: Some Fifteenth-Century Venetian Painters' Responses to the Antique'. In Gustavo Traversari, ed., *Venezia e l'archaeologia*. Rome: Bretschneider, 170–76.

(1992) '*Fatto al specchio*: Venetian Renaissance Attitudes to Self-Portraiture'. In T. Hilliard Goldfarb, ed., *Fenway Court: Imaging the Self in Renaissance Italy*. Boston: Isabella Stewart Gardner Museum, 45–60.

Floridi, Massimiliano. (2011) *Vanitas: Lotto, Caravaggio, Guercino nella Collezione Doria Pamphili*. Milan: Silvana.

Fohr, Robert. (2018) *Georges de la Tour, le maître des nuits*. Paris: Cohen & Cohen

Foister, Susan. (2004) *Holbein and England*. New Haven, CT: Yale University Press.

Foister, Susan, & Susie Nash, eds. (1996) *Robert Campin: New Directions in Scholarship*. Turnhout: Brepols.

et al., eds. (1997) *Making and Meaning: Holbein's Ambassadors*. Exhibition catalogue, London: National Gallery, 5 November 1997–1 February 1998. London: National Gallery Publications.

Fonkenell, Guillaume, et al. (2022) *Catherine de Médicis: art et pouvoir dans la France de la Renaissance*. Paris: Le Passage.

Fontana, Micol, ed. (2004) *Caravaggio, la Medusa: lo splendore degli scudi da parata del cinquecento*. Exhibition catalogue, Milan: Museo Bugatti Valsecchi, 26 March–23 May 2004. Cinisello Balsamo (Milan): Silvana.

Fontanella, Girolamo, & Rosario Contarino, eds. (1994) *Ode* (1633). Turin: Edizioni RES.

Forcione, Alban. (2009) *Majesty and Humanity: Kings and Their Doubles in the Political Drama of the Spanish Golden Age*. New Haven, CT: Yale University Press.

Ford, J. Brian. (1985) *Single Lens: The Story of the Simple Microscope*. London: Heinemann.

Forster, Leonard. (1969) *The Icy Fire: Studies in European Petrarchism*. Cambridge: Cambridge University Press.

Foster, Hal, ed. (1988) *Vision and Visuality*. New York: New Press.

Foucault, Michel. (1964). 'Les suivantes'. *Le Mercure de France*, 1221–22, 368–84.

(1970) *The Order of Things: An Archaeology of the Human Sciences*. Translated from the 1966 French edition. New York: Pantheon Books.

Fournier, Marian. (1996) *The Fabric of Life: Microscopy in the Seventeenth Century*. Baltimore: Johns Hopkins University Press.

Franits, E. Wayne. (1993) *Paragons of Virtue: Women and Domesticity in Seventeenth-Century Dutch Art*. Cambridge: Cambridge University Press.

Franits, Wayne. (2004) *Dutch Seventeenth-Century Genre Painting*. New Haven, CT: Yale University Press.

Fransen, Sietske, et al. (2023) *Antoni van Leeuwenhoek en de microwereld*. Exhibition catalogue, Leiden: Museum Boerhaave, 17 April 2023–15 January 2023. Zwolle: Wbooks.

Freedberg, David. (2002) *The Eye of the Lynx: Galileo, His Friends, and the Beginnings of Modern Natural History*. Chicago: University of Chicago Press.

Frelick, Nancy M., ed. (2016) *The Mirror in Medieval and Early Modern Culture: Specular Reflections*. Turnhout: Brepols.

(2018) 'Mirror Effects: The Narcissus Emblem in Scève's Délie'. In Angeliki Pollali & Berthold Hub, eds., *Images of Sex and Desire in Renaissance Art and Modern Historiography*. New York: Routledge, 61–79.

French, Peter J. (1972) *John Dee: The World of an Elizabethan Magus*. London: Routledge.

Freud, Sigmund. (1955) 'The Uncanny'. Translated from the 1919 German in James Strachey, ed., *The Standard Edition of the Complete Psychological Works of Sigmund Freud*, 24 vols. London: Hogarth Press, vol. 17, 219–52.

(1957) 'On Narcissism'. Translated from the 1914 German in James Strachey, ed., *The Standard Edition of the Complete Psychological Works of Sigmund Freud*, 24 vols. London: Hogarth Press, vol. 14, 67–102.

Frey, Karl, & Herman-Walther Frey, eds. (1982) *Giorgio Vasari der Literarische Nachlass* (1923). Reprint. New York: G. Olms, 1982.

Fried, Michael. (2010) *The Moment of Caravaggio*. A. W. Mellon Lectures in the Fine Arts, National Gallery of Art, Washington, DC. Bollingen Series 35:51. Princeton, NJ: Princeton University Press.

(2021) *Painting with Demons: The Art of Gerolamo Savoldo*. Amherst: Reaktion Books.

Friedman, Mira. (1989) 'The Falcon and the Hunt: Symbolic Love Imagery in Medieval and Renaissance Art'. In Mosche Lazar & Norris Lacy, eds., *Poetics of Love in the Middle Ages: Texts and Contexts*. Fairfax, VA: George Mason University Press, 157–75.

Frisius, Gemma. (1545) *De radio astronomico e geometrico*. Antwerp: G. Bontius; Louvain: P. Phalesius.

Froissart, Jean, & Anthime Fourrier. (1975) *Le Joli Buisson de Jonece*. Geneva: Droz.

Frommel, Christoph Luitpold, ed. (1998) *Pietro da Cortona*. Milan: Electa.

(2003) *La Villa Farnesina a Roma*, 2 vols. Modena: Panini Editore.

Frommel, Sabine. (1998) *Sebastiano Serlio architetto*. Milan: Electa.

ed. (2008) *Il mecenatismo di Caterina de' Medici: poesia, feste, musica, pittura, scultura, architettura*. Venice: Marsilio.

Frontisi-Ducroux, Françoise, & Jean-Pierre Vernant. (1997) *Dans l'oeil du miroir*. Paris: Odile Jacob.

Frosini, Fabio, ed. (2015) *Leonardo da Vinci on Nature: Knowledge and Representation*. Venice: Marsilio.

Fubini, Riccardo, & Anna Menci Gallorini. (1972) 'L'autobiografia di Leon Battista Alberti: studio e edizione'. *Rinascimento*, 2(12), 21–78.

Fuller, Thomas. (1662) *History of the Worthies of England*. London: Thomas Williams.

Furlotti, Barbara, & Guido Rebecchini, eds. (2022) *Giulio Romano: la forza delle cose*. Venice: Marsilio.

Furlotti, Barbara, Guido Rebecchini, & Linda Wolk Simon, eds. (2019) *Giulio Romano: Art and Desire*. Exhibition catalogue, Mantua: Palazzo Ducale, 6 October 2019–6 January 2020. Milan: Electa.

Furttenbach, Joseph. (1627) *Newer itinerarium italiae*. Ulm: J. Saurn.

Gady, Alexandre. (2019) *Jules-Hardouin Mansart, le chantier infini*. Actes du colloque internationale, Centre de recherche du château de Versailles. Paris: Le Passage.

Gady, Bénédicte, & Nicolas Milovanovic. (2016) *Charles Le Brun (1619–1690)*. Exhibition catalogue, Lens: Musée du Louvre-Lens, 18 May–29 August 2016. Paris: Lienart.

Gady, Bénédicte, & Jennifer Montagu. (2010) *L'ascension de Charles Le Brun: liens sociaux et production artistique*. Paris: Musée de l'Homme.

Gaehtgens, Thomas, Markus A. Castor, Frédéric Bussmann, & Christophe Henry. (2017) *Versailles et l'Europe: l'appartement monarchique et princier, architecture, décor, ceremonial*, 2 vols. Paris: Album Editions Montmartre.

Gal, Ofer, & Raz Chen-Morris. (2013) *Baroque Science*. Chicago: University of Chicago Press.

Galassi, Maria Clelia. (2015) 'The Reception of Italian Art in the Paintings of Jan Massys'. In Ingrid Ciulisová, ed., *Artistic Innovations and Cultural Zones* (Spectrum Slovakia Series 7). Bratislava: VEDA, 162–81.

Galassi, Cristina, & Sonia Maffei, eds. (2021). *Rivista Fontes*, 2, *L'autorappresentazione come autoconsapevolezza dell'artista*.

Galilei, Galileo. (1610) *Sidereus nuncius*. Venice: Tommaso Baglioni.

(1613) *Istoria e dimonstrazioni intorno alle macchie solari*. Rome: Accademia dei Lincei.

(1989) *Sidereus nuncius, or The Sidereal Messenger* (1610), ed. Albert van Helden. Chicago: University of Chicago Press.

Galletti, Sara. (2016) 'The Royal Gallery at the Time of Henry IV: Architecture and Ceremonial'. In Colette Navitel, ed., *Henri IV: Art et Pouvoir*. Tours: Presses universitaires de Rennes, 327–40.

Gallop, Jane. (1982/3) 'Lacan's 'Mirror Stage': Where to Begin'. *SubStance*, 11–12, 118–28.

Galluzzi, Paolo, ed. (2009) *The Universe of Galileo: Images of the Cosmos from Antiquity to the Scientific Revolution*. Exhibition catalogue, Florence: Palazzo Strozzi, 13 March–13 August 2009. Florence: Giunti.

ed. (2018) *L'acqua microscopio della natura: il codice Leicester di Leonardo da Vinci*. Exhibition catalogue, Florence: Uffizi Galleries, 30 October 2008–20 January 2019. Milan: Giunti.

Galluzzi, Paolo, & Alessandro Nova, eds. (2022) *Decoding Leonardo's Codices: Compilation, Dispersal, and Reproduction Technologies*. Venice: Marsilio.

Gamwell, Lynn, & Richard Wells, eds. (1989) *Sigmund Freud and Art: His Personal Collection of Antiquities*. New York: Harry N. Abrams.

Garland, Rosemary. (1952) *Glass*. London: Educational Supply Association.

Garrard, Mary D. (1989) *Artemisia Gentileschi: The Image of the Female Hero in Italian Baroque Art*. Princeton, NJ: Princeton University Press.

(2005) 'Artemisia's Hand'. In Judith Mann, ed., *Artemisia Gentileschi: Taking Stock*. Turnhout: Brepols Publishers, 99–120.

(2010) *Brunelleschi's Egg: Nature, Art, and Gender in Renaissance Italy*. Berkeley: University of California Press.

Garrido Pérez, Carmen, with Jonathan Brown. (1998) *Velazquez: The Technique of Genius*. New Haven, CT: Yale University Press.

Garrido Pérez, Carmen, et al. (2022) *Velázquez: el fluir expresivo de su pintura*. Lleida: Centre d'Art d'Epoca Moderna, Universitat de Lleida.

Gasché, Rodolphe. (1986) *The Tain of the Mirror: Derrida and the Philosophy of Reflection*. Cambridge, MA: Harvard University Press.

Gaskell, Ivan. (1984) 'Vermeer, Judgment, and Truth'. *Burlington Magazine*, 126, 557–61.

Gaskell, Ivan, & Michiel Jonker, eds. (1998) *Vermeer Studies*. Studies in the History of Art, Washington, DC, National Gallery of Art, 55, XXXIII. New Haven, CT: Yale University Press.

Gaukroger, Stephen. (1995) *Descartes: An Intellectual Biography*. Oxford: Oxford University Press.

Geldenhauer, Gerard. (1901), *Collectanea van. Gerard Geldenhauer Noviomagus* (1529), ed. J. Prinsen. Amsterdam: Müller.

Gelfand, Laura. (2006) 'The Devotional Portrait, the Diptych and the Manuscript Tradition'. In John Oliver Hand & Ron Spronk, eds., *Essays in Context: Unfolding the Netherlandish Diptych*. Cambridge, MA: Harvard Art Museums and Yale University Press, 46–59.

Gentil Baldrich, José Maria. (2013) 'La prospettiva: "un buco nella tavoletta"'. *Disegnare – idee: immagini*, 24, 22–29.

Gentili, Augusto, Philippe Morel, & Claudia Cieri Via, eds. (1989) *Il ritratto e la Memoria. Materiali 1, 2, 3*. Rome: Bulzoni.

Georgel, P., & Lecoq, A.-M. (1982) *La Peinture dans la peinture*. Exhibition catalogue, Dijon: Musée des Beaux Arts, 18 December 1982–28 February 1983. Dijon: Musée des Beaux Arts.

Geraerts, Marie. (2011) 'Rubens's Feast of Venus Reconsidered: The Turning of Ears to or from Love? Sensuality or Virtue?' In Karolien De Clippel, Katharina Van Cauteren, & Katlijne Van der Stighelen, eds., *The Nude and the Norm in the Early Modern Low Countries*. Turnhout: Brepols, 159–80.

Gerolemou, Maria, ed. (2020a) *Mirrors and Mirroring from Antiquity to the Early Modern Period*. Exeter: Exeter University Press.

(2020b) 'Plane and Curved Mirrors in Classical Antiquity'. In *Mirrors and Mirroring from Antiquity to the Early Modern Period*. Exeter: Exeter University Press, 157–64.

Gerstl, Doris, ed. (2005) *Georg Philipp Harsdörffer und die Künste*, Academy proceedings, *Schriftenreihe der Akademie der Bildenden Künste in Nürnberg 10*. Nürnberg: Fachverlag Hans Carl.

Gess, Nicola, Tina Hartmann, & Dominika Hens, eds. (2015) *Barocktheater als Spektakel: Maschine, Blick und Bewegung auf der Opernbühne des des Ancien Régime*. Paderborn: Fink.

Gessner, Samuel. (2019) 'The Perspective of the Instrument Maker: The Planispheric Project with Gemma Frisius and the Arsenius Workshop at Louvain'. In Sven Dupré, ed., *Perspective as Practice*. Turnhout: Brepols, 103–22.

Ghiberti, Lorenzo. (1998) *I commentari* (c. 1447), ed. Lorenzo Bartoli. Biblioteca Nazionale Centrale ms. 333. Florence: Giunti.

Ghirardi, Angela. (1994). 'Lavinia Fontana allo specchio pittrici e autoritratto nel secondo cinquecento'. In Vera Fortunati, ed., *Lavinia Fontana 1552–1614*. Exhibition catalogue, Bologna: Museo Civico, 1 October–4 December 1994. Milan: Electa, 37–52.

Gibaldi, Joseph. (1987) 'Vittoria Colonna, Child, Woman, and Poet'. In Katherine Wilson, ed., *Women Writers of the Renaissance and Reformation*. Athens: University of Georgia, 22–40.

Gibson, Walter. (1973) 'Hieronymus Bosch and the Mirror of Man: The Authorship and Iconography of the "Tabletop of the Seven Deadly Sins"'. *Oud Holland, Journal for Art in the Low Countries*, 87(4), 205–26.

Gide, André. (1948) *Journal, 1889–1939*. Paris: Gallimard.

Gifford, Melanie, et al. (2022) 'First Steps in Vermeer's Creative Process: New Findings from the National Gallery of Art'. *Journal of Historians of Netherlandish Art*, 14(2).

Gillespie, Alexandra. (2006) *Print Culture and the Medieval Author: Chaucer, Lydgate, and Their Books*. Oxford: Oxford University Press.

Gilman, B. Ernest. (1978) *The Curious Perspective: Literary and Pictorial Wit in the Eleventh Century*. New Haven, CT: Yale University Press.

Gingerich, Owen, & Albert Van Helden. (2003) 'From *occhiale* to Printed Page: The Making of Galileo's *Sidereus nuncius*'. *Journal of the History of Astronomy*, 34, 251–67.

Girard, René. (2008) *Mimesis and Theory: Essays on Literature and Criticism*, ed. Robert Doran. Stanford, CA: Stanford University Press.

Girouard, Mark. (1983) *Robert Smythson and the Elizabethan Country House*. New Haven, CT: Yale University Press.

Gisolfi, Diana. (2017) *Paolo Veronese and the Practice of Painting in Late Renaissance Venice*. New Haven, CT: Yale University Press.

Giuffrey, Jules. (1895) *Inventaire général du mobilier de la couronne sous Louis XIV (1663–1715)*, 2 vols. Paris: La Société d'Encouragement pour la Propagation des Livres d'Art.

Giusti, Giovanna, ed. (2007) *Artists' Self-Portraits from the Uffizi*. Exhibition catalogue, London: Dulwich Picture Gallery, 22 May–15 July, 2007. Milan: Skira.

Glen, Thomas. (1993) 'Should Sleeping Dogs Lie? Once Again, *Las Meninas* and the *Mise-en-Scène*'. *Source*, 12, 30–36.

Godfrind-Born, Annick, & Maximiliaan Martens. (2012) *Van Eyck in Detail*. Ghent: Ludion.

Godwin, Joscelyn. (2015) *Athanasius Kircher's Theatre of the World*. London: Thames & Hudson.

Goffen, Rona. (1991) 'Bellini's Nude with Mirror'. *Venezia Cinquecento*, 1(2), 185–99.

(1997a) *Titian's Women*. New Haven, CT: Yale University Press.

(1997b) *Titian's Venus of Urbino*. Cambridge: Cambridge University Press.

(2002) *Renaissance Rivals: Michelangelo, Leonardo, Raphael, Titian*. New Haven, CT: Yale University Press.

Goldberg, Benjamin. (1985) *The Mirror and the Man*. Charlottesville: University of Virginia Press.

Goldin, Frederick. (1967) *The Mirror of Narcissus in the Courtly Love Lyric*. Ithaca, NY: Cornell University Press.

Goldstein, Carl. (2012) *Print Culture in Early Modern France: Abraham Bosse and the Purposes of Print*. Cambridge: Cambridge University Press.

Gombrich, Ernst. (1960) *Art and Illusion: A Study in the Psychology of Pictorial Representation*. A. W. Mellon Lectures in the Fine Arts, National Gallery of Art, Washington DC, Bollingen Series. Princeton, NJ: Princeton University Press.

(1975) 'Review Lecture, Mirror and Map: Theories of Pictorial Representation'. *Philosophical Transactions of the Royal Society of London, Series B, Biological Sciences*, 270(903), 119–49.

Gomez Lopez, Susana. (2016) 'The Encounter of the Emblematic Tradition with Optics: The Anamorphic Elephant of Simon Vouet'. *Nuncius*, 31 (2), 289–331.

Gooding, David, Trevor Pinch, & Simon Schaffer, eds. (1989) *The Uses of Experiment: Studies in the Natural Sciences*. Cambridge: Cambridge University Press.

Goodman Soellner, Elise. (1983) 'Poetic Interpretations of the "Lady at Her Toilette" Theme in Sixteenth-Century Painting'. *The Sixteenth-Century Journal*, 14 (4), 426–42.

Gorman, Michael John, & Nick Wilding. (2001) 'Athanasius Kircher e la cultura barocca delle macchine.' In Eugenio Lo Sardo, ed., *Athanasius Kircher S.J. Il Museo del Mondo*. Exhibition catalogue, Rome: Palazzo Venezia, 28 February–28 April 2001. Rome: De Luca, 217–37.

Gottlieb, Carla. (1985). 'The Bewitched Reflection'. *Source: Notes in the History of Art*, special issue on mirrors, ed. Laurie Schneider, 2(3), 59–67.

Gough, Melinda. (2019) *Dancing Queen: Marie de Médicis' Ballets at the Court of Henri IV*. Toronto: University of Toronto Press.

Govi, Gilberto. (1889) 'The Compound Microscope Invented by Galileo'. *Journal of the Royal Microscopical Society*, 9, 574–98.

Grabes, Herbert. (1973) *Speculum, Mirror und Looking-Glass: Kontinuität und Originalität der Spiegelmetapher in den Buchtiteln des Mittelalters under englischen Literatur des 13. Bis 17 Jahrhunderts*. Tübingen: Max Niemeyer Verlag.

(1982) *The Mutable Glass: Mirror Imagery in Titles and Texts of the Middle Ages and English Renaissance*. Translated from the German and reprint. Cambridge: Cambridge University Press, 2009.

Grafton, Anthony. (2001a) *Cardano's Cosmos: The Worlds and Works of a Renaissance Astrologer*. Cambridge, MA: Harvard University Press.

(2001b) *Leon Battista Alberti: Master Builder of the Italian Renaissance*. London: Penguin Books.

Graham, Heather. (2008) 'Renaissance Flesh and Women's Devotion: Titian's Penitent Magdalen'. *Comitatus*, 39, 137–54.

Grave, Johannes. (2010) 'Brunelleschi's Perspective Panels: Rupture and Continuity in the History of the Image'. In Alexander Lee et al., eds., *Renaissance?: Perceptions of Continuity and Discontinuity in Europe, c. 1300–c. 1550*. Leiden: Brill, 161–80.

(2018) *Giovanni Bellini: The Art of Contemplation*. Munich: Prestel.

Grayson, Cecil. (1968) 'The Text of Alberti's *De pictura*'. *Italian Studies*, 23(1), 71–93.

Greenblatt, Stephen. (2005) *Renaissance Self-Fashioning: From More to Shakespeare*. Chicago: University of Chicago Press.

Greer, Margaret. (2017) *The Play of Power: Mythological Court Dramas of Calderón de la Barca*. Princeton, NJ: Princeton University Press.

Gregg, Robert. (1975) *Consolation Philosophy: Greek and Christian Paideia in Basil and the Two Gregories*. Cambridge, MA: Philadelphia Patristic Foundation.

Gregori, Mina, et al., eds. (1985) *The Age of Caravaggio*. Exhibition catalogue, New York: Metropolitan Museum, 5 February–14 April 1985; Naples: Capodimonte Museum, 12 May–30 June 1985. New York: Metropolitan Museum of Art; Electa/Rizzoli.

Gregory, James. (1663) *Optica promota*. London: J. Hayes for S. Thomson.

Gregory, Richard. (1997) *Mirrors in Mind*. London: Penguin Books.

Gregory the Great, *Homily on the Gospels*.

Greub, Thierry. (2015) 'Der Platz des Bildes under "Platz des Königs": Diego Velázquez' *Las Meninas* im Sommer-Arbeitszimmer Philipps IV'. *Zeitschrift für Kunstgeschichte*, 78, 441–87.

(2019) 'Reconstruyendo la "pieza del despacho de Verano", la estancia de *Las Meninas* en el Alcázar: problemas y sugerencias'. *Philostrato: Revista de Historia y Arte*, 5, 56–78.

(2001) *Las Meninas im Spiegel der Deutungen: eine Einführung in die Methoden der Kunstgeschichte*. Berlin: Reimer.

Gronau, Georg. (1928) *Spätwerke des Giovanni Bellini*. Strasburg: J. H. Heitz.

Guillaud, Jacqueline, & Maurice Guillaud. (1990) *Frescoes in the Time of Pompeii*. Paris: Guillaud Editions.

Gundestrup, Bente. (1991–95) *The Royal Danish Kunstkammer 1737*, 3 vols. Copenhagen: A. Busck; Nationalmuseet.

Gusdorf, Georges. (1956) 'Conditions et limites de l'autobiographie'. In *Formen der Selbstdarstellung: Festgabe für Fritz Neubert*. Berlin: Dunker & Humblot, 106–23.

Gutenberg Museum Mainz: A Guide to the Museum of Type and Printing. (2010) Mainz: Gutenberg Museum.

Hadfield, Andrew, ed. (2001) *The Cambridge Companion to Spenser*. Cambridge: Cambridge University Press, 2001.

Haeutle, Christian. (1881) 'Die Reisen des Augsburgers Philipp Hainhofer nack Eichstädt, München und Regensburg in den Jahren 1611, 1612, und 1613'. *Zeitschrift des HistorischenVereins für Schwaben und Neuburg*, 8, 55–148.

Hagopian van Buren, Anne. (1986) 'Reality and Literary Romance in the Park of Hesdin'. In Elisabeth B MacDougall, ed., *Medieval Gardens*, Dumbarton Oaks Colloquium on the History of Landscape Architecture, 9. Washington, DC: Dumbarton Oaks Research Library & Collection, 115–34.

Hahn, Cynthia, & Avinoam Shalem, eds. (2020) *Seeking Transparency: The Medieval Rock Crystals*. Berlin: G. Mann.

Haig Gaisser, Julia. (2008) *The Fortunes of Apuleius and The Golden Ass: A Study in Transmission and Reception*. Princeton, NJ: Princeton University Press.

Hall, Edwin. (1994) *The Arnolfini Betrothal: Medieval Marriage and the Enigma of van Eyck's Double Portrait*. Berkeley: University of California Press.

Halliwell, S. (2002) *The Aesthetics of Mimesis: Ancient Texts and Modern Problems*. Princeton, NJ: Princeton University Press.

Hallyn, Fernand. (1979–80) 'Holbein: La mort en abyme', *Gentse bijdragen tot de kunstgeschiedenis*, 25, 1–13.

Hamilka, Emilie, & Marie-Pierre Laffitte. (2009) 'L'enluminure tardive à Versailles, les manuscrits provenant du cabinet de Louis XIV à Versailles'. In Nicolas Milovanovic & Alexandre Maral, eds. *Louis XIV, l'homme et le roi*. Paris: Flammarion, 297–300.

Hamlyn, D. W. (1961). *The Psychology of Perception*. London: Routledge & Kegan Paul.

Hammond, John. (1981) *The Camera Obscura*. Bristol: Adam Hilger.

Hammond, John, & Jill Austin. (1987) *The Camera Lucida in Art and Science*. Bristol: Adam Hilger.

Hamon, Maurice. (2017) 'La manufacture royale des glaces à Versailles aux XVII et XVIII siècles'. *Versalia: Revue de la Société des Amis de Versailles*, 20, 135–56.

Hand, John Oliver. (2012) 'La Dame au Bain par François Clouet'. In Frédéric Elsig, ed., *Peindre en France à la Renaissance: Fontainebleau et son rayonnement*, 2 vols. Milan: Silvana, vol. 2, 207–16.

Hand, John Oliver, Catherine A. Metzger, & Ron Spronk. (2006) *Prayers and Portraits: Unfolding the Netherlandish Diptych*. Exhibition catalogue, Washington, DC: National Gallery of Art,

12 November 2006–4 February 2007; Koninklijk Museum voor Schone Kunsten, Antwerp, 3 March–27 May 2007. Cambridge, MA: Harvard University Art Museums; New Haven, CT: Yale University Press.

Hanley, Stephen. (2007) 'The Optical Concerns of Jan van Eyck's Painting Practice'. PhD thesis, University of York.

(2009) 'Optical Symbolism as Optical Description: A Case Study of Canon van der Paele's Spectacles'. *Journal of Historians of Netherlandish Art*, 1(1).

Hans, Pierre-Xavier. (2010) 'Du cabinet de curiosités au laboratoire: les cabinets du roi à Versailles'. In Béatrix Saule, ed., *Sciences et curiosités à la Cour de Versailles*. Exhibition catalogue, Versailles: Château de Versailles, 26 October 2010–27 February 2011. Paris: Editions RMN, 195–205.

Hardie, Philip. (2002) *Ovid's Poetics of Illusion*. Cambridge: Cambridge University Press.

Harsdörffer, Georg Philipp. (1652) *Delitiae Philosophicae et Mathematicae*. Nuremberg: Endter.

Hart, Vaughan, & Peter Hicks, eds. (1996) *Sebastiano Serlio on Architecture, vol. 1: Books I–V, 'Tutte l'opere d'architettura et prospetiva'*. New Haven, CT: Yale University Press.

eds. (2001) *Sebastiano Serlio on Architecture, vol. 2: Books VI and VII of 'Tutte l'opere d'architettura et prospetiva', with 'Castrametation of the Romans' and 'The Extraordinary Book of Doors'*. New Haven, CT: Yale University Press.

Hartlaub, G. (1951) *Zauber des Spiegels: Geschichte unde Bedeutung des Spiegels in der Kunst*. Munich: Piper.

Hasan Ibn al-Haytham. (1989) *The Optics* (c. 1010–1020). Translated from the Arabic by A. I. Sabra. London: Warburg Institute.

Haskins, Susan. (2005) *Mary Magdalen: Myth and Metaphor* (1993). Reprint. London: Pimlico.

Haudicquier de Blancourt, Jean. (1999) *Les secrets de l'art de la verrerie* (1697). Reprint. Lyon: Cosmogone Eds.

Havard, Henry. (1887) *Dictionnaire de l'ameublement et de la décoration*, 4 vols. Paris: Maison Quantin.

Hayward, J. F. (1956–58) 'The Sigman Shield'. *Journal of the Arms and Armour Society, London*, 2, 21–42.

Headlam Wells, Robert. (1983) *Spenser's Faerie Queene and the Cult of Elizabeth*. London: CroomHelm.

Healy, Fiona. (1997) *Rubens and the Judgment of Paris: A Question of Choice*. Turnhout: Brepols.

Hedin, Thomas. (2022) *The Fountain of Latona: Louis XIV, Charles Le Brun, and the Gardens of Versailles*. Philadelphia: Pennsylvania State University Press.

Heikamp, Detlef, ed. (1961) *Scritti d'arte di Federico Zuccaro*. Florence: L. S. Olschki.

(1966) 'La Medusa del Caravaggio e l'Armatura dello Scia "Abbas di Persia"'. *Paragone*, 199, 62–76.

(1986) *Studien zur Medicieschen Glaskunst*. Florence: Oschki.

Heilbron, L. John. (2010) *Galileo*. New York: Oxford University Press.

Held, Julius. (1936) 'A Diptych by Memling'. *The Burlington Magazine*, 68, 176–79.

(1982) 'Artis Pictoriae Amator' (1957). In A. W. Lowenthal et al., eds., *Rubens and His Circle*. Princeton, NJ: Princeton University Press, 35–64.

Helden, Albert van, ed. (2010) *The Origins of the Telescope*. Amsterdam: Knaw Press.

Helmholtz, Herman von. (1867) *Handbuch der Physiologischen Optik*, 3 vols. Leipzig: Voss.

Henderson, Felicity, et al., eds. (2015) *Huntington Library Quarterly*, special issue, 'Curiously Drawn: Early Modern Science as a Visual Pursuit', 78(2).

Henderson, Julian. (2013) *Ancient Glass: An Interdisciplinary Exploration*. New York: Cambridge University Press.

Hendler, Sefy. (2010) 'Entre l'ombre et ce qui fait l'ombre: le *Narcisse* de Cellini et le *paragone*'. *Studiolo*, 8, 169–84.

Hénin, Emmanuelle. (2003) *Ut pictura theatrum: théâtre et peinture de la Renaissance italienne au classicism français*. Geneva: Droz.

Hénin, Emmanuelle, & Valérie Naas. (2018) *Le mythe de l'art antique, entre anecdotes et lieux communs*. Colloque Paris, École normale supérieure, 15–17 October 2015. Paris: CNRS éditions.

Henry, Tom, Paul Joannides, et al., eds. (2013) *Late Raphael*. Exhibition catalogue, Madrid: Prado, 12 June–16 September 2012; Paris: Louvre, 11 October 2012–14 January 2013. London: Thames & Hudson

Hentzner, Paul. (1757) *A Journey into England*. London: Strawberry Hill Press.

Herlihy, David. (1985) *Medieval Households*. Cambridge, MA: Harvard University Press.

Herrmann-Fiore, Kristina. (1995) '*L'Allegoria Coniugale* di Tiziano del Louvre e le Derivazioni, Connesse con *Venere che benda Amore*'. In Maria Grazia Bernardini, ed., *Tiziano amor sacro e amor profano*. Exhibition catalogue, Rome; Palazzo delle Espositioni, 22 March–22 May 1995. Milan: Electa, 411–20.

Hesiod. (2018) *The Shield of Heracles*, trans. Glen W. Most. Cambridge, MA: Harvard University Press (LOEB).

Hesiod & Homer. 'The Homeric Hymns' (1915). In *Hesiod, Homeric Hymns, Epic Cycle, Homerica*. Translated froom the Greek by E. White. H. G. Loeb Classical Library. Cambridge, MA: Havard University Press; London: William Heinemann.

Hess, Catherine, & Karol Wight. (2005) *Looking at Glass: A Guide to Terms, Styles, and Techniques*. Los Angeles: J. Paul Getty Museum.

Hewitt, Barnard, ed. (1958) *The Renaissance Stage: Documents of Serlio, Sabbattini, Furttenbach*. Coral Gables, FL: University of Miami Press.

Heydenreich, H. Ludwig. (1954) *Leonardo da Vinci*, 2 vols. New York: Macmillan.

Heyder, Joris Corin. (2012) 'Book Illumination and Jan van Eyck's Early Years'. In Stephan Kemperdick & Friso Lammertse, eds., *The Road to Van Eyck*. Exhibition catalogue, Rotterdam: Museum Boijmans Van Beuningen, 13 October 2012–10 February 2013. Rotterdam: Museum Boijmans, 59–65.

Hills, Paul. (1999) *Venetian Colour: Marble Mosaic Painting and Glass 1250–1550*. New Haven, CT: Yale University Press.

(2006) 'Titian's Veils'. *Art History*, 29(5), 771–95.

(2018) *Veiled Presence: Body and Drapery from Giotto to Titian*. New Haven, CT: Yale University Press.

Hindman, Sandra, et al., eds. (2015) *Take This Ring: Medieval and Renaissance Rings from the Griffin Collection*. Turnhout: Brepols.

Hirsch, James. (2003) *Shakespeare and the History of Soliloquies*. Madison, NJ: Fairleigh Dickinson University Press.

Ho, Angela. (2017) *Creating Distinctions in Dutch Genre Painting: Repetition and Invention*. Amsterdam: Amsterdam University Press.

Hockney, David. (2001) *Secret Knowledge: Rediscovering the Lost Techniques of the Old Masters*. London: Thames & Hudson.

Holger, Jacob-Friesen, ed. (2019) *Hans Baldung Grien: neue Perspektiven auf sein Werk*. Berlin: Deutscher Kunstverlag.

Hollander, Martha. (2000) 'Public and Private Life in the Art of Pieter de Hooch'. *Nederlands Kunsthistorisch Jaarboek*, special issue, 'The Art of Home in the Netherlands 1500–1800', 51, 272–93.

(2002) *An Entrance for the Eyes: Space and Meaning in Seventeenth-Century Dutch Art*. Berkeley: University of California Press.

Hollstein, Friedrich W. H., Ursula Mielke, Rainer Schoch, et al. (2000) *The New Hollstein: German Engravings, Etchings and Woodcuts 1400–1700*, 76 vols. Rotterdam: Sound and Vision Publishers.

Homer. (2014) *Iliad*, trans. A. T. Murray. Cambridge, MA: Harvard University Press (LOEB).

(2015) *Odyssey*, trans. A. T. Murray. Cambridge, MA: Harvard University Press (LOEB).

Honig, Elizabeth. (2016) *Jan Brueghel and the Senses of Scale*. University Park: Penn State University Press.

Hooke, Robert, & Christopher Wren. (1665) *Micrographia*. London: Royal Society.

Hope, Charles, ed. (2012) *Il regno e l'arte: i camerini di Alfonso I d'Este*. Florence: Olschki.

ed. (2023) *Titian: Sources & Documents*, 6 vols. Cambridge: Burlington Press.

Horace. (1926) *The Art of Poetry (Ars Poetica)*, trans. H. Rushton Fairclough. Cambridge, MA: Harvard University Press (LOEB).

Houbraken, Arnold. (1718–21) *De Groote Schouburgh der Nederlantische Kunstschilders en Schilderessen*, 3 vols. Amsterdam.

Hub, Berthold. (2020). *Filarete: der Architekt der Renaissance als Demiurg und Pädagoge*. Vienna: Böhlau.

Hudson, Hugh. (2003) 'The Chronograms in the Inscription of Jan van Eyck's Portrait of Jan de Leeuw'. *Oud Holland Journal for Art in the Low Countries*, 116, 96–99.

Hui, Andrew. (2020) 'Poussin's Allegories of Ruins'. In Karen Enenkel and Walter Melion, eds., *Landscape and the Visual Hermeneutics of Place 1500–1700*. Leiden: Brill, 391–421.

Huizinga, Johan. (1984) *Erasmus and the Age of Reformation*. Princeton, NJ: Princeton University Press.

Hultèn, Pontus. (1949) 'Zu Vermeers Atelierbild'. *Konsthistorik Tidskrift*, 18, 90–98.

Humfrey, Peter. (2015) 'The Chronology of Titian's Versions of the "Venus with a Mirror" and the Lost Venus for the Emperor Charles V'. In Nebahat Avcioglu & Allison Sherman, eds., *Artistic Practices and Cultural Transfer in Early Modern Italy: Essays in Honour of Deborah Howard*. Farnham: Ashgate, 221–32.

Hunt, James L., & John Sharp. (2015) 'Decoding William Scrots' Anamorphic Portrait of Edward VI'. *BSHM Bulletin: Journal of the British Society for the History of Mathematics*, 30(3), 200–216.

Hunter, Matthew. (2013) *Wicked Intelligence: Visual Art and the Science of Experiment*. Chicago: University of Chicago Press.

Hunter, Michael, & Simon Schaffer, eds. (1989) *Robert Hooke: New Studies*. Woodbridge: British Society for the History of Science and the Boydell Press.

Hut, Margreet van der. (2020) *'Een huyshouding in 't kleyn': het poppenhuis van Petronella de la Court in het Centraal Museum Utrecht*. Steenwijk: Karel an Mander Academy Visual Heritage Series in the Netherlands.

Huygens, Christiaan. (1950) *Oeuvres complètes*. The Hague: Société Hollandaise des Sciences.

Huygens, Constantijn, & J. A. Worp. (1911–17) *De briefwisseling 1608–1687*, 6 vols. 's-Gravenhage: Nijhoff.

Ilardi, Vincent. (2007) *Renaissance Vision from Spectacles to Telescopes*. Philadelphia: American Philosophical Society.

Ilchman, Frederick, ed. (2009) *Titian, Tintoretto, Veronese: Rivals in Renaissance Venice*. Exhibition catalogue, Boston: Museum of Fine Arts, 15 March–16 August 2009; Paris: Musée du Louvre, 14 September–4 January 2010. Boston: MFA Publications.

Impey, O. R., & Arthur MacGregor, eds. (2017) *The Origins of Museums: The Cabinet of Curiosities in Sixteenth- and Seventeenth-Century Europe*. Oxford: Ashmolean.

Isager, Jacob. (2013) *Pliny on Art and Society: The Elder Pliny's Chapters on the History of Art*. New York: Routledge.

Ishikawa, Chiyo. (2004) *The 'Retablo de Isabel la Catolica' by Juan de Flandes and Michael Sittow*. Turnhout: Brepols.

Isidore of Seville. (2009) *Etymologies* (600–625). Translated by Stephen Barney. Cambridge: Cambridge University Press.

Jacobs, F. Lynn. (2012) *Opening Doors: The Early Netherlandish Triptych Reinterpreted*. University Park: Penn State University Press.

Jaffé, David, et al. (2003) *Titian*. London: National Gallery Publications.

Jansen, Anita, et al. (2019) *Pieter de Hooch in Delft: Uit de schaduw van Vermeer*. Exhibition catalogue, Museum Prinsenhof Delft, 11 October 2019–16 February 2020. Het Prinsenhof, Zwolle.

Jansen, Dieter. (1984) 'Der Kölner Provinzial des Minoritenordens Heinrich von Werl, der Werl-Altar und Robert Campin'. *Wallraf-Richartz-Jahrbuch* 45, 7–40.

Jansen, Katherine. (2000) *The Making of the Magdalen: Preaching and Popular Devotion in the Late Middle Ages*. Princeton, NJ: Princeton University Press.

Janson, Anthony F. (1985) 'The Convex Mirror as Vanitas Symbol'. *Source: Notes in the History of Art*, special issue on mirrors, ed. Laurie Schneider, 2(3), 51–54.

Jardine, Lisa. (1993) *Erasmus, Man of Letters: The Construction of Charisma in Print*. Princeton, NJ: Princeton University Press.

(1996) *Worldly Goods*. London: Macmillan.

Jay, Martin. (1993) *Downcast Eyes: The Denigration of Vision in Twentieth-Century French Thought*. Berkeley: University of California Press.

Jechova, Hana Voisine. (1994) *La visualisation des choses et la conception philosophique du monde dans l'oeuvre de Comenius*. Actes du colloque, Paris 1992. Paris: Presses de l'Université de Paris-Sorbonne.

Jolivet, Sophie. (2021) 'Chapeaux, chaperons, et autres couvre-chefs: une place de choix dans la garde-robe des ducs de Bourgogne'. In Danièle Alexandre-Bidon et al., eds., *Le vêtement au Moyen Age: de l'atelier à la garde-robe*. Actes du colloque 2016. Turnhout: Brepols, 167–83.

Jollet, Etienne. (1997) *Jean & François Clouet*. Translated from the French by D. Dusinberre. Paris: Editions de la Lagune.

Jones, Ann Rosalind, & Peter Stallybrass. (2000) *Renaissance Clothing and the Materials of Memory*. Cambridge: Cambridge University Press.

Jones, Susan Frances. (2011) *Van Eyck to Gossaert: Towards a Northern Renaissance*. Exhibition catalogue, London: National Gallery, 23 February–30 May 2011. London: National Gallery.

Jones, Susan Frances. (2017) 'Jan van Eyck's Greek, Hebrew, and Trilingual Inscriptions'. In Christina Currie et al., eds., *Van Eyck Studies: Underdrawing and Technology in Painting*. Symposium XVIII, The Royal Institute for Cultural Heritage Centre for the Study of the Flemish Primitives. Leuven: Peeters, 291–310.

Jonker, Menno. (2023) *Sofonisba Anguissola: portrettist van de Renaissance* Exhibition catalogue, Rijksmuseum, 11 February–11 June 2023. Zwolle: Waanders.

Jonson, Ben. (1608) *The Hue and Cry after Cupid*. London

(1616) *Masque of Hymen*. London: Will Stansby.

Joubert, Fabienne. (1987) *La tapisserie médiévale au Musée de Cluny*. Paris: RMN.

Joyce, Kirstin, & Shellei Addison. (1992) *Pearls: Ornament and Obsession*. London: Thames & Hudson.

Judde delaRivière, Claire. (2018) *The Revolt of Snowballs: Murano Confronts Venice, 1511*. Translated from the French by T. Cohen. London: Routledge.

Judovitz, Dalia. (2018) *Georges de la Tour and the Enigma of the Visible*. Fordham Scholarship Online.

Justi, Carl. (1889) *Velazquez and His Times*. Translated from the German by A. H. Keane. London: H. Grevel & Co.; Philadelphia: J. B. Lippincott.

(2016) *Carl Justi und die Kunstgeschichte*, ed. Bettina Marten & Roland Kanz. Frankfurt: Vervuert.

Jütte, Daniel. (2023) *Transparency: The Material History of an Idea*. New Haven, CT: Yale University Press.

Kappel, Jutta. (2017) *Elfenbeinkunst im Grünen Gewölbe zu Dresden: Geschichte einer Sammlung: Wissenschaftlicher Bestandskatalog – Statuetten, Figurengruppen, Reliefs, Gefässe, Varia, Staatliche Kunstsammlungen Dresden*. Dresden: Sandstein.

Karelis, Charles. (1985) 'The *Las Meninas* Literature and Its Lesson'. In Raphael Stern, Philip Rodman, & Joseph Cobitz, eds., *Creation and Interpretation*. New York: Haven Publications, 101–14.

Kee, Joan, & Lugli Emanuele, eds. (2015) 'Scale to Size: An Introduction'. *Art History*, special issue, 'To Scale', 38(2), 250–66.

Kelly, Philippa. (2006) 'Dialogues of Self-Reflection: Early Modern Mirrors'. In Ronald Bedford, Lloyd David, & Philippa Kelly, eds., *Early Modern Autobiography:*

Theories Genres Practices. Ann Arbor: University of Michigan Press, 62–88.

Kelso, Ruth. (1959) *Doctrine for the Lady of the Renaissance*. Urbana: University of Illinois Press.

Kemp, Martin. (1976) '"Ogni dipintore dipinge se": A Neoplatonic Echo in Leonardo's Art Theory?' In C. H. Clough, ed., *Cultural Aspects of the Italian Renaissance. Essays in Honour of Paul Oskar Kristeller*. Manchester: Manchester University Press; New York: A. F. Zambelli, 311–32.

(1977) 'Leonardo and the Visual Pyramid'. *Journal of the Warburg & Courtauld Institutes*, 40, 128–49.

(1978) 'Science, Non-Science and Nonsense: The Interpretation of Brunelleschi's Perspective'. *Art History*, 1, 134–61.

(2011) *Leonardo da Vinci: The Marvellous Works of Nature and Man* (1981). Oxford: Oxford University Press.

(1989) *Leonardo on Painting*. New Haven, CT: Yale University Press.

(1990) *The Science of Art: Optical Themes in Western Art from Brunelleschi to Seurat*. New Haven, CT: Yale University Press.

(1992) *The Science of Art: Optical Themes in Western Art from Brunelleschi to Seurat*. New Haven, CT: Yale University Press.

(2004) *Leonardo*. Oxford: Oxford University Press.

(2006) *Leonardo da Vinci: Experience, Experiment and Design*. Exhibition catalogue, London: Victoria & Albert Museum, 14 September 2006–7 January 2007. London: Victoria & Albert Museum Publications.

Kemperdick, Stephan. (2018) 'Philip the Good Bare-Headed: In Search for Original and Copy'. In Anne Dubois, Jacqueline Couvert, & Till-Holger Borchert, eds., *Technical Studies of Paintings: Problems of Attribution (15th–17th centuries)*. Leuven: Peeters, 50–59.

Kemperdick, Stephan, & Friso Lammertse. (2012) *The Road to van Eyck*. Exhibition catalogue, Rotterdam: Museum Boijmans Van Beuningen, 13 October 2012–10 February 2013. Rotterdam: Museum Boijmans van Beuningen.

Kenney, E. J. (1990) *Apuleius: Cupid and Psyche*. Cambridge: Cambridge University Press.

Kenny, A. J. P. (1970) *Descartes: Philosophical Letters*. Oxford: Oxford University Press.

Kenny, Neil. (1998) *Curiosity in Early Modern Europe: word histories*. Wiesbaden: Harrassowitz.

(2004) *The Uses of Curiosity in Early Modern France and Germany*. Oxford: Oxford University Press.

Kenseth, Joy, ed. (1991) *The Age of the Marvelous*. Exhibition catalogue, Hanover, NH: Hood Museum of Art, Dartmouth College, 1991. Chicago: University of Chicago Press.

Kepler, Johannes. (1604) *Ad vitellionem paralipomena, quibus astronomiae pars optica traditur*. Frankfurt: C. Marnius & Heirs of J. Aubrius.

(1634) *Somnium*. Frankfurt: Herzogliche Druckerei.

Kepler, Johannes, & William Donahue. (2000) *Optics: Paralipomena to Witelo and Optical Part of Astronomy*. Santa Fe, NM: Green Lion Press.

Kersten, Michiel, et al. (1996) *Delft Masters, Vermeer's Contemporaries: Illusionism through the Conquest of Light and Space*. Exhibition catalogue, Delft: Stedelijk museum het Prinsenhof, 1996. Zwolle: Waanders Publishers.

Key, Sarah. (1983) 'Love in a Mirror: An Aspect of the Imagery of Bernart de Ventadorn'. *Medium Aevum*, 52 (2), 272–85.

Kieven, Elisabeth, & Christina Strunck, eds. (2010) *Europäische Galeriebauten: Galleries in a Comparative European Perspective (1400–1800)*, Actes du colloque 2005. Munich: Hirmer.

Kircher, Athanasius. (1635) *Primitiae gnomonicae catoptricae*. Avignon: Jean Piot.

(1646) *Ars magna lucis et umbrae*. Rome: Sumptibus H. Scheus.

(1656) *Itinerarium exstaticum*. Rome: Vitale Mascardi.

Kirkbride, Robert. (2008) *Architecture and Memory: The Renaissance Studioli of Federico da Montefeltro*. New York: Columbia University Press.

Kisluk-Grosheide, Daniëlle, & Bertrand Rondot, eds. (2018) *Visitors to Versailles: From Louis XIV to the French Revolution*. Exhibition catalogue, New York: Metropolitan Museum of Art, 2018. New Haven, CT: Yale University Press.

Kitao, T. K. (1980) 'Imago and Pictura: Perspective, Camera Obscura and Kepler's Optics'. In Marisa Dalai-Emiliani, ed., *La prospettiva rinascimentale: codificazioni e transgressioni*. Florence: Centro Di, 499–510.

Klapisch-Zuber, Christiane. (1985) *Women, Family, and Ritual in Renaissance Italy*. Chicago: Chicago University Press.

Klein, Dan, & Ward Lloyd, eds. (1989) *The History of Glass*. London: Black Cat.

Klestinec, Cynthia. (2011) *Theaters of Anatomy: Students, Teachers, and Traditions of Dissection in Renaissance Venice*. Baltimore: Johns Hopkins University Press.

Knöll, Stefanie. (2019) 'Im Spiegel der Erkenntnis: Hans Memlings Diptychon Nieuwenhove im Light con Nicolaus Cusanus'. In Albert Lutz, ed., *Spiegel: Der Mensch im Widerschein*. Exhibition catalogue, Zurich: Museum Rietberg, 17 May–22 September 2019. Cologne: Wienand Verlag, 246–49.

Knoppers, Laura. (2003) 'Imagining the Death of the King: Milton, Charles I and Anamorphic Art'. In Elizabeth

Bellamy et al., eds., *Imagining Death in Spenser and Milton*. London: Palgrave Macmillan, 151–70.

Knothe, Florian. (2009) 'Depictions of Glassmaking in Diderot's *Encyclopédie*' *Journal of Glass Studies*', 51, 154–60.

Knox, Giles, & Tanya Tiffany, eds. (2017) *Velazquez Re-examined: Theory, History, Poetry, and Theatre*. Turnhout: Brepols.

Kobi, Valérie. (2021) 'On Spectacles and Magnifying Glasses: The Connoisseur in Action'. *Journal of Art Historiography*, 24, 1–15.

Koch, A. Robert. (1964) 'Flower Symbolism in the Portinari Altarpiece'. *Art Bulletin*, 46, 70–77.

Kodera, Sergius. (2014) 'The Laboratory as Stage: Giovan Battista della Porta's Experiments'. *Journal of Early Modern Studies*, 1, 15–38.

Koeppe, Wolfram, ed. (2019) *Making Marvels: Science and Splendour at the Courts of Europe*. Exhibition catalogue, Metropolitan Museum of Art New York, 25 November 2019–1 March 2020. New Haven, CT: Yale University Press.

Koerner, Joseph. (1985) 'The Mortification of the Image: Death as a Hermeneutic in Hans Baldung Grien'. *Representations*, 10, 52–101.

(1993) *The Moment of Self-Portraiture in German Renaissance Art*. Chicago: Chicago University Press.

(2006) *Dürer's Hands*. New York: Frick Collection.

(2016) *Bosch and Bruegel: From Enemy Painting to Everyday Life*. A. W. Mellon Lectures in the Fine Arts National Gallery of Art, Washington. Princeton, NJ: Princeton University Press.

Koester, Olaf. (1999) *Illusions: Gijsbrechts, Royal Master of Deception*. Exhibition catalogue, Copenhagen: Statens Museum for Kunst, 24 September–30 December 1999; London: National Gallery, 2 February–1 May 2000. Copenhagen: Statens Museum for Kunst.

Koja, Stephan. (2021) *Johannes Vermeer: On Reflection*. Exhibition catalogue, Dresden: Gemäldegalerie, 10 September 2021–2 January 2022. Dresden: Sandstein Verlag.

Koslow, Susan. (1967) 'De Wonderlijke Perspectyfkas: An Aspect of Seventeenth-Century Dutch Painting'. *Oud Holland*, 82, 35–56.

Koster, Margaret L. (2003) 'The Arnolfini Double Portrait: A Simple Solution'. *Apollo*, 158(499), 3–14.

Kowzan, Tadeusz. (2006) *Theâtre miroir: métathéâtre de l'Antiquité au XXIème siècle*. Paris: Harmattan.

Koyré, Alexandre. (1957) *From the Closed World to the Infinite Universe*. New York: Harper.

Krautheimer, Richard. (1952) *Lorenzo Ghiberti*. Princeton, NJ: Princeton University Press.

Kren, Thomas, & Scot McKendrick. (2003) *Illuminating the Renaissance: The Triumph of Flemish Manuscript Painting in Europe*. Exhibition catalogue, Los Angeles: Getty Museum, 17 June–7 September 2003. Los Angeles: J. Paul Getty Museum.

Kris, Ernst, & Otto Kurz. (1979) *Legend, Myth, and Magic in the Image of the Artist: A Historical Experiment*. New Haven, CT: Yale University Press.

Kruse, C. (1999) 'Selbsterkentnis als Medienerkenntnis: Narziß an der Quelle bei Alberti und Caravaggio'. *Marburger Jahrbuch für Kunstwissenschaft*, 26, 99–116.

Kühn, Holger. (2015) *Die leibhaftige Münze: Quentin Massys' Goldwäger und die altniederländische Malerei*. Paderborn: Willhelm Fink.

Kuhn, Thomas. (1962) *The Structure of Scientific Revolutions*. Chicago: University of Chicago Press.

Kuspitt, Donald. (1989) 'A Mighty Metaphor: The Analogy of Archaeology and Psychoanalysis'. In Lynn Gamwell & Richard Wells, eds., *Sigmund Freud and Art: His Personal Collection of Antiquities*. New York: Harry N. Abrams, 133–52.

Kyd, Thomas. (1592) *Spanish Tragedy*. London: White and Langley.

La Font de Saint-Yenne, Etienne. (1747) *Reflexions sur quelques causes de l'état présent de la peinture en France avec un examen des principaux ouvrages exposés au Louvre le mois d'août 1746*. Paris: A La Hye Chez Neaulme.

Laaser, Tilly. (2009) 'A Technical Examination of Fifteenth-Century Cassone Panels in the Courtauld Gallery'. *Zeitschrift für Kunsttechnologie und Konservierung*, 23(2), 315–26.

Lacan, Jacques. (1949) 'Le stade du miroir comme formateur de la function du Je: telle qu'elle nous est révélée dans l'experience psychanalytique'. *Revue française de psychanalyse*, October, 449–55.

(1977) 'The Mirror Stage as Formative of the Function of the "I"' (1949). Translated from the French in Alan Sheridan, ed., *Ecrits: A Selection*. London: Tavistock, 1–7.

Ladis, Andrew. (2008) *Giotto's O: Narrative, Figuration and Pictorial Ingenuity in the Arena Chapel*. University Park: Penn State University Press.

Lambrechtsen, Marine. (2005) 'Cornelis de Man (1621–1706): Een Selectie Uit het Oeuvre van Een Veelzijdige Delftse Schilder'. PhD thesis, University of Amsterdam.

Lampsonius, Domenicus. (1572) *Pictorum aliquot celebrium germaniae inferioris elogiis*. Antwerp: Hieronymous Cock.

Lane, Barbara G. (1991) 'The Patron and the Pirate: The Mystery of Memling's Gdańsk Last Judgment'. *Art Bulletin*, 73, 623–40.

(2009) *Hans Memling: Master Painter in Fifteenth-Century Bruges*. Turnout: Harvey Miller.

Langdon Forhan, Kate. (2002) *The Political Theory of Christine de Pizan*. Aldershot: Ashgate Press.

Langedijk, Karla. (1992) *Die Selbstbildnisse der holländischen und flämischen Künstler in der Galleria degli Autoritratti der Uffizien in Florenz*. Florence: Edizioni Medicea.

Lapucci, Roberta, ed. (2005) *Caravaggio and Optics*. Florence: Rest & Art.

Laqueur, Thomas. (2015) *The Work of the Dead: A Cultural History of Mortal Remains*. Princeton, NJ: Princeton University Press.

Larsen, Eric. (1977) 'The Proof of the Use of the Inverted Telescope in Dutch Seventeenth-Century Landscape Art'. *Gazette des Beaux-Arts*, 89, 172–74.

Lattis, James M. (1994) *Between Copernicus and Galileo: Christoph Clavius and the Collapse of Ptolemaic Cosmology*. Chicago: University of Chicago Press.

Laurenza, Domenico, & Martin Kemp, eds. (2019) *Leonardo da Vinci's Codex Leicester: A New Edition*, 4 vols. Oxford: Oxford University Press.

Lawson, Margaret. (2005) 'The Belles Heures of Jean, Duc de Berry: The Materials and Techniques of the Limbourg Brothers'. In Rob Dückers & Pieter Roelofs, eds., *The Limbourg Brothers: Nijmegen Masters at the French Court 1400–1416*. Exhibition catalogue, Nijmegen: Museum Het Valkhof, 28 August–20 November, 2005. Nijmegen: Ludion, 149–63.

Lazardzig, Jan, & Hole Rössler, eds. (2016) 'Technologies of Theatre: Joseph Furttenbach and the Transfer of Mechanical Knowledge in Early Modern Theatre Cultures'. *Zeitsprünge*, 20(3–4).

Le Brun, Charles. [pseud. M. Lorne] (1684) 'Explication de la Galerie de Versailles', *Mercure Galant*, ed. Jean Donneau de Visé, 12, December, 3–86.

(1698) *Conférence sur l'expression générale et particulière*. Paris: E. Picart.

Le Gillou, Jean-Claude. (2014) 'Versailles, l'ancien Appartement des Bains, de la Marquise de Montespan à la Comtesse de Toulouse'. *Versalia: Revue de la Société des Amis de Versailles*, 17, 107–34.

Ledbury, Mark, & Robert Wellington, eds. (2020) *The Versailles Effect: Objects, Lives, and Afterlives of the domaine*. New York: Bloomsbury Visual Arts.

Lee, W. Renssaeler. (1940) ''Ut pictura poesis': The Humanist Theory of Painting'. *Art Bulletin*, 22(4), 197–269.

Leeman, Fred. (1976) *Hidden Images: Games of Perception, Anamorphic Art, Illusion from the Renaissance to the Present*. New York: Abrams.

Lefèvre, Wolfgang, ed. (2003) *The Power of Images in Early Modern Science*, Basel: Birkhäuser.

ed. (2007) *Inside the Camera Obscura: Optics and Art under the Spell of the Projected Image*. Berlin: Max Planck Institute for the History of Science.

Lehman, Christine. (2010) 'Les miroirs ardents: Recherches académiques et divertissements à la cour'. In Béatrix Saule, ed., *Sciences et curiosités à la Cour de Versailles*. Exhibition catalogue, Versaille: Château de Versailles, 26 October 2010–27 February 2011. Paris: Editions RMN, 234–36.

Leibniz, Gottfried. (1710) *Théodicée*. Amsterdam: Isaac Trojel.

Leisch-Kiesl, Monika. (2021) *Die Dame Vernunft und das Schreiben von geschichte: Christine de Pizans 'Livre de la cite des dames'*. Zurich: Georg Olms.

Lemerie, Frédérique, et al. (2017) *Barbaro 500: Architecture, musique, peinture, perspective*. Conference proceedings, 13–15 November 2013, Tours, Centre d'études supérieures de la Renaissance. Turnhout: Brepols.

Leonardi, Renzo. (2019) 'Jan van Eyck and His 'Stereoscopic' Approach to Painting'. In Christina Currie et al., eds.. *Van Eyck Studies: Underdrawing and Technology in Painting*, Symposium XVIII, the Royal Institute for Cultural Heritage Centre for the Study of the Flemish Primitives. Leuven: Peeters, 327–48.

Leonardo da Vinci. (c. 1470s–1519) *Codex atlanticus*, 12 vols. Milan: Biblioteca Ambrosiana.

(1890) *Trattato della pittura di Leonardo da Vinci, Cod. Vaticano Urbinate 1270*, ed. Gaetano Milanesi. Rome: Unione Cooperativo.

(1938) *The Notebooks of Leonardo da Vinci*, 2 vols., ed. Edward MacCurdy. London: Jonathan Cape.

(1966) *Selections from the Notebooks of Leonardo da Vinci*, ed. Irma Richter. Oxford: Oxford University Press.

(1970) *The Literary Works of Leonardo da Vinci*, 2 vols., ed. Jean Paul Richter. New York: Phaidon.

(1977) *The Literary Works of Leonardo da Vinci Compiled by Jean Paul Richter*, 2 vols., ed. Jean Paul Richter & Carlo Pedretti. Oxford: Phaidon.

(1995) *Libro di pittura, edizione in facsimile del Codice Urbinate lat. 1270 nella Biblioteca Apostolica Vaticana*, 2 vols., ed. Carlo Pedretti and Carlo Vecce. Florence: Giunti.

(1999–2007) *Manuscripts of Leonardo da Vinci in the Institut de France* (1452–1519). Translated by John Verella. Milan: Ente Raccolta Vinciana.

Leoncini, Luca. (2022) 'Le metamorfosi di Filippo Parodi'. In Raffaella Besta & Margherita Priarone, eds., *I protagonisti*. Genoa: Sagep, 46–53.

LePautre, Jean. (1670) *Livre des miroirs, tables, et guéridons*. Amsterdam: Justus Danckertsz.

Lessing, Gotthold Ephraim. (1774) *Vom Alter der Olmalerey*. Braunschweig: Buchhandlung des Fürstlichen Waysenhauses.

Leurechon, Jean (pseud. H. van Etten) (1642) *Récréations mathématiques* (1624). Lyon: Claude Prost.

Leuschner, Eckhard. (2014) 'Cesare Ripa et les masques de l'imitation'. In Françoise Viatte et al., eds., *Masques, Mascarades, Mascarons*. Exhibition catalogue, Paris: Musée du Louvre, 19 June–22 September 2014. Paris: Louvre Editions, 167–78.

Levkoff, Mary. (2015). 'Remarks on Glass Eyes in Polychromed European Sculptures of the Seventeenth and Eighteenth Centuries'. In *The Eternal Baroque: Studies in Honour of Jennifer Montagu*, ed. Carolyn Miner. Milan: Skira, 467–82.

Liedtke, Walter. (1979) 'Perspective, Optics, and Delft Artists around 1650 (Outstanding Dissertations in the Fine Arts by Arthur Wheelock)'. *Art Bulletin* 61, September, 490–96.

(2000) *A View of Delft: Vermeer and His Contemporaries*. Zwolle: Waanders.

et al. (2001) *Vermeer and the Delft School*. Exhibition catalogue, New York: Metropolitan Museum of Art, 8 March–27 May 2001; London: National Gallery, 20 June–16 September 2001. New Haven, CT: Yale University Press.

Liefkes, Reino. (1997) *Glass*. London: V & A Publications.

Lincoln, Evelyn. (2000) *The Invention of the Italian Renaissance Printmaker*. New Haven, CT: Yale University Press, 2000.

Lindberg, David. (1976) *Theories of Vision: From al-Kindi to Kepler*. Chicago: University of Chicago Press.

Lipking, Lawrence. (2014) *What Galileo Saw: Imaging the Scientific Revolution*. Ithaca, NY: Cornell University Press.

Lo Bianco, Anna. (2004) *La volta di Pietro da Cortona*. Rome: Galleria Nazionale d'Arte Antica di Palazzo Barberini. Milan: Electa.

Lo Sardo, Eugenio, ed. (2001) *Athanasius Kircher S.J. Il Museo del Mondo*. Exhibition catalogue, Rome: Palazzo Venezia, 28 February–28 April 2001. Rome: De Luca.

Löcher, Kurt. (1999) *Barthel Beham: Ein Maler aus dem Dürerkreis*. Munich: Deutscher Kunstverlag.

Locker, M. Jesse. (2015) *Artemisia Gentileschi: The Language of Painting*. New Haven, CT: Yale University Press.

Loh, Maria. (2007) *Titian Remade: Repetition and the Transformation of Early Modern Italian Art*. Los Angeles: Getty Publications.

Loire, Stéphane, ed. (1992) *Simon Vouet: Nouvelles precisions et perspectives de recherches*. Actes du colloque de l'École du Louvre, Paris: Grand Palais, 5–7 February 1991. Paris: La Documentation française.

Lomazzo, Giovanni Paolo. (1584) *Trattato dell' arte della pittura, scultura et architettura*, 7 books. Milano: Paolo Gottardo.

(1590) *Idea del tempio della pittura*. Milan: Paolo Gottardo Pontio.

Long, Pamela. (2004) *Openness, Secrecy, Authorship: Technical Arts and the Culture of Knowledge from Antiquity to the Renaissance*. Baltimore: Johns Hopkins University Press.

Lopez-Rey, José. (1996) *Velázquez: Painter of Painters*, 2 vols. Paris: Wildenstein Institute & Taschen.

Lopez Vizcaino, Pilar, & Angel Mario Carreño. (2007) *Juan Carreño Miranda: Vita y obra*. Oviedo: Edicion Cajastur.

Lothe, José. (2008) *L'oeuvre gravé d'Abraham Bosse, graveur parisien du XVIIe siècle*. Paris: Paris Musées.

Loughman, John, & John Michael Montias. (2000) *Public and Private Spaces: Works of Art in Seventeenth-Century Dutch Houses*. Zwolle: Waanders Publishers.

Louw, Hentie. (1991) 'Window-Glass Making in Britain c. 1660–c. 1860 and Its Architectural Impact'. *Construction History*, 7, 47–68.

(2003) 'The Windows of Perrault's Observatory in Paris (1667–1683): The Legacy of a Proto-modern Architectural Inventor'. *Construction History*, 19, 19–46.

Lübbeke, Isolde. (1991) *The Thyssen-Bornemisza Collection: Early German Painting 1350–1550*. London: Sotheby's Publications.

Lucco, Mauro. (2004) 'Bellini and Flemish Painting'. In Peter Humfrey, ed., *The Cambridge Companion to Giovanni Bellini*. Cambridge: Cambridge University Press, 75–94.

Lucco, Mauro, & Giovanni Carlo Federico Villa. (2008) *Giovanni Bellini*. Exhibition catalogue, Rome: Scuderie del Quirinale, 30 September 2008–11 January 2009. Cinisello Balsamo (Milan): Silvana.

Lucian of Samosata. (1913a) *Affairs of the Heart (Amores| Erotes)*, trans. A. M. Harmon. Cambridge, MA: Harvard University Press (LOEB).

Lucian of Samosata. (1913b) *Essays in Portraiture (Imagines| Eikones)*, trans. A. M. Harmon. Cambridge, MA: Harvard University Press (LOEB).

Lucian of Samosata. (1913c) *A True Story (Verae historiae)*, trans. A. M. Harmon. Cambridge, MA: Harvard University Press (LOEB).

Lucretius. (1975) *De rerum natura*, trans. W. H. D. Rouse. Cambridge, MA: Harvard University Press (LOEB).

Luigini, Federico. (1554) *Libro della bella donna*. Venice: Plinio Pietrasanta.

Lukehart, Peter, ed. (2009). *The Accademia Seminars: The Accademia di San Luca in Rome, c. 1590–1635*. NGA Washington VIII. New Haven, CT: Yale University Press.

Luther, Martin. (1883–1929) *Wochenpredigten über das Deuteronomium*. (1529). In *D. Martin Luthers Werke: kritische Gesammtausgabe, Weimarer Ausgabe*, 121 vols. Weimar: Hermann Böhlaus Nochfolger.

Lüthy, Christoph. (1996) 'Atomism, Lynceus, and the Fate of Seventeenth-Century Microscopy'. *Early Science and Medicine I*, 1, 1–27.

et al., eds. (2018) *Image, Imagination, and Cognition: Medieval and Early Modern Theory and Practice*. Leiden: Brill.

Luzón Nogué, José Maria. (2022) *Velázquez en Italia*. Exhibition catalogue, Madrid: Real Academía de bellas artes de San Fernando, 1 June–4 September 2022. Madrid: Real Academía de bellas artes de San Fernando.

Lymant, Brigitte. (1994) 'Entflammen und Loschen: Zur Ikonographie des Liebeszaubers vom Meister des Bonner Diptychons'. *Zeitschrift für Kunstgeschichte* 57 (1), 111–22.

Maassen, Irmgard, & William St Clair, eds. (2000) *Conduct Literature for Women*. London: Pickering & Chatto.

Maaz, Bernard. (2010) '"Der 'Elefant im Glas"?: Eine Anamorphose nach Simon Vouet und Hans Troschel'. *Dresdener Kunstblatter*, 54(3), 140–50.

Mabille, Gérard. (2009a) 'Le mobilier de Louis XIV'. In Nicolas Milovanovic & Alexandre Maral, eds., *Louis XIV: L'homme & le roi*. Exhibition catalogue, Versailles: Château de Versailles, 20 October 2009–7 February 2010. Paris: Skira/Flammarion, 72–83.

(2009b) 'Louis XIV ou le roi jardinier'. In Nicolas Milovanovic & Alexandre Maral, eds., *Louis XIV: L'homme & le roi*. Exhibition catalogue, Versailles: Château de Versailles, 20 October 2009–7 February 2010. Paris: Skira/Flammarion, 124–33.

(2009c) 'Orfèvrerie et mobilier dans les collections de Louis XIV'. In Nicolas Milovanovic & Alexandre Maral, eds. *Louis XIV: L'homme & le roi*. Exhibition catalogue, Versailles: Château de Versailles, 20 October 2009–7 February 2010. Paris: Skira/Flammarion, 236–41.

Machiavelli, Niccolò. (1532) *Il principe*. Florence: Bernardo di Giunta.

MacPhail, Eric, ed. (2023) *Companion to Erasmus*. The Renaissance Society of America, 20. Leiden: Brill.

Madersbacher, Lukas. (2017) 'Fatto alla spera' ? Das Porträt des Leon Battista Alberti aus den Orti Oricellari'. *Mitteilungen des Kunsthistorischen Institutes in Florenz*, 58(3), 318–47.

Madou, M., et al. (2010) *Juan de Flandes en het 'Mirafloresretabel': Gesignaleerd en Opgespoord*. Exhibition catalogue, Antwerp: Museum Mayer van den Bergh, 11 September–7 November 2010. Antwerp: Ludion.

Magnani, Lauro. (1988) *La scultura a Genova e in Liguria*. Genoa.

(2006) 'Filippo Parodi, natura e meraviglia'. *FMR [Franco Maria Ricci]* 15, 99–110.

Mahon, Denis. (1947) *Studies in Seicento Art and Theory*. London: Studies of the Warburg Institute.

Maignan, Emmanuel. (1648) *Perspectiva horaria, sive de orographia gnomonica tum theoretica tum practica*. Rome: Giangiacomo de' Bossi.

Maitte, Corinne. (2009) *Les chemins de verre: Les migrations des verriers d'Altare et de Venise (XVIe–XIXe siècles)*. Rennes: Presse Universitaire de Rennes.

Malfatti, Angelantoni, & Maria Giuseppina. (2015) 'Lo specchio convesso nella pittura fiamminga: Simbolismo, magia, scienza, e arte, fra realtà e trascendenza'. In Luciana Madruzzato et al., eds., *Il vetro in Italia centrale dall'antichità al contemporaneo*. Milan: Centro Culturale Mediolanense, 177–87.

Malvasia, Carlo Cesare. (2000) *Felsina Pittrice, Malvasia's Life of the Carracci* (1678). Translated and edited by Anne Summerscale. Philadelphia: Pennsylvania State Universtiy Press.

Manetti, Antonio. (1927) *Vita di Filippo Brunelleschi* (before 1497). Reprint. Florence: Rinascimento del Libro.

(1970) *The Life of Brunelleschi by Antonio di Tuccio Manetti* (before 1497), ed. Catherine Enggass & Howard Saalman. University Park: Penn State University Press.

Mann, Judith. (2005) 'The Myth of Artemisia as Chameleon: A New Look at the London *"Allegory of Painting"*'. In Judith Mann, ed., *Artemisia Gentileschi: Taking Stock*. Turnhout: Brepols Publishers, 51–77.

Mannoni, Laurent. (2000) *The Great Art of Light and Shadow: Archaeology of the Cinema*. Translated from the French by R. Crangle. Exeter: University of Exeter Press.

et al. (2004) *Eyes, Lies and Illusions: The Art of Deception*. Exhibition catalogue, London: Hayward Gallery, 7 October 2004–3 January 2005. London: Hayward Gallery Publishing.

Mansfield, Elizabeth. (2006) *Too Beautiful to Picture: Zeuxis, Myth, and Mimesis*. Minneapolis: University of Minnesota Press.

Mansfield, Lisa. (2016) *Representations of Renaissance Monarchy: Francis I and the Image-Makers*. Manchester: Manchester University Press.

Maral, Alexandre. (2007) 'Les statues antique'. In Jacques Thuillier et al., eds., *La Galerie des Glaces: Histoire et restauration*. Dijon: Editions Faton, 208–11.

(2009) 'Louis XIV et la sculpture'. In Nicolas Milovanovic & Alexandre Maral, eds., *Louis XIV: L'Homme & Le Roi*. Exhibition catalogue, Versailles: Château de Versailles, 20 October 2009–7 February 2010. Paris: Skira/Flammarion, 104–15.

Mariacher, Giovanni. (1967) *L'arte del vetro a Murano*. Venice: Arsenale.

Marías, Fernando. (1995) 'El genero de *Las Meninas*: Los servicios de la familia'. In Fernando Marías, et al., eds., *Otras Meninas*. Madrid: Siruela, 247–78.

(2003) 'Tiziano y Velàzquez, tópicos literarios y milagros del arte'. In Charles Hope et al., eds., *Tiziano*. Exhibition catalogue, Madrid: Prado Museum, 10 June–7 September 2003. New Haven, CT: Yale University Press, 111–32.

et al., eds. (1995) *Otras Meninas*. Madrid: Siruela.

Marin, Louis. (1977) *Détruire la peinture*. Paris: Éditions Galilée.

(1989) '"C'est moi que je peins . . .": Topiques et figures de l'énonciation'. *La part de l'oeil*, 5, 141–53.

(1994) 'Mimesis et description.' In Daniel Arasse et al., eds., *Sur la représentation*. Paris: Gallimard, 251–66.

(1999) 'Variations on an Absent Portrait: Poussin's Self-Portraits, 1649–50'. In *Sublime Poussin*. Translated from the French by C. Porter. Stanford, CA: Stanford University Press, 183–208.

Marinelli, Giovanni. (1562) *Ornamenti delle leggiadre donne*. Venice: Francesco de' Franceschi.

Marino, Giovanni Battista. (1620) *La Galeria*. Ancona: Cesare Scaccioppa.

Markovic, Daniel. (2020) 'The Mirror of Nature'. In Maria Gerolemou, ed., *Mirrors and Mirroring from Antiquity to the Early Modern Period*. Exeter: Exeter University Press, 119–26.

Marlier, Georges. (1954) *Erasme et la peinture Flamande de son temps*. Damme: Musée van Maerlant.

Marlowe, Christopher. (1604) *The Tragical History of Doctor Faustus*. London: John Wright.

Marolois, Samuel. (1614) *La perspective*. The Hague: Hondius.

(1625) *Opera mathematica ou Oeuvres mathematiques traictant de geometrie, perspective, architecture et fortification*. Amsterdam: Ian Ianssen.

Maroto, Pilar Silva. (2006) *Juan de Flandes*. Salamanca: Caja Duero.

Marrow, James H. (1983). '*In desen speigell*: A New Form of *Memento Mori* in Fifteenth Century Netherlandish Art'. In *Essays in Northern European Art Presented to Egbert Haverkamp-Begemann*. Groningen: Davaco, 154–63.

Marten, Bettina, & Roland Kanz, eds. (2016) *Carl Just und die Kunstgeschichte*. Frankfurt: Vervuert.

Martens, Maximiliaan. (2020a) *Het Lam Gods in Detail*. Ghent: Ludion.

(2020b) 'Jan van Eyck's Optical Revolution'. In Maximiliaan Martens et al., eds., *Jan van Eyck: An Optical Revolution*. Exhibition catalogue, Ghent: MSK, 1 February–12 March 2020. Ghent: MSK, 141–76.

et al., eds. (2020) *Van Eyck: An Optical Revolution*. Exhibition catalogue, Ghent: MSK, 1 February–12 March 2020. Ghent: MSK.

Martin, Meredith. (2015) 'Mirror Reflections: Louis XI, Phra Narai, and the Material Culture of Kingship'. *Art History*, special issue, 'Objects in Motion in the Early Modern World', ed. Daniella Bleichmar & Meredith Martin, 38(4), 652–67.

Martínez, Jusepe. (1866) *Discursos practicables del nobilísimo arte de la pintura* (ms. c. 1673), ed. Valentín Carderera. Madrid: Real Academia de San Fernando.

Martínez i Albero, Miquel. (2016) 'La imagen de la monarquía: Moda, espectáculos y política: Maria Teresa y Margarita Teresa de Austria en busca de un Nuevo Olimpo'. *Anales de Historia del Arte*, 26, 103–39.

Martínez Leiva, Gloria, & Angel Rodríguez Rebollo. (2015) *El inventario del Alcázar de Madrid de 1666: Felipe IV y su colección artistica*. Madrid: Consejo Superior de Investigaziones Cientificas.

Masheck, Joseph. (1991) 'Alberti's "Window": Art-Historiographic Notes on an Anti-modernist Misprision'. *Art Journal*, 50(1), 34–41.

Massey, Lyle. (2007) *Picturing Space, Displacing Bodies: Anamorphosis in Early Modern Theories of Perspective*. University Park: Penn State University Press.

Mattei, J.-F. (1996) *Platon et le miroir du mythe: De l'âge d'or à l'Atlantide*. Paris: Presse universitaire de France.

McCray, Patrick. (1999) *Glassmaking in Renaissance Venice: The Fragile Craft*. Aldershot: Ashgate.

McGrath, Elizabeth, et al. (2016) *Rubens: Mythological Subjects: Achilles to the Graces*. Volume 11 of Corpus Rubenianum Ludwig Burchard. Turnout: Harvey Miller Publ.

McHam, Sarah Blake. (2008) 'Reflections of Pliny in Giovanni Bellini's *Woman with a Mirror*'. *Artibus et Historiae*, 29(58), 167–71.

McKim-Smith, Gridley, Greta Anderson-Bergdoll, & Richard Newman, eds. (1988) *Examining Velazquez*. New Haven, CT: Yale University Press.

McNeil Kettering, Alison. (1997) 'Ter Borch's Ladies in Satin'. In Wayne Franits, ed., *Looking at Seventeenth-Century Dutch Art: Realism Reconsidered*. Cambridge: Cambridge University Press, 98–115.

(1998) *Gerard ter Borch en de Vrede van Munster*. Exhibition catalogue, The Hague: Mauritshuis, 3 July–11 October 1998. The Hague: Mauritshuis.

McTighe, Sheila. (1993) 'Perfect Deformity, Ideal Beauty, and the *Imaginaire* of Work: The Reception of Annibale Carracci's *Arti di Bologna* in 1646'. *Oxford Art Journal* 16(1), 75–91.

Meadow, Mark, & Bruce Robertson, eds. (2014) *The First Treatise on Museums: Samuel Quiccheberg's Inscriptiones of 1565*. Los Angeles: Getty Research Institute.

Meiss, Millard. (1945) 'Light as Form and Symbol in Some Fifteenth-Century Paintings'. *Art Bulletin*, 27, 175–81.

Melchior-Bonnet, Sabine. (2002) *The Mirror: A History*. Translated from the 1994 French by K. Jewett, preface by Jean Delumeau. London: Routledge.

Melion, Walter, & Bartholomeus Ramakers, eds. (2016) *Personification: Embodying Meaning and Emotion*. Leiden: Brill.

Ménestrier, C.-F. (1691) *La science de la noblesse, ou La nouvelle méthode du blazon*. Paris: Etienne Michallet.

Merlini, Valeria, & Daniela Storti, eds. (2010) *Donna allo Specchio: Tiziano a Milano*. Exhibition catalogue, Milan: Palazzo Marino, 3 December 2010–6 January 2012. Milan: Skira.

Mersenne, Marin. (1652) *La perspective curieuse du R. P. Niceron, avec l'optique et la catoptrique*. Paris: Veuve F. Langlois, dit Chartres.

Meulebroeck, Wendy, et al., eds. (2018) '800 Years of Fenestration History: Flat Glass and Windows in Federal Scientific Institutes'. In *Stained Glass in the 17th Century: Continuity, Invention, Twilight*, Corpus Vitrearum 29th International Colloquium, ed. Madeleine Manderyck, Isabelle Lecocq, Yvette Vanden Remden. Antwerp: Corpus Vitrearum, 169–72.

Meyers, Amy, & Therese O'Malley, eds. (2008) *The Art of Natural History: Illustrated Treatises and Botanical Paintings 1400–1850*. New Haven, CT: Yale University Press.

Michiel, Marcantonio ('Anonimo'). (1800) *Notizie d'opere del disegno*. Jacopo Morelli, ed. and publisher. Bassano.

Mieder, Wolfgang, ed. (2004) *The Netherlandish Proverbs: An International Symposium on the Pieter Brueg(h)els*. Supplement Series of Proverbium: Yearbook of International Proverb Scholarship, 16. Burlington: University of Vermont.

Miller, J. (1998) *On Reflection*. Exhibition catalogue, London: National Gallery, 1998. New Haven, CT: Yale University Press.

Milliot, Vincent. (1995) *Les cris de Paris ou le peuple travesty: Les representations des petits métiers parisien (XVIe–XVIIIe siècles)*. Paris: Publications de la Sorbonne.

Milovanovic, Nicolas, ed. (2005) *Les grands appartements de Versailles sous Louis XIV*. Paris: Editions RMN.

(2007) 'La Galerie des Glaces: Un décor exemplaire'. In Milovanovic, Nicholas & Alexander Maral, eds., *La Galerie des Glaces: Charles Le Brun maitre d'oeuvre*. Exhibition catalogue, Versaille: Château de Versailles, 24 September–16 December 2007. Paris: Édicion de la Réunion des Musées Nationaux, 14–19.

(2009) 'Le roi soleil'. In Nicolas Milovanovic & Alexandre Maral, eds., *Louis XIV: L'homme & le roi*. Exhibition catalogue, Versailles, 20 October 2009–7 February 2010. Paris: Skira/Flammarion, 179–84.

(2010) 'Les sciences dans les décors de Versailles'. In Béatrix Saule, ed., *Sciences et curiosités à la Cour de Versailles*. Exhibition catalogue, Versailles: Château de Versailles, 26 October 2010–27 February 2011. Paris: Editions RMN, 98–103.

Milovanovic, Nicholas, & Alexander Maral. (2007) *La Galerie des Glaces: Charles Le Brun maitre d'oeuvre*. Exhibition catalogue, Versaille: Château de Versailles, 24 September–16 December 2007. Paris: Édicion de la Réunion des Musées Nationaux.

Milovanovic, Nicolas, & Alexandre Maral, eds. (2009) *Louis XIV: L'homme et le roi*. Paris: Flammarion.

Milovanovic, Nicolas, & Nathalie Volle, eds. (2013) *La Galerie des Glaces apres sa restauration: Contexte et restitution*. Actes du colloque, Ecole du Louvre 2008. Paris: Ecole du Louvre.

Mino, Gabriele, Cristina Galassi, & Roberto Guerrini, eds. (2013) *L'iconologia di Cesare Ripa: Fonti letterarie e figurative dall'Antichita al Rinascimento*. Atti Convegno Internazionale di Studi, Certosa di Pontignano, 3–4 May 2012. Florence: Olschki.

Milton, John. (1644) *Aeropagitica*. London: for the Liberty of Unlicenc'd Printing.

(1674) *Paradise Lost*, 12 books. London: Samuel Simmons.

Mirami, Rafael. (1582) *Compendiosa introduttione alla prima parte della specularia, cioè della scienza de gli specchi*. Ferrara: Heirs of Francesco de' Rossi and Paolo Tortorino.

Mitchell Havelock, Christine. (1995) *The Aphrodite of Knidos and Her Successors*. Ann Arbor: University of Michigan Press.

Moffitt, John. (1983) 'Velazquez in the Alcazar in 1656: The Meaning of the *Mise-en-Scène* of *Las Meninas*'. *Art History*, 6, 271–301.

(1984) '"Più tondo che l'O di Giotto": Giotto, Vasari, and Rembrandt's Kenwood House Self-Portrait'. *Paragone: Arte*, 35(407), 63–70.

(2002) 'Capable of Infinite Extension: From the Arabic Interlace to Alberti's *velo* via Occam's razor'. *Source*, 21 (4), 25–35.

Monnas, Lisa. (2012) *Renaissance Velvets*. London: V&A Publishing.

Montagu, Jennifer. (1983) 'Velazquez Marginalia: His Slave Juan de Pareja and His Illegitimate Son Antonio'. *Burlington Magazine*, 125, 683–85.

Montaigne, Michel de. (1588) *Essais*, 3 books. Paris: Abel L'Angelier.

(1983) *Montaigne's Travel Journal, 1580–81* (1580–81), ed. Donald Frame. Translated from the French. San Francisco: North Point Press. https://archive.org/details/journalduvoyagedo1mont.

Montias, Michael J. (1990) 'Socio-economic Aspects of Netherlandish Art from the Fifteenth to the

Seventeenth Century: A Survey'. *Art Bulletin*, 72(3), 358–73.

Morán, Miguel. (2004) 'La Venus del Espejo'. In Fernando Checa Cremades, ed., *Velázquez, Rubens y Tiziano: Arte Barroco e Ideal Clásico*. Ciclo de Conferentias, Rome, May–June 2003. Rome: Sociedad Estatal para la Acción Cultural Exterior Conferencias, 43–67.

(2014) 'It Was an Astonishing Ending. Still, It Was an Ending'. In Javier Portús, ed., *Velazquez: Las Meninas and the Late Royal Portraits*. Exhibition catalogue, Madrid: Prado Museum, 8 October 2013–9 February 2014. Translated from the Spanish by W. Matthews and L. Suffield. London: Thames & Hudson, 75–91.

Morel, Philippe, ed. (2012) *Le miroir et l'éspace du prince dans l'art italien de la Renaissance*. Tours: Presses universitaires François-Rabelais de Tours.

Morera, Raphaël. (2010) 'Amener les eaux: Entre techniques, sciences, et politique'. In Béatrix Saule, ed., *Sciences et curiosités à la Cour de Versailles*. Exhibition catalogue, Versaille: Château de Versailles, 26 October 2010–27 February 2011. Paris: Editions RMN, 87–93.

Moss, Ann. (1999) *Printed Commonplace Books and the Structuring of Renaissance Thought*. Oxford: Clarendon Press.

Müller, Heidi A. (2007) *Good Housekeeping: A Domestic Ideal in Miniature. The Nuremberg Doll Houses of the 17th Century in the Germanisches Nationalmuseum*. Nürnberg: Germanisches Nationalmuseum.

Muller, Jeffrey M. (1981–82) 'The Perseus and Andromeda on Rubens's House'. *Simiolus*, 12(2–3), 131–46.

(1989) *The Artist as Collector*. Princeton, NJ: Princeton University Press.

Müller-Hofstede, Justus. (1984) '"Non saturator oculus visu": sur "Allegorie des Gesichts" von Peter Paul Rubens und Jan Brueghel d. A.'. In Herman Vekeman and Justus Müller-Hofstede, eds., *Wort und Bild in der Niederlandischen Kunst und Literatur des 16. und 17. Jahrhunderts*. Erfstadt: Lukassen Verlag, 243–89.

Munck, (de) Bert, et al. (2018) 'Clear Window Glass in the House Archives of Printer Families Plantin and Moretus in Antwerp'. In *Stained Glass in the 17th Century: Continuity, Invention, Twilight*, Corpus Vitrearum 29th International Colloquium, eds. Madeleine Manderyck, Isabelle Lecocq, & Yvette Vanden Remden. Antwerp: Corpus Vitrearum, 165–68.

Muraro Vaiani, Luisa. (1978) *Giambattista della Porta mago e scienziato*. Milan: Feltrinelli.

Murphy, Caroline. (2003) *Lavinia Fontana: A Painter and Her Patrons in Sixteenth-Century Bologna*. New Haven, CT: Yale University Press.

Murphy, Trevor. (2004) *Pliny the Elder's 'Natural History': The Empire in the Encyclopaedia*. Oxford: Oxford University Press.

Musacchio, Jacqueline Marie. (2008) *Art Marriage and Family in the Florentine Renaissance Palace*. New Haven, CT: Yale University Press.

Naftulin, Lawrence. (1971) 'A Note on the Iconography of the van der Paele Madonna'. *Oud Holland, Journal for Art in the Low Countries*, 86, 3–8.

Nakamura, Jun. (2020) 'Seeing Outside the Box: Reexamining the Top of Samuel van Hoogstraten's London Perspective Box'. *Journal of Historians of Netherlandish Art*, 12(2).

Nash, John. (1991) *Vermeer*. London: Scala; Amsterdam: Rijksmuseum Foundation.

Nash, Susie. (2004) *Northern Renaissance Art*. Oxford: Oxford University Press.

Neer, Richard. (2017) 'Was the Knidia a Statue? Art History and the Terms of Comparison'. In Jaś Elsner, ed., *Comparativism in Art History*. New York: Routledge, 145–64.

Neidhardt, Uta. (2019) 'The Restoration of "Young Woman Reading a Letter at an Open Window" by Johannes Vermeer: An Interim Report'. *The Burlington Magazine*, 161(1395), 452–63.

Nelson, Jennifer. (2019) *Disharmony of the Spheres: The Europe of Holbein's Ambassadors*. University Park: Penn State University Press.

Neri, Antonio. (1612) *L'arte vetraria distinta in sette libri*. Florence: Giunti.

Neri, Janice. (2008) 'Between Observation and Image: Representations of Insects in Robert Hooke's Micrographia'. In Amy Meyers & Therese O'Malley, eds., *The Art of Natural History: Illustrated Treatises and Botanical Paintings 1400–1850*. New Haven, CT: Yale University Press, 82–107.

Newbery, Timothy, et al. (1990) *Italian Renaissance Frames*. Exhibition catalogue, New York: Metropolitan Museum of Art, 5 June–2 September 1990. New York: Metropolitan Museum.

Newman, William R. (2018) *Newton the Alchemist: Science, Enigma, and the Quest for Nature's 'Secret Fire'*. Princeton, NJ: Princeton University Press.

Ng, Morgan. (2017) 'Toward a Cultural Ecology of Architectural Glass in Early Modern Europe'. *Art History*, 40(3), 496–525.

Ní Mheallaigh, Karen. (2020) 'Reflections on Lucian's Lunar Mirror: *Speculum lunae* and an Ancient Telescopic Fantasy'. In Maria Gerolemou, ed., *Mirrors and Mirroring from Antiquity to the Early Modern Period*. Exeter: Exeter University Press, 165–75.

Niceron, Jean-François. (1638) *La perspective curieuse, ou Magie artificielle des effets merveilleux*. Paris: Pierre Billaine.

Niceron, Jean-François, with Marin Mersenne. (1646) *Thaumaturgus opticus*. Paris: François Langlois.

Nicolson, Marjorie. (1948) *Voyages to the Moon*. New York: Macmillan.

Nocentini, Serena. (2010) 'Specchio delle mie brame: Segreti di bellezza al tempo di Tiziano'. In Valeria Merlini & Daniela Storti, eds., *Donna allo specchio: Tiziano a Milano*. Exhibition catalogue, Milan: Palazzo Marino, 3 December 2010–6 January 2012. Milan: Skira, 121–26.

Nordenfalk, Carl. (1985) 'The Five Senses in Late Medieval and Renaissance Art'. *Journal of the Warburg & Courtauld Institutes*, 48, 1–22.

North, John. (2002) *The Ambassadors' Secret: Holbein and the World of the Renaissance*. London: Hambledon.

Nova, Alessandro. (1997) *Velázquez, Foucault, e l'enigma della rappresentazione*. Milan: Saggiatore.

(2003) *Benvenuto Cellini: Kunst und Kunsttheorie im 16. Jahrhundert*. Cologne: Böhlau.

(2007 2011) *The Book of the Wind: The Representation of the Invisible*. Montreal: McGill-Queen's University Presses.

Noyes, Ruth. (2022) *Reassessing Epistemic Images in the Early Modern World*. Amsterdam: Amsterdam University Press.

O'Bryan, Robin. (2019) *Games and Game-Playing in European Art and Literature, 16th–17th Centuries*. Amsterdam: Amsterdam University Press.

Odierna, Giovanni (1644) *L'occhio della mosca*. Palermo: D. Cirillo.

Oettinger, April. (2015) 'Vision, *Voluptas*, and the Poetics of Water in Lorenzo Lotto's *Venus and Cupid*'. In Rose Marice & Alison C. Poe, eds., *Receptions of Antiquity, Constructions of Gender in European art, 1300–1600*. Leiden: Brill, 230–63.

Oliver, Lois, Fiona Healy, Ashok Roy, & Rachel Billinge. (2005) 'The Evolution of Rubens's Judgment of Paris'. *National Gallery Technical Bulletin*, 26, 4–22.

O'Malley, Michelle, & Evelyn Welch, eds. (2010) *The Material Renaissance*. Manchester: Manchester University Press.

Onians, John. (1978) 'Art History, *Kunstgeschichte* and *Historia*'. *Art History*, 1(2), 131–33.

Orso, N. Steven. (1986) *Philip IV and the Decoration of the Alcazar in Madrid*. Princeton, NJ: Princeton University Press.

Ottonelli, D. Giulio, with Pietro Berrettini da Cortona. (1973) *Trattato della Pittura e Scultura: Uso et abuso loro* (1652). Reprint. Treviso: Canova Editore.

Ovid, *Amores*.

(1986) *Metamorphoses*. Translated by A. D. Melville. Oxford: Oxford University Press.

Pacheco, Francisco. (1649) *El arte de la peintura*. Seville: Simon Faxardo.

(2018) *Lives of Velázquez*. Translated by Nina Mallory. Los Angeles: J. Paul Getty Museum.

Padron, Mercedes, Matias Diaz, & Royo Villanova, eds. (1992) *David Teniers, Jan Brueghel y los gabinetes de pinturas*. Exhibition catalogue, Madrid: Museo del Prado, 1992. Madrid: Museo Nacional del Prado.

Page, Jutta-Annette. (2006) *The Art of Glass*. Toledo: Toledo Museum of Art.

Palatino, Giovambattista. (1540) *Libro nuovo d'imparare a scrivere*. Rome: Baldassare di Francesco Cartolari.

Palomino, Antonio de Castro y Velasco. (1795) *El museo pictórico y escala óptica* (1715–24), 3 vols. Vol. 3: *El parnaso español pittoresco laureado con las vidas de los pintores y estatuarios eminentes españoles*. Madrid: Sancha.

(1987) *Lives, of the Eminent Spanish Painters and Sculptors* (1724). Translated from the Spanish by A. Mallory. Cambridge: Cambridge University Press.

Panhans-Bühler, Ursula. (1978) *Eklektizismus und Originalität im Werk des Petrus Christus*. Vienna: Holzhausen.

Panofsky, Erwin. (1915) *Dürers Kunsttheorie: Vornehmlich in ihrem Verhältnis zur Kunsttheorie der Italianer*. Berlin: G. Reimer.

(1924) *Idea. Ein Beitrag zur Begriffsgeschichte der älteren Kunsttheorie*. Studien der Bibliothek Warburg, 5. Leipzig: B. G. Teubner.

(1934) 'Jan van Eyck's Arnolfini Portrait'. *Burlington Magazine*, 64, 117–27.

(1943) *The Life and Art of Albrecht Dürer*. Princeton, NJ: Princeton University Press.

(1953) *Early Netherlandish Painting: Its Origins and Character*, 2 vols. Cambridge, MA: Harvard University Press.

(1954) *Galileo as Critic of the Arts*. The Hague: Martinus Nijhoff.

(1956) 'More on Galileo and the Arts'. *Isis*, 47, 3–15.

(1968) *Idea: A Concept in Art Theory*. Columbia: University of South Carolina Press.

(1991) *Perspective as Symbolic Form* (1927). Translated from the German by C. S. Wood. Reprint. New York: Zone Books.

Paoli, Marco. (2012) 'Firenze e Bruges nel XV secolo: Un matrimonio di interesse'. *Art e dossier*, 27, 62–67.

Paravicini Bagliani, Agostino, ed. (2021) *Arabic and Latin Theory of Perspective*. Florence: Sismel.

Pardo, Mary. (1997) 'Veiling the Venus of Urbino'. In Rona Goffen, ed., *Titian's 'Venus of Urbino'*. Cambridge: Cambridge University Press, 108–28.

Paris Bordon e il Suo Tempo. (1987) Atti del Convegno Internazionale di Studi, Treviso, 28–30 October 1985. Treviso: Canova.

Pascal, Blaise. (1670) *Pensées*. Paris: Guillaume Desprez.

Passamani, Buno, ed. (1990) *Giovanni Gerolamo Savoldo tra Fotta, Giorgione e Caravaggio*. Exhibition catalogue, Brescia: Monastero di Santa Giulia, 3 March–31 May 1990; and Schirn Kunsthalle, Frankfurt, 8 June–3 September 1990. Milan: Electa.

Passeri, Irma. (2014) 'Gold Coins and Gold Leaf in Early Italian Paintings'. In Christy Anderson, Anne Dunlop, & Pamela H. Smith, eds., *The Matter of Art: Materials, Practices, Cultural Logics, c. 1250–1750*. Manchester: Manchester University Press, 97–117.

Pastoureau, Michel. (2009) *L'Art héraldique au Moyen Age*. Paris: Seuil.

(2013) *Vert: Histoire d'une couleur*. Paris: Seuil.

Pastoureau, Michel, & Elisabeth Taburet-Delahaye. (2013) *Les secrets de la licorne*. Paris: Réunion des Musées Nationaux.

Paviot, Jacques. (1990) 'La vie de Jan van Eyck selon les documents écrits'. *Revue des archaéologies et historiens d'art de Louvain* 23, 83–93.

Payne, Alina, ed. (2015) *Vision and Its Instruments: Art, Science, and Technology in Early Modern European Art*. University Park: Penn State University Press.

Peacock, John. (2021) *Picturing Courtiers and Nobles from Castiglione to van Dyck: Self-Representation by Early Modern Elites*. New York: Routledge Taylor & Francis.

Pendergrast, Mark. (2003) *Mirror: A History of the Human Love Affair with Reflection*. New York: Basic Books.

Penny, Nicholas, & Francis Haskell. (1981) *Taste and the Antique*. New Haven, CT: Yale University Press.

Pereda, Felipe. (2010) 'The Invisible? New World'. *The Art Bulletin*, 92(1–2), 47–52.

Pérez-Gómez, Alberto, & Louise Pelletier. (1995) *Anamorphosis: An Annotated Bibliography*. Montreal: McGill University Libraries.

Pericolo, Lorenzo. (2009) 'Love in the Mirror: A Comparative Reading of Titian's *Woman at Her Toilet* and Caravaggio's *Conversion of Mary Magdalene*'. *I Tatti Studies*, 12, 149–79.

(2015) 'What Is Metapainting? The Self-Aware Image Twenty Years Later'. In Victor Stoichita, ed., *The Self-Aware Image: An Insight into Early Modern Metapainting*. Translated by Anne-Marie Glasheen & Lorenzo Pericolo. Turnhout: Brepols-Harvey Miller, 11–32.

Perkinson, Stephen, ed. (2017) *The Ivory Mirror: The Art of Mortality in Renaissance Europe*. Exhibition catalogue, Brunswick, ME: Bowdoin College Museum of Art, 24 June–26 November 2017. New Haven, CT: Yale University Press.

Pérouse de Montclos, Jean-Marie. (1991) *Versailles*. Paris: Editions Mengès.

Perrault, Charles. (1981) *Contes: Suivis du le miroir, óu la métamorphose d'Orante, de la oeinture, poème, et du labyrinthe de Versailles* (1661). Grenoble: Jean Pierre Collinet. Reprint, Collection Folio 1281, Paris: Gallimard.

Petrarca, Francesco, Gianfranco Contini, & Daniele Ponchiroli, eds. (1964) *Canzoniere*. Torino: Einaudi.

Pfisterer, Ulrich. (2001) 'Künstlerliebe: Der Narcissus-Mythos bei Leon Battista Alberti und die Aristoteles-Lektüre der Frührenaissance'. *Zeitschrift für Kunstgeschichte*, 64(308), 324–28.

Philippe, Michel. (1998) *Naissance de la verrerie moderne XII–XVI siècles: Aspects économiques, techniques, et humains*. Turnhout: Brepols.

Philostratus (2022) *Imagines*. Translated by Arthur Fairbanks, LOEB 1931. Cambridge, MA: Harvard University Press.

Pierre de Saint-Louis. (1668) *La Madeleine*. Lyon: Jean Grégoire.

Piganiol de La Force, Jean-Aymar. (1701) *Nouvelle description des châteaux et parcs de Versailles et de Marly*. Paris: F. et P. Delaulne

Pilliod, Elizabeth. (2001) *Pontormo Bronzino Allori: A Genealogy of Florentine Art*. New Haven, CT: Yale University Press.

Pino, Paolo. (1548) *Dialogo di pittura di Messer Paolo Pino, nuovamente dato in Luce con Privilegio*. Venice: Pauolo Gherardo.

Pinto, Olga. (1971) *Nuptialia: Saggio di bibliografia di scritti italiani pubblicati per nozze dal 1484 al 1799*. Florence: Olschki.

Pisot, Sandra, ed. (2007) *Die Poesie der Venezianischen Malerei: Paris Bordone, Palma il Vecchio, Lorenzo Lotto, Tizian*. Conference publication. Munich: Hirmer.

et al., eds. (2017) *Die Poesie der Venezianischen Malerei: Paris Bordone, Palma il Vecchio, Lorenzo Lotto, Tizian*. Exhibition catalogue, Hamburg: Hamburger Kunsthalle, 24 February–21 May 2017. Munich: Hirmer Verlag; Hamburg: Hamburger Kunsthalle.

Pita Andrade, J. Manuel. (1952) 'Los Quadros di Velàzquez y Mazo que Poseyó el Séptimo Marquès del Carpio'. *Archivio Español de Arte*, 25, 223–26.

Pizzorusso, Claudio. (1982) *Ricerche su Cristofano Allori*. Florence: Olschki.

Plato. (1955) *Plato in Twelve Volumes*. Translated from the Greek by W. R. M. Lamb. Cambridge, MA: Harvard University Press.

(1986) *Alcibiades*, trans. W. R. M. Lamb. **Cambridge, MA**: Harvard University Press (LOEB).

Pliny the Elder. (1469) *Naturalis historia*. Venice: Johannes de Spira.

Plotinus. (2015) *Ennead*, trans. A. H. Armstrong. **Cambridge, MA**: Harvard University Press (LOEB).

Plutarch. (1914) *Lives*, III, *Life of Pericles*, trans. Bernadotte Perrin. **Cambridge, MA**: Harvard University Press (LOEB).

Pointon, Marcia. (2010) *Brilliant Effects: A Cultural History of Gem Stones and Jewellery*. New Haven, CT: Yale University Press.

Pollet, Christophe. (2001) *Les gravures d'Etienne Delaune (1518–1583)*. Villeneuve d'Ascq: Presses universitaires du Septentrion.

Pollitt, J. J. (1990) *The Art of Ancient Greece: Sources and Documents*. Cambridge: Cambridge University Press.

Pomian, Krzysztof. (1982) 'Collection-Microcosme et la culture de la curiosité. In Istituto Nazionale di Studi sul Rinascimento. *Scienze, Credenze Occulte, Livelli di Cultura*, Convegno internazionale di studi, Florence, 26–30 June 1980. Florence: Olschki, 535–57.

(1987) *Collectioneurs, amateurs et curieux: Paris-Venise XVIe–XVIIIe siècle*. Paris: Gallimard.

Pommier, Edouard. (1998) *Théories du portraits: De la Renaissance aux lumières*. Paris: Gallimard.

Pon, Lisa. (2004) *Raphael, Dürer, and Marcantonio Raimondi: Copying and the Italian Renaissance Print*. New Haven, CT: Yale University Press.

Porter, James, & Mark Buchan, eds. (2004) 'Before Subjectivity? Lacan and the Classics'. Special double issue. *Helios*, 31.

Portús, Javier, ed. (2014) *Velazquez: Las Meninas and the Late Royal Portraits*. Exhibition catalogue, Madrid: Prado Museum, 8 October 2013–9 February 2014. Translated from the Spanish by W. Matthews and L. Suffield. London: Thames & Hudson.

(2017a) *Meta Pintura: Un viaje a la idea del arte en España*. Exhibition catalogue, Madrid: Prado Museum, 15 November 2016–19 February 2017. Madrid: Museo Nacional del Prado.

(2017b) 'Heresy, Judaism, and Paganism in the Hall of Realms'. In Giles Knox & Tanya Tiffany, eds., *Velazquez Re-examined: Theory, History, Poetry, and Theatre*. Turnhout: Brepols, 103–20.

ed. (2018) *Velázquez: Su mundo y el maestro: Estudios dispersos*. Madrid: CEEH.

(2020) 'The Artistic Legacy of Titian's *Poesie*'. In Matthias Wivel, ed., *Titian: Love, Desire, Death*. Exhibition catalogue, London: National Gallery, 2 December 2020–17 January 2021. London: National Gallery, 91–102.

et al. (2018) *Velázquez y el siglo de oro*. Exhibition catalogue, Barcelona: CaixaForum, 16 November 2008–3 March 2009. Madrid: Madrid: Museo Nacional del Prado.

Potolsky, M. (2006) *Mimesis*. New York: Routledge.

Poulain, Hugues. (2010) *Les menuiseries de fenêtres: Du moyen age à la révolution industrielle*. Ballan Miré: Unithèque L'àpart Editions.

Prater, Andreas. (2002) *Venus at Her Mirror: Velazquez and the Art of Nude Painting*. Munich: Prestel.

Preimesberger, Rudolf. (2011) 'On Jan van Eyck's Diptych in the Thyssen-Bornemisza Collection' (1991). Reprint. In *Paragons and Paragone: Van Eyck, Raphael, Michelangelo, Caravaggio, Bernini*. Los Angeles: Getty Research Institute, 23–53.

Prinz, Wolfram. (1971) *Die Sammlung der Selbstbildnisse in den Uffizien*. Italienische Forschungen Folge 3, Bd. 5, vol. 1, *Geschichte der Sammlung*. Berlin: Mann.

(2006) *Galleria: Storia di uno spazio architectonico*, Modena: Panini.

Pullins, David. (2014) 'Techniques of the Body: Viewing the Arts and Métiers of France from the Workshop of Nicolas I and Nicolas II de Larmessin'. *Oxford Art Journal*, 37(2), 135–55.

Puppi, Lionello, ed. (2012) *Tiziano: L'epistolario*. Florence: Alinari.

Puppi, Lionello, & Serena Baccaglini. (2016) *Tiziano vanitas: Il poeta dell'immagine e l'ombra della bellezza*. Milan: Silvana.

Purrington, Robert. (2009) *The First Professional Scientist: Robert Hooke and the Royal Society of London*. Basel: Birkhäuser.

Purtle, Carol. (1982) *The Marian Paintings of Jan van Eyck*. Princeton, NJ: Princeton University Press.

Puttenham, George. (1968) *The Arte of English Poesie* (1589). Facsimile ed. Menston: Scolar Press.

Puttfarken, Thomas. (2005) *Titian and Tragic Painting: Aristotle's Poetics and the Rise of the Modern Artist*. New Haven, CT: Yale University Press.

Quevedo, Francisco de. (1670, posthumous) *Las tres musas últimas castellanas*. Madrid: Imprenta Real.

(1958) *Providencia de Dios* (1641–42), ed. Raimundo Lida. Mexico City: Fondo de Cultura.

Quiccheberg, Samuel. (1565) *Inscriptiones vel tituli theatri amplissimi*. Munich: Ex Officina Adami Berg typographi.

Ramsay, Nigel. (2022) 'Regulating Heraldry and Insignia: The Treatise *De insigniis et armis* of Bartolo da Sasso'. In Naïma Ghermani & Caroline Michel D'Annoville, eds., *Image et droit*. Rome: Collection de l'Ecole Française de Rome, 115–29.

Rank, Otto. (1971) *The Double: A Psychoanalytic Study*. Translated from the 1925 German by H. Tucker. Chapel Hill: University of North Carolina.

Rasmussen, Mary. (1995) 'The Case of the Flutes in Holbein's *The Ambassadors*'. *Early Music*, 23(1), 114–23.

Rave, Paul Ortwin. (1960) 'Das Selbstbildnis des Johannes Gumpp in den Uffizien'. *Pantheon*, 18, 28–31.

Razzall, Rosie. (2017) *Canaletto and the Art of Venice*. Exhibition catalogue, London: Royal Collection Trust, 19 May–12 November 2017. London: Royal Collection Publications.

(2019) '"What Lies Beneath": Infrared Reflectance Imaging of Canaletto's Drawings'. *Master Drawings*, 57(1).

Reeves, Eileen. (1997) *Painting the Heavens: Art and Science in the Age of Galileo*. Princeton, NJ: Princeton University Press.

(2008) *Galileo's Glassworks: The Telescope and the Mirror*. Cambridge, MA: Harvard University Press.

Reeves, Eileen, & Albert van Helden. (2010) *On Sunspots: Galileo Galilei & Christoph Scheiner*. Chicago: University of Chicago Press.

Renaudot, Théophraste, ed. (1631–53) *Gazette de France*. Paris.

Revel, Emmanuel. (1997) *L'autoportrait de Nicolas Poussin*. Paris: Musée du Louvre.

Rice, F. Eugene, Jr. (1958) *The Renaissance Idea of Wisdom*. Cambridge, MA: Harvard University Press.

Richards, Jennifer. (2001) 'Assumed Simplicity and the Critique of Nobility, or How Castiglione Read Cicero'. *Renaissance Quarterly*, 54(2, Summer), 460–86.

Ridolfi, Carlo. (1648) *Le meraviglie dell'arte*, 2 vols. Venice: Giovan Battista Sgava.

Riegl, Alois. (1902, 1999] *The Group Portraiture of Holland*. Translated from the German by Evelyn M. Kain and David Britt with introduction by W. Kemp. Los Angeles: Getty Research Center.

Riehl, Anna. (2010) *The Face of Queenship: Early Modern Representations of Elizabeth I*. New York: Palgrave Macmillan.

Rima, Beatrice. (2012) 'L'idea della pittura e la galleria degli specchi'. *Letteratura & Arte*, 10, 65–106.

Ringbom, Sixton. (1965) *Icon to Narrative. The Rise of the Dramatic Close-Up in Fifteenth-Century Devotional Painting*. Doornspijk: Davaco. Abo: Abo Academi.

Ringhieri, Innocentio. (1551) *Cento Giuochi Liberali, et d'Ingegno, nouellamente da M. Innocentio Ringhieri gentihuomo bolognese ritrovati*. Bologna: Anselmo Giaccarelli.

Ripa, Cesare. (1603) *Iconologia* (1593). Rome: Lepido Facij.

Rittgers, Ronald. (2012) *The Reformation of Suffering: Pastoral Theology and Lay Piety in Late Medieval and Early Modern Germany*. Oxford: Oxford University Press.

Roche, Serge, with Germain Courage & Pierre Devinoy. (1956) *Mirrors*. New York: Rizzoli. Translation 1985.

Rodler, Hieronymous, with Count Johann II von Simmern. (1970) *Eyn schön nützlich büchlin und underweisung der Kunst des Messens mit dem Zirkel, Richtscheidt oder Linial* (1531). Facsimile, ed. Trude Hedrian. Simmern: Hieronymous Rodler; Graz: Akademische Druck- und Verlagsanstalt.

Roelofs, Pieter, & Gregor Weber, eds. (2023) *Vermeer*. Exhibition catalogue, Rijksmuseum, 10 February–4 June 2023. London: Thames & Hudson.

Rogers, Mary, ed. (2020) *Fashioning Identities in Renaissance Art*. Aldershot: Ashgate. Ebook: London: Routledge.

Róheim, Géza. (1984) 'Magic Mirror' (1919). In Kinskő Verebély, *Selection from the Works of Géza Róheim*. Budapest: Magvető, 127–252.

Rohlmann, M. (1991) 'Im Sturm der Wogen und Geschäfte: Die Florentiner Auftraggeber von Hans Memlings Danziger "Weltgericht"'. *Frankfurter Allgemeine Zeitung*, 6 July.

Rohou, Julie, et al. (2019) *Etienne Delaune et les arts décoratifs: Graver la Renaissance*. Exhibition catalogue, Écouen, Paris: Musée national de la Renaissance, 16 October 2019–3 February 2020. Paris: Musée National de la Renaissance Ecouen and Editions RMN.

Rojewska, Oskar Jacek. (2021)*Los valets de chambre de los duques de Borgoña y sus tareas artísticas (1419–1477)*. Castelló de la Plana: Universitat Jaume I.

Rolet, Anne, & Stéphane Rolet, eds. (2013) *André Alciat: Un Humaniste au confluent des savoirs dans l'Europe de la Renaissance*. Etudes renaissantes. Turnhout: Brepols.

Roman d'Elia, Una. (2006) 'Niccolò Liburnio on the Boundaries of Portraiture in the Early Cinquecento'. *The Sixteenth Century Journal*, 37, 323–50.

Romano, Ruggiero. (2006) 'Una certa idea dell' "industria" nello studiolo di Francesco I de' Medici a Firenze'. In François Livi & Carlo Ossola, eds., *De Florence à Venise: Etudes en l'honneur de Christian Bec*. Paris: Presses de l'Université Paris-Sorbonne, 379–89.

Rombouts, Philippe-Félix, & Théodore van Lerius, eds. (1961) *De Liggeren der Antwerpsche Sint-Lucasgilde* (1864), 2 vols. Reprint. Amsterdam: Israël.

Ronchi, Vasco. (1970) *The Nature of Light: An Historical Survey*. Revised and translated from the Italian by V. Barocas. London: Heinemann.

Ronchi, Vasco, with Maria Naldini. (1962) *De telescopio: Giovan Battista della Porta*. Florence: Leo S. Olschki.

Rorty, Richard. (1979) *Philosophy and the Mirror of Nature*. Princeton, NJ: Princeton University Press.

Rosen, Edward. (1947) *The Naming of the Telescope*. New York: H. Schuman.

(1950) 'The Title of Galileo's Sidereus Nuncius'. *Isis*, 41 (3, December), 287–89.

Rosen, Valeska von. (2020) 'The Galleria degli Autoritratti in the Uffizi'. *Imagines*, 3, 156–69.

Rosenfeld, Myra Nan. (2003) 'From Bologna to Venice and Paris: The Evolution and Publication of Sebastiano Serlio's Books I and II, On Geometry and On Perspective, for Architects'. In Lyle Massey, ed., *The Treatise on Perspective, Published and Unpublished CASVA Symposium Papers XXXVI*. Washington, DC: National Gallery of Art, 281–322.

Rosenthal, Lisa. (2005) *Gender Politics and Allegory in the Art of Rubens*. Cambridge: Cambridge University Press.

Roskam, Geert, & Stefan Schorn, eds. (2018) *Concepts of Ideal Rulership from Antiquity to the Renaissance*. Turnhout: Brepols.

Roskill, Mark, ed. (1968) *Dolce's Aretino and Venetian Art Theory of the Cinquecento*. New York: CAA and New York University Press.

Rossi, Francesco. (1984) 'Armi e Cronologia in Gian Gerolamo Savoldo'. In Gaetano Panazza, ed., *Giovanni Gerolamo Savoldo Pittore Bresciano (Atti del Convegno Brescia 1983)*. Brescia: Ateneo di Brescia, 99–108.

Rossi, Paolo. (2009) *Francis Bacon: From Magic to Science* (1957). Reprint. London: Routledge.

Rothstein, Bret L. (2005) *Sight and Spirituality in Early Netherlandish Painting*. Cambridge: Cambridge University Press.

Rotman, Brian. (1987) *Signifying Nothing: The Semiotics of Zero*. Stanford CA: Stanford University Press.

Rowland, Ingrid D. (2000) *The Ecstatic Journey: Athanasius Kircher in Baroque Rome*. Exhibition catalogue, University of Chicago, Regenstein Library: Department of Special Collections, 1 February–1 April 2000. Chicago: University of Chicago Special Collections.

Rowley, Neville, ed. (2023) *Giovanni Bellini: Influences croisées*. Exhibition catalogue, Paris: Musée Jacquemart-André Paris, 3 March–17 July 2023. Brussells: Fonds Mercator.

Roy, Ashok, & Raymond White. (2000) 'Van Eyck's Technique: The Myth and the Reality (I & II)'. In Susan Foister, Sue Jones, & Delphine Cool, eds., *Investigating Jan Van Eyck*. Turnhout: Brepols, 97–106.

Rubin, Patricia Lee (2007a) *Images and Identity in Fifteenth-Century Florence*. New Haven, CT: Yale University Press.

(2007b) *Portraits by the Artist as a Young Man: Parmigianino ca. 1524*. Groningen: Gerson Lectures Foundation.

Ruby, Sigrid. (2007) 'Diane de Poitiers: Veuve et Favorite'. In Kathleen Wilson-Chevalier, ed., *Patronnes et mécènes en France à la Renaissance*. Saint-Etienne: Publications de l'Université de Saint-Etienne, 381–99.

(2017a) *Mit Macht Verbunden: Bilder der Favoritin im Frankreich der Renaissance*. Heidelberg: Universitätsbibliothek Heidelberg.

(2017b) 'Macht und Ohnmacht des Privaten: Die Gemälde der "Dames au Bain"'. In Kristina Deutsch et al., eds., *Höfische Bäder in der Frühen Neuzeit*. Berlin: De Gruyter, 204–25.

Ruestow, Edward. (1996) *The Microscope in the Dutch Republic: The Shaping of Discovery*. Cambridge: Cambridge University Press.

Ruffino, Alessandra, & Frederick Tristan. (2013) *Vanitas vs Veritas: Caravaggio, il Liuto, la Caraffa e altri Disincanti*. Turin: Allemandi.

Ruiz Gomez, Leticia (2019) *A Tale of Two Women Painters: Sofonisba Anguissola & Lavinia Fontana*. Exhibition catalogue, Madrid: Museo del Prado 22 October 2019–2 February 2020. Madrid: Prado Museum.

Russell, Malcolm. (2017) 'The Woodworker and the Redemption: The Right Shutter of the Mérode Triptych', *Simiolus*, 39(4), 335–50.

Sabellicus, Marcantonio. (1560) *Opera Omnia*, 4 books. Basel: Herwagen.

Saffioti, Tito. (2009) *Gli occhi della follia, giullari e buffoni di corte nella storia e nell'arte*. Milan: Booktime.

(2021) *Mostri graziosi e belli: I nani di corte nella storia e nell'arte*. Rimini: Bookstones.

Sales, François de. (1616) *Traité sur l'amour de Dieu*. Lyon: Pierre Rigaud.

Salmon, Dimitri, & Andrés Ubeda de los Cobos, eds. (2016) *Georges de la Tour*. Exhibition catalogue, Madrid: Prado Museum, 23 February–12 June 2016. Madrid: Museo Nacional del Prado.

Salomon, Nanette. (1983) 'Vermeer and the Balance of Destiny'. In Anne-Marie Logan, ed., *Essays in Northern European Art Presented to Egbert Haverkamp Begemann on His Sixtieth Birthday*. Doornspijk: Davaco, 216–21.

(1996) 'The Venus Pudica: Uncovering Art History's "Hidden Agendas" and Pernicious Pedigrees'. In Griselda Pollock, ed., *Generations and Geographies in the Visual Arts: Feminist Readings*. New York: Routledge, 69–87.

(1998) 'From Sexuality to Civility: Vermeer's Women.' In Ivan Gaskell & Michiel Jonker, eds., *Vermeer Studies*. Studies in the History of Art, Washington, DC, National Gallery of Art, 55, XXXIII. New Haven, CT: Yale University Press, 309–25.

Salomon, Xavier. (2011) *Le Siam à Fontainebleau: L'ambassade du 27 juin 1861*. Exhibition catalogue, Fontainbleau: Chateau de Fontainebleau, 5 November 2011–27 February 2012. Paris: Flammarion.

(2014) *Paolo Veronese*. Exhibition catalogue, London: National Gallery, 5 July–5 October 2014. London: National Gallery.

Samuel, E. R. (1963) 'Death in the Glass: A New View of Holbein's *Ambassadors*'. *Burlington Magazine*, 105 (October), 436–41.

Sanchez Canton, Francisco Javier. (1925) 'La libreria de Velázquez'. In *Homenaje ofrecido a Menéndez Pidal; Miscelánea de Estudios Lingüísticos, Literarios e Históricos*, 3 vols. Madrid: Hernando.

Sanchez Canton, Javier. (1942) 'Como vivá Velazquez: Inventario discubierto por d.f. Rodriquez Marin'. *Archivo español de arte*, 11, 69–91.

(1943) *Las Meninas y sus personajes*. Barcelona: Juventud.

Sanchez Canton, Javier. (1960) 'Inventario de los bienes que dejaron a su muerte D. Diego de Silva Velázquez y su mujer Da. Juana Pacheco'. In *Varia Velazqueña*, 2 vols. Madrid: Ministerio de Educaciòn Nacional.

Sanguineti, Daniele, ed. (2017) *Domenico Piola: Percorsi di pittura barocca*. Exhibition catalogue, Palazzo Lomellino Genoa, 13 October 2017–7 January 2018. Genoa: Sagep.

ed. (2019) *Domenico Piola e la sua bottega*. Genoa: Sagep.

Sanson, Helena, & Francesco Lucioli. (2016) *Conduct Liiterature for and about Women in Italy 1470–1900: Prescribing and Describing Life*. Paris: Classiques Garnier.

Saule, Béatrix. (2007) 'La galerie au temps de Louis XIV: De l'ordinaire à l'extraordinaire'. in *La Galerie des Glace: Histoire et restauration*. Dijon: Editions Faton, 54–73.

(2010) 'Versailles, lieu de sciences?'. In Béatrix Saule & Catherine Arminjon, eds., *Sciences et curiosités à la Cour de Versailles*. Exhibition catalogue, Versaille: Château de Versailles, 26 October 2010–27 February 2011. Paris: Editions RMN, 19–27.

(2013) 'Le mobilier d'argent dans la grande Galerie de Versailles'. Nicolas Milovanovic & Nathalie Volle, eds., *La Galerie des Glaces après sa restauration: Contexte et restitution*, XXVI Rencontres de l'Ecole du Louvre, June 2013. Paris: Ecole du Louvre, 49–60.

Saule, Béatrix, & Catherine Arminjon, eds. (2010) *Sciences et curiosités à la Cour de Versailles*. Exhibition catalogue, Versaille: Château de Versailles, 26 October 2010–27 February 2011. Paris: Editions RMN.

Scarisbrick, Diana. (1995) *Tudor and Jacobean Jewellery*. London: Tate Publishing.

(2007) *Brilliant Europe: Jewels from European Courts*. Brussels: Mercator.

Scarron, Paul. (1651) *Roman comique*, 3 vols. Paris: Touissant Quinet.

Scève, Maurice. (1544) *Délie*. Lyons,: Sulpice Sabon for Antoine Constantin.

(1562) *Microcosme*. Lyons: Ian de Tovrnes.

Schabacker, H. Peter. (1974) *Petrus Christus*. Utrecht: Haentjens Dekker & Gumbert.

Schama, Simon. (1987) *The Embarassment of Riches: An Interpretation of Dutch Culture in the Golden Age*. New York: Alfred Knopf.

Scheiner, Christoph. (1612) *Tres epistolae de maculis solaribus scriptae ad Marcum Welserum*. Augsburg: Augustae Vindelicorum Ad insigne pinus.

(1619) *Oculus hoc est*. Innsbruck: Daniel Bauer.

(1630) *Rosa Ursina sive Sol*. Bracciano: Andreas Phaeus at the Ducal Press.

Scheller, Robert. (1968) 'Als Ich Can'. *Oud Holland*, 83, 135–39.

Schickore, Jutta. (2007) *The Microscope and the Eye: A History of Reflections, 1740–1870*. Chicago: University of Chicago Press.

Schmarsow, August. (1924) *Hubert und Jan van Eyck*. Leipzig: K. W. Hiersemann.

Schneider, Laurie, ed. (1985) *Source: Notes in the History of Art*, special issue on mirrors, 2(3).

(1990) 'Leon Battista Alberti: Some Biographical Implications of the Winged Eye'. *Art Bulletin*, 72, 261–70.

Schneider, Wolfgang Christian. (2012) 'Reflection as an Object of Vision in the Ghent Altarpiece'. In Marc de Mey with Maximiliaan Martens & Cyriel Stroo, eds., *Vision & Material: Interaction between Art and Science in Jan van Eyck's Time*. Brussels: KVAB Press, 171–82.

Schoeser, Mary. (2007) *Silk*. New Haven, CT: Yale University Press.

Schott, Gaspar. (1657–59) *Magia universalis naturae et artis*, 4 vols. Würzburg: Heinrich Pigrin [Part I] Jobus Hertz [Parts II–III] for the Heirs of Johann Gottfried Schönwetter, Frankfurt.

Schott. Gaspar. (1659) *Thaumaturgis Physicus sive Magia Universalis*, 4 vols. Herbipoli [Frankfurt]: Joannis Godefridi Schönwetteri.

Schrader, Stephanie. (2010) 'Gossart's Mythological Nudes and the Shaping of Philip of Burgundy's Erotic Identity'. In Maryan Ainsworth et al., eds., *Man, Myth, and Sensual Pleasures: Jan Gossart's Renaissance*. Exhibition catalogue, New York: Metropolitan Museum of Art, 6 October 2010–17 January 2011; London: National Gallery, 23 February–30 May 2011] New Haven, CT: Yale University Press, 57–67.

Schröder, Eberhard. (1980) *Dürer, Kunst, und Geometrie: Dürers künstlerisches Schaffen aus der Sicht seiner 'Underweysung'*. Basel: Birkhäuser.

Schupbach, William. (2017) 'Some Cabinets of Curiosities within European Academic Institutions'. In O. R. Impey & Arthur MacGregor, eds., *The Origins of Museums: The Cabinet of Curiosities in Sixteenth- and Seventeenth-Century Europe*. Oxford: Ashmolean, 169–178.

Schütt, Friederike. (2021) *Quentin Massys: Bildstrategien der Affekterzeugung*, Petersburg: Michael Imhoff.

Schwartz, S. Heinrich. (1959) 'The Mirror of the Artist and the Mirror of the Devout: Observations on Some Paintings, Drawings, and Prints of the Fifteenth Century'. In *Studies in the History of Art Dedicated to William E Suida on His Eightieth Birthday*. Samuel H. Kress Foundation. London: Phaidon Press, 90–105.

(1966) 'Vermeer and the *Camera Obscura*'. *Pantheon*, 46, 170–82.

Schwendter, Daniel. (1636) *Deliciae physico-mathematicae*. Nuremberg: Jeremias Dümler.

Scott, Katie. (2013) 'Edme Bouchardon's 'Cris de Paris': Crying Food in Early Modern Paris'. *Word & Image*, 29(1), 59–91.

Scott, Philippa. (1993) *The Book of Silk*. London: Thames & Hudson.

Scoville, Warren. (2008) *Capitalism and French Glassmaking 1640–1789* (1950). Berkeley: University of California Press.

Scudéry, Madeleine de. (1684) 'Conversation de la magnificence et de la magnanimité'. In *Conversations nouvelles sur divers sujets, dédiées au roi*, vol. 1. Paris: Claude Barbin, 1–118.

Seaman, Natasha, & Joanna Woodall. (2022) *Money Matters in European Artworks and Literature, c. 1400–1750*. Amsterdam: Amsterdam University Press.

Searle, R. John. (1980) '*Las Meninas* and the Paradoxes of Pictorial Representation'. *Critical Inquiry*, 6(Spring), 477–88.

Seelig, Lorenz. (2017) 'The Munich Kunstkammer, 1565–1807'. In O. R Impey & Arthur MacGregor, eds., *The Origins of Museums: The Cabinet of Curiosities in Sixteenth- and Seventeenth-Century Europe*. Oxford: Ashmolean, 76–89.

Seidel, Linda. (1993) *Jan van Eyck's Arnolfini Portrait: Stories of an Icon*. Cambridge: Cambridge University Press.

Seipel, Wilfried, ed. (2008) *Masterpieces of the Secular Treasury*. Vienna: Kunsthistorisches Museum.

Serlio, Sebastiano. (1537) *Le regole generali di architettura*. Venice: Francesco Marcolini da Forli.

(1545) *Perspettiva*, 3 vols. Paris: J. Barbé.

Serra, Alfio (del). (1996) *Raffaello e il Ritratto di Papa Leone: Per il restauro del Leone X con due Cardinali*. Milan: Silvana.

Serrera, J. M. (1995) 'El palacio como Taller y el Taller como palacio: Una reflexion más Sobre *Las Meninas*'. In Fernando Marías et al., eds., *Otras Meninas*. Madrid: Siruela, 231–46.

Serres, Michel. (1988) 'Ambrosia and Gold'. In Norman Bryson, ed., *Calligram: Essays in New Art History from France*. Cambridge: Cambidge University Press, 116–30.

Settala, Manfredo. (1664) *Musaeum septalianum*. Tortona: Viola.

Sewell, William. (1986) 'Visions of Labour: Illustrations of the Mechanical Arts before, in, and after the *Encyclopédie*'. In Steven Kaplan & Cynthia Koepp, eds., *Work in France: Representations, Meaning, Organization and Practice*. Ithaca, NY: Cornell University Press, 258–86.

Seymour, Charles. (1964) 'Dark Chamber and Light-Filled Room: Vermeer and the Camera Obscura'. *Art Bulletin*, 46, 323–31.

Shakespeare, William. (1623 First Folio) *Mr William Shakespeare's Comedies Histories & Tragedies*. London: Isaak Iaggard and Ed Blount.

Shapin, Steven. (1996) *The Scientific Revolution*. Chicago: University of Chicago Press.

Shapin, Steven, & Simon Schaffer. (2011) *Leviathan and the Air-Pump: Hobbes, Boyle, and the Experimental Life*. Princeton, NJ: Princeton University Press.

Shearman, John. (1962) 'Leonardo's Colour and Chiaroscuro'. *Zeitschrift für Kunstgeschichte*, 25(1), 13–47.

Sherman, Bill. (2014) *Decoding the Renaissance: 500 Years of Codes and Ciphers*. Exhibition catalogue, Washington, DC: Folger Shakespeare Library, 11 November 2014–26 February 2015. Washington, DC: Folger Shakespeare Library.

Shickman, Allan. (1977) '"Turning Pictures" in Shakespeare's England'. *The Art Bulletin*, 59(1), 67–70.

Shuger, Debora. (1997) *Habits of Thought in the English Renaissance: Religion, Politics, and the Dominant Culture*. Toronto: University of Toronto Press.

(1998) 'The "I" of the Beholder: Renaissance Mirrors and the Reflexive Mind'. In Patricia Fumerton, ed., *Renaissance Culture and the Everyday*. Philadelphia: University of Pennsylvania Press, 21–41.

Shumaker, Wayne. (1978) *John Dee on Astronomy*. Berkeley: University of California Press.

Sigman, Jörg, & Angus Patterson. (2009) *Fashion and Armour in Renaissance Europe: Proud Lookes and Brave Attire*. London: V&A Publishing.

Silver, Larry. (1984) *The Paintings of Quentin Massys; with Catalogue Raisonné*. Oxford: Phaidon.

Sinisgalli, Rocco. (2011) *Leon Battista Alberti: On Painting: A New Translation and Critical Edition*. Cambridge: Cambridge University Press.

(2012) *Perspective in the Visual Culture of Classical Antiquity*. Cambridge: Cambridge University Press.

Sirén, Osvald. (1914) *Nicodemus Tessin dy's Study Trips*. Stockholm: P. A. Norstedt.

Slive, Seymour. (1964) 'Rembrandt's Self-Portrait in a Studio'. *Burlington Magazine*, 106, 483–86.

Small, Andrew. (1996) *Essays in Self-Portraiture: A Comparison of Technique in the Self-Portraits of Montaigne and Rembrandt.* New York: Peter Lang.

Smet, Rudolf De. (2002) *Les humanistes et leur bibliothèque.* Leiden: Peeters.

Smeyers, Maurits. (1998) *L'art de la miniature flamande du VIII au XVI siècle*, Leuven: La Renaissance du Livre.

Smith, Clifford H. (1914) 'The Legend of S. Eloy and S. Godeberta by Petrus Christus'. *The Burlington Magazine*, 25(138), 326–35.

(1915) *The Goldsmith and the Young Couple, or The Legend of S. Eloy and S. Godeberta by Petrus Christus.* London: Temple Sheen Press.

Smith, Mark A., ed. (2011) *Alhacen's Theory of Visual Perception: A Critical Edition with English Translation and Commentary of the First Three Books of Alhacen's De aspectibus, the Medieval Latin Version of Ibn al-Haytham's Kitab al-Manazir.* Philadelphia: American Philosophical Society.

(2014) *From Sight to Light: The Passage from Ancient to Modern Optics.* Chicago: University of Chicago Press, 2014.

(2017) *Optical Magic in the Late Renaissance: Giambattista della Porta's De refractione of 1593. Transactions of the American Philosophical Society*, 107(1).

Smith, Pamela. (2004) *The Body of the Artisan: Art and Experience in the Scientific Revolution.* Chicago: University of Chicago Press.

(2009) 'Science on the Move: Recent Trends in the History of Early Modern Science'. *Renaissance Quarterly*, 62(2), 345–75.

Smith, Pearsall Logan, ed. (1907) *The Life and Letters of Sir Henry Wotton*, 2 vols. Oxford: Clarendon Press.

Smith, Samantha. (2015) 'Blinding the Viewer: Rembrandt's 1628 Self-Portrait'. *Kunst og kultur*, 98 (3), 144–55.

Snell, Agnes. (1994) 'Reading Jacob Cats'. In Els Kloek, ed., *Women of the Golden Age: An International Debate on Women in Seventeenth-Century Holland, England, and Italy.* Hilversum: Verloren, 21–34.

Snyder, Joel. (1985) '*Las Meninas* and the Mirror of Princes'. *Critical Inquiry*, 11(4), 539–72.

Snyder, Joel, & Ted Cohen. (1980) 'Reflexions on *Las Meninas*: Paradox Lost'. *Critical Inquiry*, 7, 429–47.

Solomon, Nanette (1985). 'A Woman's Place: The Queen in *Las Meninas*'. *Source: Notes in the History of Art*, special issue on mirrors, ed. Laurie Schneider, 2(3), 72–74.

Söntgen, Beate. (2016) 'Mariology, Calvinism, Painting: Interiority in Pieter de Hooch's "Mother at a Cradle"'. In Ewa Lajer-Burcharth & Beate Söntgen, eds., *Interiors and Interiority.* Berlin: De Gruyter, 175–93.

Sparti, Donatella. (2001) 'Giovan Pietro Bellori and Annibale Carracci's Self-Portraits: From the *Vite* to the Artist's Funerary Monument'. *Mitteilungen des Kunsthistorischen Institutes in Florenz*, 45(1–2), 60–101.

Spencer, Justina. (2018) 'Illusion as Ingenuity: Dutch Perspective Boxes in the Royal Danish Kunstkammer's "Perspective Chamber"'. *Journal of the History of Collections* 30(2), 187–201.

Spenser, Edmund. (1579) *The Shepheardes Calendar.* London: William Ponsonbie.

(1595) *Amoretti and Epithalamion.* London: William Ponsonbie.

(1596) *The Faerie Queene*, 6 books. London: William Ponsonbie.

Speroni, Sperone. (1542) *Dialoghi d'amore e delle dignitá delle donne.* Venice: Aldo Manuzio.

Spezzaferro, Luigi. (1974) 'The Documentary Findings: Ottavio Costa as a Patron of Caravaggio'. *Burlington Magazine*, 116, 579–86.

Spila, Cristiano. (2009) *Mostri da salotto: I nani fra Medioevo e Rinascimento.* Naples: Liguori.

Springer, Carolyn. (2010) *Armour and Masculinity in the Italian Renaissance.* Toronto: University of Toronto Press.

Spronk, Ron. (1996) 'More than Meets the Eye: An Introduction to Technical Examination of Early Netherlandish Paintings at the Fogg Art Museum'. *Harvard University Art Museums Bulletin*, 5, 8–13.

Stafford, Barbara. (2006) 'Die "Katholisierung" der Projektionstechnologie im Zeitalter der Aufklärung'. In Helmar Schramm et al., eds., *Instrumente in Kunst und Wissenschaft zur Architektonik Kultureller Grenzen im 17. Jahrhundert.* Berlin: de Gruyter, 137–66.

Stafford, Barbara, with Frances Terpak. (2001) *Devices of Wonder: From the World in a Box to Images on a Screen.* Los Angeles: Getty Publications.

Stanley Smith, Cyril. (1965) '"The Glazier" by Jost Amman'. *Technology and Culture*, 6(1), 110–11.

Starobinski, Jean. (1965) *L'invention de la liberté, 1700–1789.* Geneva: Editions Skira.

Stauffer, Marie Therese. (2016) 'Mirror Art: Early Modern Catoptric Devices in Books, Collections, and Demonstrations'. In Lilian Zirpolo, ed., *'The Most Noble of the Senses': Anamorphosis, Trompe-l'Oeil, and Other Optical Illusions in Early Modern Art.* Ramsey, NJ: Zephyrus Scholarly Publications, 67–86.

Steadman, Philip. (2001) *Vermeer's Camera: Uncovering the Ttruth behind the Masterpieces.* Oxford: Oxford University Press.

Steinberg, Leo. (1981) 'Velazquez's *Las Meninas*'. *October*, 19, 45–54.

Steland, Dieter. (2002) 'Die Parabolae des Erasmus als Quelle von Emblemen'. In Bruno Klein & Harald

Wolter-von dem Knesebeck, eds., *Nobilis arte manus: Festschrift zum 70. Geburtstag von Antje Middeldorf Kosegarten*. Dresden: Klein, 331–61.

Stewart, Andrew. (1996) 'Reflections'. In Natalie Boymel Kampen, ed., *Sexuality in Ancient Art: Near East, Egypt, Greece, and Italy*. Cambridge: Cambridge University Press, 136–54.

(1997) *Art, Desire, and the Body in Ancient Greece*. Cambridge: Cambridge University Press.

Stewart, Susan. (1996) *On Longing: Narratives of the Miniature, the Gigantic, the Souvenir, the Collection*. Durham, NC: Duke University Press.

Stoichita, Victor. (1986) '*Imago Regis*: Kunsttheorie und Königliches Porträt in den *Meninas* von Velázquez'. *Zeitschrift für Kunstgeschichte*, 48, 165–90.

(1997) *The Self-Aware Image: An Insight into Early Modern Meta-Painting*. Translated from the 1993 French edition by A.-M. Glasheen. Cambridge: Cambridge University Press.

(2018) *Les fileuses de Velazquez: Textes, textures, images*. Paris: Collège de France.

Stradanus, Johannes. (1591) *Nova reperta*. Antwerp: Phls. Galle excud.

Strano, Giorgio, ed. (2008) *Galileo's Telescope: The Instrument That Changed the World*. Exhibition catalogue, Florence: Museo Galileo, 4 March 2008–31 January 2009. Florence: Museo Galileo.

Stratton-Pruitt, Suzanne. (2003) 'Velazquez's *Las Meninas*: An Interpretive Primer'. In Suzanne Stratton-Pruitt, ed., *Velazquez's Las Meninas*. Cambridge: Cambridge University Press, 124–49.

Straussman-Pflanzer, Eve, & Oliver Tostmann, eds. (2021) *By Her Hand: Artemisia Gentileschi and Women Artists in Italy, 1500–1800*. Exhibition catalogue, Detroit Institute of Arts & Wadsworth Atheneum Museum of Art, 30 September 2021–29 May 2022. New Haven, CT: Yale University Press

Strohl, H. G. (1904) *The Art of Heraldry: An Encyclopedia of Armory*. Translated from the German by A. Fox-Davies. London: T. C. & E. C. Jack.

Strong, Roy. (1966) 'Three Royal Jewels: The Three Brothers, the Mirror of Great Britain, and the Feather'. *The Burlington Magazine*, 108(760), 350–53.

(1969) *Tudor & Jacobean Portraits*, 2 vols. London: National Portrait Gallery.

(1987) *Gloriana: The Portraits of Elizabeth I*. London: Thames & Hudson.

(2002) *Feast: A History of Grand Eating*. London: Jonathan Cape.

Strunck, Christina, & Carolin Scheidel, eds. (2020) *Palladio, Vignola & Co.: Die Interpretation Kunsttheoretischer Texte und Illustrationen in Ubersetzungen der Frühen Neuzeit*. Berlin: Logos Verlag.

Stump, Donald. (2019) *Spenser's Heavenly Elizabeth: Providential History in 'The Faerie Queene'*. London: Palgrave Macmillan.

Sturm, Johann. (1676) *Collegium experimentale, sive curiosum*, 2 vols. Nuremberg: Wolfgang Mauritius Endteri and Johann Andreas Endteri heir.

Summers, David. (1981) *Michelangelo and the Language of Art*. Princeton, NJ: Princeton University Press.

Symons, Arthur. (1920) *Hispanic Anthology*, ed. Thomas Walsh. New York: G. P. Putnam.

Tadié, Alexis. (2014) *Francis Bacon: Le continent du savoir*. Paris: Classiques Garnier.

Tait, Hugh. (1967) '"The Devil's Looking Glass": The Magical Speculum of John Dee'. In Warren Hunting Smith, ed., *Horace Walpole: Writer, Politician, and Connoisseur*. New Haven, CT: Yale University Press, 195–212.

(1979) *The Golden Age of Venetian Glass*. London: British Museum.

ed. (1991) *Five Thousand Years of Glass*. London: British Museum Press.

Tallis, Nicola. (2023) *All the Queen's Jewels, 1445–1548: Power, Majesty, and Display*. New York: Routledge.

Tantardini, Lucia, & Rebecca Norris, eds. (2020) *From Theory to Practice: Lomazzo's Aesthetic Principles Reflected in the Art of His Time*. Leiden: Brill.

Tasso, Torquato (1581) *La Gerusalemme liberata*. Casalmaggiore: Antonio Canacci e Erasmo Viotti.

(1590) *La Gerusalemme liberata*, with illustrations by Bernardo Castello. Genoa: Girolamo Bartoli.

Taussig, M. (1993) *Mimesis and Alterity: A Particular History of the Senses*. London: Routledge.

Taws, Richard, & Genevieve Warwick, eds. (2016) *Art History*, special issue, 'Art and Technology in Early Modern Europe', 39(2), 198–209.

Taylor, Brook. (1715) *Linear Perspective*. London: Knaplock.

Taylor, Thomas. (1891) *The Eleusinian and Bacchic Mysteries*. New York: J. W. Boulton.

Teodorescu, Carmen. (2010) 'La tenture de la dame a la licorne: Nouvelle lecture des armoiries'. *Bulletin Monumentale: Société Française d'Archaéologie*, 168 (4), 355–67.

Tesauro, Emanuele. (1654) *Il cannocchiale aristotelico, o sia, Idea dell'arguta et ingeniosa elocutione: Che serue à tutta l'arte oratoria, lapidaria, et simbolica*. Turin: Giovanni Sinibaldo.

(1670) *Il cannocchiale aristotelico, o sia, Idea dell'arguta et ingeniosa elocutione: Che serue à tutta l'arte oratoria, lapidaria, et simbolica*. Turin: Bartolomeo Zavatta.

Thépaut-Cabasset, Corinne, & Pamela J. Warner. (2007–8) 'Présents du roi: An Archive at the Ministry of Foreign Affairs in Paris'. *Studies in the Decorative Arts*, 15(1), 4–18.

Thompson, Craig R., ed. (1978) *Collected Works of Erasmus*, vol. 23. Toronto: University of Toronto Press.

Thomson de Grummond, Nancy. (1981) 'Reflections on the Etruscan Mirror'. *Archaeology*, 34(5), 54–58.

Thoré-Burger, W. (1866) 'Van der Meer de Delft'. *Gazette des Beaux-Arts*, 21, 460–61.

Thorne, Alison. (2000) *Vision and Rhetoric in Shakespeare: Looking through Language*. London: Macmillan.

Thornton, Dora. (1997) *The Scholar in His Study: Ownership and Experience in Renaissance Italy*. New Haven, CT: Yale University Press.

Thornton, Peter. (1965) *Baroque and Rococo Silks*. London: Faber & Faber.

(1991) *The Italian Renaissance Interior 1400–1600*. New York: Harry N. Abrams.

Thuillier, Jacques, ed. (1972) *Georges de la Tour*. Exhibition catalogue, Paris: Orangerie, 10 May–25 September 1972. Paris: Editions des Musées Nationaux.

(1992) *Georges de la Tour*. Paris: Flammarion.

ed. (2007) *La Galerie des Glaces: Chef-d'oeuvre retrouvé*. Paris: Gallimard.

et al. (1990) *Vouet*. Exhibition catalogue, Paris: Grand Palais, 6 November 1990–11 February 1991. Paris: Editions de la Reunion des musees nationaux.

et al., eds. (2007) *La Galerie des Glaces: Histoire et restauration*. Dijon: Editions Faton.

Thürlemann, Felix. (1992) 'Das Lukas-Triptychon in Stolzenhain: Ein verlorenes Hauptwerk von Robert Campin in einer Kopie aus der Werkstatt Derick Baegerts'. *Zeitschrift für Kunstgeschichte*, 55(4), 524–64.

(2002) *Robert Campin: A Monographic Study with Critical Catalogue*. Munich: Prestel.

Tietze Conrat, Erica. (1957) *Dwarves & Jesters in Art*. London: Phaidon.

Tillander, Herbert. (1995) *Diamond Cuts in Historic Jewellery 1381–1910*. London: Art Books International.

Tolnay, Charles de. (1949) 'Velazquez' *Las Hilanderas* and *Las Meninas* (an Interpretation).' *Gazette des Beaux Arts*, 35, 21–38.

Tonelli, Luigi. (1933) *L'amore nella poesia e nel pensiero del Rinascimento*. Florence: Sansoni.

Tongiorgi Tomasi, Lucia. (2007) 'La conquista del visibile: Rimeditando Panofsky, rileggendo Galilei'. *Galilaeana*, 4, 5–46.

Torniello, Francesco. (1517) *Opera del modo de fare le littere maiuscole antique*. Milan: Gotardo da Ponte.

Tostmann, Oliver. (2021) 'The Advantages of Painting Small: Italian Women Artists and the Matter of Scale'. In Eve Straussman-Pflanzer & Oliver Tostmann, eds., *By Her Hand: Artemisia Gentileschi and Women Artists in Italy, 1500–1800*. Exhibition catalogue, Detroit Institute of Arts & Wadsworth Atheneum Museum of Art, 30 September 2021–29 May 2022. New Haven, CT: Yale University Press, 30–41.

Tournoy, Gilbert. (2002) 'The Library of Pieter Gillis'. In Rudolf de Smet, ed., *Les humanistes et leur bibliothèque*. Leuven: Peeters, 143–58.

Trachtenberg, Marvin. (1997) *Dominion of the Eye: Urbanism, Art and Power in Early Modern Florence*. Cambridge: Cambridge University Press.

Treves, Letizia. (2020) 'Artemisia Portraying Gerself'. In Letizia Treves, Sheila Barker, et al., *Artemisia*. Exhibition catalogue, London: National Gallery, 2 December 2020–25 January 2021. London: National Gallery, 64–75.

Treves, Letizia, Sheila Barker, et al. (2020) *Artemisia*. Exhibition catalogue, London: National Gallery, 2 December 2020–25 January 2021. London: National Gallery.

Trevisan, Luca, ed. (2011) *Tarsie lignee del Rinascimento in Italia*. Schio: Sassi.

Trimble, E. (2006) 'The Dark Backward and Abysm of Time: *The Tempest* and Memory'. *College Literature*, 33(1), 151–68.

Trissino, Giangiorgio. (1524) *I ritratti*. Rome: Lodovico de gli Arrighi Vicentino & Lautitio Perugino.

Trivellato, Francesca. (2000) *Fondamenta dei vetrai: Lavoro, tecnologia e mercato a Venezia tra sei e settecento*. Rome: Donzelli.

Truci, Isabella. (1976) 'Le Anamorfosi di Jean François Niceron all'Istituto e Museo di Storia della Scienza di Firenze'. *Annali dell'Istituto e Museo di Storia della Scienza di Firenze*, 1, 57–64.

Tudor, Faye (2010) '"All in him selfe as in a glass he sees": Mirrors and Vision in the Renaissance'. In John Shannon Hendrix & Charles H Carman, eds., *Renaissance Theories of Vision*. London: Routledge Taylor & Francis, 171–86.

Tufte, Virginia. (1970) *The Poetry of Marriage: The Epithalamium in Europe and its Development in England*, 2 vols. Los Angeles: Tinnon-Brown.

Turner, James Grantham. (2022) *The Villa Farnesina: Palace of Venus in Renaissance Rome*. Cambridge: Cambridge University Press.

Tuttle, Richard, Christoph Frommel, et al. (2002) *Jacopo Barozzi da Vignola*. Milan: Electa.

Un temps d'exubérance: Les arts décoratifs sous Louis XIII et Anne d'Autriche. (2002) Exhibition catalogue, Paris: Galeries nationales du Grand Palais, 9 April–8 July 2002. Paris: Réunion des Musées Nationaux.

Unger, Daniel, ed. (2022) *Titian's 'Allegory of Marriage': New Approaches*. Amsterdam: Amsterdam University Press.

Unglaub, Jonathan. (2004) 'Poussin's Reflection'. *The Art Bulletin*, 86(3), 505–28.

(2006) *Poussin and the Poetics of Painting: Pictorial Narrative and the Legacy of Tasso*. Cambridge: Cambridge University Press

Upton, Joel M. (1990) *Petrus Christus: His Place in Fifteenth-Century Flemish Painting*. University Park: Penn State University Press.

Upton, Joel. (1995) 'PETRUS XPI ME FECIT: The Transformation of a Legacy'. In Maryan Ainsworth, ed., *Petrus Christus in Renaissance Bruges: An Interdisciplinary Approach*. Turnhout: Brepols, 53–63.

Väliaho, Pasi (2022) *Projecting Spirits: Speculation, Providence, and Early Modern Optical Media*. Stanford, CA: Stanford University Press.

Van Fornenbergh, Alexander, & Theodorus Galle. (1658) *Den Antwerpschen Protheus Ofte: Cyclopschen Apelles dat is, het leven, ende konst-rijcke daden des uytnemenden, ende hoogh-beroemden, mr. Quinten Matsys*. Antwerpen: Hendrick van Soest.

Van Hoogstraten, Samuel. (1678) *Inleyding tot de Hooge Schoole der Schilderkonst: Anders de Zichtbaere Werelt*. Rotterdam: François van Hoogstraten.

(2021) *Samuel von Hoogstraten's 'Introduction to the Academy of the Art of Painting; or, The Visible World*. Translated by J. Jacobs and edited by C. Brusati. Los Angeles: Getty Research Institute Texts & Documents.

Van Hout, Nico, & Arnout Balis. (2012) *Rubens Unveiled: Notes on the Master's Painting Technique. Catalogue of the Rubens Paintings in the Antwerp Museum*. Antwerp: Koninklijk Museum.

Van Mander, Carel. (1604) *Het Schilder-boeck*. Haarlem: Pascher van Waesbusch.

Van Tilburg, Marja. (2018) 'Becoming a Woman in the Dutch Republic: Advice Literature for Young Adult Women of the Seventeenth and Eighteenth Centuries.' In Elizabeth Cohen & Margaret Reeves, eds., *The Youth of Early Modern Women*. Amsterdam: Amsterdam University Press. 255–74.

Van der Velden, Hugo. (1998) 'Defrocking St Eloy: Petrus Christus's Vocational Portrait of a Goldsmith'. *Simiolus*, 26(4), 242–76.

(2011) 'The Quatrain of the Ghent Altarpiece'. *Simiolus*, 35, 5–40.

Vanautgaerden, Alexander. (2010) *Autoportraits d'Erasme: Dürer-Holbein-Metsys-Froben. Recueils épistolaires et representations figures*. Turnhout: Brepols.

Varchi, Benedetto. (1549) *Due lezzioni di M. Benedetto Varchi, nella Prima delle Quali etc*. Florence: Lorenzo Torrentino.

Vasari, Giorgio. (1568) *Le vite de' piu eccellenti pittori, scultori e architettori*, 3 vols. Florence: Giunti.

(1986) *Vite* ... ([1550]), eds. Luciano Bellosi & Aldo Rossi. Turin: Einaudi.

Vasconi, Paola, ed. (2015) *Cristoforo Clavio e la cultura scientifica del suo tempo*. Rome: Gangemi.

Vassilopoulou, Panayiota. (2020) 'The Gaze in the Mirror: Human Self and the Myth of Dionysus in Plotinus'. *Archiv für Geschichte der Philosophie*, 20.

Vaughan, Richard. (1970) *Philip the Good, the Apogee of Burgundy*. Harlow: Longmans.

Vaulezard, Jean Louis de. (1630) *Perspective cilindrique et conique, ou Traicté des apparences veuës par le moyen des miroirs cilindriques*. Paris: Julian Jacquin.

Verardi, Donato. (2018). *La scienza e I segreti della natura a Napoli nel Rinascimento*. Florence: Florence University Press

Vergara, Alejandro (2016) *The Art of Clara Peeters*. Exhibition catalogue, Antwerp: Maison Rockox, 16 June–2 October 2016; Madrid: Prado Museum, 25 October 2016–19 February 2017. Antwerp: Koninklijk Museum voor Schone Kunsten.

Vermeir, Koen. (2007) 'Kircher's Magical Instruments: An Essay on Science, Religion, and Applied Metaphysics (1602–1680)'. *Studies in History and Philosophy of Science, Part A*, 38(2), 363–400.

Verougstraete, Hélène. (2006) 'Diptychs with Instructions for Use'. In John Oliver Hand & Ron Spronk, eds., *Essays in Context: Unfolding the Netherlandish Diptych*. Cambridge, MA: Harvard Art Museums & Yale University Press, 156–71.

Verougstraete, Hélène, & Roger Van Schoute. (2000) 'Frames and Supports of Some Eyckian Paintings'. In Susan Foister, Sue Jones, & Delphine Cool, eds., *Investigating Jan Van Eyck*. Turnhout: Brepols, 107–17.

Vickers, J. Nancy. (1982) 'The Body Re-membered: Petrarchan Lyric and the Strategies of Description'. In D. John Lyons & Stephen G. Nichols Jr., eds., *Mimesis: From Mirror to Method, Augustine to Descartes*. Hanover, NH: University Press of New England, 100–109.

Vinken, Pierre. (2000). *The Shape of the Heart*. New York: Elsevier.

Virgil. *Aeneid*.

Vitruvius. *De architectura*.

Vives, Juan Luis. (1782) *De anima et vita* (1538). In *Opera omnia*, ed. Gregorio Majáns y Siscar, 8 vols., III. Valencia: Benedict Monfort.

Vodret, Rossella. (1995) 'Il restauro del *Narciso*'. In Stefania Macioce, ed., *Michelangelo Merisi da Caravaggio: La vita e le opera attraverso I documenti (Atti del Convegno Internazionale di Studi)*. Rome: Logart Press, 167–83.

(1996) 'Il *Narciso* di Caravaggio: Ritratto di artista allo specchio'. *Art e dossier*, 11(109), 9–13.

(2010) 'Riflessioni sugli specchi nell'arte'. In Valeria Merlini & Daniela Storti, eds., *Tiziano a Milano: Donna allo specchio*. Exhibition catalogue, Milan: Palazzo Marino, 3 December 2010–6 January 2012. Milan: Skira, 27–138.

Von Berswordt-Wallrabe, Kornelia, et al., eds. (2003) *Jan Brueghels Andwerpen: Die Flamischen Gemalde in Schwerin*. Exhibition catalogue, Schwerin: Staatliches Museum Schwerin, 15 August–30 November 2003. Schwerin: Staatliches Museum Schwerin.

Von Schlosser, Julius. (1908) *Die Kunst- und Wunderkammern der Spätrenaissance: Ein Beitrag zur Geschichte des Sammelwesens*. Leipzig: Klinkhardt & Biermann.

Von Wedel, Lupold. (1895) 'Journey through England and Scotland'. Translated from the German by G. von Bülow. *Transactions of the Royal Historical Society*, 9, 223–70.

Wadum, Jørgen. (1995) 'Vermeer in Perspective'. In Arie Walert, Erma Hermens, & Maria Peck, eds., *Historical Painting Techniques, Materials, and Studio Practice*. Symposium, University of Leiden, Netherlands, 26–29 June 1995 with the Getty Conservation Institute. Oxford: Oxford University Press, 148–54.

Wagenaar, A. Willem. (1980) 'The Origins of the Lantern'. *The New Magic Lantern Journal*, 3, 10–12.

Wagener, Danièle. (2016) *Les cinq sens dans la peinture*. Exhibition catalogue, Musée d'art de la ville de Luxembourg, 19 March 2016–26 June 2016. Luxembourg: Musée d'art de la ville de Luxembourg.

Waiboer, Adriaan. (2011) *Gabriel Metsu: Life & Work*. New Haven, CT: Yale University Press.

Waiboer, Adriaan, & Wayne Franits. (2010) *Gabriel Metsu: Rediscovered Master of the Dutch Golden Age*. Exhibition catalogue, Dublin: National Gallery of Ireland, 4 September–5 December 2010; Amsterdam: Rijksmuseum, 21 December 2010–21 March 2011; Washington, DC: National Gallery, 10 April–24 July 2011. New Haven, CT: Yale University Press.

Wajcman, G. (2004) *Fênetre: Chroniques du regard et de l'intime*. Lagrasse: Verdier.

Wald, Robert. (2009) 'Tintoretto's Vienna Susannah and the Elders: History, Technique, and Restoration'. In Miguel Falomir et al., eds., *Jacopo Tintoretto: Actas del congreso internacional Jacobo Tintoretto*. Proceedings of the International Symposium, Madrid: Prado Museum, 26–27 February 2007. Madrid: Museo Nacional del Prado, 178–87.

Warburg, Aby. (1902) 'Flandrische Kunst und florentinische Frührenaissance'. *Jahrbuch der Königlich Preussischen Kunstsammlungen*, 23, 247–66.

Ward, L. John. (1994) 'Disguised Symbolism as Enactive Symbolism in van Eyck's Paintings'. *Artibus et Historiae*, 29, 9–53.

Warwick, Genevieve. (2006) 'Introduction: Caravaggio in History'. In Genevieve Warwick, ed., *Caravaggio: Realism, Reception, Rebellion*. Newark, NJ: University of Delaware Press & Associated University Presses, 13–22.

(2010) 'Soleil et nuages: Le Bernin, artiste de cour entre Rome et Paris'. In Marc Bayard, ed., *Rome-Paris 1640: Transferts culturels et renaissance d'un centre artistique* (vol. 11). Rome and Paris: Collection d'Histoire de l'Art, Académie de France a Rome, Villa Medicis, 463–80.

(2012) *Bernini: Art as Theatre*. New Haven, CT: Yale University Press.

(2014) 'The Story of the Man Who Whitened His Face: Bernini, Galileo, and the Science of Relief'. *The Seventeenth Century*, 29(1), 1–29.

(2016) 'Looking in the Mirror of Renaissance Art'. *Art History*, special issue, 'Art and Technology in Early Modern Europe', 39(2), 255–81.

(2017) 'Memory's Cut: Caravaggio's Sleeping Cupid of 1608'. *Art History*, special issue, 'Art History 40: Image and Memory', 40(4), 884–903.

(2019) 'Crying Laocoon: The Visual Arts of Translation'. *The Translator*, 25(4), 311–34.

(2021) '"Ritratto allo specchio": L'idea del autoritratto nella prima età moderna'. *Rivista Fontes*, 2, *L'autorappresentazione come autoconsapevolezza dell'artista*, ed. Cristina Galassi and Sonia Maffei, 19–44.

(2022) *Cinderella's Glass Slipper: Towards a Cultural History of Renaissance Materialities*, Cambridge: Cambridge University Press.

(forthcoming 2024) 'Filarete's Compass: Renaissance Technologies of Disegno'. *Memofonte*, special issue, ed. Vita Segreto.

Warwick, Genevieve, with Natalie Adamson. (2013) 'Editorial'. *Art History*, 36(1), 8–11.

Warwick, Genevieve, with Richard Taws. (2016) 'After Prometheus: Art and Technology in Early Modern Europe'. *Art History*, special issue, 'Art and Technology in Early Modern Europe', 39(2), 199–209.

Waterfield, Giles, et al., eds. (1988) *Mr Cartwright's Pictures: A Seventeenth-Century Collection*. Exhibition catalogue, London: Dulwich Picture Gallery, 25 November 1987–28 February 1988. London: Dulwich Picture Gallery.

Weale, W. H. James. (1908) *Hubert and Jan van Eyck: Their Life and Work*. London: J. Lane.

Weale, W. H. James, with Maurice W. Brockwell. (1928) *The Van Eycks and Their Art*. London: John Lane the Bodley Head.

Weber, Henri. (ed.) (1963) *Les amours*. Paris: Garnier.

Wedekind, Gregor. (2007) 'Wie in einem Spiegel: Porträt und Wirklichkeit in Jan van Eycks Arnolfinihochzeit'. *Zeitschrift für Kunstgeschichte*, 70(3), 325–46.

(2009) 'Jeux de vérité: Portrait et réalité dans Les Epoux Arnolfini de Jan van Eyck'. In Dominic Olariu, ed., *Le portrait individual: Réflexions autour d'une forme de représentation XIIIe–XVe siècles*. Bern: Peter Lang, 205–34.

Weiner, Annette B., & Jane Schneider. (1998) *Cloth and the Human Experience*. Washington: Smithsonian Books.

Weiss, Jessica. (2018) 'Relics of "Los Reyes Catolicos": The Retablo de Isabel and Spanish-Habsburg Dynastic Heirlooms'. In Catherine Ingersoll, Alisa McCusker, & Jessica Weiss, eds., *Imagery and Ingenuity in Early Modern Europe*. Turnhout: Brepols, 165–80.

(2019) 'Juan de Flandes and His Financial Success in Castile'. *Journal of Historians of Netherlandish Art*, 2 (1), 1–38.

Wenzel, Michael. (2020) *Philipp Hainhofer: Handeln mit Kunst und Politik*. Kunstwissenschaftliche Studien, 199. Berlin: Deutscher Kunstverlag.

Westermann, Mariët. (2000) *Art and Home: Dutch Interiors in the Age of Rembrandt*. Zwolle: Waanders.

Weststeijn, Thijs. (2008) *The Visible World: Samuel van Hoogstraten's Art Theory and the Legitimation of Painting in the Dutch Golden Age*. Amsterdam: Amsterdam University Press.

(ed.) (2013) *The Universal Art of Samuel van Hoogstraten (1627–78): Painter, Writer, and Courtier*. Amsterdam: Amsterdam University Press.

Wetering, Ernst (van de). (2005) *The Self Portraits*. Rembrandt Research Project Foundation, vol. 4. The Hague: Nijhoff.

Wethey, Harold. (1975) *The Paintings of Titian*, 3 vols. London: Phaidon.

Wheelock, Arthur, Jr. (1973) 'Carel Fabritius: Perspective and Optics in Delft'. *Nederlands Kunsthistorisch Jaarboek*, 24, 63–83.

(1977a) *Perspective, Optics & Delft Artists around 1650*. New York: Garland Publishers.

(1977b) 'Constantin Huygens and the *Camera Obscura*.' *History of Photography*, 1, 93–103.

(1988) *Vermeer and the Art of Painting*. New Haven, CT: Yale University Press.

ed. (1995) *Vermeer*. Exhibition catalogue, Washington, DC: National Gallery, 12 November 1995–11 February 1996; The Hague, Mauritshuis, 1 March–2 June 1996. New Haven, CT: Yale University Press; Zwolle: Waanders.

Wheelock, Arthur K., Jr., ed. (1998) *A Collector's Cabinet*. Exhibition catalogue, Washington, DC: National Gallery, 17 May–9 August 1998. Washington, DC: National Gallery of Art.

Jr., et al. (2004) *Gerard ter Borch*. Exhibition catalogue, Washington: National Gallery of Art, 7 November 2004–30 January 2005. New Haven, CT: Yale University Press.

White, John. (1957) *The Birth and Rebirth of Pictorial Space*. London: Faber & Faber.

Widemann, Thomas. (2010) 'Les observations astronomiques dans les residences royales'. In Béatrix Saule, ed., *Sciences et curiosités à la Cour de Versailles*. Exhibition catalogue, Versailles: Château de Versailles, 26 October 2010–27 February 2011. Paris: Editions RMN, 220–24.

Wieseman, Marjorie E. (2011) *Vermeer's Women: Secrets and Silence*. Exhibition catalogue, Washington: Fitzwilliam Museum, 5 October 2011–15 January 2012. Cambridge: Fitzwilliam Museum.

Wilding, Nick. (2014) 'Galileo's O; Bd. 3: A Galileo Forgery. Unmasking the New York Sidereus Nuncius.' *Journal für Kunstgeschichte*, 18(4), 343–47.

Willach, Rolf. (2008) *The Long Route to the Invention of the Telescope*. Philadelphia: American Philosophical Society.

Williamson, Paul, & Glyn Davies. (2014) *Medieval Ivory Carvings 1200–1550*. London: Victoria & Albert Museum.

Wilson, Catherine. (1995) *The Invisible World: Early Modern Philosophy and the Invention of the Microscope*. Princeton, NJ: Princeton University Press.

Wilson, G. R. (1969) 'The Interplay of Perception and Reflection: Mirror Imagery in Donne's Poetry'. *Studies in English Literature, 1500–1900*, Winter 1969, 107–21.

Wilson, Jean. (1998) *Painting in Bruges at the Close of the Middle Ages: Studies in Society and Visual Culture*. University Park: Penn State University Press.

Winner, Matthias. (1957) *Die Quellen der Pictura-Allegorien in gemalten Bildergalerien des 17, Jahrhunderts zu Antwerpen*. Cologne: Universität zu Köln.

(1983) 'Poussins Selbstbildnis im Louvre als kunsttheoretische Allegorie'. *Römisches Jahrbuch für Kunstgeschichte*, 20, 417–51.

(1986) 'L'autoritratto di Raffaello e la misura per il nostro occhio: Appunti sulla costruzione prospettica della Scuola d'Atene (1510–11)'. *Tecnica e stile*, 1, Florence: Villa I Tatti, 9, 83–94.

(1989) 'Annibale Carracci's Self-Portraits and the *Paragone* Debate'. In Irving Lang, ed., *World Art: Themes of Unity in Diversity. Acts of the 26th International Congress of the History of Art*, 2 vols. University Park: Penn State University Press, vol. 2, 509–15.

(2001) '"L'amore di essa pittura" in Poussins Selbstbildnis von 1650'. In Hannah Baader et al., eds., *Ars et scriptura: Festschrift für Rudolf Preimesberger*. Berlin: Mann, 180–97.

Wirth, Jean. (1979) *La jeune fille et la mort: Recherches sur les thèmes macabres dans l'art germanique de la Renaissance*. Geneva: Droz.

Witt, Robert. (1975) *Mirror within a Mirror: Ben Jonson and the Play-Within.* Salzburg: University of Salzburg.

Wivel, Matthias, ed. (2020) *Titian: Love, Desire, Death.* Exhibition catalogue, London: National Gallery, 2 December 2020–17 January 2021. London: National Gallery .

ed. (2022) *Sebastiano del Piombo and Michelangelo: The Compass and the Book.* Turnhout: Brepols.

Wolf, Bryan Jay. (2001) *Vermeer and the Invention of Seeing.* Chicago: University of Chicago Press.

Wolf, Gerhard. (1998) 'Alberti, Narziss, und die Erfindung der Malerei'. In Christine Göttler et al., eds., *Diletto e maraviglia: Festschrift für Rudolf Preimesberger.* Zurich: Imorde, 11–33.

(2002) *Schleier und Spiegel: Traditionen des Christusbildes und die Bildkonzepte der Renaissance.* Munich: Fink.

Wolohojian, Stephan, with Melinda Watt & Michael Gallagher. (2017) 'A Grand Tableau: Charles Le Brun's Portrait of the Jabach Family'. *Metropolitan Museum of Art Bulletin* 75(1, Summer).

Woltman, Alfred. (1879) 'Der heilige Eligius von Petrus Christus'. *Repertorium für Kunstwissenschaft*, 2, 298–300.

Wood, Christopher S. (2003) 'The Perspective Treatise in Ruins: Lorenz Stoer, Geometria et perspectiva, 1567'. In Lyle Massey, ed., *The Treatise on Perspective, Published and Unpublished.* Washington, DC: National Gallery of Art, 235–58.

Wood, Jeremy. (2010) *Rubens: Copies and Adaptations from Renaissance and Later Artists. Italian Artists II, Titian and North Italian Art.* Corpus Rubenianum Ludwig Burchard. London: Harvey Miller.

Woodall, Joanna. (2007) *Anthonis Mor: Art and Authority.* Studies in Netherlandish Art and Cultural History. Zwolle: Waanders.

(2015) '*De Wisselaer*: Quentin Massys's *Man Weighing Gold Coins and His Wife*, 1514'. *Netherlands Yearbook for History of Art*, 64(1), 38–75.

Woods-Marsden, Joanna. (1998) *Renaissance Self-Portraiture: The Visual Construction of Identity and the Social Status of the Artist.* New Haven, CT: Yale University Press.

ed. (2007) *Titian: Materiality, Likeness, Istoria.* Turnhout: Brepols.

Woollett, Anne, & Arianne van Suchtelen. (2006) *Rubens and Brueghel: A Working Friendship.* Exhibition catalogue, Los Angeles: Getty Museum, 5 July 2006–24 September 2006; The Hague: Mauritshuis, 21 October 2006–28 January 2007. Zwolle: Waanders Publishing, 94–99.

Woollett, Anne, et al., eds. (2021) *Holbein: Capturing Character.* Exhibition catalogue, Pierpont Morgan Library & J. Paul Getty Museum, 19 October 2021–15 May 2022. Los Angeles: J. Paul Getty Museum.

Wuestman, Gerdina, & Arie de Groot. (2017) *Emanuel de Witte: Meester van het licht.* Alkmaar: Stedelijk Museum Alkmaar, 2017

Yates, Frances. (1969) *Theatre of the World.* Chicago: University of Chicago Press.

(1972) *The Rosicrucian Enlightenment.* London: Routledge & Kegan Paul.

(2001) *The Occult Philosophy in the Elizabethan Age* (1979). Reprint. London: Routledge.

(2014) *The Art of Memory* (1966). Reprint. London: Bodley Head.

Yiu, Yvonne. (2001) *Jan van Eyck: Das Arnolfini-Doppelbildnis, Reflexionen über die Malerei.* Frankfurt: Stroemfeld.

(2005) 'Der Spiegel: Werkzeug des Künstlers oder Metapher der Malerei? Zur Deutung des Spiegels in Produktionsszenarien in der nordischen Malerei des 15. und frühen 16. Jahrhunderts'. *Zeitschrift für Kunstgeschichte*, 4, 475–88.

Zahn, Johann. (1685–86) *Oculus artificialis teledioptricus sive telescopium.* Würzburg: Quirinus Heyl.

Zamani, Daniel, et al., eds. (2019) *Visions of Enchantment: Occultism, Magic, and Visual Culture.* Lopen: Fulgur Press.

Zamora Calvo, José María. (2017) 'Myth and Exegesis in Plotinus: How to Divide and Recompose Words and Things'. *Rupkatha Journal on Interdisciplinary Studies in Humanities*, 9(2), 81–89.

Zapperi, Roberto. (1986) 'Munich Selbtbildnis und Autobiographie: Über ein Gemälde von Annibale Carracci'. In *Idea: Jahrbuch der Hamburger Kunsthalle.* Munich: Prestel, 5, 7–31.

(1991) 'Alessandro Farnese, Giovanni della Casa and Titian's Danae in Naples'. *Journal of the Warburg & Courtauld Institutes*, 54(1991), 159–71.

Zecchin, Luigi. (1986) *Il ricettario Darduin: Un codice vetrario del seicento transcritto e commentato.* Venice: Arsenale.

(1987–90) *Vetro et vetrai di Murano*, 3 vols. Studi sulla storia del vetro. Venice: Arsenale.

Zirpolo, Lilian. (2005) 'Christina of Sweden's Patronage of Bernini: The Mirror of Truth Revealed by Time'. *Woman's Art Journal*, 26(1), 38–43.

(2013) 'Embellishing the Queen's Residence: Queen Christina of Sweden's Patronage of Gian Lorenzo Bernini and Members of His Circle of Sculptors'. In Arnold Coonin, ed., *A Scarlet Renaissance: Essays in Honour of Sarah Blake McHam.* New York: Italica Press, 267–303.

ed. (2016) *'The Most Noble of the Senses': Anamorphosis, Trompe l'Oeil, and Other Optical Illusions in Early Modern Art.* Ramsey, NJ: Zephyrus.

Zoffili, Ermanno. (2011) *The First Medusa: Caravaggio.* Milan: 5 Continents Editions.

Zöllner, Frank. (1992) '*Ogni pittore dipinge sé*: Leonardo da Vinci and "automimesis"'. In *Der Künstler über sich in seinem Werk*, ed. Oskar Bätschmann et al. Weinheim: Acta Humaniora VCH, 137–60.

(2013) 'From the Face to the Aura: Leonardo da Vinci's Sfumato and Female Portraiture'. In Monika Körte et al., eds., *Inventing Faces: Rhetorics of Portraiture between Renaissance and Modernism*. Exhibition catalogue, Berlin: Gemäldegalerie, 2013. Berlin: De Gruyter, 67–83.

Zorach, Rebecca. (2001) 'Desiring Things'. *Art History*, 24 (2), 195–212.

(2005) *Blood, Milk, Ink, Gold: Abundance and Excess in the French Renaissance*. Chicago: University of Chicago Press.

Zuccaro, Federico. (1607) *Idea de' pittori, scultori, et architetti*. Turin: Agostino Disserolio.

Zwijnenberg, Robert. (1999) *The Writings and Drawings of Leonardo da Vinci: Order and Chaos in Early Modern Thought*. Translated from the Dutch by Caroline Van Eck. Cambridge: Cambridge University Press.

(2003) '*Ogni pittore dipinge sé*: On Leonardo da Vinci's *St John the Baptist*'. In Florike Egmond & Robert Zwijnenberg, eds., *Bodily Extremities*. Burlington, VT: Ashgate, 48–67.

INDEX